THE MILITARY BALANCE 2014

published by

for

The International Institute for Strategic Studies
Arundel House | 13–15 Arundel Street | Temple Place | London | WC2R 3DX | UK

THE MILITARY BALANCE 2014

The International Institute for Strategic Studies
Arundel House | 13–15 Arundel Street | Temple Place | London | WC2R 3DX | UK

This publication has been prepared by the Director-General and Chief Executive of the Institute and his Staff, who accept full responsibility for its contents. The views expressed herein do not, and indeed cannot, represent a consensus of views among the worldwide membership of the Institute as a whole.

First published February 2014

ISBN 978-1-85743-722-5
ISSN 0459-7222

Cover images: Timothy Walter/US Navy/Getty Images; Pascal Guyot/AFP/Getty Images; Manjunath Kiran/AFP/Getty Images; Alex Beltyukov; Shah Marai/AFP/Getty Images; Mark Ralston/AFP/Getty Images; US Air Force/Staff Sgt. Christopher Boitz.

The *Military Balance* (ISSN 0459-7222) is published annually by Routledge Journals, an imprint of Taylor & Francis, 4 Park Square, Milton Park, Abingdon, Oxfordshire OX14 4RN, UK. The 2014 annual subscription rate is: UK£206 (individual rate), UK£320 (institution rate) UK£280 (online only); overseas US$342 (individual rate), US$558 (institution rate), US$488 (online only).

A subscription to the institution print edition, ISSN 0459-7222, includes free access for any number of concurrent users across a local area network to the online edition, ISSN 1479-9022.

Dollar rates apply to subscribers in all countries except the UK and the Republic of Ireland where the pound sterling price applies. All subscriptions are payable in advance and all rates include postage.

Journals are sent by air to the USA, Canada, Mexico, India, Japan and Australasia. Subscriptions are entered on an annual basis, i.e. January to December. Payment may be made by sterling cheque, dollar cheque, international money order, National Giro, or credit card (Amex, Visa, Mastercard).

Please send subscription orders to: USA/Canada: Taylor & Francis Inc., Journals Department, 325 Chestnut Street, 8th Floor, Philadelphia, PA 19106, USA. UK/Europe/Rest of World: R outledge Journals, T&F Customer Services, T&F Informa UK Ltd., Sheepen Place, Colchester, Essex, CO3 3LP, UK.

The print edition of this journal is printed on ANSI conforming acid-free paper by Bell & Bain, Glasgow, UK.

Contents

Index of **TABLES**

Index of **FIGURES**

Index of **MAPS**

Editor's Introduction

Financial and strategic rebalances challenge defence planners

In 2013, a war in Mali and the threat of international military force against Syria, in response to the use there of chemical weapons, highlighted the challenge for defence planners of unanticipated events. At the same time, a range of familiar and more fundamental issues persisted, including the relative shift in the balance of military power to Asia, amid tensions in that region. Asian defence budgets rose again, as did equipment purchases. More Asian states are building their military capabilities, some of which are related to general force modernisation; others that could be used for power projection or for deterrence. Meanwhile, the Middle East and North Africa remained gripped by the consequences of the Arab Spring, including the conflict in Syria and its wider effects, continued turbulence in North Africa and the wider impact of this on Sub-Saharan Africa, as well as Iran's nuclear programme. In the region, some states continued substantial procurement programmes. Amidst all this, however, defence budgets in the West continued to contract and governments grappled with the policy requirement to balance financial imperatives with strategic priorities and risks.

For these and the following reasons, 2014 will be a significant year for many armed forces in the West. The withdrawal of most foreign military forces from Afghanistan and the end of ISAF's combat mission there mean that it is not just the United States that is viewing the end of this campaign as a 'strategic turning point', to use a phrase coined by then-US Defense Secretary Leon Panetta in 2012.

For Panetta, the forthcoming end of a decade of wars essentially fought on land gave the US a chance to reassess force structures, roles and inventories. It provided an opportunity to 'rebalance' towards the Asia-Pacific. But for Panetta's successor, Chuck Hagel, continuing uncertainty over defence budget allocations was reflected in policymakers' concern over whether sequestration or similarly severe cuts in defence spending would continue. If sequestration were to continue, according to scenarios in the Strategic Choices and Management Review ordered by Hagel, there was a danger that the Pentagon's 2012 defence strategic guidance would either 'bend' or 'break'. More detail on how the Pentagon may attempt to accommodate further cuts will probably form a central element of the Quadrennial Defense Review, due in February 2014, which will also be scrutinised for greater insight into how the US now interprets the experience of the last 12 years of war, and the degree to which it will try to institutionalise these lessons.

Similar reflection is taking place among the armed forces of many of the other countries that contributed to the campaigns in Afghanistan and Iraq. Defence spending is shrinking in European countries at a time when the reorientation of US defence policy towards the Asia-Pacific places a greater share of the burden for international security on them, particularly in Europe's fragile vicinity to the south and the east. They therefore face a loss of capability and influence, making all the more pressing initiatives – such as those from within NATO and the European Union – to maximise value from defence budgets through closer cooperation. The results of these institutional efforts have so far been lacklustre. NATO's 'Smart Defence' initiative and the EU's equipment pooling and sharing approach, both designed to increase systematic and closer defence collaboration among member states, continue to be plagued by patchy progress, while NATO's 'defence matters' initiative seemed to be met with at best a resigned shrug in many European states. While the importance of these measures may be recognised by defence policymakers in member states, total European defence spending continues to fall in real terms, by an average of 2.5% per year since 2010. As a result, finding the resources to support military capabilities will become more difficult and will place increasing importance on achieving more effective cooperation regarding future capabilities.

France's Mali operation, beginning in January 2013, highlighted the positive and negative aspects of contemporary European defence efforts. Agile, tough and operationally experienced forces deployed quickly, were able to adapt plans and tactics, fuse intelligence, surveillance and strike assets, and work well with regional and international partners. But several partners were also vital to fill shortcomings exposed in France's capabilities, such as strategic lift, airborne refuelling and persistent surveillance. France's 2013 White Paper illustrated the difficulties defence planners now face from financial pressure and continuing strategic uncertainty. However, though defence cuts will bite, Paris managed to avoid losing any capabilities in their entirety, a step that has already been taken by some European states. If reductions continue, particularly in an uncoordinated fashion, the risk is that European states may be less able to act effectively in future crises.

Crises will continue to erupt and demand attention. Turbulence in North Africa, for instance, is the latest 'new normal' for some US defence policymakers. Whether European states will be willing to act is another question. The debate over what to do about the conflict in Syria, sharpened by the chemical weapons issue, has demonstrated that the past decade's wars have left Western electorates at best unsure of their success or necessity. As well as balancing budgets, capabilities and risk, states wanting to retain the option of military intervention now also need to re-establish a convincing narrative to explain and justify the use of the armed forces in international crisis management.

NATO has tried to shape the debate on these matters, with the secretary-general saying he believed that 'without the credible threat of military force, Syria would not have agreed to the destruction of its stock of chemical weapons', and that working together in NATO offered political credibility, legitimacy and military effectiveness. But the end of combat operations in Afghanistan poses a challenge to NATO; it marks the end of an intense period of operational activity for the Alliance, and NATO is itself perhaps now at a strategic turning point. Leaders of NATO member states meeting at the Alliance's 2014 summit in the UK will face a range of pressing, though not existential, issues, notably the shape of a 'post-operational alliance'. Although NATO allies have made significant progress on interoperability as a result of operations, this will be difficult to maintain in the face of decreasing spending and the lower operational tempo expected following the 2014 ISAF drawdown. NATO has further internationalised as a result of Afghanistan; it developed close operational links with non-NATO ISAF states. Meanwhile, its agenda now includes ballistic-missile defence, cyber security and out-of-area maritime security tasks. Keeping NATO members and partner nations engaged will also prove a challenge post-2014, as defence-policy aspirations may well focus closer to home.

In the Middle East, Syria, Iran and Israel still dominate regional security calculations. In 2013, the struggle between the Assad regime and rebel forces was compounded by conflict within rebel ranks, direct intervention on the regime's side by Hizbullah, growing numbers of foreign Sunni jihadist fighters, and further refugee flows. The use of chemical weapons in Syria provoked a crisis: a threat, though hesitant, of international force, and eventual agreement following Russia's initiative on the destruction of Syria's chemical stockpile. Realising in late 2012 that much of the territory it had lost was either irretrievable or not worth the cost, the Assad regime set more realistic objectives and sought to adapt military strategy to shrinking resources and manpower. Both the number and rank of defectors fell from late 2012, reflecting a general assessment that Assad's chances of survival had improved. Among rebel forces, meanwhile, fragmentation and radicalisation continued and while the provision of foreign-funded weaponry gave rebels temporary advantage in the south, the supplies were not sustained enough to allow for such advances to be consolidated. Fear of regional escalation and missile and chemical weapon threats compelled Jordan, Israel and Turkey to enhance their air- and missile-defence systems.

Missile defence remains a key priority area for other states in the Middle East, particularly in the Gulf, where the perceived threat from Iran's missile arsenal concerns defence planners. Gulf states such as Qatar, Saudi Arabia and the UAE have bought, or are buying, the most advanced Western missile- and air-defence and strike systems, including stand-off air-launched munitions. Middle Eastern states like these have spent significantly on defence in recent years, and there remains substantial, and in some cases growing, Western military interest in the region: the West remains the source of most procurements in the Gulf; the US retains significant forces there and France – and the UK – have reinvigorated their regional defence relations with Gulf states. But though security concerns, attractive procurement deals and spending hikes in that region might lead some to perceive in this European attention something of a rebalance of their own, because of financial constraints their contributions will, in comparison with the US presence, remain modest.

While some Middle Eastern procurements might have generated headlines, like those in Asia, countries in other regions are also developing, and purchasing, more advanced weapons, though the amount and sophistication of these will depend on budgets, defence plans, and procurement and technical ambitions. States in Latin America and Africa, for instance, are buying more advanced equipment, while Russia, despite shortcomings in defence-industrial capacity, has a long history of complex weapons research and development and can produce – and sell – formidable guided weapons like *Onyx/Bastion*, *Kaliber*, and the S-350/S-400, as well as platforms like the Sukhoi T-50 combat aircraft.

Advanced military technologies are proliferating for reasons including lower technical barriers to entry, increasing application of dual-use technology and states' willingness to sell such technologies. These include capabilities previously seen almost exclusively in Western armed forces, such as unmanned systems. The use by the US of UAVs as strike assets in Pakistan and elsewhere has sharpened focus not only on the increasing inventories of unmanned systems, but also on the legal and ethical debates that accompany their use; these debates will increase with developments in autonomous control (see p. 13).

Amid pressured defence budgets and contracting defence ambitions, some states in the West may look to retain a capability edge through the pursuit of even more advanced military technologies: hypersonics is one example; active and passive multi-spectral low-observable research is another. Defence investment in the West, notably in traditionally expensive R&D, may need to be scaled in such a way that this 'edge' can be retained. Some planners might also see such capabilities as facilitating easier engagement options. However, notwithstanding any desire by policymakers to move away from the substantial ground commitments that have been central to recent Western wars, the complexities of modern conflict, explored between pp. 9–12, as well as recent history, ought to temper expectations for the effect advanced technologies can deliver.

In Asia, meanwhile, states continue to improve military capabilities against the backdrop of rising tensions among powers in the region. In real terms, Asian defence spending in 2013 was 11.6% higher than in 2010. The largest absolute spending increases occurred in East Asia, with China, Japan and South Korea accounting for more than half of all the real increases in Asian defence spending in 2013. Procurement has been wide-ranging, and in the larger Asian states (most importantly, China) indigenous defence industry has played an increasing role in providing military equipment. The growing importance of cyber was highlighted by the reported activities of China's PLA, though other Asian – and global – states continued to increase financial and material resources in this sector.

However, translating equipment into real capability – including in the space and cyber spheres – is another matter, and regional states do not yet possess the full range of operational abilities, including individual military skills and training regimes seen, for instance, in many Western armed forces that deployed to Afghanistan. Nonetheless, armed forces in the region are becoming more powerful. China's 2013 White Paper was reflective of Beijing's drive to become a major maritime power, among other military imperatives, and the paper emphasised the need for blue-water naval capabilities in protecting China's sovereignty, sea lines of communication and maritime resources. By late 2013, the Chinese aircraft carrier *Liaoning* had embarked on its third set of sea trials, including more deck landings of the J-15 naval fighter aircraft. Reports suggested that China was in the early stages of constructing in Shanghai a second 'flat-top'. Meanwhile, India launched the hull of its first domestically built carrier, while it was also introducing into service the MiG-29K combat aircraft that will be deployed on India's other new carrier, the *Vikramaditya*. Also, Japan launched its largest naval vessel since the Second World War, the helicopter carrier *Izumo*. But maritime programmes were not the only focus. Japan has bought the F-35, Singapore is likely to do the same and some analysts believe South Korea may also choose this aircraft. India is partnering with Russia in the T-50 programme, while China is continuing to revamp its air force and develop new aircraft types, including those known as the J-20 and J-31.

In this arena, with Asian states developing and procuring advanced capabilities previously dominated by Russia and the West, the contrast is stark. Europe's aerospace industry, for instance, does not have a manned combat-aircraft programme in place after current types finish production. Other sectors of Europe's defence industry are under pressure from falling orders and increased foreign competition. Amid falling budgets, European states might want to become more relevant in Asian defence but, at least individually, it is hard to see how they can do so in the way that the US can, given its established position in the region and as a defence supplier to many Asian countries. While Europe, and NATO, will want to remain globally engaged, doing so in a realistic way will probably be challenging, given reduced finances and preoccupation with Europe's unstable southern neighbourhood – leaving aside the question of whether states would be willing to act. The degree to which robust combat capabilities can be retained by Western states, as well as the degree to which those that are retained could be used, remains in doubt. As a consequence, some may look to develop more civil–military, whole-of-government approaches so that they can project stability without necessarily projecting force. Others might look to leverage potential benefits from coordinated deployments or from defence partnerships with foreign states; these are possible areas of exploitation for NATO. But as Mali showed, crises can develop quickly, in inaccessible areas against adaptable non-state (and perhaps state) adversaries, requiring the rapid use of robust military force, including the possible deployment of ground troops, and in response to policy imperatives that might not always be shared by partners. Asian states will be mindful of the same issues, as well as others such as natural disasters, but they do not face the same financial impediments as their Western counterparts. At the same time, Asia lacks security mechanisms that could defuse regional crises, and is replete with economic, political and resource competition, opposing territorial claims and long-standing flashpoints. The rapid pace of capability development and the potential for accidental conflict and escalation in Asia will continue to be a matter of concern.

Chapter One

Conflict analysis and conflict trends

Learning lessons and building capabilities

As the war in Afghanistan enters it thirteenth year, and two years after the final exit from Iraq, military thinking in the West is motivated by a range of imperatives. Some are rooted in financial stringencies; others derive from a desire to leave behind the most difficult aspects of those military experiences. That desire has also helped resurrect thinking that in future, armed conflict might be waged quickly, cheaply and efficiently, or at least without an enduring military presence.

In the United States, concepts similar to the 1990s prediction of a 'revolution in military affairs', touting advanced military technology as a means to achieve a high degree of certainty in war, have reappeared under new guises such as 'Air-Sea Battle'. Fiscal constraints and the associated need to reduce defence budgets – as well as successful unmanned aerial vehicle (UAV) strikes against terrorist cells in places like Yemen and the frontier provinces of Pakistan – have strengthened the lure of long-range strikes as a cost-effective answer to security threats.

While opinions might be mixed about the relative value of these concepts and nascent doctrines, defence planning must account for and embrace technological change; there is no doubt that rapidly developing technologies are affecting military modernisation by state and non-state actors alike. Of course, the degree to which this is the case varies according to contextual factors – such as geography, defence ambition and financial resources – but armed forces are increasingly dependent on capabilities ranging from networked systems at the high-end, to section-level hand-thrown UAVs, and even commercially available communications at the lower end. But overly high expectations of technology could leave military forces, both Western and non-Western, ill-prepared to deter conflict, respond to security threats as they emerge and cope with countermeasures that potential enemies may employ against them.

For that reason, it is increasingly important that Western defence planners look to the 'wars of 9/11' and other conflicts across the globe – as well as wider geopolitical dynamics – in order to discern whether these display continuities with the past and whether there are enduring trends that should form part of defence-planning processes. Indeed, consideration of continuities, as well as anticipated changes in geopolitical priorities, threats to international security and military capabilities are essential to the development of defence and military capability and strategy. As Sir Michael Howard observed in *The Causes of War and Other Essays* (p. 195), the challenge is to 'steer between the danger of repeating the errors of the past ... and the danger of remaining bound by theories deduced from past history although changes in conditions have rendered these theories obsolete'.

Geopolitical priorities

Since late 2011, US defence policy has emphasised change in its strategic priorities with its much-publicised 'rebalance' to the Asia-Pacific. Trends such as China's continued rise as an economic and military power, tensions over competing territorial claims in Northeast and Southeast Asia, increasing competition for resources, North Korea's development of nuclear weapons – and its frequent provocative behaviour – seem to validate that shift.

However, even as US Secretary of Defense Chuck Hagel toured Asia in September 2013, the emerging evidence of the use of chemical weapons (CW) by the regime of Bashar al-Assad in Syria highlighted the enduring threats to international security from the Middle East. The Syrian civil war is one of several interconnected conflicts that grew out of the Arab Spring and highlight the unpredictability of the region's security environment. While local dynamics vary across those conflicts, terrorists, extremists, and proxy forces have viewed them opportunistically, taking advantage of weak governance, mobilising disenfranchised youth, and exacerbating communal conflicts to advance their agendas. This is particularly true of organisations affiliated with al-Qaeda, as well as militias associated with Iran's Revolutionary Guard Corps.

The civil war in Syria has become a regional conflict contributing to large-scale communal violence in Iraq, generating vast numbers of refugees in neighbouring countries, and expanding the transnational movement of fighters, not only across the Middle East but also between the region and Western countries. While the Obama administration may remain determined to emphasise Asia-Pacific regional security, both the US and Europe are aware that the Middle East region remains a priority for improving security, as well as planning for crisis response.

The utility of prioritising security efforts mainly by region is limited due to the interconnected nature of modern conflicts. Problems in the Middle East and Africa, for example, are linked with those in Central and South Asia; this interconnection highlights the need to view security problems such as transnational terrorism holistically, while remaining sensitive to local realities.

While NATO and other ISAF partners are anxious to reduce their military commitment in Afghanistan, it will certainly continue beyond 2014. Security problems in, and emanating from, the Middle East could slow the 'rebalance' toward the Asia-Pacific, and a security collapse in Afghanistan after 2014 would generate threats far beyond the South and Central Asian region.

The stakes for international security in Afghanistan and Pakistan remain high not only because of the potential local consequences of a collapse in security there, but also because of the power that transnational terrorists could gain from control of territory and access to financial resources associated with the narcotics trade and other illicit activity.

Threats

Connections between local conflicts and transnational terrorists are found in areas as diverse as the Sinai, Mali, Nigeria, Libya, Kenya, Yemen, Somalia and Pakistan. Terrorist organisations continue to demonstrate the ability to communicate, mobilise resources, train, move freely across international boundaries and gain access to weapons – and they are increasingly using technology to do so. Alliances between these groups and transnational criminal organisations add degrees of complexity and risk. Illicit trafficking – including narcotics, weapons, money and people – strengthens criminal and insurgent groups and perpetuates state weakness in critical regions. For example, alliances of convenience between terrorist organisations, other illegal armed groups and criminal networks are prominent features of the conflict in Mali, as well as in piracy in the Indian Ocean and along the West African coast. The various Taliban-affiliated, transnational terrorist groups located in Pakistan use the narcotics trade and other trafficking to fund operations in Afghanistan, Pakistan and internationally. The diffuse and interconnected nature of these conflicts means that armed forces must remain prepared not only to conduct raids and expeditionary operations against terrorist networks, but also to integrate military intelligence and operations much more closely with law-enforcement efforts. Also important is developing partner-nation capacity in these areas, as well as in coping with illegal armed groups and organised crime.

The necessary focus on transnational threats in Western defence strategies has been accompanied by a reduced emphasis on preparedness for conflict between states; among some Western armed forces recently deployed on operations, mission priorities have meant greater focus on skills associated with counter-insurgency, to the detriment, in some cases, of combat skills associated with combined-arms manoeuvre. The withdrawal from the major wars in Iraq and Afghanistan is giving some forces the chance to rebalance back towards full-spectrum training, though in many cases this is limited by the effect of defence cuts. While focus might sharpen on inter-state conflict, Mali demonstrated that Western armed forces will need to remain prepared for operations against non-state actors. The 2013 French White Paper on Defence and National Security demonstrates this dual focus by noting Russia's rapidly expanding military budget as well as 'increasing displays of strength', but also the threat that non-state actors pose to French security interests.

A key risk to international security lies at the intersection between hostile states and terrorist organisations. The most dangerous terrorist and armed groups enjoy safe havens within the boundaries of nation-states and receive direct assistance from governments that use them as arms of their foreign policy. For example, Iran's support is a critical source of strength for Hizbullah in Lebanon and Syria, while the Pakistan military's relationship with Kashmiri groups, the Haqqani Network, Hizb-e-Islami Gulbuddin and the Quetta Shura Taliban, as well as its selective pursuit of transnational terrorist organisations such as Lashkar-e-Taiba, perpetuate threats to its own security as well as transnational threats originating from its territory.

Perhaps the greatest threat from nation-states, which could generate the greatest discontinuity with the contemporary security environment, is the proliferation of nuclear, chemical and biological weapons, including the means to deliver them at long range.

Threats to cyber security are another challenge. The nuclear threat seems particularly acute in North Korea and Iran, although the Syrian regime's use of CW highlights another hazard. Multiple Israeli strikes on Syrian and Iranian weapons transfers to Hizbullah also highlight concern over non-state actors receiving particularly destructive weapons, such as long-range surface-to-surface missiles, from hostile states. Protecting societies from terrorist threats will continue to require military forces capable of action against those organisations, as well as deterring or confronting nations that harbour and support them.

While there has been a focus on the proliferation of long-range precision missiles in potentially hostile states, more attention has arguably been given to countering the anti-access/area-denial (A2AD) problems these systems pose than to the offensive and coercive threats they represent. North Korea and Iran's nuclear programmes, for example, combined with their efforts to develop long-range delivery systems, pose threats across the globe. This contributes to the risk that other regional non-nuclear states might feel compelled to develop similar capabilities to deter that threat.

For Western armed forces, there will continue to be a focus on developing missile defences and long-range strike capabilities to deter, pre-empt or respond to aggression (though the utility of current capabilities is questionable given the difficulty of identifying and destroying targets that are possibly hardened, buried or mobile). However, there could still be a role for mobile land forces; before the international agreement that the Organisation for the Prohibition of Chemical Weapons (OPCW) could start destroying Syria's CW arsenal, there had been much talk of how Western forces could either destroy or seize the stockpile. Options included offensive air and missile operations, but discussion also focused on the potential deployment of substantial ground forces to secure suspected sites and seize CW agents and munitions.

What military capabilities?

Defence establishments in the West need to balance strategic priorities against fiscal constraints imposed on them in the wake of the financial crisis. In many cases, this is leading to reductions not just in military capability, but also in defence ambition. At the same time, it is spurring moves to develop closer defence cooperation among Western states, both bilaterally and multilaterally. While there are practical benefits to such cooperation (as demonstrated by the rapid assistance rendered by partners to France's Mali mission in early 2013), the financial benefits – including from such initiatives as pooling and sharing – are so far less certain (see p. 59).

Another outcome of the Afghanistan and Iraq wars is that Western states have become more cautious about intervention. This certainly influenced the UK Parliament's vote on Syria on 29 August 2013, with Secretary of State for Defence Philip Hammond stating that 'there is a deep well of suspicion about military involvement in the Middle East stemming largely from the experiences of Iraq'. But other states may perceive different lessons from these wars. For instance, Asian states investing heavily in their armed forces as a result of pervasive regional insecurity in the Asia-Pacific and a more positive financial situation, may look at these conflicts more in terms of specific military lessons relating to tactics and desired capabilities rather than broader questions concerning the use of force. This may also be the case for states in the turbulent Middle East and North Africa.

For Western countries, securing vital interests against a range of threats from hostile state and non-state actors will require balanced joint forces capable of combined operations in the cyber, aerospace, maritime, land and space domains. Interoperability across these domains, and between multinational forces, will remain vital. Meanwhile, the proliferation of advanced military technologies, as well as adversary efforts to counter or evade Western military strengths, will ensure that there is no easy or cheap solution to security problems.

Armed forces more broadly will continue to invest in technical-intelligence collection, long-range surveillance, and precision-strike technologies, though the level of technological sophistication of such systems will depend on financial resources and strategic priorities. Potential state and non-state adversaries will employ countermeasures that limit the effect of those technologies, including tactical countermeasures like dispersion, concealment, deception and intermingling with civilian populations. Technical countermeasures will also be employed, many of which have been categorised as A2AD capabilities, such as GPS jammers, air-defence systems, anti-ship missiles, and anti-satellite and cyber-attack capabilities. Many of these capabilities, such as anti-ship missiles and UAVs, were previously only possessed by technologically-advanced states but are already proliferating to non-state actors like Hizbullah. Networked precision-attack capabilities will remain important to armed forces, but it is not clear how those alone would deliver sufficient capability to overcome countermeasures, defeat determined adversaries or achieve political objectives.

Terrorist, insurgent and criminal organisations depend on weak state control of territory, and so Western armed forces are emphasising their ability to build partner capacity and engage in combat advisory missions, approaches that have also been spurred by budget pressures. This approach will demand strong bilateral and multilateral relationships with those partners who would bear the brunt of fighting against determined transnational non-state organisations. It will also demand management of overlapping national interests between states and, within states, of overlapping departmental responsibilities.

While Western military doctrine on security force assistance emphasises the technical aspects of these efforts, it is clear that the political dimensions of each conflict, and the associated will not only to fight but also to assist in security sector and institutional reforms, will remain fundamental determinants of success or failure. This need not be seen as analogous to the so-called 'nation-building' so criticised in the West since 9/11. Assistance could involve efforts to support military and security organisations, but could also form part of wider aid and development packages designed to bolster the resilience of fragile states. Proper consultation with partner states is required, so that diplomats and military officials can better understand what lessons the partner state has learnt from recent and continuing conflicts. They can then determine where security interests overlap, and plan cooperative efforts to strengthen regional security institutions and build durable defence and security capacities.

However, as with the drive for a technological solution to war, reliance on partner-nation forces is not a panacea. Such engagement does matter, but in security terms it is of greatest utility to the donor and recipient when it is long-term and geared towards the whole sector; as it were, from institution to infantryman or policeman. Indeed, French operations in Mali might serve as an example of what is possible through long-term security cooperation: in *Opération Serval*, France's network of regional bases and defence relationships proved vital to the successful prosecution of combat operations. That conflict provides a cautionary lesson too: Malian forces had received military assistance packages from foreign states in the past, but these had often concentrated on short-term tactical training of small sections of the armed forces; it was reported that some of these forces had joined the rebellion in 2012. The EU Training Mission (EUTM) is now processing whole battalion groups and is teaching modules that include military skills, but also human rights law. Key will be the success of 'train the trainer' initiatives and ensuring that indigenous leaders share the interests and priorities of those providing assistance.

Mali should also give pause for thought on another level; though France had prepared plans eventually to support the African-led International Support Mission to Mali (AFISMA) and EUTM military forces in Mali, it had to rapidly expedite and modify these when Bamako was threatened by jihadists, and needed material assistance, including strategic lift and intelligence, surveillance and reconnaissance (ISR). Nations cannot always choose where, when and who they will fight, or at what pace. For Western defence ministries, this means somehow, amid continuing financial constraints, trying to maintain flexible, balanced and scalable armed forces. These services must institutionalise the lessons of recent wars – as well as re-learning conventional skills that may have atrophied – and maintain joint capabilities, including deployable land, sea and air forces capable of working with indigenous forces and in multinational task forces.

Unmanned systems: capabilities develop amid continuing policy questions

In recent years the use of unmanned systems has been given increased attention by armed forces, defence ministries, defence industry, analysts and the media. The most visible capability in this area has been the unmanned aerial vehicle (UAV), attracting particular public interest because of the integration of weapons systems and the use of some platforms as strike assets in locations such as Pakistan. However, unmanned systems are making inroads into all services' inventories, in an expanding number of roles, and will also be increasingly utilised by law-enforcement agencies. The proliferation of smaller systems – particularly, but not exclusively, in the air domain – has reduced costs and barriers to entry (in terms of the technological capacity needed to operate and benefit from such systems), enabling greater use by private companies, individuals and countries possessing limited financial resources.

Legal and ethical debates have been stimulated by the state use of all forms of unmanned systems. However, the proliferation and visibility of UAVs, and their use by armed forces and government agencies, has led to these platforms dominating the debate. A range of issues have been raised; from whether attacks can be justified as self-defence by the prosecuting state, and whether they constitute a proportionate response, to the combatant – or otherwise – status of targeted individuals. These and related concerns now occupy justice and defence ministry legal departments, and animate a wider debate among jurists, defence professionals and the interested public.

Defence policymakers are also forced to consider other questions about the use of force more broadly, including whether use of unmanned systems could alter the political cost of warfare; whether state intervention becomes easier by employing them; and whether there could be greater deployment due to perceived force protection and 'increased persistence' benefits (particularly for surveillance platforms). Meanwhile, system proliferation raises a number of practical issues, such as how to integrate an increasing number of platforms – operated by a variety of state and non-state users – into national and international airspace. UAVs have been used overwhelmingly in intelligence, surveillance and reconnaissance (ISR) roles, with operators enjoying the use of effectively uncontested air space. Calculations on the utility of unmanned systems might be different were they to enter contested airspace and face active air-defence weapons.

Aspiration to field increasingly autonomous systems is sharpening these debates. Developments in the field, across all three force domains, are being driven by the need to counter problems like pressure on bandwidth in the electromagnetic spectrum and the potential for a contested electromagnetic environment. Any move towards autonomous decision-making for lethal force remains contentious. Discussions in some Western states have included reservations about the potential use of fully autonomous unmanned systems, specifically systems carrying weapons; the level of debate in this area among other nations pursuing these capabilities remains unclear. Despite these ethical and legal issues, the perceived requirement to operate unmanned systems against opponents who can attack electronic command links is likely to result in increasing degrees of autonomy in unmanned systems, though autonomous, machine-based decision-making concerning the use of lethal force will remain – to some nations at least – unacceptable.

Unmanned systems, as they are understood at present, are directed or monitored by human operators (though some UAVs incorporate autonomous navigation-by-waypoint technologies) and as such, attacks are still directed – and can be aborted – in the same way as if they were conducted by a manned combat air platform. There are, of course, degrees of autonomous control, and fully autonomous systems have raised particular concern. Some civil society groups are increasingly criticical of the development and integration of unmanned systems – and the potential removal of human decision-making from their operation; the employment of these systems has also been debated in multilateral arenas, such as the UN Human Rights Council. However, even as software-driven artificial intelligence and 'reasoning' systems become more advanced, machine-based decision-making as the basis for lethal action will remain a threshold legislatures and the public will likely be unwilling to cross.

While unmanned systems are most evident in the air domain, they are also being developed for use on land, where vehicles utilising autonomous technology are currently being tested for roles ranging from logistics to perimeter security.

The land domain

Many of the UAVs operated in the last ten years have been purchased by land forces. Large numbers have been used in Afghanistan, but less attention has been paid to a similar proliferation of unmanned ground vehicles (UGVs) for Explosive Ordnance Disposal (EOD) and other uses. Some armies are now remotely operating existing armoured vehicles, and advances in civilian technology are likely to increase the potential for wider and more ambitious use of unmanned systems on land.

Before 9/11, most UAVs were operated by a handful of air forces. Faced with unanticipated challenges in Iraq and Afghanistan, the US Army, Marine Corps (USMC) and special forces rapidly acquired large numbers of unarmed tactical UAVs for use in surveillance and base- and convoy-protection tasks. The US Army alone now has an inventory of five different UAV types. These developments have been mirrored to some extent in most of the other land forces that deployed to Iraq and Afghanistan, with the development of micro UAVs (e.g. the 16-gram Norwegian *Black Hornet* 'nano' UAV) for use at the lowest tactical levels a particular innovation.

Unmanned ground vehicles (UGVs)

Many insurgent and terrorist groups employed Improvised Explosive Devices (IEDs) during the latter half of the twentieth century. In response, armoured protective suits were developed to protect EOD operators, but casualties remained heavy. The British Army developed the 'Wheelbarrow', a remotely-operated UGV, to allow inspection and neutralisation of an IED from a safe distance; this technology was rapidly exported to other states or copied. As bomb-makers and users adapted, UGVs became more sophisticated: control links moved from wire, through radio to wireless technology; sensors improved, as did the capability of manipulator claws.

In the face of the IED threat in Iraq and Afghanistan, US, coalition and ISAF forces purchased many UGVs – in 2004 the US possessed 162; in 2005 the figure was 1,800. Small, remotely operated and soldier-transportable systems were widely used by US EOD teams in Iraq and Afghanistan. As more sophisticated systems entered service, the previous generation UGVs they replaced were often re-used as surveillance platforms by other ground units. None of these systems is known to be armed, but demonstration programmes have shown that fitting UGVs with weapons poses no technical obstacles. Israel is reported to have deployed an armed UGV designed to patrol the perimeters of military air bases.

Remote operation of existing vehicles

Bespoke EOD systems have always been small, but there is parallel development of full-size, remotely operated vehicles (ROVs) to perform the same functions as manned vehicles. For example, both the US and British army are developing ROVs that carry ground-penetrating radar for IED detection. Additionally, the Israeli army has made extensive use of armoured bulldozers to clear obstacles – a high risk activity for the crew – and, as a consequence, add-on kit to allow remote operation has been developed. The US Army has such equipment for its high-mobility excavator. The new British *Terrier* armoured engineering vehicle has a similar role of breaching obstacles under fire. Its 'drive by wire' design allows it to be operated remotely from up to 1,000m away. This is possibly the first armoured vehicle to be designed from the outset for manned or unmanned operation.

Future unmanned ground systems

Afghanistan has seen the use of existing armoured vehicles as 'motherships' for UAVs and UGVs. For example, the British Army's 'Talisman' detachments include a *Mastiff* armoured vehicle that carries both UGVs and micro-UAVs for examining suspicious objects. Using onboard unmanned systems will offer military vehicles new options in terms of visibility, surveillance or improved communications. The US Army is also experimenting with 'manned/unmanned teaming', where information is exchanged between helicopters and UAVs.

The widespread utility of UAVs means the armies who used them in Iraq and Afghanistan will seek to retain the capability after the 2014 ISAF drawdown. The technology required for simple, small UAVs is not sophisticated and they are likely to continue to be difficult for opponents to detect and – if detected – difficult to attack (though this depends on the capability of the opponent being faced at the time).

Provided costs are kept down, small UAVs and UGVs are likely to have enduring utility in land tactical operations.

All current land-based tactical UAVs and UGVs are remotely operated by soldiers. They are not autonomous. This gives forces the advantage of having a 'man in the loop' but relies on data links being uncontested. In operations against an enemy with an electronic warfare capability, such links are vulnerable to interception and jamming. Giving unmanned systems a degree of autonomy would reduce their dependence on command links and allow them to operate at greater range and in hostile electronic environments. Autonomy could also reduce the technical burden on system operators and allow the operation of more than one system at a time.

The US Army and USMC have developed the autonomous mobility appliqué system (AMAS), which allows a vehicle to either follow a manned lead vehicle in a convoy or to navigate autonomously via series of designated waypoints. Oshkosh and the USMC are experimenting with a truck employing this technology. US forces are also examining load-carrying UGVs that can follow dismounted soldiers or navigate autonomously. For logisticians, autonomy could reduce the number of trucks requiring crews, while completely unmanned logistics convoys could be used to send supplies through high-risk areas. This approach could also be applied to combat vehicles.

In the future, autonomy will probably allow the fielding of completely unmanned, full-scale ground vehicles for the full range of land warfare roles, from close-combat armoured vehicles to logistics trucks. Eliminating the crew will reduce size, weight and cost. Armies will also have the option of lower survivability levels for unmanned vehicles, for example reducing armour-plating, which would further reduce weight and cost.

At the same time, civilian technological developments in autonomous systems are likely to spin off into military applications. This could result in military unmanned systems in a wider variety of roles.

Increasing autonomy of the full range of military ground vehicles will carry with it a large number of second-order issues, including safety, moral, ethical and legal problems. But if the considerable potential of remotely-operated and autonomous technology is exploited first in civilian sectors, and these wider issues explored in a non-military context, some of these concerns could be easier for the military to address.

Unmanned maritime systems

The maritime domain poses perhaps the most physically challenging environment for unmanned vehicles. The corrosive effects of salt water, the size of vessel required for operating on the high seas, the difficulty of landing on a moving ship and of operating remotely add complications to building and operating unmanned maritime vehicles. Significant research has taken place into unmanned surface and unmanned underwater vessels (USVs and UUVs respectively). While UAVs used by navies generally fall into the ISR category, USVs and UUVs cover a wider range of roles, from patrol to anti-submarine warfare (ASW) and mine countermeasures (MCM).

Underwater vehicles

Unmanned, underwater vehicles have been used for decades, with the sub-sea oil and gas industries a primary investor, utilising the technology for underwater infrastructure construction, maintenance and repair.

The US armed forces have used unmanned systems for many years, but since the development of autonomous technology interest in UUVs has grown. Previously, all unmanned vehicles were ROVs, requiring a human operator to manipulate the machine, which were in turn tethered by a command wire. Such physical cables restricted range and ensured ROVs were unable to dive below about 1,000 metres. By the 1990s research had led to the development of untethered vehicles, which, given the difficulty of transmitting radio waves through water, operated autonomously rather than by direct human command. This has allowed the development of autonomous underwater vehicles (AUVs) that can operate at far greater depths and ranges, and without constant monitoring.

Such technology has now proliferated and is in use among most advanced navies in Europe, North America and Oceania. MCM and ASW are key roles; both of these require sustained and consistent sonar activity to gauge the movement or presence of underwater objects. Potential roles include harbour security, search and salvage, and hydrographic missions, all of which rely on significant or persistent data-gathering.

For the foreseeable future, though, the majority of UUVs are likely to be engaged in MCM tasks. Usually undertaken by larger, manned vessels, the advent of AUVs is providing a more cost-effective option for navies to fulfil the information-gathering and EOD aspects of mine warfare. UUV technology also has the ancillary benefit of being relatively immune to storms and poor weather.

With the increasingly multi-role nature of modern warships, and development of modular mission packages, relatively lightweight UUVs could, in combination with USVs and other technology, be imported into a modular warship design. The US Navy's Littoral Combat Ship is designed for just such a possibility, with Lockheed Martin developing the semi-submersible Remote Multi-Mission Vehicle as part of an MCM suite. Companies are also developing containerised solutions for MCM capabilities, suggesting a desire by suppliers to develop this market among emerging economies.

Problems with the system

There are certain drawbacks to unmanned maritime technology. Currently, the launch and recovery of UUVs is cumbersome, involving davits and/or personnel in rigid inflatable vessels hooking the vehicle and dragging it in from the water. However there are moves to improve this situation, such as enabling helicopter or maritime aircraft launch. More promisingly, automated launch and recovery systems have been trialled, which would allow for submerged recovery of the vessels, using a transponder and system that guides the UUV back to the mothership.

For AUVs in particular, loss is a further possibility. Given minimal human input once the programmed mission starts, it remains possible for the vehicle to simply run out of power, crash or for the software to fail. The experience of the Royal Netherlands Navy in Libya here is salutary: while using REMUS 100 vehicles to chart the waters around Misrata during *Operation Unified Protector* in 2011, one of the vehicles was lost and never found. (UUVs were used by other navies during the campaign, with a Royal Navy *SeaFox* I ROV destroying – with a *SeaFox* C mine disposal vehicle – one of three mines laid by the Gadhafi regime.)

Unmanned surface vehicles

To some extent, renewed interest in USVs is partially related to the growing UUV market. The creation of MCM mission packages, involving UUVs, USVs and related technology, makes the development of reliable surface vessels for the launch, recovery and tracking of underwater vessels attractive. This would allow a larger mothership to launch the entire package and have an entirely unmanned 'system of systems' undertake the mission. France's DCNS, for example, has launched the manned/unmanned catamaran *Sterenn Du*, which operates towed sonar and deploys unmanned vehicles. However, USVs have also been deployed in more kinetic roles, including harbour patrol. Israel has been a leading proponent, with its *Protector* model deployed in-country and sold to Singapore and Mexico. Although some USVs can be operated autonomously, they are more likely to be operated remotely when patrolling. However, the ability of a single user to operate more than one vessel increases their efficiency.

Beyond the West

The majority of UUV and USV research has occurred in Western navies. However, other countries are also interested in the technology. China's university sector has sought to develop a range of UUVs, from the first-generation *Hairen* 1 ROV, to the *Tansuozhe* ROV and the CR-001 AUV (based on the Russian MT-88 and developed in conjunction with Russian researchers). It is not entirely clear how many of these vehicles have made it into Chinese operations, but it is likely that the People's Liberation Army Navy (PLAN) will have utilised some for ship and harbour inspection and maintenance. The PLAN is also a current operator of the XG-2 USV, which has been utilised for targeting but, analysts believe, can also be equipped with weapons or ISR equipment. Elsewhere, countries such as South Africa, Singapore, India and South Korea have all developed separate UUVs or USVs, indicating broader interest in the technology, given its widening applications. As such, the number and range of unmanned maritime systems deployed globally in MCM, ASW, patrol and other roles is set to grow.

Military aerospace

The US Navy (USN) successfully conducted the first landing and take-off of the Northrop Grumman X-47B Unmanned Combat Air-System Demonstrator (UCAS-D) from the aircraft carrier USS *George H.W. Bush* in May 2013. This marked the latest example in a lengthening list of unmanned technology firsts. But transforming technological achievement into operational utility remains a considerable challenge at the high end of unmanned air systems.

Alongside the X-47B, other notable Unmanned Combat Air Vehicle (UCAV) projects in 2013 included the first flights of the European *Neuron* (with Dassault as prime contractor) and British *Taranis* (led by BAE Systems) programme demonstrators. *Neuron* was first flown at the end of 2012, with *Taranis* following in the third quarter of 2013. China, meanwhile, was by mid-2013 carrying out taxi trials of the Shenyang/ Hongdu *Lijian* UCAV test-bed; while at the end of May, Russia awarded a research and development (R&D) contract to MiG for a follow-on programme to its *Skat* design.

Beyond the X-47B, the USN in June 2013 issued a request for proposals for its Unmanned Carrier-Launched Airborne Surveillance and Strike system (UCLASS) to Boeing, General Atomics, Lockheed Martin and Northrop Grumman. Initial Operational Capability for UCLASS is scheduled for around 2020, with the system designed to provide low-observable ISR and strike capabilities.

The US Air Force (USAF) was a partner with the USN in the Joint Unmanned Combat Air System, a predecessor to UCAS-D, but has since remained relatively quiet about UCAV plans. This has prompted speculation about classified development programmes, although the USAF has not always been an early adopter of emerging technology; for instance, the USN led the development and fielding of *Tomahawk* cruise missiles.

Technology uptake

Irrespective of efforts by the USN, USAF and non-US forces, and the prevalence of unarmed UAVs in the battlefield, the introduction of UCAVs into air force inventories has not occurred at the pace previously envisaged by advocates of these systems.

At the beginning of the century, US legislators said it should be a goal that 'By 2010, one-third of the aircraft in the operational deep strike force fleet are unmanned'. At that point the 2010 United States' Deep Strike Force was anticipated to include the Lockheed Martin F-117, the Northrop Grumman B-2, and an as-yet-unknown UCAV. The intent, expressed in the FY2001 National Defense Authorization Act, was to be able to field a 'minimum of 30 unmanned advanced capability combat aircraft that are capable of penetrating fully-operational enemy air defense systems'. While the US has led the field in developing and operating low-observable unarmed unmanned systems in the classified world (e.g. the Lockheed Martin RQ-170 ISR system), numerous challenges, pressures and demands have conspired to slow the pace of the broader introduction of the UCAV into air force inventories.

Impetus for the rapid development and operational use of a range of unmanned systems in the ISR role, as well as the armed UAV in the shape of the MQ-1B *Predator* and MQ-9 *Reaper*, was provided by 9/11 and the ensuing decade of war. The immediate needs of the US armed forces trumped long-term R&D. Use of armed UAVs in Iraq and Afghanistan showed the utility of such systems in uncontested airspace.

Despite their obvious utility, the limitations and downsides of these platforms have also become apparent: they require significant personnel numbers for operation, support and information exploitation; they have suffered comparatively high loss rates through accidents and technical malfunction; and operators have to tackle the demands of deployment in mixed airspace, alongside crewed platforms.

UAVs can also be expensive. Cost was a reason cited by the USAF in its 2012 decision to axe its *Global Hawk* Block 30 ISR UAV purchase. In 2013 Germany abandoned its acquisition of the RQ-4E *Euro Hawk* signals-intelligence version of the *Global Hawk*, citing concerns over the costs of enabling the vehicle to be flown in controlled airspace.

A range of projects are underway to develop the capability for UAVs to be flown in controlled airspace, including 'sense and avoid' technology. This has implications for civilian aerospace, which could ultimately see such technology deployed by commercial entities.

Contested environments

In the wake of operations in Afghanistan, there is consensus among military-aerospace professionals that the need to be able to operate in more demanding threat environments will remain, if not grow.

The physical threat to UAVs in Afghanistan was limited to a small number of man-portable surface-to-air missiles (SAMs) and small-arms fire. For the air component of the campaign, considerable effort went into force protection, including minimising the threat from shoulder-launched SAMs.

Russia and China continue to develop families of short-, medium- and long-range SAM systems, with unmanned air systems part of the target set. Russia showed in June 2013 one of the latest additions to the so-called double-digit (SA-20+) SAM series, the Almaz-Antey *Vityaz* – a medium-range system that uses the Fakel 9M96 missile family intended to succeed early versions of the S-300 (SA-10 *Grumble*). State testing of the system was expected to start by the end of 2013.

The ability to operate and loiter undetected in contested airspace, faced with a capable integrated air-defence system, remains a driver for the development of very-low-observable strike and ISR unmanned platforms. Signature control in the radio frequency (RF) and infra-red spectra remain forcing factors in specifying the performance requirements of UCAV technology, with active as well as passive low-observable techniques increasingly considered. UCAVs also present particular demands with regard to propulsion, including size and power off-take requirements. As likely platforms for laser or RF-directed energy weapons, the air vehicle requires an engine capable of supporting the power demands of such systems.

Western forces have had comparatively free reign across the electromagnetic spectrum since the end of the Cold War and the collapse of the Soviet Union, but this will likely be threatened in the future. GPS has become a core element of UAV navigation and weapon guidance, as have line-of-sight and satellite data links for communications. It should not be a surprise that other military powers try to counter this advantage – to degrade or deny the ability to exploit the electromagnetic spectrum for military ends. For example, Russia and China have been developing GPS-jammer technology, while anti-satellite weaponry could pose a threat to navigation satellite constellations.

The potential vulnerability of satellite navigation systems, as well as threats to data links, has implications for UCAV development. There will be greater emphasis on navigation and targeting systems that are not GPS-dependent, while the potential for data-link interruption by enemy forces will likely see further emphasis on the ability of a UCAV to operate autonomously during certain elements of a mission.

The X-47B aircraft-carrier tests show progress being made in non-lethal elements of UCAV operation. Increasing levels of autonomy for the 'mundane' part of a mission would also reduce the number of dedicated personnel, controlling costs. As well as take-off, landing and transiting to the mission area, autonomous mission elements could include searching for possible targets and the continuation of a planned flight irrespective of data-link loss. Authority to engage and weapon-release, however, would be dependent on human operation.

For the foreseeable future, at least in Western nations, autonomy is unlikely to extend to independently prosecuting a mission through target location, identification and weapon-release without human approval. While software-driven artificial intelligence and 'reasoning' systems continue to develop, the legislature and the public could be less willing to approve machine-based decision-making as the basis for lethal action. As it is, UAV strikes in Pakistan's Federally Administered Tribal Areas are controversial, even though there is a person in the decision-making loop. Also controversial is the use of armed UAVs under the auspices of an intelligence agency rather than a military organisation. Meanwhile, concerns over autonomy have been heightened by these missions.

There is little doubt that the place of UAVs in the future inventories of the most capable air forces is assured. However, the extent to which such systems eventually replace, rather than complement, inhabited combat aircraft remains undecided.

Measuring cyber capability: emerging indicators

Coercive cyber capabilities are becoming a new instrument of state power, as countries seek to strengthen national security and exercise political influence. Military capabilities are being upgraded to monitor the constantly changing cyber domain and to launch, and to defend against, cyber attacks. Specific military enhancements to traditional capabilities include technically capable recruits, high-end intelligence and surveillance technologies, aggressive defence innovation, sophisticated doctrines and dynamic strategies for cyber operations. (For more on the challenges of defining cyber in a military context see 'Cyberspace: assessing the military dimension', *The Military Balance 2011*, pp. 27–32; see also *Cyberspace and the State: Toward a Strategy for Cyber-Power*, IISS Adelphi 424, 2011.)

While more nations are each year developing the capability to operate in the cyber realm – albeit at varying levels of sophistication – measuring national capabilities remains problematic. One reason for this is information classification. Despite heightened public interest in the subject and occasional evidence of evolving cyber-defensive (and especially cyber-offensive) capabilities, countries prefer to be secretive about their military cyber capabilities. Another challenge in measuring national cyber capabilities relates to the ubiquity and dual-use nature of computing and cyber tools, the stealth and immediacy of cyber operations and uncertainty over the responsibilities of civilian and military organisations.

Colin Gray, a professor of international relations at the University of Reading, demonstrates the difficulty in assessing the implications of cyber as a novel area of defence. He argues that the challenge posed by cyber is in fact familiar, citing the way strategists have come to terms with air power, nuclear weapons and ballistic missiles within the last 100 years. But he also points out that while cyber can, in theory, be analogous to the land/sea/air/space domains, it is as different from these domains as they are from each other: 'Indeed, because of the non-physicality of cyber power (though not the infrastructure and its human operators), this fifth domain is uniquely different technically and tactically.' (Colin S. Gray, *Making Sense of Cyber Power: Why the Sky is Not Falling*, Executive Summary; US Army War College Strategic Studies Institute, 2013.) This also reflects the strategic uncertainty that still surrounds this field. Few states have published cyber strategies, and fewer still have made public detail about their military cyber capabilities. Debates continue over what exactly cyber strategy could be, and the line between military versus civilian responsibilities is far from clear.

Understanding military cyber capabilities requires analysis of states' strategic, technological and political intentions. It also involves understanding how states themselves view the cyber domain. Nations – and also different organisations and departments within states – may have varying conceptions of the term 'cyber'. These range from information technologies that encompass some aspects of cyber, including data and the information within it, to a more strict doctrinal notion of cyber as a mainstream, cross-domain layer of physical information infrastructure, computers and networks. While some states have seen the need to create new organisations dedicated to cyber, others might not yet see cyber as requiring new structures or doctrines, and may place it within existing military disciplines, such as IW (information warfare) and EW (electronic warfare) (see 'Developing doctrines' below).

National cyber capabilities

Effective military cyber capability requires a flourishing civil and commercial information technology (IT) sector. A history of excellence in engineering education and a solid cyber-security research and development (R&D) base, for instance, could indicate the availability of domestic talent, while a high degree of Internet penetration and digital-media freedom suggests the potential for innovation and creativity. The level of advanced technology available, and legislative and political developments in the area also reflect countries' interest in the cyber domain. For example, legislative attention to cyber-security issues may indicate the maturity of social and political engagement in the subject, and an appreciation of technological power. Security alliances can also play a role: NATO is developing minimum requirements for national networks vital for NATO tasks, as well as helping states reduce critical infrastructure vulnerabilities.

The ability to operate in cyberspace requires skills and experience sometimes beyond the traditional competencies of armed forces' personnel; these include advanced computer analysis and programming abilities and forensic IT skills. As they learn to operate in the cyber domain, armed forces have also adopted relevant skills in education, training and management that have already developed in the private sector and academia. Indeed, military effectiveness in cyberspace is often predicated on non-military capabilities such as civilian, private sector R&D, and national intelligence capacities. Therefore, any discussion of cyber capabilities needs to include national-defence ambitions, current and anticipated threats and conflicts, a state's resources and the capacity of its armed forces to adapt to new challenges.

Assessing cyber warfare capabilities

Analysis of available national cyber doctrines seems to indicate that the primary requirement of cyber-warfare capability is the ability to manoeuvre in cyberspace, and to deny an adversary freedom of action within and through cyberspace. Armed forces aim to degrade, neutralise or destroy adversary combat capability while protecting their own abilities. Offensive cyber capabilities are aimed at influencing or disabling the actions of an opponent. Experts at the NATO Cooperative Cyber Defence Centre of Excellence conclude that military cyber activities encompass four different tasks: protecting a state's own defensive networks; enabling Network Centric Warfare (NCW) capabilities; battlefield or tactical cyber warfare; and strategic cyber warfare.

Resource allocation, such as financial and organisational investments devoted by states to cyber capabilities, are perhaps the clearest indicator of state cyber-warfare activity. US cyber-security spending for FY2014 is slated to jump to US$4.7bn, up 20% from US$3.9bn in FY2013, despite Pentagon plans to cut overall spending. Much of that additional cash is going into the development of offensive cyber capabilities, usually referred to as 'computer network attacks'. The UK government announced, in its Cyber Security Strategy of November 2011, a £650m (US$1.04bn) investment in a national cyber-security programme (and perhaps an additional £150m in cyber-security measures) over four years. Though Western defence budgets may be shrinking, this does not necessarily mean investment in all areas is being reduced: defence-related cyber investment is growing. However, it should be noted that state responses to perceived threats may include the actions of civil as well as military agencies, which may be reflected in the budgetary burden being shared between military and non-military cyber organisations.

Many states have announced the formation of cyber units in their armed forces, or the re-tasking of existing technical defence entities, while others are assessed by analysts as possessing such units, despite a lack of official confirmation. Other indicators of cyber activity are the recruitment of cyber-security experts; adaptating or upgrading cyber defences and military cyber-security strategies and doctrines. In 2013, the UN Institute for Disarmament Research listed more than 40 countries that possess military cyber organisations, doctrines, or policies, and almost 70 with non-military cyber policies and cyber-security bodies.

In 2013, US Cyber Command had an authorised strength of 917 active-duty military and civilian personnel, through the co-location of Cyber Command with the National Security Agency. Overall, US military cyber personnel number more than 11,000 across the armed services. Additional capability information can be gathered by assessing cyber and security decision-making, cyber unit locations and functions, as well as the relative ease with which such bodies can cooperate with the private sector, computer emergency response teams and other countries. Analysts have also applied novel ways of identifying the existence of cyber units: after identifying and studying a building and accompanying amenities in Shanghai, US cyber-security company Mandiant estimated that China's Computer Network Operations Unit 61398 'is staffed by hundreds, if not thousands of people', contending that this group occupies a high-level position in the People's Liberation Army hierarchy. Of course, unit and personnel numbers can be an indicator of a state's focus on cyberspace, but should not necessarily be taken as evidence of capability.

In cyber power and cyber capability, the US, the UK, China, Russia and France are often perceived as the 'top tier'. This reflects their global influence, their cyber ambitions and also traditional perceptions of their military power and SIGINT capabilities. Meanwhile, less developed states – though they may well understand the military potential of cyberspace – could effectively be deprived of the means to exert control over the cyber domain by a lack of technological capacity and cutting-edge innovation; developing effective cyber capacity is difficult without a well-established record of IT innovation, manufacturing and education, or established military and security traditions. Nonetheless, countries with poorly developed technology infrastructure can begin to grow capacity by formulating niche capabilities and establishing strategic alliances; for such countries' strategic requirements, a less well-developed technology infrastructure may suffice.

Non-state actors, such as insurgents, terrorists and paramilitary forces, can also develop cyber capacity for their own purposes, or they can conduct cyber activity on behalf of state sponsors. Recent examples include the Syrian Electronic Army, a pro-Assad group active on the Internet and social media. Although such groups often operate propaganda campaigns, uploading videos or hacking websites for instance, they can also be used to prosecute offensive cyber actions, such as DDOS (Distributed Denial-of-Service) attacks, designed to make a network unavailable to its users. Measuring their capability, at least in the same way that analysts may try to do for national forces, is problematic due to their independent nature and, as a result, their capability is often measured by observed action.

Defensive capability

Information assurance, or information protection, is central to cyber defence, and vital for organisations that use IT systems. Information-assurance practices and operational procedures need to be updated regularly to cope with changing threat environments. A decline in the number of successful intrusions by aggressors should demonstrate the merit of continued investment in defensive capabilities, as well as improvements to security procedures and network security architecture.

It is also important to fully understand the threat environment. Familiarity with an adversary's hardware and software can be obtained by conventional research or by information gathered by intelligence agencies, but a more effective enabler for activities such as cyber exploitation can be obtained through the export of ICT hardware and software; known vulnerabilities in these can be covertly exploited for intelligence collection or sabotage. By enabling or encouraging the use, by foreign states, of domestically manufactured computer systems, states can gain a strategic advantage in conflict: if they have a robust domestic ICT production capacity, they can gain a defence advantage over states that purchase or imitate capabilities. The picture becomes complicated, however, if hardware includes components sourced from overseas, because the assembling company may have little control over security procedures regarding the manufacture of components (in some cases, hardware components have even been shown to be recycled). Certain cyber attacks judged to have originated in China, such as those reported by Mandiant, have provided ready examples of how inadequate defences can enable a country, with the right amount of ambition and human resources, to become a military cyber power through proficiency in cyber espionage, among other factors.

Offensive cyber capability

Planning and executing offensive cyber activity requires patience, strategic thinking and planning, and sometimes luck: Russia was able to degrade Georgian tactical communications during the short war in August 2008, thanks to the Georgian armed forces' previous decision to acquire Russian radio software. Some cyber attacks may have a limited life cycle: an average 'zero-day' exploit (whereby an attack uses unanticipated system vulnerability) has a life-span of about a year. *Operation Olympic Games*, targeting nuclear enrichment centrifuges in Iran (apparently with the Stuxnet virus), reportedly employed four zero-day exploits against a hard-to-reach target. It involved a considerable amount of vision and planning, as well as a high level of confidence in the means used to integrate the exploit in the software, and in the modest level of Iran's cyber defence and security capacities.

Developing and maintaining cyber-attack capability requires national cyber forces to conduct continuous assessment of potential targets. These forces also have to stay abreast of technological developments, which can affect technical and tactical capabilities such as data mining, email hacking and DDOS attacks. They also have to maintain the ability to store and process large amounts of data and function covertly during operations. A key part of the targeting cycle is assessment, so that any necessary follow-up actions can be correctly focused. In the cyber realm, conducting such 'battle damage assessment' is perhaps more problematic than in conventional military operations where, for instance, destroyed targets can be observed. In the cyber field, damage can be difficult to observe unless information flows back from an exploited system or a state publicises an incident. Conversely, the targeted state might wish to remain quiet about any breach of its systems, so that it can eliminate the vulnerability without advertising it more widely to other potential adversaries, or exploit the situation through misinformation. More advanced capabilities include the ability to effectively conceal cyber operations; leveraging technical, tactical, operational and strategic talent; and learning how to combine cyber activities with other methods of warfare. Meanwhile, problems of cyber-attack attribution – identifying the source of attacks – persist, and although these have been called a 'declining issue' by some leading cyber powers, the ability to fuse intelligence and correlate data and incidents still presents formidable problems for less-capable states.

Developing doctrines

The British Army's *Army Doctrine Primer*, quoting the late Professor Richard Holmes, describes doctrine as 'an approved set of principles and methods, intended to provide large military organisations with a common outlook and a uniform basis for action'. Military cyber organisations require doctrine, not least because activity in this area often has to take into account the interests and activities of other government departments. The US has almost four decades of doctrine development in technical military matters, while many countries are just beginning to develop theirs. In many European states, cyber doctrine has not superseded electronic warfare (EW) or computer network operations (CNO), with many relevant units and doctrines still in use. The observable trend, however, is for states to incorporate all these capabilities, together with information warfare, in an integrated set of doctrines and systems, as indicated by ongoing doctrinal reforms in the US and China. Synchronising defensive actions, offensive actions and intelligence is an essential prerequisite of coordinated, cross-service, inter-agency and coalition cyber operations.

More broadly, education, training and exercises need to become an integral part of cyber capability for nations to operate in this domain. Cyber curricula are required at all levels of professional military education, combined with the availability of national talent drawn from top technology and engineering schools. The availability of continuing career and skills training, cyber exercises and relevant R&D at national levels also serve as indicators of military cyber potential. But fundamentally, developing defensive and offensive cyber capabilities at the state level requires the careful application of resources, and careful management of, potentially, competing imperatives and doctrines among various armed services. Therefore, joint military doctrine plays an important role in translating strategic interests into operational capabilities. Meanwhile, nations require the capacity to constantly monitor cyberspace in order to understand the threat environment. This gives armed forces situational awareness, but also informs intelligence agencies – and other branches of government that are involved with providing relevant cyber technologies – of the capacity of actual or potential adversaries. Alliances and bilateral arrangements can allow states to benefit from more advanced allied capabilities but, nonetheless, trust remains scarce in this area and, even among very close allies, cyber remains a sensitive issue, with few states willing to share what they know, and what they can do.

Table 1 **Possible Indicators of Cyber Capability**

Political	Political system
	Social stability
	National ambitions
	International standing
	Relationship of hackers with state sponsors and political aims
	Regulatory action
	Parliamentary discussions National security documentation National technical strategies
Military	Military cyber strategy and doctrine
	Organisational structure/units
	Education, training, exercises
	Known/suspected operations
	Intelligence and fusion
	Materiel, logistics, infrastructure
Economic	Defence budget/service budgets
	Programme budgets
	GDP
	Raw materials/indigenous production
	Export/import restrictions
	Acquisitions, procurements
	Patents
	R&D funding
	High-tech public companies
	Products with high R&D loads
	Manufacturing capability
Social	Maturity of information society
	Top technical universities
	Post-graduate students
	Graduation in science, engineering, manufacturing and construction
	Known hackers
	R&D intensity
	Researcher concentration
Information/ Technology	Domain control
	High-tech density
	Know-how, experience
	Innovation
	State-of-the-art technology
	Retail electronics
	Advanced technologies (unmanned systems, robotics)
Infrastructure	Military networks
	SIGINT + Platforms
	Communications
	High-speed access
	Advanced services
	Numbers of ISPs
	Space exploration capabilities
	Industrial base
Other	Manufacturers' advertisements
	Strategic purchases and sales
	Unusual policy/security attention

Chapter Two

Comparative defence statistics

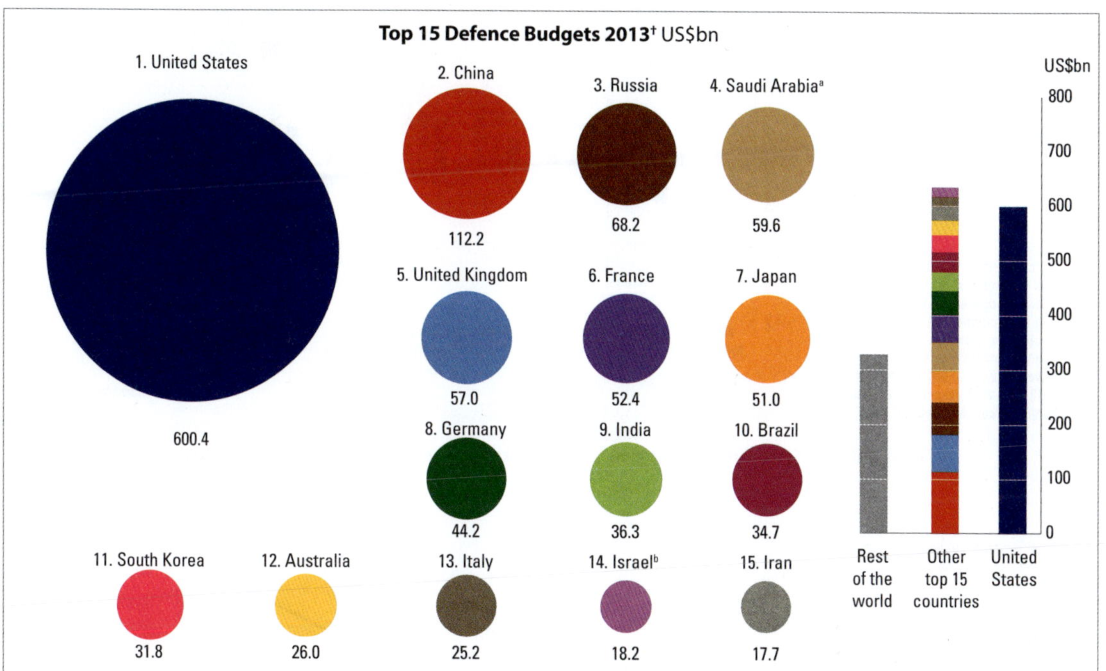

[a] Estimated spending; [b] Includes US Foreign Military Assistance

Note: US dollar totals are calculated using average market exchange-rates for 2013, derived using IMF data. The relative position of countries will vary not only as a result of actual adjustments in defence spending levels, but also due to exchange-rate fluctuations between domestic currencies and the US dollar. The use of average exchange rates reduces these fluctuations, but the effects of such movements can be significant in a small number of cases.

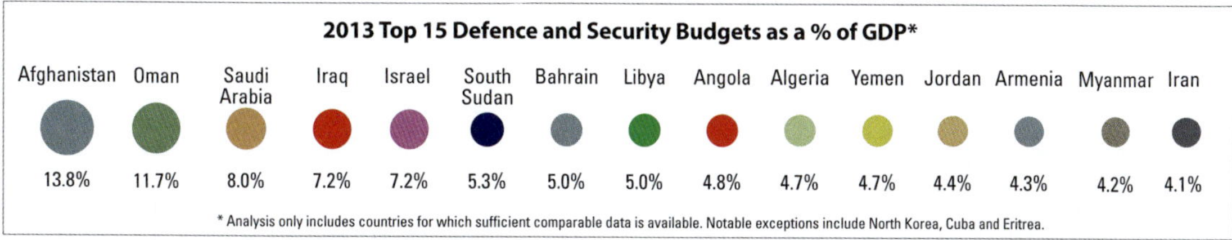

* Analysis only includes countries for which sufficient comparable data is available. Notable exceptions include North Korea, Cuba and Eritrea.

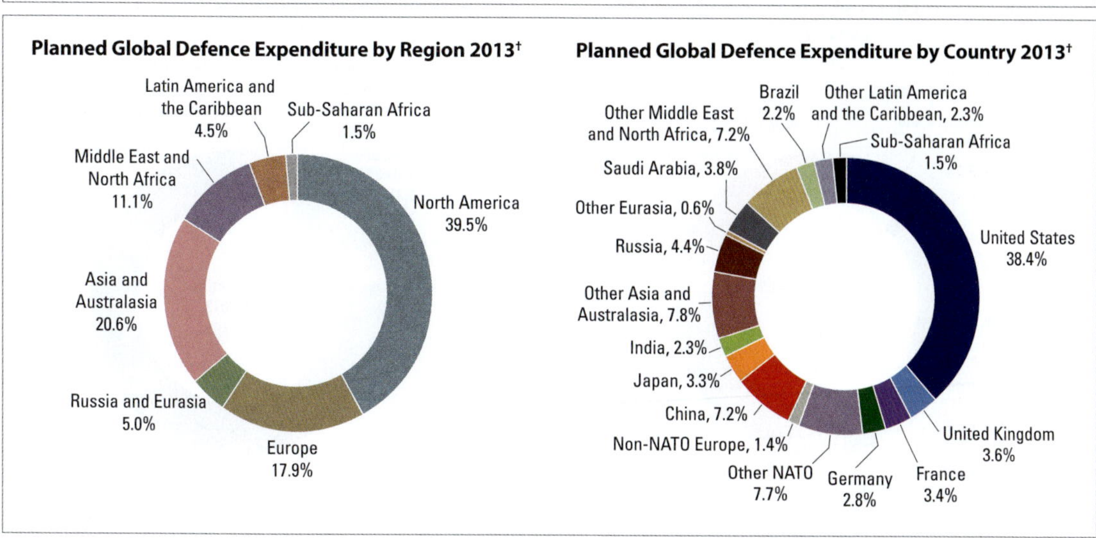

† At current prices and exchange rates.

Real Global Defence Spending Changes by Region 2011–13

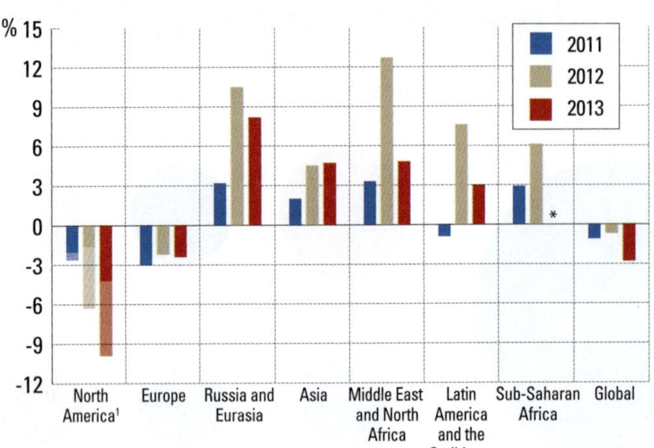

[1]Total figures for North America include real reductions in US spending on overseas operations in Afghanistan. If this is excluded, the real percentage decline in North American defence spending over the three years would be lower, at -2.0%, -1.6% and -4.2% in 2011, 2012 and 2013 respectively (indicated by the darker shaded area).

*Insufficient data

Real Defence Spending Changes in Selected States Since the 2008 Financial Crisis[1]

This graphic depicts the real change in defence spending for selected states between 2008 and 2013, relative to their spending levels in 2008. In the five years following the 2008 financial crisis, real defence spending has fallen in many advanced economies, particularly in Europe. By contrast, real spending has risen in many non-Western states, with particularly large increases seen in China and Russia.

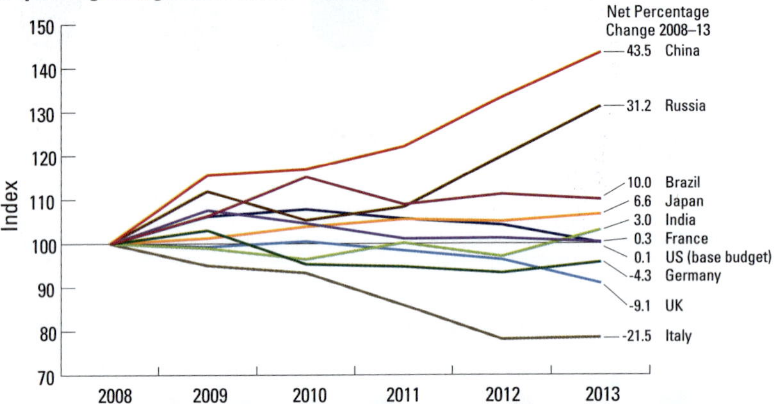

[1]For each country, defence spending levels (in local currency) were first adjusted for inflation before being rebased to a 100 index, with 2008 defence spending levels set at 100.

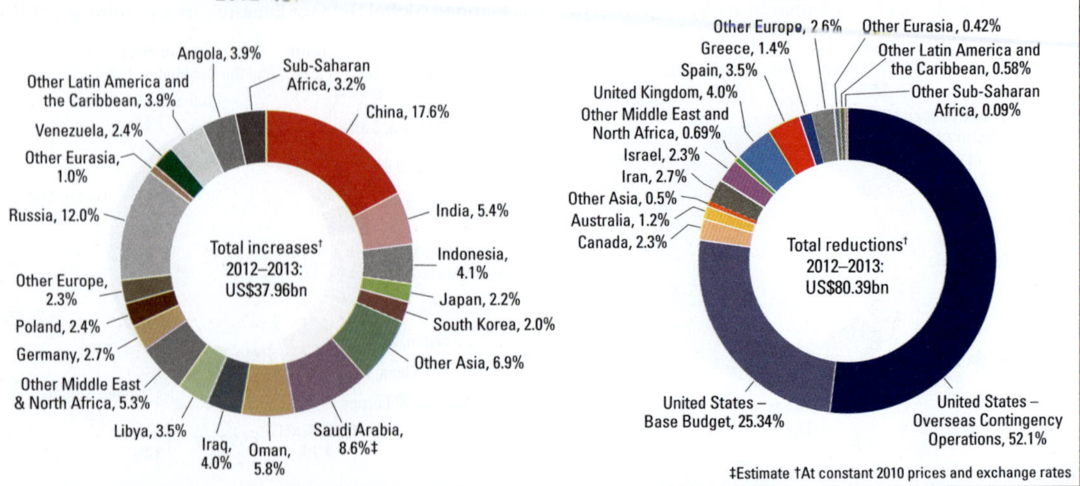

‡Estimate †At constant 2010 prices and exchange rates

Infantry and soldier modernisation

Before 9/11 the US, British and other armies had ambitious plans for major integrated soldier modernisation programmes that would not only improve protection, firepower and night-fighting capability, but which would also extend the benefits of networked wearable computers to the infantryman, especially improved situational awareness and faster command-and-control. The priority both the UK and US afforded to other capabilities for Iraq and Afghanistan means that there are now two approaches to this: incremental modernisation or integrated soldier systems.

Incremental Modernisation. The graphic below shows the major upgrades to US Army and Marine Corps infantry between 2003 and 2013. Neither service nor the UK have fielded soldier computers, navigation aids or heads-up displays. This may be a consequence of the priority both nations gave to improving protection and firepower of troops on operations. Incremental enhancements fielded by US forces have improved the survivability of infantry and their night-fighting capability. But they are yet to produce decisive advantage over the Afghan Taliban at squad and platoon level, because the high threat of IEDs constrains manoeuvre and the weight of equipment quickly leads to exhaustion.

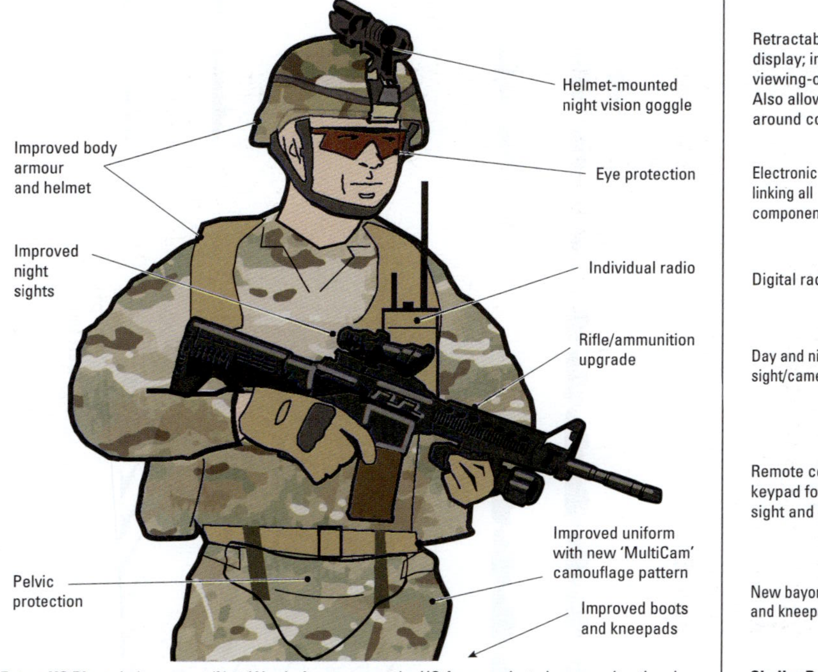

Future US Plans. In its current 'Nett Warrior' programme the US Army seeks to improve situational awareness of individual infantrymen by equipping them with individual digital radios linked to commercial smartphones, used as soldier computers running military applications. US Special Operations Command's Tactical Assault Light Operator Suit (TALOS) programme seeks to develop an integrated combat suit with 'embedded technology' including improved ballistic and flame protection, as well as generating electrical power from the soldier's movement.

Integrated Soldier System. Some countries are modernising their infantry by fielding purpose-built integrated soldier systems, such as the French FELIN, shown below in blue. It entered service in 2010 and four infantry battalion sets are being fielded each year at a reported cost of €36,000 per soldier. Based on extensive trials and use of FELIN in Afghanistan, the French assess that it greatly increases effectiveness, but also results in increased fatigue. This may partially be a result of increased cognitive demands placed on the soldier as well as the weight of body armour and batteries.

Retractable multifunction display; includes remote-viewing-of-sight images. Also allows firing around corners

Bone-vibrator headband (replaces conventional microphone and earphones)

Electronic vest linking all components

Soldier computer and messaging device

New high-performance-fabric uniform

Digital radio and GPS

New lighter body armour containing batteries

Day and night sight/camera

Remote control keypad for radio, sight and camera

Ruggedised tactical tablet computer issued to key commanders

New bayonet and kneepads

Similar Programmes. Israel is fielding a similar system ('Dominator') in a similar timescale, with two divisions already equipped. The German IDZ-2 Gladius and Norwegian NORMANS systems are in advanced development. Countries with similar requirements include Denmark, Finland, India, Italy, Jordan, Russia, South Korea, Spain, Sweden, Switzerland and Turkey.

Key defence statistics

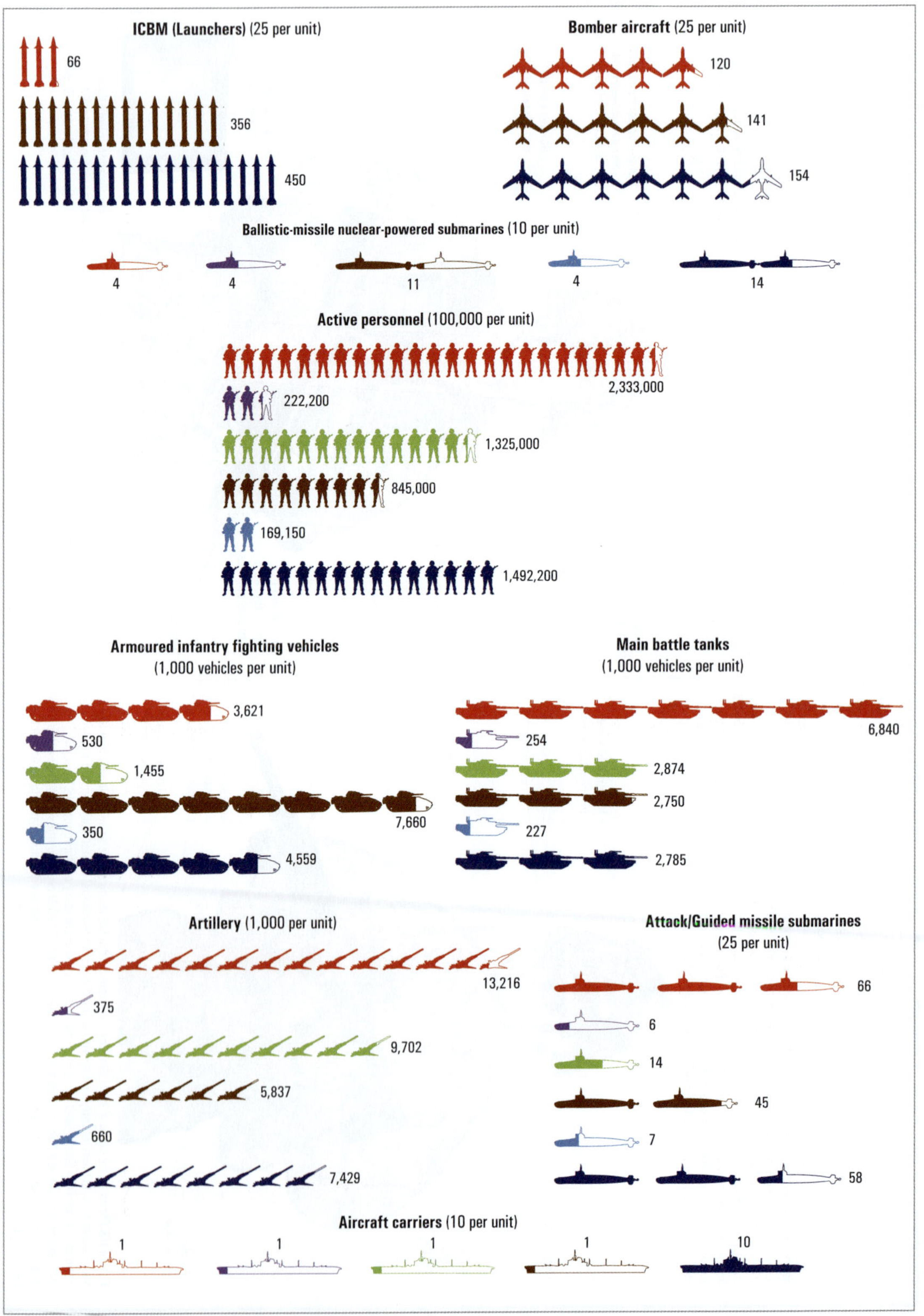

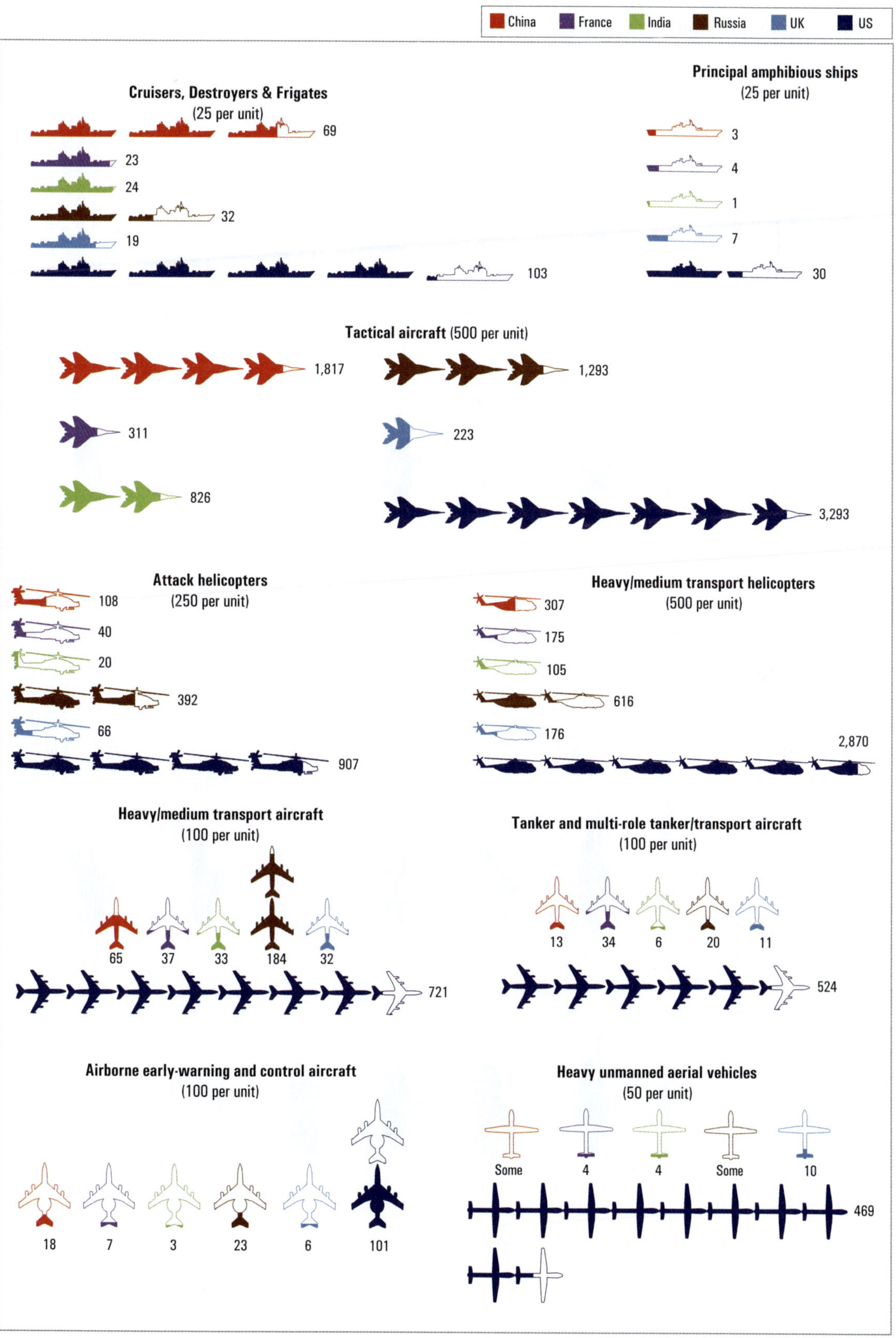
China
France
India
Russia
UK
US
Cruisers, Destroyers & Frigates
(25 per unit)
69
23
24
32
19
103
Principal amphibious ships
(25 per unit)
3
4
1
7
30
Tactical aircraft (500 per unit)
1,817
1,293
311
223
826
3,293
Attack helicopters
(250 per unit)
108
40
20
392
66
907
Heavy/medium transport helicopters
(500 per unit)
307
175
105
616
176
2,870
Heavy/medium transport aircraft
(100 per unit)
65
37
33
184
32
721
Tanker and multi-role tanker/transport aircraft
(100 per unit)
13
34
6
20
11
524
Airborne early-warning and control aircraft
(100 per unit)
18
7
3
23
6
101
Heavy unmanned aerial vehicles
(50 per unit)
Some
4
4
Some
10
469

US Army armoured fighting vehicle (AFV) modernisation

During the last decade, nations contributing troops to the Iraq and Afghanistan wars increased protection of their existing armoured vehicles. They also procured many protected patrol vehicles, including about 28,000 Mine Resistant Ambush Protected (MRAP) vehicles. As it leaves Afghanistan, the US Army plans to retain significant armoured forces. Due to its large AFV industry and level of technological innovation, among other factors, the US has since the Cold War been the leading AFV designer, manufacturer and employer. This graphic shows the way the US Army used and adapted its AFV fleet in the Iraq and Afghanistan wars, in light of unexpected operational requirements. This is representative of the way that many other Western armies employed these vehicles. It also shows Washington's plans for future capabilities. The US Army, and most NATO and European armies all face similar challenges, particularly in funding essential upgrades and replacing obsolete systems. For the US, budgetary constraints could delay the upgrade and replacement programmes, but they are unlikely to change the army's overall approach.

AFV type	Before 9/11	Modification for Iraq and Afghan wars		US Army future plans	
MBT	M1 *Abrams*	M1 *Abrams*	Included remotely operated machine guns, additional armour on sides, underbelly, turret and crew stations (incl reactive, ceramic and slat armour), jammers to counter radio-controlled IEDs, and improved electrical power generation and management.	M1 *Abrams*	Further upgraded with improved power generation and distribution, communications and data-processing power. Jammers to counter radio-controlled IEDs to be fitted as standard.
AIFV	M2 *Bradley*	M2 *Bradley*			**Ground Combat Vehicle (GCV).** *Bradley* judged to have insufficient protection and to have reached limit of growth potential. Six man squad carried judged too small. To be replaced by GCV, with higher protection, capacity for nine man squad, but less firepower.
APC (W)	*Stryker*	*Stryker*	*Strykers* in Afghanistan fitted with Double V-Hull for added protection against IEDs. Vehicle's weight increased.	*Stryker*	To be upgraded with improved protection, engine and suspension, digital data system and improved commander and driver displays.
APC (T)	M113		Protection was judged inadequate during Iraq and Afghanistan; deployments to Iraq reduced after the mid-2000s. Substitutes included armoured HMMWV and MRAPs. Now assessed to have no further growth potential.		**Armoured Multi-Purpose Vehicle (AMPV).** The AMPV will be based on an off-the-shelf AFV, and will replace – in similar numbers – the M113s employed in support and utility roles in engineer and armoured brigades.
LIGHT TACTICAL UTILITY VEHICLE	Unarmoured HMMWV	Armoured HMMWV	Vehicles fitted with light armour improvised by troops and subsequently fitted by US manufacturers. From 2006, superseded in Iraq and Afghanistan by MRAPs.		**Joint Light Tactical Vehicle (JLTV).** To replace armoured and unarmoured HMMWV. This will be armoured and have the capacity and mobility of a HMMWV. Prototypes from three different manufacturers are being trialled. A joint programme with the US Marine Corps.
MRAP	Capability not required	MRAP	From 2006 the US Army and Marine Corps procured about 28,000 MRAPs in 24 variants from six manufacturers. Optimised to protect against small arms, RPGs and IEDs. Most have little cross-country mobility.		The army has a requirement to retain 8,000 MRAPs from 2015 onwards. Three types only: Maxx Pro Dash troop carrier (shown) and ambulance vehicle and MRAP-All Terrain Vehicle with cross-country mobility.

Combat aircraft numbers reduce in European air forces

European combat aircraft fleets have sharply reduced in number since the end of the Cold War. For key European states, their fighter inventories are now around half, or less than half, of the peak total seen in the period after 1973. Changing threat perceptions and investment and procurement priorities have combined to exert downward pressure on combat aircraft numbers. The considerable reduction in the size of the Polish fleet is typical of the changes among former Warsaw Pact Eastern European states. Irrespective of the shift from single to multi-role combat aircraft between 1973 and 2013, and the greater capability of a single aircraft now, the reductions have hit European force-generation capacity. Platform numbers will likely continue to decline in European countries, where combat aircraft are not being replaced on a one-for-one basis.

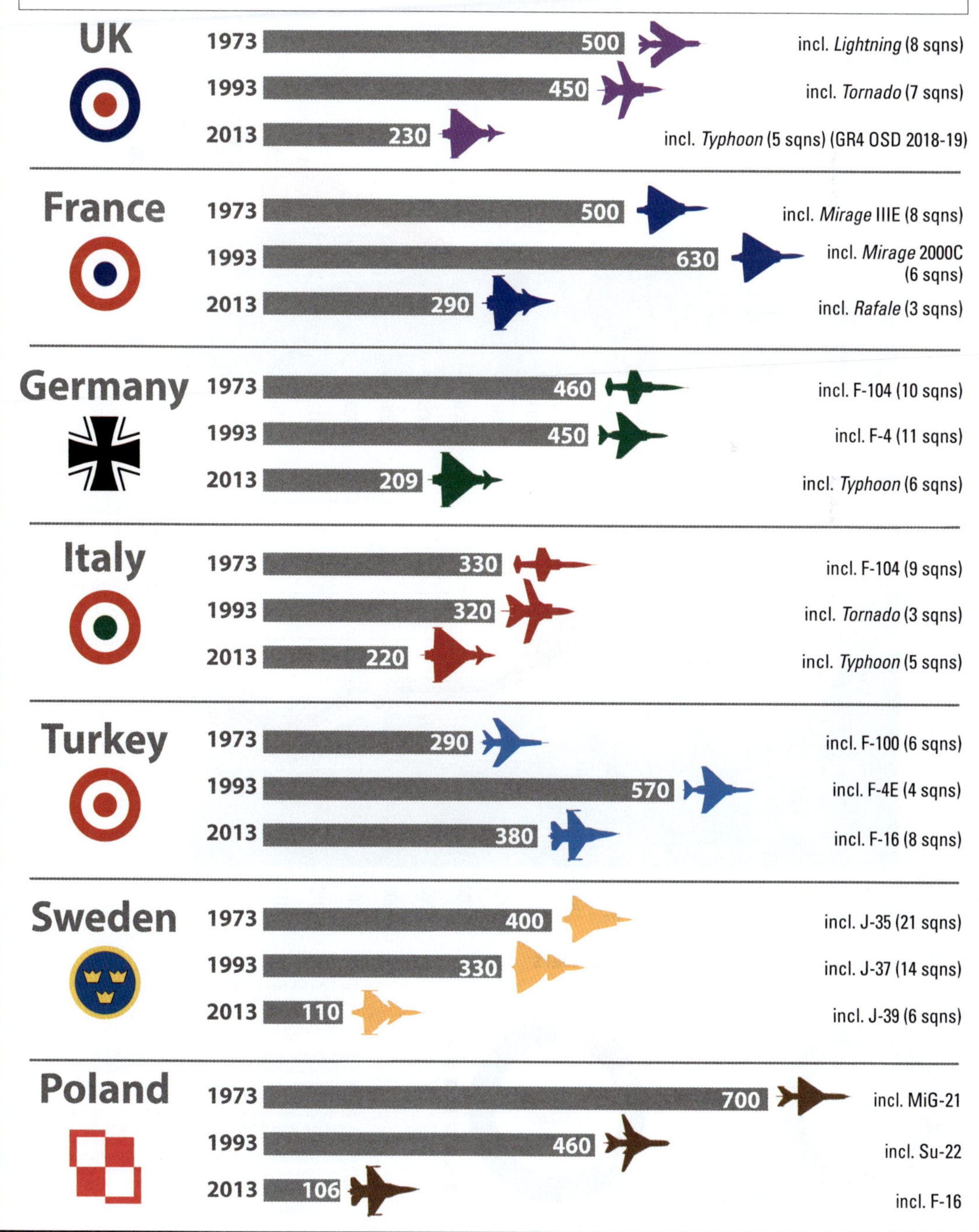

Global 'flat-top' fleets, 1964–2023

In recent years, an increasing number of nations have introduced large flat-deck vessels into their naval inventories. These vessels can include traditional aircraft carriers and other 'flat-tops', with a through-deck and a flat surface over more than 75% of the deck area. The latter vessels have become increasingly popular; they are a cheaper way for states to project naval aviation and, sometimes, amphibious capability. Countries without the resources or political will for a carrier fleet will expand the global total of 'flat-tops' in coming years. Aircraft carriers remain popular too, and here the balance of numbers has started to shift away from the US and Western Europe to other regions. However, though Western countries are gradually reducing aircraft carrier fleets, the increasing size, and number, of vessels being built elsewhere is reflected in the global full-load displacement of these vessels; this total has so far remained largely similar.

Flat-top vessels†1

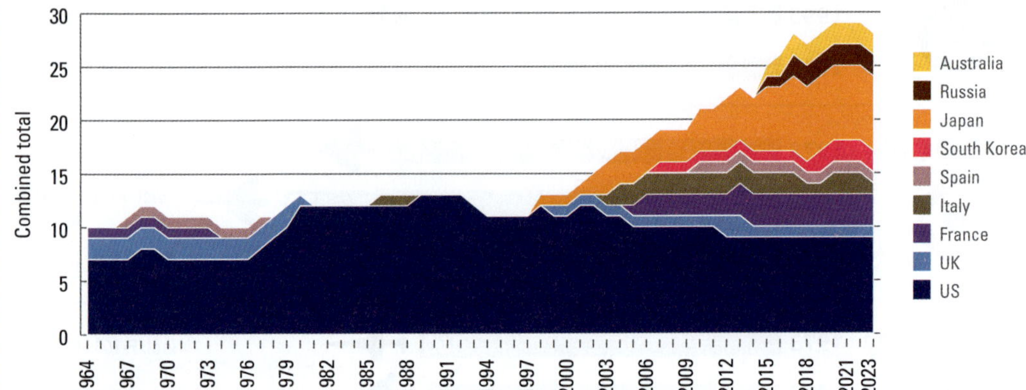

Fixed-wing aircraft carriers*

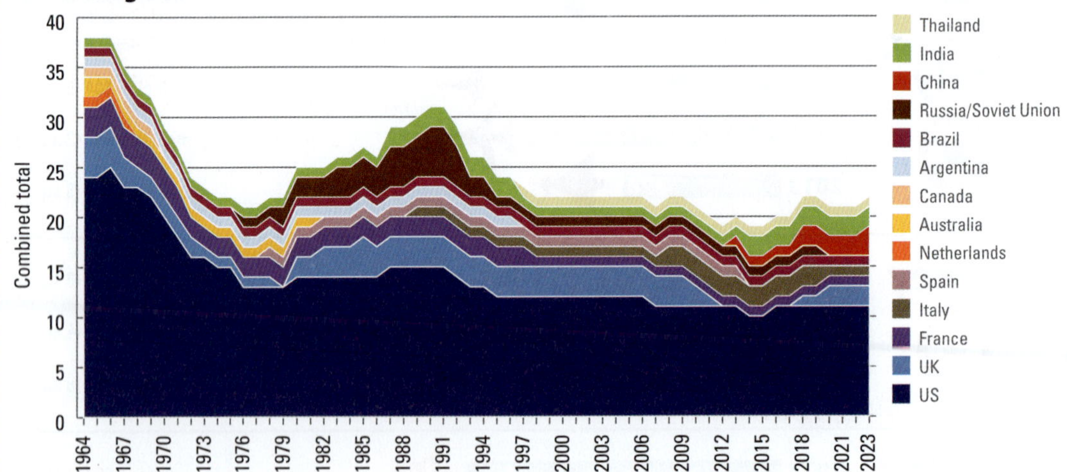

Full-load displacement for aircraft carriers

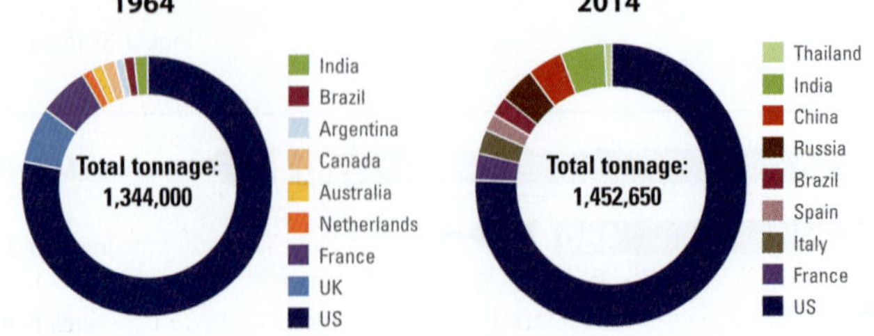

*Note: It is assumed that the UK will retain both new aircraft carriers and that China will seek to expand its carrier fleet, building one further vessel every five years. It is also assumed that Russia will not build a new carrier in the given timeframe, and that the *Admiral Kusnetzov* will either be in extended refit or be largely inoperable from 2020.

†Note: Spain's *Juan Carlos* can operate *Harriers*, but its primary function remains amphibious assault. Australia's future *Canberra*-class vessels are also included. It is presumed that the first two of Italy's replacement amphibious vessels will be delivered by 2020 and 2025. Only two of the three *San Giorgio/San Giusto*-class vessels are included as they have been refitted with larger flat-decks. The *Giuseppe Garibaldi* carrier is listed as a flat-top between 1986 and 1988 as there was a ban on naval fixed-wing aviation at this time. Russia wishes to purchase four *Mistral*-class vessels, but as it has yet to exercise the option on the latter two. They are not included.

[1] Such as amphibious assault vessels, helicopter carriers.

Chapter Three

North America

UNITED STATES

Throughout 2013, US forces remained engaged globally; on long-established and newer deployments – both short- and long-term. Combat and other missions continued in Afghanistan. Army, navy, marine-corps and air-force units were also called upon to participate in small-scale – but often high-impact – missions related to counter-terrorism imperatives, such as those in Somalia and Libya. As the drawdown from Afghanistan continued, attention was shifting towards the implications of the debate around defence funding and the impact of sequestration: particularly what effect this would have on strategic planning, force structures and inventories, should it continue.

This was unsurprising, given that so much of the domestic political debate – not just about defence – was driven by the impasse between the Executive and Congress over budgets and other policy initiatives. Nevertheless, for all the talk of weariness with the wars of 9/11 and of 'nation building at home', the fact remained that US forces were still engaged in a war in Afghanistan and would likely retain forces there for some time to come. Furthermore, announcements of a 'rebalance' to the Asia-Pacific (and Pentagon assurances that this remained Washington's intention in the midst of further crises in the Middle East); construction of missile-defence facilities in Europe; and training and other military-to-military ties with armed forces on most continents all showed that the United States was still engaged globally.

Despite concern about defence-budget cuts, which did bite, the US remained the only state with global reach across the full spectrum of operations and military capabilities. Maintaining an edge, in terms of equipment, over emerging powers' military capabilities was vital to keeping this position, as was the question of personnel. Over the past ten years, members of the US armed forces have learned new skills and adapted old ones; they are now in the process of refreshing older skills in manoeuvre warfare. As personnel numbers fall, the Pentagon's key challenges will not only be developing better equipment and doctrine, but also keeping its best personnel; institutionalising the lessons of the last 12 years; and ensuring that the forces that emerge after the period of readjustment are flexible, agile and scaleable.

Strategy developments

Sequestration went into effect in March 2013 (see p. 34). FY2013 personnel accounts were exempt from the sequester, but severe cuts to training budgets took place (except those for units going to Afghanistan). The navy cancelled a number of ship deployments and reduced some scheduled maintenance. Much attention was given to the furloughs that were applied to some defence staff, as well as the broader debate about how much more defence spending, if any, should be cut as part of deficit-reduction efforts. This had particular relevance for defence strategy.

As a prelude to the next congressionally mandated Quadrennial Defense Review (QDR), and as an educational exercise for Secretary of Defense Chuck Hagel, the Department of Defense (DoD) conducted a Strategic Choices and Management Review (SCMR) in early to mid-2013. It was released at the end of July, through press briefings and congressional testimony by then-Deputy Secretary of Defense Ashton Carter, but never codified into a public document. It was intended to provide the DoD with a range of structure and force-planning options, based on three differing budget scenarios. The SCMR identified possible savings but noted that, if the assumption was that sequestration continued, cuts could affect capability. In his testimony, Carter indicated that 'sequestration-level cuts would "break" some parts of the strategy [as defined in the Defense Strategic Guidance] no matter how the cuts were made'. Nevertheless, the Pentagon is contemplating additional cuts that could in theory achieve sequestration-level reductions in defence spending over ten years.

SCMR was not a formal plan, and was designed to inform the secretary and the DoD as they prepared the 2014 QDR, due to be released in February along with the FY2015 budget request. But its findings seemed to highlight the difficulties that the budgetary uncertainty posed for defence strategists; it was unclear, at the time of writing, how much new ground would be broken by the QDR and whether the administration would choose to accommodate prolonged sequestration or base its long-term defence-budget plan on less austere assumptions. With the president's Defense Strategic Guidance only two years old, the QDR could well focus on elements of that document, including power-projection and cyber capabilities. There may also be interest in enhancing defence value through partnerships abroad. Meanwhile, the crisis in Syria and continuing turmoil in the Middle East did not seem to affect the Obama administration's efforts to rebalance towards Asia.

The armed services

The **US Army** has just over half a million personnel in its active force; the US Marine Corps has almost 200,000. Numbers are currently being reduced in both forces to targets of 490,000 and 182,000 respectively – slightly greater than in the post-Cold War, pre-9/11 period. Since the end of the Cold War, US ground forces have been sized and shaped primarily to maintain a two-war capability. The Obama administration appeared to agree with this logic at first; its 2010 QDR stated that 'in the mid- to long-term, US military forces must plan and prepare to prevail in a broad range of operations that may occur in multiple theaters in overlapping time frames. That includes maintaining the ability to prevail against two capable nation-state aggressors'. The Defense Strategic Guidance scaled down this objective: 'even when US forces are committed to a large-scale operation in one region, *they will be capable of denying the objectives of – or imposing unacceptable costs on – an opportunistic aggressor in a second region*'. It is unclear, however, how army forces would be employed to achieve sustainable outcomes. The same review also stated that planning for large-scale stabilisation missions would no longer determine the size of US ground forces. Even so, the army was due to retain 490,000 active-duty soldiers. Since sequestration began, the debate has shifted. According to the SCMR, if sequestration continues, the total number of active-duty soldiers could drop to as low as 380,000; in this scenario, 'a large number of critical modernization programs would be at risk'. Modernisation priorities include a tactical communications network and the Ground Combat Vehicle IFV, designed to overcome limitations in firepower, protection and mobility in current vehicles such as the MRAP, *Stryker* and *Bradley*. Other possible initiatives include options for improved firepower support to light and airborne forces that could be applied to infantry and Stryker Brigade Combat Teams (BCTs).

With its rebalance to the Asia-Pacific, as well as the new defence guidance, the centre of gravity in US defence planning is partly shifting to the navy and air force, evidenced in the Air-Sea Battle concept being stressed by these two services (see *The Military Balance 2013*, pp. 29–31). Any corresponding shifts in budgetary resources, however, are likely to be modest at best.

Although the **US Navy** has increased its overseas deployment time since 9/11, it only has 285 battle-force ships – well below the official target of 306. If sequestration continues, its size could be scaled back

Developments in army BCTs

In 2003, the US Army began to transform its structure so that the brigade became its basic deployable unit of action. In order to maximise the total number of brigades available, a third manoeuvre battalion and its requisite support assets were left out of the original heavy and infantry Brigade Combat Teams (BCTs), although Stryker brigades retained three.

The demands of simultaneous campaigns in Iraq and Afghanistan led to an identified requirement to sustain 20 brigades deployed at any one time. This implied a regular component total of 40–50 brigades, an increase that, in light of manpower constraints, could only be achieved by reducing the strength of each new brigade. Results in the field tended to confirm the need for a third manoeuvre battalion, with brigade reconnaissance battalions/squadrons often required to take on this role.

Under reforms announced in June 2013, the army will add 'a third maneuver battalion, and additional engineer and fires capabilities' to armour and infantry BCTs. Total BCT numbers will fall to 33. This will reduce all ten active divisions to a three-brigade structure, with two exceptions: the 25th Infantry Division, long earmarked for operations in the Asia-Pacific, will retain four brigades, whilst the 1st Infantry Division, expected to be allocated to AFRICOM, will be reduced to two brigades. The four non-Stryker brigades based outside the continental United States (one in South Korea, one in Italy and two in Hawaii) will all keep the two-battalion structure for now, in order to save on construction costs. The Army National Guard's brigades will also retain the existing structure.

further, with one scenario postulating a fleet of just 255–60 ships by 2020. The increased wear and tear on vessels, as a result of this extended deployment time, has been exacerbated by austerity cuts to maintenance and repair budgets.

Submarine production is set to hold up; the SSBN(X) programme was listed as the chief of naval operations's top priority in testimony to Congress in September, whilst two *Virginia*-class attack submarines are projected to be purchased in each of the next five years. The surface fleet had a less positive year. The commissioning of the first of the new *Gerald R. Ford*-class aircraft carriers was postponed to February 2016 following production delays, and the first Littoral Combat Ship suffered from a series of engine and power-supply problems during her maiden deployment to the Pacific. Whilst the official objective is still to acquire 52 of these latter vessels, this may now be reduced to as few as 24.

The **US Air Force** continued to improve its legacy bomber fleet as well as pursue the acquisition of the Long-Range Strike Bomber (LRS-B). Both the B-52H and the B-1B were the focus of potential further upgrades during the course of 2013. The B-1B was used to trial a variant of the Joint Air-to-Surface Standoff Missile-Extended Range (JASSM-ER) for the Long Range Anti-Ship Missile (LRASM) requirement, while the B-52H was the focus of a data-bus upgrade

Nuclear arms control: Obama proposes more cuts

In June 2013, at the Brandenburg Gate in Berlin, US President Barack Obama proposed two new steps for US–Russia nuclear arms control. Firstly, deployed strategic nuclear arms could be cut by up to one-third below the 1,550 warhead limits both sides must meet by 2018 under the 2010 New START Treaty. He said such a voluntary reduction (which would reduce totals to about 1,000 warheads) would not undermine US security, and could be achieved by means other than a formal treaty. Secondly, the United States would work with NATO partners and Russia to seek 'bold reductions' in tactical nuclear weapons stationed in Europe. Critics question the military utility and cost-effectiveness of the approximately 180 US B61 free-fall bombs kept in Europe – the US contribution to nuclear burden-sharing with NATO allies. Regardless, NATO agreed at its May 2012 Chicago Summit to address any deployment decisions by consensus and in conjunction with how Russia deals with its much larger stockpile of tactical nuclear weapons (estimated at around 2,000 warheads).

Obama's Berlin speech was buttressed by the release, on the same day, of new presidential guidance on nuclear-weapons employment strategy. The White House described the new guidance as a step to advance 'the long-term goal of achieving the peace and security of a world without nuclear weapons'. Military plans will be aligned with the 2010 Nuclear Posture Review: nuclear weapons will only be considered for use in extreme circumstances to defend the vital interests of the US or its allies and partners. The Pentagon was also directed to reduce the role of 'launch under attack in contingency planning'.

Despite the modest proposals, Obama's political opponents condemned them as unilateral disarmament measures that would undermine US security. Supporters contended that negotiated arms cuts would enhance US security and allow for significant budget savings. The proposals found little traction in Moscow, however. Deputy Prime Minister Dmitry Rogozin said they could not be taken seriously while the US continues to pursue missile defence. Obama's cancellation, in March 2013, of Phase 4 of the European Phased Adaptive Approach for missile defence did little to change Moscow's stance; Russia insists on a iegal guarantee that US missile defences will not be targeted at Russian strategic forces, which would be politically unthinkable for Washington. Worried about China's nuclear modernisation and build-up plans, Russian officials added that other P5 countries must be included in any further nuclear arms-reduction talks. Given the poor prospects for further nuclear-arms control and other outstanding issues, Obama had little to lose in cancelling a bilateral meeting with Russian President Vladimir Putin on the margins of the August 2013 G20 meeting in St Petersburg.

Obama had no expectation that his Berlin proposals would cause states such as North Korea and Iran to curb their nuclear programmes, but he hoped to keep alive the nuclear disarmament promise of his April 2009 Prague speech. Four years later, the enthusiasm that speech had engendered has all but died. China, for example, which has an estimated 240 nuclear weapons, sees little reason to join a multilateral arms-control process while US and Russian arsenals remain several times larger. Some analysts argue that the US and Russia could reduce their total arsenals – both tactical and strategic, as well as deployed and non-deployed – to 1,000 or even 500 without undermining the credibility of their deterrence posture. However, such deep cuts are extremely unlikely in light of political dynamics in Washington, specifically resistance from Congress.

that will allow a further eight Joint Direct Attack Munitions (JDAM) to be carried on an internal rotary launcher.

In October 2013, Boeing and Lockheed Martin said they were to join together in bidding for the LRS-B programme. (B-2 manufacturer Northrop Grumman will also compete.) The air force, despite the challenges of sequestration, is aiming to acquire 80–100 of the selected designs, with the first likely fielded no sooner than the late 2020s. The B-52 and the B-1 are presently projected to remain in service until 2040, with the B-2 retained until around 2060. The B-1 and B-52 will continue to be the focus of sustainment and modernisation, the aim being to provide adequate and operationally effective legacy fleets to be used until the LRS-B enters service in sufficient numbers.

All together, the air force, navy and marine corps still plan to buy nearly 2,500 F-35 combat aircraft at a total acquisition price of more than $300bn in constant 2013 dollars. Low-level production is under way, and is due to ramp up in the next few years. However, the Pentagon's independent cost-assessment office is concerned that the average unit procurement price could be 15–20% higher than official estimates and that, once purchased, the F-35 could cost, in real terms, one-third more to operate than the aircraft which it is replacing, such as the F-16 and F/A-18.

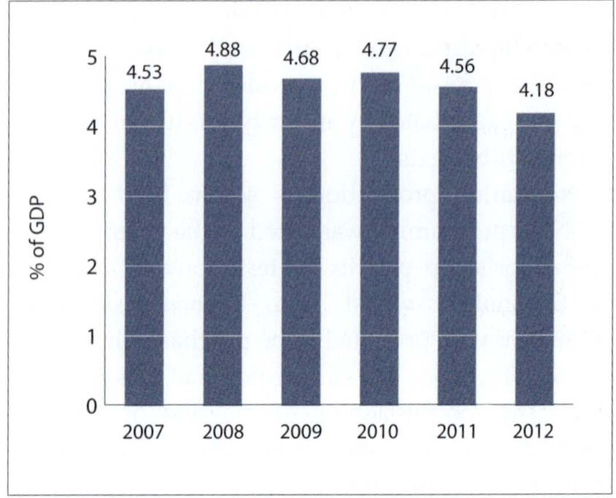

Figure 1 **US Defence Expenditure** as % of GDP

DEFENCE ECONOMICS

The US defence economy is in transition. After a decade of rapid defence-spending growth, outlays are now in decline as a result of legislative deadlock over issues including raising the US debt ceiling and healthcare reform. The lack of a negotiated settlement between Republicans and Democrats on these issues had, in March 2013, resulted in the onset of sequestration (see *The Military Balance 2013*, pp. 59–66). The caps mandated by the Budget Control Act (BCA) 2011 were set to cost the armed forces US$487bn over ten years, relative to the planned defence-budget projections that existed beforehand. In real terms, this amounted to cuts totalling US$350bn over the ten-year period. Should it continue, sequestration will cut roughly another US$500bn from defence-spending levels, also over ten years. The Obama administration's current military plan for FY2014 incorporated the caps from the first round of the BCA 2011 – the aforementioned US$487bn. It did not include possible cuts from sequestration, even though the latter is now ongoing. The Obama budget plan submitted in the spring of 2013, for FY2014 and beyond, did nevertheless envision another US$150bn in cutbacks over a ten-year period (in addition to the spending caps mandated by the BCA 2011 but less than cuts required under sequestration) – back-loaded to the post-2016 period when President Obama will have left office. When it appeared likely that sequestration, or similarly severe cuts in defence spending, would go ahead, the Strategic Choices and Management Review (SCMR), conducted in spring 2013, identified a number of areas where possible savings could be made, including nearly US$50bn in management efficiencies over ten years, another US$50bn in curbs on personnel compensation, and US$100bn in further reductions to US ground forces. The SCMR suggested additional cuts over ten years, divided into two categories: US$100bn in other force and weapons reductions that the SCMR argued would 'bend' existing strategy, and another US$250bn that would 'break' it.

Defence budget uncertainty in 2013

In contrast to the United States' traditionally high level of budgetary transparency, there was a significant degree of uncertainty in 2013 over the size and final composition of the US defence budget. Even at the end of FY2013, in late September, major elements of the 2013 defence budget remained clouded by the dearth of authoritative data. At the start of FY2014, in October 2013, no agency within the executive branch had released a complete report detailing final FY2013 defence-budget allocations. Even experienced budget analysts in the legislative branch and its investigative

Figure 2 **US National Defense Budget Function**[1]

National Defense Spending Category (US$bn)	President's Budget Request for 2013	Final 2013 Action, including Sequestration	President's Budget Request for 2014	Post-Sequestration 2014 Estimate by Congressional Budget Office
National Defense Base Budget	550.6	517.8	552.0	498.1
Overseas Contingency Operations (OCO)	88.5	82.4	88.5	84
Total	639.1	600.4	640.5	582.1

[1] The US National Defense budget function includes annual appropriations of discretionary funding for the DoD, defence activities undertaken by the Department of Energy and other 'defence-related' activities. It does not include mandatory spending, allocations to the US Coast Guard or DoD healthcare and military retirement spending included under other budget functions.

agencies (such as the Congressional Research Service) – who regularly have access to executive-branch data unavailable to the public – were uncertain about even basic elements of 2013 defence spending. The missing figures included the final allocations for the 2013 DoD base budget, funding for overseas contingency operations (OCO) and the final amounts for major procurement programmes, such as that for the F-35. In the case of the latter, data as basic as the final purchasing budget and the number of aircraft to be bought for 2013 remained unreported, and perhaps even undecided, as FY2013 drew to a close.

The confusion stemmed from two sources. Firstly, Congress imposed a 'continuing resolution' (CR) on DoD spending in the first half of FY2013, thus arbitrarily freezing accounts at 2012 levels until DoD appropriations legislation was enacted in late March (six months into the US fiscal year). Secondly, the amounts in the appropriations act were then subjected to a sequester – automatic, across-the-board reductions in specified budget accounts – stemming from the BCA 2011, which remains in effect. The post-sequester amounts for the many individual components of US defence spending, therefore, remained unreported even at the end of the fiscal year. Moreover, the six-month delay in implementing sequestration required that one year's budget reductions (totalling US$39.1bn) be effected in just six months, adding to the overall disarray.

Reflecting that confusion, different agencies and analysts reported differing amounts for 2013 allocations, or were simply unable to cite any reliable figure. However, the non-partisan Congressional Budget Office (CBO) reported late in the fiscal year that it estimated that US$517.8bn had been approved in 2013 for the 'National Defense (050)' budget function. This provides funding for the base (i.e. non-war) DoD budget; nuclear weapons activities in the Department of Energy; and miscellaneous defence-related activities. An additional US$82.4bn in OCO funding was estimated to have been made available for war operations in Afghanistan and elsewhere. However, CBO analysts privately cautioned that they expected the DoD to have effected transfers between the base and OCO budgets, thereby affecting their respective totals (although this was unlikely to change the overall allocation of US$600.4bn). Compared to President Obama's original 2013 budget request of US$641.1bn, this amounted to a 6.3% nominal reduction in annual appropriations.

The numbers for FY2014 were even more problematic. Congress again did not enact any appropriations bills by the time the fiscal year started on 1 October 2013. Instead, amid considerable political wrangling over healthcare reform and raising the federal debt limit (which precipitated a 16-day partial shutdown of the federal government in early October), on 16 October, Congress passed yet another continuing resolution freezing FY2014 spending levels at those allocated in FY2013. For the base DoD budget, this was US$20bn above the level permitted by the BCA 2011's sequestration requirement for 2014, and it would mean an increase of US$18bn if OCO funding was included. In anticipation of Congress passing a 2014 appropriations bill, the CR was planned to expire on 15 January 2014 (see below). However, it was unclear what the eventual level might be: whether it would remain at the sequestered 2013 level (US$600.4bn), or the CBO's estimated permitted level for 2014 under the BCA 2011 (US$582bn), or some other amount following congressional negotiations.

The numbers that have been released have not been without controversy. It is common for budget specialists – including those within the DoD – to make use of constant-dollar analysis when comparing defence budgets over time, in order to discount for inflation. However, the DoD's formulae for constant dollars have tended to understate cost growth and overstate inflation, thereby skewing historical

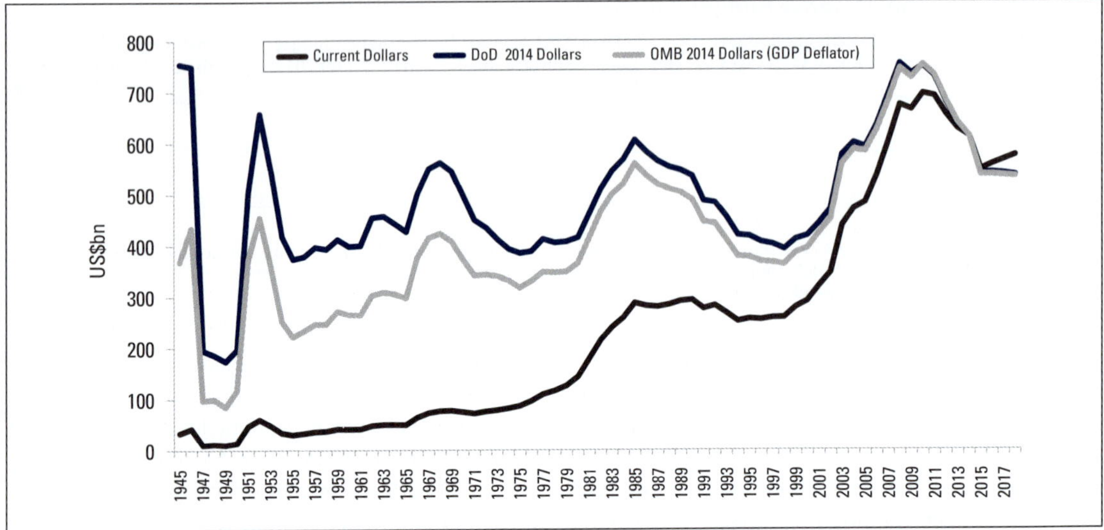

Figure 3 **DoD Budget 1945–2018 Under Various Current & Constant Dollar Calculations**

spending levels (in constant-dollar terms) so that the divergence between present spending levels and the historical average appears smaller than may in fact be the case. This is shown in Figure 3, where the defence budget calculated at DoD 2014 dollars is higher, on average, than calculations based on Office of Management and Budget (OMB) 2014 dollars. This divergence between the DoD inflation calculations and other measures increases over time, amounting to hundreds of billions of dollars when projected back to the 1980s and earlier. Discrepancies also emerge in DoD future projections. The CBO annually calculates independent estimates of future DoD budget plans. The CBO's July 2012 calculation showed that the DoD's five-year spending plan to 2017 was underfunded by US$53bn, and by US$1.2tr over the 2013–30 period. Therefore, beyond the questionable inflation estimates, future DoD spending plans include amounts that are significantly above official projections.

Paradoxes in US defence spending

US defence spending over the past decade has displayed a number of paradoxical characteristics.

Misperceptions over total US defence allocations

In order to account for defence spending not included in the DoD budget, most US budget analysts follow the so-called 'National Defense' budget function detailed in Office of Management and Budget (OMB) records. This also contains allocations for nuclear weapons-related activities undertaken by the Department of Energy, and items such as the National Defense Stockpile of war-related commodities. However, even annual appropriations under the budget function – which are 'discretionary' appropriations that require annual approval from Congress – do not constitute the total defence allocation for the broader 'National Defense' category. Each year, there is an additional US$6–8bn in 'mandatory' spending (permanent or multi-year appropriations that do not require annual congressional approval) allocated for some military retirement, healthcare and other costs. It is not uncommon for even the DoD to misreport its own budget requests without including these mandatory spending amounts.

Furthermore, some defence-related spending is omitted from both DoD and 'National Defense' budget function calculations. For example, the Department of the Treasury has expenses (of up to US$22bn in both FY2013 and FY2014) for some military retirement and DoD healthcare costs. Another common exclusion is US Coast Guard spending (roughly US$6–8bn in recent years), which is funded under the Department of Homeland Security budget. A fuller account of US defence costs would be approximately US$30bn higher than what is commonly reported as US defence-spending totals under the 'National Defense' budget function. If analysis accounts for only DoD annual appropriations, the under-reporting of total defence funding could be over US$50bn.

Foremost has been the rapid growth of the DoD base (non-war) budget, which has risen by over 40% since 2001 after adjusting for inflation, according to the CBO. This has occurred despite the fact that war-related funding for operations in Iraq and Afghanistan were meant to be channelled through the newly-created OCO budget (historically, wartime spending was channelled directly through the base budget). Moreover, the total number of active-duty personnel only increased slightly over the period (by a maximum of about 10%).

Despite increased outlays, the size of major hardware inventories (e.g. ships, submarines and combat aircraft) has shrunk and the average age of the equipment in those inventories has increased, whilst training tempos – for example, for fighter pilots – have declined. Overall, according to inflation-adjusted analysis undertaken by the CBO, hardware procurement and research and development costs (collectively termed 'acquisition costs') grew by 38% over the period. These costs for major programmes are unlikely to decline in the near future.

The costs of manpower and personnel benefit programmes also grew dramatically between 2001 and 2012, approximately doubling over the period, despite the limited increase in active-troop numbers. Between 1998 and 2010, the annual personnel cost per person grew at an average of 4.8% above the rate of inflation (roughly equivalent to a 60% real increase per active-duty service member over the period), as members of Congress awarded larger-than-requested pay rises, bonuses and benefits to service personnel each year. On average, for individuals of a given age and educational background, the US armed forces pay substantially more than the private sector. Averaged across enlisted personnel, total military compensation is about US$50,000 per annum, more than US$20,000 higher than jobs with similar educational requirements, and age and experience levels, in the civilian economy. When compared to workers in the civilian sector, based on age, experience, and educational qualifications, on average armed forces personnel earn more than 90% of civilian employees. This is generally the same for officers. Compensation per active-duty service member, according to a CBO study in 2012, increased from US$70,000 in 2000 to roughly US$100,000 in 2012, excluding spending related to military veterans. Excluding healthcare, CBO analysis of inflation-adjusted numbers showed that pay and benefits spending increased by 39% during 2001–12. Healthcare costs have also risen rapidly over the past ten years, increasing by approximately US$25bn during 2001–12, excluding additional costs in the budget of the Department of Veterans Affairs.

Thus, defence costs have escalated over the past decade due to increasing hardware acquisition and maintenance costs – for a shrinking, ageing inventory – and greater pay and benefits in the DoD's military personnel budget. Considering that both acquisition and personnel costs rose by almost 40% in real terms between 2001 and 2011, reining in these costs presents significant challenges for the DoD. Options include limiting general pay increases to the rate of inflation, with various types of bonuses used to address specific shortfalls in the force structure – measures that the CBO estimates will save about US$1.5bn per annum. Larger savings would require starker measures, such as a freeze in nominal pay for several years. While the SCMR considered such ideas, to date Congress has resisted even slowing the rate of growth in military pay levels.

In this context, a significant difference between the FY2013 and FY2014 budgets is the increased projected sequester in the National Defense budget function mandated by the BCA 2011: from US$39bn in FY2013 to US$54bn in FY2014. In FY2013, the Pentagon tended to protect major procurement programmes from cuts, instead targeting training and maintenance accounts as well as placing DoD civilian employees on furlough. It is not known whether the DoD will depart from this practice in 2014. Only when the Pentagon releases its final estimates for 2013 will it be possible to ascertain precisely which accounts were protected from, and which were subjected to, the 2013 sequester. (Note: in both FY2013 and FY2014, President Obama exempted military pay and most, but not all, benefits from sequestration.) For its part, the Pentagon insists that it will be next to impossible to achieve US$54bn in savings in 2014 as sequestration would require. Large cuts that take immediate effect are difficult to accomplish because demobilising troops, eliminating bases and cancelling weapons contracts all cost money in the short term. If required to achieve such large savings in FY2014, in addition to the US$37bn required in 2013, the Pentagon might have to consider laying off some civilian employees, curtailing training for non-deployed forces to a greater extent than it did in FY2013, further delaying equipment repairs and, with the prospect of sudden cancellation, potentially throwing various weapons-procurement plans into disarray.

Uncertain legislative outlook

During 2013, Congress considered FY2014 legislation for defence only in fits and starts. The House of Representatives passed both its policy-oriented National Defense Authorization Act and its associated funding bill, the Department of Defense Appropriations Act, but the full Senate had considered neither by the time FY2014 started. A stop-gap continuing resolution to 15 January 2014 was approved and sent to the White House on 16 October. The Senate was scheduled to debate its version of the 2014 National Defense Authorization Act in late November, but this was dependent on the resolution of the broader tax and spending impasse between Republicans and Democrats in the House and the Senate. As of mid-November, the nature and likely timing of any potential deal between the two parties remained uncertain, both to the public and to the negotiators themselves.

CANADA

Canada continued to strengthen its defence capabilities in 2013, along with efforts to fulfil new missions, in line with the 2008 *Canada First Defence Strategy*, which is being reviewed. This has been particularly evident in the shipbuilding procurements detailed in previous *Military Balance* editions. According to the new naval commander, Vice-Admiral Mark Norman, the transition to a future fleet involved 'moving forward with all dispatch on the delivery of the Arctic and Offshore Patrol Ship, the Joint Support Ship and the Canadian Surface Combatant'. Canada's non-combat ship package includes offshore science vessels for the coast guard and an icebreaker. The surface combatant vessels are designed to replace capabilities on the current fleet of *Iroquois* and *Halifax* classes. Modernisation of the *Halifax*-class fleet is due to be completed by 2017, with the fitting of a new command-and-control system, a new radar capability, a new electronic-warfare system and upgraded communications and missiles. In terms of strategy, the navy considers that maritime threats will expand, notably in 'contested littorals', so according to Norman, it needs to examine 'the acquisition of weapons, sensors and other joint capabilities that will permit the Royal Canadian Navy to contribute effectively, even decisively, to joint and combined operations ashore, even as we retain that capacity for decisive maritime action at sea'.

The *Military Balance 2013* noted the organisational change in 2012 that led to the creation of Canadian Joint Operations Command (CJOC). This was prompted, Ottawa said, by a 'logical evolution' of the 2006 transformation initiative that saw the creation of Canada Command, Canadian Expeditionary Force Command, Canadian Special Operations Forces Command and Canadian Operational Support Command. In June 2013, the defence minister established Canadian Forces Intelligence Command. According to the defence department, this was driven by a desire to strengthen defence intelligence by unifying collection capabilities under the Canadian Forces Intelligence Group in the following units: Canadian Forces Joint Imagery Centre; Canadian Forces Counter-Intelligence Unit; National Joint Meteorological Centre; Joint Task Force X; and the Mapping and Charting Establishment.

Operational and exercise activities continue, though Canada's Afghanistan deployments are due to end in March 2014, with the close of *Operation Attention*. The final rotation force numbered some 870 personnel, deployed at the time of writing to multiple locations, training the Afghan National Army, the Afghan Air Force and the Afghan National Police. (Canada had, in July 2011, ended its combat deployments to Afghanistan.) Maritime security and counter-terrorism deployments continued in the Gulf region under Combined Task Force 150 (CTF-150), as well as to the Caribbean on counter-narcotics tasks. The deployment to CTF-150 has now been extended to April 2015. Meanwhile, *Operation Nanook* – Ottawa's northern sovereignty operation and another aspect of the *Canada First* strategy – took place for the seventh time in August. The 2013 operation took place in new areas again, according to the defence department, with four locations chosen for their geographical and topographical challenges. It was also announced that an Arctic Training Centre was to be built for Canadian forces in Resolute Bay. This is intended to be a facility available to the army all-year round, as well as for joint operations.

Canada CAN

Canadian Dollar $		2012	2013	2014
GDP	CS$	1.82tr	1.87tr	
	US$	1.82tr	1.84tr	
per capita	US$	52,364	53,463	
Growth	%	1.46	2.39	
Inflation	%	1.52	1.49	
Def bdgt	CS$	18.4bn	16.6bn	
	US$	18.4bn	16.4bn	
US$1=CS$		1.00	1.02	

Population 34,568,211

Age	0 – 14	15 – 19	20 – 24	25 – 29	30 – 64	65 plus
Male	8.0%	3.1%	3.5%	3.4%	24.2%	7.4%
Female	7.6%	3.0%	3.3%	3.3%	23.9%	9.4%

Capabilities

Defence policy is based on three pillars: national defence, supporting the defence of North America, and contributing to international operations within an alliance or partnership framework. Canada provided combat forces for operations in Afghanistan from 2006 to 2011, and remaining training personnel will be withdrawn during 2014. After this, retaining hard-won experience and combat skills will likely preoccupy planners. Though the 2008 Canada First Defence Strategy still drives some exercise activity, the strategy is being updated, and the outcome of this may delay or curtail some of the procurement ambitions in the original document. A new maritime-surveillance satellite constellation is planned by 2018, in part a reflection of the increasing importance and security significance of the Arctic region. During 2013, Canada also selected the design for a new supply vessel, choosing the German navy's *Berlin*-class as the basis for two ships. Delivery of the first is due tentatively in 2018. The government continued during 2013 to review alternative options to its proposed purchase of 65 F-35 combat aircraft, while it also released the draft request for proposals for a SAR aircraft to replace the *Buffalo* (CC-115) and the C-130E (CC-130E). The S-92 (CH-148 *Cyclone*) maritime helicopter programme remained a point of contention with none yet accepted into service and the government examining its options as of the fourth quarter of 2013. (See p. 38.)

ACTIVE 66,000 **(Army 34,800 Navy 11,300 Air Force 19,900)**

CIVILIAN 4,500 **(Coast Guard 4,500)**

RESERVE 30,950 **(Army 23,150, Navy 5,450, Air 2,350)**

ORGANISATIONS BY SERVICE

Space

SATELLITES • SPACE SURVEILLANCE 1 *Sapphire*

Army 34,800

FORCES BY ROLE

COMMAND

1 (1st div) Task Force HQ

MANOEUVRE

Mechanised

1 (1st) mech bde gp (1 armd regt, 2 mech inf bn, 1 lt inf bn, 1 arty regt, 1 cbt engr regt)

2 (2nd & 5th) mech bde gp (1 armd recce regt, 2 mech inf bn, 1 lt inf bn, 1 arty regt, 1 cbt engr regt)

COMBAT SUPPORT

1 AD regt

1 engr/cbt spt regt

3 int coy

3 MP pl

COMBAT SERVICE SUPPORT

3 log bn

3 med bn

EQUIPMENT BY TYPE

MBT 120: 40 *Leopard* 2A6M; 80 *Leopard* 2A4; (61 *Leopard* 1C2 in store)

RECCE 194 LAV-25 *Coyote*

APC 1,212

APC (T) 332: 64 Bv-206; 235 M113; 33 M577

APC (W) 810: 635 LAV-III *Kodiak* (incl 33 RWS); 175 MILLAV *Bison* (incl 10 EW, 32 amb, 32 repair, 64 recovery)

PPV 70: 60 RG-31 *Nyala;* 5 *Cougar;* 5 *Buffalo*

ARTY 314

TOWED 190 **105mm** 153: 27 C2 (M101); 98 C3 (M101); 28 LG1 MK II; **155mm** 37 M777

MOR 81mm 100

SP 81mm 24 *Bison*

AT

MSL 493

SP 33 LAV-TOW

MANPATS 460: 425 *Eryx;* 35 TOW-2A/ITAS

RCL 84mm 1,075 *Carl Gustav;* M2/M3

AD • SAM • MANPAD *Starburst*

ARV 2 BPz-3 *Büffel*

UAV • ISR • Light *Skylark*

Reserve Organisations 23,150

Canadian Rangers 4,300 Reservists

The Canadian Rangers are a Reserve sub-component of the Canadian Forces, which provide a limited military presence in Canada's northern, coastal and isolated areas. They have sovereignty, public-safety and surveillance roles.

FORCES BY ROLE

MANOEUVRE

Other

5 (patrol) ranger gp (165 patrols)

Army Reserves

Most units have only coy sized establishments.

FORCES BY ROLE

COMMAND

10 bde gp HQ

MANOEUVRE
Reconnaissance
18 armd recce regt
Light
51 inf regt
COMBAT SUPPORT
14 fd arty regt
2 indep fd arty bty
1 cbt engr regt
7 engr regt
3 indep engr sqn
1 EW sqn
4 int coy
6 sigs regt
16 indep sigs sqn
COMBAT SERVICE SUPPORT
10 log bn
14 med coy
4 med det
4 MP coy

Royal Canadian Navy 11,300

EQUIPMENT BY TYPE

SUBMARINES • SSK 4:
4 *Victoria* (ex-UK *Upholder*) with 6 single 533mm TT with Mk48 *Sea Arrow* HWT (2 currently operational)

PRINCIPAL SURFACE COMBATANTS 15
DESTROYERS • DDHM 3 mod *Iroquois* with 1 Mk41 29-cell VLS with SM-2MR SAM, 2 triple 324mm ASTT with Mk46 LWT, 1 76mm gun, 1 *Phalanx* CIWS (capacity 2 SH-3 (CH-124) *Sea King* ASW hel)
FRIGATES • FFGHM 12 *Halifax* with 2 quad lnchr with RGM-84 Block II *Harpoon* AShM, 2 octuple Mk48 VLS with RIM-7P *Sea Sparrow* SAM/RIM-162 ESSM SAM, 2 twin 324mm ASTT with Mk46 LWT, 1 75mm gun, 1 *Phalanx* CIWS, (capacity 1 SH-3 (CH-124) *Sea King* ASW hel) (rolling modernisation programme until 2017)

MINE WARFARE • MINE COUNTERMEASURES • MCO 12 *Kingston*

LOGISTICS AND SUPPORT 26
AORH 2 *Protecteur* with 2 *Phalanx* CIWS, 3 SH-3 (CH-124) *Sea King* ASW hel
AGOR 1 *Quest*
AX 9: **AXL** 8 *Orca;* **AXS** 1 *Oriole*
YDT 6 (2 *Granby* MCM spt; 4 *Sechelt* diving tender/spt)
YTB 6
YTL 2

Reserves 5,430 reservists

FORCES BY ROLE
MANOEUVRE
Other
24 navy div (tasked with crewing 10 of the 12 MCO, harbour defence & naval control of shipping)

Royal Canadian Air Force (RCAF) 19,900 (plus 2,350 Primary Reservists integrated within total Air Force structure)

FORCES BY ROLE
FIGHTER/GROUND ATTACK
3 sqn with F/A-18A/B *Hornet* (CF-18AM/BM)
ANTI-SUBMARINE WARFARE
3 sqn with SH-3 *Sea King* (CH-124)
MARITIME PATROL
3 sqn with P-3 *Orion* (CP-140 *Aurora*)
SEARCH & RESCUE/TRANSPORT
4 sqn with AW101 *Merlin* (CH-149 *Cormorant*); C-130E/H/H-30/J-30 (CC-130) *Hercules*
1 sqn with DHC-5 (CC-115) *Buffalo*
TANKER/TRANSPORT
1 sqn with A310/A310 MRTT (CC-150/CC-150T)
1 sqn with KC-130H
TRANSPORT
1 sqn with C-17A (CC-177)
1 sqn with CL-600 (CC-144B)
1 (utl) sqn with DHC-6 (CC-138) *Twin Otter*
TRANSPORT HELICOPTER
5 sqn with Bell 412 (CH-146 *Griffon*)
3 (cbt spt) sqn with Bell 412 (CH-146 *Griffon)*
1 (Spec Ops) sqn with Bell 412 (CH-146 *Griffon* – OPCON Canadian Special Operations Command)
1 sqn with CH-47F (CH-147F)
RADAR
1 (NORAD Regional) HQ located at Winnipeg;
1 Sector HQ at North Bay with 11 North Warning System Long Range Radar; 36 North Warning System Short Range Radar; 4 Coastal Radar; 2 Transportable Radar

EQUIPMENT BY TYPE

AIRCRAFT 95 combat capable
FGA 77: 59 F/A-18A (CF-18AM) *Hornet;* 18 F/A-18B (CF-18BM) *Hornet*
ASW 18 P-3 *Orion* (CP-140 *Aurora)*
TKR/TPT 7: 2 A310 MRTT (CC-150T); 5 KC-130H
TPT 58: **Heavy** 4 C-17A (CC-177) *Globemaster;* **Medium** 35: 10 C-130E (CC-130) *Hercules;* 6 C-130H (CC-130) *Hercules;* 2 C-130H-30 (CC-130) *Hercules;* 17 C-130J-30 (CC-130) *Hercules;* **Light** 10: 6 DHC-5 (CC-115) *Buffalo;* 4 DHC-6 (CC-138) *Twin Otter;* **PAX** 9: 3 A310 (CC-150 *Polaris*); 6 CL-600 (CC-144B)
TRG 4 DHC-8 (CT-142)

HELICOPTERS
ASW 28 SH-3 (CH-124) *Sea King*
MRH 78 Bell 412 (CH-146 *Griffon)* (incl 10 spec ops)
TPT 19 **Heavy** 5 CH-47F (CH-147F) *Chinook;* **Medium** 14 AW101 *Merlin* (CH-149 *Cormorant*)

RADARS 53
AD RADAR • NORTH WARNING SYSTEM 47: 11 Long Range; 36 Short Range
STRATEGIC 6: 4 Coastal; 2 Transportable

MSL
ASM AGM-65 *Maverick*
AAM • IR AIM-9L *Sidewinder* **SARH** AIM-7M *Sparrow*
ARH AIM-120C AMRAAM

BOMBS
Conventional: Mk 82; Mk 83; Mk 84
Laser-Guided: GBU-10/GBU-12/GBU-16 *Paveway* II; GBU-24 *Paveway* III

NATO Flight Training Canada

EQUIPMENT BY TYPE

AIRCRAFT

TRG 45: 26 T-6A *Texan* II (CT-156 *Harvard* II); 19 *Hawk* 115 (CT-155) (advanced wpns/tactics trg)

Contracted Flying Services – Southport

EQUIPMENT BY TYPE

AIRCRAFT

TPT • Light 7 Beech C90B *King Air*

TRG 11 G-120A

HELICOPTERS

MRH 9 Bell 412 (CH-146)

TPT • Light 7 Bell 206 *Jet Ranger* (CH-139)

Canadian Special Operations Forces Command 1,500

FORCES BY ROLE

SPECIAL FORCES

1 SF regt (Canadian Special Operations Regiment)

1 SF unit (JTF2)

MANOEUVRE

Aviation

1 sqn, with Bell 412 (CH-146 *Griffon* – from the RCAF)

COMBAT SERVICE SUPPORT

1 CBRN unit (Canadian Joint Incidence Response Unit – CJIRU)

EQUIPMENT BY TYPE

RECCE 4 LAV *Bison* (NBC)

HEL • MRH Bell 412 (CH-146 *Griffon*)

Canadian Forces Joint Operational Support Group

FORCES BY ROLE

COMBAT SUPPORT

1 engr spt coy

1 (joint) sigs regt

COMBAT SERVICE SUPPORT

1 (spt) log unit

1 (movement) log unit

1 med bn

1 (close protection) MP coy

Canadian Coast Guard 4,500 (civilian)

Incl Department of Fisheries and Oceans; all platforms are designated as non-combatant.

PATROL AND COASTAL COMBATANTS 70

PSOH 1 *Leonard J Cowley*

PSO 1 *Sir Wilfred Grenfell* (with hel landing platform)

PCO 9: 2 *Cape Roger;* 1 *Gordon Reid;* 5 *Hero;* 1 *Tanu*

PCC 4: 1 *Arrow Post;* 1 *Harp;* 2 *Louisbourg*

PB 55: 4 *Point Henry;* 3 *Post;* 1 *Quebecois;* 1 *Vakta;* 4 Type-100; 10 Type-300A; 31 Type-300B; 1 *Simmonds* (on loan from RCMP)

AMPHIBIOUS • LANDING CRAFT • **LCAC** 4 Type-400

LOGISTICS AND SUPPORT 49

ABU 9

AG 8

AGB 15

AGOR 8 (coastal and offshore fishery vessels)

AGOS 9

HELICOPTERS • **TPT** 22 **Medium** 1 S-61; **Light** 21: 3 Bell 206L *Long Ranger;* 4 Bell 212; 14 Bo-105

Royal Canadian Mounted Police

In addition to the below, the RCMP also operates more than 370 small boats under 10 tonnes.

PATROL AND COASTAL COMBATANTS • **PB** 5: 2 *Inkster;* 3 *Nadon*

Cyber

Canada published its Cyber Security Strategy in October 2010. The White Paper said that the Communications Security Establishment Canada, the Canadian Security Intelligence Service and the Royal Canadian Mounted Police will investigate incidents according to their relevant mandates. Meanwhile, the armed forces will strengthen capacity to defend their networks. The Canadian Forces Network Operation Centre is the 'national operational Cyber Defence unit', permanently assigned tasks to support Canadian Forces operations.

DEPLOYMENT

AFGHANISTAN

NATO • ISAF (NTM-A) • *Operation Attention* 950; 1 inf bn (trg)

ARABIAN SEA & GULF OF ADEN

Combined Maritime Forces • CTF-150: 1 FFGHM

BOSNIA-HERZEGOVINA

OSCE • Bosnia and Herzegovina 1

CYPRUS

UN • UNFICYP (*Operation Snowgoose*) 1

DEMOCRATIC REPUBLIC OF THE CONGO

UN • MONUSCO (*Operation Crocodile*) 8 obs

EGYPT

MFO (*Operation Calumet*) 28

GERMANY

NATO (ACO) 287

HAITI

UN • MINUSTAH (*Operation Hamlet*) 39

MIDDLE EAST

UN • UNTSO (*Operation Jade*) 8 obs

SERBIA

NATO • KFOR • *Joint Enterprise* (*Operation Kobold*) 5

OSCE • Kosovo 7

OSCE • Serbia 1

SOUTH SUDAN

UN • UNMISS (*Operation Soprano*) 5; 5 obs

UNITED STATES

US CENTCOM (*Operation Foundation*) 12

US NORTHCOM/NORAD/NATO (ACT) 303

FOREIGN FORCES

United Kingdom 420; 2 trg unit; 1 hel flt with SA341 *Gazelle*

United States 130

United States US

United States Dollar $		2012	2013	2014
GDP	US$	15.7tr	16.2tr	
per capita	US$	51,248	53,328	
Growth	%	1.85	2.95	
Inflation	%	2.08	1.83	
Def bdgt	US$	655bn	600bn	612bn [a]

[a] Figures for 2014 uncertain due to lack of agreement in US Congress – see pp. 34–38.

Population 316,668,567

Age	0 – 14	15 – 19	20 – 24	25 – 29	30 – 64	65 plus
Male	10.2%	3.4%	3.6%	3.4%	22.6%	6.0%
Female	9.8%	3.2%	3.4%	3.3%	23.1%	7.8%

Capabilities

The US remains the world's most capable military power. Its forces are well trained and designed for power projection and intervention on a global scale across the whole spectrum of operations, and it is actively developing its cyber capabilities. It retains a nuclear triad with a substantial arsenal of warheads. The Pentagon continues to develop the plans for its 'rebalance' to the Asia-Pacific, as outlined in the 2012 strategic guidance. Sequestration has affected civilian and military activity; ship deployments were reduced and some exercises were cut, bar those for forces due for operational postings. The possibility of continued sequestration forced planners to develop different scenarios for deeper force reductions, and led to expressions of concern for the next Quadrennial Defense Review in early 2014. This was expected to give greater detail on future force tasks, structures and inventory plans. By December 2014 the US military presence in Afghanistan will have ended, although there will be a continuing deployment of personnel in support roles. Over the past ten years, the US armed forces have had to learn new skills and to adapt old ones; and the army is now in the process of revisiting and refreshing manoeuvre warfare skills. Institutionalising the lessons offered by its recent wars is a preoccupation for commanders, as is the refitting, upgrade or replacement of worn equipment, as well as the development of new capabilities in the cyber, space and more established domains, the latter including the long-range bomber, new armoured vehicles and multi-mission-capable naval assets. (See pp. 31–4.)

ACTIVE 1,492,200 **(Army 586,700 Navy 327,700 Air Force 337,250 US Marine Corps 199,350 US Coast Guard 41,200)**

CIVILIAN 14,000 **(US Special Operations Command 6,400 US Coast Guard 7,600)**

RESERVE 843,750 **(Army 528,500 Navy 100,750 Air Force 168,850 Marine Corps Reserve 37,550 US Coast Guard 8,100)**

ORGANISATIONS BY SERVICE

US Strategic Command

HQ at Offutt AFB (NE). Five missions: US nuclear deterrent; missile defence; global strike; info ops; ISR

US Navy

EQUIPMENT BY TYPE

SUBMARINES • STRATEGIC • SSBN 14 *Ohio* (mod) SSBN with up to 24 UGM-133A *Trident* D-5 strategic SLBM, 4 single 533mm TT with Mk48 *Sea Arrow* HWT

US Air Force • Global Strike Command

FORCES BY ROLE

MISSILE

9 sqn with LGM-30G *Minuteman* III

BOMBER

6 sqn (incl 1 AFRC) with B-52H *Stratofortress* (+1 AFRC sqn personnel only)

2 sqn with B-2A *Spirit* (+1 ANG sqn personnel only)

EQUIPMENT BY TYPE

BBR 91: 19 B-2A *Spirit*; 72 B-52H *Stratofortress*

MSL • STRATEGIC

ICBM 450 LGM-30G *Minuteman* III (capacity 1-3 MIRV Mk12/Mk12A per missile)

ALCM AGM-86B; AGM-129A

Strategic Defenses – Early Warning

North American Aerospace Defense Command (NORAD), a combined US–CAN org.

EQUIPMENT BY TYPE

SATELLITES (see Space)

RADAR

NORTH WARNING SYSTEM 15 North Warning System Long Range (range 200nm); 40 North Warning System Short Range (range 80nm)

OVER-THE-HORIZON-BACKSCATTER RADAR (OTH-B) 2: 1 AN/FPS-118 *OTH-B* (500–3,000nm) located at Mountain Home AFB (ID); 1 non-operational located at Maine (ME)

STRATEGIC 2 Ballistic Missile Early Warning System *BMEWS* located at Thule, GL and Fylingdales Moor, UK; 1 (primary mission to track ICBM and SLBM; also used to track satellites) located at Clear (AK)

SPACETRACK SYSTEM 11: 8 Spacetrack Radar located at Incirlik (TUR), Eglin (FL), Cavalier AFS (ND), Clear (AK), Thule (GL), Fylingdales Moor (UK), Beale AFB (CA), Cape Cod (MA); 3 Spacetrack Optical Trackers located at Socorro (NM), Maui (HI), Diego Garcia (BIOT)

USN SPACE SURVEILLANCE SYSTEM (NAV SPASUR) 3 strategic transmitting stations; 6 strategic receiving sites in southeast US

PERIMETER ACQUISITION RADAR ATTACK CHARACTERISATION SYSTEM (PARCS) 1 at Cavalier AFS (ND)

PAVE PAWS 3 at Beale AFB (CA), Cape Cod AFS (MA), Clear AFS (AK); 1 (phased array radar 5,500km range) located at Otis AFB (MA)

DETECTION AND TRACKING RADARS Kwajalein Atoll, Ascension Island, Antigua, Kaena Point (HI), MIT Lincoln Laboratory (MA)

GROUND BASED ELECTRO OPTICAL DEEP SPACE SURVEILLANCE SYSTEM (GEODSS) Socorro (NM), Maui (HI), Diego Garcia (BIOT)

STRATEGIC DEFENCES – MISSILE DEFENCES

SEA-BASED: *Aegis* engagement cruisers and destroyers

LAND-BASED: 26 ground-based interceptors at Fort Greely (AK); 4 ground-based interceptors at Vandenburg (CA)

Space

SATELLITES 115

COMMUNICATIONS 36: 3 AEHF; 8 DSCS-III; 2 *Milstar*-I; 3 *Milstar*-II; 2 MUOS; 1 PAN-1 (P360); 4 SDS-III; 7 UFO; 6 WGS SV2

NAVIGATION/POSITIONING/TIMING 33: 9 NAVSTAR Block II/IIA; 4 NAVSTAR Block IIF; 20 NAVSTAR Block IIR/IIRM

METEOROLOGY/OCEANOGRAPHY 6 DMSP-5

ISR 11: 2 FIA *Radar*; 5 *Evolved Enhanced/Improved Crystal* (visible and infrared imagery); 2 *Lacrosse* (*Onyx* radar imaging satellite); 1 ORS-1; 1 *TacSat*-4

ELINT/SIGINT 22: 2 *Mentor* (advanced *Orion*); 3 Advanced *Mentor*; 2 *Mercury*; 1 *Trumpet*; 2 *Trumpet*-2; 12 SBWASS (Space Based Wide Area Surveillance System); Naval Ocean Surveillance System

SPACE SURVEILLANCE 1 SBSS (Space Based Surveillance System)

EARLY WARNING 6: 4 DSP; 2 SBIRS *Geo*-1

US Army 552,100; 20,200 active ARNG; 14,500 active AR (total 586,700)

FORCES BY ROLE

Sqn are generally bn sized and tp are generally coy sized

COMMAND

3 (I, III & XVIII AB) corps HQ

SPECIAL FORCES

(see USSOCOM)

MANOEUVRE

Reconnaissance

2 (2nd & 3rd CR) cav regt (1 recce sqn, 3 mech sqn, 1 arty sqn, 1 AT tp, 1 engr tp, 1 int tp, 1 sigs tp, 1 CSS sqn)

3 (BfSB) surv bde

Armoured

1 (1st) armd div (2 (2nd & 4th ABCT) armd bde (1 armd recce sqn, 2 armd/armd inf bn, 1 SP arty bn, 1 cbt spt bn, 1 CSS bn); 1 (1st SBCT) mech bde (1 armd recce sqn, 3 mech inf bn, 1 arty bn, 1 AT coy, 1 engr coy, 1 int coy, 1 sigs coy, 1 CSS bn); 1 (3rd IBCT) lt inf bde (1 recce sqn, 2 inf bn, 1 arty bn, 1 cbt spt bn, 1 CSS bn); 1 (hy cbt avn) hel bde; 1 log bde)

1 (1st) cav div (4 (1st–4th ABCT) armd bde (1 armd recce sqn, 2 armd/armd inf bn, 1 SP arty bn, 1 cbt spt bn, 1 CSS bn); 1 (hy cbt avn) hel bde; 1 log bde)

1 (1st) inf div (2 (1st & 2nd ABCT) armd bde (1 armd recce sqn, 2 armd/armd inf bn, 1 SP arty bn, 1 cbt spt bn, 1 CSS bn); 2 (3rd & 4th IBCT) lt inf bde (1 recce sqn, 2 inf bn, 1 arty bn, 1 cbt spt bn, 1 CSS bn); 1 (cbt avn) hel bde; 1 log bde)

1 (3rd) inf div (3 (1st–3rd ABCT) armd bde (1 armd recce sqn, 2 armd/armd inf bn, 1 SP arty bn, 1 cbt spt bn, 1 CSS bn); 1 (4th IBCT) lt inf bde; (1 recce sqn, 2 inf bn, 1 arty bn, 1 cbt spt bn, 1 CSS bn); 1 (cbt avn) hel bde; 1 log bde)

1 (4th) inf div (3 (1st–3rd ABCT) armd bde (1 armd recce sqn, 2 armd/armd inf bn, 1 SP arty bn, 1 cbt spt bn, 1 CSS bn); 1 (4th IBCT) lt inf bde (1 recce sqn, 2 inf bn, 1 arty bn, 1 cbt spt bn, 1 CSS bn); 1 (hvy cbt avn) hel bde; 1 log bde)

Mechanised

1 (2nd) inf div (1 (1st ABCT) armd bde (1 armd recce sqn, 2 armd/armd inf bn, 1 SP arty bn, 1 cbt spt bn, 1 CSS bn); 3 (2nd–4th SBCT) mech bde (1 armd recce sqn, 3 mech inf bn, 1 arty bn, 1 AT coy, 1 engr coy, 1 int coy, 1 sigs coy, 1 CSS bn); 1 (cbt avn) hel bde; 1 log bde)

1 (25th) inf div (2 (1st & 2nd SBCT) mech bde (1 armd recce sqn, 3 mech inf bn, 1 arty bn, 1 AT coy, 1 engr coy, 1 int coy, 1 sigs coy, 1 CSS bn); 1 (3rd IBCT) inf bde (1 recce sqn, 2 inf bn, 1 arty bn, 1 cbt spt bn, 1 CSS bn); 1 (4th AB BCT) AB bde (1 recce bn, 2 para bn, 1 arty bn, 1 cbt spt bn, 1 CSS bn); 1 (cbt avn) hel bde; 1 log bde)

Light

1 (10th Mtn) inf div (4 (1st–4th IBCT) lt inf bde (1 recce sqn, 2 inf bn, 1 arty bn, 1 cbt spt bn, 1 CSS bn); 1 (cbt avn) hel bde; 1 log bde)

Air Manoeuvre

1 (82nd) AB div (4 (1st–4th AB BCT) AB bde (1 recce bn, 2 para bn, 1 arty bn, 1 cbt spt bn, 1 CSS bn); 1 (cbt avn) hel bde; 1 log bde)

1 (101st) air aslt div (4 (1st–4th AB BCT) AB bde (1 recce bn, 2 para bn, 1 arty bn, 1 cbt spt bn, 1 CSS bn); 2 (cbt avn) hel bde; 1 log bde)

1 (173rd AB BCT) AB bde (1 recce bn, 2 para bn, 1 arty bn, 1 cbt spt bn, 1 CSS bn)

Aviation

1 indep (hy cbt avn) hel bde

1 indep (cbt avn) hel bde

Other

1 (11th ACR) trg armd cav regt (OPFOR) (2 armd cav sqn, 1 CSS bn)

COMBAT SUPPORT

7 arty bde

1 civil affairs bde

5 engr bde

2 EOD gp (2 EOD bn)

5 AD bde

5 int bde

1 int regt

2 int gp

4 MP bde

2 NBC bde

3 (strat) sigs bde

5 (tac) sigs bde

3 (Mnv Enh) cbt spt bde

COMBAT SERVICE SUPPORT

3 log bde

3 med bde

Reserve Organisations

Army National Guard 358,200 reservists (incl 20,200 active)

Normally dual funded by DoD and states. Civil emergency responses can be mobilised by state governors. Federal government can mobilise ARNG for major domestic emergencies and for overseas operations.

FORCES BY ROLE

COMMAND
- 8 div HQ

SPECIAL FORCES
- (see USSOCOM)

MANOEUVRE

Reconnaissance
- 3 recce sqn
- 7 (BfSB) surv bde

Armoured
- 7 (ABCT) armd bde (1 armd recce sqn, 2 armd/armd inf bn, 1 SP arty bn, 1 cbt spt bn, 1 CSS bn)
- 3 armd/armd inf bn

Mechanised
- 1 (SBCT) mech bde (1 armd recce sqn, 3 mech inf bn, 1 arty bn, 1 AT coy, 1 engr coy, 1 int coy, 1 sigs coy, 1 CSS bn)

Light
- 20 (IBCT) lt inf bde (1 recce sqn, 2 inf bn, 1 arty bn, 1 cbt spt bn, 1 CSS bn)
- 11 lt inf bn

Aviation
- 2 (hy cbt avn) hel bde
- 6 (National Guard cbt avn) hel bde
- 5 (theatre avn) hel bde

COMBAT SUPPORT
- 7 arty bde
- 2 AD bde
- 7 engr bde
- 1 EOD regt
- 1 int bde
- 3 MP bde
- 1 NBC bde
- 2 sigs bde
- 16 (Mnv Enh) cbt spt bde

COMBAT SERVICE SUPPORT
- 10 log bde
- 17 (regional) log spt gp

Army Reserve 205,000 reservists (incl 16,300 active)

Reserve under full command of US Army. Does not have state emergency liability of Army National Guard.

FORCES BY ROLE

SPECIAL FORCES
- (see USSOCOM)

MANOEUVRE

Aviation
- 1 (theatre avn) hel bde

COMBAT SUPPORT
- 4 engr bde
- 4 MP bde
- 2 NBC bde
- 2 sigs bde
- 3 (Mnv Enh) cbt spt bde

COMBAT SERVICE SUPPORT
- 9 log bde
- 11 med bde

Army Standby Reserve 700 reservists

Trained individuals for mobilisation

EQUIPMENT BY TYPE

MBT 2,338 M1A1/A2 *Abrams* (ε3,500 more in store)

RECCE 1,928: 334 M7A3/SA BFIST; 545 M1127 *Stryker* RV; 134 M1128 *Stryker* MGS; 188 M1131 *Stryker* FSV; 166 M1135 *Stryker* NBCRV; 465 M1200 *Armored Knight*; 96 Tpz-1 *Fuchs*

AIFV 4,559 M2A2/A3 *Bradley*/M3A2/A3 *Bradley* (ε2,000 more in store)

APC 25,209

APC (T) ε5,000 M113A2/A3 (ε8,000 more in store)

APC (W) 2,792: 1,972 M1126 *Stryker* ICV; 348 M1130 *Stryker* CV; 168 M1132 *Stryker* ESV; 304 M1133 *Stryker* MEV

PPV 17,417: 11,658 MRAP (all models); 5,759 M-ATV

ARTY 5,899

SP 155mm 969 M109A6 (ε500 more in store)

TOWED 1,242: **105mm** 821 M119A2/3; **155mm** 421 M777A1/2

MRL 227mm 1,205: 375 M142 HIMARS; 830 M270/M270A1 MLRS (all ATACMS-capable)

MOR 2,483: **81mm** 990 M252 **120mm** 1,493: 1,076 M120/M121; 441 M1129 *Stryker* MC

AT • MSL

SP 1,512: 1,379 HMMWV TOW; 133 M1134 *Stryker* ATGM

MANPATS *Javelin*

AMPHIBIOUS 126

LCU 45: 11 LCU-1600 (capacity either 2 MBT or 350 troops); 34 LCU-2000

LC 81: 8 *Frank Besson* (capacity 15 *Abrams* MBT); 73 LCM-8 (capacity either 1 MBT or 200 troops)

AIRCRAFT

ISR 52: 11 RC-12D *Guardrail*; 6 RC-12H *Guardrail*; 9 RC-12K *Guardrail*; 13 RC-2N *Guardrail*; 4 RC-12P *Guardrail*; 9 RC-12X *Guardrail*

ELINT 9: 7 *Dash-7* ARL-M (COMINT/ELINT); 2 *Dash-7* ARL-C (COMINT)

TPT 165 **Light** 160: 113 Beech A200 *King Air* (C-12 *Huron*); 28 Cessna 560 *Citation* (UC-35A/B/C); 11 SA-227 *Metro* (C-26B/E); 8 Short 330 *Sherpa* (C-23A/B-34 more in store); **PAX** 5: 1 Gulfstream III (C-20E); 1 Gulfstream IV (C-20F); 3 Gulfstream V (C-37A)

HELICOPTERS

ATK 737: 691 AH-64D *Apache*; 46 AH-64E *Apache*

MRH 356 OH-58D *Kiowa Warrior*

ISR 90 OH-58A/C *Kiowa*

SAR 126: 26 HH-60L *Black Hawk*; 100 HH-60M *Black Hawk* (medevac)

TPT 2,787 **Heavy** 397: 208 CH-47D *Chinook*; 189 CH-47F *Chinook*; **Medium** 2,048: 885 UH-60A *Black Hawk*; 747 UH-60L *Black Hawk*; 416 UH-60M *Black Hawk*; **Light** 342: 277 EC145 (UH-72A *Lakota*); 65 UH-1H/V *Iroquois*

TRG 154 TH-67 *Creek*

UAV 323

CISR • Heavy 45 MQ-1C *Grey Eagle*

ISR 278 **Heavy** 42: 3 *I-Gnat*; 20 RQ-5A *Hunter*; 4 *Sky Warrior*; 15 *Warrior* **Medium** 236 RQ-7A *Shadow*

AD • SAM 1,296+

SP 816: 703 FIM-92A *Avenger* (veh-mounted *Stinger*); 95 M6 *Linebacker* (4 *Stinger* plus 25mm gun); 18 THAAD

TOWED 480 MIM-104 *Patriot*/PAC-2/PAC-3

MANPAD FIM-92A *Stinger*

RADAR • LAND 251: 98 AN/TPQ-36 *Firefinder* (arty); 56 AN/TPQ-37 *Firefinder* (arty); 60 AN/TRQ-32 *Teammate* (COMINT); 32 AN/TSQ-138 *Trailblazer* (COMINT); 5 AN/TSQ-138A *Trailblazer*

AEV 250 M9 ACE

ARV 1,108+: 1,096 M88A1/2 (ε1,000 more in store); 12 *Pandur*; some M578

VLB 60: 20 REBS; 40 *Wolverine* HAB

MW *Aardvark* JSFU Mk4; Hydrema 910 MCV-2; M58/M59 MICLIC; M139; *Rhino*

US Navy 322,700; 4,500 active reservists (total 327,200)

Comprises 2 Fleet Areas, Atlantic and Pacific. 5 Fleets: 3rd – Pacific, 4th – Caribbean, Central and South America, 5th – Indian Ocean, Persian Gulf, Red Sea, 6th – Mediterranean, 7th – W. Pacific; plus Military Sealift Command (MSC); Naval Reserve Force (NRF); for Naval Special Warfare Command, see US Special Operations Command

EQUIPMENT BY TYPE

SUBMARINES 72

STRATEGIC • SSBN 14 *Ohio* (mod) opcon US STRATCOM with up to 24 UGM-133A *Trident* D-5 strategic SLBM, 4 single 533mm TT with Mk48 *Sea Arrow* HWT

TACTICAL 58

SSGN 44:

4 *Ohio* (mod) with total of 154 *Tomahawk* LACM , 4 single 533mm TT with Mk48 *Sea Arrow* HWT

8 *Los Angeles* with 1 12-cell VLS with *Tomahawk* LACM; 4 single 533mm TT with Mk48 *Sea Arrow* HWT/UGM-84 *Harpoon* AShM

22 *Los Angeles* (Imp) with 1 12-cell VLS with *Tomahawk* LACM, 4 single 533mm TT with Mk48 *Sea Arrow* HWT/UGM-84 *Harpoon* AShM

10 *Virginia* with 1 12-cell VLS with *Tomahawk* LACM, 4 single 533mm TT with Mk48 ADCAP mod 6 HWT (4 additional vessels in build)

SSN 14:

11 *Los Angeles* with 4 single 533mm TT with Mk48 *Sea Arrow* HWT/UGM-84 *Harpoon* AShM

3 *Seawolf* with 8 single 660mm TT with up to 45 *Tomahawk* LACM/UGM-84C *Harpoon* AShM, Mk48 *Sea Arrow* HWT

PRINCIPAL SURFACE COMBATANTS 107

AIRCRAFT CARRIERS • CVN 10 *Nimitz* with 2–3 octuple Mk29 lnchr with RIM-7M/P *Sea Sparrow* SAM, 2 Mk49 GMLS with RIM-116 SAM, 2 *Phalanx* Mk15 CIWS, (typical capacity 55 F/A-18 *Hornet* FGA ac; 4 EA-6B *Prowler*/EA-18G *Growler* EW ac; 4 E-2C/D *Hawkeye* AEW ac; 4 SH-60F *Seahawk* ASW hel; 2 HH-60H *Seahawk* SAR hel)

CRUISERS • CGHM 22 *Ticonderoga* (*Aegis* Baseline 2/3/4) with *Aegis* C2, 2 quad lnchr with RGM-84 *Harpoon* AShM, 2 61-cell Mk41 VLS with SM-2ER SAM/*Tomahawk* LACM, 2 triple 324mm ASTT with Mk46 LWT, 2 127mm gun, 2 *Phalanx* Block 1B CIWS, (capacity 2 SH-60B *Seahawk* ASW hel); (extensive upgrade programme scheduled from 2006–2020 to include sensors and fire control systems; major weapons upgrade to include *Evolved Sea Sparrow* (ESSM), SM-3/SM-2 capability and 2 Mk45 Mod 2 127mm gun)

DESTROYERS 62

DDGHM 34 *Arleigh Burke* Flight IIA with *Aegis* C2, 1 32-cell Mk41 VLS with ASROC/SM-2ER SAM/*Tomahawk* (TLAM) LACM, 1 64-cell Mk41 VLS with ASROC ASsW/SM-2 ER SAM/*Tomahawk* LACM, 2 triple 324mm ASTT with Mk46 LWT, 1 127mm gun, 2 *Phalanx* Block 1B CIWS, (capacity 2 SH-60B *Seahawk* ASW hel), (additional ships in build)

DDGM 28 *Arleigh Burke* Flight I/II with *Aegis* C2, 2 quad lnchr with RGM-84 *Harpoon* AShM, 1 32-cell Mk41 VLS with ASROC/SM-2ER SAM/*Tomahawk* LACM, 1 64-cell Mk 41 VLS with ASROC/SM-2 ER SAM/*Tomahawk* LACM, 2 Mk49 RAM with RIM-116 RAM SAM, 2 triple 324mm ASTT with Mk46 LWT, 1 127mm gun, 2 *Phalanx* Block 1B CIWS, 1 hel landing platform

FRIGATES 13

FFHM 3:

2 *Freedom* with 1 21-cell Mk99 lnchr with RIM-116 SAM, 1 57mm gun, (capacity 2 MH-60R/S *Seahawk* hel or 1 MH-60 with 3 MQ-8 *Firescout* UAV)

1 *Independence* with 1 11-cell SeaRAM lnchr with RIM-116 SAM, 1 57mm gun, (capacity 1 MH-60R/S *Seahawk* hel and 3 MQ-8 *Firescout* UAV)

FFH 10 *Oliver Hazard Perry* with 2 triple 324mm ASTT with Mk46 LWT, 1 76mm gun, 1 *Phalanx* Block 1B CIWS (capacity 2 SH-60B *Seahawk* ASW hel)

PATROL AND COASTAL COMBATANTS 55

PCF 13 *Cyclone*

PBR 42

MINE WARFARE • MINE COUNTERMEASURES 13

MCO 13 *Avenger* with 1 SLQ-48 MCM system; 1 SQQ-32(V)3 Sonar (mine hunting)

COMMAND SHIPS • LCC 2 *Blue Ridge* with 2 *Phalanx* Mk15 CIWS, (capacity 3 LCPL; 2 LCVP; 700 troops; 1 med hel) (of which 1 vessel partially crewed by Military Sealift Command personnel)

AMPHIBIOUS

PRINCIPAL AMPHIBIOUS SHIPS 30

LHD 8 *Wasp* with 2 octuple Mk29 GMLS with RIM-7M/RIM-7P *Sea Sparrow* SAM, 2 Mk49 GMLS with RIM-116 RAM SAM, 2 *Phalanx* Mk15 CIWS (capacity: 5 AV-8B *Harrier* II FGA; 42 CH-46E *Sea Knight* hel; 6 SH-60B *Seahawk* hel; 3 LCAC(L); 60 tanks; 1,890 troops)

LHA 1 *Tarawa* with 2 Mk49 GMLS with RIM-116 RAM SAM, 2 *Phalanx* Mk15 CIWS (capacity 6 AV-8B *Harrier* II FGA ac; 12 CH-46E *Sea Knight* hel; 9 CH-53 *Sea Stallion* hel; 4 LCU; 100 tanks; 1,900 troops)

LPD 9:

1 *Austin* with 2 *Phalanx* Mk15 CIWS (capacity 6 CH-46E *Sea Knight* hel; 2 LCAC(L)/LCU; 40 tanks; 788 troops)

8 *San Antonio* with 2 21-cell Mk49 GMLS with RIM-116 SAM (capacity 1 CH-53E *Sea Stallion* hel or 2 CH-46 *Sea Knight* or 1 MV-22 *Osprey*; 2 LCAC(L); 14 AAAV; 720 troops) (3 additional vessels in build)

LSD 12:

4 *Harpers Ferry* with 2 Mk 49 GMLS with RIM-116 SAM, 2 *Phalanx* Mk15 CIWS, 1 hel landing platform (capacity 2 LCAC(L); 40 tanks; 500 troops)

8 *Whidbey Island* with 2 Mk49 GMLS with RIM-116 SAM, 2 *Phalanx* Mk15 CIWS, 1 hel landing platform (capacity 4 LCAC(L); 40 tanks; 500 troops)

LANDING CRAFT 245

LCU 32 LCU-1600 (capacity either 2 M1 *Abrams* MBT or 350 troops)

LCP 108: 75 LCPL; 33 Utility Boat

LCM 25: 10 LCM-5; 15 LCM-8

LCAC 80 LCAC(L) (capacity either 1 MBT or 60 troops; (undergoing upgrade programme))

LOGISTICS AND SUPPORT 71

AFDL 1 *Dynamic*

AGE 4: 1 MARSS; 1 *Sea Fighter*; 1 *Sea Jet*; 1 *Stiletto* (all for testing)

AGOR 6 (all leased out): 2 *Melville*; 3 *Thomas G Thompson*; 1 *Kilo Moana*

APB 3

ARD 3

AX 1 *Prevail*

AXS 1 *Constitution*

SSA 2 (for testing)

SSAN 1 (for propulsion plant training)

UUV 1 *Cutthroat* (for testing)

YDT 2

YFRT 2 *Athena* (at Naval Surface Warfare Center)

YP 25 (based at Naval Academy)

YTB 17

YTT 2 *Cape*

SF 6 DDS opcon USSOCOM

Navy Reserve Surface Forces

PRINCIPAL SURFACE COMBATANTS 6

FFH 6 *Oliver Hazard Perry* with 2 triple 324mm ASTT with Mk46 LWT, 36 SM-1 MR SAM, 1 76mm gun, (capacity 2 SH-60B *Seahawk* ASW hel)

Naval Reserve Forces 105,250 (incl 4,500 active)

Selected Reserve 62,500

Individual Ready Reserve 42,750

Naval Inactive Fleet

Under a minimum of 60–90 days notice for reactivation; still on naval vessel register

PRINCIPAL SURFACE COMBATANTS 2

AIRCRAFT CARRIERS • CV 1 *Kitty Hawk*

FRIGATES 1 **FFH**

AMPHIBIOUS 11

2 **LHA**

4 **LPD**

5 **LKA**

LOGISTICS AND SUPPORT • ATF 1 *Mohawk*

Military Sealift Command (MSC)

Combat Logistics Force

LOGISTICS AND SUPPORT 32

AEH 1 *Kilauea*

AO 15 *Henry J. Kaiser*

AOE 4 *Supply*

AKEH 12 *Lewis and Clark*

Maritime Prepositioning Program

LOGISTICS AND SUPPORT 24

AG 2: 1 *V Adm K.R. Wheeler*; 1 *Fast Tempo*

AK 4: 2 *LTC John U.D. Page*; 1 *Maj Bernard F. Fisher*; 1 *TSGT John A. Chapman*

AKEH 2 *Lewis and Clark*

AKR 11: 2 *Bob Hope*; 1 *Stockham*; 8 *Watson*

AKRH 5 *2nd Lt John P. Bobo*

Strategic Sealift Force

(At a minimum of 4 days readiness)

LOGISTICS AND SUPPORT 26

AOT 4: 1 *Champion*; 3 (long-term chartered)

AK 6: 3 *Sgt Matej Kocak*; 3 (long-term chartered, of which 1 *Mobegan*, 1 *Sea Eagle*, 1 *BBC Seattle*)

AKR 11: 5 *Bob Hope*; 2 *Gordon*; 2 *Shughart*; 1 *1st Lt Harry L Martin*; 1 *LCpl Roy M Wheat*

AP 5: 2 *Guam*; 2 *Spearhead*; 1 *Westpac Express* (chartered until Jan 2014)

Special Mission Ships

LOGISTICS AND SUPPORT 25

AGM 4: 1 *Howard O. Lorenzen*; 1 *Invincible*; 1 *Observation Island*; 1 Sea-based X-band Radar

AGOS 5: 1 *Impeccable*; 4 *Victorious*

AGS 7: 6 *Pathfinder*; 1 *Waters*

AS 9 (long-term chartered, of which 1 *C-Champion*, 1 *C-Commando*, 1 *Malama*, 1 *Dolores Chouest*, 1 *Dominator*, 4 *Arrowhead*)

Service Support Ships

LOGISTICS AND SUPPORT 14

ARS 4 *Safeguard*

AFSB 1 *Ponce* (modified *Austin*-class LPD)

AH 2 *Mercy*, with 1 hel landing platform

ARC 1 *Zeus*

AS 2 *Emory S Land*

ATF 4 *Powhatan*

US Maritime Administration Support • National Defense Reserve Fleet

LOGISTICS AND SUPPORT 39

AOT 4

ACS 3 *Keystone State*

AG 3

AGOS 3

AGS 3

AK 17: 5; 12 T-AK (breakbulk)

AKR 2

AP 4

Ready Reserve Force

Ships at readiness up to a maximum of 30 days

LOGISTICS AND SUPPORT 48:

ACS 6 *Keystone State*

AK 6: 2 *Wright* (breakbulk); 2 *Cape May* (heavy lift)

AKR 35: 1 *Adm WM M Callaghan*; 8 *Algol*; 26 *Cape Island*

AOT 1 *Petersburg*

Augmentation Force

COMBAT SERVICE SUPPORT

1 (active) Cargo Handling log bn

12 (reserve) Cargo Handling log bn

Naval Aviation 98,600

10 air wg. Average air wing comprises 8 sqns: 4 with F/A-18 (2 with F/A-18C, 1 with F/A-18E, 1 with F/A-18F); 1 with SH-60F/HH-60H/MH-60R; 1 with EA-6B/EA-18G; 1 with E-2C/D; 1 with MH-60S

FORCES BY ROLE

FIGHTER/GROUND ATTACK

11 sqn with F/A-18C *Hornet*

14 sqn with F/A-18E *Super Hornet*

10 sqn with F/A-18F *Super Hornet*

ANTI-SUBMARINE WARFARE

9 sqn with MH-60R *Seahawk*

3 sqn with SH-60B *Seahawk*

1 ASW/CSAR sqn with HH-60H *Seahawk*; SH-60F *Seahawk*

2 ASW/ISR sqn with MH-60R *Seahawk*; MQ-8B *Fire Scout*

ELINT

1 sqn with EP-3E *Aries* II

ELINT/ELECTRONIC WARFARE

3 sqn with EA-6B *Prowler*

9 sqn with EA-18G *Growler*

1 sqn (forming) with EA-18G *Growler*

MARITIME PATROL

9 sqn with P-3C *Orion*

1 sqn with P-8A *Poseidon*

2 sqn (forming) with P-8A *Poseidon*

AIRBORNE EARLY WARNING & CONTROL

10 sqn with E-2C/D *Hawkeye*

COMMAND & CONTROL

2 sqn with E-6B *Mercury*

MINE COUNTERMEASURES

2 sqn with MH-53E *Sea Dragon*

TRANSPORT

2 sqn with C-2A *Greyhound*

TRAINING

1 (FRS) sqn with EA-18G *Growler*

1 (FRS) sqn with C-2A *Greyhound*; E-2C *Hawkeye*; TE-2C *Hawkeye*

1 sqn with E-6B *Mercury*

2 (FRS) sqn with F/A-18A/A+/B/C/D *Hornet*; F/A-18E/F *Super Hornet*

1 (FRS) sqn (forming) with F-35C *Lightning* II

2 (FRS) sqn with MH-60S *Knight Hawk*; HH-60H/SH-60F *Seahawk*

1 (FRS) sqn with MH-60R *Seahawk*

1 (FRS) sqn with MH-60R/SH-60B *Seahawk*

1 sqn with P-3C *Orion*

1 (FRS) sqn with P-3C *Orion*; P-8A *Poseidon*

5 sqn with T-6A/B *Texan* II

1 sqn with T-39G/N *Sabreliner;* T-45C *Goshawk*

1 sqn T-34C *Turbo Mentor*

1 sqn with T-44A/C *Pegasus*

4 sqn with T-45A/C *Goshawk*

1 sqn with TC-12B *Huron*

3 hel sqn with TH-57B/C *Sea Ranger*

1 (FRS) UAV sqn with MQ-8B *Fire Scout*; MQ-8C *Fire Scout*

TRANSPORT HELICOPTER

14 sqn with MH-60S *Knight Hawk*

1 tpt hel/ISR sqn with MH-60S *Knight Hawk*; MQ-8B *Fire Scout*

EQUIPMENT BY TYPE

AIRCRAFT 1,089 combat capable

FGA 823: 3 F-35C *Lightning* II; 10 F/A-18A/A+ *Hornet*; 9 F/A-18B *Hornet*; 268 F/A-18C *Hornet*; 41 F/A-18D *Hornet*; 235 F/A-18E *Super Hornet*; 257 F/A-18F *Super Hornet*

ASW 151: 140 P-3C *Orion*; 11 P-8A *Poseidon*

EW 115: 30 EA-6B *Prowler**; 85 EA-18G *Growler**

ELINT 11 EP-3E *Aries* II

ISR 2: 1 RC-12F *Huron*; 1 RC-12M *Huron*

AEW&C 69: 61 E-2C *Hawkeye*; 8 E-2D *Hawkeye*

C2 16 E-6B *Mercury*

TPT • Light 68: 4 Beech A200 *King Air* (C-12C *Huron*); 20 Beech A200 *King Air* (UC-12F/M *Huron*); 35 C-2A *Greyhound*; 2 DHC-2 *Beaver* (U-6A); 7 SA-227-BC *Metro* III (C-26D)

TRG 640: 44 T-6A *Texan* II; 144 T-6B *Texan* II; 100 T-34C *Turbo Mentor*; 7 T-38C *Talon*; 5 T-39G *Sabreliner*; 13 T-39N *Sabreliner*; 55 T-44A/C *Pegasus*; 74 T-45A *Goshawk*; 171 T-45C *Goshawk*; 25 TC-12B *Huron*; 2 TE-2C *Hawkeye*

HELICOPTERS

MRH 237 MH-60S *Knight Hawk* (Multi Mission Support)

ASW 258: 178 MH-60R *Seahawk*; 50 SH-60B *Seahawk*; 30 SH-60F *Seahawk*

MCM 28 MH-53E *Sea Dragon*

ISR 3 OH-58C *Kiowa*

CSAR 11 HH-60H *Seahawk*

TPT 13 **Heavy** 2 CH-53E *Sea Stallion*; **Medium** 3 UH-60L *Black Hawk*; **Light** 8: 5 EC145 (UH-72A *Lakota*); 2 UH-1N *Iroquois*; 1 UH-1Y *Iroquois*

TRG 120: 44 TH-57B *Sea Ranger*; 76 TH-57C *Sea Ranger*

UAV • ISR 60

Heavy 25: 20 MQ-8B *Fire Scout*; 1 MQ-8C *Fire Scout*; 4 RQ-4A *Global Hawk* (under evaluation and trials)

Medium 35 RQ-2B *Pioneer*

MSL

AAM • IR AIM-9 *Sidewinder*; **IIR** AIM-9X *Sidewinder* II, **SARH** AIM-7 *Sparrow*; **ARH** AIM-120 AMRAAM

ASM AGM-65A/F *Maverick*; AGM-114B/K/M *Hellfire*; AGM-84E SLAM/SLAM-ER LACM; AGM-154A JSOW; **AShM** AGM-84D *Harpoon*; AGM-119A *Penguin* 3; **ARM** AGM-88B/C/E HARM

BOMBS
Laser-Guided: *Paveway* II (GBU-10/12/16); *Paveway* III (GBU-24)
INS/GPS guided: JDAM (GBU-31/32/38); Enhanced *Paveway* II; Laser JDAM (GBU-54)

Naval Aviation Reserve

FORCES BY ROLE
FIGHTER/GROUND ATTACK
1 sqn with F/A-18A+ *Hornet*
ANTI-SUBMARINE WARFARE
1 sqn with SH-60B *Seahawk*
ELECTRONIC WARFARE
1 sqn with EA-18G *Growler* (forming)
MARITIME PATROL
2 sqn with P-3C *Orion*
TRANSPORT
4 log spt sqn with B-737-700 (C-40A *Clipper*)
2 log spt sqn with Gulfstream III/IV (C-20A/D/G); Gulfstream V/G550 (C-37A/C-37B)
5 tactical tpt sqn with C-130T *Hercules*
1 log spt sqn with DC-9 (C-9B *Skytrain* II)
TRAINING
2 (aggressor) sqn with F-5F/N *Tiger* II
1 (aggressor) sqn with F/A-18A+ *Hornet*
TRANSPORT HELICOPTER
2 sqn with HH-60H *Seahawk*

EQUIPMENT BY TYPE
AIRCRAFT 73 combat capable
FTR 32: 2 F-5F *Tiger* II; 30 F-5N *Tiger* II
FGA 20 F/A-18A+ *Hornet*
ASW 12 P-3C *Orion*
EW 9: 4 EA-6B *Prowler** (being withdrawn); 5 EA-18G *Growler**
TPT 46: **Medium** 19 C-130T *Hercules*; **PAX** 27: 12 B-737-700 (C-40A *Clipper*); 4 DC-9 *Skytrain* II (C-9B); 3 Gulfstream III (C-20A/D); 4 Gulfstream IV (C-20G); 1 Gulfstream V (C-37A); 3 Gulfstream G550 (C-37B)
HELICOPTERS
ASW 6 SH-60B *Seahawk*
MCM 8 MH-53E *Sea Stallion*
CSAR 24 HH-60H *Seahawk*

US Marine Corps 197,300; 2,050 active reservists (total 199,350)

3 Marine Expeditionary Forces (MEF), 3 Marine Expeditionary Brigades (MEB), 7 Marine Expeditionary Units (MEU) drawn from 3 div. An MEU usually consists of a battalion landing team (1 SF coy, 1 lt armd recce coy, 1 recce pl, 1 armd pl, 1 amph aslt pl, 1 inf bn, 1 arty bty, 1 cbt engr pl), an aviation combat element (1 medium lift sqn with attached atk hel, FGA ac and AD assets) and a composite log bn, with a combined total of about 2,200 personnel. Composition varies with mission requirements.

FORCES BY ROLE
SPECIAL FORCES
(see USSOCOM)
MANOEUVRE
Reconnaissance
3 MEF recce coy
Amphibious
1 (1st) mne div (2 armd recce bn, 1 recce bn, 1 armd bn, 3 inf regt (4 inf bn), 1 amph aslt bn, 1 arty regt (4 arty bn), 1 cbt engr bn, 1 EW bn, 1 int bn, 1 sigs bn)
1 (2nd) mne div (1 armd recce bn, 1 recce bn, 1 armd bn, 3 inf regt (4 inf bn), 1 amph aslt bn, 1 arty regt (3 arty bn), 1 cbt engr bn, 1 EW bn, 1 int bn, 1 sigs bn)
1 (3rd) mne div (1 recce bn, 1 inf regt (3 inf bn), 1 arty regt (2 arty bn), 1 cbt spt bn (1 armd recce coy, 1 amph aslt coy, 1 cbt engr coy), 1 EW bn, 1 int bn, 1 sigs bn)
COMBAT SERVICE SUPPORT
3 log gp

EQUIPMENT BY TYPE
MBT 447 M1A1 *Abrams*
RECCE 252 LAV-25 *Coyote* (25mm gun, plus 189 variants)
AAV 1,311 AAV-7A1 (all roles)
APC • PPV 4,059: 2,380 MRAP; 1,679 M-ATV
ARTY 1,506
TOWED 832: **105mm**: 331 M101A1; **155mm** 501 M777A2
MRL 227mm 40 M142 HIMARS
MOR 634 **81mm** 585: 50 LAV-M; 535 M252 **120mm** 49 EFSS
AT • MSL
SP 95 LAV-TOW
MANPATS *Predator*; TOW
AD • SAM • MANPAD FIM-92A *Stinger*
UAV • Light 100 BQM-147 *Exdrone*
RADAR • LAND 23 AN/TPQ-36 *Firefinder* (arty)
AEV 42 M1 ABV
ARV 185: 60 AAVRA1; 45 LAV-R; 80 M88A1/2
VLB 6 Joint Aslt Bridge

Marine Corps Aviation 34,700

3 active Marine Aircraft Wings (MAW) and 1 MCR MAW
Flying hours 365 hrs/year on tpt ac; 248 hrs/year on ac; 277 hrs/year on hel

FORCES BY ROLE
FIGHTER
1 sqn with F/A-18A/A+ *Hornet*
6 sqn with F/A-18C *Hornet*
4 sqn with F/A-18D *Hornet*
FIGHTER/GROUND ATTACK
6 sqn with AV-8B *Harrier* II
ELECTRONIC WARFARE
3 sqn with EA-6B *Prowler*
COMBAT SEARCH & RESCUE/TRANSPORT
1 sqn with Beech A200/B200 *King Air* (UC-12B/F *Huron*); Cessna 560 *Citation Ultra/Encore* (UC-35C/D); DC-9 *Skytrain* (C-9B *Nightingale*); Gulfstream IV (C-20G); HH-1N *Iroquois*; HH-46E *Sea Knight*
TANKER
3 sqn with KC-130J *Hercules*
TRANSPORT
13 sqn with MV-22B/C *Osprey*
TRAINING
1 sqn with AV-8B *Harrier* II; TAV-8B *Harrier*
1 sqn with EA-6B *Prowler*
1 sqn with F/A-18B/C/D *Hornet*

1 sqn with F-35B *Lightning* II
1 sqn with MV-22A *Osprey*
1 hel sqn with AH-1W *Cobra*; AH-1Z *Viper*; HH-1N *Iroquois*; UH-1N *Iroquois*; UH-1Y *Venom*
1 hel sqn with CH-46E *Sea Knight*
1 hel sqn with CH-53E *Sea Stallion*

ATTACK HELICOPTER
2 sqn with AH-1W *Cobra*; UH-1N *Iroquois*
5 sqn with AH-1W *Cobra*; UH-1Y *Venom*
2 sqn with AH-1Z *Viper*; UH-1Y *Venom*

TRANSPORT HELICOPTER
2 sqn with CH-46E *Sea Knight*
8 sqn with CH-53E *Sea Stallion*
1 (VIP) sqn with MV-22B *Osprey*; VH-3D *Sea King*; VH-60N *Presidential Hawk*

ISR UAV
3 sqn with RQ-7B *Shadow*

AIR DEFENCE
2 bn with FIM-92A *Avenger*; FIM-92A *Stinger* (can provide additional heavy calibre support weapons)

EQUIPMENT BY TYPE

AIRCRAFT 394 combat capable
FGA 394: 30 F-35B *Lightning* II; 43 F/A-18A/A+ *Hornet*; 2 F/A-18B *Hornet*; 83 F/A-18C *Hornet*; 94 F/A-18D *Hornet*; 125 AV-8B *Harrier* II; 17 TAV-8B *Harrier*
EW 29 EA-6B *Prowler*
TKR 46 KC-130J *Hercules*
TPT 19 **Light** 16: 9 Beech A200/B200 *King Air* (UC-12B/F *Huron*); 7 Cessna 560 *Citation Ultra/Encore* (UC-35C/D); **PAX** 3: 2 DC-9 *Skytrain* (C-9B *Nightingale*); 1 Gulfstream IV (C-20G);
TRG 3 T-34C *Turbo Mentor*

TILTROTOR 210
TPT 30 MV-22A *Osprey*; 180 MV-22B/C *Osprey*

HELICOPTERS
ATK 158: 120 AH-1W *Cobra*; 38 AH-1Z *Viper*
SAR 9: 5 HH-1N *Iroquois*; 4 HH-46E *Sea Knight*
TPT 374 **Heavy** 145 CH-53E *Sea Stallion*; **Medium** 109: 90 CH-46E *Sea Knight*; 8 VH-60N *Presidential Hawk* (VIP tpt); 11 VH-3D *Sea King* (VIP tpt); **Light** 120: 50 UH-1N *Iroquois*; 70 UH-1Y *Iroquois*

UAV • ISR • Medium 32 RQ-7B *Shadow*

AD
SAM • SP some FIM-92A *Avenger*
MANPAD some FIM-92A *Stinger*

MSL
AAM • IR AIM-9M *Sidewinder*; **IIR** AIM-9X; **SARH** AIM-7 *Sparrow*; **ARH** AIM-120 AMRAAM
ASM AGM-65F IR *Maverick*/AGM-65E *Maverick*; AGM-114 *Hellfire*; AGM-175 *Griffin*; **AShM** AGM-84 *Harpoon*; **ARM** AGM-88 HARM

BOMBS
Conventional: CBU-59; CBU-99; MK-82 (500lb), MK-83 (1,000lb)
Laser-Guided: GBU 10/12/16 *Paveway* II (fits on Mk 82, Mk 83 or Mk 84)
INS/GPS Guided: JDAM

Reserve Organisations

Marine Corps Reserve 39,600 (incl 2,050 active)

FORCES BY ROLE

MANOEUVRE
Reconnaissance
2 MEF recce coy
Amphibious
1 (4th) mne div (1 armd recce bn, 1 recce bn, 2 inf regt (4 inf bn), 1 amph aslt bn, 1 arty regt (3 arty bn), 1 cbt engr bn, 1 int bn, 1 sigs bn)

COMBAT SERVICE SUPPORT
1 log gp

Marine Corps Aviation Reserve 11,592 reservists

FORCES BY ROLE

FIGHTER
1 sqn with F/A-18A/A+ *Hornet*

TANKER
2 sqn with KC-130T *Hercules*

TRAINING
1 sqn with F-5F/N *Tiger* II

ATTACK HELICOPTER
1 sqn with AH-1W *Cobra*; UH-1N *Iroquois*

TRANSPORT HELICOPTER
2 sqn with CH-46E *Sea Knight*
1 det with CH-53E *Sea Stallion*

ISR UAV
1 sqn with RQ-7B *Shadow*

EQUIPMENT BY TYPE

AIRCRAFT 27 combat capable
FTR 12: 1 F-5F *Tiger* II; 11 F-5N *Tiger* II
FGA 15 F/A-18A/A+ *Hornet*
TKR 28 KC-130T *Hercules*
TPT • Light 7: 2 Beech A200 *King Air* (UC-12B *Huron*); 5 Cessna 560 *Citation Ultra/Encore* (UC-35C/D)

HELICOPTERS
ATK 12 AH-1W *Cobra*
TPT 44 **Heavy** 6 CH-53E *Sea Stallion*; **Medium** 26 CH-46E *Sea Knight*; **Light** 12 UH-1N *Iroquois*

UAV • ISR • Medium 4 RQ-7B *Shadow*

Marine Stand-by Reserve 700 reservists

Trained individuals available for mobilisation

US Coast Guard 41,200 (military); 7,600 (civilian)

9 districts (4 Pacific, 5 Atlantic)

PATROL AND COASTAL COMBATANTS 159
PSOH 25: 1 *Alex Haley*; 13 *Famous*; 8 *Hamilton*; 3 *Legend*
PCO 20: 14 *Reliance* (with 1 hel landing platform); 6 *Sentinel* (one more delivered, ISD 2014)
PCC 41 *Island*
PBI 73 *Marine Protector*

LOGISTICS AND SUPPORT 377
AB 13: 1 *Cosmos*; 4 *Pamlico*; 8 *Anvil*
ABU 52: 16 *Juniper*; 4 WLI; 14 *Keeper*; 18 WLR
AGB 13: 9 *Bay*; 1 *Mackinaw*; 1 *Healy*; 2 *Polar* (of which one in reserve)
AXS 1 *Eagle*
YAG 170: 137 *Response*; 33 Utility Boat

YP 117
YTM 11

US Coast Guard Aviation

EQUIPMENT BY TYPE

AIRCRAFT

MP 14: 3 HU-25A *Guardian*; 6 HU-25C+; 5 HU-25D

SAR 27: 21 HC-130H *Hercules* (additional 4 in store); 6 HC-130J *Hercules*

TPT 16 **Light** 14 CN-235-200 (HC-144A); **PAX** 2 Gulfstream V (C-37A)

HELICOPTERS

SAR 125: 35 MH-60J/T *Jayhawk* (additional 7 in store); 90 AS366G1 (HH-65C/MH-65C/D) *Dauphin* II (additional 11 in store)

US Air Force (USAF) 329,500; 4,750 active ANG; 3,000 active AFR (total 337,250)

Flying hours Ftr 160, bbr 260, tkr 308, airlift 343

Almost the entire USAF (plus active force ANG and AFR) is divided into 10 Aerospace Expeditionary Forces (AEF), each on call for 120 days every 20 months. At least 2 of the 10 AEFs are on call at any one time, each with 10,000–15,000 personnel, 90 multi-role Ftr and bbr ac, 31 intra-theatre refuelling aircraft and 13 aircraft for ISR and EW missions.

Global Strike Command (GSC)

2 active air forces (8th & 20th); 6 wg

FORCES BY ROLE

MISSILE

9 sqn with LGM-30G *Minuteman* III

BOMBER

5 sqn (inlc 1 trg) with B-52H *Stratofortress*
2 sqn with B-2A *Spirit*

Air Combat Command (ACC)

2 active air forces (9th & 12th); 15 wg. ACC numbered air forces provide the air component to CENTCOM, SOUTHCOM and NORTHCOM.

FORCES BY ROLE

BOMBER

4 sqn with B-1B *Lancer*

FIGHTER

3 sqn with F-22A *Raptor*

FIGHTER/GROUND ATTACK

4 sqn with F-15E *Strike Eagle*
5 sqn with F-16C/D *Fighting Falcon*

GROUND ATTACK

3 sqn with A-10C *Thunderbolt* II

ELECTRONIC WARFARE

1 sqn with EA-6B *Prowler*; EA-18G *Growler* (personnel only – USN aircraft)
2 sqn with EC-130H *Compass Call*

ISR

1 sqn with Beech 350ER *King Air* (MC-12W *Liberty*)
5 sqn with OC-135/RC-135/WC-135
2 sqn with U-2S

AIRBORNE EARLY WARNING & CONTROL

4 sqn with E-3B/C *Sentry*

COMMAND & CONTROL

1 sqn with E-4B

COMBAT SEARCH & RESCUE

6 sqn with HC-130J/N/P *King*; HH-60G *Pave Hawk*

TRAINING

2 sqn with A-10C *Thunderbolt* II
1 sqn with Beech 350ER *King Air* (MC-12W *Liberty*)
1 sqn with E-3B/C *Sentry*
2 sqn with F-15E *Strike Eagle*
1 sqn with F-22A *Raptor*
1 sqn with RQ-4A *Global Hawk*; TU-2S
1 UAV sqn with MQ-1B *Predator*
3 UAV sqn with MQ-9A *Reaper*

COMBAT/ISR UAV

4 sqn with MQ-1B *Predator*
1 sqn with MQ-1B *Predator*/MQ-9A *Reaper*
1 sqn with MQ-1B *Predator*/RQ-170 *Sentinel*
2 sqn with MQ-9 *Reaper*

ISR UAV

2 sqn with RQ-4B *Global Hawk*

Pacific Air Forces (PACAF)

Provides the air component of PACOM, and commands air units based in Alaska, Hawaii, Japan and South Korea. 3 active air forces (5th, 7th, & 11th); 8 wg

FORCES BY ROLE

FIGHTER

2 sqn with F-15C/D *Eagle*
2 sqn with F-22A *Raptor* (+1 sqn personnel only)

FIGHTER/GROUND ATTACK

5 sqn with F-16C/D *Fighting Falcon*

GROUND ATTACK

1 sqn with A-10C *Thunderbolt* II

AIRBORNE EARLY WARNING & CONTROL

2 sqn with E-3B/C *Sentry*

COMBAT SEARCH & RESCUE

1 sqn with HH-60G *Pave Hawk*

TANKER

1 sqn with KC-135R (+1 sqn personnel only)

TRANSPORT

1 sqn with B-737-200 (C-40B); Gulfstream V (C-37A)
2 sqn with C-17A *Globemaster*
1 sqn with C-130H *Hercules*
1 sqn with Beech 1900C (C-12J); UH-1N *Huey*

TRAINING

1 (aggressor) sqn with F-16C/D *Fighting Falcon*

United States Air Forces Europe (USAFE)

Provides the air component to both EUCOM and AFRICOM. 1 active air force (3rd); 5 wg

FORCES BY ROLE

FIGHTER

1 sqn with F-15C/D *Eagle*

FIGHTER/GROUND ATTACK

2 sqn with F-15E *Strike Eagle*
3 sqn with F-16C/D *Fighting Falcon*

COMBAT SEARCH & RESCUE

1 sqn with HH-60G *Pave Hawk*

TANKER

1 sqn with KC-135R *Stratotanker*

TRANSPORT
1 sqn with C-130J *Hercules*
2 sqn with Gulfstream III/IV (C-20); Gulfstream V (C-37); Learjet 35A (C-21)

Air Mobility Command (AMC)

Provides strategic and tactical airlift, air-to-air refuelling and aeromedical evacuation. 1 active air force (18th); 13 wg and 1 gp

FORCES BY ROLE
TANKER
4 sqn with KC-10A *Extender*
7 sqn with KC-135R/T *Stratotanker* (+1 sqn with personnel only)
TRANSPORT
1 VIP sqn with B-737-200 (C-40B); B-757-200 (C-32A)
1 VIP sqn with Gulfstream III/IV (C-20)
1 VIP sqn with VC-25 *Air Force One*
2 sqn with C-5B/C/M *Galaxy*
11 sqn with C-17A *Globemaster* III
3 sqn with C-130H *Hercules* (+1 sqn personnel only)
3 sqn with C-130J *Hercules* (+1 sqn personnel only)
1 sqn with Gulfstream V (C-37A)
3 sqn with Learjet 35A (C-21)

Air Education and Training Command

1 active air force (2nd), 10 active air wgs

FORCES BY ROLE
TRAINING
1 sqn with C-17A *Globemaster* III
1 sqn with C-21 Learjet
1 sqn with C-130H *Hercules*
1 sqn with C-130J *Hercules*
6 sqn with F-16C/D *Fighting Falcon*
1 sqn with F-35A *Lightning* II
1 sqn with KC-135R *Stratotanker*
5 (flying trg) sqn with T-1A *Jayhawk*
10 (flying trg) sqn with T-6A *Texan* II
12 (flying trg) sqn with T-38C *Talon*
1 UAV sqn with MQ-1B *Predator*

EQUIPMENT BY TYPE
AIRCRAFT 1,438 combat capable
BBR 136: 63 B-1B *Lancer* (2 more in test); 19 B-2A *Spirit* (1 more in test); 54 B-52H *Stratofortress* (4 more in test)
FTR 275: 106 F-15C *Eagle*; 10 F-15D *Eagle*; 159 F-22A *Raptor*
FGA 823: 211 F-15E *Strike Eagle*; 469 F-16C *Fighting Falcon*; 116 F-16D *Fighting Falcon*; 27 F-35A *Lightning* II
ATK 160 A-10C *Thunderbolt* II
EW 14 EC-130H *Compass Call*
ISR 80: 42 Beech 350ER *King Air* (MC-12W *Liberty*); 2 E-9A; 2 OC-135B *Open Skies*; 27 U-2S; 5 TU-2S; 2 WC-135 *Constant Phoenix*
ELINT 22: 8 RC-135V *Rivet Joint*; 9 RC-135W *Rivet Joint*; 3 RC-135S *Cobra Ball*; 2 RC-135U *Combat Sent*
AEW&C 32 E-3B/C *Sentry* (1 more in test)
C2 4 E-4B
TKR 167: 137 KC-135R *Stratotanker*; 30 KC-135T *Stratotanker*
TKR/TPT 59 KC-10A *Extender*
CSAR 22 HC- 130J/N/P *Combat King*/*Combat King* II
TPT 431 **Heavy** 228: 33 C-5B *Galaxy*; 2 C-5C *Galaxy*; 3 C-5M *Galaxy*; 190 C-17A *Globemaster* III; **Medium** 140 C-130H/J *Hercules*; **Light** 39: 4 Beech 1900C (C-12J); 35 Learjet 35A (C-21); **PAX** 24: 2 B-737-700 (C-40B); 4 B-757-200 (C-32A); 5 Gulfstream III (C-20B); 2 Gulfstream IV (C-20H); 9 Gulfstream V (C-37A); 2 VC-25A *Air Force One*
TRG 1,130: 179 T-1A *Jayhawk*; 405 T-6A *Texan* II; 546 T-38A *Talon*
HELICOPTERS
CSAR 81 HH-60G *Pave Hawk*
TPT • Light 62 UH-1N *Huey*
UAV 248
CISR • Heavy 216: 101 MQ-1B *Predator*; 115 MQ-9A/B *Reaper*
ISR • Heavy 32+: 31 RQ-4B *Global Hawk*; 1+ RQ-170 *Sentinel*
MSL
AAM • IR AIM-9 *Sidewinder*; **IIR** AIM-9X *Sidewinder* II; **SARH** AIM-7M *Sparrow* **ARH** AIM-120B/C AMRAAM
ASM AGM-86B (ALCM) LACM (strategic); AGM-86C (CALCM) LACM (tactical); AGM-86D LACM (penetrator); AGM-130A; AGM-158 JASSM; AGM-65A *Maverick*/AGM-65B *Maverick*/AGM-65D *Maverick*/AGM-65G *Maverick*; AGM-175 *Griffin* **ARM** AGM-88A/AGM-88B HARM; **EW** MALD/MALD-J
MANPAD FIM-92 *Stinger*
BOMBS
Conventional: BLU-109/Mk 84 (2,000lb); BLU-110/Mk 83 (1,000lb); BLU-111/Mk 82 (500lb)
Laser-guided: *Paveway* II, *Paveway* III (fits on Mk82, Mk83 or Mk84)
INS/GPS guided: JDAM (GBU 31/32/38); GBU-15 (with BLU-109 penetrating warhead or Mk 84); GBU-39B Small Diameter Bomb (250lb); GBU-43B; GBU-57A/B; Enhanced *Paveway* III

Reserve Organisations

Air National Guard 105,700 reservists (incl 4,750 active)

FORCES BY ROLE
BOMBER
1 sqn with B-2A *Spirit* (personnel only)
FIGHTER
5 sqn with F-15C/D *Eagle*
1 sqn with F-22A *Raptor* (+1 sqn personnel only)
FIGHTER/GROUND ATTACK
12 sqn with F-16C/D *Fighting Falcon*
GROUND ATTACK
5 sqn with A-10C *Thunderbolt* II
ISR
3 sqn with E-8C J-STARS (mixed active force and ANG personnel)
COMBAT SEARCH & RESCUE
9 sqn with HC-130 *Hercules*/MC-130P *Combat Shadow*; HH-60G *Pave Hawk*
TANKER
16 sqn with KC-135R *Stratotanker* (+2 sqn personnel only)
3 sqn with KC-135T *Stratotanker*

TRANSPORT
1 sqn with B-737-700 (C-40C); Gulfstream G100 (C-38A)
2 sqn with C-5A *Galaxy*
3 sqn with C-17A *Globemaster* (+2 sqn personnel only)
12 sqn with C-130H *Hercules* (+1 sqn personnel only)
1 sqn with C-130H/LC-130H *Hercules*
2 sqn with C-130J *Hercules*
2 sqn with Learjet 35A (C-21A)
1 sqn with WC-130H *Hercules*
TRAINING
1 sqn with C-130H *Hercules*
1 sqn with F-15C/D *Eagle*
4 sqn with F-16C/D *Fighting Falcon*
COMBAT/ISR UAV
4 sqn with MQ-1B *Predator*
1 sqn with MQ-9A/B *Reaper* (+4 sqn personnel only)

EQUIPMENT BY TYPE

AIRCRAFT 507 combat capable
FTR 129: 92 F-15C *Eagle;* 19 F-15D *Eagle;* 18 F-22A *Raptor*
FGA 276: 254 F-16C *Fighting Falcon;* 22 F-16D *Fighting Falcon*
ATK 102 A-10C *Thunderbolt* II
ISR 17 E-8C J-STARS
ELINT 11 RC-26B *Metroliner* (being withdrawn)
CSAR 7 HC-130P/N *Combat King*
TKR 162: 138 KC-135R *Stratotanker;* 24 KC-135T *Stratotanker*
TPT 198 **Heavy** 32: 12 C-5A *Galaxy;* 20 C-17A *Globemaster* III; **Medium** 149: 111 C-130H *Hercules;* 16 C-130J *Hercules;* 10 LC-130H *Hercules;* 4 MC-130P *Combat Shadow;* 8 WC-130H *Hercules;* **Light** 10 Learjet 35A (C-21A); **PAX** 5: 3 B-737-700 (C-40C); 2 Gulfstream G100 (C-38A)
HELICOPTERS • CSAR 15 HH-60G *Pave Hawk*
UAV • CISR • Heavy 42: 36 MQ-1B *Predator;* 6 MQ-9A *Reaper*

Air Force Reserve Command 70,900 reservists (incl 3,000 active)

FORCES BY ROLE

BOMBER
1 sqn with B-52H *Stratofortress* (personnel only)
FIGHTER
2 sqn with F-22A *Raptor* (personnel only)
FIGHTER/GROUND ATTACK
2 sqn with F-16C/D *Fighting Falcon* (+2 sqn personnel only)
GROUND ATTACK
1 sqn with A-10C *Thunderbolt* II (+2 sqn personnel only)
ISR
1 (Weather Recce) sqn with WC-130H/J *Hercules*
AIRBORNE EARLY WARNING & CONTROL
1 sqn with E-3 *Sentry* (personnel only)
COMBAT SEARCH & RESCUE
3 sqn with HC-130P/N *Hercules;* HH-60G *Pave Hawk*
TANKER
4 sqn with KC-10A *Extender* (personnel only)
6 sqn with KC-135R *Stratotanker* (+2 sqn personnel only)
TRANSPORT
1 (VIP) sqn with B-737-700 (C-40C)
2 sqn with C-5A/B/M *Galaxy* (+2 sqn personnel only)
2 sqn with C-17A *Globemaster* (+8 sqn personnel only)
9 sqn with C-130H *Hercules*
1 sqn with C-130J *Hercules*
1 (Aerial Spray) sqn with C-130H *Hercules*
TRAINING
1 sqn with A-10C *Thunderbolt* II; F-15 *Eagle;* F-16 *Fighting Falcon*
1 sqn with B-52H *Stratofortress*
1 sqn with C-5A *Galaxy*
1 sqn with F-16C/D *Fighting Falcon*
5 (flying training) sqn with T-1A *Jayhawk;* T-6A *Texan* II; T-38C *Talon* (personnel only)
COMBAT/ISR UAV
2 sqn with MQ-1B *Predator*/MQ-9A *Reaper* (personnel only)
ISR UAV
1 sqn with RQ-4B *Global Hawk* (personnel only)

EQUIPMENT BY TYPE

AIRCRAFT 97 combat capable
BBR 18 B-52H *Stratofortress*
FGA 52: 49 F-16C *Fighting Falcon;* 3 F-16D *Fighting Falcon*
ATK 27 A-10C *Thunderbolt* II
ISR 10 WC-130J *Hercules* (Weather Recce)
CSAR 5 HC-130P/N *King*
TKR 62 KC-135R *Stratotanker*
TPT 142 **Heavy** 42: 8 C-5A *Galaxy;* 16 C-5B/M *Galaxy;* 18 C-17A *Globemaster* III; **Medium** 63: 51 C-130H *Hercules;* 10 C-130J *Hercules;* 2 WC-130H *Hercules;* **PAX** 4 B-737-700 (C-40C)
HELICOPTERS • CSAR 15 HH-60G *Pave Hawk*

Civil Reserve Air Fleet

Commercial ac numbers fluctuate
AIRCRAFT • TPT 37 carriers and 1,376 aircraft enrolled, including 1,273 aircraft in the international segment (990 long-range and 283 short-range), plus 37 national, 50 aeromedical evacuation segments and 4 aircraft in the Alaskan segment.

Air Force Stand-by Reserve 16,858 reservists

Trained individuals for mobilisation

US Special Operations Command (USSOCOM) 60,200; 6,400 (civilian)

Commands all active, reserve and National Guard Special Operations Forces (SOF) of all services based in CONUS.

Joint Special Operations Command

Reported to comprise elite US SF including Special Forces Operations Detachment Delta ('Delta Force'), SEAL Team 6 and integral USAF support.

US Army Special Operations Command 32,400

FORCES BY ROLE

SPECIAL FORCES
5 SF gp (3–4 SF bn, 1 spt bn)
1 ranger regt (3 ranger bn; 1 cbt spt bn)

MANOEUVRE

Aviation

1 (160th SOAR) regt (4 avn bn)

COMBAT SUPPORT

1 civil affairs bde (5 civil affairs bn)

2 psyops gp (3 psyops bn)

COMBAT SERVICE SUPPORT

1 (sustainment) log bde (1 sigs bn)

EQUIPMENT BY TYPE

APC • PPV 640 M-ATV

HELICOPTERS

MRH 50 AH-6M/MH-6M *Little Bird*

TPT 130 **Heavy** 68 MH-47G *Chinook*; **Medium** 62 MH-60K/L/M *Black Hawk*

UAV 57

ISR • Light 29: 15 XPV-1 *Tern*; 14 XPV-2 *Mako*;

TPT • Heavy 28 CQ-10 *Snowgoose*

Reserve Organisations

Army National Guard

FORCES BY ROLE

SPECIAL FORCES

2 SF gp (3 SF bn)

Army Reserve

FORCES BY ROLE

COMBAT SUPPORT

2 psyops gp

4 civil affairs comd HQ

8 civil affairs bde HQ

36 civil affairs bn (coy)

US Navy Special Warfare Command 9,500

FORCES BY ROLE

SPECIAL FORCES

8 SEAL team (total: 48 SF pl)

2 SEAL Delivery Vehicle team

EQUIPMENT BY TYPE

SF 6 DDS

Naval Reserve Force

SPECIAL FORCES

8 SEAL det

10 Naval Special Warfare det

2 Special Boat sqn

2 Special Boat unit

1 SEAL Delivery Vehicle det

US Marine Special Operations Command (MARSOC) 3,000

FORCES BY ROLE

SPECIAL FORCES

1 SF regt (3 SF bn)

COMBAT SUPPORT

1 int bn

COMBAT SERVICE SUPPORT

1 spt gp

Air Force Special Operations Command (AFSOC) 15,300

FORCES BY ROLE

GROUND ATTACK

2 sqn with AC-130H/U *Spectre*

TRANSPORT

1 sqn with An-26 *Curl*; DHC-6; M-28 *Skytruck* (C-145A); Mi-8 *Hip*; Mi-171

2 sqn with CV-22B *Osprey*

1 sqn with DHC-8; Do-328 (C-146A)

2 sqn with MC-130H *Combat Talon*

1 sqn with MC-130H *Combat Talon*; CV-22B *Osprey*

1 sqn with MC-130J *Commando* II

1 sqn with MC-130J *Commando* II; MC-130P *Combat Shadow*

1 sqn with MC-130P *Combat Shadow*

1 sqn with MC-130W *Combat Spear*

3 sqn with PC-12 (U-28A)

TRAINING

1 sqn with CV-22A/B *Osprey*

1 sqn with HC-130J *Combat King* II; MC-130J *Commando* II

1 sqn with HC-130P/N *Combat King*; MC-130H *Combat Talon* II; MC-130P *Combat Shadow*

1 sqn with Bell 205 (TH-1H *Iroquois*)

1 sqn with HH-60G *Pave Hawk*; UH-1N *Huey*

COMBAT/ISR UAV

1 sqn with MQ-1B *Predator*

1 sqn with MQ-9 *Reaper*

EQUIPMENT BY TYPE

AIRCRAFT 25 combat capable

ATK 25: 8 AC-130H *Spectre*; 17 AC-130U *Spectre*

CSAR 4: 2 HC-130N *Combat King*; 1 HC-130P *Combat King*; 1 HC-130J *Combat King* II

TPT 120 **Medium** 64: 3 C-27J *Spartan*; 20 MC-130H *Combat Talon* II; 7 MC-130J *Commando* II; 22 MC-130P *Combat Shadow*; 12 MC-130W *Combat Spear*; **Light** 56: 1 An-26 *Curl*; 1 DHC-6; 5 DHC-8; 9 Do-328 (CC-146A); 4 M-28 *Skytruck* (C-145A); 36 PC-12 (U-28A)

TILT-ROTOR 35 CV-22A/B *Osprey* (3 more in test)

HELICOPTERS

CSAR 3 HH-60G *Pave Hawk*

TPT 38 **Medium** 4: 3 Mi-8 *Hip*; 1 Mi-171; **Light** 34: 24 Bell 205 (TH-1H *Iroquois*); 10 UH-1N *Huey*

UAV • CISR • Heavy 39: 29 MQ-1B *Predator*; 10 MQ-9 *Reaper*

Reserve Organisations

Air National Guard

FORCES BY ROLE

ELECTRONIC WARFARE

1 sqn with C-130J *Hercules*/EC-130J *Commando Solo*

TRANSPORT

1 flt with B-737-200 (C-32B)

EQUIPMENT BY TYPE

AIRCRAFT

EW 3 EC-130J *Commando Solo*

TPT 5 **Medium** 3 C-130J *Hercules*; **PAX** 2 B-757-200 (C-32B)

Air Force Reserve

FORCES BY ROLE

TRANSPORT

1 sqn with M-28 *Skytruck* (C-145A)

TRAINING

1 sqn with M-28 *Skytruck* (C-145A)

COMBAT/ISR UAV

1 sqn with MQ-1B *Predator* (personnel only)

EQUIPMENT BY TYPE

AIRCRAFT

TPT • Light 5 M-28 *Skytruck* (C-145A)

Cyber

US Army Cyber Command (ARCYBER), Fleet Cyber Command (the US 10th Fleet) and the 24th Air Force deliver cyber capability for land, sea and air forces. Marine Force Cyber Command was established in 2009. These service groups are commanded by US Cyber Command (itself under US Strategic Command, and co-located with the NSA). The NSA director also heads Cyber Command. DoD's November 2011 'Cyberspace Policy Report' said that 'If directed by the President, DoD will conduct offensive cyber operations in a manner consistent with the policy principles and legal regimes that the Department follows for kinetic capabilities, including the law of armed conflict.' According to the Cyber Command chief, in March 2012 the command element had 937 staff (with an FY2013 budget request of US$182m), while service cyber staff totalled over 12,000. For Cyber Command, the government's January 2012 Defense Strategic Guidance 'means we must pay attention to the ways in which nations and non-state actors are developing asymmetric capabilities to conduct cyber espionage – and potentially cyber attacks as well – against the United States'. In October 2012, President Barack Obama signed Presidential Policy Directive 20, the purpose of which was to establish clear standards for US federal agencies in confronting threats in cyberspace. The terms of the directive are secret but are thought to include an explicit distinction between network defence and offensive cyber operations.

DEPLOYMENT

AFGHANISTAN

NATO • ISAF 60,000; 1 corps HQ; 2 div HQ; 1 armd ABCT; 2 mech inf SBCT; 5 lt inf IBCT; 1 air aslt IBCT; 2 cbt avn bde; 1 USMC MEF HQ

US Central Command • *Operation Enduring Freedom – Afghanistan* (OEF-A) ε7,000

EQUIPMENT BY TYPE (ISAF and OEF-A)

F-16C/D *Fighting Falcon*; A-10 *Thunderbolt* II; AV-8B *Harrier*; MC-12W; EC-130H *Compass Call*; C-130 *Hercules*; MV-22 *Osprey*; KC-130J *Hercules*; AH-64 *Apache*; OH-58 *Kiowa*; CH-47 *Chinook*; UH-60 *Black Hawk*; HH-60 *Pave Hawk*; AH-1 *Cobra*; CH-53 *Sea Stallion*; UH-1 *Iroquois*; RQ-7B *Shadow*; MQ-1 *Predator*; MQ-9 *Reaper*

ANTIGUA AND BARBUDA

US Strategic Command • 1 detection and tracking radar at Antigua Air Station

ARABIAN SEA

US Central Command • Navy • 5th Fleet (5th Fleet's operating forces are rotationally deployed to the region from Fleet Forces Command and/or 3rd Fleet)

EQUIPMENT BY TYPE

1 CVN; 2 CGHM; 2 DDGHM; 1 DDGM; 1 LHD; 1 LPD; 1 LSD; 1 AOE

Combined Maritime Forces • TF 53: 1 AE; 2 AKE; 1 AOH; 3 AO

ARUBA

US Southern Command • 1 Forward Operating Location at Aruba

ASCENSION ISLAND

US Strategic Command • 1 detection and tracking radar at Ascension Auxiliary Air Field

ATLANTIC OCEAN

US Northern Command • US Navy

EQUIPMENT BY TYPE

6 SSBN; 21 SSGN; 2 SSN; 3 CVN; 7 CGHM; 9 DDGHM; 12 DDGM; 8 FFH; 5 PCO; 4 LHD; 3 LPD; 6 LSD

AUSTRALIA

US Pacific Command • 170; 1 SEWS at Pine Gap; 1 comms facility at Pine Gap; 1 SIGINT stn at Pine Gap

BAHRAIN

US Central Command • 2,650; 1 HQ (5th Fleet)

BELGIUM

US European Command • 1,150

BOSNIA-HERZEGOVINA

OSCE • Bosnia and Herzegovina 10

BRITISH INDIAN OCEAN TERRITORY

US Strategic Command • 500; 1 Spacetrack Optical Tracker at Diego Garcia; 1 ground-based electro optical deep space surveillance system *(GEODSS)* at Diego Garcia

US Pacific Command • 1 MPS sqn (MPS-2 with equipment for one MEB) at Diego Garcia with 5 logistics and support ships; 1 naval air base at Diego Garcia, 1 support facility at Diego Garcia

CANADA

US Northern Command • 130

COLOMBIA

US Southern Command • 50

CUBA

US Southern Command • 850 at Guantánamo Bay

DEMOCRATIC REPUBLIC OF THE CONGO

UN • MONUSCO 3 obs

DJIBOUTI

US Africa Command • 1,200; 1 naval air base

EGYPT

MFO 700; 1 ARNG inf bn; 1 spt bn

EL SALVADOR

US Southern Command • 1 Forward Operating Location (Military, DEA, USCG and Customs personnel)

ETHIOPIA
US Africa Command • some MQ-9 *Reaper*

GERMANY
US Africa Command • 1 HQ at Stuttgart
US European Command • 43,300; 1 Combined Service HQ (EUCOM) at Stuttgart–Vaihingen
US Army 27,750
FORCES BY ROLE
1 HQ (US Army Europe (USAREUR)) at Heidelberg; 1 cav SBCT; 1 cbt avn bde; 1 engr bde; 1 int bde; 1 MP bde; 2 sigs bde; 1 spt bde; 1 (APS) armd ABCT eqpt set (transforming)
EQUIPMENT BY TYPE
M1 *Abrams;* M2/M3 *Bradley; Stryker,* M109; M777; M270 MLRS; AH-64 *Apache*; CH-47 *Chinook*; UH-60 *Black Hawk*
US Navy 480
USAF 14,200
FORCES BY ROLE
1 HQ (US Air Force Europe (USAFE)) at Ramstein AB; 1 HQ (3rd Air Force) at Ramstein AB; 1 ftr wg at Spangdahlem AB with 1 ftr sqn with 24 F-16C/D *Fighting Falcon;* 1 tpt wg at Ramstein AB with 16 C-130J *Hercules;* 2 C-20 Gulfstream; 9 C-21 Learjet; 1 C-40B
USMC 365

GREECE
US European Command • 370; 1 naval base at Makri; 1 naval base at Soudha Bay; 1 air base at Iraklion

GREENLAND (DNK)
US Strategic Command • 150; 1 ballistic missile early warning system (BMEWS) at Thule; 1 Spacetrack Radar at Thule

GUAM
US Pacific Command • 5,350; 1 air base; 1 naval base
EQUIPMENT BY TYPE
2 SSGN; 1 SSN; 1 MPS sqn (MPS-3 with equipment for one MEB) with 4 Logistics and Support vessels

GULF OF ADEN & SOMALI BASIN
NATO • *Operation Ocean Shield* 1 FFH

HAITI
UN • MINUSTAH 8

HONDURAS
US Southern Command • 400; 1 avn bn with CH-47 *Chinook*; UH-60 *Black Hawk*

ISRAEL
US Strategic Command • 1 AN/TPY-2 X-band radar at Nevatim

ITALY
US European Command • 10,950
US Army 3.450; 1 AB IBCT
US Navy 3,490; 1 HQ (US Navy Europe (USNAVEUR)) at Naples; 1 HQ (6th Fleet) at Gaeta; 1 MP sqn with 9 P-3C *Orion* at Sigonella
USAF 4,000; 1 ftr wg with 2 ftr sqn with 21 F-16C/D *Fighting Falcon* at Aviano
USMC 10

JAPAN
US Pacific Command • 50,200
US Army 2,450 1 HQ (9th Theater Army Area Command) at Zama
US Navy 19,600; 1 HQ (7th Fleet) at Yokosuka; 1 base at Sasebo; 1 base at Yokosuka
EQUIPMENT BY TYPE
1 CVN; 2 CGHM; 3 DDGHM; 4 DDGM; 1 LCC; 4 MCO; 1 LHD; 1 LPD; 2 LSD
USAF 12,650
FORCES BY ROLE
1 HQ (5th Air Force) at Okinawa – Kadena AB; 1 ftr wg at Okinawa – Kadena AB with 2 ftr sqn with 18 F-16C/D *Fighting Falcon* at Misawa AB; 1 ftr wg at Okinawa – Kadena AB with 1 AEW&C sqn with 2 E-3B *Sentry,* 1 CSAR sqn with 8 HH-60G *Pave Hawk,* 2 ftr sqn with 24 F-15C/D *Eagle;* 1 tpt wg at Yokota AB with 10 C-130H *Hercules;* 3 Beech 1900C (C-12J); 1 Special Ops gp at Okinawa – Kadena AB
USMC 15,500
FORCES BY ROLE
1 Marine div (3rd); 1 ftr sqn with 12 F/A-18D *Hornet;* 1 tkr sqn with 12 KC-130J *Hercules;* 2 tpt sqn with 12 MV-22B *Osprey*
US Strategic Command • 1 AN/TPY-2 X-band radar at Shariki

JORDAN
US Central Command • 900; 1 ANG sqn with 6 F-16C *Fighting Falcon;* 1 AD bty with MIM-104 *Patriot*

KOREA, REPUBLIC OF
US Pacific Command • 28,500
US Army 19,200
FORCES BY ROLE
1 HQ (8th Army) at Seoul; 1 div HQ (2nd Inf) located at Tongduchon; 1 armd ABCT; 1 cbt avn bde; 1 arty bde; 1 AD bde
EQUIPMENT BY TYPE
M1 *Abrams;* M2/M3 *Bradley;* M109; M270 MLRS; AH-64 *Apache;* CH-47 *Chinook;* UH-60 *Black Hawk;* MIM-104 *Patriot*/FIM-92A *Avenger;* 1 (APS) ABCT set
US Navy 250
USAF 8,800
FORCES BY ROLE
1 (AF) HQ (7th Air Force) at Osan AB; 1 ftr wg at Osan AB with 1 ftr sqn with 20 F-16C/D *Fighting Falcon;* 1 ftr sqn with 24 A-10C *Thunderbolt* II; 1 ISR sqn at Osan AB with U-2S; 1 ftr wg at Kunsan AB with 1 ftr sqn with 20 F-16C /D *Fighting Falcon;* 1 Spec Ops sqn
USMC 250

KUWAIT
US Central Command • 23,000; 1 ABCT; 1 ARNG cbt avn bde; 1 ARNG spt bde; 2 AD bty with 16 PAC-3 *Patriot;* elm 1 (APS) ABCT set

LIBERIA
UN • UNMIL 5; 4 obs

MALI
UN • MINUSMA 5

MARSHALL ISLANDS
US Strategic Command • 1 detection and tracking radar at Kwajalein Atoll

MEDITERRANEAN SEA
US European Command • US Navy • 6th Fleet

EQUIPMENT BY TYPE
1 CGHM; 1 DDGHM; 3 DDGM; 1 LCC; 1 LPD

MIDDLE EAST
UN • UNTSO 2 obs

MOLDOVA
OSCE • Moldova 3

NETHERLANDS
US European Command • 340

NORWAY
US European Command • 1 (APS) SP 155mm arty bn set

PACIFIC OCEAN
US Pacific Command • US Navy • 3rd Fleet

EQUIPMENT BY TYPE
8 SSBN; 19 SSGN; 11 SSN; 5 CVN; 10 CGHM; 18 DDGHM; 8 DDGM; 7 FFH; 3 FFHM; 3 MCO; 2 LHD; 1 LHA; 3 LPD; 4 LSD

PERSIAN GULF
US Central Command • Navy • 5th Fleet

EQUIPMENT BY TYPE
8 PCO; 6 (Coast Guard) PCC

Combined Maritime Forces • CTF-152: 6 MCO; 1 AFSB

PHILIPPINES
US Pacific Command • 180

PORTUGAL
US European Command • 750; 1 spt facility at Lajes

QATAR
US Central Command • 600; elm 1 (APS) ABCT set

SAUDI ARABIA
US Central Command • 300

SERBIA
NATO • KFOR • *Joint Enterprise* 669; 1 surv bde HQ

OSCE • Kosovo 10

OSCE • Serbia 4

SEYCHELLES
US Africa Command • some MQ-9 *Reaper* UAV; 1 DDGHM

SINGAPORE
US Pacific Command • 170; 1 log spt sqn; 1 spt facility

SOUTH SUDAN
UN • UNMISS 5

SPAIN
US European Command • 1,500; 1 air base at Morón; 1 naval base at Rota

THAILAND
US Pacific Command • 240

TURKEY
US European Command • 1,550; MQ-1B *Predator* UAV at Incirlik; 1 air base at Incirlik; 1 support facility at Ankara; 1 support facility at Izmir

US Strategic Command • 1 Spacetrack Radar at Incirlik; 1 AN/TPY-2 X-band radar at Kürecik

NATO • *Active Fence*: 2 AD bty with MIM-104 *Patriot*

UNITED ARAB EMIRATES
US Central Command • 300: 2 AD bty with MIM-104 *Patriot*

UNITED KINGDOM
US European Command • 9,500

FORCES BY ROLE
1 ftr wg at RAF Lakenheath with 1 ftr sqn with 24 F-15C/D *Eagle*, 2 ftr sqn with 23 F-15E *Strike Eagle*; 1 ISR sqn at RAF Mildenhall with OC-135/RC-135; 1 tkr wg at RAF Mildenhall with 15 KC-135R *Stratotanker*; 1 Spec Ops gp at RAF Mildenhall with 1 sqn with 5 MC-130H *Combat Talon* II; 5 CV-22B *Osprey*; 1 sqn with 1 MC-130J *Commando* II; 4 MC-130P *Combat Shadow*

US Strategic Command • 1 ballistic missile early warning system (BMEWS) and 1 Spacetrack Radar at Fylingdales Moor

FOREIGN FORCES

Canada 12 USCENTCOM; 303 NORTHCOM (NORAD)

Germany Air Force: trg units at Goodyear AFB (AZ)/ Sheppard AFB (TX) with 40 T-38 *Talon* trg ac; 69 T-6A *Texan* II; 1 trg sqn Holloman AFB (NM) with 24 *Tornado* IDS; NAS Pensacola (FL); Fort Rucker (AL) • Missile trg located at Fort Bliss (TX)

United Kingdom Army, Navy, Air Force ε480

Table 2 **Selected Arms Procurements and Deliveries, North America**

Designation	Type	Quantity (Current)	Contract Value	Prime Nationality	Prime Contractor	Order Date	First Delivery Due	Notes
Canada (CAN)								
Commando (Tactical Armoured Patrol Vehicle)	Recce	500	CAN$603m	US	Textron (Textron Marine & Land Systems)	2012	2014	Option for 100 more
Hero-class	PSOH	9	CAN$194m	CAN	Halifax Shipyard	2009	2012	For Coast Guard; fifth vessel commissioned Oct 2013
CH-148 *Cyclone*	Tpt hel	28	US$5bn	US	UTC (Sikorsky)	2004	tbd	Programme continues to suffer delay. As of late 2013, alternative options are being explored
CH-47F *Chinook*	Tpt hel	15	US$1.15bn	US	Boeing	2009	2013	Fifth delivered Oct 2013; two more due by end-2013. Delivery to be complete by Jun 2014
United States (US)								
Stryker	APC (W)	4,507	US$14.4bn	US	General Dynamics (GDLS)	2001	2002	Includes multiple variants; includes DVH (Double V-Hull) versions
Gerald R. Ford-class	CVN	2	US$15.4bn	US	Huntingdon Ingalls Industries	2008	2015	Keel of lead ship laid in 2009. Total cost for the two vessels is currently estimated at US$24.2bn
Virginia-class	SSN	18	US$50bn	US	General Dynamics (Electric Boat)	1998	2004	Ten in service by late 2013. FY14 budget would fund additional two
Zumwalt-class	CGHM	3	US$11.1bn	US	General Dynamics (BIW)/ Huntingdon Ingalls Industries	2008	2014	First vessel launched 2013; ISD due Jul 2014. Total cost for the three vessels is currently estimated at US$11.7bn
Arleigh Burke-class	DDGHM	68	US$70.1bn	US	General Dynamics (BIW)/ Huntingdon Ingalls Industries	1985	1991	62 vessels in service. FY14 budget would fund additional vessel
Freedom/ Independence-class (Littoral Combat Ship)	FFHM	14	US$7.3bn	AUS/US	Austal (Austal USA)/Lockheed Martin	2005	2008	At least 12 of each design to be built. Three currently in service; six currently in build. FY14 budget would fund additional four
America-class	LHA	2	US$6.5bn	US	Huntingdon Ingalls Industries	2007	2014	First vessel under construction. Delivery now scheduled for 2014. Third vessel planned
San Antonio-class	LPD	11	US$18.4bn	US	Huntingdon Ingalls Industries	1996	2002	Enduring problems and delays with class. Eight vessels in service by late 2013
F/A-18E/F *Super Hornet*	FGA	552	US$43.3bn	US	Boeing	1997	1998	492 delivered as of late 2013
F-35A *Lightning* II	FGA	84	US$17.3bn	US	Lockheed Martin	2007	2011	CTOL variant. 27 delivered as of late 2013. FY14 budget would fund additional 19
F-35B *Lightning* II	FGA	44	εUS$10bn	US	Lockheed Martin	2008	2011	STOVL variant. 30 delivered as of late 2013. FY14 budget would fund additional six
F-35C *Lightning* II	FGA	22	εUS$5.6bn	US	Lockheed Martin	2010	2012	CV variant. three delivered as of late 2013. FY14 budget would fund additional four
P-8A *Poseidon*	ASW ac	37	US$8.7bn	US	Boeing	2011	2012	11 delivered as of late 2013. FY14 budget would fund additional 16

Table 2 **Selected Arms Procurements and Deliveries, North America**

Designation	Type	Quantity (Current)	Contract Value	Prime Nationality	Prime Contractor	Order Date	First Delivery Due	Notes
EA-18G *Growler*	EW ac	114	US$8.9bn	US	Boeing	2003	2009	90 delivered as of late 2013. FY14 budget would fund additional 21
E-2D *Hawkeye*	AEW&C ac	64	US$8.1bn	US	Northrop Grumman	2004	2010	FY14 budget would fund additional five
C-130J *Hercules*	Tpt ac	88	US$6.9bn	US	Lockheed Martin	1995	1999	Deliveries ongoing. FY14 budget would fund additional six
CV-22 *Osprey*	Tilt Rotor ac	46	US$4bn	US	Textron (Bell)/ Boeing	2002	2006	35 delivered as of late 2013. FY14 budget would fund additional three
MV-22 *Osprey*	Tilt Rotor ac	262	US$23bn	US	Textron (Bell)/ Boeing	1997	1999	211 delivered as of late 2013. FY14 budget would fund additional 18
AH-1Z *Viper*	Atk hel	27	US$1bn	US	Textron (Bell)	2010	2013	New build; FY14 budget would fund additional 11
AH-64E *Apache Guardian*	Atk hel	101	US$2.3bn	US	Boeing	2010	2011	Ten new build and 91 remanufactured. 46 delivered by late 2013. FY14 budget would fund additional 42 remanufactured
CH-47F / MH-47G *Chinook*	Hvy tpt hel	410	εUS$10.4bn	US	Boeing	2000	2004	226 new build hel and 184 remanufactured. FY14 budget would fund an additional six and 22 respectively
UH-60M *Black Hawk*	Tpt hel	583	εUS$11.3bn	US	UTC (Sikorsky)	2004	2006	FY14 budget would fund additional 65
EC145 (UH-72A *Lakota*)	Tpt hel	305	US2bn	Int'l	EADS (EADS North America)	2006	2006	FY14 budget would fund additional ten
MH-60R *Seahawk*	ASW hel	201	US$8.6bn	US	UTC (Sikorsky)	2000	2006	178 delivered by late 2013. FY14 budget would fund additional 19
MH-60S *Knight Hawk*	MRH hel	249	US$6.2bn	US	UTC (Sikorsky)	1999	2002	237 delivered by late 2013. FY14 budget would fund additional 18
MQ-1C *Grey Eagle*	CISR UAV	103	US$2bn	US	General Atomics /ASI	2010	2011	For army. FY14 budget would fund additional 15
MQ-8B *Fire Scout*	ISR UAV	23	US$320.7m	US	Northrop Grumman	2006	2008	Delivery to be complete by end-2013
MQ-8C *Fire Scout*	ISR UAV	17	US$377.5m	US	Northrop Grumman	2012	2013	First delivered Jul 2013
MQ-9 *Reaper*	CISR UAV	228	US$3.8bn	US	General Atomics	2001	2002	132 delivered by late 2013. FY14 budget would fund additional 12
RQ-4A/B *Global Hawk*	ISR UAV	45	US$4.7bn	US	Northrop Grumman	1995	1997	Block 40 numbers reduced to fund upgrade of earlier production models. Status of final three Block 30 airframes uncertain

Chapter Four
Europe

Maintaining capability amid austerity

Since the economic and financial crisis hit Europe in 2008, the capability challenge facing European nations has been out in the open and increasingly well understood by NATO and EU member states: there will be a growing gap between security demand and capability supply. Not least because of the re-orientation of US defence policy towards the Asia-Pacific, European governments will need to assume a greater share of the burden for international security, particularly in Europe's fragile vicinity to the south and the east, at a time when defence spending is shrinking. The multinational level of ambition, as expressed in EU and NATO strategic guidance, has remained largely unchanged, while leaders recognise that they face an increasingly complex security environment. Syria also exposed another side to the capability challenge: the need for governments to define a convincing narrative for the continued use of armed forces in crisis management.

NATO's 'smart defence' initiative and the EU's equipment pooling and sharing approach, both designed to increase systematic and closer defence cooperation among the member states of these organisations, continue to be plagued by patchy progress. In July 2013, NATO allies completed one of 29 multinational smart-defence projects, developing a logistics partnership on helicopter maintenance in Afghanistan (under US leadership): the first project both launched and completed after the May 2012 Chicago Summit. The project allows allies to pool spare parts, tools and technicians to generate cost savings and reduce repair time for helicopters. Another important NATO endeavour dating back to the 2012 summit and slowly taking shape is the Connected Forces Initiative (CFI). Although NATO allies have made significant progress on interoperability as a result of operations, including those in Afghanistan, this progress will be difficult to maintain in the face of decreasing spending and the lower operational tempo many observers expect following the 2014 ISAF drawdown.

Attempts to revitalise the NATO Response Force (NRF) and a renewed focus on high-visibility live exercises will play a key part in CFI implementation. In the post-ISAF environment, the CFI is likely to concentrate on combat effectiveness, by focusing on training and exercises in particular. In this context, NATO Supreme Allied Commander Transformation (SACT), General Jean-Paul Paloméros, explained the purpose of the CFI in September 2013 as '[maintaining] military effectiveness through the preservation of our readiness and interoperability by exercising and training together and with partners'. The CFI implementation plan under development in 2013 includes a training concept for 2015–20 and recommendations on a series of exercises to be conducted from 2016–20. NATO also plans to conduct a high-visibility exercise in 2015. In this context, the NRF – a rapid-reaction formation announced in 2002 and consisting of a command-and-control element from the NATO Command Structure, a 13,000-strong Immediate Response Force (IRF), and a Response Forces Pool to supplement the IRF when necessary – is expected to regain prominence after 2014.

From the national level downward, European defence adjustments continue to take place, however, and 2013 saw key announcements from France and the Netherlands to this effect. The overdue French White Paper on Defence and National Security, published in April 2013, announced a budget freeze at €31.4bn (US$41.7bn) for three years, implying real-terms decreases in spending. The number of forces to be available for sustainable deployment will be reduced from 30,000 to 15,000. In terms of geographic focus, France will concentrate on Africa and the Mediterranean Sea. The paper amounts to a careful revision of France's overall ambitions in light of budgetary pressure (see p. 66).

In September 2013, the Dutch government published a document entitled 'In the Interest of the Netherlands', setting out major decisions on the future of the armed forces. In the paper, the government announced budget cuts in the years up to 2018 – some 2,400 military and civilian posts will be lost. As in the case of France, the personnel reductions come in addition to earlier cuts to the force structure announced in previous years. While insisting the spectrum of tasks covered by the armed forces will remain unchanged, the paper outlines that contributions to international operations will in future be of shorter duration and smaller in size. In an attempt to maintain the ability to improve future capabilities, the government 'will continue to work towards bringing its annual investment percentage back up to 20%' of the defence budget. Notable decisions include the replacement of F-16s with F-35s, beginning in 2019, and accelerated work towards establishing a cyber command.

Future agendas

A less well-understood aspect of the capability challenge is the need to define a convincing narrative for the continued use of armed forces in international crisis management. The debate over what to do regarding the Syrian conflict demonstrated that two decades of continuous and simultaneous deployments have left electorates across Europe unsure of the success and necessity of such action. Both the EU and NATO will likely have to tackle this issue in their upcoming 2013 and 2014 summits. If governments fail to define a forward-looking agenda and instead become embroiled in rehearsing the now well-understood difficulties of capability generation and provision, expectations will likely not be met.

NATO Secretary-General Anders Fogh Rasmussen argued during a speech in Brussels, on 19 September 2013, that 'NATO remains an essential source of stability in an unpredictable world'. At the same time, he warned that budget cuts were threatening European member states' ability to shape the security environment: 'the fact is that if the current trend continues, if we see continued declining defence budgets, then one day the Europeans will not be able to participate in international crisis management as we saw it in Libya, and the vacuum Europe leaves behind will be filled by the other powers in the world, for instance the emerging powers that actually invest more and more in defence and security, and eventually it means that Europe will lose influence on the international scene'.

Catherine Ashton, EU High Representative of the Union for Foreign Affairs and Security Policy, argued in her July 2013 interim report on the Common Security and Defence Policy (CSDP) that 'Europe faces rising security challenges, within a changing strategic context, while the financial crisis is increasingly affecting its security and defence capability. These developments warrant a strategic debate among heads of state and government'.

NATO's 2014 summit agenda will be heavily focused on the drawdown in Afghanistan and transition there to an assistance and mentoring mission. Meanwhile, the European Council on security and defence (19–20 December 2013) will likely be a primary means of articulating the strategic debate in the EU. Leaders will seek to address the effectiveness, visibility and impact of the CSDP; boosting capability development; and strengthening the European defence industry. Senior officials in both NATO and the EU have adopted a 'defence matters' discourse, picking up on the need for a stronger strategic narrative. Ideas on how to move forward on this agenda, however, remained scarce.

In the EU context, one player trying to expand its security- and defence-related role is the European Commission. The commission is attempting to achieve this through the use of EU-level regulations. The European defence-equipment market has remained largely unaffected by EU single-market principles, instead feeding off and perpetuating the economic distortions and inefficiencies of the European defence-industrial base. This has been enabled by governments' use of Article 346 of the Treaty of Lisbon (previously Article 296 of the Maastricht Treaty), which was intended to provide member states with the ability to circumvent the rules of the single market and European procurement law in exceptional cases where national-security considerations took precedence. Instead, recourse to Article 346 became standard practice for defence procurement, with member states invoking essential national-security interests as a matter of course.

The commission has for a number of years tried to build an economic case for making the defence-equipment market more efficient by opening it up to competition, based on the savings member-state governments could expect to generate from lower equipment prices. In July 2013, the commission outlined a strategy and action plan built on four core elements. The first deals with further deepening the internal EU market for defence and increasing its efficiency. This objective implies that market distortions – such as offsets, merger controls and state aid for industry – are tackled. Furthermore, security of supply for goods traded within the internal market is to be increased through new licensing systems. The second element is to increase the competitiveness of the European defence-industrial base through greater standardisation, common certification and fostering regional clusters of specialisation. The third is based on increased exploitation of the synergies arising from civil-military dual-use research and innovation. Finally, the commission has suggested that it might be time to introduce EU-owned dual-use capabilities to complement national assets.

Unsurprisingly, this action plan is viewed with scepticism and some direct opposition by several member governments. UK Secretary of State for Defence Philip Hammond voiced his criticism of the commission's growing role in regulating the defence market in September 2013, saying that 'interference in the export of defence equipment and government-to-government defence sales, or the creation of … "specific European standards for military products" represent a significant potential extension of the Commission's role and are not necessarily in the UK defence industry's best interests – and we will resist them'.

Despite suspicion from national capitals, the commission had been implementing elements of its strategy for several years before the 2013 publication of the document. Notably, two directives entered into force in 2009, which amount to significant regulatory reform in the defence market. The Defence Procurement Directive (Directive 2009/81/EC) deals specifically with goods and services related to security and defence. Covering contracts above a certain value, the directive establishes a principle of non-discriminatory competition and obligation to award contracts on the basis of price and performance. It also seeks to limit the use of offsets, which are required by some EU member states when they procure defence services and goods from a foreign supplier. Crucially, the directive does not apply to cooperative or collaborative procurement programmes. Although several member states were late in transposing it into national law, this process was completed in March 2013.

The second piece of EU-introduced legislation, the Directive on Transfers of Defence Related Products (Directive 2009/43/EC) provides a new licensing system for intra-EU exports, distinguishing between general, global and individual licences. Under this framework, pre-approved licences become the norm for transfers within the EU and individual licences are only used in particular instances, including one-time transfers and the protection, in individual cases, of member states' essential security interests. These transfer regulations should simultaneously improve security of defence-product supply within the EU and significantly reduce the bureaucratic burden related to transfers among member states.

Although several capitals attest to changing purchasing practices to comply with the 2009 directives, it is still too early to assess their full impact. Poland's plans, announced in May 2013, to spend some US$43bn over the coming ten years on procurement provided ample cause for commission officials to worry about member governments' willingness to take the directives seriously. Minister of National Defence Tomasz Siemoniak stressed that Poland would heavily favour local companies and bidders offering technology transfers as well as offsets: 'for us, an optimal result is to develop these big contracts in a way that we are also in the kitchen, that our engineers and scientists are taking part in an equal way. Whoever promises us a greater share of technology transfer and work in Poland will be favoured'. These are exactly the kind of market distortions EU-level emerging defence regulation seeks to avoid. Poland, buoyed by strong economic growth, has been one of the few countries in Europe able to significantly increase its spending. Measured in constant 2010 prices/exchange rates, Poland increased its defence spending by over 22% between 2006 and 2010. Despite such setbacks, the commission seems determined to introduce single-market elements into the European defence-equipment sector.

DEFENCE ECONOMICS

Regional macroeconomics

Protracted efforts by public and private sectors across Europe to deleverage – reduce debt liabilities – have meant that, five years after the 2008 financial crisis began, European growth generally remains negative or anaemic, with current expenditures reduced in order to pay down debt. The second quarter of 2013 saw economic activity in the eurozone return to the black, but this followed 18 months of recession. Output gaps remain large across the region, while high unemployment and fiscal retrenchment remain the norm for most countries. According to the IMF, only six out of 36 European states managed to run primary budget surpluses in any year since 2008, while for nearly half of them unemployment was projected to remain at double-digit levels in 2013. Unemployment in the eurozone as a whole was estimated at 12.3% in 2013. This economic stagnation notwithstanding, the financial turmoil that had affected the region since 2008 eased in 2013. In large measure, this was the product of European Central Bank (ECB) President Mario Draghi's pledge in July

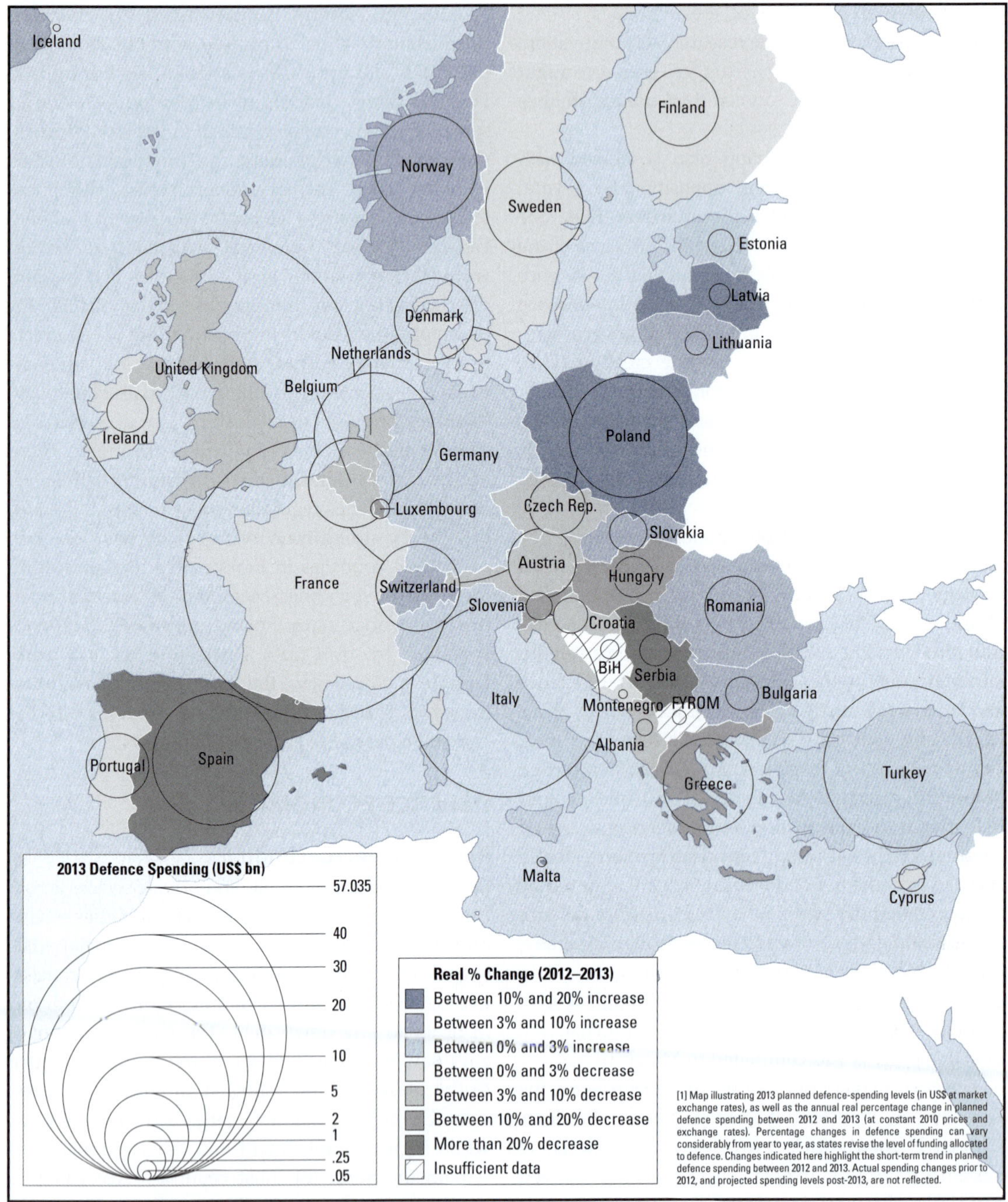

Map 1 **Europe Regional Defence Spending**[1]

Sub-regional groupings referred to in defence economics text: Central Europe (Austria, Czech Republic, Germany, Hungary, Poland, Slovakia and Switzerland), Northern Europe (Denmark, Estonia, Finland, Latvia, Lithuania, Norway and Sweden), Southern Europe (Cyprus, Greece, Italy, Malta, Portugal and Spain), Southeastern Europe (Bulgaria, Romania and Turkey), the Balkans (Albania, Bosnia–Herzegovina, Croatia, FYROM, Montenegro, Serbia and Slovenia) and Western Europe (Belgium, France, Iceland, Ireland, Luxembourg, the Netherlands and the United Kingdom).

2012 to do 'whatever it takes' to preserve the euro. The ECB subsequently announced, in September 2012, that it would consider outright monetary transactions, whereby it would purchase government securities of countries in adjustment or precautionary programmes with the European Financial Stability Facility or the European Stability Mechanism. This possible supply of potentially unlimited quantities of liquidity markedly reduced instability in financial markets in the final quarter of 2012, as risk premiums in bank and sovereign-debt markets fell sharply, and by early 2013 European equity and bond markets had risen, in some cases by as much as 20%. However, private-sector financing costs remained high due to bank balance-sheet consolidation and persistent weak demand throughout the region. Overall, in 2013 the eurozone was projected by the IMF to contract by 0.4%, while Europe as a whole was expected to only grow by 0.3%.

Regional defence spending

As discussed in *The Military Balance 2013* (pp. 92–6), the necessity of fiscal retrenchment has meant that European countries have had to reconsider the level of resources allocated towards defence. Between 2010 and 2011, nominal European defence-spending levels rose by 3.2%, from US$287bn to US$296.2bn, but then fell by 6.7% to US$276.3bn in 2012. There was a slight increase in nominal spending levels of 1.0% in 2013. However, the scale of these fluctuations was largely the product of exchange-rate volatility between the crisis-hit euro and the dollar. On average, the euro appreciated by 5% in 2011 before depreciating strongly by 8% in 2012, resulting in an inflated dollar total in 2011 and a correspondingly reduced dollar total in 2012. Discounting for such exchange-rate effects, as well as for inflation, presents a clearer perspective of the downward trajectory in European defence outlays. In 2013, real defence spending fell in more than half (57%) of European states, slightly less than the 70% and 65% of states that reduced real-terms defence outlays in 2011 and 2012 respectively. Since 2010, real defence spending has declined at a compound annual growth rate of 1.9%, with reductions of 3.0% in 2011, 2.2% in 2012 and 2.4% in 2013. Overall, real defence-spending levels in 2013 were 7.4% lower than in 2010.

Although the overall regional spending trend is negative, there has been a degree of sub-regional variation in the extent of defence austerity. As shown in Figure 4, by far the largest reductions in sub-regional defence outlays have occurred in Southern Europe and the Balkans. In both of these sub-regions, aggregate spending fell in real terms by more than one-fifth between 2010 and 2013. Particularly large reductions in these regions were seen in Greece (-42%), Slovenia (-39.2%), Hungary (-21%), Spain (-19.6%) and Italy (-15.8%). A smaller – though not insignificant – sub-regional reduction of 7.4% was also seen in Western Europe, as spending declined by 8–12% in Ireland, the Netherlands and the UK; while smaller reductions of 3–5% occurred in Belgium and France. Real

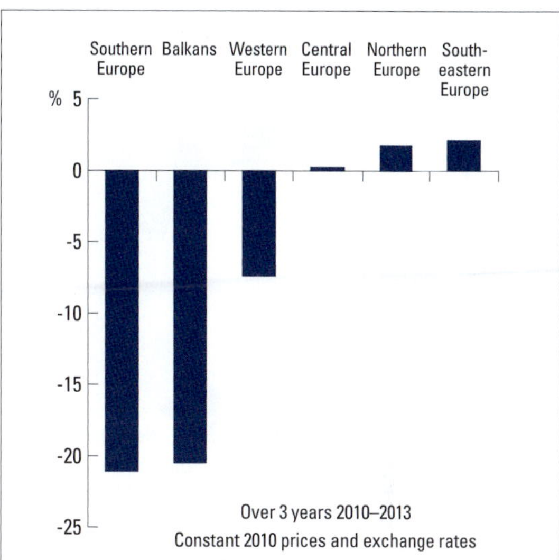

Figure 4 **Europe Real Defence Spending Changes 2010–13 by Sub-Region (%)**

spending levels remained relatively unchanged between 2010 and 2013 in Central Europe, although the aggregate figures mask significant reductions in the Czech Republic (-16%), Hungary (-21%), and, to a lesser extent, Slovakia (-6.5%). These were offset by the large increase in Polish defence spending. Real defence outlays increased in only ten out of 37 states, including Poland (14.8%), Bulgaria (10.2%), Norway (9.1%) and Turkey (5.4%).

Western Europe continues to dominate regional spending totals (see Figure 5), accounting for just under half (44.2%) of all regional outlays, while Central Europe accounted for a further 23.3%. Together, Western and Central Europe made up two-thirds of the 2013 European total, or some US$187bn. Of the remaining third, Southern Europe accounted for half of this (or 16% of total European outlays), with the other half taken up in roughly equal parts by Northern Europe (8.3% of the European total) and Southeastern Europe (Turkey, Bulgaria and Romania, at 7.3%). The Balkans accounted for less than 1% of regional spending. Overall, since 2010, real reductions in NATO European countries have fallen at a faster pace than non-NATO European states, with the former witnessing defence spending contract at an average rate of 2.6% per annum, and the latter at 1.7% per annum. In general, defence spending in Europe has been cut at a slightly faster rate than the contraction in GDP across the region; defence spending as a proportion of regional GDP has fallen steadily, from 1.58% in 2010 to 1.43% in 2013.

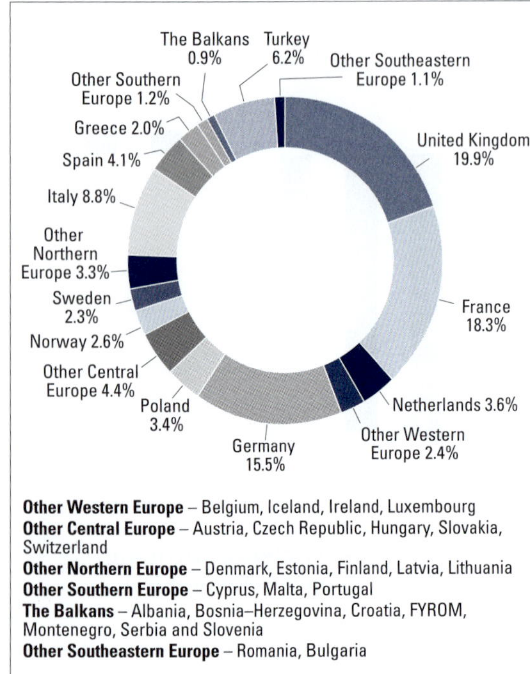

Figure 5 **Europe Defence Spending 2013 by Country**

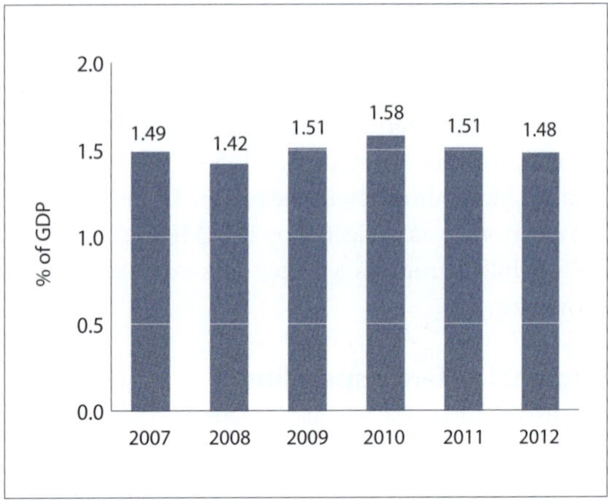

Figure 6 **Europe Regional Defence Expenditure** as % of GDP

Regional defence-spending composition

Since the 2008 crisis, there has been concern in Western states about the effect that defence austerity could have on the size, structure and capability of armed forces in Europe. Only three out of 26 NATO European states (Greece, Estonia and the UK) spend more than the NATO target of 2% of GDP on defence. Additionally, a large proportion of European defence outlays tend to be allocated to military pensions, wages and salaries, rather than on funding for training, operational readiness and capital investments in areas such as equipment acquisition and modernisation. Figure 7 depicts (on the vertical axis) the proportion of defence spending that states in the region allocated to personnel-related outlays in 2012 – principally on salaries, benefits and pensions. The horizontal axis indicates the size of states' defence budgets in dollars. As indicated, personnel-related expenses accounted for more than half of total defence outlays in 25 out of 35 states analysed. Personnel costs exceeded 40% of total defence outlays in 30 out of 35 states. On average, states allocated 60% of defence spending to personnel-related outlays. This proportion varied to some extent across sub-regions – ranging from an average of about 55% of defence outlays in Western Europe and Central Europe to 70.3% and 73.5% of outlays in the Balkans and Southern Europe respectively. That is, on average, nearly three-quarters of military spending in Southern Europe in 2012 was allocated to personnel costs. (Note: the average proportion allocated to personnel spending in 2012 was lowest in Northern Europe (43.5%), but this is an underestimate due to gaps in the dataset relating to the exclusion of military pensions as part of defence-budget totals. As such, the actual proportion for this sub-region is almost certainly higher.) Particularly high personnel spending (above 75% of the total budget) occurred in nine out of 35 states analysed, including Greece, Portugal and Italy.

The defence austerity programmes that followed the 2008 financial crash are likely to have played a role in increasing the proportion of defence budgets allocated to personnel expenses in some European states, particularly where the balance of cuts has been weighted towards reducing non-personnel expenditures, such as lower levels of equipment procurement and maintenance, research and development, base closures and reduced military-construction activities. For example, according to NATO statistics, between 2007 and 2011, the proportion of defence spending allocated to personnel-related costs rose by more than 20% in Spain, Slovenia, Bulgaria, Slovakia, Latvia and Lithuania – all of which were also hard hit by the financial crisis. However, in other European states, the proportion of defence spending allocated to personnel in 2011 and 2012 remained broadly constant between the pre- and post-crisis periods. This is the case in Portugal and Italy, where the personnel-spending proportion of the budget in 2011 has remained relatively in line with the proportion allocated in 2007

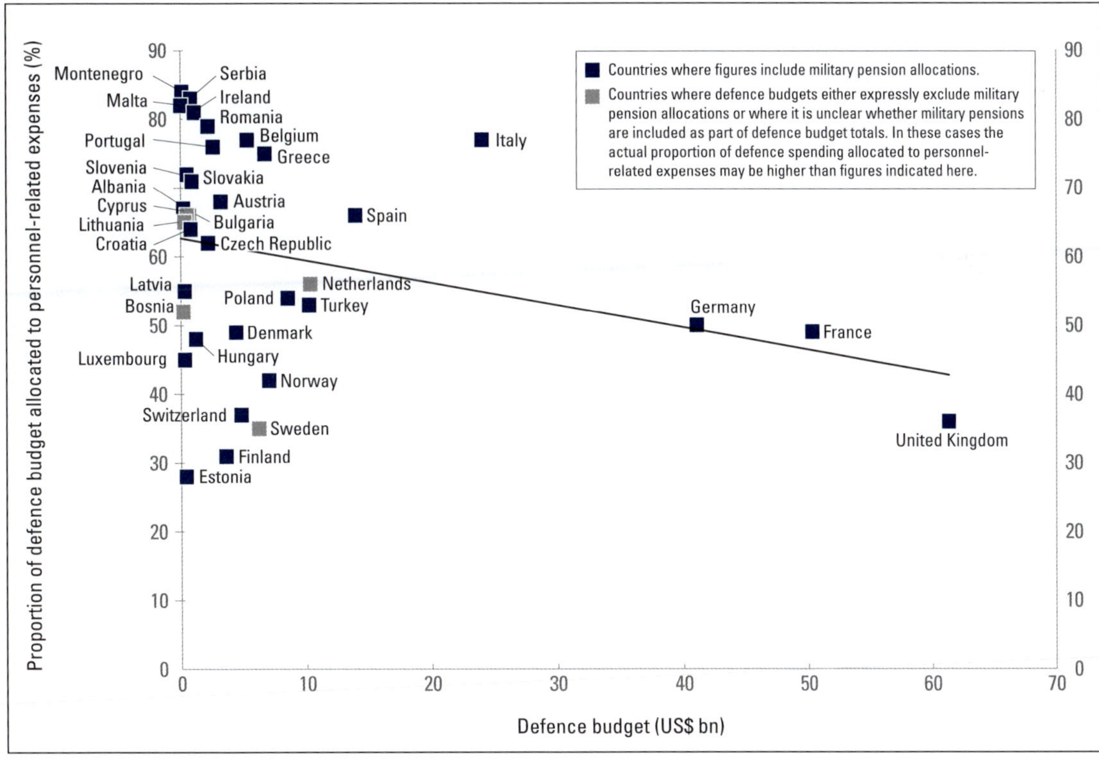

Figure 7 **Military Personnel-Related Defence Spending in Europe in 2012**

(prior to onset of the crisis), according to NATO data. In a small number of European states – notably Greece, Germany, France, Belgium and the UK – the proportion allocated to personnel costs has actually fallen from 2007 levels. For example, according to NATO statistics, personnel-related spending in France fell from 57.1% of the defence budget to 49.4% in 2011, while in Greece it fell from 79.5% to 73.9% over the same period. (Note: Figure 7 also demonstrates that, in general, the higher the defence budget, the lower the proportion of defence spending allocated to personnel costs (see downward sloping line in Figure 7).)

FRANCE

2013 was an important year for French defence policy. It began with the defence ministry initiating a rapid military deployment to Mali in the face of an imminent threat to the Malian government. The end of the year, meanwhile, was likely to see many military staff occupied with the December 2013 European Council on security and defence, to which France's contribution would be central. In late summer, France, together with the United States, played a high-profile role in the crisis over the use of chemical weapons in Syria, advocating a robust policy, including the threat of military force in response to the Syrian government's use of these weapons, and to dissuade it from doing so again. In the end, a Russian initiative to disarm the Assad regime of its chemical arsenal led to the threat of military force receding.

Amid ongoing operational deployments, contingency planning and one sharp combat mission, the government issued a new White Paper on Defence and National Security. The last paper was issued in 2008, so this document was anticipated not only for its assessment of France's current and future strategic environment but also, for instance, for detail on the degree to which the effects of the financial crisis would lead to adjustments in force structures and procurements. France was able to gather lessons not only from recent operational activities but also from other states' post-2008 defence reviews, and these factors arguably contributed to some of the key findings in the paper on force packages and capability requirements, as well as on wider themes such as retaining both the ability to act autonomously and a full spectrum of military capabilities.

Given the need for fiscal consolidation, the choices facing the Hollande administration over allocating funds were unpalatable. One was to sacrifice major programmes; the other was to reduce equipment numbers across all three services. The later 'Loi de Programmation Militaire' (LPM), the document whereby the defence ministry allocated funds to match the priorities laid out in the White Paper, focused on the latter, aiming to balance strategic priorities with financial strictures, but in such a way that major defence reductions were avoided. Notably, France decided not to cut a capability, for instance in the way that the UK had done in its 2010 Strategic Defence and Security Review (SDSR), when it relinquished carrier strike capability until new vessels, and aircraft, came into service.

Rapid reaction in Mali

Throughout 2012, the developing crisis in Mali had been closely monitored by French military planners, and an air-support mission for the Malian army and/or African Union forces had been in preparation since October. The decision to launch *Opération Serval* was taken on 10 January after an urgent request from Mali's interim president, Dioncounda Traoré, who was facing a surge towards the capital, Bamako, by hundreds of jihadist armoured vehicles, which had reached the strategically important towns of Mopti and Ségou. French combat helicopters from special forces based in Burkina Faso engaged ground targets, joined shortly afterwards by *Mirage* 2000D combat aircraft based in Chad, and the advance was rapidly thwarted. Light armour from the French contingent in Côte d'Ivoire was also deployed to Mali.

France had already developed military plans for deployment to Mali, with the goal of eventually supporting African Union-led forces and the planned EU Training Mission (EUTM) when these missions were established. These plans were quickly adapted; importantly, they meant that French forces could implement well-prepared strategies relating to areas such as tactical mobility and logistics support. Although the expectation in Paris was always that ground forces would deploy in relation to these support missions, the immediate threat to Bamako, and the parlous state of the Malian army, led to rapid deployment. In the second half of January 2013, some 4,500 troops were airlifted to Mali, where they succeeded in driving the rebels back to their northern desert redoubts. They were assisted by *Rafale* combat aircraft making the 2,500-mile, nine-hour flight from bases in eastern France. The northern towns of Gao, Timbuktu and Kidal were all cleared of jihadist forces by February and many French troops were repatriated by April. Nonetheless, some 2,800 troops remained on *Opération Serval* as of October; some of these troops also deployed on occasion as operational assistance detachments, along with Malian battalions newly trained by the EUTM. Although intermittent and mostly low-level jihadist activity continued, Mali's presidential elections passed in July and August without major incident, while parliamentary elections were due in November.

The French intervention was impressive for the speed with which contingency planning was activated and adapted; its rapid entry into theatre and establishment of reliable logistics corridors; and also the combat effectiveness of the deployed French troops. France's pre-positioned forces in the region, and those on regional operations, proved vital, as did the local knowledge that both these forces, and planners back home, had accumulated. However, during *Opération Serval's* main operational phase, France was dependent on European, Canadian and US support assets for some key tasks, mainly strategic lift, air-to-air refuelling, logistics and intelligence. This support was important not so much because of its volume, although that of course helped, but because of its immediacy: it enabled French forces to maintain a high operational tempo – crucial given the ground they had to cover, as well as a desire not to let jihadist forces regroup. There was also awareness in Paris of France's limited stocks of MALE UAVs, highlighted in Mali where persistent intelligence, surveillance and reconnaissance (ISR) was of particular utility. The UK's Royal Air Force (RAF) deployed one of its *Sentinel* R1 aircraft to Senegal to assist operations, fitted with synthetic aperture radar (SAR) and Ground Moving Target Indicator (GMTI) systems. Perhaps it was little surprise, therefore, when the US Defence Security Cooperation Agency in June issued notification of an intended French purchase of 16 *Reaper* UAVs, for US$1.6bn, with the possible sale including 40 SAR/GMTI systems. Mali has, meanwhile, requested the establishment of a permanent French base in the country – a proposal being considered by Paris.

The 2013 *Livre Blanc*

The long-awaited White Paper on Defence and National Security assessed France's threat environment, strategic options and likely force requirements,

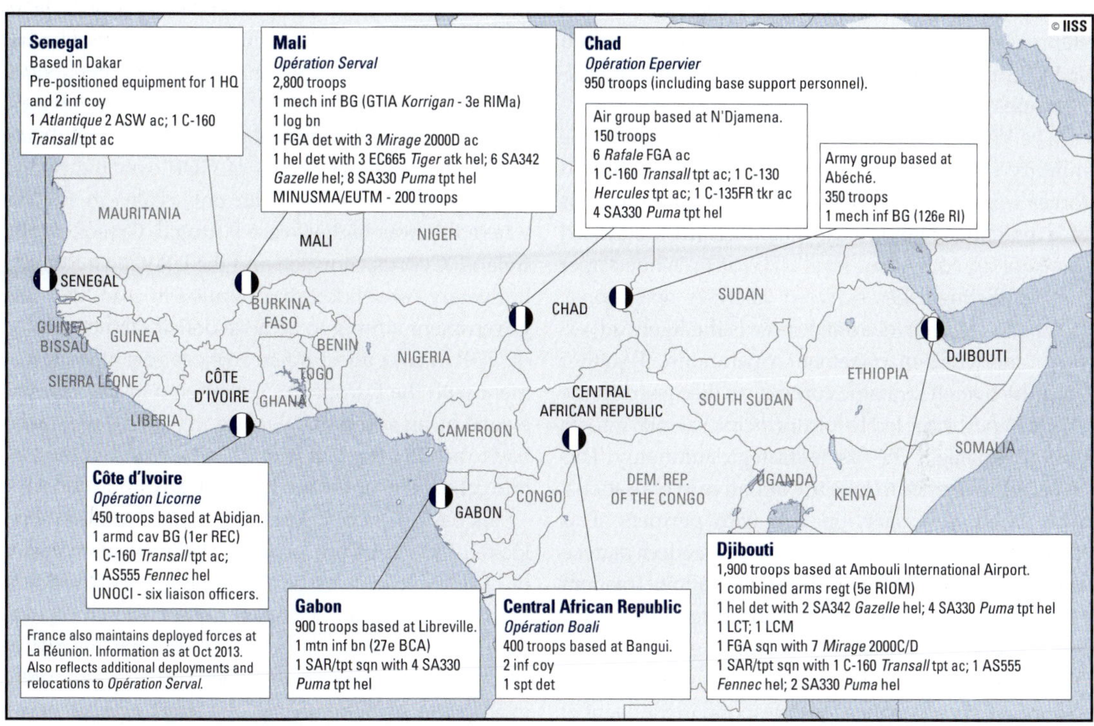

Map 2 **France: Selected Deployments in Africa**

in light of financial realities. It envisaged three types of threat: power-based threats (*menaces de la force*) emanating probably from Asia or from WMD proliferation; risks emanating from weak or failing states, above all in Africa, which are unable to exercise sovereignty, control their borders or stem migratory flows (Africa emerges in the paper as an area of ever-increasing strategic importance); and risks deriving from globalisation, such as cyber attacks, terrorism and access to, and free flow of, resources.

These threats gave rise to four main strategic priorities. The first is territorial protection, involving defence against external aggression, counter-terrorism and the protection of French citizens around the world. The second concerns collective guarantees for the security of Europe and the North Atlantic area, presented as inseparable from national defence. The White Paper discussed the relationship between France and both NATO and the EU's CSDP. France intended to play a leading and active role in NATO, but a pitch was also made for the relaunch of the EU's defence and security project. Later, the document placed this in the context of the financial crisis and the US rebalance to the Asia-Pacific. France called for this revitalisation of European defence to be enshrined by the commission, arguing that it would compensate for the EU's inadequacies in terms of external operations; foster development around pooling and sharing of the most essential military capabilities for the most plausible operations; and encourage consolidation of the European defence industry. The third strategic priority is stabilisation of Europe's neighbourhood. In the context of the US rebalance to the Asia-Pacific, Paris considers that Europeans no longer have any alternative but to consider their neighbourhood as a major strategic priority that they must manage, and for which they have to take responsibility. The fourth priority is therefore a French (and European) contribution to the stability of the Middle East and the Persian Gulf. France intends to prioritise this area (it already has a base in Abu Dhabi) in partnership with other international actors.

There are three key areas of expansion. Intelligence, which was already prioritised in the 2008 White Paper, and which has been brought more closely into focus in Libya and Mali, will be expanded, mainly through UAVs and an increased budget for the space domain. Special forces, whose role in Libya and Mali was also crucial, will be expanded. Finally, cyber defences will grow significantly. A major cyber attack will henceforth be considered an act of war and considerable new resources will be committed to an 'offensive cyber capacity'. Military cyber capacity is being stepped up with the recruitment of several hundred specialists and the creation of a dedicated and centralised operational command chain.

The White Paper also introduced a change on the military strategic level. Before 2013, France's armed forces were, it says, primarily organised on the basis of a potential high-intensity conflict with 'state-led forces of an equivalent level'. The 2013 White Paper instead distinguishes between 'coercive operations', in which a state-level armed force is the likely adversary, and crisis-management operations. Together with the overall strategic context, as discussed in the White Paper, these led to four principles which inform military strategy. The first is strategic autonomy. This 'must allow France to take the initiative in operations' and, where necessary, operate with partners. This means preserving resources that give freedom of decision and favouring capabilities that allow freedom of action, such as intelligence and targeting capacities. Second is consistency between armed forces' organisation and possible engagement scenarios. For instance, forces must be able to respond in the event of a state-level threat, but also – 'and sometimes simultaneously' – undertake long-term crisis-management operations, as well as retaining the capacity to carry out tasks such as infrastructure protection. Thirdly, forces need to be differentiated according to their specialisation, so that they are more effective in their particular role; this also would enable 'substantial savings by financing the most expensive or modern capabilities only where they are indispensable'. Analysts said this was similar thinking to the way the UK SDSR differentiated readiness levels within the Future Force 2020 construct, not least given the cost of maintaining forces at high readiness. Finally, pooling scarce and critical capabilities could allow economies in terms of allocating multi-purpose capabilities, depending on the particular mission requirement. This could also take place at the European level. Relevant capability areas include space, air transport, airborne refuelling, and surveillance and logistics.

Defence budgeting

In common with much of Europe, France saw a slowdown in economic growth after the 2008 financial crisis. After a sharp 3.1% contraction in 2009, moderate growth rates of 1.7% returned in 2010 and 2011, before the economy stagnated again in 2012 and 2013 (with growth at 0.03% and a projected -0.07% respectively). The unemployment rate exceeded 10% in 2012, while gross debt exceeded 90% of GDP in the same year. Although successive administrations made significant progress in reducing budget deficits from a high of 7.6% of GDP in 2009 to just under 4% of GDP in 2013, the general government fiscal deficit nonetheless averaged 5.6% of GDP over the period – according to the IMF, the only states in Europe where this was higher were Portugal, Greece, Spain, Ireland, Cyprus, Slovakia and the UK. Consequently, budgetary consolidation continued in 2013, with the government aiming to achieve deficit targets of 3.6% of GDP in 2014 and 2.8% in 2015, as part of an agreement with the European Commission in May 2013 to extend by an additional year (to 2015) the time France had to achieve the Maastricht Treaty requirement that budget deficits not exceed 3% of GDP.

As part of these efforts, the finance ministry had looked for significant savings. In the event, Minister of Defence Jean-Yves Le Drian persuaded President François Hollande to hold non-pension defence-budget allocations steady in nominal terms at €31.38bn from 2014 to 2016, before rising gradually in 2017 and 2018 (on average, by 0.64%) and levelling off in 2019 at €32.51bn. The maintenance of nominal spending levels between 2014 and 2016 was in part to be achieved through the realisation of 'exceptional receipts' from the sale of existing assets, such as real estate, used equipment and existing state equity holdings in major French defence companies. The state currently holds a 27% interest in Thales and Safran, 12% in EADS and 74% in shipbuilder DCNS. There was even talk of selling some state holdings in EDF and GDF SUEZ. Also important was the proposed sale of radio frequencies. Le Drian claimed that he already had €1.3bn in savings lined up for 2013 and was confident that he would find €1.8bn for 2014. These disposals (cumulatively totalling €6.1bn) were envisaged to fund 5.6% of the total defence budget in both 2014 and 2015, before declining gradually to fund 0.5% of the total in 2019. Despite the protection of nominal spending levels, however, defence spending is set to decline over the period in real terms: based on IMF deflator projections, real defence outlays are likely to decline by an average of 1.4% per annum between 2014 and 2018, with real non-pension defence-budget allocations in 2018 running at some 6.9% lower than they did in 2013. Additionally, as the economy grows over the period while nominal defence spending remains stagnant, defence spending as a proportion of GDP will fall from around 1.9% of GDP in 2013 to approximately 1.65% of GDP in 2018.

Policy implementation

On 2 August, the LPM was released, giving more detail on how France would implement, and fund, the White Paper's policy decisions. France would retain the capacity to manage a crisis such as that in Mali by projecting force to 'priority zones' – the Mediterranean, much of Africa, the Persian Gulf and the Indian Ocean. There would be 5,000 personnel at high readiness, and from this a 2,300-strong Quick Reaction Joint Force would be drawn. Up to 7,000 troops, plus air and naval assets, would be earmarked for crisis-management tasks. For major, high-intensity operations, limited in duration and with reasonable notice, envisaged assets included 15,000 troops, special forces, up to 45 combat aircraft, a carrier group and other naval assets; this was down from the 30,000-personnel total envisaged for a major multinational commitment under the 2008 White Paper. A total of 23,500 jobs would be cut from the armed forces in addition to the 10,175 job reductions remaining to be made since the findings of the 2008 White Paper. Around 7,500 soldiers would be removed from the payroll each year between 2014 and 2019, and some regiments were to disband. However, the majority of the reductions would affect support and administrative posts. These cuts were designed to save €4.4bn in salary costs.

The LPM is linked to the objective of preserving the main sectors of France's defence industry, ranging from aeronautics and communications to space and submarines. The maintenance of a viable and competitive defence industry was seen as a vital national and European interest, and the European Defence Agency was highlighted as the body responsible for promoting it. Space-based intelligence was a priority, with the optical-surveillance satellite MUSIS due to enter service in 2017 and the electronic-interception satellite CERES due in 2020. Overall, €17.1bn was set aside for equipment renewal. However, the LPM envisaged purchasing only 26 *Rafale* combat aircraft between 2014 and 2019, instead of the 11 per annum bought in recent years. Falling below 11 per year has production-cost implications, but the government hopes that exports will close this gap. However, Dassault has not, to date, secured contracts in the United Arab Emirates and Brazil, both potential overseas markets. Talks continue with India, which has selected the *Rafale* to meet a 126-aircraft requirement; French officials express confidence that the deal will be finalised. France's nuclear deterrent, comprising both air- and submarine-launched components, was still seen as the cornerstone of French security. Four ballistic-missile submarines will be retained, with the deterrent as a whole expected to cost €23bn over six years. The nuclear deterrent is explicitly stated to contribute to the security of the Atlantic Alliance and Europe.

The implications of the LPM for force structures became apparent in early October, with the first announcements concerning defence restructuring due for 2014. Among other measures, the 4th Regiment of Dragoons was to disband. The 1st Foreign Legion Cavalry Regiment, stationed at Orange in south-eastern France, was to transfer to the Dragoons' former base, with the 115th air base ensuring a continued defence presence at Orange. The air base at Dijon-Longvic was to close in 2014–15, and an air detachment at Varennes-sur-Allier to disband, as was an air-defence unit at the 116th air base at Luxeuil. The Directorate of Military Intelligence, at Creil, was to transfer to Balard, in southwest Paris, in line with a move to consolidate project staffs, departments and services into a single site. Further announcements were expected in 2014.

UNITED KINGDOM

The 2010 SDSR saw the UK government decide to reduce defence spending by 8%. Operational planning assumptions were made less demanding (see *The Military Balance 2013*, p. 107) and most non-nuclear capabilities were reduced by 20–30%. In 2013, implementation of SDSR changes continued, including reduction of civilian and military personnel. The Ministry of Defence (MoD) adopted a new management model, including decentralisation of budgets and authority for military capability moving from a much smaller ministry to the three armed services and the new Joint Forces Command (JFC). The four commands (army, navy, air force and the JFC) will now set the requirements for their force structure, equipment, personnel, training and logistics, and will manage four large, devolved budgets for this purpose.

UK forces in Afghanistan continued to be reduced, with the target of 5,000 troops remaining there by the end of 2013. Afghan forces in Helmand Province assumed security leadership and British mentors largely withdrew, although they were temporarily redeployed to support an Afghan counter-attack to evict Taliban fighters from Sangin. The unexpected French operation in Mali was supported by RAF

C-17 airlifters, a logistics team and the deployment of a *Sentinel* surveillance aircraft. UK trainers subsequently joined the EU training mission there. Royal Navy (RN) deployments to the Gulf continued and deployments of RAF *Typhoon* fighter aircraft to the UAE for training increased. These deployments, and apparent increases in training and defence-sales efforts, pointed to greater British military engagement in the region.

Cyber capability

Following direction from outgoing Chief of the Defence Staff General David Richards that the armed forces should be just as capable of manoeuvring in cyberspace as in the land, sea and air domains, Hammond announced that 'you deter people by having an offensive capability. We will build in Britain a cyber-strike capability … putting cyber alongside land, sea, air and space as a mainstream military activity. Our commanders can use cyber weapons alongside conventional weapons.' It was also announced that a Joint Cyber Reserve Unit would be established.

Armed services

Detailed plans for new **army** structures were announced in July 2013, including the withdrawal of remaining troops from Germany by 2018 and a revised role and force structure for UK reserves. This envisaged reversing a decade's decline in reserve strength by building closer relations with employers and increased investment in recruiting and training. Reserves of all services would be increased in trained strength from 29,000 to 44,000, with army-reserve trained strength set to rise to 38,000 by 2018. However, as of autumn 2013, neither regular nor reserve recruiting targets were being met, and there were no plans to bridge the gap between reduction of regular manpower by 2015 and the 2018 target for full reserve operational capability. Some critics cited the disbandment of infantry battalions, and the increase in reserve elements, as representing increased military risk.

Rebuilding the army's capability beyond 2015 depends on whether the planned withdrawal from Afghanistan remains on track, not least because the army plans to make wider use of much of the equipment purchased for that campaign, including surveillance equipment, weapons and protected patrol vehicles. Much of the army's support capability has been employed in Afghanistan, so will need to return to the UK for refurbishment before it can be used for contingency operations and training.

Reductions in Afghanistan allowed the army to begin rebuilding readiness for intervention operations, including the Air Assault Brigade's parachute capability – albeit to meet a requirement greatly reduced in the SDSR. Afghan reductions also meant that the army's high-readiness Lead Armoured Battle Group would become operational in 2014. The alignment of some brigades with overseas regions of strategic interest to the UK began, with 4 Brigade (aligned to North Africa) assigned to train tranches of Libyan security personnel (2,000 in total), though as of October 2013 this had yet to start.

A £10bn programme to upgrade UK battlefield helicopter capability progressed, as did work to define the best way to spend £5bn allocated to armoured vehicle modernisation. This programme included a funded upgrade to the *Warrior* AIFV and replacement of *Scorpion* reconnaissance vehicles with the new *Scout* vehicle. Meanwhile, deliveries of the *Terrier* armoured engineering vehicle began.

Navy personnel cuts and equipment reductions are complete, save for the expected retirement of the LPH HMS *Illustrious* in 2014, with LPH HMS *Ocean* due to return to service in early 2014 after refit. In 2013 the RN focused on improving readiness, taking equipment deliveries into service and planning future programmes. HMS *Illustrious* led the Response Force Task Group's return to the Mediterranean for *Cougar 13* exercises. Following its commitment to Afghanistan, the commando brigade was rebuilding its role as the UK's amphibious landing force.

The possibility of the navy retaining both of its *Queen Elizabeth*-class aircraft carriers in service after they are completed in 2016 and 2018 improved after Hammond commented that he supported such a policy. The Type-45 air-defence destroyer programme neared completion with the commissioning of HMS *Duncan*, with the Type-26 frigate due to enter service in 2021. Design of the Type-26 progressed and some initial contracts were awarded, with the latest iteration including new *Sea Ceptor* missiles and a 16-cell vertical-launch system. Although the lead boat of the *Astute*-class submarines suffered a number of technical problems, a second *Astute* vessel was commissioned and a sixth laid down; the class is to comprise seven in total.

The **RAF** continued to both downsize and to replace ageing aircraft types. The VC10 tanker transport retired in September 2013, with the C-130K following in October. The former is being replaced by the *Voyager*, based on the A330, with the latter likely to be replaced in the special-forces role by modified C-130Js.

Reduction of *Tornado* GR4s continued with 617 Squadron being disbanded, though it is due to reform in 2016 as the first RAF F-35 squadron. The MoD was expected to place its first production order for 12–14 F-35Bs before the end of 2013. With the last of the GR4s expected to be withdrawn in 2019, the RAF continued to pursue additional air-to-surface capability for the *Typhoon*, including the *Paveway* IV dual mode precision-guided bomb and *Storm Shadow* land-attack cruise missiles.

The RAF has been conducting an Air ISTAR Optimisation Study, which includes maritime surveillance. The UK has been without a dedicated maritime patrol aircraft since the 2010 cancellation of the *Nimrod* MRA4. Plans to withdraw the MQ-9 *Reaper* UAV and the *Sentinel* R1 by the end of 2014 were being reconsidered in light of *Reaper*'s utility in Afghanistan, and *Sentinel's* value in Libya and Mali.

Future challenges

Preparations began for a fresh SDSR in 2015, where a new government would be offered strategic choices. Much of this work re-examined familiar subjects, including NATO, European defence and regional dynamics. Hammond identified the size of the UK F-35 purchase, rebuilding maritime-patrol capability and future military cyber capabilities as key issues. Four other subjects could have strategic implications for UK defence: the future nuclear deterrent, potential Scottish independence, potential UK withdrawal from the EU and the August 2013 parliamentary veto on a military strike on Syria.

To meet a pledge made in the 2010 coalition agreement, the government published an appraisal of options for the UK's future nuclear deterrent. Unsurprisingly, it concluded that the current arrangement of four *Trident* SLBMs, with one on continuous patrol, was the most cost-effective solution. Many experts were unconvinced by statements, from coalition partners the Liberal Democrats, that whilst a deterrent was necessary it could be accomplished with fewer submarines. Whatever option was adopted, new submarines would be required in the next decade, and the history of recent submarine building led some analysts to suggest that the cost of a future deterrent might well squeeze out conventional equipment programmes.

Less than a year before the referendum on Scottish independence, the government and the House of Commons Defence Committee both assessed that the Scottish National Party's plans for security and defence of an independent Scotland were unconvincing. The MoD refused to be drawn on the potential costs of relocating the current *Trident* submarine base and conventional forces outside Scotland. Its public position was that any referendum vote for independence would need to be followed by negotiations, after which defence disengagement between the two nations would take place in an orderly fashion – so the MoD would not make contingency plans.

Prime Minister David Cameron promised a referendum on UK membership of the EU in the next parliament. However, with only France matching the UK in terms of expeditionary capability and the political and cultural willingness to engage in combat – notwithstanding the Syria vote – a British exit would greatly reduce the credibility of the EU's CSDP.

In the August 2013 parliamentary debate on Syria, a narrow majority of MPs were unconvinced by the government's case for military intervention to deter further chemical-weapon strikes by the Assad regime. Although the armed forces remained extremely popular, it appeared that, as noted by Hammond, 'there is a deep well of suspicion about military involvement in the Middle East stemming largely from the experiences of Iraq'.

MPs voting against the government were not condoning the Assad regime's chemical-weapon attacks, but they were expressing Iraq-influenced doubts about the intelligence that was presented, and reacting against being pressed into rapid action while UN inspectors were still at work in Syria – another Iraq parallel. Many doubted that the strikes being contemplated would have any useful effect. It was not clear whether the vote was an exceptional event, the beginning of the unravelling of the last two decades of broad political consensus on defence or an indication that important elements of the UK's populace and its political elite were losing confidence in the utility of force.

DEFENCE ECONOMICS

Macroeconomics

UK economic growth has remained anaemic since the 2008 financial crisis. In 2012, real GDP was still some 4% lower than pre-crisis levels and, according to the IMF, growth averaged 1.1% between 2010 and 2013. In 2013, business investment levels remained low, while inflation was still above target. Meanwhile, gross national debt more than doubled from 43.7% of GDP in 2007 to a projected 92.1% in 2013. Much of this increase was necessitated by the need to bail out the highly-indebted banking sector, along with a decline in tax revenues from that sector. Despite making progress in reducing the fiscal deficit, the weak economic recovery has required the coalition government to prolong austerity measures first announced in 2010. Originally intended to last five years, to 2015, intervening economic stagnation meant that in December 2012 the chancellor was forced to announce that deficit-reduction measures would be extended to 2018 before the budget deficit could be eliminated.

Defence spending

Significant progress had been made by May 2012 towards the government's 2010 objective of reducing real defence spending by 8% by 2015, as well as in resolving the £38bn (US$59bn) 'unfunded liabilities' gap in acquisition plans. This enabled the defence secretary to announce that the defence budget had finally been brought into balance for the first time in a decade. A revised long-term equipment plan for 2012–22 was drawn up by mid-2012, and a portion of this was provided to the National Audit Office (NAO) for independent assessment.

However, economic stagnation meant that revenue and deficit projections, which informed the decision to reduce real-terms spending by 8%, turned out to be overly optimistic. With austerity measures originally planned to last until 2015 extended to 2018 for many departments, the chancellor announced in the Autumn Statement 2012 that further defence budget reductions would occur in 2013 and 2014. Relative to the projected spending levels planned in 2010, the 2013 resource budget would be cut by 1% (£249m or US$382m) and the 2014 resource budget would be cut by 2% (£490m or US$753m). It should be noted that these percentage reductions apply only to the MoD resource budget – which finances current expenditure such as personnel and training – and not to its capital budget, which finances longer-term defence investment spending such as equipment acquisition. The reduced 2013 and 2014 figures also formed a lower baseline from which the 2015 resource budget allocation would be calculated. Funding for the multi-year equipment budget (2012–22) was agreed in mid-2012 and remains unaffected by the lower baseline.

With £11.5bn (US$17.7bn) to be reduced across government departments in 2015 as part of the austerity extension, discussions with the Treasury over the distribution of these reductions occurred over the first half of 2013. Further reductions to the 2015 defence budget were also discussed. By late 2013, it appeared that the MoD had succeeded in avoiding additional austerity measures, in part by agreeing efficiency savings in lieu of cuts. Due to larger-than-expected cost savings and improved efficiency since 2010, the MoD underspent its budget allocation in both 2012 and 2013, enabling it to carry forward these funds to help mitigate any further reductions in future non-equipment budgets.

Defence Equipment Plan 2012–22

In January 2013, the MoD published a summarised version of its Defence Equipment Plan 2012, which set out the distribution of equipment acquisition and support funding between 2012 and 2022. Of the £147.1bn (US$226bn) allocated to core equipment, just over 50% (£78bn or US$120bn) would be spent on new equipment and support costs, and the remaining £68bn (US$105bn) was allocated to supporting equipment already in service. In nominal terms, annual allocations for equipment acquisition and support are set to rise by more than one-third between 2012 and 2022.

As shown in Figure 8, almost one-quarter of the £147.1bn (24.3%; £35.8bn) was allocated to funding submarine development (including the remaining *Astute*-class submarines) and the costs associated with renewing the UK's nuclear deterrent – such as the design and production of the *Vanguard*-class ballistic-missile submarine replacement (assuming this is approved in 2015), and the costs of maintaining strategic weapons systems. When this is combined with the 11.8% of the plan allocated to naval surface combatants – such as construction of the two *Queen Elizabeth*-class aircraft carriers, Type-45 destroyer construction and Type-26 frigate development – maritime assets comprised more than one-third of the Equipment Plan (36.2%; £53.2bn). Fixed- and rotary-wing air assets made up the second-largest component (30.3%; £44.5bn), and included funds for *Typhoon* Tranche 2 and 3 and F-35 *Lightning* II programmes; UAVs; A400M and C-17 airlifters; and *Voyager* tankers. Land equipment made up the smallest portion of the Equipment Plan (8.4%; £12.3bn), although spending on new land systems was projected to rise sharply after FY2015/16 with

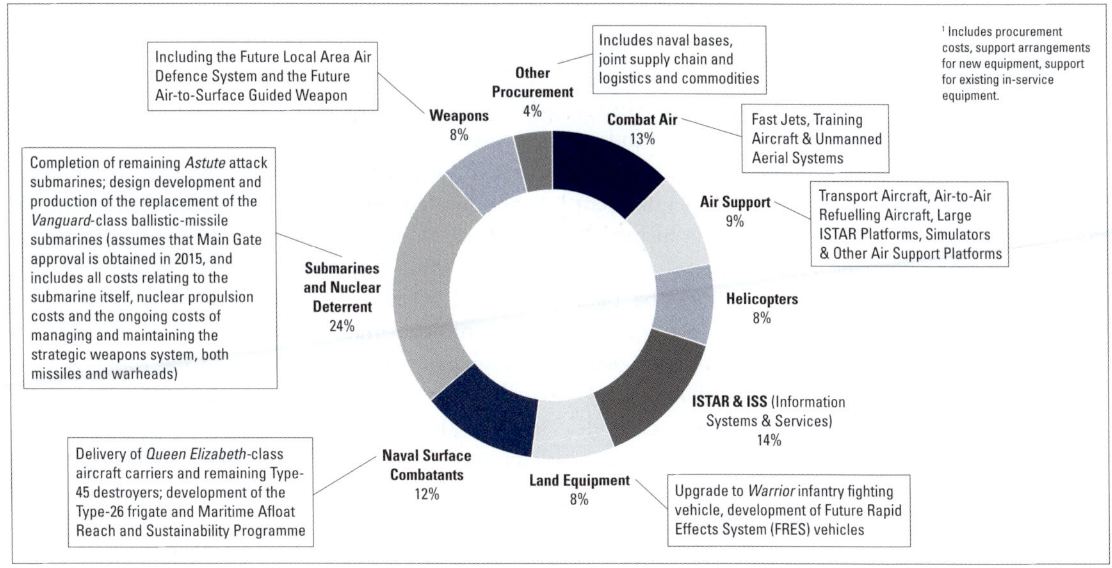

Figure 8 **Composition of the UK Multi-Year Equipment Plan 2012–22**[1]

the development of Future Rapid Effects System vehicles such as *Scout*.

Overall, combat air, air support and helicopters were prioritised during the earlier periods of the plan (until around 2016–17), while land systems, submarines and the nuclear deterrent were generally backloaded to the middle and end of the period (around 2016–22). Spending on ISR programmes (13.2%; £20.1bn) and munitions (7.5%; £11.4bn) was projected to remain relatively constant throughout the decade.

Built into these projections were two types of contingency funds, designed to guard against the kind of cost escalation that had blighted the department in the past. Firstly, £8.4bn (US$12.9bn) was built into the cost estimates of individual project budgets based on identified risks (this was included in the core £147.1bn). Secondly, £4.8bn (US$7.4bn) was allocated as centrally held contingency funding, to be distributed if costs within individual project budgets grew by more than that detailed in initial risk provisions. On top of these contingency funds, a further £8bn (US$12.3bn) was budgeted, but not allocated, so that funding could be found for high-priority items that emerge over the course of the decade. However, the Equipment Plan does not fund Urgent Operational Requirements or any net additional costs of supporting equipment in theatre, which are instead funded out of the Treasury Special Reserve. When the centrally held contingency fund and unallocated headroom are included, the total allocation for equipment procurement and support rises to £159bn over ten years.

Defence-acquisition reform

Although progress has been made towards better management of defence acquisition, it is too soon to tell if the legacy of programme delays and cost overruns has been overcome. In large measure, this is due to costing difficulties associated with the number and complexity of the elements that make up the ten-year equipment-acquisition programme. This comprises more than 400 individual cost lines relating to specific projects, involving thousands of assessments and assumptions that rely on specialist technical knowledge. The accuracy and validity of these can only be known as the plan is implemented, and assessments will need to be adjusted over time to be made more realistic. According to the NAO, 'to increase confidence in the realism of its assumptions and the consistency with which its forecasts are calculated, the Department will need to demonstrate their reasonableness over a period of years'.

In addition, the NAO was only able to assess less than half (46%) of the total value of the Equipment Plan, as the MoD has not yet been able to apply the same rigour in costing the equipment-support costs part of the plan (valued at around £86bn) as it had the equipment-procurement portion (valued at £60bn). Thus, escalation in equipment-support costs may yet prove to be problematic for the department. Overall, the NAO concluded that it could not offer a definitive view on the affordability of the Equipment Plan, and noted that that plan was highly sensitive to changes in funding assumptions. These views were echoed by the parliamentary Public Accounts Committee (PAC), which also noted assumptions in the plan over funding levels the MoD would receive from the Treasury, as well as the MoD's ability to reduce the non-equipment portion of the defence budget. Given the history of defence-cost escalation, the PAC expressed concern that the contingency measures built into the plan may be inadequate – the centrally held contingency fund amounted to just 3% of the total equipment plan. Overall, the PAC agreed with the NAO that the MoD was making progress, but that 'concerns over over-optimistic assumptions, the completeness and robustness of support cost estimates, and risks to capability mean that we cannot yet have confidence that the Equipment Plan is affordable'.

In parallel to these developments, the MoD continued with its controversial moves to restructure Defence Equipment and Support (DE&S), the agency responsible for equipment acquisition and through-life support (see *The Military Balance 2013*, pp. 109–10). In April 2013, the MoD began a 12-month study to assess whether to outsource the management of defence procurement to the private sector through reconstituting DE&S as a 'government owned, contractor operated' entity (Go-Co), or to retain DE&S within the public sector but with an overhauled management structure (termed the 'DE&S Plus' option). Three consortia were set up between the bidding companies, although by August 2013 this was reduced to two. In addition to the limited number of participants competing to operate the Go-Co, a major hurdle involved potential conflicts of interest involving the companies bidding to run DE&S, many of which already regularly enter into contracts directly with the MoD, or indirectly through other major suppliers to the MoD such as BAE Systems. Any firms operating MoD procurement tenders through a Go-Co arrangement would likely be unable to bid for these contracts in future, and may have to accept significant limits on their interactions with other major MoD suppliers. Partly in response to these concerns, in October 2013 additional resourcing was provided to the DE&S Plus team operating within the MoD. After data from both possible operating models is assessed in mid-2014, a final decision over the model to be used will be made. If the Go-Co model is approved, a contractor would be selected in the second half of 2014, and would take on the first stage of Go-Co operation in late 2014. A second stage of outsourcing would be taken over in 2016.

Albania ALB

Albanian Lek		2012	2013	2014
GDP	lek	1.41tr	1.49tr	
	US$	12.7bn	13.4bn	
per capita	US$	3,913	4,108	
Growth	%	1.30	1.80	
Inflation	%	2.02	2.17	
Def bdgt [a]	lek	19.9bn	19.3bn	16.8bn
	US$	185m	182m	
FMA (US)	US$	3m	3m	2.6m
US$1=lek		107.52	105.68	

[a] Excludes military pensions

Population 3,011,405

Age	0 – 14	15 – 19	20 – 24	25 – 29	30 – 64	65 plus
Male	10.5%	5.0%	5.0%	4.3%	19.6%	5.1%
Female	9.4%	4.6%	4.9%	4.5%	21.4%	5.7%

Capabilities

Albania has limited military capability predicated on internal security and disaster relief tasks. Efforts continue to reform its armed forces and upgrade equipment, though these are constrained by limited funding. The armed forces professionalised in 2010, one year after Albania joined NATO. Much defence activity is concerned with meeting NATO standards, including training, planning and generation of strategy documents. The 2013 Defence Directive listed full integration into NATO as a prime objective; this was achieved in October. The army, the largest of the three services, has provided troops to ISAF, for duties including surveillance and force-protection, and an EOD team to *Operation Althea*, in Bosnia. The small air brigade operates only rotary-wing and light liaison aircraft, and the country depends on NATO allies for air defence. The armed forces have no strategic lift. Albania is engaged in revising its national military strategy.

ACTIVE 14,250 (Joint Force Comd 8,150, Support Command 4,300, TRADOC 1,000, MoD and General Staff 800) Paramilitary 500

ORGANISATIONS BY SERVICE

Joint Forces Command (JFC) 8,150

Consists of a land element (comprising a rapid reaction bde, cdo regt, regional spt bde, log bn and comms bn), an air bde and naval bde. JFC units are intended to conduct and support international peace-support and humanitarian operations, and other crisis management tasks.

Land Element

FORCES BY ROLE

SPECIAL FORCES
1 cdo regt

MANOEUVRE
Light
1 (rapid reaction) lt inf bde

COMBAT SUPPORT
1 arty bn
1 cbt spt bde
1 sigs bn

COMBAT SERVICE SUPPORT
1 log bn

EQUIPMENT BY TYPE

MBT 3 Type-59
APC (T) 6 Type-5310
ARTY
TOWED 18 **152 mm**
MOR 81: **82mm** 81
AD • GUNS 42 **37mm** M-1939/S 60
ARV T-54/T-55
MW *Bozena*

Navy Element

The Albanian Navy Brigade, under the command of JFC, is organised into two naval flotillas with additional hydrographic, logistics, auxiliary and training support services.

EQUIPMENT BY TYPE

PATROL AND COASTAL COMBATANTS • PB 4: 2 *Nyryat* I; 2 *Shanghai* II† (PRC) with two single 533mm TT
MINE WARFARE • MINE COUNTERMEASURES • MSO 1 T-43† (FSU Project 254)
LOGISTICS AND SUPPORT • ARL 1; **YPT** 1 *Poluchat*

Coast Guard

FORCES BY ROLE

The Albanian Coast Guard (Roja Bregdetare) is under the command of the Navy Brigade's Coastal Defence Command.

EQUIPMENT BY TYPE

PATROL AND COASTAL COMBATANTS 34
PBF 13: 8 V-4000; 5 *Archangel*
PB 8: 3 *Iluria* (Damen Stan 4207 - 1 additional vessel to be delivered); 3 Mk3 *Sea Spectre*; 2 (other)
PBR 13: 4 Type-227; 1 Type-246; 1 Type-303; 7 Type-2010

Air Element

Flying hours at least 10–15 hrs/year.

EQUIPMENT BY TYPE

HELICOPTERS
TPT 23 **Medium** 2 AS532AL *Cougar*; **Light** 21: 1 AW109; 5 Bell 205 (AB-205); 7 Bell 206C (AB-206C); 8 Bo-105

Support Command (SC) 4,300

Consists of the logistics brigade, support regiment, infrastructure regiment, personnel and recruiting centre, military hospital, systems development centre and military police battalion.

FORCES BY ROLE

COMBAT SUPPORT
1 MP bn

COMBAT SERVICE SUPPORT
1 log bde (1 spt regt (tpt, EOD & maint)
1 fd hospital

Training and Doctrine Command (TRADOC) 1,000

Consists of the defence academy, military university, NCO academy, basic training brigade, the consolidated troops school, centre for defense analysis and training support centre.

Paramilitary ε500

DEPLOYMENT

Legal provisions for foreign deployment:
Constitution: Codified constitution (1998)
Decision on deployment of troops abroad: By the parliament upon proposal by the president (Art.171 II)

AFGHANISTAN
NATO • ISAF 105; 1 inf coy

BOSNIA-HERZEGOVINA
EU • EUFOR • *Operation Althea* 1

SERBIA
NATO • KFOR 14

FOREIGN FORCES

Italy 27 (Delegazione Italiana Esperti)

Austria AUT

Euro €		2012	2013	2014
GDP	€	318bn	329bn	
	US$	399bn	423bn	
per capita	US$	47,083	49,844	
Growth	%	0.79	0.77	
Inflation	%	2.58	2.20	
Def exp [a]	€	2.51bn		
	US$	3.23bn		
Def bdgt [a]	€	2.48bn	2.43bn	
	US$	3.19bn	3.23bn	
US$1=€		0.78	0.75	

[a] Includes military pensions

Population	8,221,646

Age	0 – 14	15 – 19	20 – 24	25 – 29	30 – 64	65 plus
Male	7.0%	2.9%	3.1%	3.1%	24.7%	8.0%
Female	6.7%	2.8%	3.0%	3.0%	24.8%	10.9%

Capabilities

The armed forces remain configured to provide territorial defence, despite the conclusion of the 2013 National Security Strategy that this is an unlikely contingency. A proposal to abandon conscription was rejected by referendum. Transformation plans were scaled back after the financial crisis, though the main tenets of a 2004 reform plan have been retained. Nonetheless, crisis management contributions are seen as essential tasks. Power projection capability is limited, and the ambition of deploying a framework brigade has been delayed until at least 2016. The level of ambition for participation in international missions has modified, with the aim now of being able to deploy concurrently up to three infantry battalions and further small contingents. Battalion- or company-sized contributions to multinational peacekeeping missions are the armed forces' primary operational activity, although some high readiness units, made up of career soldiers, have been formed for potential crisis-management tasks. Current equipment priorities are focused on aircraft and helicopter upgrades, and acquisitions to ensure interoperable units for EU Battlegroups. Training levels are high, and include regular participation in multinational exercises.

ACTIVE 22,800 (Army 11,300; Air 2,700; Support 8,800)

Conscript liability 6 months recruit trg, 30 days reservist refresher trg for volunteers; 120–150 days additional for officers, NCOs and specialists. Authorised maximum wartime strength of 55,000

RESERVE 171,400 (Joint structured 26,700; Joint unstructured 144,700)

Some 11,100 reservists a year undergo refresher trg in tranches

ORGANISATIONS BY SERVICE

Joint Command – Land Forces 11,300

FORCES BY ROLE
MANOEUVRE
Mechanised
1 (3rd) bde (1 recce/SP arty bn, 1 armd bn, 1 mech inf bn, 1 inf bn, 1 cbt engr bn, 1 CBRN defence coy, 1 spt bn)
1 (4th) bde (1 recce/SP arty bn, 1 armd bn, 1 mech inf bn, 1 inf bn, 1 CBRN defence coy, 1 spt bn)
Light
1 (6th) bde (3 inf bn, 1 cbt engr bn, 1 CBRN defence coy, 1 spt bn)
1 (7th) bde (1 recce/arty bn, 3 inf bn, 1 cbt engr bn, 1 CBRN defence coy, 1 spt bn)

EQUIPMENT BY TYPE
MBT 56 *Leopard* 2A4
RECCE 12 CBRN *Dingo*
AIFV 112 *Ulan*
APC 94
APC (W) 71 *Pandur*
PPV 23 *Dingo* II
ARTY 163
SP • 155mm 58 M109A5ÖE (to reduce to 32)
MOR • 120mm 105 M-43 (80 more in store)
AT • MSL • MANPATS PAL 2000 BILL
ARV 48: 38 4KH7FA-SB; 10 M88A1
MW 6 AID2000 Trailer

Joint Command - Air Force 2,700

The Air Force is part of Joint Forces Comd and consists of 2 bde; Air Support Comd and Airspace Surveillance Comd

Flying hours 160 hrs/year on hel/tpt ac; 110 hrs/year on ftr

FORCES BY ROLE

FIGHTER

2 sqn with *Typhoon*

ISR

1 sqn with PC-6B *Turbo Porter*

TRANSPORT

1 sqn with C-130K *Hercules*

TRAINING

1 trg sqn with Saab 105Oe*

1 trg sqn with PC-7 *Turbo Trainer*

TRANSPORT HELICOPTER

2 sqn with Bell 212 (AB-212)

1 sqn with OH-58B *Kiowa*

1 sqn with S-70A *Black Hawk*

2 sqn with SA316/SA319 *Alouette* III

AIR DEFENCE

2 bn

1 radar bn

EQUIPMENT BY TYPE

AIRCRAFT 37 combat capable

FTR 15 Eurofighter *Typhoon* Tranche 1

TPT 11: **Medium** 3 C-130K *Hercules*; **Light** 8 PC-6B *Turbo Porter*

TRG 34: 12 PC-7 *Turbo Trainer*; 22 Saab 105Oe*

HELICOPTERS

MRH 24 SA316/SA319 *Alouette* III

ISR 11 OH-58B *Kiowa*

TPT 32: **Medium** 9 S-70A *Black Hawk*; **Light** 23 Bell 212 (AB-212)

AD

SAM 24 *Mistral* (12 more in store)

GUNS • 35mm 24 Z-FIAK system (29 more in store)

MSL • AAM • IIR IRIS-T

Joint Command – Special Operations Forces

FORCES BY ROLE

SPECIAL FORCES

2 SF gp

1 SF gp (reserve)

Support 8,800

Support forces comprise Joint Services Support Command and several agencies, academies and schools.

Cyber

The MoD is developing a national-level Cyber Attack Information System (CAIS) with the goal of strengthening resilience and increasing survivability and reliability of IT structures. The national Austrian Cyber Security Strategy was approved by legislators in March 2013. The MoD's primary goal is 'cyber defence', by ensuring national defence in cyberspace as well as securing MoD ICT. The Military Cyber Emergency Readiness Team (milCERT) will be expanded to improve situational awareness and develop Computer Network Operations capabilities.

DEPLOYMENT

Legal provisions for foreign deployment:
Constitution: incl 'Federal Constitutional Law' (1/1930)
Specific legislation: 'Bundesverfassungsgesetz über Kooperation und Solidarität bei der Entsendung von Einheiten und Einzelpersonen in das Ausland' (KSE-BVG, 1997)
Decision on deployment of troops abroad: By government on authorisation of the National Council's Main Committee; simplified procedure for humanitarian and rescue tasks (Art. 23j of the 'Federal Constitutional Law'; § 2 of the KSE-BVG)

AFGHANISTAN

NATO • ISAF 3

BOSNIA-HERZEGOVINA

EU • EUFOR • *Operation Althea* 314; 1 inf bn HQ; 1 recce pl; 1 inf coy

OSCE • Bosnia and Herzegovina 1

CYPRUS

UN • UNFICYP 4

DEMOCRATIC REPUBLIC OF THE CONGO

EU • EUSEC RD Congo 1

LEBANON

UN • UNIFIL 168; 1 log coy

MALI

EU • EUTM Mali 8

MIDDLE EAST

UN • UNTSO 6 obs

SERBIA

NATO • KFOR 380; 1 mech inf coy

OSCE • Kosovo 8

OSCE • Serbia 2

WESTERN SAHARA

UN • MINURSO 2 obs

Belgium BEL

Euro €		2012	2013	2014
GDP	€	384bn	395bn	
	US$	485bn	511bn	
per capita	US$	43,686	45,687	
Growth	%	-0.20	0.16	
Inflation	%	2.62	1.73	
Def bdgt [a]	€	4.09bn	3.98bn	
	US$	5.27bn	5.29bn	
US$1=€		0.78	0.75	

[a] Includes military pensions

Population 10,444,268

Age	0–14	15–19	20–24	25–29	30–64	65 plus
Male	8.0%	2.9%	3.1%	3.1%	24.0%	7.8%
Female	7.7%	2.8%	3.0%	2.9%	23.8%	10.8%

Capabilities

The armed forces have been reduced in response to broader economic problems, and the intention was to implement most of the cuts by the end of 2013. There are concerns about their impact on some areas of operational readiness. Despite financial constraints, Belgium continues to pursue more deployable forces, with orders placed for A400M transport aircraft and NH90 NFH/TTH anti-submarine warfare/transport helicopters. A quick reaction force is maintained, and there is a limited ability for power projection, although only as part of a multinational deployment. The armed forces exercise jointly on a regular basis and also participate in a broad range of multinational training exercises. Belgian forces have deployed to ISAF since 2003. They provided air transport and force-protection support for French operations in Mali in 2013, and its troops were part of the EU training mission to Mali during the second part of 2013. The land component has been reshaped as a wheeled medium brigade and an airborne-capable light brigade. The naval component focuses on escort and mine countermeasures for littoral and blue-water operations. The air component faces a significant change in inventory around the end of this decade, when it will need to replace its F-16s.

ACTIVE 30,700 (Army 11,300 Navy 1,500 Air 6,000 Medical Service 1,400 Joint Service 10,500)

RESERVE 6,800

ORGANISATIONS BY SERVICE

Land Component 11,300

FORCES BY ROLE

SPECIAL FORCES
1 SF gp
MANOEUVRE
Reconnaissance
1 ISTAR gp (2 ISTAR coy, 1 surv coy)
Mechanised
1 (med) bde (4 mech bn)
Light
1 (lt) bde (1 cdo bn, 1 lt inf bn, 1 para bn)
COMBAT SUPPORT
1 arty gp (1 arty bty, 1 mor bty, 1 AD bty)
2 engr bn (1 cbt engr coy, 1 lt engr coy, 1 construction coy)
1 EOD unit
1 CBRN coy
1 MP coy (with 1 pl dedicated to EUROCORPS)
3 CIS sigs gp
COMBAT SERVICE SUPPORT
3 log bn

Reserves 1,400

Territorial Support Units

FORCES BY ROLE
MANOEUVRE
Light
11 inf unit

EQUIPMENT BY TYPE

MBT 16 *Leopard* 1A5
AIFV 37: 19 *Piranha* III-C DF30; 18 *Piranha* III-C DF90
APC 338
APC (W) 118: 40 *Pandur*; 64 *Piranha* III-C; 14 *Piranha* III-PC
PPV 220 *Dingo*
ARTY 105
TOWED 105mm 14 LG1 MK II
MOR 91: **81mm** 39; **120mm** 52
AD • SAM 45 *Mistral*
AEV 11: 3 *Leopard* 1; 8 *Piranha* III-C
ARV 15: 3 *Leopard* 1; 3 *Pandur*; 9 *Piranha* III-C
VLB 4 *Leguan*

Naval Component 1,500

EQUIPMENT BY TYPE

PRINCIPAL SURFACE COMBATANTS 2
FRIGATES • FFGHM 2 *Karel Doorman* each with 2 quad lnchr with *Harpoon* AShM, 1 16-cell Mk48 VLS with RIM-7P *Sea Sparrow* SAM, 4 single Mk32 324mm ASTT with Mk 46 HWT, 1 *Goalkeeper* CIWS, 1 76mm gun, (capacity 1 med hel)
MINE WARFARE • MINE COUNTERMEASURES •
MHC 6 *Flower* (*Tripartite*)
LOGISTICS AND SUPPORT 9
AG 1 *Stern* with 1 hel landing platform
AGFH 1 *Godetia* (log spt/comd) (capacity 1 *Alouette* III)
AGOR 1 *Belgica*
AXS 1 *Zenobe Gramme*
YTL 3 *Wesp*
YTM 2

Naval Aviation

(part of the Air Component)

EQUIPMENT BY TYPE
HELICOPTERS
ASW 1 NH90 NFH
MRH 3 SA316B *Alouette* III (to be replaced by NH90 NFH)

Air Component 6,000

Flying hours 165 hrs/yr on cbt ac. 300 hrs/yr on tpt ac. 150 hrs/yr on hel; 250 hrs/yr on ERJ

FORCES BY ROLE

FIGHTER/GROUND ATTACK/ISR
4 sqn with F-16AM/BM *Fighting Falcon*
SEARCH & RESCUE
1 sqn with *Sea King* Mk48
TRANSPORT
1 sqn with A330; ERJ-135 LR; ERJ-145 LR; *Falcon* 20 (VIP); *Falcon* 900B
1 sqn with C-130H *Hercules*
TRAINING
1 OCU sqn with F-16AM/BM *Fighting Falcon*
1 sqn with SF-260D/MB
1 BEL/FRA unit with *Alpha Jet**
1 OCU unit with AW109
TRANSPORT HELICOPTER
2 sqn with AW109 (ISR)

ISR UAV
1 sqn with RQ-5A *Hunter* (B-*Hunter*)

EQUIPMENT BY TYPE

AIRCRAFT 88 combat capable
FTR 59: 49 F-16AM *Fighting Falcon*; 10 F-16BM *Fighting Falcon*
TPT: 19 **Medium** 11 C-130H *Hercules*; **Light** 4: 2 ERJ-135 LR; 2 ERJ-145 LR; **PAX** 4: 1 A330; 2 *Falcon* 20 (VIP); 1 *Falcon* 900B
TRG 61: 29 *Alpha Jet**; 9 SF-260D; 23 SF-260MB

HELICOPTERS
ASW 1 NH90 NFH opcon Navy
MRH 3 SA316B *Alouette* III opcon Navy
SAR 3 *Sea King* Mk48 (to be replaced by NH90 NFH)
TPT 21 **Medium** 1 NH90 TTH; **Light** 20 AW109 (ISR)

UAV • ISR • Heavy 12 RQ-5A *Hunter* (B-*Hunter*)

MSL
AAM • IR AIM-9M/N *Sidewinder*; **ARH** AIM-120B AMRAAM

BOMBS
INS/GPS guided: GBU-31 JDAM; GBU-38 JDAM; GBU-54 (dual-mode)
Laser-Guided: GBU-10/GBU-12 *Paveway* II; GBU-24 *Paveway* III

PODS Infrared/TV: 12 *Sniper*

Cyber

The Cyber Security Strategy Belgium was approved in December 2012. An MoD Defense Cyber Strategy is due for approval before end-2013. These measures should allow, from 2013 to 2016, extension of the limited capabilities of the Federal Computer Crime Unit, CERT.be and the MoD.

DEPLOYMENT

Legal provisions for foreign deployment:
Constitution: Codified constitution (1831)
Specific legislation: 'Loi relatif à la mise en oeuvre des forces armées, à la mise en condition, ainsi qu'aux périodes et positions dans lesquelles le militaire peut se trouver' (1994)
Decision on deployment of troops abroad: By the government (Federal Council of Ministers) and the minister of defence (1994 law, Art. 88, 106, 167 of constitution)

AFGHANISTAN
NATO • ISAF 180; 6 F-16AM *Fighting Falcon*

DEMOCRATIC REPUBLIC OF THE CONGO
EU • EUSEC RD Congo 4
UN • MONUSCO 23; 1 avn flt with 1 C-130H

FRANCE
NATO • Air Component 28 *Alpha Jet* located at Cazeaux/Tours

LEBANON
UN • UNIFIL 104; 1 engr coy

LITHUANIA
NATO • Baltic Air Policing 4 F-16AM *Fighting Falcon*

MALI
EU • EUTM Mali 34

MIDDLE EAST
UN • UNTSO 2 obs

NORTH SEA
NATO • SNMCMG 1: 1 MHC

UGANDA
EU • EUTM Somalia 6

FOREIGN FORCES

United States US European Command: 1,200

Bosnia-Herzegovina BIH

Convertible Mark		2012	2013	2014
GDP	mark	27.8bn	29.3bn	
	US$	17.3bn	18.9bn	
per capita	US$	4,461	4,866	
Growth	%	-0.70	0.50	
Inflation	%	2.05	1.80	
Def bdgt	mark	352m		
	US$	231m		
FMA (US)	US$	4.5m	4.5m	4.5m
US$1=mark		1.52	1.48	

Population 3,875,723

Age	0 – 14	15 – 19	20 – 24	25 – 29	30 – 64	65 plus
Male	7.2%	3.2%	3.6%	3.8%	26.0%	5.0%
Female	6.8%	2.9%	3.4%	3.7%	26.6%	7.9%

Capabilities

Bosnia's armed forces are an uneasy amalgam of troops from all three formerly warring entities. Considerably reduced to a size that the country can afford, they likely have little capability to mount combat operations. Negotiations on NATO membership were opened in 2009, and there has been limited progress towards this ambition. Nonetheless, defence reforms have proceeded with this objective in mind, and the aim is to field small and mobile forces, including reserves, that are interoperable and compatible with NATO forces. Bosnian forces are capable of making contributions to international operations, particularly peacekeeping operations, and have identified an infantry company, a military police platoon and an EOD platoon as possible contributions. Bosnia has deployed forces to Iraq and Afghanistan.

ACTIVE 10,500 (Armed Forces 10,500)

ORGANISATIONS BY SERVICE

Armed Forces 10,500

1 ops comd; 1 spt comd

FORCES BY ROLE
MANOUEVRE
Light
3 inf bde (1 recce coy, 3 inf bn, 1 arty bn)
COMBAT SUPPORT
1 cbt spt bde (1 tk bn, 1 engr bn, 1 EOD bn, 1 int bn, 1 MP bn)
1 EOD bn
1 CBRN coy
COMBAT SERVICE SUPPORT
1 log comd (5 log bn)

EQUIPMENT BY TYPE
MBT 45 M60A3
APC • APC (T) 20 M113A2
ARTY 224
TOWED 122mm 100 D-30
MRL 122mm 24 APRA 40
MOR 120mm 100 M-75
AT
MSL
SP 60: 8 9P122 *Malyutka*; 9 9P133 *Malyutka*; 32 BOV-1; 11 M-92
MANPATS 9K11 *Malyutka* (AT-3 *Sagger*); 9K111 *Fagot* (AT-4 *Spigot*); 9K115 *Metis* (AT-7 *Saxhorn*); HJ-8; *Milan*
VLB MTU
MW Bozena

Air Force and Air Defence Brigade 800

FORCES BY ROLE
HELICOPTER
1 sqn with Bell 205; Mi-17 *Hip* H
1 sqn with Mi-8 *Hip*; Mi-8MTV *Hip*
1 sqn with Mi-8 *Hip*; SA342H/L *Gazelle* (HN-42/45M)
AIR DEFENCE
1 AD bn

EQUIPMENT BY TYPE
AIRCRAFT
FGA (7 J-22 *Orao* in store)
ATK (6 J-1 (J-21) *Jastreb*; 3 TJ-1(NJ-21) *Jastreb* all in store)
ISR (2 RJ-1 (IJ-21) *Jastreb** in store)
TRG (1 G-4 *Super Galeb* (N-62)* in store)
HELICOPTERS
MRH 13: 4 Mi-8MTV *Hip*; 1 Mi-17 *Hip* H; 1 SA-341H *Gazelle* (HN-42); 7 SA-342L *Gazelle* (HN-45M)
TPT 26 **Medium** 11 Mi-8 *Hip* **Light** 15 Bell 205 (UH-1H *Iroquois*)
TRG 1 Mi-34 *Hermit*
AD
SAM
SP 27: 1 *Strela*-10M3 (SA-13 *Gopher*); 20 2K12 *Kub* (SA-6 *Gainful*); 6 *Strela*-1 (SA-9 *Gaskin*)
MANPAD 9K34 *Strela*-3 (SA-14 *Gremlin*); 9K310 (SA-16 *Gimlet*)
GUNS 764
SP 169: **20mm** 9 BOV-3 SPAAG; **30mm** 154: 38 M53; 116 M-53-59; **57mm** 6 ZSU 57/2
TOWED 595: **20mm** 468: 32 M-55A2, 4 M38, 1 M55 A2B1, 293 M55 A3/A4, 138 M75; **23mm** 38: 29 ZU-23, 9 GSh-23; **30mm** 33 M-53; **37mm** 7 Type-55; **40mm** 49: 31 L60, 16 L70, 2 M-12

DEPLOYMENT

Legal provisions for foreign deployment:
Constitution: Codified constitution within Dayton Peace Agreement (1995)
Specific legislation: 'Law on participation of military, police, state and other employees in peacekeeping operations and other activities conducted abroad'
Decision on deployment of troops abroad: By the members of the Presidency (2003 'Defence Law' Art. 9, 13)

AFGHANISTAN
NATO • ISAF 79

DEMOCRATIC REPUBLIC OF THE CONGO
UN • MONUSCO 5 obs

SERBIA
OSCE • Kosovo 9
OSCE • Serbia 2

FOREIGN FORCES

Part of EUFOR – *Operation Althea* unless otherwise stated.
Albania 1
Armenia OSCE 2
Austria 314; 1 inf bn HQ; 1 recce pl; 1 inf coy; 3 SA316 *Allouette* III • OSCE 1
Bulgaria 18
Canada OSCE 1
Chile 15
Croatia OSCE 2
Czech Republic 2 • OSCE 2
Finland 8 • OSCE 1
France 2 • OSCE 3
Germany OSCE 3
Greece 2
Hungary 157; 1 inf coy • OSCE 1
Ireland 7 • OSCE 6
Italy OSCE 8
Kyrgyzstan OSCE 1
Luxembourg 1
Macedonia, Former Yugoslav Republic of 11
Moldova OSCE 1
Netherlands 3
Poland 34 • OSCE 2
Portugal OSCE 1
Romania 37
Russia OSCE 1
Slovakia 35 • OSCE 1
Slovenia 14
Spain 12 • OSCE 1
Sweden 2
Switzerland 20
Turkey 229; 1 inf coy
United Kingdom 4 • OSCE 5
United States OSCE 10

Bulgaria BLG

Bulgarian Lev L		2012	2013	2014
GDP	L	80.1bn	83.5bn	
	US$	51bn	54.4bn	
per capita	US$	7,033	7,582	
Growth	%	0.78	1.20	
Inflation	%	2.39	2.05	
Def exp	L	1.1bn		
	US$	723m		
Def bdgt [a]	L	1bn	1.1bn	1.1bn
	US$	659m	751m	
FMA (US)	US$	9m	9m	7m
US$1=L		1.52	1.47	

[a] Excludes military pensions

Population 6,981,642

Age	0–14	15–19	20–24	25–29	30–64	65 plus
Male	7.3%	2.3%	3.1%	3.5%	24.0%	7.6%
Female	6.9%	2.2%	2.9%	3.4%	25.5%	11.3%

Capabilities

The armed forces' tasks are territorial defence, peacetime domestic-security, and international peacekeeping and security missions. An Armed Forces Development Plan in 2010 and a new White Paper in 2011 outlined the intent to replace Soviet-era equipment, and the armed forces are due to transition to a modified force structure by the end of 2014. The aim is to achieve smaller, more balanced armed forces capable of multiple tasks. Funding shortages have curtailed or delayed some procurement, and the ambition to acquire a more modern fighter type for the air force has yet to be fulfilled. The Bulgarian armed forces contributed to ISAF, exercise regularly at the national level and also participate in NATO exercises.

ACTIVE 31,300 (Army 16,300 Navy 3,450 Air 6,700 Central Staff 4,850) Paramilitary 16,000

RESERVE 303,000 (Army 250,500 Navy 7,500 Air 45,000)

ORGANISATIONS BY SERVICE

Army 16,300

Forces are being reduced in number.

FORCES BY ROLE

SPECIAL FORCES
1 SF bde
MANOEUVRE
Reconnaissance
1 recce bn
Mechanised
2 mech bde
COMBAT SUPPORT
1 arty regt
1 engr regt
1 NBC bn
COMBAT SERVICE SUPPORT
1 log regt

EQUIPMENT BY TYPE

MBT 80 T-72
RECCE *Maritza* NBC
AIFV 160: 90 BMP-1; 70 BMP-2/3
APC 127
APC (T) 100 MT-LB
APC (W) 27: 20 BTR-60; 7 M1117 ASV
ARTY 311
SP • 122mm 48 2S1
TOWED • 152mm 24 D-20
MRL 122mm 24 BM-21
MOR 120mm 215 2S11 SP *Tundzha*
AT
MSL
SP 24 9P148 *Konkurs* (AT-5 *Spandrel*)
MANPATS 9K111 *Fagot* (AT-4 *Spigot*); 9K113 *Konkurs* (AT-5 *Spandrel*); (9K11 *Malyutka* (AT-3 *Sagger*) in store)
GUNS 126: **100mm** 126 MT-12; **85mm** (150 D-44 in store)
AD
SAM
SP 24 9K33 *Osa* (SA-8 *Gecko*)
MANPAD 9K32 *Strela*‡ (SA-7 *Grail*)
GUNS 400 **100mm** KS-19 towed/**57mm** S-60 towed/**23mm** ZSU-23-4 SP/ZU-23 towed
RADARS • LAND GS-13 *Long Eye* (veh); SNAR-1 *Long Trough* (arty); SNAR-10 *Big Fred* (veh, arty); SNAR-2/-6 *Pork Trough* (arty); *Small Fred*/*Small Yawn* (veh, arty)
AEV MT-LB
ARV T-54/T-55; MTP-1; MT-LB
VLB BLG67; TMM

Navy 3,450

EQUIPMENT BY TYPE

PRINCIPAL SURFACE COMBATANTS 4
FRIGATES 4
FFGM 3 *Drazki* (BEL *Wielingen*) with 2 twin lnchr with MM-38 *Exocet* AShM, 1 octuple Mk29 GMLS with RIM-7P *Sea Sparrow* SAM, 2 single 533mm ASTT with L5 HWT, 1 sextuple 375mm MLE 54 Creusot-Loire A/S mor, 1 100mm gun
FFM 1 *Smeli* (FSU *Koni*) with 1 twin lnchr with 2 *Osa*-M (SA-N-4 *Gecko*) SAM, 2 RBU 6000 *Smerch* 2, 2 twin 76mm gun
PATROL AND COASTAL COMBATANTS 6
PCFGM 1 *Mulnaya* (FSU *Tarantul* II) with 2 twin lnchr with P-15M *Termit*-M (SS-N-2C *Styx*) AShM, 2 quad lnchr (manual aiming) with *Strela*-2 (SA-N-5 *Grail*) SAM, 1 76mm gun
PCM 2 *Reshitelni* (FSU *Pauk* I) with 1 *Strela*-2 (SA-N-5 *Grail*) SAM (manual aiming), 4 single 406mm TT, 2 RBU 1200, 1 76mm gun
PBFG 3 *Osa* I/II† (FSU) with 4 P-15/P-15U *Termit* (SS-N-2A/B *Styx*) AShM

MINE COUNTERMEASURES 6
MHC 1 *Tsibar* (*Tripartite* – BEL *Flower*)
MSC 3 *Briz* (FSU *Sonya)*
MSI 2 *Olya,* less than 100 tonnes (FSU)
AMPHIBIOUS 1
LCU 1 *Vydra*
LOGISTICS AND SUPPORT 15: 1 **ADG**; 2 **AGS**; 2 **AOL**; 1 **AORL**; 1 **ARS**; 2 **AT**; 1 **AX**; 2 **YDT**; 1 **YPT**; 2 **YTR**

Naval Aviation
HELICOPTERS • ASW 3 AS565MB *Panther*

Air Force 6,700
Flying hours 30–40 hrs/yr

FORCES BY ROLE
FIGHTER/ISR
1 sqn with MiG-21bis/UM *Fishbed*
1 sqn with MiG-29A/UB *Fulcrum*
FIGHTER/GROUND ATTACK
1 sqn with Su-25K/UBK *Frogfoot*
TRANSPORT
1 sqn with An-30 *Clank*; C-27J *Spartan*; L-410UVP-E; PC-12M
TRAINING
1 sqn with L-39ZA *Albatros*
1 sqn with PC-9M
ATTACK HELICOPTER
1 sqn with Mi-24D/V *Hind* D/E
TRANSPORT HELICOPTER
1 sqn with AS532AL *Cougar*; Bell 206 *Jet Ranger*; Mi-17 *Hip* H

EQUIPMENT BY TYPE
AIRCRAFT 42 combat capable
FTR 16: 12 MiG-29A *Fulcrum*; 4 MiG-29UB *Fulcrum*
FGA 12: 10 MiG-21bis *Fishbed;* 2 MiG-21UM *Mongol* B (to be withdrawn by end-2014)
ATK 14: 10 Su-25K *Frogfoot*; 4 Su-25UBK *Frogfoot* (to be withdrawn by end-2014)
ISR 1 An-30 *Clank*
TPT 7: **Medium** 3 C-27J *Spartan*; **Light** 4: 1 An-2T *Colt*; 2 L-410UVP-E; 1 PC-12M
TRG 12: 6 L-39ZA *Albatros*; 6 PC-9M (basic)
HELICOPTERS
ATK 6 Mi-24D/V *Hind* D/E
MRH 6 Mi-17 *Hip* H
TPT 18: **Medium** 12 AS532AL *Cougar*; **Light** 6 Bell 206 *Jet Ranger*
UAV • EW *Yastreb*-2S
AD
SAM S-300 (SA-10 *Grumble*); S-75 *Dvina* (SA-2 *Guideline* towed); S-125 *Pechora* (SA-3 *Goa*); S-200 (SA-5 *Gammon*); 2K12 *Kub* (SA-6 *Gainful*)
MSL
AAM • IR R-3 (AA-2 *Atoll*)‡ R-73 (AA-11 *Archer*) **SARH** R-27R (AA-10 *Alamo* A)
ASM Kh-29 (AS-14 *Kedge*); Kh-23 (AS-7 *Kerry*)‡; Kh-25 (AS-10 *Karen*)

Paramilitary 16,000

Border Guards 12,000
Ministry of Interior
FORCES BY ROLE
Paramilitary 12 regt
EQUIPMENT BY TYPE
PATROL AND COASTAL COMBATANTS 26
PB 18: 1 Damen Stan 4207; 9 *Grif* (FSU *Zhuk*); 3 *Nesebar* (FSU *Neustadt*); 5 Lurssen 21
PBF 8 *Baltic*

Security Police 4,000

DEPLOYMENT
Legal provisions for foreign deployment:
Constitution: Codified constitution (1991)
Decision on deployment of troops abroad: By the president upon request from the Council of Ministers and upon approval by the National Assembly (Art. 84 XI)

AFGHANISTAN
NATO • ISAF 416; 1 mech inf coy

BOSNIA-HERZEGOVINA
EU • EUFOR • *Operation Althea* 18

LIBERIA
UN • UNMIL 2 obs

SERBIA
NATO • KFOR 11
OSCE • Kosovo 1
OSCE • Serbia 1

Croatia CRO

Croatian Kuna k		2012	2013	2014
GDP	k	336bn	351bn	
	US$	57.1bn	60.1bn	
per capita	US$	12,972	13,655	
Growth	%	-1.98	-0.20	
Inflation	%	3.43	3.16	
Def bdgt	k	4.78bn	4.55bn	4.28bn
	US$	827m	813m	
FMA (US)	US$	3m	3m	2.5m
US$1=k		5.78	5.60	

Population 4,475,611

Age	0 – 14	15 – 19	20 – 24	25 – 29	30 – 64	65 plus
Male	7.5%	3.2%	3.1%	3.4%	24.2%	7.0%
Female	7.1%	3.0%	3.0%	3.3%	25.0%	10.5%

Capabilities
Croatia continues to work on the long-term goals laid out in its 2005 defence review and the associated 2006–2015 long-term development plan, as well as the National

Security Strategy, Defence Strategy and Military Strategy; the latter details the armed forces' development and modernisation strategy. Military tasks cover national sovereignty, the defence of Croatia and its allies, the ability to participate in crisis-response operations overseas, and support to civil institutions. Croatia joined NATO in 2009 and defence-policy focus is directed at further integration into NATO structures and planning processes. In October 2012, its armed forces were formally integrated into NATO. The country contributes to ISAF and also provides support to UN missions. It has declared reaction forces to NATO and EU missions; these can deploy within Europe. Force modernisation and re-equipment plans have been hampered by the economic downturn.

ACTIVE 16,550 (Army 11,250 Navy 1,600 Air 1,850 Joint 1,850) Paramilitary 3,000

Conscript liability Voluntary conscription, 8 weeks

ORGANISATIONS BY SERVICE

Joint 1,850 (General Staff)

Army 11,250

FORCES BY ROLE

SPECIAL FORCES

1 SF bn

MANOEUVRE

Armoured

1 armd bde

Light

1 mot inf bde

Other

1 inf trg regt

COMBAT SUPPORT

1 arty/MRL regt
1 AT regt
1 ADA regt
1 engr regt
1 int bn
1 MP regt
1 NBC bn
1 sigs regt

COMBAT SERVICE SUPPORT

1 log regt

EQUIPMENT BY TYPE

MBT 75 M-84
AIFV 102 M-80
APC 139
APC (T) 15 BTR-50
APC (W) 108: 1 BOV-VP; 23 LOV OP; 84 Patria AMV
PPV 16: 4 *Cougar* HE; 12 *Maxxpro*
ARTY 215
SP 122mm 8 2S1
TOWED 64: **122mm** 27 D-30; **130mm** 19 M-46H1; **155mm** 18 M-1H1
MRL 39: **122mm** 37: 6 M91 *Vulkan* 31 BM-21 *Grad*; **128mm** 2 LOV RAK M91 R24
MOR 104: **82mm** 29 LMB M96; **120mm** 75: 70 M-75; 5 UBM 52
AT • MSL
SP 28 POLO BOV 83
MANPATS 9K11 *Malyutka* (AT-3 *Sagger*); 9K111 *Fagot* (AT-4 *Spigot*); 9K115 *Metis* (AT-7 *Saxhorn*); 9K113 *Konkurs* (AT-5 *Spandrel*); *Milan* (reported)
AD
SP 9 *Strijela*-10 CRO
GUNS 96
SP 20mm 39 BOV-3 SP
TOWED 20mm 57 M55A4
ARV M84A1; WZT-3
VLB 3 MT-55A
MW Bozena; 1 *Rhino*

Navy 1,600

Navy HQ at Split

EQUIPMENT BY TYPE

PATROL AND COASTAL COMBATANTS 5
PCGF 1 *Koncar* with 2 twin lnchr with RBS-15B AShM, 1 57mm gun
PCG 4:
2 *Helsinki* with 4 twin lnchr with RBS-15M AShM, 1 57mm gun
2 *Kralj* with 2–4 twin lnchr with RBS-15B AShM, 1 AK630 CIWS, 1 57mm gun
MINE WARFARE • MINE COUNTERMEASURES •
MHI 1 *Korcula*
AMPHIBIOUS
LCT 2 *Cetina* with 1 quad lnchr with *Strela-2* (SA-N-5 *Grail*) SAM
LCVP 3: 2 Type-21; 1 Type-22
LOGISTICS AND SUPPORT 9: **YDT** 2; **YFU** 5; **YTM** 2
MSL • TACTICAL • AShM 3 RBS-15K

Marines

FORCES BY ROLE

MANOEUVRE

Amphibious

2 indep mne coy

Coast Guard

FORCES BY ROLE

Two divisions, headquartered in Split (1st div) and Pula (2nd div).

EQUIPMENT BY TYPE

PATROL AND COASTAL COMBATANTS • PB 4 *Mirna*
LOGISTICS AND SUPPORT • AX 5

Air Force and Air Defence 1,850

Flying hours 50 hrs/year

FORCES BY ROLE

FIGHTER/GROUND ATTACK

1 (mixed) sqn with MiG-21bis/UMD *Fishbed*

TRANSPORT

1 sqn with An-32 *Cline*

TRAINING

1 sqn with PC-9M; Z-242L
1 hel sqn with Bell 206B *Jet Ranger* II

FIRE FIGHTING
1 sqn with AT-802FA *Fire Boss*; CL-415
TRANSPORT HELICOPTER
2 sqn with Mi-8MTV *Hip* H; Mi-8T *Hip* C; Mi-171Sh
EQUIPMENT BY TYPE
AIRCRAFT 10 combat capable
FGA 10: 6 MiG-21bis *Fishbed*; 4 MiG-21UMD *Fishbed*
TPT • Light 2 An-32 *Cline*
TRG 25: 20 PC-9M; 5 Z-242L
FF 11: 5 AT-802FA *Fire Boss*; 6 CL-415
HELICOPTERS
MRH 11 Mi-8MTV *Hip* H
TPT 21 **Medium** 13: 3 Mi-8T *Hip* C; 10 Mi-171Sh; **Light** 8 Bell 206B *Jet Ranger* II
UAV • ISR • Medium *Hermes* 450
AD • SAM
SP S-300 (SA-10 *Grumble*); 9K31 *Strela*-1 (SA-9 *Gaskin*)
MANPAD 9K34 *Strela*-3 (SA-14 *Gremlin*); 9K310 *Igla*-1 (SA-16 *Gimlet*)
RADAR 11: 5 FPS-117; 3 S-600; 3 PRV-11
MSL • AAM • IR R-3S (AA-2 *Atoll*)‡; R-60 (AA-8 *Aphid*)

Paramilitary 3,000

Police 3,000 armed

DEPLOYMENT

Legal provisions for foreign deployment:
Constitution: Codified constitution (2004)
Decision on deployment of troops abroad: By the parliament (Art. 7 II); simplified procedure for humanitarian aid and military exercises

AFGHANISTAN
NATO • ISAF 181

BOSNIA-HERZEGOVINA
OSCE • Bosnia and Herzegovina 2

CYPRUS
UN • UNFICYP 2

INDIA/PAKISTAN
UN • UNMOGIP 9 obs

LEBANON
UN • UNIFIL 1

LIBERIA
UN • UNMIL 2

SERBIA
NATO • KFOR 22
OSCE • Kosovo 5

WESTERN SAHARA
UN • MINURSO 7 obs

Cyprus CYP

Cypriot Pound C£		2012	2013	2014
GDP	C£	16.4bn	16bn	
	US$	23bn	21.8bn	
per capita	US$	26,389	24,706	
Growth	%	-2.43	-8.71	
Inflation	%	3.09	1.00	
Def bdgt	C£	350m	347m	319m
	US$	450m	460m	
US$1=C£		0.78	0.75	

Population 1,155,403

Age	0 – 14	15 – 19	20 – 24	25 – 29	30 – 64	65 plus
Male	8.1%	3.8%	4.8%	4.9%	24.7%	4.8%
Female	7.7%	3.3%	3.9%	4.0%	23.9%	6.2%

Capabilities

The country's national guard is predominantly a land force supplemented by small air and maritime units. It is intended to act as a deterrent to any possible Turkish incursion, and to provide enough opposition until military support can be provided by its primary ally, Greece. The air wing has a small number of rotary- and fixed-wing utility platforms, including Mi-35 attack helicopters. Key procurements include SAR helicopters and T-80U MBTs. But readiness and morale are not thought to be high. Expeditionary deployments have been limited to a few officers joining UN and EU missions. It is possible that Cyprus's economic fragility may depress capability via effects on general funding and maintenance, as well as procurement aspirations.

ACTIVE 12,000 (National Guard 12,000)
Paramilitary 750
Conscript liability 24 months

RESERVE 50,000 (National Guard 50,000)
Reserve service to age 50 (officers dependent on rank; military doctors to age 60)

ORGANISATIONS BY SERVICE

National Guard 1,300 regular; 10,700 conscript (total 12,000)

FORCES BY ROLE
SPECIAL FORCES
1 comd (regt) (1 SF bn)
MANOEUVRE
Armoured
1 lt armd bde (2 armd bn, 1 armd inf bn)
Mechanised
1 (1st) mech inf div (1 armd recce bn, 2 mech inf bn)
1 (2nd) mech inf div (1 armd recce bn, 2 armd bn, 2 mech inf bn)
Light
3 (4th, 7th & 8th) lt inf bde (2 lt inf regt)

COMBAT SUPPORT
1 arty comd (8 arty bn)
COMBAT SERVICE SUPPORT
1 (3rd) spt bde

EQUIPMENT BY TYPE

MBT 164: 82 T-80U; 30 AMX-30G; 52 AMX-30B2
RECCE 124 EE-9 *Cascavel*
AIFV 43 BMP-3
APC 294
APC (T) 168 *Leonidas*
APC (W) 126 VAB (incl variants)
ARTY 452
SP 155mm 24: 12 Mk F3; 12 *Zuzana*
TOWED 104: **100mm** 20 M-1944; **105mm** 72 M-56; **155mm** 12 TR-F-1
MRL 22: **122mm** 4 BM-21; **128mm** 18 M-63 *Plamen*
MOR 302: **81mm** 170 E-44; (70+ M1/M9 in store); **107mm** 20 M2/M30; **120mm** 112 RT61
AT
MSL
SP 33: 15 EE-3 *Jararaca* with *Milan*; 18 VAB with HOT
MANPATS 115: 70 HOT; 45 *Milan*
RCL 153: **106mm** 144 M40A1; **90mm** 9 EM-67
RL 1,000: **112mm** 1,000 APILAS
AD
SAM 48
SP 6 9K322 *Tor* (SA-15 *Gauntlet*); *Mistral*
STATIC 12 *Aspide*
MANPAD 30 *Mistral*
GUNS • TOWED 60: **20mm** 36 M-55; **35mm** 24 GDF-003 (with *Skyguard*)
ARV 2 AMX-30D; 1 BREM-1

Maritime Wing

FORCES BY ROLE

COMBAT SUPPORT
1 (coastal defence) AShM bty with MM-40 *Exocet* AShM

EQUIPMENT BY TYPE

PATROL AND COASTAL COMBATANTS 6
PBF 4: 2 Rodman 55; 2 *Vittoria*
PB 2: 1 *Esterel*; 1 *Kyrenia* (GRC *Dilos*)
MSL • AShM 24 MM-40 *Exocet*

Air Wing

AIRCRAFT
TPT • Light 2: 1 AT-802F *Air Tractor*; 1 BN-2B *Islander*
TRG 1 PC-9
HELICOPTERS
ATK 11 Mi-35P *Hind*
MRH 7: 3 AW139 (SAR); 4 SA342L1 *Gazelle* (with HOT for anti-armour role)
TPT • Light 2 Bell 206L-3 *Long Ranger*

Paramilitary 750+

Armed Police 500+

FORCES BY ROLE

MANOEUVRE
Other
1 (rapid-reaction) paramilitary unit

EQUIPMENT BY TYPE

APC (W) 2 VAB VTT
HELICOPTERS • MRH 2 Bell 412 SP

Maritime Police 250

PATROL AND COASTAL COMBATANTS 10
PBF 5: 2 *Poseidon*; 1 *Shaldag*; 2 *Vittoria*
PB 5 SAB-12

DEPLOYMENT

Legal provisions for foreign deployment:
Constitution: Codified constitution (1960)
Decision on deployment of troops abroad: By parliament, but president has the right of final veto (Art. 50)

LEBANON

UN • UNIFIL 2

FOREIGN FORCES

Argentina UNFICYP 266; 2 inf coy; 1 hel pl
Austria UNFICYP 4
Brazil UNFICYP 1
Canada UNFICYP 1
Chile UNFICYP 14
China UNFICYP 2
Croatia UNFICYP 2
Greece Army: 950; ε200 (officers/NCO seconded to Greek-Cypriot National Guard)
Hungary UNFICYP 77; 1 inf pl
Paraguay UNFICYP 14
Serbia UNFICYP 46; elm 1 inf coy
Slovakia UNFICYP 157; elm 1 inf coy; 1 engr pl
United Kingdom 2,620; 2 inf bn; 1 hel sqn with 4 Bell 412 *Twin Huey* • UNFICYP 337: 1 inf coy

TERRITORY WHERE THE GOVERNMENT DOES NOT EXERCISE EFFECTIVE CONTROL

Data here represent the de facto situation on the northern half of the island. This does not imply international recognition as a sovereign state.

Capabilities

ACTIVE 3,500 (Army 3,500) Paramilitary 150
Conscript liability 24 months

RESERVE 26,000 (first line 11,000 second line 10,000 third line 5,000)
Reserve liability to age 50.

ORGANISATIONS BY SERVICE

Army ε3,500

FORCES BY ROLE

MANOEUVRE
Light
7 inf bn

EQUIPMENT BY TYPE
ARTY • MOR • 120mm 73
AT
MSL • MANPATS 6 *Milan*
RCL • 106mm 36

Paramilitary

Armed Police ε150

FORCES BY ROLE
SPECIAL FORCES
1 (police) SF unit

Coast Guard

PATROL AND COASTAL COMBATANTS 6
PCC 5: 2 SG45/SG46; 1 *Rauf Denktash*; 2 US Mk 5
PB 1

FOREIGN FORCES

TURKEY
Army ε43,000
1 army corps HQ, 1 armd bde, 2 mech inf div, 1 avn comd

EQUIPMENT BY TYPE
MBT 348: 8 M48A2 (trg); 340 M48A5T1/2
APC (T) 627: 361 AAPC (incl variants); 266 M113 (incl variants)
ARTY
SP 155mm 90 M-44T
TOWED 102: **105mm** 72 M101A1; **155mm** 18 M-114A2; **203mm** 12 M115
MRL 122mm 6 T-122
MOR 450: **81mm** 175; **107mm** 148 M-30; **120mm** 127 HY-12
AT
MSL • MANPATS 114: 66 *Milan*; 48 TOW
RCL 106mm 192 M40A1
AD • GUNS
TOWED 20mm Rh 202; **35mm** 16 GDF-003; **40mm** 48 M1
AIRCRAFT • TPT • Light 3 Cessna 185 (U-17)
HELICOPTER • TPT 4 **Medium** 1 AS532UL *Cougar* **Light** 3 Bell 205 (UH-1H *Iroquois*)
PATROL AND COASTAL COMBATANTS 1 **PB**

Czech Republic CZE

Czech Koruna Kc		2012	2013	2014
GDP	Kc	3.92tr	4.04tr	
	US$	196bn	203bn	
per capita	US$	18,579	19,243	
Growth	%	-1.25	0.30	
Inflation	%	3.29	2.25	
Def exp	Kc	41.5bn		
	US$	2.12bn		
Def bdgt [a]	Kc	43.5bn	42bn	42bn
	US$	2.22bn	2.18bn	
FMA (US)	US$	5m	5m	3m
US$1=Kc		19.58	19.27	

[a] Includes military pensions

Population 10,162,921

Age	0–14	15–19	20–24	25–29	30–64	65 plus
Male	6.9%	2.5%	3.2%	3.4%	25.7%	7.1%
Female	6.5%	2.4%	3.0%	3.2%	25.6%	10.5%

Capabilities

According to the 2012 Defence Strategy, the Czech armed forces are intended to retain the capability to act autonomously, however Prague has earmarked a brigade-sized task force as its contribution NATO's collective defence planning. Defence cooperation with the other three members of the Visegrad group is also planned, with contributions earmarked for a multinational CBRN battalion and a manoeuvre battlegroup. The armed forces have reached a high level of capability as a result of military reform and restructuring, as well as equipment improvements and operational experience in Kosovo, Afghanistan and Iraq. But maintaining these standards will prove challenging, with the end of the ISAF mission and pressure on defence spending.

ACTIVE 23,650 (Army 13,000, Air 5,950, Other 4,850) **Paramilitary 3,100**

ORGANISATIONS BY SERVICE

Army 13,000

FORCES BY ROLE
SPECIAL FORCES
1 SF gp
MANOEUVRE
Reconnaissance
1 ISR/EW bde (1 recce bn, 1 EW bn)
Armoured
1 (7th) mech bde (1 armd bn, 2 armd inf bn, 1 mot inf bn)
Mechanised
1 (4th) rapid reaction bde (2 mech bn, 1 mot inf bn, 1 AB bn)
COMBAT SUPPORT
1 (13th) arty bde (2 arty bn)

1 engr bde (3 engr bn, 1 EOD bn)
1 CBRN bde (2 CBRN bn)
1 sigs bn
1 CIMIC pl

COMBAT SERVICE SUPPORT
1 log bde

Active Reserve

FORCES BY ROLE

COMMAND
14 (territorial defence) comd

MANOEUVRE

Armoured
1 armd coy

Light
14 inf coy (1 per territorial comd) (3 inf pl, 1 cbt spt pl, 1 log pl)

EQUIPMENT BY TYPE

MBT 30 T-72M4CZ; (93 T-72 in store)
AIFV 206: 103 BMP-2; 103 *Pandur* II (inc variants); (98 BMP-1; 82 BMP-2; 34 BPzV all in store)
APC 21:
APC (T) (17 OT-90 in store)
APC (W) (5 OT-64 in store)
PPV 21 *Dingo* 2
ARTY 146:
SP 152mm 95 M-77 *Dana* (inc 6 trg); (35 more in store)
MOR 120mm 51: 43 M-1982 (inc 3 trg); 8 SPM-85; (42 M-1982 in store);
AT • MSL • MANPATS 9P135 *Konkurs*
RADAR • LAND 3 ARTHUR
ARV 4+: MT-72; VT-72M4CZ; VPV-ARV; WPT-TOPAS; 4 *Pandur* II
VLB AM-50; MT-55A
MW UOS-155 *Belarty*

Air Force 5,950

Principal task is to secure Czech airspace. This mission is fulfilled within NATO Integrated Extended Air Defence System (NATINADS) and, if necessary, by means of the Czech national reinforced air-defence system. The air force also provides CAS for the army SAR, and performs a tpt role.

Flying hours 120hrs/yr cbt ac 150 for tpt ac

FORCES BY ROLE

FIGHTER/GROUND ATTACK
1 sqn with *Gripen* C/D
1 sqn with L-159 ALCA/L-159T

TRANSPORT
2 sqn with A319CJ; C-295M; CL-601 *Challenger*; L-410 *Turbolet*; Yak-40 *Codling*

TRAINING
1 sqn with L-39ZA*

ATTACK HELICOPTER
1 sqn with Mi-24/Mi-35 *Hind*

TRANSPORT HELICOPTER
1 sqn with Mi-17 *Hip* H; Mi-171Sh
1 sqn with Mi-8 *Hip*; Mi-17 *Hip* H; PZL W-3A *Sokol*

AIR DEFENCE
1 (25th) SAM bde (2 AD gp)

EQUIPMENT BY TYPE

AIRCRAFT 47 combat capable
FGA 14: 12 *Gripen* C (JAS 39C); 2 *Gripen* D (JAS 39D)
ATK 24: 20 L-159 ALCA; 4 L-159T
TPT 17: **Light** 14: 4 C-295M; 8 L-410 *Turbolet*; 2 Yak-40 *Codling*; **PAX** 3: 2 A319CJ; 1 CL-601 *Challenger*
TRG 26: 1 EW-97 *Eurostar*; 8 L-39C *Albatros*; 9 L-39ZA*; 8 Z-142C
HELICOPTERS
ATK 24: 6 Mi-24 *Hind* D; 18 Mi-35 *Hind* E
MRH 8 Mi-17 *Hip* H
TPT 30: **Medium** 20: 4 Mi-8 *Hip*; 16 Mi-171Sh (med tpt); **Light** 10 PZL W3A *Sokol*
AD
SAM RBS-70; 9K32 *Strela*-2 (SA-7 *Grail*) (available for trg RBS-70 gunners)
MSL
AAM • IR AIM-9M *Sidewinder*; **ARH** AIM-120 AMRAAM
BOMBS
Laser-guided: GBU *Paveway*

Joint Forces Support Units

FORCES BY ROLE

COMBAT SUPPORT
1 engr bde (3 engr bn; 2 (rescue) engr coy)
1 CIMIC/psyops coy (1 CIMIC pl; 1 psyops pl)
1 CBRN bde (2 CBRN bn)

COMBAT SERVICE SUPPORT
1 (14th) bde (1 spt bn; 1 supply bn)

Other Forces

FORCES BY ROLE

MANOEUVRE

Other
1 (presidential) gd bde (2 bn)
1 (presidential) gd coy

COMBAT SUPPORT
1 int gp
1 (central) MP comd
3 (regional) MP comd
1 (protection service) MP comd

Paramilitary 3,100

Border Guards 3,000

Internal Security Forces 100

Cyber

In 2011, a National Security Authority was established to supervise the protection of classified information and perform tasks related to communications and information-systems security. A Cyber Security Strategy was published in 2011 to coordinate government approaches to network security and create a framework for legislative developments, international cooperative activity and the development of technical means, as well as promoting network security. It also announced the creation of a national CERT agency.

DEPLOYMENT

Legal provisions for foreign deployment:
Constitution: Codified constitution (1992), Art. 39, 43
Decision on deployment of troops abroad: External deployments require approval by the parliament. As an exception, such as in urgent cases, the government can decide on such a deployment for up to 60 days with the aim of fulfilling international treaty obligations concerning collective defence.

AFGHANISTAN
NATO • ISAF 182
UN • UNAMA 2 obs

ARMENIA/AZERBAIJAN
OSCE • Minsk Conference 1

BOSNIA-HERZEGOVINA
EU • EUFOR • *Operation Althea* 2
OSCE • Bosnia and Herzegovina 2

DEMOCRATIC REPUBLIC OF THE CONGO
UN • MONUSCO 3 obs

EGYPT
MFO 3

MALI
EU • EUTM Mali 38

MOLDOVA
OSCE • Moldova 1

SERBIA
NATO • KFOR 7
OSCE • Kosovo 1
UN • UNMIK 1 obs

Denmark DNK

Danish Krone kr		2012	2013	2014
GDP	kr	1.86tr	1.92tr	
	US$	314bn	328bn	
per capita	US$	56,202	58,668	
Growth	%	-0.57	0.84	
Inflation	%	2.41	2.00	
Def exp	kr	25.6bn		
	US$	4.42bn		
Def bdgt [a]	kr	25.6bn	25.6bn	26.3bn
	US$	4.42bn	4.51bn	
US$1=kr		5.79	5.67	

[a] Includes military pensions

Population 5,556,452

Age	0–14	15–19	20–24	25–29	30–64	65 plus
Male	8.8%	3.4%	3.2%	2.8%	23.0%	8.0%
Female	8.4%	3.2%	3.1%	2.8%	23.2%	10.0%

Capabilities

Denmark's armed forces are geared towards participation in international missions. They also conduct domestic tasks, including SAR, airspace defence and surveillance, and have contributed to both the Baltic and Icelandic air policing missions. The defence agreement 2013–17 details a range of tasks for the armed forces, from war-fighting and counter-insurgency to non-combatant evacuation; and the forces themselves should be increasingly 'joint', well-trained and capable of rapid response. Some civilian-related tasks could be outsourced. Acquisition of the C-130J will aid tactical mobility, and Denmark is a partner in the F-35 programme. Notwithstanding equipment reductions, such as in long-range ATGW, the ground force has benefited from combat experience in Afghanistan. Denmark has maintained a battalion-plus deployment to ISAF and contributed to a number of UN peacekeeping missions. As with other Nordic nations, Denmark is increasingly focused on the Arctic, having formed a joint Arctic Command in 2012 in Nuuk, Greenland. Due to Denmark's 'no' vote to the Maastricht Treaty in 1992, it cannot participate in EU-led military operations or the development of EU military capabilities. It is, however, a member of NATO and involved in developing the Nordic defence co-operation grouping.

ACTIVE 17,200 (Army 7,950 Navy 3,000 Air 3,150 Joint 3,100)
Conscript liability 4–12 months, most voluntary

RESERVES 53,500 (Army 40,800 Navy 4,500 Air Force 5,300 Service Corps 2,900)

ORGANISATIONS BY SERVICE

Army 6,950; 1,000 conscript (total 7,950)

Div and bde HQ are responsible for trg only; if necessary, can be transformed into operational formations

FORCES BY ROLE
COMMAND
1 div HQ
2 bde HQ
SPECIAL FORCES
1 SF unit
MANOEUVRE
Reconnaissance
1 recce bn
1 ISTAR bn
Armoured
1 tk bn
Mechanised
5 armd inf bn
COMBAT SUPPORT
1 SP arty bn
1 cbt engr bn
1 EOD bn
1 MP bn
1 sigs regt (1 sigs bn, 1 EW coy)
COMBAT SERVICE SUPPORT
1 construction bn
1 log regt (1 spt bn, 1 log bn, 1 maint bn, 1 med bn)

EQUIPMENT BY TYPE
MBT 55 *Leopard* 2A4/5
RECCE 113: 22 *Eagle* 1; 91 *Eagle* IV
AIFV 45 CV9030 Mk II
APC 494
APC (T) 343 M113 (incl variants); (196 more in store awaiting disposal)
APC (W) 111 *Piranha* III (incl variants)
PPV 40 *Cougar*
ARTY 44
SP 155mm 24 M109
MRL 227mm (12 MLRS in store awaiting disposal)
MOR • TOWED 120mm 20 Soltam K6B1
AT
MSL • MANPATS 20 TOW
RCL 84mm 349 *Carl Gustav*
AD • SAM • MANPAD FIM-92A *Stinger*
RADAR • LAND ARTHUR
ARV 11 *Bergepanzer 2*
VLB 10 *Biber*
MW 14 910-MCV-2

Navy 2,850; 150 conscript (total 3,000)

EQUIPMENT BY TYPE
PRINCIPAL SURFACE COMBATANTS 5
DESTROYERS • DDGHM 1 *Iver Huitfeldt* with 4 quad lnchr with RGM-84 *Harpoon* Block II AShM, 1 32-cell Mk41 VLS with SM-2 IIIA SAM, 2 12-cell Mk56 VLS with RIM-162 SAM, 2 twin 324mm TT with MU90 LWT, 2 76mm guns, (capacity 1 med hel) (2 additional vessels under construction; expected ISD 2014)
FRIGATES • FFH 4 *Thetis* with 2 twin lnchr with *Stinger* SAM, 1 76mm gun, (capacity 1 *Super Lynx* Mk90B)
PATROL AND COASTAL COMBATANTS 9
PSO 2 *Knud Rasmussen* with 1 76mm gun, 1 hel landing platform
PCC 7: 1 *Agdlek*; 6 *Diana*
MINE WARFARE • MINE COUNTERMEASURES 6
MCI 4 MSF MK-I
MSD 2 *Holm*
LOGISTICS AND SUPPORT 26
ABU 2 (primarily used for MARPOL duties)
AE 1 *Sleipner*
AG 2 *Absalon* (flexible support ships) with 2 octuple VLS with RGM-84 Block 2 *Harpoon* 2 AShM, 4 twin lnchr with *Stinger* SAM, 3 12-cell Mk 56 VLS with RIM-162B *Sea Sparrow* SAM, 2 twin 324mm TT, 2 *Millenium* CIWS, 1 127mm gun (capacity 2 LCP, 7 MBT or 40 vehicles; 130 troops)
AGB 3: 1 *Thorbjørn*; 2 *Danbjørn*
AGE 1 *Dana*
AGS 3 Ska 11
AGSC 2 *Holm*
AKL 2 *Seatruck*
AX 1 *Søløven* (used as diving trainer)
AXL 2 *Holm*
AXS 2 *Svanen*
YPL 3
YTL 2

Air Force 3,050; 100 conscript (total 3,150)

Flying hours 165 hrs/yr

Tactical Air Comd

FORCES BY ROLE
FIGHTER/GROUND ATTACK
2 sqn with F-16AM/BM *Fighting Falcon*
ANTI-SUBMARINE WARFARE
1 sqn with *Super Lynx* Mk90B
SEARCH & RESCUE/TRANSPORT HELICOPTER
1 sqn with AW101 *Merlin*
1 sqn with AS550 *Fennec* (ISR)
TRANSPORT
1 sqn with C-130J-30 *Hercules*; CL-604 *Challenger* (MP/VIP)
TRAINING
1 unit with MFI-17 *Supporter* (T-17)

EQUIPMENT BY TYPE
AIRCRAFT 45 combat capable
FTR 45: 35 F-16AM *Fighting Falcon*; 10 F-16BM *Fighting Falcon* (30 operational)
TPT 7: **Medium** 4 C-130J-30 *Hercules*; **PAX** 3 CL-604 *Challenger* (MP/VIP)
TRG 27 MFI-17 *Supporter* (T-17)
HELICOPTERS
ASW 7 *Super Lynx* Mk90B
MRH 8 AS550 *Fennec* (ISR) (4 more non-operational)
TPT • Medium 14 AW101 *Merlin* (8 SAR; 6 Tpt)
MSL
AAM • IR AIM-9L; **IIR** AIM-9X; **ARH** AIM-120 AMRAAM
ASM AGM-65 *Maverick*
BOMBS
LGB/INS/GPS-guided: GBU-31 JDAM; EGBU-12/GBU-24 *Paveway* LGB

Control and Air Defence Group

1 Control and Reporting Centre, 1 Mobile Control and Reporting Centre. 4 Radar sites.

Reserves

Home Guard (Army) 40,800 reservists (to age 50)

FORCES BY ROLE
MANOEUVRE
Light
2 regt cbt gp (3 mot inf bn, 1 arty bn)
5 (local) def region (up to 2 mot inf bn)

Home Guard (Navy) 4,500 reservists (to age 50) organised into 30 Home Guard units

EQUIPMENT BY TYPE
PATROL AND COASTAL COMBATANTS 31
PB 31: 18 MHV800; 1 MHV850; 12 MHV900

Home Guard (Air Force) 5,300 reservists (to age 50)

Home Guard (Service Corps) 2,900 reservists

Cyber

Denmark has a national CERT. Within the army, the 3rd Electronic Warfare Company is in charge of exploiting and disrupting enemy communications. A cyber-warfare unit within the Defence Intelligence Service is planned, with the aim of protecting military technology.

DEPLOYMENT

Legal provisions for foreign deployment:
Constitution: Codified constitution (1849)
Decision on deployment of troops abroad: On approval by the parliament (Art. 19 II)

AFGHANISTAN
NATO • ISAF 317; 1 mech BG; 1 C-130J-30
UN • UNAMA 1 obs

DEMOCRATIC REPUBLIC OF THE CONGO
EU • EUSEC RD Congo 3

GULF OF ADEN & SOMALI BASIN
NATO • *Operation Ocean Shield* 1 CL-604 (MP)

LIBERIA
UN • UNMIL 2; 3 obs

MIDDLE EAST
UN • UNTSO 10 obs

SERBIA
NATO • KFOR 36

SOUTH SUDAN
UN • UNMISS 13; 2 obs

Estonia EST

Euro €[a]		2012	2013	2014
GDP	€	18.2bn	19.3bn	
	US$	21.9bn	24.2bn	
per capita	US$	16,320	18,027	
Growth	%	3.22	2.99	
Inflation	%	4.20	3.20	
Def bdgt[a]	€	340m	361m	387m
	US$	437m	480m	
FMA (US)	US$	2m	2.4m	2.4m
US$1=€		0.78	0.75	

[a] Includes military pensions

Population 1,266,375

Age	0–14	15–19	20–24	25–29	30–64	65 plus
Male	7.9%	2.6%	3.5%	3.8%	21.6%	6.0%
Female	7.5%	2.4%	3.4%	3.9%	25.1%	12.2%

Capabilities

Estonia's conscript-based armed forces are small and the nation's security against external threats is based on NATO membership. The country is an enthusiastic contributor to NATO organisation and missions where feasible. Estonia has contributed personnel to ISAF, as well as to UN peacekeeping operations, and is a member of the EU's Nordic Battlegroup. The armed forces are heavily land-focused, with just one offshore patrol vessel in service with the navy (and some mine countermeasures vessels), and no aircraft capable of airspace defence. Reliance is placed on a NATO Air Policing Mission for airspace defence. Following the substantial cyber attack on Estonian systems in 2007, Tallinn is the location for NATO's Cooperative Cyber Defence Centre of Excellence. This conducts theoretical and practical training for member states' personnel. Major procurement plans centre around the development of an air-defence system and radars. A new Defence Development Plan (for 2013–22) was passed in 2012 and noted Estonia's difficulties in maintaining defence spending amid the global financial crisis; nonetheless, the plan suggested that Tallinn will continue to meet its 2% of GDP spending target as required by NATO. The plan outlined an intention to double the number of infantry brigades (to two) by 2022, and to procure modern infantry fighting vehicles and armoured personnel carriers, anti-tank weapons and 155mm self-propelled howitzers.

ACTIVE 5,750 (Army 5,300 Navy 200 Air 250)
Defence League 12,000

Conscript liability 8 months, officers and some specialists 11 months. (Conscripts cannot be deployed.)

RESERVE 30,000 (Joint 30,000)

ORGANISATIONS BY SERVICE

Army 2,800; 2,500 conscript (total 5,300)

4 def region. All units except Scouts bn are reserve based

FORCES BY ROLE
MANOEUVRE
Reconnaissance
1 recce bn
Light
1 (1st) bde (2 inf bn, 1 CSS bn)
3 indep inf bn
COMBAT SUPPORT
1 arty bn
1 AD bn
1 engr bn
1 sigs bn
COMBAT SERVICE SUPPORT
1 log bn

Defence League 12,000

15 Districts

EQUIPMENT BY TYPE
APC 130
APC (W) 117: 56 XA-180 *Sisu*; 40 XA-188 *Sisu*; 21 BTR-80
PPV 13: 6 *Maxxpro*; 7 *Mamba*
ARTY 334
TOWED 98: **105mm** 32 H 61-37; **122mm** 42 D-30 (H 63); **155mm** 24 FH-70
MOR 230: **81mm** 51: 41 B455; 10 NM 95; **120mm** 179: 14 2B11; 165 41D

AT

MSL • MANPAT *Milan*; IMI MAPATS

RCL 160+ **106mm**: 30 M40A1; **84mm** *Carl Gustav*; **90mm** 130 PV-1110

AD • SAM • MANPAD *Mistral*

Navy 200

EQUIPMENT BY TYPE

PATROL AND COASTAL COMBATANTS • PB 1 *Ristna* (FIN *Rihtniemi*) with 2 RBU 1200

MINE WARFARE • MINE COUNTERMEASURES 4

MCD 1 *Tasuja* (DNK *Lindormen*)

MHC 3 *Admiral Cowan* (UK *Sandown*)

LOGISTICS AND SUPPORT • AGF 1 *Admiral Pitka* with 1 76mm gun

Air Force 250

Flying hours 120 hrs/year

FORCES BY ROLE

TRANSPORT

1 sqn with An-2 *Colt*

TRANSPORT HELICOPTER

1 sqn with R-44 *Raven* II

EQUIPMENT BY TYPE

AIRCRAFT • TPT • Light 2 An-2 *Colt*

HELICOPTERS • TPT • Light 4 R-44 *Raven* II

Paramilitary

Border Guard

The Estonian Border Guard is subordinate to the Ministry of the Interior. Air support is provided by the Estonian Border Guard Aviation Corps.

EQUIPMENT BY TYPE

PATROL AND COASTAL COMBATANTS 22

PCO 1 *Kindral Kurvits*

PCC 1 *Kou* (FIN *Silma*)

PB 9: 1 *Maru* (FIN *Viima*); 8 (other)

PBR 11

AMPHIBIOUS • LANDING CRAFT • LCU 2

LOGISTICS & SUPPORT • AGF 1 *Balsam*

AIRCRAFT • TPT • Light 2 L-410

HELICOPTERS • TPT • 3 AW139

Cyber

Estonia established CERT-ee in 2006 and has further developed its cyber-security infrastructure after the cyber attacks of 2007. It adopted a national Cyber Security Strategy in 2008. As well as domestic capacities, Tallinn hosts the NATO Cooperative Cyber Security Centre of Excellence, established in 2008 to enhance NATO's cyber-defence capability.

DEPLOYMENT

Legal provisions for foreign deployment:

Constitution: Codified constitution (1992)

Decision on deployment of troops abroad: By parliament (Art. 128). Also, International Military Cooperation Act stipulates conditions for deployment abroad. For the collective defence purposes, ratification of the North Atlantic Treaty is considered a parliamentary decision that would allow Cabinet to deploy troops. The president, chairman of the parliament and chairman of the parliament's State Defence Commission shall be immediately informed of such a decision. For other international operations, a separate parliamentary decision is necessary: the Ministry of Defence prepares a draft legal act and coordinates this with the Ministry of Foreign Affairs and the Ministry of Justice. It also asks the opinion of the chief of defence. The draft is then proposed to cabinet for approval and submission for parliamentary consideration.

AFGHANISTAN

NATO • ISAF 160; 1 mech inf coy; 1 mor det

MALI

EU • EUTM Mali 8

UN • MINUSMA 1

MIDDLE EAST

UN • UNTSO 2 obs

MOLDOVA

OSCE • Moldova 2

NORTH SEA

NATO • SNMCMG 1: 1 MHC

SERBIA

NATO • KFOR 2

Finland FIN

Euro €		2012	2013	2014
GDP	€	200bn	207bn	
	US$	250bn	265bn	
per capita	US$	46,098	48,707	
Growth	%	-0.21	0.51	
Inflation	%	3.16	2.90	
Def exp	€	2.8bn		
	US$	3.6bn		
Def bdgt	€	2.82bn	2.87bn	2.75bn
	US$	3.63bn	3.81bn	
US$1=€		0.78	0.75	

Population 5,266,114

Age	0 – 14	15 – 19	20 – 24	25 – 29	30 – 64	65 plus
Male	8.1%	3.0%	3.2%	3.1%	23.5%	8.0%
Female	7.8%	2.9%	3.1%	3.0%	23.1%	11.2%

Capabilities

The primary role of Finland's armed forces is to act as a guarantor of national sovereignty by providing territorial defence, and its combination of a conscript/reserve-based structure with a modern equipment inventory is shaped to support this aim. All the armed services exercise regularly, with an increasingly joint emphasis, and the air force and navy particularly participate in multinational exercises. There are no planned changes to the key premises of Finland's defence policy, such as territorial defence, non-alignment and general conscription. However, Finland has embarked on a wide-ranging defence reform process in a bid to reconcile defence priorities with funding and demographics (the number of available conscripts is reducing), with the process planned to complete by 2015. Current plans call for the disbandment of the Jaeger brigade, an engineer regiment, a coastal artillery battalion and two air force training wings by the end of 2014. In addition, currently independent signals, air-defence and artillery formations will be merged with existing manoeuvre brigades. The number of command levels will reduce from four to three, and the military provinces will cease to exist, with tasks divided between army command and regional offices.

ACTIVE 22,200 (Army 16,000 Navy 3,500 Air 2,700) Paramilitary 2,800

Conscript liability 6–9–12 months (12 months for officers NCOs and soldiers with special duties.) Conscript service was reduced by 15 days in early 2013.

RESERVE 354,000 (Army 285,000 Navy 31,000 Air 38,000) Paramilitary 11,500

25,000 reservists a year do refresher training: total obligation 40 days (75 for NCOs, 100 for officers) between conscript service and age 50 (NCOs and officers to age 60).

ORGANISATIONS BY SERVICE

Army 5,000; 11,000 conscript (total 16,000)

FORCES BY ROLE

Finland's army maintains a mobilisation strength of about 285,000. In support of this requirement, two conscription cycles, each for about 15,000 conscripts, take place each year. After conscript training, reservist commitment is to the age of 60. Reservists are usually assigned to units within their local geographical area. All service appointments or deployments outside Finnish borders are voluntary for all members of the armed services. All brigades are reserve based.

Reserve Organisations

60,000 in manoeuvre forces and 225,000 in territorial forces

FORCES BY ROLE

SPECIAL FORCES
1 SF bn
MANOEUVRE
Armoured
2 armd BG (regt)
Mechanised
2 (Karelia & Pori Jaeger) mech bde
Light
3 (Jaeger) bde
6 lt inf bde
Aviation
1 hel bn
COMBAT SUPPORT
1 arty bde
1 AD regt
7 engr regt
3 sigs bn
COMBAT SERVICE SUPPORT
Some log unit

EQUIPMENT BY TYPE

MBT 100 *Leopard* 2A4
RECCE 34 BMP-1TJ
AIFV 212: 110 BMP-2; 102 CV90
APC 613
APC (T) 142: 40 MT-LBu; 102 MT-LBV
APC (W) 471: 260 XA-180/185 *Sisu*; 101 XA-202 *Sisu*; 48 XA-203 *Sisu*; 62 AMV (XA-360)
ARTY 647
SP 122mm 36 2S1 (PsH 74)
TOWED 324: **122mm** 234 D-30 (H 63); **130mm** 36 K 54; **155mm** 54 K 83/K 98
MRL 227mm 22 M270 MLRS
MOR 120mm 265: 261 KRH 92; 4 XA-361 AMOS
AT • MSL 100 *Spike*; TOW 2
HELICOPTERS
MRH 7: 5 Hughes 500D; 2 Hughes 500E
TPT • Medium 16 NH90 TTH
UAV • ISR • Medium 11 ADS-95 *Ranger*
AD • SAM
SP 36 +: 16 ASRAD (ITO 05); 20 *Crotale* NG (ITO 90); 9K37 *Buk*-M1 (ITO 96)
MANPAD: 86 RBS 70 (ITO 05/05M)
GUNS 23mm; 30mm; 35mm; 57mm
AEV 6 *Leopard* 2R CEV
ARV 27: 15 MTP-LB; 12 VT-55A
VLB 15+: BLG-60M2; 6 *Leopard* 2L; 9 SISU *Leguan*
MW *Aardvark* Mk 2; KMT T-55; RA-140 DS

Navy 1,600; 1,900 conscript (total 3,500)

FORCES BY ROLE

Naval Command HQ located at Turku; with two subordinate Naval Commands (Gulf of Finland and Archipelago Sea); 1 Naval bde; 3 spt elm (Naval Materiel Cmd, Naval Academy, Naval Research Institute)

EQUIPMENT BY TYPE

PATROL AND COASTAL COMBATANTS 8
PBG 4 *Rauma* with 6 RBS-15SF3 (15SF) AShM, 1 sextuple *Sadral* lnchr with *Mistral* SAM
PCG 4 *Hamina* with 4 RBS-15 (15SF) AShM, 1 octuple VLS with *Umkhonto* SAM, 1 57mm gun
MINE WARFARE 19
MINE COUNTERMEASURES 13
MHSO 3 *Katanpää* (expected FOC 2014/15)
MSI 10: 7 *Kiiski*; 3 *Kuha*
MINELAYERS • ML 6:
2 *Hameenmaa* with 1 octuple VLS with *Umkhonto* SAM, 2 RBU 1200, up to 100–120 mines, 1 57mm gun
3 *Pansio* with 50 mines
1 *Pohjanmaa* with 2 sextruple *Sadral* lnchr with *Mistral* SAM, up to 100–150 mines, 1 57mm gun

AMPHIBIOUS • LANDING CRAFT 51
LCU 1 *Kampela*
LCP 50
LOGISTICS AND SUPPORT 33
AG 3: 1 *Louhi*; 2 *Hylje*
AGB 7 (Board of Navigation control)
AKSL 9: 2 *Hauki*; 4 *Hila*; 3 *Valas*
AX 4: 3 *Fabian Wrede*; 1 *Lokki*
YFB 8
YTM 2 *Haukipaa*

Coastal Defence

ARTY • COASTAL • 130mm 102: 30 K-53tk (static); 72 K-54 RT
MSL • TACTICAL • 4 RBS-15K AShM

Air Force 1,950; 750 conscript (total 2,700)

3 Air Comds: Satakunta (West), Karelia (East), Lapland (North)

Flying hours 90–140 hrs/year

FORCES BY ROLE
FIGHTER/GROUND ATTACK
3 sqn with F/A-18C/D *Hornet*
ISR
1 (survey) sqn with Learjet 35A
TRANSPORT
1 flt with C-295M
4 (liaison) flt with PC-12NG
TRAINING
1 sqn with *Hawk* Mk50/51A/66* (air defence and ground attack trg)
1 unit with L-70 *Vinka*

EQUIPMENT BY TYPE
AIRCRAFT 107 combat capable
FGA 62: 55 F/A-18C *Hornet*; 7 F/A-18D *Hornet*
MP 1 F-27-400M
ELINT 1 C-295M
TPT • Light 11: 2 C-295M; 3 Learjet 35A (survey; ECM trg; tgt-tow); 6 PC-12NG
TRG 73: 29 *Hawk* Mk50/51A*; 16 *Hawk* Mk66*; 28 L-70 *Vinka*
MSL • AAM • IR AIM-9 *Sidewinder*; IIR AIM-9X *Sidewinder*; **ARH** AIM-120 AMRAAM

Paramilitary

Border Guard 2,800

Ministry of Interior. 4 Border Guard Districts and 2 Coast Guard Districts

FORCES BY ROLE
MARITIME PATROL
1 sqn with Do-228 (maritime surv); AS332 *Super Puma*; Bell 412 (AB-412) *Twin Huey*; Bell 412EP (AB-412EP) *Twin Huey*;AW119KE *Koala*

EQUIPMENT BY TYPE
PATROL AND COASTAL COMBATANTS 54
PCC 3: 2 *Tursas*; 1 *Merikarhu*
PBO 3 *Telkaa*
PB 48
AMPHIBIOUS • LANDING CRAFT • LCAC 7
AIRCRAFT • TPT • Light 2 Do-228
HELICOPTERS
MRH 5: 4 Bell 412 (AB-412) *Twin Huey*; 1 Bell 412EP (AB-412EP) *Twin Huey*
TPT 7: **Medium** 3 AS332 *Super Puma*; **Light** 4 AW119KE *Koala*

Reserve 11,500 reservists on mobilisation

Cyber

Finland has a national CERT, is involved in informal CERT communities and is a member of the European Government CERTs group (EGC). The country has announced the establishment of a common secure network in 2013 to protect military, police, border guard and government confidential networks.

DEPLOYMENT

Legal provisions for foreign deployment:
Constitution: Codified constitution (2000)
Specific legislation: 'Act on Peace Support Operations' (2000); 'Act on Military Crisis Management (211/2006)'.
Decision on deployment of troops abroad: By president upon proposal by government (Art. 129 of constitution) and after formal consultation of parliamentary Foreign Affairs Committee ('Act on Peace Support Operations', Ch. 1, Section 2; 'Act on Military Crisis Management (211/2006)').

AFGHANISTAN
NATO • ISAF 100

BOSNIA-HERZEGOVINA
EU • EUFOR • *Operation Althea* 8
OSCE • Bosnia and Herzegovina 1

INDIA/PAKISTAN
UN • UNMOGIP 6 obs

LEBANON
UN • UNIFIL 192; 1 inf coy

LIBERIA
UN • UNMIL 2

MALI
EU • EUTM Mali 10
UN • MINUSMA 1

MIDDLE EAST
UN • UNTSO 16 obs

SERBIA
NATO • KFOR 21
OSCE • Kosovo 1

UGANDA
EU • EUTM Somalia 6

France FRA

Euro €		2012	2013	2014
GDP	€	2.06tr	2.12tr	
	US$	2.61tr	2.74tr	
per capita	US$	41,141	43,000	
Growth	%	0.03	-0.07	
Inflation	%	1.98	1.57	
Def bdgt [a]	€	39.1bn	39.4bn	
	US$	50.3bn	52.4bn	
US$1=€		0.78	0.75	

[a] Includes pensions

Population 65,951,611

Age	0–14	15–19	20–24	25–29	30–64	65 plus
Male	9.6%	3.0%	3.1%	3.1%	22.5%	7.6%
Female	9.1%	2.9%	3.0%	3.0%	22.9%	10.3%

Capabilities

The 2013 Livre Blanc, published in April, attempts to sustain France's ambition to retain the full spectrum of military capabilities, but with reductions in personnel and equipment. Despite cuts France remains one of the two pre-eminent defence powers in Europe, maintaining rapidly deployable armed forces, capable of self-sustainment and operation. This capacity was evident during *Opération Serval* in Mali. Also apparent were weaknesses, such as strategic lift and ISR. The size of the forces for such tasks, however, is being reduced. The 2008 Livre Blanc identified a ground force deployment of up to 30,000: the 2013 document reduces this to 15,000. Similarly, combat aircraft earmarked for rapid deployment are cut from 70 to 45. Overall platform numbers are also due to reduce; heavy armour from around 250 to 200, air force and navy combat aircraft from 300 to 225, and naval frigates from 18 to 15. Funding plans for 2014–19 reduced to 26 (from 66) the number of *Rafale* aircraft to be purchased over the period. Strategic airlift will be strengthened with the delivery of the A400M; the first aircraft was accepted by the air force in August 2013. There are also plans to acquire 12 A330-based tankers to replace the KC-135. These platforms will support France's ability to project power on a global scale. Substantial overseas deployments in Africa and Lebanon are maintained, and all of its services exercise regularly and jointly at the national level, while also participating in a broad range of international exercises. (See pp. 65–8.)

ACTIVE 222,200 (Army 119,050 Navy 37,850 Air 47,550, Other Staffs 17,750) Paramilitary 103,400

RESERVE 29,650 (Army 16,000, Navy 5,500, Air 4,750, Other Staffs 3,400) Paramilitary 40,000

ORGANISATIONS BY SERVICE

Strategic Nuclear Forces

Navy 2,200

SUBMARINES • STRATEGIC • SSBN 4
- 2 *Le Triomphant* with 16 M45 SLBM with 6 TN-75 nuclear warheads, 4 single 533mm TT with F17 Mod 2 HWT/SM-39 *Exocet* AShM
- 2 *Le Triomphant* with 16 M51 SLBM with 6 TN-75 nuclear warheads, 4 single 533mm TT with F17 Mod 2 HWT/SM-39 *Exocet* AShM

AIRCRAFT • FGA 20 *Rafale* M F3 with ASMP-A msl

Air Force 1,800

Air Strategic Forces Command

FORCES BY ROLE

STRIKE
- 1 sqn with *Mirage* 2000N with ASMP/ASMP-A msl
- 1 sqn with *Rafale* B F3 with ASMP/ASMP-A msl

TANKER
- 1 sqn with C-135FR; KC-135 *Stratotanker*

EQUIPMENT BY TYPE

AIRCRAFT 45 combat capable
- **FGA** 45: 25 *Mirage* 2000N; 20 *Rafale* B F3
- **TKR/TPT** 11 C-135FR
- **TKR** 3 KC-135 *Stratotanker*

Paramilitary

Gendarmerie 40

Space

SATELLITES 8
- **COMMUNICATIONS** 2 *Syracuse*-3 (designed to integrate with UK *Skynet* & ITA *Sicral*)
- **ISR** 4: 2 *Helios* (2A/2B); 2 *Pleiades*
- **EARLY WARNING** 2 *Spirale*

Army 119,050 (incl 7,300 Foreign Legion; 12,800 Marines)

Regt and BG normally bn size

FORCES BY ROLE

COMMAND
- 2 (task force) HQ

MANOEUVRE

Reconnaissance
- 1 ISR bde (1 recce regt, 1 UAV regt, 2 EW regt, 1 int bn)

Armoured
- 1 armd bde (2 armd regt, 2 armd inf regt, 1 MLRS regt, 1 AD regt, 1 engr regt)
- 1 armd bde (2 armd regt, 2 armd inf regt, 1 SP arty regt, 1 engr regt)

Mechanised
- 1 lt armd bde (1 armd cav regt, 2 mech inf regt, 1 SP arty regt, 1 engr regt)
- 1 (FRA/GER) mech bde (1 armd cav regt, 1 mech inf regt)
- 2 mech inf bde (1 armd cav regt, 1 armd inf regt, 1 mech inf regt, 1 SP arty regt, 1 engr regt)

1 mech BG (UAE)
1 mech regt (Djibouti)
Light
2 regt (French Guiana)
1 regt (New Caledonia)
1 coy (Mayotte)
Air Manoeuvre
1 AB bde (1 armd cav regt, 4 para regt, 1 arty regt, 1 engr regt, 1 spt regt)
1 AB regt (Réunion)
1 AB bn (Gabon)
Amphibious
1 lt armd bde (1 armd cav regt, 2 mech inf regt, 1 SP arty regt, 1 engr regt)
Mountain
1 mtn bde (1 armd cav regt, 3 mech inf regt, 1 arty regt, 1 engr regt)
Aviation
3 avn regt
Other
4 SMA regt (French Guiana, French West Indies & Indian Ocean)
3 SMA coy (French Polynesia, Indian Ocean & New Caledonia)
COMBAT SUPPORT
1 CBRN regt
1 sigs bde (5 sigs regt)
COMBAT SERVICE SUPPORT
1 log bde (5 tpt regt, 1 log regt, 1 med regt)
3 trg regt

Special Operation Forces 2,200

FORCES BY ROLE
SPECIAL FORCES
2 SF regt
MANOEUVRE
Aviation
1 avn regt

Reserves 16,000 reservists

Reservists form 79 UIR (Reserve Intervention Units) of about 75 to 152 troops, for 'Proterre' – combined land projection forces bn, and 23 USR (Reserve Specialised Units) of about 160 troops, in specialised regt.

EQUIPMENT BY TYPE
MBT 254 *Leclerc*
RECCE 2,000: 256 AMX-10RC; 110 ERC-90F4 *Sagaie*; 40 VAB Reco NBC; 1,594 VBL M-ll
AIFV 530 VBCI
APC 3,158
APC (T) 53 BvS-10
APC (W) 3,086: 3,000 VAB; 60 VAB BOA; 26 VAB NBC
PPV 19: 14 *Aravis*; 5 *Buffalo*
ARTY 375
SP 155mm 114: 37 AU-F-1; 77 CAESAR
TOWED 155mm 43 TR-F-1
MRL 227mm 26 MLRS
MOR 120mm 192 RT-F1
AT • MSL
SP 325: 30 VAB HOT; 110 VAB *Milan*; 185 VAB *Eryx*
MANPATS *Javelin*; *Milan*
AIRCRAFT • TPT • Light 16: 5 PC-6B *Turbo Porter*; 8 TBM-700; 3 TBM-700B
HELICOPTERS
ATK 40: 39 EC665 *Tiger* HAP; 1 EC665 *Tiger* HAD
MRH 140 SA341F/342M *Gazelle* (all variants)
TPT 166: **Heavy** 8 EC725AP *Caracal* (CSAR); **Medium** 122: 23 AS532UL *Cougar*; 9 NH90 TTH; 90 SA330 *Puma*; **Light** 36 EC120B *Colibri*
UAV • ISR • Medium 20 SDTI (*Sperwer*)
AD • SAM
TOWED 15 MIM-23B I-HAWK
MANPAD *Mistral*
RADAR • LAND 66: 10 *Cobra*; 56 RASIT/RATAC
AEV 71 AMX-30 EBG
ARV 154+: AMX-1-ECH; 134 AMX-30D; 20 *Leclerc* DNG; VAB-EHC
VLB 67: 39 EFA; 18 PTA; 10 SPRAT (being delivered)
MW 20+: AMX-30 B/B2; 20 *Minotaur*

Navy 37,850 (incl 2,200 opcon Strategic Nuclear Forces)

EQUIPMENT BY TYPE
SUBMARINES 10
STRATEGIC • SSBN 4:
2 *Le Triomphant* opcon Strategic Nuclear Forces with 16 M45 SLBM with 6 TN-75 nuclear warheads, 4 single 533mm TT with F17 Mod 2 HWT/SM-39 *Exocet* AShM (currently undergoing modernisation programme to install M51 SLBM; expected completion 2018)
2 *Le Triomphant* opcon Strategic Nuclear Forces with 16 M51 SLBM with 6 TN-75 nuclear warheads, 4 single 533mm TT with F17 Mod 2 HWT/SM-39 *Exocet* AShM
TACTICAL • SSN 6:
6 *Rubis* with 4 single 533mm TT with F-17 HWT/SM-39 *Exocet* AShM
PRINCIPAL SURFACE COMBATANTS 24
AIRCRAFT CARRIERS 1
CVN 1 *Charles de Gaulle* with 4 octuple VLS with *Aster* 15 SAM, 2 sextuple *Sadral* lnchr with *Mistral* SAM (capacity 35–40 *Super Etendard*/*Rafale* M/E-2C *Hawkeye*/AS365 *Dauphin*)
DESTROYERS • DDGHM 12:
2 *Cassard* with 2 quad lnchr with MM-40 *Exocet* Block 2 AShM, 1 Mk13 GMLS with SM-1MR SAM, 2 sextuple *Sadral* lnchr with *Mistral* SAM, 2 single 533mm ASTT with L5 HWT, 1 100mm gun, (capacity 1 AS565SA *Panther* ASW hel)
2 *Forbin* with 2 quad lnchr with MM-40 *Exocet* Block 3 AShM, 1 48-cell VLS with *Aster* 15/*Aster* 30 SAM, 2 twin 324mm ASTT with MU-90, 2 76mm gun, (capacity 1 NH90 TTH hel)
1 *Georges Leygues* (trg role) with 2 twin lnchr with MM-38 *Exocet* AShM, 1 octuple lnchr with *Crotale* SAM, 2 twin *Simbad* lnchr with *Mistral* SAM, 2 single 533mm ASTT with L5 HWT, 1 100mm gun, (capacity 2 *Lynx* hel)
1 *Georges Leygues* with 2 twin lnchr with MM-38 *Exocet* AShM, 1 octuple lnchr with *Crotale* SAM, 2 sextuple

Sadral lnchr with *Mistral* SAM, 2 single 533mm ASTT with L5 HWT, 1 100mm gun, (capacity 2 *Lynx* hel)

2 *Georges Leygues* with 2 quad lnchr with MM-40 *Exocet* AShM, 1 octuple lnchr with *Crotale* SAM, , 2 sextuple *Sadral* lnchr with *Mistral* SAM, 2 single 533mm ASTT with L5 HWT, 1 100mm gun, (capacity 2 *Lynx* hel)

3 *Georges Leygues* (mod) with 2 quad lnchr with MM-40 *Exocet* AShM, 1 octuple lnchr with *Crotale* SAM, 2 twin *Simbad* lnchr with *Mistral* SAM, 2 single 324mm ASTT with MU90 LWT, 1 100mm gun, (capacity 2 *Lynx* hel)

1 *Aquitaine* with 2 octuple *Sylver* A70 VLS with MdCN (SCALP Naval) LACM, 2 quad lnchr with MM-40 *Exocet* Block 3 AShM, 2 octuple *Sylver* A43 VLS with *Aster* 15 SAM, 2 twin B515 324mm ASTT with MU90 LWT, 1 76mm gun (capacity 1 NH90 NFH hel)

FRIGATES • FFGHM 11:

6 *Floreal* with 2 single lnchr with MM-38 *Exocet* AShM, 1 twin *Simbad* lnchr with *Mistral* SAM, 1 100mm gun, (capacity 1 AS565SA *Panther* hel)

5 *La Fayette* with 2 quad lnchr with MM-40 *Exocet* Block 2 AShM, 1 octuple lnchr with *Crotale* SAM, (space for fitting 2 octuple VLS lnchr for *Aster* 15/30), 1 100mm gun, (capacity 1 AS565SA *Panther*/SA321 *Super Frelon* hel)

PATROL AND COASTAL COMBATANTS 21

FSM 9 *D'Estienne d'Orves* with 1 twin *Simbad* lnchr with *Mistral* SAM, 4 single ASTT, 1 100mm gun

PCC 7: 4 *L'Audacieuse* (all deployed in the Pacific or Caribbean); 3 *Flamant*

PCO 4: 1 *Lapérouse*; 1 *Le Malin*; 1 *Fulmar*; 1 *Gowind* (owned by private company DCNS; currently operated by French Navy)

PSO 1 *Albatros*

MINE WARFARE • MINE COUNTERMEASURES 18

MCS 7: 3 *Antares* (used as route survey vessels); 4 *Vulcain* (used as mine diving tenders)

MHO 11 *Éridan*

AMPHIBIOUS

PRINCIPAL AMPHIBIOUS SHIPS 4

LHD 3 *Mistral* (capacity mixed air group of up to 16 NH90/SA330 *Puma*/AS532 *Cougar*/EC665 *Tiger* hel; 2 LCAC or 4 LCM; 60 AFVs; 450 troops)

LPD 1 *Foudre* with 2 twin *Simbad* lnchr with *Mistral* SAM, (capacity 4 AS532 *Cougar*; either 2 LCT or 10 LCM; 22 tanks; 470 troops)

LANDING SHIPS • LST 3 *Batral* (capacity 12 trucks; 140 troops)

LANDING CRAFT 42

LCT 6: 1 EDIC 700; 1 CDIC; 4 EDA-R

LCM 11 CTMS

LCVP 25

LOGISTICS AND SUPPORT 145

ABU 1 *Telenn Mor*

AE 1 *Denti*

AFS 1 *Revi*

AG 4: 1 *Lapérouse* (used as trials ships for mines and divers); 3 *Chamois*

AGE 1 *Corraline*

AGI 1 *Dupuy de Lome*

AGM 1 *Monge*

AGOR 2: 1 *Pourquoi pas?* (used 150 days per year by Ministry of Defence; operated by Ministry of Research and Education otherwise); 1 *Beautemps-beaupré*

AGS 3 *Lapérouse*

AORH 4 *Durance* with 1-3 twin *Simbad* lnchr with *Mistral* SAM (capacity 1 SA319 *Alouette* III/AS365 *Dauphin*/*Lynx*)

ATA 2 *Malabar*

AXL 12: 8 *Léopard*; 2 *Glycine*; 2 *Engageante*

AXS 4: 2 *La Belle Poule*; 2 other

YAG 2 *Phaéton* (towed array tenders)

YD 5

YDT 10: 1 *Alize*; 9 VIP 21

YFB 2 VTP

YFL 9 V14

YFRT 2 *Athos*

YFU 8

YGS 7 VH8

YTB 3 *Bélier*

YTL 34: 4 RP10; 4 PSS10; 26 PS4

YTM 21: 3 *Maïto*; 16 *Fréhel*; 2 *Esterel*

YTR 5: 3 *Avel Aber*; 2 *Las*

Naval Aviation 6,500

Flying hours 180–220 hrs/yr on strike/FGA ac

FORCES BY ROLE

STRIKE/FIGHTER/GROUND ATTACK

2 sqn with *Rafale* M F3

FIGHTER/GROUND ATTACK

1 sqn with *Super Etendard Modernisé*

ANTI-SURFACE WARFARE

1 sqn with AS565SA *Panther*

ANTI-SUBMARINE WARFARE

2 sqn (forming) with NH90 NFH

1 sqn with *Lynx* Mk4

MARITIME PATROL

2 sqn with *Atlantique* 2

1 sqn with *Falcon* 20H *Gardian*

1 sqn with *Falcon* 50MI

AIRBORNE EARLY WARNING & CONTROL

1 sqn with E-2C *Hawkeye*

SEARCH & RESCUE

1 sqn with AS365N/F *Dauphin* 2

1 sqn with EC225

TRAINING

1 sqn with SA319B *Alouette* III

1 unit with *Falcon* 10 M

1 unit with CAP 10; EMB 121 *Xingu*; MS-880 *Rallye*

EQUIPMENT BY TYPE

AIRCRAFT 77 combat capable

FGA 58: 33 *Rafale M* F3; 25 *Super Etendard Modernisé*

ASW 12 *Atlantique* 2 (10 more in store)

AEW&C 3 E-2C *Hawkeye*

SAR 1 *Falcon* 50MS

TPT 26: **Light** 11 EMB-121 *Xingu*; **PAX** 15: 6 *Falcon* 10MER; 5 *Falcon* 20H *Gardian*; 4 *Falcon* 50MI

TRG 14: 7 CAP 10; 7 MS-880 *Rallye**

HELICOPTERS

ASW 33: 22 *Lynx* Mk4; 11 NH90 NFH

MRH 52: 9 AS365N/F/SP *Dauphin* 2; 2 AS365N3; 16 AS565SA *Panther*; 25 SA319B *Alouette* III

TPT • Medium 2 EC225 *Super Puma*

MSL

AAM • IR R-550 *Magic* 2; **IIR** *Mica* IR; **ARH** *Mica* RF

AShM AM-39 *Exocet*

ASM ASMP-A; AS-30 *Laser*; AASM

Marines 2,500

Commando Units

FORCES BY ROLE

MANOEUVRE

Reconnaissance

1 recce gp

Amphibious

3 aslt gp

1 atk swimmer gp

1 raiding gp

COMBAT SERVICE SUPPORT

1 spt gp

Fusiliers-Marin 1,600

FORCES BY ROLE

MANOEUVRE

Other

9 (force protection) sy unit

14 (Naval Base) sy gp

Public Service Force

Naval personnel performing general coast guard, fishery protection, SAR, anti-pollution and traffic surveillance duties. Command exercised through Maritime Prefectures (Premar): Manche (Cherbourg), Atlantique (Brest), Méditerranée (Toulon)

FORCES BY ROLE

MARITIME PATROL

1 sqn with *Falcon* 50M; *Falcon* 200 *Gardian*

EQUIPMENT BY TYPE

PATROL AND COASTAL COMBATANTS 6

PSO 1 *Albatros*

PCO 1 *Arago*

PCC 4: 3 *Flamant*; 1 *Grèbe*

AIRCRAFT • MP 9: 4 *Falcon* 50M; 5 *Falcon* 200 *Gardian*

HELICOPTERS • MRH 4 AS365 *Dauphin* 2

Reserves 5,500 reservists

Air Force 47,550

Flying hours 180 hrs/year

Strategic Forces

FORCES BY ROLE

STRIKE

1 sqn with *Mirage* 2000N with ASMP/ASMP-A msl

1 sqn with *Rafale* B F3 with ASMP/ASMP-A msl

TANKER

1 sqn with C-135FR; KC-135 *Stratotanker*

EQUIPMENT BY TYPE

AIRCRAFT 43 combat capable

FGA 43: 23 *Mirage* 2000N; 20 *Rafale* B F3

TKR/TPT 11 C-135FR

TKR 3 KC-135 *Stratotanker*

Combat Brigade

FORCES BY ROLE

FIGHTER

1 sqn with *Mirage* 2000-5

1 sqn with *Mirage* 2000B/C

FIGHTER/GROUND ATTACK

3 sqn with *Mirage* 2000D

1 (composite) sqn with *Mirage* 2000C/D (Djibouti)

2 sqn with *Rafale* B/C F3

1 sqn with *Rafale* B/C F3 (UAE)

ISR

1 sqn with *Mirage* F-1CR *

ELECTRONIC WARFARE

1 flt with C-160G *Gabriel* (ESM)

TRAINING

1 OCU sqn with *Mirage* 2000D

1 OCU sqn with *Rafale*

1 (agressor) sqn with *Alpha Jet**

4 sqn with *Alpha Jet**

ISR UAV

1 sqn with *Harfang*

EQUIPMENT BY TYPE

AIRCRAFT 282 combat capable

FTR 67: 21 *Mirage* 2000-5; 7 *Mirage* 2000B; 39 *Mirage* 2000C

FGA 126: 61 *Mirage* 2000D; 3 *Mirage* F-1B; 2 *Mirage* F-1CT; 17 *Rafale* B F3; 43 *Rafale* C F3

ISR 17 *Mirage* F-1CR*

ELINT 2 C-160G *Gabriel* (ESM)

TRG 72 *Alpha Jet**

UAV • ISR • Heavy 4 *Harfang*

MSL

AAM • IR R-550 *Magic* 2; **IIR** *Mica* IR; **SARH** *Super* 530D; **ARH** *Mica* RF

ASM ASMP-A; AS-30L; *Apache*; AASM

LACM SCALP EG

BOMBS

Laser-guided: GBU-12 *Paveway* II

Air Mobility Brigade

FORCES BY ROLE

SEARCH & RESCUE/TRANSPORT

5 sqn with C-160 *Transall*; CN-235M; DHC-6-300 *Twin Otter*; SA330 *Puma*; AS555 *Fennec* (Djibouti, French Guiana, Gabon, Indian Ocean & New Caledonia)

TANKER/TRANSPORT

2 sqn with C-160R *Transall*

TRANSPORT

1 sqn with A310-300; A330; A340-200 (on lease)

3 sqn with A400M *Atlas*; C-130H/H-30 *Hercules*; C-160 *Transall*

2 sqn with CN-235M

1 sqn with EMB-121

1 sqn with *Falcon* 7X (VIP); *Falcon* 900 (VIP); *Falcon* 2000

3 flt with TBM-700A
1 (mixed) gp with AS532 *Cougar*; C-160 *Transall*; DHC-6-300 *Twin Otter*
TRAINING
1 OCU sqn with SA330 *Puma*; AS555 *Fennec*
1 OCU unit with C-160 *Transall*
TRANSPORT HELICOPTER
2 sqn with AS555 *Fennec*
2 sqn with AS332C/L *Super Puma*; SA330 *Puma*; EC725 *Caracal*

EQUIPMENT BY TYPE
AIRCRAFT
TKR/TPT 20 C-160R *Transall*
TPT 121: **Heavy** 2 A400M *Atlas*; **Medium** 35: 5 C-130H *Hercules*; 9 C-130H-30 *Hercules*; 21 C-160 *Transall*; **Light** 72: 19 CN-235M-100; 8 CN-235M-300; 5 DHC-6-300 *Twin Otter*; 25 EMB-121 *Xingu*; 15 TBM-700; **PAX** 12: 3 A310-300; 1 A330; 2 A340-200 (on lease); 2 *Falcon* 7X; 2 *Falcon* 900 (VIP); 2 *Falcon* 2000
HELICOPTERS
MRH 37 AS555 *Fennec*
TPT 43: **Heavy** 11 EC725 *Caracal*; **Medium** 32: 3 AS332C *Super Puma*; 4 AS332L *Super Puma*; 3 AS532UL *Cougar* (tpt/VIP); 22 SA330B *Puma*

Air Space Control Brigade

FORCES BY ROLE
SPACE
1 (satellite obs) sqn with *Helios*
AIRBORNE EARLY WARNING & CONTROL
1 (Surveillance & Control) sqn with E-3F *Sentry*
AIR DEFENCE
3 sqn with *Crotale* NG; SAMP/T
2 sqn with SAMP/T

EQUIPMENT BY TYPE
SATELLITES *see* Space
AIRCRAFT• AEW&C 4 E-3F *Sentry*
AD
SAM *Crotale* NG; SAMP/T
GUNS 20mm 76T2
SYSTEMS STRIDA (Control)

Security and Intervention Brigade

FORCES BY ROLE
SPECIAL FORCES
3 SF gp
MANOEUVRE
Other
24 protection units
30 fire fighting and rescue scn

Air Training Command

FORCES BY ROLE
TRAINING
3 sqn with CAP 10; Grob G120A-F; TB-30 *Epsilon*

EQUIPMENT BY TYPE
AIRCRAFT
TRG 48: 5 CAP 10; 18 Grob G120A-F; 25 TB-30 *Epsilon* (incl many in storage)

Reserves 4,750 reservists

Paramilitary 103,400

Gendarmerie 103,400; 40,000 reservists

EQUIPMENT BY TYPE
LT TK 28 VBC-90
APC (W) 153 VBRG-170
ARTY • MOR 157+ **60mm**; **81mm**
PATROL AND COASTAL COMBATANTS 39
PB 39: 4 *Géranium*; 1 *Glaive*; 2 VSC 14; 24 VSCM; 8 EBSLP
HELICOPTERS • TPT • Light 35: 20 EC135; 15 EC145

Customs (Direction Générale des Douanes et Droits Indirects)

EQUIPMENT BY TYPE
PATROL AND COASTAL COMBATANTS 30
PCO 2: 1 *Jacques Oudart Fourmentin*; 1 *Kermovan*
PB 28: 7 *Plascoa* 2100; 7 *Haize Hegoa*; 2 *Avel Gwalarn*; 1 *Rafale*; 1 *Arafenua*; 1 *Vent d'Amont*; 1 *La Rance*; 8 others

Coast Guard (Direction des Affaires Maritimes)

EQUIPMENT BY TYPE
PATROL AND COASTAL COMBATANTS 25
PCO 1 *Themis*
PCC 1 *Iris*
PB 23: 4 *Callisto*; 19 others
LOGISTICS AND SUPPORT • AG 7

Cyber

The French Network and Information Security Agency (ANSSI) was established in 2009 to conduct surveillance on sensitive government networks and respond to cyber attacks. The 2008 French Defence White Paper placed emphasis on cyber threats, calling for programmes in offensive and defensive cyber-war capabilities. In July 2011, the MoD produced a classified Joint Cyber Defence Concept. Ahead of the new Livre Blanc, the general secretariat on defence and national security (SGDSN) released a preparatory document stressing the strategic dimension of cyber threats and confirming the development of technical capabilities to control access to cyberspace. The 2013 White Paper marked 'a crucial new stage in recognition of cyber threats and development of cyber defence capabilities'. Cyber featured throughout the document and, 'for the first time, the armed forces model includes military cyber defence capabilities, in close liaison with intelligence and defensive and offensive planning, in preparation for or support of military operations'.

DEPLOYMENT

Legal provisions for foreign deployment:
Constitution: Codified constitution (1958)
Specific legislation: 'Order of 7 January 1959'
Decision on deployment of troops abroad: De jure: by the minister of defence, under authority of the PM and

on agreement in council of ministers ('Order of 7 January 1959', Art. 16, Art. 20-1 of constitution)

AFGHANISTAN

NATO • ISAF/OEF-A 266

ARABIAN SEA & GULF OF ADEN

Combined Maritime Forces • CTF-150: 1 FFGHM

BOSNIA-HERZEGOVINA

EU • EUFOR • *Operation Althea* (*Operation Astrée*) 2

OSCE • Bosnia and Herzegovina 3

CENTRAL AFRICAN REPUBLIC

Operation Boali 400; 2 inf coy; 1 spt det

CHAD

Operation Epervier 950; 1 mech inf BG; 1 air unit with 6 *Rafale* F3; 1 C-130H *Hercules*; 1 C-160 *Transall*; 1 C-135FR; 1 hel det with 4 SA330 *Puma*

CÔTE D'IVOIRE

Operation Licorne 450; 1 armd cav BG; 1 C-160 *Transall*; 1 AS555 *Fennec*

UN • UNOCI 6

DEMOCRATIC REPUBLIC OF THE CONGO

EU • EUSEC RD Congo 7

UN • MONUSCO 4 obs

DJIBOUTI

1,900; 1 (Marine) combined arms regt with (2 recce sqn, 2 inf coy, 1 arty bty, 1 engr coy); 1 hel det with 4 SA330 *Puma*; 2 SA342 *Gazelle*; 1 LCT; 1 LCM; 1 FGA sqn with 7 *Mirage* 2000C/D; 1 SAR/tpt sqn with 1 C-160 *Transall*; 2 SA330 *Puma*; 1 AS555 *Fennec*

EGYPT

MFO 2

FRENCH GUIANA

2,200: 1 (Foreign Legion) inf regt; 1 (Marine) inf regt; 1 SMA regt; 1 PCC; 1 tpt sqn with 1 CN-235M; 6 SA330 *Puma*; 3 AS555 *Fennec*; 3 gendarmerie coy; 1 AS350 *Ecureuil*

FRENCH POLYNESIA

1,000: (incl Centre d'Expérimentation du Pacifique); 1 SMA coy; 1 naval HQ at Papeete; 1 FFGHM; 1 LST; 1 AFS; 3 Falcon 200 *Gardian*; 1 SAR/tpt sqn with 3 CN-235M; 1 AS332 *Super Puma*; 1 AS555 *Fennec*

FRENCH WEST INDIES

1,250; 1 (Marine) inf coy; 2 SMA regt; 1 FFGHM; 1 PCC; 1 naval base at Fort de France (Martinique); 4 gendarmerie coy; 2 AS350 *Ecureuil*

GABON

900; 1 recce pl with ERC-90F4 *Sagaie*; 1 mtn inf bn; 1 SAR/tpt sqn with 4 SA330 *Puma*

GERMANY

2,000 (incl elm Eurocorps and FRA/GER bde); 1 (FRA/GER) mech bde (1 armd cav regt, 1 mech inf regt)

GULF OF GUINEA

Operation Corymbe 1 FSM

HAITI

UN • MINUSTAH 2

INDIAN OCEAN

1,900 (incl La Réunion and TAAF); 1 (Marine) para regt; 1 (Foreign Legion) inf coy; 1 SMA regt ; 1 SMA coy; 2 FFGHM; 1 PSO; 1 PCO; 1 LST; 1 LCM; 1 naval HQ at Port-des-Galets (La Réunion); 1 naval base at Dzaoudzi (Mayotte); 1 SAR/tpt sqn with 2 C-160 *Transall*; 2 AS555 *Fennec*; 5 gendarmerie coy; 1 SA319 *Alouette* III

JORDAN

Operation Tamour 80: 1 med det

LEBANON

UN • UNIFIL 863; 1 armd cav BG; *Leclerc*; AMX-10P; VBCI; PVP; VAB; CAESAR; AU-F1 155mm; *Mistral*

LIBERIA

UN • UNMIL 1

MALI

Operation Serval 2,800; 1 mech inf BG; 1 log bn; 1 hel unit with 3 EC665 *Tiger*; 8 SA330 *Puma*; 6 SA342 *Gazelle*; 1 FGA det with 3 *Mirage* 2000D

EU • EUTM Mali 207

UN • MINUSMA 19

MIDDLE EAST

UN • UNTSO 3 obs

MOLDOVA

OSCE • Moldova 1

NEW CALEDONIA

1,500; 1 (Marine) mech inf regt; 1 SMA coy; 6 ERC-90F1 *Lynx*; 1 FFGHM; 2 PCC; 1 LST; 1 base with 2 *Falcon* 200 *Gardian* at Nouméa; 1 tpt unit with 3 CN-235 MPA; 4 SA330 *Puma*; 1 AS555 *Fennec*; 4 gendarmerie coy; 2 AS350 *Ecureuil*

SENEGAL

350; 1 *Atlantique*; 1 C-160 *Transall*

SERBIA

NATO • KFOR 316; 1 armd cav sqn; 1 log coy

OSCE • Kosovo 6

OSCE • Serbia 1

UAE

700: 1 (Foreign Legion) BG (2 recce coy, 2 inf coy, 1 arty bty, 1 engr coy); 1 FGA sqn with 6 *Rafale* F3, 1 KC-135F

UGANDA

EU • EUTM Somalia 23

WESTERN SAHARA

UN • MINURSO 13 obs

FOREIGN FORCES

Belgium 29 *Alpha Jet* trg ac located at Cazaux/Tours

Germany 400 (GER elm Eurocorps)

Singapore 200; 1 trg sqn with 4 A-4SU *Super Skyhawk*; 10 TA-4SU *Super Skyhawk*; 5 M-346 *Master*

Germany GER

Euro €		2012	2013	2014
GDP	€	2.71tr	2.78tr	
	US$	3.4tr	3.6tr	
per capita	US$	41,513	44,010	
Growth	%	-0.27	2.02	
Inflation	%	2.14	1.61	
Def bdgt [a]	€	31.9bn	33.3bn	
	US$	41bn	44.2bn	
US$1=€		0.78	0.75	

[a] Includes military pensions

Population 81,147,265

Age	0–14	15–19	20–24	25–29	30–64	65 plus
Male	6.7%	2.5%	2.9%	3.1%	24.8%	9.1%
Female	6.4%	2.4%	2.8%	3.0%	24.4%	11.8%

Capabilities

The armed forces are undergoing a period of restructuring and substantial downsizing, as the 2010 defence cuts and 2011 reform agenda are implemented. With the suspension of conscription, military personnel numbers will fall and up to 20,000 civilian posts are also being cut. The army has begun its restructuring process, with one divisional headquarters disbanding in 2013 and another scheduled to follow in 2014, whilst the existing airborne forces will be consolidated into a single brigade. The air force has replaced its previous divisional structure with one based around operational and support commands and the navy is similarly being organised into capability areas. There will be base closures in Germany and reductions in equipment holdings, including battlefield helicopters. While the armed forces remain constrained politically in terms of out-of-area operations, they will increasingly have the ability for power projection, supported by the eventual introduction into service of the A400M military airlifter.

ACTIVE 186,450 (Army 62,500 Navy 16,000 Air 31,350 Joint Support Service 44,900 Joint Medical Service 19,650 Other 12,050)

Conscript liability Voluntary conscription only. Voluntary conscripts can serve up to 23 months.

RESERVE 40,320 (Army 15,350 Navy 1,850 Air 4,900 Joint Support Service 12,850 Joint Medical Service 4,950 MoD 420)

ORGANISATIONS BY SERVICE

Space

SATELLITES 7
- **COMMUNICATIONS** 2 COMSATBw (1 & 2)
- **ISR** 5 SAR-*Lupe*

Army 62,500

The German army is divided into response forces (RF) and stabilisation forces (StF).

FORCES BY ROLE

MANOEUVRE

Armoured

1 (1st) armd div (RF) (1 armd bde (1 armd recce coy, 2 armd bn, 1 armd inf bn, 1 SP arty bn, 1 engr coy, 1 log bn); 1 armd bde (1 recce coy, 1 armd bn, 1 armd inf bn, 1 SP arty bn, 1 engr coy, 1 log bn); 1 mech bde (1 recce bn, 1 armd bn, 2 armd inf bn, 1 engr bn, 1 sigs bn, 1 log bn) 1 armd recce bn; 1 arty regt; 1 engr regt; 1 sigs bn; 1 NBC bn; 1 log bn)

1 (10th) armd div (StF) (1 armd bde (1 recce bn, 1 armd bn, 2 armd inf bn, 1 engr bn, 1 sigs bn, 1 log bn); 1 mtn inf bde (1 recce bn, 3 mtn inf bn, 1 engr bn, 1 sigs bn, 1 log bn))

Light

2 bn (GER/FRA bde)

Air Manoeuvre

1 spec ops div (RF) (1 SF bde, 2 AB bde (1 recce coy, 2 para bn, 1 engr coy, 1 log bn), 1 AD coy, 1 sigs bn)

1 air mob div (RF) (1 air mob bde (1 air mob inf regt, 2 atk hel bn, 1 tpt hel bn); 1 mech bde (1 recce bn, 1 armd bn, 2 armd inf bn, 1 engr bn, 1 sigs bn, 1 log bn); 1 cbt spt bde with (1 arty regt, 1 NBC regt); 2 tpt hel regt, 1 lt tpt hel regt, 1 sigs bn)

COMBAT SUPPORT

1 arty bn (GER/FRA bde)

1 engr coy (GER/FRA bde)

COMBAT SERVICE SUPPORT

1 log bn (GER/FRA bde)

EQUIPMENT BY TYPE

MBT 322 *Leopard* 2A6

RECCE 340: 221 *Fennek* (incl 24 engr recce, 19 fires spt); 94 Tpz-1 *Fuchs* (CBRN); 25 *Wiesel* (16 recce; 9 engr)

AIFV 498: 390 *Marder* 1A2/A3; 5 *Puma* (test); 103 *Wiesel* (with 20mm gun)

APC 1,799+
- **APC (T)** 473: 177 Bv-206D/S; 296 M113 (inc variants)
- **APC (W)** 1,056: 200+ *Boxer* (inc variants); 856 TPz-1 *Fuchs* (inc variants)
- **PPV** 270 APV-2 *Dingo* II

ARTY 272
- **SP 155mm** 130 PzH 2000
- **MRL 227mm** 55 MLRS
- **MOR 120mm** 87 *Tampella*

AT • MSL
- **SP** 120 *Wiesel* (TOW)
- **MANPATS** *Milan*

AMPHIBIOUS 30 LCM (river engr)

HELICOPTERS
- **ATK** 22 EC665 *Tiger*
- **MRH/ISR** 97 Bo-105M/Bo-105P PAH-1 (with HOT)
- **TPT:** 144 **Medium** 16 NH90; **Light** 128: 76 Bell 205 (UH-1D *Iroquois*); 38 Bo-105; 14 EC135

UAV • ISR 15 **Medium** 6 KZO; **Light** 9 LUNA

RADARS 101: 8 *Cobra*; 76 RASIT (veh, arty); 17 RATAC (veh, arty)

AEV 185: 149 *Dachs*; 36 *Leopard* A1

ARV 77: 75 *Büffel*; 2 M88A1

VLB 169: 104 *Biber*; 30 M3; 35 Panzerschnellbrücke 2

MW 124+: 100 Area Clearing System; 24 *Keiler*; Minelayer 5821; *Skorpion* Minelauncher

Navy 16,000

Previous Type Comds have been merged into two Flotillas. Flotilla I combines SS, MCM, PBF and SF whilst Flotilla II comprises 2 FF and Aux squadrons.

EQUIPMENT BY TYPE

SUBMARINES • TACTICAL • SSK 4:
- 4 Type-212A with 6 single 533mm TT with 12 A4 *Seehecht* DM2 HWT (2 further vessels on order)

PRINCIPAL SURFACE COMBATANTS 18
- **DESTROYERS • DDGHM** 7:
  - 4 *Brandenburg* with 2 twin lnchr with MM-38 *Exocet* AShM, 1 16-cell Mk41 VLS with RIM-7M/P, 2 Mk49 GMLS with RIM-116 RAM SAM, 2 twin 324mm ASTT with Mk46 LWT, 1 76mm gun, (capacity 2 *Sea Lynx* Mk88A ASW hel)
  - 3 *Sachsen* with 2 quad Mk141 lnchr with RGM-84F *Harpoon* AShM, 1 32-cell Mk41 VLS with SM-2MR/RIM-162B *Sea Sparrow* SAM, 2 21-cell Mk49 GMLS with RIM-116 RAM SAM, 2 triple Mk32 324mm ASTT with MU90 LWT, 1 76mm gun, (capacity; 2 *Sea Lynx* Mk88A ASW hel)
- **FRIGATES** 11
  - **FFGHM** 6 *Bremen* (of which 1 laid up for decommissioning in Nov 2013) with 2 quad Mk141 lnchr with RGM-84A/C *Harpoon* AShM, 1 octuple Mk29 GMLS with RIM-7M/P *Sea Sparrow* SAM, 2 Mk49 GMLS with RIM-116 RAM SAM, 2 twin 324mm ASTT with Mk46 LWT, 1 76mm gun, (capacity 2 *Sea Lynx* Mk88A ASW)
  - **FFGM** 5 *Braunschweig* (K130) with 2 twin lnchr with RBS-15 AShM, 2 Mk49 GMLS each with RIM-116 RAM SAM, 1 76mm gun, 1 hel landing platform

PATROL AND COASTAL COMBATANTS • PCGM 8
- 8 *Gepard* with 2 twin lnchr with MM-38 *Exocet* AShM, 1 Mk49 GMLS with RIM-116 RAM SAM, 1 76mm gun

MINE WARFARE • MINE COUNTERMEASURES 35
- **MHO** 12: 10 *Frankenthal* (2 used as diving support); 2 *Kulmbach*
- **MSO** 5 *Ensdorf*
- **MSD** 18 *Seehund*

AMPHIBIOUS 2
- **LCU** 2 Type-520

LOGISTICS AND SUPPORT 52
- **AFH** 3 *Berlin* Type-702 (capacity 2 *Sea King* Mk41 hel; 2 RAMs)
- **AG** 5: 2 *Schwedeneck* Type-748; 3 *Stollergrund* Type-745
- **AGI** 3 *Oste* Type-423
- **AGOR** 1 *Planet* Type-751
- **AO** 2 *Walchensee* Type-703
- **AOR** 6 *Elbe* Type-404 (2 specified for PFM support; 1 specified for SSK support; 3 specified for MHC/MSC support)
- **AOT** 2 *Spessart* Type-704
- **APB** 3: 1 *Knurrhahn*; 2 *Ohre*
- **ATR** 1 *Helgoland*
- **AXS** 1 *Gorch Fock*
- **YAG** 2 (used as trials ships)
- **YDT** 4 *Wangerooge*
- **YFD** 5
- **YFRT** 4 *Todendorf* Type-905
- **YPC** 2 *Bottsand*
- **YTM** 8 *Vogelsand*

Naval Aviation 2,200

EQUIPMENT BY TYPE

AIRCRAFT 8 combat capable
- **ASW** 8 AP-3C *Orion*
- **TPT • Light** 2 Do-228 (pollution control)

HELICOPTERS
- **ASW** 22 *Lynx* Mk88A with *Sea Skua*
- **SAR** 21 *Sea King* Mk41

MSL AShM *Sea Skua*

Air Force 31,350

Flying hours 140 hrs/year (plus 40 hrs high-fidelity simulator)

FORCES BY ROLE

FIGHTER
- 2 wg (2 sqn with Eurofighter *Typhoon*)
- 1 wg (2 sqn with Eurofighter *Typhoon*) (forming)

FIGHTER/GROUND ATTACK
- 1 wg (2 sqn with *Tornado* IDS)
- 1 wg (2 sqn with Eurofighter *Typhoon*)

ISR
- 1 wg (1 ISR sqn with *Tornado* ECR/IDS; 1 UAV sqn (ISAF only) with *Heron*)

TANKER/TRANSPORT
- 1 (special air mission) wg (3 sqn with A310 MRT; A310 MRTT; A340; AS532U2 *Cougar* II; Global 5000)

TRANSPORT
- 4 wg (total: 2 sqn with CH-53G *Stallion*; 4 sqn with C-160D *Transall*; 1 sqn forming with NH90)

TRAINING
- 1 sqn located at Holloman AFB (US) with *Tornado* IDS
- 1 unit (ENJJPT) located at Sheppard AFB (US) with T-6 *Texan* II; T-38A
- 1 hel unit located at Fassberg

AIR DEFENCE
- 1 wg (3 SAM gp) with *Patriot*
- 1 AD gp with ASRAD *Ozelot*; C-RAM MANTIS
- 1 AD trg unit located at Fort Bliss (US) with ASRAD *Ozelot*; C-RAM MANTIS; *Patriot*
- 3 (tac air ctrl) radar gp

EQUIPMENT BY TYPE

AIRCRAFT 205 combat capable
- **FTR** 101 Eurofighter *Typhoon*
- **FGA** 83 *Tornado* IDS
- **EW/FGA** 21 *Tornado* ECR*
- **TKR/TPT** 4 A310 MRTT
- **TPT** 70: **Medium** 60 C-160D *Transall*; **PAX** 10: 2 A310 MRT; 2 A340 (VIP); 2 A319; 4 Global 5000
- **TRG** 109: 69 T-6 *Texan* TII, 40 T-38A

HELICOPTERS • TPT 90: **Heavy** 82 CH-53G *Stallion*; **Medium** 8: 4 AS532U2 *Cougar* II (VIP); 4 NH90

UAV • ISR • Heavy 1 *Heron*

AD • SAM
SP 30 ASRAD *Ozelot* (with FIM-92A *Stinger)*
TOWED 16: 14 *Patriot* PAC-3, 2 C-RAM MANTIS
MSL
AAM • IR AIM-9L/Li *Sidewinder*; **IIR** IRIS-T; **ARH** AIM 120A/B AMRAAM
LACM KEPD 350 *Taurus*
ARM AGM-88B HARM
BOMBS • LGB: GBU-24 *Paveway* III, GBU-54 JDAM

Joint Support Services 44,900

FORCES BY ROLE
COMBAT SUPPORT
6 MP bn
3 sigs regt
COMBAT SERVICE SUPPORT
1 log bde
2 log regt

Joint Medical Services 19,650

FORCES BY ROLE
COMBAT SERVICE SUPPORT
9 med regt (1 rapid)
5 fd hospital

Paramilitary

Border Guard 500

EQUIPMENT BY TYPE
PATROL AND COASTAL COMBATANTS 15
PCO 6: 3 *Bad Bramstedt*; 1 *Bredstedt*; 2 *Sassnitz*
PB 9: 3 *Vogtland*; 5 *Prignitz*; 1 *Rettin*

Cyber

Germany established a Department of Information and Computer Network Operations in 2009 under the guidance of the then-chief of the Bundeswehr's Strategic Reconnaissance Command. Bundeswehr units maintain organic IT monitoring capability: a Bundeswehr CERT team (CERTBw) is available. Germany issued a Cyber Security Strategy in February 2011. A National Cyber Response Centre, involving police, customs, the Federal Intelligence Service and the Bundeswehr, began operations on 1 April 2011. It reports to the Federal Office for Information Security. A National Cyber Security Council has also been established, with high-level representatives from government and, as associate members, businesses.

DEPLOYMENT

Legal provisions for foreign deployment:
Constitution: Codified constitution ('Basic Law', 1949)
Specific legislation: 'Parlamentsbeteiligungsgesetz' (2005)
Decision on deployment of troops abroad: a) By parliament: in general and in the case of military intervention; b) by government: in urgent cases of threat or emergency (parliamentary consent a posteriori), or for preparatory measures or humanitarian interventions; c) simplified procedure for 'missions of low intensity' or if the government seeks an extension of parliamentary approval (§§ 1–5 of the 2005 law).

AFGHANISTAN
NATO • ISAF 4,400; 1 div HQ; 2 inf BG; 6 *Tornado* ECR (SEAD); CH-53 tpt hel; C-160 tpt ac; *Heron* UAV
UN • UNAMA 1 obs

BOSNIA-HERZEGOVINA
OSCE • Bosnia and Herzegovina 3

DEMOCRATIC REPUBLIC OF THE CONGO
EU • EUSEC RD Congo 3

FRANCE
400 (incl GER elm Eurocorps)

GULF OF ADEN & INDIAN OCEAN
EU • *Operation Atalanta* 1 FFGHM; 1 P-3C

LEBANON
UN • UNIFIL 149; 2 PC

MALI
EU • EUTM Mali 73
UN • MINUSMA 61; 1 avn unit

MEDITERRANEAN SEA
NATO • SNMG 2: 1 DDGHM
NATO • SNMCMG 2: 1 MHO; 1 AOR

MOLDOVA
OSCE • Moldova 1

NORTH SEA
NATO • SNMCMG 1: 1 MHO

POLAND
67 (GER elm Corps HQ (multinational))

SERBIA
NATO • KFOR 741
OSCE • Kosovo 2
OSCE • Serbia 1

SOUTH SUDAN
UN • UNMISS 7; 8 obs

SUDAN
UN • UNAMID 10

TURKEY
NATO • *Active Fence*: 2 AD bty with *Patriot* PAC-3

UGANDA
EU • EUTM Somalia 21

UNITED STATES
Trg units at Goodyear AFB (AZ)/Sheppard AFB (TX) with 40 T-38 *Talon*; 69 T-6A *Texan* II; 1 trg sqn Holloman AFB (NM) with 14 *Tornado* IDS; NAS Pensacola (FL); Fort Rucker (AL) • Missile trg located at Fort Bliss (TX)

UZBEKISTAN
NATO • ISAF 100

FOREIGN FORCES

Canada NATO 226
France 2,000; 1 (FRA/GER) mech bde (1 armd cav rgt, 1 mech inf regt)

United Kingdom 16,500; 1 armd div (2 armd bde)

United States

US Africa Command: **Army**; 1 HQ at Stuttgart

US European Command: 50,500; 1 combined service HQ (EUCOM) at Stuttgart-Vaihingen

Army 35,200; 1 HQ (US Army Europe (USAREUR) at Heidelberg; 1 cav SBCT; 1 armd inf bde; 1 cbt avn bde; 1 engr bde; 1 int bde; 1 MP bde; 2 sigs bde; 1 spt bde; 1 (APS) armd HBCT eqpt. set (transforming); M1 *Abrams*; M2/M3 *Bradley*; *Stryker*; M109; M777; M270 MLRS; AH-64 *Apache*; CH-47 *Chinook*; UH-60 *Black Hawk*

Navy 485

USAF 14,450; 1 HQ (US Airforce Europe (USAFE)) at Ramstein AB; 1 HQ (3rd Air Force) at Ramstein AB; 1 ftr wg at Spangdahlem AB with (1 atk sqn with 18 A-10C *Thunderbolt* II; 1 ftr sqn with 24 F-16CJ *Fighting Falcon*); 1 airlift wg at Ramstein AB with 16 C-130E/J *Hercules*; 2 C-20 Gulfstream; 9 C-21 Learjet; 1 C-40B

USMC 365

Greece GRC

Euro €		2012	2013	2014
GDP	€	183bn	184bn	
	US$	249bn	244bn	
per capita	US$	22,055	21,645	
Growth	%	0.87	0.61	
Inflation	%	1.04	-0.80	
Def exp	€	3.83bn		
	US$	4.93bn		
Def bdgt [a]	€	5.19bn	4.27bn	3.83bn
	US$	6.68bn	5.68bn	
US$1=€		0.78	0.75	

[a] Includes military pensions and peacekeeping operations allocations

Population 10,772,967

Age	0–14	15–19	20–24	25–29	30–64	65 plus
Male	7.3%	2.5%	2.6%	3.0%	24.8%	8.8%
Female	6.8%	2.3%	2.5%	3.0%	25.2%	11.3%

Capabilities

The armed forces are tasked with assuring the territorial integrity of Greece and support to Cyprus, as well as contributing to international peacekeeping and peace-support initiatives. Regional tensions with Turkey and (FYR) Macedonia remain. A National Defence Policy was adopted in 2011 which emphasised deterrence, internal cooperation and enhanced situational awareness, as well as primary security tasks. Conscription remains in place, and is particularly important for the army; just under half of its personnel are conscripts. The armed forces have little organic ability to deploy other than regionally. Some procurement plans have been shelved as a result of economic problems – which have led to a reduction in defence spending – while cuts in military salaries, and significant reductions in training and exercises, will have depressed capability and morale.

ACTIVE 143,350 (Army 86,150, Navy 19,000 Air 26,600, Joint 11,600) **Paramilitary 4,000**

Conscript liability Up to 9 months in all services

RESERVE 216,650 (Army 177,650 Navy 5,000, Air 34,000)

ORGANISATIONS BY SERVICE

Army 48,450; 37,700 conscripts (total 86,150)

Units are manned at 3 different levels – Cat A 85% fully ready, Cat B 60% ready in 24 hours, Cat C 20% ready in 48 hours (requiring reserve mobilisation). 3 military regions.

FORCES BY ROLE

COMMAND
- 4 corps HQ (incl NDC-GR)
- 1 armd div HQ
- 3 mech inf div HQ
- 1 inf div HQ
- 1 log corps HQ

SPECIAL FORCES
- 1 comd (1 amph bde, 1 cdo/para bde)

MANOEUVRE

Reconnaissance
- 5 recce bn

Armoured
- 4 armd bde (2 armd bn, 1 mech inf bn, 1 SP arty bn)

Mechanised
- 8 mech inf bde (1 armd bn, 2 mech bn, 1 SP arty bn)

Light
- 2 inf div
- 7 inf bde (1 armd bn, 3 inf regt, 1 arty regt)

Air Manoeuvre
- 1 air mob bde

Amphibious
- 1 mne bde

Aviation
- 1 avn bde (1 hel regt with (2 atk hel bn), 2 tpt hel bn, 4 hel bn)

COMBAT SUPPORT
- 1 arty regt (1 arty bn, 2 MRL bn)
- 3 AD bn (2 with I-HAWK, 1 with *Tor* M1)
- 3 engr regt
- 2 engr bn
- 1 EW regt
- 10 sigs bn

COMBAT SERVICE SUPPORT
- 1 log div (3 log bde)

EQUIPMENT BY TYPE

MBT 1,462: 170 *Leopard* 2A6HEL; 183 *Leopard* 2A4; 526 *Leopard* 1A4/5; 208 M60A1/A3; 375 M48A5

RECCE 229 VBL

AIFV 398 BMP-1

APC 1,883

APC (T) 1,872: 89 *Leonidas* Mk1/2; 1,685 M113A1/A2; 98 M577

PPV 11 *Maxxpro*

ARTY 3,353

SP 547: **155mm** 442: 418 M109A1B/A2/A3GEA1/A5; 24 PzH 2000; **203mm** 105 M110A2

TOWED 410: **105mm** 281: 263 M101; 18 M-56; **155mm** 129 M114

MRL 147: **122mm** 111 RM-70 *Dana*; **227mm** 36 MLRS (incl ATACMS)

MOR 2,249: **81mm** 1,629; **107mm** 620 M-30 (incl 231 SP)

AT

MSL 1,108

SP 528: 196 HMMWV with 9K133 *Kornet*-E (AT-14 *Spriggan*); 42 HMMWV with *Milan*; 290 M901

MANPATS 580: 262 9K111 *Fagot* (AT-4 *Spigot*); 248 *Milan*; 70 TOW

RCL 3,927:

SP 106mm 581 M40A1

MANPATS 3,346 **84mm** 2,000 *Carl Gustav*; **90mm** 1,346 EM-67

AIRCRAFT • TPT • Light 27: 1 Beech 200 *King Air* (C-12C) 2 Beech 200 *King Air* (C-12R/AP *Huron*); 24 Cessna 185 (U-17A/B)

HELICOPTERS

ATK 29: 19 AH-64A *Apache*; 10 AH-64D *Apache*

TPT 128: **Heavy** 15: 9 CH-47D *Chinook*; 6 CH-47SD *Chinook*; **Medium** 4 NH90 TTH; **Light** 108: 95 Bell 205 (UH-1H *Iroquois*); 13 Bell 206 (AB-206) *Jet Ranger*

UAV • ISR • Medium 2 *Sperwer*

AD

SAM 614

SP 113: 21 9K331 *Tor*-M1 (SA-15 *Gauntlet*); 38 9K33 *Osa*-M (SA-8B *Gecko*); 54 ASRAD HMMWV

TOWED 42 I-HAWK

MANPAD 459 FIM-92A *Stinger*

GUNS • TOWED 727: **20mm** 204 Rh 202; **23mm** 523 ZU-23-2

RADAR • LAND 76: 3 ARTHUR, 5 AN/TPQ-36 *Firefinder* (arty, mor), 8 AN/TPQ-37(V)3; 40 BOR-A; 20 MARGOT

ARV 268: 12 *Büffel*; 43 *Leopard* 1; 95 M88A1; 113 M578

VLB 12+: 12 *Leopard* 1; *Leguan*

MW *Giant Viper*

National Guard 33,000 reservists

Internal security role

FORCES BY ROLE

MANOEUVRE

Light

1 inf div

Air Manoeuvre

1 para regt

Aviation

1 avn bn

COMBAT SUPPORT

8 arty bn

4 AD bn

Navy 16,700; 2,300 conscript; (total 19,000)

EQUIPMENT BY TYPE

SUBMARINES • TACTICAL • SSK 8:

4 *Poseidon* (GER T-209/1200) (of which 1 modernised with AIP technology) with 8 single 533mm TT with SUT HWT

3 *Glavkos* (GER T-209/1100) with 8 single 533mm TT with UGM-84C *Harpoon* AShM/SUT HWT

1 *Papanikolis* (GER T-214) with 8 single 533mm TT with UGM-84C *Harpoon* AShM/SUT HWT (5 additional vessels expected)

PRINCIPAL SURFACE COMBATANTS 13

FRIGATES • FFGHM 13:

4 *Elli* Batch I (NLD *Kortenaer* Batch 2) with 2 quad Mk141 lnchr with RGM-84A/C *Harpoon* AShM, 1 octuple Mk29 GMLS with RIM-7M/P *Sea Sparrow* SAM, 2 twin 324mm ASTT with Mk46 LWT, 1 *Phalanx* CIWS, 1 76mm gun, (capacity 2 Bell 212 (AB-212) hel)

2 *Elli* Batch II (NLD *Kortenaer* Batch 2) with 2 quad Mk141 lnchr with RGM-84A/C *Harpoon* AShM, 1 octuple Mk29 GMLS with RIM-7M/P *Sea Sparrow* SAM, 2 twin 324mm ASTT with Mk46 LWT, 1 *Phalanx* CIWS, 2 76mm gun, (capacity 2 Bell 212 (AB-212) hel)

3 *Elli* Batch III (NLD *Kortenaer* Batch 2) with 2 quad Mk141 lnchr with RGM-84A/C *Harpoon* AShM, 1 octuple Mk29 lnchr with RIM-7M/P *Sea Sparrow* SAM, 2 twin 324mm ASTT with Mk46 LWT, 1 *Phalanx* CIWS, 1 76mm gun, (capacity 2 Bell 212 (AB-212) hel)

4 *Hydra* (GER MEKO 200) with 2 quad lnchr with RGM-84G *Harpoon* AShM, 1 16-cell Mk48 Mod 5 VLS with RIM-162 ESSM SAM, 2 triple 324mm ASTT each with Mk46 LWT, 1 *Phalanx* CIWS, 1 127mm gun, (capacity 1 S-70B *Seahawk* ASW hel)

PATROL AND COASTAL COMBATANTS 33

CORVETTES • FSGM 5 *Roussen* (*Super Vita*) with 2 quad lnchr with MM-40 *Exocet* Block 2 AShM, 1 21-cell Mk49 GMLS with RIM-116 RAM SAM, 1 76mm gun (2 additional vessels in build)

PCFG 12:

5 *Kavaloudis* (FRA *La Combattante* II, III, IIIB) with 6 RB 12 *Penguin* AShM, 2 single 533mm TT with SST-4 HWT, 2 76mm gun

4 *Laskos* (FRA *La Combattante* II, III, IIIB) with 4 MM-38 *Exocet* AShM, 2 single 533mm TT with SST-4 HWT, 2 76mm gun

1 *Votsis* (FRA *La Combattante*) with 2 twin Mk-141 lnchr with RGM-84C *Harpoon* AShM, 1 76mm gun

2 *Votsis* (FRA *La Combattante* IIA) with 2 twin MM-38 *Exocet* AShM, 1 76mm gun

PCO 8:

2 *Armatolos* (DNK *Osprey*) with 1 76mm gun

2 *Kasos* with 1 76mm gun

4 *Machitis* with 1 76mm gun

PB 8: 4 *Andromeda* (NOR *Nasty*); 2 *Stamou*; 2 *Tolmi*

MINE COUNTERMEASURES 4

MHO 4: 2 *Evropi* (UK *Hunt*); 2 *Evniki* (US *Osprey*)

AMPHIBIOUS
LANDING SHIPS • LST 5:
5 *Chios* (capacity 4 LCVP; 300 troops) with 1 76mm gun, 1 hel landing platform (for med hel)
LANDING CRAFT 14
LCU 4
LCA 7
LCAC 3 *Kefallinia* (*Zubr*) with 2 AK630 CIWS, (capacity either 3 MBT or 10 APC (T); 230 troops)
LOGISTICS AND SUPPORT 49
ABU 2
AG 2 *Pandora*
AGOR 1 *Pytheas*
AGS 2: 1 *Stravon*; 1 *Naftilos*
AOR 2 *Axios* (ex-GER *Luneburg*)
AORH 1 *Prometheus* (ITA *Etna*) with 1 *Phalanx* CIWS
AOT 4 *Ouranos*
AWT 6 *Kerkini*
AXS 5
YFU 4
YNT 1 *Thetis*
YPT 3 *Evrotas*
YTM 16

Naval Aviation

FORCES BY ROLE
ANTI-SUBMARINE WARFARE
1 div with S-70B *Seahawk*; Bell 212 (AB-212) ASW; SA319 *Alouette* III
EQUIPMENT BY TYPE
AIRCRAFT • ASW (5 P-3B *Orion* in store)
HELICOPTERS
ASW 19: 8 Bell 212 (AB-212) ASW; 11 S-70B *Seahawk*
MRH 2 SA319 *Alouette* III
MSL
ASM AGM-119 *Penguin,* AGM-114 *Hellfire*

Air Force 22,050; 4,550 conscripts (total 26,600)

Tactical Air Force

FORCES BY ROLE
FIGHTER/GROUND ATTACK
1 sqn with A-7E/H *Corsair* II; TA-7C *Corsair* II
2 sqn with F-4E *Phantom* II
3 sqn with F-16CG/DG Block 30/50 *Fighting Falcon*
3 sqn with F-16CG/DG Block 52+ *Fighting Falcon*
1 sqn with F-16C/D Block 52+ ADV *Fighting Falcon*
1 sqn with *Mirage* 2000-5EG/BG Mk2
1 sqn with *Mirage* 2000EG/BG
ISR
1 sqn with RF-4E *Phantom* II
AIRBORNE EARLY WARNING
1 sqn with EMB-145H *Erieye*
EQUIPMENT BY TYPE
AIRCRAFT 277 combat capable
FGA 234: 34 F-4E *Phantom* II; 70 F-16CG/DG Block 30/50 *Fighting Falcon*: 56 F-16CG/DG Block 52+; 30 F- 16 C/D Block 52+ ADV *Fighting Falcon; 20 Mirage* 2000-5EG Mk2; 5 *Mirage* 2000-5BG Mk2; 17 *Mirage* 2000EG; 2 *Mirage* 2000BG
ATK 28: 20 A-7E/H *Corsair* II; 8 TA-7C *Corsair* II
ISR 15 RF-4E *Phantom* II*
AEW 4 EMB-145AEW (EMB-145H) *Erieye*
MSL
AAM • IR AIM-9L/P *Sidewinder*; R-550 *Magic* 2 **IIR** IRIS-T; *Mica* IR; **SARH** Super 530; **ARH** AIM-120B/C AMRAAM; *Mica* RF
ASM AGM-65A/B/G *Maverick*; AGM-154C JSOW
LACM SCALP EG
AShM AM 39 *Exocet*
ARM AGM-88 HARM
BOMBS
Conventional Mk81; Mk82; Mk83; Mk84
Electro-optical guided: GBU-8B HOBOS
Laser-guided: GBU-12/GBU-16 *Paveway* II; GBU-24 *Paveway* III
INS/GPS-guided GBU-31 JDAM

Air Defence

FORCES BY ROLE
AIR DEFENCE
6 sqn/bty with PAC-3 *Patriot* (MIM-104 A/B SOJC/D GEM)
2 sqn/bty with S-300PMU-1 (SA-10C *Grumble*)
12 bty with *Skyguard*/RIM-7 *Sparrow*/guns; *Crotale* NG/GR; *Tor*-M1 (SA-15 *Gauntlet*)
EQUIPMENT BY TYPE
AD
SAM • TOWED 61+: 36 PAC-3 *Patriot;* 12 S-300 PMU-1 (SA-10C *Grumble*); 9 *Crotale* NG/GR; 4 9K331 *Tor*-M1 (SA-15 *Gauntlet*); some *Skyguard*/*Sparrow*
GUNS 35+ 35mm

Air Support Command

FORCES BY ROLE
SEARCH & RESCUE/TRANSPORT HELICOPTER
1 sqn with AS332C *Super Puma* (SAR/CSAR)
1 sqn with AW109; Bell 205A (AB-205A) (SAR); Bell 212 (AB-212 - VIP, tpt)
TRANSPORT
1 sqn with C-27J *Spartan*
1 sqn with C-130B/H *Hercules*
1 sqn with EMB-135BJ *Legacy*; ERJ-135LR; Gulfstream V
FIRE FIGHTING
2 sqn with CL-215; CL-415
EQUIPMENT BY TYPE
AIRCRAFT
TPT 26: **Medium** 23: 8 C-27J *Spartan*; 5 C-130B *Hercules*; 10 C-130H *Hercules*; **Light** 2: 1 EMB-135BJ *Legacy*; 1 ERJ-135LR; **PAX** 1 Gulfstream V
FF 21: 13 CL-215; 8 CL-415
HELICOPTERS
TPT 31: **Medium** 11 AS332C *Super Puma;* **Light** 20: 13 Bell 205A (AB-205A) (SAR); 4 Bell 212 (AB-212) (VIP, Tpt); 3 AW109

Air Training Command

FORCES BY ROLE
TRAINING
2 sqn with T-2C/E *Buckeye*

2 sqn with T-6A/B *Texan* II
1 sqn with T-41D

EQUIPMENT BY TYPE

AIRCRAFT • TRG 104: 5 T-2C *Buckeye*; 35 T-2E *Buckeye*; 20 T-6A *Texan* II; 25 T-6B *Texan* II; 19 T-41D

Paramilitary • Coast Guard and Customs 4,000

EQUIPMENT BY TYPE

PATROL AND COASTAL COMBATANTS 122: **PCC** 3; **PBF** 54; **PB** 65

LOGISTICS AND SUPPORT • YPC 4

AIRCRAFT • TPT • Light 4: 2 Cessna 172RG *Cutlass*; 2 TB-20 *Trinidad*

DEPLOYMENT

Legal provisions for foreign deployment:
Constitution: Codified constitution (1975/1986/2001)
Specific legislation: 'Law 2295/95' (1995))
Decision on deployment of troops abroad: By the Government Council on Foreign Affairs and Defence

AFGHANISTAN
NATO • ISAF 3

BOSNIA-HERZEGOVINA
EU • EUFOR • *Operation Althea* 2

CYPRUS
Army 950 (ELDYK army); ε200 (officers/NCO seconded to Greek-Cypriot National Guard) (total 1,150)
1 mech bde (1 armd bn, 2 mech inf bn, 1 arty bn); 61 M48A5 MOLF MBT; 80 *Leonidas* APC; 12 M114 arty; 6 M110A2 arty

LEBANON
UN • UNIFIL 57; 1 PB

SERBIA
NATO • KFOR 120; 1 mech inf coy
OSCE • Kosovo 4

FOREIGN FORCES

United States US European Command: 380; 1 naval base at Makri; 1 naval base at Soudha Bay; 1 air base at Iraklion

Hungary HUN

Hungarian Forint f		2012	2013	2014
GDP	f	29.2tr	30.4tr	
	US$	127bn	133bn	
per capita	US$	12,736	13,344	
Growth	%	-6.38	-4.21	
Inflation	%	5.70	3.20	
Def exp	f	298bn		
	US$	1.32bn		
Def bdgt [a]	f	269bn	242bn	
	US$	1.2bn	1.1bn	
FMA (US)	US$	1m	1m	0.45m
US$1=f		225.02	220.31	

[a] Excludes military pensions

Population 9,939,470

Age	0–14	15–19	20–24	25–29	30–64	65 plus
Male	7.6%	2.9%	3.2%	3.2%	24.2%	6.5%
Female	7.2%	2.7%	3.1%	3.1%	25.4%	11.0%

Capabilities

Hungary's armed forces have shifted to a professional structure, with a much smaller order of battle but better-equipped and better-trained troops. With defence expenditure under pressure, however, budgetary constraints have curtailed procurement plans. Hungary's defence policy provides for operational deployments under both NATO and the EU; it has contributed troops to ISAF operations and conducts regular training exercises with bilateral and multinational partners. Hungary will contribute to the planned Visegrad CBRN battalion and manoeuvre battlegroup as part of plans for increased defence cooperation between the four Visegrad countries. The country is also host to the multinational Strategic Airlift Capability's C-17 unit. It has agreed a ten-year extension on its lease of *Gripen* fighter aircraft from Sweden.

ACTIVE 26,500 (Army 10,300, Air 5,900 Joint 10,300) **Paramilitary 12,000**

RESERVE 44,000 (Army 35,200 Air 8,800)

ORGANISATIONS BY SERVICE

Hungary's armed forces have reorganised into a joint force.

Land Component 10,300 (incl riverine element)

FORCES BY ROLE

SPECIAL FORCES
1 SF bn

MANOEUVRE

Mechanised
2 mech inf bde (total: 4 mech inf, 1 lt inf, 1 mixed bn, 2 log bn)

COMBAT SUPPORT
1 engr regt
1 EOD/rvn regt
1 CBRN bn
1 sigs regt
COMBAT SERVICE SUPPORT
1 spt bde (1 log regt)

EQUIPMENT BY TYPE
MBT 30 T-72
RECCE 24+: 24 K90 CBRN Recce; PSZH-IV CBRN Recce
AIFV 120 BTR-80A
APC (W) 260 BTR-80
ARTY 68
TOWED 152mm 18 D-20
MOR 82mm 50
AT • MSL • MANPATS 9K111 *Fagot* (AT-4 *Spigot*); 9K113 *Konkurs* (AT-5 *Spandrel*)
PATROL AND COASTAL COMBATANTS • PBR 2
AEV BAT-2
ARV BMP-1 VPV; T-54/T-55; VT-55A
VLB BLG-60; MTU; TMM

Air Component 5,900

Flying hours 50 hrs/yr

FORCES BY ROLE
FIGHTER/GROUND ATTACK
1 sqn with *Gripen* C/D
TRANSPORT
1 sqn with An-26 *Curl*
TRAINING
1 sqn with Yak-52
ATTACK HELICOPTER
1 sqn with Mi-24 *Hind*
TRANSPORT HELICOPTER
1 sqn with Mi-8 *Hip*; Mi-17 *Hip* H
AIR DEFENCE
1 regt (9 bty with *Mistral*; 3 bty with 2K12 *Kub* (SA-6 *Gainful*))
1 radar regt

EQUIPMENT BY TYPE
AIRCRAFT 14 combat capable
FGA 14: 12 *Gripen* C; 2 *Gripen* D
TPT • Light 4 An-26 *Curl*
TRG 8 Yak-52
HELICOPTERS
ATK 11: 3 Mi-24D *Hind* D; 6 Mi-24V *Hind* E; 2 Mi-24P *Hind* F
MRH 7 Mi-17 *Hip* H
TPT • Medium 10 Mi-8 *Hip*
AD • SAM 61
SP 16 2K12 *Kub* (SA-6 *Gainful*)
MANPAD *Mistral*
RADAR: 3 RAT-31DL, 6 P-18: 6 SZT-68U; 14 P-37
MSL
AAM • IR AIM-9 *Sidewinder*; R-73 (AA-11 *Archer*)
SARH R-27 (AA-10 *Alamo* A); **ARH** AIM-120C AMRAAM
ASM 250: 20 AGM-65 *Maverick*; 150 3M11 *Falanga* (AT-2 *Swatter*); 80 9K113 *Shturm*-V (AT-6 *Spiral*)

Paramilitary 12,000

Border Guards 12,000 (to reduce)

Ministry of Interior

FORCES BY ROLE
MANOEUVRE
Other
1 (Budapest) paramilitary district (7 rapid reaction coy)
11 (regt/district) paramilitary regt

EQUIPMENT BY TYPE
APC (W) 68 BTR-80

Cyber

There is no dedicated cyber organisation, but IT network management contains INFOSEC and cyber-defence elements. In February 2012, the government adopted a National Security Strategy, noting an intent to prevent and avert cyber attacks. The MoD has also developed a Military Cyber Defence concept.

DEPLOYMENT

Legal provisions for foreign deployment:
Legislation: Fundamental Law (2011)
Decision on deployment of troops abroad: Government decides on cross-border troop movements or employment, in the case of NATO (Paragraph 2.) For operations not based on NATO or EU decisions, the Fundamental Law gives parliament the prerogative to decide on the employment of Hungarian armed forces or foreign forces in, or from, Hungarian territory.

AFGHANISTAN
NATO • ISAF 354; 1 lt inf coy

BOSNIA-HERZEGOVINA
EU • EUFOR • *Operation Althea* 157; 1 inf coy
OSCE • Bosnia and Herzegovina 1

CYPRUS
UN • UNFICYP 77; 1 inf pl

DEMOCRATIC REPUBLIC OF THE CONGO
EU • EUSEC RD Congo 2

EGYPT
MFO 42; 1 MP unit

LEBANON
UN • UNIFIL 4

MALI
EU • EUTM Mali 13

SERBIA
NATO • KFOR 201; 1 inf coy (KTM)
OSCE • Kosovo 2
OSCE • Serbia 1

UGANDA
EU • EUTM Somalia 4

WESTERN SAHARA
UN • MINURSO 7 obs

Europe

Iceland ISL

Icelandic Krona K		2012	2013	2014
GDP	Kr	1.83tr	1.97tr	
	US$	13.7bn	14.5bn	
per capita	US$	41,739	44,121	
Growth	%	-1.66	-0.01	
Inflation	%	5.19	4.65	
Sy Bdgt [a]	Kr	4.11bn	4.64bn	
	US$	33m	37m	
US$1=K		125.11	126.23	

[a] Coast Guard budget

Population 315,281

Age	0–14	15–19	20–24	25–29	30–64	65 plus
Male	10.0%	3.6%	3.8%	3.4%	23.0%	6.1%
Female	9.8%	3.5%	3.7%	3.4%	22.5%	7.1%

Capabilities

The country has no armed forces, though there is a coast guard that operates ships, and fixed- and rotary-wing aircraft. A NATO member, the country is reliant on other Alliance partners for air policing and air defence.

ACTIVE NIL Paramilitary 200

ORGANISATIONS BY SERVICE

Paramilitary

Iceland Coast Guard 200

EQUIPMENT BY TYPE

PATROL AND COASTAL COMBATANTS 3
- **PSOH:** 2 *Aegir*
- **PSO** 1 *Thor*

LOGISTICS AND SUPPORT • AGS 1 *Baldur*

AIRCRAFT • TPT • **Light** 1 DHC-8-300

HELICOPTERS
- TPT • **Medium** 3 AS332L1 *Super Puma*

FOREIGN FORCES

NATO • Iceland Air Policing: Aircraft and personnel from various NATO members on a rotating basis.

Ireland IRL

Euro €		2012	2013	2014
GDP	€	167bn	174bn	
	US$	210bn	222bn	
per capita	US$	45,888	48,230	
Growth	%	1.64	1.89	
Inflation	%	1.92	1.32	
Def bdgt [a]	€	893m	901m	898m
	US$	1.15bn	1.2bn	
US$1=€		0.78	0.75	

[a] Includes military pensions and capital expenditure

Population 4,775,982

Age	0 – 14	15 – 19	20 – 24	25 – 29	30 – 64	65 plus
Male	10.9%	3.0%	3.1%	3.6%	23.8%	5.6%
Female	10.5%	2.9%	3.0%	3.7%	23.5%	6.6%

Capabilities

The armed forces' primary task is to 'defend the state against armed aggression'. They are also routinely called upon to conduct EOD operations within Ireland due to paramilitary activity, and conduct a range of security and support services such as maritime patrols and fishery protection. Irish forces also participate in UN peace-support, crisis-management and humanitarian-relief operations, most significantly in Lebanon and the Golan Heights. The army is the largest service, supported by a small air corps and naval service. During 2013, army units were consolidated within a new two-brigade structure and personnel were redeployed from support functions to operational units. Ireland's armed forces have been trimmed as a result of Dublin's economic difficulties, with further defence budget reductions planned for 2013–14, while some procurement programmes are being extended over a longer period to spread costs. A new Defence White Paper is expected to be published in 2014.

ACTIVE 9,350 (Army 7,500 Navy 1,050 Air 800)

RESERVE 4,630 (Army 4,350 Navy 260 Air 20)

ORGANISATIONS BY SERVICE

Army 7,500

FORCES BY ROLE

SPECIAL FORCES
- 1 ranger coy

MANOEUVRE
- **Reconnaissance**
  - 1 armd recce sqn
- **Mechanised**
  - 1 mech inf coy
- **Light**
  - 1 inf bde (1 cav recce sqn, 4 inf bn, 1 arty regt (3 fd arty bty, 1 AD bty), 1 fd engr coy, 1 sigs coy, 1 MP coy, 1 tpt coy)

1 inf bde (1 cav recce sqn, 3 inf bn, 1 arty regt (3 fd arty bty, 1 AD bty), 1 fd engr coy, 1 sigs coy, 1 MP coy, 1 tpt coy)

EQUIPMENT BY TYPE

LT TK 14 *Scorpion*
RECCE 15 *Piranha* IIIH
APC 94
APC (W) 67: 65 *Piranha* III; 2 XA-180 *Sisu*
PPV 27 RG-32M
ARTY 519
TOWED 24: **105mm** 24 L-118 Light Gun
MOR 495: **81mm** 400; **120mm** 95
AT
MSL • MANPATS *Javelin*
RCL 84mm *Carl Gustav*
AD
SAM • MANPAD 7 RBS-70
GUNS • TOWED 40mm 32 L/70 each with 8 *Flycatcher*
MW *Aardvark* Mk 2

Reserves 4,350 reservists (to reduce to 3,800)

FORCES BY ROLE

MANOEUVRE
Reconnaissance
1 (integrated) armd recce sqn
4 (integrated) cav tp
Mechanised
1 (integrated) mech inf coy
Light
23 (integrated) inf coy
COMBAT SUPPORT
4 (integrated) arty bty
2 engr pl
2 MP pl
COMBAT SERVICE SUPPORT
2 med det
4 tpt pl

Navy 1,050

EQUIPMENT BY TYPE

PATROL AND COASTAL COMBATANTS 8
PSOH 1 *Eithne* with 1 57mm gun
PSO 2 *Roisin* with 1 76mm gun
PCO 5: 3 *Emer*; 2 *Orla* (UK *Peacock*) with 1 76mm gun
LOGISTICS AND SUPPORT 6
AXS 2
YFL 3
YTM 1

Air Corps 800

2 ops wg; 2 spt wg; 1 trg wg; 1 comms and info sqn

EQUIPMENT BY TYPE

AIRCRAFT
MP 2 CN-235 MPA
TPT 7: **Light** 6: 5 Cessna FR-172H; 1 Learjet 45 (VIP); **PAX** 1 Gulfstream GIV
TRG 7 PC-9M
HELICOPTERS:
MRH 6 AW139
TPT • Light 2 EC135 P2 (incl trg/medevac; 1 non-operational)

DEPLOYMENT

Legal provisions for foreign deployment:
Constitution: Codified constitution (1937)
Specific legislation: 'Defence (Amendment) Act' 2006
Decision on deployment of troops abroad: a) By parliament; b) by government if scenario for deployment corresponds with conditions laid out in Art. 3 of 2006 'Defence (Amendment) Act' which exempts from parliamentary approval deployments for purposes of participation in exercises abroad; monitoring, observation, advisory or reconnaissance missions; and humanitarian operations in response to actual or potential disasters or emergencies.

AFGHANISTAN
NATO • ISAF 7

BOSNIA-HERZEGOVINA
EU • EUFOR • *Operation Althea* 7
OSCE • Bosnia and Herzegovina 6

CÔTE D'IVOIRE
UN • UNOCI 2 obs

DEMOCRATIC REPUBLIC OF THE CONGO
UN • MONUSCO 3 obs

LEBANON
UN • UNIFIL 358; 1 mech inf bn(-)

MALI
EU • EUTM Mali 8

MIDDLE EAST
UN • UNTSO 13 obs

SERBIA
NATO • KFOR 12
OSCE • Kosovo 6
OSCE • Serbia 3

SYRIA/ISRAEL
UN • UNDOF 119 obs; 1 inf coy

UGANDA
EU • EUTM Somalia 10

WESTERN SAHARA
UN • MINURSO 3 obs

Italy ITA

Euro €		2012	2013	2014
GDP	€	1.56tr	1.59tr	
	US$	2.01tr	2.08tr	
per capita	US$	33,115	34,034	
Growth	%	0.94	1.07	
Inflation	%	3.30	1.99	
Def exp	€	20.6bn		
	US$	26.5bn		
Def bdgt [a]	€	18.7bn	19bn	17.9bn
	US$	24bn	25.2bn	
US$1=€		0.78	0.75	

[a] Includes military pensions

Population 61,482,297

Age	0–14	15–19	20–24	25–29	30–64	65 plus
Male	7.1%	2.4%	2.6%	2.7%	24.6%	8.9%
Female	6.7%	2.4%	2.6%	2.8%	25.4%	11.9%

Capabilities

The armed forces' primary role is territorial defence and participation in NATO operations, with the ability for extended deployment as part of a multinational force. The services are struggling to cope with funding restrictions, with some officials voicing worry over the long-term impact of the constraints on the ability to conduct missions. Reductions up to 2025 in the size of the navy are a particular concern, however it did take delivery of the first of eight FREMM frigates in May 2013. The air force also started to receive fully-upgraded *Tornado* ECR aircraft. While the overall number of F-35s on order has been cut, the senate voted to support the programme in July 2013, approving the purchase of 60 F-35A and 30 B models. Defence expenditure remains under pressure. The armed forces have been undergoing a process of reform involving force reductions and modernised capabilities for over a decade. The air force's ability to support long-range deployment has been boosted by the belated entry into service of its four KC-767 tanker-transports. It lacks, however, a dedicated strategic airlift platform. The forces train regularly at the national and NATO Alliance levels, and support a number of overseas deployments.

ACTIVE 176,000 (Army 103,100 Navy 31,000 Air 41,900) **Paramilitary 183,500**

RESERVES 18,300 (Army 13,400 Navy 4,900)

ORGANISATIONS BY SERVICE

Space

SATELLITES 6

COMMUNICATIONS 2 *Sicral*

IMAGERY 4 *Cosmo (Skymed)*

Army 103,100

FORCES BY ROLE

COMMAND

1 (NRDC-IT) corps HQ (1 sigs bde, 1 spt regt)

MANOEUVRE

Mechanised

1 (*Friuli*) div (1 (*Ariete*) armd bde (2 tk regt, 1 mech inf regt, 1 arty regt, 1 engr regt, 1 log bn); 1 (*Pozzuolo del Friuli*) cav bde (3 cav regt, 1 amph regt, 1 arty regt); 1 (*Folgore*) AB bde (3 para regt, 1 cbt engr regt); 1 (*Friuli*) air mob bde (1 cav regt, 1 air mob regt, 2 avn regt))

1 (*Acqui*) div (1 (*Pinerolo*) mech bde (3 mech inf regt, 1 SP arty regt, 1 cbt engr regt); 1 (*Granatieri*) mech bde (1 cav regt, 2 mech inf regt, 1 SP arty regt); 1 (*Garibaldi Bersaglieri*) mech bde (1 cav regt, 1 tk regt, 2 hy mech inf regt, 1 SP arty regt, 1 cbt engr regt); 1 (*Aosta*) mech bde (1 cav regt, 3 mech inf regt, 1 SP arty regt, 1 cbt engr regt); 1 (*Sassari*) lt mech bde (3 mech inf regt, 1 cbt engr regt))

Mountain

1 (*Tridentina*) mtn div (1 (*Taurinense*) mtn bde (1 cav regt, 3 mtn inf regt, 1 arty regt, 1 mtn cbt engr regt, 1 spt bn); 1 (*Julia*) mtn bde with (3 mtn inf regt, 1 arty regt, 1 mtn cbt engr regt, 1 spt bn); 1 mtn inf trg regt))

Aviation

1 avn bde (3 avn regt, 1 avn sqn)

COMBAT SUPPORT

1 arty comd (1 hy arty regt, 2 arty regt, 1 psyops regt, 1 NBC regt)

1 AD comd (2 (HAWK) AD regt, 2 (SHORAD) AD regt)

1 engr comd (3 engr regt, 1 CIMIC regt) 1 EW/sigs comd (1 EW/ISTAR bde (1 ISTAR bn, 1 EW bn, 1 (HUMINT) int bn); 1 sigs bde with (6 sigs bn))

COMBAT SERVICE SUPPORT

1 log comd (4 (manoeuvre) log regt, 4 tpt regt)

1 spt regt

EQUIPMENT BY TYPE

MBT 200 C1 *Ariete*

RECCE 314: 300 B-1 *Centauro*; 14 VAB-RECO NBC

AIFV 308: 200 VCC-80 *Dardo*; 108 VBM 8×8 *Freccia*

APC 915

APC (T) 361: 246 Bv-206; 115 M113 (incl variants)

APC (W) 537 *Puma*

PPV 17: 6 *Buffalo*; 11 *Cougar*

AAV 16: 14 AAVP-7; 1 AAVC-7; 1 AAVR-7

ARTY 915

SP 155mm 192: 124 M109L; 68 PzH 2000

TOWED 155mm 164 FH-70

MRL 227mm 22 MLRS

MOR 537: **81mm** 212; **120mm** 325: 183 Brandt; 142 RT-F1

AT

MSL • MANPATS *Spike*; *Milan*

RCL 80mm *Folgore*

RL 110mm Pzf 3 *Panzerfaust* 3

AIRCRAFT • TPT • Light 6: 3 Do-228 (ACTL-1); 3 P-180 *Avanti*

HELICOPTERS

ATK 50 AW129CBT *Mangusta*

MRH 21 Bell 412 (AB-412) *Twin Huey*

TPT 154: **Heavy** 18 CH-47C *Chinook*; **Medium** 21 NH90 TTH; **Light** 115: 10 AW109; 56 Bell 205 (AB-205); 32 Bell 206 *Jet Ranger* (AB-206); 17 Bell 212 (AB-212)
AD
SAM
TOWED 48: 16 SAMP-T; 32 *Skyguard/Aspide*
MANPAD FIM-92A *Stinger*
GUNS • SP 25mm 64 SIDAM
AEV 40 *Leopard* 1; M113
ARV 137 *Leopard* 1
VLB 64 *Biber*
MW 2 *Miniflail*

Navy 31,000

EQUIPMENT BY TYPE
SUBMARINES • TACTICAL • SSK 6:
4 *Pelosi* (imp *Sauro*, 3rd and 4th series) with 6 single 533mm TT with Type-A-184 HWT
2 *Salvatore Todaro* (Type-U212A) with 6 single 533mm TT with Type-A-184 HWT/DM2A4 HWT (2 additional vessels under construction)
PRINCIPAL SURFACE COMBATANTS 17
AIRCRAFT CARRIERS • CVS 2:
1 *G. Garibaldi* with 2 octuple *Albatros* lnchr with *Aspide* SAM, 2 triple 324mm ASTT with Mk46 LWT, (capacity mixed air group of either 12–18 AV-8B *Harrier* II; 17 SH-3D *Sea King* or AW101 *Merlin*)
1 *Cavour* with 1 32-cell VLS with *Aster* 15 SAM, 2 76mm guns, (capacity mixed air group of 18–20 AV-8B *Harrier* II; 12 AW101 *Merlin*)
DESTROYERS • DDGHM 5:
2 *Andrea Doria* with 2 quad lnchr with *Otomat* Mk2A AShM, 1 48-cell VLS with *Aster* 15/*Aster* 30 SAM, 2 single 324mm ASTT with MU90 LWT, 3 76mm gun, (capacity 1 AW101 *Merlin*/NH90 hel)
2 *Luigi Durand de la Penne* (ex-*Animoso*) with 2 quad lnchr with *Milas AS*/*Otomat* Mk 2A AShM, 1 Mk13 GMLS with SM-1MR SAM, 1 octuple *Albatros* lnchr with *Aspide* SAM, 2 triple 324mm ASTT with Mk46 LWT, 1 127mm gun, 3 76mm gun, (capacity 2 Bell 212 (AB-212) hel)
1 *Bergamini* with 2 quad lnchr with *Otomat* Mk2A AShM, 1 11-cell VLS with *Aster* 15/*Aster* 30 SAM, 2 triple 324mm ASTT with MU90 LWT, 1 127mm gun, 1 76mm gun, (capacity 2 AW101/NH90 hel)
FRIGATES • FFGHM 10:
2 *Artigliere* with 8 single lnchr with *Otomat* Mk 2 AShM, 1 octuple *Albatros* lnchr with *Aspide* SAM, 1 127mm gun, (capacity 1 Bell 212 (AB-212) hel)
8 *Maestrale* with 4 single lnchr with *Otomat* Mk2 AShM, 1 octuple *Albatros* lnchr with *Aspide* SAM, 2 triple 324mm ASTT with Mk46 LWT, 1 127mm gun, (capacity 2 Bell 212 (AB-212) hel)
PATROL AND COASTAL COMBATANTS 20
CORVETTES 6
FSM 4 *Minerva* with 1 octuple *Albatros* lnchr with *Aspide* SAM, 1 76mm gun
FS 2 *Minerva* with 1 76mm gun (2 more in reserve)
PSOH 6:
4 *Comandante Cigala Fuligosi* with 1 76mm gun, (capacity 1 Bell 212 (AB-212)/NH90 hel)
2 *Comandante Cigala Fuligosi* (capacity 1 Bell 212 (AB-212)/NH-90 hel)
PCO 4 *Cassiopea* with 1 76mm gun (capacity 1 Bell 212 (AB-212) hel)
PB 4 *Esploratore*
MINE WARFARE • MINE COUNTERMEASURES 10
MHO 10: 8 *Gaeta*; 2 *Lerici*
AMPHIBIOUS
PRINCIPAL AMPHIBIOUS SHIPS • LPD 3:
2 *San Giorgio* with 1 76mm gun (capacity 3-5 AW101/NH90/SH3-D/Bell 212; 1 CH-47 *Chinook* tpt hel; 3 LCM 2 LCVP; 30 trucks; 36 APC (T); 350 troops)
1 *San Giusto* with 1 76mm gun (capacity 4 AW101 *Merlin*; 1 CH-47 *Chinook* tpt hel; 3 LCM 2 LCVP; 30 trucks; 36 APC (T); 350 troops)
LANDING CRAFT 30: 17 **LCVP**; 13 **LCM**
LOGISTICS AND SUPPORT 128
ABU 5 *Ponza*
AFD 19
AGE 2: 1 *Vincenzo Martellota*; 1 *Raffaele Rosseti*
AGI 1 *Elettra*
AGOR 1 *Leonardo* (coastal)
AGS 3: 1 *Ammiraglio Magnaghi* with 1 hel landing platform; 2 *Aretusa* (coastal)
AKSL 6 *Gorgona*
AORH 3: 1 *Etna* with 1 76mm gun, (capacity 1 AW101/NH90 hel); 2 *Stromboli* with 1 76mm gun, (capacity 1 AW101/NH90 hel)
AOT 7 *Depoli*
ARSH 1 *Anteo* (capacity 1 Bell 212 (AB-212) hel)
ATS 6 *Ciclope*
AT 9 (coastal)
AWT 7: 1 *Bormida*; 2 *Simeto*; 4 *Panarea*
AXL 3 *Aragosta*
AXS 8: 1 *Amerigo Vespucci*; 1 *Palinuro*; 1 *Italia*; 5 *Caroly*
YDT 2 *Pedretti*
YFT 1 *Aragosta*
YFU 2 Men 215
YPT 1 Men 212
YTB 9 *Porto*
YTM 32

Naval Aviation 2,200

FORCES BY ROLE
FIGHTER/GROUND ATTACK
1 sqn with AV-8B *Harrier* II; TAV-8B *Harrier*
ANTI-SUBMARINE WARFARE/TRANSPORT
5 sqn with AW101 ASW *Merlin*; Bell 212 ASW (AB-212AS); Bell 212 (AB-212); NH90 NFH
MARITIME PATROL
1 flt with P-180
AIRBORNE EARLY WANRING & CONTROL
1 flt with AW101 *Merlin* AEW
EQUIPMENT BY TYPE
AIRCRAFT 16 combat capable
FGA 16: 14 AV-8B *Harrier* II; 2 TAV-8B *Harrier*
MP 3 P-180

HELICOPTERS
ASW 36: 10 AW101 ASW *Merlin*; 16 Bell 212 ASW; 10 NH90 NFH
AEW 4 AW101 *Merlin* AEW
TPT 14: **Medium** 8 AW101 *Merlin*; **Light** 6 Bell 212 (AB-212)
MSL
AAM • IR AIM-9L *Sidewinder*; **ARH** AIM-120 AMRAAM
ASM AGM-65 *Maverick*
AShM *Marte* Mk 2/S

Marines 2,000

FORCES BY ROLE
MANOEUVRE
Amphibious
1 mne regt (1 SF coy, 1 aslt bn, 1 log bn)
1 landing craft gp
COMBAT SERVICE SUPPORT
1 log regt (1 log bn)
EQUIPMENT BY TYPE
APC (T) 24 VCC-2
AAV 28: 15 AAVP-7; 12 AAVC-7; 1 AAVR-7
ARTY • MOR 12: **81mm** 8 Brandt; **120mm** 4 Brandt
AT • MSL• MANPATS *Milan; Spike*
AD • SAM • MANPAD FIM-92A *Stinger*
ARV 1 AAV-7RAI

Air Force 41,900

FORCES BY ROLE
FIGHTER
4 sqn with Eurofighter *Typhoon*
FIGHTER/GROUND ATTACK
2 sqn with AMX *Ghibli*
1 (SEAD/EW) sqn with *Tornado* ECR
2 sqn with *Tornado* IDS
FIGHTER/GROUND ATTACK/ISR
1 sqn with AMX *Ghibli*
MARITIME PATROL
1 sqn (opcon Navy) with BR1150 *Atlantic*
TANKER/TRANSPORT
1 sqn with KC-767A
COMBAT SEARCH & RESCUE
1 sqn with AB-212 ICO
SEARCH & RESCUE
1 wg with AW139 (HH-139A); Bell 212 (HH-212); HH-3F *Pelican*
TRANSPORT
2 (VIP) sqn with A319CJ; AW139 (VH-139A); *Falcon* 50; *Falcon* 900 *Easy*; *Falcon* 900EX; SH-3D *Sea King*
2 sqn with C-130J/C-130J-30/KC-130J *Hercules*
1 sqn with C-27J *Spartan*
1 (calibration) sqn with P-180 *Avanti*
TRAINING
1 sqn with Eurofighter *Typhoon*
1 sqn with MB-339PAN (aerobatic team)
1 sqn with MD-500D/E (NH-500D/E)
1 sqn with *Tornado*
1 sqn with AMX-T *Ghibli*
1 sqn with MB-339A
1 sqn with MB-339CD*
1 sqn with SF-260EA
ISR UAV
1 sqn with MQ-9A *Reaper*; RQ-1B *Predator*
AIR DEFENCE
2 bty with *Spada*
EQUIPMENT BY TYPE
AIRCRAFT 245 combat capable
FTR 69 Eurofighter *Typhoon*
FGA 127: 55 *Tornado* IDS; 64 AMX *Ghibli*; 8 AMX-T *Ghibli*
EW/FGA 15 *Tornado* ECR*
ASW 6 BR1150 *Atlantic*
TKR/TPT 6: 4 KC-767A; 2 KC-130J *Hercules*
TPT 66: **Medium** 31: 9 C-130J *Hercules*; 10 C-130J-30 *Hercules*; 12 C-27J *Spartan*; **Light** 25: 15 P-180 *Avanti*; 10 S-208 (liaison); **PAX** 10: 3 A319CJ; 2 *Falcon* 50 (VIP); 2 *Falcon* 900 *Easy*; 3 *Falcon* 900EX (VIP)
TRG 103: 3 M-346; 21 MB-339A; 28 MB-339CD*; 21 MB-339PAN (aerobatics); 30 SF-260EA
HELICOPTERS
MRH 58: 10 AW139 (HH-139A/VH-139A); 2 MD-500D (NH-500D); 46 MD-500E (NH-500E)
SAR 12 HH-3F *Pelican*
TPT 31: **Medium** 2 SH-3D *Sea King* (liaison/VIP); **Light** 29 Bell 212 (HH-212)/AB-212 ICO
UAV • ISR • Heavy 11: 6 MQ-9A *Reaper*; 5 RQ-1B *Predator*
AD • SAM • TOWED *Spada*
MSL
AAM • IR AIM-9L *Sidewinder*; **IIR** IRIS-T; **ARH** AIM-120 AMRAAM
ARM AGM-88 HARM
LACM SCALP EG/*Storm Shadow*
BOMBS
Laser-guided/GPS: Enhanced *Paveway* II; Enhanced *Paveway* III

Joint Special Forces Command (COFS)

Army

FORCES BY ROLE
SPECIAL FORCES
1 SF regt (9th *Assalto paracadutisti*)
1 SF regt (185th RAO)
1 spec ops regt (4th *Alpini paracadutisti*)

Navy (COMSUBIN)

FORCES BY ROLE
SPECIAL FORCES
1 SF gp (GOI)
1 diving gp (GOS)

Air Force

FORCES BY ROLE
SPECIAL FORCES
1 sqn (17th *Stormo Incursori*)

Paramilitary

Carabinieri

FORCES BY ROLE
SPECIAL FORCES
1 spec ops gp (GIS)

Paramilitary 183,500

Carabinieri 104,200

The Carabinieri are organisationally under the MoD. They are a separate service in the Italian Armed Forces as well as a police force with judicial competence.

Mobile and Specialised Branch

FORCES BY ROLE

MANOEUVRE

Aviation

1 hel gp

Other

1 (mobile) paramilitary div (1 bde (1st) with (1 horsed cav regt, 11 mobile bn); 1 bde (2nd) with (1 (1st) AB regt, 2 (7th & 13th) mobile regt))

EQUIPMENT BY TYPE

APC 15

APC (T) 3 VCC-2

APC (W) 12 *Puma*

AIRCRAFT • TPT • Light: 1 P-180 *Avanti*

HELICOPTERS

MRH 31 Bell 412 (AB-412)

TPT • Light 19 AW109

PATROL AND COASTAL COMBATANTS • PB 68

Customs 68,100

(Servizio Navale Guardia Di Finanza)

EQUIPMENT BY TYPE

PATROL AND COASTAL COMBATANTS 179

PCF 1 *Antonio Zara*

PBF 146: 19 *Bigliani;* 24 *Corrubia;* 9 *Mazzei;* 62 V-2000; 32 V-5000/V-6000

PB 32: 24 *Buratti;* 8 *Meatini*

Coast Guard 11,200

(Guardia Costiera – Capitanerie Di Porto)

EQUIPMENT BY TYPE

PATROL AND COASTAL COMBATANTS 328

PCO 3: 2 *Dattilo;* 1 *Gregoretti*

PCC 43: 5 *Diciotti;* 1 *Saettia;* 28 200-class; 9 400-class

PB 282: 19 300-class; 3 454-class; 72 500-class; 12 600-class; 33 700-class; 94 800-class; 49 2000-class

AIRCRAFT MP 9: 6 ATR-42 MP *Surveyor,* 1 P-180GC; 2 PL-166-DL3

HELICOPTERS • MRH 13: 4 AW139; 9 Bell 412SP (AB-412SP *Griffin*)

Cyber

Overall responsibility for cyber security rests with the presidency of the Council of Ministers and the Inter-Ministerial Situation and Planning Group which includes, among others, representatives from the defence, interior and foreign affairs ministries. A Joint Integrated Concept on Computer Network Operations was approved in 2009. In 2011, an Inter-Forces Committee on Cyberspace (CIAC) was established to advise the chief of defence staff. In January 2012, an Inter-Forces Policy Directive was approved to provide a vision for both operational management (under the C4 Defence Command, the Inter-Forces Intelligence Centre and individual armed forces) and strategic direction (under the chief of defence staff (CDS) and CIAC). CDS established the Computer and Emergency Response Team (CERT-Defence) to promote the security of IT networks and share knowledge on cyber threats and cyber defence including through the collaboration with national and international CERTs.

DEPLOYMENT

Legal provisions for foreign deployment:

Constitution: Codified constitution (1949)

Decision on deployment of troops abroad: By the government upon approval by the parliament.

AFGHANISTAN

NATO • ISAF 2,825; 1 mech inf bde HQ; 1 mech inf regt; 1 para regt; AW129 *Mangusta*; CH-47; NH90; *Tornado*; C-130

UN • UNAMA 2 obs

ALBANIA

Delegazione Italiana Esperti (DIE) 27

BOSNIA-HERZEGOVINA

OSCE • Bosnia and Herzegovina 8

DEMOCRATIC REPUBLIC OF THE CONGO

EU • EUSEC RD Congo 1

EGYPT

MFO 78; 3 coastal patrol unit

GULF OF ADEN & INDIAN OCEAN

EU • *Operation Atalanta* 1 FFGHM

INDIA/PAKISTAN

UN • UNMOGIP 3 obs

LEBANON

UN • UNIFIL 1,137; 1 cav bde HQ; 1 amph bn; 1 hel flt; 1 engr coy; 1 sigs coy; 1 CIMIC coy(-)

MALI

EU • EUTM Mali 7

MALTA

26; 2 Bell 212 (HH-212)

MEDITERRANEAN SEA

NATO • SNMG 2: 1 FFGHM

NATO • SNMCMG 2: 1 MHO

MIDDLE EAST

UN • UNTSO 7 obs

SERBIA

NATO • KFOR 500; 1 MRL BG HQ;

OSCE • Kosovo 12

OSCE • Serbia 4

SOUTH SUDAN

UN • UNMISS 1 obs

UGANDA

EU • EUTM Somalia 22

WESTERN SAHARA

UN • MINURSO 5 obs

FOREIGN FORCES

United States US European Command: 11,100

Army 3,500; 1 AB IBCT; some M119A2

Navy 3,300; 1 HQ (US Navy Europe (USNAVEUR)) at Naples; 1 HQ (6th Fleet) at Gaeta; 1 MP Sqn with 9 P-3C *Orion* at Sigonella

USAF 4,200; 1 ftr wg with (2 ftr sqn with 21 F-16C/D *Fighting Falcon*) at Aviano

USMC 100

Latvia LVA

Latvian Lat L		2012	2013	2014
GDP	L	16.5bn	17.5bn	
	US$	28.4bn	31.1bn	
per capita	US$	13,900	15,285	
Growth	%	-2.37	-1.47	
Inflation	%	2.29	1.80	
Def exp	L	140m		
	US$	256m		
Def bdgt [a]	L	140m	158m	
	US$	256m	300m	
FMA (US)	US$	2.2m	2.2m	2.3m
US$1=L		0.55	0.53	

[a] Includes military pensions

Population 2,178,443

Age	0–14	15–19	20–24	25–29	30–64	65 plus
Male	7.0%	2.9%	3.8%	4.0%	23.6%	5.8%
Female	6.6%	2.7%	3.6%	3.9%	25.1%	11.0%

Capabilities

Latvia's armed forces are smaller and less well-equipped than its neighbour Estonia, despite having nearly twice the population. The small army is essentially a light infantry force, supported by a small number of utility aircraft, and the navy operates a handful of patrol and mine-countermeasures vessels. Procurement plans include air-surveillance radars and SHORAD. Latvian forces completed structural reforms in 2009–10, and now plan to improve education, supply and maintenance, as well as to develop international cooperation. Latvia's defence budget remains relatively low, at approximately 1% of GDP, with a plan to reach the NATO-required 2% only by 2020. Major development projects over the coming decade include a combat engineering capability, a mechanisation process involving the procurement of armoured personnel carriers, and replacement transport helicopters. Latvia participates in NATO and EU missions, and the country has deployed personnel with ISAF. Forces train regularly with NATO partners and in other multilateral exercises. Air policing is provided by NATO states on a rotational basis.

ACTIVE 5,310 (Army 1,250 Navy 550 Air 310 Joint Staff 2,600 National Guard 600)

RESERVE 7,850 (National Guard 7,850)

ORGANISATIONS BY SERVICE

Joint 2,600

FORCES BY ROLE

SPECIAL FORCES

1 SF unit

COMBAT SUPPORT

1 MP bn

Army 1,250

FORCES BY ROLE

MANOEUVRE

Light

1 inf bde (2 inf bn, 1 cbt spt bn HQ, 1 CSS bn HQ)

National Guard 600; 7,850 part-time (8,450 in total)

FORCES BY ROLE

MANOEUVRE

Light

11 inf bn

COMBAT SUPPORT

1 arty bn

1 AD bn

1 engr bn

1 NBC bn

COMBAT SERVICE SUPPORT

3 spt bn

EQUIPMENT BY TYPE

MBT 3 T-55 (trg)

APC • PPV 8 *Cougar* (on loan from US)

ARTY 76

TOWED 100mm 23 K-53

MOR 53: **81mm** 28 L16; **120mm** 25 M120

AT

MANPATS *Spike*-LR

RCL 84mm *Carl Gustav*

GUNS 90mm 130

AD

SAM • MANPAD RBS-70

GUNS • TOWED 40mm 24 L/70

Navy 550 (incl Coast Guard)

Naval Forces Flotilla separated into an MCM squadron and a patrol boat squadron. LVA, EST and LTU have set up a joint naval unit, BALTRON, with bases at Liepaja, Riga, Ventspils (LVA), Tallinn (EST), Klaipeda (LTU). Each nation contributes 1–2 MCMVs

EQUIPMENT BY TYPE

PATROL AND COASTAL COMBATANTS 5

PB 5: 1 *Storm* (NOR) with 1 76mm gun; 4 *Skrunda* (GER *Swath*) (1 more vessel in build)

MINE WARFARE • MINE COUNTERMEASURES 6

MHO 5 *Imanta* (NLD *Alkmaar/Tripartite*)

MCCS 1 *Vidar* (NOR)

LOGISTICS AND SUPPORT 2

AXL 2: 1 *Storm* (NOR) with 1 76mm gun; 1 *Varonis* (comd and spt ship, ex-*Buyskes*, NLD)

Coast Guard

Under command of the Latvian Naval Forces.

PATROL AND COASTAL COMBATANTS

PB 6: 1 *Astra;* 5 KBV 236 (SWE)

Air Force 310

Main tasks are air space control and defence, maritime and land SAR and air transportation.

FORCES BY ROLE

AIR DEFENCE

1 AD bn

1 radar sqn (radar/air ctrl)

AIRCRAFT • TPT • Light 4 An-2 *Colt*

HELICOPTERS

MRH 4 Mi-17 *Hip* H

TPT • Light 2 PZL Mi-2 *Hoplite*

Paramilitary

State Border Guard

PATROL AND COASTAL COMBATANTS

PB 3: 1 *Valpas* (FIN); 1 *Lokki* (FIN); 1 *Randa*

Cyber

A Cyber Defence Unit is under development within the National Guard. A National Cyber Security Strategy is also under development. Cyber defence capabilities are under development, and technical capabilities are provided according to NATO standards.

DEPLOYMENT

Legal provisions for foreign deployment:

Constitution: Codified constitution (1922)

Specific legislation: 'Law on Participation of the National Armed Forces of Latvia in International Operations' (1995) (Annex of 21 Jan 2009 allows Latvian armed forces to take part in quick response units formed by NATO/EU)

Decision on deployment of troops abroad: a) By parliament (Section 5 I of the 1995 'Law on Participation', in combination with Art. 73 of constitution); b) by cabinet, for rescue or humanitarian operations (Section 5 II of the 1995 law) or military exercises in non-NATO states (Section 9 of the 1995 law); c) by defence minister for rescue and humanitarian aid operations in NATO/EU states. Latvian units can be transferred under the control of an international organisation or another country to conduct international operations for a limited time frame only in compliance with and under conditions defined by a Parliamentary decree.

AFGHANISTAN

NATO • ISAF 141

MALI

EU • EUTM Mali 2

SERBIA

OSCE • Kosovo 12

Lithuania LTU

Lithuanian Litas L		2012	2013	2014
GDP	L	120bn	128bn	
	US$	42.2bn	45.9bn	
per capita	US$	14,018	15,358	
Growth	%	5.58	4.16	
Inflation	%	3.17	2.13	
Def exp	L	883m		
	US$	329m		
Def bdgt [a]	L	852m	925m	1.18bn
	US$	317m	355m	
FMA (US)	US$	2.55m	2.55m	2.55m
US$1=L		2.68	2.61	

[a] Excludes military pensions

Population 3,515,858

Age	0–14	15–19	20–24	25–29	30–64	65 plus
Male	7.0%	2.9%	3.8%	4.0%	23.6%	5.8%
Female	6.6%	2.7%	3.6%	3.9%	25.1%	11.0%

Capabilities

Like its Baltic neighbours Estonia and Latvia, Lithuania is a NATO member with small armed forces. The army is by far the largest of the three, supported by smaller air and naval arms. Reform and re-equipment programmes are under way, intended to provide deployable land forces drawn from a motorised infantry brigade, but continue to be slowed by funding constraints, which have also restricted training. The formation of a Lithuanian–Polish–Ukrainian army brigade was originally envisaged by autumn 2011, but as of mid-2013 had yet to materialise. The air force provides a light transport capability while the naval focus is on mine countermeasures. Lithuania was a contributor to ISAF for eight years; its mission ended in August 2013.

ACTIVE 11,800 (Army 7,350 Navy 500 Air 950 Joint 2,050) **Paramilitary 11,550**

Conscript liability 12 months

RESERVE 6,700 (Army 6,700)

ORGANISATIONS BY SERVICE

Army 3,750; 4,400 active reserves (total 8,150)

FORCES BY ROLE

MANOEUVRE

Mechanised

1 mech bde (3 mech inf bn, 1 arty bn)

Light

3 mot inf bn

COMBAT SUPPORT

1 engr bn

COMBAT SERVICE SUPPORT

1 trg regt

EQUIPMENT BY TYPE

APC (T) 126 M113A1

ARTY 48

TOWED 105mm 18 M101

MOR 120mm 30: 5 2B11; 10 M/41D; 15 M113 with Tampella

AT • MSL

SP 10 M1025A2 HMMWV with *Javelin*

MANPATS *Javelin*

RCL 84mm *Carl Gustav*

AD • SAM • MANPAD *Stinger*

AEV 8 MT-LB

ARV 4 M113

Reserves

National Defence Voluntary Forces 4,400 active reservists

FORCES BY ROLE

MANOEUVRE

Other

6 (territorial) def unit

Navy 500

LVA, EST and LTU established a joint naval unit, BALTRON, with bases at Liepaja, Riga, Ventpils (LVA), Tallinn (EST), Klaipeda (LTU)

EQUIPMENT BY TYPE

PATROL AND COASTAL COMBATANTS 4

PCC 3 *Zematis* (DNK *Flyvefisken*) with 1 76mm gun

PB 1 *Storm* (NOR) with 1 76mm gun

MINE WARFARE • MINE COUNTERMEASURES 4:

MHC 3: 1 *Sūduvis* (GER *Lindau*); 2 *Skulvis* (UK *Hunt*)

MCCS 1 *Vidar* (NOR)

LOGISTICS AND SUPPORT 4

AAR 1 *Sakiai*

YAG 1 *Lokys* (DNK)

YGS 1

YTL 1 (SWE)

Air Force 950

Flying hours 120 hrs/year

FORCES BY ROLE

AIR DEFENCE

1 AD bn

EQUIPMENT BY TYPE

AIRCRAFT

TPT 5: **Medium** 3 C-27J *Spartan;* **Light** 2 L-410 *Turbolet*

TRG 1 L-39ZA *Albatros*

HELICOPTERS • TPT • Medium 8 Mi-8 *Hip* (tpt/SAR)

AD • SAM • MANPAD FIM-92A *Stinger;* RBS-70

Special Operation Force

FORCES BY ROLE

SPECIAL FORCES

1 SF gp (1 CT unit; 1 Jaeger bn, 1 cbt diver unit)

Joint Logistics Support Command 1,300

FORCES BY ROLE

COMBAT SERVICE SUPPORT

1 log bn

Joint Training and Doctrine Command (TRADOC) 800

FORCES BY ROLE

COMBAT SERVICE SUPPORT

1 trg regt

Other Units 600

FORCES BY ROLE

COMBAT SUPPORT

1 MP bn

Paramilitary 11,550

Riflemen Union 7,550

State Border Guard Service 4,000

Ministry of Internal Affairs

Coast Guard 530

EQUIPMENT BY TYPE

PATROL AND COASTAL COMBATANTS • PB 3: 1 *Lokki* (FIN); 1 KBV 041 (SWE); 1 KBV 101 (SWE)

AMPHIBIOUS • LANDING CRAFT • UCAC 2 *Christina* (*Griffon* 2000)

Cyber

A National Electronic Information Security (cyber-security) Strategy was approved by the government in 2011. Earlier, a Cyber Security Strategy for National Defence was adopted in 2009, and is currently being implemented. To help this process, the MoD established a cyber-security division under its Communication and Information System Service the same year. In 2013 the MoD adopted a renewed Cyber Security Strategy, which defines ways of strengthening cyber security in the National Defense System.

DEPLOYMENT

Legal provisions for foreign deployment:

Constitution: Codified constitution (1992)

Decision on deployment of troops abroad: By parliament (Art. 67, 138, 142) According to legislation, the defence minister has the authority to establish the exact amount or size of contingent to be deployed, and the duration of the deployment, not exceeding the limits set out by the parliament.

AFGHANISTAN

NATO • ISAF 240

UN • UNAMA 1 obs

MALI

EU • EUTM Mali 2

SERBIA

NATO • KFOR 1

FOREIGN FORCES

Belgium NATO Baltic Air Policing 4 F-16AM *Fighting Falcon*

Luxembourg LUX

Euro €		2012	2013	2014
GDP	€	45.5bn	46.9bn	
	US$	56.7bn	60.5bn	
per capita	US$	107,206	112,135	
Growth	%	3.62	3.05	
Inflation	%	2.89	1.93	
Def exp	€			
	US$			
Def bdgt	€	207m	188m	
	US$	267m	249m	
US$1=€		0.78	0.75	

Population 514,862

Foreign citizens: ε124,000

Age	0–14	15–19	20–24	25–29	30–64	65 plus
Male	9.3%	3.2%	3.2%	3.2%	23.9%	6.4%
Female	8.7%	3.0%	3.1%	3.2%	23.8%	8.8%

Capabilities

Luxembourg maintains a small army, with no air or naval capacity. It continues to support EU anti-piracy operations by funding the Luxembourg Maritime Patrol and Reconnaissance programme. This uses contractor-operated *Merlin* IIIC maritime patrol aircraft as part of the counter-piracy *Operation Atalanta*.

ACTIVE 900 (Army 900) Paramilitary 610

ORGANISATIONS BY SERVICE

Army 900

FORCES BY ROLE

MANOEUVRE

Reconnaissance

2 recce coy (1 to Eurocorps/BEL div, 1 to NATO pool of deployable forces)

Light

1 lt inf bn

EQUIPMENT BY TYPE

APC • PPV 48 *Dingo* II

ARTY • MOR 81mm 6

AT • MSL• MANPATS 6 TOW

Paramilitary 610

Gendarmerie 610

DEPLOYMENT

Legal provisions for foreign deployment:

Constitution: Codified constitution (1868)

Specific legislation: 'Loi du 27 juillet 1992 relatif à la participation du Grand-Duché de Luxembourg à des opérations pour le maintien de la paix (OMP) dans le cadre d'organisations internationales'.

Decision on deployment of troops abroad: By government after formal consultation of relevant parliamentary committees and the Council of State (Art. 1–2 of the 1992 law).

AFGHANISTAN

NATO • ISAF 10

BOSNIA-HERZEGOVINA

EU • EUFOR • *Operation Althea* 1

DEMOCRATIC REPUBLIC OF THE CONGO

EU • EUSEC RD Congo 1

MALI

EU • EUTM Mali 1

SERBIA

NATO • KFOR 22

Macedonia, Former Yugoslav Republic FYROM

Macedonian Denar d		2012	2013	2014
GDP	d	484bn	510bn	
	US$	9.68bn	10.5bn	
per capita	US$	4,683	5,050	
Growth	%	0.11	0.05	
Inflation	%	3.31	2.50	
Def bdgt	d	6.18bn		
	US$	129m		
FMA (US)	US$	3.6m	3.6m	3.6m
US$1=d		47.83	46.29	

Population 2,087,171

Age	0 – 14	15 – 19	20 – 24	25 – 29	30 – 64	65 plus
Male	9.3%	3.7%	3.7%	3.9%	24.0%	5.2%
Female	8.6%	3.4%	3.5%	3.8%	23.9%	6.9%

Capabilities

Ambitious reform plans spelt out in the 2003 Defence Concept, and reiterated in the 2005 Defence White Paper, have so far only partly been realised, though the armed forces have been reorganised. In 2006, the services moved from a conscript-based to a professional structure. The 2003 Defence Concept called for armed forces to support territorial integrity, regional stability, peace-support missions and deployed operations. The country continues to aspire to NATO membership, having joined the NATO Membership Action Plan in 1999. The impasse with Greece over the state's name is one element that hinders progress towards full NATO status. The armed forces have a small air arm consisting mainly of transport and armed support helicopters, but have no organic fixed-wing airlift. Although forces deployed to ISAF and the EU in Bosnia are mission-capable, only a small proportion of the remaining forces are likely operationally ready.

ACTIVE 8,000 (Joint 8,000)

RESERVE 4,850

ORGANISATIONS BY SERVICE

Joint Operational Command 8,000

Army

FORCES BY ROLE
SPECIAL FORCES
1 (Special Purpose) SF regt (1 SF bn, 1 Ranger bn)
MANOEUVRE
Armoured
1 tk bn
Mechanised
1 mech inf bde
COMBAT SUPPORT
1 (mixed) arty regt
1 AD coy
1 engr bn
1 MP bn
1 NBC coy
1 sigs bn

Logistic Support Command

FORCES BY ROLE
COMBAT SUPPORT
1 engr bn (1 active coy)
COMBAT SERVICE SUPPORT
3 log bn

Reserves

FORCES BY ROLE
MANOEUVRE
Light
1 inf bde

EQUIPMENT BY TYPE
MBT 31 T-72A
RECCE 51: 10 BRDM-2; 41 M1114 HMMWV
AIFV 11: 10 BMP-2; 1 BMP-2K
APC 200
APC (T) 47: 9 *Leonidas*; 28 M113A; 10 MT-LB
APC (W) 153: 57 BTR-70; 12 BTR-80; 84 TM-170 *Hermelin*
ARTY 126
TOWED 70: **105mm** 14 M-56; **122mm** 56 M-30 M-1938
MRL 17: **122mm** 6 BM-21; **128mm** 11
MOR 39: **120mm** 39
AT • MSL • MANPATS 12 *Milan*
RCL 57mm; **82mm** M60A
AD
SAM 8 9K35 *Strela*-10 (SA-13 *Gopher*)
MANPAD 5 9K310 *Igla*-1 (SA-16 *Gimlet*)
Guns 40mm 36 L20

Marine Wing

PATROL AND COASTAL COMBATANTS 7
PCC 1 *Matsilo*
PB 6
AMPHIBIOUS • LC • LCM 1 EDIC
LOGISTICS AND SUPPORT 4:
YTB 1 *Trozona*
YTM 3

Air Wing

Air Wg is directly under Joint Operational Cmd

FORCES BY ROLE
TRANSPORT
1 (VIP) sqn with An-2 *Colt*
TRAINING
1 sqn with Bell 205 (UH-1H *Iroquois*)
1 sqn with Z-242
ATTACK HELICOPTER
1 sqn with Mi-24K *Hind* G2; Mi-24V *Hind* E
TRANSPORT HELICOPTER
1 sqn with Mi-8MTV *Hip*; Mi-17 *Hip* H

EQUIPMENT BY TYPE
AIRCRAFT
TPT • Light 1 An-2 *Colt*
TRG 5 Z-242
HELICOPTERS
ATK 4 Mi-24V *Hind* E (10: 2 Mi-24K *Hind* G2; 8 Mi-24V *Hind* E in store)
MRH 6: 4 Mi-8MTV *Hip*; 2 Mi-17 *Hip* H
TPT • Light 2 Bell 205 (UH-1H *Iroquois*)

Paramilitary

Police 7,600 (some 5,000 armed)

incl 2 SF units

EQUIPMENT BY TYPE
APC BTR APC (W)/M-113A APC (T)
HELICOPTERS 3
MRH 1 Bell 412EP *Twin Huey*
TPT • Light 2: 1 Bell 206B (AB-206B) *Jet Ranger* II; 1 Bell 212 (AB-212)

DEPLOYMENT

Legal provisions for foreign deployment of armed forces:
Constitution: Codified constitution (1991)
Specific legislation: 'Defence Law' (2005)
Decision on deployment of troops abroad: a) by the government if deployment is for humanitarian missions or military exercises; b) by the parliament if for peacekeeping operations ('Defence Law', Art. 41).

AFGHANISTAN
NATO • ISAF 158

BOSNIA-HERZEGOVINA
EU • EUFOR • *Operation Althea* 11

LEBANON
UN • UNIFIL 1

SERBIA
OSCE • Kosovo 17

Malta MLT

Maltese Lira ML		2012	2013	2014
GDP	ML	6.97bn	7.28bn	
	US$	8.69bn	9.26bn	
per capita	US$	20,852	22,193	
Growth	%	0.82	1.31	
Inflation	%	3.23	2.37	
Def exp [a]	ML	39m		
	US$	50m		
Def bdgt [a]	ML	39m	45m	
	US$	50m	60m	
US$1=ML		0.78	0.75	

[a] Excludes military pensions

Population 411,277

Age	0 – 14	15 – 19	20 – 24	25 – 29	30 – 64	65 plus
Male	7.8%	3.1%	3.5%	3.6%	24.1%	7.6%
Female	7.4%	2.9%	3.3%	3.3%	23.6%	9.6%

Capabilities

The armed forces consist of a limited number of army personnel supported by small naval and air units. Recently there have been efforts to improve maritime surveillance with the acquisition of *King Air* maritime patrol aircraft, while an AW139 is due to enter service in the search and rescue role. Malta continues to support the EU's *Operation Atalanta* counter-piracy mission, and in 2013 provided a boarding team embarked on the Dutch amphibious ship HNLMS *Johan de Witt*.

ACTIVE 1,950 (Armed Forces 1,950)

RESERVE 180 (Emergency Volunteer Reserve Force 120 Individual Reserve 60)

ORGANISATIONS BY SERVICE

Armed Forces of Malta 1,950

FORCES BY ROLE

MANOEUVRE Light

1 (1st) inf regt (3 inf coy, 1 AD/cbt spt coy)

COMBAT SUPPORT

1 (3rd) cbt spt regt (1 cbt engr sqn, 1 EOD sqn, 1 maint sqn)

1 (4th) cbt spt regt (1 CIS coy, 1 sy coy (Revenue Security Corps))

Maritime Squadron

Organised into 5 divisions: offshore patrol; inshore patrol; rapid deployment and training; marine engineering and logistics.

EQUIPMENT BY TYPE

PATROL AND COASTAL COMBATANTS 8

PCC 1 *Diciotti*

PB 7: 4 Austal 21m; 2 *Marine Protector*; 1 *Bremse* (GER)

LOGISTICS AND SUPPORT 2

AAR 2 *Cantieri Vittoria*

Air Wing

1 base party. 1 flt ops div; 1 maint div; 1 integrated log div; 1 rescue section

EQUIPMENT BY TYPE

AIRCRAFT

TPT • Light 4: 2 Beech 200 *King Air* (maritime patrol); 2 BN-2B *Islander*

TRG 3 *Bulldog* T MK1

HELICOPTERS

MRH 3 SA316B *Alouette* III

DEPLOYMENT

Legal provisions for foreign deployment:

Constitution: Codified constitution (1964)

Decision on deployment of troops abroad: The government decides on a case-by-case basis on the deployment of Maltese military personnel abroad (Malta Armed Forces Act, Chapter 220 of the Laws of Malta).

SERBIA

OSCE • Kosovo 1

UGANDA

EU • EUTM Somalia 4

FOREIGN FORCES

Italy 26; 2 Bell 212 (HH-212) hel

Montenegro MNE

Euro €		2012	2013	2014
GDP	€	3.45bn	3.58bn	
	US$	4.28bn	4.57bn	
per capita	US$	6,882	7,318	
Growth	%	0.03	1.23	
Inflation	%	3.65	2.71	
Def bdgt [a]	€	40m	40m	
	US$	52m	54m	
FMA (US)	US$	1.2m	1.2m	1.2m
US$1=€		0.78	0.75	

[a] Excludes military pensions

Population 653,474

Age	0 – 14	15 – 19	20 – 24	25 – 29	30 – 64	65 plus
Male	7.4%	2.2%	3.2%	4.4%	27.1%	5.4%
Female	7.9%	2.7%	3.2%	3.7%	24.4%	8.3%

Capabilities

In the wake of its separation from Serbia in 2006, Montenegro shifted from a conscript to a professional armed services. Force and organisational changes are under way that will likely see a further reduction in numbers, mainly in the army. The country participates in NATO's Membership Action Plan (MAP), with the aim of becoming a member of the Alliance, but its capability is limited to relatively undemanding internal security missions. Under the MAP, Montenegro has worked towards addressing sets of 'partnership goals', such as developing international defence-cooperation and training contacts. It is understood that a new Strategic Defence Review was under way in late 2013. Maintenance issues have affected operational availability of equipment.

ACTIVE 2,080 (Army 1,500 Navy 350 Air Force 230) Paramilitary 10,100

ORGANISATIONS BY SERVICE

Army 1,500

FORCES BY ROLE

SPECIAL FORCES

1 SF bde

MANOEUVRE

Reconnaissance

1 recce coy

Light

1 mot inf bde (1 SF coy, 2 inf regt (1 inf bn, 1 mtn bn), 1 arty bty, 1 cbt spt coy, 1 CBRN pl, 1 sig pl)

COMBAT SUPPORT

1 engr coy

3 sigs pl

1 MP coy

EQUIPMENT BY TYPE

APC (W) 8 BOV-VP M-86

ARTY 149

TOWED 122mm 12 D-30

MRL 128mm 18 M63/M94 *Plamen*

MOR 119: **82mm** 76; **120mm** 43

AT

SP 8 BOV-1

MSL • MANPATS 117: 71 9K111 *Fagot* (AT-4 *Spigot*); 19 9K113 *Konkurs* (AT-5 *Spandrel*); 27 9K114 *Shturm* (AT-6 *Spiral*)

Navy 350

1 Naval Cmd HQ with 4 operational naval units (patrol boat; coastal surveillance; maritime detachment and SAR) with additional sigs, log and trg units with a separate Coast Guard element. Some listed units are in the process of decommissioning.

EQUIPMENT BY TYPE

PATROL AND COASTAL COMBATANTS 5

PSO 1 *Kotor* with 1 twin 76mm gun (1 further vessel in reserve)

PCFG 2 *Rade Končar* with 2 single lnchr with P-15 *Termit* (SS-N-2B *Styx*) AShM (missiles disarmed)

PB 2 *Mirna* (Type-140) (Police units)

AMPHIBIOUS • LANDING CRAFT 5

LCU 5: 3 (Type-21); 2 (Type-22)

LOGISTICS AND SUPPORT 3

AOTL 1 *Drina*; **AET** 1 *Lubin*; **AXS** 1 *Jadran*

Air Force 230

Golubovci (Podgorica) air base under army command.

FORCES BY ROLE

TRAINING

1 (mixed) sqn with G-4 *Super Galeb*; Utva-75 (none operational)

TRANSPORT HELICOPTER

1 sqn with SA341/SA342L *Gazelle*

EQUIPMENT BY TYPE

AIRCRAFT • TRG (4 G-4 *Super Galeb* non-operational; 4 Utva-75 non-operational)

HELICOPTERS

MRH 7 SA341/SA342L *Gazelle* (8 more non-operational)

TPT • Medium (1 Mi-8T awaiting museum storage)

Paramilitary ε10,100

Montenegrin Ministry of Interior Personnel ε6,000

Special Police Units ε4,100

DEPLOYMENT

Legal provisions for foreign deployment:
Constitution: Constitution (2007)

Decision on deployment of troops abroad: The Assembly, on the proposal of the Council for Defence and Security, decide on the use of Montenegrin armed forces in international forces (Article 82, item 8).

AFGHANISTAN

NATO • ISAF 27

LIBERIA

UN • UNMIL 2 obs

SERBIA

OSCE • Kosovo 1

Multinational Organisations

Capabilities

The following represent shared capabilities held by contributors collectively rather than as part of national inventories.

ORGANISATIONS BY SERVICE

NATO AEW&C Force

Based at Geilenkirchen (GER). 12 original participating countries (BEL, CAN, DNK, GER, GRC, ITA, NLD, NOR, PRT, TUR, USA) have been subsequently joined by 5 more (CZE, ESP, HUN, POL, ROM).

FORCES BY ROLE

AIRBORNE EARLY WARNING & CONTROL

1 sqn with B-757 (trg); E-3A *Sentry* (NATO standard)

EQUIPMENT BY TYPE

AIRCRAFT

AEW&C 17 E-3A *Sentry* (NATO standard)

TPT • PAX 1 B-757 (trg)

Strategic Airlift Capability

Heavy Airlift Wing based at Papa airbase (HUN). 12 participating countries (BLG, EST, FIN, HUN, LTU, NLD, NOR, POL, ROM, SVN, SWE, USA)

EQUIPMENT BY TYPE

AIRCRAFT

TPT • Heavy 3 C-17A *Globemaster*

Strategic Airlift Interim Solution

Intended to provide strategic airlift capacity pending the delivery of A400M aircraft by leasing An-124s. 14 participating countries (BEL, CAN, CZE, DNK, FIN, FRA, GER, HUN, LUX, NOR, POL, ROM, SVK, SVN, SWE, UK)

EQUIPMENT BY TYPE

AIRCRAFT

TPT • Heavy 2 An-124-100 (4 more available on 6-9 days notice)

Netherlands NLD

Euro €		2012	2013	2014
GDP	€	609bn	624bn	
	US$	773bn	809bn	
per capita	US$	46,142	48,091	
Growth	%	-0.88	-0.53	
Inflation	%	2.82	2.82	
Def exp	€	8.07bn		
	US$	10.4bn		
Def bdgt [a]	€	8.04bn	7.79bn	7.79bn
	US$	10.3bn	10.4bn	
US$1=€		0.78	0.75	

[a] Includes military pensions

Population 16,805,037

Age	0–14	15–19	20–24	25–29	30–64	65 plus
Male	8.7%	3.0%	3.2%	3.1%	23.8%	7.6%
Female	8.3%	2.9%	3.1%	3.1%	23.7%	9.5%

Capabilities

The Netherlands is looking to meet broad security needs through its relationships with key allies, following the implementation of 2011 spending cuts and subsequent force reductions. Power projection and combat readiness have been affected by these reductions, while the organisational and personnel changes risk eroding morale. However, a late amendment to the defence budget has reduced the level of cuts and enabled the sustainment of key equipment. The intent remains to be able to field a brigade-size contribution on international operations and to provide battalion-level support for long-term stabilisation operations. The armed forces also maintain a commitment to the NATO rapid response force, including a mine-hunter, mechanised infantry and F-16s. The air force has taken delivery of two F-35A test aircraft, but these are currently in storage pending a decision on the Netherlands' future involvement in the programme. Irrespective of recent challenges, the armed forces remain a motivated and professional force capable of participating in demanding joint operations in a NATO Alliance context.

ACTIVE 37,400 (Army 20,850; Navy 8,500; Air 8,050) Military Constabulary 5,900

RESERVE 3,200 (Army 2,700; Navy 80; Air 420) Military Constabulary 80

Reserve liability to age 35 for soldiers/sailors, 40 for NCOs, 45 for officers

ORGANISATIONS BY SERVICE

Army 20,850

FORCES BY ROLE

COMMAND

elm 1 (GER/NLD) Corps HQ

SPECIAL FORCES

5 SF coy (4 land, 1 maritime)

MANOEUVRE

Reconnaissance

1 ISTAR bn (2 armd recce sqn, 1 EW coy, 1 arty bty, 1 UAV bty)

Mechanised

2 (13th & 43rd) mech bde (1 armd recce sqn, 2 armd inf bn, 1 SP arty bn (2 bty), 1 engr bn, 1 maint coy, 1 medical coy)

Air Manoeuvre

1 (11th) air mob bde (3 air mob inf bn, 1 mor coy, 1 AD coy, 1 engr coy, 1 med coy, 1 supply coy, 1 maint coy)

COMBAT SUPPORT

1 AD comd (3 AD bty)

1 CIMIC bn

1 engr bn

48 EOD teams

1 (CIS) sigs bn

1 CBRN coy

COMBAT SERVICE SUPPORT

1 med bn

5 fd hospital

3 maint coy

2 tpt bn

Reserves 2,700 reservists

National Command

Cadre bde and corps tps completed by call-up of reservists (incl Territorial Comd)

FORCES BY ROLE

MANOEUVRE

Light

3 inf bn (could be mob for territorial def)

EQUIPMENT BY TYPE

RECCE 305: 296 *Fennek;* 9 *Fuchs* Tpz-1 CBRN recce

AIFV 184 CV9035N

APC 177
APC (W) 92: 8 *Boxer* (driver trg); 14 M577A1; 70 XA-188
PPV 85 *Bushmaster* IMV
ARTY 61:
SP 155mm 18 PzH 2000
MOR 43: **81mm** 27 L16/M1 **120mm** 16 Brandt
AT
MSL
SP 40 *Fennek* MRAT
MANPATS 297 *Spike*-MR (*Gil*)
RL 1,381 Pzf
AD • SAM
SP 36: 18 *Fennek* with FIM-92A *Stinger*; 18 MB with FIM-92A *Stinger*
MANPAD 18 FIM-92A *Stinger*
RADAR • LAND 6+: 6 AN/TPQ-36 *Firefinder* (arty, mor); WALS; *Squire*
AEV 35+: 10 *Kodiak*; 20 *Leopard* 1; YPR-806 A1
ARV 77+: 25 *Büffel*; 52 *Leopard* 1; YPR-809
VLB 8 *Leopard* 1
MW Bozena

Navy 8,500 (incl Marines)

EQUIPMENT BY TYPE
SUBMARINES • TACTICAL • SSK 4:
4 *Walrus* with 4 single 533mm TT with Mk48 *Sea Arrow* HWT (equipped for UGM-84C *Harpoon* AShM, but none embarked)
PRINCIPAL SURFACE COMBATANTS 6
DESTROYERS • DDGHM 4:
4 *Zeven Provinciën* with 2 quad Mk141 lnchr with RGM-84F *Harpoon* AShM, 1 40-cell Mk41 VLS with SM-2MR/ESSM SAM, 2 twin 324mm ASTT with Mk46 LWT, 1 *Goalkeeper* CIWS, 1 127mm gun, (capacity 1 NH90 hel)
FRIGATES • FFGHM 2:
2 *Karel Doorman* with 2 quad Mk141 lnchr with RGM-84A/C *Harpoon* AShM, 1 Mk48 VLS with RIM-7P *Sea Sparrow* SAM, 2 twin 324mm ASTT with Mk46 LWT, 1 76mm gun, (capacity 1 NH90 hel)
PATROL AND COASTAL COMBATANTS • PSOH 3 *Holland* with 1 76mm gun (capacity 1 NH90 hel) (1 further vessel undergoing trials)
MINE WARFARE • MINE COUNTERMEASURES • MHO 6 *Alkmaar* (*tripartite*)
AMPHIBIOUS
PRINCIPAL AMPHIBIOUS SHIPS • LPD 2:
1 *Rotterdam* with 2 *Goalkeeper* CIWS, (capacity 4 NH90/AS532 *Cougar* hel; either 6 LCVP or 2 LCU and 3 LCVP; either 170 APC or 33 MBT; 538 troops)
1 *Johan de Witt* with 2 *Goalkeeper* CIWS, (capacity 6 NH90 hel or 4 AS532 *Cougar* hel; either 6 LCVP or 2 LCU and 3 LCVP; either 170 APC or 33 MBT; 700 troops)
LANDING CRAFT 17:
LCU 5 Mk9
LCVP 12 Mk5
LOGISTICS AND SUPPORT 32
AGS 2 *Snellius*
AK 1 *Pelikaan*
AORH 1 *Amsterdam* (capacity 2 NH90 hel) with 1 *Goalkeeper* CIWS
AOT 1 *Patria*
ASL 1 *Mercuur*
AXL 2: 1 Thetis (diving trg); 1 *Van Kingsbergen*
AXS 1 *Urania*
YDT 5: 4 *Cerberus*; 1 *Soemba*
YFL 6
YTM 5 *Linge*
YTL 7 *Breezand*

Marines 2,654 FORCES BY ROLE
MANOEUVRE
Amphibious
2 mne bn (1 integrated with UK mne bde to form UK/NLD Amphibious Landing Force)
COMBAT SUPPORT
1 amph cbt spt bn (some SF units, 1 recce coy, 1 AD pl, 2 amph beach units, 1 (Maritime Joint Effect) bty)
COMBAT SERVICE SUPPORT
1 spt bn (2 spt units, 1 sea-based spt gp, 2 medical facility)

EQUIPMENT BY TYPE
APC (T) 151: 87 Bv-206D; 73 BvS-10 *Viking*
ARTY • MOR 18: **81mm** 12 L16/M1; **120mm** 6 Brandt
AT • MSL • MANPATS 24 MRAT *Gil*
RL 84mm 144 *Pantserfaust* III Dynarange 2000
AD • SAM • MANPAD 4 FIM-92A *Stinger*
ARV 5 BvS-10
MED 4 BvS-10

Air Force 8,050

Flying hours 180 hrs/year

FORCES BY ROLE
FIGHTER/GROUND ATTACK
4 sqn with F-16AM/BM *Fighting Falcon*
ANTI-SUBMARINE WARFARE/SEARCH & RESCUE
1 sqn with NH90 NFH
SEARCH & RESCUE
1 sqn with Bell 412SP (AB-412SP *Griffin*)
TANKER/TRANSPORT
1 sqn with C-130H/C-130H-30 *Hercules*; DC-10/KDC-10; Gulfstream IV
TRAINING
1 sqn with PC-7 *Turbo Trainer*
ATTACK HELICOPTER
1 sqn with AH-64D *Apache*
TRANSPORT HELICOPTER
1 sqn with AS532U2 *Cougar* II
1 sqn with CH-47D/F *Chinook*
AIR DEFENCE
4 sqn (total: 7 AD Team. 4 AD bty with MIM-104 *Patriot* (TMD capable))

EQUIPMENT BY TYPE
AIRCRAFT 74 combat capable
FTR 72 F-16AM/BM *Fighting Falcon*
FGA 2 F-35A *Lightning* II (in test)
TKR 2 KDC-10

TPT 6: **Medium** 4: 2 C-130H *Hercules*; 2 C-130H-30 *Hercules*; **PAX** 2: 1 DC-10; 1 Gulfstream IV
TRG 13 PC-7 *Turbo Trainer*

HELICOPTERS
ATK 29 AH-64D *Apache*
ASW 8 NH90 NFH
MRH 7: 3 Bell 412 (AB-412SP *Griffin*); 4 SA316 *Alouette* III
TPT 25: **Heavy** 17: 11 CH-47D *Chinook*; 6 CH-47F *Chinook*; **Medium** 8 AS532U2 *Cougar* II

AD • SAM
TOWED 20 MIM-104 *Patriot* (TMD Capable/PAC-3 msl)
MANPAD FIM-92A *Stinger*

MSL
AAM • IR AIM-9L/M/N **ARH** AIM-120B AMRAAM
ASM AGM-114K *Hellfire*; AGM-65D/G *Maverick*

BOMBS
Conventional Mk 82; Mk 84
Laser-guided GBU-10/GBU-12 *Paveway* II; GBU-24 *Paveway* III (all supported by LANTIRN)

Paramilitary

Royal Military Constabulary 5,900

Subordinate to the Ministry of Defence, but performs most of its work under the authority of other ministries.

FORCES BY ROLE
MANOEUVRE
Other
6 paramilitary district (total: 60 paramilitary 'bde')

EQUIPMENT BY TYPE
AIFV 24 YPR-765

Cyber

In early 2011, the Dutch defence minister indicated that cyber defence would attract some of the Netherlands' declining budget and, between 2011–2015, around €30 million plus staff would be allocated, with full capability by 2016. In June 2012, the defence ministry launched a Defence Cyber Strategy to direct military cyber efforts. Among other elements, the strategy is intended to strengthen cyber defence, and 'develop the military capability to conduct cyber operations (offensive element)'. While a separate cyber service will not be established by the MoD, 'relevant cyber capabilities will be incorporated within the Defence Cyber Command, which will come under the [...] management of the [...] army'. A broader National Cyber Security Strategy was published in 2011. A National Security Centre was launched in January 2012. The Netherlands has a national CERT, is involved in informal CERT communities, and is a member of the European Government CERTs group (EGC).

DEPLOYMENT

Legal provisions for foreign deployment:
Constitution: Codified constitution (1815)
Decision on deployment of troops abroad: By the government (Art. 98)

AFGHANISTAN
NATO • ISAF 400
UN • UNAMA 1

BOSNIA-HERZEGOVINA
EU • EUFOR • *Operation Althea* 3

DEMOCRATIC REPUBLIC OF THE CONGO
EU • EUSEC RD Congo 3

GULF OF ADEN & SOMALI BASIN
NATO • *Operation Ocean Shield* 1 LPD

MIDDLE EAST
UN • UNTSO 12 obs

NORTH SEA
NATO • SNMCMG 1: 1 MHO

SERBIA
NATO • KFOR 7

SOUTH SUDAN
UN • UNMISS 7; 2 obs

SYRIA/ISRAEL
UN • UNDOF 2

TURKEY
NATO • *Active Fence*: 2 AD bty with MIM-104 *Patriot*

FOREIGN FORCES

United Kingdom Air Force 90
United States US European Command: 400

Norway NOR

Norwegian Kroner kr		2012	2013	2014
GDP	kr	3.04tr	3.16tr	
	US$	501bn	537bn	
per capita	US$	99,462	105,478	
Growth	%	2.99	2.46	
Inflation	%	0.71	1.50	
Def exp	kr	41.6bn		
	US$	7.14bn		
Def bdgt	kr	40.6bn	42.5bn	
	US$	6.97bn	7.52bn	
US$1=kr		5.82	5.65	

Population 4,722,701

Age	0–14	15–19	20–24	25–29	30–64	65 plus
Male	8.9%	3.4%	3.4%	3.0%	23.4%	7.4%
Female	8.6%	3.3%	3.3%	3.0%	23.0%	9.4%

Capabilities

Norway maintains small but capable armed forces focused largely on territorial defence, particularly in the High North. This ensures that the armed forces possess cold-weather warfare skills. Norway has been less constrained by the spending difficulties that in recent years have beset other European states and has been able to invest in acquisitions, including destroyers and equipment necessary to sustain its presence in the Arctic region

Europe

amid the retreat of seasonal sea-ice. However, these have also added a new element to the country's maritime capabilities. During the Cold War, Norway relied on small attack craft and submarines to pursue a policy of sea-denial; now, it is able to deploy further from its coast with more muscular surface platforms. The shift of the National Joint Headquarters from Jåttå to Bodø in northern Norway in August 2009 also reflected the importance of the Arctic to Oslo. Norway places importance on its alliances, particularly with European states and NATO. Given the small size of the armed forces, Norway relies on conscription for current personnel levels and reserves for crisis deployment. Conscripts comprise approximately one-third of the armed forces at any one point, affecting the level of training and readiness. Whilst Norway has made significant contributions to ISAF, this has depressed land-force readiness for other tasks.

ACTIVE 25,800 (Army 9,350, Navy 4,500, Air 3,950, Central Support 7,500, Home Guard 500)

Conscript liability 18 months maximum. Conscripts first serve 12 months from 19–21, and then up to 4–5 refresher training periods until age 35, 44, 55 or 60 depending on rank and function. Active numbers include conscripts on initial service.

RESERVE 45,940 (Army 270, Navy 320, Central Support 350, Home Guard 45,000)

Readiness varies from a few hours to several days

ORGANISATIONS BY SERVICE

Army 4,500; 4,850 conscript (total 9,350)

The mechanised brigade – Brigade North – trains new personnel of all categories and provides units for international operations. At any time around one-third of the brigade will be trained and ready to conduct operations. The brigade includes one high-readiness mechanised battalion (Telemark Battalion) with combat support and combat service support units on high readiness.

FORCES BY ROLE

MANOEUVRE

Reconnaissance

1 (Border Guard) lt bn (3 coy (HQ/garrison, border control & trg))

Mechanised

1 mech inf bde (1 ISTAR bn, 2 mech inf bn, 1 lt inf bn, 1 arty bn, 1 engr bn, 1 MP coy, 1 CIS bn, 1 spt bn, 1 med bn)

Light

1 bn (His Majesty The King's Guards)

EQUIPMENT BY TYPE

MBT 52 *Leopard* 2A4

RECCE *Fuchs* CBRN recce

AIFV 104 CV9030N

APC 410

APC (T) 315 M113 (incl variants)

APC (W) 75 XA-186 *Sisu*/XA-200 *Sisu*

PPV 20 *Dingo* II

ARTY 204

SP 155mm 18 M109A3GN

MOR 186:

SP 81mm 36: 24 M106A1; 12 M125A2

81mm 150 L-16

AT

MANPATS *Javelin*

RCL 84mm *Carl Gustav*

RADAR • LAND 12 ARTHUR

AEV 22 *Alvis*

ARV 9+: 3 M88A1; M578; 6 *Leopard* 1

VLB 35: 26 *Leguan*; 9 *Leopard* 1

MW 9 910 MCV-2

Navy 2,450; 2,050 conscripts (total 4,500)

Joint Command – Norwegian National Joint Headquarters. The Royal Norwegian Navy is organised into four elements under the command of the chief of staff of the Navy; the naval units *'Kysteskadren'*, the schools *'Sjoforsvarets Skoler'*, the naval bases and the coast guard *'Kystvakten'*.

FORCES BY ROLE

MANOEUVRE

Reconnaissance

1 ISTAR coy (Coastal Rangers)

COMBAT SUPPORT

1 EOD pl

EQUIPMENT BY TYPE

SUBMARINES • TACTICAL • SSK 6 *Ula* with 8 single 533mm TT with A3 *Seal* DM2 HWT

PRINCIPAL SURFACE COMBATANTS 5

DESTROYERS • DDGHM 5 *Fridtjof Nansen* with 2 quad lnchr with NSM AShM, 1 8-cell Mk41 VLS with ESSM SAM, 2 twin 324mm ASTT with *Sting Ray* LWT, 1 76mm gun, (capacity 1 NH90 hel)

PATROL AND COASTAL COMBATANTS • PCFGM 6 *Skjold* with 8 single lnchr with NSM AShM, 1 twin lnchr with *Mistral* SAM, 1 76mm gun

MINE WARFARE • MINE COUNTERMEASURES 6:

MSC 3 *Alta*

MHC 3 *Oksoy*

AMPHIBIOUS • LANDING CRAFT • LCP 16 S90N

LOGISTICS AND SUPPORT 20

AGI 1 *Marjata* with 1 hel landing platform

AGDS 1 *Tyr*

AGS 6: 1 *HU Sverdrup II; 4 Oljevern*; 1 *Geofjord*

ATS 1 *Valkyrien*

AXL 5: 2 *Hessa*; 2 *Kvarnen; 1 Reine*

YAC 1 *Norge*

YDT 5

Coast Guard

PATROL AND COASTAL COMBATANTS 15

PSO 8: 3 *Barentshav*; 1 *Svalbard* with 1 57mm gun, 1 hel landing platform; 1 *Harstad*; 3 *Nordkapp* with 1 57mm gun, 1 hel landing platform

PCO 7: 1 *Aalesund*; 5 *Nornen*; *1 Reine*

Air Force 2,800; 1150 conscript (total 3,950)

Joint Command – Norwegian National HQ

Flying hours 180 hrs/year

FORCES BY ROLE

FIGHTER/GROUND ATTACK
3 sqn with F-16AM/BM *Fighting Falcon*

MARITIME PATROL
1 sqn with P-3C *Orion*; P-3N *Orion* (pilot trg)

ELECTRONIC WARFARE
1 sqn with *Falcon* 20C (EW, Flight Inspection Service)

SEARCH & RESCUE
1 sqn with *Sea King* Mk43B

TRANSPORT
1 sqn with C-130J-30 *Hercules*

TRAINING
1 sqn with MFI-15 SAAB *Safari*

TRANSPORT HELICOPTER
2 sqn with Bell 412SP *Twin Huey*
1 sqn with *Lynx* Mk86
1 sqn with NH90 (forming)

AIR DEFENCE
1 bty(+) with NASAMS II

EQUIPMENT BY TYPE

AIRCRAFT 63 combat capable
FTR 57: 47 F-16AM *Fighting Falcon*; 10 F-16BM *Fighting Falcon*
ASW 6: 4 P-3C *Orion*; 2 P-3N *Orion* (pilot trg)
EW 3 *Falcon* 20C
TPT • Medium 4 C-130J-30 *Hercules*
TRG 16 MFI-15 *Safari*

HELICOPTERS
ASW 8: 5 *Lynx* Mk86 ; 3 NH90 NFH (delivery schedule of all 14 revised to an FOC of 2017)
SAR 12 *Sea King* Mk43B
MRH 18: 6 Bell 412HP; 12 Bell 412SP

AD
SAM • TOWED NASAMS II

MSL
AAM • IR AIM-9L *Sidewinder*; **IIR** IRIS-T; **ARH** AIM-120B AMRAAM

BOMBS
Laser-guided: EGBU-12 *Paveway* II
INS/GPS guided: JDAM

Special Operations Command (NORSOCOM)

FORCES BY ROLE

SPECIAL FORCES
1 (army) SF comd (2 SF gp)
1 (navy SF comd (1 SF gp)

Central Support, Administration and Command 6,500; 1,000 conscripts (total 6,500)

Central Support, Administration and Command includes military personnel in all joint elements and they are responsible for logistics and CIS in support of all forces in Norway and abroad.

Home Guard 550 (45,000 reserves)

The Home Guard is a separate organisation, but closely cooperates with all services. The Home Guard can be mobilised on very short notice for local security operations.

Land Home Guard 41,150 with reserves

11 Home Guard Districts with mobile Rapid Reaction Forces (3,000 troops in total) as well as reinforcements and follow-on forces (38,150 troops in total).

Naval Home Guard 1,900 with reserves

Consisting of Rapid Reaction Forces (500 troops), and 17 'Naval Home Guard Areas'. A number of civilian vessels can be requisitioned as required.

EQUIPMENT BY TYPE

PATROL AND COASTAL COMBATANTS • PB 11: 4 *Harek*; 2 *Gyda*; 5 Alusafe 1290

Air Home Guard 1,450 with reserves

Provides force protection and security detachments for air bases.

Cyber

The 2012 Cyber Security Strategy for Norway contains cross-governmental guidelines for cyber defence. Nor-CERT, part of the National Security Authority, is responsible for information exchange and cooperation at the operational level. Norwegian Armed Forces Cyber Defence supports the armed forces with establishing, operating and protecting networks. It is responsible for defending military networks against cyber attack.

DEPLOYMENT

Legal provisions for foreign deployment:
Constitution: Codified constitution (1814)
Decision on deployment of troops abroad: By royal prerogative exercised by the government (Art. 25, 26).

AFGHANISTAN
NATO • ISAF 111
UN • UNAMA 2 obs

EGYPT
MFO 3

GULF OF ADEN & SOMALI BASIN
NATO • *Operation Ocean Shield* 1 FFGHM

MIDDLE EAST
UN • UNTSO 13 obs

NORTH SEA
NATO • SNMCMG 1: 1 MSC

SERBIA
NATO • KFOR 4
OSCE • Serbia 2
UN • UNMIK 1

SOUTH SUDAN
UN • UNMISS 12; 4 obs

FOREIGN FORCES

United States US European Command: 1 (APS) 155mm SP Arty bn eqpt set

Poland POL

Polish Zloty z		2012	2013	2014
GDP	z	1.63tr	1.7tr	
	US$	488bn	513bn	
per capita	US$	12,538	13,075	
Growth	%	2.05	1.31	
Inflation	%	3.68	1.85	
Def bdgt [a]	z	27.8bn	31.2bn	31.7bn
	US$	8.54bn	9.83bn	
FMA (US)	US$	24m	24m	14m
US$1=z		3.26	3.17	

[a] Excludes military pensions

Population 38,383,809

Age	0–14	15–19	20–24	25–29	30–64	65 plus
Male	7.5%	2.9%	3.4%	4.1%	25.0%	5.6%
Female	7.1%	2.7%	3.3%	4.0%	25.6%	8.9%

Capabilities

Since ending conscription in 2009, Poland has restructured its armed forces, with the focus on smaller, more capable services. The 2011 Strategic Defence Review set out the general aims and development of the military over the next 25 years. NATO membership is a key pillar of Polish defence policy; it is a member of NATO's Multinational Corps Northeast, and is a regular participant in NATO and EU exercises and operations. Soviet-era equipment is being phased out as part of a broad re-equipment programme, though some projects have already fallen victim to funding pressures. Within the army, the emphasis is on expanding deployable forces, with increased helicopter support. Mobility is aided by involvement in the Strategic Airlift Capability's C-17 unit, with the air force also operating its own tactical transport aircraft. The navy is presently structured around a fleet of frigates and corvettes, with longer-term plans looking to a multi-role corvette.

ACTIVE 99,300 **(Army 48,200, Navy 7,700, Air 16,600, Special Forces 3,000, Joint 23,800)**
Paramilitary 73,400

ORGANISATIONS BY SERVICE

Land Forces Command 48,200

Land Forces Command controls airmobile bdes and their avn. Transition to lighter forces is continuing but is hampered by lack of funds.

FORCES BY ROLE

COMMAND
1 (2nd) mech corps HQ
elm 1 (MNC NE) corps HQ

MANOEUVRE

Reconnaissance
3 recce regt

Armoured
1 (11th) armd cav div (2 armd bde, 1 mech bde)

Mechanised
1 (12th) div (2 mech bde, 1 (coastal) mech bde)
1 (16th) div (2 armd bde, 2 mech bde)
1 (21st) mech bde (1 armd bn, 3 mech bn, 1 arty bn, 1 AD bn, 1 engr bn)

Air Manoeuvre
1 (6th) air aslt bde (3 air aslt bn)
1 (25th) air cav bde (3 air cav bn, 2 tpt hel bn, 1 (casevac) med unit)

Aviation
1 (1st) avn bde (2 atk hel sqn with Mi-24D/V *Hind* D/E, 1 CSAR sqn with Mi-24V *Hind* E; PZL W-3PL *Gluszec*; 2 ISR hel sqn with Mi-2URP; 2 hel sqn with Mi-2)

COMBAT SUPPORT
3 arty regt
2 engr regt
1 ptn br regt
2 chem regt
3 AD regt

EQUIPMENT BY TYPE

MBT 893: 128 *Leopard* 2A4; 232 PT-91 *Twardy*; 533 T-72/T-72M1D/T-72M1
RECCE 366: 237 BRDM-2; 37 BWR; 92 WD R-5
AIFV 1,867: 1,297 BMP-1; 570 *Rosomak*
APC • PPV 70: 40 *Cougar* (on loan from US); 30 *Maxxpro*
ARTY 783
SP 401: **122mm** 290 2S1; **152mm** 111 M-77 *Dana*
MRL **122mm** 180: 75 BM-21; 30 RM-70; 75 WR-40 *Langusta*
MOR 202: **98mm** 98 M-98; **120mm** 104 M120
AT • MSL • MANPATS 9K11 *Malyutka* (AT-3 *Sagger*); 9K111 *Fagot* (AT-4 *Spigot*); *Spike*-LR
AD
SAM
SP 64 9K33 *Osa*-AK (SA-8 *Gecko*)
MANPAD 9K32 *Strela*-2 (SA-7 *Grail*); GROM
GUNS 352
SP 23mm 28: 8 ZSU-23-4; 20 ZSU-23-4MP *Biala*
TOWED 23mm 324; 252 ZU-23-2; 72 ZUR-23-2KG/PG
RADAR • LAND 3 LIWIEC (veh, arty)
HELICOPTERS
ATK 28 Mi-24D/V *Hind* D/E
MRH 64: 7 Mi-8MT *Hip*; 4 Mi-17 *Hip* H; 2 Mi-17AE *Hip* (aeromedical); 5 Mi-17-1V *Hip*; 18 PZL Mi-2URP *Hoplite*; 24 PZL W-3W/WA *Sokol*; 4 PZL W-3PL *Gluszec* (CSAR)
TPT 41: **Medium** 14 Mi-8T *Hip*; **Light** 27: 25 PZL Mi-2 *Hoplite*; 2 PZL W-3AE *Sokol* (aeromedical)
AEV IWT; MT-LB
ARV 65+: 10 *Leopard* 1; 15 MT-LB; TRI; WPT-TOPAS; 40 WZT-3
VLB 52: 4 *Biber*; 48 BLG67M2
MW 18: 14 Bozena; 4 *Kalina* SUM

Navy 7,700

EQUIPMENT BY TYPE

SUBMARINES • TACTICAL 5:

SSK 5:

4 *Sokol* (NOR Type-207) with 8 single 533mm TT

1 *Orzel* (FSU *Kilo*) with 6 single 533mm TT each with T-53/T-65 HWT

PRINCIPAL SURFACE COMBATANTS 2

FRIGATES • FFGHM 2 *Pulaski* (US *Oliver Hazard Perry*) with 1 Mk13 GMLS with RGM-84D/F *Harpoon* AShM/ SM-1MR SAM, 2 triple 324mm ASTT with MU90 LWT, 1 *Phalanx* Block 1B CIWS, 1 76mm gun, (capacity 2 SH-2G *Super Seasprite* ASW hel) (1 vessel used as training ship)

PATROL AND COASTAL COMBATANTS 6

CORVETTES • FSM 1 *Kaszub* with 2 quad lnchr with 9K32 *Strela-2* (SA-N-5 *Grail*) SAM, 2 twin 533mm ASTT with SET-53 HWT, 2 RBU 6000 *Smerch* 2, 1 76mm gun

PCFGM 5:

3 *Orkan* (GDR *Sassnitz*) with 1 quad lnchr with RBS-15 Mk3 AShM, 1 quad lnchr (manual aiming) with *Strela-2* (SA-N-5 *Grail*) SAM, 1 AK630 CIWS, 1 76mm gun

2 *Tarantul* with 2 twin lnchr with P-21/22 *Termit*-M (SS-N-2C/D *Styx*) AShM, 1 quad lnchr (manual aiming) with 9K32 *Strela-2* (SA-N-5 *Grail*) SAM, 2 AK630 CIWS, 1 76mm gun

MINE WARFARE • MINE COUNTERMEASURES 21:

MCCS 1 Project 890

MHI 4 *Mamry*

MHO 3 *Krogulec*

MSI 13 *Goplo*

AMPHIBIOUS 8

LANDING SHIPS • LSM 5 *Lublin* (capacity 9 tanks; 135 troops)

LANDING CRAFT • LCU 3 *Deba* (capacity 50 troops)

LOGISTICS AND SUPPORT 38

AGI 2 *Moma*

AGS 8: 2 *Heweliusz*; 6 (coastal)

AORL 1 *Baltyk*

AOL 1 *Moskit*

ARS 4: 2 *Piast*; 2 *Zbyszko*

ATF 2

AX 1 *Wodnik* with 1 twin AK630 CIWS

AXS 1 *Iskra*

YDG 2 *Mrowka*

YDT 3

YFB 7

YPT 1 *Kormoran*

YTM 5

Naval Aviation 1,300

FORCES BY ROLE

ANTI SUBMARINE WARFARE/SEARCH & RESCUE

1 sqn with MI-14PL *Haze* A; MI-14PS *Haze* C

1 sqn with PZL W-3RM *Anakonda*; SH-2G *Super Seasprite*

TRANSPORT

1 sqn with An-28B1R; An-28E

1 sqn with An-28TD; Mi-17 *Hip* H; PZL Mi-2 *Hoplite*; PZL W-3RM; PZL W-3T

EQUIPMENT BY TYPE

AIRCRAFT

MP 10: 8 An-28B1R *Bryza*; 2 An-28E *Bryza* (ecological monitoring)

TPT • Light 4 An-28TD *Bryza*

HELICOPTERS

ASW 12: 8 Mi-14PL *Haze*; 4 SH-2G *Super Seasprite*

MRH 2 Mi-17 *Hip* H

SAR 9: 2 Mi-14PS *Haze* C; 7 PZL W-3RM *Anakonda*

TPT 7: **Medium** 2 PZL W-3T *Sokol*; **Light** 5 PZL Mi-2 *Hoplite*

Air Force 16,600

Flying hours 160 to 200 hrs/year

FORCES BY ROLE

FIGHTER

2 sqn with MiG-29A/UB *Fulcrum*

FIGHTER/GROUND ATTACK

3 sqn with F-16C/D Block 52+ *Fighting Falcon*

FIGHTER/GROUND ATTACK/ISR

2 sqn with Su-22M-4 *Fitter*

SEARCH AND RESCUE

1 sqn with Mi-2; PZL W-3 *Sokol*

TRANSPORT

1 sqn with C-130E; PZL M-28 *Bryza*

1 sqn with C-295M; PZL M-28 *Bryza*

1 VIP sqn with PZL M-28 *Bryza*

TRAINING

1 sqn with PZL-130 *Orlik*

1 sqn with TS-11 *Iskra*

1 hel sqn with SW-4 *Puszczyk*

TRANSPORT HELICOPTER

1 (Spec Ops) sqn with Mi-17 *Hip* H

1 (VIP) sqn with Mi-8; W-3WA *Sokol*

AIR DEFENCE

1 bde with S-125 *Neva* SC (SA-3 *Goa*); S-200C *Vega* (SA-5 *Gammon*)

EQUIPMENT BY TYPE

AIRCRAFT 106 combat capable

FTR 32: 26 MiG-29A *Fulcrum*; 6 MiG-29UB *Fulcrum*

FGA 74: 36 F-16C Block 52+ *Fighting Falcon*; 12 F-16D Block 52+ *Fighting Falcon*; 26 Su-22M-4 *Fitter*

TPT 44: **Medium** 5 C-130E *Hercules*; **Light** 39: 16 C-295M; 23 M-28 *Bryza* TD

TRG 60: 28 PZL-130 *Orlik*; 32 TS-11 *Iskra*

HELICOPTERS

MRH 4 Mi-17 *Hip* H

TPT 72: **Medium** 32: 9 Mi-8 *Hip*; 20 PZL W-3 *Sokol*; 3 PZL W-3WA *Sokol* (VIP); **Light** 40: 16 PZL Mi-2 *Hoplite*; 24 SW-4 *Puszczyk* (trg)

AD • SAM

SP 17 S-125 *Neva* SC (SA-3 *Goa*)

STATIC 1 S-200C *Vega* (SA-5 *Gammon*)

MSL

AAM • IR R-60 (AA-8 *Aphid*); R-73 (AA-11 *Archer*); AIM-9 *Sidewinder*; R-27T (AA-10B *Alamo*); **ARH** AIM-120C AMRAAM

ASM AGM-65J/G *Maverick*; Kh-25 (AS-10 *Karen*); Kh-29 (AS-14 *Kedge*)

Special Forces 3,000

FORCES BY ROLE

SPECIAL FORCES

3 SF units (GROM, FORMOZA & cdo)

COMBAT SUPPORT/

1 cbt spt unit (AGAT)

COMBAT SERVICE SUPPORT

1 spt unit (NIL)

Paramilitary 73,400

Border Guards 14,300

Ministry of Interior

Maritime Border Guard 3,700

PATROL AND COASTAL COMBATANTS 18

PCC 2 *Kaper*

PBF 6: 2 *Straznik*; 4 IC16M

PB 10: 2 *Wisloka*; 2 *Baltic* 24; 6 others

AMPHIBIOUS • LANDING CRAFT • LCAC 2 Griffon 2000TDX

Prevention Units (Police) 59,100

Anti-terrorist Operations Bureau n.k.

Ministry of Interior

Cyber

Poland has both national and government CERTs and is involved in informal CERT communities. A national cyber strategy is in the process of being drafted and Poland is an active participant in international cyber exercises.

DEPLOYMENT

Legal provisions for foreign deployment:

Constitution: Codified constitution (1997); Act on Principles of Use or External Deployment of the Polish Armed Forces (17/12/1998)

Decision on deployment of troops abroad: a) By president on request of prime minister in cases of direct threat (Art. 136);

b) in general, specified by ratified international agreement or statute (both must be passed by parliament, Art. 117)

AFGHANISTAN

NATO • ISAF 1,177; 1 air cav bde (1 inf BG); 5 Mi-24 *Hind*; 4 Mi-17 *Hip*

UN • UNAMA 1 obs

ARMENIA/AZERBAIJAN

OSCE • Minsk Conference 1

BOSNIA-HERZEGOVINA

EU • EUFOR • *Operation Althea* 34

OSCE • Bosnia and Herzegovina 2

CÔTE D'IVOIRE

UN • UNOCI 2 obs

DEMOCRATIC REPUBLIC OF THE CONGO

UN • MONUSCO 1 obs

LIBERIA

UN • UNMIL 1 obs

MALI

EU • EUTM Mali 20

MOLDOVA

OSCE • Moldova 1

NORTH SEA

NATO • SNMCMG 1: 1 MCCS

SERBIA

NATO • KFOR 228; 1 inf coy

OSCE • Kosovo 4

UN • UNMIK 1 obs

SOUTH SUDAN

UN • UNMISS 2 obs

WESTERN SAHARA

UN • MINURSO 1 obs

FOREIGN FORCES

Germany 67 (elm Corps HQ (multinational))

Portugal PRT

Euro €		2012	2013	2014
GDP	€	164bn	167bn	
	US$	213bn	218bn	
per capita	US$	20,179	20,689	
Growth	%	-3.17	-2.32	
Inflation	%	2.78	0.70	
Def bdgt	€	2.05bn	2.09bn	1.94bn
	US$	2.64bn	2.77bn	
US$1=€		0.78	0.75	

Population 10,799,270

Age	0–14	15–19	20–24	25–29	30–64	65 plus
Male	8.3%	2.9%	3.1%	3.3%	23.5%	7.5%
Female	7.7%	2.6%	2.8%	3.0%	24.4%	10.9%

Capabilities

Homeland defence, supporting NATO Article Five and UN-, EU- and NATO-led operations, along with maritime security, are core roles for the country's armed forces. As with several southern European states, Portugal has been badly affected by Europe's economic crisis. This is apparent partly in the number of procurement projects that have been cut or shelved. Armoured vehicle and rotary-wing projects have all been hit. An offshore patrol vessel programme was shelved after the delivery of the first of its class. The aim remains to be able to deploy a battalion-size force in a high-intensity conflict as part of NATO operations, while also being able to support similar-sized peace support or humanitarian missions. A brigade-level deployment could be sustained, but only for a limited period. The pressures on the armed forces have likely had a negative impact on morale, while the cuts are also hitting readiness.

ACTIVE 42,600 (Army 25,700 Navy 9,700 Air 7,200) Paramilitary 47,700

RESERVE 211,950 (Army 210,000 Navy 1,250, Air Force 700)
Reserve obligation to age 35

ORGANISATIONS BY SERVICE

Army 25,700
5 territorial comd (2 mil region, 1 mil district, 2 mil zone)

FORCES BY ROLE
SPECIAL FORCES
1 SF unit
MANOEUVRE
Reconnaissance
1 ISTAR bn
Mechanised
1 mech bde (1 cav tp, 1 tk regt, 2 mech inf bn, 1 arty bn. 1 AD bty, 1 engr coy, 1 sigs coy, 1 spt bn)
1 (intervention) bde (1 cav tp, 1 recce regt, 2 mech inf bn, 1 arty bn, 1 AD bty, 1 engr coy, 1 sigs coy, 1 spt bn)
Air Manoeuvre
1 (rapid reaction) bde (1 cav tp, 1 cdo bn, 2 para bn, 1 arty bn, 1 AD bty, 1 engr coy, 1 sigs coy, 1 spt bn)
Other
1 (Madeira) inf gp (2 inf bn, 1 AD bty)
1 (Azores) inf gp (1 inf bn, 1 AD bty)
COMBAT SUPPORT
1 STA bty
1 AD bn
1 engr bn
1 EOD unit
1 ptn br coy
1 EW coy
2 MP coy
1 CBRN coy
1 psyops unit
1 CIMIC coy (joint)
1 sigs bn
COMBAT SERVICE SUPPORT
1 construction coy
1 maint coy
1 log coy
1 tpt coy
1 med unit

Reserves 210,000
FORCES BY ROLE
MANOEUVRE
Light
3 (territorial) def bde (on mobilisation)

EQUIPMENT BY TYPE
MBT 113: 37 *Leopard* 2A6; 72 M60A3; 4 M48A5
RECCE 46: 15 V-150 *Chaimite*; 31 ULTRAV M-11
APC 458
APC (T) 261: 180 M113A1; 34 M113A2; 47 M577A2
APC (W) 197: 31 V-200 *Chaimite*; 166 *Pandur* II (all variants)
ARTY 360
SP 155mm 23: 6 M109A2; 17 M109A5
TOWED 33: **105mm** 33: 19 L-119; 9 M101; 5 M-56
COASTAL • 150mm 1
MOR 303: **81mm** 190 (incl 21 SP); **107mm** 53 M30 (incl 20 SP); **120mm** 60 *Tampella*
AT
MSL
SP 28: 18 M113 with TOW; 4 M901 with TOW; 6 ULTRAV-11 with *Milan*
MANPATS *Milan*; *Spike* LR; *Spike* MR; TOW
RCL 182: **106mm** 58 M40; **84mm** 89 *Carl Gustav*; **90mm** 35
AD
SAM • MANPAD 58: 32 *Chaparral*; 26 FIM-92A *Stinger*
AEV M728
ARV 6 M88A1, 7 *Pandur*
VLB M48

Navy 9,700 (incl 1,550 Marines)
EQUIPMENT BY TYPE
SUBMARINES • TACTICAL • SSK 2 *Tridente* (GER Type-209) with 8 533mm TT
PRINCIPAL SURFACE COMBATANTS 5
FRIGATES • FFGHM 5:
3 *Vasco Da Gama* with 2 Mk141 quad lnchr with RGM-84C *Harpoon* AShM, 1 octuple Mk 29 GMLS with RIM-7M *Sea Sparrow* SAM, 2 Mk32 triple 324mm ASTT with Mk46 LWT, 1 *Phalanx* Block 1B CIWS, 1 100mm gun, (capacity 2 *Lynx* Mk95 (*Super Lynx*) hel)
2 *Bartolomeu Dias* (ex-NLD *Karel Doorman)* with 2 quad Mk141 lnchr with RGM-84C *Harpoon* AShM, 1 Mk48 VLS with RIM-7M *Sea Sparrow* SAM, 2 Mk32 twin 324mm ASTT with Mk46 LWT, 1 *Goalkeeper* CIWS, 1 76mm gun, (capacity: 1 *Lynx* Mk95 (*Super Lynx*) hel)
PATROL AND COASTAL COMBATANTS 24
CORVETTES • FS 7:
3 *Baptista de Andrade* with 1 100mm gun, 1 hel landing platform
4 *Joao Coutinho* with 1 twin 76mm gun, 1 hel landing platform
PSO 2 *Viana do Castelo* with 1 hel landing platform
PCC 3 *Cacine*
PBR 12: 2 *Albatroz*; 5 *Argos*; 4 *Centauro*; 1 *Rio Minho*
AMPHIBIOUS • LANDING CRAFT • LCU 1 *Bombarda*
LOGISTICS AND SUPPORT 13
ABU 2: 1 *Schultz Xavier*; 1 *Guia*
AGS 4: 2 *D Carlos* I (US *Stalwart*); 2 *Andromeda*
AORL 1 *Bérrio* (ex UK *Rover*) with 1 hel landing platform (for medium hel)
AXS 3: 1 *Sagres*; 1 *Creoula*; 1 *Polar*
YGS 3

Marines 1,550
FORCES BY ROLE
SPECIAL FORCES
1 SF det
MANOEUVRE
Light
2 lt inf bn
COMBAT SUPPORT
1 mor coy 1 MP det

EQUIPMENT BY TYPE

ARTY • MOR 30 120mm

Naval Aviation

HELICOPTERS • ASW 5 *Lynx* Mk95 (*Super Lynx*)

Air Force 7,200

Flying hours 180 hrs/year on F-16 *Fighting Falcon*

FORCES BY ROLE

FIGHTER/GROUND ATTACK

2 sqn with F-16AM/BM *Fighting Falcon*

MARITIME PATROL

1 sqn with P-3C *Orion*

ISR/TRANSPORT

1 sqn with C-295M

COMBAT SEARCH & RESCUE

1 sqn with with AW101 *Merlin*

TRANSPORT

1 sqn with C-130H/C-130H-30 *Hercules*

1 sqn with *Falcon* 50

TRAINING

1 sqn with *Alpha Jet**

1 sqn with SA316 *Alouette* III

1 sqn with TB-30 *Epsilon*

EQUIPMENT BY TYPE

AIRCRAFT 42 combat capable

FTR 30: 27 F-16AM *Fighting Falcon*; 3 F-16BM *Fighting Falcon*

ASW 5 P-3C *Orion*

ISR: 7: 5 C-295M (maritime surveillance), 2 C-295M (photo recce)

TPT 14: **Medium** 6: 3 C-130H *Hercules*; 3 C-130H-30 *Hercules* (tpt/SAR); **Light** 5 C-295M; **PAX** 3 *Falcon* 50 (tpt/VIP)

TRG 23: 7 *Alpha Jet**; 16 TB-30 *Epsilon*

HELICOPTERS

MRH 12 SA316 *Alouette* III (trg, utl)

TPT • Medium 12 AW101 *Merlin* (6 SAR, 4 CSAR, 2 fishery protection)

MSL

AAM • IR AIM-9L/I *Sidewinder*; **ARH** AIM-120 AMRAAM

ASM AGM-65A *Maverick*

AShM AGM-84A *Harpoon*

BOMBS

Enhanced Paveway II; GBU-49; GBU-31 JDAM

Paramilitary 47,700

National Republican Guard 26,100

APC (W): some *Commando* Mk III (*Bravia*)

PATROL AND COASTAL COMBATANTS • PB 16

PBF 12

PB 4

HELICOPTERS • MRH 7 SA315 *Lama*

Public Security Police 21,600

DEPLOYMENT

Legal provisions for foreign deployment:

Constitution: Codified constitution (1976) (revised in 2005)

Decision on deployment of troops abroad: By government

AFGHANISTAN

NATO • ISAF 165

UN • UNAMA 1 obs

BOSNIA-HERZEGOVINA

OSCE • Bosnia and Herzegovina 1

DEMOCRATIC REPUBLIC OF THE CONGO

EU • EUSEC RD Congo 2

MALI

EU • EUTM Mali 1

SERBIA

NATO • KFOR 173; 1 AB coy (KTM)

OSCE • Kosovo 1

UGANDA

EU • EUTM Somalia 5

FOREIGN FORCES

United States US European Command: 700; 1 spt facility at Lajes

Romania ROM

New Lei		2012	2013	2014
GDP	lei	626bn	662bn	
	US$	169bn	187bn	
per capita	US$	7,935	8,775	
Growth	%	0.33	1.60	
Inflation	%	3.34	4.62	
Def bdgt [a]	lei	7.67bn	8.28bn	
	US$	2.21bn	2.47bn	
FMA (US)	US$	14m	14m	8m
US$1=lei		3.47	3.35	

[a] Includes military pensions

Population 21,790,479

Age	0–14	15–19	20–24	25–29	30–64	65 plus
Male	7.5%	2.7%	3.3%	3.9%	25.1%	6.1%
Female	7.1%	2.6%	3.2%	3.8%	25.7%	9.0%

Capabilities

NATO membership is at the heart of Romania's defence posture, and the country has moved from a conscript to a professional military as it attempts to restructure its armed forces to be able to contribute to NATO and EU missions. Since 2008, however, modernisation efforts have been hampered by funding difficulties. The army has been restructured to support deployed operations, with Romanian contingents joining NATO, EU and UN missions. An ageing fighter fleet undermines air force combat capability, with the replacement programme constrained by budget shortfalls. As of mid-2012, the favoured option was to acquire second-hand F-16s. There are a small number of tactical airlifters and Romania is a member of the Strategic Airlift Capability's C-17 unit. Romania's armed forces exercise regularly on a national and multinational basis.

ACTIVE 71,400 (Army 42,600, Navy 6,900, Air 8,400, Joint 13,500) Paramilitary 79,900

RESERVE 45,000 (Joint 45,000)

ORGANISATIONS BY SERVICE

Army 42,600

Readiness is reported as 70–90% for NATO-designated forces and 40–70% for other forces

FORCES BY ROLE

COMMAND
3 div HQ (1 NATO designated)

SPECIAL FORCES
1 SF bde

MANOEUVRE

Reconnaissance
3 recce bn

Mechanised
5 mech bde (1 NATO designated)

Light
2 inf bde (1 NATO designated)

Mountain
2 mtn inf bde (1 NATO designated)

COMBAT SUPPORT
1 arty bde
3 arty regt
3 AD regt
1 engr bde
3 engr bn
3 sigs bn
1 CIMIC bn
1 MP bn
3 CBRN bn

COMBAT SERVICE SUPPORT
4 spt bn

EQUIPMENT BY TYPE

MBT 437: 250 T-55; 42 TR-580; 91 TR-85; 54 TR-85 M1
AIFV 124: 23 MLI-84; 101 MLI-84 JDER
APC 1,609
APC (T) 75 MLVM
APC (W) 969: 69 B33 TAB *Zimbru*; 31 *Piranha* III; 367 TAB-71; 140 TAB-77; 362 TABC-79
TYPE VARIANTS 505 APC
PPV 60 *Maxxpro*
ARTY 899
SP 122mm 24: 6 2S1; 18 Model 89
TOWED 422: **122mm** 72 (M-30) M-1938 (A-19); **152mm** 350: 247 M-1981 Model 81; 103 M-1985
MRL 122mm 187: 133 APR-40; 54 LAROM
MOR 120mm 266 M-1982
AT
MSL • SP 134: 12 9P122 *Malyutka* (AT-3 *Sagger*); 74 9P133 *Malyutka* (AT-3 *Sagger*); 48 9P148 *Konkurs* (AT-5 *Spandrel*)
GUNS 100mm 232: 209 M1977 Gun 77; 23 SU-100 SP
AD • GUNS 66
SP 35mm 42 *Gepard*
TOWED • 35mm 24 GDF-203
RADARS • LAND 8 SNAR-10 *Big Fred*
ARV 3 BPz-2

Navy 6,900

EQUIPMENT BY TYPE

PRINCIPAL SURFACE COMBATANTS 3
DESTROYERS 3:
DDGH 1 *Marasesti* with 4 twin lnchr with P-15M *Termit*-M (SS-N-2C *Styx*) AShM, 2 triple 533mm ASTT with RUS 53–65 ASW, 2 RBU 6000 *Smerch* 2, 2 twin 76mm gun, (capacity 2 SA-316 (IAR-316) *Alouette* III hel)
DDH 2 *Regele Ferdinand* (ex-UK Type-22), with 2 triple 324mm TT, 1 76mm gun (capacity 1 SA330 (IAR-330) *Puma*)
PATROL AND COASTAL COMBATANTS 21
CORVETTES 4
FSH 2 *Tetal* II with 2 twin 533mm ASTT, 2 RBU 6000 *Smerch* 2, 2 AK630 CIWS, 1 76mm gun, (capacity 1 SA-316 (IAR-316) *Alouette* III hel)
FS 2 *Tetal* I with 2 twin 533mm ASTT with RUS 53-65 ASW, 2 RBU 2500 *Smerch* 1, 2 twin 76mm gun
PCFG 3 *Zborul* with 2 twin lnchr with P-15M *Termit*-M (SS-N-2C *Styx*) AShM, 2 AK630 CIWS, 1 76mm gun
PCR 8:
1 *Brutar* I with 2 BM-21 MRL, 1 100mm gun
4 *Brutar* II with 2 BM-21 MRL, 1 100mm gun
3 *Kogalniceanu* with 2 BM-21 MRL, 2 100mm gun
PBR 6 VD 141 (ex MSI now used for river patrol)
MINE WARFARE 11
MINE COUNTERMEASURES 10
MSO 4 *Musca* with 2 quad lnchr with *Strela* 2M (SA-N-5 *Grail)* SAM, 2 RBU 1200, 2 AK630 CIWS
MSI 6 VD141 (used for river MCM)
MINELAYERS • ML 1 *Corsar* with up to 100 mines, 2 RBU 1200 ASROC, 2 AK630 CIWS, 1 57mm gun
LOGISTICS AND SUPPORT 14
ADG 1 *Magnetica*
AETL 2 *Constanta* with 2 RBU 1200, 2 twin 57mm gun
AGOR 1 *Corsar*
AGS 2: 1 *Emil Racovita*; 1 *Catuneanu*
AOL 3: 1 *Tulcea*; 2 others
ATF 1 *Grozavu*
AXS 1 *Mircea*
YTL 3

Naval Infantry

FORCES BY ROLE

MANOEUVRE

Light
1 naval inf bn

EQUIPMENT BY TYPE

APC (W) 14: 11 ABC-79M; 3 TABC-79M

Air Force 8,400

Flying hours 120 hrs/year

FORCES BY ROLE

FIGHTER
- 2 sqn with MiG-21 *Lancer* C

FIGHTER/GROUND ATTACK
- 1 sqn with MiG-21 *Lancer* A/B

TRANSPORT
- 1 sqn with An-26 *Curl*; An-30 *Clank*; C-27J *Spartan*
- 1 sqn with C-130B/H *Hercules*

TRAINING
- 1 sqn with IAR-99 *Soim**
- 1 sqn with SA316B *Alouette* III (IAR-316B); Yak-52 (Iak-52)

TRANSPORT HELICOPTER
- 2 (multirole) sqn with IAR-330 SOCAT *Puma*
- 3 sqn with SA330 *Puma* (IAR-330)

AIR DEFENCE
- 1 AD bde

COMBAT SERVICE SUPPORT
- 1 engr regt

EQUIPMENT BY TYPE

AIRCRAFT 69 combat capable
- **FGA** 36: 10 MiG-21 *Lancer* A; 6 MiG-21 *Lancer* B; 20 MiG-21 *Lancer* C
- **ISR** 2 An-30 *Clank*
- **TPT** 14: **Medium** 11: 6 C-27J *Spartan*; 4 C-130B *Hercules*; 1 C-130H *Hercules*; **Light** 3 An-26 *Curl*
- **TRG** 32: 10 IAR-99 *Soim**; 10 IAR-99C *Soim**; 12 Yak-52 (Iak-52)

HELICOPTERS
- **MRH** 31: 23 IAR-330 SOCAT *Puma*; 7 SA316B *Alouette* III (IAR-316B)
- **TPT • Medium** 37: 21 SA330L *Puma* (IAR-330L); 16 SA330M *Puma* (IAR-330M)

AD • SAM 14: 6 S-75M3 *Volkhov* (SA-2 *Guideline*); 8 MIM-23 HAWK PIP III

MSL
- **AAM • IR** R-73 (AA-11 *Archer*); R-550 *Magic* 2; *Python* 3
- **ASM** *Spike*-ER

Paramilitary 79,900

Border Guards 22,900 (incl conscripts)

Ministry of Interior

EQUIPMENT BY TYPE

PATROL AND COASTAL COMBATANTS 14
- **PCO** 1 *Stefan cel Mare* (Damen OPV 900)
- **PBF** 1 *Bigliani*
- **PB** 12: 4 *Neustadt*; 3 *Mai*; 5 SNR-17

Gendarmerie ε57,000

Ministry of Interior

Cyber

Romania has a national CERT and is involved in informal CERT communities. A nationwide cyber-security policy is currently being implemented. The private sector is investing heavily in Romania with a number of international firms planning to open cyber-security facilities.

DEPLOYMENT

Legal provisions for foreign deployment:
Constitution: Codified constitution (1991)
Decision on deployment of troops abroad: By parliament (Art. 62); or b) by president upon parliamentary approval (Art. 92).

AFGHANISTAN
NATO • ISAF 1,077; 1 inf bn
UN • UNAMA 2 obs

BOSNIA-HERZEGOVINA
EU • EUFOR • *Operation Althea* 37

DEMOCRATIC REPUBLIC OF THE CONGO
EU • EUSEC RD Congo 3
UN • MONUSCO 22 obs

LIBERIA
UN • UNMIL 2 obs

MALI
NATO • EUTM Mali 1

SERBIA
NATO • KFOR 61
UN • UNMIK 1 obs

SOUTH SUDAN
UN • UNMISS 2; 4 obs

Serbia SER

Serbian Dinar d		2012	2013	2014
GDP	d	3.69tr	3.97tr	
	US$	37.4bn	42.9bn	
per capita	US$	4,943	5,667	
Growth	%	-1.76	2.00	
Inflation	%	7.35	9.57	
Def bdgt	d	73.9bn	58.7bn	61.4bn
	US$	841m	681m	
FMA (US)	US$	1.8m	1.8m	1.8m
US$1=d		87.86	86.13	

Population 7,243,007

Age	0 – 14	15 – 19	20 – 24	25 – 29	30 – 64	65 plus
Male	7.6%	3.0%	3.2%	3.5%	24.6%	6.9%
Female	7.2%	2.8%	3.0%	3.3%	25.0%	10.0%

Capabilities

2011 saw the shift from conscript to professional armed forces as part of a near decade-long restructuring process, though voluntary conscription remains. Following the conflicts of the 1990s and the political turmoil of the turn of the century, the armed forces have been reduced in size, but with the long-term aim of crafting a capable and modern force. Primary goals of Serbia's defence policy are the armed forces' transformation and professionalisation, and capability development. The land forces are built around four combined-arms brigades, supported by an army aviation unit run by the air force. The latter has a small number of combat aircraft in service, and had been aiming to procure one or two squadrons of a modern multi-role type. Funding constraints have meant that this project has been delayed. Serviceability and platform availability are likely to be a problem for the air force.

ACTIVE 28,150 **(Army 13,250, Air Force and Air Defence 5,100, Training Command 3,000, Guards 1,600; Other MoD 5,200)**
Conscript liability 6 months (voluntary)

RESERVE 50,150

ORGANISATIONS BY SERVICE

Army 13,250

FORCES BY ROLE
SPECIAL FORCES
1 SF bde (1 CT bn, 1 cdo bn, 1 para bn, 1 log bn)
MANOEUVRE
Mechanised
1 (1st) bde (1 tk bn, 2 mech inf bn, 1 inf bn, 1 SP arty bn, 1 MRL bn, 1 AD bn, 1 engr bn, 1 log bn)
3 (2nd, 3rd & 4th) bde (1 tk bn, 2 mech inf bn, 2 inf bn, 1 SP arty bn, 1 MRL bn, 1 AD bn, 1 engr bn, 1 log bn)
COMBAT SUPPORT
1 (mixed) arty bde (4 arty bn, 1 MRL bn, 1 spt bn)
2 ptn bridging bn
1 NBC bn
1 sigs bn
2 MP bn

Reserve Organisations

FORCES BY ROLE
MANOEUVRE
Light
8 (territorial) inf bde

EQUIPMENT BY TYPE
MBT 212: 199 M-84; 13 T-72
RECCE 46 BRDM-2
AIFV 323 M-80
APC 39 BOV VP M-86
ARTY 515
SP 122mm 67 2S1
TOWED 204: **122mm** 78 D-30; **130mm** 18 M-46; **152mm** 36 M-84; **155mm** 72: 66 M-1; 6 M-65
MRL 81: **128mm** 78: 18 M-63 *Plamen*; 60 M-77 *Organj*; **262mm** 3 *Orkan*
MOR 163: **82mm** 106 M-69; **120mm** 57 M-74/M-75
AT
MSL
SP 48 BOV-1 (M-83) with 9K11 *Malyutka* (AT-3 *Sagger*)
MANPATS 168: 99 9K11 *Malyutka* (AT-3 *Sagger*); 69 9K111 *Fagot* (AT-4 *Spigot*)
RCL 6: **90mm** 6 M-79
AD • SAM 156
SP 94: 77 2K12 Kub (SA-6 *Gainful*); 12 S-1M (SA-9 *Gaskin*); 5 SAVA S10M
MANPADS 62: 8 S-2M (SA-7 *Grail*)‡; 54 *Šilo* (SA-16 *Gimlet*)
GUNS 36
TOWED 40mm: 36 Bofors L70
AEV IWT
ARV M84A1; T-54/T-55
VLB MT-55; TMM

River Flotilla

The Serbian-Montenegrin navy was transferred to Montenegro upon independence in 2006, but the Danube flotilla remained in Serbian control. The flotilla is subordinate to the Land Forces.

EQUIPMENT BY TYPE
PATROL AND COASTAL COMBATANTS 5
PBR 5: 3 Type-20; 2 others
MINE WARFARE • MINE COUNTERMEASURES 4
MSI 4 *Nestin*
AMPHIBOUS • LANDING CRAFT • LCU 5 Type-22
LOGISTICS AND SUPPORT 5
ADG 1 *Šabac*
AGF 1 *Kozara*
AOL 1
YFD 1
YTL 1

Air Force and Air Defence 5,100

Flying hours: Ftr – 40 per yr

FORCES BY ROLE
FIGHTER
1 sqn with MiG-21bis *Fishbed*; MiG-29 *Fulcrum*
FIGHTER/GROUND ATTACK
1 sqn with G-4 *Super Galeb**; J-22 *Orao*
ISR
2 flt with IJ-22 *Orao* 1*; MiG-21R *Fishbed* H*
TRANSPORT
1 sqn with An-2; An-26; Do-28; Yak-40 (Jak-40); 1 PA-34 *Seneca* V
TRAINING
1 sqn with G-4 *Super Galeb** (adv trg/light atk); SA341/342 *Gazelle*; Utva-75 (basic trg)
ATTACK HELICOPTER
1 sqn with SA341H/342L *Gazelle*; (HN-42/45); Mi-24 *Hind*
TRANSPORT HELICOPTER
2 sqn with Mi-8 *Hip*; Mi-17 *Hip* H
AIR DEFENCE
1 bde (5 bn (2 msl, 3 SP msl) with S-125 *Neva* (SA-3 *Goa*); 2K12 *Kub* (SA-6 *Gainful*); 9K32 *Strela*-2 (SA-7 *Grail*); 9K310 *Igla*-1 (SA-16 *Gimlet*))
2 radar bn (for early warning and reporting)
COMBAT SUPPORT
1 sigs bn
COMBAT SERVICE SUPPORT
1 maint bn

EQUIPMENT BY TYPE
AIRCRAFT 84 combat capable
FTR 30: 20 MiG-21bis *Fishbed* L & N; 6 MiG-21UM *Mongol* B; 3 MiG-29 *Fulcrum*; 1 MiG-29UB *Fulcrum*
FGA 18 J-22 *Orao* 1
ISR 12: 10 IJ-22R *Orao* 1*; 2 MiG-21R *Fishbed* H*

TPT • Light 10: 1 An-2 *Colt*; 4 An-26 *Curl*; 2 Do-28 *Skyservant*; 2 Yak-40 (Jak-40); 1 PA-34 *Seneca* V
TRG 45: 24 G-4 *Super Galeb**; 11 Utva-75; 10 *Lasta* 95
HELICOPTERS
ATK 2 Mi-24 *Hind*
MRH 51: 2 Mi-17 *Hip* H; 2 SA341H *Gazelle* (HI-42); 34 SA341H *Gazelle* (HN-42)/SA342L *Gazelle* (HN-45); 13 SA341H *Gazelle* (HO-42)/SA342L1 *Gazelle* (HO-45)
TPT • Medium 7 Mi-8T *Hip* (HT-40)
AD
SAM 15: 6 S-125 *Pechora* (SA-3 *Goa*); 9 2K12 *Kub* (SA-6 *Gainful*)
MANPAD 156; 120 9K32 *Strela-2* (SA-7 *Grail*); 36 9K310 *Igla-1* (SA-16 *Gimlet*)
GUNS • 40mm 24 Bofors L-70
MSL
AAM • IR R-60 (AA-8 *Aphid*)
ASM AGM-65 *Maverick*; A-77 *Thunder*

Guards 1,600

MANOEUVRE
Other
1 (ceremonial) gd bde (1 gd bn, 1 MP bn, 1 spt bn)

DEPLOYMENT

Legal provisions for foreign deployment:
Constitution: Codified constitution (2006)
Decision on deployment of troops abroad: By parliament (Art. 140)

CÔTE D'IVOIRE
UN • UNOCI 3 obs

CYPRUS
UN • UNFICYP 46

DEMOCRATIC REPUBLIC OF THE CONGO
UN • MONUSCO 5; 3 obs

LEBANON
UN • UNIFIL 49

LIBERIA
UN • UNMIL 4 obs

MIDDLE EAST
UN • UNTSO 1 obs

MOLDOVA
OSCE • Moldova 1

FOREIGN FORCES

All OSCE unless specified
Austria 2
Bosnia-Herzegovina 2
Bulgaria 1
Canada 1
France 1
Germany 1
Hungary 1
Ireland 3
Italy 4
Norway 2
Russia 1
Sweden 1
Switzerland 1
United Kingdom 5
United States 4

TERRITORY WHERE THE GOVERNMENT DOES NOT EXERCISE EFFECTIVE CONTROL

Data here represent the de facto situation in Kosovo. This does not imply international recognition as a sovereign state. In February 2008, Kosovo declared itself independent. Serbia remains opposed to this, and while Kosovo has not been admitted to the United Nations, a number of states have recognised Kosovo's self-declared status.

Kosovo Security Force 2,500; reserves 800

The Kosovo Security Force was formed, in January 2009, as a non-military organisation with responsibility for crisis response, civil protection and EOD. The force is armed with small arms and light vehicles only. A July 2010 law created a reserve force.

FOREIGN FORCES

All under Kosovo Force (KFOR) comd. unless otherwise specified.
Albania 14
Armenia 36
Austria 380; 1 mech inf coy • OSCE 8
Azerbaijan OSCE 1
Bosnia-Herzegovina OSCE 9
Bulgaria 11 • OSCE 1
Canada 5 • OSCE 7
Croatia 22 • OSCE 5
Czech Republic 7 • OSCE 1 • UNMIK 1 obs
Denmark 36
Estonia 2
Finland 21 • OSCE 1
France 316; 1 armd cav sqn; 1 log coy • OSCE 6
Georgia OSCE 4
Germany 741 • OSCE 2
Greece 120; 1 mech inf coy • OSCE 4
Hungary 201; 1 inf coy (KTM) • OSCE 2
Ireland 12 • OSCE 6
Italy 500; 1 MRL BG HQ • OSCE 12
Lithuania 1
Luxembourg 22
Macedonia, Former Yugoslav Republic of OSCE 17
Malta OSCE 1
Moldova UNMIK 1 obs • OSCE 2
Montenegro OSCE 1
Morocco 169; 1 inf coy
Netherlands 7
Norway 4 • UNMIK 1 obs
Poland 228; 1 inf coy • OSCE 4 • UNMIK 1 obs

Portugal 173; 1 AB coy (KTM) • OSCE 1
Romania 61 • UNMIK 1 obs
Russia OSCE 1
Slovakia OSCE 1
Slovenia 303; 2 mot inf coy
Spain OSCE 2
Sweden 52 • OSCE 2
Switzerland 223; 1 inf coy • OSCE 1
Turkey 367; 1 inf coy • OSCE 7 • UNMIK 1 obs
Ukraine 163; 1 inf coy • OSCE 1 • UNMIK 2 obs
United Kingdom 1 • OSCE 13
United States 669; 1 surv bde HQ • OSCE 10

Slovakia SVK

Euro €		2012	2013	2014
GDP	€	74.1bn	77.3bn	
	US$	91.9bn	98.5bn	
per capita	US$	16,899	18,089	
Growth	%	2.03	1.39	
Inflation	%	3.73	1.90	
Def exp	€	790m		
	US$	1.02bn		
Def bdgt [a]	€	685m	748m	785m
	US$	881m	995m	
FMA (US)	US$	1m	1m	0.45m
US$1=€		0.78	0.75	

[a] Includes military pensions

Population 5,488,339

Age	0–14	15–19	20–24	25–29	30–64	65 plus
Male	7.9%	2.9%	3.6%	3.9%	25.1%	5.1%
Female	7.6%	2.8%	3.4%	3.8%	25.6%	8.4%

Capabilities

The Slovakian armed forces suffer from the twin pressures of low funding and the need to modernise an ageing equipment inventory. The 2013 Defence White Paper underscored the scale of the problem, noting that 70% of land force equipment was now at the end of its service life. Training remains geared towards meeting core national requirements (such as SAR), NATO requirements (air defence), or focused on participation in international operations. Discussions were reported to have restarted on the possible provision of an airlift capability.

ACTIVE 15,850 (Army 6,250, Air 3,950, Central Staff 2,550, Support and Training 3,100)
Conscript liability 6 months

ORGANISATIONS BY SERVICE

Central Staff 2,550
SPECIAL FORCES
1 (5th Special) recce regt

Army 6,250
FORCES BY ROLE
MANOEUVRE
Mechanised
1 (1st) mech bde (3 mech inf bn, 1 engr coy, 1 spt bn)
1 (2nd) mech bde (1 ISATR coy, 1 tk bn, 2 mech inf bn, 1 mixed SP arty bn, 1 engr coy, 1 spt bn)
COMBAT SUPPORT
1 MRL bn
1 engr bn
1 MP bn
1 NBC bn

EQUIPMENT BY TYPE
MBT 30 T-72M
AIFV 239: 148 BMP-1; 91 BMP-2
APC 101+
APC (T) 72 OT-90
APC (W) 22: 7 OT-64; 15 *Tatrapan* (6×6)
PPV 7+ RG-32M
ARTY 68
SP 19: **152mm** 3 M-77 *Dana;* **155mm** 16 M-2000 *Zuzana*
TOWED 122mm 19 D-30
MRL 30: **122mm** 4 RM-70; **122/227mm** 26 RM-70/85 MODULAR
AT
SP 9S428 with *Malyutka* (AT-3 *Sagger*) on BMP-1; 9P135 *Fagot* (AT-4 *Spigot*) on BMP-2; 9P148 (AT-5 *Spandrel*) on BRDM-2
MANPATS 425 9K11 *Malyutka* (AT-3 *Sagger*)/9K113 *Shturm* (AT-6 *Spandrel*)
AD
SAM
SP 48 9K35 *Strela*-10 (SA-13 *Gopher*)
MANPADS 9K32 *Strela*-2 (SA-7 *Grail*); 9K310 *Igla*-1 (SA-16 *Gimlet*)
RADAR • LAND SNAR-10 *Big Fred* (veh, arty)
ARV MT-55; VT-55A; VT-72B; WPT-TOPAS
VLB AM-50; MT-55A
MW Bozena; UOS-155 *Belarty*

Air Force 3,950
Flying hours 90 hrs/yr for MiG-29 pilots (NATO Integrated AD System); 90 hrs/yr for Mi-8/17 crews (reserved for EU & NATO)

FORCES BY ROLE
FIGHTER
1 sqn with MiG-29AS/UBS *Fulcrum*
TRANSPORT
1 flt with An-26 *Curl*
1 flt with L-410FG/T/UVP *Turbolet*
TRANSPORT HELICOPTER
1 sqn with Mi-8 *Hip*; Mi-17 *Hip* H
1 sqn with PZL MI-2 *Hoplite*
TRAINING
1 sqn with L-39CM/ZA/ZAM *Albatros*
AIR DEFENCE
1 bde with 2K12 *Kub* (SA-6 *Gainful*); 9K32 *Strela*-2 (SA-7 *Grail*); S-300 (SA-10 *Grumble*)

EQUIPMENT BY TYPE

AIRCRAFT 20 combat capable

FTR 20: 10 MiG-29AS *Fulcrum*; 2 MiG-29UBS *Fulcrum*; 8 MiG-29A/UB *Fulcrum*

TPT • Light 9: 1 An-26 *Curl*; 2 L-410FG *Turbolet*; 2 L-410T *Turbolet*; 4 L-410UVP *Turbolet*

TRG 13: 6 L-39CM *Albatros*; 5 L-39ZA *Albatros*; 2 L-39ZAM *Albatros*

HELICOPTERS

ATK (15: 5 Mi-24D *Hind* D; 10 Mi-24V *Hind* E all in store)

MRH 14 Mi-17 *Hip* H

TPT 7: **Medium** 1 Mi-8 *Hip*; **Light** 6 PZL MI-2 *Hoplite*

AD • SAM

SP S-300 (SA-10B *Grumble*); 2K12 *Kub* (SA-6 *Gainful*)

MANPAD 9K32 *Strela*-2 (SA-7 *Grail*)

MSL

AAM • IR R-60 (AA-8 *Aphid*); R-73 (AA-11 *Archer*);
SARH R-27R (AA-10A *Alamo*)

ASM S5K/S5KO (57mm rockets); S8KP/S8KOM (80mm rockets)

DEPLOYMENT

Legal provisions for foreign deployment:
Constitution: Codified constitution (1992)
Decision on deployment of troops abroad: By the parliament (Art. 86)

AFGHANISTAN

NATO • ISAF 199

BOSNIA-HERZEGOVINA

EU • EUFOR • *Operation Althea* 35

OSCE • Bosnia and Herzegovina 1

CYPRUS

UN • UNFICYP 157; elm 1 inf coy; 1 engr pl

MIDDLE EAST

UN • UNTSO 2 obs

SERBIA

OSCE • Kosovo 1

Slovenia SVN

Euro €		2012	2013	2014
GDP	€	35.1bn	36.1bn	
	US$	45.6bn	46.7bn	
per capita	US$	22,193	22,657	
Growth	%	-2.34	-2.00	
Inflation	%	2.60	1.76	
Def bdgt [a]	€	396m	357m	379m
	US$	509m	474m	
FMA (US)	US$	0.45m	0.45m	0.45m
US$1=€		0.78	0.75	

[a] Excludes military pensions

Population 1,992,690

Age	0–14	15–19	20–24	25–29	30–64	65 plus
Male	6.9%	2.4%	2.8%	3.3%	26.2%	7.0%
Female	6.5%	2.3%	2.7%	3.2%	26.0%	10.5%

Capabilities

The armed forces' role is to support territorial integrity and participate in peace-support and stabilisation operations. The 2010 Resolution on the General Long-Term Programme for the Development and Equipping of the Slovenian Armed Forces up to 2025 (Parliament, November 2010) is the main defence development and guidance document, as well as the principal long-term planning document. The Medium-Term Defence Programme 2013–2018 was developed with reference to the national budget, as well as NATO's capability target package for Slovenia. Funding limitations continue to dictate the pace of change, particularly with regard to equipment; ambitions to acquire an indigenous air-policing capability to replace the Italian air force in the role remain unfulfilled. Given limited financial resources, there will be stress on improving maintenance and readiness of existing capacities. A major reorganisation of has left the armed forces with two manoeuvre brigades, a logistics brigade, a regimental-sized air wing and a small naval division. There is no organic capability to deploy beyond Slovenia's borders.

ACTIVE 7,600 (Army 7,600) Paramilitary 5,950

RESERVE 1,500 (Army 1,500) Paramilitary 260

ORGANISATIONS BY SERVICE

Army 7,600

FORCES BY ROLE

Regt are bn sized

SPECIAL FORCES

1 SF unit (1 spec ops coy, 1 CSS coy)

MANOEUVRE

Reconnaissance

1 ISR bn (2 coy)

Mechanised

1 mech inf bde (1st) (1 mech inf regt, 1 mtn inf regt, 1 cbt spt bn)

1 mech inf bde (72nd) (2 mech inf regt, 1 cbt spt bn)
Other
1 armd trg bn (1 armd coy)
COMBAT SUPPORT
1 arty bn (2 arty bty)
1 engr bn (2 engr coy)
1 EW coy
1 MP bn (3 MP coy)
1 CBRN bn (3 CBRN coy)
1 sigs bn (3 sigs coy)
COMBAT SERVICE SUPPORT
1 log bde (1 log regt, 1 maint regt, 1 med regt)

Reserves

FORCES BY ROLE
MANOEUVRE
Mountain
2 inf regt (territorial - 1 allocated to each inf bde)

EQUIPMENT BY TYPE
MBT 46 M-84 (trg role)
RECCE 10 *Cobra* CBRN
APC (W) 115: 85 *Pandur* 6×6 (*Valuk*); 30 *Patria* 8×8 (*Svarun*)
ARTY 63
TOWED • 155mm 18 TN-90
MOR 120mm 45 MN-9
AT • MSL
SP 24: 12 BOV-3 9K11 *Malyutka* (AT-3 *Sagger*); 12 BOV-3 9K111 *Fagot* (AT-4 *Spigot*)
MANPATS 9K11 *Malyutka* (AT-3 *Sagger*); 9K111 *Fagot* (AT-4 *Spigot*)
ARV VT-55A
VLB MTU

Army Maritime Element 170

FORCES BY ROLE
MANOEUVRE
Amphibious
1 maritime det

EQUIPMENT BY TYPE
PATROL AND COASTAL COMBATANTS 2
PBF 1 *Super Dvora* MkII
PCC 1 *Triglav* III (RUS *Svetlyak*)

Air Element 650

FORCES BY ROLE
TRANSPORT
1 sqn with L-410 *Turbolet*; PC-6B *Turbo Porter*
TRAINING
1 unit with Bell 206 *Jet Ranger* (AB-206); PC-9; PC-9M*; Z-143L; Z-242L
TRANSPORT HELICOPTER
1 sqn with AS532AL *Cougar*; Bell 412 *Twin Huey* (some armed)
AIR DEFENCE
1 AD bn (2 AD bty)
COMBAT SERVICE SUPPORT
1 maint sqn

EQUIPMENT BY TYPE
AIRCRAFT 9 combat capable
TPT • Light 3: 1 L-410 *Turbolet*; 2 PC-6B *Turbo Porter*
TRG 21: 2 PC-9; 9 PC-9M*; 2 Z-143L; 8 Z-242L
HELICOPTERS
MRH 8: 5 Bell 412EP *Twin Huey*; 2 Bell 412HP *Twin Huey*; 1 Bell 412SP *Twin Huey* (some armed)
TPT 8: **Medium** 4 AS532AL *Cougar*; **Light** 4 Bell 206 *Jet Ranger* (AB-206)
AD • SAM 138
SP 6 *Roland* II
MANPAD 132: 36 9K310 *Igla*-1 (SA-16 *Gimlet*); 96 9K38 *Igla* (SA-18 *Grouse*)

Paramilitary 5,950

Police 5,950; 260 reservists

Ministry of Interior (civilian; limited elements could be prequalified to cooperate in military defence with the armed forces during state of emergency or war)
PATROL AND COASTAL COMBATANTS • PBF 1 *Ladse*
HELICOPTERS
MRH 1 Bell 412 *Twin Huey*,
TPT • Light 5: 1 AW109; 2 Bell 206 (AB-206) *Jet Ranger*; 1 Bell 212 (AB-212); 1 EC135

Cyber

An MoD Cyber concept was drawn up in 2013, defining cyber defence capabilities that comply with NATO best practices and ENISA standards. A National Cyber Strategy was expected by end-2013.

DEPLOYMENT

Legal provisions for foreign deployment:
Constitution: Codified constitution (1991)
Decision on deployment of troops abroad: By government (Art. 84 of Defence Act)

AFGHANISTAN
NATO • ISAF 60

BOSNIA-HERZEGOVINA
EU • EUFOR • *Operation Althea* 14

LEBANON
UN • UNIFIL 14; 1 inf pl

MALI
EU • EUTM Mali 3

MIDDLE EAST
UN • UNTSO 5 obs

SERBIA
NATO • KFOR 303; 2 mot inf coy

Spain ESP

Euro €		2012	2013	2014
GDP	€	1.04tr	1.06tr	
	US$	1.35tr	1.39tr	
per capita	US$	29,289	30,108	
Growth	%	-1.42	-1.56	
Inflation	%	2.44	1.94	
Def bdgt [a]	€	10.8bn	8.72bn	
	US$	13.9bn	11.6bn	
US$1=€		0.78	0.75	

[a] Includes military pensions

Population 47,370,542

Age	0–14	15–19	20–24	25–29	30–64	65 plus
Male	7.9%	2.4%	2.7%	3.2%	25.8%	7.4%
Female	7.5%	2.2%	2.5%	2.9%	25.6%	10.0%

Capabilities

Budgetary pressures continue to erode Spain's military capacity. The country's only aircraft carrier, the *Principe de Asturias*, was withdrawn from service in February 2013, while some newly-delivered *Typhoon* combat aircraft were placed in storage. The *Mirage* F-1 was also withdrawn from service during the course of 2013. The 2013–16 defence plan sets out defence requirements against the backdrop of continuing austerity. An emphasis on modernisation at the start of the last decade is now one of trying simply to retain as much of the present capability as can be funded in strained circumstances. Spain intends to join the European Air Transport Command. This will provide access to additional airlift. Although the country is a partner in the A400M, and home to the aircraft's final assembly line, it has been reported that Madrid is also looking to sell 13 of the 27 A400M airlifters it has on its order book. The number of *Pizarro* AFVs is also reduced. The armed forces are well-versed in combined operations with other countries, and Spain has been a long-term contributor to ISAF, though during 2013 it began to draw down the number of deployed personnel.

ACTIVE 134,900 (Army 70,800 Navy 22,200, Air 20,600 Joint 21,300) Paramilitary 80,700

RESERVE 14,200 (Army 3,000 Navy 9,000 Air 2,200)

ORGANISATIONS BY SERVICE

Space

SATELLITES • COMMUNICATIONS 2: 1 *Spainsat*; 1 *Xtar-Eur*

Army 70,800

The Land Forces High Readiness HQ Spain provides one NATO Rapid Deployment Corps HQ (NRDC-SP).

FORCES BY ROLE

Infantry regiments usually comprise 2 bn. Spain deploys its main battle tanks within its armd/mech inf formations, and its armd cav regt

COMMAND

1 corps HQ (CGTAD) (1 int regt, 1 MP bn)
2 div HQ

SPECIAL FORCES

1 comd (3 Spec Ops bn, 1 int coy, 1 sigs coy, 1 log bn)

MANOEUVRE

Reconnaissance

1 (2nd) bde (3 lt armd cav regt, 1 fd arty regt, 1 AD coy, 1 engr bn, 1 int coy, 1 NBC coy, 1 sigs coy, 1 log bn)

Armoured

1 (12th) bde (1 recce sqn, 1 armd inf regt, 1 mech inf regt, 1 SP arty bn, 1 AD coy, 1 engr bn, 1 int coy, 1 NBC coy, 1 sigs coy, 1 log bn)

Mechanised

2 (10th & 11th) bde (1 recce sqn, 1 armd inf bn, 1 mech inf regt, 1 SP arty bn, 1 AT coy, 1 AD coy, 1 engr bn, 1 int coy, 1 NBC coy, 1 sigs coy, 1 log bn)

Light

2 (2nd/La Legion & 7th) bde (1 recce bn, 2 inf regt, 1 fd arty bn, 1 AT coy, 1 AD coy, 1 engr bn, 1 int coy, 1 NBC coy, 1 sigs coy, 1 log bn)
1 (5th) bde (2 lt inf regt)

Air Manoeuvre

1 (6th) bde (2 para bn, 1 air mob bn, 1 fd arty bn, 1 AT coy, 1 AD coy, 1 engr bn, 1 int coy, 1 NBC coy, 1 sigs coy, 1 log bn)

Mountain

1 (1st) comd (3 mtn inf regt)

Other

1 (Canary Islands) comd (1 lt inf bde (3 lt inf regt, 1 fd arty regt, 1 AT coy, 1 engr bn, 1 int coy, 1 NBC coy, 1 sigs coy, 1 log bn); 1 spt hel bn; 1 AD regt)
1 (Balearic Islands) comd (1 inf regt)
2 (Ceuta and Melilla) comd (1 cav regt, 2 inf regt, 1 arty regt, 1 engr bn, 1 sigs coy, 1 log bn)

Aviation

1 (FAMET) avn comd (1 atk hel bn, 2 spt hel bn, 1 tpt hel bn, 1 sigs bn, 1 log unit (1 spt coy, 1 supply coy))

COMBAT SUPPORT

1 arty comd (3 arty regt; 1 coastal arty regt)
1 AD comd (5 ADA regt, 1 sigs unit)
1 engr comd (2 engr regt, 1 bridging regt)
1 EW/sigs bde with (1 EW regt, 3 sigs regt)
1 EW regt
1 NBC regt
1 railway regt
1 sigs regt
1 CIMIC bn

COMBAT SERVICE SUPPORT

1 log bde (5 log regt)
1 med bde (1 log unit, 2 med regt, 1 fd hospital unit)

EQUIPMENT BY TYPE

MBT 327: 108 *Leopard* 2A4; 219 *Leopard* 2A5E
RECCE 293: 84 B-1 *Centauro*; 209 VEC-3562 BMR-VEC
AIFV 144 *Pizarro* (incl 21 comd)

APC 875
APC (T) 453 M113 (incl variants)
APC (W) 312 BMR-600/BMR-600M1
PPV 110 RG-31
ARTY 1,894
SP 155mm 96 M109A5
TOWED 329: **105mm** 224: 56 L118 light gun; 168 Model 56 pack howitzer; **155mm** 105: 41 M114; 64 SBT 155/52 SIAC
COASTAL 155mm 19 SBT 155/52 APU SBT V07
MOR 1,450: **81mm** 989; **120mm** 461
AT • MSL
SP 116 *Milan*
MANPATS *Spike*-LR; *Milan*; TOW
HELICOPTERS
ATK 6 EC665 *Tiger* HAP-E (18 HAD-E on order)
MRH 21 Bo-105 HOT
TPT 75: **Heavy** 17 CH-47D *Chinook* (HT-17D); **Medium** 36: 16 AS332B *Super Puma* (HU-21); 14 AS532UL *Cougar*; 6 AS532AL *Cougar;* **Light** 22: 17 Bell-205 (HU-10B *Iroquois*); 5 Bell 212 (HU.18)
UAV • ISR • Medium 4 *Searcher* Mk II-J (PASI)
AD 370
SAM 279
SP 18 *Roland*
TOWED 81: 52 MIM-23B I-HAWK Phase III; 13 *Skyguard*/*Aspide;* 8 NASAMS; 8 PAC-2 *Patriot*
MANPAD *Mistral*
GUNS • TOWED 35mm 91 GDF-005
RADAR • LAND 6: 4 ARTHUR; 2 AN/TPQ-36 *Firefinder*
AEV 39 CZ-10/25E
ARV 58: 16 *Büffel*; 1 AMX-30; 1 BMR 3560.55; 4 *Centauro* REC; 22 M47-VR; 2 M578; 12 M113
VLB 19 M60

Navy 22,200 (incl Naval Aviation and Marines)

EQUIPMENT BY TYPE
SUBMARINES • TACTICAL • SSK 3:
3 *Galerna* with 4 single 533mm TT with F17 Mod 2/L5 HWT
PRINCIPAL SURFACE COMBATANTS 11
DESTROYERS • DDGHM 5:
5 *Alvaro de Bazan* with Baseline 5 *Aegis* C2, 2 quad Mk141 lnchr with RGM-84F *Harpoon* AShM, 1 48-cell Mk41 VLS (LAM capable) with SM-2MR/RIM-162B *Sea Sparrow* SAM, 2 twin 324mm ASTT with Mk46 LWT, 1 127mm gun, (capacity 1 SH-60B *Seahawk* ASW hel)
FRIGATES • FFGHM 6:
6 *Santa Maria* with 1 Mk13 GMLS with RGM-84C *Harpoon* AShM/SM-1MR SAM, 2 Mk32 triple 324mm ASTT with Mk46 LWT, 1 76mm gun, (capacity 2 SH-60B *Seahawk* ASW hel)
AMPHIBIOUS
PRINCIPAL AMPHIBIOUS SHIPS 3:
LHD 1 *Juan Carlos I* (capacity 4 LCM; 42 APC; 46 MBT; 700 troops; able to operate as platform for aviation group)
LPD 2 *Galicia* (capacity 6 Bell 212 or 4 SH-3D *Sea King* hel; 4 LCM; 130 APC or 33 MBT; 450 troops)
LANDING CRAFT 14
LCM 14 LCM 1E
LOGISTICS AND SUPPORT 2
AORH 2: 1 *Patino* (capacity 3 Bell 212 or 2 SH-3D *Sea King* hel); 1 *Cantabria* (capacity 3 Bell 212 or 2 SH-3D *Sea King* hel)

Navy – Maritime Action Force

PATROL AND COASTAL COMBATANTS 23
PSO 7:
3 *Alboran* each with 1 hel landing platform
4 *Descubierta* with 1 76mm gun
PSOH 4 *Meteoro* (*Buques de Accion Maritima* – 5 additional vessels on order, of which 3 are PSOH, 1 ASR and 1 AGS)
PCO 4 *Serviola* with 1 76mm gun
PCC 3 *Anaga* with 1 76mm gun
PB 2 *Toralla* with 1 76mm gun
PBR 3 P-101/114/201
MINE WARFARE • MINE COUNTERMEASURES 6
MHO 6 *Segura*
LOGISTICS AND SUPPORT 77
AGDS 1 *Neptuno*
AGI 1 *Alerta*
AGOR 2 (with ice-strengthened hull, for polar research duties in Antarctica)
AGS 4: 2 *Malaspina*; 2 *Castor* (1 scheduled to decommission by end-2013)
AK 2: 1 *Martin Posadillo* (with 1 hel landing platform); 1 *El Camino Español*
AP 1 *Contramaestre* (with 1 hel landing platform)
ATF 3: 1 *Mar Caribe*; 1 *Mahon*; 1 *La Grana*
AXL 8: 4 *Contramaestre*; 4 *Guardiamarina*
AXS 8
YO 22
YTM 25

Naval Aviation 800

Flying hours	150 hrs/year on AV-8B *Harrier* II FGA ac; 200 hrs/year on hel

FORCES BY ROLE
FIGHTER/GROUND ATTACK
1 sqn with AV-8B *Harrier* II; AV-8B *Harrier* II Plus **ANTI-SUBMARINE WARFARE**
1 sqn with SH-60B *Seahawk*
AIRBORNE EARLY WARNING
1 sqn with SH-3H AEW *Sea King*
TRANSPORT
1 (liaison) sqn with Cessna 550 *Citation* II; Cessna 650 *Citation* VII
TRAINING
1 sqn with Hughes 500MD8
1 flt with TAV-8B *Harrier*
TRANSPORT HELICOPTER
1 sqn with Bell 212 (HU-18)
1 sqn with SH-3D *Sea King*
EQUIPMENT BY TYPE
AIRCRAFT 17 combat capable
FGA 17: 4 AV-8B *Harrier* II; 12 AV-8B *Harrier* II Plus; 1 TAV-8B *Harrier* (on lease from USMC)
TPT • Light 4: 3 Cessna 550 *Citation* II; 1 Cessna 650 *Citation* VII

HELICOPTERS

ASW 19: 7 SH-3D *Sea King* (tpt); 12 SH-60B *Seahawk*
MRH 9 Hughes 500MD
AEW 3 SH-3H AEW *Sea King*
TPT • Light 7 Bell 212 (HA-18)

MSL

AAM • IR AIM-9L *Sidewinder*; **ARH** AIM-120 AMRAAM
ASM AGM-65G *Maverick*
AShM AGM-119 *Penguin*

Marines 5,300

FORCES BY ROLE

SPECIAL FORCES

1 spec ops unit

MANOEUVRE

Amphibious

1 mne bde (1 recce unit, 1 mech inf bn, 2 inf bn, 1 arty bn, 1 log bn)
5 mne garrison gp

EQUIPMENT BY TYPE

MBT 16 M60A3TTS
APC (W) 39 *Piranha* IIIC
AAV 18: 16 AAV-7A1/AAVP-7A1; 2 AAVC-7A1
ARTY 18
SP 155mm 6 M109A2
TOWED 105mm 12 M-56 (pack)
AT
MSL • MANPATS 24 TOW-2
RL 90mm C-90C
AD • SAM • MANPAD 12 *Mistral*
ARV 1 AAVR-7A1

Air Force 20,600

The Spanish Air Force is organised in 3 commands – General Air Command, Combat Air Command and Canary Islands Air Command

Flying hours 120 hrs/year on hel/tpt ac; 180 hrs/year on FGA/ftr

FORCES BY ROLE

FIGHTER

2 sqn with Eurofighter *Typhoon*

FIGHTER/GROUND ATTACK

5 sqn with F/A-18A/B MLU *Hornet* (EF-18A/B MLU)

MARITIME PATROL

1 sqn with P-3A/M *Orion*

ISR

1 sqn with Beech C90 *King Air*
1 sqn with Cessna 550 *Citation* V; CN-235 (TR-19A)

ELECTRONIC WARFARE

1 sqn with B-707 *Santiago*; C-212 *Aviocar*; *Falcon* 20D/E

SEARCH & RESCUE

1 sqn with AS332B/B1 *Super Puma*; CN-235 VIGMA
1 sqn with AS332B *Super Puma*; CN-235 VIGMA
1 sqn with C-212 *Aviocar*; CN-235 VIGMA; SA330J/L *Puma* (AS330)

TANKER/TRANSPORT

1 sqn with B-707/B-707 tkr
1 sqn with KC-130H *Hercules*

TRANSPORT

1 VIP sqn with A310; *Falcon* 900
1 sqn with C-130H/H-30 *Hercules*
1 sqn with C-212 *Aviocar*
2 sqn with C-295
1 sqn with CN-235

TRAINING

1 OCU sqn with Eurofighter *Typhoon*
1 OCU sqn with F/A-18A/B (EF-18A/B MLU) *Hornet*
1 sqn with Beech F33C *Bonanza*
2 sqn with C-101 *Aviojet*
1 sqn with C-212 *Aviocar*
1 sqn with T-35 *Pillan* (E-26)
2 (LIFT) sqn with F-5B *Freedom Fighter*
1 hel sqn with EC120 *Colibri*
1 hel sqn with S-76C

FIRE FIGHTING

2 sqn with CL-215; CL-415

TRANSPORT HELICOPTER

1 sqn with AS332M1 *Super Puma*; AS532UL *Cougar* (VIP)

EQUIPMENT BY TYPE

AIRCRAFT 157 combat capable
FTR 65: 45 Eurofighter *Typhoon*; 20 F-5B *Freedom Fighter*
FGA 86: 74 F/A-18A *Hornet* (EF-18A); 12 F/A-18B *Hornet* (EF-18B – 67 EF-18s being given MLU)
ASW 6: 2 P-3A *Orion*; 4 P-3M *Orion*
MP 8 CN-235 VIGMA
ISR 2 CN-235 (TR-19A)
EW 6: 1 B-707 *Santiago* (TM.17); 1 C-212 *Aviocar* (TM.12D); 2 *Falcon* 20D; 2 *Falcon* 20E
TKR 6: 5 KC-130H *Hercules*, 1 B-707 Tkr
TPT 73: **Medium** 7: 6 C-130H *Hercules*; 1 C-130H-30 *Hercules*; **Light** 57: 4 Beech C90 *King Air*; 22 Beech F33C *Bonanza*; 7 C-212 *Aviocar*; 13 C-295; 8 CN-235; 3 Cessna 550 *Citation* V (ISR); **PAX** 9: 2 A310; 2 B-707; 5 *Falcon* 900 (VIP)
TRG 103: 66 C-101 *Aviojet*; 37 T-35 *Pillan* (E-26)
FF 17: 14 CL-215; 3 CL-415

HELICOPTERS

TPT 46: **Medium** 23: 11 AS332B/B1 *Super Puma*; 4 AS332M1 *Super Puma*; 2 AS532UL *Cougar* (VIP); 4 SA330J *Puma* (AS330); 2 SA330L *Puma* (AS330); **Light** 23: 15 EC-120 *Colibri*; 8 S-76C

AD

SAM *Mistral*; R-530
TOWED *Skyguard*/*Aspide*

MSL

AAM • IR AIM-9L/JULI *Sidewinder*; **IIR** IRIS-T; **SARH** AIM-7P *Sparrow*; **ARH** AIM-120B/C AMRAAM
ARM AGM-88A HARM
ASM AGM-65G *Maverick*
AShM AGM-84C/D *Harpoon*
LACM *Taurus* KEPD 350

BOMBS

Conventional: Mk 82; Mk 83; Mk 84; BR-250; BR-500; BRP-250
Laser-guided: GBU-10/16 *Paveway* II; GBU-24 *Paveway* III; EGBU-16 *Paveway* II; BPG-2000

Emergencies Military Unit (UME)

FORCES BY ROLE
COMMAND
1 div HQ
FIRE FIGHTING
2 sqn with CL-215; CL-415 opcon Air Force
MANOEUVRE
Aviation
1 hel bn opcon Army
Other
5 Emergency Intervention bn

Paramilitary 80,700

Guardia Civil 79,950

9 regions, 56 Rural Comds

FORCES BY ROLE
SPECIAL FORCES
10 (rural) gp
MANOEUVRE
Other
17 (Tercios) paramilitary regt
6 (traffic) sy gp
1 (Special) sy bn

EQUIPMENT BY TYPE
APC (W) 18 BLR
HELICOPTERS
MRH 26 Bo-105ATH
TPT • Light 12: 8 BK-117; 4 EC-135P2

Guardia Civil Del Mar 750

PATROL AND COASTAL COMBATANTS 72
PSO 1 with 1 hel landing platform
PCC 2
PBF 40
PB 29

Cyber

Spain has established a cyber command. Spain has a national CERT and is a member of the European CERT group. The national intelligence CERT (CCN-CERT) is responsible for coordinating CERT activities.

DEPLOYMENT

Legal provisions for foreign deployment:
Constitution: Codified constitution (1978)
Specific legislation: 'Ley Orgánica de la Defensa Nacional' (2005)
Decision on deployment of troops abroad: a) By the government (Art. 6 of the 'Defence Law'); b) parliamentary approval is required for military operations 'which are not directly related to the defence of Spain or national interests' (Art. 17 of the 'Defence Law')

AFGHANISTAN
NATO • ISAF 856

BOSNIA-HERZEGOVINA
EU • EUFOR • *Operation Althea* 12
OSCE • Bosnia and Herzegovina 1

GULF OF ADEN & INDIAN OCEAN
EU • *Operation Atalanta* 1 PSO; 1 P-3A

LEBANON
UN • UNIFIL 587; 1 armd inf bde HQ; 1 mech inf BG

MALI
EU • EUTM Mali 59

MEDITERRANEAN SEA
NATO • SNMG 2 1 DDGHM

MOLDOVA
OSCE • Moldova 1

SERBIA
OSCE • Kosovo 2

UGANDA
EU • EUTM Somalia 16

FOREIGN FORCES

United States US European Command: 1,480 1 air base at Morón; 1 naval base at Rota

Sweden SWE

Swedish Krona Skr		2012	2013	2014
GDP	Skr	3.67tr	3.84tr	
	US$	526bn	576bn	
per capita	US$	55,158	60,020	
Growth	%	1.20	1.01	
Inflation	%	0.89	0.30	
Def exp [a]	Skr	40.8bn		
	US$	6.02bn		
Def bdgt [a]	Skr	41.8bn	42.3bn	43.4bn
	US$	6.17bn	6.63bn	
US$1=Skr		6.78	6.38	

[a] Excludes military pensions and peacekeeping expenditure

Population 9,119,423

Age	0 – 14	15 – 19	20 – 24	25 – 29	30 – 64	65 plus
Male	7.9%	3.0%	3.6%	3.3%	22.5%	9.2%
Female	7.5%	2.8%	3.5%	3.2%	22.2%	11.3%

Capabilities

Sweden's army and air force are relatively well-equipped, but the navy retains limited capabilities and is unable to operate beyond territorial waters and the Baltic Sea. Sweden regularly participates in peacekeeping operations, and sent troops to participate in the NATO-led coalition in Afghanistan and aircraft to *Operation Unified Protector* off Libya in 2011, even though the country remains outside NATO. Territorial defence is the primary role of the armed forces and Sweden's power-projection capabilities are limited. Two *Stockholm*-class corvettes that participated in *Operation Atalanta* in 2009 were unable to make the journey independently, and were transported by a dock ship. The air force has only one tanker to support its aircraft when on operations. Swedish forces are well-trained and professional; compulsory military service was formally abolished in July 2010. The country is moving ahead with the next generation *Gripen*, and 2014 should bring a final decision from Switzerland to also go ahead with the procurement of the *Gripen* E. Increased Russian air activity has highlighted the reduced state of round-the-clock responsiveness by the Swedish air force. Nevertheless, Sweden's armed forces will likely continue to fulfil one of their main goals of contributing small units and support to multinational coalitions.

ACTIVE 15,300 (Army 5,550 Navy 3,000 Air 3,300 Staff 3,450) Paramilitary 800 Voluntary Auxiliary Organisations 22,000

ORGANISATIONS BY SERVICE

Army 5,550

The army has been transformed to provide brigade-sized task forces depending on the operational requirement.

FORCES BY ROLE

COMMAND
1 div HQ (on mobilisation)
2 bde HQ
MANOEUVRE
Reconnaissance
1 recce bn
Armoured
3 armd coy
Mechanised
4 mech bn
Light
2 mot inf bn
1 lt inf bn
Air Manoeuvre
1 AB bn
Other
1 sy bn
COMBAT SUPPORT
2 arty bn
2 AD bn
2 engr bn
2 MP coy
COMBAT SERVICE SUPPORT
2 log bn

Reserves

FORCES BY ROLE

MANOEUVRE
Other
40 Home Guard bn

EQUIPMENT BY TYPE

MBT 132: 12 *Leopard* 2A4 (Strv-121); 120 *Leopard* 2A5 (Strv 122)
AIFV 354 CV9040 (Strf 9040)
APC 663+
APC (T) 242: 194 Pbv 302; 48 BvS10 MkII
APC (W) 161+: 23 XA-180 *Sisu* (Patgb 180); 1 XA-202 *Sisu* (Patgb 202); 136 XA-203 *Sisu* (Patgb 203); 1+ XA-360 (Patgb 360)
PPV 260 RG-32M
ARTY 195
SP 155mm 4 *Archer* being delivered
MOR 120mm 191
AT
MSL • MANPATS RB-55; RB-56 *Bill*
RCL 84mm *Carl Gustav*
AD
SAM
SP 16 RBS-70
TOWED RBS-90
MANPAD RBS-70
GUNS • SP 40mm 30 Strv 90LV
RADAR • LAND ARTHUR (arty); M113A1GE *Green Archer* (mor)
UAV • ISR • Medium 3 *Sperwer*
AEV *Kodiak*
ARV 40: 14 Bgbv 120; 26 CV90
MW *Aardvark* Mk2; 33 Area Clearing System

Navy 2,150; 850 Amphibious; (total 3,000)

EQUIPMENT BY TYPE

SUBMARINES 6
TACTICAL • SSK 5:
3 *Gotland* (AIP fitted) with 2 single 400mm TT with Tp432/Tp 451, 4 single 533mm TT with Tp613/Tp62
2 *Sodermanland* (AIP fitted) with 6 single 533mm TT with Tp432/Tp451/Tp613/Tp62
SSW 1 *Spiggen* II
PATROL AND COASTAL COMBATANTS 22
CORVETTES • FSG 5 *Visby* with 8 RBS-15 AShM, 4 single 400mm ASTT with Tp45 LWT, 1 57mm gun, 1 hel landing plaform, (all to be at FOC by mid-2014)
PCG 4:
2 *Göteborg* with 4 twin lnchr with RBS-15 Mk2 AShM, 4 single 400mm ASTT with Tp431 LWT, 4 Saab 601 A/S mor, 1 57mm gun
2 *Stockholm* with 4 twin lnchr with RBS-15 Mk2 AShM, 4 Saab 601 mortars, 4 single ASTT with Tp431 LWT, 1 57mm gun
PB 2
PBR 11 *Tapper*
MINE WARFARE • MINE COUNTERMEASURES 13
MCC 5 *Koster*
MCD 2 *Spårö*
MSD 6: 5 *Sam*; 1 *Sokaren*
AMPHIBIOUS • LANDING CRAFT 156
LCM 9 *Trossbat*
LCPL 147 Combatboat 90
LOGISTICS AND SUPPORT 46
AG 2: 1 *Carlskrona* with 2 57mm gun, 1 hel landing platform (former ML); 1 *Trosso* (spt ship for corvettes and patrol vessels but can also be used as HQ ship)
AGF 2 Combatboat 450
AGI 1 *Orion*
AGS 2 (Government Maritime Forces)
AK 1 *Loke*

ARS 2: 1 *Belos* III; 1 *Furusund* (former ML)
AX 5 *Altair*
AXS 2: 1 *Falkan*; 1 *Gladan*
YAG 16 *Trossbat*
YDT 1 *Agir*
YPT 1 *Pelikanen*
YTM 11

Amphibious 850

FORCES BY ROLE
MANOEUVRE
Amphibious
1 amph bn

EQUIPMENT BY TYPE
ARTY • MOR 81mm 12
MSL • AShM 8 RBS-17 *Hellfire*

Air Force 3,300

Flying hours 100–150 hrs/year

FORCES BY ROLE
FIGHTER/GROUND ATTACK/ISR
4 sqn with JAS 39C/D *Gripen*
SIGINT
1 sqn with Gulfstream IV SRA-4 (S-102B)
AIRBORNE EARLY WARNING & CONTROL
1 sqn with S-100B/D *Argus*
TRANSPORT
1 sqn with C-130E/H *Hercules* (Tp-84); KC-130H *Hercules* (Tp-84)
TRAINING
1 sqn with JAS-39A/B *Gripen*
1 OCU sqn with JAS-39A/B/C/D *Gripen*
1 unit with Sk-60
AIR DEFENCE
1 (fighter control and air surv) bn

EQUIPMENT BY TYPE
AIRCRAFT 134 combat capable
FGA 134 JAS39A/B/C/D *Gripen*
ELINT 2 Gulfstream IV SRA-4 (S-102B)
AEW&C 3: 1 S-100B *Argus*; 2 S-100D *Argus*
TKR 1 KC-130H *Hercules* (Tp-84)
TPT 10: **Medium** 7 C-130E/H *Hercules* (Tp-84); **Light** 2 Saab 340 (OS-100A/Tp-100C); **PAX** 1 Gulfstream 550 (Tp-102D)
TRG 80 Sk-60W
UAV • ISR • Medium 8 RQ-7 *Shadow* (AUV 3 Örnen)
MSL
ASM AGM-65 *Maverick* (RB-75)
AShM RB-15F
AAM • IR AIM-9L *Sidewinder* (RB-74); **IIR** IRIS-T (RB-98); **ARH** AIM-120B AMRAAM (RB-99)

Armed Forces Hel Wing

FORCES BY ROLE
TRANSPORT HELICOPTER
3 sqn with AS332 *Super Puma* (Hkp-10A/B/D); AW109 (Hkp 15A); AW109M (Hkp-15B); NH90 TTH (Hkp-14A); UH-60M *Black Hawk* (Hkp-16)

EQUIPMENT BY TYPE
HELICOPTERS
TPT 51: **Medium** 31: 9 AS332 *Super Puma* (Hkp-10A/B/D - SAR); 15 UH-60M *Black Hawk* (Hkp-16); 7 NH90 TTH (Hkp-14A); **Light** 20: 12 AW109 (Hkp-15A); 8 AW109M (Hkp-15B)

Paramilitary 800

Coast Guard 800

EQUIPMENT BY TYPE
PATROL AND COASTAL COMBATANTS 28
PSO 3 KBV-001
PCO 1 KBV-181 (fishery protection)
PCC 2 KBV-201
PB 22: 1 KBV-101; 4 KBV-281; 3 KBV-288; 11 KBV-301; 3 KBV-312
AMPHIBIOUS • LANDING CRAFT • LCAC 2 Griffon 2000 TDX (KBV-591)
LOGISTICS AND SUPPORT • AG 12: 8 MARPOL-CRAFT; 4 KBV-031

Air Arm

AIRCRAFT • TPT • Light 3 DHC-8Q-300

Cyber

Sweden has a national CERT, is involved in informal CERT communities, and is a member of the European Government CERTs group (EGC). A national cyber-security strategy has also been adopted. Four ministries have a cyber remit: defence, foreign affairs, justice, and enterprise and industry. The Swedish Civil Contingencies Agency (AMS), which reports to the MoD, is in charge of supporting and coordinating security across society.

DEPLOYMENT

Legal provisions for foreign deployment:
Constitution: Constitution consists of four fundamental laws; the most important is 'The Instrument of Government' (1974)
Decision on deployment of troops abroad: By the government upon parliamentary approval (Ch. 10, Art. 9)

AFGHANISTAN
NATO • ISAF 259
UN • UNAMA 2 obs

ARMENIA/AZERBAIJAN
OSCE • Minsk Conference 1

BOSNIA-HERZEGOVINA
EU • EUFOR • *Operation Althea* 2

DEMOCRATIC REPUBLIC OF THE CONGO
EU • EUSEC RD Congo 1
UN • MONUSCO 5 obs

INDIA/PAKISTAN
UN • UNMOGIP 5 obs

KOREA, REPUBLIC OF
NNSC • 5 obs

MALI
EU • EUTM Mali 16
UN • MINUSMA 6

MIDDLE EAST
UN • UNTSO 6 obs

MOLDOVA
OSCE • Moldova 1

SERBIA
NATO • KFOR 52
OSCE • Kosovo 2
OSCE • Serbia 1

SOUTH SUDAN
UN • UNMISS 2; 4 obs

UGANDA
EU • EUTM Somalia 4

Switzerland CHE

Swiss Franc fr		2012	2013	2014
GDP	fr	602bn	617bn	
	US$	632bn	648bn	
per capita	US$	79,033	80,473	
Growth	%	0.98	1.28	
Inflation	%	-0.70	-0.20	
Def exp [a]	fr	4.31bn		
	US$	4.59bn		
Def bdgt [a]	fr	4.53bn	4.69bn	4.73bn
	US$	4.83bn	5.04bn	
US$1=fr		0.94	0.93	

[a] Excludes military pensions

Population 7,996,026

Age	0 – 14	15 – 19	20 – 24	25 – 29	30 – 64	65 plus
Male	7.8%	2.8%	3.0%	3.3%	24.8%	7.5%
Female	7.4%	2.7%	3.0%	3.3%	24.6%	9.8%

Capabilities

The Swiss armed forces are almost entirely reliant on conscripts for their active personnel and reserves for full mobilisation, with professional, volunteer personnel comprising just 5% of the total armed forces. A referendum proposing an end to conscription was rejected in 2013, and with conscripts and reserves only serving for short periods of time the armed forces lack adaptability and readiness. However, Switzerland's policy of neutrality limits the missions of the armed forces to territorial defence in a benign environment and international peace-support operations, mitigating some of the problems of the conscription model. The armed forces' equipment is largely aimed at protecting Switzerland's territorial sovereignty, with limited power-projection capabilities (only light transport aircraft and no tankers). The size of the armed forces is likely to be severely reduced in forthcoming years. Current plans suggest a reduction to 100,000 personnel (still largely conscript and reserves), despite an increasing defence budget in the near term. Some of this extra funding may now be spent on replacing ageing F-5 aircraft with *Gripens* in the air-policing role after a deal was approved by parliament in late 2013, although the purchase might still face a referendum in 2014.

ACTIVE 22,650 (Joint 22,650)

Conscript liability Recruit trg of 18, 21 or 25 weeks (depending on military branch) at age 19–20, followed by 7, 6, or 5 refresher trg courses (3 weeks each) over a 10-year period between ages 20–30

RESERVE 161,250 (Army 106,900, Air 24,250, Armed Forces Logistic Organisation 14,150, Command Support Organisation 15,950)

Civil Defence 74,000

ORGANISATIONS BY SERVICE

Joint 3,350 active; 19,300 conscript (22,650 total)

Land Forces (Army) 106,900 on mobilisation

4 Territorial Regions. With the exception of military security all units are non-active.

FORCES BY ROLE
COMMAND
4 regional comd (2 engr bn, 1 sigs bn)
MANOEUVRE
Armoured
1 (1st) bde (1 recce bn, 2 armd bn, 2 armd inf bn, 1 sp arty bn, 2 engr bn, 1 sigs bn)
1 (11th) bde (1 recce bn, 2 armd bn, 2 armd inf bn, 1 inf bn, 2 SP arty bn, 1 engr bn, 1 sigs bn)
Light
1 (2nd) bde (1 recce bn, 4 inf bn, 2 SP arty bn, 1 engr bn, 1 sigs bn)
1 (5th) bde (1 recce bn, 3 inf bn, 2 SP arty bn, 1 engr bn, 1 sigs bn)
1 (7th) reserve bde (3 recce bn, 3 inf bn, 2 mtn inf bn, 1 sigs bn)
Mountain
1 (9th) bde (5 mtn inf bn, 1 SP Arty bn, 1 sigs bn)
1 (12th) bde (2 inf bn, 3 mtn inf bn, 1 (fortress) arty bn, 1 sigs bn)
1 (10th) reserve bde (1 recce bn, 2 armd bn, 3 inf bn, 2 mtn inf bn, 2 SP arty bn, 2 sigs bn)
Other
1 sy bde
COMBAT SERVICE SUPPORT
1 armd/arty trg unit
1 inf trg unit
1 engr rescue trg unit
1 log trg unit

EQUIPMENT BY TYPE
MBT 250 *Leopard* 2 (Pz-87 *Leo*)
RECCE 455: 443 *Eagle* II; 12 *Piranha* IIIC CBRN
AIFV 186: 154 CV9030; 32 CV9030 CP
APC 914

APC (T) 238 M113A2 (incl variants)
APC (W) 676: 346 *Piranha* II; 330 *Piranha* I/II/IIIC CP
ARTY 383
SP 155mm 133 M109
MOR • SP 81mm 250 M113 with M72/91
AT • MSL • SP 110 *Piranha* I TOW-2
AD • SAM • MANPAD FIM-92A *Stinger*
AEV 12 *Kodiak*
ARV 25 *Büffel*
MW 46: 26 Area Clearing System; 20 M113A2
PATROL AND COASTAL COMBATANTS • PBR 11 *Aquarius*

Air Force 24,250 (incl air defence units and military airfield guard units)

Flying hours 200–250 hrs/year

FORCES BY ROLE
FIGHTER
3 sqn with F-5E/F *Tiger* II
3 sqn with F/A-18C/D *Hornet*
TRANSPORT
1 sqn with Beech 350 *King Air*; DHC-6 *Twin Otter*; PC-6 *Turbo Porter*; PC-12
1 VIP Flt with Beech 1900D; Cessna 560XL *Citation*; *Falcon* 900EX
TRAINING
1 sqn with PC-7CH *Turbo Trainer*; PC-21
1 sqn with PC-9 (tgt towing)
1 OCU Sqn with F-5E/F *Tiger* II
TRANSPORT HELICOPTER
6 sqn with AS332M *Super Puma*; AS532UL *Cougar*; EC635
ISR UAV
1 sqn with ADS 95 *Ranger*

EQUIPMENT BY TYPE
AIRCRAFT 86 combat capable
FTR 54: 42 F-5E *Tiger* II; 12 F-5F *Tiger* II
FGA 32: 26 F/A-18C *Hornet*; 6 F/A-18D *Hornet*
TPT 22: **Light** 21: 1 Beech 350 *King Air*; 1 Beech1900D; 1 Cessna 560XL *Citation*; 1 DHC-6 *Twin Otter*; 15 PC-6 *Turbo Porter*; 1 PC-6 (owned by armasuisse, civil registration); 1 PC-12 (owned by armasuisse, civil registration); **PAX** 1 *Falcon* 900EX
TRG 44: 28 PC-7CH *Turbo Trainer*; 8 PC-9; 8 PC-21
HELICOPTERS
TPT 46: **Medium** 26: 15 AS332M *Super Puma*; 11 AS532UL *Cougar*; **Light** 20 EC635
UAV • ISR • Medium 16 ADS 95 *Ranger* (4 systems)
MSL • AAM • IR AIM-9P *Sidewinder*; **IIR** AIM-9X *Sidewinder*; **ARH** AIM-120B AMRAAM

Ground Based Air Defence (GBAD)

GBAD assets can be used to form AD clusters to be deployed independently as task forces within Swiss territory.

EQUIPMENT BY TYPE
AD
SAM
TOWED *Rapier*
MANPAD FIM-92A *Stinger*
GUNS 35mm
RADARS • AD RADARS *Skyguard*

Armed Forces Logistic Organisation 14,150 on mobilisation

FORCES BY ROLE
COMBAT SERVICE SUPPORT
1 log bde

Command Support Organisation 15,950 on mobilisation

FORCES BY ROLE
COMBAT SERVICE SUPPORT
1 spt bde

Civil Defence 74,000

(not part of armed forces)

Cyber

Five major Swiss government organisations maintain an overview of elements of cyber threats and responses: the Federal Intelligence Service; the Military Intelligence Service; the Command Support Organisation; Information Security and Facility Protection; and the Federal Office for Civil Protection. A National Cyber Defence Strategy was published in 2012.

DEPLOYMENT

Legal provisions for foreign deployment:
Constitution: Codified constitution (1999)
Decision on deployment of troops abroad:
Peace promotion (66, 66a, 66b Swiss Mil Law): UN.OSCE mandate. Decision by govt; if over 100 tps deployed or op over 3 weeks Fed Assembly must agree first, except in emergency.
Support service abroad (69, 60 Swiss Mil Law): Decision by govt; if over 2,000 tps or op over 3 weeks Fed Assembly must agree in next official session

BOSNIA-HERZEGOVINA
UN • EUFOR • *Operation Althea* 20

DEMOCRATIC REPUBLIC OF THE CONGO
UN • MONUSCO 3; 1 obs

KOREA, REPUBLIC OF
NNSC • 5 officers

MIDDLE EAST
UN • UNTSO 12 obs

MOLDOVA
OSCE • Moldova 1

SERBIA
NATO • KFOR 223 (military volunteers); 1 inf coy
OSCE • Kosovo 1
OSCE • Serbia 1

SOUTH SUDAN
UN • UNMISS 2; 2 obs

Turkey TUR

New Turkish Lira L		2012	2013	2014
GDP	L	1.57tr	1.72tr	
	US$	794bn	852bn	
per capita	US$	10,609	11,236	
Growth	%	2.62	3.43	
Inflation	%	8.91	6.64	
Def exp	L	30.7bn		
	US$	17.1bn		
Def bdgt [a]	L	18.3bn	19.8bn	22.4bn
	US$	10.2bn	10.7bn	
US$1=L		1.80	1.84	

[a] Includes funding for Undersecretariat of Defence Industries. Excludes military procurement allocations.

Population 80,694,485

Age	0–14	15–19	20–24	25–29	30–64	65 plus
Male	13.2%	4.3%	4.3%	4.3%	21.2%	3.0%
Female	12.6%	4.2%	4.1%	4.2%	20.9%	3.6%

Capabilities

Turkey has capable armed forces intended to meet national defence requirements and its NATO obligations. The role of the armed forces has been recast since the end of the Cold War, with internal security and regional instability providing challenges, as made apparent by events in Syria. The army is becoming smaller but more capable, with the aim of improving its ability to meet a full range of NATO missions while providing a highly mobile force able to fight across the spectrum of conflict. The air force is well-equipped and well-trained, and is introducing airborne early-warning aircraft. It already operates tanker aircraft and will bolster its transport fleet with the A400M airlifter. The navy is the smallest of the three services, and operates a mix of frigates, corvettes, fast-attack craft and amphibious vessels. The military has ambitious procurement plans, which will require a significant increase in funding over the period to 2016. Turkish forces are deployed to ISAF, and Ankara sent ships to take part in *Operation Unified Protector* in 2011. Single and inter-service training is carried out regularly, as is mobilisation training, and the armed forces participate in multinational exercises with NATO partners. Under NATO auspices, the US, the Netherlands and Germany deployed *Patriot* missile batteries to southern Turkey in 2013, in light of perceived threats from the conflict in Syria.

ACTIVE 510,600 (Army 402,000 Navy 48,600 Air 60,000) Paramilitary 102,200

Conscript liability 15 months. Active figure reducing.

RESERVE 378,700 (Army 258,700 Navy 55,000 Air 65,000) Paramilitary 50,000

Reserve service to age of 41 for all services.

ORGANISATIONS BY SERVICE

Space

SATELLITES • ISR 1 *Gokturk-2*

Army ε77,000; ε325,000 conscript (total 402,000)

FORCES BY ROLE

COMMAND
4 army HQ
9 corps HQ

SPECIAL FORCES
4 cdo bde
1 mtn cdo bde
1 cdo regt

MANOEUVRE

Armoured
1 (52nd) armd div (2 armd bde, 1 mech bde)
7 armd bde

Mechanised
2 (28th & 29th) mech div
14 mech inf bde

Light
1 (23rd) mot inf div (3 mot inf regt)
11 mot inf bde

Aviation
4 avn regt
4 avn bn

COMBAT SUPPORT
2 arty bde
1 trg arty bde
6 arty regt
2 engr regt

EQUIPMENT BY TYPE

MBT 2,504: 325 *Leopard* 2A4; 170 *Leopard* 1A4; 227 *Leopard* 1A3; 274 M60A1; 658 M60A3; 850 M48A5 T1/T2 (2,000 more in store)
RECCE 320+: ε250 *Akrep;* 70+ ARSV *Cobra*
AIFV 650 AIFV
APC (T) 3,643: 830 AAPC; 2,813 M113/M113A1/M113A2
ARTY 7,822+
SP 1,103: **105mm** 391: 26 M108T; 365 M-52T; **155mm** 457: 222 M-44T1; ε235 T-155 *Firtina* (K-9 *Thunder*); **175mm** 36 M107; **203mm** 219 M110A2
TOWED 760+: **105mm** 75+ M101A1; **155mm** 523: 517 M114A1/M114A2; 6 *Panter;* **203mm** 162 M115
MRL 146+: **107mm** 48; **122mm** ε36 T-122; **227mm** 12 MLRS (incl ATACMS); **302mm** 50+ TR-300 *Kasirga* (WS-1)
MOR 5,813+
SP 1,443+: **81mm**; **107mm** 1,264 M-30; **120mm** 179
TOWED 4,370: **81mm** 3,792; **120mm** 578
AT
MSL 1,363
SP 365 TOW
MANPATS 998: 80 9K123 *Kornet;* 186 *Cobra;* ε340 *Eryx;* 392 *Milan*
RCL 3,869: **57mm** 923 M18; **75mm** 617; **106mm** 2,329 M40A1

AIRCRAFT

TPT • Light 38: 5 Beech 200 *King Air*; 30 Cessna 185 (U-17B); 3 Cessna 421

TRG 74: 45 Cessna T182; 25 T-41D *Mescalero*; 4 T-42A *Cochise*

HELICOPTERS

ATK 40: 18 AH-1P *Cobra*; 12 AH-1S *Cobra*; 6 AH-1W *Cobra*; 4 TAH-1P *Cobra*

MRH 28 Hughes 300C

ISR 3 OH-58B *Kiowa*

TPT 221+: **Medium** 80+: 30 AS532UL *Cougar*; 50+ S-70A *Black Hawk*; **Light** 141: 12 Bell 204B (AB-204B); ε45 Bell 205 (UH-1H *Iroquois*); 64 Bell 205A (AB-205A); 20 Bell 206 *Jet Ranger*

UAV • ISR Heavy *Falcon 600/Firebee*; **Medium** CL-89; *Gnat*; **Light** *Harpy*

AD

SAM

SP 148: 70 *Altigan* PMADS octuple *Stinger* lnchr, 78 *Zipkin* PMADS quad *Stinger* lnchr

MANPAD 935: 789 FIM-43 *Redeye* (being withdrawn); 146 FIM-92A *Stinger*

GUNS 1,664

SP 40mm 262 M42A1

TOWED 1,402: **20mm** 439 GAI-D01; **35mm** 120 GDF-001/GDF-003; **40mm** 843: 803 L/60/L/70; 40 T-1

RADAR • LAND AN/TPQ-36 *Firefinder*

AEV 12+: 12 M48; M113A2T2

ARV 150: 12 *Leopard* 1; 105 M48T5; 33 M88A2

VLB 52 Mobile Floating Assault Bridge

MW *Tamkar*

Navy 14,100; 34,500 conscript (total 48,600 including 2,200 Coast Guard and 3,100 Marines)

EQUIPMENT BY TYPE

SUBMARINES • TACTICAL • SSK 14:

6 *Atilay* (GER Type-209/1200) with 8 single 533mm ASTT with SST-4 HWT

8 *Preveze/Gür* (GER Type-209/1400) with 8 single 533mm ASTT with UGM-84 *Harpoon* AShM/*Tigerfish* Mk2 HWT

PRINCIPAL SURFACE COMBATANTS 19

FRIGATES • FFGHM 19:

2 *Barbaros* (mod GER MEKO 200 F244 & F245) with 2 quad Mk141 lnchr with RGM-84C *Harpoon* AShM, 1 octuple Mk29 lnchr with *Aspide* SAM, 2 Mk32 triple 324mm ASTT with Mk46 LWT, 3 *Sea Zenith* CIWS, 1 127mm gun, (capacity: 1 Bell 212 (AB-212) hel)

2 *Barbaros* (mod GER MEKO 200 F246 & F247) with 2 quad Mk141 lnchr with RGM-84C *Harpoon* AShM, 1 8-cell Mk41 VLS with *Aspide* SAM, 2 Mk32 triple 324mm ASTT with Mk46 LWT, 3 *Sea Zenith* CIWS, 1 127mm gun (capacity: 1 Bell 212 (AB-212) hel)

3 *Gaziantep* (ex-US *Oliver Hazard Perry*-class) with 1 Mk13 GMLS with RGM-84C *Harpoon* AShM/SM-1MR SAM, 1 8-cell Mk41 VLS with RIM-162 SAM, 2 Mk32 triple 324mm ASTT with Mk46 LWT, 1 *Phalanx* Block 1B CIWS, 1 76mm gun, (capacity: 1 S-70B *Seahawk* ASW hel)

5 *Gaziantep* (ex-US *Oliver Hazard Perry*-class) with 1 Mk13 GMLS with RGM-84C *Harpoon* AShM/SM-1MR SAM, 2 Mk32 triple 324mm ASTT with Mk46 LWT, 1 *Phalanx* Block 1B CIWS, 1 76mm gun, (capacity: 1 S-70B *Seahawk* ASW hel)

1 *Muavenet* (ex-US *Knox*-class) with 1 octuple Mk16 lnchr with ASROC/RGM-84C *Harpoon* AShM, 2 twin 324mm ASTT with Mk46 LWT, 1 127mm gun, (capacity: 1 Bell 212 (AB-212) utl hel)

4 *Yavuz* (GER MEKO 200TN) with 2 quad Mk141 lnchr with RGM-84C *Harpoon* AShM, 1 octuple Mk29 GMLS with *Aspide* SAM, 2 Mk32 triple 324mm ASTT with Mk46 LWT, 3 *Sea Zenith* CIWS, 1 127mm gun, (capacity: 1 Bell 212 (AB-212) hel)

2 *Ada* with 2 quad lnchr with RCM-84C *Harpoon* AShM, 1 Mk49 21-cell lnchr with RIM-116 SAM, 2 Mk32 twin 324mm ASTT with Mk46 LWT, 1 76mm gun, (capacity: 1 S-70B *Seahawk* hel)

PATROL AND COASTAL COMBATANTS 60

CORVETTES • FSGM 6:

6 *Burak* (FRA *d'Estienne d'Orves*) with 2 single lnchr with MM-38 *Exocet* AShM, 4 single 324mm ASTT with Mk46 LWT, 1 Mk54 A/S mor, 1 100mm gun

PCFG 19:

8 *Dogan* (GER Lurssen-57) with 2 quad lnchr with RGM-84A/C *Harpoon* AShM, 1 76mm gun

9 *Kilic* with 2 quad Mk 141 lnchr with RGM-84C *Harpoon* AShM, 1 76mm gun

2 *Yildiz* with 2 quad lnchr with RGM-84A/C *Harpoon* AShM, 1 76mm gun

PCC 13: 6 *Tuzla*; 6 *Karamursel* (GER *Vegesack*); 1 *Trabzon*;

PBFG 8 *Kartal* (GER *Jaguar*) with 4 single lnchr with RB 12 *Penguin* AShM, 2 single 533mm TT

PBF 4: 2 *Kaan 20*; 2 MRTP22

PB 10:

4 PGM-71 with 1 Mk22 *Mousetrap* A/S mor

6 *Turk* with 1 Mk20 *Mousetrap* A/S mor

MINE WARFARE • MINE COUNTERMEASURES 28:

MCM SPT 8 (tenders)

MHO 11: 5 *Edineik* (FRA *Circe*); 6 *Aydin*

MSC 5 *Silifke* (US *Adjutant*)

MSI 4 *Foca* (US *Cape*)

AMPHIBIOUS

LANDING SHIPS • LST 5:

2 *Ertugrul* (US *Terrebonne Parish*) with 3 76mm gun, (capacity 18 tanks; 400 troops) (with 1 hel landing platform)

1 *Osman Gazi* with 1 *Phalanx* CIWS, (capacity 4 LCVP; 17 tanks; 980 troops) (with 1 hel landing platform)

2 *Sarucabey* with 1 *Phalanx* CIWS, (capacity 11 tanks; 600 troops) (with 1 hel landing platform)

LANDING CRAFT 49

LCT 33: 8 C-151; 12 C-117; 13 C-130

LCM 16 C-302

LOGISTICS AND SUPPORT 79

ABU 2: 1 AG5; 1 AG6 with 1 76mm gun

AGS 3: 2 *Cesme* (US *Silas Bent*); 1 *Cubuklu*

AKL 1 *Eregli*

AOR 2 *Akar* with 1 twin 76mm gun, 1 *Phalanx* CIWS, 1 hel landing platform

AORL 1 *Taskizak*

AOT 2 *Burak*
AOL 1 *Gurcan*
AO 4 (harbour)
AP 1 *Iskenderun*
ARS 1 *Isin*
ASR 1 *Akin*
ATA 1 *Tenace*
ATR 1 *Inebolu*
ATS 3: 1 *Akbas*; 1 *Gazal*; 1 *Darica*
AWT 9: 5; 4 (harbour)
AXL 8
AX 2 *Pasa* (GER *Rhein*)
YAG 2 *Mesaha*
YFD 13
YPB 2
YPT 3
YTM 16

Marines 3,100

FORCES BY ROLE
MANOEUVRE
Amphibious
1 mne bde (3 mne bn; 1 arty bn)

Naval Aviation

FORCES BY ROLE
ANTI-SUBMARINE WARFARE
2 sqn with Bell 212 ASW (AB-212 ASW); S-70B *Seahawk*
1 sqn with ATR-72-600; CN-235M-100; TB-20 *Trinidad*

EQUIPMENT BY TYPE
AIRCRAFT
MP 4 CN-235M-100 (2 more on order)
TPT • Light 6: 1 ATR-72-600; 5 TB-20 *Trinidad*
HELICOPTERS
ASW 29: 11 Bell 212 ASW (AB-212 ASW); 18 S-70B *Seahawk*

Air Force 60,000

2 tac air forces (divided between east and west)

Flying hours 180 hrs/year

FORCES BY ROLE
FIGHTER
1 sqn with F-4E *Phantom* II
2 sqn with F-16C/D *Fighting Falcon*
FIGHTER/GROUND ATTACK
2 sqn with F-4E *Phantom* II
8 sqn with F-16C/D *Fighting Falcon*
ISR
2 sqn with RF-4E/ETM *Phantom* II
1 unit with *King Air* 350
AIRBORNE EARLY WARNING & CONTROL
1 sqn (forming) with B-737 AEW&C
EW
1 unit with CN-235M EW
SEARCH & RESCUE
1 sqn with AS532AL/UL *Cougar*
TANKER
1 sqn with KC-135R *Stratotanker*
TRANSPORT
1 sqn with C-130B/E/H *Hercules*
1 sqn with C-160D *Transall*
1 (VIP) sqn with Cessna 550 *Citation* II (UC-35); Cessna 650 *Citation* VII; CN-235M; Gulfstream 550
3 sqn with CN-235M
10 (liaison) flt with Bell 205 (UH-1H *Iroquois*); CN-235M
TRAINING
1 sqn with F-4E *Phantom* II; F-16C/D *Fighting Falcon*
1 sqn with F-5A/B *Freedom Fighter;* NF-5A/B *Freedom Fighter*
1 OCU sqn with F-16C/D *Fighting Falcon*
1 sqn with SF-260D
1 sqn with KT-IT
1 sqn with T-38A/M *Talon*
1 sqn with T-41D *Mescalero*
AIR DEFENCE
4 sqn with MIM-14 *Nike Hercules*
2 sqn with *Rapier*
8 (firing) unit with MIM-23 HAWK
MANOEUVRE
Air Manoeuvre
1 AB bde

EQUIPMENT BY TYPE
AIRCRAFT 352 combat capable
FTR 53: 18 F-5A *Freedom Fighter;* 8 F-5B *Freedom Fighter;* 17 NF-5A *Freedom Fighter;* 10 NF-5B *Freedom Fighter* (48 F-5s being upgraded as LIFT)
FGA 299: 69 F-4E *Phantom* II (52 upgraded to *Phantom* 2020); 212 F-16C/D *Fighting Falcon* (all being upgraded to Block 50 standard); 9 F-16C Block 50 *Fighting Falcon;* 9 F-16D Block 50 *Fighting Falcon*
ISR 38: 33 RF-4E/ETM *Phantom* II; 5 Beech 350 *King Air*
EW 2+ CN-235M EW
AEW&C 1 B-737 AEW&C (3 more on order)
TKR 7 KC-135R *Stratotanker*
TPT 86 **Medium** 35: 6 C-130B *Hercules;* 12 C-130E *Hercules;* 1 C-130H *Hercules;* 16 C-160D *Transall;* **Light** 50: 2 Cessna 550 *Citation* II (UC-35 - VIP); 2 Cessna 650 *Citation* VII; 46 CN-235M; **PAX** 1 Gulfstream 550
TRG 172: 34 SF-260D; 70 T-38A/M *Talon;* 28 T-41D *Mescalero;* 40 KT-IT
HELICOPTERS
TPT 40 **Medium** 20: 6 AS532AL *Cougar* (CSAR); 14 AS532UL *Cougar* (SAR); **Light** 20 Bell 205 (UH-1H *Iroquois*)
UAV • ISR 28: **Heavy** 10 *Heron;* **Medium** 18 *Gnat* 750
AD
SAM *Rapier*
TOWED: MIM-23 HAWK
STATIC MIM-14 *Nike Hercules*
MSL
AAM • IR AIM-9S *Sidewinder; Shafrir* 2(‡); **SARH** AIM-7E *Sparrow;* **ARH** AIM-120A/B AMRAAM
ARM AGM-88A HARM
ASM AGM-65A/G *Maverick; Popeye* I
BOMBS
Conventional BLU-107;
Electro-optical guided GBU-8B HOBOS (GBU-15)
Laser-guided *Paveway* I; *Paveway* II
PODS
Infrared 80: 40 AN/AAQ-14 LANTIRN; 40 AN/AAQ-13 LANTIRN

Paramilitary

Gendarmerie/National Guard 100,000; 50,000 reservists (total 150,000)

Ministry of Interior; Ministry of Defence in war

FORCES BY ROLE

SPECIAL FORCES

1 cdo bde

MANOEUVRE

Other

1 (border) paramilitary div

2 paramilitary bde

EQUIPMENT BY TYPE

RECCE *Akrep*

APC (W) 560: 535 BTR-60/BTR-80; 25 *Condor*

AIRCRAFT

ISR Some O-1E *Bird Dog*

TPT • Light 2 Do-28D

HELICOPTERS

MRH 19 Mi-17 *Hip* H

TPT 36: **Medium** 13 S-70A *Black Hawk*; **Light** 23: 8 Bell 204B (AB-204B); 6 Bell 205A (AB-205A); 8 Bell 206A (AB-206A) *Jet Ranger*; 1 Bell 212 (AB-212)

Coast Guard 800 (Coast Guard Regular element); 1,050 (from Navy); 1,400 conscript (total 3,250)

PATROL AND COASTAL COMBATANTS 106

PSOH 2 *Dost* with 1 76mm gun (2 further vessels in build; expected ISD 2014/15)

PBF 47

PB 57

AIRCRAFT • MP 1 CN-235 MPA (2 more to be delivered)

HELICOPTERS • MRH 8 Bell 412EP (AB-412EP – SAR)

DEPLOYMENT

Legal provisions for foreign deployment:

Constitution: Codified constitution (1985)

Decision on deployment of troops abroad: a) In general, by parliament (Art. 92); b) in cases of sudden aggression and if parliament is unable to convene, by president (Art. 92, 104b)

AFGHANISTAN

NATO • ISAF 1,036; 1 inf bde HQ; 1 inf bn

UN • UNAMA 1 obs

ARABIAN SEA & GULF OF ADEN

Combined Maritime Forces • CTF-151: 1 FFGHM

BOSNIA-HERZEGOVINA

EU • EUFOR • *Operation Althea* 229; 1 inf coy

CYPRUS (NORTHERN)

ε43,000; 1 army corps HQ; 1 armd bde; 2 mech inf div; 1 avn comd; 8 M48A2 (trg;) 340 M48A5T1/T2; 361 AAPC (incl variants); 266 M113 (incl variants); 72 M101A1; 18 M114A2; 12 M115; 90 M-44T; 6 T-122; 175 81mm mor; 148 M-30; 127 HY-12; 66 *Milan*; 48 TOW; 192 M40A1; Rh 202; 16 GDF-003; 48 M1; 3 Cessna 185 (U-17); 1 AS532UL *Cougar*; 3 UH-1H *Iroquois*; 1 PB

LEBANON

UN • UNIFIL 190; 1 FFGHM

MEDITERRANEAN SEA

NATO • SNMG 2: 1 FFGHM

NATO • SNMCMG 2: 1 MHO

SERBIA

NATO • KFOR 367; 1 inf coy

OSCE • Kosovo 7

UN • UNMIK 1 obs

FOREIGN FORCES

Germany *Active Fence*: 2 bty with *Patriot* PAC-3

Netherlands *Active Fence*: 2 bty with MIM-104 *Patriot*

United States US European Command: 1,500; 4 MQ-1B *Predator* UAV at Incirlik; 1 spt facility at Izmir; 1 spt facility at Ankara; 1 air base at Incirlik• US Strategic Command: 1 Spacetrack Radar at Incirlik; 1 AN/TPY-2 X-band radar at Kürecik • *Active Fence*: 2 bty with MIM-104 *Patriot*

United Kingdom UK

British Pound £		2012	2013	2014
GDP	£	1.58tr	1.64tr	
	US$	2.44tr	2.42tr	
per capita	US$	38,589	38,002	
Growth	%	0.17	0.69	
Inflation	%	2.84	2.65	
Def bdgt [a]	£	38.7bn	37.1bn	
	US$	61.3bn	57bn	
US$1=£		0.63	0.65	

[a] Net Cash Requirement figures. These will differ from official figures based on Resource Accounting & Budgeting. Excludes military pensions covered by the Armed Forces Pension Scheme (AFPS) and the Armed Forces Compensation Scheme (AFCS).

Population 63,395,574

Age	0–14	15–19	20–24	25–29	30–64	65 plus
Male	8.9%	3.1%	3.5%	3.5%	23.0%	7.7%
Female	8.4%	2.9%	3.3%	3.4%	22.6%	9.6%

Capabilities

The UK remains, along with France, Europe's pre-eminent military force, though a mix of over-ambition, under-funding, and defence reviews have reduced the scale of the country's ability to project and sustain combat power. The 2010 Strategic Defence and Security Review was aimed at providing a balanced and affordable path to Future Force 2020, though whether this remains achievable will only become apparent following SDSR 2015. The ground force's Army 2020 review, published in 2013, detailed a cut of 20,000 regular troops by 2017, with an increasing dependence on reservists. A two-tier army structure provides a Reaction Force and an Adaptable Force, with the former providing units at high readiness. The navy received the last of its six Type-45 destroyers in September 2013, while the air force continued to receive *Voyager* tanker/transport aircraft based on the A330 as the replacement for the VC10 and *Tristar*. (See pp. 69–71.)

ACTIVE 169,150 **(Army 99,800 Navy 33,350 Air 36,000)**

RESERVE 79,100 **(Regular Reserve ε51,000 (incl 4,850 RAF); Volunteer Reserve 28,100 (Army 24,100; Navy 2,650; Air 1,350)**
Includes both trained and those currently under training within the Regular Forces, excluding university cadet units.

ORGANISATIONS BY SERVICE

Strategic Forces 1,000

Armed Forces

RADAR • STRATEGIC 1 Ballistic Missile Early Warning System (BMEWS) at Fylingdales Moor

Royal Navy

SUBMARINES • STRATEGIC • SSBN 4:
4 *Vanguard* with 4 533mm TT with *Spearfish* HWT, up to 16 UGM-133A *Trident* D-5 SLBM (Each boat will not deploy with more than 48 warheads, but each missile could carry up to 12 MIRV, some *Trident* D-5 capable of being configured for sub-strategic role)
MSL • STRATEGIC 48 SLBM (Fewer than 160 declared operational warheads)

Space

SATELLITES • COMMUNICATIONS 7: 1 NATO-4B; 3 *Skynet*-4; 3 *Skynet*-5

Army 96,600; 3,200 Gurkhas (total: 99,800)

Regt normally bn size

FORCES BY ROLE
COMMAND
1 (ARRC) corps HQ (1 sigs bde)
MANOEUVRE
Armoured
1 (1st) armd div (1 (7th) armd bde (1 armd recce regt, 1 armd regt, 1 armd inf bn, 2 inf bn, 1 sigs sqn); 1 (20th) armd bde (1 armd recce regt, 1 armd regt, 1 armd inf bn, 3 inf bn); 1 cbt spt gp (2 SP arty regt, 1 AD regt, 2 cbt engr regt, 1 ptn br regt, 1 MP regt, 2 log regt, 2 maint regt, 2 med regt); 1 sigs regt)
Mechanised
1 (3rd) mech div (1 (1st) mech bde (1 armd recce regt, 1 armd regt, 1 armd inf bn, 3 inf bn, 1 sigs sqn); 1 (4th) mech bde (1 armd recce regt, 1 armd regt, 1 armd inf bn,, 4 inf bn, 1 (Gurkha) lt inf bn, 1 sigs sqn); 1 (12th) mech bde (1 armd regt, 1 recce regt, 1 armd inf bn, 4 lt inf bn, 1 sigs sqn); 1 cbt spt gp (1 armd regt, 2 SP arty regt, 1 arty regt, 3 cbt engr regt, 1 MP regt, 3 log regt, 3 maint regt, 3 med regt); 1 sigs regt)
Light
5 lt inf bn (3 in London, 2 in Cyprus); 1 (Gurkha) lt inf bn (Brunei)
Other
1 trg BG (based on 1 armd inf bn)
COMBAT SUPPORT
1 arty bde (2 UAV regt, 1 STA regt, 1 MRL regt)
1 (opcon RAF) AD bde (1 AD regt)
1 engr bde (3 EOD regt, 1 engr regt, 1 air spt regt)
1 int bde (3 int regt)
1 sigs bde (1 EW regt, 5 sigs regt)
COMBAT SERVICE SUPPORT
3 log bde (total: 1 MP regt, 5 log regt, 1 maint reg)
1 med bde (3 bn)

Home Service Forces • Gibraltar 200 reservists; 150 active reservists (total 350)

Reserves

Territorial Army 24,100 reservists
The Territorial Army generates individuals, sub-units and some full units.

FORCES BY ROLE
MANOEUVRE
Reconnaissance
2 recce regt
Armoured
2 armd regt
Light
13 lt inf bn
Air Manoeuvre
1 para bn
Aviation
1 UAV regt
COMBAT SUPPORT
3 arty regt
1 STA regt
1 MRL regt
1 AD regt
5 engr regt;
3 engr sqn
3 EOD sqn
5 sigs regt
COMBAT SERVICE SUPPORT
14 log regt
2 maint regt
3 med regt

EQUIPMENT BY TYPE
MBT 227 *Challenger* 2
RECCE 640: 200 *Jackal*; 110 *Jackal* 2; 130 *Jackal* 2A; 200 *Scimitar*; (8 Tpz-1 *Fuchs* in store)
AIFV 350 *Warrior*
APC 2,305
APC (T) 1,260: 880 *Bulldog* Mk3; 275 FV103 *Spartan*; 105 *Warthog*
PPV 1,045: 330 *Foxhound*; 420 *Mastiff* (6×6); 170 *Ridgback*; 125 *Wolfhound* (6×6)
ARTY 610
SP 155mm 89 AS90 *Braveheart*
TOWED 105mm 126 L118 Light gun
MRL 227mm 35 M270 MLRS
MOR 81mm 360

AT • MSL
SP ε14 *Exactor* (*Spike* NLOS)
MANPATS *Javelin*
AD • SAM
SP 60 FV4333 *Stormer*
TOWED 14 *Rapier* FSC
MANPAD 24 *Starstreak* (LML)
AEV 57: 24 *Terrier*; 33 *Trojan*
ARV 155: 80 CRARRV; 35 *Samson*; 40 *Warrior* ARRV
MW 94: 64 *Aardvark*; 30 M139
VLB 71: 38 M3; 33 *Titan*
RADAR • LAND 144: 5 *Mamba*; 139 MSTAR
UAV • ISR • Medium 8 *Hermes* 450; (*Watchkeeper* in test – ISD delayed)
AMPHIBIOUS 6 **LCVP**
LOGISTICS AND SUPPORT 5 **RCL**

Royal Navy 33,350

EQUIPMENT BY TYPE
SUBMARINES 11
STRATEGIC • SSBN 4:
4 *Vanguard*, opcon Strategic Forces with up to 16 UGM-133A *Trident* D-5 SLBM, 4 single 533mm TT each with *Spearfish* HWT, (each boat will not deploy with more than 40 warheads, but each missile could carry up to 12 MIRV; some *Trident* D-5 capable of being configured for sub strategic role)
TACTICAL • SSN 7:
5 *Trafalgar* with 5 single 533mm TT with *Spearfish* HWT/*Tomahawk* tactical LACM/UGM 84 *Harpoon* AShM
2 *Astute* with 6 single 533mm TT with *Spearfish* HWT/UGM-84 *Harpoon* AShM/*Tomahawk* tactical LACM (4 additional vessels in build; 1 additional vessel on order)
PRINCIPAL SURFACE COMBATANTS 19
DESTROYERS • DDHM 6:
6 *Daring* (Type-45) with 1 48-cell VLS with *Sea Viper* SAM, 2 *Phalanx* Block 1B CIWS, 1 114mm gun, (capacity 1 *Lynx*/AW101 *Merlin* hel)
FRIGATES • FFGHM 13:
13 *Norfolk* (Type-23) with 2 quad Mk141 lnchr with RGM-84C *Harpoon* AShM, 1 32-cell VLS with *Sea Wolf* SAM, 2 twin 324mm ASTT with *Sting Ray* LWT, 1 114mm gun, (capacity either 2 *Lynx* or 1 AW101 *Merlin* hel)
PATROL AND COASTAL COMBATANTS 22
PSO 4: 3 *River*; 1 *River* (mod) with 1 hel landing platform
PB 18: 16 *Archer* (trg); 2 *Scimitar*
MINE WARFARE • MINE COUNTERMEASURES 16:
MCO 8 *Hunt* (incl 4 mod *Hunt*)
MHC 8 *Sandown* (1 decommissioned and used in trg role)
AMPHIBIOUS
PRINCIPAL AMPHIBIOUS SHIPS 4:
LPD 2 *Albion* with 2 Goalkeeper CIWS, (capacity 2 med hel; 4 LCVP; 6 MBT; 300 troops) (1 at extended readiness)
LPH 2:
1 *Ocean* with 3 *Phalanx* Block 1B CIWS, (capacity 18 hel; 4 LCU or 2 LCAC; 4 LCVP; 800 troops)
1 *Invincible* with 3 Goalkeeper CIWS, (capacity 22 hel; 600 troops) (to decommission 2014)
LANDING CRAFT 37: 10 **LCU**; 23 **LCVP**; 4 **LCAC**
LOGISTICS AND SUPPORT 10
AGB 1 *Protector* with 1 hel landing platform
AGS 3: 1 *Scott*; 2 *Echo* (all with 1 hel landing platform)
YGS 6: 1 *Gleaner*; 5 *Nesbitt*

Royal Fleet Auxiliary

Support and Miscellaneous vessels are mostly manned and maintained by the Royal Fleet Auxiliary (RFA), a civilian fleet owned by the UK MoD, which has approximately 2,500 personnel with type comd under CINCFLEET.
AMPHIBIOUS • PRINCIPAL AMPHIBIOUS SHIPS 3
LSD 3 *Bay* (capacity 4 LCU; 2 LCVP; 24 CR2 *Challenger* 2 MBT; 350 troops)
LOGISTICS AND SUPPORT 16
AORH 3: 2 *Wave*; 1 *Fort Victoria*
AOR 1 *Leaf*
AORLH 2 *Rover*
AFSH 2 *Fort Rosalie*
ARH 1 *Diligence*
AG 1 *Argus* (aviation trg ship with secondary role as primarily casualty receiving ship)
AKR 6 *Point* (not RFA manned)

Naval Aviation (Fleet Air Arm) 5,500

FORCES BY ROLE
ANTI-SUBMARINE WARFARE
3 sqn with AW101 ASW *Merlin* (HM1)
1 sqn with *Lynx* HAS3/HMA8
1 flt with *Lynx* HAS3
AIRBORNE EARLY WARNING
3 sqn with *Sea King* AEW7
SEARCH & RESCUE
1 sqn (and detached flt) with *Sea King* HU5
TRAINING
1 sqn with Beech 350ER *King Air*
1 sqn with G-115 (op under contract)
1 sqn with *Hawk* T1
1 OCU sqn with AW101 ASW *Merlin* (HM1)
1 sqn with *Lynx* HAS3
EQUIPMENT BY TYPE
AIRCRAFT 12 combat capable
TPT • Light 4 Beech 350ER *King Air*
TRG 17: 5 G-115 (op under contract); 12 *Hawk* T1*
HELICOPTERS
ASW 92: 4 AW159 *Wildcat* HMA2; 13 *Lynx* HAS3; 33 *Lynx* HMA8; 42 AW101 ASW *Merlin* (HM1/2)
AEW 13 *Sea King* AEW Mk7
TPT • Medium 16 *Sea King* HU Mk5
MSL • AShM *Sea Skua*

Royal Marines 6,850

FORCES BY ROLE
MANOEUVRE
Amphibious
1 (3rd Cdo) mne bde (1 ISTAR gp (1 EW sqn; 1 cbt spt sqn; 1 sigs sqn; 1 log sqn), 3 cdo bn; 1 amph aslt sqn; 1 (army) arty regt; 1 (army) engr regt; 1 log regt)
3 landing craft sqn opcon Royal Navy

Other
1 (Fleet Protection) sy gp

EQUIPMENT BY TYPE

APC (T) 142: 118 BvS-10 *Viking*; 24 BvS-10 Mk2 *Viking*
ARTY 50
TOWED 105mm 18 L-118
MOR 81mm 32
AT • MSL • MANPATS *Javelin*
AMPHIBIOUS • LANDING CRAFT • LCAC 4 Griffon 2400TD
AD • SAM • HVM
RADAR • LAND 4 MAMBA (*Arthur*)

Royal Marines Reserve 600

Royal Air Force 36,000

Flying hours 210/yr on fast jets; 290 on tpt ac; 240 on support hels; 90 on *Sea King*

FORCES BY ROLE

FIGHTER
2 sqn with *Typhoon* FGR4/T3
FIGHTER/GROUND ATTACK
5 sqn with *Tornado* GR4/4A
2 sqn with *Typhoon* FGR4/T3
ISR
1 sqn with *Sentinel* R1
1 sqn with *Shadow* R1
AIRBORNE EARLY WARNING & CONTROL
1 sqn with E-3D *Sentry*
SEARCH & RESCUE
2 sqn with *Sea King* HAR-3A
1 sqn with Bell 412EP *Griffin* HAR-2
TANKER/TRANSPORT
2 sqn with A330 MRTT *Voyager* KC2/3
1 sqn with *Tristar* C2/C2A/K1/KC1
TRANSPORT
1 (comms) sqn with AS355 *Squirrel*; AW109E; BAe-125; BAe-146; BN-2A *Islander* CC2
1 sqn with C-17A *Globemaster*
3 sqn with C-130J/J-30 *Hercules*
TRAINING
1 OCU sqn with *Tornado*
1 OCU sqn with *Typhoon*
1 OEU sqn with *Typhoon, Tornado*
1 OCU sqn with E-3D *Sentry*; *Sentinel* R1
1 OEU sqn with E-3D *Sentry*; *Sentinel* R1
1 OCU sqn with *Sea King* HAR-3A
1 sqn with Beech 200 *King Air*
1 sqn with EMB-312 *Tucano* (T Mk1)
3 sqn with *Hawk* T Mk1/1A/1W; *Hawk* T2
3 sqn with *Tutor*
1 hel sqn with Bell 412EP *Griffin* HT1
COMBAT/ISR UAV
2 sqn with MQ-9 *Reaper*

EQUIPMENT BY TYPE

AIRCRAFT 283 combat capable
FGA 223: 3 F-35B *Lightning* II (in test); 112 *Tornado* GR4/GR4A; 108 *Typhoon* FGR4/T3
ISR 11: 5 *Sentinel* R1 (Option to be withdrawn from role post-Afghanistan); 6 *Shadow* R1
ELINT 1 RC-135V *Rivet Joint* (IOC 2014)
AEW&C 6 E-3D *Sentry*
TKR/TPT 11: 6 A330 MRTT *Voyager* KC2/3; 1 *Tristar* K1; 4 *Tristar* KC1
TPT 59: **Heavy** 8 C-17A *Globemaster*; **Medium** 24: 10 C-130J *Hercules*; 14 C-130J-30 *Hercules*; **Light** 14: 8 Beech 200 *King Air* (on lease); 3 Beech 200GT *King Air* (on lease); 3 BN-2A *Islander* CC2; **PAX** 13: 6 BAe-125 CC-3; 4 BAe-146 CC2/C3; 2 *Tristar* C2; 1 *Tristar* C2A
TRG 290: 91 EMB-312 *Tucano* T1; 101 G-115E *Tutor*; 28 *Hawk* T2*; 32 *Hawk* T1/1A/1W* (ε40 more in store); 38 T67M/M260 *Firefly*
HELICOPTERS
MRH 5: 1 AW139; 4 Bell 412EP *Griffin* HAR-2
TPT 28 **Medium** 25 *Sea King* HAR-3A; **Light** 3 AW109E
UAV • CISR • Heavy 10 MQ-9 *Reaper*
MSL
AAM • IR AIM-9L/9L/I *Sidewinder;* **IIR** ASRAAM; **ARH** AIM-120B/C5 AMRAAM
ARM ALARM
ASM *Brimstone*; *Dual-Mode Brimstone*; AGM-65G2 *Maverick*
LACM *Storm Shadow*
BOMBS
Laser-Guided/GPS: *Paveway* II; GBU-10 *Paveway* III; Enhanced *Paveway* II/III; GBU-24 *Paveway* IV

Royal Air Force Regiment

FORCES BY ROLE

COMMAND
3 (tactical Survive To Operate (STO)) sqn
MANOEUVRE
Other
7 sy sqn
COMBAT SUPPORT
1 CBRN sqn

Tri-Service Defence Helicopter School

HELICOPTERS
MRH 11 Bell 412EP *Griffin* HT1
TPT • Light 27: 25 AS350B *Ecureuil;* 2 AW109E

Volunteer Reserve Air Forces

(Royal Auxiliary Air Force/RAF Reserve)
MANOEUVRE
Other
5 sy sqn
COMBAT SUPPORT
2 int sqn
COMBAT SERVICE SUPPORT
1 med sqn
1 (air movements) sqn
1 (HQ augmentation) sqn
1 (C-130 Reserve Aircrew) flt

Joint Helicopter Command

Includes Army, Royal Navy and RAF units

Army

FORCES BY ROLE

MANOEUVRE

Air Manoeuvre

1 (16th) air aslt bde (1 recce pl, 2 para bn, 1 air aslt bn, 2 atk hel regt (3 sqn with AH-64D *Apache*), 1 hel regt (3 sqn with *Lynx* AH7/9A), 1 arty regt, 1 engr regt, 1 MP coy, 1 log regt, 1 med regt)

Aviation

1 avn regt (1 sqn with BN-2 *Defender/Islander*; 1 sqn with SA341 *Gazelle*)

1 hel regt (2 sqn with *Lynx* AH7/9A)

1 hel sqn with *Lynx* AH7//9A

1 (test) hel sqn with *Lynx* AH7/9A

1 trg hel regt (1 sqn with AH-64D *Apache*; 1 sqn with AS350B *Ecureuil*; 1 sqn with Bell 212; *Lynx* AH7; SA341 *Gazelle*)

1 hel flt with AS365N3; SA341 *Gazelle*

1 hel flt with Bell 212 (Brunei)

1 hel flt with SA341 *Gazelle* (Canada)

Territorial Army

FORCES BY ROLE

MANOEUVRE

Aviation

1 hel regt

Royal Navy

FORCES BY ROLE

ATTACK HELICOPTER

1 lt sqn with *Lynx* AH9A

TRANSPORT HELICOPTER

2 sqn with *Sea King* HC4

TRAINING

1 hel sqn with *Sea King* HC4

Royal Air Force

FORCES BY ROLE

TRANSPORT HELICOPTER

3 hel sqn with CH-47D/SD *Chinook*

2 hel sqn with AW101 *Merlin*

2 hel sqn with SA330 *Puma*

EQUIPMENT BY TYPE

AIRCRAFT • TPT • Light 15: 9 BN-2T-4S *Defender*; 6 BN-2 *Islander*

HELICOPTERS

ATK 66 AH-64D *Apache*

MRH 110 : 5 AS365N3; 22 AW159 *Wildcat* AH1; 27 *Lynx* AH7; 22 *Lynx* AH9A; 34 SA341 *Gazelle*

TPT 152: **Heavy** 46: 32 CH-47D *Chinook* (HC2/4); 6 CH-47D *Chinook* (HC2A); 8 CH-47SD *Chinook* (HC3); **Medium** 89: 28 AW101 *Merlin* (HC3/3A); 24 SA330 *Puma* (HC1) (being upgraded to HC2 standard); 37 *Sea King* (HC4); **Light** 17: 9 AS350B *Ecureuil*; 8 Bell 212

UK Special Forces

Includes Army, Royal Navy and RAF units

FORCES BY ROLE

SPECIAL FORCES

1 (SAS) SF regt

1 (SBS) SF regt

1 (Special Reconnaissance) SF regt

1 SF BG (based on 1 para bn)

MANOEUVRE

Aviation

1 wg (includes assets drawn from 2 army avn sqn, 1 army hel flt, 1 RAF tpt sqn and 1 RAF hel sqn)

COMBAT SUPPORT

1 sigs regt

Reserve

FORCES BY ROLE

SPECIAL FORCES

2 (SAS) SF regt

Cyber

The Office of Cyber Security & Information Assurance works with the Cyber Security Operations Centre and ministries and agencies to implement cyber-security programmes. CSOC is hosted by GCHQ. The 2010 SDSR said that the country would 'establish a transformative national programme to protect ourselves in cyber space'. This 'National Cyber Security Programme' is supported by some £650m – with programme management by OSCIA – and led to a new Cyber Security Strategy, published in November 2011. A UK Defence Cyber Operations Group was set up in 2011 to place 'cyber at the heart of defence operations, doctrine and training'. This group was transferred to Joint Forces Command on this formation's establishment in April 2012. In 2013, it was announced that a new Joint Cyber Reserve Unit would be developed.

DEPLOYMENT

Legal provisions for foreign deployment:

Constitution: Uncodified constitution which includes constitutional statutes, case law, international treaties and unwritten conventions

Decision on deployment of troops abroad: By the government

AFGHANISTAN

NATO • ISAF 7,700; 1 (7th) armd bde (1 recce regt, 1 armd regt, 4 inf bn, 1 arty regt; 1 engr regt); AH-64D *Apache*; *Lynx* AH9A; *Hermes* 450; *Tornado* GR4/GR4A; C-130J *Hercules*; CH-47D *Chinook*; *Shadow* R1; MQ-9 *Reaper*

ARABIAN SEA & GULF OF ADEN

Combined Maritime Forces • CTF-150: 1 FFGHM

ARMENIA/AZERBAIJAN

OSCE • Minsk Conference 1

ASCENSION ISLAND

Air Force 20

ATLANTIC (NORTH)/CARIBBEAN
1 FFGHM

ATLANTIC (SOUTH)
1 FFGHM

BAHRAIN
20; 1 BAe-125; 1 BAe-146

BELIZE
10

BOSNIA-HERZEGOVINA
EU • EUFOR • *Operation Althea* 4
OSCE • Bosnia and Herzegovina 5

BRITISH INDIAN OCEAN TERRITORY
40; 1 Navy/Marine det

BRUNEI
550; 1 (Gurkha) lt inf bn; 1 jungle trg centre; 1 hel flt with 3 Bell 212

CANADA
420; 2 trg units; 1 hel flt with SA341 *Gazelle*

CYPRUS
2,600; 2 inf bn; 1 SAR sqn with 4 Bell 412 *Twin Huey*; 1 radar (on det)
UN • UNFICYP 337; 1 inf coy

DEMOCRATIC REPUBLIC OF THE CONGO
EU • EUSEC RD Congo 3
UN • MONUSCO 6 obs

FALKLAND ISLANDS
1,500; 1 inf coy(+); 1 AD det with *Rapier*; 1 PSO; 1 ftr flt with 4 *Typhoon* FGR4; 1 SAR sqn with *Sea King* HAR-3/3A; 1 tkr/tpt flt with C-130J *Hercules*

GERMANY
16,500; 1 armd div with (2 armd bde)

GIBRALTAR
410 (incl 175 pers of Gibraltar regt); 2 PB

GULF OF ADEN & INDIAN OCEAN
EU • *Operation Atalanta* 1 LSD

KENYA
170 (trg team)

KUWAIT
30 (trg team)

MALI
EU • EUTM Mali 40
UN • MINUSMA 2

MEDITERRANEAN SEA
NATO • SNMCMG 2: 1 MHC

MOLDOVA
OSCE • Moldova 1

NEPAL
280 (Gurkha trg org)

NETHERLANDS
90

OMAN
70; 1 *Sentinel*; 1 *Tristar* tkr

PERSIAN GULF
Combined Maritime Forces • CTF-152: 1 FFGHM; 2 MCO; 2 MHC

QATAR
4 C-130J

SERBIA
NATO • KFOR 1
OSCE • Kosovo 13
OSCE • Serbia 5

SOUTH SUDAN
UN • UNMISS 2

UGANDA
EU • EUTM Somalia 2

UNITED STATES
480

FOREIGN FORCES

United States
US European Command: 9,300; 1 ftr wg at RAF Lakenheath with (1 ftr sqn with 24 F-15C/D *Eagle*, 2 ftr sqn with 23 F-15E *Strike Eagle*); 1 ISR sqn at RAF Mildenhall with OC-135/RC-135; 1 tkr wg at RAF Mildenhall with 15 KC-135R *Stratotanker*; 1 Special Ops gp at RAF Mildenhall with (1 sqn with 5 MC-130H *Combat Talon* II; 5 CV-22B *Osprey*; 1 sqn with 1 MC-130J *Commando* II; 4 MC-130P *Combat Shadow*)
US Strategic Command: 1 Ballistic Missile Early Warning System (BMEWS) at Fylingdales Moor; 1 *Spacetrack* radar at Fylingdales Moor

Table 3 **Selected Arms Procurements and Deliveries, Europe**

Designation	Type	Quantity (Current)	Contract Value	Prime Nationality	Prime Contractor	Order Date	First Delivery Due	Notes
Belgium (BEL)								
Piranha IIIC	APC (W)	242	€700m (US$844m)	US	General Dynamics (MOWAG)	2006	2010	Delivery in progress. Option on further 104
A400M *Atlas*	Tpt ac	7	n.k.	Int'l	EADS (Airbus)	2003	2018	Five flight test aircraft now in programme. Belgium is now likely to take delivery of its aircraft 2018–19
NH90 NFH/TTH	ASW/Tpt hel	8	€293m (US$400m)	Int'l	NH Industries	2007	2012	Four TTH, four NFH. First NH90 TTH delivered Dec 2012; first NFH delivered mid-2013; option on two more NH90 TTH
Denmark (DNK)								
Iver Huitfeldt-class	DDG	3	DKK4.3bn (US$471m)	DNK	Odense Staalskibsværft	2006	2012	*Projekt Patruljeskib*. First vessel commissioned Feb 2012. Second launched Dec 2010; third laid down Dec 2009
MH-60R *Seahawk*	ASW hel	9	DKK4bn (US$686m)	US	UTC (Sikorsky)	2012	2016	To replace *Lynx*. First delivery due mid-2016
Estonia (EST)								
XA-188	APC (W)	80	€20m	NLD	Government Surplus	2010	2010	Second-hand Dutch veh. Delivery to be completed in 2015
Ground Master 403	Radar	2	n.k.	FRA/US	Thales/ Raytheon	2009	2013	First in service 2013; second due for delivery 2014
Finland (FIN)								
Norwegian Advanced Surface-to-Air Missile System (NASAMS)	SAM	n.k.	NOK3bn (US$458m)	NOR/US	Kongsberg/ Raytheon	2009	2011	To replace *Buk*-M1 (SA-11 *Gadfly*). Delivery began in 2011, following delays. Expected to become operational by 2015
Katanpaa-class	MCM	3	€244.8m (US$315m)	GER/ITA	Intermarine SpA	2006	2012	First vessel, *Katanpaa*, delivered Jun 2012; second delivered Aug 2013
NH90 TTH	Tpt hel	20	€370m	Int'l	NH Industries	2001	2008	16 delivered by late 2013
France (FRA)								
VBCI 8x8	AIFV	630	n.k.	FRA	Nexter	2000	2008	Final delivery due 2015
Barracuda-class	SSN	6	€8bn (US$10.5bn)	FRA	DCNS	2006	2016	One SSN to be delivered every two years until 2027. First to enter service 2017
Aquitaine-class (FREMM)	DDGHM	11	US$23.6bn	FRA	DCNS	2002	2012	First-of-class, FNS *Aquitaine*, commissioned Nov 2012. Second vessel launched Oct 2012; scheduled to commission May 2014
SCALP Naval	LACM	200	See notes	Int'l	MBDA	2007	2013	Original contract value €910m (US$1.2bn) for 250 msl. Test fired Mar 2010. To be deployed on *Barracuda*-class SSN (2017) and *Aquitaine*-class FFG (2014)
Rafale F3	FGA ac	180	n.k.	FRA	Dassault	1984	2006	Order increased to 180 in 2009, but annual production rate slowed
A400M *Atlas*	Tpt ac	50	n.k.	Int'l	EADS (Airbus)	2003	2013	First delivered 2013

Table 3 **Selected Arms Procurements and Deliveries, Europe**

Designation	Type	Quantity (Current)	Contract Value	Prime Nationality	Prime Contractor	Order Date	First Delivery Due	Notes
EC665 *Tiger*	Atk hel	80	n.k.	Int'l	Eurocopter	1999	2005	40 HAP, 40 HAD variant. All HAP delivered. First HAD variant delivered Apr 2013
NH90 NFH	ASW hel	27	n.k.	Int'l	NH Industries	2000	2010	For navy. Seventh hel delivered Jul 2012. Final delivery due 2019
NH90 TTH	Tpt hel	68	n.k.	Int'l	NH Industries	2007	2012	For army avn. 12 ordered 2007, 22 in 2009 and 34 in 2013. First delivery Jan 2012
Meteor	BVRAAM	200	n.k.	Int'l	MBDA	2011	2018	The first stage of missile integration work for *Rafale* began in January 2011
Germany (GER)								
Puma	AIFV	350	n.k.	GER	PSM	2007	tbd	To replace *Marder* 1A3/A4/A5 AIFVs. Order reduced from 450. To be fitted with *Spike* LR ATGW launcher. Technical defects have pushed ISD beyond 2014
Boxer (8x8)	APC (W)	272	€1.5bn (US$2.1bn)	GER/NLD	ARTEC GmbH	2006	2009	135 APC, 65 CP variants, 72 heavy armoured ambulances
IRIS-T SLS	SAM	n.k.	€123m (US$166m)	GER	Diehl BGT	2007	2012	Surface-launched variant of infra-red guided IRIS-T AAM. ISD from 2012. Secondary msl for army MEADS
Type 212A	SSK	2	n.k.	GER	TKMS (HDW)	2006	2012	U-35 and U-36. Due to enter service from 2013
Baden-Württemberg-class	DDGHM	4	€2bn	GER	TKMS	2007	2016	Final delivery due late 2018. First hull section laid down Nov 2011
Braunschweig-class	FS	5	n.k.	GER	TKMS	2001	2008	Final vessel commissioned 2013. Full operational capability expected 2014
Eurofighter EF2000 (*Typhoon*)	FGA ac	143	n.k.	Int'l	Eurofighter GmbH	1998	2003	31 aircraft Tranche 3A order signed in 2009
A400M *Atlas*	Tpt ac	53	n.k.	Int'l	EADS (Airbus)	2003	2010	First German aircraft now expected 2014. Original order cut from 60 to 53, reduction to 40 aircraft proposed in late 2011
EC665 *Tiger* (UHT variant)	Atk hel	57	n.k.	Int'l	Eurocopter	1984	2005	Order cut from 80 to 57 in early 2013
NH90 TTH	Tpt hel	80	n.k.	Int'l	NH Industries	2000	2007	Deliveries in progress to trials and test
Greece (GRC)								
M113	APC (T)	476	Free transfer	US	Government Surplus	2013	2013	Ex-US surplus. 225 M113A2, 145 M577A2 and 106 M901A2
Katsonis-class (Type-214)	SSK	6	ε€1.67bn	GER	TKMS (HDW)	2000	2010	First commissioned Dec 2010. Three further vessels launched, but commissioning stalled
NH90 TTH	Tpt hel	20	€657m	Int'l	NH Industries	2002	2011	16 tac tpt variants and four Special Op variants. Option on further 14. Delivery began June 2011

Table 3 **Selected Arms Procurements and Deliveries, Europe**

Designation	Type	Quantity (Current)	Contract Value	Prime Nationality	Prime Contractor	Order Date	First Delivery Due	Notes
Ireland (IRL)								
PV90	PSO	2	US$136m	UK	Babcock International (Babcock Marine)	2010	2014	Keel of first vessel laid in May 2012. Option for a third vessel
Italy (ITA)								
Todaro-class (Type-212A)	SSK	2	€915m (US$1.34 bn)	ITA	Fincantieri	2008	2015	Second-batch option exercised from 1996 contract. With AIP
Bergamini-class (FREMM)	DDGHM	6	€1.6bn (US$2.4bn)	FRA/ITA	Orizzonte Sistemi Navali	2002	2013	Batch 1 & 2. First vessel commissioned in 2013; second and third expected in 2014. Third batch may be cut
Typhoon	FGA ac	96	n.k.	Int'l	Eurofighter GmbH	1998	2004	21 aircraft Tranche 3A order signed in 2009
Gulfstream G550 CAEW	AEW&C ac	2	US$750m	ISR	IAI	2012	2015	Delivery due 2015
ATR-72MP	MP ac	4	€360-400m	ITA	Finmeccanica (Alenia Aeronautica)	2009	2012	To be fitted with long-range surv suite
NH90 TTH/NFH	Tpt/ASW hel	116	n.k.	Int'l	NH Industries	2000	2007	60 TTH for army; 46 NFH & ten TTH for navy
CH-47F *Chinook*	Tpt hel	16	€900m	US	Boeing	2009	2014	For army. First flight Jun 2013; delivery expected 2014. Final delivery due 2017
Luxembourg (LUX)								
A400M *Atlas*	Tpt ac	1	n.k.	Int'l	EADS (Airbus)	2003	2018	Programme delayed significantly. Delivery now expected 2018–19
NATO								
RQ-4 *Global Hawk* Block 40	ISR UAV	5	€1.3bn (US$1.7bn)	US	Northrop Grumman	2012	2015	To be based in NAS Sigonella ITA. Part of NATO's Alliance Ground Surveillance programme
Netherlands (NLD)								
Boxer (8X8)	APC (W)	200	€595m (US$747m)	GER/NLD	ARTEC GmbH	2006	2013	19 cargo/C2, 27 cargo, 55 CP variants, 58 ambulances and 41 engr. To replace YPR 765
Karel Doorman-class	AFSH	1	€364m (US$545m)	NLD	Damen Schelde (DSNS)	2009	2014	To replace HNLMS *Amsterdam*; was to have been sold, but decision reversed
NH90 NFH/TTH	ASW/Tpt hel	20	n.k.	Int'l	NH Industries	2000	2010	12 NFH, eight TTH. First NFH delivered Apr 2010. Eight NFH delivered as of late 2012
Norway (NOR)								
FH-77 BW L52 *Archer* 6x6	Arty (155mm SP)	24	GB£135m (US$200m)	UK	BAE Systems (BAE Land & Armaments)	2010	2013	Contract value is for combined 48 unit NWG/SWE order. Delivery delayed
Naval Strike Missile (NSM)	AShM	n.k.	NOK2.3bn (US$466m)	NOR	Kongsberg (KDA)	2007	2012	Final delivery due 2014. For five *Fridtjof Nansen*-class FF and six *Skjold*-class fast strike craft. First 16 rounds delivered June 2012

Table 3 **Selected Arms Procurements and Deliveries, Europe**

Designation	Type	Quantity (Current)	Contract Value	Prime Nationality	Prime Contractor	Order Date	First Delivery Due	Notes
F-35A *Lightning II*	FGA	2	n.k.	US	Lockheed Martin	2012	2015	To remain in the US for training, and to be followed by two more in 2016. Up to 48 more to be based in Norway with deliveries from 2017
NH90 NFH/TTH	ASW/Tpt hel	14	n.k.	Int'l	NH Industries	2001	2011	Six for ASW, 8 for Coast Guard. three delivered by mid-2013. FOC now expected 2017
Poland (POL)								
Rosomak	AIFV	997	US$2.2bn	FIN	Patria	2003	2004	570 delivered by late 2013. Includes addditional order for 307 in 2013
Gawron-class	PSO	2	PLN77m (US$24.8m)	POL	SMW	2004	2016	Based on GER MEKO A100. Project cancelled Feb 2012, and then restarted Sep 2012. Originally to be constructed as FFG, now to be a patrol ship
Kormoran 2-class	MCO	3	n.k.	POL	Remontowa Shipbuilding	2013	2016	–
Naval Strike Missile (NSM)	AShM	6	NOK1512m (US$234m)	NOR	Kongsberg (KDA)	2008	2012	Initial contract worth NOK800m, incl six lnchr and 12 msl, delivered Nov 2012. Contract modified in Dec 2011 to include an additional 38 msl, to be delivered between 2013 and 2015
M-28B/PT *Bryza*	Tpt ac	8	PLN399m	US	UTC (PZL Mielec)	2008	2010	Order reduced from 12 to eight ac in 2009. Seven delivered by late 2013. Final delivery due by end-2013
Romania (ROM)								
F-16AM/BM *Fighting Falcon*	FGA ac	12	US$250m	PRT	Government Surplus	2013	2016	Second-hand ac: nine PRT F-16 MLUs and three ex-USAF ac upgraded to MLU by PRT
C-27J *Spartan*	Tpt ac	7	€220m (US$293m)	ITA	Finmeccanica (Alenia Aeronautica)	2006	2010	To replace An-26. Incl log and trg support. Six in service by late 2013
Spain (ESP)								
Paz (Peace) satellite	Sat	2	€160m	ESP/Int'l	Hisdesat/EADS (CASA)	2008	2014	Launch now set for 2014
S-80A	SSK	4	n.k.	ESP	Navantia	2003	2017	Delivery further delayed by redesign; first vessel to be delivered now S-82
Typhoon	FGA ac	74	n.k.	Int'l	Eurofighter GmbH	1998	2003	21 aircraft Tranche 3A order signed 2009
A400M *Atlas*	Tpt ac	27	n.k.	Int'l	EADS (Airbus)	2003	2018	First delivery now scheduled for 2018. Current plans envisage an operational fleet of only 14 ac
EC665 *Tiger* (HAP/HAD)	Atk hel	24	€1.4bn	Int'l	Eurocopter	2003	2007	Six HAP-E delivered 2007–08. First of 18 HAD-E to be delivered by end-2013
NH90 TTH	Tpt hel	45	n.k.	Int'l	NH Industries	2007	2014	Discussions over proposed order reduction to 22 hel. First ESP assembled hel due for delivery by end-2014

Table 3 **Selected Arms Procurements and Deliveries, Europe**

Designation	Type	Quantity (Current)	Contract Value	Prime Nationality	Prime Contractor	Order Date	First Delivery Due	Notes
Sweden (SWE)								
Pansarterrängbil 360 (Patgb 360)	APC (W)	113	€240m (US$338m)	FIN	Patria	2009	2013	79 APCs and 34 other variants. Further 113 req. Was subject to contractual dispute
FH-77 BW L52 *Archer* 6x6	Arty (155mm SP)	24	GB£135m (US$200m)	UK	BAE Systems (BAE Land & Armaments)	2010	2013	Contract value is for combined 48 unit NOR/SWE order. Delivery delayed; first four delivered Sep 2013
NH90	ASW/Tpt hel	18	n.k.	Int'l	NH Industries	2001	2007	13 TTT/SAR hel and five ASW variants. Option for seven further hel
Switzerland (CHE)								
Gripen E	FGA ac	22	CHF3.1bn (US$3.3bn)	SWE	Saab	2013	2018	Funding approved by Nationalrat Sep 2013
Turkey (TUR)								
Gokturk-1	Sat	1	€270m (US$380m)	ITA/FRA	Telespazio/ Thales (Alenia Space)	2009	2014	Launch delayed until 2014
Altay	MBT	250	See notes	TUR	Otokar	2007	2014	Four initial prototypes by 2014 for approx USD500m. To be followed by an order for 250 units following testing
Firtina 155mm/52-cal	Arty (155mm SP)	350	n.k.	ROK	Samsung Techwin	2001	2003	ROK Techwin K9 *Thunder*. Total requirement of 350. Deliveries ongoing
Type-214	SSK	6	€1.96bn (US$2.9bn)	GER	MFI/TKMS (HDW)	2011	2015	To be built at Golcuk shipyard
Ada-class (MILGEM)	FFGHM	4	n.k.	TUR	Istanbul Naval Shipyard/RMK Marine	1996	2011	Second-of-class commissioned Sep 2013. Order for third and fourth vessels transferred from RMK Sep 2013. Contract for remaining four vessels to be re-tendered. Part of Milgem project which incl requirement for four F-100-class FFG
Dost-class	PSOH	4	€352.5m	TUR	RMK Marine	2007	2013	For Coast Guard. Based on *Sirio*-class PCO design. First two vessels commissioned 2013
Tuzla-class	PCC	16	€402m (US$545m)	TUR	Dearsan Shipyard	2007	2010	Nine delivered by May 2013. Final delivery due 2015
ATR-72MP	MP ac	8	€260m	ITA	Finmeccanica (Alenia Aeronautica)	2005	2013	Programme delayed; order revised in 2013 to six MP and two utility ac. First utility ac delivered Jul 2013
B-737 AEW	AEW&C ac	4	US$1bn	US	Boeing	2002	2013	*Peace Eagle* programme. Delivery delayed. First aircraft now to be delivered by end-2013
A400M *Atlas*	Tpt ac	10	n.k.	Int'l	EADS (Airbus)	2003	2013	First delivery due by end-2013
T129 (AW129 *Mangusta*)	Atk hel	60	US$3.2bn	TUR/ITA	TAI/Aselsan/ Finmeccanica (Agusta Westland)	2007	2013	Option on further 41. Initial order for 51 plus nine more ordered as interim measure. First four due for delivery by end-2013
CH-47F *Chinook*	Tpt hel	6	See notes	US	Boeing	2011	2015	Original aim to acquire 14 for US$1.2bn, but order cut to six; five for the army and one for SF Comd
Anka	ISR UAV	10	n.k.	TUR	TAI	2012	2014	–

Table 3 **Selected Arms Procurements and Deliveries, Europe**

Designation	Type	Quantity (Current)	Contract Value	Prime Nationality	Prime Contractor	Order Date	First Delivery Due	Notes
United Kingdom (UK)								
Astute-class	SSN	6	n.k.	UK	BAE Systems	1994	2010	First vessel commissioned 2010; second vessel in 2013. To be fitted with *Tomahawk* Block IV SLCM. Seventh boat not yet ordered, but contract awarded for reactor
Queen Elizabeth-class	CV	2	GB£3.9bn (US$8bn)	UK	BAE Systems	2007	2016	ISD delayed until 2018 and 2020. 2010 SDSR decision to mothball one carrier may now be reversed pending cost considerations
Tide-class	AOT	4	GB£452m	ROK	Daewoo Shipbuilding and Marine Engineering (DSME)	2012	2016	–
Typhoon	FGA ac	160	n.k.	Int'l	Eurofighter GmbH	1998	2004	40 aircraft order as part of Tranche 3A, includes 24 to replace elements of Tranche 2 order diverted to the RSAF as part of *Project Salam*
RC-135 *Rivet Joint*	ELINT ac	3	εGB£700m (US$1bn)	US	Boeing	2010	2013	First aircraft delivered in late 2013. In-service date 2014
Voyager (A330-200)	Tkr/Tpt ac	14	GB£13bn (US$26 bn)	Int'l	AirTanker Consortium	2008	2011	Six in service by mid-2013. Tenth ac in Getafe for conversion
A400M *Atlas*	Tpt ac	22	n.k.	Int'l	EADS (Airbus)	2003	2014	UK now due to take first of 22 aircraft in 2014. Original order reduced by three
AW159 *Wildcat*	MRH hel	62	GB£1bn (US$1.8bn)	ITA	Finmeccanica (Agusta Westland)	2006	2012	34 for army, 28 for navy. Option for a further four hel. Final delivery due 2015
CH-47F *Chinook* (HC6)	Tpt hel	14	GBP£1bn (US$1.6bn)	US	Boeing	2011	2013	First delivery due late 2013
Watchkeeper WK450	ISR UAV	54	GB£800m (US$1.2bn)	FRA	Thales	2005	2013	Delivery repeatedly delayed. Release to service now planned for end-2013

Chapter Five
Russia and Eurasia

RUSSIA

Just over four years after the 'New Look' defence reform process started, the Russian Defence Ministry and armed forces began 2013 with new civilian and military leaders. President Vladimir Putin appointed Sergei Shoigu as defence minister on 6 November 2012, after dismissing Anatoly Serdyukov, ostensibly over a corruption scandal. Putin said Serdyukov's removal would allow an 'objective' investigation into allegations that defence-ministry-controlled military contractor Oboronservis was selling off ministry assets at below-market prices. Serdyukov's replacement, Shoigu, is a former long-term emergencies minister and loyal Putin ally. General Nikolay Makarov, Chief of General Staff, was also removed from his post, as was First Deputy Minister of Defence Aleksandr Sukhorukov.

Despite speculation that these changes at the top might prompt a wholesale revision of the reform process spearheaded by Serdyukov and Makarov, leaders in the Kremlin and the defence ministry are still pursuing most of the key objectives. One year on, it is clear there has been a change of tack rather than direction for the military reform process.

It was signalled early on that the fundamental organisational changes begun by Serdyukov, which finally broke away from the Soviet model, are irreversible. In a much-quoted speech, Putin told the Defence Ministry board: 'Once made, decisions must not be constantly changed. This is all the more important now that we have reached the stage of polishing and fine-tuning the many components in this complex military machine.' This 'polishing and fine-tuning' (*shlifovka*) has led to several top-level organisational changes. With a new law in December 2012, the president made the General Staff directly answerable to him, as Supreme Commander-in-Chief, instead of to the defence minister. The General Staff also acquired new functions, including command of local authorities and organisations outside the defence ministry for the purpose of organising territorial defence. This reversed the concentration of power in the person of the defence minister that was seen under Serdyukov.

The new defence minister, Shoigu, reshuffled his ministry, shifting responsibilities among the deputy ministers and increasing their number from eight to ten. He also replaced those officials most closely associated with Serdyukov. Makarov was replaced as Chief of General Staff by General Valeriy Gerasimov, though Makarov was appointed to an advisory role in early 2013.

Shoigu did embark on a review of the reforms initiated by his predecessor, tackling some particularly contentious issues, such as real-estate consolidation and sale, reductions in basing, proposed cuts to central administration and mergers of military academies. Personnel cuts at defence ministry headquarters were scaled back, amid concerns from some in the armed forces that the size of the reductions had damaged command-and-control at the strategic level. Serdyukov had planned to merge military academies into ten Joint Training Centres, but this was shelved and the academies are, after a three-year break, once again taking cadets.

Shoigu also re-established the Main Directorate of Combat Training. Following its closure in 2010, unit combat training had become the responsibility of the individual services, while inter-service and operational-level training was under the authority of the General Staff. First Deputy Defence Minister General Arkady Bakhin justified the reinstatement by citing the need to improve coordination and combat effectiveness, and said this would, as Tass news agency reported, 'primarily improve combat capability of the multi-service force groupings and improve the existing regulatory framework regulating the organisation of combat training'. This is consistent with the Russian push to develop skills in joint operations, as demonstrated by major exercises during 2013.

Analysts have noted that while rearmament and related financial issues were key for Serdyukov, Shoigu is more concerned with the organisation of training and regular activities of the forces. Therefore, many of the most important decisions of the Serdyukov–Makarov era remain untouched. Despite Serdyukov's sacking, the goal continues of restructuring the armed forces away from the mass-mobilisation model intended for large-scale conflict, to professionalised armed forces at a higher state of readiness. Instead of relatively low-strength units, to be filled with mobilised personnel in time of crisis, Russia's ground forces are now mostly in mobile brigade-sized formations, more aligned with the combat requirements of low- and medium-intensity local and regional warfare. The perception of increased readiness has been reinforced by the reintroduction of surprise operational-readiness inspections at the military-district, combined-arms-unit and single-service levels, which were last carried out in the Soviet era. The presentation of a new, classified State Defence Plan early in Shoigu's tenure is evidence of continuity, since this document must have been drawn up under Shoigu and Gerasimov's predecessors.

The State Defence Plan was complemented by the publication of an Activity Plan 2013–20, which identifies intended levels of increased combat readiness, new or upgraded equipment, and increases in personnel costs for the remainder of the decade. The plan sets highly ambitious targets for manpower and the proportion of 'modern' (this term remains vague) weapons systems in service, tied in with the State Armaments Programme (see Defence Economics, p. 163). Interestingly, the plan constitutes the first official admission that the armed forces were at only 80% of planned strength in 2013, contrasting with repeated official claims that Russia has one million troops under arms. As noted in previous editions of *The Military Balance*, recruitment and staffing have been key areas of concern for some years, with ongoing challenges in securing adequate numbers of conscripts and in recruiting enough of the contract personnel expected to fill so many roles within the future armed forces.

Armed forces

Two elite **army** divisions, the 4th Tamanskaya and the 5th Kantemirovskaya divisions, were re-established in May 2013 having previously been 'reformed' into brigades. However, there was little indication during 2013 of any increase in personnel or equipment holdings to reflect this change in status, indicating that the defence ministry is not reconsidering the move to brigade-based structures more generally.

Considerable work remains to be done in establishing brigade structures within ground forces. Moves to create light, medium and heavy brigades remain at an experimental level. Nonetheless, the ministry is persisting with the plan, as analysis of combat-training exercises with these formations apparently shows that while they are far from ideal, they are better that the current 'New Look' motorised and tank brigades. The division structure is to be retained within the Airborne Forces and Strategic Missile Forces.

Air force reform and development is following three themes: improving command-and-control, modernising the combat aircraft fleet, and increasing

Personnel issues

Manpower remains a key issue for Russian military planners. Conscription targets are hard to meet, and plans for recruiting professional ('contract') servicemen to serve as NCOs and in posts requiring advanced training are falling short of targets. It has long been clear that the armed forces as a whole are understaffed. Senior Russian officers, when persuaded to admit the problem, downplay it, saying that where necessary the 'rolling deficit' (*tekushchiy nekomplekt*) can be covered by calling up reservists.

The target is still for a total of 425,000 contract servicemen by 2017 (up from a claimed 241,400 in 2013). It appears that, as with previous failed programmes to recruit contractors, Russian leaders would prefer at present to maintain the narrative that this is achievable, rather than adjust the target or institute major change to reach it. As in all discussions of Russian military manpower, information is unclear and the challenge is understated; for example, Chief of the General Staff Gerasimov said in June 2013 that the target would be met by recruiting 60,000 contractors annually – without mentioning that many more than this must be recruited to allow for those leaving the service after their contract term expires.

Stopgap measures have been put in place to keep the junior command structure functioning while these targets remain unmet. Officers continue to serve in posts that are notionally intended for NCOs under the new structure. The post of *praporshchik*, normally translated as 'warrant officer', referred to a class of long-serving specialists, usually in roles demanding technical or administrative skills. Abolished entirely under Defence Minister Serdyukov, *praporshchiki* have been reinstated under his successor Shoigu, with plans to recruit (or re-enlist) up to 50,000. However, it remains unclear how the target of achieving 100% staffing by 2014, outlined in the defence ministry's Activity Plan 2013–20, can be achieved without revising the targets radically downwards.

the types and number of air-launched precision-guided weaponry. Deliveries of fixed- and rotary-wing aircraft have increased in the past few years, allowing units to be re-equipped fully with new or upgraded platforms.

One of the most significant revisions to the Serdyukov reforms so far concerns air-force structure. Air Force Commander-in-Chief Lieutenant General Viktor Bondarev initiated a shift away from the 'air base' (*aviabaza*) approach, which often involved hosting multiple types of aircraft at single airfields, towards a 'one airfield, one regiment' formula. This will in effect reinstate a division and regiment structure. The Serdyukov reforms eliminated air armies, divisions and regiments, replacing these with the *aviabaza* as the basic unit of air-force formations. These were divided into first- and second-class categories. First-class air bases comprised 5–8 wings, while second class-bases had 1–2 wings. Each wing consisted on average of three squadrons, each with different aircraft types. Before the reforms, an air regiment consisted of not more than two squadrons, each equipped with one aircraft type.

The **navy** is in the midst of recapitalising its infrastructure, while also bringing into service more modern designs to replace ageing Soviet-era platforms due to be decommissioned. Refurbishment work is also under way at most main bases, with infrastructure upgrade and construction a key objective for shore facilities, as well as for ancillary vessels such as tugs and auxiliaries.

Mediterranean deployments also attracted attention. During the Soviet era, the navy's Fifth Squadron operated in the area and although naval vessels returned to the Mediterranean in 2012, the deployment of a Mediterranean Task Force in June 2013 was seen as a key event. Ships are to be rotated through the task force deployment, and the squadron consists of vessels from the Black Sea, Baltic Sea, Northern and, in some cases, Pacific fleets.

Russian **Airborne Forces** are due to be bolstered by the end of 2013 with three air-assault brigades from the Eastern and Southern Military Districts (under Decree 776, signed by Putin on 11 October 2013). The brigades will become the Supreme Commander-in-Chief's reserve. This shift reflects the armed forces' desire, discussed and approved by the defence ministry in May, to be able to provide rapid-deployment forces as a core capability, with airborne units used as a crisis-reaction force. Along with airborne units, rapid-deployment forces are also scheduled to include special taskforce brigades, marine units and special operations personnel. Meanwhile, a **Special Operations Command** (SOC) was established in 2013, in an attempt to unify special forces capabilities at the command level. The SOC is viewed as part of the Supreme Commander-in-Chief's reserve, alongside airborne units.

Sustaining and renewing Russia's nuclear forces remains a near-term priority. Lieutenant-General Sergey Karakayev, the **Strategic Rocket Forces** commander, claims that Russia has two new ICBM designs capable of penetrating missile-defence systems: one a solid-propellant missile, the other a long-discussed, liquid-fuelled model. Some media reports indicate that the liquid-fuelled design may be intended to replace the R36M (SS-18 *Satan*). The intent is that by 2021 almost all strategic missiles should be of new or recent design. There is also renewed interest in a rail-mobile system to succeed the *Molodets*, which was withdrawn from service in 2007. However, missile programmes continue to suffer development problems. A test firing of the *Bulava* (SS-NX-32) SLBM failed again in September 2013, prompting further concern over the project.

The **Aerospace Defence Forces** and associated air- and missile-defence systems are due to be fully integrated into the command-and-control system between 2016 and 2020. A key programme is the S-500 (*Triumf*-M) SAM system. Introduction into service of the S-500 is now promised for the beginning of 2018, but this date remains open to doubt, as the facilities for building the system are still under construction. The A-135 *Amur* ballistic-missile defence system for Moscow is also to be replaced with the A-235 *Samolyet*-M. As of the end of 2013 it appeared that the A-235 would use an improved variant of the 53T6 missile used in the A-135. The interceptor is intended to be capable of a kinetic kill, while also retaining the capacity to carry a nuclear warhead.

DEFENCE ECONOMICS

State Armaments Programme

The country's political and military leadership have shown considerable continued commitment to the ambitious State Armaments Programme to 2020, notwithstanding faltering economic performance. Spending on the programme is now nearly half of all expenditure under the 'National Defence' budget chapter, compared with less than one-third in 2005. The optimistic economic forecasts on which the programme was originally based – average annual GDP growth of at least 6% – have not been achieved. Instead, economic growth has slowed, from 4.3% in 2011 (the first year of the programme's implementation) to barely 2% in 2013. Consequently, the government has had little choice but to alter its budgetary priorities to permit a steadily growing share of defence spending as a proportion of GDP. This is now projected to rise from 2.72% of GDP in 2011 to 3.15% in 2013 (see Table 4). The draft three-year budget for 2014–16, sent to the Duma at the end of September 2013, envisaged that this share would eventually rise to 3.9% of GDP by 2016, with a significant ramping up of real defence spending over the 2012–15 period. To fund the programme, the authorities have resorted increasingly to state-guaranteed credits. This is, in effect, a non-budgetary means of increasing spending, although the finance ministry has indicated that there will be no new credits after 2015.

Defence industry restructuring

Since December 2011, the government's Military-Industrial Commission has been headed by the deputy prime minister, Dmitry Rogozin. Under his leadership, it has been transformed into a more interventionist coordinating agency, while Rogozin himself has played a prominent role in attempting to resolve issues arising from the implementation of the annual state defence order, the instrument with which the State Armaments Programme is put into effect. He has also promoted organisational restructuring, particularly through the consolidation of Russia's sprawling defence industries into large corporate structures. In addition, he has sought to boost private business involvement in the defence sector, including the use of small companies to fulfil defence contracts, though with only limited success so far.

As a result of these reforms, the defence sector is now dominated by a small number of large, predominantly state-owned corporations. The largest of these is Rostec (formerly Russian Technologies), established in 2007, which now has some 660 enterprises, both defence and civilian, employing 900,000 people. Under CEO Sergey Chemezov, there has been a concerted effort to establish an effective corporate structure, with factories grouped into a dozen or so holding companies, some playing a major role in defence work. (This development has parallels with post-war Italy, where state-owned Finmeccanica consolidated the defence and engineering assets of state holding company IRI, but eventually became a commercial business, albeit with a sizeable state shareholding.) Corporations within Rostec include: the state arms export company Rosoboronexport; Oboronprom, which includes Russian Helicopters, employing 40,000, and gas-turbine manufacturer the United Engine Corporation, employing 70,000; Radio-Electronic Technologies, comprising more than 50 enterprises employing 67,000, concerned with electronic warfare and aviation electronics, among others; Russian Electronics, responsible for most of Russia's electronics component base for military purposes; Shvabe, making military and civil optoelectronic equipment; avionics concern Aircraft Engineering; and high-precision tactical weapons firm Vysokotochnye Kompleksy.

Other major structures include the United Aviation Corporation, responsible for almost all development and production of fixed-wing aircraft, military and civil, and now employing almost 100,000; the United Shipbuilding Corporation, responsible for approximately 90% of shipbuilding, including all naval work; Almaz-Antey, responsible for almost all development and manufacture of air-defence equipment,

Table 4 **Russian National Defence Expenditure Trends (2010–16)**

Year	GDP (R bn)	Real GDP Change (%)	National Defence Expenditure (R bn)	% change in Real Defence Expenditure	National Defence as a % of GDP
2016DB	86,869.0	3.3	3,377.3	5.4	3.89
2015DB	79,725.0	3.1	3,026.9	15.7	3.80
2014DB	73,354.0	3.0	2,489.4	12.4	3.39
2013B	66,515.0	2.4	2,098.4	11.5	3.15
2012	62,599.1	3.4	1,812.3	10.2	2.90
2011	55,799.6	4.3	1,516.0	2.8	2.72
2010	46,308.5	4.5	1,276.5	-5.9	2.76

Sources: Rosstat, Ministry of Finance, Kremlin Annual Budget Laws, Ministry of Economic Development and 2014–16 draft budget. National defence expenditure figures for 2010–12 reflect actual expenditure; figures for 2013 reflect the law on the budget; and figures for 2014–16 reflect the draft national budget as of September 2013. Spending in real terms calculated using the annual GDP deflator.

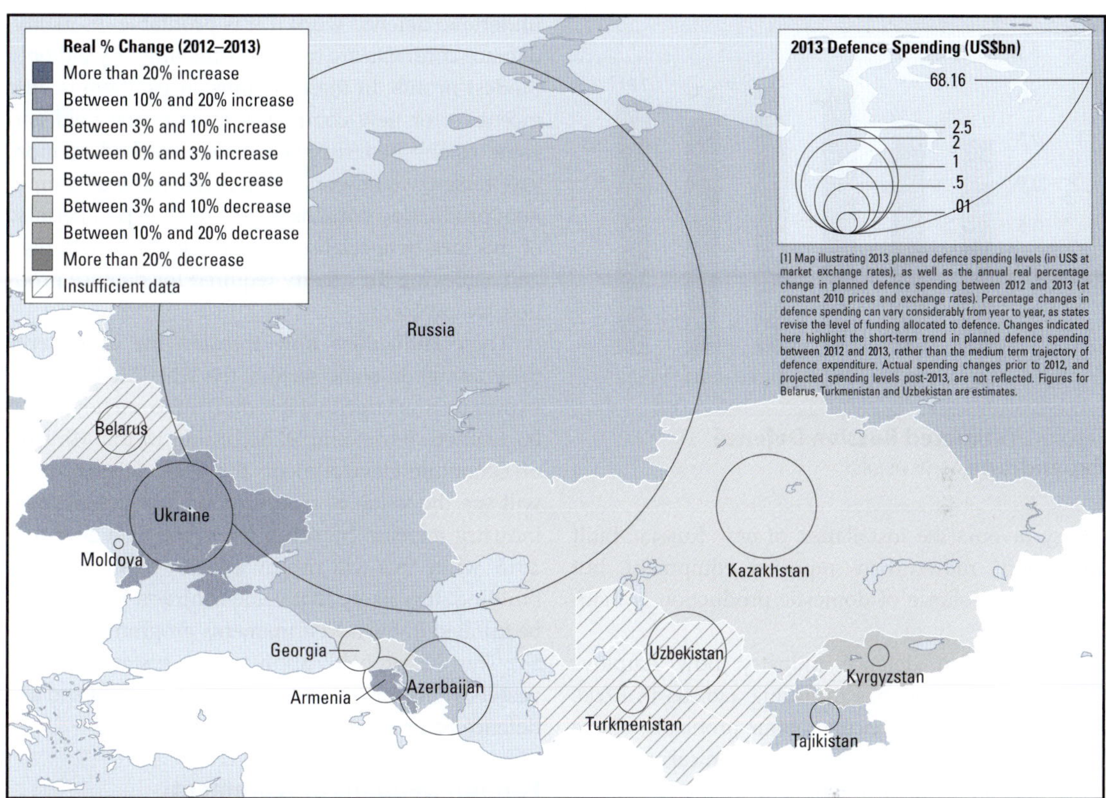

Map 3 **Russia and Eurasia Regional Defence Spending**[1]

with more than 60 enterprises employing almost 95,000; and the Tactical Missiles Corporation, uniting 25 enterprises and design organisations concerned with air-, land- and sea-based tactical missile systems. In late 2013 plans to reorganise the space-missile industry were announced, transforming the Federal Space Agency (Roskosmos) into a more effective, business-orientated, structure: the United Rocket and Space Corporation. These corporations are mostly state-owned, but the intention is to form joint-stock companies with the involvement of private capital. This is with the exception of the nuclear weapons industry, which will remain in state hands under the Rosatom state corporation.

Remaining defence-industrial challenges

The R20tr (US$610bn) State Armaments Programme to 2020 poses a major challenge for Russia's defence industry. Until its adoption, Russia's defence industry was largely dependent on foreign orders. Defence exports assisted in the recovery of the industry after the collapse of output during the 1990s. However, exports did not equally benefit all sectors. Enterprises obliged to focus on domestic orders because of the nature of their work – for example, strategic missile manufacturers – were unable to rely on foreign orders to sustain their activities, and consequently lacked investment resources and had difficulty in retaining workers because of low pay rates. As a result, industrial capabilities now vary considerably across Russia's defence sectors. Some companies face capacity constraints, and find it difficult to meet both export demand and the increased domestic orders required by the State Armament Programme. This applies in particular to Almaz-Antey, which now has to build new factories to manufacture its air-defence systems. The same applies, albeit to a lesser degree, to the construction of conventionally powered submarines and other naval systems.

In parallel with the armaments programme there is another programme focused on development of the defence industry (to 2020), with a R2–3tr (approximately US$65–98bn) budget for investment in new capacity and the refurbishment of existing production facilities. However, the rate of renewal of productive assets remains low, and many enterprises forced to use Soviet-era equipment have found it difficult to meet modern quality standards. Official

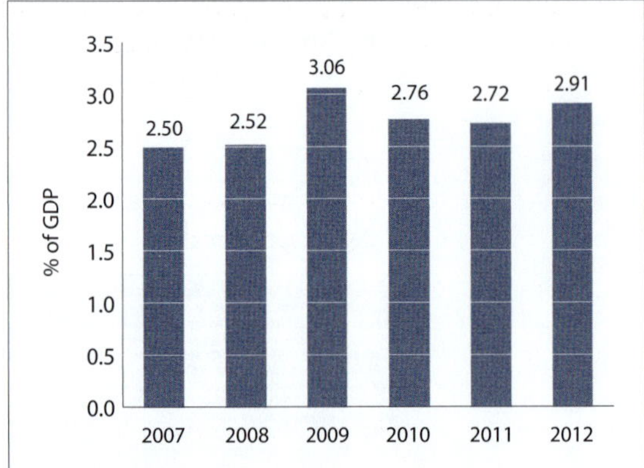

Figure 9 **Estimated Russian Defence Expenditure** as % of GDP

policy favours the installation of new Russian-built machinery, rather than imported equipment, but overall the volume of domestic production is inadequate.

The Russian defence industry now employs more than 1.3m people, including 440,000 in R&D. However, it is experiencing labour problems, above all difficulty in recruiting younger technical and R&D personnel and skilled shopfloor workers. The workforce is ageing, with a large cohort of personnel near or above the official retirement age (60) and relatively few under the age of 30. The average age of employees is reported to be 46 years at industrial enterprises and 48 in R&D. Relatively low pay is a major factor in the inability to recruit and retain. However, increased orders in recent years have enabled some companies to offer pay increases, which may be a way to reverse the negative trends of the past 20 years.

Defence companies are also experiencing difficulties in obtaining high-quality domestically produced components and systems. A feature of the Soviet defence industry was the low level of subcontracting. Many Soviet-era defence enterprises not only conducted final assembly in-house, but also manufactured a wide range of components – often using costly low-volume production methods – that in market economies are normally obtained from specialist suppliers, often small- or medium-sized companies. While this meant higher costs for in-house components, Soviet arms producers were able to minimise the supply disruptions that plagued many other sectors of the state-run economy. Today, most end-product producers are still state-owned, but specialist component suppliers, where they exist, are now often private businesses, and will only undertake defence work if it is profitable. In reality, defence contracts are often loss-making or yield only modest profits. In these circumstances, there is little incentive for new companies to enter the field and some established suppliers have switched to more profitable civilian work. Soviet-style internal component production remains widespread, in part because of this lack of specialist firms, but costs remain high and achieving the quality required for defence products is a problem.

These difficulties now threaten the armaments programme. In some sectors, the scheduled increase in output is so large that it is difficult to see how it can be realised. For example, according to the Ministry of Economic Development, the state defence order will see the value of contracts for Russia's aviation industry increase by seven times between 2012 and 2016, while this will rise by a factor of six for shipbuilding. It is likely that some contracts will have to be fulfilled in the next armaments programme (2016–25). This will probably apply to such systems as naval vessels, transport aircraft, armoured vehicles and air-defence equipment.

Foreign weapons procurement

Given the defence industry's problems, there has been interest in acquiring overseas military hardware. Importing arms and components from CIS countries, especially from Belarus, has been acceptable, but strains have developed with Ukraine, notwithstanding its significant role in the manufacture of transport aircraft, power units for ships and some types of missiles for aircraft. Serdyukov took the initiative in securing foreign supply, most prominently by buying two *Mistral*-class LPDs from France, with the option of building two more at a Russian shipyard. The two vessels are now being built at Saint-Nazaire, with the delivery of the first, the *Vladivostok* for the Pacific Fleet, scheduled for late 2014 and the second, the *Sevastopol*, at the end of 2015. However, it now seems unlikely that two more will be built in Russia. While there have been some foreign technology acquisitions, such as optical equipment from France, there have been only two other significant imports of end-product weapons: Iveco armoured vehicles from Italy and UAVs from Israel. In the latter case, some Israeli UAVs are now being assembled at a factory in Yekaterinburg.

Since Shoigu replaced Serdyukov there has been a policy change, in which Rogozin played a role. It is being stressed that Russia will no longer import assembled weapons. However, cooperation with international partners will still be welcome, provided that Russia is an equal partner with direct access to the relevant technology. For instance, UralVagonZavod is now working jointly with France's Sagem and Renault Trucks Defense on a new combat vehicle, which may be built in Russia. Foreign systems can be manufactured in Russia but only with a high degree of local sourcing; simple assembly of imported components will no longer be permitted.

Russia is now dependent on imported microelectronic components, with Belarus a major supplier. In principle, all components of foreign origin have to undergo rigorous testing before they can be accepted for use in Russian armaments. In practice, this time-consuming and costly procedure is often bypassed, leading to the use of components of inadequate quality for military purposes. This is a matter of considerable policy concern, with efforts under way to increase the domestic supply of crucial components and systems.

Russia is also committed to achieving a significant modernisation of its armed forces' armaments, with the headline goal that by 2020 at least 70% of Russian inventories will be modern equipment. However, the current armaments programme is ambitious, and does not take adequate account of the development and production constraints facing the country's defence industry. While defence-industrial renewal is gradually beginning, it is taking longer than Russia's political and military leadership would wish.

EURASIA

Military and security policy in Eurasia is driven by differing perceptions of the internal and external threat environment. Russia continues to play a key role in shaping some of the underlying assumptions regarding security, while states have divergent views about the potential security impact of the ISAF drawdown from Afghanistan. Policy development is marked by little unity of purpose, except in the relatively low-key common agreements emerging from the Collective Security Treaty Organisation (CSTO) and in the security dimension of the Shanghai Cooperation Organisation (SCO). Beyond apparent determination to combat extremism, separatism and terrorism at a multilateral level, there is little consistency in terms of planning and threat assessment linked to Afghanistan, or on prioritising transnational security threats.

Russian security policy in Central Asia demonstrates further the collapse of the US–Russia 'reset' in relations. Moscow is primarily concerned with promoting or exploiting the perception of declining Western/NATO influence in light of the 2014 withdrawal. To this end, it is using both the CSTO and SCO as instruments to present local governments with alternatives to pursuing closer relations with NATO; pushing joint air-defence policies; and offering arms to the weaker Central Asian states as a means of boosting political influence and reducing these countries' appetite for cooperating with NATO. It also wants to further develop the CSTO Collective Rapid Reaction Forces (KSOR), in case of a possible deterioration of the post-2014 security situation in Central Asia.

Security policy and the Afghan drawdown

Since the ISAF drawdown was announced, both Kazakhstan and Kyrgyzstan have issued new military doctrines. Kazakhstan's 2011 Military Doctrine confirmed that Astana's security policy has not prioritised Afghanistan, and its force structure and armed forces modernisation suggest that Kazakhstan expects no deterioration in post-2014 security environment in Central Asia.

Kyrgyzstan's new doctrine, signed into law on 5 July 2013, sets out possible threats to the state, and notes plans to reform the armed forces. The security environment is described as unpredictable, with a risk of sudden conflict; the text then refers to the Middle East and Afghanistan. The doctrine identifies potential threats to Kyrgyz security, including international terrorism and interference in its domestic affairs, only afterwards adding possible recurrences of the ethnic violence that the country experienced in June 2010.

There is no evidence in the references to military reform (section III, 31) that Kyrgyzstan is actively preparing for post-2014 Afghanistan-linked contingencies. Instead, it is said that existing structures have preserved the Soviet model which does not 'meet current requirements'. The reforms promise, among other things, a modern military with enhanced command-and-control, effective military logistics, and a modern air-defence system – adding the term 'mobilisation readiness'. In general, Kyrgyz combat readiness remains low, with large numbers of poorly trained conscripts in the armed forces. According to analysts, Bishkek is no closer to devising the force structure, doctrine, training and procurement policies that would support state security priorities.

The smaller Central Asian states, such as Kyrgyzstan and Tajikistan, are preoccupied with internal stability and limited militant activity, with less focus on the post-2014 implications of the ISAF drawdown. Tajik security forces have intermittent problems coping with armed gangs linked to drug trafficking. Given the overall weaknesses of the Tajik armed and security forces – which suffer from inadequate special forces training and personnel issues revolving around high numbers of conscripts and low planning capacity – it is likely that low-level militant activity linked to drug trafficking will continue to challenge the armed forces.

The larger and more prosperous states are more or less indifferent to the possible effects of the Afghan drawdown. Priorities for Kazakhstan include protecting the capital during EXPO 2017, deploying peace-support elements abroad in support of future UN missions, and boosting its naval forces in the Caspian Sea. Having declared neutrality in 1999 and enshrined this in its 2009 Military Doctrine, Turkmenistan is mainly focused on its naval build-up in the Caspian. President Gurbanguly Berdimuhamedov plans to strengthen the country's naval forces by 2015, and the navy has already procured coastal assets, including fast patrol boats. A low level of training for officers and enlisted personnel, lack of spare parts and insufficient numbers of trained pilots, combined with the lack of contact with foreign armed forces, limit capability.

The one exception is Uzbekistan. Although security documents are classified as a state secret in Uzbekistan, statements by senior government officials imply that this is the sole Central Asian state to now consider Afghanistan the main potential security threat (although past security issues requiring state action have mainly stemmed from domestic issues). Tashkent's focus on Afghanistan-linked contingencies means that border security, mobility and small-scale operations are central to security thinking. The Uzbek government has lobbied Washington heavily to materially benefit from the drawdown. ISAF members have dampened this appetite among Central Asian states by insisting that any hardware transfers, based on what individual countries choose to leave behind, must be collected and transported by the recipient country.

In general, Central Asian states show little sign of preparing for any negative impact on their security arising from the 2014 ISAF drawdown. This reflects a mixture of political confidence in some capitals, coupled with weak defence capacity in others. The smaller states refer to the potential threat increase post-2014 in order to extract a better security assistance package from NATO members; those states less focused on Afghanistan present requests more suited to varied security applications.

Consistent with its 2011 Military Doctrine, Kazakhstan continues to develop its peace support operation (PSO) capabilities in order to participate in UN peacekeeping operations (PKO). Legislation has been drafted that would give the defence ministry the power to send forces abroad. Kazakhstan's peacekeeping battalion (KAZBAT) functions as part of the emerging KAZBRIG peacekeeping brigade. Since 2003, this battalion has participated in annual *Steppe Eagle* exercises with US and UK forces. Other countries have recently joined the exercise, including small contingents from Kyrgyzstan and Tajikistan. *Steppe Eagle 2013*, held in southern Kazakhstan in August, included an assessment under NATO Partnership for Peace arrangements of KAZBAT/KAZBRIG PSO capabilities, partly to help deployment preparations for UN PKOs. However, supporting security forces in responding to future domestic crises remains a core focus, as does enhancing forces assigned to the CSTO and developing CIS joint air-defence, mainly with Russia.

In the South Caucasus, Russian security policy remains focused on preventing tensions flaring between Georgia and the breakaway territories of Abkhazia and South Ossetia. Moscow has relaxed trade sanctions imposed on Tbilisi after the August 2008 war, though renewing diplomatic relations is proving more difficult.

Policy is more nuanced regarding Armenia and Azerbaijan. Moscow wants to avoid any renewal of territorial conflict over Nagorno-Karabakh, yet arms sales proceed to both sides. Despite alarmist reporting on the defence policies of both Armenia and Azerbaijan, neither side appears closer to renewed conflict, with modernisation and defence reform plans progressing moderately.

Defence economics

Kyrgyzstan and Tajikistan struggle to maintain defence spending at levels high enough to support structural reforms. The larger states in the region, Kazakhstan, Turkmenistan and Uzbekistan, have greater defence-spending capacity, although precise levels are impossible to establish in Uzbekistan, because of state secrecy. Defence spending in

Turkmenistan reached 1.6% of GDP in 2012 (around US$538.9m) and in 2013 stabilised at around this figure.

Kazakhstan's cumulative 2013–15 defence budget of 1.01tr tenge (around US$6.74bn) was approved in the Law on the Republic's Budget. In 2013 it reached 348.4bn tenge (US$2.32bn, 0.95% of GDP), with year-on-year growth of 75bn tenge (approximately US$511m), reflecting overall growth in the country's GDP. Progress in improving capacity in the domestic defence industry through the joint-stock company Kazakhstan Engineering is proceeding slowly. The number of joint ventures stands at four (Exocet, Eurocopter, Cessna and Otokar) with plans to increase this in the near future. President Nursultan Nazarbayev has set a target for 70% of the armed forces' modern weapons to be manufactured domestically by 2015. Joint ventures and in-country assembly will likely be central to this aim, as part of the country's 'multi-vector' defence policy (see *The Military Balance 2013*, p. 212). Kazakhstan is diversifying its foreign military cooperation with NATO and non-NATO members, while still serving as Russia's main partner within Central Asia. Its security policy, however, limits the level of potential cooperation with NATO, which will mostly centre on small-scale activities to boost peacekeeping capabilities. In January 2013, Astana took delivery of two Airbus C-295s, with the option of a further six. The contract also envisages a service package for spare parts and ground support. Kazakhstan's defence ministry is also discussing the possible procurement of A400M. Nonetheless, these procurement developments do not signal any move away from close defence cooperation with Russia.

South Caucasus

Defence spending in the South Caucasus continues to be dominated by **Azerbaijan's** disbursements. According to President Ilham Aliyev, the country's defence budget increased from US$3bn in 2012 to US$3.7bn in 2013. This funding will enable the replacement of ageing equipment and weapons systems. Military procurement falls into three areas: diversification of Baku's foreign military cooperation; equipment purchases; and efforts to boost domestic production. Azerbaijan buys equipment from a range of suppliers, developing forms of defence cooperation with a variety of states. Ukraine was the main source of foreign equipment until a substantial 2012 deal with Russia, which will sell Baku US$4bn-worth of equipment and weapons over three years. Azerbaijan is also reportedly interested in military equipment from South Korea, although details remain unclear. Also important is a related initiative to boost domestic defence production capacity. In 2012, the volume of such production increased by 12% on 2011, and there are now some 700 defence items produced domestically. It is likely, however, that Baku will rely on foreign procurement for high-tech requirements.

Armenia's 2013 defence budget was US$447m. Although the country's fledgling domestic defence industry has developed in recent years, it is unlikely to become profitable before 2015 at the earliest, leaving Armenia's armed forces heavily reliant on a strategic partnership with Russia for upgrades, modernisation and maintenance of its predominantly Russian-manufactured inventory. Small joint ventures with Greece and Poland to modernise T-72 MBTs will mean the country is not completely reliant upon Russia, though contacts with Moscow will likely continue in relation to advanced systems, such as Armenia's S-300PM air-defence system. Yerevan is interested in enhancing its artillery capabilities, most recently demonstrated by an agreement to procure the Chinese A100 300mm MRL. (A military parade in 2006 showcased an earlier version of this MRL, which appears to have entered service in the 1990s.) Military-technical cooperation with China is unlikely to weaken Moscow's grip on this market, particularly given Yerevan's membership of the CSTO and its decision in September 2013 to enter the Customs Union of Belarus, Kazakhstan and Russia.

Armenia ARM

Armenian Dram d		2012	2013	2014
GDP	d	3.98tr	4.33tr	
	US$	10.1bn	10.3bn	
per capita	US$	2,991	3,037	
Growth	%	7.18	4.30	
Inflation	%	2.51	4.20	
Def bdgt	d	159bn	188bn	
	US$	402m	447m	
FMA (US)	US$	2.7m	2.7m	2.7m
US$1=d		395.54	419.66	

Population 2,974,184

Age	0 – 14	15 – 19	20 – 24	25 – 29	30 – 64	65 plus
Male	9.2%	3.8%	5.2%	5.0%	20.2%	3.6%
Female	8.0%	3.5%	5.1%	5.1%	24.9%	6.2%

Capabilities

Armenia's armed forces focus on territorial defence, given continuing tensions with neighbouring Azerbaijan. While overall military doctrine remains influenced strongly by Russian thinking, Armenia's overseas deployments, which include support to ISAF in Afghanistan, enable the troops serving in the Pul-e Khumri PRT to learn lessons from their NATO counterparts. The ISAF contribution increased in 2011. In November 2011, Armenia signed a new Individual Partnership Action Plan with NATO. While conscription continues, there is a growing cohort of professional officers. The country's armed forces are generally held to be at least competent and well-motivated. Serviceability and maintenance have been a problem for the air force, and Russia provides national air defence from a leased base. The army exercises regularly, and aims to be able to deploy and sustain a battalion-sized contingent by 2015 as part of a multinational mission. To inform these developments, Armenia completed a Strategic Defense Review in May 2011.

ACTIVE 44,800 (Army 41,850 Air/AD Aviation Forces (Joint) 1,100 other Air Defence Forces 1,850) Paramilitary 4,300

Conscript liability 24 months.

RESERVES some mob reported, possibly 210,000 with military service within 15 years.

ORGANISATIONS BY SERVICE

Army 22,900; 18,950 conscripts (total 41,850)

FORCES BY ROLE

SPECIAL FORCES
1 SF regt

MANOEUVRE

Mechanised
1 (1st) corps (1 recce bn, 1 tk bn, 2 MR regt, 1 maint bn)
1 (2nd) corps (1 recce bn, 1 tk bn, 2 MR regt, 1 lt inf regt, 1 arty bn)
1 (3rd) corps (1 recce bn, 1 tk bn, 4 MR regt, 1 lt inf regt, 1 arty bn, 1 MRL bn, 1 sigs bn, 1 maint bn)
1 (4th) corps (4 MR regt; 1 SP arty bn; 1 sigs bn)
1 (5th) corps (with 2 fortified areas) (1 MR regt)

Other
1 indep MR trg bde

COMBAT SUPPORT
1 arty bde
1 MRL bde
1 AT regt
1 AD bde
2 AD regt
1 (radiotech) AD regt
1 engr regt

EQUIPMENT BY TYPE

MBT 109: 3 T-54; 5 T-55; 101 T-72
AIFV 98: 75 BMP-1; 6 BMP-1K; 5 BMP-2; 12 BRM-1K
APC (W) 130: 8 BTR-60; 100 look-a-like; 18 BTR-70; 4 BTR-80
ARTY 232
SP 38: **122mm** 10 2S1; **152mm** 28 2S3
TOWED 131: **122mm** 69 D-30; **152mm** 62: 26 2A36; 2 D-1; 34 D-20
MRL 51: **122mm** 47 BM-21; **273mm** 4 WM-80
MOR 120mm 12 M120
AT • MSL 22
SP 22: 9 9P148 *Konkurs*; 13 9P149 MT-LB *Spiral*
AD
SAM
SP 2K11 *Krug* (SA-4 *Ganef*); 2K12 *Kub* (SA-6 *Gainful*); 9K33 *Osa* (SA-8 *Gecko*)
TOWED S-75 *Dvina* (SA-2 *Guideline*); S-125 *Pechora* (SA-3 *Goa*)
MANPAD *Igla*-1 (SA-16 *Gimlet*); *Igla* (SA-18 *Grouse*)
GUNS
SP ZSU-23-4
TOWED 23mm ZU-23-2
UAV Light 15 *Krunk*
RADAR • LAND 6 SNAR-10
MSL • TACTICAL • SSM 12: 8 9K72 *Elbrus* (SS-1C *Scud* B); 4 9K79 *Tochka* (SS-21 *Scarab*)
AEV MT-LB
ARV BREhM-D; BREM-1

Air and Air Defence Aviation Forces 1,100

1 Air & AD Joint Command

FORCES BY ROLE

GROUND ATTACK
1 sqn with Su-25/Su-25UBK *Frogfoot*

EQUIPMENT BY TYPE

AIRCRAFT 15 combat capable
ATK 15: 13 Su-25 *Frogfoot*; 2 Su-25UBK *Frogfoot*
TPT 3 **Heavy** 2 Il-76 *Candid*; **PAX** 1 A319CJ
TRG 14: 4 L-39 *Albatros*; 10 Yak-52
HELICOPTERS
ATK 8 Mi-24P *Hind*
ISR 4: 2 Mi-24K *Hind*; 2 Mi-24R *Hind* (cbt spt)
MRH 10 Mi-8MT (cbt spt)
C2 2 Mi-9 *Hip* G (cbt spt)

TPT • Light 7 PZL Mi-2 *Hoplite*
SAM • SP S-300/S-300PM (SA-10 *Grumble*)

Paramilitary 4,300

Ministry of Internal Affairs

FORCES BY ROLE
MANOEUVRE
Other
4 paramilitary bn
EQUIPMENT BY TYPE
AIFV 55: 5 BMD-1; 44 BMP-1; 1 BMP-1K; 5 BRM-1K
APC (W) 24 BTR-60/BTR-70/BTR-152

Border Troops

Ministry of National Security
EQUIPMENT BY TYPE
AIFV 43: 5 BMD-1; 35 BMP-1; 3 BRM-1K
APC (W) 23: 5 BTR-60; 18 BTR-70

DEPLOYMENT

Legal provisions for foreign deployment:
Constitution: Codified constitution (1995, amended 2005)
Specific legislation: 'Law on Defence of the Republic of Armenia'
Decision on deployment of troops abroad: by the president, in accordance with 'Law on Defence of the Republic of Armenia' (Article 5 (2) (1)). Also, under Art. 55 (13) of constitution, president can call for use of armed forces (and National Assembly shall be convened). (Also Art. 81 (3) of constitution.)

AFGHANISTAN
NATO • ISAF 131

BOSNIA-HERZEGOVINA
OSCE • Bosnia and Hezegovina 2

LEBANON
UN • UNIFIL 1

SERBIA
NATO • KFOR 36

FOREIGN FORCES

OSCE figures represent total Minsk Conference mission personnel in both Armenia and Azerbaijan
Bulgaria OSCE 1
Czech Republic OSCE 1
Poland OSCE 1
Russia 3,303: 1 MR bde; 74 MBT; 201 AIFV; 84 arty; (12 MRL; 72 SP/towed): 1 ftr sqn with 18 MiG-29 *Fulcrum*; 2 SAM bty with S-300V (SA-12 *Gladiator/Giant*); 1 SAM bty with 2K12 *Kub* (SA-6 *Gainful*)
Sweden OSCE 1
Ukraine OSCE 1
United Kingdom OSCE 1

Azerbaijan AZE

Azerbaijani New Manat m		2012	2013	2014
GDP	m	54bn	58.9bn	
	US$	68.8bn	77.2bn	
per capita	US$	7,450	8,297	
Growth	%	2.16	4.14	
Inflation	%	1.08	3.37	
Def bdgt [a]	m	1.38bn	1.53bn	1.64bn
	US$	1.76bn	2bn	
FMA (US)	US$	2.7m	2.7m	2.7m
US$1=m		0.78	0.76	

[a] Official budget

Population 9,590,159

Age	0 – 14	15 – 19	20 – 24	25 – 29	30 – 64	65 plus
Male	12.1%	4.2%	5.2%	4.8%	20.7%	2.4%
Female	10.5%	3.9%	5.0%	4.6%	22.7%	3.9%

Capabilities

While the armed forces have yet to successfully transition from a Soviet-era model, increasing defence expenditure has provided the opportunity to acquire some more capable military equipment. Rising oil revenues have provided the financial headroom for acquisitions, including the S-300 SAM system, but it is unclear whether the potential benefits brought by these modern systems have been felt in terms of operational capability. The armed forces still rely on conscription, and readiness within the services varies considerably between units. Peacekeeping deployments have included a small number of personnel in Afghanistan. Azerbaijan maintains defence relationships with NATO through an IPAP, and has a close relationship with Turkey. With NATO support, the Internal Troops are developing a police support unit to be available for NATO-led operations. US military assistance has included support to maritime-security operations in the Caspian Sea. The air force suffers from training and maintenance problems. The armed forces cannot organically support external deployments.

ACTIVE 66,950 (Army 56,850 Navy 2,200 Air 7,900)
Paramilitary 15,000

Conscript liability 17 months, but can be extended for ground forces.

RESERVE 300,000

Some mobilisation reported, 300,000 with military service within 15 years

ORGANISATIONS BY SERVICE

Army 56,850

FORCES BY ROLE
COMMAND
5 corps HQ
MANEOEUVRE
Mechanised
4 MR bde

Light
19 MR bde
Other
1 sy bde
COMBAT SUPPORT
1 arty bde
1 arty trg bde
1 MRL bde
1 AT bde
1 engr bde
1 sigs bde
COMBAT SERVICE SUPPORT
1 log bde

EQUIPMENT BY TYPE
MBT 433: 95 T-55; 244 T-72; 94 T-90S
AIFV 211: 20 BMD-1; 43 BMP-1; 33 BMP-2; 100 BMP-3; 15 BRM-1
APC 575
APC (T) 336 MT-LB
APC (W) 149: 10 BTR-60; 132 BTR-70; 7 BTR-80A
PPV 90: 45 *Marauder*; 45 *Matador*
ARTY 542
SP 87: **122mm** 46 2S1; **152mm** 24: 6 2S3; 18 2S19 *Msta-S*; **155mm** 5 ATMOS-2000; **203mm** 12 2S7
TOWED 207: **122mm** 129 D-30; **130mm** 36 M-46; **152mm** 42: 18 2A36; 24 D-20
GUN/MOR 120mm 36: 18 2S9 NONA; 18 2S31 *Vena*
MRL 100+: **122mm** 52+: 43 BM-21; 9+ IMI *Lynx*; **128mm** 12 RAK-12; **220mm** 6 TOS-1A; **300mm** 30 9A52 *Smerch*
MOR 120mm 112: 5 CARDOM; 107 PM-38
AT • MSL • MANPATS 9K11 *Malyutka* (AT-3 *Sagger*); 9K111 *Fagot* (AT-4 *Spigot*); 9K113 *Konkurs* (AT-5 *Spandrel*); 9K115 *Metis* (AT-7 *Saxhorn*); *Spike*-LR
AD • SAM • SP 9K35 *Strela*-10 (SA-13 *Gopher*); 2K11 *Krug* (SA-4 *Ganef*): 9K33 *Osa* (SA-8 *Gecko*)‡
MANPAD 9K32 *Strela* (SA-7 *Grail*;) 9K34 *Strela-3*; (SA-14 *Gremlin*); 9K310 *Igla*-1 (SA-16 *Gimlet*); 9K338 *Igla*-S (SA-24 *Grinch*)
MSL • SSM ε4 9M79 *Tochka* (SS-21 *Scarab*)
RADAR • LAND SNAR-1 *Long Trough*/SNAR-2/-6 *Pork Trough* (arty); *Small Fred/Small Yawn*/SNAR-10 *Big Fred* (veh, arty); GS-13 *Long Eye* (veh)
UAV • ISR • Medium 3 *Aerostar*
AEV MT-LB
MW *Bozena*

Navy 2,200

EQUIPMENT BY TYPE
PATROL AND COASTAL COMBATANTS 8
CORVETTES • FS 1 *Petya II* with 2 RBU 6000 *Smerch* 2, 2 twin 76mm gun
PSO 1 *Luga* (*Woodnik* 2 Class) (FSU Project 888; additional trg role)
PCC 3: 2 *Petrushka* (FSU UK-3; additional trg role); 1 *Shelon* (FSU Project 1388M)
PB 3: 1 *Bryza* (FSU Project 722); 1 *Turk* (TUR AB 25); 1 *Poluchat* (FSU Project 368)
MINE WARFARE • MINE COUNTERMEASURES 4
MHC 4: 2 *Yevgenya* (FSU Project 1258); 2 *Yakhont* (FSU *Sonya*)
AMPHIBIOUS 6
LSM 3: 1 *Polnochny A* (FSU Project 770) (capacity 6 MBT; 180 troops); 2 *Polnochny B* (FSU Project 771) (capacity 6 MBT; 180 troops)
LCU 1 *Vydra*† (FSU) (capacity either 3 AMX-30 MBT or 200 troops)
LCM 2 T-4 (FSU)
LOGISTICS AND SUPPORT 5
AGS 1 (FSU Project 10470)
ARS 1 *Iva* (FSU *Vikhr*)
YTB 2
YTD 1

Air Force and Air Defence 7,900

FORCES BY ROLE
FIGHTER
1 sqn with MiG-29 *Fulcrum*
FIGHTER/GROUND ATTACK
1 regt with MiG-21 *Fishbed*; Su-17 *Fitter*; Su-24 *Fencer*; Su-25 *Frogfoot*; Su-25UB *Frogfoot* B
TRANSPORT
1 sqn with An-12 *Cub*; Yak-40 *Codling*
ATTACK/TRANSPORT HELICOPTER
1 regt with Mi-8 *Hip*; Mi-24 *Hind*; Mi-35M *Hind*; PZL Mi-2 *Hoplite*

EQUIPMENT BY TYPE
AIRCRAFT 44 combat capable
FTR 14 MiG-29 *Fulcrum*
FGA 11: 4 MiG-21 *Fishbed* (1 more in store); 4 Su-17 *Fitter*; 1 Su-17U *Fitter*; 2 Su-24 *Fencer*†
ATK 19: 16 Su-25 *Frogfoot*; 3 Su-25UB *Frogfoot* B
TPT 4: **Medium** 1 An-12 *Cub*; **Light** 3 Yak-40 *Codling*
TRG 40: 28 L-29 *Delfin*; 12 L-39 *Albatros*
HELICOPTERS
ATK 42: 26 Mi-24 *Hind*; 16 Mi-35M *Hind*
MRH: 20+ Mi-17-IV *Hip*
TPT 20: **Medium** 13 Mi-8 *Hip*; **Light** 7 PZL Mi-2 *Hoplite*
UAV • ISR • Medium 4 *Aerostar*
AD • SAM S-75 *Dvina* (SA-2 *Guideline*); S-125 *Neva* (SA-3 *Goa*); /S-200 *Vega* (SA-5 *Gammon*) static; S-300PM/PMU2 (SA-10 *Grumble*/SA-20 *Gargoyle*)
MSL • AAM • IR R-60 (AA-8 *Aphid*); R-73 (AA-11 *Archer*)
IR/SARH R-27 (AA-10 *Alamo*)

Paramilitary ε15,000

Border Guard ε5,000

Ministry of Internal Affairs
AIFV 168 BMP-1/2
APC (W) 19 BTR-60/70/80

Coast Guard

The Coast Guard was established in 2005 as part of the State Border Service.

EQUIPMENT BY TYPE
PATROL AND COASTAL COMBATANTS 10
PBF 6: 1 *Osa* II (FSU Project 205); 2 Silver Ships 48ft; 3 *Stenka*
PB 4: 2 Baltic 150; 1 *Point* (US); 1 *Grif* (FSU *Zhuk*)

Militia 10,000+

Ministry of Internal Affairs

APC (W) 7 BTR-60/BTR-70/BTR-80

DEPLOYMENT

Legal provisions for foreign deployment:

Constitution: Codified constitution (1995)

Decision on deployment of troops abroad: By parliament upon proposal by president (Art. 109, No. 28)

AFGHANISTAN

NATO • ISAF 94

SERBIA

OSCE • Kosovo 1

FOREIGN FORCES

OSCE figures represent total Minsk Conference mission personnel in both Armenia and Azerbaijan

Bulgaria OSCE 1

Czech Republic OSCE 1

Poland OSCE 1

Sweden OSCE 1

Ukraine OSCE 1

United Kingdom OSCE 1

TERRITORY WHERE THE GOVERNMENT DOES NOT EXERCISE EFFECTIVE CONTROL

Data presented here represent an assessment of the de facto situation. Nagorno-Karabakh was part of the Azerbaijani Soviet Socialist Republic (SSR), but mostly populated by ethnic Armenians. In 1988, when inter-ethnic clashes between Armenians and Azeris erupted in Azerbaijan, the local authorities declared their intention to secede from Azerbaijan and join the Armenian SSR. Baku rejected this and armed conflict erupted. A ceasefire was brokered in 1994. All ethnic Azeris had been expelled from Nagorno-Karabakh and almost all ethnic Armenians were forced to leave Azerbaijan. Since 1994, Armenia has controlled most of Nagorno-Karabakh, and also seven adjacent regions of Azerbaijan, often called the 'occupied territories'. While Armenia provides political, economic and military support to Nagorno-Karabakh, the region has declared itself independent – although this has not been recognised by any other state, including Armenia. Azerbaijan claims, and the rest of the international community generally regards, Nagorno-Karabakh and the occupied territories as part of Azerbaijan. (See IISS Strategic Comment, *Medvedev momentum falters in Nagorno-Karabakh*, August 2011.)

Available estimates vary with reference to military holdings in Nagorno-Karabakh. Main battle tanks are usually placed at around 200–300 in number, with similar numbers for armoured combat vehicles and artillery pieces, with small numbers of fixed- and rotary-wing aviation. Available personnel number estimates are between 18,000–20,000.

Belarus BLR

Belarusian Ruble r		2012	2013	2014
GDP	r	527tr	698tr	
	US$	63.3bn	72.9bn	
per capita	US$	6,739	7,807	
Growth	%	1.50	2.11	
Inflation	%	59.22	20.50	
Def bdgt	r	4.61tr		
	US$	552m		
US$1=r		8336.92	9573.73	

Population 9,625,888

Age	0 – 14	15 – 19	20 – 24	25 – 29	30 – 64	65 plus
Male	7.8%	2.7%	3.7%	4.3%	23.7%	4.4%
Female	7.4%	2.5%	3.5%	4.2%	26.3%	9.6%

Capabilities

The primary role of the armed forces is to protect territorial integrity. Much of Belarus's military inventory consists of ageing Soviet-era equipment. High inflation during 2011 is believed to have adversely affected morale within the conscript-based armed forces; these have reduced in size. As of late-2013 the fate of the air force's Su-27 *Flankers* remained unclear. This threatened to leave the MiG-29 *Fulcrum* as the country's only fighter aircraft. Air combat capabilities could be bolstered by the creation of a Russian air base in Belarus. Moscow is Minsk's main ally. Early 2013 saw a second *Tor*-M2 battery enter service, with an additional S-300 (SA-10/20) battery now expected in 2014. Belarusian forces exercise with their Russian counterparts regularly and could support notionally a regional joint operation with Moscow, though the actual combat capacity of its ground forces is limited. Alongside its close bilateral defence and security ties to Russia, through the CSTO and the Belarus, Kazakhstan, Russia Customs Union, Belarus is also developing a relationship with China, and has defence-industrial ties with Ukraine. Belarus hosted in September 2013 the CSTO's Rapid Reaction Forces *Zapad*-13 exercise, to which it contributes an air assault brigade.

ACTIVE 48,000 (Army 22,500 Air 15,000 Joint 10,500) Paramilitary 110,000

RESERVE 289,500 (Joint 289,500 with mil service within last 5 years)

ORGANISATIONS BY SERVICE

Joint 10,500 (Centrally controlled units and MoD staff)

Army 22,500

FORCES BY ROLE

COMMAND

2 comd HQ (West & North West)

Russia and Eurasia

SPECIAL FORCES
1 SF bde
MANOEUVRE
Mechanised
1 (mobile) armd inf bde
1 (mobile) mech bde
4 mech bde
COMBAT SUPPORT
2 arty bde
1 arty gp
1 MRL bde
2 MRL regt
2 SSM bde
2 AD bde
2 engr bde
2 engr regt
1 EW unit
1 NBC regt
1 ptn bridging regt
2 sigs bde

EQUIPMENT BY TYPE

MBT 515: 446 T-72; 69 T-80
AIFV 1,111: 100 BMD-1; 875 BMP-2; 136 BRM-1
APC 264
APC (T) 72: 22 BTR-D; 50 MT-LB
APC (W) 192: 39 BTR-70; 153 BTR-80
ARTY 1,005
SP 434: **122mm** 198 2S1; **152mm** 236: 108 2S3; 116 2S5; 12 2S19 *Farm*
TOWED 228: **122mm** 48 D-30; **152mm** 180: 48 2A36; 132 2A65
GUN/MOR 120mm 48 2S9 NONA
MRL 234: **122mm** 126 BM-21; **220mm** 72 9P140 *Uragan*; **300mm** 36 9A52 *Smerch*
MOR 120mm 61 2S12
AT • MSL
SP 236: 126 9P148 *Konkurs*; 110 9P149 *Shturm*
MANPATS 9K111 *Fagot* (AT-4 *Spigot*); 9K113 *Konkurs* (AT-5 *Spandrel*); 9K114 *Shturm* (AT-6 *Spiral*); 9K115 *Metis* (AT-7 *Saxhorn*)
AD • SAM • SP 350 9K37 *Buk* (SA-11 *Gadfly*); S-300V(SA-12A *Gladiator*/SA-12B *Giant*); 9K35 *Strela*-10 (SA-13 *Gopher*); 9K33 *Osa* (SA-8 *Gecko*) (700–2,100 eff.); *Tor*-M2E (SA-15 *Gauntlet*)
RADAR • LAND GS-13 *Long Eye*/SNAR-1 *Long Trough*/SNAR-2/-6 *Pork Trough* (arty); some *Small Fred*/*Small Yawn*/SNAR-10 *Big Fred* (veh, arty)
MSL • TACTICAL • SSM 96: 36 FROG/SS-21 *Scarab* (*Tochka*); 60 *Scud*
AEV MT-LB
VLB MTU

Air Force and Air Defence Forces 15,000

Flying hours 15 hrs/year

FORCES BY ROLE

FIGHTER
2 sqn with MiG-29S/UB *Fulcrum*
GROUND ATTACK
2 sqn with Su-25K/UBK *Frogfoot* A/B
TRANSPORT
1 base with An-12 *Cub*; An-24 *Coke*; An-26 *Curl*; Il-76 *Candid*; Tu-134 *Crusty*
TRAINING
Some sqn with L-39 *Albatros*
ATTACK HELICOPTER
Some sqn with Mi-24 *Hind*
TRANSPORT HELICOPTER
Some (cbt spt) sqn with Mi-6 *Hook*; Mi-8 *Hip*; Mi-24K *Hind* G2; Mi-24R *Hind* G1; Mi-26 *Halo*

EQUIPMENT BY TYPE

AIRCRAFT 72 combat capable
FTR 38 MiG-29S/UB *Fulcrum*
FGA (21 Su-27P/UB *Flanker* B/C poss. non-operational)
ATK 34 Su-25K/UBK *Frogfoot* A/B
TPT 13: **Heavy** 2 Il-76 *Candid* (+9 civ Il-76 available for mil use); **Medium** 3 An-12 *Cub*; **Light** 8: 1 An-24 *Coke*; 6 An-26 *Curl*; 1 Tu-134 *Crusty*
TRG Some L-39 *Albatros*
HELICOPTERS
ATK 49 Mi-24 *Hind*
ISR 20: 8 Mi-24K *Hind* G2; 12 Mi-24R *Hind* G1
TPT 168: **Heavy** 43: 29 Mi-6 *Hook*; 14 Mi-26 *Halo*; **Medium** 125 Mi-8 *Hip*
MSL
ASM Kh-25 (AS-10 *Karen*); Kh-29 (AS-14 *Kedge*)
ARM Kh-58 (AS-11 *Kilter*)
AAM • IR R-60 (AA-8 *Aphid*); R-73 (AA-11 *Archer*)
SARH R-27R (AA-10 *Alamo* A)

Air Defence

AD data from Uzal Baranovichi EW radar

FORCES BY ROLE

AIR DEFENCE
1 bde (2 AD bn)

EQUIPMENT BY TYPE

AD • SAM S-300PS (SA-10B *Grumble*); S-125 *Pechora* (SA-3 *Goa*); S-200 (SA-5 *Gammon*)

Paramilitary 110,000

Border Guards 12,000

Ministry of Interior

Militia 87,000

Ministry of Interior

Ministry of Interior Troops 11,000

DEPLOYMENT

LEBANON

UN • UNIFIL 5

SOUTH SUDAN

UN • UNMISS 4 obs

FOREIGN FORCES

Russia: Military Air Forces: 4 SAM units with S-300 (SA-10 *Grumble* (quad))

Georgia GEO

Georgian Lari		2012	2013	2014
GDP	lari	26.3bn	28.9bn	
	US$	15.9bn	17bn	
per capita	US$	3,543	3,763	
Growth	%	6.55	5.98	
Inflation	%	-0.94	0.96	
Def bdgt	lari	651m	660m	711m
	US$	394m	389m	
FMA (US)	US$	14m	14m	12m
US$1=lari		1.65	1.70	

Population 4,555,911

Age	0 – 14	15 – 19	20 – 24	25 – 29	30 – 64	65 plus
Male	8.2%	3.2%	4.0%	3.9%	22.0%	6.4%
Female	7.2%	2.9%	3.9%	4.0%	24.5%	9.7%

Capabilities

Georgia's armed forces continue to make efforts to address lessons from the conflict with Russia in 2008, while tensions with Moscow remain. The brief war revealed significant shortcomings in key areas, including anti-armour and air-defence capabilities, though performance in air defence was better. It has also acquired the Israeli *Spyder* short-range air-defence system. A substantial number of Georgia's T-72 MBTs were destroyed during the short conflict. Current plans call for the small air force – comprising Soviet-era ground-attack aircraft and combat-support helicopters as well as transport and utility helicopters – to merge with the army. Georgia currently deploys personnel to ISAF in Afghanistan, and has aspirations for NATO membership. Training activity involves international forces, including the US. Moves are under way to generate a pool of four-year contract servicemen to boost professionalisation.

ACTIVE 20,650 (Army 17,750 Air 1,300 National Guard 1,600) Paramilitary 11,700

Conscript liability 18 months

ORGANISATIONS BY SERVICE

Army 14,000; 3,750 conscript (total 17,750)

FORCES BY ROLE

SPECIAL FORCES

1 SF bde

MANOEUVRE

Light

5 inf bde

Amphibious

2 mne bn (1 cadre)

COMBAT SUPPORT

2 arty bde

1 engr bde

1 sigs bn

1 SIGINT bn

1 MP bn

COMBAT SERVICE SUPPORT

1 med bn

EQUIPMENT BY TYPE

MBT 123: 23 T-55; 100 T-72

RECCE 4+ *Didgori-2*

AIFV 72: 25 BMP-1; 46 BMP-2; 1 BRM-1K

APC 199+

APC (T) 69+: 3+ *Lazika*; 66 MT-LB

APC (W) 120+: 25 BTR-70; 19 BTR-80; 8+ *Didgori-1*; 3+ *Didgori-3*; 65 *Ejder*

PPV 10 *Cougar*

ARTY 240

SP 67 **152mm** 66: 32 DANA; 20 2S1; 13 2S3; 1 2S19; **203mm** 1 2S7

TOWED 71: **122mm** 58 D-30; **152mm** 13: 3 2A36; 10 2A65

MRL 122mm 37: 13 BM-21; 6 GRADLAR; 18 RM-70

MOR 120mm 65: 14 2S12; 33 M-75; 18 M120

AT ε50

MSL ε10

GUNS ε40

AD • SAM • SP 9K35 *Strela-10* (SA-13 *Gopher*); *Spyder*

MANPAD *Grom*; 9K32 *Strela-2* (SA-7 *Grail*)‡; 9K36 *Strela-3* (SA-14 *Gremlin*); 9K310 *Igla-1* (SA-16 *Gimlet*)

Air Force 1,300 (incl 300 conscript)

1 avn base, 1 hel air base

AIRCRAFT 12 combat capable

ATK 12: 3 Su-25 *Frogfoot*; 7 Su-25K *Frogfoot* A; 2 Su-25UB *Frogfoot* B

TPT • Light 9: 6 An-2 *Colt*; 1 Tu-134A *Crusty* (VIP); 2 Yak-40 *Codling*

TRG 9 L-29 *Delfin*

HELICOPTERS

ATK 6 Mi-24 *Hind*

TPT 29 **Medium** 17 Mi-8T *Hip*; **Light** 12 Bell 205 (UH-1H *Iroquois*)

UAV • ISR • Medium 1+ *Hermes* 450

AD • SAM 1–2 bn 9K37 *Buk*-M1 (SA-11 *Gadfly*), 8 9K33 *Osa*-AK (SA-8B *Gecko*) (two bty), 6-10 9K33 *Osa*-AKM updated SAM systems.

National Guard 1,600 active reservists opcon Army

FORCES BY ROLE

MANOEUVRE

Light

1 inf bde

Paramilitary 11,700

Border Guard 5,400

Coast Guard

HQ at Poti. The Navy was merged with the Coast Guard in 2009 under the auspices of the Georgian Border Guard, within the Ministry of the Interior.

PATROL AND COASTAL COMBATANTS 16

PBF 2: 1 *Kaan 33*; 1 *Kaan 20*

Russia and Eurasia

PB 14: 7 *Zhuk* (3 ex-UKR); 2 *Point*; 2 *Dauntless*; 2 *Dilos* (ex-GRC); 1 *Akhmeta* (up to 20 patrol launches also in service)

AMPHIBIOUS • LANDING CRAFT • LCU 1 *Vydra* (ex-BUL)

LOGISTIC AND SUPPORT • YTL 1

Ministry of Interior Troops 6,300

DEPLOYMENT

Legal provisions for foreign deployment of armed forces:

Constitution: Codified constitution (1995)

Decision on deployment of troops abroad: By the presidency upon parliamentary approval (Art. 100)

AFGHANISTAN

NATO • ISAF 1,561; 2 inf bn

SERBIA

OSCE • Kosovo 4

TERRITORY WHERE THE GOVERNMENT DOES NOT EXERCISE EFFECTIVE CONTROL

Following the August 2008 war between Russia and Georgia, the areas of Abkhazia and South Ossetia declared themselves independent. Data presented here represents the de facto situation and does not imply international recognition as sovereign states.

FOREIGN FORCES

Russia Army 7,000; 1 MR bde at Gudauta (Abkhazia); 1 MR bde at Djava/Tskhinvali (S. Ossetia)

Kazakhstan KAZ

Kazakhstani Tenge t		2012	2013	2014
GDP	t	29.3tr	32.2tr	
	US$	196bn	214bn	
per capita	US$	11,773	12,708	
Growth	%	5.04	5.50	
Inflation	%	5.12	7.22	
Def bdgt	t	340bn	348bn	377bn
	US$	2.28bn	2.32bn	
FMA (US)	US$	1.8m	1.8m	1.5m
US$1=t		149.11	150.28	

Population 17,736,896

Ethnic groups: Kazakh 51%; Russian 32%; Ukrainian 5%; German 2%; Tatar 2%; Uzbek 13%

Age	0–14	15–19	20–24	25–29	30–64	65 plus
Male	12.4%	3.9%	4.7%	4.6%	19.9%	2.3%
Female	12.3%	3.8%	4.6%	4.6%	22.3%	4.5%

Capabilities

The Soviet origins of Kazakhstan's conscript-based armed forces remain. The 2011 Military Doctrine identified both internal and external security concerns, and risks from regional instability. There were few force structure changes in that document, with much focus on the development of Kazakhstan's indigenous defence industry. Kazakhstan is a member of the CSTO and also participates in Shanghai Cooperation Organisation military exercises. Moscow and Astana signed an agreement on the creation of a joint regional air-defence system at the beginning of 2013. As of mid-2013, it appeared that delivery of the S-300PMU-1, under discussion since 2010, had not yet begun. The services are at varying levels of preparedness. In the army, air mobile units are held at the highest level of readiness, with other units at considerably lower levels. There are ongoing efforts to improve the navy and the air force, with modest procurement projects underway. Rotary- and fixed-wing transport is being improved, while some combat aircraft have also been upgraded. The air force reportedly struggles to keep its aircraft airworthy, although air-defence fighters fare better than strike aircraft. Tactical airlift is being bolstered with the purchase of the C-295; deliveries began in 2013. Ukraine is also emerging as a defence-industrial partner, with collaboration on armoured vehicle production.

ACTIVE 39,000 (Army 20,000 Navy 3,000 Air 12,000 MoD 4,000) Paramilitary 31,500

Conscript liability 12 months

ORGANISATIONS BY SERVICE

Army 20,000

4 regional comd: Astana, East, West and Southern

FORCES BY ROLE

MANOEUVRE

Armoured

1 tk bde

Mechanised

4 mech bde

Air Manoeuvre

4 air aslt bde

COMBAT SUPPORT

3 arty bde

1 SSM unit

3 cbt engr bde

EQUIPMENT BY TYPE

MBT 300 T-72

RECCE 100: 40 BRDM; 60 BRM

AIFV 652: 500 BMP-2; 107 BTR-80A; 43 BTR-82A; 2 BTR-3E

APC 357

APC (T) 150 MT-LB

APC (W) 207: 190 BTR-80; 17 *Cobra*

ARTY 602

SP 246: **122mm** 126: 120 2S1; 6 *Semser*; **152mm** 120 2S3

TOWED 150: **122mm** 100 D-30; **152mm** 50 2A65; (**122mm** up to 300 D-30 in store)

GUN/MOR 120mm 25 2S9 *Anona*
MRL 118: **122mm** 100 BM-21 *Grad*; **300mm** 18 *Lynx* (with 50 msl); (**122mm** 100 BM-21 *Grad*; **220mm** 180 9P140 *Uragan* all in store)
MOR 63 **SP 120mm** 18 CARDOM **120mm** 45 2B11/M120
AT
MSL
SP 3 BMP-T
MANPATS 9K111 *Fagot* (AT-4 *Spigot*); 9K113 *Konkurs* (AT-5 *Spandrel*); 9K115 *Metis* (AT-6 *Spiral*)
GUNS 100mm 68 MT-12/T-12
MSL • SSM 12 9K79 *Tochka* (SS-21 *Scarab*)
AEV MT-LB

Navy 3,000

PATROL AND COASTAL COMBATANTS 17
PCG 1 *Kazakhstan* with 2 quad lnchr with 3424 *Uran* (SS-N-25 *Switchblade*) AShM, 1 *Ghibka* lnchr with SA-N-10 *Gimlet* SAM
PBF 5: 3 *Sea Dolphin;* 2 *Saygak;*
PB 15: 4 *Almaty;* 1 *Dauntless;* 1 *Turk* (AB25); 2 *Zhuk* (of which 1 may be operational); 4 *Sardar;* 3 *Archangel;*
LOGISTICS AND SUPPORT • AGS 1 *Zhaik*

Coastal Defence

MANOEUVRE
Other
1 coastal defence bde

Air Force 12,000 (incl Air Defence)

Flying hours 100 hrs/year

FORCES BY ROLE
FIGHTER
1 sqn with MiG-29/MiG-29UB *Fulcrum*
2 sqn with MiG-31/MiG-31BM *Foxhound*
FIGHTER/GROUND ATTACK
2 sqn with MiG-27 *Flogger* D; MiG-23UB *Flogger* C
2 sqn with Su-27/Su-27UB *Flanker*
GROUND ATTACK
1 sqn with Su-25 *Frogfoot*
TRANSPORT
1 unit with Tu-134 *Crusty;* Tu-154 *Careless,*
1 sqn with An-12 *Cub,* An-26 *Curl,* An-30 *Clank,* An-72 *Coaler*
TRAINING
1 sqn with L-39 *Albatros*
ATTACK HELICOPTER
5 sqn with Mi-24V *Hind*
TRANSPORT HELICOPTER
Some sqn with Bell 205 (UH-1H); EC145; Mi-8 *Hip;* Mi-17V-5 *Hip;* Mi-26 *Halo*
AIR DEFENCE
Some regt with S-75M *Volkhov* (SA-2 *Guideline*); S-125 *Neva* (SA-3 *Goa*); S-300 (SA-10 *Grumble*); 2K11 *Krug* (SA-4 *Ganef*); S-200 *Angara* (SA-5 *Gammon*); 2K12 *Kub* (SA-6 *Gainful*)

EQUIPMENT BY TYPE
AIRCRAFT 121 combat capable
FTR 55: 12 MiG-29 *Fulcrum;* 2 MiG-29UB *Fulcrum;* 41 MiG-31/MiG-31BM *Foxhound*
FGA 53: 24 MiG-27 *Flogger* D; 4 MiG-23UB *Flogger* C; 21 Su-27 *Flanker;* 4 Su-27UB *Flanker*
ATK 14: 12 Su-25 *Frogfoot;* 2 Su-25UB *Frogfoot*
ISR 1 An-30 *Clank*
TPT 15: **Medium** 2 An-12 *Cub*: **Light** 12; 6 An-26 *Curl,* 2 An-72 *Coaler;* 2 C-295; 2 Tu-134 *Crusty;* **PAX** 1 Tu-154 *Careless*
TRG 17 L-39 *Albatros*
HELICOPTERS
ATK 40+ Mi-24V *Hind* (first 9 upgraded)
MRH 20 Mi-17V-5 *Hip*
TPT 64 **Heavy** 2 Mi-26 *Halo;* **Medium** 50 Mi-8 *Hip;* **Light** 12: 6 Bell-205 (UH-1H); 6 EC145
AD • SAM 147+
SP 47+: 20 2K12 *Kub* (SA-6 *Gainful*); 27+ 2K11 *Krug* (SA-4 *Ganef*)/S-200 *Angara* (SA-5 *Gammon*); static; S-300 (SA-10 *Grumble*)
TOWED 100 S-75M *Volkhov* (SA-2 *Guideline*); S-125 *Neva* (SA-3 *Goa*)
MSL
ASM Kh-23 (AS-7 *Kerry*)‡; Kh-25 (AS-10 *Karen*); Kh-29 (AS-14 *Kedge*)
ARM Kh-28 (AS-9 *Kyle*); Kh-27 (AS-12 *Kegler*); Kh-58 (AS-11 *Kilter*)
AAM • IR R-60 (AA-8 *Aphid*); R-73 (AA-11 *Archer*) **IR/SARH** R-27 (AA-10 *Alamo*) **SARH** R-33 (AA-9 *Amos*)
ARH R-77 (AA-12 *Adder* – on MiG-31BM)

Paramilitary 31,500

Government Guard 500

Internal Security Troops ε20,000

Ministry of Interior

Presidential Guard 2,000

State Border Protection Forces ε9,000

Ministry of Interior
HEL • TPT • Medium 1 Mi-171

Kyrgyzstan KGZ

Kyrgyzstani Som s		2012	2013	2014
GDP	s	304bn	348bn	
	US$	6.47bn	7.23bn	
per capita	US$	1,158	1,282	
Growth	%	-0.90	7.37	
Inflation	%	2.77	8.61	
Def bdgt [a]	s	4.95bn	4.91bn	4.87bn
	US$	105m	102m	
FMA (US)	US$	1.5m	1.5m	1.5m
US$1=s		47.02	48.11	

[a] Expenses on Ministry of Defence & Ministry of Interior.

Population 5,548,042

Ethnic groups: Kyrgyz 56%; Russian 17%; Uzbek 13%; Ukrainian 3%

Age	0–14	15–19	20–24	25–29	30–64	65 plus
Male	15.2%	4.7%	5.2%	4.8%	17.3%	1.9%
Female	14.5%	4.5%	5.1%	4.7%	19.1%	3.0%

Capabilities

A new military doctrine was enacted in July 2013, setting out possible threats to the state and plans to reform the armed forces. The security environment is characterised as being marked by unpredictability and the sudden emergence of conflict. The reform plans promise, among other things, a modern military with enhanced C2, effective military logistics and a modern air-defence system, adding the term 'mobilisation readiness'. In general, combat readiness remains low with large numbers of poorly trained conscripts within the armed forces and, according to analysts, Bishkek is no closer to devising the force structure, doctrine, training and procurement policies that would support state security priorities. Kyrgyzstan is a member of the CSTO and the Shanghai Cooperation Organisation. In mid-2013 the army conducted an anti-terrorist exercise with Russian air force units from Kant air base. The US and Russia have a base each in the country, though the agreement allowing the US to use Manas expires in 2014.

ACTIVE 10,900 (Army 8,500 Air 2,400) Paramilitary 9,500

Conscript liability 18 months

ORGANISATIONS BY SERVICE

Army 8,500

FORCES BY ROLE

SPECIAL FORCES

1 SF bde

MANOEUVRE

Mechanised

2 MR bde

1 (mtn) MR bde

COMBAT SUPPORT

1 arty bde

1 AD bde

EQUIPMENT BY TYPE

MBT 150 T-72

RECCE 30 BRDM-2

AIFV 320: 230 BMP-1; 90 BMP-2

APC (W) 35: 25 BTR-70; 10 BTR-80

ARTY 246

SP 122mm 18 2S1

TOWED 141: **100mm** 18 M-1944; **122mm** 107: 72 D-30; 35 M-30 (M-1938); **152mm** 16 D-1

GUN/MOR 120mm 12 2S9 *Anona*

MRL 21: **122mm** 15 BM-21; **220mm** 6 9P140 *Uragan*

MOR 120mm 54: 6 2S12; 48 M-120

AT • MSL • MANPATS 9K11 (AT-3 *Sagger*); 9K111 (AT-4 *Spigot*); 9K113 (AT-5 *Spandrel*)

RCL 73mm SPG-9

GUNS 100mm 18 MT-12/T-12

AD • SAM • MANPAD 9K32 *Strela-2* (SA-7 *Grail*)‡

GUNS 48

SP 23mm 24 ZSU-23-4

TOWED 57mm 24 S-60

Air Force 2,400

FORCES BY ROLE

FIGHTER

1 regt with L-39 *Albatros**

FIGHTER/TRANSPORT

1 (comp avn) regt with MiG-21 *Fishbed*; An-2 *Colt*; An-26 *Curl*

ATTACK/TRANSPORT HELICOPTER

1 regt with Mi-24 *Hind*; Mi-8 *Hip*

AIR DEFENCE

Some regt with S-125 *Pechora* (SA-3 *Goa*); S-75 *Dvina* (SA-2 *Guideline*)

EQUIPMENT BY TYPE

AIRCRAFT 33 combat capable

FGA 29 MiG-21 *Fishbed*

TPT • Light 6: 4 An-2 *Colt*; 2 An-26 *Curl*

TRG 4 L-39 *Albatros**

HELICOPTERS

ATK 2 Mi-24 *Hind*

TPT • Medium 8 Mi-8 *Hip*

AD • SAM

SP 2K11 *Krug* (SA-4 *Ganef*)

TOWED S-75 *Dvina* (SA-2 *Guideline*); S-125 *Pechora* (SA-3 *Goa*)

Paramilitary 9,500

Border Guards 5,000 (KGZ conscript, RUS officers)

Interior Troops 3,500

National Guard 1,000

DEPLOYMENT

BOSNIA-HERZEGOVINA

OSCE • Bosnia and Herzegovina 1

LIBERIA

UN • UNMIL 3 obs

SOUTH SUDAN

UN • UNMISS 2 obs

SUDAN

UN • UNAMID 2 obs

FOREIGN FORCES

Russia ε500 Military Air Forces: 5 Su-25 *Frogfoot*; 2 Mi-8 *Hip*

Moldova MDA

Moldovan Leu L		2012	2013	2014
GDP	L	87.8bn	96.9bn	
	US$	7.25bn	7.89bn	
per capita	US$	2,037	2,218	
Growth	%	-0.82	4.00	
Inflation	%	4.66	4.64	
Def bdgt [a]	L	270m	292m	330m
	US$	22m	24m	
FMA (US)	US$	1.25m	1.25m	1.25m
US$1=L		12.11	12.29	

[a] Includes military pensions

Population 3,619,925

Age	0 – 14	15 – 19	20 – 24	25 – 29	30 – 64	65 plus
Male	9.1%	3.4%	4.3%	4.7%	23.0%	4.0%
Female	8.5%	3.2%	4.0%	4.4%	24.6%	6.7%

Capabilities

Moldova is a neutral state with limited military capability. Its conscript-based army's primary focus is on the disputed territory of Transdniestr, though the country is also looking to develop further the capacity to contribute to peacekeeping and crisis management missions in a multinational context. Political upheaval during the first half of 2013 may have delayed its ambitions to sign an association agreement with the European Union, though this could be initialled at November's Eastern Partnership Summit in Vilnius. Russia continues to support an army garrison as well as a peacekeeping contingent in Transdniestr. Moldova's air capability is limited to a small fixed- and rotary-wing transport fleet. Implementing the recommendations of the Strategic Defence Review, carried out with UK support in 2011, is a priority, though funding problems mean this could prove a challenge. Moldovan forces are deployed in small numbers on UN operations.

ACTIVE 5,350 **(Army 3,250 Air 800 Logistic Support 1,300) Paramilitary 2,400**

RESERVE 58,000 **(Joint 58,000)**

ORGANISATIONS BY SERVICE

Army 1,300; 1,950 conscript (total 3,250)

FORCES BY ROLE

SPECIAL FORCES

1 SF bn

MANOEUVRE

Light

3 mot inf bde

1 mot inf bn

Other

1 gd bn

COMBAT SUPPORT

1 arty bn

1 engr bn

1 NBC coy

1 sigs coy

EQUIPMENT BY TYPE

RECCE 5 BRDM-2

AIFV 44 BMD-1

APC 164

APC (T) 64: 9 BTR-D; 55 MT-LB

APC (W) 100: 11 BTR-80; 89 TAB-71

ARTY 148

TOWED 69: **122mm** 17 (M-30) *M-1938*; **152mm** 52: 21 2A36; 31 D-20

GUN/MOR • SP 120mm 9 2S9 *Anona*

MRL 220mm 11 9P140 *Uragan*

MOR 59: **82mm** 52; **120mm** 7 M-120

AT

MSL • MANPATS 9K111 *Fagot* (AT-4 *Spigot*); 9K113 *Konkurs* (AT-5 *Spandrel*); 9K114 *Shturm* (AT-6 *Spiral*)

RCL 73mm SPG-9

GUNS 100mm 36 MT-12

AD • GUNS • TOWED 39: **23mm** 28 ZU-23; **57mm** 11 S-60

RADAR • LAND 4: 2 ARK-1; 2 SNAR-10

Air Force 800 (incl 250 conscripts)

FORCES BY ROLE

TRANSPORT

2 sqn with An-2 *Colt*; An-26 *Curl*; An-72 *Coaler*; Mi-8PS *Hip*; Yak-18

AIR DEFENCE

1 regt with S-125 *Neva* (SA-3 *Goa*)

EQUIPMENT BY TYPE

AIRCRAFT

TPT • Light 6: 2 An-2 *Colt*; 1 An-26 *Curl*; 2 An-72 *Coaler* 1 Yak-18

HELICOPTERS

MRH 4 Mi-17-1V *Hip* H

TPT • Medium 2 Mi-8PS *Hip*

AD • SAM 12 S-125 *Neva* (SA-3 *Goa*)

Paramilitary 2,400

Ministry of Interior

OPON 900 (riot police)

Ministry of Interior

DEPLOYMENT

Legal provisions for foreign deployment:

Constitution: Codified constitution (1994)

Decision on deployment of troops abroad: By the parliament (Art. 66)

BOSNIA-HERZEGOVINA

OSCE • Bosnia and Herzegovina 1

CÔTE D'IVOIRE

UN • UNOCI 3 obs

LIBERIA

UN • UNMIL 2 obs

SERBIA
OSCE • Kosovo 1
OSCE • Serbia 1
UN • UNMIK 1 obs

SOUTH SUDAN
UN • UNMISS 3 obs

FOREIGN FORCES

Czech Republic OSCE 1
Estonia OSCE 2
France OSCE 1
Germany OSCE 1
Poland OSCE 1
Russia ε1,500 (including 350 peacekeepers) Military Air Forces 7 Mi-24 *Hind*/Mi-8 *Hip*
Serbia OSCE 1
Spain OSCE 1
Sweden OSCE 1
Switzerland OSCE 1
Ukraine 10 mil obs (Joint Peacekeeping Force)
United Kingdom OSCE 1
United States OSCE 3

Russia RUS

Russian Rouble r		2012	2013	2014
GDP	r	62.4tr	68.1tr	
	US$	2.02tr	2.21tr	
	US$ [a]	2.52tr	2.64tr	
per capita	US$	14,247	15,650	
Growth	%	3.40	3.37	
Inflation	%	5.07	6.86	
Def bdgt	r	1.81tr	2.1tr	2.49tr
	US$	58.8bn	68.2bn	
	US$ [a]	73bn	81.4bn	
US$1=r	MER	30.84	30.78	
	PPP	24.81	25.81	

[a] PPP estimate

Population 142,500,482

Ethnic groups: Tatar 4%; Ukrainian 3%; Chuvash 1%; Bashkir 1%; Belarussian 1%; Moldovan 1%; Other 8%

Age	0–14	15–19	20–24	25–29	30–64	65 plus
Male	8.2%	2.4%	3.5%	4.4%	23.7%	4.0%
Female	7.8%	2.3%	3.3%	4.4%	26.8%	9.1%

Capabilities

Russia remains a significant continental military power, and is in the process of renewing its nuclear arsenal. The first of the *Borey*-class SSBNs, the *Yury Dolgoruky*, formally joined the fleet at the beginning of 2013, and is intended as part of a broader recapitalisation of the country's nuclear capability. The Russian armed forces are undergoing a reform process, begun by Defence Minister Anatoly Serdyukov in 2008. His replacement by Sergey Shoigu in November 2012 raised questions about the future of the reform process. However, main elements, such as the initiative to transform the army towards a combined arms brigade-based structure, appear to continue. Though pay rates were increased in 2012, the recruitment of contract personnel in adequate numbers remains a challenge, particularly for NCOs and specialist roles; this is also a reflection of demographic issues. The warrant officer rank cut by the Serdyukov reforms – a class of long-serving specialists usually in roles demanding technical or administrative skills – was reinstated and an ambitious 50,000 recruitment target set. Conventional re-equipment continues with all three services taking delivery of modern combat systems, if sometimes in modest numbers. Force restructuring – such as the establishment of the Special Operations Command – is intended to improve capability amid smaller armed forces. The deployment of the Russian Mediterranean Task Force in response to the 2013 Syria crisis and the Western naval presence was a significant show of maritime power. Deployments in Eurasia and on UN missions continue. (See pp. 161–3.)

ACTIVE 845,000 **(Army 250,000 Airborne 35,000 Navy 130,000 Air 150,000 Strategic Deterrent Forces 80,000 Command and Support 200,000) Paramilitary 519,000**

Conscript liability 12 months conscription.

RESERVE 2,000,000 **(all arms)**

Some 2,000,000 with service within last 5 years; Reserve obligation to age 50.

ORGANISATIONS BY SERVICE

Strategic Deterrent Forces ε80,000 (incl personnel assigned from the Navy and Air Force)

Navy

SUBMARINES • STRATEGIC • SSBN 11
3 *Kalmar* (*Delta* III) with 16 RSM-50 (SS-N-18 *Stingray*) strategic SLBM
6 *Delfin* (*Delta* IV) with 16 R-29RMU *Sineva* (SS-N-23 *Skiff*) strategic SLBM (of which 1 vessel in repair following a fire; expected return to service 2014)
1 *Akula* (*Typhoon*)† in reserve with capacity for 20 *Bulava* (SS-N-X-32) strategic SLBM (trials/testing)
1 *Borey* with capacity for 16 *Bulava* (SS-N-X-32) SLBM (missiles not yet operational), (2 additional units completed sea trials with a notional ISD 2014; 2 further units in build)

Strategic Rocket Force Troops

3 Rocket Armies operating silo and mobile launchers organised in 12 divs (reducing to 8). Launcher gps normally with 10 silos (6 for RS-20/SS-18), or 9 mobile lnchr, and one control centre

MSL • STRATEGIC 356
ICBM 356: 54 RS-20 (SS-18 *Satan*) (mostly mod 5, 10 MIRV per msl); 160 RS-12M (SS-25 *Sickle*) (mobile single warhead); 40 RS-18 (SS-19 *Stiletto*) (mostly mod

3, 6 MIRV per msl.); 60 RS-12M2 *Topol*-M (SS-27M1) silo-based (single warhead); 18 RS-12M2 *Topol*-M (SS-27M1) road mobile (single warhead); 24 RS-24 *Yars* (SS-27M2; ε3 MIRV per msl)

Long-Range Aviation Command

FORCES BY ROLE

BOMBER

1 sqn with Tu-160 *Blackjack*

3 sqn with Tu-95MS *Bear*

EQUIPMENT BY TYPE

AIRCRAFT

BBR 78: 16 Tu-160 *Blackjack* each with up to 12 Kh-55 SM (AS-15A/B *Kent*) nuclear ALCM; 31 Tu-95MS6 (*Bear* H-6) each with up to 6 Kh-55/SM (AS-15A/B *Kent*) nuclear ALCM; 31 Tu-95MS16 (*Bear* H-16) each with up to 16 Kh-55 (AS-15A *Kent*) nuclear ALCM; (Kh-102 likely now in service on Tu-95MS)

Warning Forces 3rd Space and Missile Defence Army

ICBM/SLBM launch-detection capability: 3 operational satellites

RADAR (9 stations) 1 ABM engagement system located at Sofrino (Moscow). Russia leases ground-based radar stations in Baranovichi (Belarus); Balkhash (Kazakhstan). It also has radars on its own territory at Lekhtusi, (St Petersburg); Armavir, (southern Russia); Olenegorsk (northwest Arctic); Pechora (northwest Urals); Mishelevka (east Siberia).

MISSILE DEFENCE 1,996: 68 53T6 (ABM-3 *Gazelle*); 1,800 S-300 (SA-10 *Grumble*); 96 S-400 (SA-21 *Growler*); (32 51T6 (ABM-4 *Gorgon*) in store; possibly destroyed)

Space Forces 40,000

Formations and units to detect missile attack on the RF and its allies, to implement BMD, and to be responsible for military/dual-use spacecraft launch and control. May become part of new Air-Space Defence Command.

SATELLITES 63

COMMUNICATIONS 24: 2 Mod *Globus* (*Raduga*-1M); 11 *Strela*; 8 *Rodnik* (*Gonets*-M); 3 *Meridian*

NAVIGATION/POSITIONING/TIMING 32 GLONASS

ELINT/SIGINT 4: 1 *Kondor*; 1 *Liana* (*Lotos*-S); 1 *Persona*; 1 *Tselina*-2;

EARLY WARNING 3 *Oko*

Army ε205,000 (incl 35,000 AB); ε80,000 conscript (total 285,000)

Transformation process continues; previous 6 Military Districts have been consolidated into 4 (West (HQ St Petersburg), Centre (HQ Yekaterinburg), South (HQ Rostov-on-Don) & East (HQ Khabarovsk), each with a unified Joint Strategic Command. Current plans call for the establishment of 28 new bdes (6 MR; 2 air aslt; 1 engr; 1 AD & 18 army avn), and for the restructuring of the existing MR brigades into new light, medium and heavy formations.

FORCES BY ROLE

COMMAND

10 army HQ

SPECIAL FORCES

7 (Spetsnaz) SF bde

1 (AB Recce) SF regt

MANOEUVRE

Reconnaissance

1 recce bde

Armoured

1 (4th) tk div (1 armd recce bn; 3 tk bn; 1 MR bn; 1 arty bn; 1 MRL bn; 2 AD bn; 1 engr bn; 1 EW coy; 1 NBC coy)

3 tk bde (1 armd recce bn; 3 tk bn; 1 MR bn; 1 arty bn; 1 MRL bn; 2 AD bn; 1 engr bn; 1 EW coy; 1 NBC coy)

Mechanised

1 (5th) MR div (1 recce bn; 1 tk bn; 3 MR bn; 2 arty bn; 1 MRL bn; 1 AT bn; 2 AD bn; 1 engr bn; 1 EW coy; 1 NBC coy)

1 (201st) MR div

30 MR bde (1 recce bn; 1 tk bn; 3 MR bn; 2 arty bn; 1 MRL bn; 1 AT bn; 2 AD bn; 1 engr bn; 1 EW coy; 1 NBC coy)

2 MR bde (4—5 MR bn; 1 arty bn; 1 AD bn; 1 engr bn)

3 (lt/mtn) MR bde (1 recce bn; 2 MR bn; 1 arty bn)

1 (18th) MGA div (2 MGA regt; 1 arty regt; 1 tk bn; 2 AD bn)

Air Manoeuvre

4 AB div (2 para/air aslt regt; 1 arty regt; 1 AD regt)

1 indep AB bde

3 air aslt bde

COMBAT SUPPORT

8 arty bde

4 MRL bde

2 MRL regt

2 SSM bde with *Iskander*-M (SS-26 *Stone*)

7 SSM bde with *Tochka* (SS-21 *Scarab* — to be replaced by *Iskander*-M)

10 AD bde

4 engr bde

1 MP bde

EQUIPMENT BY TYPE

MBT 2,550: 1,400 T-72B/BA; 150 T-72B3; 650 T-80BV/U; 350 T-90/T-90A; (18,000 in store: 2,800 T-55; 2,500 T-62; 2,000 T-64A/B; 7,500 T-72/T-72A/B; 3,000 T-80B/BV/U; 200 T-90)

RECCE 1,200+: 100+ *Dozor*, 100+ *Tigr*, 1,000 BRDM-2/2A; (1,000+ BRDM-2 in store)

AIFV 7,360+: 700 BMD-1; 600 BMD-2; 100 BMD-3; 60+ BMD-4; 1,000 BMP-1; 3,500 BMP-2; 500+ BMP-3; 700 BRM-1K; 200+ BTR-80A/82A; (8,500 in store: 7,000 BMP-1; 1,500 BMP-2)

APC 9,700+

APC (T) 5,700+: some BMO-T; 700 BTR-D; 5,000 MT-LB; (2,000 MT-LB in store)

APC (W) 4,000+ BTR-60/70/80; (4,000 BTR-60/70 in store)

ARTY 5,436+

SP 1,820: **122mm** 400 2S1; **152mm** 1,400: 800 2S3; 150 2S5; 450 2S19; **203mm** 20 2S7; (4,050 in store: **122mm** 1,800 2S1; **152mm** 1,950: 1,000 2S3; 800 2S5; 150 2S19; **203mm** 300 2S7)

TOWED 550: **122mm** 400 D-30; **152mm** 150 2A65; (12,215 in store: **122mm** 7,950: 4,200 D-30; 3,750 M-30 *M-1938*; **130mm** 650 M-46; **152mm** 3,575: 1,100 2A36; 600 2A65; 1,075 D-20; 700 D-1 M-1943; 100 ML-20 M-1937; **203mm** 40 B-4M)

GUN/MOR 970+
SP 120mm 870+: 790 2S9 NONA-S; 30 2S23 NONA-SVK; 50+ 2S34
TOWED 120mm 100 2B16 NONA-K
MRL 1,106+ **122mm** 800 BM-21; **220mm** 200 9P140 *Uragan*; some TOS-1A; **300mm** 106 9A52 *Smerch;* (2,920 in store: **122mm** 2,120: 1,700 BM-21; 420 9P138; **132mm** 100 BM-13; **220mm** 700 9P140 *Uragan*)
MOR 990
SP 240mm 20 2S4; (410 2S4 in store)
TOWED 970+: **120mm** 970: 50+ 2B23; 920 2S12; (2,100 in store: **120mm** 1,800: 900 2S12; 900 PM-38; **160mm** 300 M-160)
AT
MSL
SP BMP-T with 9K120 *Ataka* (AT-9 *Spiral* 2); 9P149 with 9K114 *Shturm* (AT-6 *Spiral*); 9P157-2 with 9K123 *Khrisantema* (AT-15 *Springer*)
MANPATS 9K11/9K14 *Malyutka* (AT-3 *Sagger*); 9K111 *Fagot* (AT-4 *Spigot*); 9K112 *Kobra* (AT-8 *Songster*); 9K113 *Konkurs* (AT-5 *Spandrel*); 9K114 *Shturm* (AT-6 *Spiral*); 9K115 *Metis* (AT-7 *Saxhorn*); 9K115-1 *Metis*-M (AT-13 *Saxhorn* 2); 9K116 *Bastion/Basnya* (AT-10 *Stabber*); 9K119 *Reflex/Svir* (AT-11 *Sniper*); 9K135 *Kornet* (AT-14 *Spriggan*)
RCL 73mm SPG-9
RL 105mm RPG-29
GUNS 562+
SP: 125mm 36+ 2S25
TOWED 100mm 526 MT-12; (**100mm** 2,000 T-12/MT-12 in store)
AD • SAM 1,570+
SP 1,320+: 350+ 9K37/9K317 *Buk* (SA-11 *Gadfly*); 400 9K33M3 *Osa*-AKM (SA-8 *Gecko*); 400 9K35M3 *Strela*-10 (SA-13 *Gopher*); 120+ 9K330/9K331 *Tor* (SA-15 *Gauntlet*)
SPAAGM 250+ 2K22 *Tunguska* (SA-19 *Grison*)
MANPAD *Igla*-1 (SA-16 *Gimlet*); 9K38 *Igla* (SA-18 *Grouse*): 9K338 *Igla*-S (SA-24 *Grinch*); 9K34 *Strela*-3 (SA-14 *Gremlin*)
GUNS
SP 23mm ZSU-23-4
TOWED 23mm ZU-23-2; **57mm** S-60
UAV • Heavy Tu-143 *Reys*; Tu-243 *Reys*/Tu-243 *Reys* D; Tu-300 *Korshun* **Light** BLA-07; *Pchela*-1; *Pchela*-2
MSL • SSM 200+: 200 *Tochka* (SS-21 *Scarab*); some *Iskander*-M (SS-26 *Stone*); (some FROG in store; some *Scud* in store)
AEV BAT-2; IMR; IMR-2; IRM; MT-LB
ARV BMP-1; BREM-1/64/D/K/L; BREhM-D; BTR-50PK(B); M1977; MTP-LB; RM-G; T-54/55; VT-72A
VLB KMM; MT-55A; MTU; MTU-20; MTU-72; PMM-2
MW BMR-3M; GMX-3; MCV-2 (reported); MTK; MTK-2

Reserves

Cadre formations, on mobilisation form
MANOEUVRE
Armoured
1 tk bde
Mechanised
13 MR bde

Navy ε130,000

4 major fleet organisations (Northern Fleet, Pacific Fleet, Baltic Fleet, Black Sea) and Caspian Sea Flotilla

EQUIPMENT BY TYPE
SUBMARINES 64
STRATEGIC • SSBN 11:
3 *Kalmar* (*Delta* III) with 16 R-29R *Volna* (SS-N-18 *Stingray*) strategic SLBM
6 *Delfin* (*Delta* IV) with 16 R-29RMU *Sineva* (SS-N-23 *Skiff*) strategic SLBM (of which 1 vessel in repair following a fire; expected return to service 2014)
1 *Akula* (*Typhoon*)† in reserve for training with capacity for 20 *Bulava* (SS-N-X-32) strategic SLBM (trials/testing - 2 more awaiting decommissioning)
1 *Borey* with capacity for 16 *Bulava* (SS-N-X-32) SLBM (missiles not yet operational), (2 additional units completed sea trials with expected ISD 2014; 2 further units in build)
TACTICAL 45
SSGN 8:
8 *Antyey* (*Oscar* II) (of which 3 in reserve) with 2 single 650mm TT each with T-65 HWT, 4 single 553mm TT with 3M45 *Granit* (SS-N-19 *Shipwreck*) AShM
SSN 17:
2 *Schuka*-B (*Akula* II) with 4 single 533mm TT each with 3M10 *Granat* (SS-N-21 *Sampson*) SLCM, 4 single 650mm TT with T-65 HWT (one further boat leased to India for 10 years from 2012)
8 *Schuka*-B (*Akula* I) (of which 2 in reserve) with 4 single 533mm TT with 3M10 *Granat* (SS-N-21 *Sampson*) SLCM, 4 single 650mm TT with T-65 HWT
2 *Kondor* (*Sierra* II) with 4 single 533mm TT each with 3M10 *Granat* (SS-N-21 *Sampson*) SLCM, 4 single 650mm TT with T-65 HWT
1 *Barracuda* (*Sierra* I) with 4 single 533mm TT with 3M10 (SS-N-21 *Sampson*) SLCM, RPK-2 (SS-N-15 *Starfish*) and T-53 HWT, 4 single 650mm TT with RPK-7 (SS-N-16 *Stallion*) AShM and T-65 HWT
4 *Schuka* (*Victor* III) (of which 1 in reserve) with 4 single 533mm TT each with 3M10 *Granat* (SS-N-21 *Sampson*) SLCM, 2 single 650mm TT with T-65 HWT
(1 *Yasen* (*Graney*) in sea trials; expected ISD 2014; 2 more units in build)
SSK 20:
15 *Paltus* (*Kilo*) with 6 single 533mm TT with T-53 HWT
4 *Varshavyanka* (*Kilo*) with 6 single 533mm TT (3 additional vessels under construction)
1 *Lada* with 6 single 533mm TT (2 additional vessels in build)
SUPPORT 8
SSAN 7: 1 *Orenburg* (*Delta III* Stretch); 1 *Losharik* (one further vessel under construction); 2 Project 1851 (*Paltus*); 3 *Kashalot* (*Uniform*)
SSA 1 *Sarov*

PRINCIPAL SURFACE COMBATANTS 33

AIRCRAFT CARRIERS • CV 1 *Orel (Kuznetsov)* with 1 12-cell VLS with 3M45 *Granit* (SS-N-19 *Shipwreck*) AShM, 4 sextuple VLS with 3K95 *Kindzhal* (SA-N-9 *Gauntlet*) SAM, 2 RBU 12000 *Udav* 1, 8 CADS-N-1 *Kashtan* CIWS with 9M311 (SA-N-11 *Grison*) SAM, 6 AK630 CIWS, (capacity 18-24 Su-33 *Flanker D* FGA ac; 4 Su-25UTG *Frogfoot* ac, 15 Ka-27 *Helix* ASW hel, 2 Ka-31R *Helix* AEW hel)

CRUISERS 5

CGHMN 1:

1 *Orlan* (*Kirov*) with 10 twin VLS with 3M45 *Granit* (SS-N-19 *Shipwreck*) AShM, 2 twin lnchr with *Osa*-M (SA-N-4 *Gecko*) SAM, 12 single VLS with *Fort*/*Fort* M (SA-N-6 *Grumble*/SA-N-20 *Gargoyle*) SAM, 2 octuple VLS with 3K95 *Kindzhal* (SA-N-9 *Gauntlet*) SAM, 10 single 533mm ASTT, 1 RBU 12000 *Udav* 1, 2 RBU 1000 *Smerch* 3, 6 CADS-N-1 *Kashtan* CIWS with 9M311 (SA-N-11 *Grison*) SAM, 1 twin 130mm gun, (capacity 3 Ka-27 *Helix* ASW hel) (2nd *Orlan* undergoing extensive refit currently non operational; expected return to service in 2017)

CGHM 4:

1 *Berkot*-B (*Kara*)† (scheduled to be decommissioned), with 2 quad lnchr with *Rastrub* (SS-N-14 *Silex*) AShM/ASW, 2 twin lnchr with 4K60 *Shtorm* (SA-N-3 *Goblet*) SAM, 2 twin lnchr with *Osa*-M (SA-N-4 *Gecko*) SAM, 2 quintuple 533mm ASTT, 2 RBU 6000, 2 twin 76mm gun, (capacity 1 Ka-27 *Helix* ASW hel)

3 *Atlant* (*Slava*) with 8 twin lnchr with *Vulkan* (SS-N-12 mod 2 *Sandbox*) AShM, 8 octuple VLS with *Fort*/*Fort* M (SA-N-6 *Grumble*/SA-N-20 *Gargoyle*) SAM, 2 single lnchr with *Osa*-M (SA-N-4 *Gecko*) SAM, 2 quintuple 533mm ASTT, 2 RBU 6000 *Smerch* 2, 6 AK650 CIWS, 1 twin 130mm gun, (capacity 1 Ka-27 *Helix* ASW hel) (one *Atlant* entered repairs in June 2011, currently non-operational; expected return to service in 2014)

DESTROYERS 18

DDGHM 17:

8 *Sarych* (*Sovremenny*) (of which 3 in reserve) with 2 quad lnchr with 3M80 *Moskit* (SS-N-22 *Sunburn*) AShM, 2 twin lnchr with 3K90 *Uragan*/9K37 *Yezh* (SA-N-7 *Gadfly*/SA-N-12 *Grizzly*) SAM, 2 twin 533mm TT, 2 RBU 1000 *Smerch* 3, 4 AK630 CIWS, 2 twin 130mm gun, (capacity 1 Ka-27 *Helix* ASW hel)

8 *Fregat* (*Udaloy* I) each with 2 quad lnchr with *Rastrub* (SS-N-14 *Silex*) AShM/ASW, 8 octuple VLS with 3K95 *Kindzhal* (SA-N-9 *Gauntlet* SAM), 2 quad 533mm ASTT, 2 RBU 6000 *Smerch* 2, 4 AK630 CIWS, 2 100mm gun, (capacity 2 Ka-27 *Helix* ASW hel)

1 *Fregat* (*Udaloy* II) with 2 quad lnchr with 3M80 *Moskit* (SS-N-22 *Sunburn*) AShM, 8 octuple VLS with 3K95 *Kindzhal* (SA-N-9 *Gauntlet*) SAM, 2 CADS-N-1 *Kashtan* CIWS with 9M311 (SA-N-11 *Grison*) SAM, 10 single 533mm ASTT, 2 RBU 6000 *Smerch* 2, 2 130mm gun, (capacity 2 Ka-27 *Helix* ASW hel)

DDGM 1:

1 *Komsomolets Ukrainy* (*Kashin* mod) with 2 quad lnchr with 3M24 *Uran* (SS-N-25 *Switchblade*) AShM, 2 twin lnchr with *Volnya* (SA-N-1 *Goa*) SAM, 5 single 533mm ASTT, 2 RBU 6000 *Smerch* 2, 1 twin 76mm gun

FRIGATES 9

FFGHM 5:

2 *Jastreb* (*Neustrashimy*) with 2 quad lnchr with 3M24 *Uran* (SS-N-25 *Switchblade*) AShM, 4 octuple VLS with 3K95 *Kindzhal* (SA-N-9 *Gauntlet*) SAM, 4 single 533mm ASTT, 1 RBU 12000, 2 CADS-N-1 *Kashtan* CIWS with 9M311 (SA-N-11 *Grison*) SAM, 1 100mm gun, (capacity 1 Ka-27 *Helix* ASW) (3rd vessel launched, but production halted in 1997; unclear status)

1 *Steregushchiy* with 2 quad lnchr with 3M24 *Uran* (SS-N-25 *Switchblade)* AShM, 2 quad 324mm ASTT, 1 CADS-N-1 *Kashtan* CIWS with 9M311 (SA-N-11 *Grison*) SAM, 2 AK630 CIWS, 1 100mm gun

2 *Steregushchiy* with 2 quad lnchr with 3M24 *Uran* (SS-N-25 *Switchblade)* AShM, 1 12-cell VLS with 9M96 *Redut* SAM, 2 quad 324mm ASTT, 1 CADS-N-1 *Kashtan* CIWS with 9M311 (SA-N-11 *Grison*) SAM, 2 AK630 CIWS, 1 100mm gun (5 additional vessels in build, of which two are improved *Steregushchiy* II)

FFGM 4:

1 *Gepard* with 2 quad lnchr with 3M24 *Uran* (SS-N-25 *Switchblade*) AShM, 1 twin lnchr with *Osa*-M (SA-N-4 *Gecko*) SAM, 2 AK630 CIWS, 1 76mm gun

1 *Gepard* with 1 8-cell VLS with 3M14 (SS-N-30 *Kaliber*) LACM, 2 quad lnchr with 3M24 *Uran* (SS-N-25 *Switchblade*) AShM, 1 twin lnchr with *Osa*-M (SA-N-4 *Gecko*) SAM, 1 AK630 CIWS, 1 76mm gun

1 *Burevestnik* (*Krivak* I mod)† with 1 quad lnchr with *Rastrub* (SS-N-14 *Silex*) AShM/ASW, 1 twin lnchr with *Osa*-M (SA-N-4 *Gecko*) SAM, 2 quad 533mm ASTT, 2 RBU 6000 *Smerch* 2, 2 twin 76mm gun

1 *Burevestnik* M (*Krivak* II) each with 1 quad lnchr with RPK-3 *Rastrub* (SS-N-14 *Silex*) AShM/ASW, 2 twin lnchr with 10 *Osa*-M (SA-N-4 *Gecko* SAM), 2 quad 533mm ASTT, 2 RBU 6000 *Smerch* 2, 2 100mm gun

PATROL AND COASTAL COMBATANTS 82

CORVETTES 46:

FSGM 15:

2 *Sivuchi* (*Dergach*) with 2 quad lnchr with 3M80 *Moskit* (SS-N-22 *Sunburn*) AShM, 1 twin lnchr with *Osa*-M (SA-N-4 *Gecko*) SAM, 2 AK630 CIWS, 1 76mm gun

12 *Ovod* (*Nanuchka* III) with 2 triple lnchr with P-120 *Malakhit* (SS-N-9 *Siren*) AShM, 1 twin lnchr with *Osa*-M (SA-N-4 *Gecko*), 1 76mm gun

1 *Ovod* (*Nanuchka* IV) with 2 triple lnchr with 3M55 *Onix* (SS-N-26) AShM, 1 twin lnchr with *Osa*-M (SA-N-4 *Gecko*), 1 76mm gun

FSM 31:

3 *Albatros* (*Grisha* III) with 1 twin lnchr with *Osa*-M (SA-N-4 *Gecko*) SAM, 2 twin 533mm ASTT, 2 RBU 6000 *Smerch* 2. 2 twin 57mm gun

21 *Albatros* (*Grisha* V) with 1 twin lnchr with Osa-M (SA-N-4 *Gecko*) SAM, 2 twin 533mm ASTT, 1 RBU 6000 *Smerch 2*, 1 76mm gun

7 *Parchim* II with 2 quad lnchr with *Strela*-2 (SA-N-5 *Grail*) SAM, 2 twin 533mm ASTT, 2 RBU 6000 *Smerch 2*, 1 AK630 CIWS, 1 76mm gun

PCFG 25:

6 *Molnya* (*Tarantul* II) with 2 twin lnchr with P-15M *Termit* (SS-N-2C/D *Styx*) AShM, 1 quad lnchr (manual aiming) with *Strela*-2 (SA-N-5 *Grail*) SAM, 2 AK630 CIWS, 1 76mm gun

19 *Molnya* (*Tarantul* III) with 2 twin lnchr with 3M80 *Moskit* (SS-N-22 *Sunburn*) AShM, 1 quad lnchr (manual aiming) with *Strela*-2 (SA-N-5 *Grail*) SAM, 2 AK630 CIWS, 1 76mm gun

PCM 6:

3 *Astrakhan* (*Buyan*) with some 9K310 *Igla*-1 (SA-16 *Gimlet*) SAM, 2 AK630 CIWS, 1 100mm gun (6 improved *Buyan*-M vessels under construction)

3 *Grachonok* with 4 9K38 *Igla* (SA-18 *Grouse*) SAM (original design was as diving tender)

PHG 4 *Vekhr* (*Matka*) with 2 single lnchr with P-15M *Termit* (SS-N-2C/D *Styx*) AShM, 1 AK630 CIWS, 1 76mm gun

PHT 1 *Sokol* (*Mukha*) with 2 quad 406mm TT, 2 AK630 CIWS, 1 76mm gun (damaged in 2007 and laid up since; unclear status)

MINE WARFARE • MINE COUNTERMEASURES 53

MHO 2 *Rubin* (*Gorya*) with 2 quad lnchr with *Strela-2* (SA-N-5 *Grail*) SAM, 1 AK630 CIWS, 1 76mm gun

MSO 11: 10 *Akvamaren* (*Natya*); *1 Agat* (*Natya* II) (all with 2 quad lnchr (manual aiming) with *Strela*-2 (SA-N-5 *Grail*) SAM, 2 RBU1200 *Uragan*, 2 twin AK230 CIWS

MSC 25: 23 *Yakhont* (*Sonya*) with 4 AK630 CIWS (some with 2 quad lnchr with *Strela*-2 (SA-N-5 *Grail*) SAM); 2 Project 1258 (*Yevgenya*)

MHI 15: 9 *Sapfir* (*Lida*) with 1 AK630 CIWS; 3 Project 696 (*Tolya*); 3 *Malakhit* (*Olya*)

AMPHIBIOUS

LANDING SHIPS • LST 20:

4 *Tapir* (*Alligator*) with 2-3 twi lnchr with *Strela*-2 (SA-N-5 *Grail*) SAM, 2 twin 57mm guns, (capacity 20 tanks; 300 troops)

12 Project 775 (*Ropucha* I) with 2 twin 57mm guns, (capacity either 10 MBT and 190 troops or 24 APC (T) and 170 troops)

3 Project 775M (*Ropucha* II) with 2 AK630 CIWS, 2 twin 57mm guns, (capacity either 10 MBT and 190 troops or 24 APC (T) and 170 troops)

1 *Tapir* (*Alligator* (mod)) with 2 AK630 CIWS, 1 76mm gun, (capacity 1 Ka-29 *Helix* B; 13 MBT; 300 troops) (vessel launched in 2012; expected ISD end-2013))

LANDING CRAFT 19

LCU 5:

1 *Dyugon* (4 more in build)

4 Project 11770 (*Serna*) (capacity 100 troops)

LCM 7 *Akula* (*Ondatra*) (capacity 1 MBT)

LCAC 7:

2 *Dzheryan* (*Aist*) with 2 twin AK630 CIWS (capacity 4 lt tk)

2 *Pomornik* (*Zubr*) (capacity 230 troops; either 3 MBT or 10 APC (T)

3 *Kalmar* (*Lebed*) (capacity 2 lt tk)

LOGISTICS AND SUPPORT 636

ABU 12: 8 *Kashtan*; 4 *Sura*

AE 2: 1 *Muna*; 1 *Dubnyak*

AEM 3: 2 *Amga*; 1 *Lama*

AG 3: 2 *Vytegrales*; 1 *Potok*

AGB 4 *Dobrynya Mikitich*

AGE 2: 1 *Tchusovoy*; 1 *Zvezdochka* (2 more vessels under construction)

AGI 11: 2 *Alpinist*; 1 *Balzam*; 3 *Moma*; 5 *Vishnya*

AGM 1 *Marshal Nedelin*

AGOR 6: 1 *Akademik Krylov*; 2 *Sibiriyakov*, 2 *Vinograd*; 1 *Seliger*

AGS 21: 3 BGK-797; 6 *Kamenka*; 9 *Onega*; 3 *Vaygach*

AGSH 4: 1 *Samara*; 3 *Vaygach*

AGSI 52: 8 *Biya*; 25 *Finik*; 7 *Moma*; 14 *Yug*

AH 3 *Ob* †

AK 2 *Bira*

AOL 13: 2 *Dubna*; 5 *Uda*; 6 *Altay* (mod)

AOR 5 *Boris Chilikin*

AORL 3: 1 *Kaliningradneft*; 2 *Olekma*

AOS 1 *Luza*

AR 13 *Amur*

ARC 7: 4 *Emba*; 3 *Klasma*

ARS 14: 4 *Mikhail Rudnitsky*; 10 *Goryn*

AS 1 Project 2020 (*Malina*)

ASR 2: 1 *Nepal*; 1 *Alagez*

ATF 61: 2 *Baklazhan*; 5 *Katun*; 3 *Ingul*; 2 *Neftegaz*; 14 *Okhtensky*; 18 *Prometey*; 1 *Prut*; 3 *Sliva*; 13 *Sorum*

AWT 2 *Manych*

AXL 12: 10 *Petrushka*; 2 *Smolny*

YDG 15 *Bereza*

YDT 104: 40 *Flamingo*; 20 *Nyryat 2*; 28 *Yelva*; 3 Project 11980; 13 *Pelym*

YGS 60 GPB-480

YO 36: 5 *Khobi*; 30 *Toplivo*; 1 *Konda*

YPB 30 *Bolva*

YPT 43: 12 *Shelon*; 31 *Poluchat*

YTB 46: 11 *Stividor*; 35 *Sidehole*

YTR 42: 27 *Pozharny*; 15 *Morkov*

Naval Aviation ε28,000

4 Fleet Air Forces; most combat aircraft previously assigned to Naval Aviation were transfered to Air Force command by end-2011.

Flying hours 60+ hrs/year

FORCES BY ROLE

FIGHTER

2 sqn with Su-33 *Flanker* D; Su-25UTG *Frogfoot*

ANTI-SURFACE WARFARE/ISR

2 sqn with Su-24M/MR *Fencer*

ANTI-SUBMARINE WARFARE

2 sqn with Il-20RT *Coot* A; Il-38 *May**

8 sqn with Ka-27/Ka-29 *Helix*

1 sqn with Mi-14 *Haze* A

2 sqn with Tu-142M/MR *Bear* F/J*

1 unit with Ka-31R

MARITIME PATROL/ELECTRONIC WARFARE
1 sqn with An-12 *Cub*; Be-12 *Mail**; Mi-8 *Hip*
TRANSPORT
3 sqn with An-12 *Cub*; An-24 *Coke*; An-26 *Curl*; Tu-134

EQUIPMENT BY TYPE
AIRCRAFT 104 combat capable
FTR 18 Su-33 *Flanker* D
FGA 18 Su-24M *Fencer*
ATK 5 Su-25UTG *Frogfoot*
ASW 27 Tu-142M/MR *Bear* F/J
MP 32: 6 Be-12 *Mail**; 26 Il-38 *May**
ISR 4 Su-24MR *Fencer* E*
EW • ELINT 7: 2 Il-20RT *Coot* A; 5 An-12 *Cub*
TPT 38 An-12 *Cub*/An-24 *Coke*/An-26 *Curl*/An-140/Tu-134
HELICOPTERS
ASW 90: 70 Ka-27 *Helix*; 20 Mi-14 *Haze* A
EW 8 Mi-8 *Hip* J
AEW 2 Ka-31R *Helix*
SAR 62: 22 Ka-25PS *Hormone* C/Ka-27PS *Helix* D; 40 Mi-14PS *Haze* C
TPT 50 **Heavy** 10 Mi-6 *Hook*; **Medium** 40: 28 Ka-29 *Helix*; 12 Mi-8 *Hip*
MSL
ASM Kh-25 (AS-10 *Karen*); Kh-59 (AS-13 *Kingbolt*)
ARM Kh-58 (AS-11 *Kilter*); Kh-25MP (AS-12 *Kegler*)
AShM Kh-22 (AS-4 *Kitchen*)
AAM • IR R-27T/ET (AA-10B/D *Alamo*); R-60 (AA-8 *Aphid*); R-73 (AA-11 *Archer*); **SARH** R-27R/ER (AA-10A/C *Alamo*)

Naval Infantry (Marines) ε20,000

FORCES BY ROLE
SPECIAL FORCES
1 (fleet) SF bde (1 para bn, 2–3 underwater bn, 1 spt unit)
2 (fleet) SF bde (cadre) (1 para bn, 2–3 underwater bn, 1 spt unit)
MANOEUVRE
Mechanised
2 MR bde
1 MR regt
3 indep naval inf bde
2 indep naval inf regt
COMBAT SUPPORT
1 arty bde
3 SAM regt

EQUIPMENT BY TYPE
MBT 200 T-72/T-80
RECCE 60 BRDM-2 each with 9K11 (AT-3 *Sagger*)
AIFV 300 BMP-2
APC 800
APC (T) 300 MT-LB
APC (W) 500 BTR-80
ARTY 365
SP 263: **122mm** 113: 95 2S1; 18 2S19; **152mm** 150: 50 2A36; 50 2A65; 50 2S3
GUN/MOR 66
SP 120mm 42: 12 2S23 NONA-SVK; 30 2S9 NONA-S
TOWED 120mm 24 2B16 NONA-K
MRL 122mm 36 BM-21
AT
MSL
SP 9P149 with 9K114 *Shturm* (AT-6 *Spiral*)
MANPATS 9K11 (AT-3 *Sagger*); 9K113 (AT-5 *Spandrel*)
GUNS 100mm T-12
AD
SAM
SP 70: 20 9K33 *Osa* (SA-8 *Gecko*); 50 *Strela*-1/*Strela*-10 (SA-9 *Gaskin*/SA-13 *Gopher*)
MANPAD 9K32 *Strela*-2 (SA-7 *Grail*)
GUNS 23mm 60 ZSU-23-4

Coastal Missile and Artillery Troops 2,000

FORCES BY ROLE
COMBAT SUPPORT
3 AShM bde
2 AShM regt
1 indep AShM bn

EQUIPMENT BY TYPE
ARTY • SP 130mm ε36 A-222 *Bereg*
AShM 36+: 24 3K60 *Bal* (SSC-6 *Sennight*); 12 K-300P *Bastion* (SSC-5 *Stooge*); some 4K44 *Redut* (SSC-1 *Sepal*); some 4K51 *Rubezh* (SSC-3 *Styx*)

Military Air Forces ε150,000 (incl conscripts — reducing to 148,000)

Flying hours 60 to 100 hrs/year (combat aircraft)
120+ (tranpsort aircraft)

HQ at Balashikha, near Moscow. A joint CIS Unified Air Defence System covers RUS, ARM, BLR, KAZ, KGZ, TJK, TKM, UKR and UZB. The Russian Air Force is currently undergoing a period of restructuring, both in terms of general organisation as well as air base and unit structure.

FORCES BY ROLE
BOMBER
4 sqn with Tu-22M3/MR *Backfire* C
3 sqn with Tu-95MS *Bear*
1 sqn with Tu-160 *Blackjack*
FIGHTER
8 sqn with MiG-29 *Fulcrum*
3 sqn with MiG-29SMT *Fulcrum*
11 sqn with MiG-31/MiG-31BM *Foxhound*
10 sqn with Su-27 *Flanker*
4 sqn with Su-27SM2 *Flanker*; Su-30M2
FIGHTER/GROUND ATTACK
1 sqn with Su-27SM3 *Flanker*; Su-30M2
GROUND ATTACK
11 sqn with Su-24M/M2 *Fencer*
13 sqn with Su-25/Su-25SM *Frogfoot*
2 sqn with Su-34 *Fullback*
1 sqn with Su-34 *Fullback* (forming)
GROUND ATTACK/ISR
1 sqn with Su-24M/MR *Fencer**
ELECTRONIC WARFARE
1 sqn with Mi-8PPA *Hip*
ISR
1 sqn with MIG-25RB *Foxbat**

8 sqn with Su-24MR *Fencer**
1 flt with An-30 *Clank*

AIRBORNE EARLY WARNING & CONTROL
1 sqn with A-50/A-50U *Mainstay*

TANKER
1 sqn with Il-78/Il-78M *Midas*

TRANSPORT
7 (mixed) sqn with An-12 *Cub*/An-24 *Coke*/An-26 *Curl*/Mi-8 *Hip*/Tu-134 *Crusty*/Tu-154 *Careless*
2 sqn with An-124 *Condor*
1 flt with An-12BK *Cub*
1 sqn with An-22 *Cock*
13 sqn with Il-76MD *Candid*

ATTACK HELICOPTER
2 sqn with Ka-52A *Hokum* B
12 sqn with Mi-24 *Hind*
2 sqn with Mi-28N *Havoc* B
1 sqn with Mi-28N *Havoc* B (forming)

TRANSPORT HELICOPTER
17 sqn with Mi-8 *Hip*/Mi-26 *Halo*

AIR DEFENCE
35 regt with S-300PS (SA-10 *Grumble*); S-300PM (SA-20 *Gargoyle*)
6 regt with S-400 (SA-21 *Growler*); 96K6 *Pantsir*-S1 (SA-22 *Greyhound*)

EQUIPMENT BY TYPE

AIRCRAFT 1,389 combat capable
BBR 141: 63 Tu-22M3/MR *Backfire* C; 31 Tu-95MS6 *Bear*; 31 Tu-95MS16 *Bear*; 16 Tu-160 *Blackjack*
FTR 580: 150 MiG-29 *Fulcrum*; 40 MiG-29UB *Fulcrum*; 120 MiG-31B/31BS *Foxhound*; 40 MiG-31B/31BS *Foxhound*; 200 Su-27 *Flanker*; 30 Su-27UB *Flanker*
FGA 343: 28 MiG-29SMT *Fulcrum*; 6 MiG-29UBT *Fulcrum*; 150 Su-24M *Fencer*; 50 Su-24M2 *Fencer*; 47 Su-27SM2 *Flanker*; 12 Su-27SM3; 4 Su-30M2; 6 Su-30SM; 28 Su-34 *Fullback*; 12 Su-35S *Flanker*
ATK 215: 150 Su-25 *Frogfoot*; 50 Su-25SM *Frogfoot*; 15 Su-25UB *Frogfoot*
ISR 114: 4 An-30 *Clank*; 10 MiG-25RB *Foxbat**; 100 Su-24MR *Fencer**
ELINT 22 Il-22 *Coot* B
AEW&C 23: 19 A-50/A-50U *Mainstay*; 4 Il-76SKIP (Be-976 – telemetry aircraft)
C2 6: 2 Il-76VKP; 4 Il-86VKP *Maxdome*
TKR 20 Il-78/Il-78M *Midas*
TPT 390: **Heavy** 134: 12 An-124 *Condor*; 4 An-22 *Cock*; 118 Il-76MD/MF *Candid*; **Medium** 50 An-12/An-12BK *Cub*; **Light** 205: 25 An-24 *Coke*; 80 An-26 *Curl*; 15 An-72 *Coaler*; 5 An-140; 40 L-410; 30 Tu-134 *Crusty*; 10 Yak-40 *Codling*; **PAX** 1 Tu-154 *Careless*
TRG 220: 190 L-39 *Albatros*; 30 Yak-130 *Mitten*

HELICOPTERS
ATK 392+: 12 Ka-50 *Hokum*; 30+ Ka-52A *Hokum* B; 290 Mi-24D/V/P *Hind*; 50+ Mi-28N *Havoc* B; 10+ Mi-35 *Hind*
EW 54: 50 Mi-8PPA *Hip*; 4 Mi-8TRP-1 *Hip*
TPT 566: **Heavy** 32 Mi-26 *Halo*; **Medium** 534 Mi-17 (Mi-8MT) *Hip* H/Mi-8 *Hip*
TRG 30: 10 Ka-226; 20 Ansat-U

UAV • ISR Light some *Pchela*-1T
AD • SAM • SP 1,900+ S-300PS (SA-10 *Grumble*)/S-300PM (SA-20 *Gargoyle*)/S-400 (SA-21 *Growler*); 96K6 *Pantsir*-S1 (SA-22 *Greyhound*)

MSL
AAM • IR R-27T/ET (AA-10 *Alamo* B/D); R-73 (AA-11 *Archer*); R-60T (AA-8 *Aphid*); **SARH** R-27R/ER (AA-10 *Alamo* A/C); R-33/33S (AA-9 *Amos* A/B); **ARH** R-77/R-77-1 (AA-12 *Adder*); K-37M (AA-13 *Axehead*); **PRH** R-27P/EP (AA-10 *Alamo* E/F)
ARM Kh-58 (AS-11 *Kilter*); Kh-25MP (AS-12 *Kegler*); Kh-15P (AS-16 *Kickback*) Kh-31P/PM (PM entering production) (AS-17A *Krypton*)
ASM Kh-25 (AS-10 *Karen*); Kh-59/Kh-59M (AS-13 *Kingbolt*/AS-18 *Kazoo*); Kh-29 (AS-14 *Kedge*); Kh-31A/AM (AM entering production) (AS-17B *Krypton*); Kh-38 (trials underway)
LACM Kh-22/32 (AS-4 *Kitchen*); Kh-55/55SM (AS-15A/B *Kent*); Kh-101; Kh-102; Kh-555 (AS-15C *Kent*)

BOMBS • Laser-guided KAB-500; KAB-1500L; **TV-guided** KAB-500KR; KAB-1500KR; KAB-500OD;UPAB 1500

Russian Military Districts

Western Military District

(ex-Leningrad & Moscow Military Districts & Kaliningrad Special Region) HQ at St Petersburg

Army

FORCES BY ROLE

COMMAND
2 army HQ

SPECIAL FORCES
2 (Spetsnaz) bde
1 (AB Recce) bn

MANOEUVRE
Armoured
1 tk div
1 tk bde
Mechanised
1 MR div
5 MR bde
Air Manoeuvre
3 (VdV) AB div

COMBAT SUPPORT
2 arty bde
1 MRL bde
1 SSM bde with *Iskander*-M
2 SSM bde with *Tochka* (SS-21 *Scarab*)
2 AD bde
1 engr bde
1 MP bde

Reserves

FORCES BY ROLE

MANOEUVRE
Armoured
1 tk bde
Mechanised
2 MR bde

Northern Fleet

EQUIPMENT BY TYPE

SUBMARINES 41

STRATEGIC 10 **SSBN** (1 SSBN's *Bulava* SLBM not yet operational)

TACTICAL 23: 3 **SSGN**; 13 **SSN**; 7 **SSK**

SUPPORT 8: 7 **SSAN** (other roles); 1 **SSA**

PRINCIPAL SURFACE COMBATANTS 10: 1 **CV**; 1 **CGHMN**; 1 **CGHM** (in repair); 7 **DDGHM** (of which 1 in refit)

PATROL AND COASTAL COMBATANTS 12: 3 **FSGM**; 9 **FSM**

MINE WARFARE 12: 1 **MHSO** (in repair); 3 **MSO**; 8 **MSC**

AMPHIBIOUS 4 **LST**

Naval Aviation

FORCES BY ROLE

FIGHTER

2 sqn with Su-33 *Flanker* D; Su-25UTG *Frogfoot*

ANTI-SUBMARINE WARFARE

1 sqn with Il-20RT *Coot* A; Il-38 *May**; Tu-134

3 sqn with Ka-27/Ka-29 *Helix*

1 sqn with Tu-142M/MR *Bear* F/J

EQUIPMENT BY TYPE

AIRCRAFT

FTR 18 Su-33 *Flanker* D

ATK 5 Su-25UTG *Frogfoot*

ASW 13 Tu-142M/MR *Bear* F/J

EW • ELINT Il-20RT *Coot* A

MP 14 Il-38 *May**

TPT Tu-134

HELICOPTERS

ASW Ka-27 *Helix* A

TPT Ka-29 *Helix* B; Mi-8 *Hip*

Naval Infantry

FORCES BY ROLE

MANOEUVRE

Mechanised

1 MR bde

1 naval inf bde

1 naval inf regt

Coastal Artillery and Missile Troops

FORCES BY ROLE

COMBAT SUPPORT

1 AShM bde

Baltic Fleet

EQUIPMENT BY TYPE

SUBMARINES • TACTICAL 3 **SSK**: 1 *Lada*; 2 *Paltus* (*Kilo*)

PRINCIPAL SURFACE COMBATANTS 7: 2 **DDGHM**; 5 **FFGHM**

PATROL AND COASTAL COMBATANTS 20: 4 **FSGM**; 8 **FSM**; 7 **PCFG**; 1 **PCM**

MINE WARFARE • MINE COUNTERMEASURES 15: 4 **MSC**; 11 **MHI**

AMPHIBIOUS 11: 4 **LST**; 5 **LCM**; 2 **LCAC**

Naval Aviation

FORCES BY ROLE

ANTI-SUBMARINE WARFARE

1 sqn with Ka-27/Ka-29 *Helix*

TRANSPORT

1 sqn with An-24 *Coke*; An-26 *Curl*; Tu-134 *Crusty*

EQUIPMENT BY TYPE

AIRCRAFT

TPT An-24 *Coke*/An-26 *Curl*/Tu-134 *Crusty*

HELICOPTERS

ASW Ka-27 *Helix*

TPT • Medium Ka-29 *Helix*

Naval Infantry

FORCES BY ROLE

MANOEUVRE

Mechanised

1 MR bde

1 MR regt

1 naval inf bde

COMBAT SUPPORT

1 arty bde

1 SAM regt

Coastal Artillery and Missile Troops

FORCES BY ROLE

COMBAT SUPPORT

1 AShM regt

Military Air Forces

1st Air Force & Air Defence Command

(ex-6th & 16th Air Army)

FORCES BY ROLE

FIGHTER

1 sqn with MiG-29 *Fulcrum*

2 sqn with MiG-29SMT *Fulcrum*

4 sqn with MiG-31 *Foxhound*

8 sqn with Su-27/Su-27UB *Flanker*

GROUND ATTACK

2 sqn with Su-24M/M2 *Fencer*

2 sqn with Su-34 *Fullback*

GROUND ATTACK/ISR

1 sqn with Su-24M/MR *Fencer**

ISR

1 flt with A-30 *Clank*

1 sqn with MiG-25RB *Foxbat**

2 sqn with Su-24MR *Fencer* E

ELECTRONIC WARFARE

1 sqn with Mi-8PPA *Hip*

TRANSPORT

1 sqn with An-12 *Cub*; An-26 *Curl*; Tu-134 *Crusty*

ATTACK HELICOPTER

6 sqn with Mi-24 *Hind*

TRANSPORT HELICOPTER

6 sqn with Mi-8 *Hip*

EQUIPMENT BY TYPE

AIRCRAFT

FTR 180: 20 MiG-29 *Fulcrum*; 51 MiG-31 *Foxhound*; 109 Su-27/Su-27UB *Flanker*

FGA 98: 28 MiG-29SMT *Fulcrum*; 6 MiG-29UBT *Fulcrum*; 44 Su-24M/M2 *Fencer*; 20+ Su-34 *Fullback*
ISR 42+: 4 An-30 *Clank*; 10+ MiG-25RB *Foxbat** 28 Su-24MR *Fencer**
TPT 12 An-12/An-26/Tu-134
HELICOPTERS
ATK 60 Mi-24 *Hind*
EW 10 Mi-8PPA *Hip*
TPT • Medium 60 Mi-8 *Hip*
AD • SAM 1,125 incl S-300V

Central Military District

(ex-Volga-Ural & part ex-Siberia Military Districts) HQ at Yekaterinburg

Army

FORCES BY ROLE
COMMAND
2 army HQ
SPECIAL FORCES
1 (Spetsnaz) SF bde
MANOEUVRE
Armoured
1 tk bde
Mechanised
1 (201st) MR div
7 MR bde
Air Manoeuvre
1 (VdV) AB bde
COMBAT SUPPORT
1 arty bde
1 MRL regt
2 SSM bde with *Tochka* (SS-21 *Scarab*)
2 AD bde
1 engr bde

Reserves

FORCES BY ROLE
MANOEUVRE
Mechanised
3 MR bde

Military Air Force

2nd Air Force & Air Defence Command

(ex-5th & elm ex-14th Air Army)

FORCES BY ROLE
FIGHTER
4 sqn with MiG-31 *Foxhound*
GROUND ATTACK
2 sqn with Su-24 *Fencer*
ISR
1 sqn with Su-24MR *Fencer* E
TRANSPORT
3 sqn with An-12 *Cub*; An-24 *Coke*; Il-86; Tu-134 *Crusty*; Tu-154; Mi-8 *Hip*
ATTACK HELICOPTER
2 sqn with Mi-24 *Hind*
TRANSPORT HELICOPTER
3 sqn with Mi-8 *Hip*/Mi-26 *Halo*

EQUIPMENT BY TYPE
AIRCRAFT
FTR 73 MiG-31 *Foxhound*
FGA 26 Su-24M *Fencer*
ISR 13 Su-24MR *Fencer* E
TPT 36 An-12/An-24 *Coke*/Tu-134 *Crusty*/Tu-154 *Careless*
HELICOPTERS
ATK 24 Mi-24 *Hind*
TPT 46: 6 Mi-26 *Halo*; 40 Mi-8 *Hip*
AD • SAM S-300 (SA-10 *Grumble*)

Southern Military District

(ex-North Caucasus Military District – including Trans-Caucasus Group of Forces (GRVZ)) HQ located at Rostov-on-Don

Army

FORCES BY ROLE
COMMAND
2 army HQ
SPECIAL FORCES
2 (Spetsnaz) SF bde
MANOEUVRE
Reconnaissance
1 recce bde
Mechanised
6 MR bde
2 MR bde (Armenia)
1 MR bde (Abkhazia)
1 MR bde (South Ossetia)
3 (lt/mtn) MR bde
Air Manoeuvre
1 (VdV) AB div
1 (army) air aslt bde
COMBAT SUPPORT
1 arty bde
1 MRL bde
1 MRL regt
1 SSM bde with *Tochka* (SS-21 *Scarab*)
2 AD bde
1 engr bde

Black Sea Fleet

The RUS Fleet is leasing bases in Sevastopol and Karantinnaya Bay, and is based, jointly with UKR warships, at Streletskaya Bay.

EQUIPMENT BY TYPE
SUBMARINES • TACTICAL 1 **SSK** (also 1 *Som* (*Tango*) in reserve)
PRINCIPAL SURFACE COMBATANTS 5: 2 **CGHM**; 1 **DDGM**; 2 **FFGM**
PATROL AND COASTAL COMBATANTS 19: 4 **FSGM**; 6 **FSM**; 1 **PHM**; 5 **PCFG**; 2 **PCM**; 1 **PHT**
MINE WARFARE • MINE COUNTERMEASURES 9: 1 **MCO**; 6 **MSO**; 2 **MSC**
AMPHIBIOUS 9: 8 **LST**; 1 **LCU**

Naval Aviation

FORCES BY ROLE
FIGHTER
ANTI-SURFACE WARFARE/ISR
2 sqn with Su-24M/MR *Fencer*
ANTI-SUBMARINE WARFARE
1 sqn with Ka-27 *Helix*
1 sqn with Mi-14 *Haze*
MARITIME PATROL/ELECTRONIC WARFARE
1 sqn with An-12 *Cub*; Be-12 *Mail**; Mi-8

EQUIPMENT BY TYPE
AIRCRAFT
FGA 18 Su-24M *Fencer*
ISR 4 Su-24MR *Fencer* E
MP 9 Be-12 *Mail**
EW • ELINT An-12 *Cub*
TPT An-12; An-26
HELICOPTERS
ASW Ka-27 *Helix*
TPT • Medium Mi-8 *Hip* (MP/EW/Tpt)

Naval Infantry

FORCES BY ROLE
MANOEUVRE
Mechanised
1 naval inf bde
COMBAT SUPPORT
1 SAM regt

Coastal Artillery and Missile Troops

FORCES BY ROLE
1 AShM bde
1 indep AShM bn

Caspian Sea Flotilla

EQUIPMENT BY TYPE
PRINCIPAL SURFACE COMBATANTS 2 **FFGM**
PATROL AND COASTAL COMBATANTS 6: 2 **PCFG**; 3 **PHM**; 1 **PCM**
MINE WARFARE • MINE COUNTERMEASURES 7: 5 **MSC**; 2 **MHI**
AMPHIBIOUS 11: 2 **LCM**; 4 **LCU**; 5 **LCAC**

Military Air Force

4th Air Force & Air Defence Command

(ex 4th Air Army)

FORCES BY ROLE
FIGHTER
3 sqn with MiG-29 *Fulcrum*
1 sqn with MiG-29 *Fulcrum* (Armenia)
3 sqn with Su-27 *Flanker*
FIGHTER/GROUND ATTACK
1 sqn with Su-27SM3 *Flanker*; Su-30M2
GROUND ATTACK
3 sqn with Su-24M *Fencer*
6 sqn with Su-25 *Frogfoot*
1 sqn with Su-34 *Fullback* (forming)
ISR
2 sqn with Su-24MR *Fencer* E
TRANSPORT
1 sqn with An-12 *Cub*/Mi-8 *Hip*
ATTACK HELICOPTER
3 sqn with Mi-24 *Hind*
2 sqn with Mi-28N *Havoc* B (forming)
TRANSPORT HELICOPTER
6 sqn with Mi-8 *Hip*/Mi-26 *Halo*

EQUIPMENT BY TYPE
AIRCRAFT
FTR 121: 63 MiG-29 *Fulcrum*; 58 Su-27 *Flanker*
FGA 80+: 62 Su-24M *Fencer;* 12 Su-27SM3 *Flanker*; 2 Su-30M2; 4+ Su-34 *Fullback*
ATK 129 Su-25 *Frogfoot*
ISR 24 Su-24MR *Fencer**
TPT 12 An-12 *Cub*
HELICOPTERS
ATK 36: 24 Mi-24 *Hind;* 12+ Mi-28N *Havoc* B
TPT 72 **Heavy** 10 Mi-26 *Halo* **Medium** 28 Mi-8 *Hip*

Eastern Military District

(ex-Far East & part ex-Siberia Military Districts) HQ located at Khabarovsk

Army

FORCES BY ROLE
COMMAND
4 army HQ
SPECIAL FORCES
2 (Spetsnaz) SF bde
MANOEUVRE
Armoured
1 tk bde
Mechanised
10 MR bde
1 MGA div
Air Manoeuvre
2 (army) air aslt bde
COMBAT SUPPORT
4 arty bde
2 MRL bde
3 SSM bde with *Tochka* (SS-21 *Scarab*)
4 AD bde
1 engr bde

Reserves

FORCES BY ROLE
MANOEUVRE
Mechanised
8 MR bde

Pacific Fleet

EQUIPMENT BY TYPE
SUBMARINES 21
STRATEGIC 3 **SSBN**
TACTICAL 18: 5 **SSGN**; 4 **SSN**; 9 **SSK**
PRINCIPAL SURFACE COMBATANTS 9: 1 **CGHM**; 8 **DDGHM** (of which one in reserve)
PATROL AND COASTAL COMBATANTS 23: 4 **FSGM**; 9 **FSM**; 10 **PCFG**
MINE WARFARE 7: 2 **MSO**; 5 **MSC**
AMPHIBIOUS 4 **LST**

Russia and Eurasia

Naval Aviation

FORCES BY ROLE

ANTI-SUBMARINE WARFARE

3 sqn with Ka-27/Ka-29 *Helix*
1 sqn with Il-38 *May**
1 sqn with Tu-142M/MR *Bear* F/J*

TRANSPORT

2 sqn with An-12 *Cub*; An-26 *Curl*

EQUIPMENT BY TYPE

AIRCRAFT

ASW 14 Tu-142M/MR *Bear* F/J*
MP 15 Il-38 *May**
TPT An-12 *Cub* (MR/EW); An-26 *Curl*

HELICOPTERS

ASW Ka-27 *Helix*
TPT • Medium Ka-29 *Helix*; Mi-8 *Hip*

Naval Infantry

FORCES BY ROLE

MANOEUVRE

Mechanised
1 naval inf bde
1 naval inf regt

COMBAT SUPPORT

1 SAM regt

Coastal Artillery and Missile Troops

FORCES BY ROLE

COMBAT SUPPORT

1 AShM bde
1 AShM regt

Military Air Force

3rd Air Force & Air Defence Command

(ex 11th & elms 14th AF and AD Army)

FORCES BY ROLE

FIGHTER

3 sqn with MiG-29 *Fulcrum*
3 sqn with MiG-31 *Foxhound*
4 sqn with Su-27SM2 *Flanker*; Su-30M2

GROUND ATTACK

4 sqn with Su-24M/M2 *Fencer*
5 sqn with Su-25 *Frogfoot*

ISR

3 sqn with Su-24MR *Fencer* E

TRANSPORT

2 sqn with An-12 *Cub*/An-24 *Coke*/An-26 *Curl*/Tu-134 *Crusty*/Tu-154 *Careless*

ATTACK HELICOPTER

2 sqn with Mi-24 *Hind*
1 sqn (forming) with Ka-52A *Hokum* B

TRANSPORT HELICOPTER

6 sqn with Mi-8 *Hind*/Mi-26 *Halo*

EQUIPMENT BY TYPE

AIRCRAFT

FTR 104: 60 MiG-29 *Fulcrum*; 44 MiG-31 *Foxhound*
FGA 103: 44 Su-24M *Fencer*; 10 Su-24M2 *Fencer*; 47 Su-27SM2 *Flanker*; 2 Su-30M2
ATK 72 Su-25 *Frogfoot*
ISR 28 Su-24MR *Fencer* E
TPT 22 An-12 *Cub*/An-24 *Coke*/An-26 *Curl*; 1 Tu-134 *Crusty*; 1 Tu-154 *Careless*

HELICOPTERS

ATK 32: 8 Ka-52A *Hokum* B; 24 Mi-24 *Hind*
TPT 60 **Heavy** 4 Mi-26 *Halo*; **Medium** 56 Mi-8 *Hip*

AD • SAM S-300P (SA-10 *Grumble*)

Direct Reporting Commands

Long-Range Aviation Command

Flying hours: 80–100 hrs/yr

FORCES BY ROLE

BOMBER

4 sqn with Tu-22M3/MR *Backfire* C
3 sqn with Tu-95MS *Bear*
1 sqn with Tu-160 *Blackjack*

EQUIPMENT BY TYPE

AIRCRAFT

BBR 141: 63 Tu-22M3/MR *Backfire* C; 31 Tu-95MS6 *Bear*; 31 Tu-95MS16 *Bear*; 16 Tu-160 *Blackjack*

Transport Aviation Command

Flying hours 60 hrs/year

FORCES BY ROLE

TRANSPORT

2 sqn with An-124 *Condor*
1 flt with An-12BK *Cub*
1 sqn with An-22 *Cock*
13 sqn with Il-76MD *Candid*

EQUIPMENT BY TYPE

AIRCRAFT • TPT 140 **Heavy** 134: 12 An-124 *Condor*; 4 An-22 *Cock* (Under MoD control); 118 Il-76MD/MF *Candid* **Medium** 6 An-12BK *Cub*

Paramilitary 519,000

Federal Border Guard Service ε160,000

Directly subordinate to the president; now reportedly all contract-based personnel

FORCES BY ROLE

10 regional directorates

MANOEUVRE

Other
7 frontier gp

EQUIPMENT BY TYPE

AIFV/APC (W) 1,000 BMP/BTR
ARTY • SP 90: **122mm** 2S1; **120mm** 2S12; **120mm** 2S9 *Anona*

PRINCIPAL SURFACE COMBATANTS

FRIGATES • FFHM 3 *Nerey* (*Krivak* III) with 1 twin lnchr with *Osa*-M (SA-N-4 *Gecko*) SAM, 2 quad 533mm TT lnchr, 2 RBU 6000 *Smerch* 2 lnchr, 1 100mm gun (capacity 1 Ka-27 *Helix* A ASW hel)

PATROL AND COASTAL COMBATANTS 203

PCM 46:
2 *Molnya* II (*Pauk* II) with 1 quad lnchr with *Strela*-2 (SA-N-5 *Grail* SAM), 2 twin 533mm TT lnchr, 2 RBU 1200 lnchr, 1 AK630 CIWS, 1 76mm gun
27 *Svetljak* (*Svetlyak*) with 1 quad lnchr with *Strela*-2 (SA-N-5 *Grail* SAM), 2 single 406mm TT, 1 76mm gun

17 *Molnya* I (*Pauk* I) with 1 quad lnchr with *Strela*-2 (SA-N-5 *Grail* SAM), 4 single 406mm TT, 1 AK630 CIWS, 1 76mm gun
PHT 2 *Antares* (*Muravey*)
PCO 15: 8 Project 503 (*Alpinist*); 1 *Sprut*; 3 *Rubin* with 1 AK630 CIWS; 2 *Antur*; 1 *Purga*
PSO 4 *Komandor*
PCC 13 *Tarantul* (*Stenka*) with 4 406mm TT, 2 twin AK630 CIWS
PB 45: 3 Project 14310 (*Mirazh*); 13 Type 1496; 12 *Grif* (*Zhuk*); 17 *Kulik*
PBR 25: 3 *Ogonek* with 2 AK630 CIWS; 8 *Piyavka* with 1 AK630 CIWS; 5 *Shmel* with 1 76mm gun; 6 *Moskit* (*Vosh*); 2 *Slepen* (*Yaz*) with 2 115mm guns; 1 *Gornostay*
PBF 53: 1 A-125; 2 *Bogomol* with 2 twin AK630 CIWS, 1 76mm gun; 17 *Mangust*; 4 *Mustang* (Project 18623); 15 *Saygak*; 12 *Sobol*; 2 *Sokzhoi*
AMPHIBIOUS • LC • LCAC 7 *Tsaplya* (used for patrol duties)
LOGISTICS AND SUPPORT 41
AGB 5 *Ivan Susanin* (primarily used as patrol ships)
AGS 2 *Yug* (primarily used as patrol ships)
AK 8 *Neon Antonov*
AKSL 6 *Kanin*
AO 2: 1 *Baskunchak*; 1 Project 1510
ATF 18 *Sorum* (primarily used as patrol ships)
AIRCRAFT • TPT ε86: 70 An-24 *Coke*/An-26 *Curl*/An-72 *Coaler*/Il-76 *Candid*/Tu-134 *Crusty*/Yak-40 *Codling*; 16 SM-92
HELICOPTERS: ε200 Ka-28 (Ka-27) *Helix* ASW/Mi-24 *Hind* Atk/Mi-26 *Halo* Spt/Mi-8 *Hip* Spt

Federal Agency for Special Construction (MOD) ε50,000

Federal Communications and Information Agency ε55,000

FORCES BY ROLE
MANOEUVRE
Other
4 paramilitary corps
28 paramilitary bde

Federal Protection Service ε10,000–30,000 active

Org include elm of ground forces (mech inf bde and AB regt)

FORCES BY ROLE
MANOEUVRE
Mechanised
1 mech inf regt
Air Manoeuvre
1 AB regt
Other
1 (Presidential) gd regt

Federal Security Service ε4,000 active (armed)

FORCES BY ROLE
MANOEUVRE
Other
Some cdo unit (including Alfa and Vympel units)

Interior Troops ε170,000

FORCES BY ROLE
7 Regional Commands: Central, Urals, North Caucasus, Volga, Eastern, North-Western and Siberian
MANOEUVRE
Other
3 (55th, 59th & ODON) paramiltiary div (2–5 paramilitary regt)
18 (OBRON) paramilitary bde (3 mech bn, 1 mor bn)
2 indep paramilitary bde (OBR/OSMBR)
102 paramilitary regt/bn (incl special motorised units)
11 (special) paramilitary unit
Aviation
8 sqn
COMBAT SUPPORT
1 arty regt
EQUIPMENT BY TYPE
MBT 9
AIFV/APC (W) 1,650 BMP-1/BMP-2/BTR-80
ARTY 35
TOWED 122mm 20 D-30
MOR 120mm 15 PM-38
AIRCRAFT TPT 23: **Heavy** 9 Il-76 *Candid*; **Medium** 2 An-12 *Cub*; **Light** 12 An-26 *Curl*; 6 An-72 *Coaler*
HELICOPTERS • TPT 70: **Heavy** 10 Mi-26 *Halo*; **Medium** 60 Mi-8 *Hip*

Railway Troops (MOD) ε50,000

Cyber

Until 2003, activities within the cyber domain were the responsibility of the Russian SIGINT agency, FAPSI. In 2003, this agency was abolished and its responsibilities divided between the Defence Ministry and the internal security service FSB, with the latter having responsibility for investigating cyber crime. Moscow State University's Institute for Information Security Issues conducts research on technical issues, including cryptography, and counts the General Staff and the FSB among its clients. In March 2012, Dmitry Rogozin, deputy prime minister with responsibility for the defence industry, said Russia was considering establishing a 'Cyber Security Command' in the armed forces, though there is scant detail. The first official doctrinal statement on the role of the Russian military in cyberspace, the 'Conceptual Views on the Activity of the Russian Federation Armed Forces in Information Space', was released at the end of 2011, and described cyber force tasks with little correlation to those of equivalent commands in the West. In particular, the document contains no mention of the possibility of offensive cyber activity. The document is entirely defensive in tone, and focuses on force protection and prevention of information war, including allowing for a military role in negotiating international treaties governing information security. Following mixed performance in the information aspects of the armed conflict with Georgia in 2008, there was discussion about creating 'Information Troops', whose role would include cyber capability; but this initiative was publicly scotched by the FSB. In January 2012, then-CGS Makarov gave a different picture of the three main tasks for any new command: 'disrupting adversary information systems, including by introducing harmful software; defending our own communications and command systems'; and 'working on domestic and foreign public opinion using the media, Internet and more'. The third task is a reminder that, unlike some other nations with advanced cyber capabilities, Russia deals in cyber warfare as an integral component of information warfare.

DEPLOYMENT

ARMENIA
3,214; 1 MR bde; 74 MBT; 201 AIFV; 72 SP/towed arty; 12 MRL; 1 sqn with 18 MiG-29 *Fulcrum*; 2 AD bty with S-300V (SA-12 *Gladiator/Giant*); 1 AD bty with 2K12 *Kub* (SA-6 *Gainful*)

BELARUS
1 radar station at Baranovichi (*Volga* system; leased); 1 Naval Communications site

CÔTE D'IVOIRE
UN • UNOCI 6 obs

DEMOCRATIC REPUBLIC OF THE CONGO
UN • MONUSCO 1; 27 obs

GEORGIA
7,000; Abkhazia 1 MR bde; South Ossetia 1 MR bde; some atk hel; some S-300 SAM

GULF OF ADEN
1 CGHM; 1 AORL; 1 ATF

KAZAKHSTAN
1 radar station at Balkash (Dnepr system; leased)

KYRGYZSTAN
ε500; 5 Su-25 *Frogfoot*; 2 Mi-8 *Hip* spt hel

LIBERIA
UN • UNMIL 4 obs

MIDDLE EAST
UN • UNTSO 5 obs

MOLDOVA/TRANSDNIESTR
ε1,500 (including 350 peacekeepers); 2 MR bn; 100 MBT/AIFV/APC; 7 Mi-24 *Hind*; some Mi-8 *Hip*

SOUTH SUDAN
UN • UNMISS 4; 3 obs

SUDAN
UN • UNISFA 2 obs

SYRIA
1 naval facility at Tartus

TAJIKISTAN
5,000; 1 mil base with (1 (201st) MR div(-); 54 T-72; 300 BMP-2/BTR-80/MT-LB; 100 2S1/2S3/2S12/9P140 *Uragan*; 5 Su-25 *Frogfoot*; 4 Mi-8 *Hip*

UKRAINE
13,000; 102 AIFV/APC: 24 arty; 1 Fleet HQ located at Sevastopol; 2 radar stations located at Sevastopol (*Dnepr* system, leased) and Mukachevo (*Dnepr* system, leased).

WESTERN SAHARA
UN • MINURSO 16 obs

Tajikistan TJK

Tajikistani Somoni Tr		2012	2013	2014
GDP	Tr	36.2bn	41.8bn	
	US$	7.59bn	8.56bn	
per capita	US$	953	1,052	
Growth	%	7.50	7.00	
Inflation	%	5.80	7.72	
Def bdgt [a]	Tr	808m	923m	
	US$	170m	189m	
FMA (US)	US$	0.8m	0.8m	1.5m
US$1=Tr		4.76	4.88	

[a] Defence and law enforcement expenses

Population 7,910,041

Ethnic groups: Tajik 67%; Uzbek 25%; Russian 2%; Tatar 2%

Age	0–14	15–19	20–24	25–29	30–64	65 plus
Male	17.0%	5.0%	5.4%	5.1%	16.0%	1.3%
Female	16.4%	4.8%	5.2%	5.0%	17.0%	1.9%

Capabilities

Internal and border security is a particular concern for Tajikistan, with the country sharing an extended border with Afghanistan. Tajik security forces have intermittent problems with groups of armed gangs linked to drug trafficking. Given the overall weaknesses of the armed and security forces – which include inadequate special forces training and personnel issues revolving around high numbers of conscripts and low planning capacity – it is likely that low-level militant activity linked to drug trafficking will continue to burden and challenge the armed forces. Most military equipment is of Soviet origin. The country has little capacity to deploy other than token forces, though the armed forces are an active participant in CSTO and SCO military exercises. Russia maintains a military base in the country, though this was the source of friction between the two as signature of a lease extension was delayed by Tajikistan during the first half of 2013. India, which also has basing interests in Tajikistan, has offered to provide Mi-8/17 helicopters.

ACTIVE 8,800 **(Army 7,300, Air Force/Air Defence 1,500) Paramilitary 7,500**
Conscript liability 24 months

ORGANISATIONS BY SERVICE

Army 7,300

FORCES BY ROLE
MANOEUVRE
Mechanised
3 MR bde

Air Manoeuvre
1 air aslt bde

COMBAT SUPPORT
1 arty bde
1 SAM regt

EQUIPMENT BY TYPE

MBT 37: 30 T-72; 7 T-62
AIFV 23: 8 BMP-1; 15 BMP-2
APC (W) 23 BTR-60/BTR-70/BTR-80
ARTY 23
TOWED 122mm 10 D-30
MRL 122mm 3 BM-21
MOR 120mm 10
AD • SAM 20+
TOWED 20 S-75 *Dvina* (SA-2 *Guideline*); S-125 *Pechora-2M* (SA-3 *Goa*)
MANPAD 9K32 *Strela-2* (SA-7 *Grail*)‡

Air Force/Air Defence 1,500

FORCES BY ROLE

TRANSPORT
1 sqn with Tu-134A *Crusty*

ATTACK/TRANSPORT HELICOPTER
1 sqn with Mi-24 *Hind*; Mi-8 *Hip*; Mi-17TM *Hip* H

EQUIPMENT BY TYPE

AIRCRAFT
TPT • Light 1 Tu-134A *Crusty*
TRG 4+: 4 L-39 *Albatros*; some Yak-52

HELICOPTERS
ATK 4 Mi-24 *Hind*
TPT • Medium 11 Mi-8 *Hip*/Mi-17TM *Hip* H

Paramilitary 7,500

Interior Troops 3,800

National Guard 1,200

Emergencies Ministry 2,500

Border Guards

DEPLOYMENT

MALI
UN • MINUSMA 1

FOREIGN FORCES

India Air Force: 1 Fwd Op Base located at Farkhar
Russia 5,000 Army: 1 mil base (subord Central MD) with (1 (201st) MR div(-); 54 T-72; 300 BMP-2/BTR-80/MT-LB; 100 2S1/2S3/2S12/9P140 *Uragan* • Military Air Forces: 5 Su-25 *Frogfoot*; 2 Mi-8 *Hip*

Turkmenistan TKM

Turkmen New Manat TMM		2012	2013	2014
GDP	TMM	96bn	115bn	
	US$	33.7bn	40.2bn	
per capita	US$	5,999	7,051	
Growth	%	10.97	7.71	
Inflation	%	4.87	5.64	
Def bdgt	TMM	ε1.54bn		
	US$	ε538.9m		
FMA (US)	US$			0.69m
USD1=TMM		2.85	2.85	

Population 5,113,040

Ethnic groups: Turkmen 77%; Uzbek 9%; Russian 7%; Kazak 2%

Age	0–14	15–19	20–24	25–29	30–64	65 plus
Male	13.5%	5.1%	5.3%	5.0%	18.8%	1.8%
Female	13.2%	5.0%	5.3%	5.0%	19.6%	2.4%

Capabilities

Turkmenistan declared neutrality in 1999 and enshrined this principle in its 2009 Military Doctrine. A military reform programme is under way, intended to improve Turkmenistan's conscript-based armed forces. These continue to rely on Soviet-era equipment and doctrine. Delivery of around 30 T90S MBTs, ordered from Russia in 2011, is yet to take place. The air force has a limited number of fixed-wing combat aircraft and helicopters, though the level of availability is uncertain. Internal security and counter-narcotics are priorities. There are plans to strengthen coastal naval forces by 2015, and some assets have already been procured. Military capability is believed to be limited by low levels of training and availability of spare parts.

ACTIVE 22,000 (Army 18,500 Navy 500 Air 3,000)
Conscript liability 24 months

ORGANISATIONS BY SERVICE

Army 18,500

5 Mil Districts

FORCES BY ROLE

MANOEUVRE
Mechanised
3 MR div
2 MR bde
Air Manouvre
1 air aslt bn
Other
1 MR trg div

COMBAT SUPPORT
1 arty bde
1 MRL regt
1 AT regt
1 SSM bde with *Scud*

2 SAM bde
1 engr regt

EQUIPMENT BY TYPE †

MBT 680: 10 T-90S; 670 T-72
RECCE 170 BRDM/BRDM-2
AIFV 942: 930 BMP-1/BMP-2; 12 BRM
APC (W) 829 BTR-60/BTR-70/BTR-80
ARTY 570
SP 56: **122mm** 40 2S1; **152mm** 16 2S3
TOWED 269: **122mm** 180 D-30; **152mm** 89: 17 D-1; 72 D-20
GUN/MOR 120mm 17 2S9 *Anona*
MRL 131: **122mm** 65: 9 9P138; 56 BM-21; **220mm** 60 9P140 *Uragan*; **300mm** 6 BM 9A52 *Smerch*
MOR 97: **82mm** 31; **120mm** 66 PM-38
AT
MSL • MANPATS 100 9K11 (AT-3 *Sagger*); 9K111 (AT-4 *Spigot*); 9K113 (AT-5 *Spandrel*); 9K115 (AT-6 *Spiral*)
GUNS 100mm 72 MT-12/T-12
AD • SAM 53+
SP 53: 40 9K33 *Osa* (SA-8 *Gecko*); 13 9K35 *Strela-10* (SA-13 *Gopher*)
MANPAD 9K32 *Strela-2* (SA-7 *Grail*)‡
GUNS 70
SP 23mm 48 ZSU-23-4
TOWED 57mm 22 S-60
MSL • SSM 10 SS-1 *Scud*

Navy 500

EQUIPMENT BY TYPE

PATROL AND COASTAL COMBATANTS 19
PCFG 2 *Edermen* (RUS *Molnya*) with 4 quad lnchr with 3M24E *Uran* AShM, 1 quad lnchr (manual aiming) with 9K32 *Strela-2* (SA-N-5 *Grail*) SAM, 1 76mm gun
PCC 4 *Arkadag*
PBF 12: 5 *Grif*-T; 5 Dearsan 14: 2 *Sobol*
PB 1 *Point*

Air Force 3,000

FORCES BY ROLE

FIGHTER/GROUND ATTACK
2 sqn with MiG-29 *Fulcrum*; MiG-29UB *Fulcrum*; Su-17 *Fitter*; Su-25MK *Frogfoot*
TRANSPORT
1 sqn with An-26 *Curl*; Mi-8 *Hip*; Mi-24 *Hind*
TRAINING
1 unit with Su-7B *Fitter* A; L-39 *Albatros*
AIR DEFENCE
Some sqn with S-75 *Dvina* (SA-2 *Guideline*); S-125 *Pechora* (SA-3 *Goa*); S-200 *Angara* (SA-5 *Gammon*)

EQUIPMENT BY TYPE

AIRCRAFT 94 combat capable
FTR 24: 22 MiG-29 *Fulcrum*; 2 MiG-29UB *Fulcrum*
FGA 68: 3 Su-7B *Fitter* A; 65 Su-17 *Fitter* B
ATK 2 Su-25MK *Frogfoot* (41 more being refurbished)
TPT • Light 1 An-26 *Curl*
TRG 2 L-39 *Albatros*
HELICOPTERS
ATK 10 Mi-24 *Hind*
TPT • Medium 8 Mi-8 *Hip*
AD • SAM 50 S-75 *Dvina* (SA-2 *Guideline*)/S-125 *Pechora* (SA-3 *Goa*)/S-200 *Angara* (SA-5 *Gammon*)

Ukraine UKR

Ukrainian Hryvnia h		2012	2013	2014
GDP	h	1.41tr	1.48tr	
	US$	176bn	182bn	
per capita	US$	3,877	4,015	
Growth	%	0.15	0.36	
Inflation	%	0.57	0.48	
Def bdgt	h	16.4bn	19.7bn	25.8bn
	US$	2.05bn	2.42bn	
FMA (US)	US$	7m	7m	4.2m
US$1=h		7.99	8.15	

Population 44,573,205

Age	0 – 14	15 – 19	20 – 24	25 – 29	30 – 64	65 plus
Male	7.1%	2.7%	3.5%	4.3%	23.3%	5.1%
Female	6.7%	2.6%	3.4%	4.2%	26.8%	10.5%

Capabilities

The armed forces are tasked with ensuring territorial integrity and having the capability to participate in international peace-keeping operations. There is at least a notional ability for limited force projection using air-mobile troops. However, the armed forces have suffered from inadequate finances and a 2006–11 defence programme was significantly underfunded. Procurement targets were missed and plans to end conscription by 2011 were not achieved. A reform programme covering the period to 2017 has been drafted by the ministry, which includes the objective of increasing the number of contract personnel. The services continue to operate mainly Soviet-era equipment, which increasingly needs replacement, such as much of the SAM inventory. Aircraft availability and serviceability remain low, as do flying hours. Funding restrictions have constrained naval ambitions, though the programme to re-equip the fleet with a new class of corvette is proceeding slowly. The navy is also attempting to return its one *Foxtrot*-class submarine to service condition, after more than a decade of inactivity. The armed forces take part in national and multinational exercises, and also provide personnel for UN peacekeeping operations. Ukraine has an industrial relationship with China in certain areas of defence technology. The Russian Black Sea Fleet continues to use leased facilities at Sevastopol.

ACTIVE 129,950 (Army 64,750 Navy 13,950 Air 45,250 Airborne 6,000) Paramilitary 84,900

Conscript liability Army, Air Force 18 months, Navy 2 years. During the Autumn 2013 draft, authorities indicated that concription could be suspended in 2014. Contract servicemen comprise just over 50% of the armed forces.

RESERVE 1,000,000 (Joint 1,000,000)

Military service within 5 years

ORGANISATIONS BY SERVICE

Ground Forces (Army) 64,750

Transformation due to be completed by 2015.

FORCES BY ROLE:

COMMAND
3 corps HQ
SPECIAL FORCES
2 SF regt
MANOEUVRE
Armoured
2 tk bde
Mechanised
8 mech bde
1 mech regt
Aviation
3 avn regt
COMBAT SUPPORT
3 arty bde
3 MRL regt
1 SSM bde
3 AD regt
4 engr regt
1 EW regt
1 CBRN regt
4 sigs regt

EQUIPMENT BY TYPE

MBT 1,110: 10 T-84 *Oplot* (development complete); 1,100 T-64; (165 T-80; 600 T-72; 650 T-64; 20 T-55 all in store)
RECCE 600+ BRDM-2
AIFV 1,484: 15 BMD-1, 15 BMD-2; 250 BMP-1; 1,050 BMP-2; 4 BMP-3; 150 BRM-1K
APC 490
APC (T) 15 BTR-D
APC (W) 475: up to 10 BTR-4; 15 BTR-60; 300 BTR-70; 150 BTR-80
ARTY 1,952
SP 733: **122mm** 300 2S1; **152mm** 334: 40 2S19 *Farm*; 270 2S3; 24 2S5; **203mm** 99 2S7
TOWED 595: **122mm** 100 D-30; **152mm** 495: 200 2A36; 165 2A65; 130 D-20
GUN/MOR • 120mm • TOWED 2 2B16 NONA-K
MRL 372: **122mm** 220: 20 9P138; 200 BM-21; **132mm** 2 BM-13; **220mm** 70 9P140 *Uragan*; **300mm** 80 9A52 *Smerch*
MOR 120mm 250: 210 2S12; 40 PM-38
AT
MSL • MANPATS 9K111 *Fagot* (*Spigot*); 9K113 *Konkurs* (AT-5 *Spandrel*); 9K114 *Shturm* (AT-6 *Spiral*)
GUNS 100mm ε500 MT-12/T-12
HELICOPTERS
ATK 139 Mi-24 *Hind*
TPT • Medium 38 Mi-8 *Hip*
AD
SAM • SP 435: 60 9K37 *Buk* (SA-11 *Gadfly*); ε150 9K35 *Strela*-10(SA-13 *Gopher*); 100 2K11 *Krug* (SA-4 *Ganef*); 125 9K33 *Osa* (SA-8 *Gecko*); S-300V (SA-12 *Gladiator*)
GUNS 470:
SP 30mm 70 2S6
TOWED 57mm ε400 S-60
RADAR • LAND *Small Fred*/*Small Yawn*/SNAR-10 *Big Fred* (arty)
MSL • SSM 212: 50 FROG; 90 *Tochka* (SS-21 *Scarab*); 72 *Scud*-B
AEV 53 BAT-2; MT-LB
ARV BREM-2; BREM-64; T-54/T-55
VLB MTU-20

Navy 11,950; 2,000 conscript (total 13,950 incl Naval Aviation and Naval Infantry)

After intergovernmental agreement in 1997, the Russian Federation Fleet currently leases bases in Sevastopol and Karantinnaya Bays and also shares facilities jointly with UKR warships at Streletskaya Bay. The overall serviceability of the fleet is assessed as low.

EQUIPMENT BY TYPE

SUBMARINES • TACTICAL • SSK 1 *Foxtrot* (T-641) with 10 533mm TT
PRINCIPAL SURFACE COMBATANTS 1
FRIGATES • FFHM 1 *Hetman Sagaidachny* (RUS *Krivak* III) with 1 twin lnchr with *Osa*-M (SA-N-4 *Gecko*) SAM, 2 quad 533mm ASTT with T-53 HWT, 1 100mm gun, (capacity 1 Ka-27 *Helix* ASW hel)
PATROL AND COASTAL COMBATANTS 10
CORVETTES • FSM 3 *Grisha* (II/V) with 1 twin lnchr with *Osa*-M (SA-N-4 *Gecko*) SAM, 2 twin 533mm ASTT with SAET-60 HWT, 1 to 2 RBU 6000 *Smerch* 2, 1 76mm gun
PCFGM 2 *Tarantul* II (FSU *Molnya*) with 2 twin lnchr with P-15 Termit-R (SS-N-2D *Styx*) AShM; 1 quad lnchr (manual aiming) with 9K32 *Strela*-2 (SA-N-5 *Grail*); 1 76mm gun
PHG 2 *Matka* (FSU *Vekhr*) with 2 single lnchr with P-15 *Termit*-M/R (SS-N-2C/D *Styx*) AShM, 1 76mm gun
PCMT 2 *Pauk* I (FSU *Molnya* II) with 1 quad lnchr (manual aiming) with 9K32 Strela-2 (SA-N-5 *Grail*) SAM, 4 single 406mm TT, 2 RBU-1200, 1 76mm gun
PB 1 *Zhuk* (FSU *Grif*)
MINE WARFARE • MINE COUNTERMEASURES 5
MHI 1 *Yevgenya* (FSU *Korund*)
MSO 2 *Natya* with 2 RBU 1200
MSC 2 *Sonya* (FSU *Yakhont*)
AMPHIBIOUS
LANDING SHIPS 2
LSM 1 *Polnochny* C (capacity 6 MBT; 180 troops)
LST 1 *Ropucha* with 4 quad lnchr with 9K32 Strela-2 (SA-N-5 *Grail*) SAM, 2 twin 57mm guns, (capacity either 10 MBT or 190 troops; either 24 APC (T) or 170 troops)
LANDING CRAFT 3
LCAC 1 *Pomornik* (*Zubr*) with 2 quad lnchr with 9K32 *Strela*-2 (SA-N-5 *Grail*) SAM, (capacity 230 troops; either 3 MBT or 10 APC (T))
LCU 2
LOGISTICS AND SUPPORT 34
ABU 1 *Shostka*
ADG 1 *Bereza*
AGI 2 *Muna*
AGF 2: 1 *Bambuk* (fitted with 2 quad lnchr with SA-N-5/8 *Grail* SAM (manual aiming)); 1 *Amur* (can also act as a spt ship for surface ships and submarines)
AGS 2: 1 *Moma* (mod); 1 *Biya*

AWT 1 *Sudak*
AXL 3 *Petrushka*
YDT 13: 1 *Yelva*; 12 other
YTM 6
YTR 2 *Pozharny*
YY 1 *Sokal*

Naval Aviation ε2,500

AIRCRAFT 10 combat capable
ASW 10 Be-12 *Mail*
TPT 16: **Medium** 5 An-12 *Cub*; **Light** 10: 1 An-24 *Coke*; 8 An-26 *Curl*; 1 Tu-134 *Crusty*; **PAX** 1 Il-18 *Coot*
HELICOPTERS
ASW 72: 28 Ka-25 *Hormone*; 2 Ka-27E *Helix*; 42 Mi-14 *Haze*
TPT • Heavy 5 Mi-6 *Hook*

Naval Infantry 3,000

FORCES BY ROLE
MANOEUVRE
Mechanised
1 mech inf bde
COMBAT SUPPORT
1 arty bde
EQUIPMENT BY TYPE
MBT 40 T-64
AIFV 75 BMP-2
APC (W) 100: 50 BTR-70; 50 BTR-80
ARTY 90
SP • 122mm 12 2S1
TOWED 36: **122mm** 18 D-30; **152mm** 18 2A36
MRL • 122mm 18 BM-21
MOR 120mm 24 2S12

Air Forces 45,250

Flying hours 40 hrs/yr
FORCES BY ROLE
FIGHTER
5 bde with MiG-29 *Fulcrum*; Su-27 *Flanker*
FIGHTER/GROUND ATTACK
2 bde with Su-24M *Fencer*; Su-25 *Frogfoot*
ISR
2 sqn with Su-24MR *Fencer* E*
TRANSPORT
3 bde with An-24; An-26; An-30; Il-76 *Candid*; Tu-134 *Crusty*
TRAINING
Some sqn with L-39 *Albatros*
TRANSPORT HELICOPTER
Some sqn with Mi-8; Mi-9; PZL Mi-2 *Hoplite*
EQUIPMENT BY TYPE
AIRCRAFT 221 combat capable
FTR 126: 90 MiG-29 *Fulcrum*; 36 Su-27 *Flanker*
FGA 36 Su-24 *Fencer*
ATK 36 Su-25 *Frogfoot*
ISR 26: 3 An-30 *Clank*; 23 Su-24MR *Fencer* E*
TPT 46: **Heavy** 20 Il-76 *Candid*; **Light** 26: 3 An-24 *Coke*; 21 An-26 *Curl*; 2 Tu-134 *Crusty*
TRG 39 L-39 *Albatros*
HELICOPTERS
C2 4 Mi-9
TPT 34: **Medium** 31 Mi-8 *Hip*; **Light** 3 PZL Mi-2 *Hoplite*
AD • SAM 825 S-300PS (SA-10 *Grumble*)/SA-11 *Gadfly*/S-75 Volkhov (SA-2 *Guideline*) (towed)/S-125 *Pechora* (SA-3 *Goa*) (towed)/S-200V *Angara* (SA-5 *Gammon*) (static)/9K37M *Buk*-M1 (SA-11 *Gadfly*)
MSL
ASM: Kh-25 (AS-10 *Karen*); Kh-59 (AS-13 *Kingbolt*); Kh-29 (AS-14 *Kedge*);
ARM: Kh-58 (AS-11 *Kilter*); Kh-25MP (AS-12 *Kegler*); Kh-28 (AS-9 *Kyle*)
AAM • IR R-60 (AA-8 *Aphid*); R-73 (AA-11 *Archer*)
SARH R-27 (AA-10A *Alamo*)

Airborne Forces 6,000

FORCES BY ROLE:
MANOEUVRE
Air Manoeuvre
1 AB bde
2 air mob bde
1 air mob regt
EQUIPMENT BY TYPE
AIFV 98: 35 BMD-1; 63 BMD-2
APC 180
APC (T) 25 BTR-D
APC (W) 155: 5 BTR-60; 150 BTR-80
ARTY 128
TOWED • 122mm 54 D-30
GUN/MOR • SP • 120mm 50 2S9 *Anona*
MOR 120mm 24 2S12

Paramilitary

MVS ε39,900 active

(Ministry of Internal Affairs)
FORCES BY ROLE
MANOEUVRE
Other
4 paramilitary tp
COMBAT SUPPORT
1 (Internal Security) MP tp

Border Guard 45,000 active

Maritime Border Guard

The Maritime Border Guard is an independent subdivision of the State Commission for Border Guards and is not part of the navy.

FORCES BY ROLE
PATROL
4 (cutter) bde
2 rvn bde
MINE WARFARE
1 MCM sqn
TRANSPORT
3 sqn
TRANSPORT HELICOPTER
1 sqn

COMBAT SERVICE SUPPORT
1 trg div
1 (aux ships) gp

EQUIPMENT BY TYPE

PATROL AND COASTAL COMBATANTS 27
PCFT 6 *Stenka* with 4 single 406mm TT
PCT 3 *Pauk* I with 4 single 406mm TT, 2 RBU-1200, 1 76mm gun
PHT 1 *Muravey* with 2 single 406mm TT, 1 76mm gun
PB 13: 12 *Zhuk;* 1 *Orlan* (seven additional vessels under construction)
PBR 4 *Shmel*

LOGISTICS AND SUPPORT • AGF 1

AIRCRAFT • TPT Medium An-8 *Camp;* **Light** An-24 *Coke;* An-26 *Curl;* An-72 *Coaler*

HELICOPTERS • ASW: Ka-27 *Helix* A

Civil Defence Troops 9,500+ (civilian)

(Ministry of Emergency Situations)

FORCES BY ROLE

MANOEUVRE
Other
4 paramilitary bde
4 paramilitary regt

DEPLOYMENT

Legal provisions for foreign deployment:
Constitution: Codified constitution (1996)
Specific legislation: 'On the procedures to deploy Armed Forces of Ukraine units abroad' (1518-III, March 2000).
Decision on deployment of troops abroad: Parliament authorised to approve decision to provide military assistance, deploy troops abroad and allow foreign military presence in Ukraine (Art. 85, para 23); Also, in accordance with Art. 7 of the specific legislation (above), president is authorised to take a decision to deploy troops abroad and at the same time to submit a draft law to the Parliament of Ukraine for approval.

AFGHANISTAN
NATO • ISAF 26

ARMENIA/AZERBAIJAN
OSCE • Minsk Conference 1

CÔTE D'IVOIRE
UN • UNOCI 38; 1 atk hel flt

DEMOCRATIC REPUBLIC OF THE CONGO
UN • MONUSCO 254; 11 obs; 2 atk hel sqn

GULF OF ADEN & SOMALI BASIN
NATO • *Operation Ocean Shield* 1 FFHM

LIBERIA
UN • UNMIL 238; 2 obs; 1 hel sqn

MOLDOVA
10 obs

SERBIA
NATO • KFOR 163; 1 inf coy
OSCE • Kosovo 1
UN • UNMIK 2 obs

SOUTH SUDAN
UN • UNMISS 1; 3 obs

SUDAN
UN • UNISFA 2 obs

FOREIGN FORCES

Russia ε13,000 Navy 1 Fleet HQ at Sevastopol; 1 indep naval inf bde; 102 AIFV/APC (T)/APC (W); 24 arty

Uzbekistan UZB

Uzbekistani Som s		2012	2013	2014
GDP	s	96.7tr	117tr	
	US$	51.2bn	56.5bn	
per capita	US$	1,737	1,895	
Growth	%	8.00	7.00	
Inflation	%	12.06	10.94	
Def bdgt	s	ε2.75tr		
	US$	ε1.46bn		
FMA (US)	US$	2.7m	2.7m	1.15m
US$1=s		1889.24	2078.74	

Population 28,661,637

Ethnic groups: Uzbek 73%; Russian 6%; Tajik 5%; Kazakh 4%; Karakalpak 2%; Tatar 2%; Korean <1%; Ukrainian <1%

Age	0–14	15–19	20–24	25–29	30–64	65 plus
Male	13.0%	5.2%	5.5%	5.2%	18.9%	2.0%
Female	12.3%	5.0%	5.4%	5.1%	19.6%	2.7%

Capabilities

Uzbekistan's conscript-based armed forces are the most capable in Central Asia, and better-equipped than those of its immediate neighbours. Uzbekistan is a member of the SCO, but suspended its membership of the CSTO in mid-2012. It maintains bilateral defence ties with Russia, and relations with Moscow improved following a heads-of-state meeting in the second quarter of 2013. Security issues after the ISAF drawdown from Afghanistan were part of the discussion. As part of an agreement covering transit rights for US and UK military equipment being returned from Afghanistan, the Uzbek armed forces will receive some military equipment, although the type and amount were unclear at November 2013. Air force flying hours are reported to be low, with significant logistical and maintenance shortcomings affecting the availability of aircraft.

ACTIVE 48,000 (Army 24,500 Air 7,500 Joint 16,000)
Paramilitary 20,000

Conscript liability conscription 12 months

ORGANISATIONS BY SERVICE

Army 24,500

4 Mil Districts; 2 op comd; 1 Tashkent Comd

FORCES BY ROLE

SPECIAL FORCES

1 SF bde

MANOEUVRE

Armoured

1 tk bde

Mechanised

11 MR bde

Air Manoeuvre

1 air aslt bde

1 AB bde

Mountain

1 lt mtn inf bde

COMBAT SUPPORT

3 arty bde

1 MRL bde

EQUIPMENT BY TYPE

MBT 340: 70 T-72; 100 T-64; 170 T-62

RECCE 19: 13 BRDM-2; 6 BRM

AIFV 399: 120 BMD-1; 9 BMD-2; 270 BMP-2

APC 309

APC (T) 50 BTR-D

APC (W) 259: 24 BTR-60; 25 BTR-70; 210 BTR-80

ARTY 487+

SP 83+: **122mm** 18 2S1; **152mm** 17+: 17 2S3; 2S5 (reported); **203mm** 48 2S7

TOWED 200: **122mm** 60 D-30; **152mm** 140 2A36

GUN/MOR 120mm 54 2S9 *Anona*

MRL 108: **122mm** 60: 24 9P138; 36 BM-21; **220mm** 48 9P140 *Uragan*

MOR 120mm 42: 5 2B11; 19 2S12; 18 PM-120

AT • MSL • MANPATS 9K11 (AT-3 *Sagger*); 9K111 (AT-4 *Spigot*)

GUNS 100mm 36 MT-12/T-12

Air Force 7,500

FORCES BY ROLE

FIGHTER

1 regt with MiG-29/MiG-29UB *Fulcrum*; Su-27/Su-27UB *Flanker*

FIGHTER/GROUND ATTACK

1 regt with Su-24 *Fencer*; Su-24MP *Fencer* F* (ISR)

GROUND ATTACK

1 regt with Su-25/Su-25BM *Frogfoot*; Su-17M (Su-17MZ) *Fitter* C/Su-17UM-3 (Su-17UMZ) *Fitter* G

ELINT/TRANSPORT

1 regt with An-12/An-12PP *Cub*; An-26/An-26RKR *Curl*

TRANSPORT

Some sqn with An-24 *Coke*; Tu-134 *Crusty*

TRAINING

Some sqn with L-39 *Albatros*

ATTACK/TRANSPORT HELICOPTER

1 regt with Mi-24 *Hind* (attack); Mi-26 *Halo* (tpt); Mi-8 *Hip* (aslt/tpt);

1 regt with Mi-6 *Hook* (tpt); Mi-6AYa *Hook* C (C2)

EQUIPMENT BY TYPE

AIRCRAFT 135 combat capable

FTR 30 MiG-29/MiG-29UB *Fulcrum*

FGA 74: 26 Su-17M (Su-17MZ)/Su-17UM-3 (Su-17UMZ) *Fitter* C/G; 23 Su-24 *Fencer*; 25 Su-27/Su-27UB *Flanker*

ATK 20 Su-25/Su-25BM *Frogfoot*

EW/Tpt 26 An-12 *Cub* (med tpt)/An-12PP *Cub* (EW)

ELINT 11 Su-24MP *Fencer* F*

ELINT/Tpt 13 An-26 *Curl* (lt tpt)/An-26RKR *Curl* (ELINT)

TPT • Light 2: 1 An-24 *Coke*; 1 Tu-134 *Crusty*

TRG 5 L-39 *Albatros* (9 more in store)

HELICOPTERS

ATK 29 Mi-24 *Hind*

C2 2 Mi-6AYa *Hook* C

TPT 79 **Heavy** 27: 26 Mi-6 *Hook*; 1 Mi-26 *Halo*; **Medium** 52 Mi-8 *Hip*

AD • SAM 45

TOWED S-75 *Dvina* (SA-2 *Guideline*); S-125 *Pechora* (SA-3 *Goa*)

STATIC S-200 *Angara* (SA-5 *Gammon*)

MSL

ASM Kh-23 (AS-7 *Kerry*); Kh-25 (AS-10 *Karen*)

ARM Kh-25P (AS-12 *Kegler*); Kh-28 (AS-9 *Kyle*); Kh-58 (AS-11 *Kilter*)

AAM • IR R-60 (AA-8 *Aphid*); R-73 (AA-11 *Archer*); **IR/SARH** R-27 (AA-10 *Alamo*)

Paramilitary up to 20,000

Internal Security Troops up to 19,000

Ministry of Interior

National Guard 1,000

Ministry of Defence

FOREIGN FORCES

Germany 100; some C-160 *Transall*

Table 5 **Selected Arms Procurements and Deliveries, Russia and Eurasia**

Designation	Type	Quantity (Current)	Contract Value	Prime Nationality	Prime Contractor	Order Date	First Delivery Due	Notes
Armenia (ARM)								
A100	MRL (300mm)	n.k.	n.k.	PRC	China Academy of Launch Vehicle Technology	2013	n.k.	–
Azerbaijan (AZE)								
Mi-35M *Hind*	Atk hel	24	n.k.	RUS	Rosvertol	2010	2011	First four delivered Dec 2011; 12 delivered by Aug 2012
Mi-17-1V *Hip*	MRH hel	40	n.k.	RUS	Rosvertol	2010	2010	–
Belarus (BLR)								
Tor-M2 (SA-15 *Gauntlet*)	SAM	12	n.k.	RUS	Almaz-Antey	2011	2011	Second bty delivered Dec 2012; third due in 2013
Yak-130	Trg ac	4	n.k.	RUS	UAC (Irkut)	2012	2015	–
Kazakhstan (KAZ)								
C-295	Tpt ac	2	n.k.	Int'l	EADS (CASA)	2013	2014	Follow on to original 2012 order for two. Part of an eight ac MoU
Russia (RUS)								
Bulava (SS-NX-30)	SLBM	n.k.	n.k.	RUS	MITT	n.k.	2009	In development. For *Borey*-class SSBN
BTR-82A	APC (W)	n.k.	n.k.	RUS	VPK	n.k.	n.k.	–
Buk-M2 (SA-17 *Grizzly*)	SAM	n.k.	n.k.	RUS	Almaz-Antey	n.k.	n.k.	One bde set delivered. May be succeeded by *Buk*-M3
S-400 *Triumf* (SA-21 *Growler*)	SAM	18 bn	n.k.	RUS	Almaz-Antey	n.k.	2007	Five regt deployed by late 2013
S-300V4 (SA-23 *Gladiator/Giant*)	SAM	12	n.k.	RUS	Almaz-Antey	2012	n.k.	Three battalions
Pantsir-S1	AD	n.k.	n.k.	RUS	KBP Insturment Design Bureau	n.k.	2010	Delivery in progress to S-400 regiments
Borey-class	SSBN	3	n.k.	RUS	Sevmash Shipyard	1996	2012	Lead vessel delivered Dec 2012. Second vessel in sea trials; third vessel launched Dec 2012. 16 launch tubes
Borey-A-class	SSBN	5	n.k.	RUS	Sevmash Shipyard	2012	2015	Construction delayed by price dispute. Contract signed in May 2012, although pricing dispute continues and will be reviewed in 2015. 20 launch tubes
Yasen-class	SSN	5	n.k.	RUS	Sevmash Shipyard	1993	2014	Construction of third vessel began Jun 2013. Delayed for financial reasons
Kilo-class	SSK	6	n.k.	RUS	Admiralty Shipyards	2010	2014	First three due for delivery 2014
Lada-class	SSK	3	n.k.	RUS	Admiralty Shipyards	1997	2010	First vessel launched in 2010. Construction on further two boats suspended in 2011 but resumed in 2012/13
Admiral Gorshkov-class	FFGHM	6	US$400m	RUS	Severnaya Verf Shipyard	2005	2013	First-of-class ISD expected Nov 2013 with Northern Fleet
Steregushchiy-class	FFGHM	6	n.k.	RUS	Severnaya Verf Shipyard/ Komosololsk Shipyard	2001	2008	Third vessel delivered to Baltic Fleet May 2013; fourth vessel launched. Two more in build for Pacific Fleet

Table 5 **Selected Arms Procurements and Deliveries, Russia and Eurasia**

Designation	Type	Quantity (Current)	Contract Value	Prime Nationality	Prime Contractor	Order Date	First Delivery Due	Notes
Improved *Steregushchiy*-class	FFGHM	2	n.k.	RUS	Severnaya Verf Shipyard	2011	2015	First-of-class laid down Feb 2012
Admiral Grigorovich-class (*Krivak* IV)	FFGHM	6	n.k.	RUS	Yantar Shipyard	2010	2014	Four vessels in build for Black Sea Fleet. Two more ordered. First ISD expected 2014
Buyan-M-class	FSG	6	n.k.	RUS	Zelenodolsk Shipyard	2010	2013	For Caspian Flotilla. To be fitted with *Kalibr*-NK msl. First and second vessels to commission by end 2013
Vladivostock-class	LHD	2	US$1.2bn	FRA/RUS	DCNS/STX/USC	2011	2014	Contract signed in 2011 for two vessels. A further two vessels are expected
Ivan Gren-class	LST	1	n.k.	RUS	Yantar Shipyard	2004	2013	Launched May 2012. Delivery currently planned for 2013. Up to four more vessels planned
Seliger-class	AGOR	2	n.k.	RUS	Yantar Shipyard	2009	2012	For Baltic Fleet. First vessel commissioned Jan 2013
Igor Belousov-class	AGOR	2	n.k.	RUS	Admiralty Shipyards	2005	2014	R11.5bn contract signed in Nov 2011 for completion. Launched Oct 2012
Admiral Yuri Ivanov-class	AGI	2	n.k.	RUS	Severnaya Verf Shipyard	n.k.	2013	First intelligence vessel to be constructed since the Soviet era. First vessel now scheduled for delivery in Nov 2013 after slippage
MiG-29K *Fulcrum* D	Ftr ac	24	n.k.	RUS	UAC (MiG)	2012	2013	20 MiG-29K and four MiG-29KUB. For navy. First ac in flight test late 2013
Su-30SM	FGA ac	30	n.k.	RUS	UAC (Sukhoi)	2012	2012	Six delivered by late 2013. Order to be complete by end-2015
Su-34 *Fullback*	FGA ac	92	n.k.	RUS	UAC (Sukhoi)	2008	2010	28 delivered by late 2013
Su-35S *Flanker*	FGA ac	48	See notes	RUS	UAC (Sukhoi)	2009	2012	Part of combined order for 48 Su-35S, 12 Su-27SM3 and four Su-30, worth US$2.5bn. 12 delivered by late 2013
An-140	Tpt ac	11	n.k.	UKR	Antonov	2011	2012	Ten for air force, four for navy. Four delivered to air force, one to navy
An-148-100	Tpt ac	15	US$450m	RUS	VASO	2013	2013	First delivery due 2013
Yak-130	Trg ac	55	n.k.	RUS	UAC (Irkut)	2012	2012	To replace current L-39. 30 delivered by late-2013
Turkmenistan (TKM)								
T-90S	MBT	30	n.k.	RUS	UKBTM	2011	n.k.	–
Ukraine (UKR)								
Gaiduck-class	FFGHM	4	UAH16.2bn (US$2.01bn)	UKR	Chernomorsky Shipbuilding	2011	2015	First keel laid down 2011. All vessels expected to be delivered by 2016

Chapter Six

Asia

Across Asia, continuing efforts to strengthen military capabilities have taken place against rising strategic tensions among major powers in the region, including the United States. China's efforts to improve its military capabilities in 2012–13 were wide-ranging and reflected, among other factors, its continued economic growth. Chinese sources also expressed concern over the military dimensions of the US 'rebalance' to the Asia-Pacific, which was widely interpreted – in the region, as well as in Beijing – as a thinly disguised effort to contain and balance China's growing power and strategic extroversion (see p. 206).

While there was much regional and international interest in China's potential use of its growing military power in relation to maritime disputes, the primary focus of the People's Liberation Army (PLA) for force development and operational planning almost certainly remained Taiwan. In October, Taiwan's 2013 National Defense Report highlighted the impact of China's growing military strength on US ability to assist the island should Beijing decide to mount an offensive: indeed, the report claimed that by 2020 China could be in a position to invade and occupy Taiwan. Meanwhile, Taiwan's defence budget was strained by the dual imperatives of military reform (including the establishment of all-volunteer armed forces, scheduled for late 2016) and major procurement programmes. The most important of these has been the upgrade of 145 F-16A/Bs, procured in the 1990s, with new equipment, including active electronically scanned array radars.

China's diplomatic pressure and deployment of maritime paramilitary forces in support of its claim to the Japanese-controlled Senkaku/Diaoyu islands, along with continuing concern in Tokyo over North Korea's nuclear and missile programmes and aggressive behaviour, contributed significantly to a more assertive Japanese posture on security matters, particularly after the landslide election victory in December 2012 of Shinzo Abe's Liberal Democratic Party. The domestic economy was Abe's first priority and extra defence funding for 2013 amounted to a mere 0.8% increase, sufficient only to sustain existing programmes. Nevertheless, the new government continued to stress the 'dynamic defence force' concept, which included the continued reorientation of the Ground Self-Defense Force towards the south-west of Japan, as well as an emphasis on developing amphibious warfare capability. In August 2013, the first of two 27,000-tonne helicopter carriers, the *Izumo*, due for commission in March 2015, was launched. This was Japan's largest naval vessel since the Second World War. Along with the two 18,000-tonne *Hyuga*-class helicopter carriers, the larger vessels will form the core of Japan's four flotillas in the future. Japan's growing interest in amphibious capability was also demonstrated by its participation in *Exercise Dawn Blitz*, in California in June 2013.

South Korea's most pressing security concern remained North Korea, with its Mid-Term Defense Plan 2013–17 emphasising the development of deterrent and defensive systems. President Park Geun-hye, who took office in February 2013, promised a strong reaction to any military provocations from the North, alongside efforts to re-establish dialogue with Pyongyang. In September 2013, the largest military

The ADMM–Plus

The ten members of the Association of Southeast Asian Nations (ASEAN) and eight ASEAN dialogue partners were represented in Brunei in August 2013, when defence ministers (or deputies) came together for the second meeting of the ASEAN Defence Ministers' Meeting–Plus (ADMM–Plus). Although the ADMM–Plus has focused on fostering cooperation in 'lowest common denominator' spheres such as Humanitarian and Disaster Relief (HADR), military medicine and maritime security, even some of its detractors acknowledge that it appears to have fostered closer cooperation among armed forces in the Asia-Pacific. In June 2013, the ADMM–Plus organised a HADR/military-medicine exercise in Brunei, back-to-back with the first ASEAN armed forces HADR exercise; participating countries deployed 3,200 personnel and various platforms. At their August meeting, ADMM–Plus ministers agreed to support practical measures to de-escalate and prevent conflict, such as setting up a hotline to defuse maritime tensions. In future, the ADMM–Plus will meet biennially at ministerial level.

parade in Seoul for a decade provided an opportunity to display new equipment, including the *Hyunmu*-2 ballistic missile and the *Hyunmu*-3 cruise missile. Another key procurement project has been the third stage of the F-X combat aircraft programme, which was prolonged in September 2013 after the air force rejected an advanced version of the F-15 in favour of a new fifth-generation platform competition.

South Korea's defence policy is by no means entirely focused on the Korean Peninsula, however, and wider considerations – including the protection of the country's sea-lanes, rivalry with Japan (including a major dispute over the Dokdo/Takeshima features) and a dispute with China over the Yellow Sea's Socotra Rock – have influenced the development of its navy. In August 2013, Seoul launched its fourth *Son Won-il*-class (German Type-214) submarine; a further five are on order. Other continuing naval procurement programmes include a class of up to 24 FFX frigates and additional *Dokdo*-class helicopter carriers, the second of which is under construction.

Southeast Asian states' defence programmes are smaller than those of Northeast Asia, but some are making serious efforts to enhance capabilities. This is particularly true in Singapore, where the primary focus this year was strengthening the air force. In March 2013, based on a request to the US for weapons and support systems, analysts believe Singapore probably ordered 12 more F-15SG long-range strike aircraft, perhaps indicating replacement of the remaining F-5S fighters. In September 2013, Defence Minister Dr Ng Eng Hen announced the choice of *Aster*-30 (already deployed on Singapore's frigates) as the new upper-tier land-based air-defence system, the upgrading of F-16C/Ds with improved radars and other new systems, and a plan to expand facilities at Changi East air base (while closing the Paya Lebar base). It was apparent that Singapore had postponed its long-anticipated order for the F-35 (probably the F-35B in the first instance); however, Dr Ng said that Singapore continued to evaluate the F-35, and an order still seemed inevitable. Another important programme concerned modernising Singapore's submarine flotilla, with the second *Archer*-class (modernised Swedish A-17-class) boat, *Swordsman*, commissioned in April 2013.

Improving naval and air-force capabilities continued to be important for Vietnam, one of the main contestants of China's claims in the South China Sea. In April 2013, navy personnel began training in Russia on the first of six Project 636 *Kilo*-class submarines ordered in 2009; the boat is due for delivery in November 2013. Also in August, Vietnam continued its incremental air force modernisation by ordering an additional 12 Su-30MK2 combat aircraft from Russia.

Malaysia's government has stressed the importance of maintaining close relations with Beijing, and cabinet ministers have claimed not to be worried by Chinese naval deployments within their country's Exclusive Economic Zone. However, the defence ministry and armed forces have been concerned about the potential for conflict in the South China Sea, where Malaysia is a claimant. Malaysia also watches Indonesian naval development and deployments closely, especially after the two countries had a naval stand-off in June 2009 over ownership of the potentially oil- and gas-rich 'Ambalat block'. Because of these maritime concerns, developing the navy and air force feature strongly in Malaysia's continuing modernisation plans. A decision on the competition for a Multi-Role Combat Aircraft was delayed by the May 2013 general election. Though Defence Minister Hishammuddin Hussein confirmed in September 2013 that the programme would proceed, he declined to say when his ministry might issue a request for proposals.

The Philippines particularly felt the pressure from China's growing power and assertiveness in the South China Sea. However, budgetary constraints limited the scale of the armed forces' modernisation. A framework agreement between the Philippine government and the Moro Islamic Liberation Front in October 2012 promised to bring greater security to the country's Muslim-majority south, but the agreement effectively sidelined other Muslim insurgents. In September 2013, internal discontent within the Moro National Liberation Front erupted when one faction mounted a three-week siege on Zamboanga City. The conflict showed that internal security concerns were likely to remain significant for the armed forces, in parallel with increased emphasis on external defence.

Thailand's defence budget for FY2014 was little changed from the 2013 figure, though this level of funding is apparently sufficient to provide for major procurement projects focused on improving maritime and air defences. There is still an operational requirement for at least three submarines. Though financial constraints have prevented an order for boats, construction of infrastructure, including a submarine squadron headquarters and command training school, is due for completion in 2014. Thai

Australia's defence: continuity or change?

Australia's former Labor government, unseated in the September 2013 election, had placed considerable emphasis on developing Australian Defence Force (ADF) capabilities against the backdrop of unfolding changes in the postures and military capabilities of other powers in the Asia-Pacific. The May 2013 Defence White Paper considered in detail the implications of evolving strategic circumstances, notably the rapid growth of Asian economies, the US rebalance to the Asia-Pacific and enhanced defence cooperation with Australia, as well as the ADF's operational drawdowns from Afghanistan, Timor-Leste and the Solomon Islands. The White Paper emphasised Labor's continuing commitment to deliver core ADF capabilities outlined in the preceding 2009 White Paper, stressing particularly plans to replace the *Collins*-class submarines with 12 new conventional boats and to acquire F-35A combat aircraft. The White Paper also revealed an impending order for 12 EA-18G *Growler* aircraft for the SEAD role. However, doubts remained over Australia's capacity to fund these improvements, particularly after defence-funding cuts were announced in May 2012.

The new Liberal–National coalition government made an election promise to increase defence spending to 2% of GDP (a figure that Labor had also claimed it was aiming for), but beyond a stated commitment to proceed with the F-35A, details of the new government's defence programme were unclear. It appeared possible that it might alter elements of its predecessor's plans in a promised new Defence White Paper, but this was unlikely to be tabled before mid-2014.

naval personnel have also been sent to Germany, South Korea and Spain to study submarine technologies and operations. In September, following the delivery of the last three of 12 *Gripen* combat aircraft, the air force commissioned its *Gripen* Integrated Air Defence System, which also involves two Saab 340 AEW aircraft. In December 2012, Air Chief Marshal Prajin Jantong had announced plans to replace and modernise ground-based radars and communications systems, and to network the air force's new equipment with naval vessels and army units. This was to facilitate future joint operations under the 'Network Centric' plan due for completion in 2014.

In Thailand's far south, attacks by ethnic Malay rebels from the Barisan Revolusi Nasional (BRN) continued, despite a deal in February 2013 to begin peace talks. The agreement, brokered by Malaysia, was soon criticised as a 'dead end' on the grounds that the BRN had little influence over the insurgents, who belonged to a specific militant faction. In addition, Thailand's army was concerned that the talks might lend legitimacy to the insurgents. However, in July the National Security Council was reported to have begun parallel, but secret, talks with other insurgent groups.

Myanmar's large, army-dominated armed forces, the Tatmadaw, remained heavily engaged in internal security operations, particularly against the Kachin Independence Army. Although the government continued to allocate more than 20% of the overall state budget to the Tatmadaw, the defence allocation for FY2013/14 was slightly smaller than in the previous year. However, the Law on Special Funds adopted in 2011 allowed the armed forces to use income from the businesses they control and it was likely that this income grew through exploitation of natural gas and other natural resources.

DEFENCE ECONOMICS

Regional macroeconomics

Growth in Asia remained solid in 2013, although a larger-than-expected slowdown in China's economic expansion (down to around 8% from 10.4% in 2010) adversely affected emerging market supply chains across the region. Economic activity also slowed in India, where supply-side constraints caused 2013 growth to fall to 3.8%, just over one-third of the 10.6% growth rate in 2010. Resilient domestic demand in most states – combined with generally supportive fiscal and/or monetary policies – meant the region was expected to grow by a healthy 5.2% in 2013. Many developing economies grew at rates exceeding 6%, including the Philippines (6.0%), Myanmar (6.5%) and Cambodia (6.7%). By contrast, many advanced regional economies grew by less than 3%, including South Korea (2.8%), Australia (3.1%) and Japan (1.6%). The latter embarked on an ambitious new economic policy in January 2013, called 'Abenomics', after Prime Minister Abe. This centred on monetary easing, flexible fiscal policies and structural reforms aimed at lifting Japan out of the 'liquidity trap' that has resulted in more than two decades of economic stagnation, deflationary pressures and rising debt. Overall, the IMF projected that almost all states in the region would grow by more than 2% in 2013, which continues the positive economic trajectory recently seen in Asia: between 2010 and 2013, Japan was the only country out of 26 regional states to experience economic contraction. Average rates of economic growth in Asia have generally exceeded 5% since 2010, although the rate of expansion has been gradually falling, from 6.7% in 2010 to 4.9% in 2013.

Regional defence spending

Nominal defence spending in Asia has risen by 23% since 2010, from around US$261.7 billion to US$321.8bn in 2013. Much of this increase occurred between 2010 and 2011 (when nominal spending rose by 12% to US$293.1bn), although this mainly reflected the elevated inflation rates and strong currency appreciation that occurred across the region at the time, which served to inflate US dollar totals of regional defence outlays. These pressures abated over 2012 and 2013, dampening nominal increases in defence spending (in US dollar terms), which rose by 5.8%, from US$293.1bn in 2011 to US$309.9bn in 2012, and 3.8% in 2013, to US$321.8bn. Discounting for these exchange-rate and inflationary effects, the rate of real defence-spending increases in the region has accelerated since 2010, rising by 2.0% in 2011, 4.5% in 2012 and 4.7% in 2013. In real terms, Asian defence spending in 2013 was 9.4% higher than it was in 2011, equivalent to a compound annual growth rate of 3%. However, the rate of real regional defence-spending increases has trailed behind regional economic growth: the average rate of regional GDP growth between 2011 and 2013 was 5.4%, whereas the average rate of real defence-spending increases was 3.7% over the same period.

Real defence spending in 2013 rose most quickly in Southeast Asia, by 8.7% overall, with large year-on-year increases in Indonesia (26.5%), the Philippines (16.8%) and Cambodia (10.3%). All countries in Southeast Asia, except Singapore and Timor-Leste, increased real spending in 2013. Vietnam, the Philippines and Indonesia increased outlays on equipment procurement. In December 2012, the Philippines allocated PHP75bn (around US$1.8bn) of extra funding for equipment acquisition over 2013–18, through the armed forces' Capability Upgrade Programme. Indonesia has boosted real defence spending since 2010 by a compound annual growth rate of 12.4%, in large measure to finance a multi-year acquisition programme. Since 2010, real defence spending in Southeast Asia has grown on average at around 6% per annum, and was almost one-fifth higher in 2013 than it was in 2010 (the fastest sub-regional rise across Asia), rising in nominal terms from US$28.3bn in 2010 to US$38.7bn in 2013.

Real defence spending in East Asia also rose rapidly, with real 2013 defence outlays 13.2% higher than in 2010. Real spending increases averaged 4.2% over this time, rising from US$165.7bn in 2010 to US$205.4bn in 2013. East Asia continues to dominate Asian defence spending, accounting for 63.8% of the regional total. It was also the sub-region where some of the largest absolute increases in defence outlays occurred, with 57% of the total real increase in 2013 Asian defence spending accounted for by China (46%), Japan (5.7%) and South Korea (5.2%) (see Figure 10) – the remaining 40% was roughly equally split between Southeast Asia and South Asia. In February 2013, Japan announced the first percentage increase in its nominal defence budget in 11 years, to ¥4.75tr (US$50.9bn), while a month later China revealed that it would continue augmenting nominal defence outlays at the double-digit rate of increase seen for more than a decade (to RMB718bn or US$112bn), which was the largest absolute spending rise in Asia (see p. 209). Real defence spending rose by 2.8% in South Korea, while in Taiwan the defence budget fell by an equivalent proportion.

Real defence spending also rose strongly in South Asia in 2013, with large real increases in Afghanistan (36.5%) and Sri Lanka (13.1%) contributing to a 7.2%

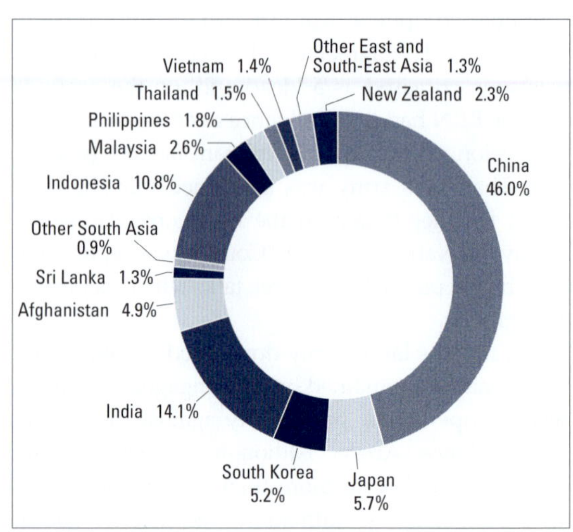

Figure 10 **Composition of Real Defence Spending Increases 2012–13**

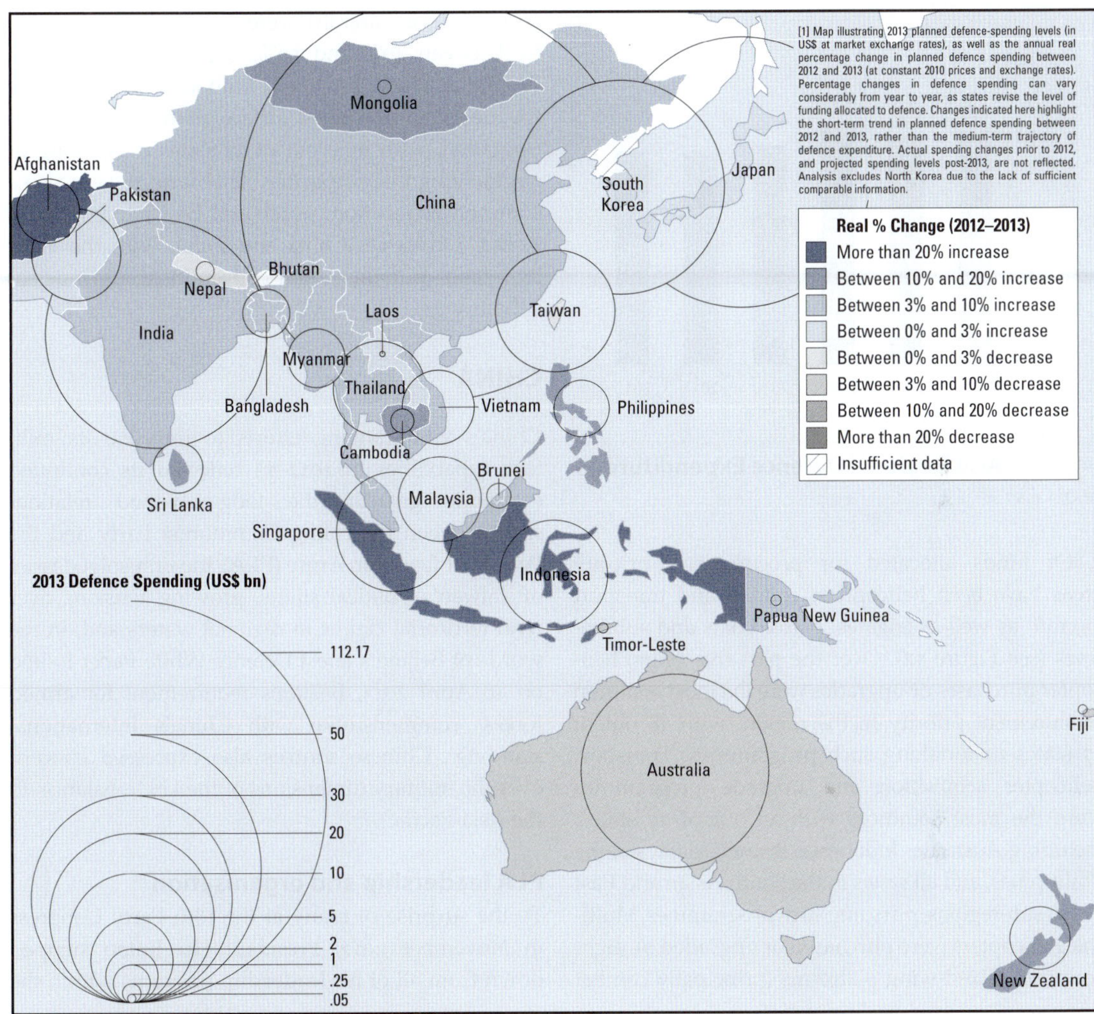

Map 4 **Asia Regional Defence Spending**[1]

overall uplift in defence outlays, although this came after a 2.4% real reduction in 2012 when India revised its initial budgetary allocation for defence downwards. Indian defence-budget growth continued to be constrained by poor economic performance in 2013, with nominal defence spending limited to a 5.3% increase over the original allocation for the previous year. Significant real reduction in spending occurred in Australia (-4.3%), as Canberra cut back on defence capital investment as part of the government's efforts to achieve a federal budgetary surplus. The new government discussed raising spending to 2% of GDP, but its precise defence aspirations remain unclear. In New Zealand, the successful implementation of previous defence austerity measures allowed a 17.2% real increase in the 2013 defence budget.

Regional defence procurement

The composition of defence budgets varies widely across Asian states. Some spend high proportions on personnel, such as Afghanistan (85% of the total budget in 2013) and Fiji (82%), with others such as Australia further down the list at 35–40%. China, meanwhile, is believed to spend around 30%. In between these lie Pakistan (43%), Japan (44%), India (45%) and Brunei (59%), although a lack of defence budget transparency in many other Asian states makes these proportions difficult to evaluate. Nevertheless, it is clear that in recent years a large proportion of budgetary outlays have prioritised equipment procurement, as states recapitalise ageing inventories, invest in new technologies, and reorientate capabilities from internal to external threats.

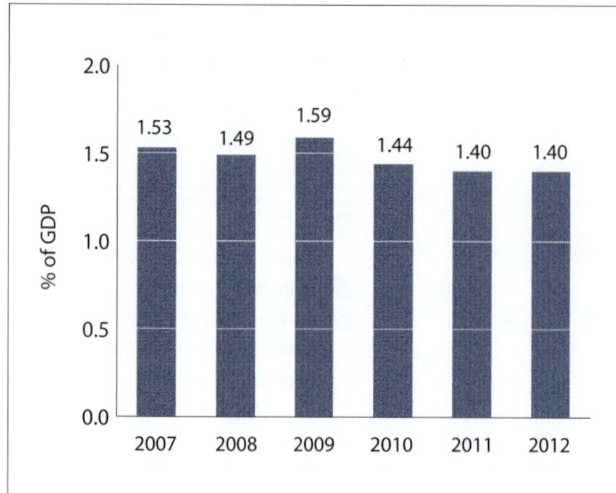

Figure 11 **Asia Regional Defence Expenditure** as % of GDP

Of funds allocated for procurement, priority areas have been helicopters, combat and transport aircraft, as well as frigates, patrol boats and submarines (see Figure 12). Over the past five years, helicopter purchases or upgrades were the most common procurement priority in the region, with 18 out of 27 states undertaking such programmes. Transport helicopter acquisition and upgrade programmes were the most common, with 15 out of 27 states, including Australia, Indonesia, Brunei, Malaysia, the Philippines, and all states in the South Asian and East Asian sub-regions, pursuing such programmes. Multi-role helicopters were purchased or upgraded by eight countries. Fixed-wing platforms (principally combat and transport aircraft) were acquired or upgraded by between 40% and 50% of states, among them Australia, China, India and Indonesia. Frigates were the most common naval surface platform acquired or upgraded, with nine out of 27 states developing or augmenting their capacities. Submarines were also a common acquisition, purchased by Vietnam, South Korea, Indonesia, China and India, with the latter two states pursuing both conventional and nuclear submarines.

CHINA

China's wide-ranging efforts to improve its military capabilities in 2012–13 reflected its continued economic growth, the long-entwined relationship between the ruling Communist Party and the People's Liberation Army (PLA), the unresolved issue of Taiwan's political status, growing tensions over rival territorial claims in regional waters and, in the words of Beijing's latest Defence White Paper issued on 16 April 2013, Beijing's requirement for armed forces 'commensurate with China's international standing'. Chinese sources also expressed concern over the military dimensions of the US 'rebalance' to the Asia-Pacific.

PLA leadership and organisation

To the surprise of many at the 18th Party Congress in November 2012, President Hu Jintao stepped down from all of his leadership positions within the

Figure 12 **Asia: Selected Procurement & Upgrade Priorities Since 2009**[1]

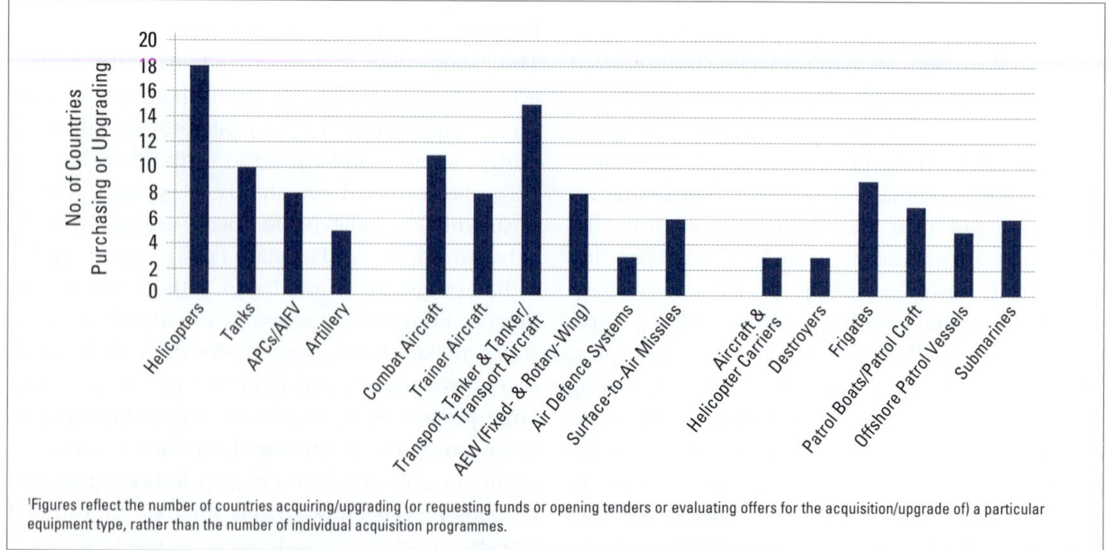

[1]Figures reflect the number of countries acquiring/upgrading (or requesting funds or opening tenders or evaluating offers for the acquisition/upgrade of) a particular equipment type, rather than the number of individual acquisition programmes.

Chinese Communist Party, including the chair of the Central Military Commission (CMC). The CMC is the supreme military decision-making body in China, commanding the PLA and the paramilitary People's Armed Police (PAP). It is the nerve centre of the armed element of the Communist Party. Like the civilian party leadership, it is subject to an overhaul at the Party Congress every five years. With a chairman, two vice chairmen and a further eight members, the CMC commands the four general headquarters of the PLA: the General Staff, Political, Armament and Logistics departments. The commission also directly controls the Ministry of Defense, the military area commands and the navy, air force and 2nd Artillery HQ.

Gaining control of the CMC at the start of his leadership, Hu's successor Xi Jinping has set about a campaign of political resilience within the armed forces, promoting a cohort of officers from the PLA's political commissariat. This may reflect the rising influence of the General Political Department. Xi promoted the commanders of the Nanjing and Guangzhou military areas to General in August. The remainder of the promotions all included political commissars; later Xi promoted more senior political officers serving with the PLA's Hong Kong garrison.

White Paper

Entitled 'The Diversified Employment of China's Armed Forces', the April 2013 Defence White Paper differs from previous versions by taking a subject-based rather than a systematic doctrinal approach and dispensing with much formulaic jargon. The media were most interested in revelations on PLA infrastructure, however, perhaps more notable is the way its authors have tried to incorporate some of the concerns driving the strategic debate in China over the US rebalance to the Asia-Pacific. The paper could be described as a reaction to increased rivalry between China and its neighbours in the last two years and is perhaps reflective of the change in leadership; there has been speculation that it bears the hallmarks of Xi's influence within the CMC as vice chair, before Hu Jintao stepped down. Japan is described as 'making trouble' over the Senkaku/Diaoyu territorial dispute and the US military rebalance makes the regional situation in Asia more tense, according to the document. Echoing Hu's discourse on the historic mission of the PLA a decade ago and reflective of China's drive to become a major maritime power, the paper emphasises the need for blue-water naval capabilities in protecting China's sovereignty, sea lines of communication and maritime resources.

Armed forces

In the latest phase of the PLA's **ground forces** restructuring, eight of the nine remaining armoured divisions have been broken up, and two regiments from each used as the basis for 16 new brigades – eight armoured and eight mechanised. One of the new mechanised brigades has been designated the PLA's first dedicated OPFOR formation. By contrast, the mechanised infantry divisions – and the Beijing-based 6th Armoured Division – remain untouched; these unreformed formations will continue to provide an insurance policy of sorts for the PLA as it gradually adapts to a brigade-based structure. These organisational changes have also seen a considerable redistribution of new and existing equipment in an attempt to standardise tank, armoured vehicle and artillery holdings in the new brigades. Surplus armoured vehicles have been used to upgrade some previously motorised brigades to light mechanised status. Armoured vehicle production appears to have settled into two streams, with the high-end Type-99A MBT, Type-04A AIFV and Type-09 APC being built in smaller numbers for select units, and the Type-96A MBT, Type-86A AIFV and Type-92 APC allocated to the rest. Given the scale of the task, it is likely that the ageing Type-59 MBT and Type-63 APC will continue to form a substantial part of the PLA's AFV inventory for some time. The appearance of a new light tank, which seems to be a combination of Type-99A-style turret with a smaller chassis and main gun, could herald the final retirement of the Type-62.

The PLA had also begun to address its long-standing deficiency in rotary lift. Continuing production of the Z-10 and Z-19 attack helicopters, and the Z-8B transport helicopter, has allowed the expansion of several aviation regiments into full brigades with larger inventories.

The **PLA Navy** (PLAN) is undergoing a qualitative revolution in its equipment as Beijing moves away from the last two decades of 'leap-frog' shipbuilding development. This allowed China to develop technically without the expense of mass producing different classes. For instance, four classes of vessels were built with just one or two ships each. Now, China appears to be increasingly satisfied with the quality of its vessels, with six of the Type-052C destroyer built, and three of the new Type-052D ships already launched in 2013, with the class likely to exceed the Type-052Cs in number. The Type-052Ds constitute a significant capability increase. While there has been little change to hull design, the new variant includes further development of the *Dragon Eye* radar and a 64-cell VLS that will allow for the deployment of anti-air, anti-ship and even land-attack cruise missiles. Meanwhile, the littoral patrol fleet is being overhauled, with the rapidly produced new Type-056 corvette replacing the outdated Type-037 patrol craft, in a bid to fill the anti-submarine warfare gap that has long plagued the PLAN.

In sub-surface capabilities, China continues to develop its strategic deterrent, but continuing difficulties with the JL-2 SLBM and the sclerotic production of nuclear-powered submarines means progress on new submarine designs is slow. Despite widespread speculation about a new-generation Type-095 nuclear attack submarine and Type-096 ballistic-missile submarine, including in the annual Pentagon report, there has been no sign yet of these boats. Rather, there has been an evolution in design of the Type-093, with one modified Type-093A in the water. A new class of conventional submarine, the Type-032, was launched in 2010 but only confirmed in 2013. Although it is probably a single-ship ballistic-missile test bed, the Type-032 reflects the trend towards indigenisation of submarine production within China, albeit strongly influenced by the Russian submarines purchased previously.

A naval aviation platform is in early production in Shanghai. This may be a second aircraft carrier (and the first to be built in China) or a large amphibious assault vessel. From available imagery, its dimensions seem smaller than the *Liaoning*, making it difficult to assess whether Beijing is trying to develop its indigenous carrier production with a scaled-down version, or it is starting production of a new landing helicopter dock that has also been offered to Turkey. The *Liaoning* anchored at its new home port near Qingdao in early 2013, and embarked on its third set of sea trials for the year in August 2013, including more J-15 deck landings. The tempo of tests has reduced since the *Liaoning*'s commissioning in 2012, but duration and complexity have increased.

Developments in PLA training

Over the past 15 years, PLA units have undergone major structural changes and received significant amounts of new equipment. A new doctrine has also been introduced, emphasising joint operations using all units, with both old and new equipment, and integrating new capabilities from all services. Missions have expanded from the mainland and the coast to well beyond. The PLA has focused on attracting better-educated personnel and is building a professional NCO corps. These developments require realistic unit training so personnel are able to command, execute and sustain modern operations; they will also likely require extra funding in future military budgets, unless the force is substantially reduced in size.

Unit training in all services has increased in intensity and tempo under the slogan 'train as you fight and fight as you train'. Force-on-force, confrontational training is now common. Much training remains experimental, seeking to improve 'warfighting capabilities based on information systems', according to China's 2013 White Paper. Training is constrained, however, because most units still use a mix of old and new equipment and because the PLA has not conducted an external campaign for more than 30 years. According to domestic media reports, PLA leaders have seen improvements on previous capabilities, but recognise that their services lag considerably behind most advanced armed forces.

The army has conducted dispersed, transregional operations within China, incorporating support from naval, air force and non-nuclear Second Artillery assets. It seeks to improve the integration of special operations, helicopter, UAV and electronic warfare in its manoeuvre and firepower capabilities. Exercises have displayed the ability to deploy multiple divisions and brigades within China, but not significantly further beyond its borders. The navy has doubled the number of exercises it undertakes, in the past five years taking its surface task forces farther out to sea than before. Extended submarine patrols are also reportedly increasing. Complex, multi-service exercises such as the Jinan Military Region's 'Joint' exercises between 2006 and 2010 have improved area air-defence and anti-submarine capabilities, as have new ships and aircraft. Meanwhile, coastal-defence operations by land-based anti-ship cruise missile, aviation, surface and sub-surface forces are practised routinely. The aircraft carrier *Liaoning* will likely first concentrate on developing its own capabilities before it joins surface task forces for more distant operations. Air force exercises have become larger, combining multiple aircraft types over dispersed areas, including operations over water. Pilots are being given greater freedom of manoeuvre and units are developing procedures for complex operations such as aerial refuelling and airborne command-and-control.

Exemplifying the transition underway in Chinese **military aerospace**, 2013 saw final deliveries of two older fighter types designed originally in the 1950s. Production of the Q-5 *Fantan* and the J-7 has come to an end; the former was based on the Mikoyan MiG-19 *Farmer*, the latter on the MiG-21 *Fishbed*. The types have been mainstays of the PLA Air Force (PLAAF) fleet for decades. At the same time, Beijing continued flight testing two future combat aircraft with low-observable characteristics. Two prototypes of the Chengdu J-20 heavy fighter continued in flight test, as did the single example of the smaller Shenyang J-31.

Imagery of J-20 flight trials in 2013 showed the captive carriage of at least two new air-to-air missile (AAM) designs. An imaging infrared-guided AAM, possibly linked to the PL-10 designation, was seen carried in one of the aircraft's two shoulder bays. A larger active-radar guided weapon, photographed in the main internal weapons bay, was first seen carried by a J-11B and may be associated with the PL-15. The exact developmental status of both AAMs remained unclear as of late 2013. While this imagery supports the supposition that a key task of the J-20 is air superiority, it does not rule out an air-to-surface role. It may be that strike weapons will simply be earmarked for test and integration after the AAM element of the programme.

Along with new indigenous designs, and upgrades to in-service combat aircraft – such as the Chengdu J-10 and the Shenyang J-11 family – China turned again to Russia for combat aircraft. Beijing last placed an order with Sukhoi in 1995 (for the Su-27); 2013 saw continuing negotiations for a batch of Su-35 *Flankers*. The Su-35 is the latest iteration of the basic Su-27 *Flanker*, boasting improved avionics, radar, weapons and engines. There has been speculation that the deal may have been prompted by China's continuing difficulty in developing military turbofan engines to a level suitable for its latest generation of airframes, and its desire to have as advanced an engine design as possible.

The Xian aircraft firm is also undertaking test flights of the prototype of its Y-20 heavy transport aircraft. Should it enter service in significant numbers, this type will improve markedly the air force's ability to support long-range power-projection operations.

Defence economics

Macroeconomics

Chinese economic growth in 2012 slowed to its lowest level in 13 years, down to 7.8%, from 9.3% in 2011, due to deterioration in the external economic environment and weakened internal demand. Measures undertaken to cool economic overheating in 2011 – including a property-market bubble – such as the tightening of monetary policy and restrictions on the purchase of investment property, had been effective in stabilising prices. House prices settled and the 2.6% inflation rate seen in 2012 was less than half the 5.4% of 2011. However, these measures also resulted in a decline in real estate investment across the country, which acted as a drag on overall economic activity. Nonetheless, lower inflation combined with salary and pension increases to boost real income across the country: according to the Asian Development Bank, real income grew on average by 9.5% in urban areas and 10.7% in rural areas. Consequently, consumption exceeded investment expenditure in 2012, supporting the government's continued attempts to move the economy away from an export-orientated model, towards greater domestic demand.

With inflation in check, the central bank was able to continue with the expansionary actions it first commenced in late 2011, and in 2012 it engaged in open market operations, on top of cutting both interest rates and reserve ratios. However, strong growth in credit issuance and non-traditional lending sources (such as bank acceptance bills) resulted in a disproportionate rise in liquidity and indebtedness, particularly at the local government level. This meant that by early 2013 the central bank had begun to taper off some of its liquidity injections. More generally, in 2012 China embarked on a gradual, multi-year policy of capital account, interest rate and exchange rate liberalisation, as part of the central government's aims of advancing renminbi internationalisation and rebalancing the economy towards consumption-led growth. These measures contributed to the renminbi's appreciation in 2012, by an average of 2.4% against the dollar and 10.6% against the euro.

Defence spending

On 5 March, China released its 2013 defence budget. It was set at RMB718bn (US$112bn), an increase of 10.7% over 2012. Over the past decade, China has seen a rapid acceleration in its official defence-spending levels (see Figure 13), with rates of increase comparable to the expansion of the Chinese economy. Additionally, as noted each year in *The Military Balance*, official Chinese defence budget figures probably underestimate true defence spending. Although official figures include personnel, operations and

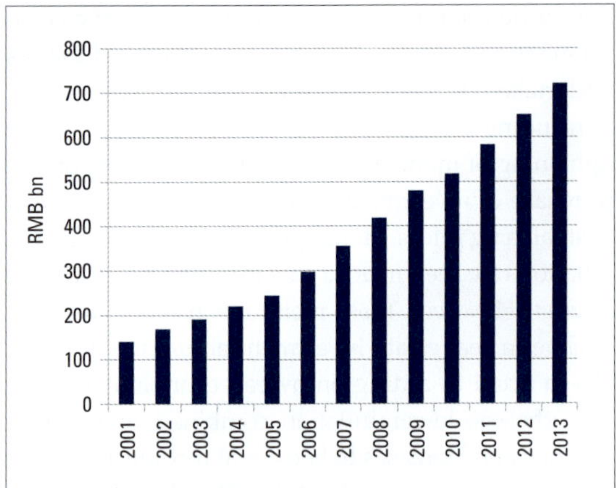

Figure 13 **Official PLA Budget 2001–13 (RMB bn)**

equipment expenditure, it is widely held that other military-related expenditures are omitted, such as R&D and overseas weapons purchases. A fuller account of China's true military spending levels should also include funding allocated to the People's Armed Police (PAP). If estimates of these extra items are included, Chinese defence spending typically rises to about 1.4 to 1.5 times official figures.

However, the after-effects of the financial and debt crises that in 2008 hit advanced Western economies, China's main export destination, call into question Beijing's export-orientated industrial growth model. China's announced growth target for 2013 is, at 7.5%, lower than the 2012 figure. Unless China can decouple from advanced economies and successfully rebalance towards a domestic-demand-driven model, its GDP growth – and by extension, its defence spending growth – will in part continue to be constrained by the ill-health of advanced economies. Chinese real defence spending growth rates may have started to fall in the five years since the crisis. In 2009–13, average real defence-spending growth was 7.6% per annum, compared to an average 10.4% per annum in the five years before the crisis (2003–07) (see Figure 14).

Economic development & defence industries

Increased funding is not the only way in which China's broader economic development has shaped its defence economy. For example, the sustained success of economic reforms meant that by the late 1990s these were being applied to China's protected state monopolies – including those in the defence sector – to reorganise them along more corporate structures and create new competition-based frameworks. Since the mid-2000s, state-owned defence firms have tapped China's developing domestic financial markets for alternative sources of funding through bond issuance and privatisation. Additionally, China's integration into global trade and production networks has increased the potential for spillover effects from civilian to military sectors. This provided opportunities for the closer integration of state-owned firms with the country's growing civilian and military R&D apparatus.

Figure 14 **China Real GDP & Defence Budget Growth (%)**

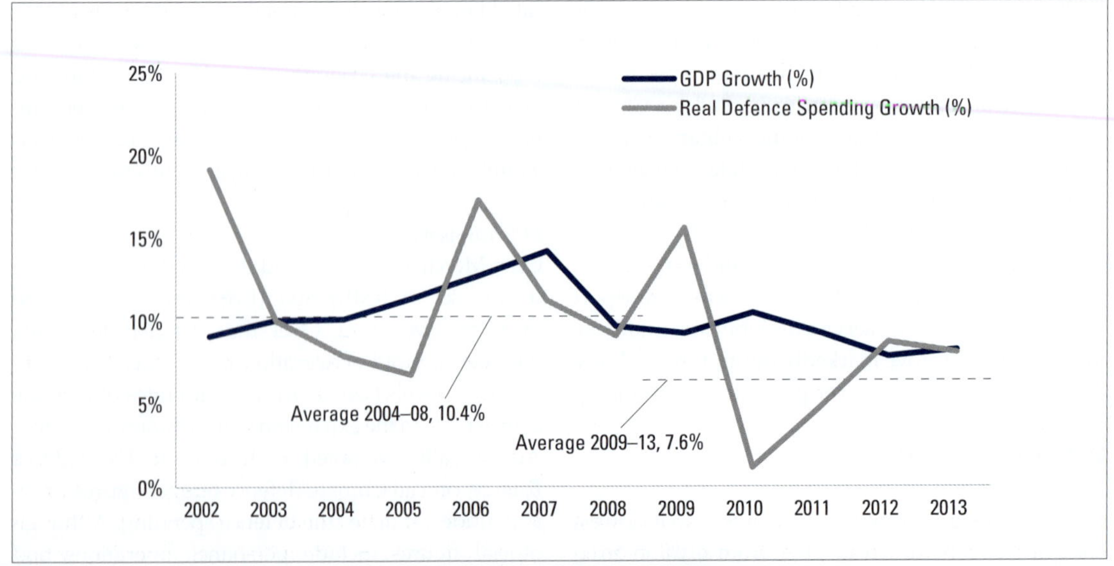

Privatising state-owned defence industries

Despite a rising defence budget, Chinese officials often assert that inadequate investment funding has constrained the growth of the defence sector and the pace of technological progress. So instead of relying solely on relatively limited PLA procurement budgets and the small proportion of state defence conglomerate profits that are reinvested in R&D, since the mid-2000s the authorities have encouraged defence firms to tap into China's growing financial markets for the capital they need to boost R&D. The practice of 'financial repression' in China for much of the 2000s (real interest rates on bank deposits moved from 1.52% in 2002, to -4.08% in 2007, to -7.28% in 2008) meant that there has been a ready pool of capital for most of the past decade. Secondary effects of this process included improved market competition and market discipline within the defence sector.

To facilitate the listing of defence companies on stock exchanges, SASTIND (China's defence industry regulator) released a set of policy requirements in 2007 regulating defence-sector initial public offerings, private placements, bond issuance and bank lending. By 2013, more than 70 defence firms had been listed on exchanges; around one-third were subsidiaries of AVIC, China's state-owned military aerospace monopoly, which had aimed to list 80% of all its assets by 2012. The government had intended that state defence conglomerates be restructured as shareholding entities by 2013, but market turbulence accompanying the financial crisis increased investor risk-aversion. Instead, defence conglomerates took advantage of China's major economic stimulus package unveiled in late 2008 (see *The Military Balance 2012*, p. 214), raising capital through borrowing from and issuing corporate debt to the state-owned banking sector. By 2013, only around 25% of the ten largest defence conglomerates' total assets (estimated at RMB2tr, or US$312.6bn) had been privatised.

Expansion of this process is an important aspect of the current 12th Five-Year Plan (2011–15); according to the government's 2010 'Guiding Opinions' document on defence industrial development, structural reorganisation of defence conglomerates was to be completed by 2015. Additional guidelines were issued in July 2012, aimed at augmenting the involvement of private capital in the defence sector. Diversifying and increasing R&D funding has been a major driver in opening capital markets to the defence sector, but it is also intended to increase market discipline and competition between these firms. As part of the listing process, they have to undertake reforms to increase transparency in order to comply with stock exchange listing and update requirements. Once listed, firms would be scrutinised and compared against each other by market analysts, the results of which would be reflected in their share prices, thereby providing an independent indicator of the firms' performance and further incentivising the adoption of best practices. Increased competition is also a likely benefit of this process, as successful private civilian firms are better able to access capital to diversify their operations into the defence arena. It would also boost competition within the existing R&D sector around securing seed capital from venture capital funds, on top of the new civilian entrants to the defence R&D sector.

Integrating R&D sectors to boost dual-use spillovers

China's integration into global trade and production networks has increased the potential for spillover effects from civilian to military sectors. Since 2007 a particular emphasis has been placed on improving civil–military integration (CMI), and the removal of barriers separating the defence Research, Development, Testing and Evaluation (RDT&E) system from the broader civilian RDT&E sector. CMI is the process of integrating the defence and civilian industrial bases, such that manufacturing processes and facilities, among others, can be used for both military and civilian commercial purposes. In its most basic form, it involves the direct use of mature, commercial off-the-shelf items in military systems, allowing armed forces to use key civilian technological advances – for instance in such areas as information technology, communications, microelectronics and sensors.

More complex approaches to CMI include varying degrees of collaboration (from partial cooperation through to combined activities in shared facilities) between government agencies, state defence conglomerates and civilian entities, in areas such as dual-use R&D and the maintenance of military equipment and facilities. Most broadly, CMI could involve both the military and civilian elements of an industrial sector using the same set of R&D activities, technologies and production processes for both military and commercial product development. Until the mid-1990s, much of China's CMI was from the military sector to the civilian sector. As the authorities began placing less priority on defence spending in the 1980s and 1990s, defence conglomerates increasingly branched out into civilian commercial activities.

However, this was targeted at the low-value, basic production-and-assembly end of the technology spectrum, leading to few benefits for defence industries in terms of, for instance, improved design capabilities. So while there was 'spin-off' from the defence sector, there was little 'spin-on' from the civilian sector. As a consequence, the 10th Five-Year Plan (2001–05) placed less emphasis on the use of defence-sector facilities for civilian output, and more stress on the development of dual-use civil-to-military 'spin-on' technologies, notably in areas like IT, microelectronics and materials.

Nonetheless, the complexity of the technologies involved means that CMI is hard to achieve, and a major effort is under way to develop an institutional framework to enable CMI development. A Civil–Military Integration Promotion Department was created in 2008 and given the task of establishing a coordinated and integrated system of technical standards for both military and civilian products. Meanwhile, SASTIND was absorbed by the civilian Ministry of Industry and Information Technology (MIIT), and defence R&D institutes, CMI bureaux and defence industry offices across China, right down to the provincial level, are being reassigned to civilian economic management departments.

The PLA's General Armaments Department and SASTIND are also increasing the funds available for military and dual-use research activities. Various measures have been enacted to further incentivise CMI, including the use of preferential tax policies favouring CMI-related R&D activities. Selected cities (such as Mianyang in Sichuan Province) with clusters of industries demonstrating CMI promise (such as composites and aviation) have been classed as CMI Science and Technology zones. Expert testimony before the US–China Economic & Security Review Commission in May 2010 said that a goal was a new geographical structure for civilian aviation, based on specialised clusters in South and East China and another centred on Tianjin. More specialised areas were a commercial engine base in Shanghai and 'generation aviation operations' at Zhuhai. 'These new clusters', the testimony continued 'are intended to complement the existing military-intensive aviation industrial complex that was built in the Maoist era and is concentrated in the country's interior, such as Chengdu, Xian, Shenyang, Guizhou, and Harbin.'

But as noted above, the complexity of implementing CMI means it will be some time before this reform starts to yield results. Much of the civilian sector consists of small and medium-sized enterprises that have only a limited ability to access capital to finance their activities. This inhibits these firms' willingness and ability to undertake more risky projects. Greater maturity and consolidation within the civilian sector itself could assist the process, along with institutional and legal mechanisms to protect and enforce intellectual property rights.

INDIA

India is paying close attention to the withdrawal of most US and allied forces from Afghanistan and the effect this may have on regional security. Other security concerns range from internal and regional counter-insurgency issues to the rise of China, as well as managing long-standing tensions with Pakistan. All of these have contributed to continuing efforts to upgrade and modernise the country's armed forces and their equipment inventories.

Armed forces

While counter-insurgency and domestic security remain important, the **army**'s re-equipment programme reflects an abiding concern that the armed forces need to be able to wage high-intensity land warfare against a state adversary. Heavy armour units are being equipped with Russian T-90S, while the previously purchased T-72 is being upgraded. Testing of the Mark II variant of the nationally-developed *Arjun* MBT continued during 2013. The army is also trying to replace many of its tactical air defences, the bulk of which remain Soviet-era missile systems. Efforts to acquire a light reconnaissance and surveillance helicopter to replace the army's ageing *Chetak* fleet led to the selection of the AS550 *Fennec*, though no contract had been signed by the end of 2013.

As the **navy** increasingly sees itself as a bastion against China's growing presence in the Indian Ocean, it is also embarked on a procurement drive. On 12 August, Delhi launched the hull of its first indigenous aircraft carrier, the 40,000-tonne INS *Vikrant*. Building its own carrier before China has been a point of pride for a service troubled by a heavily delayed and costly programme to acquire a former Soviet carrier from Russia – which was finally due to launch in November 2013 as the INS *Vikramaditya*, almost a decade after her purchase.

After nearly 30 years of development, India also took a significant step towards becoming only the sixth country to design, build and operate a nuclear-powered ballistic-missile submarine when the reactor on its first indigenous SSBN, INS *Arihant*, was activated on 10 August. When in operation, the boat will carry a short-range ballistic missile, the K-15 *Sagarika*.

But the broader submarine programme suffered a blow on 14 August when the recently upgraded conventional submarine INS *Sindhurakshak* sank in a Mumbai dockyard after an on-board explosion. The *Kilo*-class boat had just undergone a US$80m two-and-a-half year refit in Russia, following a fire in 2010, and analysts thought it highly unlikely that it would be recovered. The sinking came amid delays to the purchase of six French *Scorpene* submarines, with deliveries planned to start in 2012 now pushed back to 2016. In a scathing 2013 report, the comptroller and auditor general noted that the navy was holding just '67% of the submarines envisaged in its 1985 Maritime Perspective Plan' and that 'the average operational availability between January 2002 and December 2006 of the existing boats was as low as 48%'.

Programmes to deliver new frigates, destroyers and offshore patrol ships are transforming the navy's surface capabilities. Naval air power is being bolstered by the first deliveries of the P-8I anti-submarine warfare and maritime patrol aircraft, and by the introduction into service of the MiG-29K combat aircraft (which will form the fixed-wing complement of the INS *Vikramaditya*). Because of rivalry with China, ambitious naval procurement is likely to continue. However, delivery problems will continue to blight the navy's operational readiness and prestige.

Air force upgrade

India's **air force** is due to upgrade or replace the bulk of its combat-aircraft fleet over the next ten years. Much of this ongoing modernisation is being driven by air-power developments in China and, to a lesser extent, in Pakistan. However, it is causing substantial challenges in managing the number of procurement projects, including infrastructure upgrades. It also means sustaining some aircraft types well beyond their original lifespan.

By the third quarter of 2013, the defence ministry had still to conclude an agreement with Dassault to buy 126 *Rafale* to meet the air force's long-running Medium Multi-Role Combat Aircraft (MMRCA) requirement. The aircraft will enter service no earlier than 2017, at least three years behind the target date of 2014 for an already-proven, foreign-designed platform. Even when the MMRCA selection enters service, and the air force completes the acquisition of further Su-30MKI *Flankers*, squadron strength could fall further because of the retirement of other types.

The MMRCA delays are relatively minor when compared to the ongoing challenge of bringing the Hindustan Aeronautics (HAL) *Tejas* light combat aircraft into the inventory. This indigenous fighter aircraft is edging towards service entry, though with little apparent enthusiasm from the air force or navy. The *Tejas* project is not only of great importance to the aerospace industry; with HAL state-owned, it also remains an issue of national prestige. Cost overruns and development delays on other HAL projects are of concern to senior officers. HAL is intended to be the lead on final assembly of the MMRCA and on the air force's Fifth Generation Fighter Aircraft, a version of the Sukhoi T-50. It is also leading the Advanced Medium Combat Aircraft project, a national industrial project to develop a fifth-generation combat aircraft.

While revamping its combat-aircraft fleet, the air force is also bolstering its airlift capability. Delivery of the Boeing C-17 began in 2013, with a follow-up order to the initial ten still possible. A further six Lockheed Martin C-130Js for special forces were expected to be ordered by the end of the year. For its tanker transport capability, the air force opted for the Airbus A330 Multi-role Tanker Transport in preference to additional Ilyushin Il-78 *Midas* tankers.

Defence economics

After registering a high GDP growth of 9.3% in 2010, the Indian economy slowed, with growth falling in 2012 to its lowest level for a decade (4%). In 2013, it is projected to be a marginally better 5.7%. The government has implemented several market reforms and initiatives in response, including a plan to progressively reduce fuel subsidies, the establishment of a high-level committee to fast-track large projects and relaxing restrictions on foreign direct investment (FDI) in certain sectors. Nevertheless, high inflation (9.3% in 2012 and 10.8% in 2013) and low levels of business confidence continue to constrain growth prospects. India's trade deficit was US$191bn in 2012, and remained under stress in the first quarter of 2013 with a contraction in exports and a rise in imports. The current account deficit reached a record high of 4.8% of GDP in 2012.

Faced with this gloomy economic picture, the government restricted nominal defence budget growth in FY2013/14 to 5.3% at INR2.04tr (US$36.3bn). The allocation for FY2012/13 was also the subject of budgetary reductions. The revised FY2012/13 budget (INR1.79tr or US$33.4bn) was 7.7% lower than the original allocation of INR1.93tr (US$36.2bn). Double-digit inflation means the FY2013/14 defence budget is 2% below the previous year's original allocation in real terms, although it represented a real increase of 6.2% compared to the revised FY2012/13 figure. Depreciation of the rupee has further reduced the Ministry of Defence's purchasing power, a substantial portion of which is spent on foreign procurement and priced in dollars. This comes as the share of 'contractual liabilities' (arising out of contracts already signed) in the armed forces' modernisation budget is rising (96% in 2013/14 compared with 92% in 2012/13), leaving little room for new contracts.

Defence industry

India has built up a vast defence-industrial base and series of research laboratories (see *The Military Balance 2013*, pp. 261–2). Until 2001, when the industry was opened up to both Indian private-sector and foreign companies, India's defence production was confined to government-owned Defence Public Sector Undertakings (DPSUs) and ordnance factories (OFs), which retain a dominant role.

Self-reliance has driven the creation of this defence-industrial base, but the country remains largely dependent on external suppliers for military hardware. In August 2013, the defence minister revealed that India's arms imports had amounted to INR495.9bn (around US$10bn) between FY2010/11 and FY2012/13. This does not include 'indirect' arms imports, such as components and raw materials. According to analysis undertaken by the Institute for Defence Studies and Analyses, between 2006/07 and 2010/11 India's defence self-reliance index varied between 36% and 48%, well below the 70% India had planned to achieve by 2005.

Defence-industrial reform measures

India has implemented a host of initiatives to encourage higher indigenous defence production since its Defence Production Policy (DPP) in January 2011 (see *The Military Balance 2012*, p. 220). The DPP has four broad objectives: achieving 'substantive' indigenous capability in designing, developing and producing armaments; increasing private-sector involvement; enhancing the participation of small and medium enterprises; and expanding the country's defence R&D base. In February 2012, guidelines were released for establishing public-private joint ventures between DPSUs and private firms (see *The Military Balance 2013*, p. 262).

To try to further streamline offset policies, the MoD also announced that, with effect from 1 August 2012, it would allow both technology and equipment transfer as valid offset mechanisms. It detailed the objectives of the offset policy for the first time, including developing an 'internationally competitive' defence industry, enhancing domestic R&D, and creating a 'synergistic' dual-use industrial base. Other modifications to existing policy included extending the banking period for offset provisions to seven years. The new policy also replaced the widely criticised Defence Offset Facilitation Agency with a more powerful Defence Offset Management Wing, now responsible for post-offset contract monitoring and implementation.

To inform domestic companies about capability requirements early in the acquisition process, the MoD in April 2013 released a Technology Perspective and Capability Roadmap. This is based on the armed forces' 15-year Long-Term Integrated Perspective Plan 2012–27, and is intended to help domestic companies make the necessary long-term planning and investment provisions required for product development and production.

Further reforms were unveiled in April 2013 by the Defence Acquisition Council, the MoD's highest decision-making body. Most were formally incorporated in the revised DPP, issued in June 2013. Among other changes, DPP 2013 introduced a 'preferred order of categorisation' that places domestic-orientated procurement categories above import-orientated ones. The armed forces, which are responsible for initiating procurement proposals and suggesting initial sources of procurement, are now required to provide justification for excluding indigenous options. The MoD expects this to increase pressure on procurement authorities to seek Indian solutions first, providing additional impetus to domestic industry. DPP 2013 also simplified the 'Buy and Make (Indian)' procurement category, whereby Indian firms can establish joint ventures with foreign firms. Additionally, DPP 2013 includes measures to simplify the existing 'Make' category, which gives exclusive rights to Indian industry for design and development of 'high-technology complex systems', for which the MoD is committed to share up to 80% of development costs.

Constraints on industry

India's defence industries continue to suffer from low investment in defence R&D, organisational deficiencies, low private-sector participation and a lack of foreign investment. Compared to the US and China, which spend more than 10% of their defence budget on R&D, India's R&D spending – as measured by the Defence Research and Development Organisation (DRDO) – was only 5.2% in FY2013/14. The DRDO's limited budget, along with negligible R&D spending by domestic industry, has constrained India's defence technological progress.

Poor performance also stems from a lack of reform in the state-owned defence-industrial sector. Several high-level committees have suggested DRDO, DPSU and OF efficiency and accountability reforms. For instance, in 2008 the DRDO Review Committee recommended the creation of a Defence Technology Commission, which would lead India's self-reliance efforts by providing policy direction, setting out R&D targets and monitoring indigenous projects, but this has yet to be implemented. Similarly, there has been little progress on the 'corporatisation' of OFs and listing of DPSUs on the stock market (to help accountability and efficiency).

With less experience than DPSUs and OFs, the Indian private sector continues to play a marginal role in the defence sector. Analysts also claim there is an uneven playing field, arguing that the MoD's Department of Defence Production takes an interest in ensuring that DPSUs and OFs have a constant flow of orders, whereas the private sector enjoys no such privileges. Preferential licensing and tax regimes further inhibit meaningful private-sector participation.

By May 2013, cumulative FDI inflows into India's defence industry reached just US$4.94m. Nonetheless, India decided in July 2013 to keep its cap on FDI in defence at 26%, with any increase beyond that to be approved by the Cabinet Committee on Security on a 'case-to-case basis', subject to 'access to modern and state-of-the-art technology'.

NORTH KOREA

Nuclear weapons

The third test of a nuclear device on 12 February 2013 increased North Korea's confidence in the reliability of its nuclear designs, but whether the weapons can be successfully delivered remains unclear. The test produced a yield of 4–8 kilotonnes, larger than the previous tests in October 2006 (0.5kt) and May 2009 (about 4kt). North Korea claimed success in making its nuclear weapons 'smaller, lighter, and diversified', but it could not be ascertained whether 'diversified' meant the latest device was made from highly enriched uranium rather than plutonium as in the previous tests – or perhaps even a combination of the two. The xenon gases detected in Japan two months after the test had deteriorated too much to clarify what fissile material was used. The status of North Korea's enriched uranium also remains unclear. The only clear reference point came when North Korea displayed the plant to a team from Stanford University in November 2010. In August 2013, satellite imagery showed that the roof of the enrichment facility had doubled in size, which could indicate that enrichment capacity has increased.

More is known about the plutonium programme. In April 2013, Pyongyang announced that it would revive the aged reactor that once produced almost all of the country's plutonium, before its cooling tower was destroyed in July 2007 under a now-defunct diplomatic deal. In mid-September, steam from a replacement cooling system indicated the reactor had been restarted. North Korea has enough plutonium from previous production for 4–10 weapons.

Some analysts, including in the US Defense Intelligence Agency, believe that, after working on weaponisation for more than 20 years, North Korea is likely to have the ability to miniaturise and mount a nuclear weapon on its medium-range *Nodong* missiles. These have a range of some 900km if armed with a one-tonne warhead. *Nodongs* have been tested for ten years, but never with a dummy nuclear warhead to test atmospheric re-entry. The consensus of the US intelligence community is that North Korea 'has not yet demonstrated the full range of capabilities necessary for a nuclear armed missile'. Nor could its ageing aircraft penetrate South Korean or Japanese air defences with a nuclear weapon. A nuclear suicide mission by a mini-submarine cannot be ruled out, however.

Missiles

In April 2013, after weeks of threats against South Korea and the US, Pyongyang appeared ready to increase tensions by testing *Musudan* road-mobile intermediate-range missiles. Several of the missiles were transported to a site near Dongham Bay on the east coast. US government sources indicate they might have a range of 4,000km, putting US facilities at Guam in range, but they are more likely to have the 2,400km range of the Soviet systems upon which they were based. Ultimately, because the *Musudan* has not been flight-tested, its capabilities and operational readiness are uncertain. Tensions subsided when the missiles were quietly withdrawn in early May. It is unknown whether this was because of technical trouble or concern over US and South Korean surveillance, or whether it was a political decision to follow advice from Beijing and avoid additional sanctions.

Further threats in spring 2013 included the release of an operations-centre photo purportedly showing missile-strike options against US cities. North Korea is probably five or more years away from being able to produce an intercontinental ballistic missile, even though valuable lessons will have been learnt from the successful December 2012 launch of a satellite by the three-stage *Unha*-3 rocket. The missile programme appeared to have suffered a set-back when construction of the Tonghae rocket launch site on the north-east coast was observed to have stopped in late 2012. Facilities at Tonghae would have been capable of handling missiles larger than the *Unha*. Construction was likely stopped to give priority to the Sohae rocket launch site on the west coast, where the December 2012 launch took place. The Sohae site was also used for rocket-engine tests in spring 2013, possibly for longer-range missiles. If work at Tonghae resumes, the new facilities would not be ready before 2017.

Meanwhile, North Korea's short-range *Scud* missiles pose the greatest threat to South Korea. The North has about 300–500 *Scud*-B and -C variants (with ranges of 300km and 500km respectively). Their diameter is smaller than that of the *Nodong*, which would make it harder to carry nuclear weapons, though they can be armed with chemical agents.

Conventional and asymmetric capabilities

In mid-May North Korea carried out three successive days of tests of improved multiple rocket launchers (MRLs) from the area where the *Musudan* had been observed. First reports claimed a new 300mm rocket was tested. It is more likely, however, that it was a modified 70km-range version of the 60km-range 240mm MRLs that are already in place along the border. The 240mm models supplement North Korea's 107mm MRLs, which have a maximum range of 40km (or 54km when specially equipped). North Korea is estimated to have approximately 5,000 MRLs in total.

Given Seoul's proximity to the border, North Korea's long-range artillery pieces present a threat. They are capable of delivering chemical and biological agents, although it is not known if North Korea's research on biological weapons has resulted in production. North Korea is known to have an active chemical weapons (CW) programme, with probably the third largest CW arsenal in the world. North Korea's asymmetric capabilities also include the world's largest special-operations forces as well as electronic warfare units that are frequently used against South Korean government departments, banks and media outlets through 'distributed denial-of-service' and hacking incidents. Such cyber attacks took place in March and June 2013.

There are some indications that North Korea has assisted Syria in its CW programme. In April 2013, a Libyan-flagged ship – apparently bound for Syria – was intercepted in Turkey carrying gas masks from North Korea, along with arms and ammunition. In 2009, a North Korean ship carrying CW protective clothing to Syria was similarly interdicted. Press reports that North Korea has also sent experts to Syria to assist with synthesising chemical agents and chemical warhead manufacture cannot be confirmed.

Pyongyang continues to update its armoured and mechanised units, replacing Soviet-era T-54 and T-55 MBTs with the locally-produced *Chonma* version of the T-62. North Korea has close to twice as many tanks as South Korea. However, most of North Korea's conventional military equipment is outdated, and although it has nearly twice the number of personnel, chronic shortages of fuel and foodstuffs impede training, operational capability and the readiness of its forces. Military morale may also be affected by the growing marketisation of the economy and pervasive corruption that has weakened the general population's loyalty to the regime.

The poor state of North Korea's equipment came to light after one of its ships, the *Chong Chon Gang*, was intercepted in Panama carrying arms from Cuba, in violation of UN Security Council resolutions. Cuba claimed the equipment, which included two outdated anti-aircraft missile systems, nine missiles and spare parts, two MiG-21 combat aircraft, and 15 MiG-21 engines, was being sent to North Korea for repair and return to Cuba. It appeared more likely, however, that the items, which also included RPG ammunition and conventional artillery in near mint condition, were being sent to North Korea for its own use.

The interdictions in Panama and Turkey were proof of the effectiveness of international sanctions and interdiction measures designed to prevent North

Korea from exporting or importing military goods, although these measures are not watertight, especially for dual-use items. Fuselage parts from North Korea's December 2012 rocket launch, recovered underwater by South Korea, included foreign-procured common commercial products. To avoid interdiction, North Korea has increasingly shipped military exports on DPRK-owned vessels and used non-stop cargo aircraft. According to a 2012 UN report, North Korea 'has continued to provide missiles, components and technology to certain countries including Iran and Syria'. The UN Security Council resolution adopted after the February 2013 nuclear test tightened up several loopholes in previous sanctions, including calling on states to prevent the transfer of any items that the state determines 'could contribute' to North Korea's illicit programmes. Under this unqualified catch-all, China should prevent the further sale of the off-road multi-axle chassis that North Korea used as transporter erector launchers to parade new intermediate-range missiles in April 2012. Although six such chassis were exported, Beijing blocked the sale of four more. Demonstrating a new spirit of compliance with sanctions, in late September 2013, China released a 236-page list of technologies and goods banned for export to North Korea.

Purges and the party

Two weeks before Panama stopped the *Chong Chon Gang*, Kim Kyok-sik, the chief of the general staff of the Korean People's Army (KPA), visited Havana to oversee the shipment. Shortly after the interdiction, he disappeared from public view, replaced by his former deputy, Ri Yong-gil. The sacking of Kim Kyok-sik was but one of a series of unprecedented personnel shifts among North Korea's top brass. In the first 18 months after Kim Jong-un succeeded his father, North Korea had four ministers of defence and four chiefs of the KPA General Staff. The four top military leaders at the time of Kim Jong-il's funeral were all purged within a year. Below them, dozens of other commanders were removed to make room for younger officers, who presumably are more loyal to the new leader. Three generals who were promoted to vice marshall by Kim Jong-un had this title rescinded, seemingly on a whim.

In fact, under Kim Jong-un, the KPA has lost its former dominant position in North Korean politics and its control over revenue-generating enterprises. Instead, the Korean Workers' Party, nearly dormant during part of Kim Jong-il's reign, has reasserted control. Party official Choe Ryong-hae was given top military rank and put in charge of the KPA Politburo. Although Choe himself was among the vice marshalls to lose a star, he remains a key player, as exemplified by his choice as Kim Jong-un's emissary to Beijing in May 2013. Choe is a protégé of the leader's uncle, Jang Song-taek, who is thought to be pulling the strings on personnel and policy.

The military purges have strengthened Kim Jong-un's power base without any apparent signs of having provoked the sort of unrest that could spark a coup attempt. Nor has the emphasis on loyalty led to any noticeable military recklessness. Whether the replacement of senior military officers has any policy implications is unclear. The departed generals were hardliners, but it is difficult to identify generals in North Korea who are not.

The party's renewed dominance over the military could mean a gradual diminution of the *Songun* (military-first) policy that became a national ideology under Kim Jong-il, although it is still accorded reverence. Stripping the armed forces of their economic management role does not necessarily mean a change in emphasis away from military strength and the dominance of the defence sector. The military budget increased in 2013, albeit only slightly. It accounts for about 22% of GDP.

In April 2013, a new national slogan was introduced: *byungjin*, meaning the simultaneous development of the nuclear programme and the economy. But as long as North Korea pursues nuclear weapons, it will remain under international sanctions that preclude the foreign trade and investment needed to lift the nation out of poverty. And the few economic reforms announced under Kim Jong-un have seen limited implementation. While nuclear and missile development has seen success, economic policy directives still rest on exhortations to 'work harder'.

PAKISTAN

Pakistan's armed forces are concerned that the challenge from al-Qaeda and Taliban insurgents could grow after 2014, when ISAF forces end their combat mission in Afghanistan. The US will rely principally on a land route via Pakistan for withdrawing military equipment from Afghanistan, through routes that have proved vulnerable to attack in the past. The Pakistan government is seeking financial compensation for wear and tear on infrastructure along the route, as well as the cost of guarding it.

Since the start of the conflict in Afghanistan in 2001, Pakistan's armed forces have been countering Taliban and al-Qaeda militants across the seven tribal agencies along the Afghan border that make up the Federally Administered Tribal Areas (FATA). Roughly one-third of the army, or 150,000 troops, remains deployed in that region, alongside 30,000 troops of the paramilitary Frontier Corps. About half of all strike and support missions are carried out by AH-1F/S *Cobras* operated by the Army Aviation Corps. The resistance put up by Tehrik-e-Taliban Pakistan and associated groups presents the biggest insurgency-related challenge to Pakistan's army. These long counter-insurgency campaigns, with intensive use of air–ground operations, have led to considerable tactical adaptation in the army and air force.

Foreign defence relations

Pakistan shows no signs of wishing to break off its defence and security relationship with the United States, despite tensions over Afghanistan–Pakistan border incidents, including strikes by US-operated UAVs in FATA. Pakistan has received generous, although sometimes interrupted, US security assistance and economic development aid since 2004, when Washington named it a 'major non-NATO ally'.

Indeed, the US–Pakistan Strategic Dialogue process, which was derailed by several 2011 incidents, was formally resumed after a visit to Islamabad by US Secretary of State John Kerry in August 2013. Relations between the two countries had soured after the US sent special forces to the Pakistani city of Abbottabad in May 2011 to kill Osama bin Laden without notifying Pakistani authorities. They worsened with the later suspension of US military aid. In November 2011, 24 Pakistani soldiers were killed at an army post at Salala near the Afghan border in an engagement by US aircraft, causing the government to close the land route used by ISAF for transporting supplies in and out of Afghanistan. Ground routes were reopened in July 2012 and US security assistance was again approved in principle, although it was not cleared for resumption by Congress until September 2013. (Relations came under further strain in November 2013, with the death of Pakistan Taliban leader Hakimullah Mehsud after a US UAV strike.)

Pakistan is now keen to use the renewed strategic dialogue mechanism for discussions on future US economic and military assistance beyond 2014, when the drawdown from Afghanistan will also end US payments to Pakistan under Coalition Support Fund arrangements. In July–August 2013 the Pentagon told Congress it wanted to transfer two deferred tranches of military aid, of US$295m and US$386m, to Pakistan. In August another two requests amounting to US$705m were made. In October, all of these were approved and allocation was expected to begin in early 2014, to assist in counter-insurgency and general internal security operations.

Two other areas are of interest to Islamabad; firstly, Washington's continued use of UAVs to attack suspected Islamist militants in FATA, notably in North Waziristan where strongholds of the Haqqani militant group have been targeted, and secondly, potential transfers of materiel. Pakistan's armed forces are open to offers of ISAF equipment declared as Excess Defence Articles, to reduce capital expenditure. However, much depends on the type and sustainability of the materiel.

Pakistan's cordial relations with China remain important for military planning and equipment procurement, as well as major domestic infrastructure projects, including operation of the major Chinese-built port at Gwadar. In addition to missile development, defence cooperation has included joint production of MBTs, combat aircraft and major naval vessels, and is expected to continue.

Armed forces

Beijing is working with Pakistan's **air force** to provide some 250 JF-17 *Thunder* multi-role fighter, jointly built by China's Chengdu Aircraft Industries, with final assembly at the Pakistan Aeronautical Complex facility. Forty-five Block 1 aircraft have been delivered. The air force is obviously interested in obtaining China's J-10 fighter but, given IMF strictures and other financial limits, any decision on acquisition is unlikely to be soon. The US completed delivery of 18 new F-16D Block 52s in 2012 and is assisting in an upgrade of older aircraft in Turkey through its Foreign Military Assistance Programme.

Pakistan's **navy** continues to rely on US-supplied P-3C *Orion* aircraft for maritime patrol and anti-submarine warfare. Further co-production with China of *Zulfiquar*-class guided-missile frigates and *Azmat*-class guided-missile corvettes is possible, and there have been reports that Chinese submarines could be acquired after talks for the purchase of German Type-214 submarines stalled over costs. Although the least-funded armed service, the navy is viewed by

Afghanistan

The June 2013 announcement of 'Milestone 13' saw Afghan forces assume military leadership of the campaign against the Taliban. Drawdown of international forces continued, and by mid-year ISAF comprised 87,000 troops, 60,000 of them from the US. Plans for ISAF's combat mission to cease at the end of 2014 were on track, although some forces could remain on training and counter-terrorism duties if the US and Afghanistan finalise a bilateral security agreement.

Well-planned insurgent attacks continued against ISAF bases and prestige targets in Kabul. The Taliban attacked outlying Afghan National Security Forces (ANSF) posts, some of which were temporarily overrun. These attacks were all successfully counter-attacked by the ANSF, usually with few or no NATO ground troops. However, the fighting season saw heavy ANSF casualties, with deaths peaking at 100 per week, double the peak of 2012's fighting season. This reflects both Afghan forces' lead role in the fighting and their lower counter-IED capability and skills. Insider attacks greatly reduced, however.

The ANSF almost reached their planned strength of 352,000, except for a small shortfall in police numbers. There was still reliance on NATO for artillery and air strikes and airborne intelligence gathering, and for help in logistics and administration. NATO's training mission concentrated on building these areas and medical, counter-IED, and intelligence capabilities.

The Afghan Army is probably capable enough to continue to hold the main cities and the key rural areas largely cleared of insurgents. ISAF commander General Joseph Dunford assessed, however, that NATO is 'lagging some years in developing the police', while improvements in the whole machinery of justice, including courts, lawyers and prisons, was further behind. The Afghan Air Force is unlikely to achieve full capability before 2018, due to a shortage of sufficiently educated and literate personnel to fill technical and engineering posts. The service also suffers from corruption.

Once US and NATO troops depart, it is unclear if the Taliban will still be able to rely on the notion that they are fighting to expel 'infidels' from Afghanistan. The Afghan endgame will be greatly influenced by the results of the 2014 Afghan presidential election. The new president will have a key role in endorsing US plans for a residual counter-terrorism mission and NATO's follow-on training and advisory mission, *Operation Resolute Support*.

Map 5 **Afghan Forces Assume Security Lead**

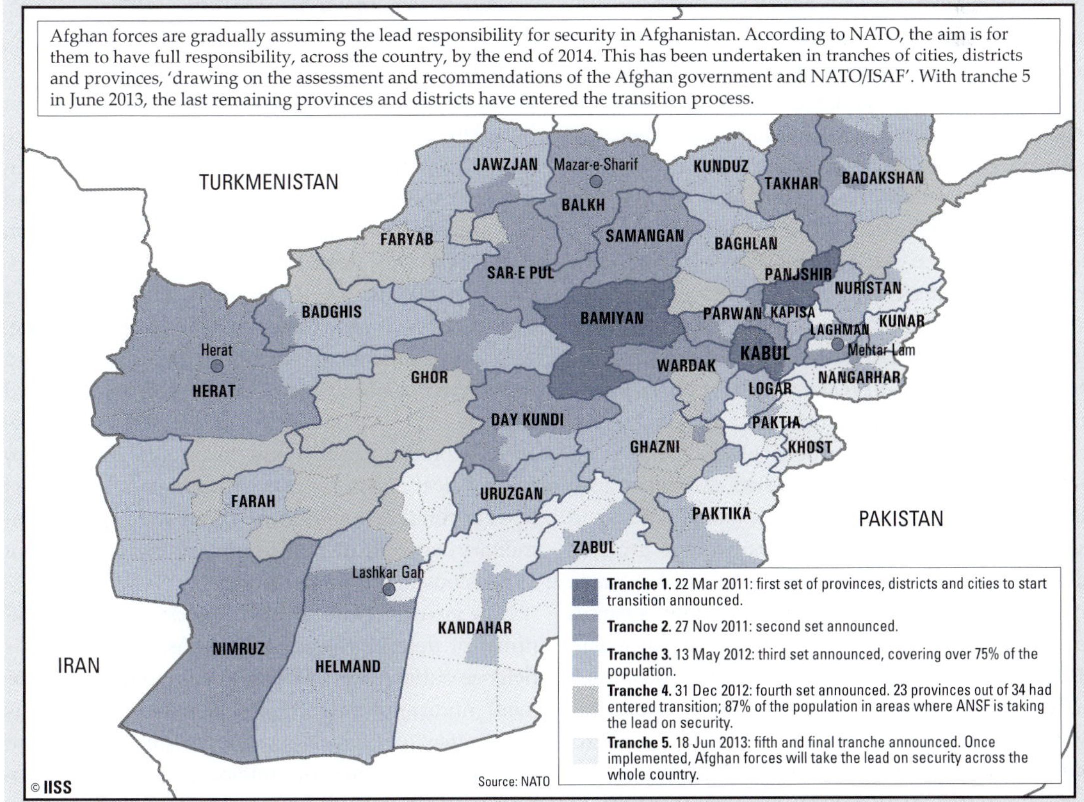

Asia

analysts as competent and capable of presenting an adequate defence of territorial waters.

The **army** remains engaged in counter-insurgency operations in the west of the country and has concentrated on re-equipping and retraining formations and units to fit them for service. When units were first committed on a large scale in 2008 they suffered casualties, as training had been almost solely focused on the conventional warfare skills necessary for possible operations along the frontier with India. Emphasis on IED awareness, protection and neutralisation continues, in addition to convoy drills, helicopter assault and specialised operations in built-up areas. Improved air–ground coordination between the air force and army's integral attack helicopters has been a notable tactical development. Operating costs have risen markedly due to the demands of aerial troop transport and resupply, and because of difficulties in ground logistics in the remote and poorly served FATA. Movement of equipment of all types to rear bases for maintenance has proved a major challenge.

Nuclear developments

Having tested its first nuclear weapon in 1998, Pakistan has the world's fastest growing nuclear arsenal, adding about ten weapons per year to an estimated stockpile in 2013 of 100–120. Two plutonium-producing reactors at Khushab will soon be joined by two more. Given the estimated increase in plutonium production, along with the ongoing uranium-enrichment programme, Pakistan could have the world's fifth largest arsenal by 2020, overtaking the UK. The need for more fissile material and warheads is driven by new platforms and deterrence strategy. The potential nuclear air-delivery capability provided by *Mirage* and F-16 squadrons has been supplemented by short- and medium-range ballistic missiles, the *Hatf*-II (*Abdali*), *Hatf*-III (*Ghaznavi*), *Hatf*-IV (*Shaheen*) and *Hatf*-V (*Ghauri*), with ranges of 180km, 300km, 700km and 900–1,200km respectively.

More recently, Pakistan tested a short-range ballistic missile, the 60km *Hatf*-IX (*Nasr*) MRL, and dual-use cruise missiles, the 700km-range ground-launched *Hatf*-VII (*Babur*) and the 350km-range air-launched *Hatf*-VIII (*Ra'ad*). The new systems contribute to 'full-spectrum deterrence'. In particular, the *Nasr* battlefield-use nuclear weapon is considered a deterrent to a potential Indian incursion across the border, in line with its reported 'Cold Start' or 'proactive defence' doctrine. Sea-based systems are also under development, including the potential purchase from China of six *Qing*-class diesel submarines, which would enhance Pakistan's second-strike capability.

The lowering of Pakistan's nuclear threshold is seen in many capitals as of greater concern than the prospect for nuclear terrorism that makes media headlines. The possibility of nuclear theft or diversion by jihadi elements increases with the growing amount of fissile material produced. Yet Pakistan's nuclear arsenal is well protected by the Army's 20,000-strong Strategic Plans Division, which insists that in a crisis command and control of even short-range systems will remain with the National Command Authority.

Defence economics

To obtain favourable terms on a US$6.6bn loan from the IMF, Pakistan had to agree in September 2013 to a wide range of measures constricting its ability to raise and disburse funds. While defence was not specifically mentioned in the joint Memorandum on Economic and Financial Policies (MEFP), it is clear that the loan under the IMF's Extended Fund Facility depends on disbursement restrictions that will curb major defence-equipment acquisitions. The MEFP indicated, among other initiatives, that there would be privatisation of 65 Public Sector Enterprises, but no mention was made of defence factories.

Budgeting and expenditure

Estimates provided in the annual budget suggest that defence expenditure remained constant in the five years before 2013, with annual increases only in line with inflation. In 2013, however, Pakistan raised its defence FY2013/14 budget by 15% to Rps627.2bn (US$6.45bn), up from Rps545.3bn (US$6.12bn) allocated in FY2012/13 – although actual spending exceeded this, at approximately Rps570bn (US$6.40bn).

Major elements of spending in 2013 included Rs271.2bn (US$2.79bn) for employee-related expenses (43.2%), Rs162.2bn (US$1.67bn) for operating expenses (25.9%) and Rs131.3bn (US$1.35bn) for physical assets (20.9%). A separate allocation of Rps132.7bn (US$1.36bn) was also made under a non-military expenditure budgetary heading, for payment of pensions to retired personnel.

The government does not provide a public breakdown of defence-related allocations, and Pakistan's defence outlays remain opaque even to most government ministers and officials. The Public Accounts Committee of the National Assembly has also noted that 'at times the military was very uncomfortable with the scrutiny by this committee'. The prime concern is that army and air force operations in the west of the country may become so costly as to require expenditure cuts in other fields, such as training and equipment acquisition for conventional operations. This could also reduce the navy's ability to acquire major assets, especially submarines, which it considers its highest priority.

Procurement and industry

There is no ministry with responsibility for defence procurement. The chairman of the Joint Chiefs of Staff Committee has a small staff but no role in operational or procurement decisions. Similarly, the Ministry of Defence Production has only an advisory role on defence-materiel acquisition. As a result, equipment is acquired depending on agreement between the services and on their respective capital equipment budget allocations by the government.

Expenditure on operations against militants and on protecting the border with Afghanistan remains largely immune from IMF-imposed measures, but spending on, or even commitment to, future outlays on capital equipment programmes seems impractical. It may be possible to negotiate further contracts with China, given the attractive terms likely to be offered by Beijing. There is unlikely to be a repeat of China's cut-price provision of 50 JF-17s (some reports even indicated that they were a gift), but repayment of overall project costs, as already agreed, will not present an unbearable strain on the normal defence budget, given China's generous attitude.

Pakistan has a large and capable defence manufacturing industry, which is the responsibility of the Ministry of Defence Production; the secretary and the additional secretary of the ministry are usually retired senior officers. The ministry is heavily influenced by individual service headquarters, all of which have directorates tasked with placing their priorities before government. Facilities include Pakistan Ordnance Factories, Heavy Industries Taxila, Karachi Shipyard and Engineering Works, and the Pakistan Aeronautical Complex. Wider private-sector involvement in defence production has foundered on the reluctance by the armed forces to accept civilian input, and an unwillingness to provide information concerning requirements, citing security concerns. There is no question of privatising of any of these facilities. Despite the quality of products, exports are modest, given the dominance of Western defence manufacturers in the region.

Afghanistan AFG

New Afghan Afghani Afs		2012	2013	2014
GDP	Afs	1.01tr	1.1tr	
	US$	19.9bn	21bn	
per capita	US$	622	636	
Growth	%	10.21	3.10	
Inflation	%	4.45	6.11	
Def bdgt [a]	Afs	106bn	152bn	
	US$	2.08bn	2.9bn	
US$1=Afs		50.92	52.57	

[a] Security expenditure. Includes expenditure on Ministry of Defence, Ministry of Interior, Ministry of Foreign Affairs, National Security Council and the General Directorate of National Security. Includes US DoD funds to Afghan Ministry of Defence & Ministry of Interior.

Population 31,108,077

Ethnic groups: Pashtun 38%; Tajik 25%; Hazara 19%; Uzbek 12%; Aimaq 4%; Baluchi 0.5%

Age	0–14	15–19	20–24	25–29	30–64	65 plus
Male	21.6%	6.2%	5.0%	3.8%	12.9%	1.2%
Female	21.0%	6.0%	4.8%	3.7%	12.6%	1.3%

Capabilities

The Afghan National Army (ANA) now leads combat operations against the Taliban, though mostly alongside ISAF forces whilst improvements to capability are made. With the planned defence force structure now almost fully staffed, the priority is to develop combat support, logistic leadership and technical expertise. Plans call for the ANA to reach full capability as a counter-insurgency force in time for the Afghan assumption of security leadership by the end of 2014, by which time all ANA units should be operating independently. Already some elements – notably special forces – are highly rated by ISAF. Although there are plans and funding to give the air force fixed- and rotary-wing lift capability, as well as ISR, attack helicopters and turboprop light strike fighters, corruption and a shortage of sufficiently educated personnel to undertake pilot training mean the air force is unlikely to reach full capability before 2015 (see p. 219). NATO's ongoing training and advisory mission, *Operation Resolute Support*, is focused on building medical, counter-IED and intelligence capabilities.

ACTIVE 185,800 (Army 179,000 Air Force 6,800)
Paramilitary 152,350

ORGANISATIONS BY SERVICE

Afghan National Army (ANA) 179,000

5 regional comd.

FORCES BY ROLE

SPECIAL FORCES

1 spec ops div (1 SF gp; 2 cdo bde (total: 5 cdo bn))

MANOEUVRE

Mechanised

2 mech bde HQ
5 mech inf bn (2 more forming)

Light

1 (201st) corps (1 cdo bn, 2 inf bde, 1 mech bde, 1 EOD coy)
3 (207th, 209th & 215th) corps (1 cdo bn, 3 inf bde, 1 EOD coy)
2 (203rd & 205th) corps (1 cdo bn, 4 inf bde, 1 EOD coy)
1 (111st Capital) div (2 inf bde)

COMBAT SUPPORT

1 int bn
1 sigs bn

EQUIPMENT BY TYPE

APC 673
APC (T) 173 M113A2†
APC(W) ε500 MSFV (inc variants)

ARTY 214
TOWED 109: **122mm** 85 D-30†; **155mm** 24 M114A1†
MOR 82mm 105 M-69†

MSL • SSM SS-1 *Scud*†

MW Bozena

Afghan Air Force (AAF) 6,800

EQUIPMENT BY TYPE

AIRCRAFT

TPT 37: **Medium** 2 C-130H *Hercules*; **Light** 35: 6 Cessna 182; 26 Cessna 208B; 3 PC-12
TRG 2 L-39 *Albatros*†

HELICOPTERS

ATK 11 Mi-35
MRH 46+: 6 MD-530F; 40+ Mi-17

Paramilitary 152,350

Afghan National Police 152,350

Under control of Interior Ministry. Includes 85,000 Afghan Uniformed Police (AUP), 15,000 Afghan National Civil Order Police (ANCOP), 23,000 Afghan Border Police (ABP), Police Special Forces (GDPSU) and Afghan Anti-Crime Police (AACP).

FOREIGN FORCES

All under ISAF comd unless otherwise specified. ISAF HQ resembles a static HQ with contributing NATO countries filling identified posts.

Albania 105; 1 inf coy
Armenia 131
Australia 1,031; 1 inf BG with (1 mot inf coy; 1 armd recce sqn); 1 UAV det with RQ-7B *Shadow* 200; 1 UAV det with *Heron* • UNAMA 4 obs
Austria 3
Azerbaijan 94
Belgium 180; 6 F-16 *Fighting Falcon*
Bosnia-Herzegovina 79
Bulgaria 416; 1 mech inf coy
Canada 950; 1 inf bn (trg)
Croatia 181
Czech Republic 182 • UNAMA 2 obs

Denmark 317; 1 mech inf BG • UNAMA 1 obs

El Salvador 24

Estonia 160; 1 mech inf coy; 1 mor det

Finland 100

France 226

Georgia 1,561; 2 inf bn

Germany 4,400; 1 div HQ; 2 inf BG; CH-53G *Stallion*; 6 *Tornado* ECR; C-160 *Transall* • UNAMA 1 obs

Greece 3

Hungary 354; 1 lt inf coy

Ireland 7

Italy 2,825; 1 mech inf bde HQ; 1 mech inf regt; 1 para regt; AW129 *Mangusta*; CH-47 *Chinook*; NH90; RQ-1 *Predator*; C-27J *Spartan*; C-130 *Hercules*; • UNAMA 2 obs

Jordan *Operation Enduring Freedom – Afghanistan* 720; 1 ranger bn

Korea, Republic of 50

Latvia 141

Lithuania 240 • UNAMA 1 obs

Luxembourg 10

Macedonia, Former Yugoslav Republic of 158

Malaysia 2

Mongolia 40 • UNAMA 1 obs

Montenegro 27

Netherlands 400 • UNAMA 1 obs

New Zealand 11 • UNAMA 1 obs

Norway 111 • UNAMA 2 obs

Poland 1,177; 1 air cav bde HQ; 1 inf BG; 6 Mi-24; 4 Mi-17 • UNAMA 1 obs

Portugal 165 • UNAMA 1 obs

Romania 1,077; 1 inf bn; • UNAMA 2 obs

Slovakia 199

Slovenia 60

Spain 856

Sweden 259 • UNAMA 2 obs

Turkey 1,036; 1 inf bde HQ; 2 inf bn • UNAMA 1 obs

Ukraine 26

United Arab Emirates 35

United Kingdom 7,700; 1 (7th) armd bde HQ (1 recce regt, 1 armd regt, 4 lt inf bn, 1 arty regt; 1 engr regt); AH-64D *Apache*; *Lynx* AH9A; *Hermes* 450; MQ-9 *Reaper*; *Tornado* GR4; C-130J *Hercules*; CH-47D *Chinook*; *Shadow* R1

United States 60,000; 1 corps HQ; 2 div HQ; 1 armd ABCT; 2 mech inf SBCT(-); 5 lt inf IBCT(-); 1 air aslt IBCT(-); 2 cbt avn bde; 1 MEF HQ; F-16C/D *Fighting Falcon*; A-10 *Thunderbolt* II; AV-8B *Harrier*; MC-12W; EC-130H *Compass Call*, C-130 *Hercules*, MV-22 *Osprey*, KC-130J *Hercules*, AH-64 *Apache*; OH-58 *Kiowa*; CH-47 *Chinook*; UH-60 *Black Hawk*; HH-60 *Pave Hawk*; AH-1 *Cobra*, CH-53 *Sea Stallion*; UH-1 *Iroquois*; RQ-7B *Shadow*; MQ-1 *Predator*; MQ-9 *Reaper* • *Operation Enduring Freedom – Afghanistan* ε7,000

Australia AUS

Australian Dollar A$		2012	2013	2014
GDP	A$	1.49tr	1.55tr	
	US$	1.54tr	1.59tr	
per capita	US$	67,723	68,939	
Growth	%	3.58	2.96	
Inflation	%	1.76	2.46	
Def exp	A$	27.3bn		
	US$	28.3bn		
Def bdgt	A$	26.2bn	25.3bn	
	US$	27.1bn	26bn	
US$1=A$		0.97	0.98	

Population 22,262,501

Age	0–14	15–19	20–24	25–29	30–64	65 plus
Male	9.3%	3.3%	3.6%	3.7%	23.5%	6.8%
Female	8.8%	3.1%	3.4%	3.5%	23.1%	7.9%

Capabilities

Australia has a strong military tradition and its relatively compact armed forces' considerable operational experience, together with the country's high levels of technological expertise, defence-industrial base, and international defence relationships (particularly with the US) contribute substantially to its military capabilities. Continuing modernisation of all three services seems likely to ensure that the sophistication of the ADF's equipment at least matches, and in many cases continues to surpass, that of nations in Australia's immediate region. Notable planned future procurement includes up to 100 F-35 Joint Strike Fighters, and new conventional submarines to replace the *Collins*-class. Two *Canberra*-class LHDs are also under construction. ADF units have high training standards and participate frequently in joint-service exercises at the national, bilateral and multinational levels. The ADF trains with a view to future operational deployments in Southeast Asia and possibly further afield, as well as in defence of Australia. As Canberra completes its drawdown from Afghanistan, Solomon Islands and Timor-Leste, the ADF is intensifying engagement with the armed forces of states in Australia's immediate region (notably Indonesia). The May 2013 White Paper considered in detail the implications of issues including the rapid growth of Asian economies, the US rebalance to the Asia-Pacific and enhanced defence cooperation with Australia, as well the ADF's operational drawdowns. Though it emphasised commitment to earlier plans to boost capabilities, doubts remained over the capacity to fund these improvements, particularly after defence funding cuts were announced in May 2012.

ACTIVE 56,200 (Army 28,600 Navy 13,550 Air 14,050)

RESERVE 28,550 (Army 16,200 Navy 8,200 Air 4,150)

The High-Readiness Reserve of 1,050 army and 240 air-force personnel is intended to strengthen the Australian

Defence Force (ADF) with members trained to the same skill levels as the Regular Force. Integrated units are formed from a mix of reserve and regular personnel. All ADF operations are now controlled by Headquarters Joint Operations Command (HQJOC).

ORGANISATIONS BY SERVICE

Space

SATELLITES • COMMUNICATIONS 1 *Optus* C1 (dual use for civil/mil comms)

Army 28,600

Forces Command

FORCES BY ROLE

COMMAND

1 (1st) div HQ

MANOEUVRE

Reconnaissance

3 (regional force) surv unit (integrated)

Mechanised

3 (1st, 3rd & 7th) mech inf bde (1 armd cav regt, 2 mech inf bn, 1 arty regt, 1 cbt engr regt, 1 sigs regt, 1 CSS bn)

Amphibious

1 (6th RAR) amph bn

Aviation

1 (16th) avn bde (1 regt (2 ISR hel sqn), 1 regt (3 tpt hel sqn), 1 regt (1 spec ops hel sqn, 1 avn sqn))

COMBAT SUPPORT

1 (6th) cbt spt bde (1 STA regt (1 STA bty, 1 UAV bty, 1 CSS bty), 1 AD/FAC regt (integrated), 1 int bn)

1 EW regt

COMBAT SERVICE SUPORT

1 (17th) CSS bde (3 log bn, 3 med bn, 1 MP bn)

1 engr regt (2 (construction) engr sqn, 1 (topographic) engr sqn)

Special Operations Command

FORCES BY ROLE

SPECIAL FORCES

1 (SAS) SF regt

1 (SF Engr) SF regt

2 cdo bn

COMBAT SUPPORT

3 sigs sqn (incl 1 reserve sqn)

COMBAT SERVICE SUPPORT

1 CSS sqn

Reserve Organisations

Force Command 16,200 reservists

FORCES BY ROLE

COMMAND

1 (2nd) div HQ

MANOEUVRE

Light

6 inf bde (total: 5 recce regt, 12 inf bn, 3 arty regt, 3 arty bty, 3 cbt engr regt, 3 cbt engr sqn, 5 sigs sqn, 6 CSS bn, 2 construction bn)

EQUIPMENT BY TYPE

MBT 59 M1A1 *Abrams*

AIFV 257 ASLAV-25 (all variants)

APC 1,431

APC (T) 431 M113AS4

PPV 1,000 *Bushmaster* IMV

ARTY 356

TOWED 171: **105mm** 101 L-118 Light Gun; **155mm** 70: 35 M198; 35 M777A2

MOR 81mm 185

AT

MSL • MANPATS *Javelin*

RCL • 84mm *Carl Gustav*

AMPHIBIOUS 15 LCM-8 (capacity either 1 MBT or 200 troops)

HELICOPTERS

ATK 22 EC665 *Tiger*

TPT 107: **Heavy** 6 CH-47D *Chinook*; **Medium** 60: 25 NH90 TTH (MRH90 TTH); 35 S-70A *Black Hawk*; **Light** 41 Bell 206B-1 *Kiowa*

UAV • ISR • Medium 10 RQ-7B *Shadow* 200

AD • SAM • MANPAD 42: 2 CRAM; 40 RBS-70

RADAR • LAND 38: 7 AN/TPQ-36 *Firefinder* (arty, mor); 31 LCMR

ARV 18+: 10 ASLAV-F; 1 ASLAV-R; 7 M88A2; M806A1

VLB 5 *Biber*

MW 11: 3 *Chubby*; 8 ST-AT/V

Navy 13,550

Fleet Comd HQ located at Stirling; Naval Systems Comd located at Canberra

EQUIPMENT BY TYPE

SUBMARINES • TACTICAL • SSK 6 *Collins* with 6 single 533mm TT each with Mk48 *Sea Arrow* ADCAP HWT/UGM-84C *Harpoon* AShM

PRINCIPAL SURFACE COMBATANTS 12

FRIGATES • FFGHM 12

4 *Adelaide* (Mod) with 1 Mk13 GMLS with RGM-84C *Harpoon* AShM/SM-2 MR SAM, 1 8 cell Mk41 VLS with RIM-162 *Evolved Sea Sparrow* SAM, 2 triple Mk32 324mm ASTT with MU90 LWT, 1 *Phalanx* Block 1B CIWS, 1 76mm gun, (capacity 2 S-70B *Seahawk* ASW hel)

8 *Anzac* (GER MEKO 200) with 2 quad Mk141 lnchr with RGM-84C *Harpoon* AShM, 1 8 cell Mk41 VLS with RIM-162 *Evolved Sea Sparrow* SAM, 2 triple 324mm ASTT with MU90 LWT, 1 127mm gun, (capacity 1 S-70B *Seahawk* ASW hel), (capability upgrades in progress)

PATROL AND COASTAL COMBATANTS • PHSC 14 *Armidale*

MINE WARFARE • MINE COUNTERMEASURES • MHO 6 *Huon*

AMPHIBIOUS

PRINCIPAL AMPHIBIOUS SHIPS 2

LSD 1 *Choules* (UK *Bay*) (capacity 4 LCU; 2 LCVP; 24 MBT; 350 troops)

LSL 1 *Tobruk*; 2 LCM; 2 LCVP; 40 APC and 18 MBT; 500 troops)

LANDING CRAFT 8
LCH 3 *Balikpapan* (capacity 3 MBT or 13 APC - to decommission end-2014)
LCVP 5
LOGISTICS AND SUPPORT 37
AGSH 2 *Leeuwin*
AGS 4 *Paluma*
AORH 1 *Success*
AOR 1 *Sirius*
The following vessels are operated by a private company, DMS Maritime:
AE 3 *Wattle*
AOL 4 *Warrigal*
ASR 3
AX 2: 1 **AXL**; 1 **AXS**
YDT 4
YPT 3
YTL 4
YTM 6

Naval Aviation 1,350

FORCES BY ROLE
ANTI SUBMARINE WARFARE
1 sqn with NH90 (MRH90)
1 sqn with S-70B-2 *Seahawk*
TRAINING
1 sqn with AS350BA *Ecureuil*; Bell 429
EQUIPMENT BY TYPE
HELICOPTERS
ASW 13 S-70B-2 *Seahawk*
TPT 22 **Medium** 6 NH90 (MRH90); **Light** 16: 13 AS350BA *Ecureuil*; 3 Bell 429

Air Force 14,050

Flying hours 175 hrs/year on F/A-18 *Hornet*

FORCES BY ROLE
FIGHTER/GROUND ATTACK
3 sqn with F/A-18A/B *Hornet*
2 sqn with F/A-18F *Super Hornet*
ANTI SUBMARINE WARFARE
2 sqn with AP-3C *Orion*
AIRBORNE EARLY WARNING & CONTROL
1 sqn with B-737-700 *Wedgetail* (E-7A)
TANKER/TRANSPORT
1 sqn with A330 MRTT (KC-30A)
TRANSPORT
1 VIP sqn with B-737BBJ; CL-604 *Challenger*
1 sqn with Beech 350 *King Air*
1 sqn with C-17A *Globemaster*
1 sqn with C-130J-30 *Hercules*
TRAINING
1 sqn with Beech 350 *King Air*
2 (LIFT) sqn with *Hawk* MK127*
1 sqn with PC-9/A(F)
ISR UAV
1 flt with *Heron*
EQUIPMENT BY TYPE
AIRCRAFT 142 combat capable
FGA 95: 55 F/A-18A *Hornet*; 16 F/A-18B *Hornet*; 24 F/A-18F *Super Hornet*
ASW 18 AP-3C *Orion*
AEW&C 6 B-737-700 *Wedgetail* (E-7A)
TKR/TPT 5 A330 MRTT (KC-30A)
TPT 39: **Heavy** 6 C-17A *Globemaster*; **Medium** 12 C-130J-30 *Hercules*; **Light** 16 Beech 300 *King Air*; **PAX** 5: 2 B-737BBJ (VIP); 3 CL-604 *Challenger* (VIP)
TRG 96: 33 *Hawk* Mk127*; 63 PC-9/A (incl 4 PC-9/A(F) for tgt marking)
UAV • ISR • Heavy 4 *Heron*
RADAR • AD RADAR 7
OTH-B 3 *Jindalee*
Tactical 4 AN/TPS-77
MSL
AAM • IIR AIM-9X *Sidewinder*; ASRAAM; **ARH** AIM-120 AMRAAM
ASM AGM-154 JSOW
AShM AGM-84A *Harpoon*
LACM AGM-158 JASSM
BOMBS
Conventional Mk 82; Mk 83; Mk 84; BLU-109/B
Laser-guided *Paveway* II/IV; Laser JDAM (being delivered)
INS/GPS guided JDAM; JDAM-ER (in development)

Paramilitary

Border Protection Command

Has responsibility for operational coordination and control of both civil and military maritime enforcement activities within Australia's EEZ. At any one time, 7 *Armidale*-class patrol boats, 1 major fleet unit and 3 AP-3C *Orion* aircraft are assigned to BPC activities.

EQUIPMENT BY TYPE
PATROL AND COASTAL COMBATANTS 12
PSO 1 *Ocean Protector* with 1 hel landing platform
PCO 2: 1 *Triton* with 1 hel landing platform; 1 *Cape* (8 vessels to be commissioned)
PCC 9: 1 *Ashmore Guardian*; 8 *Bay* (to be replaced by *Cape*-class from 2015)
AIRCRAFT
TPT • Light 12: 10 DHC-8; 2 F-406 *Caravan* II
HELICOPTERS • TPT 2 **Medium** 1 Bell 214; **Light** 1 AS350

Cyber

Canberra published a Cyber Security Strategy in 2009, and the issue featured heavily in the 2009 and 2013 Defence White Papers, and in the 2013 National Security Strategy. A Cyber Security Operations Centre (CSOC) was established in the Australian Signals Directorate (DSD), while CERT Australia was established in the Attorney General's Department. It was announced in 2013, as part of the National Security Strategy, that an Australian Cyber Security Centre would be set up, combining existing capabilities across the Defence Department (such as CSOC), the Attorney General's Department, as well as in ASIO, the AFP and Australian Crime Commission. Within the Department of Defence, routine Computer Network Defence is managed by the Chief Information Officer Group, which also runs the network. The function is carried out by the Australian Defence Force Computer Incident Response Team, located at the Defence Network Operations Centre.

DEPLOYMENT

Legal provisions for foreign deployment:
Constitution: Constitution (1900)
Decision on deployment of troops abroad: By Government exercising its executive power under Section 61 of the Australian Constitution.

AFGHANISTAN
NATO • ISAF 1,031; 1 inf BG; 1 UAV det with RQ-7B *Shadow* 200; 1 UAV det with *Heron*
UN • UNAMA 4 obs

ARABIAN SEA
Combined Maritime Forces • CTF-151 1 FFGHM

EGYPT
MFO (*Operation Mazurka*) 25

IRAQ
UN • UNAMI 2 obs

MALAYSIA
130; 1 inf coy (on 3-month rotational tours); 1 AP-3C *Orion* (on occasion)

MIDDLE EAST
UN • UNTSO 12 obs

PAPUA NEW GUINEA
38; 1 trg unit; 1 LSD

SOUTH SUDAN
UN • UNMISS 11; 4 obs

UNITED ARAB EMIRATES
300; 1 tpt det with 3 C-130J *Hercules*; 1 C-17A (on occasion); 1 MP det with 2 AP-3C *Orion*

FOREIGN FORCES

New Zealand 9 (air navigation trg)
Singapore 230: 1 trg sqn at Pearce with PC-21 trg ac; 1 trg sqn at Oakey with 12 AS332 *Super Puma*; AS532 *Cougar*
United States US Pacific Command: 180; 1 SEWS at Pine Gap; 1 comms facility at NW Cape; 1 SIGINT stn at Pine Gap

Bangladesh BGD

Bangladeshi Taka Tk		2012	2013	2014
GDP	Tk	9.76tr	11tr	
	US$	123bn	135bn	
per capita	US$	818	891	
Growth	%	6.05	6.01	
Inflation	%	8.72	6.54	
Def bdgt	Tk	122bn	135bn	145bn
	US$	1.54bn	1.65bn	
FMA (US)	US$	2.2m	2.2m	2.5m
US$1=Tk		79.55	81.73	

Population 163,654,860

Religious groups: Muslim 90%; Hindu 9%; Buddhist 1%

Age	0–14	15–19	20–24	25–29	30–64	65 plus
Male	16.7%	4.8%	4.0%	3.5%	17.2%	2.4%
Female	16.3%	5.2%	4.8%	4.3%	18.4%	2.5%

Capabilities

Bangladesh has a limited military capability, optimised for border and domestic security. It has shown itself capable of mobilising and deploying quickly to counter internal threats, albeit with considerable use of lethal force. According to media reports, the armed forces retain extensive business interests, reportedly in control of real estate, banks and other businesses. In 2009, a pay dispute sparked a rebellion by a group of the Bangladesh Rifles paramilitary force and, though this did not directly affect the armed forces, the longer-term effect on the subsequently renamed Border Guard Bangladesh is harder to gauge. Meanwhile, the after-effects have lingered: in late 2013 over 150 of the mutineers were sentenced to death. Inter-service cooperation is limited. Bangladesh's long record of service in UN missions has brought considerable peacekeeping experience. Modest efforts to improve its inventory are underway across all three services. Mid-2012 saw the country request four second hand C-130E *Hercules* from the US.

ACTIVE 157,050 (Army 126,150 Navy 16,900 Air 14,000) Paramilitary 63,900

ORGANISATIONS BY SERVICE

Army 126,150

FORCES BY ROLE
COMMAND
7 inf div HQ
SPECIAL FORCES
1 cdo bn
MANOEUVRE
Armoured
1 armd bde
6 indep armd regt
Light
18 inf bde
1 (composite) bde

Aviation
1 avn regt (1 avn sqn; 1 hel sqn)

COMBAT SUPPORT
20 arty regt
1 AD bde
1 engr bde
1 sigs bde

EQUIPMENT BY TYPE
MBT 245+: 174 Type-59; 58 Type-69/Type-69G; 13+ Type-90-II (MBT-2000)
LT TK 8 Type-62
RECCE 5+ BOV M11
AIFV 155 BTR-80A
APC 151
APC (T) 134 MT-LB
APC (W) 17 *Cobra*
ARTY 836+
SP 155mm 1+ NORA B-52
TOWED 363+: **105mm** 170: 56 Model 56A1; 114 Model 56/L 10A1 pack howitzer; **122mm** 131: 57 Type-54/54-1 (M-30); 20 Type-83; 54 Type-96 (D-30), **130mm** 62 Type-59-1 (M-46)
MOR 472: **81mm** 11 M29A1; **82mm** 366 Type-53/87/M-31 (M-1937); **120mm** 95 MO-120-AM-50 M67/UBM 52
AT • RCL 106mm 238 M40A1
AIRCRAFT • TPT • Light 6: 5 Cessna 152; 1 PA-31T *Cheyenne*
HELICOPTERS
MRH 2 AS365N3 *Dauphin*
TPT • Light 3 Bell 206L-4 *Long Ranger*
AD • SAM
SP FM-90
MANPAD QW-2; HN-5A (being replaced by QW-2)
GUNS • TOWED 166: **37mm** 132 Type-65/74; **57mm** 34 Type-59 (S-60)
AEV MT-LB
ARV 3+: T-54/T-55; Type-84; 3 Type-654
VLB MTU

Navy 16,900

EQUIPMENT BY TYPE
PRINCIPAL SURFACE COMBATANTS • FRIGATES 4
FFGHM 2:
1 *Bangabandhu* (ROK *Modified Ulsan*) with 2 twin lnchr with *Otomat* Mk2 AShM, 1 octuple HQ-7 SAM, 2 triple 324mm TT with A244 LWT, 1 76mm gun (capacity: 1 AW109E hel)
1 *Somudro Joy* (ex-USCG *Hero*) with 2 quad lnchr with C-802 AShM, 1 octuple HQ-7 SAM, 2 triple 324mm ASTT with A244 LWT, 1 Type 730B CIWS, 1 76mm gun,
FFG 1 *Osman* (PRC *Jianghu* I) with 2 quad lnchr with YJ-82 (C-802) AShM, 2 RBU 1200, 2 twin 100mm gun, 2 RBU 1200
FF 1 *Umar Farooq*† (UK *Salisbury* – trg role) with 3 *Squid*, 1 twin 115mm gun
PATROL AND COASTAL COMBATANTS 45
FSG 2 *Durjoy* with 2 twin lnchr with C-704 AShM, 1 76mm gun
PSOH 2 *Bijoy* (UK *Castle*) with 2 twin lnchr with C-704 AShM, 1 76mm gun, 1 hel landing platform
PCFG 4 *Durdarsha* (PRC *Huangfeng*) with 4 single lnchr with HY-2 (CSS-N-2) *Silkworm* AShM
PCO 6: 1 *Madhumati* (*Sea Dragon*) with 1 57mm gun; 5 *Kapatakhaya* (UK *Island*)
PCC 5:
2 *Meghna* with 1 57mm gun (fishery protection)
1 *Nirbhoy* (PRC *Hainan*) with 4 RBU 1200; 2 twin 57mm gun
2 *Padma* (3 more vessels under construction)
PBFG 5 *Durbar* (PRC *Hegu*) with 2 single lnchr with SY-1 AShM
PBFT 4 *Huchuan* (PRC) with 2 single 533mm TT each with YU 1 Type-53 HWT
PBF 4 *Titas (ROK Sea Dolphin)*
PB 13: 1 *Akshay*; 1 *Barkat* (PRC *Shanghai III*); 1 *Bishkali*; 2 *Karnaphuli*; 1 *Salam* (PRC *Huangfen*); 7 *Shaheed Daulat (PRC Shanghai II)*
MINE WARFARE • MINE COUNTERMEASURES 5
MSO 5: 1 *Sagar*; 4 *Shapla* (UK *River*)
AMPHIBIOUS
LANDING SHIPS • LSL 1
LANDING CRAFT 10:
LCU 2†
LCVP 3†
LCM 5 *Yuchin*
LOGISTICS AND SUPPORT 11
AG 1
AGHS 2: 1 *Agradoot*; 1 *Anushandhan*
AOR 2 (coastal)
AR 1†
ATF 1†
AX 1 *Shaheed Ruhul Amin*
YTM 3

Naval Aviation

EQUIPMENT BY TYPE
AIRCRAFT • TPT • Light 2 Do-228NG (MP)
HELICOPTERS • TPT • Light 2 AW109E *Power*

Air Force 14,000

FORCES BY ROLE
FIGHTER
1 sqn with MiG-29B/UB *Fulcrum*
FIGHTER/GROUND ATTACK
1 sqn with F-7MB/FT-7B *Airguard*
1 sqn with F-7BG/FT-7BG *Airguard*
GROUND ATTACK
1 sqn with A-5C (Q-5III) *Fantan*; FT-6 (MiG-19UTI) *Farmer*
TRANSPORT
1 sqn with An-32 *Club*
1 sqn with C-130B *Hercules*
TRAINING
1 (OCU) sqn with L-39ZA *Albatros**
1 sqn with PT-6
TRANSPORT HELICOPTER
2 sqn with Mi-17 *Hip* H; Mi-17-1V *Hip* H; Mi-171Sh
1 sqn with Bell 212
1 trg sqn with Bell 206L *Long Ranger*

EQUIPMENT BY TYPE†

AIRCRAFT 86 combat capable

FTR 61: 10 F-7MB *Airguard*; 11 F-7BG *Airguard*; 12 F-7BGI *Airguard* (being delivered); 5 FT-7B *Airguard*; 4 FT-7BG *Airguard*; 4 FT-7BGI *Airguard* (being delivered); 7 FT-6 *Farmer*; 6 MiG-29 *Fulcrum*; 2 MiG-29UB *Fulcrum*

ATK 18 A-5C *Fantan*

TPT 7: **Medium** 4 C-130B *Hercules*; **Light** 3 An-32 *Cline*†

TRG 17: 7 L-39ZA *Albatros**; 10 PT-6

HELICOPTERS

MRH 14: 12 Mi-17 *Hip* H; 2 Mi-17-1V *Hip* H (VIP)

TPT 9: **Medium** 3 Mi-171Sh; **Light** 6: 2 Bell 206L *Long Ranger*; 4 Bell 212

MSL • AAM • IR R-3 (AA-2 *Atoll*)‡; R-73 (AA-11 *Archer*); PL-5; PL-7; **SARH** R-27R (AA-10A *Alamo*)

Paramilitary 63,900

Ansars 20,000+

Security Guards

Armed Police 5,000

Rapid action force (forming)

Border Guard Bangladesh 38,000

FORCES BY ROLE

MANOEUVRE

Other

41 paramilitary bn

Coast Guard 900

EQUIPMENT BY TYPE

PATROL AND COASTAL COMBATANTS 9

PB 4: 1 *Ruposhi Bangla*; 1 *Shaheed Daulat*; 2 *Shetgang*

PBR 5 *Pabna*

DEPLOYMENT

CÔTE D'IVOIRE

UN • UNOCI 2,168; 13 obs; 2 mech inf bn; 1 avn coy; 1 engr coy; 1 sigs coy; 1 log coy; 1 fd hospital

DEMOCRATIC REPUBLIC OF THE CONGO

UN • MONUSCO 2,542; 17 obs; 2 mech inf bn; 1 avn coy; 2 hel coy; 1 engr coy

LEBANON

UN • UNIFIL 326; 1 FFG; 1 PCO

LIBERIA

UN • UNMIL 529; 13 obs; 2 engr coy; 1 log coy; 1 fd hospital

MALI

UN • MINUSMA 5

SOUTH SUDAN

UN • UNMISS 278; 3 obs; 1 engr coy

SUDAN

UN • UNAMID 196; 17 obs; 1 inf coy

WESTERN SAHARA

UN • MINURSO 19; 7 obs; 1 fd hospital

Brunei BRN

Brunei Dollar B$		2012	2013	2014
GDP	B$	20.8bn	20.4bn	
	US$	16.6bn	16.5bn	
per capita	US$	41,703	40,647	
Growth	%	1.30	1.19	
Inflation	%	0.46	1.50	
Def bdgt	B$	513m	516m	
	US$	411m	416m	
US$1=B$		1.25	1.24	

Population 415,717

Ethnic groups: Malay, Kedayan, Tutong, Belait, Bisaya, Dusun, Murut 66.3%; Chinese 11.2%; Iban, Dayak, Kelabit 6%; Other 11.8%

Age	0–14	15–19	20–24	25–29	30–64	65 plus
Male	12.7%	4.3%	4.3%	4.7%	21.8%	1.9%
Female	11.9%	4.3%	4.6%	5.1%	22.4%	2.0%

Capabilities

The Royal Brunei Armed Forces (RBAF) are an important source of employment in this oil-rich state. Despite these small, professional forces being well-trained, they could offer little resistance on their own to a determined aggressor. However, the sultanate has long-established defence relations with the UK and Singapore, with which its forces train. It has deployed small contingents, under Malaysian command, to Lebanon (UNIFIL) and the southern Philippines (IMT).

ACTIVE 7,000 (Army 4,900 Navy 1,000 Air 1,100)
Paramilitary 2,250

RESERVE 700 (Army 700)

ORGANISATIONS BY SERVICE

Army 4,900

FORCES BY ROLE

MANOEUVRE

Light

3 inf bn

COMBAT SUPPORT

1 cbt spt bn (1 armd recce sqn, 1 engr sqn)

Reserves 700

FORCES BY ROLE

MANOEUVRE

Light

1 inf bn

EQUIPMENT BY TYPE

LT TK 20 *Scorpion* (16 to be upgraded)

APC (W) 45 VAB

ARTY • MOR 81mm 24

ARV 2 *Samson*

Navy 1,000

FORCES BY ROLE

SPECIAL FORCES

1 SF sqn

EQUIPMENT BY TYPE

PATROL AND COASTAL COMBATANTS 11

PSO 3 *Darussalam* with 1 57mm gun

PCC 4 *Ijtihad*

PBF 1 *Mustaed*

PB 3 *Perwira*

AMPHIBIOUS • LANDING CRAFT • LCU 4: 2 *Teraban*; 2 *Cheverton Loadmaster*

Air Force 1,100

FORCES BY ROLE

MARITIME PATROL

1 sqn with CN-235M

TRAINING

1 sqn with PC-7; Bell 206B *Jet Ranger* II

TRANSPORT HELICOPTER

1 sqn with Bell 212; Bell 214 (SAR)

1 sqn with Bo-105

1 sqn with S-70A *Black Hawk*

AIR DEFENCE

1 sqn with *Rapier*

1 sqn with *Mistral*

EQUIPMENT BY TYPE

AIRCRAFT

MP 1 CN-235M

TRG 4 PC-7

HELICOPTERS

TPT 23 **Medium** 5: 1 Bell 214 (SAR); 4 S-70A *Black Hawk*; **Light** 18: 2 Bell 206B *Jet Ranger* II; 10 Bell 212; 6 Bo-105 (armed, 81mm rockets)

AD • SAM 12+: *Rapier*; 12 *Mistral*

Paramilitary ε2,250

Gurkha Reserve Unit 400-500

FORCES BY ROLE

MANOEUVRE

Light

2 inf bn(-)

Royal Brunei Police 1,750

EQUIPMENT BY TYPE

PATROL AND COASTAL COMBATANTS • PB 10: 3 *Bendaharu*; 7 PDB-type

DEPLOYMENT

LEBANON

UN • UNIFIL 30

PHILIPPINES

IMT 9

FOREIGN FORCES

Singapore 1 trg camp with infantry units on rotation; 1 trg school; 1 hel det with AS332 *Super Puma*

United Kingdom 550; 1 Gurhka bn; 1 trg unit; 1 hel flt with 3 hel

Cambodia CAM

Cambodian Riel r		2012	2013	2014
GDP	r	57.5tr	63.4tr	
	US$	14.2bn	15.7bn	
per capita	US$	934	1,017	
Growth	%	6.45	6.68	
Inflation	%	2.93	3.07	
Def bdgt	r	1.4tr	1.59tr	
	US$	346m	394m	
FMA (US)	US$	0.8m	0.8m	1m
US$1=r		4039.07	4045.10	

[a] Includes public security expenditure disbursed by the Ministry of Interior. Excludes defence capital expenditure.

Population 15,205,539

Ethnic groups: Khmer 90%; Vietnamese 5%; Chinese 1%

Age	0–14	15–19	20–24	25–29	30–64	65 plus
Male	16.0%	4.9%	5.6%	5.0%	15.5%	1.5%
Female	15.8%	5.0%	5.7%	5.1%	17.5%	2.4%

Capabilities

Despite their name, which reflects Cambodia's formal status as a constitutional monarchy, and their integration, (in the early 1990s) of two non-communist resistance armies, the Royal Cambodian Armed Forces (RCAF) are essentially the modern manifestation of the armed forces of the former People's Republic of Kampuchea, established in 1979 following Vietnam's invasion. The army is organised into many under-strength 'divisions', and is top-heavy with senior officers. Minor skirmishes on the border with Thailand since 2008 provide little indication of the RCAF's capacity for high-intensity combat, which is probably limited. Peacekeeping troops are deployed in Lebanon and South Sudan.

ACTIVE 124,300 (Army 75,000 Navy 2,800 Air 1,500 Provincial Forces 45,000) Paramilitary 67,000

Conscript liability Authorised but not implemented since 1993

ORGANISATIONS BY SERVICE

Army ε75,000

6 Military Regions (incl 1 special zone for capital)

FORCES BY ROLE

SPECIAL FORCES

1 AB/SF regt

MANOEUVRE

Reconnaissance

Some indep recce bn

Armoured

3 armd bn

Light
12 inf div(-)
3 indep inf bde
9 indep inf regt
Other
1 (70th) sy bde (4 sy bn)
17 (border) sy bn
COMBAT SUPPORT
2 arty bn
1 AD bn
4 fd engr regt
COMBAT SERVICE SUPPORT
1 (construction) engr regt

EQUIPMENT BY TYPE
MBT 200+: 50 Type-59; 150+ T-54/T-55
LT TK 20+: Type-62; 20 Type-63
RECCE 4+ BRDM-2
AIFV 70 BMP-1
APC 230+
APC (T) M113
APC (W) 230: 200 BTR-60/BTR-152; 30 OT-64
ARTY 433+
TOWED 400+ **76mm** ZIS-3 (M-1942)/**122mm** D-30/**122mm** M-30 (M-1938)/**130mm** Type-59-I
MRL 33+: **107mm** Type-63; **122mm** 13: 8 BM-21; **5 RM-70; 132mm** BM-13-16 (BM-13); **140mm** 20 BM-14-16 (BM-14)
MOR 82mm M-37; **120mm** M-43; **160mm** M-160
AT • RCL 82mm B-10; **107mm** B-11
AD
MSL • MANPAD 50 FN-6; FN-16 (reported)
GUNS • TOWED 14.5mm ZPU-1/ZPU-2/ZPU-4; **37mm** M-1939; **57mm** S-60
ARV T-54/T-55
MW Bozena; RA-140 DS

Navy ε2,800 (incl 1,500 Naval Infantry)

EQUIPMENT BY TYPE
PATROL AND COASTAL COMBATANTS 15
PBF 2 *Stenka*
PB 11: 4 (PRC 46m); 3 (PRC 20m); 2 *Shershen*; 2 *Turya*
PBR 2 *Kaoh Chhlam*
AMPHIBIOUS • CRAFT
LCU 1

Naval Infantry 1,500

FORCES BY ROLE
MANOEUVRE
Light
7 inf bn
COMBAT SUPPORT
1 arty bn

Air Force 1,500

FORCES BY ROLE
ISR/TRAINING
1 sqn with P-92 *Echo*; L-39 *Albatros**
TRANSPORT
1 VIP sqn (reporting to Council of Ministers) with An-24RV *Coke*; AS350 *Ecureuil*; AS355F2 *Ecureuil* II
1 sqn with BN-2 *Islander*; Y-12 (II)
TRANSPORT HELICOPTER
1 sqn with Mi-26 *Halo*; Mi-17 *Hip* H; Mi-8 *Hip*; Z-9

EQUIPMENT BY TYPE
AIRCRAFT 5 combat capable
TPT • Light 10: 2 An-24RV *Coke*; 1 BN-2 *Islander*; 5 P-92 *Echo* (pilot trg/recce); 2 Y-12 (II)
TRG 5 L-39 *Albatros**
HELICOPTERS
MRH 5+: 3 Mi-17 *Hip* H; 2+ Z-9
TPT 10: **Heavy** 2 Mi-26 *Halo*; **Medium** 4 Mi-8 *Hip*; **Light** 4: 2 AS350 *Ecureuil*; 2 AS355F2 *Ecureuil* II

Provincial Forces 45,000+

Reports of at least 1 inf regt per province, with varying numbers of inf bn (with lt wpn)

Paramilitary

Police 67,000 (including gendarmerie)

DEPLOYMENT

LEBANON
UN • UNIFIL 219; 1 engr coy

SOUTH SUDAN
UN • UNMISS 147; 3 obs; 1 MP coy; 1 fd hospital

SUDAN
UN • UNAMID 3 obs
UN • UNISFA 2 obs

China, People's Republic of PRC

Chinese Yuan Renminbi Y		2012	2013	2014
GDP	Y	51.9tr	57.7tr	
	US$	8.23tr	9.02tr	
	US$ [a]	12.4tr	13.6tr	
per capita	US$	6,076	6,629	
Growth	%	7.80	8.04	
Inflation	%	2.65	3.01	
Def exp	Y	ε923bn		
	US$	ε146bn		
	US$ [a]	221bn		
Def bdgt [b]	Y	648bn	718bn	
	US$	103bn	112bn	
US$1=Y	MER	6.31	6.40	
	PPP	4.19	4.24	

[a] PPP estimate

[b] Includes central government expenditure only.

Population 1,356,768,562

Ethnic groups: Tibetan, Uighur and other non-Han 8%

Age	0–14	15–19	20–24	25–29	30–64	65 plus
Male	9.2%	3.7%	4.4%	4.2%	25.4%	4.5%
Female	7.9%	3.3%	4.0%	4.0%	24.4%	4.9%

Capabilities

The PLA is engaged in a modernisation programme fuelled by the country's rapid economic development that has seen it surpass the armed forces of less developed countries in Asia. However, a lack of war-fighting experience, questions over training and morale, and key capability weaknesses in areas such as C4ISTAR and ASW, mean that it remains qualitatively inferior, in some respects, to more technologically advanced armed forces in the region – such as South Korea and Japan – and it lags far behind the US. The armed forces' range of roles is gradually expanding to include humanitarian assistance and disaster response, non-combatant evacuation operations and counter-piracy. The 2013 defence white paper includes such missions as 'protecting overseas interests' and 'safeguarding maritime rights'. In line with the growth in missions is a broad, full-spectrum procurement programme. While much investment since the early 1990s has been in anti-access/area denial capabilities, now more power projection and area control capabilities are being developed. China's first aircraft carrier was commissioned in 2012, however the country has yet to demonstrate the capabilities that would enable carrier battle group operations. The PLA is increasingly able to deploy internally and can complicate rivals' operations in its littoral waters, but it would struggle with a sustained conflict within the region and currently has little capability to deploy beyond East Asia. (See pp. 206–12.)

ACTIVE 2,333,000 (Army 1,600,000 Navy 235,000 Air Force 398,000 Strategic Missile Forces 100,000) Paramilitary 660,000

Conscript liability Selective conscription; all services 2 years

RESERVE ε510,000

Overall organisation: army leadership is exercised by the four general headquarters/departments. A military region exercises direct leadership over the army units under it. The navy, air force and Second Artillery Force each have a leading body consisting of the headquarters, political department, logistics department and armaments department. These direct the military, political, logistical and equipment work of their respective troops, and take part in the command of joint operations.

ORGANISATIONS BY SERVICE

Strategic Missile Forces (100,000+)

Offensive

The Second Artillery Force organises and commands its own troops to launch nuclear counterattacks with strategic missiles and to conduct operations with conventional missiles. Org as launch bdes subordinate to 6 army-level msl bases (1 in Shenyang & Beijing MR, 1 in Jinan MR, 1 in Nanjing MR, 2 in Gunagzhou MR and 1 in Lanzhou MR). Org varies by msl type. The DF-16 MRBM is reported to be in service, but it is not yet clear which formation it has been assigned to.

FORCES BY ROLE

MISSILE

1 ICBM bde with DF-4
3 ICBM bde with DF-5A
1 ICBM bde with DF-31
2 ICBM bde with DF-31A
1 IRBM bde with DF-3A
1 MRBM bde with DF-16 (reported)
1 MRBM bde with DF-21
6 MRBM bde with DF-21A
2 MRBM bde with DF-21C
1 MRBM bde forming with DF-21D (reported)
4 SRBM bde with DF-11A
4 SRBM bde with DF-15
2 SSM bde with DH-10
2 SSM trg bde

MSL • STRATEGIC 458

ICBM 66: ε10 DF-4 (CSS-3); ε20 DF-5A (CSS-4 Mod 2); ε12 DF-31 (CSS-10 Mod 1); ε24 DF-31A (CSS-10 Mod 2)
IRBM ε6 DF-3A (CSS-2 Mod)
MRBM 134: ε12 DF-16 (CSS-11); ε80 DF-21/DF-21A (CSS-5 Mod 1/2); ε36 DF-21C (CSS-5 Mod 3); ε6 DF-21D (CSS-5 Mod 4 - ASBM) reported
SRBM 252: ε108 DF-11A/M-11A (CSS-7 Mod 2); ε144 DF-15/M-9 (CSS-6)
LACM ε54 DH-10

Navy

EQUIPMENT BY TYPE

SUBMARINES • STRATEGIC • SSBN 4:
1 *Xia* with 12 JL-1 (CSS-N-3) strategic SLBM
3 *Jin* with up to 12 JL-2 (CSS-NX-4) strategic SLBM (operational status unknown; 1 additional vessel in build)

Air Force

FORCES BY ROLE

BOMBER

2 regt with H-6K

EQUIPMENT BY TYPE

AIRCRAFT • BBR ε20 H-6K
LACM CJ-10/CJ-20 (reported)

Defensive

RADAR • STRATEGIC: some phased array radar; some detection and tracking radars (covering Central Asia and Shanxi on the northern border) located in Xinjiang province

Space

SATELLITES 59

COMMUNICATIONS 5 *Zhongxing* (dual use telecom satellites for civ/mil comms)
NAVIGATION/POSITIONING/TIMING 17: 2 *Beidou*-1; 5 *Beidou*-2(M); 5 *Beidou*-2(G); 5 *Beidou*-2 (IGSO)
ISR 25: 1 *Haiyang* 2A; 22 *Yaogan Weixing* (remote sensing); 2 *Zhangguo Ziyuan* (ZY-2 - remote sensing)
ELINT/SIGINT 12: 8 *Shijian* 6 (4 pairs - reported ELINT/SIGINT role); 4 *Shijian* 11 (reported ELINT/SIGINT role)

People's Liberation Army ε800,000; ε800,000 conscript (total ε1,600,000)

7 military region commands are sub-divided into a total of 28 military districts.

FORCES BY ROLE

COMMAND
- 7 mil region
- 18 (Group) army HQ

SPECIAL FORCES
- 9 SF unit

MANOEUVRE

Armoured
- 1 armd div (3 armd regt, 1 arty regt, 1 AD regt)
- 16 armd bde

Mechanised
- 1 mech inf div (1 armd regt, 3 mech inf regt, 1 arty regt, 1 AD regt)
- 6 mech inf div (1 armd regt, 2 mech inf regt, 1 arty regt, 1 AD regt)
- 2 (high alt) mech inf div (1 armd regt, 2 mech inf regt, 1 arty regt, 1 AD regt)
- 17 mech inf bde
- 1 (high alt) mech inf bde
- 2 indep mech inf regt

Light
- 1 mot inf div (1 armd regt, 3 mot inf regt, 1 arty regt, 1 AD regt)
- 9 mot inf div (1 armd regt, 2 mot inf regt, 1 arty regt, 1 AD regt)
- 3 (high alt) mot inf div (1 armd regt, 2 mot inf regt, 1 arty regt, 1 AD regt)
- 1 (jungle) mot inf div (1 armd regt, 2 mot inf regt, 1 arty regt, 1 AD regt)
- 14 mot inf bde
- 2 (high alt) mot inf bde

Amphibious
- 1 amph armd bde
- 2 amph mech div

Mountain
- 2 mtn inf bde

Other
- 1 (OPFOR) mech inf bde
- 1 mech gd div (1 armd regt, 2 mech inf regt, 1 arty regt, 1 AD regt)
- 1 sy gd div (4 sy regt)

Aviation
- 5 avn bde
- 5 avn regt
- 4 trg avn regt

COMBAT SUPPORT
- 2 arty div (4 arty regt, 1 MRL regt)
- 17 arty bde
- 9 (coastal defence) AShM regt
- 21 AD bde
- 1 indep AD regt
- 1 engr bde
- 20 engr regt
- 10 EW regt
- 50 sigs regt

Reserves

FORCES BY ROLE

MANOEUVRE

Armoured
- 2 armd regt

Light
- 18 inf div
- 4 inf bde
- 3 indep inf regt

COMBAT SUPPORT
- 3 arty div
- 7 arty bde
- 17 AD div
- 8 AD bde
- 8 AD regt
- 15 engr regt
- 1 ptn br bde
- 3 ptn br regt
- 10 chem regt
- 10 sigs regt

COMBAT SERVICE SUPPORT
- 9 log bde
- 1 log regt

EQUIPMENT BY TYPE

MBT 6,840: 2,200 Type-59; 550 Type-59-II; 650 Type-59D; 300 Type-79; 500 Type-88A/B; 1,000 Type-96; 1,000 Type-96A; 40 Type-98A; 500 Type-99; 100 Type-99A

LT TK 750: 350 Type-05 AAAV (ZTD-05); 350 Type-62; 50 Type-63A

RECCE 200 Type-09 (ZTL-09)

AIFV 3,450: 500 Type-04 (ZBD-04); 250 Type-04A (ZBD-04A); 300 Type-05 AAAV (ZBD-05); 600 Type-86; 650 Type-86A; 600 Type-92; 550 Type-92B

APC 4,350

APC (T) 3,150: 1,650 Type-63/Type-63C; 1,500 Type-89

APC (W) 1,200: 400 Type-09 (ZBL-09); 700 Type-92A; 100 WZ-523

ARTY 13,014+

SP 2,180: **122mm** 1,550: 750 Type-89; 300 Type-07 (PLZ-07); 150 Type-07B (PLZ-07B); 250 Type-09 (PLC-09); 100 Type-09 (PLL-09); **152mm** 360 Type-83; **155mm** 270 Type-05 (PLZ-05)

TOWED 6,140: **122mm** 3,800 Type-54-1 (M 1938)/Type-83/Type-60 (D-74)/Type-96 (D-30); **130mm** 234 Type-59 (M-46)/Type-59-I; **152mm** 2,106 Type-54 (D-1)/Type-66 (D-20)

GUN/MOR 120mm 266+: 200+ Type-05 (PLL-05); 66 Type-05A (PLZ-05A)

MRL 1,842+

SP 1,788+: **107mm** some **122mm** 1,638+: 1,620 Type-81/Type-89; 18+ Type-10 (PHZ-10); **300mm** 150 Type-03 (PHL-03)

TOWED • **107mm** 54 Type-63

MOR 2,586

TOWED 82mm Type-53 (M-37)/Type-67/Type-82/Type-87; **100mm** Type-89

AT

MSL

SP 400 HJ-9 *Red Arrow* 9

MANPATS HJ-73A/B/C; HJ-8A/C/E

RCL 3,966: **75mm** Type-56; **82mm** Type-65 (B-10)/Type-78; **105mm** Type-75; **120mm** Type-98
GUNS 1,888:
SP 580 **100mm** 350 Type-02 (PTL-02); **120mm** 230 Type-89 (PLZ-89)
TOWED • 100mm 1,308 Type-73 (T-12)/Type-86
AIRCRAFT • TPT 8 **Medium** 4 Y-8; **Light** 4 Y-7
HELICOPTERS
ATK 108: 60+ Z-10; 48+ Z-19
MRH 351: 22 Mi-17 *Hip* H; 3 Mi-17-1V *Hip* H; 38 Mi-17V-5 *Hip* H; 25 Mi-17V-7 *Hip* H; 8 SA342L *Gazelle*; 21 Z-9A; 31 Z-9W; 10 Z-9WA; 193 Z-9WZ
TPT 304+ **Heavy** 53+: 4 Mi-26 *Halo*; 9 Z-8A; 40+ Z-8B; **Medium** 183+: 50 Mi-8T *Hip*; 114+ Mi-171; 19 S-70C2 (S-70C) *Black Hawk* **Light** 68: 53 AS350 *Ecureuil*; 15 EC120
UAV • ISR • Heavy BZK-005; BZK-009; WZ-5 **Medium** ASN-105; ASN-206; BZK-006; BZK-007; **Light** ASN-104; W-50
AD
SAM 278+:
SP 278: 200 HQ-7A; 24 9K331 *Tor*-M1 (SA-15 *Gauntlet*); 30 HQ-6D *Red Leader*; 24 HQ-16A
MANPAD HN-5A/HN-5B *Hong Nu;* FN-6/QW-1/QW-2
GUNS 7,700+
SP 25mm Type-04A; **35mm** Type-07; **37mm** Type-88
TOWED 25mm Type-87; **35mm** Type-99 (GDF-002); **37mm** Type-55 (M-1939)/Type-65/Type-74; **57mm** Type-59 (S-60); **100mm** Type-59 (KS-19)
RADAR • LAND *Cheetah*; RASIT; Type-378
MSL
AShM HY-1 (CSS-N-2) *Silkworm*; HY-2 (CSS-C-3) *Seersucker*; HY-4 (CSS-C-7) *Sadsack*
ASM KD-10
ARV Type-73; Type-84; Type-85; Type-97; Type-654
VLB KMM; MTU; TMM; Type-84A
MW Type-74; Type-79; Type-81-II; Type-84

Navy ε200,000; 35,000 conscript (total 235,000)

The PLA Navy is organised into five service arms: submarine, surface, naval aviation, coastal defence and marine corps, as well as other specialised units. There are three fleets, the Beihai Fleet (North Sea), Donghai Fleet (East Sea) and Nanhai Fleet (South Sea).

EQUIPMENT BY TYPE

SUBMARINES 70
STRATEGIC • SSBN 4:
1 *Xia* (Type-092) with 12 JL-1 (CSS-N-3) strategic SLBM
3 *Jin* (Type-094) with up to 12 JL-2 (CSS-NX-4) strategic SLBM (operational status unknown; 1 additional vessel in build)
TACTICAL 66
SSN 5:
3 *Han* (Type-091) with YJ-82 AShM, 6 single 533mm TT
2 *Shang* (Type-093) with 6 single 533mm TT (operational status unknown)
SSK 60:
12 *Kilo* (2 Project 877, 2 Project 636, 8 Project 636N) with 3M54 *Klub* (SS-N-27B *Sizzler*) ASCM; 6 single 533mm TT
20 *Ming* (4 Type-035, 12 Type-035G, 4 Type-035B) with 8 single 533mm TT
16 *Song* (Type-039/039G) with YJ-82 (CSS-N-8) *Saccade* ASCM, 6 single 533mm TT
4 *Yuan* (Type-039A) with 6 533mm TT
up to 8 *Yuan* II (Type-039B) with 6 533mm TT
SSB 1 *Qing* (Type-032) (SLBM trials)
PRINCIPAL SURFACE COMBATANTS 70
AIRCRAFT CARRIERS • CV 1
1 *Liaoning* with 4 18-cell FL3000N SAM, 2 RBU 6000 *Smerch* 2, 3 Type 1030 CIWS (capacity 18-24 J-15 ac; 17 Ka-28/Ka-31/Z-8S/Z-8JH/Z-8AEW hel)
DESTROYERS 15
DDGHM 13:
2 *Hangzhou* (RUS *Sovremenny*) with 2 quad lnchr with 3M80/3M82 *Moskit* (SS-N-22 *Sunburn*) AShM, 2 3K90 *Uragan* (SA-N-7 *Grizzly*) SAM, 2 twin 533mm ASTT, 2 RBU 1000 *Smerch* 3, 2 CADS-N-1 *Kashtan* CIWS, 2 twin 130mm gun, (capacity 1 Z-9C/Ka-28 *Helix* A hel)
2 *Hangzhou* (RUS *Sovremenny*) with 2 quad lnchr with 3M80/3M82 *Moskit* (SS-N-22 *Sunburn*) AShM, 2 3K90 *Uragan* (SA-N-7 *Grizzly*) SAM, 2 twin 533mm ASTT, 2 RBU 1000 *Smerch* 3, 4 AK630 CIWS, 2 twin 130mm gun, (capacity 1 Z-9C/Ka-28 *Helix* A hel)
2 *Luyang* (Type-052B) with 4 quad lnchr with YJ-82/83 AShM, 2 single lnchr with 3K90 *Uragan* (SA-N-7 *Grizzly*) SAM, 2 triple 324mm TT with Yu-7 LWT, 2 Type 730 CIWS, 1 100mm gun, (capacity 1 Ka-28 *Helix* A hel)
4 *Luyang* II (Type-052C) with 2 quad lnchr with YJ-62 AShM, 8 sextuple VLS with HHQ-9 SAM, 2 triple 324mm TT with Yu-7 LWT, 2 Type 730 CIWS, 1 100mm gun, (capacity 2 Ka-28 *Helix* A hel) (2 additional vessels; expected ISD 2014)
1 *Luhai* (Type-051B) with 4 quad lnchr with YJ-83 AShM, 1 octuple lnchr with HQ-7 SAM, 2 triple 324mm ASTT with Yu-7 LWT, 1 twin 100mm gun, (capacity 2 Z-9C/Ka-28 *Helix* A hel)
2 *Luhu* (Type-052) with 4 quad lnchr with YJ-82/83 AShM, 1 octuple lnchr with HQ-7 SAM, 2 triple 324mm ASTT with Yu-7 LWT, 2 FQF 2500, 2 Type 730 CIWS, 1 twin 100mm gun, (capacity 2 Z-9C hel)
DDGM 2:
2 *Luzhou* (Type-051C) with 2 quad lnchr with YJ-82/83 AShM; 6 sextuple VLS with SA-N-20 *Grumble* SAM, 2 Type 730 CIWS, 1 100mm gun, 1 hel landing platform
FRIGATES 54
FFGHM 31:
2 *Jiangkai* (Type-054) with 2 quad lnchr with YJ-82/83 AShM, 1 octuple lnchr with HQ-7 SAM, 2 triple 324mm TT with Yu-7 LWT, 2 RBU 1200, 4 AK630 CIWS, 1 100mm gun, (capacity 1 Ka-28 *Helix* A/Z-9C hel)
15 *Jiangkai* II (Type-054A) with 2 quad lnchr with YJ-82/83 AShM, 1 32-cell VLS with HQ-16 SAM (reported), 2 triple 324mm TT with Yu-7 LWT, 2 RBU 1200, 2 Type 730 CIWS, 1 76mm gun, (capacity 1 Ka-28 *Helix* A/Z-9C hel) (4 additional vessels launched)

4 *Jiangwei* I (Type-053H2G) with 2 triple lnchr with YJ-82/83 AShM, 1 sextuple lnchr with HQ-61 (CSA-N-2) SAM, 2 RBU 1200, 1 twin 100mm gun, (capacity 2 Z-9C hel)
10 *Jiangwei* II (Type-053H3) with 2 quad lnchr with YJ-82/83 AShM, 1 octuple lnchr with HQ-7 SAM, 2 RBU 1200, 1 twin 100mm gun, (capacity 2 Z-9C hel)
FFGH 1:
1 *Jianghu* IV (Type-053H1Q - trg role) with 1 triple lnchr with HY-2 (CSS-N-2) AShM, 4 RBU 1200, 1 100mm gun, (capacity 1 Z-9C hel)
FFGM 4:
2 *Luda* III (Type-051DT) with 4 quad lnchr with YJ-82/83 AShM, 1 octuple lnchr with HQ-7 SAM, 2 FQF 2500, 2 130mm gun, 3 twin 57mm gun
2 *Luda* III (Type-051G) with 4 quad lnchr with YJ-82/83 AShM, 1 octuple lnchr with HQ-7 SAM, 2 FQF 2500, 2 triple 324mm ASTT, 2 twin 100mm gun
FFG 18:
2 *Jianghu* I (Type-053H) with 2 triple lnchr with SY-1 (CSS-N-2) AShM, 4 RBU 1200, 2 100mm gun
6 *Jianghu* II (Type-053H1) with 2 triple lnchr with HY-2 (CSS-N-2) AShM, 2 RBU 1200, 1 twin 100mm gun, (capacity 1 Z-9C hel)
1 *Jianghu* III (Type-053H2) with 2 twin lnchr with YJ-82/83 AShM, 2 RBU 1200, 2 twin 100mm gun
6 *Jianghu* V (Type-053H1G) with 2 quad lnchr with YJ-82/83 AShM, 2 RBU 1200, 2 twin 100mm gun
3 *Luda* II (Type-051) with 2 triple lnchr with HY-2 (CSS-N-2) *Seersucker* AShM, 2 triple 324mm ASTT, 2 FQF 2500, 2 twin 130mm gun, (mine-laying capability)
PATROL AND COASTAL COMBATANTS 216+
CORVETTES • FSGM 8:
8 *Jiangdao* (Type-056) with 2 twin lnchr with YJ-83 AShM, 1 8-cell GMLS with FL3000N SAM, 2 triple ASTT, 1 76mm gun, 1 hel landing platform
PCFG 76+
65+ *Houbei* (Type-022) with 2 quad lnchr with YJ-82/83 AShM
11 *Huangfen* (Type-021) with 2 twin lnchr with HY-2 (CSS-N-3) AShM
PCG 26
6 *Houjian* (Type-037/II) with 2 triple lnchr with YJ-8 (CSS-N-4) AShM
20 *Houxin* (Type-037/IG) with 2 twin lnchr with YJ-8 (CSS-N-4) AShM
PCC 72
2 *Haijiu* (Type-037/I) with 4 RBU 1200, 1 twin 57mm gun
48 *Hainan* (Type-037) with ε4 RBU 1200, 2 twin 57mm gun
22 *Haiqing* (Type-037/IS) with 2 Type-87
PB 34+ *Haizui/Shanghai* III (Type-062/I)
MINE WARFARE 53
MINE COUNTERMEASURES 52
MCO 10: 8 *Wochi*; 2 *Wozang*
MSO 16 T-43
MSC 16 *Wosao*
MSD 10: 4 *Futi* (Type-312 - 42 more in reserve); 6 Type-529
MINELAYERS • ML 1 *Wolei*
AMPHIBIOUS
PRINCIPAL AMPHIBIOUS VESSELS • LPD 3 *Yuzhao* (Type-071) with 4 AK630 CIWS, 1 76mm gun, (capacity 2 LCAC or 4 UCAC plus supporting vehicles; 500–800 troops; 2 hel)
LANDING SHIPS 85
LSM 59:
10 *Yubei* (Type-074A) (capacity 10 tanks or 150 troops)
1 *Yudeng* (Type-073) with 1 twin 57mm gun, (capacity 6 tk; 180 troops)
10 *Yuhai* (Type-074) (capacity 2 tk; 250 troops)
28 *Yuliang* (Type-079) (capacity 5 tk; 250 troops)
10 *Yunshu* (Type-073A) (capacity 6 tk)
LST 26:
7 *Yukan* with 1 twin 57mm gun (capacity 10 tk; 200 troops)
9 *Yuting* (capacity 10 tk; 250 troops; 2 hel)
10 *Yuting* II (capacity 4 LCVP; 10 tk; 250 troops)
LANDING CRAFT 152
LCU 120 *Yunnan*
LCM 20 *Yuchin*
LCAC 2: 1 *Yuyi*; 1 *Zubr*
UCAC 10
LOGISTICS AND SUPPORT 212
ABU 7 *Yannan*
AG 6: 4 *Qiongsha* (capacity 400 troops); 2 *Qiongsha* (hospital conversion)
AGI 2: 1 *Dadie*; 1 Type-813
AGM 5 (space and missile tracking)
AGOR 8: 3 *Dahua*; 2 *Kan*; 1 *Bin Hai*; 1 *Shuguang*; 1 other
AGS 5: 4 *Yenlai*; 1 *Ganzhu*
AH 1 *Daishan*
AK 23: 2 *Yantai*; 2 *Dayun*; 6 *Danlin*; 7 *Dandao*; 6 *Hongqi*
AOL 5 *Guangzhou*
AORH 7: 2 *Fuqing*; 2 *Fuchi* (Type-903); 2 *Fuchi* mod (Type-903A); 1 *Nanyun*
AOT 50: 7 *Danlin*; 20 *Fulin*; 2 *Shengli*; 3 *Jinyou*; 18 *Fuzhou*
ARS 2: 1 *Dadong*; 1 *Dadao*
AS 8: 1 *Dazhi*; 5 *Dalang*; 2 *Dazhou*
ASR 6: 3 *Dajiang* (capacity 2 Z-8); 3 *Dalao*
ATF 51: 4 *Tuzhong*; 10 *Hujiu*; 1 *Daozha*; 17 *Gromovoy*; 19 *Roslavl*
AWT 18: 10 *Leizhou*; 8 *Fuzhou*
AX 3: 1 *Shichang*; 1 *Daxin*; 1 other
YDG 5 *Yen Pai*
MSL • AShM 72 YJ-62 (coastal defence) (3 regt)

Naval Aviation 26,000

FORCES BY ROLE
BOMBER
1 regt with H-6DU/G
1 regt with H-6G
FIGHTER
1 regt with J-7E
1 regt with J-8F
FIGHTER/GROUND ATTACK
1 regt with J-10A/S
2 regt with J-11B/BS
1 regt with Su-30MK2

ATTACK
2 regt with JH-7
3 regt with JH-7A
ELINT/ISR/AEW
1 regt with Y-8J/JB/W/X
TRANSPORT
1 regt with Y-7; Y-7H; Y-8
1 regt with Y-7; Y-8; Z-8; Z-9
TRAINING
1 regt with CJ-6A
2 regt with HY-7
1 regt with JL-8
1 regt with JL-9
1 regt with Mi-8 *Hip*; Z-9C
1 regt with Y-5
HELICOPTER
1 regt with Mi-8; Ka-28; Ka-31
1 regt with SH-5; AS365; Ka-28; Z-9; Z-8A/JH/S

EQUIPMENT BY TYPE
AIRCRAFT 332 combat capable
BBR 30 H-6G
FTR 48: 24 J-7E *Fishbed*; 24 J-8F *Finback*
FGA 216: 120 JH-7/JH-7A; 16 J-10A; 8 J-10S; 48 J-11B/BS; 24 Su-30MK2 *Flanker*
ASW 3 SH-5
ELINT 7: 4 Y-8JB *High New* 2; 3 Y-8X
AEW&C 10: 4 Y-8J; 6 Y-8W *High New* 5
ISR 7 HZ-5
TKR 3 H-6DU
TPT 66: **Medium** 4 Y-8; **Light** 62: 50 Y-5; 4 Y-7; 6 Y-7H; 2 Yak-42
TRG 106+: 38 CJ-6; 5 HJ-5*; 21 HY-7; 14 JJ-6*; 4 JJ-7*; 12 JL-8*; 12+ JL-9
HELICOPTERS
ASW 44: 19 Ka-28 *Helix* A; 25 Z-9C
AEW 10+: 9 Ka-31; 1+ Z-8 AEW
SAR 6: 4 Z-8JH; 2 Z-8S
TPT 43 **Heavy** 35: 15 SA321 *Super Frelon*; 20 Z-8/Z-8A; **Medium** 8 Mi-8 *Hip*
UAV • ISR Heavy BZK-005; **Medium** BZK-007
MSL
AAM • IR PL-5; PL-8; PL-9; R-73 (AA-11 *Archer*) **SARH** PL-11 **IR/SARH** R-27 (AA-10 *Alamo*) **ARH** R-77 (AA-12 *Adder*); PL-12
ASM Kh-31A (AS-17B *Krypton*); KD-88
AShM YJ-61; YJ-8K; YJ-83K
ARM YJ-91
BOMBS
Conventional: Type-200-4/Type-200A
Laser-Guided: LS-500J
TV-Guided: KAB-500KR; KAB-1500KR

Marines ε10,000

FORCES BY ROLE
MANOEUVRE
Amphibious
2 mne bde (1 spec ops bn, 1 SF amph recce bn, 1 recce bn, 1 tk bn, 2 mech inf bn, 1 arty bn, 1 AT/AD bn, 1 engr bn, 1 sigs bn)

EQUIPMENT BY TYPE
LT TK 73 Type-05 AAAV (ZTD-05)
APC (T) 152 Type-05 AAAV (ZBD-05)
ARTY 40+
SP 122mm 40+: 20+ Type-07; 20+ Type-89
MRL 107mm Type-63
MOR 82mm
AT
MSL • MANPATS HJ-73; HJ-8
RCL 120mm Type-98
AD • SAM • MANPAD HN-5

Air Force 398,000

The PLAAF organises its command through seven military-region air forces (MRAF) – Shenyang, Beijing, Lanzhou, Jinan, Nanjing, Guangzhou and Chengdu – five corps deputy leader-grade command posts (Datong, Kunming, Wuhan, Xian, and Fuzhou); four corps deputy leader-grade bases (Nanning, Urumqi, Shanghai, and Dalian); and four division leader-grade command posts (Lhasa, Hetian, Zhangzhou, and Changchun). Each MRAF, CP, and base is responsible for all subordinate combat organizations (aviation, SAM, AAA, and radar) in its area of operations. The regiments of four air divisions have been reorganised into new brigades, and MRAF training formations have been consolidated into three new flying academies.

Flying hours Ftr, ground attack and bbr pilots average 100–150 hrs/yr. Tpt pilots average 200+ per year. Each regt has two quotas to meet during the year – a total number of hours, and the percentage of flight time dedicated to tactics trg.

FORCES BY ROLE
BOMBER
1 regt with H-6A/M
3 regt with H-6H
2 regt with H-6K
FIGHTER
7 regt with J-7 *Fishbed*
6 regt with J-7E *Fishbed*
4 regt with J-7G *Fishbed*
1 regt with J-8B *Finback*
1 regt with J-8F *Finback*
2 regt with J-8H *Finback*
1 regt with Su-27SK/UBK *Flanker*
6 regt with J-11/Su-27UBK *Flanker*
2 regt with J-11B/BS
2 bde with J-7/J-7G *Fishbed*
FIGHTER/GROUND ATTACK
2 regt with Su-30MKK *Flanker*
7 regt with J-10/J-10A/J-10S
2 bde with J-7E *Fishbed*; J-11B/BS; Q-5D/E *Fantan*
2 bde with J-8H *Finback*; J-11B/BS; JH-7A
FIGHTER/GROUND ATTACK/ISR
2 bde with J-7E *Fishbed*; J-8H *Finback*; JZ-8F *Finback** Su-30MKK
GROUND ATTACK
4 regt with JH-7A
4 regt with Q-5C/D/E *Fantan*
ELECTRONIC WARFARE
1 regt with Y-8CB/G/XZ
1 regt with Y-8CB/G

ISR
1 regt with JZ-8F *Finback**
1 regt with Y-8H1
AIRBORNE EARLY WARNING & CONTROL
1 regt with KJ-200; KJ-2000; Y-8T
COMBAT SEARCH & RESCUE
1 regt with Mi-171; Z-8
TANKER
1 regt with H-6U
TRANSPORT
1 (VIP) regt with B-737; CRJ-200/700
1 (VIP) regt with B-737; Tu-154M; Tu-154M/D
2 regt with Il-76MD/TD *Candid*
1 regt with Mi-17V-5; Y-7
2 regt with Y-7
1 regt with Y-8
1 regt with Y-8; Y-9
TRAINING
2 regt with J-7; JJ-7
5 bde with CJ-6/6A/6B; JL-8*; Y-5; Y-7; Z-9
TRANSPORT HELICOPTER
1 regt with AS332 *Super Puma* (VIP)
AIR DEFENCE
3 SAM div
2 mixed SAM/ADA div
9 SAM bde
2 mixed SAM/ADA bde
2 ADA bde
9 indep SAM regt
1 indep ADA regt
4 indep SAM bn

EQUIPMENT BY TYPE
AIRCRAFT 2,193 combat capable
BBR 90: ε70 H-6A/H/M; ε20 H-6K
FTR 842: 216 J-7 *Fishbed*; 192 J-7E *Fishbed*; 120 J-7G *Fishbed*; 24 J-8B *Finback*; 24 J-8F *Finback*; 96 J-8H *Finback*; 95 J-11; 43 Su-27SK *Flanker*; 32 Su-27UBK *Flanker*
FGA 543+: 78 J-10; 122+ J-10A; 40 J-10S; 110+ J-11B/BS; 120 JH-7A; 73 Su-30MKK *Flanker*
ATK 120 Q-5C/D/E *Fantan*
EW 13: 4 Y-8CB *High New* 1; 7 Y-8G *High New* 3; 2 Y-8XZ *High New* 7
ELINT 4 Tu-154M/D *Careless*
ISR 51: 24 JZ-8 *Finback**; 24 JZ-8F *Finback**; 3 Y-8H1
AEW&C 8+: 4+ KJ-200; 4 KJ-2000
C2 5: 2 B-737; 3 Y-8T *High New* 4
TKR 10 H-6U
TPT 327+ **Heavy** 16+ Il-76MD/TD *Candid*; **Medium** 41+: 40 Y-8; 1+ Y-9; **Light** 239: 170 Y-5; 41 Y-7/Y-7H; 20 Y-11; 8 Y-12 **PAX** 31: 9 B-737 (VIP); 5 CRJ-200; 5 CRJ-700; 12 Tu-154M *Careless*
TRG 950: 400 CJ-6/6A/6B; 200 JJ-7*; 350 JL-8*
HELICOPTERS
MRH 22: 20 Z-9; 2 Mi-17V-5 *Hip* H
TPT 28+: **Heavy** 18+ Z-8 (SA321) **Medium** 10+: 6+ AS332 *Super Puma* (VIP); 4+ Mi-171
UAV • ISR • Heavy CH-1 *Chang Hong*; *Chang Kong* 1; *Firebee*; **Light** *Harpy*
AD
SAM 600+
SP 300+: 24 HD-6D; 60+ HQ-7; 32+ HQ-9; 24 HQ-12 (KS-1A); 32 S-300PMU (SA-10B *Grumble*); 64 S-300PMU1 (SA-20 *Gargoyle*); 64 S-300PMU2 (SA-20 *Gargoyle*)
TOWED 300+ HQ-2 (SA-2) *Guideline* Towed/HQ-2A/HQ-2B(A)
GUNS 16,000 **100mm/85mm**
MSL
AAM • IR PL-2B‡; PL-5B/C; PL-8; R-73 (AA-11 *Archer*); **SARH** PL-11; **IR/SARH** R-27 (AA-10 *Alamo*); **ARH** PL-12; R-77 (AA-12 *Adder*)
ASM KD-88; Kh-29 (AS-14 *Kedge*); Kh-31A/P (AS-17 *Krypton*); Kh-59 (AS-18 *Kazoo*); YJ-91 (Domestically produced Kh-31P variant)
LACM YJ(KD)-63; CJ-10/CJ-20 (reported)

15th Airborne Corps

FORCES BY ROLE
SPECIAL FORCES
1 SF unit
MANOEUVRE
Reconnaissance
1 recce regt
Air Manoeuvre
2 AB div (2 AB regt; 1 arty regt)
1 AB div (1 AB regt; 1 arty regt)
Aviation
1 hel regt
COMBAT SUPPORT
1 sigs gp
COMBAT SERVICE SUPPORT
1 log gp

EQUIPMENT BY TYPE
AIFV 171 Type-03 (ZBD-03)
APC (T) 4 Type-04 (ZZZ04)
ARTY 162+
TOWED • 122mm ε54 Type-96 (D-30)
MRL • TOWED • 107mm ε54 Type-63
MOR • 82mm some **100mm** 54
AT • SP some HJ-9 *Red Arrow* 9
AD
SAM • MANPAD QW-1
GUNS • TOWED 25mm 54 Type-87
HELICOPTERS
CSAR 8 Z-8KA
MRH 22 Z-9WZ

Military Regions

This represents the geographical disposition of the PLA's group armies, fleets and air divisions within China, as opposed to a joint-service command structure. Designated Rapid Reaction Units (RRU) are indicated.

Shenyang MR (North East)

Land Forces

(Heilongjiang, Jilin, Liaoning MD)
16th Group Army
(1 armd bde, 3 mech inf bde, 2 mot inf div, 1 arty bde, 1 AD bde, 1 engr regt)
39th Group Army
(1 SF unit, 1 armd bde, 1 mech inf div, 2 mech inf bde,

1 mot inf div; 1 avn regt, 1 arty bde, 1 AD bde, 1 engr regt, 1 EW regt)
40th Group Army
(1 armd bde, 3 mot inf bde, 1 arty bde, 1 AD bde, 1 engr regt)

North Sea Fleet Naval Aviation
Other Forces
(1 trg regt with CJ-6A; 1 trg regt with HY-7; 1 trg regt with Y-5)

Shenyang MRAF
1st Fighter Division
(1 ftr regt with J-11B; 1 FGA regt with J-10/J-10A/J-10S; 1 ftr regt with J-8F)
11th Attack Division
(1 atk regt with JH-7A; 1 atk regt with Q-5)
16th Special Mission Division
(1 EW regt with Y-8CB/G; 1 ISR regt with JZ-8F; 1 tpt regt with Y-8)
21st Fighter Division
(1 ftr regt with J-7E; 1 ftr regt with J-8H; 1 ftr regt with J-7H)
Dalian Base
(2 FGA bde with J-7E; J-11B; Q-5)
Harbin Flying Academy
(2 trg bde with CJ-6; JL-8; Y-5; Y-7)
Other Forces
(1 (mixed) SAM/ADA bde; 1 SAM bde)

Beijing MR (North)

Land Forces
(Beijing, Tianjin Garrison, Inner Mongolia, Hebei, Shanxi MD)
27th Group Army
(1 armd bde, 2 mech inf bde, 2 mot inf bde, 1 arty bde, 1 AD bde, 1 engr regt)
38th Group Army
(1 SF unit, 1 armd div, 2 mech inf div, 1 avn bde, 1 arty bde, 1 AD bde, 1 engr regt)
65th Group Army
(1 armd bde, 1 mech inf div, 1 (OPFOR) mech inf bde, 2 mot inf bde, 1 arty bde, 1 AD bde, 1 engr regt)
Other Forces
(2 (Beijing) gd div; 1 avn regt)

North Sea Fleet Naval Aviation
2nd Naval Air Division
(1 tpt regt with Y-7/Y-8)
Other Forces
(1 trg regt with JL-9; 1 trg regt with HY-7; 1 trg regt with JL-8; 1 trg regt with Mi-8; Z-9)

Beijing MRAF
7th Fighter Division
(1 ftr regt with J-11; 1 ftr regt with J-7G; 1 ftr regt with J-7)
15th Fighter/Attack Division
(1 FGA regt with J-10A/S; 1 ftr regt with J-7; 1 atk regt with Q-5C)
24th Fighter Division
(1 ftr regt with J-7G; 1 FGA regt with J-10/J-10A/J-10S)
Shijiazhuang Flying Academy
(1 trg bde with CJ-6; JL-8; Y-5; Y-7)
Other Forces
(1 Flight Test Centre; 3 SAM div; 1 (mixed) SAM/ADA div)

Other Forces
34th VIP Transport Division
(1 tpt regt with B-737; CRJ200/700; 1 tpt regt with B-737; Tu-154M; Tu-154M/D; 1 tpt regt with Y-7; 1 hel regt with AS332)

Lanzhou MR (West)

Land Forces
(Ningxia, Shaanxi, Gansu, Qing-hai, Xinjiang, South Xinjiang MD)
21st Group Army
(1 SF unit, 1 armd bde, 1 mech inf bde, 1 mot inf div (RRU), 1 arty bde, 1 AD bde, 1 engr regt, 1 EW regt)
47th Group Army
(1 armd bde, 1 mech inf bde, 2 (high alt) mot inf bde, 1 arty bde, 1 AD bde, 1 engr regt)
Xinjiang MD
(1 SF unit, 1 (high alt) mech div, 1 indep mech inf regt, 3 (high alt) mot div, 1 avn bde, 1 arty bde, 1 AD bde, 1 engr regt, 1 EW regt)

Lanzhou MRAF
6th Fighter Division
(1 ftr regt with J-11; 1 ftr regt with J-7E; 1 ftr regt with J-7)
36th Bomber Division
(1 surv regt with Y8H-1; 1 bbr regt with H-6M; 1 bbr regt with H-6H)
Urumqi Base
(2 FGA bde with J-8H; J-11B; JH-7A)
Xi'an Flying Academy
(2 trg bde with CJ-6; JL-8; Y-7; Z-9)
Other Forces
(1 (mixed) SAM/ADA div; 1 SAM bde; 4 indep SAM regt)

Jinan MR (Centre)

Land Forces
(Shandong, Henan MD)
20th Group Army
(1 armd bde, 2 mech inf bde, 1 arty bde, 1 AD bde, 1 engr regt)
26th Group Army
(1 SF unit, 1 armd bde, 1 mech inf bde, 3 mot inf bde, 1 avn regt, 1 arty bde, 1 AD bde, 1 engr regr, 1 EW rgt)
54th Group Army
(1 armd bde, 2 mech inf div (RRU), 1 mech bde, 1 avn regt, 1 arty bde, 1 AD bde, 1 engr regt)

North Sea Fleet
Coastal defence from DPRK border (Yalu River) to south of Lianyungang (approx 35°10′N); equates

Asia

to Shenyang, Beijing and Jinan MR, and to seaward; HQ at Qingdao; support bases at Lushun, Qingdao. 9 coastal-defence districts
3 **SSBN**; 3 **SSN**; 20 **SSK**; 2 **DDGHM**; 2 **DDGM**; 8 **FFGHM**; 2 **FFGM**; 1 **FFGH**; 3 **FFG**; 2 **FSGM**; ε22 **PCFG/PCG**; ε28 **PCC**; 9 **LS**; 1 **ML**; ε7 **MCMV**

North Sea Fleet Naval Aviation

2nd Naval Air Division
(1 EW/ISR/AEW regt with Y-8J/JB/W/X; 1 MP/hel regt with SH-5; AS365; Ka-28; SA321; Z-8; Z-9)
5th Naval Air Division
(2 FGA regt with JH-7A; 1 ftr regt with J-8F)

Jinan MRAF

5th Attack Division
(1 atk regt with Q-5E; 1 atk regt with JH-7A)
12th Fighter Division
(1 ftr regt with J-10A/S; 1 ftr regt with J-8B; 1 ftr regt with J-7G)
19th Fighter Division
(1 ftr regt with Su-27SK; 1 ftr regt with J-7; 1 trg regt with J-7/JJ-7)
32nd Fighter Division
(1 ftr regt with J-11B; 1 trg regt with J-7/JJ-7)
Other Forces
(1 Flight Instructor Training Base with CJ-6; JL-8; 4 SAM bn)

Nanjing MR (East)

Land Forces

(Shanghai Garrison, Jiangsu, Zhejiang, Fujian, Jiangxi, Anhui MD)
1st Group Army
(1 armd bde, 1 amph mech div, 1 mech inf bde, 1 mot inf bde, 1 avn bde, 1 arty div, 1 AD bde, 1 engr regt, 1 EW regt)
12th Group Army
(1 armd bde, 2 mech inf bde, 2 mot inf bde (1 RRU), 1 arty bde, 1 AD bde, 1 engr regt)
31st Group Army
(1 SF unit, 1 (amph) armd bde, 2 mot inf div (incl 1 RRU), 1 mot inf bde, 1 avn regt, 1 arty bde, 1 AD bde, 1 engr regt, 1 EW regt)

East Sea Fleet

Coastal defence from south of Lianyungang to Dongshan (approx 35°10′N to 23°30′N); equates to Nanjing Military Region, and to seaward; HQ at Ningbo; support bases at Fujian, Zhoushan, Ningbo. 7 coastal defence districts
17 **SSK**; 6 **DDGHM**; 16 **FFGHM**; 5 **FFG**; 2 **FSGM**; ε34 **PCFG/PCG**; ε22 **PCC**; 27 **LS**; ε22 **MCMV**

East Sea Fleet Naval Aviation

4th Naval Aviation Division
(1 FGA regt with Su-30MK2; 1 FGA regt with J-10A)
6th Naval Aviation Division
(2 FGA regt with JH-7; 1 bbr regt with H-6G)
Other Forces
(1 hel regt with Mi-8; Ka-28; Ka-31)

Nanjing MRAF

3rd Fighter Division
(1 ftr regt with J-7G; 1 FGA regt with J-10/J-10A/J-10S; 1 FGA regt with Su-30MKK)
10th Bomber Division
(1 bbr regt with H-6H; 1 bbr regt with H-6K)
14th Fighter Division
(2 ftr regt with J-11; 1 ftr regt with J-7E)
26th Special Mission Division
(1 AEW&C regt with KJ-200/KJ-2000/Y-8T; 1 CSAR regt with M-171/Z-8)
28th Attack Division
(2 atk regt with JH-7A; 1 atk regt with Q-5D/E)
Shanghai Base
(2 FGA/ISR bde with J-7E; J-8H; JZ-8F; Su-30MKK)
Other Forces
(3 SAM bde; 1 ADA bde; 2 indep SAM regt)

Guangzhou MR (South)

Land Forces

(Hubei, Hunan, Guangdong, Guangxi, Hainan MD)
41st Group Army
(1 armd bde, 1 mech inf div (RRU), 1 mot inf div, 1 arty bde, 1 AD bde, 1 engr regt)
42nd Group Army
(1 SF unit, 1 armd bde, 1 amph mech div (RRU), 1 mot inf div, 1 avn bde, 1 arty div, 1 AD bde, 1 engr regt, 1 EW regt)
Other Forces
(1 mot inf bde; 1 (composite) mot inf bde (Composed of units drawn from across the PLA and deployed to Hong Kong on a rotational basis))

South Sea Fleet

Coastal defence from Dongshan (approx 23°30′N) to VNM border; equates to Guangzhou MR, and to seaward (including Paracel and Spratly Islands); HQ at Zuanjiang; support bases at Yulin, Guangzhou
1 **SSBN**; 2 **SSN**; 18 **SSK**; 5 **DDGHM**; 7 **FFGHM**; 12 **FFG**; 4 **FSGM**; ε42 **PCFG/PCG**; ε20 **PCC**; 2 **LPD**; 51 **LS**; ε10 **MCMV**

South Sea Fleet Naval Aviation

8th Naval Aviation Division
(1 FGA regt with J-11B; 1 bbr regt with H-6G; 1 ftr regt with J-7E)
9th Naval Aviation Division
(1 ftr regt with J-8H, 1 FGA regt with JH-7A; 1 tpt regt with Y-7; Y-8; Z-8; Z-8JH/S; Z-9)

Guangzhou MRAF

2nd Fighter Division
(1 ftr regt with J-8H; 1 FGA regt with J-10/J-10S; 1 ftr regt with J-11)
8th Bomber Division
(1 tkr regt with H-6U; 1 bbr regt with H-6H; 1 bbr regt with H-6K)
9th Fighter Division
(1 FGA regt with J-10A/S; 2 ftr regt with J-7E)
13th Transport Division
(1 tpt regt with Y-8; 2 tpt regt with Il-76MD/TD)

18th Fighter Division
(1 ftr regt with J-7; 1 FGA regt with Su-30MKK)
Nanning Base
(2 ftr bde with J-7/J-7G *Fishbed*)
Other Forces
(4 SAM Bde, 1 ADA bde, 1 indep ADA regt)

Other Forces

Marines
(2 mne bde)
15th Airborne Corps
(3 AB div)

Chengdu MR (South-West)

Land Forces

(Chongqing Garrison, Sichuan, Guizhou, Yunnan, Tibet MD)
13th Group Army
(1 SF unit, 1 armd bde, 1 (high alt) mech inf div (RRU), 1 mot inf div, 1 avn bde, 1 arty bde, 1 AD bde, 1 engr regt, 1 EW regt)
14th Group Army
(1 armd bde, 1 (jungle) mot inf div, 1 mot inf div, 1 arty bde, 1 AD bde, 1 engr regt)
Xizang Military District
(1 SF unit; 1 (high alt) mech inf bde; 2 mtn inf bde; 1 arty regt, 1 AD regt, 1 engr regt, 1 EW regt)

Chengdu MRAF

4th Transport Division
(1 tpt regt with Y-8/Y-9; 1 tpt regt with Y-7; 1 tpt regt with Mi-17V-5/Y-7)
20th Special Mission Division
(1 tpt regt with Y-7; 1 EW regt with Y-8CB/G/XZ)
33rd Fighter Division
(1 ftr regt with J-7E; 1 ftr regt with J-11)
44th Fighter Division
(1 ftr regt with J-7; 1 FGA regt with J-10/J-10A/J-10S)
Other Forces
(1 (mixed) SAM/ADA bde; 3 indep SAM regt)

Paramilitary 660,000+ active

People's Armed Police ε660,000

Internal Security Forces ε400,000

FORCES BY ROLE
MANOEUVRE
Other
14 (mobile) paramilitary div
22 (mobile) indep paramilitary regt
Some (firefighting/garrison) unit

Border Defence Force ε260,000

FORCES BY ROLE
COMMAND
30 div HQ
MANOEUVRE
Other
110 (border) paramilitary regt
20 (marine) paramilitary regt

China Coast Guard

In March 2013, four of China's maritime law enforcement agencies were unified under the State Oceanic Administration and renamed the China Coast Guard

EQUIPMENT BY TYPE
PATROL AND COASTAL COMBATANTS 370+
PSO 18
PCO 48
PB/PBF 304+

Maritime Safety Administration (MSA)

Various tasks including aid to navigation

EQUIPMENT BY TYPE
PATROL AND COASTAL COMBATANTS 214+
PSO 4
PCO 10
PB 200+

Cyber

The PLA has devoted much attention to information warfare over the past decade, both in terms of battlefield EW and wider, cyber-warfare capabilities. The main doctrine is the 'Integrated Network Electronic Warfare' document, which guides PLA computer-network operations. PLA thinking appears to have moved beyond INEW towards a new concept of 'information confrontation' (*xinxi duikang*) which aims to integrate both electronic and non-electronic aspects of information warfare within a single command authority. PLA thinking sees warfare under informationised conditions as characterised by opposing sides using complete systems of ground, naval, air, space and electromagnetic forces. It aspires to link all service branches to create a system of systems to improve battlespace situational awareness. Three PLA departments – Informatisation, Strategic Planning and Training – have either been established or re-formatted to help enable this transformation. Since 2008, major PLA military exercises, including *Kuayue 2009* and *Lianhe 2011*, have all had cyber and information operations components that have been both offensive and defensive in nature. China's cyber assets fall under the command of two main departments of the General Staff Department. Computer network attacks and EW would, in theory, come under the 4th Department (ECM), and computer network defence and intelligence gathering come under the 3rd Department (SIGINT). The 3rd Department (3PLA) is supported by a variety of 'militia units' comprising both military cyber-warfare personnel and civilian hackers. In a February 2013 report, US security company Mandiant described a secret Chinese military unit, 'Unit 61398', subordinate to 3PLA that had, Mandiant alleged, systematically exfiltrated substantial amounts of data from 141 companies since its facility was built, in 2007, in Shanghai.

DEPLOYMENT

CÔTE D'IVOIRE
UN • UNOCI 6 obs

CYPRUS

UN • UNFICYP 2

DEMOCRATIC REPUBLIC OF THE CONGO

UN • MONUSCO; 220; 10 obs; 1 engr coy; 1 fd hospital

GULF OF ADEN

1 FFGHM; 1 LPD; 1 AORH

LEBANON

UN • UNIFIL 343; 1 engr coy; 1 fd hospital

LIBERIA

UN • UNMIL 564; 2 obs; 1 engr coy; 1 tpt coy; 1 fd hospital

MIDDLE EAST

UN • UNTSO 4 obs

SOUTH SUDAN

UN • UNMISS 340; 3 obs; 1 engr coy; 1 fd hospital

SUDAN

UN • UNAMID 233; 1 engr coy

WESTERN SAHARA

UN • MINURSO 10 obs

Fiji FJI

Fijian Dollar F$		2012	2013	2014
GDP	F$	7.19bn	7.67bn	
	US$	4bn	4.16bn	
per capita	US$	4,445	4,600	
Growth	%	2.08	2.22	
Inflation	%	4.33	3.02	
Def bdgt	F$	113m	107m	101m
	US$	62m	58m	
US$1=F$		1.80	1.85	

Population 896,758

Ethnic groups: Fijian 51%; Indian 44%; European/Others 5%

Age	0–14	15–19	20–24	25–29	30–64	65 plus
Male	14.5%	4.5%	4.3%	4.3%	20.5%	2.6%
Female	13.9%	4.3%	4.1%	4.1%	19.7%	3.0%

Capabilities

The Republic of Fiji Military Forces (RFMF) are small, but have substantial operational experience. They have participated in international peacekeeping missions in Lebanon, the Sinai and Iraq, operations which have also provided an important revenue source for Fiji's government. Since the 1980s, however, the RFMF has also been heavily involved in domestic politics, mounting a coup for the third time in 2006. This intervention disrupted relations with Fiji's traditional military partners, Australia and New Zealand, leading the military-controlled government to emphasise the potential of defence ties with China, India and South Korea. In 2011, the RFMF Engineers Regiment received a gift of major civil engineering equipment from China, allowing an expansion of its developmental role. The RFMF's small naval unit operates patrol boats, primarily in EEZ-protection and search-and-rescue roles. Though it has operated helicopters in the past, the RFMF presently has no aircraft.

ACTIVE 3,500 (Army 3,200 Navy 300)

RESERVE ε6,000

(to age 45)

ORGANISATIONS BY SERVICE

Army 3,200 (incl 300 recalled reserves)

FORCES BY ROLE

SPECIAL FORCE

1 spec ops coy

MANOEUVRE

Light

3 inf bn

COMBAT SUPPORT

1 arty bty

1 engr bn

COMBAT SUPPORT

1 log bn

Reserves 6,000

FORCES BY ROLE

MANOEUVRE

Light

3 inf bn

EQUIPMENT BY TYPE

ARTY 16

TOWED 85mm 4 25-pdr (ceremonial)

MOR 81mm 12

Navy 300

EQUIPMENT BY TYPE

PATROL AND COASTAL COMBATANTS • PB 5: 3 *Kula;* (AUS *Pacific*) 2 *Levuka*

DEPLOYMENT

EGYPT

MFO 338; 1 inf bn

IRAQ

UN • UNAMI 168; 2 sy unit

SOUTH SUDAN

UN • UNMISS 4: 2 obs

SYRIA/ISRAEL

UN • UNDOF 500; 1 inf bn

India IND

Indian Rupee Rs		2012	2013	2014
GDP	Rs	97.5tr	111tr	
	US$	1.82tr	1.97tr	
per capita	US$	1,492	1,592	
Growth	%	3.99	5.68	
Inflation	%	9.31	10.82	
Def bdgt [a]	Rs	1.79tr	2.04tr	
	US$	33.4bn	36.3bn	
US$1=Rs		53.44	56.11	

[a] Excludes military pensions

Population 1,220,800,359

Religious groups: Hindu 80%; Muslim 14%; Christian 2%; Sikh 2%

Age	0–14	15–19	20–24	25–29	30–64	65 plus
Male	15.3%	5.0%	4.6%	4.3%	19.9%	2.7%
Female	13.5%	4.4%	4.2%	4.0%	19.0%	3.0%

Capabilities

India has the third-largest armed forces in the world and is making serious efforts to improve their capabilities. The armed forces regularly carry out combined arms and joint-service exercises, and have joined international exercises with France, Singapore, the UK and the US, among others. India is among the largest providers of personnel for UN peacekeeping operations. It has ambitious procurement programmes aimed at modernising inventories, although this procurement, particularly from the inefficient indigenous defence industry, has often been hampered by delays imposed by top-heavy and old fashioned defence ministry bureaucracy. In late-2013, the air force had still to conclude an agreement over the purchase of 126 French *Rafale* to meet its MMRCA requirement. Current procurement programmes, including new airlifters, air tankers and aircraft carriers, promise to improve India's power projection capabilities substantially over the next decade. The navy's carrier aviation capability will be bolstered by the (late) arrival of the *Vikramaditya* from Russia. As well as successful test firings of the *Agni*-V ballistic missile, India is in the process of developing the last element of its nuclear capabilities with a first-generation submarine-launched ballistic missile. The army is modernising one of the world's largest fleets of armoured vehicles, and is forming a new mountain corps specifically for operations along its land border with China. But it is unclear if all the services' aspirations are affordable. (See pp. 212–15.)

ACTIVE 1,325,000 (Army 1,129,900, Navy 58,350 Air 127,200, Coast Guard 9,550) Paramilitary 1,403,700

RESERVE 1,155,000 (Army 960,000 Navy 55,000 Air 140,000) Paramilitary 987,800

Army first-line reserves (300,000) within 5 years of full time service, further 500,000 have commitment to the age of 50.

ORGANISATIONS BY SERVICE

Strategic Forces Command

Strategic Forces Command (SFC) is a tri-service command established in 2003. The commander-in-chief of SFC, a senior three-star military officer, manages and administers all strategic forces through separate army and air force chains of command.

FORCES BY ROLE

MISSILE
- 1 gp with *Agni* I
- 1 gp with *Agni* II
- 1 gp (reported forming) with *Agni* III
- 2 gp with SS-150/250 *Prithvi* I/II

EQUIPMENT BY TYPE

MSL • STRATEGIC 54
- **ICBM** *Agni* V (in test)
- **IRBM** 24+: ε12 *Agni* I (80–100 msl); ε12 *Agni* II (20–25 msl); some *Agni* III (entering service); *Agni* IV (in test)
- **SRBM** 30+: ε30 SS-150 *Prithvi* I/SS-250 *Prithvi* II; some SS-350 *Dhanush* (naval testbed)
- **LACM** *Nirbhay* (likely nuclear capable; in development)

Some Indian Air Force assets (such as *Mirage* 2000H or Su-30MKI) may be tasked with a strategic role

Space

SATELLITES 5
- **COMMUNICATIONS** 2 GSAT
- **ISR** 3: 1 *Cartosat* 2A; 2 RISAT

Army 1,129,900

6 Regional Comd HQ (Northern, Western, Central, Southern, Eastern, South Western), 1 Training Comd (ARTRAC)

FORCES BY ROLE

COMMAND
- 3 (strike) corps HQ
- 10 (holding) corps HQ

MISSILE
- 2 msl gp with *Agni* I/II
- 2 msl gp with SS-150/250 *Prithvi* I/II

SPECIAL FORCES
- 8 SF bn

MANOEUVRE

Armoured
- 3 armd div (2–3 armd bde, 1 SP arty bde (1 medium regt, 1 SP arty regt))
- 8 indep armd bde

Mechanised
- 4 (RAPID) mech inf div (1 armd bde, 2 mech inf bde, 1 arty bde)
- 2 indep mech bde

Light
- 17 inf div (2–5 inf bde, 1 arty bde)
- 7 indep inf bde

Air Manoeuvre
- 1 para bde

Mountain
- 12 mtn div (3-4 mtn inf bde, 3–4 art regt)
- 2 indep mtn bde

Aviation
14 hel sqn
COMBAT SUPPORT
3 arty div (2 arty bde (3 med art regt, 1 STA/MRL regt))
8 AD bde
2 SSM regt with PJ-10 *Brahmos*
4 engr bde

Reserve Organisations

Reserves 300,000 reservists (first- line reserve within 5 years full time service); 500,000 reservists (commitment until age of 50) (total 800,000)

Territorial Army 160,000 reservists (only 40,000 regular establishment)

FORCES BY ROLE
MANOEUVRE
Light
25 inf bn
COMBAT SUPPORT
20 ADA regt
COMBAT SERVICE SUPPORT
6 ecological bn
37 (non-departmental) unit (raised from government ministries)

EQUIPMENT BY TYPE
MBT 2,874+ 124 *Arjun*; 1,950 T-72M1; 800+ T-90S; (ε1,100 various models in store)
RECCE 110 BRDM-2 with 9K111 *Fagot* (AT-4 *Spigot*)/9K113 *Konkurs* (AT-5 *Spandrel*); *Ferret* (used for internal security duties along with some indigenously built armd cars)
AIFV 1,455+: 350+ BMP-1; 980 *Sarath* (BMP-2); 125 BMP-2K
APC 336+
APC (W) 157+ OT-62/OT-64;
PPV 179: 165 *Casspir*; 14 *Yukthirath* MPV (of 327 order)
ARTY 9,702+
SP 20+: **130mm** 20 M-46 *Catapult*; **152mm** 2S19 *Farm* (reported)
TOWED 2,970+: **105mm** 1,350+: 600+ IFG Mk1/Mk2/Mk3 (being replaced); up to 700 LFG; 50 M-56; **122mm** 520 D-30; **130mm** ε600 M-46; (500 in store) **155mm** 500: ε300 FH-77B; ε200 M-46 (mod)
MRL 192: **122mm** ε150 BM-21/LRAR **214mm** 14 *Pinaka* (non operational) **300mm** 28 9A52 *Smerch*
MOR 6,520+
SP 120mm E1
TOWED 6,520+: **81mm** 5,000+ E1 **120mm** ε1,500 AM-50/E1 **160mm** 20 M-58 *Tampella*
AT • MSL
SP 9K111 *Fagot* (AT-4 *Spigot*); 9K113 *Konkurs* (AT-5 *Spandrel*)
MANPATS 9K11 *Malyutka* (AT-3 *Sagger*) (being phased out); 9K111 *Fagot* (AT-4 *Spigot*); 9K113 *Konkurs* (AT-5 *Spandrel*); *Milan* 2
RCL 84mm *Carl Gustav*; **106mm** 3,000+ M40A1 (10 per inf bn)
HELICOPTERS
MRH 264+: 70 *Dhruv*; 12 *Lancer*; 2+ *Rudra*; 120 SA315B *Lama* (*Cheetah*); 60 SA316B *Alouette III* (*Chetak*)
UAV • ISR • Medium 26: 14 *Nishant*; 12 *Searcher* Mk I/II
AD
SAM 3,300+
SP 680+: 180 2K12 *Kub* (SA-6 *Gainful*); 50+ 9K33 *Osa* (SA-8B *Gecko*); 200 9K31 *Strela*-1 (SA-9 *Gaskin*); 250 9K35 *Strela*-10 (SA-13 *Gopher*); *Akash*
MANPAD 2,620+: 620 9K32 *Strela*-2 (SA-7 *Grail* – being phased out)‡; 2,000+ 9K31 *Igla*-1 (SA-16 *Gimlet*); 9K38 Igla (SA-18 *Grouse*)
GUNS 2,395+
SP 155+: **23mm** 75 ZSU-23-4; ZU-23-2 (truck-mounted); **30mm** 20-80 2S6 *Tunguska*
TOWED 2,240+: **20mm** Oerlikon (reported); **23mm** 320 ZU-23-2; **40mm** 1,920 L40/70
RADAR • LAND 38+: 14 AN/TPQ-37 *Firefinder*; BSR Mk.2; 24 *Cymbeline*; EL/M-2140; M113 A1GE *Green Archer* (mor); MUFAR; *Stentor*
AMPHIBIOUS 2 **LCVP**
MSL
IRBM 24+: ε12 *Agni*-I (80-100 msl); ε12 *Agni*-II (20-25 msl); some *Agni*-III (successfully tested)
SRBM 30: ε30 SS-150 *Prithvi* I/SS-250 *Prithvi* II
LACM 8–10 PJ-10 *Brahmos*
AEV BMP-2; FV180
ARV T-54/T-55; VT-72B; WZT-2; WZT-3
VLB AM-50; BLG-60; BLG T-72; *Kartik*; MTU-20; MT-55; *Sarvatra*
MW 910 MCV-2

Navy 58,350 (incl 7,000 Naval Avn and 1,200 Marines)

Fleet HQ New Delhi; Commands located at Mumbai, Vishakhapatnam, Kochi & Port Blair

EQUIPMENT BY TYPE
SUBMARINES • TACTICAL 14
SSN 1 *Chakra* (RUS *Nerpa*) with 4 single 533mm TT with 3M54 *Klub* (SS-N-27 *Sizzler*) SLCM, 4 single 650mm TT with T-65 HWT; (RUS lease agreement)
SSK 13:
4 *Shishumar* (GER T-209/1500) with 8 single 533mm TT
4 *Sindhughosh* (FSU *Kilo*) with 6 single 533mm TT (undergoing refit with 3M54 *Klub* (SS-N-27 *Sizzler*) SLCM by 2015)
5 *Sindhughosh* (FSU *Kilo*) with 6 single 533mm TT with 3M54 *Klub* (SS-N-27 *Sizzler*) SLCM
PRINCIPAL SURFACE COMBATANTS 25
AIRCRAFT CARRIERS 1
CVS 1 *Viraat* (UK *Hermes*) with 2 octuple VLS with *Barak*-1 SAM, 2 twin AK230 CIWS (capacity 30 *Sea Harrier* FRS 1 (*Sea Harrier* FRS MK51) FGA ac; 7 Ka-27 *Helix* ASW hel/*Sea King* Mk42B ASW hel)
DESTROYERS 11
DDGHM 6:
3 *Delhi* with 4 quad lnchr with 3M24 *Uran* (SS-N-25 *Switchblade*) AShM, 2 single lnchr with 3K90 *Uragan* (SA-N-7 *Gadfly*) SAM, 4 octuple VLS with *Barak*-1 SAM, 5 single 533mm ASTT, 2 AK630 CIWS, 1 100mm gun, (capacity either 2 *Dhruv* hel/ *Sea King* Mk42A ASW hel)
3 *Shivalik* with 1 octuple VLS with 3M54 *Klub* (SS-N-27 *Sizzler*) ASCM, 1 octuple VLS with *Barak*-1

SAM, 1 single lnchr with 3K90 *Uragan* (SA-N-7 *Gadfly*) SAM, 2 triple 324mm ASTT, 2 RBU 6000, *Smerch 2*, 2 AK630 CIWS, 1 76mm gun, (capacity 1 *Sea King* Mk42B ASW hel)

DDGM 5:

2 *Rajput* (FSU *Kashin*) with 2 twin lnchr with R-15M *Termit* M (SS-N-2C *Styx*) AShM, 2 twin lnchr with M-1 *Volna* (SA-N-1 *Goa*) SAM, 5 single 533mm ASTT, 2 RBU 6000 *Smerch 2*, 2 AK630 CIWS, 1 76mm gun, (capacity 1 Ka-25 *Hormone*/Ka-28 *Helix A* hel)

1 *Rajput* (FSU *Kashin*) with 2 twin lnchr with *Brahmos* AShM, 2 single lnchr with R-15M *Termit* M (SS-N-2C *Styx*) AShM, 2 twin lnchr with M-1 *Volna* (SA-N-1 *Goa*) SAM, 5 single 533mm ASTT, 2 RBU 6000 *Smerch 2*, 2 AK630 CIWS, 1 76mm gun, (capacity 1 Ka-25 *Hormone*/Ka-28 *Helix A* hel)

2 *Rajput* (FSU *Kashin*) with 1 octuple VLS with *Brahmos* AShM, 2 twin lnchr with R-15M *Termit* M (SS-N-2C *Styx*) AShM, 2 octuple VLS with *Barak* SAM. 1 twin lnchr with M-1 *Volna* (SA-N-1 *Goa*) SAM, 5 single 533mm ASTT, 2 RBU 6000 *Smerch 2*, 2 AK630 CIWS, 1 76mm gun, (capacity 1 Ka-25 *Hormone*/Ka-28 *Helix* A hel)

FRIGATES 13:

FFGHM 12:

3 *Brahmaputra* with 4 quad lnchr with 3M24 *Uran* (SS-N-25 *Switchblade*) AShM, 3 octuple VLS with *Barak* SAM, 2 triple 324mm ASTT, 1 76mm gun, (capacity 2 SA316B *Alouette* III (*Chetak*)/*Sea King* Mk42 ASW hel)

3 *Godavari* with 4 single lnchr with R-15 *Termit* M (SS-N-2D *Styx*) AShM, 1 octuple VLS with *Barak* SAM, 2 triple 324mm ASTT, 1 76mm gun, (capacity 2 SA316B *Alouette* III (*Chetak*)/*Sea King* Mk42 ASW hel)

3 *Talwar* I with 1 octuple VLS with 3M54 *Klub* (SS-N-27 *Sizzler*) AShM, 6 single lnchr with 3K90 *Uragan* (SA-N-7 *Gadfly*) SAM, 2 twin 533mm ASTT, 2 RBU 6000 *Smerch 2*, 2 CADS-N-1 *Kashtan* CIWS, 1 100mm gun, (capacity 1 *Dhruv*/Ka-31 *Helix* B AEW hel/Ka-28 *Helix* A ASW hel)

3 *Talwar* II with 1 octuple VLS with *Brahmos*/3M54 Klub (SS-N-27 *Sizzler*) AShM, 6 single lnchr with 3K90 *Uragan* (SA-N-7 *Gadfly*) SAM, 2 twin 533mm ASTT, 2 RBU 6000 *Smerch 2*, 2 CADS-N-1 *Kashtan* CIWS, 1 100mm gun, (capacity 1 *Dhruv*/Ka-31 *Helix* B AEW hel/Ka-28 *Helix* A ASW hel)

FFH 1:

1 *Nilgiri* with 2 triple 324mm ASTT, 2 twin AK630 CIWS, 2 twin 114mm gun (capacity 1 SA316B *Alouette III* (*Chetak*) hel/*Sea King* Mk42 ASW hel)

PATROL AND COASTAL COMBATANTS 84

CORVETTES 24

FSGM 20:

4 *Khukri* with 2 twin lnchr with R-15M *Termit* M (SS-N-2C *Styx*) AShM, 2 twin lnchr (manual aiming) with 9K32M *Strela*-2M (SA-N-5 *Grail*) SAM, 2 AK630 CIWS, 1 76mm gun, 1 hel landing platform (for *Dhruv*/SA316 *Alouette* III (*Chetak*))

4 *Kora* with 4 quad lnchr with 3M24 *Uran* (SS-N-25 *Switchblade*) AShM, 1 quad lnchr (manual aiming) with 9K32M *Strela*-2M (SA-N-5 *Grail*) SAM, 2 AK630 CIWS, 1 76mm gun, 1 hel landing platform (for *Dhruv*/SA316 *Alouette* III (*Chetak*))

10 *Veer* (FSU *Tarantul*) with 4 single lnchr with R-15 *Termit* M (SS-N-2D *Styx*) AShM, 2 quad lnchr (manual aiming) with 9K32M *Strela*-2M (SA-N-5 *Grail*), 1 76mm gun

2 *Prabal* (mod *Veer*) each with 4 quad lnchr with 3M24 *Uran* (SS-N-25 *Switchblade*) AShM, 1 quad lnchr (manual aiming) with 9K32M *Strela*-2M (SA-N-5 *Grail*) SAM, 2 AK630 CIWS, 1 76mm gun

FSM 4:

4 *Abhay* (FSU *Pauk* II) with 1 quad lnchr (manual aiming) with 9K32M *Strela*-2M (SA-N-5 *Grail*) SAM, 2 twin 533mm ASTT, 2 RBU 1200, 1 76mm gun

PSOH 8: 2 *Saryu* with 2 AK630 CIWS, 1 76 mm gun (capacity 1 *Dhruv* – 2 more vessels in build); 6 *Sukanya* with 4 RBU 2500 (capacity 1 SA316 *Alouette* III (*Chetak*))

PCC 16: 10 *Car Nicobar*; 6 *Trinkat* (SDB Mk5)

PBF 21: 5 *Super Dvora; 16 Solar Marine Interceptor* (additional vessels in build)

PB 15 *Plascoa* 1300 (SPB)

MINE WARFARE • MINE COUNTERMEASURES 8

MSO 7 *Pondicherry* (FSU *Natya*)

AMPHIBIOUS

PRINCIPAL AMPHIBIOUS VESSELS 1

LPD 1 *Jalashwa* (US *Austin*) (capacity up to 6 med spt hel; either 9 LCM or 4 LCM and 2 LCAC; 4 LCVP; 930 troops)

LANDING SHIPS 9

LSM 4 *Kumbhir* (FSU *Polnocny* C) (capacity 5 MBT or 5 APC; 160 troops)

LST 5:

2 *Magar* (capacity 15 MBT or 8 APC or 10 trucks; 500 troops)

3 *Magar* mod (capacity 11 MBT or 8 APC or 10 trucks; 500 troops)

LANDING CRAFT 30

LCM 4 LCM-8 (for use in *Jalashwa*)

LCU 6 *Vasco de Gama* Mk2/3 LC (capacity 2 APC; 120 troops)

LCVP 20 (for use in *Magar*)

LOGISTICS AND SUPPORT 55

AGOR 1 *Sagardhwani*

AGHS 8 *Sandhayak*

AGS 2 *Makar*

AH 1

AK 2

AOL 7: 6 *Poshak*; 1 *Ambika*

AOR 1 *Jyoti* with 1 hel landing platform

AORH 3: 1 *Aditya* (mod *Deepak*); 2 *Deepak* with 4 AK630 CIWS

AP 3 *Nicobar*

ASR 1

ATF 1

AWT 2

AX 4: 1 *Tir*; 3 AXS

YPT 1

Asia

YDT 3
YTL/YTM 15

Naval Aviation 7,000

Flying hours 125–150 hrs/year on *Sea Harrier*

FORCES BY ROLE

FIGHTER/GROUND ATTACK
1 sqn with MiG-29K/KUB *Fulcrum*
1 sqn with *Sea Harrier* FRS 1 (Mk51); *Sea Harrier* T-4N (T-60)

ANTI SUBMARINE WARFARE
4 sqn with Ka-25 *Hormone*; Ka-28 *Helix* A; SA316B *Alouette* III (*Chetak*); *Sea King* Mk42A/B

MARITIME PATROL
2 sqn with BN-2 *Islander*; Do-228-101; Il-38 *May*; Tu-142M *Bear* F

AIRBORNE EARLY WARNING & CONTROL
1 sqn with Ka-31 *Helix* B

SEARCH & RESCUE
1 sqn with SA316B *Alouette* III (*Chetak*); *Sea King* Mk42C
1 sqn with *Dhruv*

TRANSPORT
1 (comms) sqn with Do-228
1 sqn with HS-748M (HAL-748M)

TRAINING
1 sqn with HJT-16 *Kiran* MkI/II , *Hawk* Mk132

TRANSPORT HELICOPTER
1 sqn with UH-3H *Sea King*

ISR UAV
1 sqn with *Heron*; *Searcher* MkII

EQUIPMENT BY TYPE

AIRCRAFT 40 combat capable
FTR 16 MiG-29K/KUB *Fulcrum*
FGA 10: 8 *Sea Harrier* FRS 1 (Mk51); 2 *Sea Harrier* T-4N (T-60)
ASW 10: 5 Il-38 *May*; 4 Tu-142M *Bear* F; 1 P-8I *Poseidon*
MP 14 Do-228-101
TPT 37: **Light** 27: 17 BN-2 *Islander*; 10 Do-228; **PAX** 10 HS-748M (HAL-748M)
TRG 16: 6 HJT-16 *Kiran* MkI; 6 HJT-16 *Kiran* MkII; 4 *Hawk* Mk132*

HELICOPTERS
ASW 54: 7 Ka-25 *Hormone*; 12 Ka-28 *Helix* A; 21 *Sea King* Mk42A; 14 *Sea King* Mk42B
MRH 58: 10 *Dhruv*; 25 SA316B *Alouette* III (*Chetak*); 23 SA319 *Alouette* III
AEW 9 Ka-31 *Helix* B
TPT • Medium 11: 5 *Sea King* Mk42C; up to 6 UH-3H *Sea King*

UAV • ISR 11 **Heavy** 4 *Heron;* **Medium** 7 *Searcher* Mk II

MSL
AShM Kh-35 (*Bear* and *May* ac cleared to fire); *Sea Eagle* (service status unclear); *Sea Skua*
ASCM PJ-10 *Brahmos*
AAM • IR R-550 *Magic/Magic* 2; R-73 (AA-11 *Archer*) **IR/SARH** R-27 (AA-10 *Alamo*); **ARH** *Derby*; R-77 (AA-12 *Adder*)

Marines ε1,200 (Additional 1,000 for SPB duties)

After the Mumbai attacks, the Sagar Prahari Bal (SPB), with 80 PBF, was established to protect critical maritime infrastructure.

FORCES BY ROLE

SPECIAL FORCES
1 (marine) cdo force

MANOEUVRE
Amphibious
1 amph bde

Air Force 127,200

5 regional air comds: Western (New Delhi), Southwestern (Gandhinagar), Eastern (Shillong), Central (Allahabad), Southern (Trivandrum). 2 support comds: Maintenance (Nagpur) and Training (Bangalore)

Flying hours 180 hrs/year

FORCES BY ROLE

FIGHTER
3 sqn with MiG-29 *Fulcrum*; MiG-29UB *Fulcrum*

FIGHTER/GROUND ATTACK
4 sqn with *Jaguar* IB/IS
8 sqn with MiG-21bis/*Bison*
3 sqn with MiG-21M/MF *Fishbed*
6 sqn with MiG-27ML *Flogger*
3 sqn with *Mirage* 2000E/ED (2000H/TH - secondary ECM role)
9 sqn with Su-30MKI *Flanker*

ANTI SURFACE WARFARE
1 sqn with *Jaguar* IM with *Sea Eagle* AShM

ISR
1 unit with Gulfstream IV SRA-4
AIRBORNE EARLY WARNING & CONTROL 1 sqn with EMB-145AEW; Il-76TD *Phalcon*

TANKER
1 sqn with Il-78 *Midas*

TRANSPORT
1 sqn with C-130J-30 *Hercules*
1 sqn (forming) with C-17A *Globemaster* III
5 sqn with An-32/An-32RE *Cline*
1 (comms) sqn with B-737; B-737BBJ; EMB-135BJ 4 sqn with Do-228; HS-748
2 sqn with Il-76MD *Candid*
1 flt with HS-748

TRAINING
1 sqn with *Tejas*
Some units with An-32; Do-228; *Hawk* Mk 132*; HJT-16 *Kiran* MkI/II; *Jaguar* IS/IM; MiG-21bis; MiG-21FL; MiG-21M/MF; MiG-27ML; PC-7 *Turbo Trainer* MkII; SA316B *Alouette* III (*Chetak*)

ATTACK HELICOPTER
2 sqn with Mi-25 *Hind*; Mi-35 *Hind*

TRANSPORT HELICOPTER
5 sqn with *Dhruv*
7 sqn with Mi-8 *Hip*
7 sqn with Mi-17/Mi-17-1V *Hip* H
4 sqn with Mi-17V-5 *Hip* H
2 sqn with SA316B *Alouette* III (*Chetak*)
1 flt with Mi-8 *Hip*

1 flt with Mi-26 *Halo*
2 flt with SA315B *Lama* (*Cheetah*)
2 flt with SA316B *Alouette* III (*Chetak*)
ISR UAV
5 sqn with *Searcher* MkII
AIR DEFENCE
25 sqn with S-125 *Pechora* (SA-3B *Goa*)
6 sqn with 9K33 *Osa*-AK (SA-8B *Gecko*)
2 sqn with *Akash*
10 flt with 9K38 *Igla*-1 (SA-18 *Grouse*)

EQUIPMENT BY TYPE

AIRCRAFT 866 combat capable
FTR 62: 55 MiG-29 *Fulcrum* (incl 12+ MiG-29UPG); 7 MiG-29UB *Fulcrum*
FGA 738: 14 *Jaguar* IB; 81 *Jaguar* IS; 10 *Jaguar* IM; 31 MiG-21bis; 116 MiG-21 *Bison*; 54 MiG-21M *Fishbed*; 16 MiG-21MF *Fishbed*; 40 MiG-21U/UM *Mongol*; 126 MiG-27ML *Flogger* J2; 40 *Mirage* 2000E (2000H); 10 *Mirage* 2000ED (2000TH); ε200 Su-30MKI *Flanker*
ISR 3 Gulfstream IV SRA-4
AEW&C 3: 1 EMB-145AEW (2 more on order); 2 Il-76TD *Phalcon* (1 more on order)
TKR 6 Il-78 *Midas*
TPT 241 **Heavy** 27: 3 C-17A *Globemaster* III; 24 Il-76MD *Candid*; **Medium** 6 C-130J-30 *Hercules*; **Light** 144: 90 An-32; 15 An-32RE *Cline*; 35 Do-228; 4 EMB-135BJ; **PAX** 64: 1 B-707; 4 B-737; 3 B-737BBJ; 56 HS-748
TRG 265: 66 *Hawk* Mk132*; 120 HJT-16 *Kiran* MkI; 55 HJT-16 *Kiran* MkII; 24 PC-7 *Turbo Trainer* MkII

HELICOPTERS
ATK 20 Mi-25/Mi-35 *Hind*
MRH 292: 52 *Dhruv*; 80 Mi-17/Mi-17-1V *Hip* H; ε60 Mi-17V-5 *Hip* H; 60 SA315B *Lama* (*Cheetah*); 40 SA316B *Alouette* III (*Chetak*)
TPT 94 **Heavy** 4 Mi-26 *Halo*; **Medium** 90 Mi-8

UAV • ISR • Medium some *Searcher* MkII

AD • SAM S-125 *Pechora* (SA-3B *Goa*)
SP 9K33 *Osa*-AK (SA-8B *Gecko*); *Akash*
MANPAD 9K38 *Igla*-1 (SA-18 *Grouse*)

MSL
AAM • IR R-60 (AA-8 *Aphid*); R-73 (AA-11 *Archer*) R-550 *Magic*; **IR/SARH** R-27 (AA-10 *Alamo*); **SARH** Super 530D **ARH** R-77 (AA-12 *Adder*)
AShM AM-39 *Exocet*; *Sea Eagle*
ASM AS-11; AS-11B (ATGW); Kh-29 (AS-14 *Kedge*); Kh-59 (AS-13 *Kingbolt*); Kh-59M (AS-18 *Kazoo*); Kh-31A (AS-17B *Krypton*); AS-30; Kh-23 (AS-7 *Kerry*)‡
ARM Kh-25MP (AS-12 *Kegler*); Kh-31P (AS-17A *Krypton*)
LACM *Nirbhay* (likely nuclear capable; in development)

Coast Guard 9,550

EQUIPMENT BY TYPE

PATROL AND COASTAL COMBATANTS 85
PSOH 12: 2 *Sankalp* (additional vessels in build); 4 *Samar* with 1 76mm gun; 3 *Samudra*; 3 *Vishwast*
PCO 6 *Vikram*
PCC 28: 8 *Priyadarshini*; 8 *Rajshree*; 5 *Rani Abbakka* (7 additional vessels in build); 7 *Sarojini Naidu*
PCF 2 *Cochin* 50 (additional vessels in build)
PBF 18: 13 *Interceptor*; 5 (various)
PB 19: 3 *Jija Bai* mod 1; 6 *Tara Bai*; 10 (various)

AMPHBIBIOUS • LCAC 12 Griffon 8000

AIRCRAFT • TPT • Light 24 Do-228

HELICOPTERS • MRH 17 SA316B *Alouette* III (*Chetak*)

Paramilitary 1,403,700

Rashtriya Rifles 65,000

Ministry of Defence. 15 sector HQ

FORCES BY ROLE

MANOEUVRE
Other
65 paramilitary bn

Assam Rifles 63,900

Ministry of Home Affairs. Security within north-eastern states, mainly army-officered; better trained than BSF

FORCES BY ROLE

Equipped to roughly same standard as an army inf bn
COMMAND
7 HQ
MANOEUVRE
Other
46 paramilitary bn

EQUIPMENT BY TYPE

ARTY • MOR 81mm 252

Border Security Force 230,000

Ministry of Home Affairs.

FORCES BY ROLE

MANOEUVRE
Other
170+ paramilitary bn

EQUIPMENT BY TYPE

Small arms, lt arty, some anti-tank weapons
ARTY • MOR 81mm 942+
AIRCRAFT • TPT some (air spt)

Central Industrial Security Force 134,100 (lightly armed security guards)

Ministry of Home Affairs. Guards public-sector locations

Central Reserve Police Force 229,700

Ministry of Home Affairs. Internal security duties, only lightly armed, deployable throughout the country.

FORCES BY ROLE

MANOEUVRE
Other
198 paramilitary bn
10 (rapid action force) paramilitary bn
10 (CoBRA) paramilitary bn
3 (Mahila) paramilitary bn (female)

Defence Security Corps 31,000

Provides security at Defence Ministry sites

Indo-Tibetan Border Police 36,300

Ministry of Home Affairs. Tibetan border security SF/ guerrilla warfare and high-altitude warfare specialists; 49 bn.

Asia

National Security Guards 7,350
Anti-terrorism contingency deployment force, comprising elements of the armed forces, CRPF and Border Security Force.

Railway Protection Forces 70,000

Sashastra Seema Bal 73,350
Guards the borders with Nepal and Bhutan

Special Frontier Force 10,000
Mainly ethnic Tibetans

Special Protection Group 3,000
Protection of ministers and senior officials

State Armed Police 450,000
For duty primarily in home state only, but can be moved to other states. Some bn with GPMG and army standard infantry weapons and equipment.

FORCES BY ROLE

MANOEUVRE

Other

24 (India Reserve Police) paramilitary bn (cdo trained)

Reserve Organisations

Civil Defence 500,000 reservists
Operate in 225 categorised towns in 32 states. Some units for NBC defence

Home Guard 487,800 reservists (515,000 authorised str)
In all states except Arunachal Pradesh and Kerala; men on reserve lists, no trg. Not armed in peacetime. Used for civil defence, rescue and fire-fighting provision in wartime; 6 bn (created to protect tea plantations in Assam).

Cyber
National agencies include the Computer and Emergency Response Team (CERT-In), which has authorised designated individuals to carry out penetration tests against infrastructure. The Defence Information Assurance and Research Agency (DIARA) is mandated to deal with cyber security-related issues of the armed services. All services have their own cyber security policies and CERT teams, and headquarters maintain information-security policies. The Indian Army, in 2005, raised the Army Cyber Security Establishment and, in April 2010, set up the Cyber Security Laboratory at the Military College of Telecommunications Engineering (under the Corps of Signals). The Department of Electronics and Information Technology has outlined a cyber-security strategy, and, in 2013, there was reporting that the same department was to set up a National Cyber Coordination Centre.

DEPLOYMENT

AFGHANISTAN

300 (Indo-Tibetan Border Police paramilitary: facilities protection)

CÔTE D'IVOIRE

UN • UNOCI 8 obs

DEMOCRATIC REPUBLIC OF THE CONGO

UN • MONUSCO 3,731; 36 obs; 3 mech inf bn; 1 inf bn; 1 hel coy; 1 fd hospital

GULF OF ADEN

1 FFGHM

LEBANON

UN • UNIFIL 896; 1 mech inf bn; elm 1 fd hospital

SOUTH SUDAN

UN • UNMISS 1,991; 5 obs; 2 inf bn; 1 fd hospital

SUDAN

UN • UNISFA 2: 2 obs

SYRIA/ISRAEL

UN • UNDOF 194; 1 log bn(-)

FOREIGN FORCES
Total numbers for UNMOGIP mission in India and Pakistan

Chile 2 obs

Croatia 9 obs

Finland 6 obs

Italy 3 obs

Korea, Republic of 8 obs

Philippines 4 obs

Sweden 5 obs

Thailand 3 obs

Uruguay 2 obs

Indonesia IDN

Indonesian Rupiah Rp		2012	2013	2014
GDP	Rp	8,242tr	9,250tr	
	US$	878bn	946bn	
per capita	US$	3,592	3,817	
Growth	%	6.23	6.30	
Inflation	%	4.26	5.57	
Def bdgt	Rp	61.2tr	81.8tr	83.4tr
	US$	6.52bn	8.37bn	
FMA (US)	US$	14m	14m	14m
US$1=Rp		9384.97	9773.90	

Population 251,160,124

Ethnic groups: Javanese 45%; Sundanese 14%; Madurese 8%; Malay 8%; Chinese 3%; other 22%

Age	0–14	15–19	20–24	25–29	30–64	65 plus
Male	13.6%	4.5%	4.2%	4.1%	20.9%	2.8%
Female	13.1%	4.4%	4.0%	3.9%	21.0%	3.6%

Capabilities
Indonesia's army remains the country's dominant military force – a legacy of the 1940s' independence struggle

and the army's subsequent involvement in domestic politics. Even under civilian rule, the army's 'territorial structure' continues to deploy military personnel throughout the country down to village level. Within the army, the better-trained and -equipped Strategic Command (KOSTRAD) and Special Forces Command (KOPASSUS) units are trained for deployment nationwide and for exercises with other countries' armed forces. In West Papua, where resistance to Indonesian rule continues, the army still deploys operationally and has faced accusations of serious human-rights abuses. Efforts to improve armed forces' capabilities are guided by the notion of a Minimum Essential Force (MEF), a concept developed in the wake of concern that defence funding levels in the 2000s had fallen below acceptable levels. Rising defence spending has permitted improved pay and allowances and modest equipment purchases for all three services, particularly the air force and navy. Indonesia buys equipment from diverse sources, while using technology-transfer agreements with foreign suppliers to develop national defence industry. The armed forces lack the capacity for significant autonomous military deployments beyond national territory, but in July–August 2012 the air force contributed Su-27/-30 combat aircraft to the annual *Pitch Black* exercise in Australia and, in 2013, took part in a range of bilateral and multilateral military exercises.

ACTIVE 395,500 **(Army 300,400 Navy 65,000 Air 30,100) Paramilitary 281,000**

Conscription liability 2 years selective conscription authorised

RESERVE 400,000

Army cadre units; numerical str n.k., obligation to age 45 for officers

ORGANISATIONS BY SERVICE

Army ε300,400

Mil Area Commands (KODAM)

13 comd (I, II, III, IV, V, VI, VII, IX, XII, XVI, XVII, Jaya & Iskandar Muda)

FORCES BY ROLE

MANOEUVRE

Mechanised

3 armd cav bn

6 cav bn

Light

1 inf bde (1 cav bn, 3 inf bn)

3 inf bde (1 cdo bn, 2 inf bn)

4 inf bde (3 inf bn)

45 indep inf bn

8 cdo bn

Aviation

1 composite avn sqn

1 hel sqn

COMBAT SUPPORT

12 fd arty bn

1 AD regt (2 ADA bn, 1 SAM unit)

6 ADA bn

3 SAM unit

7 cbt engr bn

COMBAT SERVICE SUPPORT

4 construction bn

Special Forces Command (KOPASSUS)

FORCES BY ROLE

SPECIAL FORCES

3 SF gp (total: 2 cdo/para unit, 1 CT unit, 1 int unit)

Strategic Reserve Command (KOSTRAD)

FORCES BY ROLE

COMMAND

2 div HQ

MANOEUVRE

Mechanised

2 armd cav bn

Light

3 inf bde (total: 4 cdo bn; 4 inf bn)

Air Manoeuvre

3 AB bde (3 AB bn)

COMBAT SUPPORT

2 fd arty regt (total: 6 arty bn)

1 arty bn

2 AD bn

2 cbt engr bn

EQUIPMENT BY TYPE

MBT 2+ *Leopard* 2A4

LT TK 350: 275 AMX-13 (partially upgraded); 15 PT-76; 60 *Scorpion* 90

RECCE 142: 55 *Ferret* (13 upgraded); 69 *Saladin* (16 upgraded); 18 VBL

AIFV 24+: 22 BMP-2; 2 + *Marder* 1A3

APC 549+

APC (T) 90: 75 AMX-VCI; 15 FV4333 *Stormer*

APC (W) 459: 14 APR-1; ε150 *Anoa*; 22 *Black Fox*; 40 BTR-40; 34 BTR-50PK; 22 *Commando Ranger*; 45 FV603 *Saracen* (14 upgraded); 100 LAV-150 *Commando*; 32 VAB-VTT

PPV *Barracuda*; *Casspir*

ARTY 1,097+

TOWED 133+: **105mm** 110+: some KH-178; 60 M101; 50 M-56; **155mm** 23: 5 FH-88; 18 KH-179

MOR 955: **81mm** 800; **120mm** 155: 75 Brandt; 80 UBM 52

MLR 70mm 9 NDL-40

AT

MSL SS.11; 100 *Milan*; 9M14M (AT-3 *Sagger*)

RCL 135: **106mm** 45 M40A1; **90mm** 90 M67

RL 89mm 700 LRAC

AIRCRAFT • TPT • Light 9: 1 BN-2A *Islander*; 6 C-212 *Aviocar* (NC-212); 2 *Turbo Commander* 680

HELICOPTERS

ATK 6 Mi-35P *Hind*

MRH 35: 18 Bell 412 *Twin Huey* (NB-412); 17 Mi-17V-5 *Hip* H

TPT • Light 30: 8 Bell 205A; 20 Bo-105 (NBo-105); 2 EC120B *Colibri*

TRG 12 Hughes 300C

AD

SAM

SP 2 *Kobra* (with 125 GROM-2 msl); TD-2000B (*Giant Bow II*)

Asia

TOWED 93: 51 *Rapier*; 42 RBS-70
MANPAD QW-3
GUNS • TOWED 411: **20mm** 121 Rh 202; **23mm** *Giant Bow*; **40mm** 90 L/70; **57mm** 200 S-60
ARV 11+: 2 AMX-13; 6 AMX-VCI; 3 BREM-2; *Stormer*; T-54/T-55
VLB 12+: 10 AMX-13; *Leguan*; 2 *Stormer*

Navy ε65,000 (including Marines and Aviation)

Two fleets: East (Surabaya), West (Jakarta). It is currently planned to change to three commands: Riau (West); Papua (East); Makassar (Central). Two Forward Operating Bases at Kupang (West Timor) and Tahuna (North Sulawesi)

EQUIPMENT BY TYPE

SUBMARINES • TACTICAL • SSK 2 *Cakra*† with 8 single 533mm TT with SUT HWT
PRINCIPAL SURFACE COMBATANTS 11
FRIGATES 11
FFGHM 7
4 *Ahmad Yani* with 2 quad Mk 141 lnchr with RGM-84A *Harpoon* AShM, 2 SIMBAD twin lnchr (manual) with *Mistral* SAM, 2 triple 324mm ASTT with Mk46 LWT, 1 76mm gun, (capacity 1 Bo-105 (NBo-105) hel)
1 *Ahmad Yani* with 2 twin-cell VLS with 3M55 *Yakhont* (SS-N-26 *Strobile*) AShM; 2 SIMBAD twin lnchr (manual) with *Mistral* SAM, 2 triple 324mm ASTT with Mk46 LWT, 1 76mm gun, (capacity 1 Bo-105 (NBo-105) hel)
1 *Ahmad Yani* with 4 single lnchr with C-802 AShM, 2 SIMBAD twin lnchr (manual) with *Mistral* SAM, 2 triple 324mm ASTT with Mk46 LWT, 1 76mm gun, (capacity 1 Bo-105 (NBo-105) hel)
1 *Hajar Dewantara* (trg role) with 2 twin lnchr with MM-38 *Exocet* AShM, 2 single 533mm ASTT with SUT HWT, 1 57mm gun, (capacity 1 Bo-105 (NBo-105) hel)
FFGM 4:
4 *Diponegoro* with 2 twin lnchr with MM-40 *Exocet* Block II AShM, 2 quad *Tetral* lnchr with *Mistral* SAM, 2 triple 324mm ASTT with MU90 LWT, 1 76mm gun, 1 hel landing platform
PATROL AND COASTAL COMBATANTS 72
CORVETTES 18:
FSGH 1:
1 *Nala* with 2 twin lnchr with MM-38 *Exocet* AShM, 1 twin 375mm A/S mor, 1 120mm gun (capacity 1 lt hel)
FSG 2:
2 *Fatahillah* with 2 twin lnchr with MM-38 *Exocet* AShM, 2 triple B515 *ILAS*-3/Mk32 324mm ASTT with A244/Mk46 LWT, 1 twin 375mm A/S mor, 1 120mm gun
FSM 15 *Kapitan Patimura*† (GDR *Parchim* I) with 2 quad lnchr with 9K32M *Strela*-2 (SA-N-5 *Grail*) SAM, 4 single 400mm ASTT, 2 RBU 6000 *Smerch* 2, 1 twin 57mm gun
PCFG 4 *Mandau* with 4 single lnchr with MM-38 *Exocet* AShM, 1 57mm gun
PCT 4 *Singa* with 2 single 533mm TT, 1 57mm gun
PCC 8: 4 *Kakap*; 4 *Todak* with 1 57mm gun
PBG 5:
3 *Clurit* with 2 twin lnchr with C-705 AShM
2 *Waspada* with 2 twin lnchr with MM-38 *Exocet* AShM
PB 33: 1 *Cucut*; 13 *Kobra*; 1 *Krait*; 8 *Sibarau*; 10 *Viper*
MINE WARFARE • MINE COUNTERMEASURES 11
MCO 2 *Pulau Rengat*
MSC 9 *Palau Rote*†
AMPHIBIOUS
PRINCIPAL AMPHIBIOUS VESSELS • LPD 5: 1 *Dr Soeharso* (Ex-*Tanjung Dalpele*; capacity 2 LCU/LCVP; 13 tanks; 500 troops; 2 AS332L *Super Puma*); 4 *Makassar* (capacity 2 LCU/LCVP; 13 tanks; 500 troops; 2 AS332L *Super Puma*)
LANDING SHIPS • LST 20
1 *Teluk Amboina* (capacity 16 tanks; 200 troops);
11 *Teluk Gilimanuk*
2 *Teluk Langsa* (capacity 16 tanks; 200 troops);
6 *Teluk Semangka* (capacity 17 tanks; 200 troops)
LANDING CRAFT 55
LCM 20
LCU 5
LCVP 30
LOGISTICS AND SUPPORT 32
AGF 1 *Multatuli*
AGOR 7: 5 *Baruna Jaya*; 1 *Jalanidhi*; 1 *Burujulasad*
AGSH 1
AKSL 4
AOL 1
AORLH 1 *Arun* (UK *Rover*)
AOT 3: 2 *Khobi*; 1 *Sorong*
ATF 2
AXS 2
AP 7: 1 *Tanjung Kambani* (troop transport); 2 *Tanjung Nusanive* (troop transport); 4 *Karang Pilang* (troop transport)
YTM 3

Naval Aviation ε1,000

EQUIPMENT BY TYPE

AIRCRAFT
MP 23: 3 CN-235 MPA; 14 N-22B *Searchmaster* B; 6 N-22SL *Searchmaster* L
TPT • Light 28: 21 C-212-200 *Aviocar*; 2 DHC-5D *Buffalo*; 3 TB-9 *Tampico*; 2 TB-10 *Tobago*
HELICOPTERS
MRH 4 Bell 412 (NB-412) *Twin Huey*
TPT 15: **Medium** 3 AS332L *Super Puma* (NAS322L); **Light** 12: 3 EC120B *Colibri*; 9 Bo-105 (NBo-105)

Marines ε20,000

FORCES BY ROLE

SPECIAL FORCES
1 SF bn
MANOEUVRE
Amphibious
2 mne gp (1 cav regt, 3 mne bn, 1 arty regt, 1 cbt spt regt, 1 CSS regt)
1 mne bde (3 mne bn)

EQUIPMENT BY TYPE
LT TK 55 PT-76†
RECCE 21 BRDM
AIFV 83: 24 AMX-10P; 10 AMX-10 PAC 90; 37 BMP-3F; 12 BTR-80A
AAV 10 LVTP-7A1
APC (W) 100 BTR-50P
ARTY 59+
TOWED 50: **105mm** 22 LG1 MK II; **122mm** 28 M-38
MRL 122mm 9 RM-70
MOR 81mm
AD • GUNS 150: **40mm** 5 L/60/L/70; **57mm** S-60

Air Force 30,100

2 operational comd (East and West) plus trg comd.

FORCES BY ROLE
FIGHTER
1 sqn with F-5E/F *Tiger* II
1 sqn with F-16A/B *Fighting Falcon*
FIGHTER/GROUND ATTACK
1 sqn with Su-27SK/SKM *Flanker*; Su-30MK/MK2 *Flanker*
3 sqn with *Hawk* MK53*/Mk109*/Mk209*
GROUND ATTACK
1 sqn (forming) with EMB-314 (A-29) *Super Tucano**
MARITIME PATROL
1 sqn with B-737-200; CN-235M-220 MPA
TANKER/TRANSPORT
1 sqn with C-130B/KC-130B *Hercules*
TRANSPORT
1 VIP sqn with B-737-200; C-130H/H-30 *Hercules*; L-100-30; F-27-400M *Troopship*; F-28-1000/3000; AS332L *Super Puma* (NAS332L); SA330SM *Puma* (NAS300SM)
1 sqn with C-130H/H-30 *Hercules*; L-100-30
1 sqn with C-212 *Aviocar* (NC-212)
1 sqn with CN-235M-110; F-27-400M *Troopship*
TRAINING
1 sqn with AS-202 *Bravo*
1 sqn with KT-1B; T-34C *Turbo Mentor*
1 sqn with SF-260M; SF-260W *Warrior*
TRANSPORT HELICOPTER
2 sqn with AS332L *Super Puma* (NAS332L); SA330J/L *Puma* (NAS330J/L); EC120B *Colibri*

EQUIPMENT BY TYPE
Only 45% of ac op
AIRCRAFT 78 combat capable
FTR 22: 8 F-5E *Tiger* II; 4 F-5F *Tiger* II; 7 F-16A *Fighting Falcon*; 3 F-16B *Fighting Falcon*
FGA 16: 2 Su-27SK *Flanker*; 3 Su-27SKM *Flanker*; 2 Su-30 MK *Flanker*; 9 Su-30MK2 *Flanker*
MP 5: 3 B-737-200; 2 CN-235M-220 MPA
TKR 1 KC-130B *Hercules*
TPT 39 **Medium** 15: 4 C-130B *Hercules*; 3 C-130H *Hercules*; 6 C-130H-30 *Hercules*; 2 L-100-30; **Light** 19: 2 C-295 (7 more on order); 6 C-212 *Aviocar* (NC-212); 5 CN-235-110; 6 F-27-400M *Troopship*; **PAX** 5: 1 B-737-200; 1 B-737-800BBJ;1 F-28-1000; 2 F-28-3000
TRG 122: 39 AS-202 *Bravo*; 4 EMB-314 (A-29) *Super Tucano** (12 more on order); 4 Grob 120TP (14 more on order); 6 *Hawk* Mk53*; 7 *Hawk* Mk109*; 23 *Hawk* Mk209*; 11 KT-1B; 10 SF-260M; 7 SF-260W *Warrior*; 15 T-34C *Turbo Mentor*
HELICOPTERS
TPT 31 **Medium** 19: 10 AS332 *Super Puma* (NAS332L) (VIP/CSAR); 1 SA330SM *Puma* (NAS330SM) (VIP); 4 SA330J *Puma* (NAS330J); 4 SA330L *Puma* (NAS330L); **Light** 12 EC120B *Colibri*
MSL • TACTICAL ASM AGM-65G *Maverick*
AAM • IR AIM-9P *Sidewinder*; R-73 (AA-11 *Archer*) **IR/SARH** R-27 (AA-10 *Alamo*)
ARM Kh-31P (AS-17A *Krypton*)

Special Forces (Paskhasau)

FORCES BY ROLE
SPECIAL FORCES
3 (PASKHASAU) SF wg (total: 6 spec ops sqn)
4 indep SF coy

Paramilitary ε281,000 active

Naval Auxiliary Service

EQUIPMENT BY TYPE
PATROL AND COASTAL COMBATANTS • PB 71: 6 *Carpentaria*; 65 *Kal Kangean*

Customs

EQUIPMENT BY TYPE
PATROL AND COASTAL COMBATANTS 65
PBF 15
PB 50

Marine Police

EQUIPMENT BY TYPE
PATROL AND COASTAL COMBATANTS 37
PSO 2 *Bisma*
PCC 5
PBF 3 *Gagak*
PB 27: 14 *Bango*; 13 (various)
LOGISTICS AND SUPPORT • AP 1

Police ε280,000 (including 14,000 police 'mobile bde' (BRIMOB) org in 56 coy, incl CT unit (Gegana))

EQUIPMENT BY TYPE
APC (W) 34 *Tactica*
AIRCRAFT • TPT • Light 5: 2 Beech 18; 2 C-212 *Aviocar* (NC-212); 1 *Turbo Commander* 680
HELICOPTERS • TPT • Light 22: 3 Bell 206 *Jet Ranger*; 19 Bo-105 (NBo-105)

KPLP (Coast and Seaward Defence Command)

Responsible to Military Sea Communications Agency

EQUIPMENT BY TYPE
PATROL AND COASTAL COMBATANTS 28
PCO 4: 2 *Arda Dedali*; 2 *Trisula*
PB 24: 4 *Golok* (SAR); 5 *Kujang*; 15 (various)
LOGISTICS AND SUPPORT • ABU 1 *Jadayat*

Reserve Organisations

Kamra People's Security ε40,000 (report for 3 weeks' basic training each year; part time police auxiliary)

DEPLOYMENT

DEMOCRATIC REPUBLIC OF THE CONGO
UN • MONUSCO 177; 15 obs; 1 engr coy

HAITI
UN • MINUSTAH 169; 1 engr coy

LEBANON
UN • UNIFIL 1,288; 1 mech inf bn; 1 MP coy; elm 1 fd hospital; 1 FFGM

LIBERIA
UN • UNMIL 1 obs

SOUTH SUDAN
UN • UNMISS 3 obs

SUDAN
UN • UNAMID 1; 7 obs

Japan JPN

Japanese Yen ¥		2012	2013	2014
GDP	¥	476tr	480tr	
	US$	5.96tr	5.15tr	
per capita	US$	46,736	40,442	
Growth	%	2.00	1.58	
Inflation	%	-0.04	0.06	
Def bdgt	¥	4.71tr	4.75tr	
	US$	59.1bn	51bn	
US$1=¥		79.79	93.25	

Population 127,253,075

Ethnic groups: Korean <1%

Age	0–14	15–19	20–24	25–29	30–64	65 plus
Male	6.9%	2.6%	2.4%	2.7%	23.2%	10.7%
Female	6.4%	2.3%	2.4%	2.8%	23.4%	14.1%

Capabilities

Japan's Self-Defense Forces (SDF) are the most modern Asian armed forces in terms of equipment, despite a historically low defence-spending-to-GDP ratio and a pacifistic constitution. Despite constitutional restrictions, Tokyo's 2010 National Defense Programme Guidelines set the goal of creating a 'dynamic defense force' that would be more responsive and deployable militarily in contrast to the 'static deterrence' of previous years. The primary objective of Japan's new defence posture will be to deter North Korea and China more effectively, but HADR operations, counter-piracy and counter-terrorism will also be key. Concern over China is driving fundamental shifts in posture, with greater weight being given to deployments in, and protection of, the country's southwestern islands. Further subtle shifts in Japan's defence posture are likely as Prime Minister Shinzo Abe seeks to alter the country's restrictions on collective self-defence. Equally, while the 2012 defence white paper outlined the limits to the use of force, it also clarified that the denial of the 'right of belligerency' in the constitution did not preclude retaliatory strikes on a rival's territory if attacked. In line with the very gradual normalisation of Japan's defence posture, the country is also purchasing greater power-projection capabilities, such as two DDH22 helicopter carriers, which will augment the capability introduced in 2009 by the smaller *Hyuga*-class. However, economic and constitutional constraints will continue to hamper Japanese military modernisation in the medium-term.

ACTIVE 247,150 (Ground Self-Defense Force 151,050; Maritime Self- Defense Force 45,500; Air Self-Defense Force 47,100; Central Staff 3,500) **Paramilitary 12,650**

RESERVE 56,100 (General Reserve Army (GSDF) 46,000; Ready Reserve Army (GSDF) 8,200; Navy 1,100; Air 800)

ORGANISATIONS BY SERVICE

Space

EQUIPMENT BY TYPE
SATELLITES • ISR 4: IGS 1/3/4/5

Ground Self-Defense Force 151,050

FORCES BY ROLE
COMMAND
5 army HQ (regional comd)
SPECIAL FORCES
1 spec ops unit (bn)
MANOEUVRE
Armoured
1 (7th) armd div (1 armd recce sqn, 3 tk regt, 1 armd inf regt, 1 avn sqn, 1 SP arty regt, 1 AD regt, 1 cbt engr bn, 1 sigs bn, 1 NBC bn, 1 log regt)
Mechanised
1 (2nd) inf div (1 armd recce sqn, 1 tk regt, 1 mech inf regt, 2 inf regt, 1 avn sqn, 1 SP arty regt, 1 AT coy, 1 AD bn, 1 cbt engr bn, 1 sigs bn, 1 NBC bn, 1 log regt)
1 (4th) inf div (1 armd recce sqn, 1 tk bn, 1 mech inf regt, 3 inf regt, 1 inf coy, 1 avn sqn, 1 arty regt, 1 AT coy, 1 AD bn, 1 cbt engr bn, 1 sigs bn, 1 NBC bn, 1 log regt)
1 (9th) inf div (1 armd recce sqn, 1 tk bn, 2 mech inf regt, 1 inf regt, 1 avn sqn, 1 arty regt, 1 AD bn, 1 cbt engr bn, 1 sigs bn, 1 NBC bn, 1 log regt)
2 (5th & 11th) inf bde (1 armd recce sqn, 1 tk bn, 3 mech inf regt, 1 avn sqn, 1 SP arty bn, 1 AD coy, 1 cbt engr coy, 1 sigs coy, 1 NBC coy, 1 log bn)
Light
1 (8th) inf div (1 recce sqn, 1 tk bn, 4 inf regt, 1 avn sqn, 1 arty regt, 1 AD bn, 1 cbt engr bn, 1 sigs bn, 1 NBC bn, 1 log regt)
4 (1st, 3rd, 6th & 10th) inf div (1 recce sqn, 1 tk bn, 3 inf regt, 1 avn sqn, 1 arty regt, 1 AD bn, 1 cbt engr bn, 1 sigs bn, 1 NBC bn, 1 log regt)
1 (13th) inf bde (1 recce sqn, 1 tk coy, 3 inf regt, 1 avn sqn, 1 arty bn, 1 AD coy, 1 cbt engr coy, 1 sigs coy, 1 log bn)

1 (14th) inf bde (1 recce sqn, 1 tk coy, 2 inf regt, 1 avn sqn, 1 arty bn, 1 AD coy, 1 cbt engr coy, 1 sigs coy, 1 log bn)
1 (15th) inf bde (1 recce sqn, 1 inf regt, 1 avn sqn, 1 AD bn, 1 cbt engr coy, 1 EOD coy, 1 sigs coy, 1 log bn)
Air Manoeuvre
1 (1st) AB bde (3 AB bn, 1 arty bn, 1 cbt engr coy, 1 sigs coy, 1 log bn)
1 (12th) air mob inf bde (1 recce sqn, 4 inf regt, 1 avn sqn, 1 SP arty bn, 1 AD coy, 1 cbt engr coy, 1 sigs coy, 1 log bn)
Aviation
1 hel bde
5 avn gp (1 atk hel bn, 1 hel bn)
COMBAT SUPPORT
1 arty bde
2 arty unit (bde)
2 AD bde
4 AD gp
4 engr bde
1 engr unit
1 EW bn
5 int bn
1 MP bde
1 sigs bde
COMBAT SERVICE SUPPORT
5 log unit (bde)
5 trg bde

EQUIPMENT BY TYPE
MBT 777: 26 Type-10; 410 Type-74; 341 Type-90
RECCE 152: 105 Type-87; 47 Chemical Reconnaissance Vehicle
AIFV 68 Type-89
APC 803
APC (T) 254 Type-73
APC (W) 549: 227 Type-82; 322 Type-96
ARTY 1,773
SP 167: **155mm** 100: 22 Type-75; 78 Type-99; **203mm** 67 M110A2
TOWED 155mm 422 FH-70
MRL 227mm 99 M270 MLRS
MOR 1,085
SP 120mm 24 Type-96
TOWED 1,061: **81mm** 639 L16 **120mm** 422
AT
MSL
SP 30 Type-96 MPMS
MANPATS 1,610: 140 Type-79 *Jyu*-MAT; 440 Type-87 *Chu*-MAT; 1,030 Type-01 LMAT
RCL • 84mm 2,712 *Carl Gustav*
RL 89mm 200
AIRCRAFT
TPT • Light 12: 5 MU-2 (LR-1); 7 Beech 350 *King Air* (LR-2)
HELICOPTERS
ATK 109: 73 AH-1S *Cobra*; 10 AH-64D *Apache*; 26 OH-1
ISR 80 OH-6D
TPT 238 **Heavy** 55: 34 CH-47D *Chinook* (CH-47J); 21 CH-47JA *Chinook*; **Medium** 33: 3 EC225LP *Super Puma* MkII+ (VIP); 30 UH-60L *Black Hawk* (UH-60JA); **Light** 150: 140 Bell-205 (UH-1J); 10 Enstrom 480B (TH-480B)
AD
SAM 700
SP 180: 20 Type-03 *Chu*-SAM; 50 Type-81 *Tan*-SAM; 110 Type-93 *Kin*-SAM
TOWED 160 MTM-23B I-HAWK
MANPAD 360 Type-91 *Kin*-SAM
GUNS • SP 35mm 52 Type-87 SP
MSL • AShM 90 Type-88
AEV Type-75
ARV 70: 41 Type-78; 29 Type-90
VLB Type-67; Type-70; Type-81; Type-91 **MW** Type-82; Type-92

Maritime Self- Defense Force 45,500

Surface units organised into 4 Escort Flotillas with a mix of 7–8 warships each. Bases at Yokosuka, Kure, Sasebo, Maizuru, Ominato. SSK organised into two flotillas with bases at Kure and Yokosuka. Remaining units assigned to five regional districts.

EQUIPMENT BY TYPE
SUBMARINES • TACTICAL • SSK 18:
2 *Harushio* (trg role) with 6 single 533mm TT with T-89 HWT/UGM-84C *Harpoon* AShM
11 *Oyashio* with 6 single 533mm TT with T-89 HWT/UGM-84C *Harpoon* AShM
5 *Soryu* (AIP fitted) with 6 single 533mm TT with T-89 HWT/UGM-84C *Harpoon* AShM (additional vessels in build)
PRINCIPAL SURFACE COMBATANTS 47
AIRCRAFT CARRIERS • CVH 2 *Hyuga* with 1 16-cell Mk41 VLS with ASROC/RIM-162/ESSM *Sea Sparrow*, 2 triple 324mm TT with Mk46 LWT, 2 *Phalanx* Block 1B CIWS, (normal ac capacity 3 SH-60 *Seahawk* ASW hel; plus additional ac embarkation up to 7 SH-60 *Seahawk* or 7 MCH-101)
CRUISERS • CGHM 2 *Atago* (*Aegis* Base Line 7) with 2 quad lnchr with SSM-1B AShM, 1 64-cell Mk41 VLS with SM-2 MR SAM/ASROC, 1 32-cell Mk41 VLS with SM-2 MR SAM, 2 triple 324mm ASTT with Mk46 LWT, 2 *Phalanx* Block 1B CIWS, 1 127mm gun, (capacity 1 SH-60 *Seahawk* ASW hel)
DESTROYERS 32:
DDGHM 24:
8 *Asagiri* with 2 quad Mk141 lnchr with RGM-84C *Harpoon* AShM, 1 octuple Mk29 lnchr with *Sea Sparrow* SAM, 2 triple 324mm ASTT with Mk46 LWT, 1 octuple Mk112 lnchr with ASROC, 2 *Phalanx* CIWS, 1 76mm gun, (capacity 1 SH-60 *Seahawk* ASW hel)
2 *Akizuki* with 2 quad lnchr with SS-1B AShM, 1 32-cell Mk41 VLS with ASROC/ESSM *Sea Sparrow* SAM, 2 triple 324mm ASTT with Mk46 LWT, 2 *Phalanx* Block 1B CIWS, 1 127mm gun (capacity 1 SH-60 *Seahawk* ASW hel)
9 *Murasame* with 2 quad lnchr with SSM-1B AShM, 1 16-cell Mk48 VLS with RIM-7M *Sea Sparrow* SAM, 2 triple 324mm TT with Mk46 LWT, 1 16-cell Mk41 VLS with ASROC, 2 *Phalanx* CIWS, 2 76mm gun, (capacity 1 SH-60 *Seahawk* ASW hel)

Asia

5 *Takanami* (improved *Murasame*) with 2 quad lnchr with SSM-1B AShM, 1 32-cell Mk41 VLS with ASROC/RIM-7M/ESSM *Sea Sparrow* SAM, 2 triple 324mm TT with Mk46 LWT, 2 *Phalanx* CIWS, 1 127mm gun, (capacity 1 SH-60 *Seahawk* ASW hel)

DDGM 6:

2 *Hatakaze* with 2 quad Mk141 lnchr with RGM-84C *Harpoon* AShM, 1 Mk13 GMLS with SM-1 MR SAM, 2 triple 324mm ASTT with Mk46 LWT, 1 octuple Mk112 lnchr with ASROC, 2 *Phalanx* CIWS, 2 127mm gun, 1 hel landing platform

4 *Kongou* (*Aegis* Baseline 4/5) with 2 quad Mk141 lnchr with RGM-84C *Harpoon* AShM, 1 29-cell Mk41 VLS with SM-2/3 SAM/ASROC, 1 61-cell Mk41 VLS with SM-2/3 SAM/ASROC, 2 triple 324mm ASTT, 2 *Phalanx* Block 1B CIWS, 1 127mm gun

DDHM 2 *Shirane* with 1 octuple Mk112 lnchr with ASROC, 1 octuple Mk29 lnchr with RIM-7M *Sea Sparrow* SAM, 2 triple ASTT with Mk46 LWT, 2 *Phalanx* CIWS, 2 127mm gun, (capacity 3 SH-60 *Seahawk* ASW hel)

FRIGATES 11:

FFGHM 5 *Hatsuyuki* with 2 quad Mk141 lnchr with RGM-84C *Harpoon* AShM, 1 octuple Mk29 lnchr with RIM-7F/M *Sea Sparrow* SAM, 2 triple ASTT with Mk46 LWT, 1 octuple Mk112 lnchr with ASROC, 2 *Phalanx* CIWS, 1 76mm gun, (capacity 1 SH-60 *Seahawk* ASW hel)

FFGM 6 *Abukuma* with 2 quad Mk141 lnchr with RGM-84C *Harpoon* AShM, 2 triple ASTT with Mk 46 LWT, 1 Mk112 octuple lnchr with ASROC, 1 *Phalanx* CIWS, 1 76mm gun

PATROL AND COASTAL COMBATANTS 6

PBFG 6 *Hayabusa* with 4 SSM-1B AShM, 1 76mm gun

MINE WARFARE • MINE COUNTERMEASURES 36

MCM SPT 4:

2 *Nijma*

2 *Uraga* with 1 hel landing platform (for MH-53E)

MSO 26: 3 *Hirashima*; 12 *Sugashima*; 6 *Uwajima*; 3 *Yaeyama*; 2 *Enoshima*

MSD 6

AMPHIBIOUS

LANDING SHIPS • LST 4:

3 *Osumi* with 1 hel landing platform (for 2 CH-47 hel) (capacity 10 Type-90 MBT; 2 LCAC(L) ACV; 330 troops)

1 *Yura* (capacity 70 troops)

LANDING CRAFT 20

LCU 2 *Yusotei*

LCM 12

LCAC 6 LCAC(L) (capacity either 1 MBT or 60 troops)

LOGISTICS AND SUPPORT 80

AG 1 *Asuka* with 1 8-cell VLS (wpn trials)

AGB 1 *Shirase*

AGOS 2 *Hibiki*

AGS 4: 1 *Futami*; 1 *Nichinan*; 1 *Shonan*; 1 *Suma*

AOE 5: 2 *Mashu*; 3 *Towada*

ARC 1 *Muroto*

ASR 2: 1 *Chihaya*; 1 *Chiyoda*

ATF 26

AX 8: 1 *Kashima*; 3 *Shimayuki* with 2 quad lnchr with RGM-84 *Harpoon* AShM, 1 octuple Mk29 lnchr with RIM-7M *Sea Sparrow* SAM, 1 octuple Mk112 lnchr with ASROC, 2 triple 324mm ASTT with Mk46 LWT, 2 *Phalanx* CIWS, 1 76mm gun; 1 *Tenryu* (trg spt ship); 1 *Kurobe* with 1 76mm gun (trg spt ship); 2 (various)

YAC 1 *Hashidate*

YDT 6

YG 5 *Hiuchi*

YTM 16

YTR 2

Naval Aviation ε9,800

7 Air Groups

FORCES BY ROLE

ANTI SUBMARINE/SURFACE WARFARE

7 sqn (shipboard/trg) with SH-60B (SH-60J)/SH-60K *Seahawk*

MARITIME PATROL

6 sqn (incl 1 trg) with P-3C *Orion*

ELECTRONIC WARFARE

1 sqn with EP-3 *Orion*

MINE COUNTERMEASURES

1 sqn with MH-53E *Sea Dragon*; MCH-101

SEARCH & RESCUE

1 sqn with *Shin Meiwa* US-1A/US-2

2 sqn with UH-60J *Black Hawk*

TRANSPORT

1 sqn with AW101 *Merlin* (CH-101); Beech 90 *King Air* (LC-90); YS-11M

TRAINING

1 sqn with EC135 (TH-135); OH-6DA

3 sqn with T-5; Beech 90 *King Air* (TC-90)

EQUIPMENT BY TYPE

AIRCRAFT 78 combat capable

ASW 80: 2 P-1; 78 P-3C *Orion*

ELINT 5 EP-3C *Orion*

SAR 7: 2 *Shin Meiwa* US-1A; 5 *Shin Meiwa* US-2

TPT • Light 28: 3 YS-11M; 5 Beech 90 *King* Air (LC-90); 20 Beech 90 *King Air* (TC-90)

TRG 32 T-5

HELICOPTERS

ASW 87: 49 SH-60B *Seahawk* (SH-60J); 37 SH-60K *Seahawk*; 1 USH-60K *Seahawk*

MCM 12: 7 MH-53E *Sea Dragon*; 5 MCH-101

ISR 4 OH-6DA

SAR 19 UH-60J *Black Hawk*

TPT 12 **Medium** 2 AW101 *Merlin* (CH-101) (additional ac being delivered); **Light** 10 EC135 (TH-135)

Air Self-Defense Force 47,100

Flying hours 150 hrs/year

7 cbt wg

FORCES BY ROLE

FIGHTER

7 sqn with F-15J *Eagle*

2 sqn with F-4EJ (F-4E) *Phantom* II

3 sqn with Mitsubishi F-2

ELECTRONIC WARFARE

2 sqn with Kawasaki EC-1; YS-11E

ISR
1 sqn with RF-4EJ (RF-4E) *Phantom II**
AIRBORNE EARLY WARNING & CONTROL
2 sqn with E-2C *Hawkeye*; E-767
SEARCH & RESCUE
1 wg with U-125A *Peace Krypton*; MU-2 (LR-1); UH-60J *Black Hawk*
TANKER
1 sqn with KC-767J
TRANSPORT
1 (VIP) sqn with B-747-400
3 sqn with C-1; C-130H *Hercules*; YS-11
Some (liaison) sqn with Gulfstream IV (U-4); T-4*
TRAINING
1 (aggressor) sqn with F-15J *Eagle*
TEST
1 wg with F-15J *Eagle*; T-4*
TRANSPORT HELICOPTER
4 flt with CH-47 *Chinook*

EQUIPMENT BY TYPE
AIRCRAFT 552 combat capable
FTR 201 F-15J *Eagle*
FGA 139: 76 F-2A/B; 63 F-4E *Phantom* II (F-4EJ)
EW 3: 1 Kawasaki EC-1; 2 YS-11EA
ISR 17: 13 RF-4E *Phantom* II* (RF-4J); 4 YS-11EB
AEW&C 17: 13 E-2C *Hawkeye*; 4 E-767
SAR 28 U-125A *Peace Krypton*
TKR 4 KC-767J
TPT 66 **Medium** 16 C-130H *Hercules*; **PAX** 50: 2 B-747-400; 13 Beech T-400; 26 C-1; 5 Gulfstream IV (U-4); 4 YS-11
TRG 248: 199 T-4*; 49 T-7
HELICOPTERS
SAR 41 UH-60J *Black Hawk*
TPT • **Heavy** 15 CH-47 *Chinook*
MSL
ASM ASM-1 (Type-80); ASM-2 (Type-93)
AAM • **IR** AAM-3 (Type-90); AIM-9 *Sidewinder*; **IIR** AAM-5 (Type-04); **SARH** AIM-7 *Sparrow*; **ARH** AAM-4 (Type-99)

Air Defence
Ac control and warning. 4 wg; 28 radar sites

FORCES BY ROLE
AIR DEFENCE
6 SAM gp (total: 24 SAM bty with MIM-104 *Patriot*)
1 (Air Base Defence) AD gp with Type-81 *Tan*-SAM; Type-91 *Kei*-SAM; M167 *Vulcan*

EQUIPMENT BY TYPE
AD
SAM
SP Type-81 *Tan*-SAM
TOWED 120 MIM-104 *Patriot*
MANPAD Type-91 *Kei*-SAM
GUNS • **TOWED 20mm** M167 *Vulcan*

Paramilitary 12,650

Coast Guard
Ministry of Land, Transport, Infrastructure and Tourism (no cbt role)

EQUIPMENT BY TYPE
PATROL AND COASTAL COMBATANTS 389+
PSOH 13: 2 *Mizuho*; 1 *Shikishima*; 10 *Soya*
PSO 26: 3 *Hida*; 1 *Izu*; 1 *Kojima* (trg); 1 *Miura*; 1 *Nojima*; 7 *Ojika*; 10 *Shiretoko*; 2 *Kunigami*
PCO 29: 3 *Aso*; 2 *Bihoro*; 9 *Hateruma*; 2 *Takatori*; 13 *Teshio*
PCC 25: 4 *Amani*; 21 *Tokara*
PBF 44: 17 *Hayagumo*; 5 *Mihashi*; 14 *Raizan*; 2 *Takatsuki*; 6 *Tsuruugi*
PB 252+: 8 *Akizuki*; 4 *Asogiri*; 200+ CL-Type; 15 *Hayanami*; 1 *Matsunami*; 7 *Murakumo*; 2 *Natsugiri*; 3 *Shimagiri*; 10 *Yodo*; 2 *Katonami*
LOGISTICS AND SUPPORT 37
ABU 1 *Teshio*
AGS 12
AKSL 7
YAG 5
YPC 3
YTR 9
AIRCRAFT
MP 2 *Falcon* 900 MPA
ISR 2 Beech 200T
TPT 21 **Light** 12: 10 Beech 350 *King Air* (LR-2); 1 Cessna 206 *Stationair* (U-206G); 1 YS-11A; **PAX** 9: 3 CL-300; 2 Gulfstream V (MP); 4 Saab 340B
HELICOPTERS
MRH 7 Bell 412 *Twin Huey*
TPT 39 **Medium** 6: 4 AS332 *Super Puma*; 2 EC225 *Super Puma*; **Light** 33: 5 AW139; 4 Bell 206B *Jet Ranger II*; 20 Bell 212; 4 S-76C

Cyber
The Self-Defense Forces (SDF) established a Command Control Communication Computer Systems Command in 2008. According to the government's 'Secure Japan 2009' document, the Ministry of Defense was to be involved in investigating the latest technological trends in cyber attacks. In order to analyse attacks on MoD information systems and response capabilities, government agencies were to 'study the basics of illegal access monitoring and analysis technology, cyber attack analysis technology, and active defense technology'. Further, the 'Information Security 2010' document stated that 'at the end of FY2010, a cyber planning and coordination officer (provisional title) will be stationed in the Joint Staff Office of the Ministry of Defense to enhance … preparedness against cyber attacks'. In the FY2013 defence budget, the MoD is creating a 'cyber defense group' in order to develop operational infrastructure.

DEPLOYMENT

DJIBOUTI
200; 2 P-3C *Orion*

GULF OF ADEN & INDIAN OCEAN
2 DDGHM

SOUTH SUDAN
UN • UNMISS 271; 1 engr coy

FOREIGN FORCES

United States

US Pacific Command: 36,700

Army 2,500; 1 HQ (9th Theater Army Area Command) at Zama

Navy 6,750; 1 CVN; 2 CG; 8 DDG; 1 LCC; 2 MCM; 1 LHD; 2 LSD; 1 base at Sasebo; 1 base at Yokosuka

USAF: 12,500; 1 HQ (5th Air Force) at Okinawa–Kadena AB; 1 ftr wg at Okinawa–Kadena AB (2 ftr sqn with 18 F-16C/D *Fighting Falcon* at Misawa AB); 1 ftr wg at Okinawa–Kadena AB (1 SAR sqn with 8 HH-60G *Pave Hawk*, 1 AEW sqn with 2 E-3B *Sentry*, 2 ftr sqn with total of 24 F-15C/D *Eagle*); 1 airlift wg at Yokota AB with 10 C-130E *Hercules*; 2 C-21J; 1 spec ops gp at Okinawa–Kadena AB

USMC 14,950; 1 Marine div (3rd); 1 ftr sqn with 12 F/A-18D *Hornet*; 1 tkr sqn with 12 KC-130J *Hercules*; 2 tpt sqn with 12 MV-22B *Osprey*;

US Strategic Command: 1 AN/TPY-2 X-band radar at Shariki

Korea, Democratic People's Republic of DPRK

North Korean Won		2012	2013	2014
GDP	US$			
per capita	US$			
Def exp	won			
	US$			

US$1=won

*definitive economic data not available

Population 24,720,407

Age	0–14	15–19	20–24	25–29	30–64	65 plus
Male	11.0%	4.1%	4.2%	3.8%	22.1%	3.2%
Female	10.7%	4.1%	4.1%	3.6%	22.8%	6.3%

Capabilities

North Korea maintains the world's fourth-largest standing armed forces. However, equipment is mainly in a poor state, and training, morale and operational readiness all remain questionable. Incremental improvements in North Korean equipment continue to be developed, such as a new 122mm multiple-launch rocket system tested in 2013, and an apparently improved *Sang-O*-class submarine, developed in 2011. Nevertheless, Pyongyang relies on weight of numbers, asymmetric capabilities (including electronic and cyber warfare) and the deployment of short-range *Scud* missiles to deter its southern neighbour, with whom North Korea is still officially at war. North Korea is actively pursuing a nuclear-weapons capability, with three devices tested in 2006, 2009 and 2013; a second route to nuclearisation was opened up by the uranium enrichment programme revealed in 2010; and a ballistic-missile programme that has deployed hundreds of short- and medium-range missiles. However, there is no proof that North Korea has successfully weaponised a nuclear device. The ideological 'military-first' construct ensures that the armed forces will continue to have prioritised access to resources. However, under Kim Jong-un, the armed forces have lost their former dominant position in North Korean politics and their control over revenue-generating enterprises. The Korean Workers Party, which had become nearly dormant during part of Kim Jong-il's reign, has instead reasserted control. A range of high-profile sackings have strengthened Kim Jong-un's power base without any apparent signs of having provoked unrest. The party's renewed dominance over the military could mean a gradual diminution of the *Songun* 'military-first' policy that became a national ideology under Kim Jong-il. (See pp. 215–17.)

ACTIVE 1,190,000 (Army ε1,020,000 Navy 60,000 Air 110,000) Paramilitary 189,000

Conscript liability Army 5–12 years, Navy 5–10 years, Air Force 3–4 years, followed by compulsory part-time service to age 40. Thereafter service in the Worker/Peasant Red Guard to age 60.

RESERVE ε600,000 (Armed Forces ε600,000), Paramilitary 5,700,000

Reservists are assigned to units (see also Paramilitary)

ORGANISATIONS BY SERVICE

Strategic Forces

North Korea's *Nodong* missiles and H-5 (Il-28) bombers could in future be used to deliver nuclear warheads or bombs. At present, however, there is no conclusive evidence to suggest that North Korea has successfully produced a warhead or bomb capable of being delivered by either of these systems.

Army ε1,020,000

FORCES BY ROLE

COMMAND

2 mech corps HQ
9 inf corps HQ
1 (Capital Defence) corps HQ

MANOEUVRE

Armoured

1 armd div
15 armd bde

Mechanised

4 mech div

Light

27 inf div
14 inf bde

COMBAT SUPPORT

1 arty div
21 arty bde
9 MRL bde
1 SSM bde with *Scud*
1 SSM bde with FROG-7
5–8 engr river crossing / amphibious regt
1 engr river crossing bde

Special Purpose Forces Command 88,000

FORCES BY ROLE

SPECIAL FORCES

8 (Reconnaissance General Bureau) SF bn

MANOEUVRE

Reconnaissance

17 recce bn

Light

9 lt inf bde

6 sniper bde

Air Manoeuvre

3 AB bde

1 AB bn

2 sniper bde

Amphibious

2 sniper bde

Reserves 600,000

FORCES BY ROLE

MANOEUVRE

Light

40 inf div

18 inf bde

EQUIPMENT BY TYPE (ε)

MBT 3,500+ T-34/T-54/T-55/T-62/Type-59/*Chonma*/*Pokpoong*

LT TK 560+: 560 PT-76; M-1985

APC 2,500+

APC (T) Type-531 (Type-63); VTT-323

APC (W) 2,500 BTR-40/BTR-50/BTR-60/BTR-80A/BTR-152/BTR look-a-like

ARTY 21,100+

SP/TOWED 8,500: **SP 122mm** M-1977/M-1981/M-1985/M-1991; **130mm** M-1975/M-1981/M-1991; **152mm** M-1974/M-1977; **170mm** M-1978/M-1989

TOWED 122mm D-30/D-74/M-1931/37; **130mm** M-46; **152mm** M-1937/M-1938/M-1943

GUN/MOR 120mm (reported)

MRL 5,100: **107mm** Type-63; **122mm** BM-11/M-1977 (BM-21)/M-1985/M-1992/M-1993; **200mm** BMD-20; **240mm** BM-24/M-1985/M-1989/M-1991; **300mm** some (reported)

MOR 7,500: **82mm** M-37; **120mm** M-43; **160mm** M-43

AT • MSL

SP 9K11 *Malyutka* (AT-3 *Sagger*)

MANPATS 2K15 *Shmel* (AT-1 *Snapper*); 9K111 *Fagot* (AT-4 *Spigot*); 9K113 *Konkurs* (AT-5 *Spandrel*)

RCL 82mm 1,700 B-10

AD

SAM

SP some 9K35 *Strela*-10 (SA-13 *Gopher*)

MANPAD 9K310 *Igla*-1 (SA-16 *Gimlet*)/9K32 *Strela*-2 (SA-7 *Grail*)‡

GUNS 11,000

SP 14.5mm M-1984; **23mm** M-1992; **37mm** M-1992; **57mm** M-1985

TOWED 11,000: **14.5mm** ZPU-1/ZPU-2/ZPU-4; **23mm** ZU-23; **37mm** M-1939; **57mm** S-60; **85mm** M-1939 *KS*-12; **100mm** KS-19

MSL

SSM 64+: 24 FROG-3/FROG-5/FROG-7; KN-08 (in development); some *Musudan*; ε10 *Nodong* (ε90+ msl); 30+ *Scud*-B/*Scud*-C (ε200+ msl)

Navy ε60,000

EQUIPMENT BY TYPE

SUBMARINES • TACTICAL 72

SSK 20 PRC Type-031/FSU *Romeo*† with 8 single 533mm TT with 14 SAET-60 HWT

SSC 32+:

30 *Sang-O* with 2 single 533mm TT with Type-53–65 HWT;

2+ *Sang-O* II with 4 single 533mm TT with Type-53–65 HWT;

SSW 20† (some *Yugo* with 2 single 406mm TT; some *Yeono* with 2 single 533mm TT)

PRINCIPAL SURFACE COMBATANTS 3

FRIGATES • FFG 3:

2 *Najin* with 2 single lnchr with P-15 *Termit* (SS-N-2) AShM, 2 RBU 1200, 2 100mm gun , 2 twin 57mm gun

1 *Soho* with 4 single lnchr with P-15 *Termit* (SS-N-2) AShM, 2 RBU 1200, 1 100mm gun, 1 hel landing platform (for med hel)

PATROL AND COASTAL COMBATANTS 382

PCG 18:

8 *Osa* I with 4 single lnchr with P-15 *Termit* (SS-N-2) AShM, 2 twin AK230 CIWS

10 *Soju* with 4 single lnchr with P-15 *Termit* (SS-N-2) AShM

PCO 5: 4 *Sariwon* with 2 twin 57mm gun; 1 *Tral* with 1 85mm gun

PCC 18:

6 *Hainan* with 4 RBU 1200, 2 twin 57mm gun

7 *Taechong* I with 2 RBU 1200, 1 85mm gun, 1 twin 57mm gun

5 *Taechong* II with 2 RBU 1200, 1 100mm gun, 1 twin 57mm gun

PBFG 16:

4 *Huangfen* with 4 single lnchr with P-15 *Termit* (SS-N-2) AShM, 2 twin AK230 CIWS

6 *Komar* with 2 single lnchr with P-15 *Termit* (SS-N-2) AShM

6 *Sohung* with 2 single lnchr with P-15 *Termit* (SS-N-2) AShM

PBF 229: 54 *Chong-Jin* with 1 85mm gun; 142 *Ku Song*/*Sin Hung*/*Sin Hung (mod)*; 33 *Sinpo*

PB 96:

59 *Chaho*

6 *Chong-Ju* with 2 RBU 1200, 1 85mm gun

13 *Shanghai* II

18 SO-1 with 4 RBU 1200, 2 twin 57mm gun

MINE WARFARE • MINE COUNTERMEASURES 24: 19 *Yukto* I; 5 *Yukto* II

AMPHIBIOUS

LANDING SHIPS • LSM 10 *Hantae* (capacity 3 tanks; 350 troops)

LANDING CRAFT 257

LCPL 96 *Nampo* (capacity 35 troops)

LCM 25
LCVP 136 (capacity 50 troops)
LOGISTICS AND SUPPORT 23:
AGI 14 (converted fishing vessels)
AS 8 (converted cargo ships)
ASR 1 *Kowan*

Coastal Defence

FORCES BY ROLE

COMBAT SUPPORT
2 AShM regt with HY-1 (CSS-N-2) (6 sites, and probably some mobile launchers)

EQUIPMENT BY TYPE

ARTY • TOWED 122mm M-1931/37; **152mm** M-1937
COASTAL 130mm M-1992; SM-4-1
MSL • AShM HY-1 (CSS-N-2); KN-01 (in development)

Air Force 110,000

4 air divs. 1st, 2nd and 3rd Air Divs (cbt) responsible for N, E and S air defence sectors respectively; 8th Air Div (trg) responsible for NE sector. The AF controls the national airline.

Flying hours 20 hrs/year on ac

FORCES BY ROLE

BOMBER
3 (lt) regt with H-5†

FIGHTER
1 regt with F-7B *Airguard*
6 regt with J-5
4 regt with J-6
5 regt with J-7
1 regt with MiG-23ML/P *Flogger*
1 regt with MiG-29 *Fulcrum*

FIGHTER/GROUND ATTACK
1 regt with Su-7 *Fitter*

GROUND ATTACK
1 regt with Su-25 *Frogfoot*

TRANSPORT
Some regt with Y-5 (to infiltrate 2 air-force sniper brigades deep into ROK rear areas), but possibly grounded; An-24 *Coke*; Il-18 *Coot*; Il-62M *Classic*; Tu-134 *Crusty*; Tu-154 *Careless*

TRAINING
Some regt with CJ-6; FT-2; MiG-21 *Fishbed*

ATTACK HELICOPTER
1 regt with Mi-24 *Hind*

TRANSPORT HELICOPTER
Some regt with Hughes 500D†; Mi-8 *Hip*/Mi-17 *Hip* H; PZL Mi-2 *Hoplite*; Z-5

AIR DEFENCE
19 bde with S-125 *Pechora* (SA-3 *Goa*); S-75 *Dvina* (SA-2 *Guideline*); S-200 *Angara* (SA-5 *Gammon*); 9K36 *Strela-3* (SA-14 *Gremlin*); 9K310 *Igla-1* (SA-16 *Gimlet*); 9K32 *Strela-2* (SA-7 *Grail*)‡; (KN-06 SAM system shown in 2010)

EQUIPMENT BY TYPE

AIRCRAFT 603 combat capable
BBR 80 H-5†
FTR 441+: 40 F-7B *Airguard*; 107 J-5; 100 J-6; 120 J-7†; 46 MiG-23ML *Flogger*; 10 MiG-23P *Flogger*; 18+ MiG-29A/S *Fulcrum*
FGA 48: 30 MiG-21bis *Fishbed*†; 18 Su-7 *Fitter*
ATK 34 Su-25 *Frogfoot*
TPT 217: **Light** 208: 6 An-24 *Coke*; 2 Tu-134 *Crusty*; ε200 Y-5 **PAX** 9: 2 Il-18 *Coot*; 2 Il-62M *Classic*; 4 Tu-154 *Careless*; 1 Tu-204-300
TRG 215: 180 CJ-6; 35 FT-2

HELICOPTERS
ATK 20 Mi-24 *Hind*
MRH 80 Hughes 500D†
TPT 202 **Medium** 63: 15 Mi-8 *Hip*/Mi-17 *Hip* H; 48 Z-5 **Light** 139 PZL Mi-2 *Hoplite*

UAV • ISR • Light *Pchela*-1 (*Shmel*)

AD • SAM 3,390+
TOWED 312+: 179+ S-75 *Dvina* (SA-2 *Guideline*); 133 S-125 *Pechora* (SA-3 *Goa*)
STATIC/SHELTER 38 S-200 (SA-5 *Gammon*)
MANPAD 3,050+ 9K32 *Strela*-2 (SA-7 *Grail*)‡; 9K36 *Strela*-3 (SA-14 *Gremlin*); 9K310 *Igla*-1 (SA-16 *Gimlet*)

MSL
ASM Kh-23 (AS-7 *Kerry*); Kh-25 (AS-10 *Karen*)
AShM KN-01
AAM • IR R-3 (AA-2 *Atoll*)‡; R-60 (AA-8 *Aphid*); R-73 (AA-11 *Archer*); PL-5; PL-7; **SARH** R-23/24 (AA-7 *Apex*); R-27R/ER (AA-10 A/C *Alamo*)

Paramilitary 189,000 active

Security Troops 189,000 (incl border guards, public safety personnel)

Ministry of Public Security

Worker/Peasant Red Guard ε5,700,000 reservists

Org on a provincial/town/village basis; comd structure is bde–bn–coy–pl; small arms with some mor and AD guns (but many units unarmed)

Cyber

Since the 1970s, the North Korean military (the Korean People's Army – KPA) has maintained a modest electronic warfare (EW) capability. As a result of strategic reviews following *Operation Desert Storm*, the KPA established an information warfare (IW) capability under the concept of 'electronic intelligence warfare' (EIW). Complementing these EIW developments, the KPA is believed to have expanded its EW capabilities with the introduction of more modern ELINT equipment, jammers and radars. In 1998, Unit 121 was reportedly established within the Reconnaissance Bureau of the General Staff Department to undertake offensive cyber operations. Staff are trained in North Korea but some also receive training in Russia and China. In early 2012, activity attributed to Pyongyang included jamming the global positioning systems of aircraft using Seoul's main international airports, as well as those of vessels in nearby waters for two weeks. North Korea also continued to launch distributed denial of service attacks on South Korean institutions and pursue cyber infiltration against military and other government agencies.

Korea, Republic of ROK

South Korean Won		2012	2013	2014
GDP	won	1,302tr	1,367tr	
	US$	1.16tr	1.26tr	
per capita	US$	23,113	25,051	
Growth	%	2.02	2.85	
Inflation	%	2.19	2.36	
Def bdgt	won	33tr	34.6tr	36.2tr
	US$	29.3bn	31.8bn	
US$1=won		1126.53	1086.47	

Population 48,955,203

Age	0–14	15–19	20–24	25–29	30–64	65 plus
Male	7.6%	3.6%	3.6%	3.5%	26.7%	5.0%
Female	7.0%	3.2%	3.1%	3.1%	26.3%	7.2%

Capabilities

More than half a century of tailoring its defence posture around the possibility of an invasion from its northern neighbour has left South Korea with some of the best-equipped and most capable armed forces in East Asia. The country's rapid economic growth has encouraged a broader ambition to procure power projection capabilities and build a blue-water navy. The *Aegis*-equipped *Sejong the Great*-class destroyers, the third of which was commissioned in 2012, are among the most capable platforms developed as part of this strategy. The aggressive behaviour of its northern neighbour ensures that Seoul is unable to divorce its defence strategy from North Korea, which in early 2013 rejected the 1953 Armistice Agreement. The 2012 defence white paper was notable for describing, for the first time, the western maritime border shared with North Korea and highlighting the goal of defending it from instability. As such, while South Korea has demonstrated a willingness to deploy forces overseas in support of international coalitions and operations, such as the Cheonghae Counter-piracy Unit that has operated in the Indian Ocean since April 2009, more immediate security concerns will continue to occupy the South Korean armed forces for the foreseeable future.

ACTIVE 655,000 (Army 522,000 Navy 68,000 Air 65,000) **Paramilitary 4,500**

Conscript liability Army, Navy and Air Force 26 months

RESERVE 4,500,000

Reserve obligation of three days per year. First Combat Forces (Mobilisation Reserve Forces) or Regional Combat Forces (Homeland Defence Forces) to age 33.

Paramilitary 3,000,000

Being reorganised

ORGANISATIONS BY SERVICE

Army 522,000

FORCES BY ROLE

COMMAND

2 army HQ
8 corps HQ
1 (Capital Defence) comd HQ

SPECIAL FORCES

1 (Special Warfare) SF comd
7 SF bde

MANOEUVRE

Armoured
5 armd bde

Mechanised
6 mech inf div (1 recce bn, 1 armd bde, 2 mech inf bde, 1 fd arty bde, 1 engr bn)

Light
16 inf div (1 recce bn, 1 tk bn, 3 inf regt, 1 arty regt (4 arty bn), 1 engr bn)
2 indep inf bde

Air Manoeuvre
1 air aslt bde

Other
3 (Counter Infiltration) bde

Aviation
1 (army avn) comd

COMBAT SUPPORT

3 SSM bn
1 ADA bde
5 ADA bn
6 engr bde
5 engr gp
1 CBRN defence bde
8 sigs bde

COMBAT SERVICE SUPPORT

4 log cpt cmd
5 sy regt

EQUIPMENT BY TYPE

MBT 2,414: 1,000 K1; 484 K1A1; 253 M48; 597 M48A5; 80 T-80U; (400 M47 in store)

AIFV 290: 40 BMP-3; ε250 K21

APC 2,790
- **APC (T)** 2,560: 300 Bv 206; 1,700 KIFV; 420 M113; 140 M577
- **APC (W)** 220; 20 BTR-80; 200 KM-900/-901 (Fiat 6614)
- **PPV** 10 *MaxxPro*

ARTY 11,038+
- **SP** 1,353+: **155mm** 1,340: ε300 K9 *Thunder;* 1,040 M109A2 (K55/K55A1); **175mm** some M107; **203mm** 13 M110
- **TOWED** 3,500+: **105mm** 1,700 M101/KH-178; **155mm** 1,800+ KH-179/M114/M115
- **MRL** 185: **130mm** 156 *Kooryong*; **227mm** 29 MLRS (all ATACMS capable)
- **MOR** 6,000: **81mm** KM-29 (M29); **107mm** M30

AT
- **MSL • MANPATS** 9K115 *Metis* (AT-7 *Saxhorn*); TOW-2A
- **RCL 57mm; 75mm; 90mm** M67; **106mm** M40A2
- **GUNS** 58
  - **SP 90mm** 50 M36
  - **TOWED 76mm** 8 M18 *Hellcat* (AT gun)

HELICOPTERS
ATK 60 AH-1F/J *Cobra*
MRH 175: 130 Hughes 500D; 45 MD-500
TPT 232+ **Heavy** 23: 17 CH-47D *Chinook*; 6 MH-47E *Chinook*; **Medium** 97+: 10+ KUH-1 *Surion*; 87 UH-60P *Black Hawk*; **Light** 112: ε100 Bell-205 (UH-1H *Iroquois*); 12 Bo-105
AD
SAM 780+
SP *Chun Ma* (*Pegasus*)
MANPAD 780+: 60 FIM-43 *Redeye*; ε200 FIM-92A *Stinger*; 350 *Javelin*; 170 *Mistral*; 9K31 *Igla*-1 (SA-16 *Gimlet*)
GUNS 330+
SP 170: **20mm** ε150 KIFV *Vulcan* SPAAG; **30mm** 20 BIHO *Flying Tiger*
TOWED 160: **20mm** 60 M167 *Vulcan*; **35mm** 20 GDF-003; **40mm** 80 L/60/L/70; M1
RADAR • LAND AN/TPQ-36 *Firefinder* (arty, mor); AN/TPQ-37 *Firefinder* (arty); RASIT (veh, arty)
MSL
SRBM 30 *Hyonmu* I/IIA/IIB
LACM *Hyonmu* III
AEV 207 M9
ARV 238: 200 K1; K288A1; M47; 38 M88A1
VLB 56 K1

Reserves

FORCES BY ROLE
COMMAND
1 army HQ
MANOEUVRE
Light
24 inf div

Navy 68,000 (incl marines)

Naval HQ (CNOROK) located at Gyeryongdae, with an Operational Cmd HQ (CINCROKFLT) located at Jinhae with three separate fleet elements; 1st Fleet Donghae (Sea of Japan (East Sea)); 2nd Fleet Pyeongtaek (West Sea/Yellow Sea); 3rd Fleet Busan (South Sea/Korea Strait); additional three flotillas (incl SF, mine warfare, amphibious and spt elements) and 1 Naval Air Wing (3 gp plus Spt gp).

EQUIPMENT BY TYPE
SUBMARINES • TACTICAL 23
SSK 12:
6 *Chang Bogo* with 8 single 533mm TT with SUT HWT
3 *Chang Bogo* with 8 single 533mm TT with SUT HWT/UGM-84B *Harpoon* AShM
3 *Son Won-ill* (KSS-2; AIP fitted) with 8 single 533mm TT with SUT HWT (additional vessels in build)
SSC 11:
9 *Cosmos*
2 *Dolgorae* (KSS-1) with 2 single 406mm TT
PRINCIPAL SURFACE COMBATANTS 22
CRUISERS • CGHM 3:
3 *Sejong* (KDX-3) with 2 quad Mk141 lnchr with RGM-84 *Harpoon* AShM, 1 48-cell Mk41 VLS with SM-2MR SAM, 1 32-cell Mk41 VLS with SM-2MR SAM, 1 Mk49 GMLS with RIM-116 SAM, 2 triple Mk32 324mm ASTT with K745 LWT, 1 32-cell VLS with ASROC, 1 *Goalkeeper* CIWS, 1 127mm gun, (capacity 2 *Lynx* Mk99 hel)
DESTROYERS • DDGHM 6:
6 *Chungmugong Yi Sun-Jhin* (KDX-2) with 2 quad Mk141 lnchr with RGM-84C *Harpoon* AShM (some may be fitted with *Hae Sung* AShM), 1 or 2 32-cell Mk41 VLS with SM-2 MR SAM/ASROC, 1 Mk49 GMLS with RIM-116 SAM, 2 triple Mk32 324mm ASTT with Mk46 LWT, 1 *Goalkeeper* CIWS, 1 127mm gun (capacity 1 *Lynx* Mk99 hel)
FRIGATES 13
FFGHM 4:
3 *Gwanggaeto Daewang* (KDX-1) with 2 quad Mk141 lnchr with RGM-84 *Harpoon* AShM, 1 16 cell Mk48 VLS with *Sea Sparrow* SAM, 2 triple Mk32 324mm ASTT with Mk46 LWT, 1 *Goalkeeper* CIWS, 1 127mm gun, (capacity 1 *Lynx* Mk99 hel)
1 *Incheon* with 2 quad lnchr with *Hae Sung* AShM, 1 21-cell Mk49 lnchr with RIM-116 SAM, 2 triple 324mm ASTT with K745 *Blue Shark* LWT, 1 Mk15 1B *Phalanx* CIWS, 1 127 mm gun (2 further vessels under construction)
FFGM 9:
9 *Ulsan* with 2 quad Mk141 lnchr with RGM-84C *Harpoon* AShM, 2 triple Mk32 324mm ASTT with Mk46 LWT, 2 76mm gun
PATROL AND COASTAL COMBATANTS 110
CORVETTES • FSG 30:
9 *Gumdoksuri* with 2 twin lnchr with RGM-84 *Harpoon* AShM, 1 76mm gun (additional vessel in build)
2 *Po Hang* with 2 single lnchr with MM-38 *Exocet* AShM, 2 triple ASTT with Mk 46 LWT, 1 76mm gun
19 *Po Hang* with 2 twin lnchr with RGM-84 *Harpoon* AShM, 2 triple ASTT with Mk46 LWT, 2 76mm gun
PBF 80 *Sea Dolphin*
MINE WARFARE 10
MINE COUNTERMEASURES 9
MHO 6 *Kan Kyeong*
MSO 3 *Yang Yang*
MINELAYERS • ML 1 *Won San* with 2 triple Mk32 ASTT, 1 76mm gun
AMPHIBIOUS
PRINCIPAL AMPHIBIOUS SHIPS 1
LPD 1 *Dokdo* with 1 Mk49 GMLS with RIM-116 SAM, 2 Goalkeeper CIWS (capacity 2 LCAC; 10 tanks; 700 troops; 10 UH-60 hel)
LANDING SHIPS • LST 4 *Alligator* (capacity 20 tanks; 300 troops)
LANDING CRAFT 41
LCAC 5: 3 *Tsaplya* (capacity 1 MBT; 130 troops); 2 LSF-II
LCM 10 LCM-8
LCT 6
LCVP 20
LOGISTICS AND SUPPORT 24
AG 1 *Sunjin* (trials spt)
AGOR 17 (civil manned, funded by the Ministry of Transport)
AORH 3 *Chun Jee*
ARS 1
ATS 2

Naval Aviation

AIRCRAFT 16 combat capable
ASW 16: 8 P-3C *Orion;* 8 P-3CK *Orion*
TPT • Light 5 Cessna F406 *Caravan* II
HELICOPTERS
ASW 24: 11 *Lynx* Mk99; 13 *Lynx* Mk99-A
MRH 3 SA319B *Alouette* III
TPT 15 **Medium** 8 UH-60P *Black Hawk* **Light** 7 Bell 205 (UH-1H *Iroquois*)

Marines 27,000

FORCES BY ROLE
MANOEUVRE
Amphibious
2 mne div (1 recce bn, 1 tk bn, 3 mne regt, 1 amph bn, 1 arty regt, 1 engr bn)
1 mne bde
COMBAT SUPPORT
Some cbt spt unit
EQUIPMENT BY TYPE
MBT 100: 50 K1A1; 50 M48
AAV 166 AAV-7A1
ARTY TOWED: **105mm**; **155mm**
AT • MSL • SP 2 *Spike* NLOS
MSL • AShM RGM-84A *Harpoon* (truck mounted)

Air Force 65,000

4 Comd (Ops, Southern Combat, Logs, Trg)
FORCES BY ROLE
FIGHTER/GROUND ATTACK
3 sqn with F-4E *Phantom* II
11 sqn with F-5E/F *Tiger* II
3 sqn with F-15K *Eagle*
10 sqn with F-16C/D *Fighting Falcon* (KF-16C/D)
ISR
1 wg with KO-1
1 sqn with RF-4C *Phantom* II*
SIGINT
1 sqn with Hawker 800RA/XP
SEARCH & RESCUE
2 sqn with AS332L *Super Puma*; Bell 412EP; HH-47D *Chinook;* HH-60P *Black Hawk;* Ka-32 *Helix* C
TRANSPORT
1 VIP sqn with B-737-300; B-747; CN-235-220; S-92A *Superhawk;* VH-60P *Black Hawk* (VIP)
3 sqn (incl 1 Spec Ops) with C-130H *Hercules*
2 sqn with CN-235M-100/220
TRAINING
2 sqn with F-5E/F *Tiger* II
1 sqn with F-16C/D *Fighting Falcon*
1 sqn with *Hawk* Mk67
4 sqn with KT-1
1 sqn with Il-103
3 sqn with T-50/TA-50 *Golden Eagle**
TRANSPORT HELICOPTER
1 sqn with UH-60P *Black Hawk* (Spec Ops)
AIR DEFENCE
3 AD bde (total: 3 SAM bn with I-HAWK; 2 SAM bn with *Patriot* PAC-2)

EQUIPMENT BY TYPE
AIRCRAFT 568 combat capable
FTR 174: 142 F-5E *Tiger* II; 32 F-5F *Tiger* II
FGA 294: 70 F-4E *Phantom* II; 60 F-15K *Eagle;* 118 F-16C *Fighting Falcon* (KF-16C); 46 F-16D *Fighting Falcon* (KF-16D); (some F-4D *Phantom* II in store)
AEW&C 4 B-737 AEW
ISR 41: 4 Hawker 800RA; 20 KO-1; 17 RF-4C *Phantom* II*
SIGINT 4 Hawker 800SIG
TPT 34 **Medium** 12: 8 C-130H *Hercules;* 4 C-130H-30 *Hercules;* **Light** 20: 12 CN-235M-100; 8 CN-235M-220 (incl 2 VIP); **PAX** 2: 1 B-737-300; 1 B-747
TRG 189: 15 *Hawk* Mk67*; 23 Il-103; 83 KT-1; 49 T-50 *Golden Eagle**; 9 T-50B *Black Eagle** (aerobatics); 10 TA-50 *Golden Eagle**
HELICOPTERS
SAR 16: 5 HH-47D *Chinook;* 11 HH-60P *Black Hawk*
MRH 3 Bell 412EP
TPT • Medium 30: 2 AS332L *Super Puma;* 8 Ka-32 *Helix* C; 3 S-92A *Superhawk;* 7 UH-60P *Black Hawk;* 10 VH-60P *Black Hawk* (VIP)
UAV • ISR 103+ **Medium** 3+: some *Night Intruder;* 3 *Searcher* **Light** 100 *Harpy*
AD • SAM 206
SP 48 *Patriot* PAC-2
TOWED 158 MIM-23B I-HAWK
MSL
ASM AGM-65A *Maverick;* AGM-84H SLAM-ER
AShM AGM-84 *Harpoon;* AGM-130; AGM-142 *Popeye*
ARM AGM-88 HARM
AAM • IR AIM-9 *Sidewinder;* **IIR** AIM-9X *Sidewinder;* **SARH** AIM-7 *Sparrow;* **ARH** AIM-120B/C5 AMRAAM

Paramilitary ε4,500 active

Civilian Defence Corps 3,000,000 reservists (to age 50)

Coast Guard ε4,500

PATROL AND COASTAL COMBATANTS 50
PSO 5: 1 *Sumjinkang;* 3 *Mazinger;* 1 *Sambongho*
PCO 16: 1 *Han Kang* with 1 76mm gun; 15 *Tae Geuk*
PCC 20: 4 *Bukhansan;* 6 (430 tonne); 10 *Hae Uri*
PB 9: 5 Hyundai Type; ε4 (various)
LOGISTICS AND SUPPORT • ARS 30+
AIRCRAFT
MP 5: 1 C-212-400 MP; 4 CN-235-110 MPA
TPT • PAX 1 CL-604
HELICOPTERS
MRH 8: 6 AS365 *Dauphin* II; 1 AW139; 1 Bell 412SP
TPT • Medium 8 Ka-32 *Helix* C

Cyber

South Korea established a Cyber Warfare Command Centre in early 2010, with over 200 personnel, in the wake of a substantial distributed denial of service attack in 2009. The new centre responds to the attention given to cyber and information security by the National Intelligence Service and the Defense Security Command. South Korea published an 'Internet White Paper' in 2009.

DEPLOYMENT

AFGHANISTAN
NATO • ISAF 50

ARABIAN SEA
Combined Maritime Forces • CTF-151: 1 DDGHM

CÔTE D'IVOIRE
UN • UNOCI 2 obs

HAITI
UN • MINUSTAH 2

INDIA/PAKISTAN
UN • UNMOGIP 8 obs

LEBANON
UN • UNIFIL 321; 1 mech inf bn

LIBERIA
UN • UNMIL 1; 1 obs

SOUTH SUDAN
UN • UNMISS 273; 2 obs; 1 engr coy

SUDAN
UN • UNAMID 2

UAE
150 (trg activities at UAE Spec Ops School)

WESTERN SAHARA
UN • MINURSO 4 obs

FOREIGN FORCES

Sweden NNSC: 5 obs
Switzerland NNSC: 5 obs
United States US Pacific Command: 28,500
Army 19,200; 1 HQ (8th Army) at Seoul; 1 div HQ (2nd Inf) at Tongduchon; 1 armd HBCT with M1 *Abrams*; M2/M3 *Bradley*; M109; 1 cbt avn bde with AH-64 *Apache*; CH-47 *Chinook*; UH-60 *Black Hawk*; 1 arty (fires) bde with M270 MLRS; 1 AD bde with MIM 104 *Patriot*/FIM-92A *Avenger*
Navy 250
USAF 8,800; 1 HQ (7th Air Force) at Osan AB; 1 ftr wg at Kunsan AB (1 ftr sqn with 20 F-16C/D *Fighting Falcon*); 1 ftr wg at Kunsan AB (1 ftr sqn with 20 F-16C/D *Fighting Falcon*, 1 ftr sqn with 24 A-10C *Thunderbolt* II at Osan AB)
USMC 250

Laos LAO

New Lao Kip		2012	2013	2014
GDP	kip	74.8tr	86.2tr	
	US$	9.22bn	10.3bn	
per capita	US$	1,446	1,587	
Growth	%	8.31	8.03	
Inflation	%	4.26	7.32	
Def bdgt	kip	160bn	172bn	
	US$	20m	21m	
US$1=kip		8112.46	8396.51	

Population **6,695,166**

Ethnic groups: Lao 55%; Khmou 11%; Hmong 8%

Age	0–14	15–19	20–24	25–29	30–64	65 plus
Male	17.9%	5.5%	5.1%	4.3%	15.2%	1.7%
Female	17.6%	5.5%	5.2%	4.3%	15.7%	2.1%

Capabilities

The Lao People's Armed Forces (LPAF) have considerable historical military experience from the Second Indo-China War and the 1988 border war with Thailand. However, Laos is one of the world's poorest countries and the defence budget and military procurement have been extremely limited for more than 20 years. The armed forces remain closely linked to the ruling Communist Party, and their primary orientation is towards internal security, with operations continuing against Hmong rebel remnants. Contacts with the Chinese and Vietnamese armed forces continue, but the LPAF have made no international deployments and have little capacity for sustained high intensity operations.

ACTIVE 29,100 (Army 25,600 Air 3,500) **Paramilitary 100,000**
Conscript liability 18 months minimum

ORGANISATIONS BY SERVICE

Army 25,600

FORCES BY ROLE
4 Mil Regions
MANOEUVRE
Armoured
1 armd bn
Light
5 inf div
7 indep inf regt
65 indep inf coy
Aviation
1 (liaison) flt
COMBAT SUPPORT
5 arty bn
9 ADA bn
1 engr regt
2 (construction) engr regt

EQUIPMENT BY TYPE
MBT 25: 15 T-54/T-55; 10 T-34/85
LT TK 10 PT-76
APC (W) 50: 30 BTR-40/BTR-60; 20 BTR-152
ARTY 62+
TOWED 62: **105mm** 20 M101; **122mm** 20 D-30/M-30 M-1938; **130mm** 10 M-46; **155mm** 12 M114
MOR 81mm; 82mm; 107mm M-1938/M-2A1; **120mm** M-43
AT • RCL 57mm M18/A1; **75mm** M20; **106mm** M40; **107mm** B-11
AD • SAM • MANPAD 9K32 *Strela*-2 (SA-7 *Grail*)‡; 25 9K310 *Igla*-1 (SA-16 *Gimlet*)
GUNS
SP 23mm ZSU-23-4
TOWED 14.5mm ZPU-1/ZPU-4; **23mm** ZU-23; **37mm** M-1939; **57mm** S-60
ARV T-54/T-55
VLB MTU

Army Marine Section ε600
PATROL AND COASTAL COMBATANTS 52
PBR 52†
AMPHIBIOUS LCM 4†

Air Force 3,500
FORCES BY ROLE
TRANSPORT
1 sqn with An-2 *Colt*; An-26 *Curl*; An-74 *Coaler*; Y-7; Y-12; Yak-40 *Codling* (VIP)
TRAINING
1 sqn with Yak-18 *Max*
TRANSPORT HELICOPTER
1 sqn with Ka-32T *Helix* C; Mi-6 *Hook*; Mi-8 *Hip*; Mi-17 *Hip* H; Mi-26 *Halo*; SA360 *Dauphin*
EQUIPMENT BY TYPE
AIRCRAFT
TPT • Light 15: 4 An-2 *Colt*; 3 An-26 *Curl*; 1 An-74 *Coaler*; 5 Y-7; 1 Y-12; 1 Yak-40 *Codling* (VIP)
TRG 8 Yak-18 *Max*
HELICOPTERS
MRH 12 Mi-17 *Hip* H
TPT 15 **Heavy** 2: 1 Mi-6 *Hook;* 1 Mi-26 *Halo* **Medium** 10: 1 Ka-32T *Helix* C (5 more on order); 9 Mi-8 *Hip* **Light** 3 SA360 *Dauphin*
MSL • AAM • IR R-3 (AA-2 *Atoll*)†

Paramilitary

Militia Self-Defence Forces 100,000+
Village 'home guard' or local defence

Malaysia MYS

Malaysian Ringgit RM		2012	2013	2014
GDP	RM	938bn	1tn	
	US$	304bn	328bn	
per capita	US$	10,304	10,946	
Growth	%	5.61	5.10	
Inflation	%	1.66	2.20	
Def bdgt	RM	13.7bn	15.3bn	
	US$	4.44bn	5bn	
US$1=RM		3.09	3.05	

Population 29,628,392

Ethnic groups: Malay and other indigenous (Bunipatre) 64%; Chinese 27%; Indian 9%

Age	0–14	15–19	20–24	25–29	30–64	65 plus
Male	15.0%	4.5%	4.2%	4.1%	20.6%	2.5%
Female	14.1%	4.3%	4.1%	4.1%	19.9%	2.8%

Capabilities

Malaysia's armed forces have considerable historical experience of counter-insurgency. Over the last 30 years, however, substantial equipment modernisation programmes have helped to develop their capacity for external defence. Malaysian army units have deployed on UN peacekeeping operations, and the navy has achieved well-publicised successes with its anti-piracy patrols in the Gulf of Aden. There is considerable emphasis on joint-service operations. Malaysia regularly participates in Five Power Defence Arrangements exercises. The armed forces' personnel are disproportionately drawn from the Malay community, with few ethnic-Chinese Malaysians and members of other ethnic minorities. While this ethnic homogeneity may reinforce military morale, it may also have implications for the armed forces' capabilities (particularly because of problems recruiting sufficient technical personnel), and for the government's ability to sustain national support for military operations.

ACTIVE 109,000 (Army 80,000 Navy 14,000 Air 15,000) Paramilitary 24,600

RESERVE 51,600 (Army 50,000, Navy 1,000 Air Force 600) Paramilitary 244,700

ORGANISATIONS BY SERVICE

Army 80,000 (to be 60–70,000)
2 mil region, 4 area comd (div)
FORCES BY ROLE
SPECIAL FORCES
1 SF bde (3 SF bn)
MANOEUVRE
Armoured
1 tk regt (with 5 armd bn)
Mechanised
5 armd regt
1 mech inf bde (3 mech bn, 1 cbt engr sqn)

Light
9 inf bde (total: 36 inf bn)
Air Manoeuvre
1 (Rapid Deployment Force) AB bde (1 lt tk sqn, 3 AB bn, 1 lt arty regt, 1 engr sqn)
Aviation
1 hel sqn
COMBAT SUPPORT
9 arty regt
1 arty locator regt
1 MRL regt
3 ADA regt
1 cbt engr sqn
3 fd engr regt (total: 7 cbt engr sqn, 3 engr spt sqn)
1 int unit
4 MP regt
1 sigs regt
COMBAT SERVICE SUPPORT
1 const regt

EQUIPMENT BY TYPE
MBT 48 PT-91M *Twardy*
LT TK 21 *Scorpion-90*
RECCE 296: 130 AML-60/90; 92 *Ferret* (60 mod); K216A1 (as CBRN recce); 74 SIBMAS (some †)
AIFV 44: 31 ACV300 *Adnan (25mm Bushmaster);* 13 ACV300 *Adnan* AGL
APC 787
APC (T) 265: 149 ACV300 *Adnan* (incl 69 variants); 13 FV4333 *Stormer* (upgraded); 63 K-200A; 40 K-200A1
APC (W) 522: 32 *Anoa*; 300 *Condor* (incl variants); 150 LAV-150 *Commando*; 30 M3 Panhard; 10 VBL
ARTY 424
TOWED 134: **105mm** 100 Model 56 pack howitzer; **155mm** 34: 12 FH-70; 22 G-5
MRL 36 ASTROS II (equipped with 127mm SS-30)
MOR 254: **81mm SP** 14: 4 K281A1; 10 ACV300-S; **120mm SP** 8 ACV-S **81mm**: 232
AT • MSL
SP 8 ACV300 *Baktar Shikan*; K263
MANPATS 60+: 18 9K115 *Metis* (AT-7 *Saxhorn*); 9K115-2 *Metis*-M (AT-13 Saxhorn 2); 24 *Eryx*; 18 *Baktar Shihan* (HJ-8); C90-CRRB; SS.11
RCL 260: **84mm** 236 *Carl Gustav*; **106mm** 24 M40
AMPHIBIOUS • LCA 165 Damen Assault Craft 540 (capacity 10 troops)
HELICOPTERS • TPT • Light 11 AW109
AD
SAM 15 *Jernas* (*Rapier* 2000)
MANPAD 88+: *Anza*; HY-6 (FN-6); 40 9K38 *Igla* (SA-18 *Grouse*); QW-1 *Vanguard*; 48 *Starburst*
GUNS • TOWED 52: **35mm** 16 GDF-005; **40mm** 36 L40/70
AEV 9: 3 MID-M; 6 WZT-4
ARV 41+: *Condor*; 15 ACV300; 4 K-288A1; 22 SIBMAS
VLB 5+: *Leguan*; 5 PMCz-90

Reserves

Territorial Army
Some paramilitary forces to be incorporated into a re-organised territorial organisation.

FORCES BY ROLE
MANOEUVRE
Mechanised
4 armd sqn
Light
16 inf regt (3 inf bn)
Other
1 (border) sy bde (5 bn)
5 (highway) sy bn
COMBAT SUPPORT
5 arty bty
2 fd engr regt
1 int unit
3 sigs sqn
COMBAT SUPPORT
4 med coy
5 tpt coy

Navy 14,000
3 Regional Commands; Kuantan (East Coast); Kinabalu (Borneo) & Langkawi (West Coast)

EQUIPMENT BY TYPE
SUBMARINES • TACTICAL • SSK 2 *Tunku Abdul Rahman* (*Scorpene*) with 6 single 533mm TT with WASS *Black Shark* HWT/SM-39 *Exocet* AShM
PRINCIPAL SURFACE COMBATANTS 10
FRIGATES 10
FFGHM 2:
2 *Lekiu* with 2 quad lnchr with MM-40 *Exocet* Block II AShM, 1 16-cell VLS with *Sea Wolf* SAM, 2 B515 ILAS-3 triple 324mm ASTT with *Sting Ray* LWT, 1 57mm gun, (capacity 1 *Super Lynx* hel)
FFG 2:
2 *Kasturi* with 2 twin lnchr with MM-40 *Exocet* Block II AShM, 1 twin 375mm A/S mor, 1 100mm gun, 1 57m gun, 1 hel landing platform
FF 6:
6 *Kedah* (MEKO) with 1 76mm gun, 1 hel landing platform, (fitted for MM-40 *Exocet* AShM & RAM CIWS)
PATROL AND COASTAL COMBATANTS 37
CORVETTES • FSGM 4:
4 *Laksamana* with 3 twin lnchr with Mk 2 *Otomat* AShM, 1 *Albatros* quad lnchr with *Aspide* SAM, 2 B515 *ILAS*-3 triple 324mm TT with A244 LWT, 1 76mm gun
PCFG 4 *Perdana* (*Combattante* II) with 2 single lnchr with MM-38 *Exocet* AShM, 1 57mm gun
PBG 4 *Handalan* (*Spica*-M) with 2 twin lnchr with MM-38 *Exocet* AShM , 1 57mm gun
PBF 17 *Tempur* (SWE CB90)
PB 8: 6 *Jerong* (Lurssen 45) with 1 57mm gun; 2 *Sri Perlis*
MINE WARFARE • MINE COUNTERMEASURES
MCO 4 *Mahamiru*
AMPHIBIOUS
LANDING CRAFT 115 **LCM/LCU**
LOGISTICS AND SUPPORT 16
AG 2 *Bunga Mas Lima*
AGS 2
AP 2 *Sri Gaya*
AOR 2 with 1 or 2 57mm gun

ASR 1 *Mega Bakti*
ATF 2
AX 3: 1 *Hang Tuah* with 1 57mm gun; 2 *Samudera*
AXS 1
YTM 1

Naval Aviation 160

HELICOPTERS
ASW 6 *Super Lynx* 300
MRH 6 AS555 *Fennec*
MSL • AShM *Sea Skua*

Special Forces

FORCES BY ROLE
SPECIAL FORCES
1 (mne cdo) SF unit

Air Force 15,000

1 Air Op HQ, 2 Air Div, 1 trg and Log Cmd, 1 Intergrated Area Def Systems HQ

Flying hours 60 hrs/year

FORCES BY ROLE
FIGHTER
2 sqn with MiG-29/MiG-29UB *Fulcrum*
FIGHTER/GROUND ATTACK
1 sqn with F/A-18D *Hornet*
1 sqn with Su-30MKM *Flanker*
2 sqn with *Hawk* Mk108*/Mk208*
FIGHTER/GROUND ATTACK/ISR
1 sqn with F-5E/F *Tiger* II; RF-5E *Tigereye**
MARITIME PATROL
1 sqn with Beech 200T
TANKER/TRANSPORT
2 sqn with KC-130H *Hercules*; C-130H *Hercules*; C-130H-30 *Hercules*; Cessna 402B
TRANSPORT
1 (VIP) sqn with A319CT; AW109; B-737-700 BBJ; BD700 *Global Express*; F-28 *Fellowship*; *Falcon* 900
1 sqn with CN-235
TRAINING
1 unit with PC-7; SA316 *Alouette* III
TRANSPORT HELICOPTER
4 (tpt/SAR) sqn with S-61A-4 *Nuri*; S-61N; S-70A *Black Hawk*
AIR DEFENCE
1 sqn with *Starburst*
SPECIAL FORCES
1 (Air Force Commando) unit (airfield defence/SAR)

EQUIPMENT BY TYPE
AIRCRAFT 67 combat capable
FTR 21: 8 F-5E *Tiger* II; 3 F-5F *Tiger* II; 8 MiG-29 *Fulcrum* (MiG-29N); 2 MiG-29UB *Fulcrum* (MIG-29NUB) (MiG-29 to be withdrawn from service)
FGA 26: 8 F/A-18D *Hornet*; 18 Su-30MKM
ISR 6: 4 Beech 200T; 2 RF-5E *Tigereye**
TKR 4 KC-130H *Hercules*
TPT 32 **Medium** 10: 2 C-130H *Hercules*; 8 C-130H-30 *Hercules*; **Light** 17: 8 CN-235M-220 (incl 2 VIP); 9 Cessna 402B (2 modified for aerial survey) **PAX** 5: 1 A319CT; 1 B-737-700 BBJ; 1 BD700 *Global Express*; 1 F-28 *Fellowship*; 1 *Falcon* 900
TRG 80: 6 *Hawk* Mk108*; 12 *Hawk* Mk208*; 8 MB-339C; 7 MD3-160 *Aero Tiga*; 30 PC-7; 17 PC-7 Mk II *Turbo Trainer*
HELICOPTERS
MRH 17 SA316 *Alouette* III
TPT 37 **Heavy** 4 EC725 *Super Cougar*; **Medium** 32: 28 S-61A-4 *Nuri*; 2 S-61N; 2 S-70A *Black Hawk*; **Light** 1 AW109
UAV • ISR • Medium *Aludra*
AD • SAM •MANPAD *Starburst*
MSL
AAM • IR AIM-9 *Sidewinder*; R-73 (AA-11 *Archer*) **IR/SARH** R-27 (AA-10 *Alamo*); **SARH** AIM-7 *Sparrow*; **ARH** AIM-120C AMRAAM; R-77 (AA-12 *Adder*)
ASM AGM-65 *Maverick*
AShM AGM-84D *Harpoon*

Paramilitary ε24,600

Police-General Ops Force 18,000

FORCES BY ROLE
COMMAND
5 bde HQ
SPECIAL FORCES
1 spec ops bn
MANOEUVRE
Other
19 paramilitary bn
2 (Aboriginal) paramilitary bn
4 indep paramilitary coy

EQUIPMENT BY TYPE
RECCE ε100 S52 *Shorland*
APC (W) 170: 140 AT105 *Saxon*; ε30 SB-301

Malaysian Maritime Enforcement Agency (MMEA) ε4,500

Controls 5 Maritime Regions (Northern Peninsula; Southern Peninsula; Eastern Peninsula; Sarawak; Sabah), sub-divided into a further 18 Maritime Districts. Supported by one provisional MMEA Air Unit.

EQUIPMENT BY TYPE
PATROL AND COASTAL COMBATANTS 189:
PSO 2 *Langkawi* with 1 57mm gun, 1 hel landing platform
PBF 57: 18 *Penggalang 17* (TUR MRTP 16); 2 *Penggalang 18*; 6 *Penyelamat 20*; 16 *Penggalang 16*; 15 *Tugau*
PB 130: 15 *Gagah*; 4 *Malawali*; 2 *Nusa*; 3 *Nusa 28*; 1 *Peninjau*; 7 *Ramunia*; 2 *Rhu*; 4 *Semilang*; 15 *Sipadan* (ex-*Kris/Sabah*); 8 *Icarus 1650*; 10 *Pengawal*; 10 *Pengawal 13*; 27 *Pengawal 23*; 4 *Penyelamat*; 9 *Sipadan Steel*; 9 *Sipadan Kayu*
LOGISTICS AND SUPPORT • AX 1 *Marlin*
AIRCRAFT • MP 2 Bombardier 415MP
HELICOPTERS
MRH 3 AS365 *Dauphin*

Marine Police 2,100

EQUIPMENT BY TYPE
PATROL AND COASTAL COMBATANTS 132

PBF 12: 6 *Sangitan;* 6 Stan Patrol 1500
PB/PBR 120

Police Air Unit
AIRCRAFT
TPT • Light 17: 4 Cessna 206 *Stationair;* 6 Cessna 208 *Caravan;* 7 PC-6 *Turbo-Porter*
HELICOPTERS
TPT • Light 3: 1 Bell 206L *Long Ranger;* 2 AS355F *Ecureuil* II

Area Security Units (R) 3,500
(Auxiliary General Ops Force)
FORCES BY ROLE
MANOEUVRE
Other
89 paramilitary unit

Border Scouts (R) 1,200
in Sabah, Sarawak

People's Volunteer Corps 240,000 reservists (some 17,500 armed)
RELA

Customs Service
PATROL AND COASTAL COMBATANTS 23
PBF 10
PB 13

DEPLOYMENT

AFGHANISTAN
NATO • ISAF 2

DEMOCRATIC REPUBLIC OF THE CONGO
UN • MONUSCO 9; 7 obs

LEBANON
UN • UNIFIL 829; 1 mech inf bn; 1 mech inf coy

LIBERIA
UN • UNMIL 6 obs

PHILIPPINES
IMT 13

SUDAN
UN • UNAMID 12; 3 obs
UN • UNISFA 1 obs

WESTERN SAHARA
UN • MINURSO 12 obs

FOREIGN FORCES
Australia 130; 1 inf coy (on 3-month rotational tours); 1 AP-3C *Orion* on occasion

Mongolia MNG

Mongolian Tugrik t		2012	2013	2014
GDP	t	13.9tr	17tr	
	US$	10.3bn	12.1bn	
per capita	US$	3,627	4,213	
Growth	%	12.28	14.04	
Inflation	%	15.00	11.14	
Def bdgt	t	155bn	187bn	
	US$	114m	133m	
FMA (US)	US$	3m	3m	2.4m
US$1=t		1359.35	1405.87	

Population 3,226,516

Ethnic groups: Khalka 80%; Kazakh 6%

Age	0–14	15–19	20–24	25–29	30–64	65 plus
Male	13.7%	4.6%	5.1%	5.1%	19.8%	1.7%
Female	13.2%	4.4%	5.0%	5.0%	20.2%	2.3%

Capabilities

Mongolia's armed forces are small and generally under-equipped. The army fields largely obsolete armoured vehicles while its air force operates only transport aircraft and helicopters. Mongolia has nevertheless contributed to international operations, and since 2011 an infantry battalion has served in a peacekeeping role in South Sudan. However, the armed forces possess no logistical capabilities for power projection or for supporting and sustaining forces deployed internationally. Attempts are being made to modernise the armed forces. An annual simulation exercise, and collaboration with international partners, including China, European states, Japan, Russia and the US, ensures continued training. Improving the equipment and capability of Mongolia's armed forces would require substantially greater investment than the defence budget currently provides.

ACTIVE 10,000 (Army 8,900 Air 800 Construction Troops 300) Paramilitary 7,200
Conscript liability One year for males aged 18–25

RESERVE 137,000 (Army 137,000)

ORGANISATIONS BY SERVICE

Army 5,600; 3,300 conscript (total 8,900)
FORCES BY ROLE
MANOEUVRE
Mechanised
6 MR regt(-)
Light
1 (rapid deployment) lt inf bn (2nd bn to form)
Air Manoeuvre
1 AB bn
COMBAT SUPPORT
1 arty regt

EQUIPMENT BY TYPE
MBT 420: 370 T-54/T-55; 50 T-72A
RECCE 120 BRDM-2
AIFV 310 BMP-1
APC (W) 210: 150 BTR-60; 40 BTR-70M; 20 BTR-80
ARTY 570
TOWED ε300: **122mm** D-30/M-30 (M-1938); **130mm** M-46; **152mm** ML-20 (M-1937)
MRL 122mm 130 BM-21
MOR 140: **120mm**; **160mm**; **82mm**
AT • GUNS 200: **85mm** D-44/D-48; **100mm** M-1944/MT-12
AD • SAM 2+ S-125 *Pechora* 2M (SA-3B *Goa*)
ARV T-54/T-55

Air Force 800

FORCES BY ROLE
TRANSPORT
1 sqn with An-24 *Coke*; An-26 *Curl*
ATTACK/TRANSPORT HELICOPTER
1 sqn with Mi-8 *Hip*; Mi-171
AIR DEFENCE
2 regt with S-60/ZPU-4/ZU-23
EQUIPMENT BY TYPE
AIRCRAFT • TPT • Light 3: 2 An-24 *Coke*; 1 An-26 *Curl*
HELICOPTERS
TPT • Medium 13: 11 Mi-8 *Hip*; 2 Mi-171
AD • GUNS • TOWED 150: **14.5mm** ZPU-4; **23mm** ZU-23; **57mm** S-60

Paramilitary 7,200 active

Border Guard 1,300; 4,700 conscript (total 6,000) Internal Security Troops 400; 800 conscript (total 1,200)

FORCES BY ROLE
MANOEUVRE
Other
4 gd unit

Construction Troops 300

DEPLOYMENT

AFGHANISTAN
NATO • ISAF 40
UN • UNAMA 1 obs

DEMOCRATIC REPUBLIC OF THE CONGO
UN • MONUSCO 2 obs

SOUTH SUDAN
UN • UNMISS 857; 1 inf bn; 1 engr coy

SUDAN
UN • UNAMID 70; 1 fd hospital
UN • UNISFA 2 obs

WESTERN SAHARA
UN • MINURSO 4 obs

Myanmar MMR

Myanmar Kyat K		2012	2013	2014
GDP	K	44.8tr	50.3tr	
	US$	53.1bn	57.4bn	
per capita	US$	835	884	
Growth	%	6.30	6.47	
Inflation	%	6.10	6.50	
Def bdgt	K	1.88tr	2.1tr	
	US$	2.23bn	2.4bn	
US$1=K		843.01	876.02	

Population 55,167,330

Ethnic groups: Burman 68%; Shan 9%; Karen 7%; Rakhine 4%; Chinese 3+%; Other Chin, Kachin, Kayan, Lahu, Mon, Palaung, Pao, Wa, 9%

Age	0–14	15–19	20–24	25–29	30–64	65 plus
Male	13.6%	4.7%	4.7%	4.6%	19.9%	2.3%
Female	13.1%	4.6%	4.6%	4.5%	20.6%	2.9%

Capabilities

Myanmar's large, army-dominated armed forces have, since the country's independence struggle in the 1940s, been intimately involved in domestic politics, which they still dominate despite the advent of a nominally civilian government in March 2011. Their focus has always been on holding together this ethnically-diverse state, particularly in the face of the world's longest-running insurgencies, conducted by the Karen, Kachin, Mon, Shan and other minority groups around the country's perimeter. However, ceasefires with most of the rebel groups have for the last two decades contributed to a decline in the army's operational experience. Morale among ordinary soldiers (mainly poorly-paid conscripts) is reportedly low. While the army grew substantially after the military seized power in 1988, its counter-insurgency focus means that it has remained essentially a light infantry force. Nevertheless, since the 1990s, large-scale military procurement has resulted in new armoured vehicles, air-defence weapons, artillery, combat aircraft and naval vessels from China, Russia and other diverse sources entering service, and it remains unclear whether Myanmar will be able to soon vary its supplier list.

ACTIVE 406,000 (Army 375,000 Navy 16,000 Air 15,000) Paramilitary 107,250

ORGANISATIONS BY SERVICE

Army ε375,000

12 regional comd, 4 regional op comd, 14 military op comd, 34 tactical op comd (TDC)
FORCES BY ROLE
MANOEUVRE
Armoured
10 armd bn

Light
10 lt inf div
100 inf bn
337 inf bn (regional comd)
COMBAT SUPPORT
7 arty bn
37 indep arty coy
7 AD bn
6 cbt engr bn
54 fd engr bn
40 int coy
45 sigs bn

EQUIPMENT BY TYPE
MBT 185+: 10 T-55; 50 T-72S; 25+ Type-59D; 100 Type-69-II
LT TK 105 Type-63 (ε60 serviceable)
RECCE 115: 45 *Ferret*; 40 Humber *Pig*; 30 Mazda
APC 371+
APC (T) 331: 26 MT-LB; 250 Type-85; 55 Type-90
APC (W) 30+: 10+ BTR-3U; 20 Hino; some Type-92
PPV 10 MPV
ARTY 410+
SP 155mm 36: 30 NORA B-52; 6 SH-1
TOWED 264+: **105mm** 132: 36 M-56; 96 M101; **122mm** 100 D-30; **130mm** 16 M-46; **140mm**; **155mm** 16 *Soltam*
MRL 30+: **107mm** 30 Type-63; **122mm** BM-21 (reported); **240mm** M-1991 (reported)
MOR 80+: **82mm** Type-53 (M-37); **120mm** 80+: 80 *Soltam*; Type-53 (M-1943)
AT
RCL 1,000+: **106mm** M40A1; **84mm** ε1,000 *Carl Gustav*
GUNS 84
SP 100mm 24 PTL-02
TOWED 60: **57mm** 6-pdr; **76.2mm** 17-pdr
AD • SAM • MANPAD HN-5 *Hong Nu/Red Cherry* (reported); 9K310 *Igla*-1 (SA-16 *Gimlet*)
GUNS 46
SP 57mm 12 Type-80
TOWED 34: **37mm** 24 Type-74; **40mm** 10 M1
MSL • SSM some *Hwasong*-6 (reported)
ARV Type-72

Navy ε16,000

EQUIPMENT BY TYPE
PRINCIPAL SURFACE COMBATANTS • FRIGATES 4
FFGH 1 *Aung Zeya* with 2 twin lnchr with YJ-62 (C-602) AShM, 4 AK630 CIWS, 1 76mm gun, (capacity 1 med hel)
FFG 3:
1 *Aung Zeya* with 2 twin lnchr with YJ-62 (C-602) AShM, 1 76mm gun
2 *Mahar Bandoola* (PRC Type-053H1) with 2 triple lnchr with HY-2 (C-201) *Seersucker* AShM, 2 RBU 1200, 2 twin 100mm gun
PATROL AND COASTAL COMBATANTS 113
CORVETTES • FSG 3 *Anawrahta* with 2 twin lnchr with YJ-82 (C-802) AShM; 1 76mm gun
PCG 7: 6 *Houxin* with 2 twin lnchr with C-801 (CSS-N-4 *Sardine*) AShM; 1 (other) with 2 twin YJ-82 (C-802) AShM
PCO 2 *Indaw*
PCC 9 *Hainan* with 4 RBU 1200, 2 twin 57mm gun
PBG 4 *Myanmar* with 2 twin lnchr with C-801 (CSS-N-4 *Sardine*) AShM
PB 31: 3 PB-90; 6 PGM 401; 6 PGM 412; 13 *Myanmar*; 3 *Swift*
PBR 57: 4 *Sagu*; 9 Y-301†; 1 Y-301 (Imp); 43 (various)
AMPHIBIOUS • CRAFT 18: 8 **LCU** 10 **LCM**
LOGISTICS AND SUPPORT 18
ABU 1; **AGS** 1; **AK** 1; **AKSL** 5; **AP** 9; **YAC**

Naval Infantry 800

FORCES BY ROLE
MANOEUVRE
Light
1 inf bn

Air Force ε15,000

FORCES BY ROLE
FIGHTER
4 sqn with F-7 *Airguard*; FT-7; MiG-29B *Fulcrum*; MiG-29UB *Fulcrum*
GROUND ATTACK
2 sqn with A-5M *Fantan*
TRANSPORT
1 sqn with An-12 *Cub*; F-27 *Friendship*; FH-227; PC-6A/B *Turbo Porter*
TRAINING
2 sqn with G-4 *Super Galeb**; PC-7 Turbo Trainer*; PC-9*
1 (trg/liaison) sqn with Cessna 550 *Citation* II; Cessna 180 *Skywagon*; K-8 *Karakorum**
TRANSPORT HELICOPTER
4 sqn with Bell 205; Bell 206 *Jet Ranger*; Mi-17 *Hip* H; Mi-35P *Hind*; PZL Mi-2 *Hoplite*; PZL W-3 *Sokol*; SA316 *Alouette* III

EQUIPMENT BY TYPE
AIRCRAFT 156 combat capable
FTR 89: 49 F-7 *Airguard*; 10 FT-7; 18 MiG-29 *Fulcrum*; 6 MiG-29SE *Fulcrum*; 6 MiG-29UB *Fulcrum*
ATK 22 A-5M *Fantan*
TPT 19 **Medium** 2 An-12 *Cub*; **Light** 13: 4 Cessna 180 *Skywagon*; 1 Cessna 550 *Citation* II; 3 F-27 *Friendship*; 5 PC-6A/B *Turbo Porter*; **PAX** 4 FH-227
TRG 45+: 12 G-4 *Super Galeb**; 12+ K-8 *Karakorum**; 12 PC-7 *Turbo Trainer**; 9 PC-9*
HELICOPTERS
ATK 7 Mi-35P *Hind*
MRH 20: 11 Mi-17 *Hip* H; 9 SA316 *Alouette* III
TPT 46: **Medium** 10 PZL W-3 *Sokol*; **Light** 36: 12 Bell 205; 6 Bell 206 *Jet Ranger*; 18 PZL Mi-2 *Hoplite*
MSL • AAM • IR PL-5; R-73 (AA-11 *Archer*) **IR/SARH** R-27 (AA-10 *Alamo*)

Paramilitary 107,250

People's Police Force 72,000

People's Militia 35,000

People's Pearl and Fishery Ministry ε250

PATROL AND COASTAL COMBATANTS • PBR 6 *Carpentaria*

Nepal NPL

Nepalese Rupee NR		2012	2013	2014
GDP	NR	1.56tr	1.76tr	
	US$	19.4bn	20.4bn	
per capita	US$	626	646	
Growth	%	4.63	3.01	
Inflation	%	8.31	9.62	
Def exp	NR	22.5bn		
	US$	281m		
Def bdgt [a]	NR	19.1bn	ε20.5bn	27.4bn
	US$	238m	ε238m	
FMA (US)	US$	1.24m	1.24m	1.3m
US$1=NR		80.20	86.31	

Population 30,430,267

Religious groups: Hindu 90%; Buddhist 5%; Muslim 3%

Age	0–14	15–19	20–24	25–29	30–64	65 plus
Male	16.6%	6.1%	5.2%	4.0%	15.2%	2.1%
Female	16.0%	6.0%	5.3%	4.4%	16.8%	2.4%

Capabilities

Nepal's armed forces are dominated by the army, though a small air wing provides transport and support capability. Following a 2006 peace accord with the Maoist People's Liberation Army, and the subsequent transition from monarchy to republic, Maoist personnel entered a process of demobilisation, or integration into the regular forces. It was reported that this concluded in late 2013. A 2011 draft national-security policy focused on territorial integrity. Mobility remains a challenge, due to limited transport assets and the country's mountainous terrain. The military has no power projection capability but is extensively involved in UN peace-support operations, particularly in Africa and the Middle East. Training support is provided by several countries, including the US, India and China.

ACTIVE 95,750 (Army 95,750) Paramilitary 62,000

ORGANISATIONS BY SERVICE

Army 95,750

FORCES BY ROLE

COMMAND
- 6 inf div HQ
- 1 (valley) comd

SPECIAL FORCES
- 1 bde (1 SF bn, 1 AB bn , cdo bn, 1 ranger bn, 1 mech inf bn)

MANOEUVRE

Light
- 16 inf bde (total: 63 inf bn)
- 32 indep inf coy

COMBAT SUPPORT
- 4 arty regt
- 2 AD regt
- 4 indep AD coy
- 5 engr bn

EQUIPMENT BY TYPE

RECCE 40 *Ferret*

APC 253
- **APC (W)** 13: 8 OT-64C; 5 WZ-551
- **PPV** 240: 90 *Casspir*; 150 MPV

ARTY 92+
- **TOWED 105mm** 22: 8 L118 Lt Gun; 14 Pack Howitzer (6 non-operational)
- **MOR** 70+: **81mm; 120mm** 70 M-43 (est 12 op)

AD • GUNS • TOWED 32+: **14.5mm** 30 Type-56 (ZPU-4); **37mm** (PRC); **40mm** 2 L/60

Air Wing 320

AIRCRAFT • TPT 4 **Light** 3: 1 BN-2T *Islander*; 2 M-28 *Skytruck*; **PAX** 1 BAe-748

HELICOPTERS
- **MRH** 9: 1 *Dhruv*; 2 *Lancer*; 3 Mi-17-1V *Hip* H; 1 SA315B *Lama (Cheetah)*; 2 SA316B *Alouette* III
- **TPT** 3 **Medium** 1 SA330J *Puma*; **Light** 2 AS350B2/B3 *Ecureuil*

Paramilitary 62,000

Armed Police Force 15,000

Ministry of Home Affairs

Police Force 47,000

DEPLOYMENT

CÔTE D'IVOIRE

UN • UNOCI 1; 3 obs

DEMOCRATIC REPUBLIC OF THE CONGO

UN • MONUSCO 1,029; 20 obs; 1 inf bn; 1 engr coy

HAITI

UN • MINUSTAH 363; 2 inf coy

IRAQ

UN • UNAMI 77; 1 sy unit

LEBANON

UN • UNIFIL 869; 1 inf bn

LIBERIA

UN • UNMIL 18; 2 obs; 1 MP sect

MIDDLE EAST

UN • UNTSO 3 obs

SOUTH SUDAN

UN • UNMISS 858; 4 obs; 1 inf bn

SUDAN

UN • UNAMID 365; 20 obs; 1 SF coy; 1 inf coy

UN • UNISFA 2; 3 obs

SYRIA/ISRAEL

UN • UNDOF 71; 1 inf coy

WESTERN SAHARA

UN • MINURSO 4 obs

FOREIGN FORCES

United Kingdom 280 (Gurkha trg org)

New Zealand NZL

New Zealand Dollar NZ$		2012	2013	2014
GDP	NZ$	209bn	220bn	
	US$	170bn	183bn	
per capita	US$	38,222	40,884	
Growth	%	2.54	2.74	
Inflation	%	1.06	1.39	
Def exp	NZ$	2.72bn		
	US$	2.21bn		
Def bdgt	NZ$	2.72bn	3.26bn	
	US$	2.21bn	2.71bn	
US$1=NZ$		1.23	1.20	

Population 4,365,113

Ethnic groups: NZ European 58%; Maori 15%; Other European 13%; Other Polynesian 5% ; Chinese 2%; Indian 1%; Other 6%

Age	0–14	15–19	20–24	25–29	30–64	65 plus
Male	10.3%	3.5%	3.7%	3.2%	22.6%	6.4%
Female	9.8%	3.3%	3.5%	3.2%	22.8%	7.5%

Capabilities

The New Zealand Defence Force (NZDF) is small, but draws on a strong national military tradition. New Zealand has contributed forces to almost every conflict in which the country's larger allies have been involved over the last century, minor contingents remain deployed overseas, and the forces exercise regularly with international counterparts. Despite funding shortfalls and capability losses, including the withdrawal from service of jet combat aircraft in 2001, the NZDF is characterised by high training standards, professionalism and morale. The November 2010 Defence White Paper promised to maintain and enhance existing capabilities, and to provide some additional elements (such as short-range maritime air patrol aircraft). However, there was no promise of any significant increase in defence spending.

ACTIVE 8,550 (Army 4,300 Navy 1,900 Air 2,350)

RESERVE 2,290 (Army 1,800 Navy 300 Air Force 190)

ORGANISATIONS BY SERVICE

Army 4,300

FORCES BY ROLE

SPECIAL FORCES

1 SF gp

MANOEUVRE

Light

1 inf bde (1 armd recce regt, 2 lt inf bn, 1 arty regt (2 arty bty, 1 AD tp), 1 engr regt(-), 1 MI coy, 1 MP coy, 1 sigs regt, 2 log bn, 1 med bn)

COMBAT SUPPORT

1 EOD sqn

EQUIPMENT BY TYPE

AIFV 105 NZLAV-25

ARTY 74

TOWED 105mm 24 L-118 Light Gun

MOR 81mm 50

AT • MSL 24 *Javelin*

RCL 84mm 42 *Carl Gustav*

AD • SAM • MANPAD 12 *Mistral*

AEV 7 NZLAV

ARV 3 LAV-R

Reserves

Territorial Force 1,800 reservists

Responsible for providing trained individuals for augmenting deployed forces

FORCES BY ROLE

COMBAT SERVICE SUPPORT

3 (Territorial Force Regional) trg regt

Navy 1,900

Fleet HQ at Auckland

EQUIPMENT BY TYPE

PRINCIPAL SURFACE COMBATANTS • FRIGATES • FFHM 2:

2 *Anzac* with 1 octuple Mk41 VLS with RIM-7M *Sea Sparrow* SAM, 2 triple Mk32 324mm TT, 1 Mk15 *Phalanx* Block 1B CIWS, 1 127mm gun, (capacity 1 SH-2G (NZ) *Super Seasprite* ASW hel)

PATROL AND COASTAL COMBATANTS 6

PSOH 2 *Otago* (capacity 1 SH-2G *Super Seasprite* ASW hel)

PCC 4 *Rotoiti*

AMPHIBIOUS • LANDING CRAFT • LCM 2

LOGISTICS AND SUPPORT 4

AKRH 1 *Canterbury* (capacity 4 NH90 tpt hel; 1 SH-2G *Super Seasprite* ASW hel; 2 LCM; 16 NZLAV; 14 NZLOV; 20 trucks; 250 troops)

AOR 1 *Endeavour*

YDT 1 *Manawanui*

Air Force 2,350

Flying hours 190

FORCES BY ROLE

MARITIME PATROL

1 sqn with P-3K/K2 *Orion*

TRANSPORT

1 sqn with B-757-200 (upgraded); C-130H *Hercules* (being progressively upgraded)

ANTI SUBMARINE/SURFACE WARFARE

1 (RNZAF/RNZN) sqn with SH-2G *Super Seasprite* (SH-2G(NZ))

TRAINING

1 sqn with CT-4E *Airtrainer* (leased);

1 sqn with Beech 200 *King Air* (leased);

1 (transition) hel unit with AW109; NH90

TRANSPORT HELICOPTER
1 sqn with Bell 205 (UH-1H *Iroquois*) (to be replaced by NH90)

EQUIPMENT BY TYPE

AIRCRAFT 6 combat capable
ASW 6: 3 P-3K *Orion*; 3 P-3K2 *Orion*
TPT 12 **Medium** 5 C-130H *Hercules* (being upgraded) **Light** 5 Beech 200 *King Air* (leased, to be replaced) **PAX** 2 B-757-200 (upgraded)
TRG 13 CT-4E *Airtrainer* (leased)

HELICOPTERS
ASW 5 SH-2G *Super Seasprite* (SH-2G(NZ))
TPT 22 **Medium** 4 NH90 (1 more used for spares - further 4 on order); **Light** 18: 5 AW109 (1 more used for spares); 13 Bell 205 (UH-1H *Iroquois*) (being replaced by NH90)

MSL • ASM AGM-65B/G *Maverick*

DEPLOYMENT

AFGHANISTAN
NATO • ISAF 11
UN • UNAMA 1 obs

EGYPT
MFO 28; 1 trg unit; 1 tpt unit

IRAQ
UN • UNAMI 1 obs

MIDDLE EAST
UN • UNTSO 8 obs

SOUTH SUDAN
UN • UNMISS 1; 2 obs

Pakistan PAK

Pakistani Rupee Rs		2012	2013	2014
GDP	Rs	20.7tr	23.2tr	
	US$	232bn	239bn	
per capita	US$	1,296	1,309	
Growth	%	3.68	3.51	
Inflation	%	11.01	8.16	
Def bdgt [a]	Rs	518bn	573bn	634bn
	US$	5.81bn	5.89bn	
FMA (US) [b]	US$	80m	80m	300m
US$1=Rs		89.07	97.22	

[a] Includes budget for Ministry of Defence Production

[b] FMA figure does not include the Pakistan Counter-Insurgency Capability Fund, the 2013 request for which amounted to US$850m.

Population 193,238,868

Religious groups: Hindu less than 3%

Age	0–14	15–19	20–24	25–29	30–64	65 plus
Male	17.5%	5.8%	5.4%	4.6%	16.1%	2.0%
Female	16.5%	5.4%	5.0%	4.3%	15.1%	2.3%

Capabilities

Pakistan's nuclear and conventional forces have traditionally been orientated and structured against a prospective threat from India. Since 2008, however, a priority for the army has been counter-insurgency operations, mainly in the FATA, against Islamist groups such as Tehrik-e-Taliban Pakistan, which have seen forces redeployed from the Indian border. These operations have usually been tactically successful but the Pakistani Taliban is a continued threat to the state. Friction with Afghanistan continued in 2013, with cross-border shelling. The potential power vacuum left by the 2014 ISAF drawdown, and use of the route through Pakistan for equipment transportation, is of concern to senior officials. The air force is modernising its combat aircraft inventory with procurements from China and the US, while also improving its precision strike and ISR capabilities. However, the May 2011 US helicopter-borne attack on Osama bin Laden's compound outside Abbottabad called into question the effectiveness of Pakistan's air defences. The navy's submarine force is currently too small to sustain a long campaign against enemy vessels equipped with ASW capabilities. Internationally, the navy has contributed to international efforts to counter Indian Ocean piracy. Pakistan's armed forces have greatly reduced their domestic political role, allowing a successful election and democratic transition. The army continues to contribute to UN peacekeeping operations. (See pp. 217–21.)

ACTIVE 643,800 **(Army 550,000 Navy 23,800 Air 70,000) Paramilitary 304,000**

ORGANISATIONS BY SERVICE

Strategic Forces

Operational control rests with the National Command Authority (NCA); army and air force strategic forces are responsible for technical aspects, training and administrative control of the services' nuclear assets.

Army Strategic Forces Command 12,000-15,000

Commands all land-based strategic nuclear forces.

MSL • STRATEGIC 60+
MRBM ε30 *Ghauri*/*Ghauri* II (*Hatf*-5)/*Shaheen*-2 (*Hatf*-6 – in test)
SRBM 30+: ε30 *Ghaznavi* (*Hatf*-3 - PRC M-11)/*Shaheen*-1 (*Hatf*-4); some *Abdali* (*Hatf*-2)
LACM *Babur* (*Hatf*-7); *Ra'ad* (*Hatf*-8 – in test)
ARTY • MRL *Nasr* (*Hatf*-9 – likely nuclear capable; in development)

Air Force

1-2 sqn of F-16A/B or *Mirage* 5 may be assigned a nuclear strike role

Army 550,000

FORCES BY ROLE

COMMAND
9 corps HQ
1 (area) comd
SPECIAL FORCES
2 SF gp (total: 4 SF bn)
MANOEUVRE
Armoured
2 armd div
7 indep armd bde
Mechanised
2 mech inf div
1 indep mech bde
Light
18 inf div
5 indep inf bde
Aviation
1 VIP avn sqn
5 (composite) avn sqn
10 hel sqn
COMBAT SUPPORT
9 (corps) arty bde
5 indep arty bde
1 AD comd (3 AD gp (total: 8 AD bn))
7 engr bde

EQUIPMENT BY TYPE

MBT 2,501+: 355 *Al-Khalid* (MBT 2000); 320 T-80UD; 51 T-54/T-55; 1,100 Type-59/*Al-Zarrar*; 400 Type-69; 275+ Type-85; (270 M48A5 in store)
APC 1,390
APC (T) 1,260: 1,160 M113/*Talha*; ε100 Type-63
APC (W) 120 BTR-70/BTR-80
PPV 10 *Dingo* II
ARTY 4,472+
SP 375: **155mm** 315: 200 M109A2; ε115 M109A5 **203mm** 60 M110/M110A2
TOWED 1,659: **105mm** 329: 216 M101; 113 M-56; **122mm** 570: 80 D-30 (PRC); 490 Type-54 M-1938; **130mm** 410 Type-59-I; **155mm** 322: 144 M114; 148 M198; ε30 *Panter*; **203mm** 28 M115
MRL 88+ **107mm** Type-81; **122mm** 52+: 52 *Azar* (Type-83); some KRL-122; **300mm** 36 A100
MOR 2,350+: **81mm**; **120mm** AM-50; M-61
AT
MSL
SP M901 TOW
MANPATS 11,100: 10,500 HJ-8/TOW; 600 9K119 *Refleks* (AT-11 *Sniper*)
RCL 75mm Type-52; **106mm** M40A1
RL 89mm M20
GUNS 85mm 200 Type-56 (D-44)
AIRCRAFT
ISR 30 Cessna O-1E *Bird Dog*
TPT • Light 14: 1 Beech 200 *King Air*; 1 Beech 350 *King Air*; 3 Cessna 208B; 1 Cessna 421; 1 Cessna 550 *Citation*; 1 Cessna 560 *Citation*; 2 *Turbo Commander* 690; 4 Y-12(II)
TRG 90 Saab 91 *Safir* (50 obs; 40 liaison)
HELICOPTERS
ATK 42: 25 AH-1F *Cobra* with TOW; 16 AH-1S *Cobra*; 1 Mi-24 *Hind*
MRH 114+: 10 AS550 *Fennec*; 6 AW139; 26 Bell 412EP *Twin Huey*; 40+ Mi-17 *Hip* H; 12 SA315B *Lama*; 20 SA319 *Alouette* III
TPT 59 **Medium** 36: 31 SA330 *Puma*; 4 Mi-171; 1 Mi-172; **Light** 23: 5 Bell 205 (UH-1H *Iroquois*); 5 Bell 205A-1 (AB-205A-1); 13 Bell 206B *Jet Ranger* II
TRG 22: 12 Bell 47G; 10 Hughes 300C
UAV • ISR • Light *Bravo*; *Jasoos*; *Vector*
AD
SAM
SP some M113 with RBS-70
MANPAD 2,990+: 2,500 Mk1/Mk2; 60 FIM-92A *Stinger*; HN-5A; 230 *Mistral*; 200 RBS 70
GUNS • TOWED 1,933: **14.5mm** 981; **35mm** 248 GDF-002/GDF-005 (with 134 *Skyguard* radar units); **37mm** 310 Type-55 (M-1939)/Type-65; **40mm** 50 L/60; **57mm** 144 Type-59 (S-60); **85mm** 200 Type-72 (M-1939) KS-12
RADAR • LAND AN/TPQ-36 *Firefinder* (arty, mor); RASIT (veh, arty); SLC-2
MSL
STRATEGIC
MRBM ε30 *Ghauri*/*Ghauri* II (*Hatf*-5); some *Shaheen*-2 (*Hatf*-6 - in test)
SRBM ε30 *Ghaznavi* (*Hatf*-3 – PRC M-11)/*Shaheen*-1 (*Hatf*-4); some *Abdali* (*Hatf*-2)
LACM some *Babur* (*Hatf*-7)
TACTICAL • SRBM 105 *Hatf*-1
ARV 117+: 65 Type-653; *Al-Hadeed*; 52 M88A1; T-54/T-55
VLB M47M; M48/60
MW *Aardvark* Mk II

Navy 23,800 (incl ε3,200 Marines and ε2,000 Maritime Security Agency (see Paramilitary))

EQUIPMENT BY TYPE

SUBMARINES • TACTICAL 8

SSK 5:

2 *Hashmat* (FRA *Agosta* 70) with 4 single 533mm ASTT with F17P HWT/UGM- 84 *Harpoon* AShM

3 *Khalid* (FRA *Agosta* 90B – 1 with AIP) with 4 single 533mm ASTT with F17 Mod 2 HWT/SM-39 *Exocet* AShM

SSI 3 MG110 (SF delivery) each with 2 single 533mm TT

PRINCIPAL SURFACE COMBATANTS • FRIGATES 11

FFGHM 4 *Sword* (PRC Type-054) with 2 quad lnchr with YJ-83 (C-802) AShM, 1 octuple lnchr with HQ-7 SAM, 2 triple 324mm ASTT with Mk 46 LWT, 2 sextuple Type 87 A/S mor, 1 Type 730B CIWS, 1 76mm gun, (capacity 1 Z-9C *Haitun* hel)

FFGH 3:

2 *Tariq* (UK *Amazon*) with 2 twin Mk141 lnchr with RGM-84D *Harpoon* AShM, 2 triple 324mm ASTT with Mk 46 LWT, 1 *Phalanx* Block 1B CIWS, 1 114mm gun, (capacity 1 hel)

1 *Tariq* (UK *Amazon*) with 2 quad Mk141 lnchr with RGM-84D *Harpoon* AShM, 2 single TT with TP 45 LWT, 1 *Phalanx* Block 1B CIWS, 1 114mm gun, (capacity 1 hel)

FFHM 3 *Tariq* (UK *Amazon*) with 1 sextuple lnchr with LY-60 (*Aspide*) SAM, 2 single TT with TP 45 LWT, 1 *Phalanx* Block 1B CIWS, 1 114mm gun, (capacity 1 hel)

FFH 1 *Alamgir* (US *Oliver Hazard Perry*) with 2 triple 24mm ASTT with Mk46 LWT, 1 *Phalanx* CIWS, 1 76mm gun

PATROL AND COASTAL COMBATANTS 18

PCG 2 *Azmat* (PRC *Houjian* mod) with 2 quad lnchr with YJ-83 (C-802A) AShM, 1 AK630 CIWS

PBFG 2 *Zarrar* each with 4 single each with RGM-84 *Harpoon* AShM

PBG 4:

2 *Jalalat* II with 2 twin lnchr with C-802 (CSS-N-8 *Saccade*) AShM

2 *Jurrat* with 2 twin lnchr with C-802 (CSS-N-8 *Saccade*) AShM

PBFG 2 *Kaan 33* with 1 quad lnchr with RGM-84 *Harpoon* AShM

PBF 2 *Kaan 15*

PB 6: 1 *Larkana;* 1 *Rajshahi*; 4 LCP

MINE WARFARE • MINE COUNTERMEASURES

MHC 3 *Munsif* (FRA *Eridan*)

AMPHIBIOUS

LANDING CRAFT • UCAC 4 Griffon 2000

LOGISTICS AND SUPPORT 14

AGS 1 *Behr Paima*

AOL 2 *Madagar*

AORH 2:

1 *Fuqing* with 1 *Phalanx* CIWS (capacity 1 SA319 *Alouette* III hel)

1 *Moawin* with 1 *Phalanx* CIWS (capacity 1 *Sea King* Mk45 ASW hel)

AOT 3: 1 *Attock*; 2 *Gwadar*

AXS 1

YTM 5

Marines ε3,200

FORCES BY ROLE

SPECIAL FORCES

1 cdo gp

MANOEUVRE

Amphibious

3 mne bn

COMBAT SUPPORT

1 AD bn

Naval Aviation

AIRCRAFT 10 ac combat capable

ASW 10: 3 *Atlantic*; 7 P-3C *Orion*

MP 6 F-27-200 MPA

TPT 3 **Light** 2 ATR-72-500 (MP); **PAX** 1 Hawker 850XP

HELICOPTERS

ASW 12: 5 *Sea King* Mk45; 7 Z-9C *Haitun*

MRH 6 SA319B *Alouette* III

MSL • AShM AM-39 *Exocet*

Air Force 70,000

3 regional comds: Northern (Peshawar) Central (Sargodha) Southern (Masroor). The Composite Air Tpt Wg, Combat Cadres School and PAF Academy are Direct Reporting Units.

FORCES BY ROLE

FIGHTER

2 sqn with F-7P/FT-7P *Skybolt*

3 sqn with F-7PG/FT-7PG *Airguard*

1 sqn with F-16A/B *Fighting Falcon*

1 sqn with *Mirage* IIID/E (IIIOD/EP)

FIGHTER/GROUND ATTACK

1 sqn with JF-17 *Thunder* (FC-1)

1 sqn (forming) with JF-17 *Thunder* (FC-1)

1 sqn with F-16C/D Block 52 *Fighting Falcon*

3 sqn with *Mirage* 5 (5PA)

ANTI SURFACE WARFARE

1 sqn with *Mirage* 5PA2/5PA3 with AM-39 *Exocet* AShM

ELECTRONIC WARFARE/ELINT

1 sqn with *Falcon* 20F

AIRBORNE EARLY WARNING & CONTROL

1 sqn with Saab 2000; Saab 2000 *Erieye*

1 sqn with ZDK-03

SEARCH & RESCUE

1 sqn with Mi-171Sh (SAR/liaison)

6 sqn with SA316 *Alouette* III

TANKER

1 sqn with Il-78 *Midas*

TRANSPORT

1 sqn with C-130B/E *Hercules*; CN-235M-220; L-100-20

1 VIP sqn with B-707; Cessna 560XL *Citation Excel*; CN-235M-220; F-27-200 *Friendship*; *Falcon* 20E; Gulfstream IVSP

1 (comms) sqn with EMB-500 *Phenom* 100; Y-12 (II)

TRAINING

2 OCU sqn with F-7P/FT-7P *Skybolt*

1 OCU sqn with *Mirage* III/*Mirage* 5

1 OCU sqn with F-16A/B *Fighting Falcon*

2 sqn with K-8 *Karakorum**

2 sqn with MFI-17
2 sqn with T-37C *Tweet*

AIR DEFENCE

1 bty with CSA-1 (SA-2 *Guideline*); 9K310 *Igla*-1 (SA-16 *Gimlet*)
6 bty with *Crotale*
10 bty with SPADA 2000

EQUIPMENT BY TYPE

AIRCRAFT 422 combat capable

FTR 199: 51 F-7PG *Airguard*; 74 F-7P *Skybolt*; 24 F-16A *Fighting Falcon*; 21 F-16B *Fighting Falcon* (undergoing mid-life update) 21 FT-7; 6 FT-7PG; 2 *Mirage* IIIB

FGA 174: 12 F-16C Block 52 *Fighting Falcon*; 6 F-16D Block 52 *Fighting Falcon*; 33+ JF-17 *Thunder* (FC-1 - 150+ to be acquired); 7 *Mirage* IIID (*Mirage* IIIOD); 63 *Mirage* IIIE (IIIEP); 40 *Mirage* 5 (5PA)/5PA2; 3 *Mirage* 5D (5DPA)/5DPA2; 10 *Mirage* 5PA3 (ASuW)

ISR 10 *Mirage* IIIR* (*Mirage* IIIRP)

ELINT 2 *Falcon* 20F

AEW&C 3: 1 Saab 2000 *Erieye* (2 more non-op); 2 ZDK-03

TKR 4 Il-78 *Midas*

TPT 34: **Medium** 16: 5 C-130B *Hercules*; 10 C-130E *Hercules*; 1 L-100-20 **Light** 13: 1 Cessna 560XL *Citation Excel*; 4 CN-235M-220; 4 EMB-500 *Phenom* 100; 1 F-27-200 *Friendship*; 2 Y-12 (II) **PAX** 5: 1 B-707; 1 *Falcon* 20E; 2 Gulfstream IVSP; 1 Saab 2000

TRG 143: 39 K-8 *Karakorum**; 80 MFI-17B *Mushshak*; 24 T-37C *Tweet*

HELICOPTERS

MRH 15 SA316 *Alouette* III

TPT • Medium 4 Mi-171Sh

AD • SAM 190+

TOWED 190: 6 CSA-1 (SA-2 *Guideline*); 144 *Crotale*; ε40 SPADA 2000

MANPAD 9K310 *Igla*-1 (SA-16 *Gimlet*)

RADAR • LAND 51+: 6 AR-1 (AD radar low level); some *Condor* (AD radar high level); some FPS-89/100 (AD radar high level)

MPDR 45 MPDR/MPDR 60 MPDR 90 (AD radar low level)

TPS-43G Type-514 some (AD radar high level)

MSL

ASM: AGM-65 *Maverick*; CM-400AKG (reported); *Raptor* II

AShM AM-39 *Exocet*

LACM *Ra'ad* (in test)

ARM MAR-1

AAM • IR AIM-9L/P *Sidewinder*; *U-Darter*; PL-5; **SARH** Super 530; **ARH** PL-12 (SD-10 – likely on order for the JF-17); AIM-120C AMRAAM

Paramilitary up to 304,000 active

Coast Guard

PATROL AND COASTAL COMBATANTS 5

PBF 4

PB 1

Frontier Corps up to 65,000 (reported)

Ministry of Interior

FORCES BY ROLE

MANOEUVRE

Reconnaissance

1 armd recce sqn

Other

11 paramilitary regt (total: 40 paramilitary bn)

EQUIPMENT BY TYPE

APC (W) 45 UR-416

Maritime Security Agency ε2,000

PRINCIPAL SURFACE COMBATANTS

DESTROYERS 1

DD 1 *Nazim* (US *Gearing*) with 2 triple 324mm TT, 1 twin 127mm gun

PATROL AND COASTAL COMBATANTS 15

PCC 4 *Barkat*

PBF 5

PB 6: 2 *Subqat* (PRC *Shanghai II*); 1 *Sadaqat* (ex-PRC *Huangfen*); 3 *Guns*

National Guard 185,000

Incl Janbaz Force; Mujahid Force; National Cadet Corps; Women Guards

Northern Light Infantry ε12,000

FORCES BY ROLE

MANOEUVRE

Other

3 paramilitary bn

Pakistan Rangers up to 40,000

Ministry of Interior

DEPLOYMENT

ARABIAN SEA & GULF OF ADEN

Combined Maritime Forces • CTF-150: 1 FFGHM

CÔTE D'IVOIRE

UN • UNOCI 1,391; 11 obs; 1 inf bn; 1 engr coy; 1 tpt coy

DEMOCRATIC REPUBLIC OF THE CONGO

UN • MONUSCO 3,715; 43 obs; 3 mech inf bn; 1 inf bn; 1 hel coy

LIBERIA

UN • UNMIL 1,987; 9 obs; 2 inf bn; 2 engr coy; 1 fd hospital

SUDAN

UN • UNAMID 505; 6 obs; 1 engr coy; 1 med pl

WESTERN SAHARA

UN • MINURSO 10 obs

FOREIGN FORCES

Unless specified, figures represent total numbers for UNMOGIP mission in India and Pakistan

Chile 2 obs

Croatia 9 obs

Finland 6 obs

Italy 3 obs

Korea, Republic of 8 obs
Philippines 4 obs
Sweden 5 obs
Thailand 3 obs
United Kingdom some (fwd mounting base) air elm located at Karachi
Uruguay 2 obs

Papua New Guinea PNG

Papua New Guinea Kina K		2012	2013	2014
GDP	K	33.5bn	37.5bn	
	US$	15.8bn	17.4bn	
per capita	US$	2,313	2,491	
Growth	%	9.09	4.43	
Inflation	%	3.96	7.94	
Def bdgt [a]	K	162m	180m	
	US$	76m	84m	
US$1=K		2.12	2.15	

[a] Includes defence allocations to the Public Sector Development Programme (PSDP), including funding to the Defence Division and the Defence Production Division.

Population 6,431,902

Age	0–14	15–19	20–24	25–29	30–64	65 plus
Male	18.0%	5.3%	4.6%	4.0%	17.3%	2.0%
Female	17.4%	5.2%	4.5%	3.9%	16.1%	1.8%

Capabilities

In view of chronic funding problems, since 1999 the government has reduced the size of the Papua New Guinea Defence Force (PNGDF) to its current strength of roughly 1,900 personnel. This compact force includes small air and naval elements and receives financial and training support from Australia and, to a lesser extent, China, France, Germany and New Zealand. Alhough it has engaged in internal security operations and minor regional deployments, the PNGDF would be stretched to provide comprehensive border security, let alone defend national territory, without substantial Australian support. In February 2013, the defence minister announced plans to increase personnel strength to 10,000, but this ambition was widely criticised as unrealistic. The government is expected to clarify its defence plans in a white paper, the release of which was imminent in late 2013.

ACTIVE 1,900 **(Army 1,600 Maritime Element 200 Air 100)**

ORGANISATIONS BY SERVICE

Army ε1,600

FORCES BY ROLE

MANOEUVRE

Light

2 inf bn

COMBAT SUPPORT

1 engr bn

1 EOD unit

1 sigs sqn

EQUIPMENT BY TYPE

ARTY • **MOR** 3+: **81mm**; **120mm** 3

Maritime Element ε200

1 HQ located at Port Moresby

EQUIPMENT BY TYPE

PATROL AND COASTAL COMBATANTS • **PB** 4 *Pacific*

AMPHIBIOUS • LANDING SHIPS • **LSM** 2 *Salamaua*

Air Force ε100

FORCES BY ROLE

TRANSPORT

1 sqn with CN-235M-100; IAI-201 *Arava*

TRANSPORT HELICOPTER

1 sqn with Bell 205 (UH-1H *Iroquois*)†

EQUIPMENT BY TYPE

AIRCRAFT • TPT • **Light** 5: 2 CN-235M-100; 3 IAI-201 *Arava*

HELICOPTERS • TPT • **Light** 7: 4 Bell 205 (UH-1H *Iroquois*)†; 2 Bell 412 (leased); 1 Bell 212 (leased)

DEPLOYMENT

SOUTH SUDAN

UN • UNMISS 2 obs

FOREIGN FORCES

Australia 38; 1 trg unit; 1 LSD

Philippines PHL

Philippine Peso P		2012	2013	2014
GDP	P	10.6tr	11.5tr	
	US$	250bn	284bn	
per capita	US$	2,614	2,918	
Growth	%	6.59	6.02	
Inflation	%	3.13	3.06	
Def bdgt [a]	P	74.4bn	89.5bn	92.9bn
	US$	1.76bn	2.21bn	
FMA (US)	US$	27m	27m	50m
US$1=P		42.20	40.60	

[a] Excludes military pensions

Population 105,720,644

Age	0–14	15–19	20–24	25–29	30–64	65 plus
Male	17.3%	5.1%	4.7%	4.3%	16.8%	1.9%
Female	16.7%	4.9%	4.5%	4.2%	17.2%	2.5%

Capabilities

The Armed Forces of the Philippines (AFP), particularly the army and marines, are deployed extensively in an internal security role in the face of continuing challenges from the Abu Sayyaf Group and other Muslim insurgents in the country's south. Until the withdrawal of the US military presence in 1992, the Philippines had largely relied on Washington to provide for its external defence, and since then perennially low defence budgets have thwarted efforts to develop any significant capacity for conventional warfighting or deterrence. While the government of Benigno Aquino III has promised, since 2011, that it will provide a stronger military defence of its South China Sea claims in the face of Chinese pressure, military modernisation budgets have consistently failed to provide the resources needed to fulfil the armed forces' procurement plans. The damage wrought by Typhoon Haiyan in November highlighted limited lift capability and, though AFP C-130s were used, the capability and number of larger platforms provided by other states, like C-17s, and assets including deployable field hospitals and military air traffic controllers, were vital.

ACTIVE 125,000 (Army 86,000 Navy 24,000 Air 15,000) Paramilitary 40,500

RESERVE 131,000 (Army 100,000 Navy 15,000 Air 16,000) Paramilitary 40,000 (to age 49)

ORGANISATIONS BY SERVICE

Army 86,000

5 Area Unified Comd (joint service), 1 National Capital Region Comd

FORCES BY ROLE

SPECIAL FORCES

1 spec ops comd (1 Scout Ranger regt, 1 SF regt, 1 lt reaction bn)

MANOEUVRE

Mechanised

1 lt armd div with (2 mech bde (total: 3 lt armd sqn; 7 armd cav tp; 4 mech inf bn; 1 cbt engr coy; 1 avn bn; 1 cbt engr coy, 1 sigs coy))

Light

10 div (each: 3 inf bde; 1 arty bn, 1 int bn, 1 sigs bn)

Other

1 (Presidential) gd gp

COMBAT SUPPORT

1 arty regt HQ

5 engr bde

EQUIPMENT BY TYPE

LT TK 7 *Scorpion*

AIFV 36: 2 YPR-765; 34 M113A1 FSV

APC 299

APC (T) 76: 6 ACV300; 70 M113

APC (W) 223: 77 LAV-150 *Commando*; 146 *Simba*

ARTY 254+

TOWED 214: **105mm** 204 M101/M102/M-26/M-56 **155mm** 10 M114/M-68

MOR 40+: **81mm** M-29; **107mm** 40 M-30

AT • RCL 75mm M20; **90mm** M67; **106mm** M40A1

AIRCRAFT

TPT • Light 4: 1 Beech 80 *Queen Air*; 1 Cessna 170; 1 Cessna 172; 1 Cessna P206A

UAV • ISR • Medium *Blue Horizon*

ARV ACV-300; *Samson*; M578

Navy 24,000

EQUIPMENT BY TYPE

PRINCIPAL SURFACE COMBATANTS • FRIGATES

FF 1 *Rajah Humabon* (ex-US *Cannon*) with 3 76mm gun

PATROL AND COASTAL COMBATANTS 62

PSOH 2 *Gregorio del Pilar* (ex-US *Hamilton*) with 1 76mm gun, (capacity 1 Bo 105)

PCF 1 *General Mariano Alvares* (ex-US *Cyclone*)

PCO 11:

3 *Emilio Jacinto* (ex-UK *Peacock*) with 1 76mm gun

6 *Miguel Malvar* (ex-US) with 1 76mm gun

2 *Rizal* (ex-US *Auk*) with 2 76mm gun

PBF 16: 3 *Conrado Yap* (ex-ROK *Sea Hawk*); 7 *Tomas Batilo* (ex-ROK *Chamsuri*); 6 MPAC (3 more vessels on order)

PB 32: 2 *Aguinaldo*; 22 *Jose Andrada*; 2 *Kagitingan*; 2 *Point*; 4 *Swift* Mk3 (ex-US)

AMPHIBIOUS

LANDING SHIPS • LST 6

2 *Bacolod City* (US *Besson*) with 1 hel landing platform (capacity 32 tanks; 150 troops)

4 *Zamboanga del Sur* (capacity 16 tanks; 200 troops)

LANDING CRAFT 30: 12 **LCU**; 2 **LCVP**; 16 **LCM**

LOGISTICS AND SUPPORT 15: **AFD** 4; **AK** 1; **AOL** 2; **AP** 1; **AR** 1; **AWT** 2; **YTL** 3; **YTM** 1

Naval Aviation

AIRCRAFT • TPT • Light 6: 4 BN-2A *Defender*; 2 Cessna 177 *Cardinal*

HELICOPTERS • TPT 8 **Medium** 4 Mi-171Sh; **Light** 4 Bo-105

Marines 8,300

FORCES BY ROLE

MANOEUVRE

Amphibious

4 mne bde (total: 12 mne bn)

COMBAT SUPPORT

1 CSS bde (6 CSS bn)

EQUIPMENT BY TYPE

APC (W) 42 19 LAV-150 *Commando*; 23 LAV-300

AAV 85: 30 LVTP-5; 55 LVTP-7

ARTY 31+

TOWED 105mm 31: 23 M101; 8 M-26

MOR 107mm M-30

Air Force 15,000

FORCES BY ROLE

FIGHTER

1 sqn with S-211*

GROUND ATTACK

1 sqn with OV-10A/C *Bronco**

ISR
1 sqn with *Turbo Commander* 690A
SEARCH & RESCUE
4 (SAR/Comms) sqn with Bell 205 (UH-1M *Iroquois*); AUH-76
TRANSPORT
1 sqn with C-130B/H *Hercules*; L-100-20
1 sqn with N-22B *Nomad*; N-22SL *Searchmaster*
1 sqn with F-27-200 MPA; F-27-500 *Friendship*
1 VIP sqn with F-28 *Fellowship*
TRAINING
1 sqn with SF-260F/TP
1 sqn with T-41B/D/K *Mescalero*
ATTACK HELICOPTER
1 sqn with MD-520MG
TRANSPORT HELICOPTER
1 sqn with AUH-76
1 sqn with W-3 *Sokol*
4 sqn with Bell 205 (UH-1H *Iroquois*)
1 (VIP) sqn with Bell 412EP *Twin Huey*; S-70A *Black Hawk* (S-70A-5)

EQUIPMENT BY TYPE
AIRCRAFT 22 combat capable
MP 2: 1 F-27-200 MPA; 1 N-22SL *Searchmaster*
ISR 10 OV-10A/C *Bronco**
TPT 9 **Medium** 5: 1 C-130B *Hercules*; 3 C-130H *Hercules*; 1 L-100-20; **Light** 3: 1 F-27-500 *Friendship*; 1 N-22B *Nomad*; 1 *Turbo Commander* 690A; **PAX** 1 F-28 *Fellowship* (VIP)
TRG 40: 12 S-211*; 8 SF-260F; 10 SF-260TP; 10 T-41B/D/K *Mescalero*
HELICOPTERS
MRH 27: 8 W-3 *Sokol*; 3 AUH-76; 3 Bell 412EP *Twin Huey*; 2 Bell 412HP *Twin Huey*; 11 MD-520MG
TPT 40 **Medium** 1 S-70A *Black Hawk* (S-70A-5); **Light** 39 Bell 205 (UH-1H *Iroquois*)
UAV • ISR • Medium 2 *Blue Horizon* II

Paramilitary

Philippine National Police 40,500
Department of Interior and Local Government. 15 regional & 73 provincial comd. 62,000 auxiliaries.

EQUIPMENT BY TYPE
PATROL AND COASTAL COMBATANTS • **PB** 14 : 10 Rodman 101; 4 Rodman 38
AIRCRAFT
TPT • Light 5: 2 BN-2 *Islander*; 3 Lancair 320

Coast Guard
PATROL AND COASTAL COMBATANTS 58
PCO 5: 4 *San Juan*; 1 *Balsam*
PCC 2 *Tirad*
PB 40: 3 *De Haviland*; 4 *Ilocos Norte*; 1 *Palawan*; 12 PCF 50 (US *Swift* Mk1/2); 10 PCF 46; 10 PCF 65 (US *Swift* Mk3)
PBR 11
AMPHIBIOUS • LANDING CRAFT 2
LCM 1
LCVP 1
LOGISTICS AND SUPPORT • **ABU** 3
HELICOPTERS 3 SAR

Citizen Armed Force Geographical Units
50,000 reservists
MANOEUVRE
Other
56 militia bn (part-time units which can be called up for extended periods)

DEPLOYMENT

CÔTE D'IVOIRE
UN • UNOCI 1; 3 obs

HAITI
UN • MINUSTAH 157; 1 HQ coy

INDIA/PAKISTAN
UN • UNMOGIP 4 obs

LIBERIA
UN • UNMIL 109; 1 inf coy

SUDAN
UN • UNISFA 1

SYRIA
UN • UNDOF 337; 1 inf bn

FOREIGN FORCES
Brunei IMT 9
Malaysia IMT 13
United States US Pacific Command: 180

Singapore SGP

Singapore Dollar S$		2012	2013	2014
GDP	S$	346bn	359bn	
	US$	277bn	287bn	
per capita	US$	51,162	52,179	
Growth	%	1.32	2.01	
Inflation	%	4.58	4.01	
Def bdgt	S$	12.3bn	12.3bn	
	US$	9.84bn	9.86bn	
US$1=S$		1.25	1.25	

Population 5,460,302

Ethnic groups: Chinese 76%; Malay 15%; Indian 6%

Age	0–14	15–19	20–24	25–29	30–64	65 plus
Male	7.0%	3.8%	5.2%	5.2%	24.2%	3.7%
Female	6.7%	3.7%	5.5%	5.7%	24.9%	4.4%

Capabilities

The Singapore Armed Forces (SAF) are the best-equipped military force in Southeast Asia, and have benefited since the late 1960s from steadily increasing defence spending and the gradual development of a substantial national defence industry capable of producing and modifying equipment for specific national requirements. The SAF is organised essentially along Israeli lines; the air force and navy being staffed mainly by professional personnel while, apart from a small core of regulars, the much larger army is based on conscripts and reservists. Much training is routinely carried out overseas, notably but not only in Australia, Brunei, Taiwan, Thailand and the United States. The SAF also engages in multilateral exercises through the Five Power Defence Arrangements. Singapore's government has traditionally been reluctant to make public details of its strategic outlook or military doctrine, but it is widely presumed that the SAF has been developed primarily with a view to deter attacks from near-neighbours or impingements on its vital interests (such as its water supply from Malaysian reservoirs). Since the 1990s, however, the SAF has increasingly become involved – albeit on a relatively small-scale – in multinational peace-support operations. While these deployments have provided some operational experience, and SAF training and operational readiness are high by international standards, the army's reliance on conscripts and reservists limits its capacity for sustained operations away from Singapore.

ACTIVE 72,500 (Army 50,000 Navy 9,000 Air 13,500) Paramilitary 75,100

Conscription liability 24 months

RESERVE 312,500 (Army 300,000 Navy 5,000 Air 7,500) Paramilitary 44,000

Annual trg to age of 40 for army other ranks, 50 for officers

ORGANISATIONS BY SERVICE

Army 15,000; 35,000 conscript (total 50,000)

FORCES BY ROLE

SPECIAL FORCES

1 cdo bn

MANOEUVRE

Reconnaissance

4 lt armd/recce bn

Armoured

1 armd bn

Mechanised

3 combined arms div (mixed active/reserve formations (1 recce bn, 1 armd bde, 2 inf bde (3 inf bn), 2 arty bn, 1 (air force) AD bn, 1 engr bn, 1 sigs bn, 1 log spt cmd)

Light

1 rapid reaction div (mixed active/reserve formations) (1 inf bde, 1 air mob bde, 1 amph bde (3 amph bn), 1 (air force) AD bn, 1 engr bn, 1 sigs bn, 1 log spt cmd)

8 inf bn

COMBAT SUPPORT

4 arty bn

4 engr bn

1 int bn

1 CBRN coy

Reserves

9 inf bde incl in mixed active/inactive reserve formations listed above; 1 op reserve div with additional inf bde; People's Defence Force Comd (homeland defence) with inf bn 12

FORCES BY ROLE

SPECIAL FORCES

1 cdo bn

MANOEUVRE

Reconnaissance

6 lt armd/recce bn

Mechanised

6 mech inf bn

Light

ε56 inf bn

COMBAT SUPPORT

ε12 arty bn

ε8 engr bn

EQUIPMENT BY TYPE

MBT 96 *Leopard* 2SG; (80–100 *Tempest* (upgraded *Centurion)* in store)

LT TK ε350 AMX-13 SM1

RECCE 22 AMX-10 PAC 90

AIFV 457+: 22 AMX-10P; 135 AV-81 *Terrex*; 250 IFV-25 *Bionix*; 50+ M113A1/A2 (some with 40mm AGL, some with 25mm gun)

APC 1,645+

APC (T) 1,350+: 250 IFV-40/50; 700+ M113A1/M113A2; 400+ ATTC *Bronco*

APC (W) 280: 250 LAV-150 *Commando*/V-200 *Commando*; 30 V-100 *Commando*

PPV 15 *MaxxPro Dash*

ARTY 798+

SP 155mm 54 SSPH-1 *Primus*

TOWED 88: **105mm** (37 LG1 in store); **155mm** 88: 18 FH-2000; ε18 *Pegasus*; 52 FH-88

MRL 227mm 18 HIMARS

MOR 638+

SP 90+ **81mm**; **120mm** 90: 40 on *Bronco*; 50 on M113

TOWED 548 **81mm** 500 **120mm** 36 M-65; **160mm** 12 M-58 *Tampella*

AT • MSL • MANPATS 60: 30 *Milan*; 30 *Spike* MR

RCL 290: **84mm** ε200 *Carl Gustav*; **106mm** 90 M40A1

UAV • ISR • Light *Skylark*

RADAR • LAND AN/TPQ-36 *Firefinder*; AN/TPQ-37 *Firefinder* (arty, mor); 3 ARTHUR (arty)

AEV 80: 18 CET; 54 FV180; 8 M728

ARV *Bionix*; *Büffel*; LAV-150; LAV-300

VLB *Bionix*; LAB 30; *Leguan*; M2; M3; 12 M60

MW 910-MCV-2; *Trailblazer*

Navy 3,000; 1,000 conscript; ε5,000 active reservists (total 9,000)

EQUIPMENT BY TYPE

SUBMARINES • TACTICAL • SSK 6:

3 *Challenger* with 4 single 533mm TT

1 *Challenger* (trg role) with 4 single 533mm TT

2 *Archer* (SWE *Västergötland*-class) (AIP fitted) with 6 single 533mm TT for WASS *Black Shark* LWT

PRINCIPAL SURFACE COMBATANTS 6:

FRIGATES • FFGHM 6 *Formidable* with 2 quad lnchr with RGM-84 *Harpoon* AShM, 4 octuple VLS with *Aster* 15 SAM, 2 triple 324mm ASTT with A244 LWT, 1 76mm gun, (capacity 1 S-70B *Sea Hawk* hel)

PATROL AND COASTAL COMBATANTS 35
CORVETTES • FSGM 6 *Victory* with 2 quad Mk140 lnchr with RGM-84C *Harpoon* AShM, 2 octuple lnchr with *Barak* SAM, 2 triple 324mm ASTT with A244 LWT, 1 76mm gun
PCO 11 *Fearless* with 2 sextuple *Sadral* lnchr with *Mistral* SAM, 1 76mm gun
PBF 6
PB 12
MINE WARFARE • MINE COUNTERMEASURES
MHC 4 *Bedok*
AMPHIBIOUS
PRINCIPAL AMPHIBIOUS SHIPS • LPD 4 *Endurance* with 2 twin lnchr with *Mistral* SAM, 1 76mm gun (capacity 2 hel; 4 LCVP; 18 MBT; 350 troops)
LANDING CRAFT 34 **LCU** 100 **LCVP**
LOGISTICS AND SUPPORT 2
AR 1 *Swift Rescue*
AX 1

Air Force 13,500 (incl 3,000 conscript)

5 comds

FORCES BY ROLE
FIGHTER/GROUND ATTACK
1 sqn with F-5S/T *Tiger* II
1 sqn with F-15SG *Eagle*
3 sqn with F-16C/D *Fighting Falcon* (some used for ISR with pods)
MARITIME PATROL/TRANSPORT
1 sqn with F-50
AIRBORNE EARLY WARNING & CONTROL
1 sqn with G550-AEW
TANKER
1 sqn with KC-135R *Stratotanker*
TANKER/TRANSPORT
1 sqn with KC-130B/H *Hercules*; C-130H *Hercules*
TRAINING
1 (France-based) sqn with A-4SU/TA-4SU *Super Skyhawk*; M-346 *Master*
4 (US-based) units with AH-64D *Apache*; CH-47D *Chinook*; F-15SG: F-16C/D
1 (Australia-based) sqn with PC-21
ATTACK HELICOPTER
1 sqn with AH-64D *Apache*
TRANSPORT HELICOPTER
1 sqn with CH-47SD *Super D Chinook*
2 sqn with AS332M *Super Puma*; AS532UL *Cougar*
ISR UAV
2 sqn with *Searcher* MkII
1 sqn with *Hermes* 450
AIR DEFENCE
1 AD bn with *Mistral* opcon Army
3 AD bn with RBS-70; 9K38 *Igla* (SA-18 *Grouse*) opcon Army
1 ADA sqn with Oerlikon
1 AD sqn with MIM-23 HAWK
1 AD sqn with *Spyder*
1 radar sqn with radar (mobile)
1 radar sqn with LORADS
MANOEUVRE
Other
4 (field def) sy sqn

EQUIPMENT BY TYPE
AIRCRAFT 132 combat capable
FTR 29: 20 F-5S *Tiger* II; 9 F-5T *Tiger* II
FGA 84: 24 F-15SG *Eagle*; 20 F-16C *Fighting Falcon*; 40 F-16D *Fighting Falcon* (incl reserves)
ATK 14: 4 A-4SU *Super Skyhawk*; 10 TA-4SU *Super Skyhawk*
MP 5 F-50 *Maritime Enforcer**
AEW&C 4 G550-AEW
TKR 5: 1 KC-130H *Hercules*; 4 KC-135R *Stratotanker*
TKR/TPT 4 KC-130B *Hercules*
TPT 9 **Medium** 5 C-130H *Hercules* (2 ELINT); **PAX** 4 F-50
TRG 24: 5 M-346 *Master*; 19 PC-21
HELICOPTERS
ATK 19 AH-64D *Apache*
ASW 6 S-70B *Seahawk*
TPT 46 **Heavy** 16: 6 CH-47D *Chinook*; 10 CH-47SD *Super D Chinook*; **Medium** 30: 18 AS332M *Super Puma* (incl 5 SAR); 12 AS532UL *Cougar*
TRG 5 EC120B *Colibri* (leased)
UAV • ISR • Medium 45: 5 *Hermes* 450; 40 *Searcher* MkII
AD
SAM
SP *Spyder*; *Mistral*; RBS-70; 9K38 *Igla* (SA-18 *Grouse*) (on V-200/M113)
TOWED *Mistral*; RBS-70; MIM-23 HAWK
MANPAD 9K38 *Igla* (SA-18 *Grouse*)
GUNS 34
SP 20mm GAI-C01
TOWED 34 **20mm** GAI-C01; **35mm** 34 GDF (with 25 *Super-Fledermaus* fire control radar)
MSL • TACTICAL
ASM: AGM-65B/G *Maverick*; *Hellfire*
AShM AGM-84 *Harpoon*; AM-39 *Exocet*
ARM AGM-45 *Shrike*
AAM • IR AIM-9N/P *Sidewinder*; *Python* 4 (reported); **IIR** AIM-9X *Sidewinder*; **SARH** AIM-7P *Sparrow*; **ARH** (AIM-120C AMRAAM in store in US)

Paramilitary 19,900 active

Civil Defence Force 5,600 (incl conscripts); 500 auxiliaries; (total 6,100)

Singapore Police Force (including Coast Guard) 8,500; 3,500 conscript (total 12,000)

EQUIPMENT BY TYPE
PATROL AND COASTAL COMBATANTS 99
PBF 78: 10 *Shark*; 68 (various)
PB 21: 2 *Manta Ray*; 19 (various)

Singapore Gurkha Contingent (under police) 1,800

FORCES BY ROLE
MANOEUVRE
Other
6 paramilitary coy

Asia

Cyber

The Singapore Ministry of Defence has long identified the potential damage that could be caused by cyber attacks, with this concern perhaps more acute following its adoption of the Integrated Knowledge-based Command and Control (IKC2) doctrine, designed to aid the transition of Singapore's Armed Forces to a 'third generation' force. Meanwhile, Singapore established the Singapore Infocomm Technology Security Authority (SITSA) on 1 October 2009, as a division within the Internal Security Department of the Ministry of Home Affairs (MHA). Its main responsibilities will be dealing with cyber terrorism and cyber espionage, as well as operational IT security development.

DEPLOYMENT

AUSTRALIA

2 trg schools – 1 with 12 AS332 *Super Puma*/AS532 *Cougar* (flying trg) located at Oakey; 1 with PC-21 (flying trg) located at Pearce. Army: prepositioned AFVs and heavy equipment at Shoalwater Bay training area.

BRUNEI

1 trg camp with inf units on rotation; 1 hel det with AS332 *Super Puma*

FRANCE

200: 1 trg sqn with 4 A-4SU *Super Skyhawk*; 10 TA-4SU *Super Skyhawk*; 5 M-346 *Master*

TAIWAN

3 trg camp (incl inf and arty)

THAILAND

1 trg camp (arty, cbt engr)

UNITED STATES

Trg units at Luke AFB (AZ) with F-16C/D; Mountain Home AFB (ID) with F-15SG; AH-64D *Apache* at Marana (AZ); 6+ CH-47D *Chinook* hel at Grand Prairie (TX)

FOREIGN FORCES

United States US Pacific Command: 150; 1 naval spt facility at Changi naval base; 1 USAF log spt sqn at Paya Lebar air base

UK and NZ minor support elements

Sri Lanka LKA

Sri Lankan Rupee Rs		2012	2013	2014
GDP	Rs	7.58tr	8.57tr	
	US$	59.4bn	65.3bn	
per capita	US$	2,873	3,134	
Growth	%	6.41	6.25	
Inflation	%	7.54	7.89	
Def bdgt	Rs	196bn	235bn	247bn
	US$	1.53bn	1.79bn	
FMA (US)	US$	0.5m	0.5m	0.45m
US$1=Rs		127.63	131.24	

[a] Includes all funds allocated to the Ministry of Defence & Urban Development except those disbursed to the following departments: Police, Immigration & Emigration, Registration of Persons, Coast Conservation and Civil Security.

Population 21,675,648

Age	0–14	15–19	20–24	25–29	30–64	65 plus
Male	12.6%	3.8%	3.8%	3.9%	21.2%	3.6%
Female	12.1%	3.7%	3.8%	3.9%	22.8%	4.8%

Capabilities

Internal security was the main focus for Sri Lanka's armed forces during the protracted campaign against the Tamil Tigers (LTTE), and both military and paramilitary personnel numbers and equipment holdings reached high levels. Since the defeat of the LTTE, the armed forces have been reorientating to a peacetime internal security role, amid continuing allegations concerning the conduct of forces in the final push against the LTTE. In July 2013 the armed forces were authorised to become involved in public order, though how this correlates to civilian police authority remained unclear. The army is reducing in size, but its plans are unclear. Soldiers and units are being employed in the tourist commercial sectors. There does not appear to have been any spending on new equipment since the end of the war and Sri Lanka has little capacity for force projection beyond national territory, apart from sending about 1,000 troops on a variety of UN missions. The navy has a littoral protection capability and is equipped with fast-attack and patrol vessels. It also has experience gained from numerous sea battles with LTTE naval commando units, and experience of coordinating with foreign navies in exercise scenarios. There appears to have been little spending on new equipment since the end of the war.

ACTIVE 160,900 (Army 200,000 Navy 15,000 Air 28,000) Paramilitary 62,200

RESERVE 5,500 (Army 1,100 Navy 2,400 Air Force 2,000) Paramilitary 30,400

ORGANISATIONS BY SERVICE

Army 160,000; 40,00 active reservists (recalled) (total 200,000)

Regt are bn sized

FORCES BY ROLE

COMMAND
12 div HQ
SPECIAL FORCES
1 indep SF bde
MANOEUVRE
Reconnaissance
3 armd recce regt
Armoured
1 armd bde (under strength)
Light
34 inf bde
1 cdo bde
Air Manoeuvre
1 air mob bde
COMBAT SUPPORT
9 arty regt
1 MRL bty
4 engr regt
5 sigs regt

EQUIPMENT BY TYPE

MBT 62 T-55AM2/T-55A
RECCE 15 *Saladin*
AIFV 62: 13 BMP-1; 49 BMP-2
APC 211+
APC (T) 30+: some Type-63; 30 Type-85; some Type-89
APC (W) 181: 25 BTR-80/BTR-80A; 31 *Buffel*; 20 Type-92; 105 *Unicorn*
ARTY 908
TOWED 96: **122mm** 20; **130mm** 30 Type-59-I; **152mm** 46 Type-66 (D-20)
MRL 122mm 28: 6 KRL-122; 22 RM-70 *Dana*
MOR 784: **81mm** 520; **82mm** 209; **120mm** 55 M-43
AT • RCL 40: **105mm** ε10 M-65; **106mm** ε30 M40
GUNS 85mm 8 Type-56 (D-44)
UAV • ISR • Medium 1 *Seeker*
RADAR • LAND 4 AN/TPQ-36 *Firefinder* (arty)
ARV 16 VT-55
VLB 2 MT-55

Navy 15,000 (incl 2,400 recalled reservists)

EQUIPMENT BY TYPE

PATROL AND COASTAL COMBATANTS 135
PSOH 1 *Sayura* (IND *Vigraha*)
PCG 2 *Nandimithra* (ISR *Sa'ar* 4) with 3 single lnchr with *Gabriel II* AShM, 1 76mm gun
PCO 2: 1 *Samadura* (ex-US *Reliance*); 1 *Sagara* (IND *Vikram*)
PCC 1 *Jayesagara*
PBF 84: 26 *Colombo*; 3 *Dvora*; 3 *Killer* (ROK); 6 *Shaldag*; 14 *Super Dvora* (Mk1/II/III); 5 *Trinity Marine*; 27 *Wave Rider*
PB 18: 4 *Cheverton*; 2 *Prathapa* (PRC mod *Haizhui*); 3 *Ranajaya* (PRC *Haizhui*); 1 *Ranarisi* (PRC mod *Shanghai* II); 5 *Weeraya* (PRC *Shanghai II*); 3 (various)
PBR 27
AMPHIBIOUS
LANDING SHIPS • LSM 1 *Shakthi* (PRC *Yuhai*) (capacity 2 tanks; 250 troops)
LANDING CRAFT 9
LCAC 1
LCM 2
LCP 3 *Hansaya*
LCU 2 *Yunnan*
UCAC 1 M 10 (capacity 56 troops)
LOGISTICS AND SUPPORT 2: 1 **AP**; 1 **AX**

Air Force 28,000 (incl SLAF Regt)

FORCES BY ROLE

FIGHTER
1 sqn with F-7BS/G; FT-7
FIGHTER/GROUND ATTACK
1 sqn with MiG-23UB *Flogger* C; MiG-27M *Flogger* J2
1 sqn with *Kfir* C-2/C-7/TC-2
1 sqn with K-8 *Karakorum**
TRANSPORT
1 sqn with An-32B *Cline*; C-130K *Hercules*; Cessna 421C *Golden Eagle*
1 sqn with Beech B200 *King Air*; Y-12 (II)
TRAINING
1 wg with PT-6, Cessna 150L
ATTACK HELICOPTER
1 sqn with Mi-24V *Hind* E; Mi-35P *Hind*
TRANSPORT HELICOPTER
1 sqn with Mi-17 *Hip* H
1 sqn with Bell 206A/B (incl basic trg), Bell 212
1 (VIP) sqn with Bell 212; Bell 412 *Twin Huey*
ISR UAV
1 sqn with *Blue Horizon*-2
1 sqn with *Searcher* II
MANOEUVRE
Other
1 (SLAF) sy regt

EQUIPMENT BY TYPE

AIRCRAFT 30 combat capable
FTR 8: 3 F-7BS; 4 F-7GS; 1 FT-7
FGA 15: 4 *Kfir* C-2; 2 *Kfir* C-7; 2 *Kfir* TC-2; 6 MiG-27M *Flogger* J2; 1 MiG-23UB *Flogger* C (conversion trg)
TPT 23 **Medium** 2 C-130K *Hercules*; **Light** 21: 5 An-32B *Cline*; 6 Cessna 150L; 1 Cessna 421C *Golden Eagle*; 7 Y-12 (II); 2 Y-12 (IV)
TRG 14: 7 K-8 *Karakoram**; 7 PT-6
HELICOPTERS
ATK 11: 6 Mi-24P *Hind*; 3 Mi-24V *Hind* E; 2 Mi-35V *Hind*
MRH 18: 6 Bell 412 *Twin Huey* (VIP); 2 Bell 412EP (VIP); 10 Mi-17 *Hip* H
TPT • Light 12: 2 Bell 206A *Jet Ranger*; 2 Bell 206B *Jet Ranger*; 8 Bell 212
UAV • ISR • Medium 2+: some *Blue Horizon*-2; 2 *Searcher* II
AD • GUNS • TOWED 27: **40mm** 24 L/40; **94mm** 3 (3.7in)

Paramilitary ε62,200

Home Guard 13,000

National Guard ε15,000

Police Force 30,200; 1,000 (women) (total 31,200) 30,400 reservists

Ministry of Defence Special Task Force 3,000

Anti-guerrilla unit

Coast Guard n/k

EQUIPMENT BY TYPE

PATROL AND COASTAL COMBATANTS • PB 7

DEPLOYMENT

DEMOCRATIC REPUBLIC OF THE CONGO

UN • MONUSCO 4 obs

HAITI

UN • MINUSTAH 861; 1 inf bn

LEBANON

UN • UNIFIL 151; 1 inf coy

SOUTH SUDAN

UN • UNMISS 2 obs

SUDAN

UN • UNISFA 1; 5 obs

WESTERN SAHARA

UN • MINURSO 3 obs

Taiwan (Republic of China) ROC

New Taiwan Dollar NT$		2012	2013	2014
GDP	NT$	14tr	14.7tr	
	US$	474bn	495bn	
per capita	US$	20,328	21,141	
Growth	%	1.26	2.96	
Inflation	%	1.93	2.00	
Def bdgt	NT$	310bn	307bn	
	US$	10.5bn	10.3bn	
US$1=NT$		29.62	29.78	

Population 23,299,716

Ethnic groups: Taiwanese 84%; mainland Chinese 14%

Age	0–14	15–19	20–24	25–29	30–64	65 plus
Male	7.4%	3.5%	3.5%	3.7%	26.4%	5.4%
Female	6.9%	3.3%	3.3%	3.6%	26.7%	6.2%

Capabilities

Taiwan's armed forces are well-trained and operate some advanced technology, but their relatively small size, lack of combat experience and the age of some equipment – as well as China's rapid and substantial military modernisation – have reduced any previous military advantage. The current government has proposed modernisation of the armed forces, and continues to aim to move towards an all-volunteer recruitment system. Compulsory basic training would remain for adult males, with the term reduced to a four-month period for those born after 1994. This could create a more professional dedicated armed forces, albeit at significant financial cost. A reduction to 220,000 personnel is planned, with most cuts coming from the army. The result will be a relatively small professional force that will continue to benefit from close defence relations with the US in terms of training. However, the capacity of such a small armed forces to withstand a concerted Chinese offensive is doubtful. Moreover, a growing reluctance on the part of the US to furnish Taiwan with the most advanced military equipment means that China is rapidly closing the technology gap. Taiwan is currently finding particular difficulty in procuring F-16C/D aircraft and diesel-electric submarines. Taipei is emphasising the procurement of early-warning and missile-defence systems to enable the island to withstand an assault until US intervention can occur. In 2013 the first of four new *Patriot* PAC-3 missile batteries was delivered, and three existing batteries were in the process of being upgraded from PAC-2 to PAC-3 configuration.

ACTIVE 290,000 (Army 200,000 Navy 45,000 Air 45,000) Paramilitary 17,000

Conscript liability 12 months

RESERVE 1,657,000 (Army 1,500,000 Navy 67,000 Air Force 90,000)

Some obligation to age 30

ORGANISATIONS BY SERVICE

Space

SATELLITES • ISR 1 Rocsat-2

Army ε200,000 (incl MP)

FORCES BY ROLE

COMMAND

5 defence HQ

3 corps HQ

SPECIAL FORCES/AVIATION

1 SF/avn comd (2 spec ops gp, 2 avn bde)

MANOEUVRE

Armoured

4 armd bde

Mechanised

3 mech inf bde

Light

8 inf bde

COMBAT SUPPORT

3 arty gp

1 (coastal defence) AShM bn

3 engr gp

3 CBRN gp

3 sigs gp

Reserves

FORCES BY ROLE

MANOEUVRE

Light

21 inf bde

EQUIPMENT BY TYPE

MBT 565: 200 M60A3; 100 M48A5; 265 M48H *Brave Tiger*

LT TK 625 M41/Type-64; (230 M24 *Chaffee* (90mm gun); in store)

RECCE 48+: BIDS (CBRN recce); 48 K216A1 (CBRN recce); KM453 (CBRN recce)

AIFV 225 CM-25 (M113 with 20–30mm cannon)

APC 1,022
APC (T) 650 M113
APC (W) 372: ε72 CM-32 *Yunpao*; 300 LAV-150 *Commando*
ARTY 2,254
SP 492: **105mm** 100 M108; **155mm** 318: 225 M109A2/A5; 48 M44T; 45 T-69; **203mm** 70 M110; **240mm** 4
TOWED 1,060+: **105mm** 650 T-64 (M101); **155mm** 340+: 90 M-59; 250 T-65 (M114); M-44; XT-69 **203mm** 70 M115
COASTAL 127mm ε50 US Mk 32 (reported)
MRL 330: **117mm** 120 *Kung Feng* VI; **126mm** 210: 60 *Kung Feng* III/*Kung Feng* IV; 150 RT 2000 *Thunder* (KF towed and SP)
MOR 322+
SP 162+: **81mm** 72+: M-29; 72 M125; **107mm** 90 M106A2
TOWED 81mm 160 M-29; T75; **107mm** M30; **120mm** K5; XT-86
AT • MSL
SP TOW
MANPATS 60 *Javelin*; TOW
RCL 500+: **90mm** M67; **106mm** 500+: 500 M40A1; Type-51
HELICOPTERS
ATK 73: 67 AH-1W *Cobra*; 6 AH-64E *Apache*
MRH 38 OH-58D *Kiowa Warrior*
TPT 84 **Heavy** 8 CH-47SD *Super D Chinook*; **Light** 76 Bell 205 (UH-1H *Iroquois*)
TRG 29 TH-67 *Creek*
UAV • ISR • Light *Mastiff* III
AD
SAM 137
SP 76: 74 FIM-92A *Avenger*; 2 M48 *Chaparral*
MANPAD FIM-92A *Stinger*
GUNS 400
SP 40mm M-42
TOWED 20: 35mm 20 GDF-001 (30 systems with 20 guns) **40mm** L/70
MSL • AShM *Ching Feng*
RADAR 1 TPQ-37 *Firefinder*
AEV 18 M9
ARV CM-27/A1; 37 M88A1
VLB 22 M3; M48A5

Navy 45,000

3 district; 1 (ASW) HQ located at Hualien; 1 Fleet HQ located at Tsoying; 1 New East Coast Fleet

EQUIPMENT BY TYPE
SUBMARINES • TACTICAL • SSK 4:
2 *Hai Lung* with 6 single 533mm TT with SUT HWT
2 *Hai Shih* (ex-US *Guppy* II - trg role) with 10 single 533mm TT (6 fwd, 4aft) with SUT HWT
PRINCIPAL SURFACE COMBATANTS 26
CRUISERS • CGHM 4 *Keelung* (ex-US *Kidd*) with 1 quad lnchr with RGM-84L *Harpoon* AShM, 2 twin Mk26 lnchr with SM-2MR SAM, 2 triple Mk32 324mm ASTT with Mk46 LWT, 2 *Phalanx* Block 1B CIWS, 2 127mm gun, (capacity 1 S-70 ASW hel)
FRIGATES 22
FFGHM 20:
8 *Cheng Kung* with 2 quad lnchr with *Hsiung Feng* II/III AShM, 1 Mk13 GMLS with SM-1MR SAM, 2 triple 324mm ASTT with Mk 46 LWT, 1 *Phalanx* Block 1B CIWS, 1 76mm gun, (capacity 2 S-70C ASW hel)
6 *Chin Yang* (ex-US *Knox*) with 1 octuple Mk112 lnchr with ASROC/RGM-84C *Harpoon* AShM, 2 triple lnchr with SM-1 MR SAM, 2 twin lnchr with SM-1 MR SAM, 2 twin 324mm ASTT with Mk 46 LWT, 1 *Phalanx* Block 1B CIWS, 1 127mm gun, (capacity 1 MD-500 hel)
6 *Kang Ding* with 2 quad lnchr with *Hsiung Feng* II AShM, 1 quad lnchr with *Sea Chaparral* SAM, 2 triple 324mm ASTT with Mk 46 LWT, 1 *Phalanx* Block 1B CIWS, 1 76mm gun, (capacity 1 S-70C ASW hel)
FFGH 2:
2 *Chin Yang* (ex-US *Knox*) with 1 octuple Mk112 lnchr with ASROC/RGM-84C *Harpoon* AShM, 2 twin 324mm ASTT with Mk 46 LWT, 1 *Phalanx* Block 1B CIWS, 1 127mm gun, (capacity 1 MD-500 hel)
PATROL AND COASTAL COMBATANTS 51
PCG 12:
10 *Jin Chiang* with 1 quad lnchr with *Hsiung Feng* II/III AShM
2 *Jin Chiang* with 1 quad lnchr with *Hsiung Feng* III AShM, 1 76mm gun
PBG 31 *Kwang Hua* with 2 twin lnchr with *Hsiung Feng* II AShM
PBF 8 *Ning Hai*
MINE WARFARE • MINE COUNTERMEASURES 14
MHC 2 *Yung Jin* (US *Osprey*)
MSC 8: 4 *Yung Chuan*; 4 *Yung Feng*
MSO 4 *Yung Yang* (ex-US *Aggressive*)
COMMAND SHIPS • LCC 1 *Kao Hsiung*
AMPHIBIOUS
PRINCIPAL AMPHIBIOUS SHIPS • LSD 1 *Shiu Hai* (ex-US *Anchorage*) with 2 *Phalanx* CIWS, 1 hel landing platform (capacity either 2 LCU or 18 LCM; 360 troops)
LANDING SHIPS
LST 12:
10 *Chung Hai* (capacity 16 tanks; 200 troops)
2 *Chung Ho* (ex-US *Newport*) with 1 *Phalanx* CIWS , 1 hel landing platform (capacity 3 LCVP, 400 troops)
LANDING CRAFT 278: 8 **LCU**; 100 **LCVP**; 170 **LCM**
LOGISTICS AND SUPPORT 13
AGOR 1 *Ta Kuan*
AK 1 *Wu Kang* with 1 hel landing platform (capacity 1,400 troops)
AOE 1 *Wu Yi* with 1 hel landing platform
ARS 6
YFD 6
YTL 10
YTM 12

Marines 15,000

FORCES BY ROLE
MANOEUVRE
Amphibious
3 mne bde
COMBAT SUPPORT
Some cbt spt unit
EQUIPMENT BY TYPE
AAV 202: 52 AAV-7A1; 150 LVTP-5A1

Asia

ARTY • TOWED 105mm; 155mm
AT • RCL 106mm
ARV 2 AAV-7R

Naval Aviation

FORCES BY ROLE
ANTI SUBMARINE WARFARE
3 sqn with S-70C *Seahawk* (S-70C *Defender*)
EQUIPMENT BY TYPE
HELICOPTERS • ASW 20 S-70C *Seahawk* (S-70C *Defender*)

Air Force 55,000

Flying hours 180 hrs/year

FORCES BY ROLE
FIGHTER
3 sqn with *Mirage* 2000-5E/D (2000-5EI/DI)
FIGHTER/GROUND ATTACK
3 sqn with F-5E/F *Tiger* II
6 sqn with F-16A/B *Fighting Falcon*
5 sqn with F-CK-1A/B *Ching Kuo*
ANTI SUBMARINE WARFARE
1 sqn with S-2T *Turbo Tracker*
ELECTRONIC WARFARE
1 sqn with C-130HE *Tien Gian*
ISR
1 sqn with RF-5E *Tigereye*; RF-16A *Fighting Falcon*
AIRBORNE EARLY WARNING & CONTROL
1 sqn with E-2T *Hawkeye*
SEARCH & RESCUE
1 sqn with EC225; S-70C *Black Hawk*
TRANSPORT
2 sqn with C-130H *Hercules*
1 (VIP) sqn with B-727-100; B-737-800; Beech 1900; F-50
TRAINING
1 sqn with AT-3A/B *Tzu-Chung**
1 sqn with Beech 1900
1 (basic) sqn with T-34C *Turbo Mentor*
TRANSPORT HELICOPTER
1 sqn with CH-47 *Chinook*; S-70C *Black Hawk*; S-62A (VIP)
EQUIPMENT BY TYPE
AIRCRAFT 485 combat capable
FTR 288: 87 F-5E/F *Tiger* II (some in store); 145 F-16A/B *Fighting Falcon*; 9 *Mirage* 2000-5D (2000-5DI); 47 *Mirage* 2000-5E (2000-5EI)
FGA 128 F-CK-1A/B *Ching Kuo*
ASW 12: 11 S-2T *Tracker*; 1 P-3C *Orion*
EW 1 C-130HE *Tien Gian*
ISR 7 RF-5E *Tigereye*
AEW&C 6 E-2T *Hawkeye*
TPT 34 **Medium** 20 C-130H *Hercules*; **Light** 10 Beech 1900; **PAX** 4: 1 B-737-800; 3 F-50
TRG 99: 57 AT-3A/B *Tzu-Chung**; 42 T-34C *Turbo Mentor*
HELICOPTERS
TPT 23: **Heavy** 3 CH-47 *Chinook*; **Medium** 20: 3 EC225; 1 S-62A (VIP); 16 S-70C *Black Hawk*
MSL
ASM AGM-65A *Maverick*
AShM AGM-84 *Harpoon*
ARM *Sky Sword* IIA
AAM • IR AIM-9J/P *Sidewinder*; R-550 *Magic 2*; *Shafrir*; *Sky Sword* I; **IR/ARH** MICA; **ARH** AIM-120C AMRAAM; *Sky Sword* II
AD • SAM *Antelope*

Missile Command

FORCES BY ROLE
COMBAT SUPPORT
3 SSM bty with *Hsiung Feng* IIE
AIR DEFENCE
2 AD/SAM gp (total: 13 bty with MIM-23 HAWK; 4 bty with *Patriot* PAC-3; 6 bty with Tien Kung I *Sky Bow*/Tien Kung II *Sky Bow*)
EQUIPMENT BY TYPE
MSL • LACM ε12 *Hsiung Feng* IIE
AD • SAM • TOWED 624+: 24+ *Patriot* PAC-3; 100 MIM-23 HAWK; ε500 *Tien Kung* I *Sky Bow*/*Tien Kung* II *Sky Bow*

Paramilitary 17,000

Coast Guard 17,000

EQUIPMENT BY TYPE
PATROL AND COASTAL COMBATANTS 138
PSO 7: 2 *Ho Hsing*; 3 *Shun Hu 7*; 2 *Tainan*
PCO 14: 1 *Teh Hsing*; 2 *Kinmen*; 2 *Mou Hsing*; 1 *Shun Hu 1*; 2 *Shun Hu 2/3*; 4 *Taichung*; 2 *Taipei*
PBF 83 (various)
PB 34: 1 *Shun Hu 5*; 1 *Shun Hu 6*; 32 (various)

Directorate General (Customs)

EQUIPMENT BY TYPE
PATROL AND COASTAL COMBATANTS 9
PCO 1 *Yun Hsing*
PB 8: 4 *Hai Cheng*; 4 *Hai Ying*

Cyber

Although Taiwan has a highly developed civilian IT sector, the Taiwanese government has been relatively slow to exploit this advantage for national-defence purposes. But for the past decade, Taipei has worked on its *Po Sheng* – Broad Victory – C4ISR programme, an all-hazards defence system with a significant defence component located in the Hengshan Command Center, which also houses the Tri-Service Command. The main focus of the military component of this programme is on countering PLA IW and EW attacks. Taiwanese civilian hackers are thought to be responsible for many of the viruses infecting Chinese computers but it is unclear to what extent, if at all, such activities benefit from government direction. Responsible authorities for cyber activity include the National Security Bureau (NSB), the defence ministry, and the Research, Development and Evaluation Commission (RDEC). Among other projects, the Chungshan Institute of Science and Technology (a government R&D house) plans to invest finance on a project to 'display and confirm' Taiwan's latest 'cyber offensive system' between 2013 and 2015.

FOREIGN FORCES

Singapore 3 trg camp (incl inf and arty)

Thailand THA

Thai Baht b		2012	2013	2014
GDP	b	11.4tr	12.3tr	
	US$	366bn	425bn	
per capita	US$	5,678	6,572	
Growth	%	6.44	5.88	
Inflation	%	3.02	3.00	
Def bdgt [a]	b	169bn	180bn	183bn
	US$	5.43bn	6.21bn	
FMA (US)	US$	1.2m	1.2m	1m
US$1=b		31.08	29.05	

[a] Excludes military pensions

Population 67,448,120

Ethnic and religious groups: Thai 75%; Chinese 14%; Muslim 4%

Age	0–14	15–19	20–24	25–29	30–64	65 plus
Male	9.8%	3.9%	3.8%	3.7%	23.8%	4.4%
Female	9.4%	3.7%	3.7%	3.6%	24.9%	5.4%

Capabilities

Thailand's armed forces have benefited from substantially increased funding since reasserting their central political role in a 2006 coup. However, despite increased resources, and other positive indications such as continuing involvement in multinational exercises and significant international deployments, the armed forces' entanglement in domestic politics often appears to overshadow efforts to sustain and modernise operational capability. The army remains the dominant service, its commander-in-chief wielding considerably greater authority than the chief of defence forces. While the army prevailed in clashes with Red-Shirt protesters in Bangkok in May 2010, the confrontation revealed potential splits in the service, particularly in light of many ordinary soldiers' origins in relatively poor northern and northeastern provinces where Red-Shirt support is strong. Subsequently, the army played a high-profile role in flood relief operations during 2011. Operations against Malay-Muslim insurgents in the three southernmost provinces continue, but ineffectively: the low-intensity war there remains stalemated. Sporadic border clashes with Cambodia in 2008–11 were essentially small-scale skirmishes involving infantry supported by mortar and artillery fire. Thailand's air force is one of the best-equipped and -trained in Southeast Asia, and benefits from regular exercises with its US, Australian and Singapore counterparts. The induction into service of *Gripen* combat aircraft and Saab 340 AEW platforms, which will have data-links to ground-based air defences, naval vessels and army units under the air force's Network Centric plan (due for completion in 2014–15), promises to boost the effectiveness of Thailand's air power significantly.

ACTIVE 360,850 (Army 245,000 Navy 69,850 Air 46,000) Paramilitary 92,700
Conscription liability 2 years

RESERVE 200,000 Paramilitary 45,000

ORGANISATIONS BY SERVICE

Army 130,000; ε115,000 conscript (total 245,000)

FORCES BY ROLE
COMMAND
4 (regional) army HQ
3 corps HQ
SPECIAL FORCES
1 SF div
1 SF regt
MANOEUVRE
Mechanised
3 cav div
1 mech inf div
Light
8 inf div
1 Rapid Reaction force (1 bn per region forming)
Aviation
Some hel flt
COMBAT SUPPORT
1 arty div
1 ADA div (6 bn)
1 engr div
COMBAT SERVICE SUPPORT
4 economic development div

EQUIPMENT BY TYPE
MBT 283: 53 M60A1; 125 M60A3; (50 Type-69 in store); 105 M48A5
LT TK 194: 24 M41; 104 *Scorpion* (50 in store); 66 *Stingray*
RECCE 32+: 32 S52 Mk 3; M1114 HMMWV
AIFV 119 BTR-3E1 (incl variants)
APC 1,140
APC (T) 880: *Bronco*; 430 M113A1/A3; 450 Type-85
APC (W) 160: 18 *Condor*; 142 LAV-150 *Commando*
PPV 100 *Reva*
ARTY 2,623+
SP 155mm 26: 6 CAESAR; 20 M109A5
TOWED 619: **105mm** 340: 24 LG1 MkII; 12 M-56; 200 M101/-Mod; 12 M102; 32 M618A2; 60 L119; **155mm** 277: 90 GHN-45 A1; 48 M114; 118 M198; 21 M-71
MRL 78: **130mm** 60 Type-85; **302mm** 18 DTI-1
MOR 1,900+
SP 33+: **81mm** 21 M125A3; **107mm** M106A3; **120mm** 12 M1064A3
TOWED 1,867: **81mm**; **107mm**; **120mm**
AT
MSL 318+
SP 18+ M901A5 (TOW); 6 BTR-3RK
MANPATS 300 M47 *Dragon*
RCL 180: **75mm** 30 M20; **106mm** 150 M40
AIRCRAFT
TPT • Light 19: 2 Beech 200 *King Air*; 2 Beech 1900C; 1 C-212 *Aviocar*; 10 Cessna A185E (U-17B); 2 ERJ-135LR; 2 *Jetstream* 41
TRG 33: 11 MX-7-235 *Star Rocket*; 22 T-41B *Mescalero*
HELICOPTERS
ATK 7 AH-1F *Cobra*
MRH 10: 7 AS550 *Fennec*; 3 Mi-17V-5 *Hip* H

Asia

TPT 201 **Heavy** 5 CH-47D *Chinook*; **Medium** 6 UH-60L *Black Hawk*; **Light** 190: 94 Bell 205 (UH-1H *Iroquois*); 28 Bell 206 *Jet Ranger*; 52 Bell 212 (AB-212); 16 Enstrom 480B
TRG 54 Hughes 300C
UAV • ISR • Medium *Searcher*; *Searcher* II
AD • SAM
SP 8 *Starstreak*
STATIC *Aspide*
MANPAD 54 9K338 *Igla*-S (SA-24 *Grinch*)
GUNS 202+
SP 54: **20mm** 24 M163 *Vulcan*; **40mm** 30 M1/M42 SP
TOWED 148+: **20mm** 24 M-167 *Vulcan*; **37mm** 52 Type-74; **40mm** 48 L/70; **57mm** 24+: ε6 Type-59 (S-60); 18+ non-operational
RADAR • LAND AN/TPQ-36 *Firefinder* (arty, mor); RASIT (veh, arty)
ARV 48: 5 BTR-3BR; 22 M88A1; 6 M88A2; 10 M113; 5 Type-653; WZT-4
VLB Type-84
MW Bozena; *Giant Viper*

Reserves

FORCES BY ROLE
COMMAND
1 inf div HQ

Navy 44,000 (incl Naval Aviation, Marines, Coastal Defence); 25,850 conscript (total 69,850)

EQUIPMENT BY TYPE
PRINCIPAL SURFACE COMBATANTS 11
AIRCRAFT CARRIERS • CVH 1:
1 *Chakri Naruebet* with 2 sextuple *Sadral* lnchr with *Mistral* SAM (capacity 6 S-70B *Seahawk* ASW hel)
FRIGATES 10
FFGHM 2:
2 *Naresuan* with 2 quad Mk141 lnchr with RGM-84A *Harpoon* AShM, 1 8 cell Mk41 VLS with RIM-7M *Sea Sparrow* SAM, 2 triple Mk32 324mm TT, 1 127mm gun, (capacity 1 *Super Lynx* 300 hel)
FFGM 4:
2 *Chao Phraya* with 4 twin lnchr with C 801 (CSS-N-4 *Sardine*) AShM, 2 twin lnchr with HQ-61 (CSA-N-2) SAM (non-operational), 2 RBU 1200, 2 twin 100mm gun
2 *Kraburi* with 4 twin lnchr with C-801 (CSS-N-4 *Sardine*) AShM, 2 twin lnchr with HQ-61 (CSA-N-2) SAM, 2 RBU 1200, 1 twin 100mm gun, 1 hel landing platform
FFGH 2:
2 *Phuttha Yotfa Chulalok* (ex-US *Knox*, leased) with 1 octuple Mk112 lnchr with RGM-84C *Harpoon* AShM/ASROC, 2 twin 324mm ASTT with Mk 46 LWT, 1 *Phalanx* CIWS, 1 127mm gun, (capacity 1 Bell 212 (AB-212) hel)
FF 2:
1 *Makut Rajakumarn* with 2 triple 34mm ASTT, 2 114mm gun
1 *Pin Klao* (trg role) with 6 single 324mm ASTT, 3 76mm gun

PATROL AND COASTAL COMBATANTS 80
CORVETTES 7
FSG 2 *Rattanakosin* with 2 quad Mk140 lnchr with RGM-84A *Harpoon* AShM, 1 octuple *Albatros* lnchr with *Aspide* SAM, 2 triple Mk32 324mm ASTT with *Stingray* LWT, 1 76mm gun
FS 5:
3 *Khamronsin* with 2 triple 324mm ASTT with *Stingray* LWT, 1 76mm gun
2 *Tapi* with 6 single 324mm ASTT with Mk46 LWT, 1 76mm gun
PSO 1 *Krabi* (UK *River* mod) with 1 76mm gun
PCFG 6:
3 *Prabparapak* with 2 single lnchr w1ith *Gabriel I* AShM, 1 triple lnchr with *Gabriel I* AShM, 1 57mm gun
3 *Ratcharit* with 2 twin lnchr with MM-38 *Exocet* AShM, 1 76mm gun
PCOH 2 *Pattani* with 1 76mm gun
PCO 3 *Hua Hin* with 1 76mm gun
PCC 9: 3 *Chon Buri* with 2 76mm gun; 6 *Sattahip* with 1 76mm gun
PBF 4
PB 48: 7 T-11; 4 *Swift*; 3 T-81; 9 T-91; 3 T-210; 13 T-213; 3 T-227; 3 T-991; 3 T-994
MINE WARFARE • MINE COUNTERMEASURES 17
MCM SPT 1 *Thalang*
MCO 2 *Lat Ya*
MCC 2 *Bang Rachan*
MSR 12
AMPHIBIOUS
PRINCIPAL AMPHIBIOUS SHIPS 1
LPD 1 *Anthong* (SIN *Endurance*) with 1 76mm gun (capacity 2 hel; 19 MBT; 500 troops)
LANDING SHIPS 2
LST 2 *Sichang* with 2 hel landing platform (capacity 14 MBT; 300 troops)
LANDING CRAFT 56
LCU 13: 3 *Man Nok*; 6 *Mataphun* (capacity either 3–4 MBT or 250 troops); 4 *Thong Kaeo*
LCM 24
LCVP 12
LCA 4
LCAC 3 Griffon 1000TD
LOGISTICS AND SUPPORT 16
ABU 1
AGOR 1
AGS 2
AOL 5: 4 *Prong*; 1 *Samui*
AOR 1 *Chula*
AORH 1 *Similan* (capacity 1 hel)
AWT 1
YTL 2
YTM 2
YTR 2

Naval Aviation 1,200

AIRCRAFT 3 combat capable
ASW 2 P-3A *Orion* (P-3T)
ISR 9 *Sentry* O-2-337
MP 1 F-27-200 MPA*

TPT • Light 15: 7 Do-228-212*; 2 ERJ-135LR; 2 F-27-400M *Troopship;* 3 N-24A *Searchmaster;* 1 UP-3A *Orion* (UP-3T)

HELICOPTERS

ASW 8: 6 S-70B *Seahawk;* 2 *Super Lynx* 300

TPT 13 **Medium** 2 Bell 214ST (AB-214ST); **Light** 11: 6 Bell 212 (AB-212); 5 S-76B

MSL • AShM AGM-84 *Harpoon*

Marines 23,000

FORCES BY ROLE

COMMAND

1 mne div HQ

MANOEUVRE

Reconnaissance

1 recce bn

Light

2 inf regt (total: 6 bn)

Amphibious

1 amph aslt bn

COMBAT SUPPORT

1 arty regt (3 fd arty bn, 1 ADA bn)

EQUIPMENT BY TYPE

APC (W) 24 LAV-150 *Commando*

AAV 33 LVTP-7

AIFV 14 BTR-3E1

ARTY • TOWED 48: **105mm** 36 (reported); **155mm** 12 GC-45

AT • MSL 24+

TOWED 24 HMMWV TOW

MANPATS M47 *Dragon;* TOW

AD • GUNS 12.7mm 14

ARV 1 AAVR-7

Air Force ε46,000

4 air divs, one flying trg school

Flying hours 100 hrs/year

FORCES BY ROLE

FIGHTER

2 sqn with F-5E/5F *Tiger II*

3 sqn with F-16A/B *Fighting Falcon*

FIGHTER/GROUND ATTACK

1 sqn with *Gripen* C/D

GROUND ATTACK

1 sqn with *Alpha Jet**

1 sqn with AU-23A *Peacemaker*

1 sqn with L-39ZA *Albatros**

ELINT/ISR

1 sqn with DA42 MPP *Guardian;* IAI-201 *Arava*

AIRBORNE EARLY WARNING & CONTROL

1 sqn with Saab 340B; Saab 340 *Erieye*

TRANSPORT

1 (Royal Flight) sqn with A310-324; A319CJ; B-737-800

1 sqn with ATR-72; BAe-748

1 sqn with BT-67; N-22B *Nomad*

1 sqn with C-130H/H-30 *Hercules*

TRAINING

1 sqn with L-39ZA *Albatros**

1 sqn with CT-4A/B *Airtrainer;* T-41D *Mescalero*

1 sqn with CT-4E *Airtrainer*

1 sqn with PC-9

TRANSPORT HELICOPTER

1 sqn with Bell 205 (UH-1H *Iroquois*)

1 sqn with Bell 412 *Twin Huey;* S-92A

EQUIPMENT BY TYPE

AIRCRAFT 134 combat capable

FTR 79: 1 F-5B *Freedom Fighter;* 21 F-5E *Tiger* II; 3 F-5F *Tiger* II (F-5E/F being upgraded); 39 F-16A *Fighting Falcon;* 15 F-16B *Fighting Falcon*

FGA 12: 8 *Gripen* C; 4 *Gripen* D

ATK 17 AU-23A *Peacemaker*

EW 2 IAI-201TH *Arava*

ISR 5 DA42 MPP *Guardian*

AEW&C 2 Saab 340 *Erieye*

TPT 59 **Medium** 14: 6 C-130H *Hercules;* 6 C-130H-30 *Hercules;* 2 Saab 340B; **Light** 36: 3 ATR-72; 3 Beech 200 *King Air;* 8 BT-67; 1 *Commander* 690; 6 DA42M; 4 N-22B *Nomad;* **PAX** 10: 1 A310-324; 1 A-319CJ; 1 B-737-800; 5 BAe-748

TRG 119: 16 *Alpha Jet**; 13 CT-4A *Airtrainer;* 6 CT-4B *Airtrainer;* 20 CT-4E *Airtrainer;* 27 L-39ZA *Albatros**; 21 PC-9; 7 T-41D *Mescalero*

HELICOPTERS

MRH 11: 2 Bell 412 *Twin Huey;* 2 Bell 412SP *Twin Huey;* 1 Bell 412HP *Twin Huey;* 6 Bell 412EP *Twin Huey*

TPT 20 **Medium** 3 S-92A *Super Hawk* **Light** 17 Bell 205 (UH-1H *Iroquois*)

MSL

AAM • IR AIM-9B/J *Sidewinder; Python* III; **ARH** AIM-120 AMRAAM

ASM AGM-65 *Maverick*

Paramilitary ε92,700 active

Border Patrol Police 20,000

Marine Police 2,200

PATROL AND COASTAL COMBATANTS 92

PCO 1 *Srinakrin*

PCC 2 *Hameln*

PB 43: 1 *Burespadoongkit;* 2 *Chasanyabadee;* 3 *Cutlass;* 1 *Sriyanont;* 1 *Yokohama;* 35 (various)

PBR 46

National Security Volunteer Corps 45,000 – Reserves

Police Aviation 500

AIRCRAFT 6 combat capable

ATK 6 AU-23A *Peacemaker*

TPT 16 **Light** 15: 2 CN-235; 8 PC-6 *Turbo-Porter;* 3 SC-7 3M *Skyvan;* 2 Short 330UTT; **PAX** 1 F-50

HELICOPTERS

MRH 6 Bell 412 *Twin Huey*

TPT • Light 61: 27 Bell 205A; 14 Bell 206 *Jet Ranger;* 20 Bell 212 (AB-212)

Provincial Police 50,000 (incl est. 500 Special Action Force)

Thahan Phran (Hunter Soldiers) 21,000

Volunteer irregular force

FORCES BY ROLE

MANOEUVRE

Other

22 paramilitary regt (total: 275 paramilitary coy)

DEPLOYMENT

Legal provisions for foreign deployment:

Constitution: In addition to the below, Government has to ensure no violation of Para. 1 and 2 of Provision 190 of the Constitution of the Kingdom of Thailand, BE 2550

Decision on deployment of troops abroad: Depends on operation. In case of PSO or HADR, cabinet resolution endorsing deployment and defence council concurrence would constitute legislation. Legal provisions for foreign deployment generally under the Defence Act, BE 2551 (2008). Justification for overseas missions is in accordance with following sections of the Act: Provision 37, Art. 4: Minister of Defence has exclusive authority to arrange and deploy armed forces to areas considered appropriate; Provision 38, Art. 4: Employment of armed forces for peace operations shall be endorsed by council of ministers with concurrence of defence council. No terms of reference on 'the foreign deployment of forces for combat operations in [a] conventional war area are stipulated' in the Act, so deployment purpose and operation type should be clearly determined.

INDIA/PAKISTAN

UN • UNMOGIP 3 obs

SUDAN

UN • UNAMID 10; 9 obs

FOREIGN FORCES

United States US Pacific Command: 120

Timor-Leste TLS

US$		2012	2013	2014
GDP	US$	4.17bn	4.24bn	
per capita	US$	3,730	3,704	
Growth	%	10.00	10.00	
Inflation	%	11.80	8.00	
Def bdgt	US$	64m	67m	69m
FMA (US)	US$			0.3m

Population 1,172,390

Age	0–14	15–19	20–24	25–29	30–64	65 plus
Male	22.0%	5.4%	4.5%	3.4%	13.2%	1.7%
Female	20.7%	5.2%	4.6%	3.8%	13.6%	1.9%

Capabilities

The Timor-Leste Defence Force was formed in 2001 from the former Falintil insurgent army. However, it soon became clear that the new force suffered from poor morale and weak discipline. In 2006, these problems culminated in the dismissal of large numbers of personnel who had protested over poor conditions and alleged discrimination on regional lines, which precipitated the collapse of both the defence force and the national police. These circumstances forced the government to call for an international intervention, and a mainly Australian International Stabilisation Force remained in the country until early 2013. Meanwhile, the government has attempted to rebuild the defence force. Long-term plans outlined in the Force 2020 document, made public in 2006, call for an expanded defence force, conscription, the establishment of an air component, and acquisition of modern weapons. The defence force continues to depend heavily on foreign assistance and training, notably from Australia, Portugal and Brazil.

ACTIVE 1,330 (Army 1,250 Naval Element 80)

ORGANISATIONS BY SERVICE

Army 1,250

Training began in January 2001 with the aim of deploying 1,500 full-time personnel and 1,500 reservists. Authorities are engaged in developing security structures with international assistance.

FORCES BY ROLE

MANOEUVRE

Light

2 inf bn

COMBAT SUPPORT

1 MP pl

COMBAT SERVICE SUPPORT

1 log spt coy

Naval Element 80

PATROL AND COASTAL COMBATANTS 7

PB 7: 2 *Albatros*; 2 *Dili*; 2 *Shanghai* II; 1 *Sea Dolphin* (ROK *Chamsuri*)

DEPLOYMENT

SOUTH SUDAN

UN • UNMISS 2 obs

Vietnam VNM

Vietnamese Dong d		2012	2013	2014
GDP	d	2,933tr	3,396tr	
	US$	138bn	156bn	
per capita	US$	1,528	1,705	
Growth	%	5.02	5.24	
Inflation	%	9.10	8.80	
Def bdgt	d	70tr	82.7tr	
	US$	3.3bn	3.8bn	
FMA (US)	US$	2.3m	2.3m	3m
US$1=d		21243.90	21775.93	

Population **92,477,857**

Ethnic groups: Kinh 86%, Tay 2%, Thai 2%, Muang 1%, Khmei 1%, Mong 1%, Nung 1%, Hua 1%, Dao 1%, Other 4%

Age	0–14	15–19	20–24	25–29	30–64	65 plus
Male	12.9%	4.5%	5.0%	4.9%	20.5%	2.1%
Female	11.7%	4.2%	4.7%	4.7%	21.3%	3.4%

Capabilities

Communist Vietnam has a stronger military tradition and much more operational experience than any of its Southeast Asian counterparts. Although the Vietnam People's Army (VPA) remains a central element of the political system led by the Vietnam Worker's Party, following the cessation of Soviet military aid with the end of the Cold War, the armed forces suffered from much-reduced budgets and only limited procurement. With Vietnam's rapid economic growth over the last decade, however, defence spending has increased, and particular efforts have been made to re-equip the navy and air force, apparently with a view to deterring Chinese military pressure in the disputed Spratly Islands. While Vietnam cannot hope to balance China's power on its own, acquisition of a submarine capability during the present decade, with six *Kilo*-class boats ordered from Russia in 2009, may complicate Beijing's naval options, as may an order for more Su-30MK2 aircraft due for delivery by 2015. The conscript-based armed forces have broad popular support, particularly in the context of current tensions with China.

ACTIVE 482,000 (Army 412,000 Navy 40,000 Air 30,000) Paramilitary 40,000

Conscript liability 2 years Army and Air Defence, 3 years Air Force and Navy, specialists 3 years, some ethnic minorities 2 years

RESERVES 5,000,000

ORGANISATIONS BY SERVICE

Army ε412,000

8 Mil Regions (incl capital)

FORCES BY ROLE

COMMAND

4 corps HQ

SPECIAL FORCES

1 SF bde (1 AB bde, 1 demolition engr regt)

MANOEUVRE

Armoured

6 armd bde

3 armd regt

Mechanised

2 mech inf div

Light

23 inf div

COMBAT SUPPORT

13 arty bde

1 arty regt

11 AD bde

10 engr bde

1 engr regt

1 EW unit

3 sigs bde

2 sigs regt

COMBAT SERVICE SUPPORT

9 economic construction div

1 log regt

1 med unit

1 trg regt

Reserve

MANOEUVRE

Light

9 inf div

EQUIPMENT BY TYPE

MBT 1,270: 70 T-62; 350 Type-59; 850 T-54/T-55; (45 T-34 † in store)

LT TK 620: 300 PT-76; 320 Type-62/Type-63

RECCE 100 BRDM-1/BRDM-2

AIFV 300 BMP-1/BMP-2

APC 1,380

APC (T) 280: 200 M113 (to be upgraded); 80 Type-63

APC (W) 1,100 BTR-40/BTR-50/BTR-60/BTR-152

ARTY 3,070+

SP 30+: **152mm** 30 2S3; **175mm** M107

TOWED 2,300 **100mm** M-1944; **105mm** M101/M102; **122mm** D-30/Type-54 (M-1938)/Type-60 (D-74); **130mm** M-46; **152mm** D-20; **155mm** M114

GUN/MOR 120mm 30 2S9 NONA-S (reported)

MRL 710+: **107mm** 360 Type-63; **122mm** 350 BM-21; **140mm** BM-14

MOR 82mm; **120mm** M-43; **160mm** M-43

AT • MSL • MANPATS 9K11 (AT-3 *Sagger*)

RCL 75mm Type-56; **82mm** Type-65 (B-10); **87mm** Type-51

GUNS

SP 100mm Su-100; **122mm** Su-122

TOWED 100mm T-12 (arty)

AD • SAM • MANPAD 9K32 *Strela*-2 (SA-7 *Grail*)‡; 9K310 *Igla*-1 (SA-16 *Gimlet*); 9K38 *Igla* (SA-18 *Grouse*)

GUNS 12,000

SP 23mm ZSU-23-4

TOWED 14.5mm/30mm/37mm/57mm/85mm/100mm

MSL • SSM *Scud*-B/C (reported)

Navy ε40,000 (incl ε27,000 Naval Infantry)

EQUIPMENT BY TYPE

SUBMARINES • TACTICAL • SSI 2 *Yugo*† (DPRK)

PRINCIPAL SURFACE COMBATANTS 2

FRIGATES • FFGM 2

2 *Dinh Tien Hoang* (RUS *Gepard* mod) with 2 quad lnchr with Kh-35 *Uran* (SS-N-25 *Switchblade*), 1 *Palma* lnchr with *Sosna*-R SAM, 2 twin 533mm TT, 2 AK630 CIWS, 1 76mm gun

PATROL AND COASTAL COMBATANTS 68

CORVETTES • FSG 6:

1 BPS-500 with 2 quad lnchr with 3M24 *Uran* (SS-N-25 *Switchblade*) AShM, 9K32 *Strela*-2M (SA-N-5 *Grail*) SAM (manually operated), 2 twin 533mm TT, 1 RBU-1600, 1 AK630 CIWS, 1 76mm gun

3 *Petya* II (FSU) with 1 quintuple 406mm ASTT, 4 RBU 6000 *Smerch 2*, 2 twin 76mm gun

2 *Petya* III (FSU) with 1 triple 533mm ASTT, 4 RBU 2500 *Smerch 1*, 2 twin 76mm gun

PCFGM 8:

4 *Tarantul* (FSU) with 2 twin lnchr with P-15 *Termit* (SS-N-2D *Styx*) AShM, 1 quad lnchr with SA-N-5 *Grail* SAM (manually operated), 2 AK630 CIWS, 1 76mm gun

4 *Tarantul* V with 4 quad lnchr with 3M24 *Uran* (SS-N-25 *Switchblade*) AShM; 1 quad lnchr with SA-N-5 *Grail* SAM (manually operated), 2 AK630 CIWS, 1 76mm gun

PCC 9: 6 *Svetlyak* with 1 AK630 CIWS, 1 76mm gun; 3 TT-400TP wiht 2 AK630 CIWS, 1 76mm gun

PBFG 8 *Osa* II with 4 single lnchr with 1 SS-N-2 AShM

PBFT 2 *Shershen*† (FSU) with 4 single 533mm TT

PHT 3 *Turya*† with 4 single 533mm TT, 1 twin 57mm gun

PH 2 *Turya*† with 1 twin 57mm gun

PB 26: 2 *Poluchat* (FSU); 14 *Zhuk*†; 4 *Zhuk* (mod); 6 (various)

PBR 4 *Stolkraft*

MINE WARFARE • MINE COUNTERMEASURES 13

MSO 2 *Yurka*

MSC 4 *Sonya*

MHI 2 *Yevgenya*

MSR 5 K-8

AMPHIBIOUS

LANDING SHIPS 8

LSM 5:

1 *Polnochny* A† (capacity 6 MBT; 180 troops)

2 *Polnochny* B† (capacity 6 MBT; 180 troops)

2 *Nau Dinh*

LST 3 LST-510-511 (US) (capacity 16 tanks; 200 troops)

LANDING CRAFT 30: 15 **LCU**; 12 **LCM**; 3 **LCVP**

LOGISTICS AND SUPPORT 29:

AFD 2; **AGS** 1; **AGSH** 1; **AKSL** 18; **AP** 1; **AT** 2; **YDT** 2; **YTM** 2

Naval Infantry ε27,000

Navy Air Wing

FORCES BY ROLE

ASW/SAR

1 regt with EC225; Ka-28 (Ka-27PL) *Helix* A; Ka-32 *Helix* C

EQUIPMENT BY TYPE

AIRCRAFT • TPT • Light 2 DHC-6-400 *Twin Otter*

HELICOPTERS

ASW 10 Ka-28 *Helix* A

TPT • Medium 4: 2 EC225; 2 Ka-32 *Helix* C

Air Force 30,000

3 air div, 1 tpt bde

FORCES BY ROLE

FIGHTER

4 regt with MiG-21bis *Fishbed* L; MiG-21UM *Mongol* B

FIGHTER/GROUND ATTACK

1 regt with Su-22M3/M4/UM *Fitter* (some ISR)
1 regt with Su-27SK/Su-27UBK *Flanker*
1 regt with Su-27SK/Su-27UBK *Flanker*; Su-30MK2
1 regt with Su-30MK2

TRANSPORT

2 regt with An-2 *Colt*; An-26 *Curl*; Bell 205 (UH-1H *Iroquois*); Mi-8 *Hip*; Mi-17 *Hip H*; M-28 *Bryza*

TRAINING

1 regt with L-39 *Albatros*
1 regt with Yak-52

ATTACK/TRANSPORT HELICOPTER

2 regt with Mi-8 *Hip*; Mi-17 *Hip* H; Mi-171; Mi-24 *Hind*

AIR DEFENCE

4 ADA bde
Some (People's Regional) force (total: ε1,000 AD unit, 6 radar bde with 100 radar stn)

EQUIPMENT BY TYPE

AIRCRAFT 97 combat capable

FGA 97: 25 MiG-21bis *Fishbed* L & N; 8 MiG-21UM *Mongol* B; 30 Su-22M3/M4/UM *Fitter* (some ISR); 6 Su-27SK *Flanker*; 5 Su-27UBK *Flanker*; 23 Su-30MK2 *Flanker*

TPT • Light 18: 6 An-2 *Colt*; 12 An-26 *Curl*; 1 M-28 *Bryza*

TRG 48: 18 L-39 *Albatros*; 30 Yak-52

HELICOPTERS

ATK 26 Mi-24 *Hind*

MRH 6 Mi-17 *Hip* H

TPT 30 **Medium** 18: 14 Mi-8 *Hip*; 4 Mi-171; **Light** 12 Bell 205 (UH-1H *Iroquois*)

AD • SAM

SP 12+: 2K12 *Kub* (SA-6 *Gainful*); 12 S-300PMU1 (SA-20 *Gargoyle*)

TOWED S-75 *Dvina* (SA-2 *Guideline*); S-125 *Pechora* (SA-3 *Goa*)

MANPAD 9K32 *Strela*-2 (SA-7 *Grail*)‡; 9K310 *Igla*-1 (SA-16 *Gimlet*)

GUNS 37mm; **57mm**; **85mm; 100mm**; **130mm**

MSL

ASM Kh-29T/L (AS-14 *Kedge*); Kh-31A (AS-17B *Krypton*); Kh-59M (AS-18 *Kazoo*)

ARM Kh-28 (AS-9 *Kyle*); Kh-31P (AS-17A *Krypton*)

AAM • IR R-3 (AA-2 *Atoll*)‡; R-60 (AA-8 *Aphid*); R-73 (AA-11 *Archer*); **IR/SARH** R-27 (AA-10 *Alamo*)

Paramilitary 40,000+ active

Border Defence Corps ε40,000

Coast Guard

EQUIPMENT BY TYPE

PATROL AND COASTAL COMBATANTS 34+

PSO 1 Damen 9014 (one more vessel on order)

PCO 1+

PCC 4 TT-400TP

PBF 2 *Shershen*

PB 26: 12 TT-200; 13 TT-120; 1 other

LOGISTICS AND SUPPORT • ATF 4

AIRCRAFT • MP 3 C-212-400 MPA

Local Forces ε5,000,000 reservists

Incl People's Self-Defence Force (urban units), People's Militia (rural units); comprises of static and mobile cbt units, log spt and village protection pl; some arty, mor and AD guns; acts as reserve.

Table 6 **Selected Arms Procurements and Deliveries, Asia**

Designation	Type	Quantity	Contract Value (Current)	Supplier Country	Prime Contractor	Order Date	First Delivery Due	Notes
Afghanistan (AFG)								
Mobile Strike Force Vehicle (MSFV)	APC (W)	634	n.k.	US	Textron (Textron Marine & Land Systems)	2011	2012	Modified *Commando Select*. Includes additional 135 ordered in 2013. Delivery to be complete by Feb 2014
C-130H *Hercules*	Tpt ac	4	n.k.	US	Government Surplus	2013	2013	Ex-USAF surplus. First two delivered Oct 2013. Second pair due 2014
EMB-314 *Super Tucano*	Trg ac	20	US$427m	BRZ	Embraer	2013	n.k.	USAF Light Air Support (LAS) programme. Delivery to be complete by Apr 2015
Australia (AUS)								
M777A2	Arty (155mm towed)	19	A$70m	UK	BAE Systems (BAE Land & Armaments)	2012	2013	Follow on from previous order for 35
Hobart-class	DDGHM	3	US$8bn	AUS/ESP	AWD Alliance	2007	2016	A.k.a. Air Warfare Destroyer (AWD). Delivery of first vessel delayed to Mar 2016. Second vessel now to be delivered Sep 2017; third Mar 2019. Option on fourth. All to be fitted with *Aegis* system
Canberra-class	LHD	2	A$3.1bn (US$2.8bn)	AUS/ESP	Navantia	2007	2014	To replace HMAS *Tobruk* and *Kanimbla*-class. First vessel launched 2011; second in 2012
F-35A *Lightning* II	FGA ac	2	n.k.	US	Lockheed Martin	2012	2014	First two test and trg ac
EA-18G *Growler*	EW ac	12	n.k.	US	Boeing	2013	n.k.	IOC planned for 2018
C-27J *Spartan*	Tpt ac	10	A$1.4bn (US$1.4bn)	ITA	Finmeccanica (Alenia Aermacchi)	2012	2015	To replace DHC-4s. Contract price includes logistics support and training
MH-60R *Seahawk*	ASW hel	24	US$3bn+	US	UTC (Sikorsky)	2011	2013	To replace navy's S-70Bs. First two to be delivered Dec 2013; seven in 2014; seven in 2015 and final eight in 2016
NH90	Tpt hel	47	A$2bn (US$1.47bn)	Int'l	NH Industries	2005	2007	12 ordered 2005, 34 more in 2006 and one hel added in 2013. First four built in Europe; remainder in AUS
CH-47F *Chinook*	Tpt hel	7	A$755m (US$670m)	US	Boeing	2010	2014	All to be operational by 2017. To replace CH-47Ds
Bangladesh (BGD)								
MBT-2000	MBT	44	Tk 1,201 crore	PRC	NORINCO	2011	2012	Order also includes three ARVs. First delivered 2012
NORA B-52	Arty (155mm SP)	18	n.k.	SER	Yugoimport	2011	2013	First shipment Sep 2013
Padma-class	PCC	5	US$42m	BNG	Khulna Shipyard	2010	2013	First vessel commissioned Jan 2013; second in May 2013. Remaining three vessels to be delivered by Dec 2013
Brunei (BRN)								
S-70i	Tpt hel	12	n.k.	US	UTC (Sikorsky)	2011	2013	Option for additional ten. First delivery due end-2013

Table 6 **Selected Arms Procurements and Deliveries, Asia**

Designation	Type	Quantity	Contract Value (Current)	Supplier Country	Prime Contractor	Order Date	First Delivery Due	Notes
China (PRC)								
JL-2 (CSS-NX-5)	SLBM	n.k.	n.k.	PRC	n.k.	1985	2009	In development; range 8,000km. Reportedly to equip new Type-094 SSBN. IOC anticipated in 2014
Type-96A	MBT	n.k.	n.k.	PRC	NORINCO	n.k.	2006	Delivery in progress
Type-99A	MBT	n.k.	n.k.	PRC	NORINCO	n.k.	2011	In limited production
Type-05 (ZBD-05)	AIFV	n.k.	n.k.	PRC	NORINCO	n.k.	2006	Amphibious assault veh family. Issued to marine and amph army units
Type-04A (ZBD-04A)	AIFV	n.k.	n.k.	PRC	NORINCO	n.k.	2011	Infantry Fighting Vehicle Family. Improved version of Type-04 with extra armour
Type-09 (ZBL-09)	APC (W)	n.k.	n.k.	PRC	NORINCO	n.k.	2010	Veh family including aslt gun (ZTL-09) and 122mm SP how (PLL-09) variants. Being issued to lt mech units
Type-07 (PLZ-07)	Arty (122mm SP)	n.k.	n.k.	PRC	NORINCO	n.k.	2007	122mm tracked SP howitzer; first displayed in public at 2009 parade
Type-09 (PLC-09)	Arty (122mm SP)	n.k.	n.k.	PRC	n.k.	n.k.	2009	Truck mounted 122mm howitzer
Type-05 (PLZ-05)	Arty (155mm SP)	n.k.	n.k.	PRC	NORINCO	n.k.	2008	155mm tracked SP howitzer; first displayed in public at 2009 parade
Type-03 (PHL-03)	Arty (300mm MRL)	n.k.	n.k.	PRC	NORINCO	n.k.	n.k.	8x8 truck mounted MRL
HQ-16A	SAM	n.k.	n.k.	PRC	ALIT	n.k.	2011	First delivered to 39th Group Army in 2011
Type-07 (PGZ-07)	SPAAG	n.k.	n.k.	PRC	n.k.	n.k.	2011	Twin 35mm-armed tracked SPAAG
Jin-class (Type-094)	SSBN	5	n.k.	PRC	Huludao Shipyard	1985	2008	Commissioning status unclear; three vessels belived to be in service; at least one more awaiting commissioning
Shang II-class (Type-093 mod)	SSN	ε4	n.k.	PRC	Bohai Shipyard	n.k.	n.k.	First vessel launched early 2013
Yuan II-class (Type-039B)	SSK	+8	n.k.	PRC	Wuchang Shipyard/ Jiangnan Shipyard	n.k.	2011	Follow on to Type-039A *Yuan*-class
Luyang II-class (Type-052C)	DDGHM	6	n.k.	PRC	Jiangnan Shipyard	2002	2004	Final two vessels awaiting commissioning
Luyang III-class (Type-052D)	DDGHM	4	n.k.	PRC	Jiangnan Shipyard	n.k.	2014	First vessel on sea trials late 2013
Jiangkai II-class (Type-054A)	FFGHM	20	n.k.	PRC	Huangpu Shipyard/ Hudong Shipyard	2005	2008	15 commissioned by late 2013. Four more in build or awaiting commissioning
Jiangdao-class (Type-056)	FSG	20	n.k.	PRC	Huangpu Shipyard/ Hudong Shipyard/ Wuchang Shipyard/ Liaonan Shipyard	n.k.	2013	First vessel commissioned Feb 2013. Replacing *Hainan*-class PCCs

Table 6 **Selected Arms Procurements and Deliveries, Asia**

Designation	Type	Quantity	Contract Value (Current)	Supplier Country	Prime Contractor	Order Date	First Delivery Due	Notes
J-10A/S	FGA ac	n.k.	n.k.	PRC	AVIC (CAC)	n.k.	2004	In service with PLAAF and PLANAF. Improved J-10B variant currently in flight test
J-11B/BS	FGA ac	n.k.	n.k.	PRC	AVIC (SAC)	n.k.	2007	Upgraded J-11; now fitted with indigenous WS-10 engines. In service with PLAAF and PLANAF
J-15/J-15S	FGA ac	n.k.	n.k.	PRC	AVIC (SAC)	n.k.	2012	Test unit forming
Y-9	Tpt ac	n.k.	n.k.	PRC	AVIC (Shaanxi)	n.k.	2012	–
Z-10	Atk hel	n.k.	n.k.	PRC	Harbin	n.k.	2010	Deliveries underway
Mi-171E	Tpt hel	52	n.k.	RUS	Russian Helicopters (Mil)	2012	2012	Delivery to be complete in 2014
India (IND)								
Agni V	ICBM	n.k.	n.k.	IND	DRDO	n.k.	2012	In development. Est 5,000km range
K-15 *Sagarika*	SLBM	n.k.	n.k.	IND	Bharat Dynamics	1991	n.k.	Test firing programme underway. Est 700km range with 1 tonne payload
BrahMos Block II (Land Attack)	AShM/ LACM	n.k.	US$1.73bn	IND/RUS	Brahmos Aerospace	2010	n.k.	To equip additional two regiments
Nirbhay	ALCM	n.k.	n.k.	IND	DRDO	n.k.	n.k.	In development
T-90S *Bhishma*	MBT	1,893	n.k.	IND/RUS	Ordnance Factory Board/ UKBTM	2001	n.k.	–
Arjun II	MBT	124	n.k.	IND	CVRDE	2010	2014	Upgraded variant. Currently in trials. To be delivered by 2016.
Akash	SAM	180	n.k.	IND	DRDO	2009	2012	To equip eight air force AD sqn and two army regt. Delivery in progress
Medium-range SAM	SAM	18 units	US$1.4bn	ISR	IAI	2009	2016	For air force. Development and procurement contract for a medium-range version of the *Barak* naval AD system
Arihant-class	SSBN	5	n.k.	IND	DRDO	n.k.	2014	INS *Arihant* on sea trials 2013; expected ISD 2014
Scorpene-class	SSK	6	INR235.62bn	FRA	DCNS	2005	2016	Built under licence in IND. First delivery delayed again; now expected end-2016. Option for a further six SSK
Kiev-class (*Admiral Gorshkov*)	CV	1	US$2.5bn	RUS	Severnaya Verf Shipyard	1999	2014	Incl 16 MiG-29K. To be renamed INS *Vikramaditya*. Delivery delayed repeatedly. ISD now expected Jan 2014
Vikrant-class	CV	1	US$730m	IND	Cochin Shipyard	2001	2015	Formerly known as Air Defence Ship (ADS). Launched Aug 2013. Expected ISD has slipped to 2015. Second vessel of class anticipated
Improved *Shivalik*-class	DDGHM	7	INR450bn (US$9.24 bn)	IND	Mazagon Dock/ GRSE	2009	2017	Follow up to Project 17. Requires shipyard upgrade. Construction expected to begin in 2013
Kolkata-class	DDGHM	3	US$1.75bn	IND	Mazagon Dock	2000	2014	First-of-class launched 2006; second launched in 2009; third launched in 2010. First delivery delayed again; now expected in early 2014

Table 6 **Selected Arms Procurements and Deliveries, Asia**

Designation	Type	Quantity	Contract Value (Current)	Supplier Country	Prime Contractor	Order Date	First Delivery Due	Notes
Project-15B	DDGHM	4	US$6.5bn	IND	Mazagon Dock	2011	2017	Follow-on from *Kolkata*-class with increased stealth capabilites
Kamorta-class	FFGHM	4	INR70bn	IND	GRSE	2003	2013	ASW role. First-of-class expected to be commissioned by end-2013; second launched 2011; third launched Mar 2013. One more in build
Saryu-class	PSOH	4	n.k.	IND	Goa Shipyard	2006	2013	Two launched in 2009; third and fourth in 2010. First commissioned Jan 2013; second Oct 2013
Su-30MKI	FGA ac	272	n.k.	IND/RUS	UAC (Sukhoi)/ HAL	2000	2004	Includes at least 140 delivered in kit form and completed in IND under licence
MiG-29K *Fulcrum* D	FGA ac	29	US$1.5bn	RUS	UAC (MiG)	2010	2012	First delivery 2012
Tejas	FGA ac	20	INR20bn (US$445m)	IND	HAL	2005	2011	Limited series production. To be delivered in initial op config. Option for a further 20 in full op config
P-8I *Poseidon*	ASW ac	8	US$2.1bn	US	Boeing	2009	2013	To replace current Tupolev Tu-142M. First delivered May 2013. Two more due by end-2013
EMB-145	AEW&C ac	3	US$210m	BRZ	Embraer	2008	2014	Part of a INR18bn (US$400m) AEW&C project. Aircraft due to enter into service with the air force in 2014
C-17A *Globemaster* III	Tpt ac	10	US$4.1bn	US	Boeing	2011	2013	First four delivered Jun–Oct 2013. One more due in 2013; remaining five in 2014
C-130J-30 *Hercules*	Tpt ac	6	n.k.	US	Lockheed Martin	2013	n.k.	–
HJT-36 *Sitara*	Trg ac	85	n.k.	IND	HAL	2003	2014	12 limited series production and 73 more full series
Hawk Mk132 Advanced Jet Trainer	Trg ac	57	US$780m	IND	HAL	2010	2013	40 for air force and 17 for navy. First four delivered late 2013. Delivery to be complete by 2016
PC-7 *Turbo Trainer* Mk II	Trg ac	75	INR29bn	CHE	Pilatus	2012	2013	To replace HPT-32s. First delivered early 2013. Option for 37 more
Dhruv	MRH hel	159	n.k.	IND	HAL	2004	2004	132 reported delivered by late 2013
Rudra	MRH hel	76	n.k.	IND	HAL	2012	2013	Armed version of *Dhruv* hel. Was *Dhruv*-WSI. 60 for army and 16 for air force
Mi-17V-5 *Hip*	MRH hel	139	εINR144bn (US$2.7bn)	RUS	Russian Helicopters (Mil)	2008	2011	2008 and 2012 orders. Cost includes 12 Mi-17V-5s for the Ministry of Home Affairs.To replace current air force Mi-8/ Mi-17 fleet
Indonesia (IDN)								
Leopard 2	MBT	102	See notes	GER	Rheinmetall	2012	2013	Ex-Bundeswehr surplus. Part of US$290m deal including 42 *Marder* 1A3 AIFVs. First two delivered Sep 2013
BMP-3F	AIFV	37	US$100m	RUS	Kurgan-mashzavod	2012	2013	For marines; second order following delivery of 17 in Nov 2010

Table 6 **Selected Arms Procurements and Deliveries, Asia**

Designation	Type	Quantity	Contract Value (Current)	Supplier Country	Prime Contractor	Order Date	First Delivery Due	Notes
Marder 1A3	AIFV	42	See notes	GER	Rheinmetall	2012	2013	Ex-Bundeswehr surplus. Part of US$290m deal including 102 *Leopard* 2 MBTs. First two delivered Sep 2013
Anoa 6x6	APC (W)	31	Rp250bn	IDN	PT Pindad	2012	n.k.	–
CAESAR	Arty (155mm SP)	37	€108m	FRA	Nexter	2012	2014	–
Type-209/1200	SSK	3	US$1.1bn	ROK/IDN	DSME/PT PAL	2012	2015	First to be built in ROK; second to be partially assembled in IDN and third to be largely built in IDN
SIGMA 10514	FFGHM	2	n.k.	NLD	Damen Schelde Naval Shipbuilding	2012	2017	Option on second vessel exercised 2013. Delivery of both vessels expected 2017
KCR-60	PCGM	3	n.k.	IDN	PT PAL	2011	2013	Construction begun mid-2012. First delivery due Dec 2013
CN-235-220 MPA	MP ac	3	US$80m	IDN	PT Dirgantara	2009	2013	First delivered Oct 2013
C-295	Tpt ac	9	US$325m	Int'l	EADS (CASA)	2012	2012	First two ac delivered late 2012. Final ac due mid-2014
C-130H *Hercules*	Tpt ac	9	Free transfer	AUS	Government Surplus	2012	2013	AUS surplus aircraft. First delivery due Oct 2013
EMB-314 *Super Tucano*	Trg ac	8	US$142m	BRZ	Embraer	2012	2014	Second batch of eight. All ac to be delivered in 2014
T-50 *Golden Eagle*	Trg ac	16	US$400m	ROK	KAI	2011	2013	First two ac delivered Sep 2013
AH-64E *Apache Guardian*	Atk hel	8	US$500m	US	Boeing	2013	2014	First two due 2014
Japan (JPN)								
Type 10	MBT	68	Y55.1bn (US$679m)	JPN	MHI	2010	2011	–
Soryu-class	SSK	9	n.k.	JPN	KHI/MHI	2004	2009	Fifth vessel delivered Mar 2013
Izumo-class	CVH	2	US$1.3bn	JPN	IHI Marine United	2010	2015	First vessel launched Aug 2013; ISD expected 2015
Akizuki -class	DDGHM	4	Y84.8 bn (US$700m)	JPN	MHI	2007	2012	To replace the oldest 5 *Hatsuyuki*-class. Second vessel commissioned 2013; remaining two ISD expected 2014
Enoshima-class	MSO	3	n.k.	JPN	Universal Shipbuilding Corporation	2008	2012	Improved *Hirashima*-class. Second vessel commissioned 2013
Republic of Korea (ROK)								
K2	MBT	297	n.k.	ROK	Hyandai Rotem	2007	2014	Production delayed again due to continuing problems with engine and transmission
K21	AIFV	ε500	US$3.5 m per unit	ROK	Doosan Infracore	2008	2009	Delivery resumed after accident investigation
Son Won-il class	SSK	6	εUS$3bn	ROK	DSME	2008	2014	A second batch of six KSS-II (with AIP). First boat launched Aug 2013; expected ISD 2014
Incheon-class	FFGHM	6	KRW1.7bn (US$1.8bn)	ROK	Hyandai Heavy Industries	2006	2013	To replace current *Ulsan*-class FFG. First vessel commissioned Jan 2013. Fourth and fifth vessels contracted to STX Marine. Up to 15 vessels may be built

Table 6 **Selected Arms Procurements and Deliveries, Asia**

Designation	Type	Quantity	Contract Value (Current)	Supplier Country	Prime Contractor	Order Date	First Delivery Due	Notes
LST II	LPD	4	n.k.	ROK	Hanjin Heavy Industries	2011	2014	–
FA-50	FGA ac	60	εUS$1.6bn	ROK	KAI	2012	2012	To replace F-5E/F. Initial order for 20 plus additional ε40 ordered 2013
Falcon 2000LX	ELINT ac	2	n.k.	FRA	Dassault	2012	n.k.	To replace Hawker 800SIGs
C-130J-30 *Hercules*	Tpt ac	4	US$500m	US	Lockheed Martin	2011	2014	First ac in test; delivery scheduled for 2014
AH-64E *Apache Guardian*	Atk hel	36	KRW1.8tr (US$1.6bn)	US	Boeing	2013	2016	Deliveries to commence late 2016
AW159 *Wildcat*	MRH hel	8	€270m (US$358m)	ITA	Finmeccanica (Agusta Westland)	2013	2015	Part of US$560m contract including support and training
Surion	Tpt hel	up to 242	up to KRW8bn	ROK	KAI	2012	2013	24 to be delivered by end-2013
Malaysia (MYS)								
AV8 *Pars* 8x8	APC (W)	257	US$559m	TUR	FNSS	2010	2013	Letter of intent signed Apr 2010. To include 12 variants. Prototype delivered 2013
Second Generation Patrol Vessel (SGPV)	FF	6	MYR9bn (US$2.8bn)	MYS	Boustead Naval Shipyard	2011	2019	Licence-built DCNS *Gowind* 100m design. Delivery now expected to begin 2019
A400M *Atlas*	Tpt ac	4	n.k.	Int'l	EADS (Airbus)	2006	2016	First deliveries delayed until at least 2016
EC725 *Super Cougar*	Tpt hel	12	MYR1.6bn (US$500m)	Int'l	Eurocopter	2010	2012	Contract reinstated Apr 2010. Eight for air force, four for army. First two delivered Dec 2012
New Zealand (NZL)								
NH90 TTH	Tpt hel	9	NZ$771m (US$477m)	Int'l	NH Industries	2006	2011	Eight operational and one attrition airframe. Five delivered; two more due by end-2013. Final two hel due Apr 2014
Pakistan (PAK)								
Hatf 8 (*Ra'ad*)	ALCM	n.k.	n.k.	PAK	n.k.	n.k.	n.k.	In development. Successfully test fired
Al Khalid (MBT 2000)	MBT	400+	n.k.	PAK	Heavy Industries Taxila	1999	2001	–
Azmat-class	FSG	2	n.k.	PRC/PAK	Xinggang Shipyard/ KS&EW	2010	2012	First vessel built in PRC and commissioned May 2012. Second (PNS *Dehshat*) built in PAK and launched Aug 2012
JF-17 (FC-1)	FGA ac	150	n.k.	PAK/PRC	PAC	2006	2008	150 currently on order; ε40 Block 1 delivered by mid-2013. Block 2 in development
Singapore (SGP)								
Littoral Mission Vessel	PCO	8	n.k.	SGP	ST Engineering	2013	2016	To replace *Fearless*-class PCOs
M-346 *Master*	Trg ac	12	SGD543m (US$411m)	ITA/SGP	ST Aerospace	2010	2012	To be based at Cazaux in France. Five delivered by mid-2013

Table 6 **Selected Arms Procurements and Deliveries, Asia**

Designation	Type	Quantity	Contract Value (Current)	Supplier Country	Prime Contractor	Order Date	First Delivery Due	Notes
Sri Lanka (LKA)								
Mi-171	Tpt hel	12	n.k.	RUS	Russian Helicopters (Mil)	2012	2013	Part of order funded by US$300m ten year loan from Russia; order includes two Mi-171s for VIP use. First four delivered Jun 2013
Taiwan (ROC)								
CM-32 *Yunpao*	APC (W)	up to 650	n.k.	ROC	Ordnance Readiness Development Centre	2010	2011	To replace existing M113s. First veh delivered late 2011
Patriot PAC-3	AD	24	US$6bn	US	Raytheon	2009	2013	Four batteries. Three existing batteries also being upgraded from PAC-2 to PAC-3. Two more batteries requested in 2010
P-3C *Orion*	ASW ac	12	US$1.3bn	US	Lockheed Martin	2010	2013	Refurbished by Lockheed Martin. First delivered Sep 2013
AH-64E *Apache Guardian*	Atk hel	30	US$2.5bn	US	Boeing	2010	2013	First six delivered Nov 2013
Thailand (THA)								
T-84 *Oplot*	MBT	54	THB7bn (US$241m)	UKR	KMP	2011	2013	First five handed over Oct 2013. Delivery now due Dec 2013
BTR-3E1 8x8	AIFV	223	εUS$400m	UKR	KMDB	2007	2010	Initial order for 96 increased to 102. Subsequent order for 121 in 2011
DW3000H	FFGHM	1	KRW520bn (US$464m)	ROK	DSME	2013	2018	Order for second vessel anticipated. Based on KDX-1 derivative
AS550C3 *Fennec*	MRH hel	8	THB1.59bn	Int'l	Eurocopter	2011	2013	For army
EC725 *Super Cougar*	Tpt hel	4	εUS$130m	Int'l	Eurocopter	2012	n.k.	SAR configuration
Vietnam (VNM)								
VNREDSat-1	Sat	1	US$100m	FRA/VNM	EADS (Astrium)/ VAST	2009	2014	Remote sensing; launch delayed until 2014
Kilo-class	SSK	6	US$1.8bn	RUS	Admiralty Shipyards	2009	2013	First boat handed over Nov 2013; commissioning due early 2014
Gepard	FFGM	2	n.k.	RUS	Zelenodolsk Shipyard	2011	2016	Follow on order form original 2005 contract. To be delivered 2016 and 2017. Reportedly to be fitted for ASW
Su-30MK2	FGA ac	12	US$600m	RUS	UAC (Sukhoi)	2013	2014	_

Chapter Seven
Middle East and North Africa

SYRIA: IMPLICATIONS FOR REGIONAL ARMED FORCES

The Syrian civil war grew more complex during 2013. The main armed struggle, between the Assad regime and rebel forces, was compounded by conflict within rebel ranks, direct intervention by Hizbullah, growing numbers of foreign Sunni jihadi fighters, and regional and global tensions. By the end of the year, the death toll had approached 120,000 and one-third of the total population was either displaced internally or had sought refuge abroad. The use of chemical weapons by Assad forces in August provoked an international outcry and the threat of force by the US and France.

Regime regroups

Realising in late 2012 that much of the territory it had lost was either irretrievable or not worth the cost, the Assad regime set new, more realistic objectives and sought to adapt military strategy to shrinking resources and manpower. It focused on clearing a central corridor from Damascus to Homs, and on to Aleppo and then the coastal regions; and on securing its western flank bordering Lebanon, from which rebel fighters and their foreign allies operated. There, the regime established checkpoints manned by regular and auxiliary forces, and focused on isolating remaining rebel pockets and cutting supply routes. Securing this corridor meant sealing the border with Lebanon, primarily in cooperation with Hizbullah.

At the same time, the armed forces began a process of transformation, both organisationally and doctrinally, to fight an insurgency in a largely urban environment. Tactics alternated between ground operations and artillery-dominated assaults. Large units were broken down into smaller formations, old commanders were retired, and greater command responsibility was devolved to junior officers. Defections, desertions and casualties all degraded the regular forces, and morale suffered. However, both the number and rank of defectors fell from late 2012, reflecting a general assessment that Assad's chances of survival had improved, and concern among would-be deserters about their prospects amid an increasingly fragmented and radicalised rebellion.

Army strength remained about 50% of its pre-war size, with casualties being replenished by enlisting loyalist volunteers and low-strength brigades being disbanded or merged. It experienced difficulty in supplying besieged small bases, like Maarat al-Numan, and used helicopters to reach more important ones, like Taftanaz. Nevertheless the regime's elite units, notably the 4th Armoured Division, the Republican Guard, and its special forces (primarily, but not exclusively, deployed around the capital) maintained a high degree of readiness and operational capability. Salaries continued to be paid on time, and troops were still given leave. Despite rising fuel prices, the regime's mechanised and armoured assets seemed adequately supplied. While degraded, the regime's air force remained dominant in the skies.

The financial and material support provided by Iran remained considerable and arguably contributed to improving the regime's bleak prospects in late 2012. Early in the uprising, which began in March 2011, Iran had provided communications and Internet-monitoring equipment. Starting in 2012, Iran dispatched members of its Iranian Revolutionary Guards Corps (IRGC) to advise Syrian troops in urban and counter-insurgency warfare and, in some cases, to take part in the fighting. Iran also trained hundreds of Shia militiamen at the Amir Al-Momenin camp outside Tehran.

The Syrian regime also funded and deployed the National Defence Force (NDF), an array of militias locally recruited among Alawite and other minorities. Many Shabbiha units (mainly composed of Alawites) were folded into the NDF, though others, such as the Popular Front for the Liberation of Iskenderun/Syrian Resistance of Ali Kayali (operating in Latakia Province) maintained autonomy. Pro-regime militias often comprised young and middle-aged men, with military training acquired during conscription. Such units, costing less to field, were primarily used to hold territory, provide local intelligence and contribute to localised fighting; this 'militia-fication' process also served to tie the fate of loyalists even more to that of the regime.

The results of this transformation, underwritten in large part by Iran through funding, weapons shipments and military advice from the IRGC Quds Force, became apparent in February 2013: the regime was able to fend off a rebel build-up in the eastern and southern suburbs of Damascus. Over the spring, it recovered lost territory in and around the key city of Homs. Notably, the regime re-established control over the town of Qusayr, a major rebel logistical hub south of Homs and close to the Lebanese border, though it struggled in other parts of the country. In the eastern and southern suburbs of Damascus, the Yarmouk and Islam brigades, benefitting from mostly Saudi-supplied weaponry and joined by smaller units of defectors, posed a strong challenge. These suburbs, close to major airports and regime sites, eventually became the target of a large chemical-weapons (CW) attack on 21 August.

According to the UK's Joint Intelligence Committee, 14 previous CW attacks had been recorded since 2012. The 21 August attack was on a different scale, with 1,400 killed, including more than 400 children, as a result of exposure to the nerve agent sarin. In response, Western and Arab countries considered the use of force. The US announced its intention to conduct limited military strikes; the use of CW had been designated the previous year by President Barack Obama as a 'red line', the crossing of which would prompt American intervention in Syria. But, as noted in the IISS Strategic Comment *Syria Chemical Plan Faces Multiple Challenges*, 27 September 2013, 'advocates of the use of force to punish the Assad regime for its actions, such as Obama and French President François Hollande, failed to persuade Syria's ally Russia firstly that the Assad regime was behind the attack and secondly that military intervention would improve the situation'. After a Russian initiative persuaded Assad to give up his CW stockpile for destruction, a US–Russia framework agreement – to be overseen by inspectors from the Organisation for the Prohibition of Chemical Weapons (OPCW) – was endorsed by the United Nations. The destruction began on 6 October, with a tight nine-month deadline for completion. There was no indication that the regime had lost control of the units (the Scientific Research Centre, Unit 450, Brigades 104 and 155 of the 4th Division, and Air Force Intelligence) that maintain both the chemical agents and their delivery systems.

Hizbullah assumed a larger role in the war. Around 2,000 of its personnel spearheaded the attack against a mix of Syrian insurgents and foreign fighters in the battle for Qusayr. Ironically, the resort to Hizbullah highlighted the Syrian military's eroding capabilities. Hizbullah assumed other missions, including training local militias in Aleppo and securing now-endangered supply lines into Lebanon, but the difficulty of sustaining personnel outside Lebanon – and the priority given to securing areas close to the border both for propaganda and strategic reasons – shaped its operations.

Rebel forces

Among rebel forces, fragmentation and radicalisation continued. As many as 1,200 armed factions existed, but three umbrella groups conducted most of the fighting: the Supreme Military Council of the Free Syrian Army (FSA); the Syrian Islamic Front; and the Syrian Islamic Liberation Front. The first alliance, a prime interlocutor of Western governments, grouped factions close to Saudi Arabia, Qatar and Turkey; the latter two included Islamist and Salafist groups that played an increasingly pivotal role across the country. Two al-Qaeda-linked organisations, Jabhat al-Nusra (JN) and the Islamic State of Iraq and Syria (ISIS), took part in key battles, but also sought to impose strict Islamic rule on regions they seized. The presence of foreign fighters was primarily felt in the north, where they joined ISIS and JN, though tensions with local civilians, rebels and Kurdish militias grew in 2013.

Rebel factions continued to acquire weapons from a multitude of sources: Chinese-made FN-6 shoulder-launched surface-to-air missiles and Soviet-era 9M113 *Konkurs* (AT-5 *Spandrel*) anti-tank missiles have been observed. The provision of foreign-funded weaponry gave rebels a temporary advantage in the south, but the supplies were not sustained enough to allow for such advances to be consolidated. A US decision in June to supply limited quantities of weaponry to select rebel units suffered political and logistical delays, though the US ran military training programmes in Jordan for small numbers of vetted rebels.

Rebels controlled much of Syria's north and east. Though they seized much of the region of Idlib and the areas surrounding Aleppo, including the air bases of Minnigh and Taftanaz, they failed to liberate its western and southern neighbourhoods. As rebel groups competed to consolidate their authority over liberated areas, they also faced in the east often-superior Kurdish organisations, such as those of the Democratic Union Party. This resulted in a series of clashes with FSA and Islamist units. The Kurdish

Egypt: the military resumes power

Egypt's armed forces have for decades maintained extensive interests throughout the state economy (see p. 306). Since toppling King Farouk in 1952, and until the 2011 ouster of Hosni Mubarak and subsequent elections, they also provided the country's leaders. In July 2013, the military resumed this position, removing – in the wake of widespread protests against him – the elected president, Muhammad Morsi, and forming an interim government. Morsi had earlier in 2012 removed key military leaders and nullified constitutional rules put in place by the armed forces limiting the powers of the president. However, his actions did not challenge the military's core corporate interests.

Protests erupted against Morsi's overthrow, with the Muslim Brotherhood calling for a 'day of anger'. Violence continued in a number of cities in the following months, with hundreds reported killed and the courts eventually banning the 'activities', according to media reports, of the Muslim Brotherhood.

The armed forces are facing challenges on other fronts. In recent years, instability in the Sinai Peninsula has led to increasingly substantive troop deployments and military operations. With large parts of the Sinai now closed, military zones, troops and police face 'near-daily attacks', according to the BBC, and after 2011 the Sinai – which for years had seen low-level lawlessness and illicit activity – experienced a growing security vacuum, as well as a growth in Islamist activity. There was an increasing number of small-arms, rocket and bomb attacks on security forces in 2013, including one in September that targeted the interior minister. The armed forces have engaged in a series of operations against militants, with media reports indicating that around 22,000 personnel are deployed in the region.

At the same time, Egypt's relationship with the US has come under strain. Washington has in recent years been a key security partner, sending US$1.3bn in military assistance to Egypt every year. Defence ties extend to training and procurement, with the Egyptian armed forces operating a range of equipment of US origin, as well as maintaining factories co-producing M1A1 *Abrams* tanks.

This relationship came under strain after Morsi's ouster. As a result, a delivery of F-16s (part of an order for 20) was delayed and the biennial *Bright Star* exercise was cancelled. There was also a funding review, leading to 'a recalibration of assistance': as of October, while US assistance in non-military areas such as healthcare, as well as security assistance relating to counter-terrorism, would remain in place, it suspended significant military aid. A State Department spokeswoman said the US would 'continue to hold the delivery of certain large-scale military systems and cash assistance to the government pending credible progress toward an inclusive, democratically elected civilian government through free and fair elections'.

factions regularly prevailed, benefitting from superior training, organisation and weaponry. Arab rebel units suffered, by comparison, from internal disorganisation and disunity: FSA and Islamist groups rarely collaborated effectively.

Fear of regional escalation compelled neighbouring armed forces to increase their readiness and prepare contingency plans. To face missile and CW threats, Jordan, Israel and Turkey each upgraded their air- and missile-defence systems. Jordan received US support, including *Patriot* batteries and small numbers of F-16 fighter aircraft; Israel maintained high readiness on the Golan Heights; while NATO allies deployed *Patriot* batteries to Turkey. In July, a Russian shipment of *Bastion* (SSC-5 *Stooge*) anti-ship missiles to Latakia was reportedly attacked in an Israeli strike, damaging the regime's anti-ship capabilities. Israel was earlier reported to have conducted air strikes to destroy suspected missile shipments (understood to include M-600 rockets) in Damascus, amid concerns that Hizbullah would acquire more advanced weaponry. Border security was bolstered to manage refugee flows and to monitor cross-border trade and movements of jihadi fighters and government agents. While Jordan could still count on a capable intelligence service and armed forces, Lebanon's overstretched and unevenly capable military and security services struggled to deal with the pressure.

LIBYA

The security situation in Libya continued to deteriorate in 2013. A wave of attacks against diplomatic and political targets underscored the challenge from local, tribal, Islamist and radical militias. Stalled attempts to incorporate existing militias into national institutions underlined the weakness of a central government already facing a contentious transitional process.

Political, regional and tribal interests stood in the way of security reform. As part of its Demobilisation, Disarmament and Reintegration (DDR) plan, the government established a Warriors' Affairs Commission to facilitate the individual integration of militiamen into national-security forces, offer educational and vocational training, or find alternative public-sector jobs.

After 2011, in an attempt to organise existing militias under nominal state control before DDR, two umbrella organisations were formed: the Supreme Security Committee (SSC) under the interior ministry, and Libya Shield, under army command. The goal was to gradually transform these militias into paid auxiliary units for the armed forces, as a first step before integrating them not only into the national armed forces but also into a newly constituted National Guard. However, security reform remained more an aspiration than a plan: the strategic, jurisdictional and operational framework presented serious political and operational deficiencies. Osama al-Juwali, appointed defence minister in 2011, was himself the former head of the powerful Zintan Brigade.

Even while they ostensibly reported to the government, many militias retained some autonomy and territorial control. Incentives, whether political or material, failed to alter loyalties significantly. Militias saw the conventional armed forces as a remnant of the Gadhafi regime and were concerned that integration into the security forces based on individuals rather than groups was designed to weaken them. Meanwhile, salaries paid to members of the armed forces and police remained lower than those paid to SSC and Libya Shield by the interior and defence ministries. At the same time, the armed forces viewed with scepticism plans to integrate militiamen.

Distrust of central institutions and DDR processes was apparent in militia behaviour. Some mounted operations in Tripoli to influence the transitional process. This culminated in May 2013 with militias coercing the General National Congress into adopting a broad ban on the participation in government and political life of those who had worked for the former regime, including senior military and police officers. Various security incidents and the inability to restore government control led to the resignation of senior security officials. There was also a backlash against the militias. In June, civilians protested in Benghazi against Libya Shield, demanding the deployment of regular forces. The government proved unable to capitalise on popular rejection of these groups, and militias retained relative freedom of action, highlighted by the brief kidnap of Libya's prime minister in early October.

In parallel, the Libyan government announced the creation of a 20,000-strong general-purpose force (GPF), recruiting non-militia personnel to try to ensure loyalty and with a focus on small-unit training. It would also rely on foreign assistance; several NATO and EU countries (such as the US, the UK, Turkey and Italy) have offered to train troops, as well as specialist counter-terrorism, border-security and gendarmerie forces. But the planned force is proving controversial: some fear it could be used as a counterbalance to local militias or as a regime-protection force. Meanwhile, the regular Libyan army remains in place, though in a much reduced state; the future relationship between the GPF and the army remains unclear.

Basic mobility and protection remains a problem for official military forces, with much equipment either destroyed in 2011, under the control of militia forces or in poor repair. This was partially addressed in 2013 by the arrival of *Nimr* light armoured vehicles, the Italian gift of 20 *Puma* armoured personnel carriers, and reported shipments of three variants of HMMWV. It is unclear which units will field these vehicles, what kinds of facilities will support them, and what other assets are under government control.

IRAN: MISSILE DEVELOPMENTS

Since the mid-1990s, Iran has prioritised the acquisition and development of ballistic missiles capable of striking Israel. These efforts began with the purchase of the liquid-fuelled *Nodong* missile from North Korea. Dubbed the *Shahab*-3 by Iran, the missile underwent modifications, beginning around 2004, to extend its maximum range from approximately 900km to roughly 1,600km. The longer-range variant has taken a number of names since 2007, but is generally recognised as the *Ghadr* missile.

Iranian engineers leveraged a solid-propellant production infrastructure acquired from China for the manufacture of large artillery rockets, to develop a large, two-stage *Sajjil* missile, starting in the early 2000s. These efforts were rewarded in November 2008 when the *Sajjil* underwent its first successful flight test. Three additional development flights of the 2,000km-range *Sajjil* occurred over the following 13 months. But, inexplicably, the *Sajjil* has been flown only once since December 2009, suggesting that the programme has encountered technical difficulties that have stalled development. A half-dozen or more flight tests are needed before the missile reaches operational status. Iran could deploy the *Sajjil* prematurely, though its reliability and military utility would at best be questionable.

More recently, Tehran, apparently satisfied with its capacity to threaten Israel with its stockpile of *Ghadr* missiles, has shifted its development efforts to focus on improving its short-range missiles and defeating missile defences. The *Fateh*-110, a quasi-guided missile with a range of about 250km has reportedly undergone several enhancements to improve its accuracy. One version of the *Fateh*-110, renamed *Khalij Fars*, is said to be equipped with optical guidance sensors to enable maritime targeting, though the practical effect on the system's capability is unclear. Despite Iran's boasts of being able to hit targets with precision, evidence from military exercises in 2012 – where a mock airfield was targeted – indicated that the *Fateh*-110 was no more accurate than the *Scud*-B missile, which has a circular error probable of around 1km.

In May, Defence Minister Brigadier General Ahmad Vahidi unveiled about 30 transporter-erector-launch vehicles for Iran's medium-range missiles, which were later seen at a September military parade. It is unclear whether the Iranian military has trained 30 additional crews to operate the new launchers. However, the appearance of nearly three dozen medium-range missile launchers indicates that Iran might intend to overwhelm an adversary's defences by firing missiles in large salvos, an operational strategy that has been practised using short-range rockets and missiles during recent military drills.

Russia's decision not to transfer the S-300 air-defence system to Iran was a setback to Tehran's effort to defend its airspace. Air-defence forces have tried to compensate for the loss of the S-300 by a combination of leveraging Chinese-supplied radars, à la carte acquisition of other Russian systems and the modernisation of existing air-defence components. *Pantsir*-S1 (SA-22) and *Tor*-M1 (SA-15) provide point defence protection of Iran's nuclear facilities and other strategic sites. Components of the Russian 9K37 *Buk* (SA-11 or SA-17), possibly acquired by Syria, have been spotted in Iran. The operational status of the newly acquired missiles, dubbed *Ra'ad*, is unknown. Longer-range defences are provided by older Russian systems, including the S-200 (SA-5), S-75 (SA-2) and

GCC: cooperative defence and Iran

The Gulf Cooperation Council, established in 1981, is a consultative body that actively promotes social and economic initiatives aimed at strengthening cohesion across member states. Yet to date the GCC has failed to agree on a common strategic vision to guide the integration of military forces or establish a collective defence system capable of meeting the security requirements of member states. Divergent threat perceptions, parochial interests of individual states, issues of sovereignty, lingering fears of Saudi dominance, border disputes among member states, and a general distrust of Arab military competence have all contributed to the failure of the GCC to create the viable and coherent institutions needed to sustain a meaningful cooperative security system.

Iraq's invasion of Kuwait in August 1990 posed the greatest threat to the GCC. The alliance's failure to deter the invasion, and fears that it could not prevent or halt an Iraqi incursion into parts or all of Saudi Arabia, exposed the fragility of the GCC and its military component, the Peninsula Shield force. Recognising this weakness, member states sought to secure bilateral security agreements with external powers, including basing rights and lavish military-acquisition programmes, primarily with the United States, the UK and France.

Growing concern that the US and its Western partners could begin to withdraw from the region, combined with fears of a rising Iran and a worsening Sunni–Shia divide might compel individual states within the GCC to seek greater coordination and independence. Maritime security cooperation – including a number of combined task forces to combat piracy, prevent the proliferation of weapons of mass destruction, and secure freedom of navigation in and south of the Gulf – has been successful. However, US-led efforts to construct an integrated air- and missile-defence architecture in the Gulf have stalled, and show few signs of improving substantively, despite the threat posed by Iran's growing ballistic-missile capabilities.

Sovereignty issues, internecine rivalries and fragmented procurement policies have all stymied the development of a seamless defensive system across the GCC. The unwillingness of states to subordinate their individual interests to those of the alliance has also prevented the GCC from constructing and implementing a coherent strategy for arming the rebels in Syria. For the foreseeable future, the Gulf states will continue to rely on bilateral defence pacts with external powers for their security at the expense of forging a meaningful and coherent collective defence alliance.

modified *Hawk* units, renamed *Mersad*. Iran claims to have domestically developed an improved version of the S-300, known locally as *Bavar* 373, though the veracity of such claims is unclear. Also, it is not known how well Iran has integrated individual air-defence components, making assessments of overall effectiveness problematic.

DEFENCE ECONOMICS

Regional macroeconomics

Continued social and political instability in many Middle Eastern states dampened regional economic activity in 2013, with the International Monetary Fund (IMF) estimating that average growth rates in the region would halve to 4.6% in 2013, down from 9.3% in 2012. Sustained economic stagnation in one of the region's major trading partners, the eurozone, meant that export growth remained sluggish, while instability in several countries and uncertainty over the regional effects of the Syrian conflict weighed heavily on business confidence and foreign direct investment. Nonetheless, growth rates of 3–6% were achieved by most states in 2013, with only Iran and Syria experiencing economic contraction. By contrast, post-conflict reconstruction and development efforts in Libya and Iraq saw their economies grow by 20.2% and 9% respectively, though in the Libyan case this was from an admittedly low base. However, fiscal deficits and public debt rose in most states in 2013, as governments continued to respond to high levels of domestic unemployment by expanding the state sector and increasing food and energy subsidies.

Defence budget transparency

Detailed official defence budget documentation can be hard to obtain for regional states. This stems from factors such as perceived security requirements applying to defence-related information, varying degrees of legislative oversight over defence matters, as well as generally weak budgetary oversight mechanisms. Few states publish more than headline defence-spending figures, and some – such as Qatar and the United Arab Emirates – do not even release these. For example, while Qatar includes revenues derived from oil and petrochemical exports in its annual budgets, it generally holds off-budget its largest revenue streams derived from liquefied natural gas sales, which are used to fund non-transparent areas of expenditure, such as royal expenses, defence outlays and allocations to its sovereign wealth fund, the Qatar Investment Authority. Similarly, the UAE channels an undisclosed portion of its hydrocarbon revenues directly into its sovereign wealth funds, thereby bypassing the budgetary process.

Defence budget transparency has deteriorated since the start of the Arab Spring, as political

Map 6 **Middle East and North Africa Regional Defence Spending[1]**

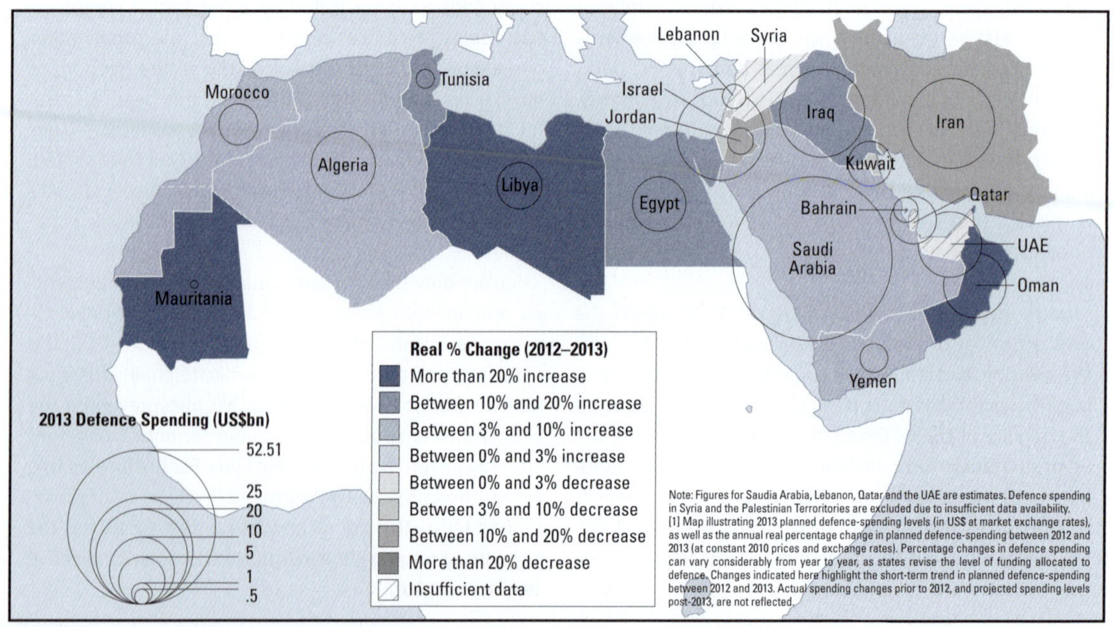

Note: Figures for Saudia Arabia, Lebanon, Qatar and the UAE are estimates. Defence spending in Syria and the Palestinian Terroritories are excluded due to insufficient data availability.
[1] Map illustrating 2013 planned defence-spending levels (in US$ at market exchange rates), as well as the annual real percentage change in planned defence-spending between 2012 and 2013 (at constant 2010 prices and exchange rates). Percentage changes in defence spending can vary considerably from year to year, as states revise the level of funding allocated to defence. Changes indicated here highlight the short-term trend in planned defence-spending between 2012 and 2013. Actual spending changes prior to 2012, and projected spending levels post-2013, are not reflected.

upheaval in Tunisia and Egypt, and civil war in Libya and Syria, have increased uncertainty over the true level of defence outlays in the region. One exception to this trend is Mauritania, which in late 2012 published an official defence budget for the first time since 2009. However, increasingly fraught civil–military relations in many countries have heightened mistrust and led to greater levels of secrecy and sensitivity over defence funding levels. In addition, the long-established and extensive involvement of military-owned businesses in civilian commercial sectors further obscures the origins and distribution of military finances (see textbox, p. 306). As a result, defence-spending levels and real-term spending trends for many states in the region have to be estimated (see Map 6), and in some cases – e.g. Syria and the Palestinian Territories – lack of data leads to exclusion from analysis entirely.

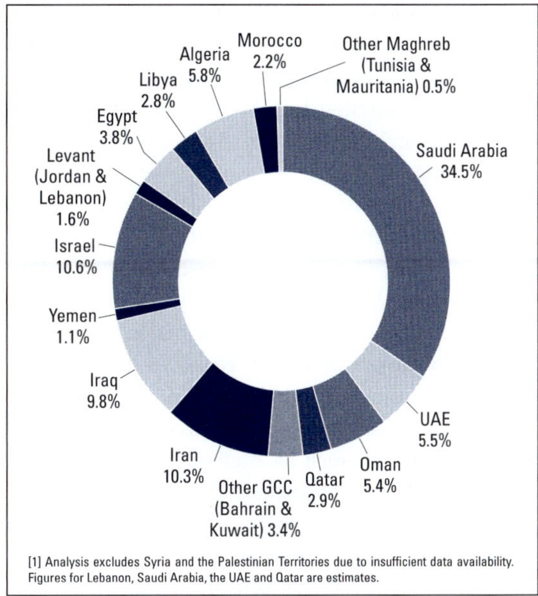

[1] Analysis excludes Syria and the Palestinian Territories due to insufficient data availability. Figures for Lebanon, Saudi Arabia, the UAE and Qatar are estimates.

Figure 15 **Estimated MENA Defence Expenditure 2013: Sub-Regional Breakdown**

Estimated defence-spending trends

Nominal defence spending in the region is estimated to have risen by 39.8% since 2010, from around US$123.5bn in 2010 to approximately US$172.7bn in 2013. After increases of 18.4% and 15.7% in 2011 and 2012 respectively, in 2013 nominal defence spending is estimated to have risen by just 2%. However, this was partly the result of a massive depreciation in the Iranian rial, which lost more than two-thirds of its value over the course of 2012 and 2013 as US and EU economic and financial sanctions implemented in those years precipitated a flight from the currency, serving to reduce the dollar value of Iran's military spending totals in 2013. (The nominal increase in regional spending would otherwise have been 9%, when calculated using 2012 rial–dollar exchange rates.) Discounting for exchange rate and inflationary effects, real defence spending growth in the region spiked in 2012 when it rose by an estimated 11.9%, before reducing to 4.9% in 2013. This latter figure is more in line with the medium-term regional trend: over the past four years the real compound growth rate is estimated at 4.9%. Overall, military spending in the region is progressively taking up a larger share of economic resources: regional defence spending as a proportion of GDP rose from 4.75% in 2010 to 5.15% in 2013.

In 2013, significant real increases in defence spending occurred in ten out of the 14 states for which reliable statistics were available. Particularly large increments were observed in Libya (63.1%), Oman (39%), Bahrain (36.7%) and Mauritania (26.8%), though again, in the Libyan case, this rise has to be set against the low levels seen over the previous two years. Real increases of between 10% and 15% occurred in Iraq (14%), Tunisia (10.7%) and Egypt (10.7%) and, lower down the scale, real increases below 10% were seen in Algeria (8.9%), Yemen (5.9%) and Morocco (4.1%). In many of these states, spending increases were due to major equipment-acquisition programmes. For example, Libya's transitional government pledged to allocate at least 10% of its budget towards defence, in order to address the country's extensive equipment recapitalisation requirements following regime change in 2011. Similarly, Mauritania raised equipment funding to counter Islamist activity in the Sahel.

By contrast, sizeable reductions occurred in Kuwait (-6%), Israel (-9.6%), Iran (-11.2%) and Jordan (-20%). The decline in Israel reflected parliamentary attempts to curb a widening budget deficit, though coming after a 13.9% spending hike in 2012 this perhaps indicates a return to Israel's historical defence-spending trajectory. In Jordan, 2013 defence outlays were squeezed due to the country's dire fiscal position. This stemmed in part from large deficit spending in 2012 on food and fuel subsidies after the start of the Arab Spring.

The large real reduction in Iranian outlays partly resulted from rampant inflation after domestic subsidies stopped in late 2010 and sanctions were implemented. Nonetheless, the 2013 reduction in defence outlays came after a real uplift in 2012 of 14.7%. This saw large nominal increases in budgetary allocations (in many cases exceeding 100%) for Iran's defence electronics industries, military academies, universities and research centres, as well as military construction activities.

Regional defence procurement

In many states, large increases in defence spending partly reflected higher procurement funding. There has been a rise in the number of major arms deals across the region in recent years, as post-conflict states such as Iraq seek to re-equip forces, Gulf states upgrade their combat capabilities, and states with ageing platforms, such as Algeria, seek to upgrade or replace existing inventories. As shown below, the aerospace sector has grown significantly over the last five years, with nearly half of the region's states buying air assets. Other priority acquisition areas have been patrol vessels, as well as armoured vehicles, with eight states (including Algeria, Iraq and Morocco) purchasing main battle tanks, armoured personnel carriers and/or armoured infantry fighting vehicles.

Notably large fighter aircraft orders have been placed by Saudi Arabia, as discussed in *The Military Balance 2013* (pp. 357, 369). Among other deals, Riyadh has signed several contracts to purchase or upgrade Eurofighter *Typhoon* and F-15SA *Strike Eagle* aircraft. Oman also selected the *Typhoon* (12 units) in December 2012. A number of states have acquired or are in the process of acquiring F-16C/Ds, including Iraq (36) and Morocco (17). Egypt was due to receive 20 in total, but deliveries of the remaining 12 were halted in August 2013 as a result of the domestic political situation. Other states interested in acquiring new airframes include the UAE (up to 25 F-16E/Fs), Israel (20 F-35As, for delivery commencing 2016), and Algeria (16 Su-30MKA). In terms of airlift and tankers, 26 C-130Js have since 2009 been ordered by or delivered to the UAE, Iraq, Oman, Qatar, Israel and Tunisia; meanwhile Egypt and Oman acquired 14 C-295 tactical transports between them – a third batch of six aircraft to Egypt was suspended in August 2013. Saudi Arabia and the UAE ordered the A330 multi-role tanker transport, with Kuwait opting for the KC-130J.

Since 2011, sales of – and negotiations for – air-defence systems to Gulf states have grown. In 2011, Saudi Arabia signed a US$1.7bn contract to upgrade its PAC-2 batteries to PAC-3 configuration, while the UAE ordered from the US two Terminal High-Altitude Area Defence (THAAD) batteries with 96 missiles for US$4.3bn. The UAE followed up with a US$1.135bn request for an additional 48 interceptors and nine launchers in November 2012, while Qatar also requested a US$6.5bn purchase of THAAD that month. Earlier, in July 2012, Kuwait requested additional PAC-3 missiles and other equipment for its existing *Patriot* systems. In May 2013, Oman signed a

Figure 16 **Middle East and North Africa: Selected Procurement & Upgrade Priorities Since 2009**[1]

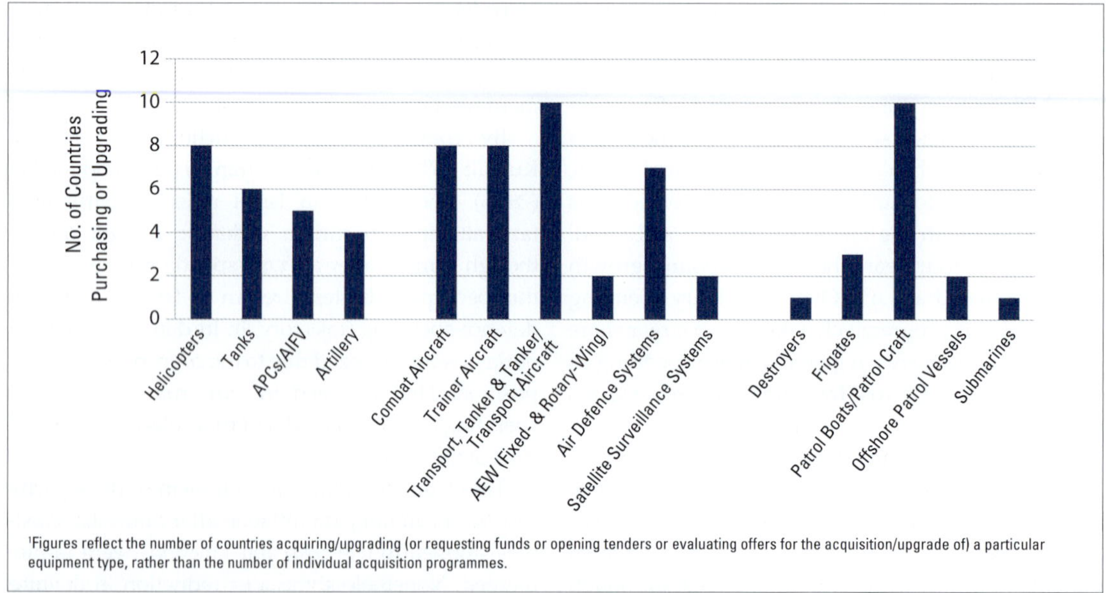

[1]Figures reflect the number of countries acquiring/upgrading (or requesting funds or opening tenders or evaluating offers for the acquisition/upgrade of) a particular equipment type, rather than the number of individual acquisition programmes.

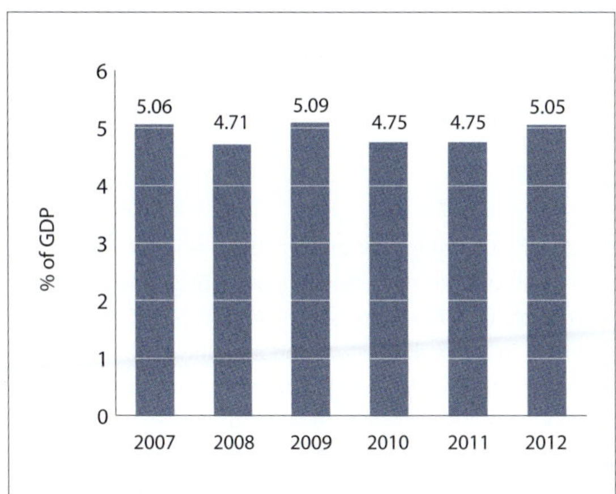

Figure 17 **Middle East and North Africa Regional Defence Expenditure** as % of GDP

US$2.1bn deal to purchase ground-based air-defence systems from Raytheon, while in July 2013 Qatar requested the sale of an AN/FPS-132 Block 5 early-warning radar. In September 2013, the UAE placed a US$2bn order for additional THAAD interceptors and related equipment. However, these purchases were not part of any coordinated multinational missile-defence effort within the Gulf (see textbox p. 301).

Naval platform acquisition has been particularly significant for North African states such as Algeria and Morocco; the UAE has also been active in this area. As shown in Figure 16, the most common types acquired have been patrol vessels, with ten countries acquiring, upgrading or taking delivery of these since 2009. Many of the larger contracts have featured European suppliers, particularly Italy (Fincantieri) and France (DCNS and STX France), while Germany has sold *Dolphin*-class submarines to Israel. Indigenous naval defence-industrial capacities remain nascent, although there have been significant advances in the UAE in the past few years.

Major arms-trade developments in 2012 and 2013

The past two years have seen record armaments deals signed with regional states. Notable sales include those by the US to Saudi Arabia, the UAE, Israel and Iraq. The largest-ever US foreign military sale to any country was signed with Saudi Arabia in January 2012. Worth more than US$60bn in full-life costs over 15–20 years, it is to provide 84 F-15SA combat aircraft, 190 helicopters, up to 12,000 missiles and 15,000 bombs, and to upgrade the existing Saudi air force fleet of 68 F-15S to the F-15SA configuration.

In April 2013, US Secretary of Defense Chuck Hagel confirmed that a complex US$10bn arms deal involving Israel, Saudi Arabia and the UAE had been agreed after a year of negotiations. This would see the supply of unspecified stand-off weapons to Saudi Arabia and the UAE for the first time, while simultaneously maintaining Israel's qualitative military edge within the region. As part of the package, Israel would receive an unconfirmed number of Bell-Boeing V-22 *Osprey* transport aircraft, Boeing KC-135 tankers, advanced fighter aircraft radars and anti-radiation missiles. Nearly half the value of the deal was said to consist in the UAE's planned F-16E/F purchase, which, if implemented, would augment its existing E/F fleet, in service since 2004.

Iraq has also been involved in major arms purchases in recent years, principally from the US but also Russia, as the country invests in systems to protect its airspace. Iraq ordered 36 F-16IQ Block 52s (for around US$6.6bn) in 2011 and 2012. In 2013, integrated air-defence systems were a priority. A request was submitted to the US in August for US$2.4bn-worth of *Stinger* missiles, truck-mounted launchers, *Sentinel* radars, and HAWK XXI missile systems. Meanwhile, the US was negotiating the sale of 50 M1135 *Stryker* nuclear, chemical and biological reconnaissance vehicles following the Iraqi defence ministry's announcement in June 2013 that it had detained an al-Qaeda cell at an advanced stage of manufacturing sarin and mustard-gas agents. In addition, the US and Iraq were working towards a five-year logistics contract to maintain thousands of US-made vehicles operated by the Iraqi armed forces but which were falling into disrepair due to problems with Iraq's logistics support structures.

In October 2012, Baghdad announced it would purchase 24 Aero Vodochody L-159 advanced trainers from the Czech Republic, although talks reportedly later stalled after an offer from Korean Aerospace Industries for its TA-50 *Golden Eagle*. In the same month, Iraq also finalised a US$4.2bn deal with Moscow for 30 Mi-28 attack helicopters and 42 *Pantsir* S-1 mobile air-defence systems. Although this deal was called into question in November 2012 owing to corruption allegations, by mid-2013 it appeared that it would go ahead.

Moscow is also attempting to resume arms supplies to the Libyan government, but faces significant competition from arms suppliers in the NATO countries that overthrew the Gadhafi regime. Meanwhile, the US, France and the UK continue to compete over the UAE's *Mirage* 2000 replacement contract, while in December 2012 the UK's BAE Systems won a contract to supply Eurofighter *Typhoon* aircraft to Oman and continued to negotiate with Saudi Arabia over additional *Typhoons*.

Military commercial activities

Many regional armed forces are active in the commercial sectors of domestic economies through extensive military-owned business networks and holding companies. In many cases, these activities developed during the Cold War as a hybrid form of socialism and state capitalism to promote national economic self-sufficiency in the production of goods and services. However, these organisations' ownership structures and internal accounts remain shrouded in secrecy, partly to preserve profits by restricting competition, but also to protect powerful stakeholders and vested interests from public scrutiny. In common with the general lack of defence-budget transparency in the region, there are few reliable statistics concerning the proportion of individual economies under the control of armed forces. Nevertheless, the examples of Egypt and Iran are illustrative.

In Egypt, military industries are estimated to comprise 5–40% of national output. In part, this reflects government actions after the 1979 peace treaty with Israel, when Cairo chose to reassign personnel to newly opened military factories and business ventures rather than demobilise them. More recently, military-economic ties have grown through privatisation programmes that allowed the officer class to purchase state assets at heavily discounted rates. As a result, the army is heavily involved in construction, including large infrastructure projects, as well as the manufacture of consumer durables. It is also active in the agricultural sector, developing from the early 1980s an extensive network of farms. Other military-owned entities reportedly provide banking, tourism and healthcare services. These activities are divided among a plethora of subsidiaries and overseen by vast holding companies, such as the National Service Products Organisation, the al-Nasr Company for Services and Maintenance, the Arab Organisation for Industrialisation, alongside others administered by the Ministry of Military Production. The armed forces consume some of this output, but surpluses and services are also sold to the public commercially, with profits being returned to the armed forces, without disclosure in the state budget. As a result, the armed forces command considerable resources, as exemplified by the army's ability to provide emergency funds to the Ministry of Finance in 2011.

Similarly, the Iranian Revolutionary Guard Corps (IRGC) is a major player in Iran's economy. According to some reports, the IRGC controls between one-third and two-thirds of domestic economic activity and as many as half of all government-owned companies. Though it is impossible to verify these proportions, the IRGC is heavily involved in Iran's domestic economy and civilian industries through expansive networks of holding companies, subsidiaries, affiliates and tax-exempt, government-subsidised foundations (*bonyads*), which themselves control vast swathes of the civilian economy. Bonyad Mostazafan, for instance, controls more than 170 subsidiaries.

Originally intended to bolster military finances during the Iran–Iraq war in the 1980s, the IRGC's commercial activities grew during the post-war reconstruction period under then-president Akbar Hashemi Rafsanjani in the 1990s. A notable example of this is the IRGC-owned Khatam al-Anbia, a massive conglomerate (possibly Iran's largest company) with more than 800 subsidiaries both within Iran and abroad. Since the early 1980s this has undertaken major infrastructure development and engineering projects including the construction of dams, highways, tunnels, water-supply systems and oil-pipeline networks. These commercial activities increased under Mahmoud Ahmadinejad from the mid-2000s onwards, as the company diversified from construction into the development and extraction of Iran's oil and gas reserves, and as foreign energy companies either slowed or abandoned their activities in Iran's segment of the South Pars gas fields in response to US pressure.

Overall, IRGC economic ventures span the breadth of Iran's economy, ranging from agriculture and banking to telecommunications, mining and petrochemicals. IRGC ownership over commercial assets has been augmented since 2006 by extensive privatisation of state assets to parastatal entities, which enabled the IRGC to incorporate some of these divestitures into its conglomerates. Current economic and financial sanctions have tended to reinforce the IRGC's role as a major conduit for much of Iran's international trade thanks to its experience with circumventing sanctions. Although newly elected President Hassan Rouhani in September 2013 seemed to commence a process of repositioning the IRGC away from Iran's economic sectors, saying that 'the IRGC is not a rival to the people and the private sector', it will be difficult to break up the vast networks of foundations, cooperatives and other entities that IRGC commanders have established, not least since the IRGC reports to the supreme leader rather than the president.

ALGERIA

Algerian defence- and security-policy priorities remain dominated by the effects of the seven-year-long civil war of the 1990s, as well as the continuing fight against internal and regional terrorist activity. The long-running dispute with Morocco over Western Sahara also remains a point of focus, and a likely prompt for capability procurements.

Though political initiatives led to an effective end to the bloody civil war by the early 2000s, low-level violence continued, perpetrated, among others, by the Salafist Group for Preaching and Combat, which in early 2007 changed its name to al-Qaeda in the Islamic Maghreb. This group has attacked security forces, civilians and wider infrastructure, and is involved in smuggling and terrorist training.

Persistent terrorist activity, manifesting itself most notably in the audacious attack in January 2013 at the Tiguentourine gas-production facility near In Amenas, means that counter-terrorism will remain a policy imperative. Other issues that dictate policy priorities, and the armed forces' structure and deployments, include: the conflict in Mali; instability in Libya; the continuing effects of the Arab Spring; and porous eastern and southern borders. Long-standing tensions with Morocco – centred on the dispute over Western Sahara – also shape Algeria's conventional defence policy and acquisitions.

Algeria was not immune to the effects of the Arab Spring. In response to demonstrations, 'the government's initial response was to lower food prices, invest in housing, distribute cash hand-outs and increase public-sector salaries' (IISS *Strategic Survey 2011*, p. 93). In February 2011, the regime lifted a 19-year-long state of emergency and the following month announced reforms to the armed forces' terms of service. All men over 30 were now exempt from conscription. The regime also reformed political laws, and in June 2012 a three-year retrospective decree was enacted enabling a 40% rise in military salaries. In November, the government re-evaluated military retirement, seen by some analysts – in tandem with the earlier pay rise – as designed to defuse resentment among personnel who may have looked unfavourably on pay rises in 2010 for police and customs officers. The 2014 elections have the potential to change the country's political make-up, but security priorities, coupled with the pivotal role the armed forces will probably retain post-election, make it unlikely there will be significant modification to the overall direction of Algeria's defence policies.

Recent initiatives

Policy priorities and concerns have motivated an increase in military spending, with a particular focus on structural modification and professionalisation, equipment modernisation and procurement, as well as the need to meet the cost of ongoing operations. To this end, Algeria has dispatched a number of personnel abroad on training and 'train the trainer' courses, and has deepened its defence-related academic outreach.

The counter-terrorism focus that emerged after 1992 consumed substantial resources and slowed defence modernisation. However, instability is now increasingly regional, and the nature of the threat has changed: adaptive adversaries are now engaged in terrorism, arms smuggling and drug trafficking. This has heightened awareness of the need for continuing investment not just in equipment but in people and training. It has also highlighted the stress that has been placed on civilian security forces in recent years, and on the requirement for conventional military forces to adapt operational capabilities both to the use of modern, sophisticated equipment and to new types of missions.

Improving flexibility, mobility and rapid deployment in counter-insurgency and anti-terrorism operations is a priority, particularly as the country's size and significant desert area pose logistical problems for internal security and border protection. These conditions have led Algeria to boost the technical sophistication of systems at its disposal, to become more pragmatic in its procurement policy, to try to diversify suppliers, and to develop its own defence-industrial capacity (see p. 310).

The importance of counter-terrorism has been reflected in a number of administrative reorganisations: in June 2011 the defence ministry took responsibility for all counter-terrorism forces, including auxiliary units formerly under the authority of the interior ministry. In July 2013, the defence ministry took over the fight against drug trafficking, which had been the responsibility of the Gendarmerie Nationale, as well as customs and border patrols. Though trafficking is of particular concern along border areas, the Algerian authorities are conscious that such activity – notably in the type of groups and contraband involved – can also have a direct impact on national security. These concerns are driving some recent procurement decisions, such as the interest in establishing an electronic border surveillance system. Nevertheless, many of the procurements under way owe as much to general military modernisation imperatives – such as recapitalising ageing fleets – as they do to broader regional security concerns.

Regional and border defence

Continuing terrorist incidents, as well as general border-security concerns related to smuggling and other illicit activity, led to the establishment of an active/passive border-surveillance system, backed up by enhanced aerial and ground surveillance. Meanwhile, in July 2012, the authorities created two new sub-regions. The first – within the Fourth Military Region (Ouargla) – contains the Hassi Messaoud oil field and was the site of a suicide attack on gendarmerie barracks in June 2012. The second is located in the vast southern area under the Sixth Military Region (Tamanrasset), the subject of an earlier attack on gendarmerie barracks in March 2012. In 2013, a Seventh Military Region was announced, headquartered in the southeastern city of Illizi. Plans include a larger deployment of forces on the southern and eastern borders (where tens of thousands of troops are already stationed) and the construction of new facilities and bases for the security forces near the oil and gas fields in and around Hassi Messaoud, Tin Fouyé Tabankort, In Amenas and Adrar.

Coming after the terrorist attack at the Tiguentourine gas facility, these initiatives are perhaps as reflective of the difficulties of rapidly deploying forces to remote areas as of the need for standing garrisons to maintain overwatch in remote areas. Additionally, the response to the Tiguentourine attack showed the tactical approach that the Algerian security forces can take to such incidents (in this case perhaps also a reflection of the facility's importance to national gas production), and displayed some of the lessons – both operational and political – that the security establishment has absorbed from its long-running counter-terrorist campaign.

The mountainous region of Djebel Chaambi, bordering Tunisia, is another security concern. Algerian authorities are working with the Tunisians to secure the shared border by establishing 20 military zones and deploying 60,000 troops (as at May 2013), in order to prevent arms smuggling and infiltration by terrorist groups. This is part of a joint security plan that includes the establishment of a military cooperation committee in charge of intelligence sharing. Additional resources have also been sent south: in 2012, along the southern border with Libya, Mali and Niger, Algeria established 30 new gendarmerie garrisons and a new air base. This air base will enable greater areas of the Sahel region bordering Algeria to be monitored, and allow for more rapid deployments of personnel and equipment.

Counter-terrorism and international cooperation

Since the turn of the century, closer ties with European and US military advisers, as well as training activity with the US, have somewhat diluted established Soviet-era military doctrine, certainly with regard to specialist counter-terrorism tasks. In broader military and security terms, Algeria has invested heavily in forensic sciences as part of its counter-terrorism agenda. It also joined NATO's Mediterranean Partnership in March 2000, and in 2006 it became an observer in *Operation Active Endeavour*. There is more consistent military engagement in the maritime domain. In 2013, the Algerian navy was one of the eight North African navies to take part in the 8th *Phoenix Express* exercise, designed to improve cooperation and to increase maritime safety and security in the Mediterranean. But these wider ties should not necessarily be taken as heralding a more activist regional role for Algeria or a desire to see more muscular external participation in regional security. (Ties with NATO waned after its 2011 intervention in Libya.)

A constitutional provision forbidding Algerian forces from taking part in military action outside its own territory remains in place, but defence contacts do take place. Just before the Mali crisis erupted, Algeria pledged to provide logistical support to Malian counter-terrorism army units stationed near their shared border and to train Malian troops and police officers at bases in Tamanrasset. However, Algeria had withdrawn its military advisers from Mali and halted military assistance at the end of 2011 when conflict was imminent.

Algeria hosts the African Union's African Centre for Study and Research into Terrorism and also hosts the Joint Chief of Staff Operational Military Committee, established in Tamanrasset in April 2010 in light of concerns over transnational threats in the Sahel. However, this body suffers from a lack of consensus, including disagreement about the absence of Morocco, Libya and Chad. Meanwhile, the Western Sahara dispute and the closure of the Moroccan–Algerian border since 1994 continue to act as a brake on security cooperation in North Africa.

Defence economics

The past few years have seen Algeria experience steady rates of economic growth, averaging 2.83% between 2010 and 2012. In 2013, the IMF expected overall growth to rise to 3.3%. Hydrocarbons have traditionally been the backbone of the economy, accounting for some 70% of public revenue and virtually all of the country's export earnings. However, long-running civil conflicts, an over-reliance on resource extraction and a heavily statist developmental model have meant that infrastructure in other areas (e.g. housing, healthcare, transport) and the private sector remain underdeveloped. Unemployment continues to be high (estimated by the IMF at 9.7% in 2012), although this has fallen steadily over the past decade (at an average rate of 1.55% per annum), down from a peak of 29.5% in 2000. In order to quell popular unrest in early 2011, the government undertook expansionary fiscal policies targeted at public-sector salary increments (many applied retrospectively), as well as the expansion of food subsidies and grant programmes. These led to a widening of government fiscal deficits, though high oil prices in recent years in excess of US$100 per barrel have helped finance these elevated levels of public expenditure. (Algeria's oil stabilisation fund is automatically allocated any oil revenues earned above a reference level of US$37 per barrel.) Abundant hard-currency export earnings also provided ample funding for the purchase of military equipment from abroad. (Algeria's foreign reserves stood at approximately US$150bn in 2011.)

Defence spending

Algeria's military spending has grown rapidly over the past decade, rising by a factor of five relative to nominal spending levels in 2002. Increases have been particularly large since 2010, nearly doubling in nominal terms from D421.9bn (US$5.67bn) in 2010 to D825.9bn (US$9.96bn) in 2013. In real terms, defence spending in 2013 was 46.3% higher than it was in 2010, equivalent to a compound annual growth rate of 10%.

These increases have in part been driven by increased outlays on equipment modernisation and procurement, as well as on operational expenditure for counter-terrorist activities. Increased funding has also been required to finance the expansion in the number of organisations under defence ministry authority (see p. 307). In addition, military pay levels were hiked by 40% in June 2012 and backdated for the preceding three years. This came after a 34% increase accorded to civil servants in the same year, as well as an increment for police and customs officials in 2011. As a result of these developments, defence has seen a steady rise in its share of total government budget allocations – from 14.8% in 2010 to 15.04% in 2011, 15.69% in 2012, and 19.04% in 2013. Defence was the single largest item of expenditure in the 2013 budget.

Defence-spending levels are likely to remain elevated in the medium-term. In the coming years, Algeria's procurement requirements are expected to include areas such as C4ISR (command, control, communications, computers, intelligence, surveillance and reconnaissance) systems and other surveillance equipment (certainly in relation to the proposed border-monitoring system), unmanned aerial vehicles, satellites, combat aircraft and attack helicopters, submarines, landing platform docks, and associated naval dockyard infrastructure, as well as armoured vehicles. An international tender for the procurement, development and implementation of the border surveillance system was issued in late 2012. Although the initial plan to upgrade surveillance in the Sahel dates back to 2006, the government has prioritised it following the conflict in Mali, continuing instability in Libya and the transnational activity of groups engaged in terrorism, smuggling and other forms of trafficking.

Defence procurement

Algeria has historically maintained strong procurement links with Russia, which remains its largest supplier, and some deliveries from the last major arms package – signed between the two states in 2006, and estimated at US$7.5bn – are still under way. It included 44 Su-30MKA combat aircraft, two Project-636 *Kilo*-class submarines, an estimated three S-300PMU-2 air-defence missile batteries and T-90S main battle tanks. Smaller orders were placed in subsequent years.

In recent years, Algeria has sought to diversify its supplier base as it modernises. A growing number of non-Russian defence companies have been engaged in commercial deals, including suppliers from Western Europe and the US. These include a C-130H upgrade programme from Lockheed Martin and a military air-traffic communications system – for operations in remote locations – from Harris Corporation. Procurements from other states include three MEKO A-200 frigates from Germany's ThyssenKrupp Marine Systems, and *Fuchs* armoured personnel carriers from Rheinmetall; Spain's Navantia is currently modernising two LSTs; and in 2011 the Algerian defence ministry ordered an LSD from Italy's Orizzonte Sistemi Navali, due for delivery in 2015. AgustaWestland is also supplying six *Super Lynx* anti-surface warfare helicopters. Algeria has additionally looked to non-traditional suppliers of defence equipment to fulfil its requirements, such as China and GCC states. In May 2012, a deal with the China Shipbuilding Trading Company for three C28A frigates was reportedly signed, while in August 2012 Algeria agreed to procure some 200 armoured vehicles (to be produced at a factory in Algeria) from Nimr Automotive, a subsidiary of UAE-based Tawazun Holding.

Defence-industrial organisation

Algeria has intensified efforts to develop its own defence-industrial base. Motivating factors include high levels of youth unemployment (estimated at around 21.5%) and a desire to diversify from a hydrocarbon-dependent economy towards the development of higher value-added, technology-intensive sectors. In 2010, President Abdelaziz Bouteflika announced the establishment of two state-owned companies to manufacture all-terrain vehicles and electronic systems for the army.

The ambition is to achieve a degree of defence-industrial capacity that allows local firms to meet domestic procurement requirements and generate earnings through exports. However, these remain long-term aspirations; at present Algeria's capabilities are mainly limited to licensed production of Russian and Chinese small arms and consumables. In addition, the army has developed its own maintenance facilities for military aircraft (both fixed- and rotary-wing) and armoured fighting vehicles, though the precise level of engineering activity at these facilities remains unclear.

It is hoped that opening the defence market to increased foreign participation will intensify competition in the sector, which remains predominantly state-owned, as well as inject foreign expertise, technologies and capital through the formation of partnerships and joint ventures. Assisting these objectives are Algeria's compulsory finance laws promulgated in 2009 and 2010, which require 51% Algerian ownership of any new foreign investment and which mandate that foreign bidders who win contracts have to invest in a joint venture with a local partner. However, the burdensome regulatory environment in Algeria, profit repatriation limits and restrictive exchange controls continue to serve as disincentives to foreign investment.

Nonetheless, since the passage of these laws, Algeria has entered into agreements with various foreign defence and investment companies, following high-level diplomatic visits by several countries. In March 2011, the UAE's Aabar Investments and German firms Daimler, Deutz AG and MTU Friedrichshafen agreed to establish three joint-venture companies to manufacture army vehicles and refurbish engines in Rouiba, a suburb of Algiers. In November 2011, a US$400m agreement to establish three small-arms and ammunition production factories was made with Serbian firm Yugoimport. Subsequently, in July 2012, the state-owned Groupement de la promotion de l'Industrie mécanique and the UAE's Tawazun Group announced the creation of a joint-stock company called Nimr-Algérie to build armoured vehicles in Khenchela. Meanwhile, as part of the deal for procurement of *Fuchs* armoured vehicles, Germany's Rheinmetall is looking at establishing a joint venture so that kits can be assembled locally. A further joint venture with the Chinese state ordnance manufacturer Norinco to assemble anti-tank mines in a factory located in Khemis-Miliana was being discussed as of mid-2013.

Algeria currently lacks a formal offset policy, although informal systems do exist. As part of the 2006 arms deal with Russia, it was agreed that US$4.7bn-worth of existing Algerian debt to the former USSR would be written off. But there are moves to formalise offset policy, and Algeria has held talks with some GCC countries to establish offset programmes. Unless such policies are tightly formulated and closely monitored, they run the risk of providing opportunities for financial impropriety, particularly as the awarding of defence contracts has in the past been marred by a lack of transparency. Oversight mechanisms are weak, and while the corruption-prevention law of 2006 calls for addressing off-budget expenditure, there is scant evidence that such expenditures are controlled.

Algeria ALG

Algerian Dinar D		2012	2013	2014
GDP	D	16.1tr	17.5tr	
	US$	208bn	211bn	
per capita	US$	5,694	5,683	
Growth	%	2.53	3.33	
Inflation	%	8.89	5.00	
Def bdgt	D	723bn	826bn	
	US$	9.32bn	9.96bn	
US$1=D		77.55	82.94	

Population 38,087,812

Age	0–14	15–19	20–24	25–29	30–64	65 plus
Male	14.4%	4.4%	4.9%	4.9%	19.8%	2.3%
Female	13.7%	4.2%	4.6%	4.7%	19.3%	2.8%

Capabilities

Algeria's armed and security forces have substantial counter-insurgency experience, although recent procurement has been focused on conventional weaponry for state-on-state contingencies. Policy priorities, and the armed forces' structure and deployments, have been affected by the conflict in Mali, instability in Libya and the continuing effects of the Arab Spring, as well as terrorist activity and porous eastern and southern borders. Having taken responsibility for counter-terrorism tasks in 2011, the MoD took over the fight against drug trafficking in 2013. Nonetheless, Algeria has been a leading proponent of combined training with regional powers, partially to build capacity in neighbouring states to combat al-Qaeda in the Islamic Maghreb. There is limited experience of tri-service joint operations, and few training exercises have focused on this. However, the armed forces have completed a small number of training courses abroad in order to raise their professionalism and 'train the trainer'. The MoD has also been increasing its foreign academic studies in order to bring intellectual rigour and depth to technical understanding and, as a consequence, procurement. The army maintains a division-sized rapid-reaction force, although the fact that two-thirds of the army is conscript-based reduces expertise and the ability to deploy quickly. Mobility is enhanced by a large fleet of light armoured vehicles and helicopters. A modest power-projection capability is also apparent in the transport and air tanker fleet, although limits to this capability were reflected in the decision to create new military regions and establish more garrisons in outlying areas. (See pp. 307–10.)

ACTIVE 130,000 (Army 110,000 Navy 6,000 Air 14,000) **Paramilitary 187,200**

Conscript liability 18 months, only in the army (6 months basic, 12 months wth regular army often involving civil projects)

RESERVE 150,000 (Army 150,000) to age 50

ORGANISATIONS BY SERVICE

Army 35,000; 75,000 conscript (total 110,000)

FORCES BY ROLE

6 Mil Regions; re-org into div structure on hold

MANOEUVRE

Armoured

2 (1st & 8th) armd div (3 tk regt; 1 mech regt, 1 arty gp)

1 indep armd bde

Mechanised

2 (12th & 40th) mech div (1 tk regt; 3 mech regt, 1 arty gp)

3 indep mech bde

Light

2 indep mot bde

Air Manoeuvre

1 AB div (4 para regt; 1 SF regt)

COMBAT SUPPORT

2 arty bn

7 AD bn

4 engr bn

EQUIPMENT BY TYPE

MBT 1,195: 300 T-90S; 325 T-72; 300 T-62; 270 T-54/T-55

RECCE 134: 44 AML-60; 26 BRDM-2; 64 BRDM-2M with 9M133 *Kornet* (AT-14 *Spriggan*)

AIFV 1,089: 100 BMP-3; 304 BMP-2M with 9M133 *Kornet* (AT-14 *Spriggan*); 685 BMP-1

APC 707

APC (W) 705: 250 BTR-60; 150 BTR-80; 150 OT-64; 55 M3 Panhard; 100 *Fahd*

PPV 2 *Marauder*

ARTY 1,037

SP 170: **122mm** 140 2S1; **152mm** 30 2S3

TOWED 393: **122mm** 345 160 D-30; 25 D-74; 100 M-1931/37; 60 M-30; **130mm** 10 M-46; **152mm** 20 ML-20 M-1937; **155mm** 18 Type-88 (PLL-01)

MRL 144: **122mm** 48 BM-21; **140mm** 48 BM-14/16; **240mm** 30 BM-24; **300mm** 18 9A52 *Smerch*

MOR 330: **82mm** 150 M-37; **120mm** 120 M-1943; **160mm** 60 M-1943

AT

MSL • MANPATS *Milan*; 9K133 *Kornet*-E (AT-14 *Spriggan*); 9K115-2 *Metis*-M1 (AT-13 *Saxhorn*-2); 9K11 (AT-3 *Sagger*); 9K111 (AT-4 *Spigot*); 9K113 (AT-5 *Spandrel*)

RCL 180: **107mm** 60 B-11; **82mm** 120 B-10

GUNS 250: **57mm** 160 ZIS-2 M-1943; **85mm** 80 D-44: **100mm** 10 T-12; (50 SU-100 SP in store)

AD

SAM 288+

SP 132+: ε48 9K33 *Osa* (SA-8 *Gecko*); ε20 9K31 *Strela*-1 (SA-9 *Gaskin*); *Pantsir*-S1 (SA-22 *Greyhound*)

MANPAD 200+: ε200 9K32 *Strela*-2 (SA-7A/B *Grail*)

GUNS ε830

SP ε225 ZSU-23-4

TOWED ε605: **14.5mm** 100: 60 ZPU-2; 40 ZPU-4 **23mm** 100 ZU-23 **37mm** ε150 M-1939 **57mm** 75 S-60 **85mm** 20 M-1939 *KS-12* **100mm** 150 KS-19 **130mm** 10 KS-30

Navy ε6,000

EQUIPMENT BY TYPE

SUBMARINES • TACTICAL • SSK 4:
- 2 *Kilo* (FSU *Paltus*) with 6 single 533mm TT with Test-71ME HWT/3M54 *Klub*-S (SS-N-27B) AShM
- 2 Improved *Kilo* (RUS *Varshavyanka*) with 6 single 533mm TT with Test-71ME HWT/3M54 *Klub*-S (SS-N-27B) AShM

PRINCIPAL SURFACE COMBATANTS 3

FRIGATES • FFM 3:
- 3 *Mourad Rais* (FSU *Koni*) with 2 twin 533mm TT, 2 RBU 6000 *Smerch* 2, 2 twin 76mm gun

PATROL AND COASTAL COMBATANTS 24

CORVETTES 6
- **FSGM** 3 *Rais Hamidou* (FSU *Nanuchka* II) with 2-4 quad lnchr with 3M24 *Uran* (SS-N-25 *Switchblade*) AShM, 1 twin lnchr with 9M33 *Osa*-M (SA-N-4 *Gecko*) SAM, 1 AK630 CIWS, 1 twin 57mm gun
- **FSG** 3 *Djebel Chenona* with 2 twin lnchr with C-802 (CSS-N-8 *Saccade*) AShM, 1 AK630 CIWS, 1 76mm gun

PBFG 9 *Osa* II (3†) with 4 single lnchr with P-15 *Termit* (SS-N-2B *Styx*) AShM

PB 9 *Kebir* with 1 76mm gun

AMPHIBIOUS • LS 3:
- **LSM** 1 *Polnochny* B with 1 twin AK230 CIWS (capacity 6 MBT; 180 troops)
- **LST** 2 *Kalaat beni Hammad* (capacity 7 tanks; 240 troops) with 1 med hel landing platform

LOGISTICS AND SUPPORT 11
- **AGS** 1 *El Idrissi*
- **AX** 1 *Daxin* with 2 twin AK230 CIWS, 1 76mm gun
- **YGS** 2 *Ras Tara*
- **YPT** 1 *Poluchat I* (used for SAR)
- **YTB** 6: 1 *El Chadid*; 1 *Kader*; 4 *Mazafran*

Naval Aviation

EQUIPMENT BY TYPE

HELICOPTERS
- **SAR** 10: 6 AW101 SAR; 4 *Super Lynx* Mk130

Coast Guard ε500

PATROL AND COASTAL COMBATANTS 55
- **PBF** 6 *Baglietto* 20
- **PB** 49: 6 *Baglietto Mangusta*; 12 *Jebel Antar*; 21 *Deneb*; 4 *El Mounkid*; 6 *Kebir* with 1 76mm gun

LOGISTICS AND SUPPORT 8
- **ARL** 1 *El Mourafek*
- **AXL** 7 *El Mouderrib* (PRC *Chui-E*) (2 in reserve†)

Air Force 14,000

Flying hours 150 hrs/year

FORCES BY ROLE

FIGHTER
- 1 sqn with MiG-25PDS/RU *Foxbat*
- 4 sqn with MiG-29C/UB *Fulcrum*

FIGHTER/GROUND ATTACK
- 2 sqn with Su-24M/MK *Fencer* D
- 3 sqn with Su-30MKA *Flanker*

ELINT
- 1 sqn with Beech 1900D

MARITIME PATROL
- 2 sqn with Beech 200T/300 *King Air*

ISR
- 1 sqn with Su-24MR *Fencer* E*; MiG-25RBSh *Foxbat* D*

TANKER
- 1 sqn with Il-78 *Midas*

TRANSPORT
- 1 sqn with C-130H/H-30 *Hercules*; L-100-30
- 1 sqn with C-295M
- 1 sqn with Gulfstream IV-SP; Gulfstream V
- 1 sqn with Il-76MD/TD *Candid*

TRAINING
- 2 sqn with Z-142
- 1 sqn with Yak-130 *Mitten*
- 2 sqn with L-39C/ZA *Albatros*
- 1 hel sqn with PZL Mi-2 *Hoplite*

ATTACK HELICOPTER
- 3 sqn with Mi-24 *Hind*

TRANSPORT HELICOPTER
- 1 sqn with AS355 *Ecureuil*
- 5 sqn with Mi-8 *Hip*; Mi-17 *Hip* H
- 1 sqn with Ka-27PS *Helix* D; Ka-32T *Helix*

AIR DEFENCE
- 3 ADA bde
- 3 SAM regt with S-75 *Dvina* (SA-2 *Guideline*)/S-125 *Neva* (SA-3 *Goa*)/2K12 *Kub* (SA-6 *Gainful*); S-300PMU2 (SA-20 *Gargoyle*)

EQUIPMENT BY TYPE

AIRCRAFT 121 combat capable
- **FTR** 35: 12 MiG-25 *Foxbat*; 23 MiG-29C/UB *Fulcrum*
- **FGA** 78: 44 Su-30MKA; 34 Su-24M/MK *Fencer* D
- **ISR** 8: 4 MiG-25RBSh *Foxbat* D*; 4 Su-24MR *Fencer* E*
- **TKR** 6 Il-78 *Midas*
- **TPT** 68 **Heavy** 12: 3 Il-76MD *Candid* B; 9 Il-76TD *Candid*; **Medium** 18: 9 C-130H *Hercules*; 7 C-130H-30 *Hercules*; 2 L-100-30; **Light** 32: 3 Beech C90B *King Air*; 5 Beech 200T *King Air*; 6 Beech 300 *King Air*; 12 Beech 1900D (electronic surv); 5 C-295M; 1 F-27 *Friendship*; **PAX** 6: 1 A340; 4 Gulfstream IV-SP; 1 Gulfstream V
- **TRG** 99: 36 L-39ZA *Albatros*; 7 L-39C *Albatros*; 16 Yak-130 *Mitten*; 40 Z-142

HELICOPTERS
- **ATK** 33 Mi-24 *Hind*
- **SAR** 3 Ka-27PS *Helix* D
- **MRH** 3 Bell 412EP
- **MRH/TPT** 75 Mi-8 *Hip* (med tpt)/Mi-17 *Hip* H
- **TPT** 40 **Medium** 4 Ka-32T *Helix*; **Light** 36: 8 AS355 *Ecureuil*; 28 PZL Mi-2 *Hoplite*

UAV • ISR • Medium *Seeker* II

AD
- **SAM** S-75 *Dvina* (SA-2 *Guideline*); S-125 *Pechora*-M (SA-3 *Goa*); 2K12 *Kvadrat* (SA-6 *Gainful*) SP; S-300PMU2 (SA-20 *Gargoyle*)
- **GUNS** 725 **100mm/130mm/85mm**

MSL
- **ASM** Kh-25 (AS-10 *Karen*); Kh-29 (AS-14 *Kedge*); Kh-23 (AS-7 *Kerry*); Kh-31P/A (AS-17A/B *Krypton*); Kh-59ME (AS-18 *Kazoo*): ZT-35 *Ingwe*

ARM Kh-25MP (AS-12 *Kegler*)
AAM • IR R-3 (AA-2 *Atoll*)‡; R-60 (AA-8 *Aphid*); R-73 (AA-11 *Archer*); **IR/SARH** R-40/46 (AA-6 *Acrid*); R-23/24 (AA-7 *Apex*); R-27 (AA-10 *Alamo*); **ARH** R-77 (AA-12 *Adder*)

Paramilitary ε187,200

Gendarmerie 20,000

Ministry of Defence control; 6 regions

EQUIPMENT BY TYPE
RECCE AML-60
APC (W) 210: 100 *Fahd*; 110 M-3 Panhard
HELICOPTERS • TPT • Light Some PZL Mi-2 *Hoplite*

National Security Forces 16,000

Directorate of National Security. Small arms

Republican Guard 1,200

EQUIPMENT BY TYPE
RECCE AML-60
APC (T) M-3

Legitimate Defence Groups ε150,000

Self-defence militia, communal guards (60,000)

DEPLOYMENT

DEMOCRATIC REPUBLIC OF THE CONGO
UN • MONUSCO 5 obs

Bahrain BHR

Bahraini Dinar D		2012	2013	2014
GDP	D	10.2bn	10.6bn	
	US$	27bn	28.1bn	
per capita	US$	23,477	23,930	
Growth	%	3.85	4.15	
Inflation	%	1.20	2.55	
Def bdgt [a]	D	383m	524m	566m
	US$	1.02bn	1.39bn	
FMA (US)	US$	10m	10m	10m
US$1=D		0.38	0.38	

[a] Includes expenditure on National Guard in 2012. Excludes funds allocated to the Ministry of the Interior.

Population 1,281,332

Ethnic groups: Nationals 64%; Asian 13%; other Arab 10%; Iranian 8%; European 1%

Age	0–14	15–19	20–24	25–29	30–64	65 plus
Male	10.2%	3.9%	5.0%	6.7%	33.6%	1.3%
Female	9.8%	3.4%	3.6%	4.0%	17.1%	1.4%

Capabilities

Bahrain retains moderately well-trained and -equipped forces, but their small size limits their effectiveness. While in general focused on the possibility of state-to-state conflict, their role in internal security has become more apparent since 2011. The armed forces' primary role is defence of the island from an amphibious invasion and/or aerial assault from Iran. Bahrain could mount a sturdy defence though it would eventually be overwhelmed by concerted operations. The kingdom therefore relies on the security umbrella offered by the Gulf Cooperation Council and the deterrent effect provided by the presence of the US through Fifth Fleet/NAVCENT. Bahrain retains close alliances with the US and the UK, and participates in GCC military exercises. The GCC's defence obligations were invoked in 2011, reflecting the Bahraini armed forces' inability to quell protests. Following a series of crackdowns on protesters, a state of emergency was declared and Saudi, Qatari and Emirati personnel were deployed as part of the GCC's Peninsula Shield force. Washington suspended arms transfers in the wake of this security crackdown, though the suspension was partially lifted in May 2012. The deployment was a tacit admission by Manama that its security forces needed assistance in the internal security role and suggested greater training and improved rules of engagement might be required for similar future operations. The primary procurement priority in the short term is likely to be replacement of the F-5E/F *Tiger* II, delivered in the 1980s; the Eurofighter *Typhoon* is a possible candidate.

ACTIVE 8,200 (Army 6,000 Navy 700 Air 1,500)
Paramilitary 11,260

ORGANISATIONS BY SERVICE

Army 6,000

FORCES BY ROLE
SPECIAL FORCES
1 SF bn
MANOEUVRE
Armoured
1 armd bde(–) (1 recce bn, 2 armd bn)
Mechanised
1 inf bde (2 mech bn, 1 mot bn)
Light
1 (Amiri) gd bn
COMBAT SUPPORT
1 arty bde (1 hvy arty bty, 2 med arty bty, 1 lt arty bty, 1 MRL bty)
1 AD bn (1 ADA bty, 2 SAM bty)
1 engr coy
COMBAT SERVICE SUPPORT
1 log coy
1 tpt coy
1 med coy

EQUIPMENT BY TYPE
MBT 180 M60A3
RECCE 30: 22 AML-90; 8 S52 *Shorland*; (8 *Ferret* & 8 *Saladin* in store)
AIFV 25 YPR-765 (with 25mm)
APC 375
APC (T) 200 M113A2
APC (W) 120: 10 AT105 *Saxon*; 110 M3 Panhard
PPV 55: 49 *Cobra*; 6 *Nimer*-1

Middle East and North Africa

ARTY 151
SP 82: **155mm** 20 M109A5; **203mm** 62 M110A2
TOWED 36: **105mm** 8 L118 Light Gun; **155mm** 28 M198
MRL 227mm 9 M270 MLRS (with 30 ATACMS)
MOR 24: **SP 120mm** 12 M113A2; **81mm** 12 L16
AT • MSL • MANPATS 75: 60 *Javelin*; 15 BGM-71A TOW
RCL 31: **106mm** 25 M40A1; **120mm** 6 MOBAT
AD • SAM 91
SP 7 *Crotale*
TOWED 6 MIM-23B I-HAWK
MANPAD 78: 18 FIM-92A *Stinger*; 60 RBS-70
GUNS 24: **35mm** 12 Oerlikon; **40mm** 12 L/70
ARV 53 *Fahd* 240

Navy 700

EQUIPMENT BY TYPE
PRINCIPAL SURFACE COMBATANTS 1
FRIGATES • FFGHM 1 *Sabha* (US *Oliver Hazard Perry*) with 1 Mk13 GMLS with SM-1MR SAM/RGM-84C *Harpoon* AShM, 2 triple 324mm Mk32 ASTT with Mk46 LWT, 1 *Phalanx* Block 1B CIWS, 1 76mm gun, (capacity 1 Bo-105 hel)
PATROL AND COASTAL COMBATANTS 12
CORVETTES • FSG 2 *Al Manama* (GER Lurssen 62m) with 2 twin lnchr with MM-40 *Exocet* AShM, 1 76mm gun, 1 hel landing platform
PCFG 4 *Ahmed el Fateh* (GER Lurssen 45m) with 2 twin lnchr with MM-40 *Exocet* AShM, 1 76mm gun
PB 4: 2 *Al Jarim* (US *Swift* FPB-20); 2 *Al Riffa* (GER Lurssen 38m)
PBF 2 Mk V SOC
AMPHIBIOUS • LANDING CRAFT 9
LCU 7: 1 *Loadmaster*; 4 *Mashtan*; 2 ADSB 42m
LCVP 2 *Sea Keeper*
LOGISTICS AND SUPPORT 2
YFL 1 *Tighatlib*
YFU 1 *Ajeera*

Naval Aviation

EQUIPMENT BY TYPE
HELICOPTERS • TPT • Light 2 Bo-105

Air Force 1,500

FORCES BY ROLE
FIGHTER
2 sqn with F-16C/D *Fighting Falcon*
FIGHTER/GROUND ATTACK
1 sqn with F-5E/F *Tiger* II
TRANSPORT
1 (Royal) flt with B-727; B-747; BAe-146; Gulfstream II; Gulfstream IV; Gulfstream 450; Gulfstream 550; S-92A
TRAINING
1 sqn with *Hawk* Mk129*
1 sqn with T-67M *Firefly*
ATTACK HELICOPTER
2 sqn with AH-1E/F *Cobra*; TAH-1P *Cobra*
TRANSPORT HELICOPTER
1 sqn with Bell 212 (AB-212)
1 sqn with UH-60M *Black Hawk*
1 (VIP) sqn with Bo-105; S-70A *Black Hawk*; UH-60L *Black Hawk*
EQUIPMENT BY TYPE
AIRCRAFT 39 combat capable
FTR 12: 8 F-5E *Tiger* II; 4 F-5F *Tiger* II
FGA 21: 17 F-16C *Fighting Falcon*; 4 F-16D *Fighting Falcon*
TPT • PAX 10: 1 B-727; 2 B-747; 1 Gulfstream II; 1 Gulfstream IV; 1 Gulfstream 450; 1 Gulfstream 550; 3 BAe-146
TRG 9: 6 *Hawk* Mk129*; 3 T-67M *Firefly*
HELICOPTERS
ATK 28: 16 AH-1E *Cobra*; 12 AH-1F *Cobra*
TPT 27 **Medium** 13: 3 S-70A *Black Hawk*; 1 S-92A (VIP); 1 UH-60L *Black Hawk*; 8 UH-60M *Black Hawk*; **Light** 14: 11 Bell 212 (AB-212); 3 Bo-105
TRG 6 TAH-1P *Cobra*
MSL
ASM AGM-65D/G *Maverick*
AAM • IR AIM-9P *Sidewinder*; **SARH** AIM-7 *Sparrow*; **ARH** AIM-120 AMRAAM
AT • MSL some TOW

Paramilitary ε11,260

Police 9,000

Ministry of Interior
EQUIPMENT BY TYPE
RECCE *Cobra*; *Shorland*
APC (W) Otokar ISV
HELICOPTERS
MRH 2 Bell 412 *Twin Huey*
ISR 2 Hughes 500
TPT • Light 1 Bo-105

National Guard ε2,000

FORCES BY ROLE
MANOEUVRE
Other
3 paramilitary bn
EQUIPMENT BY TYPE
APC (W) *Arma* 6x6

Coast Guard ε260

Ministry of Interior
PATROL AND COASTAL COMBATANTS 50
PBF 21: 4 *Jaris*; 6 *Saham*; 6 *Fajr*; 5 *Jarach*
PB 29: 6 *Haris*; 1 *Al Muharraq*; 10 *Deraa* (of which 4 *Halmatic* 20, 2 *Souter* 20, 4 Rodman 20); 10 *Saif* (of which 4 *Fairey Sword*, 6 *Halmatic* 160); 2 *Hawar*
AMPHIBIOUS • LANDING CRAFT • LCU 1 *Loadmaster* II
LOGISTICS AND SUPPORT • YAG 1 *Safra*

DEPLOYMENT

AFGHANISTAN
NATO • ISAF 95

FOREIGN FORCES

Saudi Arabia GCC (SANG): Peninsula Shield ε1,000

United Kingdom Air Force 1 BAe-125 CC-3; 1 BAe-146 MKII

United States US Central Commmand: 2,100; 1 HQ (5th Fleet)

Egypt EGY

Egyptian Pound E£		2012	2013	2014
GDP	E£	1.54tr	1.72tr	
	US$	257bn	265bn	
per capita	US$	3,112	3,146	
Growth	%	2.22	2.01	
Inflation	%	8.60	8.24	
Def exp	E£	27.5bn		
	US$	4.58bn		
Def bdgt	E£	27.5bn	34.3bn	38bn
	US$	4.58bn	5.28bn	
FMA (US)	US$	1.3bn	1.3bn	1.3bn
US$1=E£		6.01	6.50	

Population 85,294,388

Age	0–14	15–19	20–24	25–29	30–64	65 plus
Male	16.5%	4.7%	4.5%	4.7%	18.0%	2.2%
Female	15.8%	4.5%	4.3%	4.4%	17.8%	2.6%

Capabilities

Egypt's armed forces resumed power in July 2013, after ousting President Muhammad Morsi in the wake of protests against his rule. After the overthrow, violence erupted and continued in a number of cities throughout the following months, with hundreds reported killed and the courts eventually in September banning the 'activities', according to media reports, of the Muslim Brotherhood. The armed forces are facing other challenges: in recent years instability in Sinai has led to a growing security vacuum, greater Islamist activity and increasingly substantive troop deployments and military operations. Egypt's relationship with the US came under strain after Morsi's exit, and a delivery of F-16s (part of an order for 20) was delayed and the *Bright Star* exercise cancelled. In late October, it was announced that the delivery of several large-scale military systems, and cash assistance would be suspended. Before this, Cairo had received US$1.3bn annually in US military aid, and had long been upgrading its inventories with US systems. That Cairo might widen its list of suppliers is not inconceivable in some capability areas, and there have been some reports of Russian contact. However, since 1980, US equipment has increasingly replaced ageing Soviet-era kit. While training will be at a high standard for many within the military, it is harder to judge effectiveness across the entire force, given the level of conscription and the tasks that some conscripts are reported to undertake, in relation to the Egyptian armed forces' extensive domestic business and industrial interests. (See p. 299.)

ACTIVE 438,500 (Army 310,000 Navy 18,500 Air 30,000 Air Defence Command 80,000) **Paramilitary 397,000**

Conscription liability 12 months–3 years (followed by refresher training over a period of up to 9 years)

RESERVE 479,000 (Army 375,000 Navy 14,000 Air 20,000 Air Defence 70,000)

ORGANISATIONS BY SERVICE

Army 90,000–120,000; 190,000–220,000 conscript (total 310,000)

FORCES BY ROLE

SPECIAL FORCES
- 5 cdo gp
- 1 counter-terrorist unit

MANOEUVRE

Armoured
- 4 armd div (2 armd bde, 1 mech bde, 1 arty bde)
- 4 indep armd bde
- 1 Republican Guard bde

Mechanised
- 8 mech div (1 armd bde, 2 mech bde, 1 arty bde)
- 4 indep mech bde

Light
- 1 inf div
- 2 indep inf bde

Air Manoeuvre
- 2 air mob bde
- 1 para bde

COMBAT SUPPORT
- 15 arty bde
- 1 SSM bde with FROG-7
- 1 SSM bde with *Scud*-B
- 6 engr bde (3 engr bn)
- 2 spec ops engr bn
- 6 salvage engr bn
- 24 MP bn
- 18 sigs bn

COMBAT SERVICE SUPPORT
- 36 log bn
- 27 med bn

EQUIPMENT BY TYPE

MBT 2,497: 1,087 M1A1 *Abrams*; 300 M60A1; 850 M60A3; 260 *Ramses* II (mod T-54/55); (840 T-54/T-55 in store); (500 T-62 in store)

RECCE 412: 300 BRDM-2; 112 *Commando Scout*

AIFV 390 YPR-765 (with 25mm); (220 BMP-1 in store)

APC 3,560

APC (T) 2,000 M113A2/YPR-765 (incl variants); (500 BTR-50/OT-62 in store)

APC (W) 1,560: 250 BMR-600P; 250 BTR-60S; 410 *Fahd*-30/TH 390 *Fahd*; 650 *Walid*

ARTY 4,468

SP 492: **122mm** 124 SP 122; **155mm** 368: 164 M109A2; 204 M109A5

Middle East and North Africa

TOWED 962: **122mm** 526: 190 D-30M; 36 M-1931/37; 300 M-30; **130mm** 420 M-46; **155mm** 16 GH-52
MRL 450: **122mm** 356: 96 BM-11; 60 BM-21; 50 *Sakr*-10; 50 *Sakr*-18; 100 *Sakr*-36; **130mm** 36 *Kooryong*; **140mm** 32 BM-14; **227mm** 26 M270 MLRS; **240mm** (48 BM-24 in store)
MOR 2,564
SP 136: **107mm** 100: 65 M106A1; 35 M106A2 **120mm** 36 M1064A3
81mm 50 M125A2; **82mm** 500; **120mm** 1,848: 1,800 M-1943; 48 Brandt; **160mm** 30 M160
AT • MSL
SP 262: 52 M-901, 210 YPR 765 PRAT
MANPATS 2,100: 1,200 9K11 *Malyutka* (AT-3 *Sagger*) (incl BRDM-2); 200 *Milan*; 700 TOW-2
UAV • ISR • Medium R4E-50 *Skyeye*; ASN-204
AD
SAM
SP 96: 50 FIM-92A *Avenger*; 26 M48 *Chaparral*; 20 9K31 *Strela*-1 (SA-9 *Gaskin*)
MANPAD 2,764: 2,000 *Ayn al-Saqr*/9K32 *Strela-2* (SA-7 *Grail*)‡; 164 FIM-92A *Stinger*; 600 *Igla* (SA-18 *Grouse*)
GUNS
SP 355: **23mm** 165: 45 *Sinai*-23; 120 ZSU-23-4; **37mm** 150; **57mm** 40 ZSU-57-2
TOWED 700: **14.5mm** 300 ZPU-4; **23mm** 200 ZU-23-2; **57mm** 200 S-60
RADAR • LAND AN/TPQ-36 *Firefinder*; AN/TPQ-37 *Firefinder* (arty/mor)
MSL • TACTICAL • SSM 42+: 9 FROG-7; 24 *Sakr*-80; 9 *Scud*-B
ARV 355+: *Fahd* 240; GMR 3560.55; 220 M88A1; 90 M88A2; M113 ARV; 45 M578; T-54/55 ARV
VLB KMM; MTU; MTU-20
MW *Aardvark* JFSU Mk4

Navy ε8,500 (incl 2,000 Coast Guard); 10,000 conscript (total 18,500)

EQUIPMENT BY TYPE
SUBMARINES • TACTICAL • SSK 4 *Romeo*† (PRC Type-033) with 8 single 533mm TT with UGM-84C *Harpoon* AShM/Mk 37 HWT
PRINCIPAL SURFACE COMBATANTS 8
FRIGATES 8
FFGHM 4 *Mubarak* (US *Oliver Hazard Perry*) with 1 Mk13 GMLS with RGM-84C *Harpoon* AShM/SM-1MP SAM, 2 triple 324 mm ASTT with Mk 46 LWT, 1 *Phalanx* CIWS, 1 76mm gun, (capacity 2 SH-2G *Super Seasprite* ASW hel)
FFGH 2 *Damyat* (US *Knox*) with 1 octuple Mk16 GMLS with RGM-84C *Harpoon* AShM/ASROC, 2 twin 324mm Mk 32 TT with Mk 46 LWT, 1 *Phalanx* CIWS 1 127mm gun, (capacity 1 SH-2G *Super Seasprite* ASW hel)
FFG 2 *Najim Al Zaffer* (PRC *Jianghu* I) with 2 twin lnchr with HY-2 (CSS-N-2 *Silkworm*) AShM, 2 RBU 1200, 2 twin 57mm guns
PATROL AND COASTAL COMBATANTS 56
CORVETTES • FSGM 2:
2 *Abu Qir* (ESP *Descubierta* – 1†) with 2 quad Mk141 lnchr with RGM-84C *Harpoon* AShM, 1 octuple lnchr with *Aspide* SAM, 2 triple 324mm with *Sting Ray* LWT, 1 twin 375mm A/S mor, 1 76mm gun
PCFG 11:
6 *Ramadan* with 4 single lnchr with *Otomat* MkII AShM, 1 76mm gun
5 *Tiger* with 2 twin lnchr with MM-38 *Exocet* AShM, 1 76mm gun
PCC 5:
5 *Hainan* (PRC – 3 more in reserve†) with 2 triple 324mm TT, 4 RBU 1200, 2 twin 57mm guns
PBFG 18:
1 *Ezzat* (US *Ambassador* IV) with 2 quad lnchr with RGM-84L *Harpoon* Block II AShM, 1 21-cell Mk49 lnchr with RAM Block 1A SAM, 1 Mk15 Mod 21 Block 1B *Phalanx* CIWS, 1 76mm gun (3 additional vessels in build, of which 2 completed and awaiting delivery)
4 *Hegu* (PRC – *Komar* type) with 2 single lnchr with SY-1 AShM (2 additional vessels in reserve)
5 *October* (FSU *Komar* – 1†) with 2 single lnchr with *Otomat* MkII AShM (1 additional vessel in reserve)
8 *Osa* I (FSU – 3†) with 1 9K32 *Strela*-2 (SA-N-5 *Grail*) SAM (manual aiming), 4 single lnchr with P-15 *Termit* (SS-N-2A *Styx*) AShM
PBFM 4:
4 *Shershen* (FSU) with 1 9K32 *Strela*-2 (SA-N-5 *Grail*) SAM (manual aiming), 1 12-tube BM-24 MRL
PBF 10:
6 *Kaan* (TUR MRTP20)
4 *Osa* II (FSU)
PB 6:
4 *Shanghai* II (PRC)
2 *Shershen* (FSU – 1†) with 4 single 533mm TT, 1 8-tube BM-21 MRL
MINE WARFARE • MINE COUNTERMEASURES 14
MHC 5: 2 *Osprey*; 3 *Dat Assawari* (US Swiftships)
MSI 2 *Safaga* (US Swiftships)
MSO 7: 3 *Assiout* (FSU T-43 class); 4 *Aswan* (FSU *Yurka*)
AMPHIBIOUS 12
LANDING SHIPS • LSM 3 *Polnochny* A (FSU) (capacity 6 MBT; 180 troops)
LANDING CRAFT • LCU 9 *Vydra* (capacity either 3 AMX-30 MBT or 100 troops)
LOGISTICS AND SUPPORT 32
AOT 7 *Toplivo* (1 additional in reserve)
AE 1 *Halaib* (*Westerwald*-class)
AKR 3 *Al Hurreya*
ARL 1 *Shaledin* (*Luneberg*-class)
ARS 2 *Al Areesh*
ATA 5† *Okhtensky*
AX 5: 1 *El Fateh*† (UK 'Z' class); 1 *El Horriya* (also used as the presidential yacht); 1 *Al Kousser*; 1 *Intishat*; 1 other
YDT 2 *Nyryat I* (Project 522)
YPT 2 *Poluchat 1*
YTL 4 *Galal Desouky* (Damen Stan 2208)

Coastal Defence

Army tps, Navy control

EQUIPMENT BY TYPE
ARTY • COASTAL 100mm; **130mm** SM-4-1; **152mm**
MSL • AShM 4K87 (SSC-2B *Samlet*); *Otomat* MkII AShM

Naval Aviation

All aircraft operated by Air Force

AIRCRAFT • TPT • Light 4 Beech 1900C (Maritime Surveillance)

HELICOPTERS

ASW 10 SH-2G *Super Seasprite* with Mk 46 LWT

MRH 5 SA342L *Gazelle*

UAV • ISR • Light 2 *Camcopter* 5.1

Coast Guard 2,000

PATROL AND COASTAL COMBATANTS 77

PBF 15: 6 *Crestitalia*; 6 *Swift Protector*; 3 *Peterson*

PB 62: 5 *Nisr*; 12 *Sea Spectre* MkIII; 12 Swiftships (three additional vessels in build); 21 *Timsah*; 3 Type-83; 9 *Peterson*

LOGISTICS AND SUPPORT • YTL 4 *Khoufou*

Air Force 30,000 (incl 10,000 conscript)

FORCES BY ROLE

FIGHTER

1 sqn with F-16A/B *Fighting Falcon*

8 sqn with F-16C/D *Fighting Falcon*

4 sqn with J-7/MiG-21 *Fishbed*/MiG-21U *Mongol* A

2 sqn with *Mirage* 5D/E

1 sqn with *Mirage* 2000B/C

FIGHTER/GROUND ATTACK

2 sqn with F-4E *Phantom* II

1 sqn with *Mirage* 5E2

ANTI-SUBMARINE WARFARE

1 sqn with SH-2G *Super Seasprite*

MARITIME PATROL

1 sqn with Beech 1900C

ELECTRONIC WARFARE

1 sqn with Beech 1900 (ELINT); *Commando* Mk2E (ECM)

ELECTRONIC WARFARE/TRANSPORT

1 sqn with C-130H/VC-130H *Hercules*

AIRBORNE EARLY WARNING

1 sqn with E-2C *Hawkeye*

SEARCH & RESCUE

1 unit with AW139

TRANSPORT

1 sqn with An-74TK-200A

1 sqn with C-130H/C-130H-30 *Hercules*

1 sqn with C-295M

1 sqn with DHC-5D *Buffalo*

1 sqn with B-707-366C; B-737-100; Beech 200 *Super King Air*; *Falcon* 20; Gulfstream III; Gulfstream IV; Gulfstream IV-SP

TRAINING

1 sqn with *Alpha Jet**

1 sqn with DHC-5 *Buffalo*

3 sqn with EMB-312 *Tucano*

1 sqn with Grob 115EG

ε6 sqn with K-8 *Karakorum**

1 sqn with L-39 *Albatros*; L-59E *Albatros**

ATTACK HELICOPTER

2 sqn with AH-64D *Apache*

2 sqn with SA-342K *Gazelle* (with HOT)

1 sqn with SA-342L *Gazelle*

TRANSPORT HELICOPTER

1 sqn with CH-47C/D *Chinook*

2 sqn with Mi-8 *Hip*

1 sqn with S-70 *Black Hawk*; UH-60A/L *Black Hawk*

UAV

Some sqn with R4E-50 *Skyeye*; Teledyne-Ryan 324 *Scarab*

EQUIPMENT BY TYPE

AIRCRAFT 569 combat capable

FTR 62: 26 F-16A *Fighting Falcon*; 6 F-16B *Fighting Falcon*; ε30 J-7

FGA 310: 29 F-4E *Phantom* II; 127 F-16C *Fighting Falcon*; 38 F-16D *Fighting Falcon*; 3 *Mirage* 2000B; 15 *Mirage* 2000C; 36 *Mirage* 5D/E; 12 *Mirage* 5E2; ε50 MiG-21 *Fishbed*/MiG-21U *Mongol* A

ELINT 2 VC-130H *Hercules*

ISR 6 *Mirage* 5R (5SDR)*

AEW&C 7 E-2C *Hawkeye*

TPT 61 **Medium** 24: 21 C-130H *Hercules*; 3 C-130H-30 *Hercules*; **Light** 26: 3 An-74TK-200A; 1 Beech 200 *King Air*; 4 Beech 1900 (ELINT); 4 Beech 1900C; 5 C-295M; 9 DHC-5D *Buffalo* **PAX** 11: 1 B-707-366C; 3 *Falcon* 20; 2 Gulfstream III; 1 Gulfstream IV; 4 Gulfstream IV-SP

TRG 329: 36 *Alpha Jet**; 54 EMB-312 *Tucano*; 74 Grob 115EG; 120 K-8 *Karakorum**; 10 L-39 *Albatros*; 35 L-59E *Albatros**

HELICOPTERS

ATK 35 AH-64D *Apache*

ASW 10 SH-2G *Super Seasprite* (opcon Navy)

ELINT 4 *Commando* Mk2E (ECM)

MRH 72: 2 AW139 (SAR); 65 SA342K *Gazelle* (some with HOT); 5 SA342L *Gazelle* (opcon Navy)

TPT 93: **Heavy** 19: 3 CH-47C *Chinook*; 16 CH-47D *Chinook*; **Medium** 74: 2 AS-61; 24 *Commando* (of which 3 VIP); 40 Mi-8 *Hip*; 4 S-70 *Black Hawk* (VIP); 4 UH-60L *Black Hawk* (VIP)

TRG 17 UH-12E

UAV • ISR • Medium R4E-50 *Skyeye*; Teledyne-Ryan 324 *Scarab*

MSL

ASM AGM-65A/D/F/G *Maverick*; AGM-114 *Hellfire*; AS-30L; HOT

AShM AGM-84 *Harpoon*; AM-39 *Exocet*;

ARM *Armat*; Kh-25MP (AS-12 *Kegler*)

AAM • IR R-3 (AA-2 *Atoll*)‡; AIM-9FL/P *Sidewinder*; R-550 *Magic*; **SARH** AIM-7E/F/M *Sparrow*; R530

Air Defence Command 80,000 conscript; 70,000 reservists (total 150,000)

FORCES BY ROLE

AIR DEFENCE

5 AD div (geographically based) (total: 12 SAM bty with M48 *Chaparral*, 12 radar bn, 12 ADA bde (total: 100 ADA bn), 12 SAM bty with MIM-23B I-HAWK, 14 SAM bty with *Crotale*, 18 SAM bn with *Skyguard*, 110 SAM bn with S-125 *Pechora*-M (SA-3A *Goa*); 2K12 *Kub* (SA-6 *Gainful*); S-75M *Volkhov* (SA-2 *Guideline*))

EQUIPMENT BY TYPE

AD

SYSTEMS 72+: Some *Amoun* with RIM-7F *Sea Sparrow* SAM, 36+ quad SAM, *Skyguard* towed SAM, 36+ twin 35mm guns

SAM 702+
SP 130+: 24+ *Crotale*; 50+ M48 *Chaparral*; 56+ SA-6 *Gainful*
TOWED 572+: 78+ MIM-23B I-HAWK; S-75M *Volkhov* (SA-2 *Guideline*) 282+ *Skyguard*; 212+ S-125 *Pechora*-M (SA-3A *Goa*)
GUNS 1,566+
SP • 23mm 266+: 36+ *Sinai*-23 (SPAAG) with *Ayn al-Saqr* MANPAD, Dassault 6SD-20S land; 230 ZSU-23-4
TOWED 57mm 600 S-60; **85mm** 400 M-1939 *KS-12;* **100mm** 300 KS-19

Paramilitary ε397,000 active

Central Security Forces 325,000
Ministry of Interior; Includes conscripts
APC (W) 100+: 100 *Hussar; Walid*

National Guard 60,000
Lt wpns only
FORCES BY ROLE
MANOEUVRE
Other
8 paramilitary bde (cadre) (3 paramilitary bn)
EQUIPMENT BY TYPE
APC (W) 250 *Walid*

Border Guard Forces 12,000
Ministry of Interior; lt wpns only
FORCES BY ROLE
MANOEUVRE
Other
18 Border Guard regt

DEPLOYMENT

CÔTE D'IVOIRE
UN • UNOCI 175; 1 engr coy

DEMOCRATIC REPUBLIC OF THE CONGO
UN • MONUSCO 1,006; 21 obs; 1 SF coy; 1 mech inf bn

LIBERIA
UN • UNMIL 7 obs

SOUTH SUDAN
UN • UNMISS 3 obs

SUDAN
UN • UNAMID 1,055; 32 obs; 1 inf bn; 1 tpt coy

WESTERN SAHARA
UN • MINURSO 21 obs

FOREIGN FORCES

Australia MFO (*Operation Mazurka*) 25
Canada MFO 28
Colombia MFO 354; 1 inf bn
Czech Republic MFO 3
Fiji MFO 338; 1 inf bn
France MFO 2
Hungary MFO 42; 1 MP unit
Italy MFO 78; 3 coastal ptl unit
New Zealand MFO 28 1 trg unit; 1 tpt unit
Norway MFO 3
United States MFO 700; 1 inf bn; 1 spt bn (1 EOD coy, 1 medical coy, 1 hel coy)
Uruguay MFO 58 1 engr/tpt unit

Iran IRN

Iranian Rial r		2012	2013	2014
GDP	r	6729tr	8857tr	
	US$	549bn	429bn	
per capita	US$	7,211	5,568	
Growth	%	-1.88	-1.25	
Inflation	%	30.60	27.20	
Def bdgt	r	310tr	366tr	
	US$	25.2bn	17.7bn	
US$1=r		12260.00	20634.79	

Population **79,853,900**

Ethnic groups: Persian 51%; Azeri 24%; Gilaki/Mazandarani 8%; Kurdish 7%; Arab 3%; Lur 2%; Baloch 2%; Turkman 2%

Age	0–14	15–19	20–24	25–29	30–64	65 plus
Male	12.2%	4.4%	5.8%	5.8%	20.2%	2.4%
Female	11.6%	4.1%	5.5%	5.5%	19.8%	2.7%

Capabilities

The Iranian Revolutionary Guard Corps (IRGC) is a capable organisation well-versed in a variety of different operations. There has been some division of labour between the regular armed forces and IRGC, with the IRGC Navy assuming greater responsibility for operations in the Persian Gulf and the navy assuming a greater extra-regional role. Although the armed forces suffer from a generally outdated arsenal, exacerbated by the imposition of a UN weapons embargo in June 2010, innovative and cost-effective tactics and techniques (particularly the use of asymmetric warfare) mean that Iran is able to present a challenge to most potential adversaries, especially its weaker neighbours. The inability to offer effective deterrence to an advanced force such as the United States may be a motivation for Iran's pursuit of dual-use nuclear programmes. The Iran–Iraq War of the 1980s and various counter-insurgency campaigns mean the armed forces are battle-hardened and, perhaps now true more for mid-level and senior staff, combat-experienced. Police and paramilitary forces remain engaged against limited insurgent and smuggling activity along the eastern border. The air force's ageing fleets of combat aircraft are of limited value and many may already have been cannibalised. Although Tehran has attempted, with partial success, to invigorate its domestic defence industry, it relies on foreign state support for high-tech equipment, including anti-ship missiles and advanced air-defence platforms. In 2012, Iran dispatched Revolutionary Guards to advise Syrian troops in urban and counter-insurgency warfare; in some cases it is believed they took part in the fighting. (See pp. 300–02.)

ACTIVE 523,000 (Army 350,000 Iranian Revolutionary Guard Corps 125,000 Navy 18,000 Air 30,000) Paramilitary 40,000

Armed Forces General Staff coordinates two parallel organisations: the regular armed forces and the Revolutionary Guard Corps

RESERVE 350,000 (Army 350,000, ex-service volunteers)

ORGANISATIONS BY SERVICE

Army 130,000; 220,000 conscript (total 350,000)

FORCES BY ROLE
5 corps-level regional HQ
COMMAND
1 cdo div HQ
4 armd div HQ
2 mech div HQ
4 inf div HQ
SPECIAL FORCES
1 cdo div (3 cdo bde)
6 cdo bde
1 SF bde
MANOEUVRE
Armoured
7 armd bde
Mechanised
16 mech bde
Light
12 inf bde
Air Manoeuvre
1 AB bde
Aviation
Some avn gp
COMBAT SUPPORT
5 arty gp

EQUIPMENT BY TYPE
Totals incl those held by IRGC Ground Forces. Some equipment serviceability in doubt
MBT 1,663+: ε150 *Zulfiqar*; 480 T-72Z; 150 M60A1; 75+ T-62; 100 *Chieftain* Mk3/Mk5; 540 T-54/T-55/Type-59/*Safir-74*; 168 M47/M48
LT TK 80+: 80 *Scorpion*; *Towsan*
RECCE 35 EE-9 *Cascavel*
AIFV 610: 210 BMP-1; 400 BMP-2 with 9K111 *Fagot* (AT-4 *Spigot*)
APC 640+
APC (T) 340+: 140 *Boragh* with 9K111 *Fagot* (AT-4 *Spigot*); 200 M113; BMT-2 *Cobra*
APC (W) 300+: 300 BTR-50/BTR-60; *Rakhsh*
ARTY 8,798+
SP 292+: **122mm** 60+: 60 2S1; *Raad*-1 (*Thunder* 1); **155mm** 150+: 150 M109; *Raad*-2 (*Thunder* 2); **170mm** 30 M-1978; **175mm** 22 M107; **203mm** 30 M110
TOWED 2,030+; **105mm** 150: 130 M101A1; 20 M-56; **122mm** 640: 540 D-30; 100 Type-54 (M-30); **130mm** 985 M-46; **152mm** 30 D-20; **155mm** 205: 120 GHN-45; 70 M114; 15 Type-88 WAC-21; **203mm** 20 M115
MRL 1,476+: **107mm** 1,300: 700 Type-63; 600 HASEB *Fadjr* 1; **122mm** 157: 7 BM-11; 100 BM-21; 50 *Arash/Hadid/Noor*; **240mm** 19: ε10 *Fadjr* 3; 9 M-1985; **330mm** *Fadjr* 5
MOR 5,000: **60mm**; **81mm**; **82mm**; **107mm** M-30; **120mm** M-65
AT
MSL • MANPATS 9K11 *Malyutka* (AT-3 *Sagger*/I-*Raad*); 9K111 *Fagot* (AT-4 *Spigot*); 9K113 *Konkurs* (AT-5 *Spandrel*/*Towsan*-1); *Saeqhe* 1; *Saeqhe* 2; *Toophan*; *Toophan* 2
RCL 200+: **75mm** M-20; **82mm** B-10; **106mm** ε200 M-40; **107mm** B-11
AIRCRAFT • TPT 17 **Light** 16: 10 Cessna 185; 2 F-27 *Friendship*; 4 *Turbo Commander* 690; **PAX** 1 *Falcon* 20
HELICOPTERS
ATK 50 AH-1J *Cobra*
TPT 173: **Heavy** 20 CH-47C *Chinook*; **Medium** 75: 50 Bell 214; 25 Mi-171; **Light** 78: 68 Bell 205A (AB-205A); 10 Bell 206 *Jet Ranger* (AB-206)
UAV • ISR • Medium *Mohajer* 3/4; **Light** *Mohajer* 2; *Ababil*
AD • SAM
SP HQ-7 (reported)
MANPAD 9K36 *Strela*-3 (SA-14 *Gremlin*); 9K32 *Strela*-2 (SA-7 *Grail*)‡; *Misaq 1* (QW-1 *Vanguard*); *Misaq 2* (QW-11); *Igla-S* (SA-24 *Grinch* - reported); HN-54
GUNS 1,122
SP 180: **23mm** 100 ZSU-23-4; **57mm** 80 ZSU-57-2
TOWED 942 **14.5mm** ZPU-2; ZPU-4; **23mm** 300 ZU-23-2; **35mm** 92 *Skyguard*; **37mm** M-1939; **40mm** 50 L/70; **57mm** 200 S-60; **85mm** 300 M1939
MSL • TACTICAL • SSM ε30 CSS-8 (175 msl); *Shahin*-1/*Shahin*-2; *Nazeat*; *Oghab*
ARV 20+: BREM-1 reported; 20 *Chieftain* ARV; M578; T-54/55 ARV reported
VLB 15: 15 *Chieftain* AVLB
MW *Taftan* 1

Iranian Revolutionary Guard Corps 125,000+

Iranian Revolutionary Guard Corps Ground Forces 100,000+

Controls Basij paramilitary forces. Lightly manned in peacetime. Primary role: internal security; secondary role: external defence, in conjunction with regular armed forces.

FORCES BY ROLE
COMMAND
31 provincial corps HQ (2 in Tehran)
MANOEUVRE
Light
31 indep bde (each bde allocated 10 Basij militia bn for ops)

Iranian Revolutionary Guard Corps Naval Forces 20,000+ (incl 5,000 Marines)

FORCES BY ROLE
COMBAT SUPPORT
Some arty bty
Some AShM bty with HY-2 (CSS-C-3 *Seersucker*) AShM

Middle East and North Africa

EQUIPMENT BY TYPE

In addition to the vessels listed the IRGC operates a substantial number of patrol boats with a full-load displacement below 10 tonnes, including ε40 *Boghammar*-class vessels and small *Bavar*-class wing-in-ground effect air vehicles.

PATROL AND COASTAL COMBATANTS 113

PBFG 46:

5 *China Cat* with 2 twin lnchr with C-701/*Kosar* AShM

10 *Thondor* (PRC *Houdong*) with 2 twin lnchr with C-802 (CSS-N-4 *Sardine*) AShM , 2 twin AK230 CIWS

25 *Peykaap* II (IPS-16 mod) with 2 single lnchr with C-701 (*Kosar*) AShM, 2 single 324mm TT

6 *Zolfaghar* (*Peykaap* III/IPS-16 mod) with 2 single lnchr with C-701 (*Kosar*)/C-704 (*Nasr*) AShM

PBF 35: 15 *Peykaap I* (IPS -16) with 2 single 324mm TT; 10 *Tir* (IPS 18); ε10 *Pashe* (MIG-G-1900)

PB ε 20 *Ghaem*

PTG 12

AMPHIBIOUS

LANDING SHIPS • LST 4:

2 *Hejaz* (mine-laying capacity)

2 MIG-S-5000 (*Hejaz* design for commercial use)

LOGISTICS AND SUPPORT • AP 3 *Naser*

MSL • TACTICAL • AShM C-701 (*Kosar*); C-704 (*Nasr*); C-802; HY-2 (CSS-C-3 *Seersucker*)

Iranian Revolutionary Guard Corps Marines 5,000+

FORCES BY ROLE

MANOEUVRE

Amphibious

1 marine bde

Iranian Revolutionary Guard Corps Air Force

Controls Iran's strategic missile force.

FORCES BY ROLE

MISSILE

ε1 bde with *Shahab*-1/2

ε1 bn with *Shahab*-3; *Ghadr*-1; *Sajjil*-2 (in devt)

EQUIPMENT BY TYPE

MISSILE • TACTICAL

MRBM 12+: 12+ *Shahab*-3/*Ghadr*-1; some *Sajjil*-2 (in devt)

SRBM 18+: some *Fateh* 110; 12-18 *Shahab*-1/2 (ε200–300 msl)

SSM Some *Zelzal*

Navy 18,000

HQ at Bandar-e Abbas

EQUIPMENT BY TYPE

In addition to the vessels listed the Iranian Navy operates a substantial number of patrol boats with a full-load displacement below 10 tonnes.

SUBMARINES 29

TACTICAL 21

SSK 3 *Kilo* (RUS Type 877EKM) with 6 single 533mm TT

SSC 1 *Fateh* (in build; expected ISD 2014)

SSW 17: 16 *Qadir* with 2 single 533mm TT (additional vessels in build); 1 *Nahang*

SDV 8: 5 *Al Sabehat* (SF insertion and mine-laying capacity); 3 other

PATROL AND COASTAL COMBATANTS 69 (+ε50 small craft under 10 tonnes)

CORVETTES 6

FSGM 1 *Jamaran* (UK Vosper Mk 5 – 1 undergoing sea trials; 1 more under construction at Bandar Abbas, expected ISD 2014/15) with 2 twin lnchr with C-802 (CSS-N-4 *Sardine*) AShM, 2 lnchr with SM-1 SAM, 2 triple 324mm Mk32 ASTT, 1 76mm gun, 1 hel landing platform

FSG 4:

3 *Alvand* (UK Vosper Mk 5) with 2 twin lnchr with C-802 (CSS-N-4 *Sardine*) AShM, 2 triple Mk32 324mm ASTT, 1 114mm gun

1 *Bayandor* (US PF-103) with 2 twin lnchr with C-802 AShM, 2 triple 324mm Mk32 ASTT, 1 76mm gun

FS 1 *Bayandor* (US PF-103) with 2 76mm gun

PCFG 14 *Kaman* (FRA *Combattante* II) with 1–2 twin lnchr with C-802 AShM, 1 76 mm gun

PBFG 8:

ε4 Mk13 with 2 single lnchr with C-704 (*Nasr*) AShM, 2 single 324mm TT

4 *China Cat* with 2 single lnchr with C-701 (*Kosar*) AShM

PBF 16: 15 *Kashdom* II; 1 MIL55

PB 22: 3 *Kayvan*; 6 MkII; 10 MkIII; 3 *Parvin* with 2 single lnchr with C-704 (*Nasr*) AShM

PTF 3 *Kajami* (semi-submersible)

MINE WARFARE • MINE COUNTERMEASURES 5

MSC 3: 2 Type-292; 1 *Shahrokh* (in Caspian Sea as trg ship)

MSI 2 *Riazi* (US *Cape*)

AMPHIBIOUS

LANDING SHIPS 13

LSM 3 *Farsi* (ROK) (capacity 9 tanks; 140 troops)

LST 4 *Hengam* (capacity 9 tanks; 225 troops)

LSL 6 *Fouque*

LANDING CRAFT 11

LCAC 8: 6 *Wellington*; 2 *Tondar* (UK *Winchester*)

LCT 2

LCU 1 *Liyan 110*

LOGISTICS AND SUPPORT 47

AB 12 *Hendijan* (also used for coastal patrol) with 2 twin lnchr with C-802 (*Noor*) AShM

AE 2 *Delvar*

AFD 2 *Dolphin*

AG 1 *Hamzah* with 2 single lnchr with C802 (*Noor*) AShM

AK 3 *Delvar*

AORH 3: 2 *Bandar Abbas*; 1 *Kharg* with 1 76 mm gun

AWT 5: 4 *Kangan*; 1 *Delvar*

AX 2 *Kialas*

YTB 17

MSL • AshM C-701 (*Kosar*); C-704 (*Nasr*); C-802/A (*Noor*/*Ghader*); *Ra'ad* (reported; coastal defence)

Marines 2,600

FORCES BY ROLE

MANOEUVRE

Amphibious

2 marine bde

Naval Aviation 2,600

EQUIPMENT BY TYPE

AIRCRAFT 3 combat capable

ASW 3 P-3F *Orion*

TPT 16 **Light** 13: 5 Do-228; 4 F-27 *Friendship*; 4 *Turbo Commander* 680; **PAX** 3 *Falcon* 20 (ELINT)

HELICOPTERS

ASW ε10 SH-3D *Sea King*

MCM 3 RH-53D *Sea Stallion*

TPT • Light 17: 5 Bell 205A (AB-205A); 2 Bell 206 *Jet Ranger* (AB-206); 10 Bell 212 (AB-212)

Air Force 30,000 (incl 12,000 Air Defence)

FORCES BY ROLE

Serviceability probably about 60% for US ac types and about 80% for PRC/Russian ac. Includes IRGC Air Force equipment.

FIGHTER

1 sqn with F-7M *Airguard*; JJ-7 *Mongol* A*

2 sqn with F-14 *Tomcat*

2 sqn with MiG-29A/UB *Fulcrum*

FIGHTER/GROUND ATTACK

1 sqn with *Mirage* F-1E; F-5E/F *Tiger* II

1 sqn with Su-24MK *Fencer* D

5 sqn with F-4D/E *Phantom* II

3 sqn with F-5E/F *Tiger* II

MARITIME PATROL

1 sqn with P-3MP *Orion**

ISR

1 (det) sqn with RF-4E *Phantom* II*

SEARCH & RESCUE

Some flt with Bell-214C (AB-214C)

TANKER/TRANSPORT

1 sqn with B-707; B-747; B-747F

TRANSPORT

1 sqn with B-707; *Falcon* 50; L-1329 *Jetstar*; Bell 412

2 sqn with C-130E/H *Hercules*

1 sqn with F-27 *Friendship*; *Falcon* 20

1 sqn with Il-76 *Candid*; An-140 (Iran-140 *Faraz*)

TRAINING

1 sqn with Beech F33A/C *Bonanza*

1 sqn with F-5B *Freedom Fighter*

1 sqn with PC-6

1 sqn with PC-7 *Turbo Trainer*

Some units with EMB-312 *Tucano*; MFI-17 *Mushshak*; TB-21 *Trinidad*; TB-200 *Tobago*

TRANSPORT HELICOPTER

1 sqn with CH-47 *Chinook*

Some units with Bell 206A *Jet Ranger* (AB-206A); *Shabaviz* 2-75; *Shabaviz* 2061

AIR DEFENCE

16 bn with MIM-23B I-HAWK/*Shahin*

5 sqn with FM-80 (*Crotale*); *Rapier*; *Tigercat*; S-75M *Volkhov* (SA-2 *Guideline*); S-200 *Angara* (SA-5 *Gammon*); FIM-92A *Stinger*; 9K32 *Strela*-2 (SA-7 *Grail*)‡; 9K331 *Tor*-M1 (SA-15 *Gauntlet*) (reported)

EQUIPMENT BY TYPE

AIRCRAFT 334 combat capable

FTR 184+: 20 F-5B *Freedom Fighter*; 55+ F-5E/F *Tiger* II 24 F-7M *Airguard*; 43 F-14 *Tomcat*; 36 MiG-29A/U/UB *Fulcrum*; up to 6 *Azarakhsh* reported

FGA 111: 65 F-4D/E *Phantom* II; 10 *Mirage* F-1E; 30 Su-24MK *Fencer* D; up to 6 *Saegheh* reported

ATK 13: 7 Su-25K *Frogfoot*; 3 Su-25T *Frogfoot*; 3 Su-25UBK *Frogfoot*

ASW 5 P-3MP *Orion*

ISR: 6+ RF-4E *Phantom* II*

TKR/TPT 3: ε1 B-707; ε2 B-747

TPT 117: **Heavy** 12 Il-76 *Candid*; **Medium** ε19 C-130E/H *Hercules*; **Light** 75: 11 An-74TK-200; 5 An-140 (Iran-140 *Faraz*) (45 projected); 10 F-27 *Friendship*; 1 L-1329 *Jetstar*; 10 PC-6B *Turbo Porter*; 8 TB-21 *Trinidad*; 4 TB-200 *Tobago*; 3 *Turbo Commander* 680; 14 Y-7; 9 Y-12; **PAX** 11: 2 B-707; 1 B-747; 4 B-747F; 1 *Falcon* 20; 3 *Falcon* 50

TRG 151: 25 Beech F33A/C *Bonanza*; 15 EMB-312 *Tucano*; 15 JJ-7*; 25 MFI-17 *Mushshak*; 12 *Parastu*; 15 PC-6; 35 PC-7 *Turbo Trainer*; 9 T-33

HELICOPTERS

MRH 2 Bell 412

TPT 34+: **Heavy** 2+ CH-47 *Chinook*; **Medium** 30 Bell 214C (AB-214C); **Light** 2+: 2 Bell 206A *Jet Ranger* (AB-206A); some *Shabaviz* 2-75 (indigenous versions in production); some *Shabaviz* 2061

AD • SAM 529+: 250 FM-80 (*Crotale*); 30 *Rapier*; 15 *Tigercat*; 150+ MIM-23B I-HAWK/*Shahin*; 45 S-75 *Dvina* (SA-2 *Guideline*); 10 S-200 *Angara* (SA-5 *Gammon*); 29 9K331 *Tor*-M1 (SA-15 *Gauntlet*) (reported)

MANPAD FIM-92A *Stinger*; 9K32 *Strela*-2 (SA-7 *Grail*)‡

GUNS • TOWED 23mm ZU-23; **37mm** Oerlikon

MSL

ASM AGM-65A *Maverick*; Kh-25 (AS-10 *Karen*); Kh-29 (AS-14 *Kedge*); C-801K AShM

ARM Kh-58 (AS-11 *Kilter*)

AAM • IR PL-2A‡; PL-7; R-60 (AA-8 *Aphid*); R-73 (AA-11 *Archer*): AIM-9 *Sidewinder*; **IR/SARH** R-27 (AA-10 *Alamo*) **SARH** AIM-54 *Phoenix*†; AIM-7 *Sparrow*

Air Defence Command

Established to co-ordinate army, air force and IRGC air-defence assets. Precise composition unclear.

Paramilitary 40,000–60,000

Law-Enforcement Forces 40,000–60,000 (border and security troops); 450,000 on mobilisation (incl conscripts)

Part of armed forces in wartime

PATROL AND COASTAL COMBATANTS • PB ε90

AIRCRAFT • TPT • Light 2+: 2 *An*-140; some Cessna 185/Cessna 310

HELICOPTERS • UTL ε24 AB-205 (Bell 205)/AB-206 (Bell 206) *Jet Ranger*

Basij Resistance Force up to ε1,000,000 on mobilisation

Paramilitary militia, with claimed membership of 12.6 million; perhaps 1 million combat capable; in the process of closer integration with IRGC Ground Forces.

FORCES BY ROLE

MANOEUVRE

Other

2,500 militia bn (claimed, limited permanent membership)

Cyber

Iran is believed to have a developed capacity for cyber operations. The precise relationship of groups such as the 'Iranian Cyber Army' to regime and military organisations is unclear, but the former has launched hacking attacks against a number of foreign organisations. In 2011, it was reported by state-sponsored media that Iran was stepping up its cyber defences and conducting exercises in this area, and that Iran was establishing its own cyber command. In 2011/2012, Tehran established a Joint Chiefs of Staff Cyber Command with emphasis on thwarting attacks against Iranian nuclear facilities. In June 2012, the head of the Civil Defence Organisation announced that plans to develop a cyber-defence strategy were under way.

DEPLOYMENT

GULF OF ADEN AND SOMALI BASIN

Navy: 1 FSG; 1 AORH

SUDAN

UN • UNAMID 2 obs

Iraq IRQ

Iraqi Dinar D		2012	2013	2014
GDP	D	248tr	272tr	
	US$	213bn	233bn	
per capita	US$	6,305	6,708	
Growth	%	8.43	9.04	
Inflation	%	6.09	4.30	
Def bdgt [a]	D	17.2tr	19.7tr	
	US$	14.7bn	16.9bn	
US$1=D		1166.00	1166.00	

[a] Defence and security budget

Population 31,858,481

Ethnic and religious groups: Arab 75–80% (of which Shia Muslim 55%, Sunni Muslim 45%) Kurdish 20–25%

Age	0–14	15–19	20–24	25–29	30–64	65 plus
Male	18.9%	5.3%	4.7%	4.5%	15.7%	1.5%
Female	18.3%	5.1%	4.6%	4.4%	15.3%	1.7%

Capabilities

Iraq's armed forces are heavily land-focused. Baghdad has presently no combat aircraft and a navy largely focused on coastal security and EEZ patrol. In conjunction with the police and other security services, the Iraqi Army's prime role is to provide internal security. The speed with which the army was reconstituted after 2003 meant that up to 70% of old, pre-regime-change officers were eventually reintegrated into the new officer corps. To counter this, Iraq's ruling elite have inserted so-called *dimaj* officers into the senior ranks. These political appointments were either militia leaders or had no military experience. Beyond political interference, a broad set of problems continue to plague the army, including weaknesses in management, logistics and strategic planning. There have been reports of defections from the armed forces in 2013. The unwillingness of senior military officials to delegate responsibility down the chain of command stifles innovation and independent decision-making at a junior level. The withdrawal of all US troops and NATO trainers has greatly reduced external training assistance and mentoring. However, continued investment in equipment is improving capabilities; in 2013, requests were made for US$2bn-worth of Bell 412EP helicopters, M1135 *Stryker* NBC-variant APCs and maintenance for the variety of US-origin vehicles that have been delivered in recent years. Airlift capacity has increased with C-130J deliveries. As such, the Iraqi forces' ability to provide effective security is still growing, but the continuation of a terrorist campaign by Sunni and al-Qaeda insurgents points to continuing deficiencies across wider security-force tactics and leadership.

ACTIVE 271,400 (Army 193,400 Navy 3,600 Air 5,050 Support 69,350) Ministry of Interior 531,000

ORGANISATIONS BY SERVICE

Military Forces

Figures for Iraqi security forces reflect ongoing changes in organisation and manpower.

Army 193,400

FORCES BY ROLE

SPECIAL FORCES

2 SF bde

MANOEUVRE

Armoured

1 armd div (2 armd bde, 2 mech bde, 1 engr bn, 1 sigs regt, 1 log bde)

Mechanised

3 mech div (4 mech inf bde, 1 engr bn, 1 sigs regt, 1 log bde)

2 mech div (2 mech inf bde, 2 inf bde, 1 engr bn, 1 sigs regt, 1 log bde)

Light

2 mot div (1 mech bde, 3 mot inf bde, 1 engr bn, 1 sigs regt, 1 log bde)

1 mot div (4 mot inf bde, 1 engr bn, 1 sigs regt, 1 log bde)

1 inf div (1 armd bde, 3 lt inf bde, 1 engr bn, 1 sigs regt, 1 log bde)
2 inf div (4 lt inf bde, 1 engr bn, 1 sigs regt, 1 log bde)
1 inf div (3 lt inf bde, 1 air mob bde, 1 engr bn, 1 sigs regt, 1 log bde)
1 cdo div (4 lt inf bde, 1 engr bn, 1 sigs regt, 1 log bde)

Other
2 (presidential) sy bde

Aviation
1 sqn with Bell 205 (UH-1H *Huey* II)
1 sqn with Bell 206; OH-58C *Kiowa*
1 sqn with Bell T407
3 sqn with Mi-17 *Hip* H; Mi-171
1 sqn with SA342M *Gazelle*

EQUIPMENT BY TYPE
MBT 336+: 140 M1A1 *Abrams;* 120+ T-72; 76 T-55;
RECCE 73: 18 BRDM 2; 35 EE-9 *Cascavel;* 20 *Fuchs* NBC
AIFV 188+: 100 BMP-1; 88+ BTR-4 (inc variants)
APC 3,688+
APC (T) 1,494+: 100 FV 103 *Spartan;* 850+ M113A2; 500 MT-LB; 44 *Talha*
APC (W) 860: 570 *Akrep/Scorpion;* 60 AT-105 *Saxon;* 100 BTR-80; 10 *Cobra;* 50 M3 Panhard; 60 *Mohafiz;* 10 VCR-TT
PPV 1,334: 12 *Barracuda;* 600 *Dzik-3;* 607 ILAV *Cougar;* 115 *Mamba*
ARTY 1,386+
SP 48+: **152mm** 18+ Type-83; **155mm** 30: 6 M109A1; 24 M109A5
TOWED 138+: **130mm** 18+ M-46; **155mm** 120 M198
MLRS 122mm some BM-21
MOR 1,200: **81mm** 650 M252; **120mm** 550 M120
ARV 215+: 180 BREM; 35+ M88A1/2; T-54/55 ARV; Type-653; VT-55A
HELICOPTERS
MRH 30+: 26 Mi-17 *Hip* H; 4+ SA342 *Gazelle*
ISR 10 OH-58C *Kiowa*
TPT 58: **Medium** 8 Mi-171Sh; **Light** 50: 16 Bell 205 (UH-1H *Huey* II); 10 Bell 206B3 *Jet Ranger;* 24 Bell T407

Navy 3,600

Iraqi Coastal Defence Force (ICDF)

EQUIPMENT BY TYPE
PATROL AND COASTAL COMBATANTS 32+:
PCO 2 *Al Basra* (US *River Hawk)*
PCC 4 *Fateh* (ITA *Diciotti*)
PB 20: 12 Swiftships 35; 5 *Predator* (PRC-27m); 3 *Al Faw*
PBR 6: 2 Type-200; 4 Type-2010

Iraqi Air Force 5,050

FORCES BY ROLE
ISR
1 sqn with CH-2000 *Sama;* SB7L-360 *Seeker*
1 sqn with Cessna 208B *Grand Caravan;* Cessna AC-208B *Combat Caravan**
1 sqn with Beech 350 *King Air*
TRANSPORT
1 sqn with An-32B *Cline*
1 sqn with C-130E/J-30 *Hercules*
TRAINING
1 sqn with Cessna 172, Cessna 208B
1 sqn with *Lasta*-95
1 sqn with T-6A

EQUIPMENT BY TYPE
AIRCRAFT 3 combat capable
ISR 10: 3 Cessna AC-208B *Combat Caravan**; 2 SB7L-360 *Seeker;* 5 Beech 350ER *King Air*
TPT 32: **Medium;** 15: 3 C-130E *Hercules;* 6 C-130J-30 *Hercules;* 6 An-32B *Cline;* **Light** 17: 1 Beech 350 *King Air;* 8 Cessna 208B *Grand Caravan;* 8 Cessna 172
TRG 33+: 8 CH-2000 *Sama;* 10+ *Lasta*-95; 15 T-6A
MSL
ASM AGM-114 *Hellfire*

Ministry of Interior Forces 531,000

Iraqi Police Service 302,000 (incl Highway Patrol)

Iraqi Federal Police 44,000

Facilities Protection Service 95,000

Border Enforcement 60,000

Oil Police 30,000

FOREIGN FORCES

Australia UNAMI 2 obs
Fiji UNAMI 168; 2 sy unit
Nepal UNAMI 77; 1 sy unit
New Zealand UNAMI 1 obs

Israel ISR

New Israeli Shekel NS		2012	2013	2014
GDP	NS	928bn	977bn	
	US$	241bn	254bn	
per capita	US$	31,296	32,248	
Growth	%	3.10	3.56	
Inflation	%	1.71	1.64	
Def bdgt	NS	65bn	58.4bn	57.7bn
	US$	16.9bn	15.2bn	
FMA (US)	US$	3.08bn	3.08bn	3.1bn
US$1=NS		3.85	3.85	

Population 7,707,042

Age	0–14	15–19	20–24	25–29	30–64	65 plus
Male	14.0%	4.1%	3.9%	3.8%	19.8%	4.6%
Female	13.3%	3.9%	3.7%	3.6%	19.4%	5.9%

Capabilities

The Israel Defense Forces (IDF) remain the most capable force in the region, with the motivation, equipment and training to considerably overmatch the conventional capability of other regional armed forces. Currently able to contain the threats posed by Hamas and Hizbullah they have conducted precision air or missile strikes deep into Syria, retaliated to cross border fire on the Golan Heights and stepped up security on their southern border with Egypt. But the requirement to make significant budget savings and the apparent decline in the conventional threat posed by its neighbours have triggered a defence review that will make significant structural, personnel and capability changes. There will be increased emphasis on maintaining Israel's technological superiority, especially in missile defence, intelligence gathering, precision weapons and cyber capabilities. There will still be a requirement for ground manoeuvre, but army capability reductions include all M60 and *Merkava* 1 tanks (to eventually be replaced by *Merkava* IVs) and an artillery brigade. Two corvettes, about 50 F-16A/B combat aircraft and all AH-1 *Cobra* attack helicopters will be retired. The IDF will also dispose of bases in Israel's cities and consolidate elsewhere on Israel's periphery, particularly in the less populated Negev desert, where forces have already relocated in recent years. Some 4–5,000 professional personnel, about 10% of the force, will be made redundant. Reductions in the size of the standing army are possible. These changes could be made over the next two to four years.

ACTIVE 176,500 **(Army 133,000 Navy 9,500 Air 34,000) Paramilitary 8,000**

Conscript liability officers 48 months, other ranks 36 months, women 24 months (Jews and Druze only; Christians, Circassians and Muslims may volunteer)

RESERVE 465,000 **(Army 400,000 Navy 10,000 Air 55,000)**

Annual trg as cbt reservists to age 40 (some specialists to age 54) for male other ranks, 38 (or marriage/pregnancy) for women

ORGANISATIONS BY SERVICE

Strategic Forces

Israel is widely believed to have a nuclear capability – delivery means include ac, *Jericho* 1 SRBM and *Jericho* 2 IRBM, and, reportedly, *Dolphin*-class SSKs with LACM.

FORCES BY ROLE

MISSILE

3 sqn with *Jericho* 1/2

EQUIPMENT BY TYPE

MSL • STRATEGIC

IRBM: *Jericho* 2

SRBM: *Jericho* 1

Strategic Defences

FORCES BY ROLE

AIR DEFENCE

3 bty with *Arrow*/*Arrow* 2 ATBM with *Green Pine*/*Super Green Pine* radar and *Citrus Tree* command post.

6 bty with *Iron Dome*

17 bty with MIM-23B I-HAWK

6 bty with MIM-104 *Patriot*

Space

SATELLITES 8

COMMUNICATIONS 4 *Amos*

ISR 4: 3 *Ofeq* (5, 7 & 9); 1 TecSAR-1 (*Polaris*)

Army 26,000; 107,000 conscript; (total 133,000)

Organisation and structure of formations may vary according to op situations. Equipment includes that required for reserve forces on mobilisation.

FORCES BY ROLE

COMMAND

3 (regional comd) corps HQ

2 armd div HQ

4 (territorial) inf div HQ

SPECIAL FORCES

3 SF bn

MANOEUVRE

Reconnaissance

1 indep recce bn

Armoured

3 armd bde (1 armd recce coy, 3 armd bn, 1 AT coy, 1 cbt engr bn)

Mechanised

3 mech inf bde (3 mech inf bn, 1 cbt spt bn,1 sigs coy)

1 mech inf bde (6 mech inf bn)

1 indep mech inf bn

Light

1 indep inf bn

Air Manoeuvre

1 para bde (3 para bn,1 cbt spt bn. 1 sigs coy)

Other

1 armd trg bde (3 armd bn)

COMBAT SUPPORT

3 arty bde

3 engr bn

1 EOD coy

1 CBRN bn

3 int bn

2 MP bn

Reserves 400,000+ on mobilisation

FORCES BY ROLE

COMMAND

5 armd div HQ

1 AB div HQ

MANOEUVRE

Armoured

13 armd bde

Mechanised

8 mech inf bde

Light

14 (territorial/regional) inf bde

Air Manoeuvre

4 para bde

Mountain

1 mtn inf bn

COMBAT SUPPORT

4 arty bde

COMBAT SERVICE SUPPORT

6 log unit

EQUIPMENT BY TYPE

MBT 480: ε120 *Merkava* MkII; ε160 *Merkava* MkIII; ε200 *Merkava* MkIV (ε440 *Merkava* Mk1; ε330 *Merkava* MkII; ε270 *Merkava* MkIII; ε160 *Merkava* MkIV; 111 *Magach-7*; 711 M60/M60A1/M60A3 all in store)

RECCE 308: ε300 RBY-1 RAMTA; ε8 Tpz-1 *Fuchs* (NBC)

APC 1,265

APC (T) 1,165: ε65 *Namer*; ε200 *Achzarit* (modified T-55 chassis); 500 M113A2; ε400 *Nagmachon* (*Centurion* chassis); *Nakpadon* (5,000 M113A1/A2 in store)

APC (W) 100 *Ze'ev*

ARTY 530

SP 250: **155mm** 250 M109A5 (**155mm** 148 L-33; 30 M109A1; 50 M-50; **175mm** 36 M107; **203mm** 36 M110 all in store)

TOWED (**122mm** 5 D-30; **130mm** 100 M-46; **155mm** 171: 40 M-46; 50 M-68/M-71; 81 M-839P/M-845P all in store)

MRL 30: **227mm** 30 M270 MLRS (**122mm** 58 BM-21; **160mm** 50 LAR-160; **227mm** 30 M270 MLRS; **240mm** 36 BM-24; **290mm** 20 LAR-290 all in store)

MOR 250 **81mm** 250 (**81mm** 1,100; **120mm** 650 **160mm** 18 Soltam M-66 all in store)

AT • MSL

SP M113 with *Spike*; *Tamuz* (*Spike* NLOS)

MANPATS IMI MAPATS; *Spike* MR/LR/ER

AD • SAM

SP 20 *Machbet*

MANPAD FIM-92A *Stinger*

RADAR • LAND AN/PPS-15 (arty); AN/TPQ-37 *Firefinder* (arty); EL/M-2140 (veh)

MSL 100

STRATEGIC ε100 *Jericho* 1 SRBM/*Jericho* 2 IRBM

TACTICAL • SSM (7 *Lance* in store)

AEV D9R; *Puma*

ARV *Centurion* Mk2; *Eyal*; *Merkava*; M88A1; M113 ARV

VLB *Alligator* MAB; M48/60; MTU

Navy 7,000; 2,500 conscript (total 9,500)

EQUIPMENT BY TYPE

SUBMARINES

TACTICAL

SSK 3 *Dolphin* (GER Type-212 variant) with 6 single 533mm TT with UGM-84C *Harpoon* AShM/HWT, 4 single 650mm TT (3 additional vessels under construction; ISD 2014–15)

SDV 20 *Alligator* (semi-submersible)

PATROL AND COASTAL COMBATANTS 55

CORVETTES • FSGHM 3 *Eilat* (*Sa'ar* 5) with 2 quad Mk140 lnchr with RGM-84C *Harpoon* AShM, 2 32-cell VLS with *Barak* SAM (being upgraded to *Barak*-8 by 2014), 2 triple 324mm TT with Mk 46 LWT, 1 *Sea Vulcan* CIWS, 1 76mm gun (capacity either 1 AS565SA *Panther* ASW hel)

PCGM 8 *Hetz* (*Sa'ar* 4.5) with 6 single lnchr with *Gabriel* II AShM, 2 twin Mk140 lnchr with RGM-84C *Harpoon* AShM, 1 16-32-cell Mk56 VLS with *Barak* SAM, 1 *Vulcan* CIWS, 1 *Typhoon* CIWS, 1 76mm gun

PCG 2 *Reshef* (*Sa'ar* 4) with 4–6 single lnchr with *Gabriel* II AShM, 1 twin or quad Mk140 lnchr with RGM-84C *Harpoon* AShM, 2 triple 324mm TT, 1 *Phalanx* CIWS

PBFT 13: 9 *Super Dvora* MkI with 2 single 324mm TT with Mk 46 LWT (AShM may also be fitted); 4 *Super Dvora* MkII with 2 single 324mm TT with Mk 46 LWT (AShM may also be fitted)

PBT 11 *Dabur* with 2 single 324mm TT with Mk 46 LWT

PBF 18: 5 *Shaldag* with 1 *Typhoon* CIWS; 3 *Stingray*; 10 *Super Dvora* MK III (AShM & TT may be fitted)

AMPHIBIOUS • LANDING CRAFT • LCT 3: 1 *Ashdod*; 2 others

LOGISTICS AND SUPPORT 3

AG 2 *Bat Yam* (ex German Type-T45)

AX 1 *Queshet*

Naval Commandos ε300

Air Force 34,000

Responsible for Air and Space Coordination

FORCES BY ROLE

FIGHTER & FIGHTER/GROUND ATTACK

1 sqn with F-15A/B/D *Eagle*

1 sqn with F-15B/C/D *Eagle*

1 sqn with F-15I *Ra'am*

6 sqn with F-16A/B/C/D *Fighting Falcon*

4 sqn with F-16I *Sufa*

(3 sqn with A-4N *Skyhawk*/F-4 *Phantom* II/*Kfir* C-7 in reserve)

ANTI-SUBMARINE WARFARE

1 sqn with AS565SA *Panther* (missions flown by IAF but with non-rated aircrew)

MARITIME PATROL/TANKER/TRANSPORT

1 sqn with IAI-1124 *Seascan*; KC-707

ELECTRONIC WARFARE

2 sqn with RC-12D *Guardrail*; Beech A36 *Bonanza* (*Hofit*); Beech 200 *King Air*; Beech 200T *King Air*; Beech 200CT *King Air*

AIRBORNE EARLY WARNING & CONTROL

1 sqn with Gulfstream G550 *Eitam*; Gulfstream G550 *Shavit*

TANKER/TRANSPORT

1 sqn with C-130E/H *Hercules*; KC-130H *Hercules*

1 sqn (forming) with C-130J-30 *Hercules*

TRAINING

1 OPFOR sqn with F-16A/B *Fighting Falcon*

1 sqn with A-4N/TA-4H/TA-4J *Skyhawk*

ATTACK HELICOPTER

1 sqn with AH-64A *Apache*

1 sqn with AH-64D *Apache*

TRANSPORT HELICOPTER

2 sqn with CH-53D *Sea Stallion*

2 sqn with S-70A *Black Hawk*; UH-60A *Black Hawk*

1 medevac unit with CH-53D *Sea Stallion*

UAV

1 ISR sqn with *Hermes* 450

1 ISR sqn with *Searcher* MkII

1 ISR sqn with *Heron* (*Shoval*); *Heron* TP (*Eitan*)

AIR DEFENCE

3 bty with *Arrow*/*Arrow* 2

6 bty with *Iron Dome*

17 bty with MIM-23 I-HAWK

6 bty with MIM-104 *Patriot*

EQUIPMENT BY TYPE

AIRCRAFT 440 combat capable

FTR 143: 16 F-15A *Eagle*; 6 F-15B *Eagle*; 17 F-15C *Eagle*; 11 F-15D *Eagle*; 77 F-16A *Fighting Falcon*; 16 F-16B *Fighting Falcon*

FGA 251: 25 F-15I *Ra'am*; 78 F-16C *Fighting Falcon*; 49 F-16D *Fighting Falcon*; 99 F-16I *Sufa*

ATK 46: 20 A-4N *Skyhawk*; 10 TA-4H *Skyhawk*; 16 TA-4J *Skyhawk*

FTR/FGA/ATK (200+ A-4N *Skyhawk*/F-4 *Phantom* II/F-15A *Eagle*/F-16A/B *Fighting Falcon*/*Kfir* C-7 in store)

MP 3 IAI-1124 *Seascan*

ISR 6 RC-12D *Guardrail*

ELINT 4: 1 EC-707; 3 Gulfstream G550 *Shavit*

AEW 4: 2 B-707 *Phalcon*; 2 Gulfstream G550 *Eitam* (1 more on order)

TKR/TPT 11: 4 KC-130H *Hercules*; 7 KC-707

TPT 59: **Medium** 12: 5 C-130E *Hercules*; 6 C-130H *Hercules*; 1 C-130J-30 *Hercules*; **Light** 47: 3 AT-802 *Air Tractor*; 9 Beech 200 *King Air*; 8 Beech 200T *King Air*; 5 Beech 200CT *King Air*; 22 Beech A36 *Bonanza* (*Hofit*)

TRG 37: 17 Grob G-120; 20 T-6A

HELICOPTERS

ATK 77: 33 AH-1E/F *Cobra*; 27 AH-64A *Apache*; 17 AH-64D *Apache* (*Sarat*)

ASW 7 AS565SA *Panther* (missions flown by IAF but with non-rated aircrew)

ISR 12 OH-58B *Kiowa*

TPT 81: **Heavy** 26 CH-53D *Sea Stallion*; **Medium** 49: 39 S-70A *Black Hawk*; 10 UH-60A *Black Hawk*; **Light** 6 Bell 206 *Jet Ranger*

UAV • **ISR** 24+: **Heavy** 2+: *Heron* (*Shoval*); 3 *Heron* TP (*Eitan*); RQ-5A *Hunter*; **Medium** 22+: *Hermes* 450; *Hermes* 900; 22 *Searcher* MkII (22+ in store); **Light** *Harpy*

AD

SAM 24+: 24 *Arrow*/*Arrow* 2; some *Iron Dome*; some MIM-104 *Patriot*; some MIM-23 I-HAWK

GUNS 920

SP 165: **20mm** 105 M163 *Machbet Vulcan*; **23mm** 60 ZSU-23-4

TOWED 755: **23mm** 150 ZU-23; **20mm/37mm** 455 M167 *Vulcan* towed 20mm/M-1939 towed 37mm/TCM-20 towed 20mm; **40mm** 150 L/70

MSL

ASM AGM-114 *Hellfire*; AGM-62B *Walleye*; AGM-65 *Maverick*; *Popeye* I/*Popeye* II; *Delilah* AL

AAM • **IR** AIM-9 *Sidewinder*; *Python* 4; **IIR** *Python* 5; **ARH** *Derby*; AIM-120C AMRAAM

BOMB • **PGM** • JDAM (GBU-31); *Spice, Lizard, Opher, Griffon*

Airfield Defence 3,000 active (15,000 reservists)

Paramilitary ε8,000

Border Police ε8,000

Cyber

Israel is widely reported to have developed capacity for cyber operations. Some reporting has highlighted a 'Unit 8200' believed responsible for ELINT, and reportedly cyber, operations. The IDF's Intelligence and C4I Corps are also concerned with cyber-related activity, with the C4I Corps having telecommunications and EW within its purview. According to the IDF, 'the IDF cyber staff was established [in early 2011], and works to recruit qualified soldiers building an integrative body that will cooperate with other technologically-affiliated units.' The IDF has, it says, 'been engaged in cyber activity consistently and relentlessly, gathering intelligence and defending its own cyber space. Additionally if necessary the cyber space will be used to execute attacks and intelligence operations.' In early 2012, the Israel National Cyber Bureau (INCB) was created in the prime minister's office, to develop technology, human resources and international collaboration. In late October 2012, the INCB and the MoD's Directorate for Research and Development announced a dual cyber-security programme, called MASAD, 'to promote R&D projects that serve both civilian and defense goals at the national level'.

FOREIGN FORCES

UNTSO unless specified. UNTSO figures represent total numbers for mission in Israel, Syria & Lebanon

Argentina 4 obs

Australia 12 obs Austria 6 obs

Belgium 2 obs

Canada 8 obs

Chile 3 obs

China 4 obs

Denmark 10 obs

Estonia 2 obs

Finland 16 obs

France 3 obs

Ireland 13 obs

Italy 7 obs

Nepal 3 obs

Netherlands 12 obs

New Zealand 8 obs

Norway 13 obs

Russia 5 obs

Serbia 1 obs

Slovakia 2 obs

Slovenia 5 obs

Sweden 6 obs

Switzerland 12 obs

United States 2 obs • US Strategic Command; 1 AN/TPY-2 X-band radar at Nevatim

Jordan JOR

Jordanian Dinar D		2012	2013	2014
GDP	D	22.1bn	24.2bn	
	US$	31.2bn	34.1bn	
per capita	US$	4,879	5,207	
Growth	%	2.80	3.25	
Inflation	%	4.77	5.89	
Def exp	D	62bn		
	US$	87.4bn		
Def bdgt [a]	D	1.08bn	862m	899m
	US$	1.52bn	1.22bn	
FMA (US)	US$	300m	300m	300m
US$1=D		0.71	0.71	

[a] Excludes expenditure on public order and safety

Population 6,482,081

Ethnic groups: Palestinian ε50–60%

Age	0–14	15–19	20–24	25–29	30–64	65 plus
Male	17.8%	5.3%	4.9%	4.3%	16.0%	2.4%
Female	16.8%	5.0%	4.6%	4.1%	16.0%	2.6%

Capabilities

Although Jordan does not face conventional threats from its neighbours Israel, Saudi Arabia or Iraq, overspill from the Syrian war poses a variety of destabilising threats, and is putting some strain on the country. As a result, border security has been boosted, and it was decided to retain in Jordan a US HQ and F-16 detachment, after a bilateral exercise. The main roles of Jordan's fully professional armed forces are border and internal security, and the services are capable of combat and contributing to international expeditionary operations. Regular exercises take place with foreign forces. Personnel are well-trained, particularly aircrew and special forces, who are highly regarded, and have served alongside ISAF forces in Afghanistan and participate in various UN missions. The country has developed a bespoke SF training centre, and regularly plays host to various SF contingents, affording its forces opportunity to develop their capability. Jordanian forces deploy on UN peacekeeping missions, and its combat aircraft escorted Jordanian C-130s flying humanitarian aid to Libya.

ACTIVE 100,500 (Army 74,000 Navy 500 Air 12,000 Special Operations 14,000) Paramilitary 15,000

RESERVE 65,000 (Army 60,000 Joint 5,000)

ORGANISATIONS BY SERVICE

Army 74,000

FORCES BY ROLE

MANOEUVRE

Armoured

1 (strategic reserve) armd div (3 armd bde, 1 arty bde, 1 AD bde)

1 armd bde

Mechanised

5 mech bde

Light

3 lt inf bde

COMBAT SUPPORT

3 arty bde

3 AD bde

1 MRL bn

EQUIPMENT BY TYPE

MBT 752: 390 CR1 *Challenger* 1 (*Al Hussein*); 274 FV4030/2 *Khalid*; 88 M60 *Phoenix*; (292 *Tariq Centurion*; 115 M60A1A3; 23 M47/M48A5 in store)

LT TK (19 *Scorpion*; in store)

RECCE 153: 103 *Scimitar*; 50 *Ferret*

AIFV 452: 31 BMP-2; 321 *Ratel*-20; 100 YPR-765

APC 784+

APC (T) 634+: 100 M113A1; 300 M113A2 Mk1J; some *Temsah*; 234 YPR-765

PPV 150: 25 *Marauder*; 25 *Matador*; 100 *MaxxPro*

ARTY 1,441+

SP 568: **105mm** 30 M52; **155mm** 390: 370 M109A1/A2; 20 M-44; **203mm** 148 M110A2

TOWED 100: **105mm** 72: 54 M102; 18 MOBAT; **155mm** 28: 10 M1/M59; 18 M114; **203mm** (4 M115 in store)

MRL 14+: **227mm** 12 HIMARS **273mm** 2+ WM-80

MOR 759:

SP 81mm 50

TOWED 709: **81mm** 359; **107mm** 50 M30; **120mm** 300 Brandt

AT • MSL 975

SP 115: 70 M901; 45 YPR-765 with *Milan*

MANPATS *Javelin*; M47 *Dragon*; TOW/TOW-2A; 9K123 *Kornet* (AT-14 *Spriggan*)

RL 112mm 2,300 APILAS

AD

SAM 930+

SP 140: 92 9K35 *Strela*-10 (SA-13 *Gopher*); 48 9K33 *Osa*-M (SA-8 *Gecko*)

MANPAD 790+: 250 FIM-43 *Redeye*; 9K32M *Strela*-2M (SA-7B *Grail*); 300 9K36 *Strela*-3 (SA-14 *Gremlin*); 240 9K310 *Igla*-1 (SA-16 *Gimlet*); 9K38 *Igla*/*Igla*-1 (SA-18 *Grouse*)

GUNS • SP 356: **20mm** 100 M163 *Vulcan*; **23mm** 40 ZSU-23-4; **40mm** 216 M-42 (not all op)

RADAR • LAND 7 AN/TPQ-36 *Firefinder*/AN/TPQ-37 *Firefinder* (arty, mor)

ARV 137+: *Al Monjed*; 55 *Chieftain* ARV; *Centurion* Mk2; 20 M47; 32 M88A1; 30 M578; YPR-806

MW 12 *Aardvark* Mk2

Navy ε500

EQUIPMENT BY TYPE

PATROL AND COASTAL COMBATANTS 7 (+ 12 patrol boats under 10 tonnes)

PB 7: 3 *Al Hussein* (UK Vosper 30m); 4 *Abdullah* (US *Dauntless*)

Air Force 12,000

Flying hours 180 hrs/year

FORCES BY ROLE

FIGHTER

1 sqn with F-16A/B ADF *Fighting Falcon*

FIGHTER/GROUND ATTACK

2 sqn with F-16AM/BM *Fighting Falcon*

FIGHTER/GROUND ATTACK/ISR

1 sqn with F-5E/F *Tiger* II

TRANSPORT

1 sqn with C-130E/H *Hercules*; CN-235; C-295M
1 sqn with Cessna 208B; EC635
1 unit with Il-76MF *Candid*

TRAINING

1 OCU with F-5E/F *Tiger* II
1 sqn with C-101 *Aviojet*
1 sqn with T-67M *Firefly*
1 hel sqn with AS350B3; Hughes 500

ATTACK HELICOPTER

2 sqn with AH-1F *Cobra* (with TOW)

TRANSPORT HELICOPTER

1 sqn with AS332M *Super Puma*
1 sqn with Bell 205 (UH-1H *Iroquois*)
1 (Royal) flt with S-70A *Black Hawk*; UH-60L/M *Black Hawk*

AIR DEFENCE

1 comd (5–6 bty with PAC-2 *Patriot*; 5 bty with MIM-2BB Phase III I-HAWK; 6 bty with *Skyguard*/*Aspide*)

EQUIPMENT BY TYPE

AIRCRAFT 85 combat capable
FTR 46: 30 F-5E/F *Tiger* II; 16 F-16A/B ADF *Fighting Falcon*
FGA 39 F-16AM/BM *Fighting Falcon*
TPT 18: **Heavy** 2 Il-76MF *Candid*; **Medium** 7: 3 C-130E *Hercules*; 4 C-130H *Hercules*; **Light** 9: 2 C-295M; 2 CN-235; 5 Cessna 208B
TRG 25: 15 T-67M *Firefly*; 10 C-101 *Aviojet*

HELICOPTERS
ATK 25 AH-1F *Cobra*
MRH 13 EC635 (Tpt/SAR)
TPT 70: **Medium** 20: 12 AS332M *Super Puma*; 3 S-70A *Black Hawk*; 3 UH-60L *Black Hawk*; 2 UH-60M *Black Hawk*; **Light** 50: 36 Bell 205 (UH-1H *Iroquois*); 8 Hughes 500D; 6 AS350B3

AD • SAM 64: 24 MIM-23B Phase III I-HAWK; 40 PAC-2 *Patriot*

MSL
ASM AGM-65D *Maverick*; BGM-71 TOW
AAM • IR AIM-9J/N/P *Sidewinder*; R-550 *Magic*; **SARH** AIM-7 *Sparrow*; R-530; **ARH** AIM-120C AMRAAM

Joint Special Operations Command 14,000

FORCES BY ROLE

SPECIAL FORCES

1 spec ops bde (2 SF bn, 2 AB bn, 1 AB arty bn, 1 psyops unit)
1 ranger bde (1 SF bn, 3 ranger bn)

MANOEUVRE

Other

1 (Royal Guard) sy bde (1 SF regt, 3 sy bn)

TRANSPORT

1 sqn with An-32B

TRANSPORT HELICOPTER

1 sqn with MD-530F
1 sqn with UH-60L *Black Hawk*

EQUIPMENT BY TYPE

AIRCRAFT
TPT Light 3 An-32B

HELICOPTERS
MRH 6 MD-530F
TPT • Medium 8 UH-60L *Black Hawk*

Paramilitary 15,000 active

Gendarmerie ε15,000 active

3 regional comd

FORCES BY ROLE

SPECIAL FORCES

2 SF unit

MANOEUVRE

Other

10 sy bn

EQUIPMENT BY TYPE

LT TK: *Scorpion*
APC (W) 55+: 25+ EE-11 *Urutu*; 30 FV603 *Saracen*

Reserve Organisations 35,000 reservists

Civil Militia 'People's Army' ε35,000 reservists

Men 16–65, women 16–45

DEPLOYMENT

AFGHANISTAN

Operation Enduring Freedom–Afghanistan 720; 1 ranger bn

CÔTE D'IVOIRE

UN • UNOCI 1,067; 7 obs; 1 SF coy; 1 inf bn

DEMOCRATIC REPUBLIC OF THE CONGO

UN • MONUSCO 230; 17 obs; 1 SF coy; 1 fd hospital

HAITI

UN • MINUSTAH 252; 1 inf coy

IRAQ

UN • UNAMI 2 obs

LIBERIA

UN • UNMIL 120; 4 obs; 1 med coy

MALI

UN • MINUSMA 1

SOUTH SUDAN

UN • UNMISS 3; 3 obs

SUDAN

UN • UNAMID 14; 13 obs

FOREIGN FORCES

France *Operation Tamour* 80; 1 med det
United States Central Command 900: 1 FGA sqn with 6 F-16C *Fighting Falcon*; 1 AD bty with MIM-104 *Patriot*

Kuwait KWT

Kuwaiti Dinar D		2012	2013	2014
GDP	D	48.2bn	48.2bn	
	US$	173bn	173bn	
per capita	US$	45,824	44,585	
Growth	%	5.08	1.06	
Inflation	%	2.93	3.33	
Def exp	D	911m		
	US$	3.28bn		
Def bdgt	D	1.32bn	1.23bn	
	US$	4.76bn	4.43bn	
US$1=D		0.28	0.28	

Population 2,695,316

Ethnic groups: Nationals 35%; other Arab 35%; South Asian 9%; Iranian 4%; other 17%

Age	0–14	15–19	20–24	25–29	30–64	65 plus
Male	13.3%	3.4%	5.1%	7.6%	28.3%	1.0%
Female	12.3%	3.1%	3.8%	4.5%	16.5%	1.1%

Capabilities

Kuwait's armed forces have been transformed since they failed to prevent an Iraqi invasion in 1991. A more professional officer corps now exists, with better training, greater joint force capabilities and a higher state of readiness. However, the force remains too small to deter a resolute threat from its larger neighbours, and the country relies on its membership of the GCC and relationship with the US to guarantee its security. A close defence relationship with the US has afforded Kuwait access to high-tech weapons systems and combined training exercises. This has allowed Kuwait to develop a professional, relatively well-equipped, land-focused force. The US maintains substantial forces in the country. The navy is small, with patrol boats capable of ensuring maritime security and defence against small flotillas entering Kuwaiti waters. The air force regularly deploys aircraft to GCC air exercises and flew humanitarian flights during the 2011 Libya conflict. Plans to acquire two C-17 *Globemaster* IIIs and three KC-130J tanker transports will provide the country with hitherto absent airlift capabilities.

ACTIVE 15,500 (Army 11,000 Navy 2,000 Air 2,500)
Paramilitary 7,100

RESERVE 23,700 (Joint 23,700)

Reserve obligation to age 40; 1 month annual trg

ORGANISATIONS BY SERVICE

Army 11,000

FORCES BY ROLE

SPECIAL FORCES
- 1 SF unit (forming)

MANOEUVRE
- **Reconnaissance**
- 1 mech/recce bde
- **Armoured**
- 3 armd bde
- **Mechanised**
- 2 mech inf bde
- **Light**
- 1 cdo bn
- **Other**
- 1 (Amiri) gd bde

COMBAT SUPPORT
- 1 arty bde
- 1 engr bde
- 1 MP bn

COMBAT SERVICE SUPPORT
- 1 log gp
- 1 fd hospital

Reserve

FORCES BY ROLE

MANOEUVRE
- **Mechanised**
- 1 bde

EQUIPMENT BY TYPE

MBT 293: 218 M1A2 *Abrams*; 75 M-84 (75 more in store)
RECCE 11 TPz-1 *Fuchs* NBC
AIFV 432: 76 BMP-2; 120 BMP-3; 236 *Desert Warrior*† (incl variants)
APC 260
- **APC (T)** 260: 230 M113A2; 30 M577
- **APC (W)** (40 TH 390 *Fahd* in store)

ARTY 218
- **SP 155mm** 106: 37 M109A3; 18 (AMX) Mk F3; 51 PLZ45; (18 AU-F-1 in store)
- **MRL 300mm** 27 9A52 *Smerch*
- **MOR** 78: **81mm** 60; **107mm** 6 M-30; **120mm** ε12 RT-F1

AT • MSL 118+
- **SP** 74: 66 HMMWV TOW; 8 M901
- **MANPATS** 44+: 44 TOW-2; M47 *Dragon*
- **RCL 84mm** ε200 *Carl Gustav*

AD • SAM 60+
- **STATIC/SHELTER** 12 *Aspide*
- **MANPAD** 48 *Starburst*; *Stinger*
- **GUNS • TOWED 35mm** 12+ Oerlikon

ARV 24+: 24 M88A1/2; Type-653A; *Warrior*
MW *Aardvark* Mk2

Navy ε2,000 (incl 500 Coast Guard)

EQUIPMENT BY TYPE

PATROL AND COASTAL COMBATANTS 17
- **PCFG** 2:
  - 1 *Al Sanbouk* (GER Lurssen TNC-45) with 2 twin lnchr with MM-40 *Exocet* AShM, 1 76mm gun
  - 1 *Istiqlal* (GER Lurssen FPB-57) with 2 twin lnchr with MM-40 *Exocet* AShM, 1 76mm gun
- **PBF** 10 *Al Nokatha* (US Mk V *Pegasus*)
- **PBG** 8 *Um Almaradim* (FRA P-37 BRL) with 2 twin lnchr with *Sea Skua* AShM, 1 sextuple lnchr (lnchr only)

LOGISTICS AND SUPPORT • AG 1 *Sawahil*

Air Force 2,500

Flying hours 210 hrs/year

FORCES BY ROLE

FIGHTER/GROUND ATTACK

2 sqn with F/A-18C/D *Hornet*

TRANSPORT

1 sqn with L-100-30

TRAINING

1 unit with EMB-312 *Tucano* (*Tucano* Mk52)*; *Hawk* Mk64*

ATTACK HELICOPTER

1 sqn with AH-64D *Apache*

1 atk/trg sqn with SA342 *Gazelle* with HOT

TRANSPORT HELICOPTER

1 sqn with AS532 *Cougar*; SA330 *Puma*; S-92

AIR DEFENCE

1 comd (5–6 SAM bty with PAC-2 *Patriot*; 5 SAM bty with MIM-23B I-HAWK Phase III; 6 SAM bty with *Skyguard/Aspide*)

EQUIPMENT BY TYPE

AIRCRAFT 66 combat capable

FGA 39: 31 F/A-18C *Hornet*; 8 F/A-18D *Hornet*

TPT • Medium 3 L-100-30

TRG 27: 11 *Hawk* Mk64*; 16 EMB-312 *Tucano* (*Tucano* Mk52)*

HELICOPTERS

ATK 16 AH-64D *Apache*

MRH 13 SA342 *Gazelle* with HOT

TPT • Medium 13: 3 AS532 *Cougar*; 7 SA330 *Puma*; 3 S-92

MSL

ASM AGM-65G *Maverick*; AGM-114K *Hellfire*

AShM AGM-84A *Harpoon*

AAM • IR AIM-9L *Sidewinder*; R-550 *Magic*; **SARH** AIM-7F *Sparrow*; **ARH** AIM-120C7 AMRAAM

AD • SAM 76: 40 PAC-2 *Patriot*; 24 MIM-23B I-HAWK Phase III; 12 *Skyguard/Aspide*

Paramilitary ε7,100 active

National Guard ε6,600 active

FORCES BY ROLE

SPECIAL FORCES

1 SF bn

MANOEUVRE

Reconnaissance

1 armd car bn

Other

3 security bn

COMBAT SUPPORT

1 MP bn

EQUIPMENT BY TYPE

RECCE 20 VBL

APC (W) 97+: 5+ *Desert Chameleon*; 70 *Pandur*; 22 S600 (incl variants)

ARV *Pandur*

Coast Guard 500

PATROL AND COASTAL COMBATANTS 32

PBF 12 *Manta*

PB 20: 3 *Al Shaheed*; 4 *Inttisar* (Austal 31.5m); 3 *Kassir* (Austal 22m); 10 *Subahi*

AMPHIBIOUS • LANDING CRAFT • LCU 4: 2 *Al Tahaddy*; 1 *Saffar*; 1 other

LOGISTICS AND SUPPORT • AG 1 *Sawahil*

FOREIGN FORCES

United Kingdom 35

United States Central Command: 23,000; 1 ABCT; 1 ARNG cbt avn bde; 1 ARNG spt bde; 2 AD bty with total of 16 PAC-3 *Patriot*; elm 1 (APS) ABCT eqpt set.

Lebanon LBN

Lebanese Pound LP		2012	2013	2014
GDP	LP	62.3tr	66.1tr	
	US$	41.3bn	43.8bn	
per capita	US$	10,311	10,793	
Growth	%	1.50	2.00	
Inflation	%	6.57	6.66	
Def exp	LP	2.62tr		
	US$	1.74bn		
Def bdgt	LP	1.73tr		
	US$	1.15bn	1.22bn	
FMA (US)	US$	75m	75m	75m
US$1=LP		1507.48	1507.50	

Population 4,131,583

Ethnic and religious groups: Christian 30%; Druze 6%; Armenian 4%, excl ε300,000 Syrians and ε350,000 Palestinian refugees

Age	0–14	15–19	20–24	25–29	30–64	65 plus
Male	11.3%	4.3%	4.6%	4.5%	19.9%	4.3%
Female	10.8%	4.1%	4.5%	4.4%	22.2%	5.1%

Capabilities

2013 saw considerable overspill into Lebanon from the conflict in Syria, including bombings, kidnappings and clashes between Islamists and the armed forces. This has aggravated political and sectarian divisions, leading to institutional paralysis and outbreaks of violence. However, Lebanon has so far avoided a descent into a fresh civil war of its own. An ambitious five-year plan to modernise Lebanese Armed Forces (LAF) capabilities was announced in September 2013. The LAF are viewed with suspicion by large segments of the population, especially in the Sunni community, but it has played a key role in containing localised violence and mediating between rival groups across the country. Reflecting rather than transcending Lebanon's divisions, the armed forces are afflicted by severe logistical, operational and political problems. Delicate domestic missions undertaken since 2005 have overstretched and exhausted the force. Despite Western aid, it remains ill-equipped, while some experts have cast doubt on leadership quality. In 2013 Hizbullah provided advice and training to Syrian government forces as well as security to lines of communication and an expeditionary force of around 2,000 fighters. Inside Lebanon, it has sought to isolate Sunni towns in the Bekaa Valley and dismantle rebel support networks. Hizbullah forces appear more tactically effective than Syrian government troops, but they have suffered increasing numbers of casualties.

ACTIVE 60,000 (Army 56,600 Navy 1,800 Air 1,600) Paramilitary 20,000

ORGANISATIONS BY SERVICE

Army 56,600

FORCES BY ROLE

5 regional comd (Beirut, Bekaa Valley, Mount Lebanon, North, South)

SPECIAL FORCES

1 cdo regt

MANOEUVRE

Armoured

2 armd regt

Mechanised

11 mech inf bde

Air Manoeuvre

1 AB regt

Amphibious

1 mne cdo regt

Other

1 Presidential Guard bde

5 intervention regt

2 border sy regt

COMBAT SUPPORT

2 arty regt

1 cbt spt bde (1 engr rgt, 1 AT regt, 1 sigs regt)

1 MP bde

COMBAT SERVICE SUPPORT

1 log bde

1 med regt

1 construction regt

EQUIPMENT BY TYPE

MBT 324: 92 M48A1/A5; 185 T-54; 47 T-55

RECCE 55 AML

AIFV 16 AIFV-B-C25

APC 1,330

APC (T) 1,244 M113A1/A2 (incl variants)

APC (W) 86 VAB VCT

ARTY 487

TOWED 201: **105mm** 13 M101A1; **122mm** 35: 9 D-30; 26 M-30; **130mm** 15 M-46; **155mm** 138: 18 M114A1; 106 M198; 14 Model-50

MRL 122mm 11 BM-21

MOR 275: **81mm** 134; **82mm** 112; **120mm** 29 Brandt

AT

MSL • MANPATS 38: 26 *Milan*; 12 TOW

RCL 106mm 113 M40A1

RL 73mm 11 M-50; **90mm** 8 M-69

AD

SAM • MANPAD 83 9K32 *Strela*-2/2M (SA-7A *Grail*/SA-7B *Grail*)‡

GUNS • TOWED 77: **20mm** 20; **23mm** 57 ZU-23

ARV M113 ARV; T-54/55 ARV reported

VLB MTU-72 reported

MW Bozena

UAV • ISR • Medium 8 *Mohajer* 4

Navy 1,800

EQUIPMENT BY TYPE

In addition to the vessels listed, the Lebanese Navy operates a further 22 vessels with a full-load displacement below ten tonnes.

PATROL AND COASTAL COMBATANTS 13

PCC 1 *Trablous*

PB 11: 1 *Aamchit* (GER *Bremen*); 1 *Al Kalamoun* (FRA *Avel Gwarlarn*); 7 *Tripoli* (UK *Attacker*/*Tracker* Mk 2); 1 *Naquora* (GER *Bremen*); 1 *Tabarja* (GER *Bergen*)

PBF 1

AMPHIBIOUS • LANDING CRAFT • LCT 2 *Sour* (FRA *Edic* – capacity 8 APC; 96 troops)

Air Force 1,600

4 air bases

FORCES BY ROLE

FIGHTER/GROUND ATTACK

1 sqn with *Hunter* Mk6/Mk9/T66; Cessna AC-208 *Combat Caravan**

ATTACK HELICOPTER

1 sqn with SA342L *Gazelle*

TRANSPORT HELICOPTER

4 sqn with Bell 205 (UH-1H)

1 sqn with AS330/IAR330SM *Puma*

1 trg sqn with R-44 *Raven* II

EQUIPMENT BY TYPE

AIRCRAFT 9 combat capable

FGA 4: 3 *Hunter* Mk6/Mk9; 1 *Hunter* T66

ISR 3 Cessna AC-208 *Combat Caravan**

TRG (3 *Bulldog*; could be refurbished)

HELICOPTERS

MRH 9: 1 AW139; 8 SA342L *Gazelle* (plus 5 unserviceable – could be refurbished); (5 SA316 *Alouette* III unserviceable – 3 could be refurbished); (1 SA318 *Alouette* II unserviceable – could be refurbished)

TPT 29: **Medium** 13: 3 S-61N (fire fighting); 10 AS330/IAR330 *Puma*; **Light** 16: 12 Bell 205 (UH-1H *Huey*) (11 more unserviceable); 4 R-44 *Raven* II (basic trg); (7 Bell 212 unserviceable – 6 could be refurbished)

Paramilitary ε20,000 active

Internal Security Force ε20,000

Ministry of Interior

FORCES BY ROLE

Other Combat Forces

1 (police) judicial unit

1 regional sy coy

1 (Beirut Gendarmerie) sy coy

EQUIPMENT BY TYPE

APC (W) 60 V-200 *Chaimite*

Customs

PATROL AND COASTAL COMBATANTS 7

PB 7: 5 *Aztec*; 2 *Tracker*

Middle East and North Africa

FOREIGN FORCES

Unless specified, figures refer to UNTSO and represent total numbers for the mission in Israel, Syria & Lebanon.

Argentina 4 obs
Armenia UNIFIL 1
Australia 12 obs
Austria 6 obs • UNIFIL 168: 1 log coy
Bangladesh UNIFIL 326: 1 FFG; 1 PCO
Belarus UNIFIL 5
Belgium 2 obs • UNIFIL 104: 1 engr coy
Brazil UNIFIL 260: 1 FFGHM
Brunei UNIFIL 30
Cambodia UNIFIL 219: 1 engr coy
Canada 8 obs (*Op Jade*)
Chile 3 obs
China, People's Republic of 4 obs • UNIFIL 343: 1 engr bn; 1 fd hospital
Croatia UNIFIL 1
Cyprus UNIFIL 2
Denmark 10 obs
El Salvador UNIFIL 52: 1 inf pl
Estonia 2 obs
Finland 16 obs • UNIFIL 192; 1 inf coy
France 3 obs • UNIFIL 863: 1 armd cav BG; *Leclerc*; AMX-10P; PVP; VAB; CAESAR; AU-F1; *Mistral*
Germany UNIFIL 149: 2 PC
Ghana UNIFIL 869: 1 mech inf bn
Greece UNIFIL 57: 1 PB
Guatemala UNIFIL 1
Hungary UNIFIL 4
India UNIFIL 896: 1 mech inf bn; elm 1 fd hospital
Indonesia UNIFIL 1,288: 1 mech inf bn; 1 MP coy; elm 1 fd hospital; 1 FFGM
Ireland 13 obs • UNIFIL 358: 1 inf bn(-)
Italy 7 obs • UNIFIL 1,137: 1 cav bde HQ; 1 amph bn; 1 hel flt; 1 engr coy; 1 sigs coy; 1 CIMIC coy
Kenya UNIFIL 1
Korea, Republic of UNIFIL 321: 1 mech inf bn
Macedonia, Former Yugoslav Republic of UNIFIL 1
Malaysia UNIFIL 829: 1 mech inf bn; 1 mech inf coy
Nepal 3 obs • UNIFIL 869: 1 inf bn
Netherlands 12 obs
New Zealand 8 obs
Nigeria UNIFIL 1
Norway 13 obs
Qatar UNIFIL 3
Russia 5 obs
Serbia 1 obs • UNIFIL 49
Sierra Leone UNIFIL 3
Slovakia 2 obs
Slovenia 5 obs • UNIFIL 14; 1 inf pl
Spain UNIFIL 587: 1 armd inf bde HQ; 1 mech inf BG
Sri Lanka UNIFIL 151: 1 inf coy
Sweden 6 obs
Switzerland 12 obs
Tanzania UNIFIL 158; 2 MP coy
Turkey UNIFIL 190: 1 FFGH
United States 2 obs

Libya LBY

Libyan Dinar D		2012	2013	2014
GDP	D	103bn	121bn	
	US$	81.9bn	96.4bn	
per capita	US$	12,778	14,761	
Growth	%	104.48	20.19	
Inflation	%	6.07	2.00	
Def exp	D	3.77bn		
	US$	2.99bn		
Def bdgt	D	3.77bn	6bn	
	US$	2.99bn	4.77bn	
US$1=D		1.26	1.26	

Population 6,002,347

Age	0–14	15–19	20–24	25–29	30–64	65 plus
Male	14.0%	4.7%	5.0%	5.4%	20.8%	2.0%
Female	13.3%	4.4%	4.5%	4.8%	19.2%	1.9%

Capabilities

Attacks against diplomatic and political targets underscored the challenge from militias, while stalled attempts to incorporate militias into national institutions underlined the weakness of the central government. It remains unclear whether the General National Congress has any meaningful authority over the former rebels. These still consist of a large number of 'brigades', most of which have little formal structure of command and control. Political, regional and tribal interests impede security reform. As part of its DDR plan, the government established a Warriors' Affairs Commission to enable individual integration of militiamen. Meanwhile, in an attempt to organise existing militias under nominal state control before DDR, two umbrella organisations were formed: the Supreme Security Committees (SSC) under the Ministry of Interior and Libya Shield, under army command. However, salaries paid to members of the armed forces and police remained lower than those paid to the SSC and Libya Shield by the interior and defence ministries and, even while they ostensibly reported to the government, many militias retained some autonomy and territorial control. In parallel, Tripoli announced the creation of a 20,000-strong general purpose force, recruiting non-militia personnel to circumvent possible loyalty issues. Italy, the UK and the US were among those who offered to train troops. Only some Gadhafi-regime weapons were destroyed in 2011, but precise ownership of remaining equipment remains in doubt, as does serviceability. It is possible to estimate remaining warships and military aircraft but it is not clear if Libya retains any credible air or maritime capability. (See pp. 299–300.)

ACTIVE 7,000

ORGANISATIONS BY SERVICE

Army up to 7,000

FORCES BY ROLE

SPECIAL FORCES
1 SF bn
MANOEUVRE
Armoured
1 armd bn
Light
Some mot inf bn
Other
1 sy unit
COMBAT SUPPORT
1+ AD bn

EQUIPMENT BY TYPE

Most of the equipment that survived the 2011 conflict in a salvageable condition is still awaiting reactivation.
MBT 18: 7+ T-55; 11+ T-72
RECCE 4+ BRDM-2
AIFV 7+ BMP-1
APC 11+
APC (T) 4+ M113;
APC (W) 7+ BTR-60PB
AT • MSL
SP some 9P122 *Malyutka*; 10 9P157-2 *Khryzantema*-S
MANPATS some: 9K11 *Malyutka* (AT-3 *Sagger*); 9K11 *Fagot* (AT-4 *Spigot*); 9K113 *Konkurs* (AT-5 *Spandrel*); *Milan*
RCL some: **106mm** M40A1; **84mm** *Carl Gustav*
AD • SAM • SP: 9K338 *Igla*-S (SA-24 *Grinch*)
GUNS
SP 23mm some ZSU-23-4
TOWED: **14.5mm** some ZPU-2
MSL • TACTICAL • SSM some: *Scud*-B

Navy (incl Coast Guard) not known

EQUIPMENT BY TYPE

SUBMARINES • TACTICAL • SSK 2 *Khyber*† (FSU *Foxtrot*) each with 10 533mm TT (6 fwd, 4 aft)
PRINCIPAL SURFACE COMBATANTS 1
FRIGATES • FFGM 1 *Al Hani*† (FSU *Koni*) with 2 twin lnchr (with P-15 *Termit*-M (SS-N-2C *Styx*) AShM, 1 twin lnchr with 9K33 *Osa*-M (SA-N-4 *Gecko*) SAM, 2 twin 406mm ASTT with USET-95 Type-40 LWT, 1 RBU 6000 *Smerch 2*, 2 twin 76mm gun
PATROL AND COASTAL COMBATANTS 17
CORVETTES • FSGM 1 *Tariq Ibin Ziyad* (FSU *Nanuchka* II) with 4 single lnchr with P-15 *Termit*-M (SS-N-2C *Styx*) AShM, 1 twin lnchr with SA-N-4 *Gecko* SAM
PBFG 5:
4 *Al Zuara* (FSU *Osa* II) with 4 single lnchr with P-15 *Termit*-M (SS-N-2C *Styx*) AShM
1 *Sharaba* (FRA *Combattante* II) with 4 single lnchr with *Otomat* Mk2 AShM, 1 76mm gun (3 further vessels may be non-operational)
PB: 11: 8 *Burdi* (Damen Stan 1605); 2 *Ikrimah* (FRA RPB20); 1 *Hamelin*
MINE WARFARE • MINE COUNTERMEASURES 4
MSO 4 *Ras al Gelais* (FSU *Natya*)
AMPHIBIOUS
LANDING SHIPS • LST 2 *Ibn Harissa* (capacity 1 hel; 11 MBT; 240 troops)
LANDING CRAFT 5
LCAC 2 *Slingsby* SAH 2200
LCT 3† C107
LOGISTICS AND SUPPORT 11
AFD 2
ARS 1 *Al Munjed* (YUG *Spasilac*)
YDT 1 *Al Manoud* (FSU *Yelva*)
YTB 7

Coastal Defence

EQUIPMENT BY TYPE

PBF 5 *Bigliani*
PB 6 PV30

Air Force not known

EQUIPMENT BY TYPE

A small number of aircraft inherited from the previous regime continue to be operated, though the air force needs to be rebuilt. Maintainability likely an issue.
AIRCRAFT 21 combat capable
FTR 8: 6 MiG-23MLD *Flogger*; 2 MiG-23UB *Flogger*
FGA 9+: 4+ MiG-21bis *Fishbed*; 3 MiG-21UM *Fishbed*; 2 *Mirage* F-1E (F-1ED); (up to 10 more *Mirage* F-1E in store)
TPT 7: **Heavy** 2 Il-76TD *Candid*; **Medium** 3: 2 C-130H *Hercules*; 1 L-100-30; **Light**: 2 An-26 *Curl*
TRG 11: 4 G-2 *Galeb*; 3 L-39ZO *Albatros*; 4 SF-260WL *Warrior**
HELICOPTERS
ATK 3: 3 Mi-25 *Hind* D;
TPT 9+: **Heavy** 2 CH-47C *Chinook*; **Medium** 5 Mi-8T *Hip*; **Light** 2+: 1+ Bell 206 *Jet Ranger* (AB-206); 1 PZL Mi-2 *Hoplite*
MSL
ASM 9M17 (AT-2 *Swatter*)
ARM Kh-58 (AS-11 *Kilter*)
AAM • IR R-3 (AA-2 *Atoll*)‡; R-60 (AA-8 *Aphid*); R-550 *Magic*; **IR/SARH** R-23/24 (AA-7 *Apex*)

Mauritania MRT

Mauritanian Ouguiya OM		2012	2013	2014
GDP	OM	1.24tr	1.4tr	
	US$	4.2bn	4.55bn	
per capita	US$	1,157	1,224	
Growth	%	6.36	5.91	
Inflation	%	4.90	4.67	
Def exp	OM	33.1bn	44.5bn	
	US$	112m	145m	
FMA (US)	US$	0.2m		
US$1=OM		296.18	307.42	

Population 3,437,610

Age	0–14	15–19	20–24	25–29	30–64	65 plus
Male	20.0%	5.3%	4.5%	3.8%	13.1%	1.5%
Female	19.8%	5.4%	4.8%	4.2%	15.5%	2.0%

Capabilities

While Mauritania's armed forces may be able to cope with some internal security contingencies, limited airlift capacity means the military lacks mobility across the country's extensive territory. Force readiness appears low, with little combat experience. Much of the armed forces' equipment is outdated. Investment in new equipment is sporadic, although a focus on the air force and navy has marginally improved resource-protection capabilities and light transport. Patrol craft donated by the EU have been key to the navy's improvement. Limited capability to secure territory and resources, combined with the perceived regional threat from al-Qaeda in the Islamic Maghreb, has encouraged the US to provide training to the armed forces through the *Flintlock* Joint Combined Exchange Training programme as well as other military-to-military exercises (in 2012 these included the *Seaborder* 2012 maritime exercise in Algeria). This also seems integral in spurring the government to purchase new capabilities: the first EMB-314 *Super Tucanos* were delivered in 2012, and there were reports of Mauritanian interest in AW-109 helicopters during the 2013 Paris Air Show.

ACTIVE 15,850 (Army 15,000 Navy 600 Air 250)
Paramilitary 5,000

Conscript liability 24 months authorised

ORGANISATIONS BY SERVICE

Army 15,000

FORCES BY ROLE

6 mil regions

MANOEUVRE

Reconnaissance

1 armd recce sqn

Armoured

1 armd bn

Light

7 mot inf bn

8 (garrison) inf bn

Air Manoeuvre

1 cdo/para bn

Other

2 (camel corps) bn

1 gd bn

COMBAT SUPPORT

3 arty bn

4 ADA bty

1 engr coy

EQUIPMENT BY TYPE

MBT 35 T-54/T-55

RECCE 70: 20 AML-60; 40 AML-90; 10 *Saladin*

APC

APC (W) 25: 5 FV603 *Saracen*; ε20 M3 Panhard

ARTY 202

TOWED 80: **105mm** 36 HM-2/M101A1; **122mm** 44: 20 D-30; 24 D-74

MRL 8: **107mm** 4 Type-63; **122mm** 4 Type-81

MOR 114: **60mm** 24; **81mm** 60; **120mm** 30 Brandt

AT • MSL • MANPATS 24 *Milan*

RCL 114: **75mm** ε24 M20; **106mm** ε90 M40A1

AD • SAM 104

SP ε4 SA-9 *Gaskin* (reported)

MANPAD ε100 9K32 *Strela-2* (SA-7 *Grail*)‡

GUNS • TOWED 82: **14.5mm** 28: 16 ZPU-2; 12 ZPU-4; **23mm** 20 ZU-23-2; **37mm** 10 M-1939; **57mm** 12 S-60; **100mm** 12 KS-19

ARV T-54/55 ARV reported

Navy ε600

EQUIPMENT BY TYPE

PATROL AND COASTAL COMBATANTS 18

PCO 1 *Voum-Legleita*

PCC 5: 1 *Abourbekr Ben Amer* (FRA OPV 54); 1 *Arguin*; 2 *Conjera*; 1 *Limam El Hidran* (PRC *Huangpu)*

PB 12: 1 *El Nasr*† (FRA *Patra*); 4 *Mandovi*; 1 *Yacoub Ould Rajel* (FRA RPB18); 2 Rodman 55M; 2 *Saeta*-12; 2 *Megsem Bakkar* (FRA RPB20 – for SAR duties)

Air Force 250

EQUIPMENT BY TYPE

AIRCRAFT 4 combat capable

TPT 8: **Light** 7: 2 BN-2 *Defender*; 1 C-212; 2 PA-31T *Cheyenne* II; 2 Y-12(II); **PAX** 1 Basler BT-67

TRG 11: 3 EMB-312 *Tucano*; 4 EMB-314 *Super Tucano**; 4 SF-260E

HELICOPTERS

MRH 3: 1 SA313B *Alouette* II; 2 Z-9

Paramilitary ε5,000 active

Gendarmerie ε3,000

Ministry of Interior

FORCES BY ROLE

MANOEUVRE

Other

6 regional sy coy

National Guard 2,000

Ministry of Interior

Aux 1,000

Customs

PATROL AND COASTAL COMBATANTS • PB 2: 1 *Dah Ould Bah* (FRA *Amgram* 14); 1 *Yaboub Ould Rajel* (FRA RPB18)

DEPLOYMENT

MALI

UN • MINUSMA 4

Morocco MOR

Moroccan Dirham D		2012	2013	2014
GDP	D	840bn	899bn	
	US$	97.5bn	107bn	
per capita	US$	2,999	3,260	
Growth	%	2.99	4.52	
Inflation	%	1.30	2.47	
Def exp	D	29.4bn		
	US$	3.41bn		
Def bdgt	D	29.4bn	31.3bn	
	US$	3.41bn	3.73bn	
FMA (US)	US$	8m	8m	7m
US$1=D		8.62	8.39	

Population 32,649,130

Age	0–14	15–19	20–24	25–29	30–64	65 plus
Male	13.8%	4.5%	4.4%	4.5%	19.2%	2.8%
Female	13.3%	4.5%	4.5%	4.7%	20.3%	3.4%

Capabilities

Morocco's armed forces are well-trained and enjoy a good relationship with US and French armed forces. The armed forces have gained extensive experience in counter-insurgency operations in Western Sahara. This has given them expertise in desert warfare and combined air–land operational experience, although there is little capability to launch tri-service operations. The country has taken part in many peacekeeping operations, providing overseas experience for thousands of its troops. However, there has been little experience in state-on-state warfare. The military is relatively mobile, relying on mechanised infantry, supported by a modest fleet of medium lift, fixed-wing transport aircraft and various transport helicopters. Air force equipment is ageing, with the bulk of the combat fleet procured in the 1970s and 1980s, although this has been partially rectified by delivery, in 2012, of 24 F-16s. This is a tangible benefit of the closer relationship with the US, amid a shared concern over non-state threats. The navy has traditionally been the least favoured and used of the three services, with a moderately sized but ageing fleet of patrol and coastal craft that is incapable of preventing fast-boat smuggling across the Mediterranean. Nonetheless, more significant investment is now being seen in the fleet, with three SIGMA frigates delivered and a FREMM destroyer on sea trials in late 2013, which will provide much-improved sea-control capability.

ACTIVE 195,800 (Army 175,000 Navy 7,800 Air 13,000) **Paramilitary 50,000**

Conscript liability 18 months authorised; most enlisted personnel are volunteers

RESERVE 150,000 (Army 150,000)

Reserve obligation to age 50

ORGANISATIONS BY SERVICE

Army ε75,000; 100,000 conscript (total 175,000)

FORCES BY ROLE

2 comd (Northern Zone, Southern Zone)

MANOEUVRE

Armoured

12 armd bn

Mechanised

3 mech inf bde

Mechanised/Light

8 mech/mot inf regt (2–3 bn)

Light

1 lt sy bde
3 (camel corps) mot inf bn
35 lt inf bn
4 cdo unit

Air Manoeuvre

2 para bde
2 AB bn

Mountain

1 mtn inf bn

COMBAT SUPPORT

11 arty bn
7 engr bn
1 AD bn

Royal Guard 1,500

FORCES BY ROLE

MANOEUVRE

Other

1 gd bn
1 cav sqn

EQUIPMENT BY TYPE

MBT 434: 40 T-72, 220 M60A1; 120 M60A3; 54 Type-90-II (MBT-2000) (reported); (ε200 M48A5 in store)
LT TK 116: 5 AMX-13; 111 SK-105 *Kuerassier*
RECCE 384: 38 AML-60-7; 190 AML-90; 80 AMX-10RC; 40 EBR-75; 16 *Eland*; 20 M1114 HMMWV
AIFV 70: 10 AMX-10P; 30 MK III-20 *Ratel*-20; 30 MK III-90 *Ratel*-90
APC 851
APC (T) 486: 400 M113A1/A2; 86 M577A2
APC (W) 365: 45 VAB VCI; 320 VAB VTT
ARTY 2,141
SP 282: **105mm** 5 Mk 61; **155mm** 217: 84 M109A1/A1B; 43 M109A2; 90 (AMX) Mk F3; **203mm** 60 M110
TOWED 118: **105mm** 50: 30 L118 Light Gun; 20 M101; **130mm** 18 M-46; **155mm** 50: 30 FH-70; 20 M114
MRL 35 BM-21
MOR 1,706
SP 56: **106mm** 32–36 M106A2; **120mm** 20 (VAB APC)
TOWED 1,650: **81mm** 1,100 Expal model LN; **120mm** 550 Brandt
AT • MSL
SP 80 M901
MANPATS 9K11 *Malyutka* (AT-3 *Sagger*); M47 *Dragon*; *Milan*; TOW
RCL 106mm 350 M40A1

RL 89mm 200 M20
GUNS 36
SP 100mm 8 SU-100
TOWED 90mm 28 M-56
UAV • Heavy R4E-50 *Skyeye*
AD • SAM
SP 49: 12 2K22M *Tunguska*-M (SA-19 *Grison*) SPAAGM; 37 M48 *Chaparral*
MANPAD 9K32 *Strela*-2 (SA-7 *Grail*)‡
GUNS 407
SP 60 M163 *Vulcan*
TOWED 347: **14.5mm** 200: 150-180 ZPU-2; 20 ZPU-4; **20mm** 40 M167 *Vulcan*; **23mm** 75-90 ZU-23-2; **100mm** 17 KS-19
RADAR • LAND: RASIT (veh, arty)
ARV 48+: 10 *Greif*; 18 M88A1; M578; 20 VAB-ECH

Navy 7,800 (incl 1,500 Marines)

EQUIPMENT BY TYPE
PRINCIPAL SURFACE COMBATANTS
FRIGATES 5
FFGHM 3 *Tarik ben Ziyad* (NLD SIGMA 9813/10513) with 4 single lnchr with MM-40 *Exocet* Block II/III AShM, 2 sextuple lnchr with MICA SAM, 2 triple 324 mm ASTT with Mu-90 LWT, 1 76mm gun (capacity 1 AS565SA *Panther*)
FFGH 2 *Mohammed V* (FRA *Floreal*) with 2 single lnchr with MM-38 *Exocet* AShM, 1 76mm gun (can be fitted with *Simbad* SAM if 20mm guns replaced) (capacity 1 AS565SA *Panther*)
PATROL AND COASTAL COMBATANTS 50
CORVETTES • FSGM 1
1 *Lt Col Errhamani* (ESP *Descubierto*) with 2 twin lnchr with MM-38 *Exocet* AShM, 1 octuple *Albatros* lnchr with *Aspide* SAM, 2 triple 324mm ASTT with Mk 46 LWT, 1 76mm gun
PSO 1 *Bin an Zaran* (OPV 70) with 1 76mm gun
PCG 4 *Cdt El Khattabi* (ESP *Lazaga* 58m) with 4 single lnchr with MM-38 *Exocet* AShM, 1 76mm gun
PCO 5 *Rais Bargach* (under control of fisheries dept)
PCC 12:
4 *El Hahiq* (DNK *Osprey* 55, incl 2 with customs)
6 *LV Rabhi* (ESP 58m B-200D)
2 *Okba* (FRA PR-72) each with 1 76mm gun
PB 27: 6 *El Wacil* (FRA P-32); 10 VCSM (RPB 20); 10 Rodman 101; 1 other (UK *Bird*)
AMPHIBIOUS 5
LANDING SHIPS 4:
LSM 3 *Ben Aicha* (FRA *Champlain* BATRAL) (capacity 7 tanks; 140 troops)
LST 1 *Sidi Mohammed Ben Abdallah* (US *Newport*) (capacity 3 LCVP; 400 troops)
LANDING CRAFT • LCM 1 CTM (FRA CTM-5)
LOGISTICS AND SUPPORT 9
AGOR 1 *Abou Barakat Albarbari* (ex-US *Robert D. Conrad*)
AGS 1 Stan 1504
AK 2
AX 1 *Essaouira*
AXS 2
YDT 1
YTB 1

Marines 1,500

FORCES BY ROLE
MANOEUVRE
Amphibious
2 naval inf bn

Naval Aviation

EQUIPMENT BY TYPE
HELICOPTERS • ASW/ASUW 3 AS565SA *Panther*

Air Force 13,000

Flying hours 100 hrs/year on *Mirage* F-1/F-5E/F *Tiger* II/F-16C/D *Fighting Falcon*

FORCES BY ROLE
FIGHTER/GROUND ATTACK
2 sqn with F-5E/F-5F *Tiger* II
3 sqn with F-16C/D *Fighting Falcon*
1 sqn with *Mirage* F-1C (F-1CH)
1 sqn with *Mirage* F-1E (F-1EH)
ELECTRONIC WARFARE
1 sqn with EC-130H *Hercules*; *Falcon* 20 (ELINT)
MARITIME PATROL
1 flt with Do-28
TANKER/TRANSPORT
1 sqn with C-130/KC-130H *Hercules*
TRANSPORT
1 sqn with CN-235
1 VIP sqn with B-737BBJ; Beech 200/300 *King Air*; *Falcon* 50; Gulfstream II/III/V-SP
TRAINING
1 sqn with *Alpha Jet**
1 sqn T-6C
ATTACK HELICOPTER
1 sqn with SA342L *Gazelle* (Some with HOT)
TRANSPORT HELICOPTER
1 sqn with Bell 205A (AB-205A); Bell 206 *Jet Ranger* (AB-206); Bell 212 (AB-212)
1 sqn with CH-47D *Chinook*
1 sqn with SA330 *Puma*

EQUIPMENT BY TYPE
AIRCRAFT 92 combat capable
FTR 22: 19 F-5E *Tiger* II; 3 F-5F *Tiger* II
FGA 51: 16 F-16C *Fighting Falcon*; 8 F-16D *Fighting Falcon*; 16 *Mirage* F-1C (F-1CH); 11 *Mirage* F-1E (F-1EH)
ELINT 1 EC-130H *Hercules*
TKR/TPT 2 KC-130H *Hercules*
TPT 47: **Medium** 17: 4 C-27J *Spartan*; 13 C-130H *Hercules*; **Light** 21: 4 Beech 100 *King Air*; 2 Beech 200 *King Air*; 1 Beech 200C *King Air*; 2 Beech 300 *King Air*; 3 Beech 350 *King Air*; 7 CN-235; 2 Do-28; **PAX** 9: 1 B-737BBJ; 2 *Falcon* 20; 2 *Falcon* 20 (ELINT); 1 *Falcon* 50 (VIP); 1 Gulfstream II (VIP); 1 Gulfstream III; 1 Gulfstream V-SP
TRG 81: 12 AS-202 *Bravo*; 19 *Alpha Jet**; 2 CAP-10; 25 T-6C *Texan*; 9 T-34C *Turbo Mentor*; 14 T-37B *Tweet*
FF 4 CL-415
HELICOPTERS
MRH 19 SA342L *Gazelle* (7 with HOT, 12 with cannon)

TPT 70: **Heavy** 7 CH-47D *Chinook*; **Medium** 24 SA330 *Puma*; **Light** 39: 25 Bell 205A (AB-205A); 11 Bell 206 *Jet Ranger* (AB-206); 3 Bell 212 (AB-212)

MSL

AAM • **IR** AIM-9B/D/J *Sidewinder*; R-550 *Magic*; **IIR** (AIM-9X *Sidewinder* on order); **SARH** R-530; **ARH** (AIM-120 AMRAAM on order)

ASM AASM (on order); AGM-62B *Walleye* (for F-5E); HOT

Paramilitary 50,000 active

Gendarmerie Royale 20,000

FORCES BY ROLE

MANOEUVRE

Air Manoeuvre

1 para sqn

Other

1 paramilitary bde

4 (mobile) paramilitary gp

1 coast guard unit

TRANSPORT HELICOPTER

1 sqn

EQUIPMENT BY TYPE

PATROL AND COASTAL COMBATANTS • **PB** 15 Arcor 53

AIRCRAFT • **TRG** 2 R-235 *Guerrier*

HELICOPTERS

MRH 14: 3 SA315B *Lama*; 2 S316 *Alouette* III; 3 SA318 *Alouette* II; 6 SA342K *Gazelle*

TPT 8: **Medium** 6 SA330 *Puma*; **Light** 2 SA360 *Dauphin*

Force Auxiliaire 30,000 (incl 5,000 Mobile Intervention Corps)

Customs/Coast Guard

PATROL AND COASTAL COMBATANTS • **PB** 36: 4 *Erraid*; 18 *Arcor* 46; 14 (other SAR craft)

DEPLOYMENT

CÔTE D'IVOIRE

UN • UNOCI 726; 1 inf bn

DEMOCRATIC REPUBLIC OF THE CONGO

UN • MONUSCO 844; 1 obs; 1 mech inf bn; 1 fd hospital

SERBIA

NATO • KFOR 169; 1 inf coy

Oman OMN

Omani Rial R		2012	2013	2014
GDP	R	29.4bn	30.3bn	
	US$	76.5bn	78.8bn	
per capita	US$	24,765	24,729	
Growth	%	5.02	4.16	
Inflation	%	2.94	3.33	
Def bdgt	R	2.59bn	3.56bn	
	US$	6.72bn	9.25bn	
FMA (US)	US$	8m	8m	8m
US$1=R		0.38	0.38	

Population 3,154,134

Expatriates: 27%

Age	0–14	15–19	20–24	25–29	30–64	65 plus
Male	15.7%	5.1%	5.5%	6.1%	20.7%	1.6%
Female	14.9%	4.8%	4.8%	4.8%	14.4%	1.6%

Capabilities

Oman's armed forces, although small in comparison to regional neighbours, are well-staffed, with a strong history of cooperation and training with UK armed forces. It retains an effective inventory managed by well-trained personnel. Despite a lack of war-fighting experience, a good state of readiness is maintained. The armed forces remain well-funded, ensuring a steady flow of new equipment, primarily from the UK and the US. Although focused on territorial defence, there is some special forces and amphibious capability, a relatively high proportion of airlift and modest sealift, and the Royal Guard brigade, which reports directly to the sultan and carries out internal security and ceremonial functions. Oman is attempting to significantly bolster its air-defence capabilities, ordering AIM-120C-7 air-to-air missiles in conjunction with Saudi Arabia and considering the purchase of PAC-2 air defence systems, to integrate with other Gulf countries, such as Saudi Arabia and Kuwait, that operate *Patriot* batteries. The navy is also seeing investment, with an order for three Project Khareef frigates that began to arrive in 2013. In 2013, the air force placed an order for 12 *Typhoon* combat aircraft. However, there are also capability gaps, such as in ASW, and greater training and equipment (particularly ISR systems) are required to cope more effectively with security issues such as smuggling across the Strait of Hormuz. Oman is a GCC member.

ACTIVE 42,600 (Army 25,000 Navy 4,200 Air 5,000 Foreign Forces 2,000 Royal Household 6,400) Paramilitary 4,400

ORGANISATIONS BY SERVICE

Army 25,000

FORCES BY ROLE
(Regt are bn size)
MANOEUVRE
Armoured
1 armd bde (2 armd regt, 1 recce regt)
Light
1 inf bde (5 inf regt, 1 arty regt, 1 fd engr regt, 1 engr regt, 1 sigs regt)
1 inf bde (3 inf regt, 2 arty regt)
1 indep inf coy (Musandam Security Force)
Air Manoeuvre
1 AB regt
COMBAT SUPPORT
1 ADA regt (2 ADA bty)
COMBAT SERVICE SUPPORT
1 tpt regt

EQUIPMENT BY TYPE
MBT 117: 38 CR2 *Challenger* 2; 6 M60A1; 73 M60A3
LT TK 37 *Scorpion*
RECCE 137: 13 *Sultan*; 124 VBL
APC 206
APC (T) 16: 6 FV 103 *Spartan*; 10 FV4333 *Stormer*
APC (W) 190: 175 *Piranha* (incl variants); 15 AT-105 *Saxon*
ARTY 233
SP 155mm 24 G-6
TOWED 108: **105mm** 42 ROF lt; **122mm** 30 D-30; **130mm** 24: 12 M-46; 12 Type-59-I; **155mm** 12 FH-70
MOR 101: **81mm** 69; **107mm** 20 M-30; **120mm** 12 Brandt
AT • MSL 88
SP 8 VBL (TOW)
MANPATS 80: 30 *Javelin*; 32 *Milan*; 18 TOW/TOW-2A
AD • SAM
SP 8 *Mistral* 2
MANPAD *Javelin*; 9K32 *Strela*-2 (SA-7 *Grail*)‡
GUNS 26: **23mm** 4 ZU-23-2; **35mm** 10 GDF-005 (with *Skyguard*); **40mm** 12 L/60 (Towed)
ARV 11: 4 *Challenger*; 2 M88A1; 2 *Piranha*; 3 *Samson*

Navy 4,200

EQUIPMENT BY TYPE
SUBMARINES • SDV 2 Mk 8
PRIMARY SURFACE COMBATANTS 1
FFGHM 1 *Al-Shamikh* with 2 quad lnchr with MM-40 *Exocet* Block III AShM, 2 sextuple lnchr with VL MICA SAM, 2 DS 30M CIWS, 1 76mm gun (two additional vessels under construction)
PATROL AND COASTAL COMBATANTS 13
CORVETTES • FSGM 2:
2 *Qahir Al Amwaj* with 2 quad lnchr with MM-40 *Exocet* AShM, 1 octuple lnchr with *Crotale* SAM, 1 76mm gun, 1 hel landing platform
PCFG 4 *Dhofar* with 2 quad lnchr with MM-40 *Exocet* AShM, 1 76mm gun
PCC 3 *Al Bushra* (FRA P-400) with 1 76mm gun
PB 4 *Seeb* (UK Vosper 25m, under 100 tonnes)
AMPHIBIOUS 6
LANDING SHIPS • LST 1 *Nasr el Bahr* (with hel deck) (capacity 7 tanks; 240 troops)
LANDING CRAFT 5: 1 **LCU**; 3 **LCM**; 1 **LCT**
LOGISTICS AND SUPPORT 7
AK 1 *Al Sultana*
AP 2 *Shinas* (commercial tpt - auxiliary military role only) (capacity 56 veh; 200 tps)
AX 1 *Al Mabrukah* (with hel deck, also used in OPV role)
AXS 1 *Shabab Oman*

Air Force 5,000

FORCES BY ROLE
FIGHTER/GROUND ATTACK
1 sqn with F-16C/D Block 50 *Fighting Falcon*
1 sqn with *Hawk* Mk103; *Hawk* Mk203
2 sqn with *Jaguar* S (OS)/*Jaguar* B (OB)
TRANSPORT
1 sqn with C-130H/J-30 *Hercules*
1 sqn with SC.7 3M *Skyvan* (radar-equipped, for MP)
TRAINING
1 sqn with MFI-17B *Mushshak*; PC-9*; Bell 206 (AB-206) *Jet Ranger*
TRANSPORT HELICOPTER
4 (med) sqn; Bell 212 (AB-212); NH-90; *Super Lynx* Mk300 (maritime/SAR)
AIR DEFENCE
2 sqn with *Rapier*; *Blindfire*; S713 *Martello*

EQUIPMENT BY TYPE
AIRCRAFT 52 combat capable
FGA 24: 8 F-16C Block 50 *Fighting Falcon*; 4 F-16D Block 50 *Fighting Falcon*; 10 *Jaguar* S (OS); 2 *Jaguar* B (OB)
TPT 14: **Medium** 4: 3 C-130H *Hercules*; 1 C-130J-30 *Hercules* (VIP); **Light** 8: 1 C-295M; 7 SC.7 3M *Skyvan* (radar-equipped, for MP); **PAX** 2 A320-300
TRG 36: 4 *Hawk* Mk103*; 12 *Hawk* Mk203*; 8 MFI-17B *Mushshak*; 12 PC-9*
HELICOPTERS
MRH 15 *Super Lynx* Mk300 (maritime/SAR)
TPT 36+ **Medium** 12+ NH90 TTH; **Light** 25: 19 Bell 205 (possibly wfu); 3 Bell 206 (AB-206) *Jet Ranger*; 3 Bell 212 (AB-212)
AD • SAM 40 *Rapier*
RADAR • LAND 6+: 6 *Blindfire*; S713 *Martello*
MSL
AAM • IR AIM-9N/M/P *Sidewinder*; **ARH** AIM-120C AMRAAM
ASM AGM-65 *Maverick*
AShM AGM-84D *Harpoon*

Royal Household 6,400

(incl HQ staff)
FORCES BY ROLE
SPECIAL FORCES
2 SF regt

Royal Guard bde 5,000

FORCES BY ROLE
MANOEUVRE
Light
1 gd bde (2 gd regt, 1 armd sqn, 1 cbt spt bn)

EQUIPMENT BY TYPE
LT TK (9 VBC-90 in store)
RECCE 9 *Centauro* MGS

APC (W) 73: ε50 Type-92; 14 VAB VCI; 9 VAB VDAA
ARTY • MRL 122mm 6 Type-90A
AT • MSL • MANPATS *Milan*
AD • SAM • MANPAD 14 *Javelin*
GUNS • SP 9: **20mm** 9 VAB VDAA

Royal Yacht Squadron 150

LOGISTICS AND SUPPORT 3
AP 1 *Fulk Al Salamah* (also veh tpt) with up to 2 AS332 *Super Puma* hel
YAC 2: 1 *Al Said*; 1 *Zinat Al Bihaar* (Royal Dhow)

Royal Flight 250

AIRCRAFT • TPT • PAX 5: 2 B-747SP; 1 DC-8-73CF; 2 Gulfstream IV
HELICOPTERS • TPT • Medium 6: 3 SA330 (AS330) *Puma*; 2 AS332F *Super Puma*; 1 AS332L *Super Puma*

Paramilitary 4,400 active

Tribal Home Guard 4,000

org in teams of ε100

Police Coast Guard 400

PATROL AND COASTAL COMBATANTS 33 (+20 *Cougar Enforcer* 33 PBF under 10 tonnes)
PCO 2 *Haras*
PBF 3 *Haras* (US Mk V *Pegasus*)
PB 28: 3 Rodman 101; 1 *Haras* (SWE CG27); 3 *Haras* (SWE CG29); 14 Rodman 58; 2 D59116; 5 *Zahra*

Police Air Wing

AIRCRAFT • TPT • Light 4: 1 BN-2T *Turbine Islander*; 2 CN-235M; 1 Do-228
HELICOPTERS • TPT • Light 5: 2 Bell 205A; 3 Bell 214ST (AB-214ST)

FOREIGN FORCES

United Kingdom Army 30; Navy 20; Air Force 30; 1 *Tristar* tkr; 1 *Sentinel*

Palestinian Territories PT

New Israeli Shekel NS		2011	2012	2013
GDP	US$			
per capita	US$			
Growth	%			
Inflation	%			

*definitive economic data unavailable

US$1=NS	3.55	3.85	3.85

Population 4,440,127

Age	0–14	15–19	20–24	25–29	30–64	65 plus
Male	19.5%	5.7%	5.3%	4.2%	14.9%	1.4%
Female	18.5%	5.4%	5.1%	4.0%	14.2%	1.9%

Capabilities

The Palestinian Authority's National Security Force (NSF) is a paramilitary organisation intended to provide internal security support within Gaza and the West Bank. The NSF only has real authority within the West Bank, where it has proved capable of maintaining internal security. It would have little effect against any Israeli incursion. Since 2007, the Gaza strip has been run by Hamas. The Izz ad-Din al-Qassam Brigades, Hamas's military wing, is seen by the organisation as its best-trained and most disciplined force. It has a strong well-developed rocket artillery capability, including manufacturing, development and testing, but this is increasingly countered by Israel's *Iron Dome* missile-defence system. It is seeking to improve its command-and-control structure, the acquisition of better weapons and the creation of a training programme. The revolution in Egypt has reduced security in the Sinai. Smuggling tunnels continue to function between Sinai and Gaza, which likely benefit military holdings in the territory. In the November 2012 hostilities, Iranian-developed *Fajr*-5 rockets were used, putting Tel Aviv and Jerusalem within range of rocket fire. Israel's military actions, meanwhile, will have degraded the command-and-control, as well as physical infrastructure, of Hamas forces.

ACTIVE 0 Paramilitary 56,000

Precise personnel strength figures for the various Palestinian groups are not known.

ORGANISATIONS BY SERVICE

There are few data available on the status of the organisations mentioned below. Following internal fighting in June 2007, Gaza is under the de facto control of Hamas, while the West Bank is controlled by the Palestinian Authority.

Paramilitary

National Forces ε56,000 (reported)

GENERAL SECURITY
Presidential security 3,000
SF 1,200
Police 9,000
Preventative Security n.k.
Civil Defence 1,000

AD • SAM • MANPAD 9K32 *Strela*-2 (SA-7 *Grail*)‡

The **al-Aqsa Brigades** profess loyalty to the Fatah group that dominates the Palestinian Authority. The strength of this group is not known.

Hamas groupings include internal-security groupings such as the **Executive Force** (est strength: 10–12,000; major equipment include: artillery rockets, mortars, SALW) and the **al-Qassam Brigades** (est strength: 10,000; major equipment include: mines and IEDs, artillery rockets, mortars, SALW).

Qatar QTR

Qatari Riyal R		2012	2013	2014
GDP	R	667bn	687bn	
	US$	183bn	189bn	
per capita	US$	99,731	98,737	
Growth	%	6.58	5.20	
Inflation	%	1.86	3.02	
Def exp	R	ε13.6bn		
	US$	ε3.73bn		
US$1=R		3.64	3.64	

Population 2,042,444

Ethnic groups: Nationals 25%; Expatriates 75% of which Indian 18%; Iranian 10%; Pakistani 18%

Age	0–14	15–19	20–24	25–29	30–64	65 plus
Male	6.3%	2.7%	7.5%	12.4%	47.5%	0.5%
Female	6.2%	1.6%	2.1%	3.0%	9.9%	0.3%

Capabilities

Qatar maintains small armed forces with limited capability, although its equipment is relatively modern and its personnel are well-trained and motivated. As with other small Gulf states, Qatar relies on its international alliances, primarily with the US and through the GCC, to guarantee its security. However, a high proportion of government spending goes on defence, so, despite the forces' small size an adequate defence capability has been maintained. Some equipment, particularly main battle tanks and fast missile craft, are ageing, but high-tech weapons, such as *Exocet* anti-ship missiles, make these platforms capable of fulfilling their primary role of border and maritime security. The armed forces suffer from a number of capability gaps, particularly in air defence, and the age of some equipment may hamper its ability to perform in high-tempo operations. The air force has been a priority for procurement in recent years, with the arrival of C-17s, which – along with *Mirage* 2000 aircraft – were deployed on operations over Libya in 2011. Later that year, the chief of staff also admitted that Qatar deployed 'hundreds' of ground troops to conduct liaison duties. Adequate funding exists, and recent procurement requests have included the sale of *Patriot* and THAAD missile-defence batteries from the US, up to 24 AH-64 *Apache* attack helicopters and up to 72 combat aircraft. In mid-2013, a request was made for an A/N FPS-132 Block 5 Early Warning Radar.

ACTIVE 11,800 (Army 8,500 Navy 1,800 Air 1,500)

ORGANISATIONS BY SERVICE

Army 8,500

FORCES BY ROLE

SPECIAL FORCES
1 SF coy

MANOEUVRE

Armoured
1 armd bde (1 tk bn, 1 mech inf bn, 1 AT bn, 1 mor sqn)

Mechanised
3 mech inf bn

Light
1 (Royal Guard) bde (3 inf regt)

COMBAT SUPPORT
1 fd arty bn

EQUIPMENT BY TYPE

MBT 30 AMX-30
RECCE 68: 12 AMX-10RC; 20 EE-9 *Cascavel*; 12 *Ferret*; 8 V-150 *Chaimite*; 16 VBL
AIFV 40 AMX-10P
APC 226
APC (T) 30 AMX-VCI
APC (W) 196: 36 *Piranha* II; 160 VAB
ARTY 89
SP 155mm 28 (AMX) Mk F3
TOWED 155mm 12 G-5
MRL 4 ASTROS II
MOR 45
SP • 81mm 4 VAB VPM 81
81mm 26 L16
120mm 15 Brandt
AT • MSL 148
SP 24 VAB VCAC HOT
MANPATS 124: 24 HOT; 100 *Milan*
RCL 84mm ε40 *Carl Gustav*
ARV 3: 1 AMX-30D; 2 *Piranha*

Navy 1,800 (incl Coast Guard)

EQUIPMENT BY TYPE

PATROL AND COASTAL COMBATANTS 10
PCFG 7:
4 *Barzan* (UK *Vita*) with 2 quad lnchr with MM-40 *Exocet* Block III AShM, 1 sextuple lnchr with *Mistral* SAM, 1 *Goalkeeper* CIWS 1 76mm gun
3 *Damsah* (FRA *Combattante* III) with 2 quad lnchr with MM-40 *Exocet* AShM, 1 76mm gun
PB 3 Q-31 series
AMPHIBIOUS • LANDING CRAFT • LCT 1 *Rabha* (capacity 3 MBT; 110 troops)
LOGISTICS AND SUPPORT • YTB 2 *Al Jaroof* (Damen Stan 1907)

Coast Guard

EQUIPMENT BY TYPE

PATROL AND COASTAL COMBATANTS 12
PBF 4 DV 15
PB 8: 4 *Crestitalia* MV-45; 3 *Halmatic* M160; 1 other

Coastal Defence

FORCES BY ROLE

MISSILE
1 bty with 3 quad lnchr with MM-40 *Exocet* AShM

EQUIPMENT BY TYPE

MSL • AShM 12 MM-40 *Exocet* AShM

Air Force 1,500

FORCES BY ROLE

FIGHTER/GROUND ATTACK
1 sqn with *Alpha Jet**
1 sqn with *Mirage* 2000ED; *Mirage* 2000D

TRANSPORT
1 sqn with C-17A; C-130J-30
1 sqn with A-340; B-707; B-727; *Falcon* 900
ATTACK HELICOPTER
1 ASuW sqn with *Commando* Mk3 with *Exocet*
1 sqn with SA341 *Gazelle;* SA342L *Gazelle* with HOT
TRANSPORT HELICOPTER
1 sqn with *Commando* Mk2A; *Commando* Mk2C
1 sqn with AW139

EQUIPMENT BY TYPE
AIRCRAFT 18 combat capable
FGA 12: 9 *Mirage* 2000ED; 3 *Mirage* 2000D
TPT 12: **Heavy** 2 C-17A *Globemaster;* **Medium** 4 C-130J-30 *Hercules;* **PAX** 6: 1 A340; 2 B-707; 1 B-727; 2 *Falcon* 900
TRG 6 *Alpha Jet**
HELICOPTERS
ASuW 8 *Commando* Mk3
MRH 31: 18 AW139 (3 more being delivered); 2 SA341 *Gazelle;* 11 SA342L *Gazelle*
TPT • Medium 4: 3 *Commando* Mk2A; 1 *Commando* Mk2C
AD • SAM 75: 24 *Mistral*
SP 9 *Roland* II
MANPAD 42: 10 *Blowpipe;* 12 FIM-92A *Stinger;* 20 9K32 *Strela*-2 (SA-7 *Grail*)‡
MSL
ASM AM-39 *Exocet; Apache;* HOT
AAM • IR R-550 *Magic* 2; **ARH** *Mica*

DEPLOYMENT

LEBANON
UN • UNIFIL 3

FOREIGN FORCES

United Kingdom Air Force: 4 C-130J
United States US Central Command: 600; elm 1 (APS) HBCT set; USAF CAOC

Saudi Arabia SAU

Saudi Riyal R		2012	2013	2014
GDP	R	2.73tr	2.8tr	
	US$	727bn	746bn	
per capita	US$	25,085	25,163	
Growth	%	6.81	4.39	
Inflation	%	2.86	3.74	
Def exp	R	213bn	ε223bn	
	US$	56.7bn	ε59.6bn	
US$1=R		3.75	3.75	

Population 26,939,583

Ethnic groups: Nationals 73% of which Bedouin up to 10%, Shia 6%, Expatriates 27% of which Asians 20%, Arabs 6%, Africans 1%, Europeans <1%

Age	0–14	15–19	20–24	25–29	30–64	65 plus
Male	14.4%	4.9%	5.6%	6.0%	22.0%	1.6%
Female	13.7%	4.5%	4.6%	4.7%	16.4%	1.5%

Capabilities

Saudi Arabia has the best-equipped armed forces in the Gulf region, and is a GCC member. Its inventory is generally more modern and better maintained than its neighbours'. However, coordination and cooperation between the regular armed forces remains poor and decision making at the highest levels is hampered by inter-service competition as well as the age and infirmity of senior ministers. Air force priorities are air defence and deterrence, whilst the navy maintains advanced destroyers, but rarely operates beyond Saudi Arabia's EEZ. Land forces are configured to meet threats such as border instability. The ability to effectively utilise the country's advanced inventory was questioned by operations against Houthi rebels in late 2009 and early 2010. Saudi Arabia relies on overseas partners to ultimately guarantee its security and to assist its military development. The Saudi armed forces maintain a good relationship with overseas forces, in particular those of the US, the UK and France, which affords combined training possibilities as well as access to equipment. The country's air-defence network is extensive and highly capable, and a good range of airlift enables deployment across the country and a moderate power-projection capability. In November 2012, Saudi Arabia requested the sale of 20 C-130Js and 5 KC-130J tankers, as an upgrade to its existing C-130H fleet; sealift is currently inadequate to sustain a large force overseas for any period of time.

ACTIVE 233,500 (Army 75,000 Navy 13,500 Air 20,000 Air Defence 16,000 Industrial Security Force 9,000 National Guard 100,000) **Paramilitary 15,500**

ORGANISATIONS BY SERVICE

Army 75,000

FORCES BY ROLE
MANOEUVRE
Armoured
4 armd bde (1 recce coy, 3 tk bn, 1 mech bn, 1 fd arty bn, 1 AD bn, 1 AT bn,1 engr coy, 1 log bn, 1 maint coy, 1 med coy)
Mechanised
5 mech bde (1 recce coy, 1 tk bn, 3 mech bn, 1 fd arty bn, 1 AD bn, 1 AT bn, 1 engr coy, 1 log bn, 1 maint coy, 1 med coy)
Light
1 (Royal Guard) regt (3 lt inf bn)
Air Manoeuvre
1 AB bde (2 AB bn, 3 SF coy)
Aviation
1 comd (1 atk hel bde, 1 tpt hel bde)
COMBAT SUPPORT
1 arty bde (5 fd arty bn, 2 MRL bn, 1 msl bn)

EQUIPMENT BY TYPE
MBT 600: 200 M1A2/A2S *Abrams* (173 more in store); 400 M60A3; (145 AMX-30 in store)
RECCE 300 AML-60/AML-90
AIFV 780: 380 AMX-10P; 400 M2A2 *Bradley*
APC 1,423

APC (T) 1,200 M113A1/A2/A3 (incl variants)
APC (W) 150 M3 Panhard; (ε40 AF-40-8-1 *Al-Fahd* in store)
PPV 73 *Aravis*
ARTY 771
SP 155mm 224: 60 AU-F-1; 110 M109A1B/A2; 54 PLZ-45
TOWED 50: **105mm** (100 M101/M102 in store); **155mm** 50 M114; (60 M198 in store); **203mm** (8 M115 in store)
MRL 60 ASTROS II
MOR 437
SP 220: **81mm** 70; **107mm** 150 M30
TOWED 217: **81mm/107mm** 70 incl M30 **120mm** 147: 110 Brandt; 37 M12-1535
AT • MSL 2,240+
SP 290+: 90+ AMX-10P (HOT); 200 VCC-1 ITOW
MANPATS 1950: 1,000 M47 *Dragon*; 950 TOW-2A
RCL 450: **84mm** 300 *Carl Gustav*; **106mm** 50 M40A1; **90mm** 100 M67
RL 112mm ε200 APILAS
AD • SAM 1,000+
SP *Crotale*
MANPAD 1,000: 500 FIM-43 *Redeye*; 500 FIM-92A *Stinger*
RADAR • LAND AN/TPQ-36 *Firefinder*/AN/TPQ-37 *Firefinder* (arty, mor)
MSL • TACTICAL • SSM 10+ CSS-2 (40 msl)
AEV 15 M728
ARV 283+: 8 ACV ARV; AMX-10EHC; 55 AMX-30D; *Leclerc* ARV; 130 M88A1; 90 M578
VLB 10 AMX-30
MW *Aardvark* Mk2
HELICOPTERS
ATK 12 AH-64 *Apache*
MRH 21: 6 AS365N *Dauphin* 2 (medevac); 15 Bell 406CS *Combat Scout*
TPT • Medium 58: 12 S-70A-1 *Desert Hawk*; 22 UH-60A *Black Hawk* (4 medevac); 24 UH-60L *Black Hawk*

Navy 13,500

Navy HQ at Riyadh; Eastern Fleet HQ at Jubail; Western Fleet HQ at Jeddah

EQUIPMENT BY TYPE
PRINCIPAL SURFACE COMBATANTS 7
DESTROYERS • DDGHM 3 *Al Riyadh* (FRA *La Fayette* mod) with 2 quad lnchr with MM-40 *Exocet* Block II AShM, 2 8-cell VLS with *Aster* 15 SAM, 4 single 533mm TT with F17P HWT, 1 76mm gun (capacity 1 AS365N *Dauphin* 2 hel)
FRIGATES • FFGHM 4 *Madina* (FRA F-2000) with 2 quad lnchr with *Otomat* Mk 2 AShM, 1 octuple lnchr with *Crotale* SAM, 4 single 533mm ASTT with F17P HWT, 1 100mm gun (capacity 1 AS365N *Dauphin* 2 hel)
PATROL AND COASTAL COMBATANTS 69
CORVETTES • FSG 4 *Badr* (US *Tacoma*) with 2 quad Mk140 lnchr with RGM-84C *Harpoon* AShM, 2 triple 324mm ASTT with Mk 46 LWT, 1 *Phalanx* CIWS, 1 76mm gun
PCFG 9 *Al Siddiq* (US 58m) with 2 twin Mk140 lnchr with RGM-84C *Harpoon* AShM, 1 *Phalanx* CIWS, 1 76mm gun
PB 56: 17 (US *Halter Marine*); 39 *Simmoneau* 51
MINE WARFARE • MINE COUNTERMEASURES 7
MCC 4 *Addriyah* (US MSC-322)
MHC 3 *Al Jawf* (UK *Sandown*)
AMPHIBIOUS 8
LCU 4 1610 (capacity 120 troops)
LCM 4 LCM 6 (capacity 80 troops)
LOGISTICS AND SUPPORT 17
AORH 2 *Boraida* (mod FRA *Durance*) (capacity either 2 AS365F *Dauphin* 2 hel or 1 AS332C *Super Puma*)
YAC 2
YTB 2
YTM 11 *Radhwa*

Naval Aviation

HELICOPTERS
MRH 34: 6 AS365N *Dauphin* 2; 15 AS565 with AS-15TT AShM; 13 Bell 406CS *Combat Scout*
TPT • Medium 12 AS332B/F *Super Puma* with AM-39 *Exocet* AShM

Marines 3,000

FORCES BY ROLE
MANOEUVRE
Amphibious
1 inf regt with (2 inf bn)
EQUIPMENT BY TYPE
APC (W) 140 BMR-600P

Air Force 20,000

FORCES BY ROLE
FIGHTER
1 sqn with F-15S *Eagle*
4 sqn with F-15C/D *Eagle*
FIGHTER/GROUND ATTACK
2 sqn with F-15S *Eagle*
3 sqn with *Tornado* IDS; *Tornado* GR1A
2 sqn with *Typhoon*
AIRBORNE EARLY WARNING & CONTROL
1 sqn with E-3A *Sentry*
ELINT
1 sqn with RE-3A/B; Beech 350ER *King Air*
TANKER
1 sqn with KE-3A
TANKER/TRANSPORT
1 sqn with KC-130H *Hercules* (tkr/tpt)
1 sqn forming with A330 MRTT
TRANSPORT
3 sqn with C-130H *Hercules*; C-130H-30 *Hercules*; CN-235; L-100-30HS (hospital ac)
2 sqn with Beech 350 *King Air* (forming)
TRAINING
3 sqn with *Hawk* Mk65*; *Hawk* Mk65A*
1 sqn with *Jetstream* Mk31
1 sqn with Cessna 172; MFI-17 *Mushshak*
2 sqn with PC-9
TRANSPORT HELICOPTER
4 sqn with AS532 *Cougar* (CSAR); Bell 212 (AB-212); Bell 412 (AB-412) *Twin Huey* (SAR)
EQUIPMENT BY TYPE
AIRCRAFT 305 combat capable
FTR 81: 56 F-15C *Eagle*; 25 F-15D *Eagle*
FGA 172: 71 F-15S *Eagle*; 69 *Tornado* IDS; 32 *Typhoon*
ISR 14+: 12 *Tornado* GR1A*; 2+ Beech 350ER *King Air*

AEW&C 5 E-3A *Sentry*
ELINT 2: 1 RE-3A; 1 RE-3B
TKR/TPT 10: 3 A330 MRTT (3 more on order); 7 KC-130H *Hercules*
TKR 7 KE-3A
TPT 56+ **Medium** 36: 30 C-130H *Hercules*; 3 C-130H-30 *Hercules*; 3 L-100-30; **Light** 20+: 2+ Beech 350 *King Air*; 13 Cessna 172; 4 CN-235; 1 *Jetstream* Mk31
TRG 100: 24 *Hawk* Mk65* (incl aerobatic team); 16 *Hawk* Mk65A*; 20 MFI-17 *Mushshak*; 40 PC-9
HELICOPTERS
MRH 15 Bell 412 (AB-412) *Twin Huey* (SAR)
TPT 30: **Medium** 10 AS532 *Cougar* (CSAR); **Light** 20 Bell 212 (AB-212)
MSL
ASM AGM-65 *Maverick*
AShM *Sea Eagle*
LACM *Storm Shadow*
ARM ALARM
AAM • **IR** AIM-9P/L/X *Sidewinder*; **SARH** AIM-7 *Sparrow*; AIM-7M *Sparrow*; **ARH** AIM-120 AMRAAM

Royal Flt

AIRCRAFT • **TPT** 24; **Medium** 8: 5 C-130H *Hercules*; 3 L-100-30; **Light** 3: 1 Cessna 310; 2 Learjet 35; **PAX** 13: 1 A340; 1 B-737-200; 2 B-737BBJ; 2 B-747SP; 4 BAe-125-800; 2 Gulfstream III; 1 Gulfstream IV
HELICOPTERS • **TPT** 3+; **Medium** 3: 2 AS-61; 1 S-70 *Black Hawk*; **Light** Some Bell 212 (AB-212)

Air Defence Forces 16,000

FORCES BY ROLE
AIR DEFENCE
16 bty with PAC-2; 17 bty with *Shahine*/AMX-30SA; 16 bty with MIM-23B I-HAWK; 73 units (static defence) with *Crotale*/*Shahine*

EQUIPMENT BY TYPE
AD • **SAM** 1,805
SP 581: 40 *Crotale*; 400 FIM-92A *Avenger*; 73 *Shahine*; 68 *Crotale*/*Shahine*
TOWED 224: 128 MIM-23B I-HAWK; 96 PAC-2
MANPAD 500 FIM-43 *Redeye*
NAVAL 500 *Mistral*
GUNS 1,070
SP 942: **20mm** 92 M163 *Vulcan*; **30mm** 850 AMX-30SA
TOWED 128: **35mm** 128 GDF Oerlikon; **40mm** (150 L/70 in store)
RADARS • **AD RADAR** 80: 17 AN/FPS-117; 28 AN/TPS-43; AN/TPS-59; 35 AN/TPS-63; AN/TPS-70

Industrial Security Force 9,000+

The force is part of a new security system that will incorporate surveillance and crisis management.

National Guard 75,000 active; 25,000 (tribal levies) (total 100,000)

FORCES BY ROLE
MANOEUVRE
Mechanised
4-5 mech bde (4 combined arms bn, 1 SP arty bn)
Light
5 inf bde (3 combined arms bn, 1 arty bn, 1 log bn)
Other
2–3 (Special Security) sy bde (3 sy bn)
1 (ceremonial) cav sqn
COMBAT SUPPORT
1 MP bn

EQUIPMENT BY TYPE
RECCE 214 LAV-AG (90mm)
AIFV 648 LAV-25
APC • **APC (W)** 808: 119 LAV-A; 30 LAV-AC; 296 LAV-CC; 73 LAV-PC; 290 V-150 *Commando* (810 in store)
ARTY 333+
SP 155mm ε116 CAESAR (16 more on order)
TOWED 108: **105mm** 50 M102; **155mm** 58 M198
MOR 109+ **81mm some; 120mm** 119 LAV-M
AT
MSL
SP 183 LAV-AT
MANPATS TOW-2A; M47 *Dragon*
RCL • **106mm** M40A1
AD • **GUNS** • **TOWED** 160: **20mm** 30 M167 *Vulcan*; **90mm** 130 M2
AEV 58 LAV-E
ARV 111 LAV-R; V-150 ARV

Paramilitary 15,500+ active

Border Guard 10,500

FORCES BY ROLE
Subordinate to Ministry of Interior. HQ in Riyadh. 9 subordinate regional commands
MANOEUVRE
Other
Some mobile def (long range patrol/spt) units
2 border def (patrol) units
12 infrastructure def units
18 harbour def units
Some coastal def units
COMBAT SUPPORT
Some MP units

Coast Guard 4,500

EQUIPMENT BY TYPE
PATROL AND COASTAL COMBATANTS 14 (100+ small patrol boats are also in service)
PBF 6: 4 *Al Jouf*; 2 *Sea Guard*
PB 8: 6 *StanPatrol 2606*; 2 *Al Jubatel*
AMPHIBIOUS • **LANDING CRAFT** 8: 3 **UCAC**; 5 **LCAC** *Griffin* 8000
LOGISTICS AND SUPPORT 4: 1 **AXL**; 3 **AO**

General Civil Defence Administration Units

HELICOPTERS • **TPT** • **Medium** 10 Boeing Vertol 107

Special Security Force 500

APC (W): UR-416

DEPLOYMENT

BAHRAIN
GCC • *Peninsula Shield* ε1,000 (National Guard)

FOREIGN FORCES

United States US Central Command: 270

Syria SYR

Syrian Pound S£		2012	2013
GDP	S£		
	US$		
per capita	US$		
Growth	%		
Inflation	%		
Def exp	S£		
	US$		
US$1=S£			

*definitive economic data unavailable

Population 22,457,336

Age	0–14	15–19	20–24	25–29	30–64	65 plus
Male	17.4%	5.4%	5.2%	4.8%	16.2%	1.8%
Female	16.5%	5.2%	5.0%	4.6%	15.9%	2.1%

Capabilities

Accurately estimating force levels of the various actors in Syria is problematic, and complicated by both government and rebel militias comprising many part-time fighters. By November 2013 Syrian rebels, comprising over 1,200 different groups of varying size, controlled large areas of countryside and enclaves of major cities. They continued to use light weapons, MANPADs, IEDs and some captured armour, and received arms supplies from a number of external parties. During the year rebel groups affiliated to the Free Syrian Army decreased in influence and effectiveness, at the expense of jihadist groups. The regime continued to rely heavily on stand-off firepower, particularly from artillery and tanks. The army sustained the brunt of the fighting with significant losses of armour, while the air force lost some combat aircraft and helicopters. The navy remained largely untouched. The strength of the army remained at about 50% of its pre-war size, with casualties being replenished by enlistment of loyalist volunteers and low-strength brigades being disbanded or merged. The most capable and most reliable army units comprised about 50,000 troops, including the mainly Alawite Special Forces – largely employed in and around Damascus. The Republican Guard and the elite 3rd and 4th divisions formed the regime's strike force. Previously disparate groups of loyalist militia were combined into a unified 'National Defence Force'. Formed bodies of Hizbullah troops deployed into western Syria to protect regime lines of communication and disrupt rebel supply lines. Some 2–3,000 Shia volunteers from other countries were also serving with the regime, the majority from Iraq. (See pp. 297–99.)

ACTIVE 178,000 (Army 110,000 Navy 5,000 Air 27,000 Air Defence 36,000) Paramilitary n.k.

Conscript liability 30 months

RESERVE n.k.

ORGANISATIONS BY SERVICE

Army ε110,000 (incl conscripts)

FORCES BY ROLE

Most formations are now understrength. Some brigades are reported to have been disbanded because of either political unreliability or heavy casualties.

COMMAND

3 corps HQ

SPECIAL FORCES

2 SF div (total: 11 SF regt; 1 tk regt)

MANOEUVRE

Armoured

6 armd div (3 armd bde, 1 mech bde, 1 arty regt)

1 (4th) armd div (1 SF regt, 2 armd bde, 2 mech bde, 1 arty regt, 1 SSM bde (3 SSM bn with *Scud*-B/C))

Mechanised

3 mech div (1 armd bde, 3 mech bde, 1 arty regt)

1 (Republican Guard) mech div (3 mech bde, 2 sy regt, 1 arty regt)

Light

2 indep inf bde

5 (Border Guard) lt inf bde (under command of the General Security Directorate for border sy)

COMBAT SUPPORT

2 arty bde

2 AT bde

1 SSM bde (3 SSM bn with FROG-7)

1 SSM bde (3 SSM bn with SS-21)

Reserves

FORCES BY ROLE

COMMAND

1 armd div HQ

MANOEUVRE

Armoured

4 armd bde

2 tk regt

Light

31 inf regt

COMBAT SUPPORT

3 arty regt

EQUIPMENT BY TYPE

Equipment numbers represent pre-war holdings, and have significantly reduced during the civil war.

MBT 4,950: 1,500–1,700 T-72/T-72M; 1,000 T-62K/T-62M; 2,250 T-55/T-55MV (some in store)

RECCE 590 BRDM-2

AIFV up to 2,450 BMP-1/BMP-2/BMP-3

APC (W) 1,500: 500 BTR-152; 1,000 BTR-50/BTR-60/BTR-70

ARTY up to 3,440+

SP 500+: **122mm** 450+: 400 2S1; 50+ D-30 (mounted on T34/85 chassis); **152mm** 50 2S3

TOWED 2,030: **122mm** 1,150: 500 D-30; 150 (M-30) M1938; 500 in store (no given designation); **130mm** 700-800 M-46; **152mm** 70 D-20/ML-20 M1937; **180mm** 10 S23

MRL 500: **107mm** up to 200 Type-63; **122mm** up to 300 BM-21 (*Grad*); **140mm** BM-14; **330mm** some (reported)

MOR 410+: **82mm**; **120mm** circa 400 M-1943; **160mm** M-160 (hundreds); **240mm** up to 10 M-240

AT • MSL 2,600

SP 410 9P133 BRDM-2 *Sagger*

MANPATS 2190+: 150 AT-4 9K111 *Spigot*; 40 AT-5 9K113 *Spandrel*; AT-7 9K115 *Saxhorn*; 800 AT-10 9K116 *Stabber*; 1,000 AT-14 9M133 *Kornet*; 200 *Milan*

RL 105mm RPG-29

AD

SAM

SP 84: 14 9K33 *Osa* (SA-8 *Gecko*); 20 9K31 *Strela*-1 (SA-9 *Gaskin*); 20 9K37 *Buk* (SA-11 *Gadfly*); 30 9K35 *Strela*-10 (SA-13 *Gopher*); 96K6 *Pantsir*-S1 (SA-22 *Greyhound*); 9K317 *Buk*-M2 (SA-17 *Grizzly*)

MANPAD 9K32 *Strela*-2 (SA-7 *Grail*)‡; 9K38 *Igla* (SA-18 *Grouse*); 9K36 *Strela*-3 (SA-14 *Gremlin*); 9K338 *Igla-S* (SA-24 *Grinch*)

GUNS 1,225+

SP ZSU-23-4

TOWED 23mm 600 ZU-23; **37mm** M-1939; **57mm** 600 S-60; **100mm** 25 KS-19

MSL • TACTICAL • SSM 84+: 18 *Scud*-B/*Scud*-C/*Scud*-D; 30 look-a-like; 18 FROG-7; 18+ SS-21 *Tochka* (*Scarab*)

ARV BREM-1 reported; T-54/55

VLB MTU; MTU-20

UAV • ISR • Medium *Mohajer* 3/4 **Light** *Ababil*

Navy ε5,000

EQUIPMENT BY TYPE

PATROL AND COASTAL COMBATANTS 32:

CORVETTES • FS 2 *Petya* III (1†) with 1 triple 533mm ASTT with SAET-60 HWT, 4 RBU 2500 *Smerch* 1†, 2 twin 76mm gun

PBFG 22:

16 *Osa* I/II with 4 single lnchr with P-15M *Termit*-M (SS-N-2C *Styx*) AShM

6 *Tir* with 2 single lnchr with C-802 (CSS-N-8 *Saccade*) AShM

PB 8 *Zhuk*†

MINE WARFARE • MINE COUNTERMEASURES 7

MHC 1 *Sonya* with 2 quad lnchr with 9K32 *Strela*-2 (SA-N-5 *Grail*) SAM, 2 AK630 CIWS

MSO 1 *Natya* with 2 quad lnchr with 9K32 *Strela*-2 (SA-N-5 *Grail*) SAM

MSI 5 *Yevgenya*

AMPHIBIOUS • LANDING SHIPS • LSM 3 *Polnochny* B (capacity 6 MBT; 180 troops)

LOGISTICS AND SUPPORT 2

AX 1 *Al Assad*

YDT 1 *Palmyra*

Coastal Defence

FORCES BY ROLE

COMBAT SUPPORT

1 (coastal defence) AShM bde with P-35 (SS-C-1B *Sepal*); P-15M *Termit*-R (SS-C-3 *Styx*); C-802; K-300P *Bastion* (SS-C-5 *Stooge*)

EQUIPMENT BY TYPE

MSL • AShM 10+: 4 P-35 (SS-C-1B *Sepal*); 6 P-15M *Termit*-R (SS-C-3 *Styx*); C-802; K-300P *Bastion* (SS-C-5 *Stooge*)

Naval Aviation

HELICOPTER

ASW 13: 2 Ka-28 *Helix* A (air force manned); 11 Mi-14 *Haze*

Air Force ε20,000

FORCES BY ROLE

FIGHTER

2 sqn with MiG-23 MF/ML/UM *Flogger*

2 sqn with MiG-29A/U *Fulcrum*

FIGHTER/GROUND ATTACK

4 sqn with MiG-21MF/bis *Fishbed*; MiG-21U *Mongol* A

2 sqn with MiG-23BN/UB *Flogger*

4 sqn with Su-22 *Fitter* D

1 sqn with Su-24 *Fencer*

TRANSPORT

1 sqn with An-24 *Coke*; An-26 *Curl*; Il-76 *Candid*

1 sqn with *Falcon* 20; *Falcon* 900

1 sqn with Tu-134B-3

1 sqn with Yak-40 *Codling*

TRAINING

1 sqn with L-39 *Albatros**

ATTACK HELICOPTER

3 sqn with Mi-25 *Hind* D

2 sqn with SA342L *Gazelle*

TRANSPORT HELICOPTER

6 sqn with Mi-8 *Hip*/Mi-17 *Hip* H

EQUIPMENT BY TYPE

The level of readiness of a significant element of the air force's combat aircraft inventory is likely poor. Equipment numbers represent pre-war holdings, and have significantly reduced during the civil war.

AIRCRAFT 295 combat capable

FTR 70: 40 MiG-23MF/ML/UM *Flogger*; 30 MiG-29A/SM/UB *Fulcrum*

FGA 205: 80 MiG-21MF/bis *Fishbed*; 15 MiG-21U *Mongol* A; 50 MiG-23BN/UB *Flogger*; 40 Su-22 *Fitter* D; 20 Su-24 *Fencer*

TPT 23: **Heavy** 3 Il-76 *Candid*; **Light** 13: 1 An-24 *Coke*; 6 An-26 *Curl*; 2 PA-31 *Navajo*; 4 Yak-40 *Codling*; **PAX** 7: 2 *Falcon* 20; 1 *Falcon* 900; 4 Tu-134B-3

TRG 61: 20 L-39 *Albatros**; 35 MBB-223 *Flamingo* (basic); 6 MFI-17 *Mushshak*

HELICOPTERS

ATK 25 Mi-25 *Hind* D

MRH 70: 30 Mi-17 *Hip* H; 30 SA342L *Gazelle*

TPT • Medium 30 Mi-8 *Hip*

MSL

AAM • IR R-3 (AA-2 *Atoll*)‡; R-60 (AA-8 *Aphid*); R-73 (AA-11 *Archer*); **IR/SARH**; R-23/24 (AA-7 *Apex*); R-27 (AA-10 *Alamo*)

ASM Kh-25 (AS-7 *Kerry*); HOT

ARM Kh-31P (AS-17A *Krypton*)

Air Defence Command ε36,000

FORCES BY ROLE

AIR DEFENCE

2 AD div (total: 25 AD bde (total: 150 SAM bty with S-125 *Pechora* (SA-3 *Goa*); 2K12 *Kub* (SA-6 *Gainful*); S-75 *Dvina* (SA-2 *Guideline*); some ADA bty with 9K32 *Strela*-2/M (SA-7A *Grail*/SA-7B *Grail*)‡)
2 AD regt (2 SAM bn with (2 SAM bty with S-200 *Angara* (SA-5 *Gammon*))

EQUIPMENT BY TYPE

AD • SAM 4,707
SP 195 2K12 *Kub* (SA-6 *Gainful*)
TOWED 468: 320 S-72 *Dvina* (SA-2 *Guideline*); 148 S-125 *Pechora* (SA-3 *Goa*)
STATIC/SHELTER 44 S-200 *Angara* (SA-5 *Gammon*)
MANPAD 4,000 9K32 *Strela*-2/2M (SA-7A *Grail*/SA-7B *Grail*)‡

Paramilitary not known

Gendarmerie

Ministry of Interior

Popular Committees

Local security organisations

National Defence Force

Comprising pro-government militia groups, including the *Shabbiha*

Coast Guard

EQUIPMENT BY TYPE

PATROL AND COASTAL COMBATANTS 6
PBF 2 *Mawani*
PB 4

FOREIGN FORCES

UNTSO unless specified. UNTSO figures represent total numbers for mission in Israel, Syria and Lebanon.

Argentina 4 obs
Australia 12 obs
Austria 6 obs
Belgium 2 obs
Canada 8 obs
Chile 3 obs
China, People's Republic of 4 obs
Denmark 10 obs
Estonia 2 obs
Fiji UNDOF 500; 1 inf bn
Finland 16 obs
France 3 obs
India UNDOF 194; 1 log bn(-)
Ireland 13 obs • UNDOF 119; 1 inf coy
Italy 7 obs
Japan UNDOF 31; elm 1 log bn
Nepal 3 obs • UNDOF 71; 1 inf coy
Netherlands 12 obs • UNDOF 2
New Zealand 8 obs
Norway 13 obs
Philippines UNDOF 337; 1 inf bn
Russia 5 obs • naval facility reportedly under renovation at Tartus
Serbia 1 obs
Slovakia 2 obs
Slovenia 5 obs
Sweden 6 obs
Switzerland 12 obs
United States 2 obs

Tunisia TUN

Tunisian Dinar D		2012	2013	2014
GDP	D	71.7bn	79.4bn	
	US$	45.6bn	49.5bn	
per capita	US$	4,232	4,533	
Growth	%	3.60	4.00	
Inflation	%	5.58	6.00	
Def exp	D	1.11bn		
	US$	705m		
Def bgt	D	1.05bn	1.23bn	
	US$	666m	769m	
FMA (US)	US$	18m	18m	20m
US$1=D		1.57	1.60	

Population 10,835,873

Age	0–14	15–19	20–24	25–29	30–64	65 plus
Male	11.9%	4.1%	4.2%	4.3%	21.5%	3.8%
Female	11.1%	4.0%	4.3%	4.5%	22.4%	3.9%

Capabilities

Small and relatively poorly equipped by regional standards, Tunisia's armed forces are reliant on conscripts, and much of the equipment across the three services is outdated and, in some cases, approaching obsolescence. In terms of internal security, the military's role is limited as the National Guard, arguably better-trained and designed to act as a counterbalance to the armed forces, takes the lead on domestic stability. Nonetheless, the army was integral to the Jasmine Revolution of January–February 2011, as it refused to fire on protesters and verbally leant its support to the demonstrations. The military was also utilised during the Libyan uprising in 2011, with the army and air force able to patrol the borders relatively successfully and the navy competently dealing with migrant flows and search-and-rescue operations in Tunisian waters. Tunisia's armed forces were well-suited to these constabulary roles, with more traditional military roles, such as high-tempo war fighting, largely beyond their current capabilities. Military modernisation programmes may be undermined by the 2011 revolution. As such, the country will most probably continue to rely on surplus stocks of US, French and Italian equipment for its arsenal.

ACTIVE 35,800 (Army 27,000 Navy 4,800 Air 4,000)
Paramilitary 12,000
Conscript liability 12 months selective

ORGANISATIONS BY SERVICE

Army 5,000; 22,000 conscript (total 27,000)

FORCES BY ROLE
SPECIAL FORCES
1 SF bde
1 (Sahara) SF bde
MANOEUVRE
Reconnaissance
1 recce regt
Mechanised
3 mech bde (1 armd regt, 2 mech inf regt, 1 arty regt, 1 AD regt, 1 engr regt, 1 sigs regt, 1 log gp)
COMBAT SUPPORT
1 engr regt

EQUIPMENT BY TYPE
MBT 84: 30 M60A1; 54 M60A3
LT TK 48 SK-105 *Kuerassier*
RECCE 60: 40 AML-90; 20 *Saladin*
APC 268
APC (T) 140 M113A1/A2
APC (W) 128: 18 EE-11 *Urutu*; 110 Fiat 6614
ARTY 276
TOWED 115: **105mm** 48 M101A1/A2; **155mm** 67: 12 M114A1; 55 M198
MOR 161: **81mm** 95; **107mm** 48 (some SP); **120mm** 18 Brandt
AT • MSL 590
SP 35 M901 ITV TOW
MANPATS 555: 500 *Milan*; 55 TOW
RL 89mm 600: 300 LRAC; 300 M20
AD • SAM 86
SP 26 M48 *Chaparral*
MANPAD 60 RBS-70
GUNS 127
SP 40mm 12 M-42
TOWED 115: **20mm** 100 M-55; **37mm** 15 Type-55 (M-1939)/Type-65
RADAR • LAND RASIT (veh, arty)
AEV 2 *Greif*
ARV 3 *Greif*; 6 M88A1

Navy ε4,800

EQUIPMENT BY TYPE
PATROL AND COASTAL COMBATANTS 25
PCFG 3 *La Galite* (FRA *Combattante* III) with 2 quad Mk140 lnchr with MM-40 *Exocet* AShM, 1 76mm gun
PCG 3 *Bizerte* (FRA P-48) with 8 SS 12M AShM
PCF 6 *Albatros* (GER Type-143B) with 2 single 533mm TT, 2 76mm guns
PB 13: 3 *Utique* (mod PRC *Haizhui* II); 4 *Istiklal*; 6 V Series
LOGISTICS AND SUPPORT 10:
ABU 3: 2 *Tabarka* (ex-US *White Sumac*); 1 *Sisi Bou Said*
AGE 1 *Hannibal*
AGS 1 *Khaireddine* (ex-US *Wilkes*)
AWT 1 *Ain Zaghouan* (ex-ITA *Simeto*)
AX 1 *Salambo* (ex-US *Conrad*, survey)
YDT 2
YTB 1 *Sidi Daoud* (ex-ITA *Porto d'Ischia*)

Air Force 4,000

FORCES BY ROLE
FIGHTER/GROUND ATTACK
1 sqn with F-5E/F-5F *Tiger* II
TRANSPORT
1 sqn with C-130B/H/J *Hercules*; G-222; L-410 *Turbolet*
1 liaison unit with S-208A
TRAINING
2 sqn with L-59 *Albatros**; MB-326B; SF-260
1 sqn with MB-326K; MB-326L
TRANSPORT HELICOPTER
2 sqn with AS350B *Ecureuil*; AS365 *Dauphin* 2; AB-205 (Bell 205); SA313; SA316 *Alouette* III; UH-1H *Iroquois*; UH-1N *Iroquois*
1 sqn with HH-3E

EQUIPMENT BY TYPE
AIRCRAFT 24 combat capable
FTR 12: 10 F-5E *Tiger* II; 2 F-5F *Tiger* II
ATK 3 MB-326K
TPT 18: **Medium** 13: 6 C-130B *Hercules*; 1 C-130H *Hercules*; 1 C-130J *Hercules*; 5 G-222; **Light** 5: 3 L-410 *Turbolet*; 2 S-208A
TRG 30: 9 L-59 *Albatros**; 4 MB-326B; 3 MB-326L; 14 SF-260
HELICOPTERS
MRH 10: 1 AS365 *Dauphin 2*; 6 SA313; 3 SA316 *Alouette* III
SAR 11 HH-3 *Sea King*
TPT • Light 33: 6 AS350B *Ecureuil*; 15 Bell 205 (AB-205); 10 Bell 205 (UH-1H *Iroquois*); 2 Bell 212 (UH-1N *Iroquois*)
MSL • AAM • IR AIM-9P *Sidewinder*

Paramilitary 12,000

National Guard 12,000

Ministry of Interior
PATROL AND COASTAL COMBATANTS 23
PCC 6 *Rais el Blais* (ex-GDR *Kondor* I)
PCI 15: 5 *Breitla* (ex-GDR *Bremse*); 4 *Gabes*; 4 *Rodman* 38; 2 *Socomena*
PBF 2 *Patrouiller*
HELICOPTERS • MRH 8 SA318 *Alouette* II/SA319 *Alouette* III

DEPLOYMENT

CÔTE D'IVOIRE
UN • UNOCI 3; 7 obs

DEMOCRATIC REPUBLIC OF THE CONGO
UN • MONUSCO 33 obs

United Arab Emirates UAE

Emirati Dirham D		2012	2013	2014
GDP	D	1.32tr	1.36tr	
	US$	359bn	369bn	
per capita	US$	64,840	64,780	
Growth	%	3.91	3.14	
Inflation	%	0.67	1.59	
Def bdgt	D	ε34.2bn		
	US$	ε9.32bn		
US$1=D		3.67	3.67	

Population 5,473,972

Ethnic groups: Nationals 24%; Expatriates 76% of which Indian 30%, Pakistani 20%; other Arab 12%; other Asian 10%; UK 2%; other European 1%

Age	0–14	15–19	20–24	25–29	30–64	65 plus
Male	10.6%	2.8%	5.4%	10.7%	38.6%	0.6%
Female	10.1%	2.4%	3.2%	4.1%	11.3%	0.4%

Capabilities

Although objectively few in number, the UAE's armed forces comprise a relatively large percentage of the population (about 1%), and maintain an extensive array of high quality equipment. Arms purchases will continue in the near future, particularly for the navy, which is undertaking a modernisation programme. In common with other regional states, and perhaps in line with regional threat perceptions, the UAE has expanded its air-defence capabilities with purchases in recent years of *Patriot* missile systems and an order for THAAD batteries and missiles. The air force has also seen significant investment, with discussions over a potential order of 25 more F-16 Block 60s beginning in 2013, and a separate competition to replace the UAE's current *Mirage* 2000 fleet. A GCC member, the UAE comprises seven separate emirates joined in a federation, each retaining influence within the overall command structure through regional commands; essentially nominally independent forces maintained by three emirates (in 1976, the Abu Dhabi Defence Force became the Western Command, the Dubai Defence Force became the Central Command and the Ras al-Khaimah Mobile Force became the Northern Command). Under the aegis of the federal Union Defence Force, this situation leads to greater autonomy and influence from these emirates on procurement and organisation. The country was one of the leading proponents of Arab participation in operations in Libya in 2011, sending six F-16s and six *Mirage* combat aircraft in support.

ACTIVE 51,000 (Army 44,000 Navy 2,500 Air 4,500)

The Union Defence Force and the armed forces of the UAE (Abu Dhabi, Dubai, Ras al-Khaimah, Fujairah, Ajman, Umm al-Qawayn and Sharjah) were formally merged in 1976 and headquartered in Abu Dhabi. Dubai still maintains independent forces, as do other emirates to a lesser degree.

ORGANISATIONS BY SERVICE

Space

SATELLITES • COMMUNICATIONS 2 *Yahsat*

Army 44,000 (incl Dubai 15,000)

FORCES BY ROLE

GHQ Abu Dhabi

MANOEUVRE

Armoured

1 armd bde

Mechanised

3 mech bde

Light

2 inf bde

Aviation

1 bde with AH-64D *Apache*; CH-47F *Chinook*; UH-60L/M *Black Hawk*

Other

1 Royal Guard bde

COMBAT SUPPORT

1 arty bde (3 arty regt)

1 engr gp

Dubai Independent Forces

FORCES BY ROLE

MANOEUVRE

Mechanised

2 mech inf bde

EQUIPMENT BY TYPE

MBT 471: 390 *Leclerc*; 36 OF-40 Mk2 (*Lion*); 45 AMX-30

LT TK 76 *Scorpion*

RECCE 105: 49 AML-90; 24 VBL; 32 TPz-1 *Fuchs* (NBC); (20 *Ferret* in store); (20 *Saladin* in store)

AIFV 605: 15 AMX-10P; 590 BMP-3

APC 1,642

APC (T) 136 AAPC (incl 53 engr plus other variants)

APC (W) 756: 90 BTR-3U *Guardian*; 120 EE-11 *Urutu*; 370 M3 Panhard; 80 VCR (incl variants); 20 VAB

PPV 826: 750 M-ATV; 76 RG-31 *Nyala*

ARV 46

ARTY 561+

SP 155mm 221: 78 G-6; 125 M109A3; 18 Mk F3

TOWED 93: **105mm** 73 ROF lt; **130mm** 20 Type-59-I

MRL 92+: **70mm** 18 LAU-97; **122mm** 48+: 48 Firos-25 (est 24 op); Type-90 (reported); **227mm** 20 HIMARS being delivered; **300mm** 6 9A52 *Smerch*

MOR 155: **81mm** 134: 20 Brandt; 114 L16; **120mm** 21 Brandt

AT • MSL 305+

SP 20 HOT

MANPATS 285+: 30 HOT; 230 *Milan*; 25 TOW; (*Vigilant* in store)

RCL 262: **84mm** 250 *Carl Gustav*; **106mm** 12 M40

AD • SAM • MANPAD 40+: 20+ *Blowpipe*; 20 *Mistral*

GUNS 62

SP 20mm 42 M3 VDAA

TOWED 30mm 20 GCF-BM2

MSL • TACTICAL • SSM 6 *Scud*-B (up to 20 msl)

AEV 53 ACV-AESV

ARV 143: 8 ACV-AESV Recovery; 4 AMX-30D; 85 BREM-L; 46 *Leclerc* ARV

HELICOPTERS

ATK 30 AH-64D *Apache*

TPT 45+ **Heavy** 4 CH-47F *Chinook;* **Medium** 41+: 11 UH-60L *Black Hawk;* 30+ UH-60M *Black Hawk*
UAV • ISR • Medium *Seeker* II

Navy ε2,500

EQUIPMENT BY TYPE
SUBMARINES • SDV ε10
PATROL AND COASTAL COMBATANTS 25
CORVETTES 7
FSGHM 3:
2 *Baynunah* with 2 quadruple lnchr with MM-40 *Exocet* Block III AShM, 1 8-cell Mk 56 VLS with RIM-162 ESSM SAM, 1 21-cell MR49 GMLS with RIM 116B SAM, 1 76mm gun (four additional vessels under construction)
1 *Abu Dhabi* with 2 quad lnchr with MM-40 *Exocet* Block III AShM, 1 76mm gun
FSGM 4:
2 *Muray Jib* (GER Lurssen 62m) with 2 quad lnchr with MM-40 *Exocet* Block II AShM, 1 octuple lnchr with *Crotale* SAM, 1 *Goalkeeper* CIWS, 1 76mm gun, 1 hel landing platform
2 *Ganthoot* with 2 twin lnchr with MM-40 *Exocet* Block III AShM, 2 triple lnchr with VL *Mica* SAM, 1 76mm gun, 1 hel landing platform
PCFGM 2 *Mubarraz* (GER Lurssen 45m) with 2 twin lnchr with MM-40 *Exocet* AShM, 1 sextuple lnchr with *Mistral* SAM, 1 76mm gun
PCFG 6 *Ban Yas* (GER Lurssen TNC-45) with 2 twin lnchr with MM-40 *Exocet* Block III AShM, 1 76mm gun
PBFG 4 *Al Bazam* (*Ghannatha* mod) with 4 single lncher with *Marte* Mk2/N AShM
PB 6 *Ardhana* (UK Vosper 33m)
MINE WARFARE • MINE COUNTERMEASURES 2:
MHO 2 *Al Murjan* (*Frankenthal*-class Type-332)
AMPHIBIOUS 29
LANDING SHIPS • LS 1 *Sir Bunuer*
LANDING CRAFT 28
LCP 16: 12 *Ghannatha* (capacity 40 troops; currently undergoing modernisation to include weapons mounts); 4 (Fast Supply Vessel multi-purpose
LCU 5: 3 *Al Feyi* (capacity 56 troops); 2 (capacity 40 troops and additional vehicles)
LCT 7
LOGISTICS AND SUPPORT 4: 1 **YDT**; 1 **YTB**; 2 **YTM**

Naval Aviation

AIRCRAFT • TPT • Light 2 Learjet 35A
HELICOPTERS
ASW 7 AS332F *Super Puma* (5 in ASuW role)
MRH 11: 7 AS565 *Panther*; 4 SA316 *Alouette* III
MSL • AShM AS-15TT; AM-39 *Exocet*

Air Force 4,500

Flying hours 110 hrs/year

FORCES BY ROLE
FIGHTER/GROUND ATTACK
3 sqn with F-16E/F Block 60 *Fighting Falcon*
3 sqn with *Mirage* 2000-9DAD/EAD/RAD
GROUND ATTACK
1 sqn with AT802 *Air Tractor*
SEARCH & RESCUE
2 flt with AW109K2; AW139
TRANSPORT
1 sqn with C-130H/C-130H-30 *Hercules*; L-100-30
1 sqn with CN-235M-100
1 (Spec Ops) sqn with AS365F *Dauphin* 2; AS550C3 *Fennec*; AW139; Cessna 208B *Grand Caravan*; CH-47C *Chinook*; DHC-6-300 *Twin Otter*
TRAINING
1 sqn with Grob 115TA
1 sqn with *Hawk* Mk63A/C*
1 sqn with *Hawk* Mk102*
1 sqn with PC-7 *Turbo Trainer*; PC-21
TRANSPORT HELICOPTER
1 sqn with Bell 412 *Twin Huey*
EQUIPMENT BY TYPE
AIRCRAFT 201 combat capable
FGA 138: 54 F-16E Block 60 *Fighting Falcon* (*Desert Eagle*); 24 F-16F Block 60 *Fighting Falcon* (13 to remain in US for trg); 16 *Mirage* 2000-9DAD; 44 *Mirage* 2000-9EAD
ISR 7 *Mirage* 2000 RAD*
AEW&C 2 Saab 340 *Erieye*
TPT/TKR 3 A330 MRTT
TPT 58 **Heavy** 6 C-17 *Globemaster* III; **Medium** 6: 3 C-130H *Hercules*; 1 C-130H-30 *Hercules*; 2 L-100-30; **Light** 46: 2 Beech 350 *King Air*; 8 Cessna 208B *Grand Caravan*; 7 CN-235M-100; 1 DHC-6-300 *Twin Otter*; 4 DHC-8 *Dash* 8 (MP); 24 AT802 *Air Tractor**
TRG 99: 12 Grob 115TA; 20 *Hawk* Mk63A/C*; 12 *Hawk* Mk102*; 30 PC-7 *Turbo Trainer*; 25 PC-21
HELICOPTERS
MRH 39: 4 AS365F *Dauphin* 2 (VIP); 18 AS550C3 *Fennec*; 8 AW139 (incl 2 VIP); 9 Bell 412 *Twin Huey*
TPT 22 **Heavy** 18: 12 CH-47C *Chinook* (SF); 6 CH-47F *Chinook*; **Light** 4: 3 AW109K2; 1 Bell 407
MSL
AAM • IR AIM-9L *Sidewinder*; R-550 *Magic*; **IIR/ARH** *Mica*; **ARH** AIM-120 AMRAAM
ASM AGM-65G *Maverick*; AGM-114 *Hellfire*; *Hydra-70*; *Hakeem* 1/2/3 (A/B); HOT
ARM AGM-88 HARM
LACM *Black Shaheen* (*Storm Shadow*/SCALP EG variant)

Air Defence

FORCES BY ROLE
AIR DEFENCE
2 AD bde (3 bn with MIM-23B I-HAWK; *Patriot* PAC-3)
3 (short range) AD bn with *Crotale*; *Mistral*; *Rapier*; RB-70; *Javelin*; 9K38 *Igla* (SA-18 *Grouse*); *Pantsir*-S1
EQUIPMENT BY TYPE
AD • SAM
SP *Crotale*; RB-70; 50 *Pantsir*-S1
TOWED MIM-23B I-HAWK; *Patriot* PAC-3; *Rapier*
MANPAD *Javelin*; 9K38 *Igla* (SA-18 *Grouse*)
NAVAL *Mistral*

Paramilitary

Coast Guard

Ministry of Interior
PATROL AND COASTAL COMBATANTS 62

PBF 9: 6 *Baglietto* GC23; 3 *Baglietto* 59
PB 53: 2 *Protector;* 16 (US Camcraft 65); 5 (US Camcraft 77); 6 *Watercraft* 45; 12 *Halmatic Work;* 12 *Al Saber*

UAE National Infrastructure Authority
PATROL AND COASTAL COMBATANTS 45
PBF ε30 MRTP 16 (a further 14 are in build); 15 DV-15

DEPLOYMENT

AFGHANISTAN
NATO • ISAF 35

FOREIGN FORCES

Australia 313; 1 tpt det with 3 C-130 *Hercules;* 1 MP det with 2 AP-3C *Orion*
France 700: 1 (Foreign Legion) BG (2 recce sqn, 2 inf sqn, 1 aty bty, 1 engr coy); 6 *Rafale,* 1 KC-135F
Korea, Republic of: 150 (trg activities at UAE Spec Ops School)
United States: 175; 2 bty with MIM-104 *Patriot*

Yemen, Republic of YEM

Yemeni Rial R		2012	2013	2014
GDP	R	7.64tr	8.54tr	
	US$	35.6bn	39bn	
per capita	US$	1,377	1,461	
Growth	%	0.14	4.39	
Inflation	%	10.98	7.50	
Def bdgt	R	350bn	397bn	397bn
	US$	1.63bn	1.81bn	
FMA (US)	US$	20m	20m	20m
US$1=R		214.48	219.18	

Population 25,408,288

Ethnic groups: Majority Arab, some African and South Asian

Age	0–14	15–19	20–24	25–29	30–64	65 plus
Male	21.4%	5.7%	5.0%	4.4%	13.0%	1.2%
Female	20.6%	5.5%	4.9%	4.2%	12.7%	1.4%

Capabilities

Yemen's armed forces are under-equipped, poorly-trained, and, given internal military and political conflict, have problems with morale across the forces. Despite a relatively high level of defence spending compared to GDP, the country's underdeveloped economic status means that the state is unable to exercise full control over internal security. The army is the best-equipped of the services, but still relies on Soviet-era equipment. The importance of tribal ties combined with the reintroduction of conscription in 2007 creates difficulties in encouraging loyalty to the armed forces. Restructuring in 2012, which led to the formation of a new Presidential Protection force, financially and administratively independent of the armed forces, was an attempt to resolve loyalty issues. A further restructure in December 2012 disbanded the Republican Guard and the 1st Armoured Division, while in April 2013 two key generals were moved from their posts and five regional military commands were reorganised into seven. The air force and navy are unable to fulfil their core roles of defending territorial sovereignty, with insufficient equipment and training. Airlift is almost non-existent, leading to severe problems in rapid mobility within the large country. Some combat aircraft – particularly the aged MiG-21s – are unreliable. The navy's Chinese-supplied *Hounan*-class patrol boats may well be unserviceable and, while international maritime forces on counter-piracy duties do liaise with representatives from the Yemeni coast guard, the rest of the small naval force faces challenges in monitoring and securing the country's extensive coastline.

ACTIVE 66,700 (Army 60,000 Navy 1,700 Air Force 3,000, Air Defence 2,000) **Paramilitary 71,200**
Conscript liability 2 years

ORGANISATIONS BY SERVICE

Army 60,000 (incl conscripts)
7 regional comd
FORCES BY ROLE
SPECIAL FORCES
1 SF bde
MANOEUVRE
Armoured
12 armd bde
Mechanised
11 mech bde
Light
22 inf bde
Air Manoeuvre
3 cdo/AB bde
Mountain
5 mtn inf bde
Other
1 (Presidential Protection) gd force (2 armd bde, 2 sy bde)
3 (border gd) sy bde
COMBAT SUPPORT
3 arty bde
1 SSM bde
2 AD bn
EQUIPMENT BY TYPE
MBT 880: 50 M60A1; 70 T-72; 80 T-80; 200 T-62; 450 T-54/T-55; 30 T-34
RECCE 130+: 80 AML-90; 50 BRDM-2; *Ratel*
AIFV 200: 100 BMP-1; 100 BMP-2
APC 258
APC (T) 60 M113A2
APC (W) 180: 60 BTR-40; 100 BTR-60; 20 BTR-152; (470 BTR-40/BTR-60/BTR-152 in store)
PPV 18 YLAV *Cougar*
ARTY 1,307
SP 122mm 25 2S1
TOWED 310: **105mm** 25 M101A1; **122mm** 200: 130 D-30; 30 M-1931/37; 40 M-30 M-1938; **130mm** 60 M-46; **152mm** 10 D-20; **155mm** 15 M114
COASTAL 130mm 36 SM-4-1
MRL 294: **122mm** 280 BM-21 (150 op); **140mm** 14 BM-14

MOR 642: **81mm** 250; **82mm** 144 M-43; **107mm** 12; **120mm** 136; **160mm** ε100

AT

MSL • MANPATS 71: 35 9K11 *Malyutka* (AT-3 *Sagger*); 24 M47 *Dragon*; 12 TOW

RCL 75mm M-20; **82mm** B-10; **107mm** B-11

GUNS 50+

SP 100mm 30 SU-100

TOWED 20+: **85mm** D-44; **100mm** 20 M-1944

AD

SAM ε800

SP 9K31 *Strela*-1 (SA-9 *Gaskin*); 9K35 *Strela*-10 (SA-13 *Gopher*)

MANPAD 9K32 *Strela*-2 (SA-7 *Grail*)‡; 9K36 *Strela*-3 (SA-14 *Gremlin*)

GUNS 530

SP 70: **20mm** 20 M163 *Vulcan*; **23mm** 50 ZSU-23-4

TOWED 460: **20mm** 50 M167 *Vulcan*; **23mm** 100 ZU-23-2; **37mm** 150 M-1939; **57mm** 120 S-60; **85mm** 40 M-1939 *KS-12*

MSL • TACTICAL • SSM 28: 12 FROG-7; 10 SS-21 *Scarab* (*Tochka*); 6 *Scud*-B (ε33 msl)

ARV T-54/55 reported

VLB MTU reported

Navy 1,700

EQUIPMENT BY TYPE

PATROL AND COASTAL COMBATANTS 22

PCO 1 *Tarantul*† with 2 twin lnchr (fitted for P-15 *Termit*-M (SS-N-2C *Styx*) AShM), 1 quad lnchr (manual aiming) with 9K32 *Strela*-2 (SA-N-5 *Grail*) SAM, 2 AK630 CIWS, 1 76mm gun

PBF 6 *Baklan*

PB 15: 3 *Hounan*† with 4 single lnchr (fitted for C-801 (CSS-N-4 *Sardine*) AShM), 2 twin AK230 CIWS; 10 P-1000 (Austal 37.5m); 2 *Zhak* (FSU *Osa* II) (1†)

MINE WARFARE • MINE COUNTERMEASURES 1:

MSO 1 *Natya* (FSU) with 2 RBU1200 RL

AMPHIBIOUS 4:

LANDING SHIPS • LSM 1 NS-722 (capacity 5 MBT; 110 troops)

LANDING CRAFT • LCU 3 *Deba*

LOGISTICS AND SUPPORT 2: 1 **AFD;** 1 **AGS**

Air Force 3,000

FORCES BY ROLE

FIGHTER

3 sqn with F-5E *Tiger* II; MiG-21 *Fishbed*; MiG-29SMT/MiG-29UBT *Fulcrum*

FIGHTER/GROUND ATTACK

1 sqn with Su-22 *Fitter* D/Su-22UMS *Fitter* G

MARITIME PATROL

1 unit with DHC-8 MPA

ISR

1 unit with Cessna 208B (forming)

TRANSPORT

1 sqn with An-12 *Cub*; An-26 *Curl*; C-130H *Hercules*; Il-76 *Candid*

ATTACK/TRANSPORT HELICOPTER

3 sqn with Bell 205 (UH-1H); Bell 212; Ka-27; Mi-8 *Hip*; Mi-17 *Hip* H; Mi14PS; Mi-35 *Hind*

EQUIPMENT BY TYPE

AIRCRAFT 75 combat capable

FTR 10 F-5E *Tiger* II

FGA 65: 15 MiG-21 *Fishbed*; 3 MiG-21U *Mongol* A*; 15 MiG-29SMT *Fulcrum*; 1 MiG-29UBT; 27 Su-22 *Fitter* D; 4 Su-22UM3 *Fitter* G

MP 2 DHC-8 MPA

TPT 13: **Heavy** 3 Il-76 *Candid*; **Medium** 4: 2 An-12 *Cub*; 2 C-130H *Hercules*; 1 CN235-300 **Light** 3 An-26 *Curl*; 2 Cessna 208B

TRG 36: 24 L-39C; 12 Z-242

HELICOPTERS

ATK 8 Mi-35 *Hind*

ASW 1 Ka-27 (tpt role)

MRH 10 Mi-17 *Hip* H

TPT 14: **Medium** 8 Mi-8 *Hip*; **Light** 6: 2 Bell 212; 4 Bell 205 (UH-1H)

MSL • IR R-3 (AA-2 *Atoll*)‡; R-60 (AA-8 *Aphid*); AIM-9 *Sidewinder*; **IR/SARH** R-27 (AA-10 *Alamo*)

Air Defence 2,000

AD • SAM:

SP 2K12 *Kub* (SA-6 *Gainful*); 9K31 *Strela*-1 (SA-9 *Gaskin*); 9K35 *Strela*-10 (SA-13 *Gopher*)

TOWED S-75 *Dvina* (SA-2 *Guideline*); S-125 *Pechora* (SA-3 *Goa*)

MANPAD 9K32 *Strela*-2 (SA-7 *Grail*); 9K36 *Strela*-3 (SA-14 *Gremlin*)

Paramilitary 71,200+

Ministry of the Interior Forces 50,000

Tribal Levies 20,000+

Yemeni Coast Guard Authority ε1,200

PATROL AND COASTAL COMBATANTS 17

PBF 4 *Archangel* (US)

PB 13: 2 *Marine Patrol*; 11 various

DEPLOYMENT

CÔTE D'IVOIRE

UN • UNOCI 1; 9 obs

DEMOCRATIC REPUBLIC OF THE CONGO

UN • MONUSCO 5 obs

LIBERIA

UN • UNMIL 1

MALI

UN • MINUSMA 2

SOUTH SUDAN

UN • UNMISS 3; 4 obs

SUDAN

UN • UNAMID 5; 49 obs

UN • UNISFA 2; 2 obs

WESTERN SAHARA

UN • MINURSO 11 obs

Table 7 **Selected Arms Procurements and Deliveries, Middle East and North Africa**

Designation	Type	Quantity (Current)	Contract Value	Prime Nationality	Prime Contractor	Order Date	First Delivery Due	Notes
Algeria (ALG)								
Fuchs 2	APC (W)	54	n.k.	GER	Rheinmetall	2011	2013	–
S-300PMU-2	SAM	32	US$1bn	RUS	Almaz-Antey	2006	2008	Eight bty. First bty delivered 2008
Pantsir-S1	AD	38	US$500m	RUS	KBP Insturment Design Bureau	2006	2010	Delivery underway
MEKO A200	FFGHM	2	See notes	GER	TKMS	2012	2016	Part of US$3.3bn (€2.5bn) deal including six *Super Lynx* 300 hel
C28A	FFGHM	3	n.k.	PRC	Hudong-Zhonghua Shipbuilding	2012	2015	–
Kalaat Beni Abbes-class	LPD	1	€400m	ITA	Fincantieri	2011	2014	Based on *San Giorgio*-class. 8,800 tonne FLD reported
Super Lynx 300	MRH hel	6	See notes	ITA	Finmeccanica (Agusta Westland)	2012	n.k.	Part of US$3.3bn (€2.5bn) deal including 2 MEKO A200 FFGHM
Egypt (EGY)								
F-16C/D *Fighting Falcon*	FGA ac	20	n.k.	US	Lockheed Martin	2010	2013	16 F-16C and 4 F-16D. First eight ac delivered Jan 2013. Further deliveries put on hold following removal of President Morsi
C-295	Tpt ac	6	n.k.	Int'l	EADS (CASA)	2013	tbd	Third order; were to be delivered from late 2013, but delivery suspended in Aug
Iran (IRN)								
Jamaran-class	FSGM	3	n.k.	IRN	n.k.	n.k.	2010	Second vessel in series launched at Bandar Anzali in Mar 2013; third expected late 2013. For third Naval District on Caspian Sea
Iraq (IRQ)								
BTR-4	APC (W)	420	US$2.5bn	UKR	KMDB	2010	2011	Contract value includes six An-32 tpt ac. At least 88 delivered by early 2013, but subsequent batch of 42 refused in mid-2013
Pantsir-S1	AD	up to 50	n.k.	RUS	KBP Insturment Design Bureau	2012	n.k.	Total number on order unclear
F-16C/D *Fighting Falcon* Block 52	FGA ac	36	n.k.	US	Lockheed Martin	2011	2014	24 C and 12 D models
Mi-28NE *Havoc*	Atk hel	up to 36	n.k.	RUS	Russian Helicopters (Kamov)	2012	2013	Total number on order unclear. Delivery to begin late 2013
Mi-35M *Hind*	Atk hel	6	US$250m	RUS	Russian Helicopters (Mil)	2013	2013	First four delivered Nov 2013
Israel (ISR)								
Merkava Mk IV	MBT	Up to 400	n.k.	ISR	MANTAK	2001	2003	Deliveries continue
Dolphin-class (Type 800)	SSK	3	ε€1.4bn (US$1.7bn)	GER	TKMS (HDW)	2006	2014	With Air-Independent Propulsion (AIP) system. First handed over May 2012; ISD expected mid-2014

Table 7 **Selected Arms Procurements and Deliveries, Middle East and North Africa**

Designation	Type	Quantity (Current)	Contract Value	Prime Nationality	Prime Contractor	Order Date	First Delivery Due	Notes
F-35A *Lightning* II	FGA ac	20	US$2.75bn	US	Lockheed Martin	2010	2016	Option for a further 75
M-346 *Master*	Trg ac	30	US$1bn	ITA	Finmeccanica (Alenia Aeronautica)	2012	2014	Part of a deal under which Italy agrees to purchase US$1bn of military equipment from Israeli suppliers
Jordan (JOR)								
YPR-765	AIFV	510	n.k.	NLD	Government Surplus	2010	2011	Order includes 69 M577s and unknown number of YPR-806s. Deliveries to be complete by 2014
Kuwait (KWT)								
KC-130J *Hercules*	Tkr ac	3	US$245m	US	Lockheed Martin	2010	2013	Deliveries to be complete in early 2014
Morocco (MOR)								
Mohammed VI-class (FREMM)	DDGHM	1	€470m (US$676m)	FRA	DCNS	2008	2013	Launched Sep 2011; delivery delayed until Nov 2013
Bin an Zaran-class	PSO	4	US$140m	FRA	STX Shipbuilding	2008	2011	First vessel delivered 2011
Oman (OMN)								
Al-Shamikh-class	FFG	3	GB£400m (US$785m)	UK	BAE Systems (BAE Maritime)	2007	2013	First vessel *(Al-Shamikh)* delivered Jul 2013
Fearless-class	PCO	4	US$880m (€535m)	SGP	ST Engineering (ST Marine)	2012	2015	–
Eurofighter *Typhoon*	FGA ac	12	See notes	Int'l	Eurofighter GmbH (BAE Systems)	2013	2017	Part of UK£2.5bn deal including eight *Hawk* Mk128. Nine single-seat and three twin-seat
C-130J-30 *Hercules*	Tpt ac	2	n.k.	US	Lockheed Martin	2010	2013	Delivery due in 2013 and 2014
C-295	Tpt ac	8	n.k.	Int'l	EADS (CASA)	2012	2013	For air force. Five in tpt and three in MP configuration. First delivered 2013
Hawk Mk128 Advanced Jet Trainer	Trg ac	8	See notes	UK	BAE Systems	2012	n.k.	Part of UK£2.5bn deal including 12 Eurofighter *Typhoon*
NH90 TTH	Tpt hel	20	n.k.	Int'l	NH Industries	2004	2010	12 delivered by early 2013
Qatar (QTR)								
Leopard 2A7	MBT	62	See notes	GER	KMW	2013	2015	Part of €1.89bn (US$2.47bn) contract incl 24 PzH 2000
PzH 2000	Arty (155mm SP)	24	See notes	GER	KMW	2013	2015	Part of €1.89bn (US$2.47bn) contract incl 62 *Leopard* 2A7
Saudi Arabia (SAU)								
CAESAR	Arty (155mm SP)	132	n.k.	FRA	Nexter	2006	2010	For SAU National Guard; to replace M198. 100 delivered 2010–11. Additional order for 32 signed in 2012 for delivery by end 2014

Table 7 **Selected Arms Procurements and Deliveries, Middle East and North Africa**

Designation	Type	Quantity (Current)	Contract Value	Prime Nationality	Prime Contractor	Order Date	First Delivery Due	Notes
Eurofighter *Typhoon*	FGA ac	72	GB£4.43bn (US$8.9bn)	Int'l	Eurofighter GmbH	2005	2008	*Project Salam*. First 24 delivered by Sep 2011. Original plan to final assemble remaining 48 in SAU dropped; deliveries from UK started 2013
F-15E *Strike Eagle*	FGA ac	84	US$11.4bn	US	Boeing	2012	2015	F-15SA variant. Part of a package including F-15S upgrades, AH-64 and AH-6i helicopters that could total US$24bn
Saab 2000 *Erieye*	AEW&C ac	1	US$670m	SWE	Saab	2010	n.k.	Ac, believed to be for SAU, in test in SWE 2013
KC-130J *Hercules*	Tkr ac	2	US$180m	US	Lockheed Martin	2013	n.k.	Initial two aircraft pending agreement of larger order
A330 MRTT	Tkr/Tpt ac	6	US$600m	FRA	EADS	2008	2011	First three ac delivered. Three more purchased July 2009 for undisclosed fee; delivery due to begin by end-2014
PC-21	Trg ac	55	n.k.	CHE	Pilatus	2012	2014	To replace PC-9s
Hawk Mk128 Advanced Jet Trainer	Trg ac	22	n.k.	UK	BAE Systems	2012	2016	–
Syria (SYR)								
Yak-130	Trg ac	36	US$550m	RUS	UAC (Irkut)	2012	2013	–
Tunisia (TUN)								
C-130J *Hercules*	Tpt ac	2	n.k.	US	Lockheed Martin	2010	2013	First ac delivered Apr 2013. Second due in 2014
United Arab Emirates (UAE)								
Falcon Eye	ISR Satellite	2	€800m (US$1.1bn)	Int'l	EADS/Thales	2013	2017	First satellite due to launch 2017; second 2018
Agrab Mk2 *(Scorpion)* MMS	Arty (120mm SP Mor)	72	US$214m	RSA/SGP/ UAE/UK	IGG	2011	2014	–
Patriot Advanced Capability (PAC) 3	AD System	10 fire units, 172 msl	US$3.3bn	US	Raytheon	2008	2012	To replace HAWK. Incl 172 PAC-3 msl and 42 launcher mod packs, plus some GEM-T msl. First bty delivered 2012
Baynunah-class	FSGHM	6	AED3bn (US$820m)	FRA/UAE	ADSB	2003	2006	First-of-class built in FRA, others to be built in UAE. Delivery expected to be complete by 2014

Chapter Eight
Latin America and the Caribbean

Drugs and insecurity

Organised crime and insurgencies continue to pose strategic threats to Latin American countries. In South America, insurgents and criminal groups presented serious challenges for state forces, particularly in Colombia, Venezuela and Peru. Heavy pressure from security forces in Colombia pushed powerful criminal groups to seek new routes for drug trafficking; Venezuela deployed its armed forces to the streets of the capital, Caracas; and Brazil, in response to increasing drug flows into the country, deployed troops internally in the country's largest military deployment since the Second World War. In some countries, these challenges have spurred moves to enhance inventories and personnel numbers. Specifically tailored responses continue, often combining military and law-enforcement authorities. These still include military deployments in urban areas; they also include the creation of specialist units designed to combat criminal networks.

New forces and tailored responses

Last year's *Military Balance* detailed the security response to criminal violence in Mexico (pp. 417–9). There, and in some Central American cities, the armed forces remain deployed to combat gangs.

In December 2012, the new Mexican government of President Enrique Peña Nieto promised a new approach in the fight against criminal violence, with more emphasis on social and economic policies. However, the administration then announced that a new National Gendarmerie would be established to counter organised crime. The force was due to deploy in late 2013 with 10,000 personnel, but this was postponed until July 2014, and numbers reduced to 5,000. Though the gendarmerie will be a division of the federal police, it will also receive some military training. This has led some analysts to question whether the government's security policies represent a substantial change from the military-led approach of the previous administration under Felipe Calderón. Meanwhile, the Public Security Secretariat – which was responsible for the federal police, among other units – was dissolved. The Interior Ministry absorbed its security responsibilities, with the aim of increasing cooperation between government agencies.

Honduras and Guatemala continue to experience high levels of violent crime, but both states created new units and procured light attack aircraft to boost their capabilities. In Honduras, high levels of violence again saw military units deployed onto the streets, while the government later sought to bolster security by creating new forces. Measures to reform the police continued – given a public perception of police corruption – though plans to scrutinise members of security-related agencies with, among other methods, polygraphs and drug testing progressed slowly. In June, Congress agreed that 1,000 personnel be recruited to form a new police unit, known by the acronym TIGRES. This force is intended to be highly trained and well-equipped, to help counter criminal groups that often possess more firepower than the police. In early August, a new community police force was announced, together with a reorganisation of existing police jurisdictions, and later in the month Congress announced the formation of a new Public Order Military Police unit. These units should add to security capability, though effectively generating, deploying and coordinating the varying security forces could, given continuing criminal violence and ongoing efforts to improve national police capacity, prove a challenge for the new administration.

In April, Guatemalan authorities raised Task Force Tecún Umán, with a view to countering illicit activity in border areas. Initially comprising 250 recruits from the army's Mountain Infantry Brigade, numbers are expected to rise to 750. Personnel have also received training, and reportedly some funding, from the United States as part of SOUTHCOM's ongoing partnership activities. The government also increased personnel numbers, and broadened territorial deployments with the posting of more than 1,500 soldiers to three departments along the south-western coast and the eastern border with Honduras. These border deployments signal continuing concern over the activity of transnational criminal organisations. Guatemala became the first Central American country to order the EMB-314 *Super Tucano*; an order for six was announced in April. Neighbouring El Salvador opted for ten second-hand Chilean A-37s, instead of EMB-314s. Some analysts have questioned the decision. Although El Salvador already operates the A-37, and will have established support facilities, operating costs will likely be higher than for the turboprop EMB-314.

Regional and external actors remained involved in efforts to address regional security issues. The Central American Integration System (SICA) announced new initiatives, mostly financed by the EU and US, to improve security coordination. During a foreign ministers' summit in June 2013, SICA announced a Regional Treaty for Border Security, to coordinate security initiatives and draft joint border-security plans. Ongoing efforts to limit small-arms proliferation continue through the SICA/UNDP Central American Programme for the Control of Small Arms. The US, meanwhile, continued its strategy of focusing aid to strengthen regional institutions through the Central America Regional Security Initiative (CARSI), the budget for which rose 26% (to US$162m) for FY2014. *Operation Martillo* (see *The Military Balance* 2013, p. 416) continued in 2013, with rotational deployments of personnel, ships and aircraft. The operation, spearheaded by the US Joint Interagency Task Force South (JIATFS), aims to weaken the capabilities of criminal groups operating along the Pacific and Atlantic coasts.

Insurgency and criminality in the Andean region

Colombia and Peru both took measures to boost their security forces and acquired more equipment for riverine and coastal operations as part of measures against the FARC and Shining Path guerrilla groups. In **Colombia**, the armed forces continued the 'Sword of Honour' campaign, initially implemented in 2012, in which mobile task forces are deployed to areas of high FARC activity. Both FARC and the country's second-largest guerrilla group, the National Liberation Army (ELN), continued attacks in 2013, despite being under severe pressure from the Colombian armed forces.

FARC and ELN insurgents engage in drug trafficking alongside, and sometimes with, organised crime groups known in Colombia as *bacrim* (*bandas criminales*). To help combat the movement of these criminal and guerrilla networks, the air force established a seventh Air Combat Command (CACOM-7) in February 2013. This has responsibility for the southwestern departments of Valle del Cauca, Nariño, Cauca and Huila – strategic locations for the international drug trade and the location of FARC's 6th, 29th and 60th fronts. In July, a new Naval Force East was established to patrol around 5,000km of river systems that include areas bordering Brazil and Venezuela. This 1,800-strong organisation will coordinate assets, including a range of patrol boats and other riverine capabilities with forces including the 5th Marine Brigade. Riverine capabilities were also due to be strengthened by the arrival of eight Griffon 2000TD hovercraft, ordered earlier in the year.

Despite continued fighting in 2013, Colombia retains its intention to diversify the activities of its armed forces. On 25 June, Defence Minister Juan Carlos Pinzón signed an information and security cooperation agreement with NATO. During a lecture at The International Institute for Strategic Studies two days later, Pinzón explained that cooperation will include the exchange of knowledge and experience in fighting terrorism and drug trafficking. He made it clear that Colombia does not wish to join NATO as an official member.

In **Peru**, Shining Path may hold only a fraction of the power it had in the 1990s, but it still conducts

Regional defence initiatives

UNASUR's South American Defence Council (CDS) announced progress on the development of a joint multi-role training aircraft, known as UNASUR I or IA-73. Argentina's Aircraft Factory (FAdeA) is leading the project, and Argentina's vice-minister for defence announced in May that several UNASUR countries were offering to assemble different parts. The other of UNASUR's two main cooperation initiatives, a joint UAV project led by Brazil, is facing delays with other member countries, such as Argentina and Venezuela, pursuing their own UAV development programmes. During an 8 May CDS meeting, defence authorities from Argentina, Brazil and Ecuador announced support for a South American Defence School. The objective would be to encourage joint regional approaches to defence and strategy.

Meanwhile, the KC-390 military transport aircraft concluded its critical design review in 2013. Led by Embraer, the main project partners are Argentina, Chile and Colombia. In April 2013 Embraer announced that the construction of the first two prototypes, and a sales campaign, were to start. It estimates the model could sell 728 aircraft in 77 countries.

hit-and-run attacks against government forces and sabotage against extractive industries in the impoverished jungle region known as the Apurímac, Ene and Mantaro River Valleys (VRAEM). Although weakened by the arrest or death of senior leaders in recent years, the group staged bold assaults against army bases in the region during 2013. In response, the government more than doubled the budget for security investment in the VRAEM in 2013 to US$300m.

Given the inaccessibility of some areas, especially the lower Urabamba river basin where Shining Path leaders are thought to be based, the navy has boosted its riverine capabilities with a second *Clavero*-class PCR and four additional hovercraft. Rotary-wing capabilities remain vital, and in March 2013 the defence ministry announced a plan to buy 24 Russian Mi-171Sh helicopters, to be delivered in 2014 and 2015. The government also began the construction of four police stations and refurbished three military bases in the VRAEM, promising to build ten more military outposts. More controversially, the government announced on 21 March that it would reimpose the military draft, abolished in 1998, to meet a shortage of 30,000 recruits. Although the government gave assurances in the media that these recruits would not participate in combat roles in the VRAEM, it faced accusations of elitism, since young men selected in the draft lottery could opt out by paying US$715 – double the average monthly income for young people in the capital. The initial draft, which would have selected 12,500 men, was cancelled by a Peruvian court in June.

Internal security was a key challenge for the new administration in **Venezuela**. President Hugo Chávez died in March 2013, leaving behind a United Socialist Party (PSUV) dealing with an increasingly problematic economy as well as persistently high homicide rates linked to drug-trafficking groups. The new president, former foreign minister Nicolás Maduro, was sworn in on 19 April, and shortly afterwards announced the deployment of 3,000 troops from the army, navy and air force to the capital, Caracas.

Maduro's position within Venezuela's political and military circles is weaker than that enjoyed by Chávez. Despite being his anointed successor, Maduro lacks the support of officers closely linked to National Assembly Speaker Diosdado Cabello, a former army colleague of Chávez. Maduro announced concessions to the armed forces on 25 April, nearly one week after being sworn in. He declared a 'special mission' to give more social benefits to members of the armed forces, including food subsidies and loans. Additionally, he proposed the creation of military business enterprises. Under these plans, the armed forces would control a TV station (TV-FANB) and a bank (Banco-FANB), and in August details of the bank appeared in the official gazette; Maduro reportedly announced an initial capital injection of some Bs170m. Plans were also announced for a military-run transport business and an agricultural concern to produce food for the armed forces. Around the same time, Maduro resorted to the creation of more citizen militias, an instrument used by Chávez to generate armed groups loyal directly to the president and the Bolívarian Revolution. Maduro announced a new Bolívarian Workers' Militia to 'defend the homeland [and] the stability of the Bolívarian Revolution'; although details remain scant, it is reported that this will be an arm of the existing Bolívarian Militia.

REGIONAL DEFENCE ECONOMICS

Regional macroeconomics

Economic growth rates across Latin America in 2012 and 2013 were generally positive, though they varied considerably between countries. In the face of a weakened external environment, with continued economic stagnation in advanced countries and growth moderation in major emerging economies, the strongest group of performers was Mexico,

Cuban weapons shipment uncovered

On 12 July 2013, authorities in Panama boarded the North Korean vessel *Chong Chon Gang*, travelling from Cuba through the canal. Searching for drugs, they instead found military equipment hidden beneath a cargo of sugar. Pictures revealed by Panamanian President Ricardo Martinelli and the media showed a RSN-75 *Fan Song* radar, used with the S-75M *Volkov* (SA-2 *Guideline*) SAM system. The ship also contained two MiG-21 fighter aircraft and 15 jet engines, plus two anti-aircraft systems, nine missiles and spare parts. Cuba claimed that the equipment was obsolete and was being sent to North Korea for upgrade, while others posited that the shipment was an attempt by North Korea to acquire defensive systems in response to continued international sanctions. It was also unclear whether previous shipments had taken place. (See p. 216.)

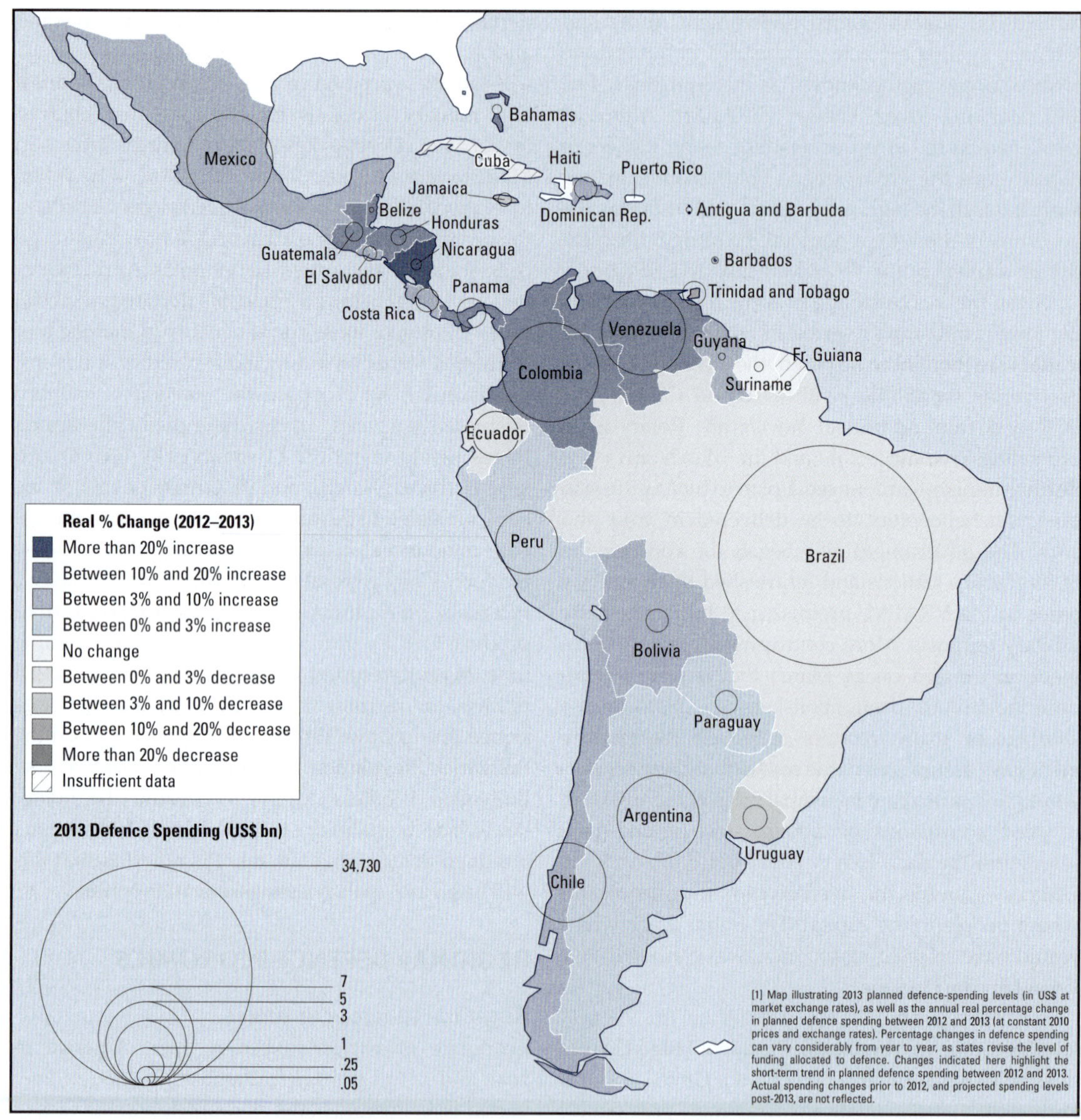

Map 7 **Latin America and the Caribbean Regional Defence Spending[1]**

Chile, Peru and Colombia – all financially integrated commodity-exporting economies. These states experienced favourable domestic credit conditions, elevated commodity prices, FDI inflows (particularly in the mining sector) and strong consumer and business confidence, all of which supported domestic demand, and resulted in growth rates of 4–6%. An exception to this trend was Brazil, where rising domestic costs and supply-side constraints led to heightened business uncertainty over the country's short- to medium-term trajectory. The result was a decline in private investment and a sharp deceleration in 2012 growth (0.9% – down from 7.5% in 2010 and 2.7% in 2011), although economic activity was expected to rebound to around 3% in 2013. Growth also slowed among less financially integrated commodity exporters, such as Argentina, Venezuela, Bolivia, Ecuador and Paraguay, although Paraguay rebounded from a -1.2% economic contraction in 2012 as its soft-commodity sector recovered from a severe drought. Argentina and Venezuela experienced economic volatility in 2012 and 2013. Both countries pursued heavily expansionary fiscal and monetary policies, which resulted in capital outflows, currency depreciation and the use of price controls in an attempt to curb high inflation.

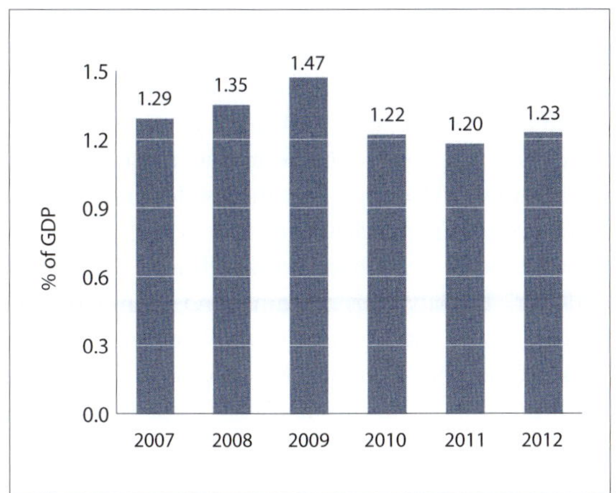

Figure 18 **Latin America and the Caribbean Regional Defence Expenditure** as % of GDP

By contrast, economic activity was relatively healthy in Central America. Output rose in 2012 and 2013 by 3–5.5% in Nicaragua, Costa Rica, Honduras and Guatemala. In the Caribbean, commodity-exporting economies such as Belize, Guyana, Suriname and Trinidad and Tobago saw growth average around 3.5% in 2012, while post-crisis stagnation continued in the tourism-dependent economies, with 2012 growth averaging less than 0.5%. Overall, regional growth moderated from 6.1% in 2010 to 3% in 2012, and an estimated 3.4% in 2013.

Regional defence spending

From 2010, nominal defence spending in Latin America rose by 15.6%, from around US$61.3bn in 2010 to US$70.9bn in 2013. Much of this increase occurred between 2010 and 2011, when nominal spending rose by 8.8% to US$66.7bn. In the main, it was a reflection of the elevated inflation rates and strong currency appreciation seen across the region at the time, which served to inflate US dollar conversions of regional defence outlays. These pressures gradually abated during 2012 and 2013, dampening nominal increases in defence spending – in US dollar terms at least. Between 2011 and 2012, spending rose by 6.1%, from US$66.7bn to US$70.8bn. In 2013, it rose by just 0.2%, to US$70.9bn. Discounting these exchange rate and inflationary effects, real defence spending increased at a moderate 3.04% in 2013, a figure much in line with the 3–3.5% regional growth rates for 2012 and 2013 outlined above. However, regional defence spending growth appears to be slowing. The 3.04% real increase in 2013 was less than half the 7.6% real increase seen in 2012, indicating that despite the region's relative economic buoyancy, concerns over the economic outlook have meant that, in general, states have been unwilling to expand defence outlays beyond increases in their GDP. For example, between 2011 and 2013, average economic growth in the region was 3.8%, while the real compound annual growth rate for defence spending was 3.5% over the same period.

In 2013, real defence spending rose fastest in Mexico and Central America – by 6.9% overall. Large year-on-year increases were seen in Nicaragua (27%), Guatemala (18.3%), Honduras (17.8%), Belize (12.9%), Panama (10.7%) and Costa Rica (9.6%). All Central American countries increased real spending levels in 2013, as several states established new security forces (see p. 355) and increased investment to purchase more advanced equipment (principally helicopters and fast patrol craft), improve coastal/border surveillance systems and construct new bases to combat narco-trafficking and organised crime.

By contrast, real defence budgets in South America grew by just 2.8% in 2013, with the largest increases in Venezuela (12.4%), Colombia (11.6%) and Bolivia (8.0%). Increases in Venezuela were partly driven by military procurement (see below) and expansion of the marine corps. Defence investment in Colombia rose by over 50% in 2013, including funds to build a new coast guard station, in addition to the establishment of new air and naval commands (see p. 356). Smaller real spending increases of 2–3%, were seen in Paraguay, Argentina and Peru. Lima increased funds for military intelligence, salaries, equipment and infrastructure, while in March 2013 Buenos Aires was forced to raise personnel salaries, particularly for junior officers, due to the threat of industrial action by the gendarmerie and coast guard. However, funding for training and capital investment remains stretched in Argentina. Air force flying hours were reportedly cut by nearly half in 2013, while equipment acquisition and repair timetables have been delayed. For example, funding constraints have hampered development of the *Pampa* II fighter/trainer and the *Patrullera Oceanica Multipropósito* offshore patrol vessel (OPV) programmes, as well as delayed repairs to the *Almirante Irizar* ice-breaker.

Real defence outlays fell in Uruguay (-4.1%, principally due to higher inflation) as well as Brazil (-1.1%), where the Rouseff administration aimed for a primary surplus target of 2.3% of GDP for 2013 and reorientated its spending priorities towards the

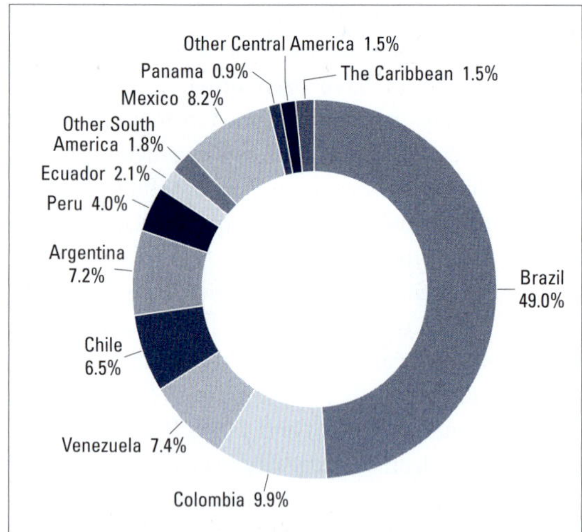

Figure 19 **Latin America & the Caribbean Defence Spending by Country & Sub-Region**

social, education and construction sectors following large-scale protests in June 2013. As a result, a total of R4.2bn (US$2.15bn) was pruned from Brazil's 2013 defence budget, with the R3.3bn (US$1.73bn) in defence reductions negotiated in May 2013 increased by a further R919.4m (US$471m) in July 2013 (see p. 363). These reductions were focused on non-mandatory areas of expenditure, particularly on administrative expenses. Defence spending also declined by 4.5% in the Caribbean in 2013, following a slight increase of 2.4% in 2012, as real defence spending levels fell in all states except the Dominican Republic and the Bahamas.

Regional defence procurement

Most defence spending in the majority of Latin American states is allocated to personnel costs and pensions, rather than to capital expenditure on equipment and infrastructure. For example, in 2008 Brazil allocated 79.5% of military spending to salaries and pensions. While this proportion has fallen over recent years, as the country's defence aspirations have increased, personnel and pension costs still accounted for 68.3% of Brazil's total defence budget in 2013. Similarly, personnel costs accounted for around 78% of Argentine defence spending in 2012, with similar figures for Chile (73%), Uruguay (74%) and Paraguay (about 70%). Even in Colombia, where the proportion of the defence budget allocated to personnel costs tends to be lower due to higher operational expenditures, only around 16% of 2012 outlays were allocated to actual equipment procurement.

Platforms that can be utilised in counter-narcotics and internal/border security operations have dominated regional procurement programmes (see Figure 20). Over the past five years, helicopter purchases and upgrades were the most common procurement in the region, with 14 states undertaking such programmes, including orders for multi-role helicopters in Argentina, Bolivia, Brazil, Colombia, Ecuador, El Salvador, Panama and Trinidad and Tobago; transport helicopters in Argentina, Bolivia, Brazil, Colombia, Ecuador, Mexico, Peru; and attack helicopters in Brazil, Peru and Venezuela. In 2013, the Chilean army opened tenders for attack and transport helicopters, while the Bolivian and Chilean air forces were separately studying the acquisition of additional multi-role helicopters. Coastal and jungle surveillance systems continue to feature in national procurement priorities, with several states pursuing programmes to purchase or upgrade such systems: Brazil, Mexico, Chile and Paraguay for long-range unmanned systems for wide-area surveillance; Mexico, Panama and Ecuador for radar systems; and Brazil and Chile for maritime patrol aircraft. Maritime priorities include OPVs in Argentina, Brazil, Colombia, Panama, Peru, Uruguay and Mexico, and riverine patrol craft in Brazil, Colombia and Peru. Hovercraft procurements continued, with Peru receiving five Griffon 2000TDs and announcing further procurements in July. Earlier, in January, Colombia ordered an initial batch of the same type.

With a continuing regional focus on air mobility, many states looked to acquire transport aircraft, and programmes to rejuvenate ageing fleets are under way in Mexico, Colombia, Argentina and Chile, among others. In the case of Chile, transport assets were prioritised from late 2012, when it emerged that much of the army's fixed-wing transport fleet was grounded due to a lack of maintenance and spare parts. In 2013, Paraguay considered upgrading its Air Transport Group's capacity with Airbus CN235 or CN295 transport aircraft to better fulfil its revived role in providing – through the Military Air Transport Service – passenger and cargo flights to rural areas. Venezuela took delivery of another two Shaanxi Y-8 transport aircraft from China's AVIC; eight were ordered in late 2011.

In March 2013, Venezuela took delivery of another batch of BMP-3s from Russia and Belarus (first ordered in 2011), and in April 2013 received the first deliveries of the Russian-manufactured S-300VM air-defence system. Other regional vehicle procurements

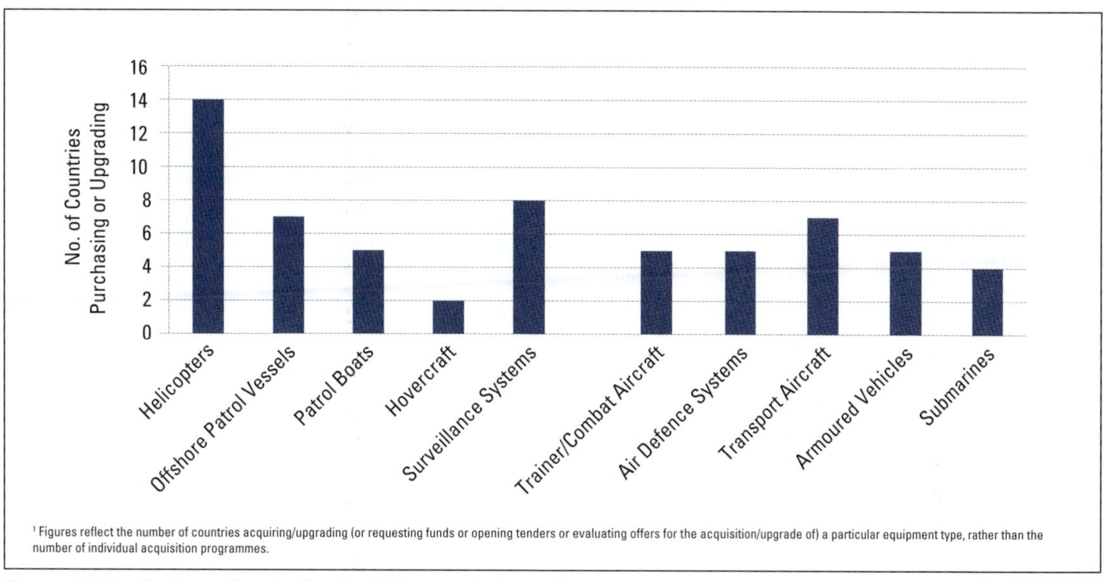

[1] Figures reflect the number of countries acquiring/upgrading (or requesting funds or opening tenders or evaluating offers for the acquisition/upgrade of) a particular equipment type, rather than the number of individual acquisition programmes.

Figure 20 **Latin America & the Caribbean: Selected Procurement & Upgrade Priorities Since 2009**[1]

include Brazil's long-running purchase of Iveco *Guarani* APCs and Colombia's acquisition of General Dynamics LAV III and Textron *Commando* APCs.

Several countries plan to upgrade their trainer and combat aircraft fleets. While some states, like Chile, Colombia and Ecuador, have purchased second-hand aircraft (many of which were upgraded prior to delivery), budgetary uncertainties have meant that many countries remain cautious about committing funds for aircraft acquisition. For example, Brazil's F-X2 programme remains stalled, while funding limits revealed in December 2012 forced Chile to reconsider its purchase of advanced jet trainers, instead turning to the second-hand market. Exceptions were Peru and El Salvador, which agreed purchases of 20 KT-1 turboprop trainers from Korea Aerospace Industries and ten second-hand Cessna A-37s from Chile respectively (see pp. 355–56).

BRAZIL

Brazil in 2013 stepped up efforts to patrol its extensive land frontiers in light of continuing activity by criminal and narco-trafficking groups. The government launched new joint military and police operations in border regions and continued to procure surveillance equipment. These efforts are part of Brazil's 2011 Strategic Border Plan.

Despite criticism from some in Congress that the plan was having little permanent effect on the border regions, on 18 May the government launched the latest *Operation Ágata*. Six of these had taken place since June 2011 (see *The Military Balance* 2013, p. 426). Led by the Ministry of Defence, they combine armed forces and federal police personnel and have primarily been aimed at combatting drug smuggling. While previous *Ágata* operations were relatively small-scale, under *Ágata* 7, personnel were dispatched to multiple border areas over 19 days.

The operation resulted in the seizure of 657kg of drugs. Around 33,000 military personnel were deployed – the largest mobilisation of the armed forces since the Second World War. As with previous operations, the security effort was accompanied by social programmes, with a key objective of strengthening state presence in remote communities. *Operation Sentinel*, a permanent law-enforcement effort led by the Ministry of Justice, is also part of the Strategic Border Plan. Although the authorities announced substantial seizures of drugs and suspects between June 2011 and November 2012, opposition congressmen said the measures were insufficient.

Armed services

Growing reliance on the armed forces for law-enforcement operations in the western and northwestern Amazon region has led to a reorganisation of the army's land battalions. A new Northern Military Command was activated on 7 March 2013, covering the northeastern states of Pará, Maranhão and Amapá, previously part of the Amazon Military Command. The authorities assess different threats in these states than in western regions, where law-enforcement concerns predominate, and a key task of the new command will be natural resource protection.

Because of the scale of Brazil's borders, the army continues to stress that the Integrated Border Monitoring System (SISFRON) remains one of its most important projects. In June 2013, Embraer subsidiary SAVIS, the lead company in the consortium implementing the system, finalised selection of the main suppliers for SISFRON's initial phase. According to Embraer, SISFRON will monitor about 650km of borders in Mato Grosso and Mato Grosso do Sul, which includes the borders with Bolivia and Paraguay. Brazil also expanded its UAV fleet. The air force received two additional *Hermes*-450s MALE UAVs, destined for the 1st squadron (Horus Squadron) of the 12th Aviation Group. This specialist UAV reconnaissance squadron was established in 2011 and is located at Santa Maria Air Base in Rio Grande do Sul state. In May 2013, along the southwestern frontier, the air force carried out its first joint counter-narcotics operation using UAVs. This was conducted with the federal police, which is integrating UAV output into its Intelligence and Strategic Analysis Police Centre, set up to gather information about organised crime using both human sources and technology.

The navy has also been involved in law-enforcement operations in the Amazon region. While the naval modernisation programme is focused on the Atlantic Coast, it has included the procurement of some riverine assets, such as the four LPR-40 Mk II patrol boats (two for the navy, two for the army) ordered from Colombian shipbuilder COTECMAR. Deliveries are due to end in March 2014.

Most of the procurements are geared towards the acquisition of surface vessels, such as through the PROSUPER and PROSUB programmes (see *The Military Balance 2013*, p. 425). These programmes are aimed at protecting the Atlantic, or 'Blue Amazon', Coast, as well as Brazil's oil reserves. But Brazilian strategy is broader. The 2008 National Defence Strategy noted a desire for the country to 'reach its deserved spot in the world', as it aims to be recognised as a major political and economic player in the region. In February 2013, the government announced it will request exclusive rights of exploration for the mineral-rich Rio Grande underwater mountain range located 1,000km from Rio de Janeiro. Terrorism, piracy and drug-trafficking groups are considered threats to the growing trade links between Brazil and West Africa. Consequently, security cooperation initiatives with African states are on the rise, especially with Namibia, Angola, Liberia and Senegal. On 8 May 2013, Defence Minister Celso Amorim voiced concern that instability could occur in West African coastal areas due to the presence of extremist groups in Mali.

Despite significant budget cuts during the year (see p. 363), procurements included two new *Amazonas*-class PSOs from BAE Systems making a total of three. However, most patrol capabilities will be developed domestically. Rio de Janeiro shipbuilder Eisa, for instance, is building additional *Macaé*-class PCCs to add to the three in service, and the navy is in negotiations with the National Development Bank to finance the construction of 20 more patrol vessels.

PROSUB is considered a strategic priority and remains exempt from budget cuts. On 1 March 2013, construction finished on the Metal Structures

Brazil's cyber defence policy

Following a report by *O Globo* newspaper in July that Brazil had been the target of cyber espionage by the US National Security Agency (NSA) in the wake of leaks by former NSA contractor Edward Snowden, the armed forces asked for faster development of the Geostationary Satellite for Defence and Strategic Communication (SGDC). This is intended to provide the state with the capability to control sensitive communications. Developed by Telebras and Embraer, its launch is currently scheduled for 2015. Brazil also intends to construct domestic Internet Exchange Points. Currently, all information exchanged internationally by Brazilian internet users passes through the US and, to a lesser extent, Europe and Japan. The Exchange Points would, according to the Communications Ministry, decrease the cost of broadband internet, though the project is also viewed as a way of reducing the risk of cyber-espionage by a foreign government.

On 27 December 2012, the defence ministry published its Cyber Defence Policy, a document outlining measures to improve information security and inter-agency coordination. It specifies the standard procedures to be followed by defence-related agencies and the creation of a new agency – the Military System for Cyber Defence (SMDC), comprising personnel from all three services – to coordinate cyber-security initiatives, including intelligence gathering and the creation of doctrines for cyberspace.

Manufacturing Unit in Itaguaí. This will assemble some parts of the four conventional *Scorpene*-class submarines and one nuclear vessel (see *The Military Balance 2013*, p. 425). Sections of the first conventional submarine are being manufactured by DCNS in Cherbourg but will be assembled in Itaguaí, with the first submarine due for delivery in 2017.

In contrast to the progress made by the navy, the air force is still waiting for a decision on the F-X2 jet fighter programme. The potential for a gap in air-defence capabilities has increased with the announcement that the Anápolis-based *Mirage*-2000 B/C fleet is to be decommissioned on 31 December 2013. These were purchased in 2005 to provide an air-defence capability until completion of the F-X2 programme. Originally lifed until 2011, the air force said they had already been extended by two years and are no longer fit for use. Up to 12 F-5 *Tiger* IIs are scheduled to be relocated to Anápolis in early 2014.

BRAZIL DEFENCE ECONOMICS

Macroeconomics

Brazil's economy gradually regained momentum in 2013 after a severe slowdown in 2012, when GDP grew by just 0.9%. There was a gradual increase in private-sector investment, encouraged by tax incentives enacted in 2012 and 2013 for some industries. This partially compensated for a sharp deceleration in the pace of consumer spending. To boost domestic demand, tax reductions totalling R46bn (US$23.6bn) were announced in 2012 and 2013. Nonetheless, private-sector investment remained at the relatively low level of 18.6% of GDP in the second quarter of 2013. The resultant reduction in tax revenue affected public-sector accounts, causing the government to revise its target for a 2013 primary budget surplus (the excess of revenue over expenditure, excluding debt service payments) downwards in May from 3.1% to 2.3%, a difference of R72.1bn (US$36.9bn). Finance Minister Guido Mantega said this was part of counter-cyclical measures to stimulate the sluggish economy.

Defence spending

Despite the reduction of some taxes, the government remained cautious about expanding spending levels, repeating in 2013 its practice of freezing large portions of the investment budget for many ministries (see *The Military Balance 2013*, pp. 427–9). As in 2011 and 2012, the defence portfolio was heavily affected, suffering one of the largest emergency restrictions. A net total R3.38bn (US$1.73bn) in discretionary spending was suspended in 2013. Mantega announced the first batch of these 'contingency measures' for the 2013 budgetary cycle in May and another in July, citing concerns over meeting the primary surplus target, even though this had earlier been revised downwards. However, in common with previous years, these restrictions were only applied to the investment and maintenance portion of the budget (i.e. discretionary defence spending), originally forecast to reach R18.5bn (US$9.5bn). The majority of Brazil's defence budget is allocated to salaries, pensions and benefits. These protected mandatory outlays accounted for R46.3bn (US$23.7bn) out of a total 2013 budget of R67.8bn (US$34.7bn). By October 2013, R1.2bn (US$600m) of the R3.38bn (US$1.73bn) in restrictions had been gradually unfrozen, bringing investment and maintenance funds to R16.3bn (US$8.35bn).

Defence procurement

A key change in the defence ministry's investment strategy in 2013 was the decision to channel four of the largest procurement projects through the Accelerated Growth Programme (PAC), Brazil's economy-wide infrastructure and major projects programme. Projects formally included under PAC can be excluded from government expenses factored into the primary budget surplus. More importantly, PAC programmes are exempt from cuts and restrictions, resulting in greater stability. The projects included, such as PROSUB (see p. 362) and the navy's development of nuclear fuel, had been priorities for some years. In total, R2.6bn (US$1.33bn) was allocated to these projects in 2013. Embraer's KC-390 military tanker/transport aircraft programme was given R1.18bn (US$600m) as part of a development contract signed with the Brazilian Air Force. The final project was the HX-BR helicopter programme, for which Eurocopter subsidiary Helibras is manufacturing 50 EC-725s in the state of Minas Gerais. The inclusion of these four programmes in PAC has allowed the companies involved a greater degree of financial stability than in previous years.

Defence industry

The PROSUB and nuclear-fuel projects progressed during 2013: a manufacturing and assembly facility was opened in Itaguaí in March and later in July a new state-run company called Blue Amazon Defence Technologies – a joint development between French

DCNS and Brazilian firm Odebrecht – was created to manage and develop technologies associated with the nuclear-powered submarine. The objective of the company is 'promoting, developing, absorbing, transferring and maintaining technologies needed for the nuclear activities of the Brazilian navy and the Brazilian nuclear programme'. This also reflects Brazil's emphasis on technology transfer.

In 2013, the KC-390 was the only other programme with a budget over R1bn (US$513m). The manufacturing phase for prototypes started in March 2013, after Embraer announced the completion of the critical design review. Embraer had announced in 2012 a deal whereby Boeing could market the aircraft in the US, the UK and some, as yet unspecified, Middle Eastern countries.

The government made no new announcements about F-X2, the air force's other major procurement project. Competitors Boeing, Dassault and Saab moved ahead with partnerships to demonstrate their willingness to share and transfer technology. Boeing signed a memorandum of understanding with the state of Pernambuco for training and technology transfer related to the construction of ships. In May 2012, Saab acquired a 15% stake in Brazilian engineering company Akaer and invited a Brazilian naval officer to fly a simulated maritime mission. The navy expects to buy the same fighter aircraft as the air force to equip its current and future carrier capability.

In February 2013, Embraer's EMB-314 *Super Tucano* won the US Air Force's Afghan Light Air Support competition. Other *Super Tucano* sales included six aircraft to Guatemala, another six to Angola and three to Senegal, highlighting the growing importance of Embraer's Defence and Security division, which increased its share of total company revenue to 23% in the first quarter of 2013, from approximately 18% in mid-2012.

Another Brazilian aerospace company, Avibras, is developing an upgrade to its *Astros* MRL product line, *Astros 2020*, after a contract was signed with the Brazilian army on 29 November 2012. The programme is forecast to cost R1.26bn (US$645m).

Whilst Embraer and Avibras are major players in Brazil's domestic aerospace industry, its defence industrial sector as a whole is gradually expanding due to government support and pro-growth policies. Tax-exemption legislation and benefits in government procurement programmes were part of the Special Taxation Regime for the Defence Industry, contained in March 2012's Law 12,598, though they only came into effect on 1 April 2013. The measure exempts 'strategic defence companies' from three taxes – PIS, Pasep and COFINS – that would normally fall on sales revenues, including cases of equipment sales to the armed forces (see *The Military Balance 2013*, pp. 427–9). According to a note released by the defence ministry shortly after the publication of the law, the government's aim is to benefit sectors and skills of strategic importance. According to the director of products of the defence ministry, General Aderico Mattioli, this is to be achieved through Special Bids – auctions for defence projects that will take into account not just technical criteria such as price but also strategic and geopolitical considerations. The law itself does not specify which strategic considerations will be prioritised. In practice, it means that products offered by Brazilian companies would win armed-forces auctions even when they are up to 25% more expensive than imported products. But that also means companies will remain dependent on public-sector capacity to invest in new equipment, which in recent years has been seriously compromised by the special budget restrictions noted above.

With key industry executives voicing concern over the slow pace of fiscal stimulus measures, the government appealed to state funding institutions to provide assistance to the sector. A new credit line of R2.9bn (US$1.5bn) for the aerospace sector, the *Inova Aerodefesa* initiative, was launched in April 2013, aimed at innovative projects in the fields of aerospace, defence and security. This was financed mainly by the Studies and Projects Funding Body (FINEP), with R500m (US$256m) of the total being provided by the state development bank. FINEP received bids amounting to four times the total level of resources being offered. The loan initiative represents a new level of commitment by state funding mechanisms to the defence and security sectors, and was part of a wider Company Innovation plan (*Inova Empresa*) launched by President Dilma Rousseff in March 2013. This included a R32.9bn (US$16.9bn) state venture capital fund to offer concessional loans, provide subsidies, fund partnerships and take equity stakes in domestic firms active in the defence and space sectors, as part of an attempt to increase the proportion of high-tech products in the country's export base.

Antigua and Barbuda ATG

East Caribbean Dollar EC$		2012	2013	2014
GDP	EC$	3.18bn	3.33bn	
	US$	1.18bn	1.23bn	
per capita	US$	13,429	14,057	
Growth	%	1.59	1.65	
Inflation	%	3.39	2.98	
Def bdgt [a]	EC$	76m	70m	
	US$	28m	26m	
US$1=EC$		2.70	2.70	

[a] Budget for the Ministry of National Security & Labour. Includes funds for labour, immigration, passport and citizenship departments, in addition to the prison service, police and Barbuda Defence Force.

Population 90,156

Age	0–14	15–19	20–24	25–29	30–64	65 plus
Male	12.6%	4.5%	3.8%	3.4%	20.0%	3.1%
Female	12.2%	4.5%	4.0%	3.9%	24.0%	4.1%

Capabilities

Antigua and Barbuda lacks any conventional external security threat, though the activity of illicit narcotics smugglers poses security concerns. Overall, security is bolstered by the presence of a US Air Force satellite tracking station in Antigua, though the future of the base is now in doubt, as it was confirmed in 2013 that the C-band radar hosted there would be removed and relocated to Holt Naval Communication Station in Australia. The force lacks the capability to deploy at reach, due to its size and equipment inventory, and it lacks an air component. Key duties include internal security, counter-narcotics and HA/DR tasks. Despite this, small numbers of personnel have contributed to peacekeeping operations in both Haiti and Grenada. It is an active participant in regional security initiatives, and, in 2011, hosted the *Tradewinds* exercise with the US and other regional states, focusing on peacekeeping and countering illicit trafficking.

ACTIVE 180 (Army 130 Navy 50)

(all services form combined Antigua and Barbuda Defence Force)

RESERVE 80 (Joint 80)

ORGANISATIONS BY SERVICE

Army 130

Navy 50

EQUIPMENT BY TYPE

PATROL AND COASTAL COMBATANTS • PB 2: 1 *Dauntless*; 1 *Swift*

FOREIGN FORCES

United States US Strategic Command: 1 detection and tracking radar at Antigua Air Station

Argentina ARG

Argentine Peso P		2012	2013	2014
GDP	P	2.16tr	2.57tr	
	US$	475bn	499bn	
per capita	US$	11,576	12,019	
Growth	%	1.90	2.77	
Inflation	%	10.04	9.84	
Def bdgt [a]	P	22.1bn	26.3bn	
	US$	4.86bn	5.1bn	
US$1=P		4.55	5.16	

[a] Excludes funds allocated to the Ministry of Security.

Population 42,610,981

Age	0–14	15–19	20–24	25–29	30–64	65 plus
Male	12.8%	4.0%	4.0%	3.8%	19.9%	4.7%
Female	12.2%	3.8%	3.9%	3.8%	20.3%	6.6%

Capabilities

Argentina's armed forces remain configured towards state-on-state war, though there has also been increased attention to counter-narcotics tasks. A programme to restructure and re-equip the services is under way; however, procurement has been funded inadequately so far. This leaves the armed forces with ageing equipment that is increasingly difficult and expensive to maintain, and results in low availability and often low levels of operational readiness. By the end of 2012, the air force's *Dagger* fighter aircraft had been in service for 40 years, and though the type has seen limited system upgrades in past decades, the fleet is showing its age. Army procurement projects include upgrading the TAM medium tank, and a prototype of the intended platform was completed during the first quarter of 2013. Replacing elements of the army's light armoured vehicle fleet is also targeted. The Brazilian *Guarani* is a candidate for some of the light armoured vehicle requirement. The navy struggles with maintenance, with both its surface fleet and its air component suffering. The armed forces have an increasingly limited capability for modest power projection, however infantry and helicopter unit contributions have been made to UN missions in Cyprus and Haiti.

ACTIVE 73,100 (Army 38,500 Navy 20,000 Air 14,600) Paramilitary 31,250

ORGANISATIONS BY SERVICE

Army 38,500; 7,000 civilian

Regt and gp are usually bn-sized

FORCES BY ROLE

SPECIAL FORCES
1 SF gp

MANOEUVRE

Mechanised

1 (1st) div (1 armd bde (4 tk regt, 1 mech inf regt, 1 SP arty gp, 1 cbt engr bn, 1 int coy, 1 sigs coy, 1 log coy),

Latin America and the Caribbean

1 jungle bde (3 jungle inf regt, 1 arty gp, 1 engr bn, 1 int coy, 1 sigs coy, 1 log coy, 1 med coy), 2 engr bn, 1 sigs bn, 1 log coy)
1 (3rd) div (1 mech bde (1 armd recce regt, 1 tk regt, 2 mech inf regt,1 SP arty gp, 1 cbt engr bn, 1 int coy, 1 sigs coy, 1 log coy), 1 mech bde (1 armd recce tp, 1 tk regt, 2 mech inf regt, 1 SP arty gp, 1 cbt engr bn, 1 int coy, 1 sigs coy, 1 log coy), 1 int bn, 1 sigs bn, 1 log coy)
1 (Rapid Deployment) force (1 armd bde (1 recce sqn, 3 tk regt, 1 mech inf regt, 1 SP arty gp, 1 cbt engr coy, 1 int coy, 1 sigs coy, 1 log coy), 1 mech bde (1 armd recce regt, 3 mech inf regt, 1 arty gp, 1 cbt engr coy, 1 int coy, 1 sigs coy,1 log coy), 1 AB bde (1 recce tp, 2 para regt, 1 arty gp, 1 cbt engr coy, 1 sigs coy, 1 log coy), 1 AD gp (2 AD bn))

Light
1 mot cav regt (presidential escort)

Air Manoeuvre
1 air aslt regt

Mountain
1 (2nd) div (2 mtn inf bde (1 armd recce regt, 3 mtn inf regt, 2 arty gp, 1 cbt engr bn, 1 sigs coy, 1 log coy), 1 mtn inf bde (1 armd recce bn, 2 mtn inf regt, 1 jungle inf regt, 2 arty gp, 1 cbt engr bn, 1 sigs coy, 1 construction coy, 1 log coy), 1 AD gp, 1 sigs bn)

Aviation
1 avn gp (bde)

COMBAT SUPPORT
1 arty gp (bn)
1 engr bn
1 sigs gp (1 EW bn, 1 sigs bn, 1 maint bn)
1 sigs bn
1 sigs coy

COMBAT SERVICE SUPPORT
5 maint bn

EQUIPMENT BY TYPE

MBT 213: 207 TAM, 6 TAM S21
LT TK 123: 112 SK-105A1 *Kuerassier;* 6 SK-105A2 *Kuerassier;* 5 *Patagón*
RECCE 81: 47 AML-90; 34 M1025A2 HMMWV
AIFV 377: 263 VCTP (incl variants); 114 M113A2 (20mm cannon)
APC (T) 294: 70 M113A1-ACAV; 224 M113A2
ARTY 1,103
SP 155mm 37: 20 Mk F3; 17 VCA 155 *Palmaria*
TOWED 179: **105mm** 70 M-56 (Oto Melara); **155mm** 109: 25 CITEFA M-77/CITEFA M-81; 84 SOFMA L-33
MRL 105mm 4 SLAM *Pampero*
MOR 883: **81mm** 492; **120mm** 353 Brandt
SP 38: 25 M106A2; 13 TAM-VCTM
AT
MSL • SP 3 HMMWV with total of 18 TOW-2A
RCL 150 M-1968
RL 78mm MARA
AIRCRAFT
ISR 1+ OV-10 *Mohawk*
TPT • Light 15: 1 Beech 80 *Queen Air;* 1 C-212-200 *Aviocar;* 3 Cessna 207 *Stationair;* 1 Cessna 500 *Citation* (survey); 2 DHC-6 *Twin Otter;* 3 SA-226 *Merlin* IIIA; 3 SA-226AT *Merlin* IVA; 1 *Sabreliner* 75A (*Gaviao* 75A)
TRG 5 T-41 *Mescalero*
HELICOPTERS
MRH 5: 4 SA315B *Lama;* 1 Z-11
TPT 47 **Medium** 3 AS332B *Super Puma;* **Light** 44: 1 Bell 212; 25 Bell 205 (UH-1H *Iroquois* - 6 armed); 5 Bell 206B3; 13 UH-1H-II *Huey* II
TRG 8 UH-12E (possibly wfu)
AD
SAM 6 RBS -70
GUNS • TOWED 411: **20mm** 230 GAI-B01; **30mm** 21 HS L81; **35mm** 12 GDF Oerlikon (*Skyguard* fire control); **40mm** 148: 24 L/60 training, 40 in store; 76 L/60; 8 L/70
RADAR • AD RADAR 11: 5 Cardion AN/TPS-44; 6 *Skyguard*
LAND 18+: M113A1GE *Green Archer* (mor); 18 RATRAS (veh, arty)
ARV *Greif*

Navy 20,000; 7,200 civilian

Commands: Surface Fleet, Submarines, Naval Avn, Marines

EQUIPMENT BY TYPE

SUBMARINES • TACTICAL • SSK 3:
1 *Salta* (GER T-209/1200) with 8 single 533mm TT with Mk 37/SST-4 HWT
2 *Santa Cruz* (GER TR-1700) with 6 single 533mm TT with SST-4 HWT
PRINCIPAL SURFACE COMBATANTS 11
DESTROYERS 5
DDGHM 4 *Almirante Brown* (GER MEKO 360) with 2 quad lnchr with MM-40 *Exocet* AShM, 1 octuple *Albatros* lnchr with *Aspide* SAM, 2 triple B515 ILAS-3 324mm TT with A244 LWT, 1 127mm gun, (capacity 1 AS555 *Fennec*/SA316B *Alouette* III hel)
DDH 1 *Hercules* (UK Type-42 – utilised as a fast troop transport ship), with 1 114mm gun, (capacity 1 SH-3H *Sea King* hel)
FRIGATES • FFGHM 6:
6 *Espora* (GER MEKO 140) with 2 twin lnchr with MM-38 *Exocet* AShM, 2 triple B515 ILAS-3 324mm ASTT with A244 LWT, 1 76mm gun (capacity either 1 SA319 *Alouette* III hel or 1 AS555 *Fennec* hel)
PATROL AND COASTAL COMBATANTS 17
CORVETTES • FSG 3 *Drummond* (FRA A-69) with 2 twin lnchr with MM-38 *Exocet* AShM, 2 triple Mk32 324mm ASTT with A244 LWT, 1 100mm gun
PSO 3:
2 *Irigoyen* (US *Cherokee* AT)
1 *Teniente Olivieri* (ex-US oilfield tug)
PCO 3:
2 *Murature* (US *King* - trg/river patrol role) with 3 105mm gun
1 *Sobral* (US *Sotoyomo* AT)
PCGT 1 *Intrepida* (GER Lurssen 45m) with 2 single lnchr with MM-38 *Exocet* AShM, 2 single 533mm TT with SST-4 HWT, 1 76mm gun

PCT 1 *Intrepida* (GER Lurssen 45m) with 2 single 533mm TT with SST-4 HWT, 1 76mm gun
PB 6: 4 *Baradero* (*Dabur*); 2 *Point*
AMPHIBIOUS 18 **LCVP**
LOGISTICS AND SUPPORT 28
ABU 3 *Red*
AFD 1
AGB 1 *Almirante Irizar* (damaged by fire in 2007; expected to return to service in 2014)
AGE 2
AGHS 1 *Puerto Deseado* (ice breaking capability, used for polar research)
AGOR 1 *Commodoro Rivadavia*
AK 3 *Costa Sur*
AOR 1 *Patagonia* (FRA *Durance*) with 1 hel platform
AORL 1 *Ingeniero Julio Krause*
AX 2 *King* with 4 105mm guns
AXS 1 *Libertad*
YTB 11

Naval Aviation 2,000

AIRCRAFT 23 combat capable
FGA 2 *Super Etendard* (9 more in store)
ATK 1 AU-23 *Turbo Porter*
ASW 10: 4 S-2T *Tracker*; 6 P-3B *Orion*
TPT 9 **Light** 7 Beech 200F/M *King Air*; **PAX** 2 F-28 *Fellowship*
TRG 10 T-34C *Turbo Mentor**
HELICOPTERS
ASW 6 SH-3H (ASH-3H) *Sea King*
MRH 4 AS555 *Fennec*
TPT • **Medium** 4 UH-3H *Sea King*
MSL
AAM • **IR** R-550 *Magic*
ASM AS-25K CITEFA *Martin Pescador*‡
AShM AM-39 *Exocet*

Marines 2,500

FORCES BY ROLE
MANOEUVRE
Amphibious
1 (fleet) force (1 cdo gp, 1 (AAV) amph bn, 1 mne bn, 1 arty bn, 1 ADA bn)
1 (fleet) force (2 mne bn, 2 navy det)
1 force (1 mne bn)
EQUIPMENT BY TYPE
RECCE 52: 12 ERC-90F *Sagaie*; 40 M1097 HMMWV
APC (W) 24 Panhard VCR
AAV 17: 10 LARC-5; 7 LVTP-7
ARTY 100
TOWED 105mm 18: 6 M101; 12 Model 56 pack howitzer
MOR 82: 70 **81mm**; 12 **120mm**
AT
MSL • **MANPATS** 50 *Cobra*/RB-53 *Bantam*
RCL 105mm 30 M-1974 FMK-1
RL 89mm 60 M-20
AD
SAM 6 RBS-70
GUNS 30mm 10 HS-816; **35mm** GDF-001
ARV AAVR 7

Air Force 14,600; 6,900 civilian

4 Major Comds – Air Operations, Personnel, Air Regions, Logistics, 8 air bde

Air Operations Command

FORCES BY ROLE
FIGHTER/GROUND ATTACK
1 sqn with *Mirage* IIID/E (*Mirage* IIIDA/EA)
1 sqn with *Nesher* S/T (*Dagger* A/B)
GROUND ATTACK
2 sqn with A-4/OA-4 (A-4AR/OA-4AR) *Skyhawk*
2 (tac air) sqn with IA-58 *Pucara*; EMB-312 *Tucano* (on loan for border surv/interdiction)
ISR
1 sqn with Learjet 35A
SEARCH & RESCUE/TRANSPORT HELICOPTER
2 sqn with Bell 212; Bell 212 (UH-1N); Mi-171, SA-315B *Lama*,
TANKER/TRANSPORT
1 sqn with C-130B/E/H *Hercules*; KC-130H *Hercules*; L-100-30
TRANSPORT
1 sqn with B-707
1 sqn with DHC-6 *Twin Otter*; Saab 340
1 sqn with F-27 *Friendship*
1 sqn with F-28 *Fellowship*; Learjet 60
1 (Pres) flt with B-757-23ER; S-70A *Black Hawk*, S-76B
TRAINING
1 sqn with AT-63 *Pampa*
1 sqn with EMB-312 *Tucano*
1 sqn with Grob 120TP
1 hel sqn with Hughes 369; SA-315B *Lama*,
TRANSPORT HELICOPTER
1 sqn with Hughes 369; MD-500; MD500D
EQUIPMENT BY TYPE
AIRCRAFT 100 combat capable
FGA 18: 8 *Mirage* IIID/E (*Mirage* IIIDA/EA); 7 *Nesher* S (*Dagger* A), 3 *Nesher* T (*Dagger* B);
ATK 62: 30 A-4 (A-4AR) *Skyhawk*; 2 OA-4 (OA-4AR) *Skyhawk*; 21 IA-58 *Pucara*; 9 IA-58M *Pucara*
ELINT 1 Cessna 210
TKR 2 KC-130H *Hercules*
TPT 37: **Medium** 7: 1 C-130B *Hercules*; 1 C-130E *Hercules*; 4 C-130H *Hercules*; 1 L-100-30; **Light** 22: 1 Cessna 310; 8 DHC-6 *Twin Otter*; 4 F-27 *Friendship*; 4 Learjet 35A (test and calibration); 1 Learjet 60; 4 Saab 340; **PAX** 8: 1 B-757-23ER; 7 F-28 *Fellowship*
TRG 43: 20 AT-63 *Pampa** (LIFT); 19 EMB-312 *Tucano*; 4 Grob 120TP
HELICOPTERS
MRH 25: 15 Hughes 369; 3 MD-500; 4 MD-500D; 3 SA315B *Lama*
TPT 11 **Medium** 3: 2 Mi-171E; 1 S-70A *Black Hawk*; **Light** 8: 7 Bell 212; 1 S-76B
MSL
AAM • **IR** AIM-9L *Sidewinder*; R-550 *Magic*; *Shafrir* II‡
AD
GUNS 88: **20mm**: 86 Oerlikon/Rh-202 with 9 Elta EL/M-2106 radar; **35mm**: 2 Oerlikon GDF-001 with *Skyguard* radar

RADAR 6: 5 AN/TPS-43; 1 BPS-1000

Paramilitary 31,250

Gendarmerie 18,000

Ministry of Interior

FORCES BY ROLE

COMMAND

5 regional comd

MANOEUVRE

Other

16 paramilitary bn

EQUIPMENT BY TYPE

RECCE S52 *Shorland*

APC (W) 87: 47 *Grenadier*; 40 UR-416

ARTY • MOR 81mm

AIRCRAFT

TPT • Light 12: 3 Cessna 152; 3 Cessna 206; 1 Cessna 336; 1 PA-28 *Cherokee*; 2 PC-6B *Turbo Porter*; 2 PC-12

HELICOPTERS

MRH 2 MD-500C

TPT • Light 16: 5 Bell 205 (UH-1H *Iroquois*); 7 AS350 *Ecureuil*; 1 EC135; 3 R-44 *Raven* II

TRG 1 S-300C

Prefectura Naval (Coast Guard) 13,250

PATROL AND COASTAL COMBATANTS 66

PCO 6: 1 *Delfin*; 5 *Mantilla* (F30 *Halcón*)

PCC 1 *Mandubi*

PB 58: 1 *Dorado*; 25 *Estrellemar*; 2 *Lynch* (US *Cape*); 18 *Mar del Plata* (Z-28); 1 *Surel*; 8 Damen Stan 2200; 3 Stan Tender 1750

PBR 1 *Tonina*

LOGISTICS & SUPPORT 16

AG 2

AX 4

YTL 10

AIRCRAFT

TPT • Light 6: 5 C-212 *Aviocar*; 1 Beech *King Air* 350

TRG 2 Piper PA-28 *Archer* III

HELICOPTERS

SAR 3 AS565MA *Panther*

MRH 1 AS365 *Dauphin 2*

TPT 4 **Medium** 2 SA330L (AS330L) *Puma*; **Light** 2 AS355 *Ecureuil* II

TRG 4 S-300C

DEPLOYMENT

CYPRUS

UN • UNFICYP 266; 2 inf coy; 1 hel pl; 2 Bell 212

HAITI

UN • MINUSTAH 571; 1 inf bn; 1 hel coy; 1 spt coy; 1 fd hospital

MIDDLE EAST

UN • UNTSO 4 obs

WESTERN SAHARA

UN • MINURSO 3 obs

Bahamas BHS

Bahamian Dollar B$		2012	2013	2014
GDP	B$	8.04bn	8.37bn	
	US$	8.04bn	8.37bn	
per capita	US$	22,833	23,485	
Growth	%	2.50	2.70	
Inflation	%	2.30	2.00	
Def exp	B$	55m		
	US$	55m		
Def bdgt	B$	57m	64m	87m
	US$	57m	64m	
US$1=B$		1.00	1.00	

Population 319,031

Age	0–14	15–19	20–24	25–29	30–64	65 plus
Male	12.0%	4.4%	4.4%	3.8%	21.7%	2.6%
Female	11.6%	4.3%	4.3%	3.8%	22.9%	4.2%

Capabilities

The Bahamas Defence Force (BDF) has a limited territorial defence role, but has not engaged in active combat in the past 30 years. A key task is combating narcotics trafficking in the surrounding waters, though some marines were in 2013 deployed internally to assist in policing duties after a crime wave. Though the BDF is one of the more capable armed forces among the small Caribbean nations, it remains a coast guard-type organisation with some very limited amphibious capability provided by an attached infantry battalion. Capability is due to be boosted by an order made in 2013 for eight long-range patrol craft and a landing craft, while the US also gifted a smaller 41-foot boat to the police forces in 2013, as part of US efforts to support counter-narcotics activities. Media reporting has indicated a plan to modestly increase personnel strength by mid-2014. The country is a regular participant in the US SOUTHCOM-sponsored *Tradewinds* exercise series.

ACTIVE 850

ORGANISATIONS BY SERVICE

Royal Bahamian Defence Force 850

FORCES BY ROLE

MANOEUVRE

Amphibious

1 mne coy (incl marines with internal and base security duties)

EQUIPMENT BY TYPE

PATROL AND COASTAL COMBATANTS 16 (additional 7+ patrol boats under 10 tonnes)

PCC 2 *Bahamas*

PBF 6 Nor-Tech

PB 8: 2 *Dauntless*; 1 *Eleuthera*; 1 *Protector*; 2 Sea Ark 12m; 2 Sea Ark 15m

AIRCRAFT • TPT • Light 3: 1 Beech A350 *King Air*; 1 Cessna 208 *Caravan*; 1 P-68 *Observer*

FOREIGN FORCES

Guyana Navy: Base located at New Providence Island

Barbados BRB

Barbados Dollar B$		2012	2013	2014
GDP	B$	8.98bn	9.37bn	
	US$	4.49bn	4.68bn	
per capita	US$	16,152	16,804	
Growth	%	0.00	0.50	
Inflation	%	4.62	4.89	
Def bdgt	B$	65m	66m	
	US$	33m	33m	
US$1=B$		2.00	2.00	

[a] Defence & security expenditure

Population 288,725

Age	0–14	15–19	20–24	25–29	30–64	65 plus
Male	9.3%	3.2%	3.7%	3.6%	24.6%	4.0%
Female	9.3%	3.2%	3.6%	3.6%	25.7%	6.2%

Capabilities

The Barbados Defence Force is a small coast guard- and constabulary-style force with a very limited regional deployment capability for peacekeeping within the Caribbean. Its primary role has been to provide support to the Royal Barbados Police Force and to participate in disaster-relief efforts. In recent years, it has suffered from recruitment problems. The country is a regular participant in the US SOUTHCOM-sponsored *Tradewinds* exercise series, hosting the 2012 iteration.

ACTIVE 610 (Army 500 Navy 110)

RESERVE 430 (Joint 430)

ORGANISATIONS BY SERVICE

Army 500

FORCES BY ROLE

MANOEUVRE

Light

1 inf bn (cadre)

Navy 110

HQ located at HMBS Pelican, Spring Garden

EQUIPMENT BY TYPE

PATROL AND COASTAL COMBATANTS • PB 6: 1 *Dauntless*; 2 *Enterprise* (Damen Stan 1204); 3 *Trident* (Damen Stan 4207)

LOGISTICS & SUPPORT • AX 1

Belize BLZ

Belize Dollar BZ$		2012	2013	2014
GDP	BZ$	3.11bn	3.22bn	
	US$	1.55bn	1.61bn	
per capita	US$	4,536	4,620	
Growth	%	5.29	2.50	
Inflation	%	1.41	1.31	
Def bdgt [a]	BZ$	31m	36m	
	US$	16m	18m	
FMA (US)	US$	0.2m	0.2m	1m
US$1=BZ$		2.00	2.00	

[a] Excludes funds allocated to Coast Guard and Police Service

Population 334,297

Age	0–14	15–19	20–24	25–29	30–64	65 plus
Male	18.3%	5.6%	5.2%	4.5%	15.4%	1.7%
Female	17.5%	5.4%	5.0%	4.3%	15.2%	1.9%

Capabilities

The Belize Defence Force (BDF) has national sovereignty and internal-security roles, principally countering narcotics smuggling. It deployed combat engineers to assist Haiti in 2010. Although well-trained in jungle operations, the relatively small size of the BDF means that its capabilities are limited to countering relatively minor threats. Until 2011, British infantry units used Belize for jungle training, and some British units still train in-country.

ACTIVE ε1,050 (Army ε1,050)

RESERVE 700 (Joint 700)

ORGANISATIONS BY SERVICE

Army ε1,050

FORCES BY ROLE

MANOEUVRE

Light

3 inf bn (each 3 inf coy)

COMBAT SERVICE SUPPORT

1 spt gp

EQUIPMENT BY TYPE

MOR 81mm 6

RCL 84mm 8 *Carl Gustav*

Air Wing

EQUIPMENT BY TYPE

AIRCRAFT

TPT • Light 3: 1 BN-2A *Defender*; 1 BN-2B *Defender*; 1 Cessna 182 *Skylane*

TRG 1 T-67M-200 *Firefly*

Reserve

FORCES BY ROLE

MANOEUVRE

Light

3 inf coy

Latin America and the Caribbean

Paramilitary 150

Coast Guard 150

EQUIPMENT BY TYPE

Approx 10 small craft under 10 tonnes

FOREIGN FORCES

United Kingdom Army 10

Bolivia BOL

Bolivian Boliviano B		2012	2013	2014
GDP	B	188bn	202bn	
	US$	27.4bn	29.5bn	
per capita	US$	2,532	2,674	
Growth	%	5.24	4.80	
Inflation	%	4.52	4.63	
Def bdgt	B	2.3bn	2.56bn	
	US$	336m	373m	
US$1=B		6.86	6.86	

Population 10,461,053

Age	0–14	15–19	20–24	25–29	30–64	65 plus
Male	17.2%	5.2%	4.9%	4.5%	15.6%	2.1%
Female	16.6%	5.0%	4.8%	4.5%	16.9%	2.7%

Capabilities

Counter-narcotics, and internal and border security are the main tasks of the Bolivian armed forces, and modest procurement programmes are intended to improve the services' ability to meet these roles. The country has limited independent power-projection capacity, and such a capability would be contrary to the stated defence policy. The army and air force are receiving new or upgraded equipment, though in small numbers. Six Chinese H425 medium helicopters (paid for with a PRC loan) were due for delivery in 2013, providing a combat-capable rotary-wing capacity for the army. Tactical airlift is provided by a variety of aircraft, including a handful of C-130 *Hercules*. The armed forces have taken part in recent UN peacekeeping missions.

ACTIVE 46,100 (Army 34,800 Navy 4,800 Air 6,500) Paramilitary 37,100

ORGANISATIONS BY SERVICE

Army 9,800; 25,000 conscript (total 34,800)

FORCES BY ROLE

COMMAND
- 6 mil region HQ
- 10 div HQ

SPECIAL FORCES
- 3 SF regt

MANOEUVRE

Reconnaissance
- 1 mot cav gp

Armoured
- 1 armd bn

Mechanised
- 1 mech cav regt
- 2 mech inf regt

Light
- 1 (aslt) cav gp
- 5 (horsed) cav gp
- 3 mot inf regt
- 21 inf regt
- 1 (Presidential Guard) inf regt

Air Manoeuvre
- 2 AB regt (bn)

Aviation
- 2 avn coy

COMBAT SUPPORT
- 6 arty regt (bn)
- 1 ADA regt
- 6 engr bn
- 1 int coy
- 1 MP bn
- 1 sigs bn

COMBAT SERVICE SUPPORT
- 2 log bn

EQUIPMENT BY TYPE

LT TK 54: 36 SK-105A1 *Kuerassier*; 18 SK-105A2 *Kuerassier*

RECCE 24 EE-9 *Cascavel*

APC 152+
- **APC (T)** 87+: 50+ M113, 37 M9 half-track
- **APC (W)** 61: 24 EE-11 *Urutu*; 22 MOWAG *Roland*; 15 V-100 *Commando*

ARTY 311+
- **TOWED** 61: **105mm** 25 M101A1; **122mm** 36 M-30 (M-1938)
- **MOR** 250+: **81mm** 250 M29; Type-W87; **107mm** M30; **120mm** M120

AT • MSL• MANPATS 50+ HJ-8 (2 SP on *Koyak*)
- **RCL 106mm** M40A1; **90mm** M67
- **RL 89mm** 200+ M20

AIRCRAFT
- **TPT • Light** 4: 1 Fokker F-27-200; 1 Beech 90 *King Air*; 1 C-212 *Aviocar*; 1 Cessna 210 *Centurion*

HELICOPTERS
- **TRG** 1 Robinson R55

AD • GUNS • TOWED 37mm 18 Type-65

ARV 4 4K-4FA-SB20 *Greif*; M578

Navy 4,800

Organised into six naval districts with HQ located at Puerto Guayaramerín.

EQUIPMENT BY TYPE

PATROL AND COASTAL COMBATANTS • PBR 3: 1 *Santa Cruz*; 2 others (additional five patrol boats and 30-40 small craft under 10 tonnes)

LOGISTICS AND SUPPORT 27:
- **AG** 1
- **AH** 2
- **YFL** 10 (river transports)
- **YTL** 14

Marines 1,700 (incl 1,000 Naval Military Police)

FORCES BY ROLE
MANOEUVRE
Mechanised
1 mech inf bn
Amphibious
6 mne bn (1 in each Naval District)
COMBAT SUPPORT
4 (naval) MP bn

Air Force 6,500 (incl conscripts)

FORCES BY ROLE
GROUND ATTACK
2 sqn with AT-33AN *Shooting Star*
1 sqn with K-8WB *Karakorum*
ISR
1 sqn with Cessna 206; Cessna 402; Learjet 25B/25D (secondary VIP role)
SEARCH & RESCUE
1 sqn with AS332B *Super Puma*; AS350B3 *Ecureuil*; EC145
TRANSPORT
1 sqn with BAe-146-100; CV-580; MA60
1 (TAB) sqn with C-130A *Hercules*; DC-10
1 sqn with C-130B/H *Hercules*
1 sqn with F-27-400M *Troopship*
1 (VIP) sqn with Beech 90 *King Air*; Beech 200 *King Air* Beech 1900; *Falcon* 900EX; *Sabreliner* 60
6 sqn with Cessna 152/206; IAI-201 *Arava*; PA-32 *Saratoga*; PA-34 *Seneca*
TRAINING
1 sqn with DA40; T-25
1 sqn with Cessna 152/172
1 sqn with PC-7 *Turbo Trainer*
1 hel sqn with R-44 *Raven* II
TRANSPORT HELICOPTER
1 (anti-drug) sqn with Bell 205 (UH-1H *Iroquois*)
AIR DEFENCE
1 regt with Oerlikon; Type-65

EQUIPMENT BY TYPE
AIRCRAFT 39 combat capable
ATK 15 AT-33AN *Shooting Star*
TPT 86: **Medium** 4: 1 C-130A *Hercules*; 2 C-130B *Hercules*; 1 C-130H *Hercules*; **Light** 70: 1 *Aero Commander* 690; 3 Beech 90 *King Air*; 2 Beech 200 *King Air*; 1 Beech 1900; 5 C-212-100; 10 Cessna 152; 2 Cessna 172; 19 Cessna 206; 1 Cessna 402; 1 CV-580; 9 DA40; 3 F-27-400M *Troopship*; 4 IAI-201 *Arava*; 2 Learjet 25B/D; 2 MA60; 1 PA-32 *Saratoga*; 3 PA-34 *Seneca*; 1 *Sabreliner* 60 **PAX** 12: 1 B-727; 3 B-737-200; 5 BAe-146-100; 2 DC-10; 1 *Falcon* 900EX (VIP)
TRG 30: 6 K-8W *Karakorum**; 6 T-25; 18 PC-7 *Turbo Trainer**
HELICOPTERS
MRH 1 SA316 *Alouette* III
TPT 30 **Medium** 1 AS332B *Super Puma*; **Light** 29: 2 AS350B3 *Ecureuil*; 19 Bell 205 (UH-1H *Iroquois*); 2 EC145; 6 R-44 *Raven* II
AD•GUNS 18+: **20mm** Oerlikon; **37mm** 18 Type-65

Paramilitary 37,100+

National Police 31,100+

FORCES BY ROLE
MANOEUVRE
Other
27 frontier sy unit
9 paramilitary bde
2 (rapid action) paramilitary regt

Narcotics Police 6,000+

FOE (700) - Special Operations Forces

DEPLOYMENT

CÔTE D'IVOIRE
UN • UNOCI 3 obs

DEMOCRATIC REPUBLIC OF THE CONGO
UN • MONUSCO 10 obs

HAITI
UN • MINUSTAH 208; 1 mech inf coy

LIBERIA
UN • UNMIL 1; 2 obs

SOUTH SUDAN
UN • UNMISS 3 obs

SUDAN
UN • UNAMID 2 obs
UN • UNISFA 1; 3 obs

Brazil BRZ

Brazilian Real R		2012	2013	2014
GDP	R	4.4tr	4.8tr	
	US$	2.4tr	2.46tr	
per capita	US$	12,079	12,291	
Growth	%	0.87	3.02	
Inflation	%	5.40	6.13	
Def bdgt [a]	R	64.8bn	67.8bn	
	US$	35.3bn	34.7bn	
US$1=R		1.84	1.95	

[a] Includes military pensions

Population 201,009,622

Age	0–14	15–19	20–24	25–29	30–64	65 plus
Male	12.3%	4.3%	4.2%	4.4%	21.1%	3.1%
Female	11.9%	4.1%	4.1%	4.3%	22.0%	4.2%

Capabilities

Brazil has the largest defence budget in South America, and it is the region's most capable military power. Brasilia continues to develop its armed forces, with ambitions to enhance power projection capability. Moves to develop its industrial base continue, with additional research and technology funding for the defence aerospace sector.

Police units were deployed during civil unrest in mid-2013, sparked initially by a protest over rises in public transport costs, while the army deployed to border areas on counter-narcotics operations. Security of the Amazon region and coastal waters remains a priority as part of the armed forces' broader role of assuring territorial integrity. Substantial recapitalisation of the equipment inventory is required to fully support the ambitions of the National Defence Strategy and the white paper. Procurement, however, remains patchwork. Brazil continues to purchase air-defence systems, in part to meet security requirements for the 2014 World Cup and the 2016 Olympics. The air force's long-running fighter replacement program continued to be delayed during the first half of 2013, leaving the air force with a mostly ageing fighter fleet. Airlift capabilities will be enhanced with the delivery of the KC-390 from domestic manufacturer Embraer. The country's submarine development programme is emblematic of the navy's long-term blue water ambition, and the government's desire to take a more global role commensurate with its economic strength. The armed forces participate in domestic and international exercises, and deploy on peacekeeping missions. Brazil is actively developing its cyber defence capabilities. (See pp. 361–64.)

ACTIVE 318,500 (Army 190,000 Navy 59,000 Air 69,500) Paramilitary 395,000

Conscript liability 12 months (can go to 18; often waived)

RESERVE 1,340,000

ORGANISATIONS BY SERVICE

Army 120,000; 70,000 conscript (total 190,000)

FORCES BY ROLE

COMMAND

8 mil comd HQ
12 mil region HQ
7 div HQ (2 with regional HQ)

SPECIAL FORCES

1 SF bde (1 SF bn, 1 cdo bn)
1 SF coy

MANOEUVRE

Reconnaissance

3 mech cav regt

Armoured

1 (5th) armd bde (1 mech cav sqn, 2 armd bn, 2 armd inf bn, 1 SP arty bn, 1 engr bn, 1 sigs coy, 1 log bn)
1 (6th) armd bde (1 mech cav sqn, 2 armd bn, 2 armd inf bn, 1 SP arty bn, 1 AD bty, 1 engr bn, 1 sigs coy, 1 log bn)

Mechanised

3 (1st, 2nd & 4th) mech cav bde (1 armd cav bn, 3 mech cav bn, 1 arty bn, 1 engr coy, 1 sigs coy, 1 log bn)
1 (3rd) mech cav bde (1 armd cav bn, 2 mech cav bn, 1 arty bn, 1 engr coy, 1 sigs coy, 1 log bn)

Light

1 (3rd) mot inf bde (1 mech cav sqn, 2 mot inf bn, 1 inf bn, 1 arty bn, 1 engr coy, 1 sigs coy, 1 log bn)
1 (4th) mot inf bde (1 mech cav sqn, 1 mot inf bn, 1 inf bn, 1 mtn inf bn, 1 arty bn, 1 sigs coy, 1 log bn)
1 (7th) mot inf bde (3 mot inf bn, 1 arty bn)
1 (8th) mot inf bde (1 mech cav sqn, 3 mot inf bn, 1 arty bn, 1 log bn)
1 (10th) mot inf bde (1 mech cav sqn, 4 mot inf bn, 1 inf coy, 1 arty bn, 1 engr coy, 1 sigs coy)
1 (13th) mot inf bde (1 mot inf bn, 2 inf bn, 1 inf coy, 1 arty bn)
1 (14th) mot inf bde (1 mech cav sqn, 3 inf bn, 1 arty bn)
1 (15th) mot inf bde (3 mot inf bn, 1 arty bn, 1 engr coy, 1 log bn)
1 (11th) lt inf bde (1 mech cav regt, 3 inf bn, 1 arty bn, 1 engr coy, 1 sigs coy, 1 MP coy, 1 log bn)
11 inf bn

Air Manoeuvre

1 AB bde (1 cav sqn, 3 AB bn, 1 arty bn, 1 engr coy, 1 sigs coy, 1 log bn)
1 (12th) air mob bde (1 cav sqn, 3 air mob bn, 1 arty bn, 1 engr coy, 1 sigs coy, 1 log bn)

Jungle

1 (1st) jungle inf bde (1 mech cav sqn, 2 jungle inf bn, 1 arty bn)
3 (2nd, 16th & 17th) jungle inf bde (3 jungle inf bn)
1 (23rd) jungle inf bde (1 cav sqn, 4 jungle inf bn, 1 arty bn, 1 sigs coy, 1 log bn)
2 jungle inf bn

Other

1 (9th) mot trg bde (3 mot inf bn, 1 arty bn, 1 log bn)
1 (18th) sy bde (2 sy bn, 2 sy coy)
1 sy bn
7 sy coy
3 gd cav regt
1 gd inf bn

Aviation

1 avn bde (3 hel bn, 1 maint bn)
1 hel bn

COMBAT SUPPORT

3 SP arty bn
6 fd arty bn
1 MRL bn
1 ADA bde (5 ADA bn)
6 engr bn
1 EW coy
1 int coy
6 MP bn
3 MP coy
4 sigs bn
2 sigs coy

COMBAT SERVICE SUPPORT

1 engr gp (1 engr bn, 4 construction bn)
1 engr gp (4 construction bn, 1 construction coy)
2 construction bn
5 log bn
1 tpt bn
4 spt bn

EQUIPMENT BY TYPE

MBT 393: 128 *Leopard* 1A1BE; 220 *Leopard* 1A5BR; 45 M60A3/TTS
LT TK 152 M41B/C
RECCE 408 EE-9 *Cascavel*

APC 857
APC (T) 584 M113
APC (W) 273: 223 EE-11 *Urutu*; ε50 VBTP-MR *Guarani*
ARTY 1,805
SP 109: **105mm** 72 M7/108; **155mm** 37 M109A3
TOWED 431
105mm 336: 233 M101/M102; 40 L-118 Light Gun; 63 Model 56 pack howitzer
155mm 95 M114
MRL 20+: **70mm** SBAT-70; **127mm** 20 ASTROS II
MOR 1,245: **81mm** 1,168: 453 Royal Ordnance L-16, 715 M936 AGR; **120mm** 77 M2
AT
MSL • MANPATS *Eryx*; *Milan*; MSS-1.2 AC
RCL 343: **106mm** 194 M40A1; **84mm** 149 *Carl Gustav*
HELICOPTERS
MRH 49: 32 AS565 *Panther* (HM-1); 17 AS550U2 *Fennec* (HA-1 – armed)
TPT 31 **Heavy** 4 EC725 *Super Cougar* (HM-4); **Medium** 12: 8 AS532 *Cougar* (HM-3); 4 S-70A-36 *Black Hawk* (HM-2); **Light** 15 AS350L1 *Ecureuil* (HA-1)
AD
SAM • MANPAD 9K38 *Igla* (SA-18 *Grouse)*
GUNS 74:
SP 35mm 8 *Gepard* 1A2
TOWED 66 **35mm** 39 GDF-001 towed (some with *Super Fledermaus* radar); **40mm** 27 L/70 (some with BOFI)
RADAR: 5 SABER M60
AEV 4+: *Greif*; HART; 4+ *Leopard* 1; M578
ARV *Leopard* 1
VLB 4+: XLP-10; 4 *Leopard* 1

Navy 59,000

FORCES BY ROLE

Organised into 9 districts with HQ I Rio de Janeiro, HQ II Salvador, HQ III Natal, HQ IV Belém, HQ V Rio Grande, HQ VI Ladario, HQ VII Brasilia, HQ VIII Sao Paulo, HQ IX Manaus.

EQUIPMENT BY TYPE

SUBMARINES • TACTICAL • SSK 5:
4 *Tupi* (GER T-209/1400) with 8 single 533mm TT with Mk48 HWT
1 *Tikuna* with 8 single 533mm TT with Mk48 HWT
PRINCIPAL SURFACE COMBATANTS 15
AIRCRAFT CARRIERS • CV 1:
1 *Sao Paulo* (FRA *Clemenceau*) with 2 sextuple *Sadral* lnchr with *Mistral* SAM, (capacity 15–18 A-4 *Skyhawk* atk ac; 4–6 SH-3D/A *Sea King* ASW hel; 3 AS355F/AS350BA *Ecureuil* hel; 2 AS532 *Cougar* hel)
DESTROYERS • DDGHM 3:
3 *Greenhalgh* (UK *Broadsword*, 1 low readiness) with 4 single lnchr with MM-40 *Exocet* Block II AShM, 2 sextuple lnchr with *Sea Wolf* SAM, 6 single STWS Mk2 324mm ASTT with Mk 46 LWT, (capacity 2 *Super Lynx* Mk21A hel)
FRIGATES 11
FFGHM 6 *Niteroi* with 2 twin lnchr with MM-40 *Exocet* Block II AShM, 1 octuple *Albatros* lnchr with *Aspide* SAM, 2 triple Mk32 324mm ASTT with Mk 46 LWT, 1 twin 375mm A/S mor, 1 115mm gun, (capacity 1 *Super Lynx* Mk21A hel)
FFGH 5:
4 *Inhauma* with 2 twin lnchr with MM-40 *Exocet* Block II AShM, 2 triple Mk32 324mm ASTT with Mk 46 LWT, 1 115mm gun, (1 *Super Lynx* Mk21A hel)
1 *Barroso* with 2 twin lnchr with MM-40 *Exocet* Block II AShM, 2 triple 324mm ASTT with Mk 46 LWT, 1 *Sea Trinity* CIWS, 1 115mm gun, (capacity 1 *Super Lynx* Mk21A hel)
PATROL AND COASTAL COMBATANTS 47
PSO 3 *Amazonas*
PCO 7: 4 *Bracui* (UK *River*); 2 *Imperial Marinheiro* with 1 76mm gun; 1 *Parnaiba* with 1 hel landing platform
PCC 3 *Macaé* (2 additional vessels under construction)
PCR 5: 2 *Pedro Teixeira*; 3 *Roraima*
PB 28: 12 *Grajau*; 6 *Marlim*; 6 *Piratini* (US PGM); 4 *Tracker* (Marine Police)
PBR 1 LPR-40 (3 additional vessels under construction)
MINE WARFARE • MINE COUNTERMEASURES •
MSC 6 *Aratu* (GER *Schutze*)
AMPHIBIOUS
PRINCIPAL AMPHIBIOUS SHIPS • LSD 1:
1 *Ceara* (US *Thomaston*) with 3 twin 76mm guns (capacity either 21 LCM or 6 LCU; 345 troops)
LANDING SHIPS 3:
LST 1 *Mattoso Maia* (US *Newport*) with 1 *Phalanx* CIWS (capacity 3 LCVP; 1 LCPL; 400 troops)
LSLH 2: 1 *Garcia D'Avila* (UK *Sir Galahad*) (capacity 1 hel; 16 MBT; 340 troops); 1 *Almirante Saboia* (UK *Sir Bedivere*) (capacity 1 med hel; 18 MBT; 340 troops)
LANDING CRAFT 27: 3 **LCU**; 8 **LCVP**; 16 **LCM**
LOGISTICS AND SUPPORT 96+
ABU 35+: 4 *Comandante Varella*; 1 *Faroleiro Mario Seixas*; 30+ others
ABUH 1 *Almirante Graca Aranah* (lighthouse tender)
AFD 4
AGHS 4 *Rio Tocantin*
AGOB 2: 1 *Ary Rongel* (1 hel landing platform); 1 *Almirante Maximiano* (1 hel landing platform)
AGS 6: 1 *Aspirante Moura*; 1 *Cruzeiro do Sul*; 1 *Antares*; 3 *Amorim Do Valle* (UK *Rover*)
AGSC 4
AGSH 1 *Sirius*
AH 5: 2 *Oswaldo Cruz* (1 hel landing platform); 1 *Dr Montenegro*; 1 *Tenente Maximianol* (1 hel landing platform); 1 *Soares de Meirelles*
AK 5
AOR 2: 1 *Gastao Motta*; 1 *Marajo*
AP 7: 1 *Paraguassu*; 1 *Piraim*; 1 *Para* (all river transports); 4 *Rio Pardo*
ASR 1 *Felinto Perry* (NOR *Wildrake*) (1 hel landing platform)
ATF 5: 3 *Tritao*; 2 *Almirante Guihem*
AX 1 *Brasil* (1 hel landing platform)
AXL 3 *Nascimento*
AXS 1 *Cisne Barco*
YTB 8
YPT 1

Naval Aviation 2,500

FORCES BY ROLE

GROUND ATTACK

1 sqn with A-4/4M (AF-1) *Skyhawk*; TA-4/4M (AF-1A) *Skyhawk*

ANTI SURFACE WARFARE

1 sqn with *Super Lynx* Mk21A

ANTI SUBMARINE WARFARE

1 sqn with SH-3G/H *Sea King*; S-70B *Seahawk* (MH-16)

TRAINING

1 sqn with Bell 206B3 *Jet Ranger* III

TRANSPORT HELICOPTER

1 sqn with AS332 *Super Puma*; AS532 *Cougar*

4 sqn with AS350 *Ecureuil* (armed); AS355 *Ecureuil* II (armed)

EQUIPMENT BY TYPE

AIRCRAFT 12 combat capable

ATK 12: 9 A-4/4M (AF-1/1B) *Skyhawk*; 3 TA-4/4M (AF-1A) *Skyhawk*

HELICOPTERS

ASW 20: 12 *Super Lynx* Mk21A; 4 SH-3G/H *Sea King* (being withdrawn); 4 S-70B *Seahawk* (MH-16)

TPT 47: **Heavy** 2 EC725 *Super Cougar* (UH-15); **Medium** 7: 5 AS332 *Super Puma*; 2 AS532 *Cougar* (UH-14); **Light** 38: 15 AS350 *Ecureuil* (armed); 8 AS355 *Ecureuil* II (armed); 15 Bell 206B3 *Jet Ranger* III (IH-6B)

MSL • AShM: AM-39 *Exocet*; *Sea Skua*; AGM-119 *Penguin* (on order)

Marines 15,000

FORCES BY ROLE

SPECIAL FORCES

1 SF bn

MANOEUVRE

Amphibious

1 (Fleet Force) div (1 comd bn, 3 inf bn, 1 arty gp)

8+ (regional) mne gp

3 mne inf bn

COMBAT SUPPORT

1 engr bn

EQUIPMENT BY TYPE

LT TK 18 SK-105 *Kuerassier*

APC 56

APC (T) 30 M113A1 (incl variants)

APC (W) 26 *Piranha* IIIC (additional 4 on order)

AAV 25: 13 AAV-7A1; 12 LVTP-7

ARTY 59

TOWED 41: **105mm** 33: 18 L118 Light Gun; 15 M101; **155mm** 8 M114

MOR 18 **81mm**

AT

MSL• MANPATS RB-56 *Bill*; MSS-1.2 AC

RL 89mm M20

AD • GUNS 40mm 6 L/70 (with BOFI)

AEV 1 AAVR7

Air Force 69,500

Brazilian air space is divided into 7 air regions, each of which is responsible for its designated air bases. Air assets are divided among four designated air forces (I, II, III & V) for operations (IV Air Force temporarily deactivated).

FORCES BY ROLE

FIGHTER

1 gp with *Mirage* 2000B/C (being retired end 2013)

4 sqn with F-5EM/FM *Tiger* II

FIGHTER/GROUND ATTACK

2 sqn with AMX (A-1A/B)

GROUND ATTACK/ISR

4 sqn with EMB-314 *Super Tucano* (A-29A/B)*

MARITIME PATROL

1 sqn with EMB-111 (P-95A/P-95B)/P-3AM *Orion*

2 sqn with EMB-111 (P-95A/P-95B)

ISR

1 sqn with AMX-R (RA-1)*

1 sqn with Learjet 35 (R-35A); EMB-110B (R-95)

AIRBORNE EARLY WARNING & CONTROL

1 sqn with EMB-145RS (R-99); EMB-145SA (E-99)

TANKER/TRANSPORT

1 sqn with C-130H/KC-130H *Hercules*

TRANSPORT

1 VIP sqn with A319 (VC-1A); EMB-190 (VC-2); AS332M *Super Puma* (VH-34); AS355 *Ecureuil* II (VH-55); EC635 (VH-35)

1 VIP sqn with EMB-135BJ (VC-99B); ERJ-135LR (VC-99C); ERJ-145LR (VC-99A); Learjet 35A (VU-35); Learjet 55C (VU-55C)

2 sqn with C-130E/H *Hercules*

2 sqn with C-295M (C-105A)

7 (regional) sqn with Cessna 208/208B (C-98); Cessna 208-G1000 (C-98A); EMB-110 (C-95); EMB-120 (C-97)

1 sqn with ERJ-145 (C-99A)

1 sqn with EMB-120RT (VC-97), EMB-121 (VU-9)

TRAINING

1 sqn with EMB-110 (C-95)

2 sqn with EMB-312 *Tucano* (T-27) (incl 1 air show sqn)

1 sqn with T-25A/C

ATTACK HELICOPTER

1 sqn with Mi-35M *Hind* (AH-2)

TRANSPORT HELICOPTER

1 sqn with AS332M *Super Puma* (H-34)

1 sqn with AS350B *Ecureuil* (H-50); AS355 *Ecureuil* II (H-55)

1 sqn with Bell 205 (H-1H); EC725 *Super Cougar* (H-36)

2 sqn with UH-60L *Black Hawk* (H-60L)

ISR UAV

1 sqn with *Hermes* 450

EQUIPMENT BY TYPE

AIRCRAFT 234 combat aircraft

FTR 57: 6 F-5E *Tiger* II; 51 F-5EM/FM *Tiger* II

FGA 61: 38 AMX (A-1); 11 AMX-T (A-1B); 12 *Mirage* 2000B/C (to be retired by Dec 2013)

ASW 7 P-3AM *Orion* (2 more on order)

MP 19: 10 EMB-111 (P-95A *Bandeirulha*)*; 9 EMB-111 (P-95B *Bandeirulha*)*

ISR: 8: 4 AMX-R (RA-1)*; 4 EMB-110B (R-95)

ELINT 6: 3 EMB-145RS (R-99); 3 Learjet 35A (R-35A)

AEW&C 5 EMB-145SA (E-99)
SAR 5: 4 EMB-110 (SC-95B), 1 SC-130E *Hercules*
TKR/TPT 2 KC-130H
TPT 200 **Medium** 20: 4 C-130E *Hercules*; 16 C-130H *Hercules*; **Light** 172: 12 C-295M (C-105A); 7 Cessna 208 (C-98); 9 Cessna 208B (C-98); 13 Cessna 208-G1000 (C-98A); 53 EMB-110 (C-95A/B/C/M); 16 EMB-120 (C-97); 4 EMB-120RT (VC-97); 5 EMB-121 (VU-9); 7 EMB-135BJ (VC-99B); 3 EMB-201R *Ipanema* (G-19); 2 EMB-202A *Ipanema* (G-19A); 2 ERJ-135LR (VC-99C); 7 ERJ-145 (C-99A); 1 ERJ-145LR (VC-99A); 9 Learjet 35A (VU-35); 1 Learjet 55C (VU-55); 9 PA-34 *Seneca* (U-7); 12 U-42 *Regente*; **PAX** 8: 1 A319 (VC-1A); 3 EMB-190 (VC-2); 4 Hawker 800XP (EU-93A- calibration)
TRG 265: 101 EMB-312 *Tucano* (T-27); 39 EMB-314 *Super Tucano* (A-29A)*; 44 EMB-314 *Super Tucano* (A-29B)*; 81 T-25A/C

HELICOPTERS
ATK 9 Mi-35M *Hind* (AH-2 - 3 more due)
TPT 83: **Heavy** 3 EC725 *Super Cougar* (H-36); **Medium** 26: 10 AS332M *Super Puma* (H-34/VH-34); 16 UH-60L *Black Hawk* (H-60L); **Light** 54: 24 AS350B *Ecureuil* (H-50); 4 AS355 *Ecureuil* II (H-55/VH-55); 24 Bell 205 (H-1H); 2 EC635 (VH-35)

UAV • ISR • Medium 4 *Hermes* 450
MSL • AAM • IR MAA-1 *Piranha*; *Magic* 2; *Python* III; **IIR** *Python* IV; **SARH** Super 530F; **ARH** *Derby*
ARM MAR-1 (in development)

Paramilitary 395,000 opcon Army

Public Security Forces 395,000

State police organisation technically under army control. However, military control is reducing, with authority reverting to individual states.

EQUIPMENT BY TYPE

UAV • ISR • Heavy 3 *Heron* (deployed by Federal Police for Amazon and border patrols)

Cyber

Cyber was a key component of the 2008 National Defence Strategy and the July 2012 Defence White Paper. The Federal Police, focused on internal law enforcement, has opened a 24-hour cyber-crime monitoring centre. In 2011, the army inaugurated Brazil's cyber-defence centre (CDCiber) to coordinate the existing activities of the army, navy and air force. In February 2012, Brazil's military cyber chief said that the country only had a 'minimum' level of preparedness to defend against theft and large-scale cyber attacks, such as a large cyber attack on government websites in June 2011, but he hoped a new anti-virus system and cyber-attack simulator, bought in January 2012, would improve readiness. Allegations by former NSA contractor Edward Snowden of cyber exploitation of Brazilian systems sharpened focus on cyber defence. (See p. 362.)

DEPLOYMENT

CÔTE D'IVOIRE
UN • UNOCI 3; 4 obs

CYPRUS
UN • UNFICYP 1

DEMOCRATIC REPUBLIC OF THE CONGO
UN • MONUSCO 6

HAITI
UN • MINUSTAH 1,403; 1 inf bn; 1 engr coy

LEBANON
UN • UNIFIL 260; 1 FFGHM

LIBERIA
UN • UNMIL 2; 2 obs

SOUTH SUDAN
UN • UNMISS 3; 1 obs

SUDAN
UN • UNISFA 1; 3 obs

WESTERN SAHARA
UN • MINURSO 9 obs

Chile CHL

Chilean Peso pCh		2012	2013	2014
GDP	pCh	130tr	140tr	
	US$	268bn	286bn	
per capita	US$	15,410	16,273	
Growth	%	5.47	4.94	
Inflation	%	3.01	2.14	
Def bdgt [a]	pCh	2.08tr	2.25tr	
	US$	4.27bn	4.59bn	
US$1=pCh		486.49	490.12	

[a] Includes military pensions

Population 17,216,945

Age	0–14	15–19	20–24	25–29	30–64	65 plus
Male	10.7%	4.1%	4.4%	4.0%	22.0%	4.0%
Female	10.3%	3.9%	4.2%	3.9%	22.9%	5.6%

Capabilities

Assuring sovereignty and territorial integrity are the core roles for the armed forces, as is internal security. There has been a focus on restructuring and re-equipment projects in the services. The army has shifted to a brigade structure with an increased emphasis on mobility, while its heavy armour inventory has been bolstered by the acquisition of second-hand *Leopard* 2s. The country has an amphibious assault capability built around its marine corps. Second-hand purchases have also been used to revamp the navy's frigate inventory over the past ten years. The air force has a modest tactical airlift fleet, though its overall operational reach has been improved by the acquisition of three KC-135 tanker aircraft. A mix of surplus and new-build F-16s has been acquired since 2005 to improve the air force's combat aircraft fleet. There is also interest in improving rotary-wing airlift with additional medium helicopters, along with additional fixed-wing airlift. Tenders were opened in 2013 for attack and transport helicopters. Replacing the air force's ageing jet trainers is also increasingly pressing. Slower economic growth, however, will likely impact the timing and nature of some plans. The services train regularly on a national basis, and also participate routinely in exercises with international and regional partners. Morale amongst the services is generally held to be high. The country has a significant interest in Antarctic security.

ACTIVE 61,400 (Army 34,650 Navy 18,700 Air 8,050) Paramilitary 44,700

Conscript liability Army 1 year; Navy 21 months; Air Force 18 months. Legally, conscription can last for 2 years

RESERVE 40,000 (Army 40,000)

ORGANISATIONS BY SERVICE

Space

SATELLITES

ISR 1 SSOT (Sistema Satelital del la Observación del la Tierra)

Army 34,650

6 military administrative regions.

FORCES BY ROLE

Currently being reorganised into 4 armd, 2 mot, 2 mtn and 1 SF brigade. Standard regt/gp are single bn strength, reinforced regt comprise multiple bn.

COMMAND

6 div HQ

SPECIAL FORCES

1 SF bde (1 SF bn, 1 (mtn) SF Gp, 1 para bn, 1 cdo coy, 1 log coy)
2 cdo coy

MANOEUVRE

Reconnaissance
1 armd recce pl
3 cav sqn
4 recce pl

Armoured
3 (1st, 2nd & 3rd) armd bde (1 armd recce pl, 1 armd cav gp, 1 mech inf bn, 1 arty gp, 1 AT coy, 1 engr coy, 1 sigs coy)
1 (4th) armd bde (1 armd recce pl, 1 armd cav gp, 1 mech inf bn, 1 arty gp, 1 engr coy)

Mechanised
1 (1st) mech inf regt

Light
1 (1st) reinforced regt (1 mot inf bn, 1 arty gp, 2 AT coy, 1 engr bn)
1 (4th) reinforced regt (1 mot inf bn, 1 MRL gp, 1 mor coy, 1 AT coy, 1 engr bn)
1 (5th) reinforced regt (1 armd cav gp, 1 mech inf coy, 1 arty gp, 1 engr coy)
1 (7th) reinforced regt (1 mot inf bn, 1 arty gp, 1 sigs coy)
1 (10th) reinforced regt (1 mot inf bn, 1 AT coy, 1 engr bn, 1 sigs bn)
2 (11th & 24th) reinforced mot inf regt (1 mot inf bn, 1 arty gp, 1 AT coy)
1 (14th) reinforced mot inf regt (1 mot inf bn, 1 sigs coy, 1 AT coy)
7 mot inf regt

Mountain
1 (3rd) reinforced mtn regt (1 mtn inf bn, 1 arty gp, 1 engr coy)
1 (9th) reinforced mtn regt (1 mtn inf bn, 1 engr bn)
1 (17th) reinforced mtn regt (1 mtn inf bn, 1 engr coy)
2 mtn inf regt

Aviation
1 avn bde (1 tpt avn bn, 1 hel bn, 1 maint bn, 1 spt bn, 1 log coy)

COMBAT SUPPORT

3 arty regt
1 engr regt
2 sigs regt
1 int regt
1 MP bn

COMBAT SERVICE SUPPORT

1 log div (2 log regt)
4 log regt
6 log coy
1 maint div (1 maint regt)

EQUIPMENT BY TYPE

MBT 260: 129 *Leopard* 1; 131 *Leopard* 2A4
AIFV 191: 173 *Marder*; 18 YPR-765
APC 426
  APC (T) 247 M113A1/A2
  APC (W) 179 Cardoen *Piranha*
ARTY 1,170
  SP 155mm 36: 24 M109A3; 12 M109A5+
  TOWED 233: **105mm** 193: 89 M101; 104 Mod 56; **155mm** 40 M-68
  MRL 160mm 12 LAR-160
  MOR 889:
    81mm 635: 300 M-29; 150 Soltam; 185 FAMAE; **120mm** 170: 110 FAMAE; 60 Soltam M-65
    SP 120mm 84: 36 FAMAE (on *Piranha* 6x6); 48 M-5L1A
AT
  MSL • MANPATS *Spike*
  RCL 106mm M40A1; **84mm** *Carl Gustav*
AIRCRAFT
  TPT 10 **Light** 8: 2 C-212 *Aviocar*; 3 Cessna 208 *Caravan*; 3 CN-235; **PAX** 2; 1 Cessna 680 *Sovereign*; 1 Cessna 650 *Citation* III
HELICOPTERS
  ISR 9 MD-530F *Lifter* (armed)
  TPT 17 **Medium** 12: 8 AS532AL *Cougar*; 4 SA330 *Puma*; **Light** 5: 4 AS350B3 *Ecureuil*; 1 AS355F *Ecureuil* II
AD
  SAM • MANPAD 24 *Mistral*
  GUNS 41:
    SP 16: **20mm** 16 *Piranha*/TCM-20
    TOWED 25: **20mm** 25 M167 *Vulcan*
AEV 8 *Leopard* 1
ARV 21 *Leopard* 1
VLB 13 *Leopard* 1
MW 3 *Leopard* 1

Navy 18,700

5 Naval Zones; 1st Naval Zone and main HQ at Valparaiso; 2nd Naval Zone at Talcahuano; 3rd Naval Zone at Punta Arenas; 4th Naval Zone at Iquique; 5th Naval Zone at Puerto Montt.

EQUIPMENT BY TYPE

SUBMARINES • TACTICAL • SSK 4:
- 2 *O'Higgins* (*Scorpene*) with 6 single 533mm TT with A-184 *Black Shark* HWT/SUT HWT/SM-39 *Exocet* Block II AShM
- 2 *Thompson* (GER T-209/1300) with 8 single 533mm TT A-184 *Black Shark* HWT/SUT HWT/SM-39 *Exocet* Block II AShM

PRINCIPAL SURFACE COMBATANTS 8
- **DESTROYERS • DDGHM** 1 *Almirante Williams* (UK Type-22) with 2 quad Mk141 lnchr with RGM-84 *Harpoon* AShM, 2 octuple VLS with *Barak* SAM; 2 triple 324mm ASTT with Mk46 LWT, 1 76mm gun (capacity 1 AS532SC *Cougar*)
- **FRIGATES** 7:
  - **FFGHM** 5:
    - 3 *Almirante Cochrane* (UK *Duke*-class Type-23*)* with 2 quad Mk141 lnchr with RGM-84C *Harpoon* AShM, 1 32-cell VLS with *Sea Wolf* SAM, 2 twin 324mm ASTT with Mk46 Mod 2 LWT, 1 114mm gun, (capacity 1 AS-532SC *Cougar*)
    - 2 *Almirante Riveros* (NLD *Karel Doorman*-class) with 2 twin lnchr with RGM-84 *Harpoon* AShM, 1 octuple Mk48 lnchr with RIM-7P *Sea Sparrow* SAM, 4 single Mk32 Mod 9 324mm ASTT with Mk46 Mod 5 HWT, 1 76mm gun, (capacity 1 AS532SC *Cougar*)
  - **FFGM** 2:
    - 2 *Almirante Lattore* (NLD *Jacob Van Heemskerck*-class) with 2 quad Mk141 lnchr with RGM-84 *Harpoon* AShM, 1 Mk13 GMLS with SM-1MR SAM, 1 octuple Mk48 lnchr with RIM-7P *Sea Sparrow* SAM, 2 twin Mk32 324mm ASTT with Mk46 LWT, 1 *Goalkeeper* CIWS

PATROL AND COASTAL COMBATANTS 12
- **PCG** 6:
  - 3 *Casma* (ISR *Sa'ar* 4) with 4 GI *Gabriel I* AShM, 2 76mm gun
  - 3 *Tiger* (GER Type-148) with 4 single lnchr with MM-38 *Exocet* AShM, 1 76mm gun
- **PCO** 6 *Micalvi*

AMPHIBIOUS
- **PRINCIPAL AMPHIBIOUS SHIPS**
  - **LPD** 1 *Sargento Aldea* (FRA *Foudre*) with 3 twin *Simbad* lnchr with *Mistral* SAM
- **LANDING SHIPS** 3
  - **LSM** 1 *Elicura*
  - **LST** 2 *Maipo* (FRA *Batral* - capacity 7 tanks; 140 troops)
- **LANDING CRAFT** 3
  - **LCT** 1 CDIC (for use in *Sargento Aldea*)
  - **LCM** 2 (for use in *Sargento Aldea*)

LOGISTICS AND SUPPORT 18
- **ABU** 1 *George Slight Marshall* (1 hel landing platform)
- **AFD** 3
- **AGOR** 1 *Cabo de Hornos*
- **AGP** 1 *Almirante Jose Toribio Merino Castro* (also used as general spt ship) (1 hel landing platform)
- **AGS** 1 Type-1200 (ice strengthened hull, ex-CAN) (1 hel landing platform)
- **AOR** 2: 1 *Almirante Montt* (1 hel landing platform); 1 *Araucano*
- **AP** 1 *Aguiles* (1 hel landing platform)
- **ATF** 2 *Veritas*
- **AXS** 1 *Esmeralda*
- **YFB** 2
- **YTB** 3

MSL • AShM MM-38 *Exocet*

Naval Aviation 600

EQUIPMENT BY TYPE

AIRCRAFT 23 combat capable
- **ASW** 6: 3 C-295ASW *Persuader*; 3 P-3ACH *Orion*
- **MP** 4: 1 C-295MPA *Persuader*; 3 EMB-111 *Bandeirante**
- **ISR** 7 Cessna O-2A *Skymaster**
- **TPT • Light** 3 C-212A *Aviocar*
- **TRG** 7 PC-7 *Turbo Trainer**

HELICOPTERS
- **ASW** 5 AS532SC *Cougar*
- **MRH** 9: 8 AS365 *Dauphin*; 1 Bell 412HP
- **TPT • Light** 10: 5 Bell 206 *Jet Ranger*; 5 Bo-105S

MSL • AShM AM-39 *Exocet*

Marines 3,600

FORCES BY ROLE

MANOEUVRE

Amphibious

1 amph bde (4 inf bn, 4 fd arty bty, 1 SSM bty (Excalibur Central Defence System), 4 ADA bty, 2 trg bn)

4 sy det

EQUIPMENT BY TYPE

LT TK 15 *Scorpion*

APC (W) 25 MOWAG *Roland*

ARTY 34
- **TOWED** 18: **105mm** 4 KH-178; **155mm** 14 G-5
- **MOR 81mm** 16

AD • SAM • SP 18: 4 M998 HMMWV; 4 M1151A HMMWV; 10 M1097 HMMWV *Avenger*

Coast Guard

Integral part of the Navy

EQUIPMENT BY TYPE

PATROL AND COASTAL COMBATANTS 60+
- **PSOH** 2 *Piloto Pardo* (1 additional vessel in build)
- **PBF** 20+ *Archangel*
- **PB** 38: 18 *Alacalufe* (*Protector*-class); 7 *Grumete Diaz* (*Dabor*-class); 6 *Pelluhue*; 5 *Archangel*; 1 *Maullin*; 1 *Ona*

Air Force 8,050

Flying hours 100 hrs/year

FORCES BY ROLE

FIGHTER

1 sqn with F-5E/F *Tiger* III+

2 sqn with F-16AM/BM *Fighting Falcon*

FIGHTER/GROUND ATTACK
1 sqn with F-16C/D Block 50 *Fighting Falcon* (*Puma*)
ISR
1 (photo) flt with; DHC-6-300 *Twin Otter*; Learjet 35A
AIRBORNE EARLY WARNING
1 flt with B-707 *Phalcon*
TANKER/TRANSPORT
1 sqn with B-737-300; C-130B/H *Hercules*; KC-135
TRANSPORT
3 sqn with Bell 205 (UH-1H *Iroquois*); C-212-200/300 *Aviocar*; Cessna O-2A; Cessna 525 *Citation* CJ1; DHC-6-100/300 *Twin Otter*; PA-28-236 *Dakota*; Bell 205 (UH-1H *Iroquois*)
1 VIP flt with B-737-500 (VIP); Gulfstream IV
TRAINING
1 sqn with EMB-314 *Super Tucano**
1 sqn with PA-28-236 *Dakota*; T-35A/B *Pillan*
TRANSPORT HELICOPTER
1 sqn with Bell 205 (UH-1H *Iroquois*); Bell 206B (trg); Bell 412 *Twin Huey*; Bo-105CBS-4; S-70A *Black Hawk*
AIR DEFENCE
1 AD regt (5 AD sqn) with *Mygale*; *Mistral*; M163/M167 *Vulcan*; GDF-005 Oerlikon; *Crotale*

EQUIPMENT BY TYPE
AIRCRAFT 79 combat capable
FTR 48: 10 F-5E *Tigre* III+; 2 F-5F *Tigre* III+; 29 F-16AM *Fighting Falcon*; 7 F-16BM *Fighting Falcon*
FGA 10: 6 F-16C Block 50 *Fighting Falcon*; 4 F-16D Block 50 *Fighting Falcon*
ATK 9 C-101CC *Aviojet* (A-36 *Halcón*)
ISR 2 Cessna O-2A
AEW&C 1 B-707 *Phalcon*
TKR 3 KC-135
TPT 37 **Medium** 3: 1 C-130B *Hercules*; 2 C-130H *Hercules*; **Light** 30: 2 C-212-200 *Aviocar*; 1 C-212-300 *Aviocar*; 4 Cessna 525 *Citation* CJ1; 3 DHC-6-100 *Twin Otter*; 7 DHC-6-300 *Twin Otter*; 2 Learjet 35A; 11 PA-28-236 *Dakota*; **PAX** 4: 1 B-737-300; 1 B-737-500; 1 B-767-300ER; 1 Gulfstream IV
TRG 42: 12 EMB-314 *Super Tucano**; 30 T-35A/B *Pillan*
HELICOPTERS
MRH 12 Bell 412EP *Twin Huey*
TPT 22: **Medium** 1 S-70A *Black Hawk*; **Light** 21: 13 Bell 205 (UH-1H *Iroquois*); 5 Bell 206B (trg); 2 BK-117; 1 Bo-105CBS-4
UAV • ISR Medium 3 *Hermes* 900
AD
SYSTEMS *Mygale*
SAM *Mistral*
SP 5 *Crotale*
GUNS • TOWED 20mm M163/M167 *Vulcan*; **35mm** GDF-005 Oerlikon
MSL
AAM • IR AIM-9J/M *Sidewinder*; *Python* III; *Python* IV; *Shafrir*‡; **ARH** AIM-120C AMRAAM; *Derby*
ASM AGM-65G *Maverick*
BOMBS
INS/GPS guided JDAM
Laser-guided *Paveway* II

Paramilitary 44,700

Carabineros 44,700
Ministry of Interior; 15 zones, 36 districts, 179 *comisaria*
EQUIPMENT BY TYPE
APC (W) 20 MOWAG *Roland*
ARTY • MOR 60mm; 81mm
AIRCRAFT
TPT • Light 4: 1 Beech 200 *King Air*; 1 Cessna 208; 1 Cessna 550 *Citation* V; 1 PA-31T *Cheyenne* II
HELICOPTERS • TPT • Light 15: 5 AW109E *Power*; 1 Bell 206 *Jet Ranger*; 2 BK 117; 5 Bo-105; 2 EC135

Cyber
The Joint Staff coordinates cyber-security policies for the Ministry of Defense and the Armed Forces. Each service has a cyber-security organisation within their security structure. The Ministry of Interior and Public Security (Internal Affairs) is the national coordination authority for cyber security and is currently developing a National Cyber Security Strategy.

DEPLOYMENT
Legal provisions for foreign deployment:
Constitution: Constitution (1980, since amended)
Decision on deployment of troops abroad: Article 63, number 13 of the Constitution, concerning matters of law, states that the procedures for foreign deployment are a matter that must be established by law by Congress. Law Number 19.067 regulates matters concerning the foreign deployment of Chilean troops and deployment of foreign troops in Chile. It states that the government needs to request congressional approval.

BOSNIA-HERZEGOVINA
EU • EUFOR • *Operation Althea* 15

CYPRUS
UN • UNFICYP 14

HAITI
UN • MINUSTAH 464; 1 mech inf bn; 1 hel coy; elm 1 engr coy

INDIA/PAKISTAN
UN • UNMOGIP 2 obs

MIDDLE EAST
UN • UNTSO 3 obs

Colombia COL

Colombian Peso pC		2012	2013	2014
GDP	pC	655tr	700tr	
	US$	366bn	388bn	
per capita	US$	7,855	8,238	
Growth	%	4.00	4.09	
Inflation	%	3.17	2.22	
Def bdgt [a]	pC	11tr	12.6tr	
	US$	6.21bn	7.02bn	
FMA (US)	US$	40m	40m	29m
US$1=pC		1789.64	1802.27	

[a] Excludes decentralised expenditures & expenditure on National Police

Population 45,745,783

Age	0–14	15–19	20–24	25–29	30–64	65 plus
Male	13.2%	4.7%	4.6%	4.2%	20.0%	2.7%
Female	12.6%	4.5%	4.5%	4.1%	21.2%	3.8%

Capabilities

While Colombia's security and defence requirements continue to be dominated by counter-insurgency and counter-narcotics, recent successes in both are beginning to see the armed forces consider broader horizons. The state has recorded notable gains in its campaign against FARC, a conflict now in its fifth decade. Peace talks announced in 2012 continued into 2013, however a new air combat command was established to confront FARC fronts in the southwest. To combat drug-trafficking, a new naval force was announced, with an order made for five fast boats built by local company COTECMAR, to be deployed in Caribbean waters. Colombia enjoys considerable support from the US in terms of training and equipment provision, to bolster its counter-narcotics effort. Army special forces have received training, while the air force operates a large fleet of US helicopter types to provide tactical mobility for the army. Fixed-wing tactical transport has also been enhanced, with an additional two C-295s delivered in 2013, while the air force has upgraded and received additional *Kfir* fighters. The air force took part in the US *Red Flag* exercises in 2012. The navy has a littoral warfare capacity only. Morale in the air force and navy is at least adequate, similarly within the army's special forces. An eventual end to the hostilities with FARC would likely see a modest shift in procurement to support a more general force structure, rather than one focused on counter-insurgency.

ACTIVE 281,400 (Army 221,500, Navy 46,150 Air 13,750) **Paramilitary 159,000**

RESERVE 61,900 (Army 54,700 Navy 4,800 Air 1,200 Joint 1,200)

ORGANISATIONS BY SERVICE

Army 221,500

FORCES BY ROLE

SPECIAL FORCES

1 anti-terrorist SF bn

MANOEUVRE

Mechanised

1 (1st) div (1 (2nd) mech bde (2 mech inf bn, 1 mtn inf bn, 1 engr bn, 1 MP bn, 1 cbt spt bn, 1 log bn, 1 Gaula anti-kidnap gp); 1 (10th) mech bde (1 (med) tk bn, 1 mech cav bn, 1 mech inf bn, 1 mtn inf bn, 1 fd arty bn, 1 engr bn, 1 cbt spt bn, 2 Gaula anti-kidnap gp); 2 sy bn; 1 log bn)

Light

1 (2nd) div (1 (5th) lt inf bde (3 lt inf bn, 1 fd arty bn, 1 AD bn, 1 engr bn, 1 cbt spt bn, 1 Gaula anti-kidnap gp); 1 (30th) lt inf bde (1 cav recce bn, 2 lt inf bn, 1 sy bn, 1 arty bn, 1 engr bn, 1 cbt spt bn, 1 log bn); 1 rapid reaction force (3 mobile sy bde, 1 fixed sy bde))

1 (3rd) div (1 (3rd) lt inf bde (2 lt inf bn, 1 mtn inf bn, 1 COIN bn, 1 arty bn, 1 engr bn, 1 cbt spt bn, 1 MP bn, 1 log bn, 1 Gaula anti-kidnap gp); 1 (23rd) lt inf bde (1 cav gp, 1 lt inf bn, 1 jungle inf bn, 1 cbt spt bn, 1 log bn); 1 (29th) mtn bde (1 mtn inf bn, 1 lt inf bn, 2 COIN bn, 1 cbt spt bn, 1 log bn); 2 rapid reaction force (total: 7 mobile sy bde))

1 (4th) div (1 (7th) air mob bde (2 air mob inf bn, 1 lt inf bn, 1 COIN bn, 1 engr bn, 1 cbt spt bn, 1 log bn, 1 Gaula anti-kidnap gp); 1 (22nd) jungle bde (1 air mob inf bn, 1 lt inf bn, 1 jungle inf bn, 1 COIN bn, 1 cbt spt bn, 1 log bn; 1 (31st) jungle bde (1 lt inf bn, 1 jungle inf bn))

1 (5th) div (1 (6th) lt inf bde (2 lt inf bn,1 mtn inf bn, 2 COIN bn, 1 cbt spt bn, 1 log bn, 1 Gaula anti-kidnap gp); 1 (8th) lt inf bde (1 lt inf bn, 1 mtn inf bn, 1 arty bn, 1 engr bn, 1 cbt spt bn, 1 Gaula anti-kidnap gp); 1 (9th) lt inf bde (1 SF bn, 2 lt inf bn, 1 arty bn, 1 COIN bn, 1 cbt spt bn, 1 sy bn, 1 log bn, 1 Gaula anti-kidnap gp); 1 (13th) lt inf bde (2 cav recce bn, 1 airmob inf bn, 3 lt inf bn, 1 COIN bn, 1 arty bn, 1 engr bn, 1 cbt spt bn, 2 MP bn, 1 log bn, 2 Gaula anti-kidnap gp); 1 rapid reaction force (3 mobile sy bde))

1 (6th) div (1 (12th) lt inf bde (2 lt inf bn, 2 jungle inf bn, 1 COIN bn, 1 engr bn, 1 cbt spt bn, 1 Gaula anti-kidnap gp); 1 (13th) mobile sy bde (4 COIN bn); 1 (26th) jungle bde (1 lt jungle inf bn, 1 COIN bn, 1 cbt spt bn); 1 (27th) lt inf bde (2 lt inf bn, 1 jungle inf bn, 1 sy bn, 1 arty bn, 1 cbt spt bn, 1 log bn))

1 (7th) div (1 (4th) lt inf bde (1 cav recce bn, 3 lt inf bn, 1 sy bn, 1 arty bn, 1 engr bn, 1 MP bn, 1 cbt spt bn, 1 log bn); 1 (11th) lt inf bde (2 lt inf bn, 1 sy bn, 1 engr bn, 1 cbt spt bn); 1 (14th) lt inf bde (2 lt inf bn, 1 sy bn, 1 engr bn, 1 cbt spt bn, 1 log bn); 1 (15th) jungle bde (1 ilt inf bn, 1 COIN bn, 1 engr bn, 1 log bn); 1 (17th) lt inf bde (2 lt inf bn, 1 COIN bn, 1 engr bn, 1 cbt spt bn, 1 log bn); 1 rapid reaction force (1 (11th) mobile sy bde (3 COIN bn)))

1 (8th) div (1 (16th) lt inf bde (1 mech cav recce bn, 1 lt inf bn, 1 log bn, 1 Gaula anti-kidnap gp); 1 (18th) lt inf bde (1 air mob gp, 1 sy bn, 1 arty bn, 1 engr bn, 1 cbt spt bn, 1 log bn); 1 (28th) jungle bde (2 inf, 2 COIN, 1 cbt spt bn); 1 rapid reaction force (1 (5th) mobile sy bde (3 COIN bn); 1 (31st) mobile sy bde (5 COIN bn)))

3 COIN mobile bde (each: 4 COIN bn, 1 cbt spt bn)

Other
1 indep rapid reaction force (1 SF bde; 3 mobile sy bde)
Aviation
1 air aslt div (1 SF bde (2 SF bn); 1 counter-narcotics bde (3 counter-narcotics bn, 1 spt bn); 1 (25th) avn bde (4 hel bn; 5 avn bn; 1 avn log bn); 1 (32nd) avn bde (1 avn bn, 2 maint bn, 1 trg bn, 1 spt bn); 1 SF avn bn)
COMBAT SUPPORT
1 cbt engr bde (1 SF engr bn, 1 (emergency response) engr bn, 1 EOD bn, 1 construction bn, 1 demining bn, 1 maint bn)
1 int bde (2 SIGINT bn, 1 kog bn, 1 maint bn)
COMBAT SERVICE SUPPORT
2 spt/log bde (each: 1 spt bn, 1 maint bn, 1 supply bn, 1 tpt bn, 1 medical bn, 1 log bn)

EQUIPMENT BY TYPE
RECCE 222: 119 EE-9 *Cascavel*; 6 M8 (anti-riot vehicle); 8 M8 with TOW; 39 M1117 *Guardian*; 50 VCL
APC 114
APC (T) 54: 28 M113A1 (TPM-113A1); 26 M113A2 (TPM-113A2)
APC (W) 56 EE-11 *Urutu*
PPV 4 RG-31 *Nyala*
ARTY 710
TOWED 121: **105mm** 106: 20 LG1 MkIII; 86 M101; **155mm** 15 155/52 APU SBT-1
MOR 589: **81mm** 141: 125 M1; 16 M125A1 (SP) **107mm** 148 M2; **120mm** 300: 210 Brandt, 38 HY12; 52 AM50
AT
MSL • SP 8+: 8 TOW; *Nimrod*
MANPATS 10+: 10 TOW; *Spike*-ER; APILAS
RCL 106mm 63 M40A1
RL 15+: **89mm** 15 M20; **90mm** C-90C; **106mm** SR-106
AD
SAM • TOWED 3 *Skyguard/Sparrow*
GUNS 39+
SP 12.7mm 18 M8/M55
TOWED 21+: **35mm** GDF Oerlikon; **40mm** 21 M1A1 (with 7 *Eagle Eye* radar)
AIRCRAFT
ELINT 3: 2 Beech B200 *King Air*; 1 Beech 350 *King Air*
TPT • Light 21: 2 An 32B; 2 Beech 350 *King Air*; 2 Beech 200 *King Air* (Medevac); 1 Beech C90 *King Air*; 2 C-212 *Aviocar* (Medevac); 1 Cessna 206; 6 Cessna 208B *Grand Caravan*; 2 PA-34 *Seneca*; 3 *Turbo Commander* 695A
HELICOPTERS
MRH 21: 8 Mi-17-1V *Hip*; 8 Mi-17MD; 5 Mi-17V-5 *Hip*
TPT 111 **Medium** 55: 48 UH-60L *Black Hawk*; 7 S-70i *Black Hawk*; **Light** 56: 29 Bell 205 (UH-1H *Iroquois*); 27 Bell 212 (UH-1N *Twin Huey*)

Navy 46,150; (incl 7,200 conscript)

HQ (Tri-Service Unified Eastern Command HQ) located at Puerto Carreño.

EQUIPMENT BY TYPE
SUBMARINES • TACTICAL • SSK 4:
2 *Pijao* (GER T-209/1200) each with 8 single 533mm TT each with HWT
2 *Intrepido* (GER T-206A) each with 8 single 533mm TT each with HWT
PRINCIPAL SURFACE COMBATANTS 4
FRIGATES • FFG 4 *Almirante Padilla* with 2 twin lnchr with MM-40 *Exocet* AShM, 2 twin *Simbad* lnchr with *Mistral* SAM, 2 triple B515 *ILAS-3* 324mm ASTT each with A244 LWT, 1 76mm gun, (capacity 1 Bo-105/AS555SN *Fennec* hel)
PATROL AND COASTAL COMBATANTS 49
PSOH 1 *20 de Julio* (1 additional vessel to be delivered Dec 2013)
PCO 2: 1 *Valle del Cauca Durable* (ex-US *Reliance*) with 1 hel landing platform; 1 *San Andres* (ex-US *Balsam*)
PCR 13: 2 *Arauca* with 2 76mm guns; 8 *Nodriza* (PAF-II) with hel landing platform; 3 LPR-40 (additional vessels on order)
PBF 1 *Quitasueño* (US *Asheville*) with 1 76mm gun
PB 12: 1 *11 de Noviembre* (CPV-40) with 1 *Typhoon* CIWS; 2 *Castillo Y Rada* (*Swiftships* 105); 2 *Jaime Gomez*; 1 *José Maria Palas* (*Swiftships* 110); 4 *Point*; 2 *Toledo*
PBR 20: 6 *Diligente*; 3 *Swiftships*; 9 *Tenerife*; 2 PAF-L
AMPHIBIOUS 13
LCAC 3 Griffon 2000TD (5 further vessels on order)
LCM 3 LCM-8 (there are more than 200 small assault RHIBs also in service)
LCU 7 *Morrosquillo* (LCU 1466)
LOGISTICS AND SUPPORT 20
ABU 1 *Quindio*
AG 2 *Luneburg* (ex-GER, depot ship for patrol vessels)
AGOR 2 *Providencia*
AGP 1 *Inirida*
AGS 1 *Gorgona*
AXS 1 *Gloria*
YTL 12

Naval Aviation 146

AIRCRAFT
MP 3 CN-235 MPA *Persuader*
ISR 1 PA-31 *Navajo* (upgraded for ISR)
TPT • Light 10: 1 C-212 (Medevac); 4 Cessna 206; 2 Cessna 208 *Caravan*; 1 PA-31 *Navajo*; 1 PA-34 *Seneca*; 1 Beech 350 *King Air*
HELICOPTERS
MRH 5: 2 AS555SN *Fennec*; 3 Bell 412 *Twin Huey*
TPT • Light 10: 1 Bell 212; 6 Bell 212 (UH-1N); 1 BK-117; 2 Bo-105

Marines 27,000

FORCES BY ROLE
SPECIAL FORCES
1 SF bde (forming)
1 SF bn
2 (river) SF gp
MANOEUVRE
Amphibious
1 mne bde (3 mne bn, 2 COIN bn, 1 comd/spt bn)
1 rvn bde (3 mne bn)
1 rvn bde (3 mne bn, 3 mne aslt bn, 1 comd/spt bn)
1 rvn bde (4 mne bn)
COMBAT SERVICE SUPPORT
1 log bde (forming)
1 trg bde (3 trg bn)

EQUIPMENT BY TYPE

AIFV 8 BTR-80A

ARTY • MOR • 81mm 20

Air Force 13,750

6 Combat Air Commands (CACOM) plus CACOM 7 (former Oriental Air Group) responsible for air ops in specific geographic area. Flts can be deployed or 'loaned' to a different CACOM.

FORCES BY ROLE

FIGHTER GROUND ATTACK

1 sqn with *Kfir* C-10/C-12/TC-12

GROUND ATTACK/ISR

1 sqn with A-37B/OA-37B *Dragonfly*

1 sqn with AC-47T; Hughes 369

1 sqn with EMB-312 *Tucano**

2 sqn with EMB-314 *Super Tucano** (A-29)

1 Sqn with OV-10A *Bronco*

EW/ELINT

2 sqn with Beech 350 *King Air*; Cessna 208; Cessna 560; C-26B *Metroliner*; SA 2-37

MARITIME PATROL/SEARCH & RESCUE

1 sqn with Bell 212, EMB-110P1 (C-95)

TRANSPORT

1 (Presidential) sqn with B-707 Tkr; B-727; B-737BBJ; EMB-600 *Legacy*; KC-767; Bell 212; Bell 412; F-28 *Fellowship*

1 sqn with C-130B/H *Hercules*; C-295M

1 sqn with Beech C90 *King Air*; C-212; CN-235M; Do-328; IAI *Arava*

TRAINING

1 (primary trg) sqn with Bell 205 (UH-1H *Iroquois*); PA-42 *Cheyenne*

1 (basic trg) sqn with T-34 *Mentor*

1 sqn with T-37B

2 hel sqn with Bell 206B3

HELICOPTER

1 sqn with AH-60L *Arpia* III

1 sqn with UH-60L *Black Hawk* (CSAR)

1 sqn with MD500; Bell 205 (UH-1H)

1 sqn with Hughes 369

1 sqn with Bell 205 (UH-1H); Hughes 369

1 sqn with Bell 206B3; Hughes 369

EQUIPMENT BY TYPE

AIRCRAFT 88 combat capable

FGA 22: 10 *Kfir* C-10; 10 *Kfir* C-12; 2 *Kfir* TC-12

ATK 27: 4 A-37B *Dragonfly*; 8 OA-37B *Dragonfly*; 8 AC-47T *Spooky* (*Fantasma*); 7 OV-10A *Bronco*

ISR 13: 1 C-26B *Metroliner*; 5 Cessna 560 *Citation* V; 6 SA 2-37; 1 Beech C90 *King Air*

ELINT 3: 1 Beech 350 *King Air*; 2 Cessna 208 *Grand Caravan*

TKR/TPT 2: 1 B-707 Tkr; 1 KC-767

TPT 72 **Medium** 8: 4 C-130B *Hercules* (3 more in store); 3 C-130H *Hercules*; 1 B-737F; **Light** 59: 5 ATR-42; 2 ATR-72; 2 Beech 300 *King Air*; 5 Beech 350C *King Air*; 2 Beech C90 *King Air*; 4 C-212; 5 C-295M; 1 Cessna 182R; 12 Cessna 208B (medevac); 1 Cessna 337G; 1 Cessna 337H; 1 Cessna 550; 3 CN-235M; 6 Do-328; 2 EMB-110P1 (C-95); 1 EMB-170-100LR; 1 IAI-201 *Arava*; 1 L-410UVP *Turbolet*; 2 PA-42 *Cheyenne*; 2 *Turbo Commander* 695; **PAX** 5: 1 B-727; 1 B-737BBJ; 1 EMB-600 *Legacy*; 1 F-28-1000 *Fellowship*; 1 F-28-3000 *Fellowship*

TRG 78+: 14 EMB-312 *Tucano**; 25 EMB-314 *Super Tucano* (A-29)*; 10+ Lancair *Synergy* (T-90 - 15 more on order); 9 T-34 *Mentor*; 20 T-37B

HELICOPTERS

ISR 20 OH-58 *Kiowa*

MRH 17: 12 AH-60L *Arpia* III; 2 Bell 412 *Twin Huey*; 2 Hughes 500M; 1 MD-500E

TPT 62 **Medium** 18 UH-60L *Black Hawk*; **Light** 45: 21 Bell 205 (UH-1H *Iroquois*); 12 Bell 206B3 *Jet Ranger* III; 11 Bell 212

MSL • IR *Python* III; R-530 (possibly wfu); **IIR** *Python* IV

ARH *Derby*

Paramilitary 159,000

National Police Force 159,000

AIRCRAFT

ELINT 3: 1 Cessna 208B, 2 C-26B *Metroliner*

TPT • Light 59: 15 AT-802; 1 ATR-42; 3 Beech 200 *King Air*; 3 Beech 300 *King Air*; 2 Beech 1900; 1 Beech C99; 4 BT-67; 5 C-26 *Metroliner*; 2 Cessna 152; 3 Cessna 172; 7 Cessna 206; 5 Cessna 208 *Caravan*; 2 DHC 6 *Twin Otter*; 1 DHC-8; 4 PA-31 *Navajo*

HELICOPTERS

MRH 4: 1 Bell 412EP; 1 MD-500D; 2 Hughes 369

TPT 56 **Medium** 10 UH-60L *Black Hawk*; **Light** 46: 25 Bell 205 (UH-1H-II *Huey II*); 3 Bell 206B; 7 Bell 206L *Long Ranger*; 10 Bell 212; 1 Bell 407

DEPLOYMENT

EGYPT

MFO 354; 1 inf bn

FOREIGN FORCES

United States US Southern Command: 60

Costa Rica CRI

Costa Rican Colon C		2012	2013	2014
GDP	C	22.7tr	24.9tr	
	US$	45.1bn	48.9bn	
per capita	US$	9,673	10,363	
Growth	%	5.00	4.20	
Inflation	%	4.49	4.67	
Sy Bdgt [a]	C	175bn	202bn	
	US$	349m	397m	
FMA (US)	US$	1m	1m	1m
US$1=C		502.91	508.47	

[a] No armed forces. Paramilitary budget

Population 4,695,942

Age	0–14	15–19	20–24	25–29	30–64	65 plus
Male	12.2%	4.4%	4.6%	4.6%	21.2%	3.1%
Female	11.6%	4.3%	4.5%	4.5%	21.3%	3.7%

Capabilities

Military forces were constitutionally abolished in 1949. Costa Rica relies on a series of moderately-sized paramilitary-style organisations for internal security and regional peacekeeping operations. Some force elements, such as the special operations unit, have received training in some capability areas by outside states, including the US.

Paramilitary 9,800

ORGANISATIONS BY SERVICE

Paramilitary 9,800

Special Intervention Unit

FORCES BY ROLE
SPECIAL FORCES
1 spec ops unit

Public Force 9,000

FORCES BY ROLE
MANOEUVRE
Other
1 (tac) police *comisaria*
6 (provincial) paramilitary *comisaria*
7 (urban) paramilitary *comisaria*
2 (border) sy comd (8 *comisaria*)
8 paramilitary comd

Coast Guard Unit 400

EQUIPMENT BY TYPE
PATROL AND COASTAL COMBATANTS 8:
PB 8: 2 *Cabo Blanco* (US *Swift* 65); 1 *Isla del Coco* (US *Swift* 105); 3 *Point*; 1 *Primera Dama* (US *Swift* 42); 1 *Puerto Quebos* (US *Swift* 36)

Air Surveillance Unit 400

AIRCRAFT • TPT • Light 15: 4 Cessna T210 *Centurion*; 4 Cessna U206G *Stationair*; 1 DHC-7 *Caribou*; 2 PA-31 *Navajo*; 2 PA-34 *Seneca*; 1 Piper PA-23 *Aztec*; 1 Cessna 182RG
HELICOPTERS • MRH : 3 2 MD-500E; 1 MD 600N

Cuba CUB

Cuban Peso P		2012	2013	2014
GDP	P			
	US$			
per capita	US$			
Growth	%			
Inflation	%			
Def bdgt	P			
	US$			
Exchange Rate				

*definitive economic data unavailable

Population 11,061,886

Age	0–14	15–19	20–24	25–29	30–64	65 plus
Male	8.5%	3.3%	3.8%	3.7%	24.8%	5.5%
Female	8.1%	3.1%	3.6%	3.5%	25.2%	6.8%

Capabilities

Numerically the strongest in the Caribbean, the effectiveness of the Cuban armed forces is restricted by their largely outdated equipment holdings and maintenance problems resulting from US sanctions on Cuba and the collapse of the Soviet Union. They have focused on a national-defence role after the end of the Cold War, and lack recent experience of either combat or significant operational deployment. They do, however, retain strong ties with some regional militaries, particularly Venezuela, with which Cuba has signed several defence production agreements and to which advisers and medical personnel have been deployed. Links to military forces further afield also exist, demonstrated by the seizure of a cargo ship transporting missile, radar and aircraft components to North Korea in July 2013. Though Cuba's equipment inventory and industrial capability is degraded such that the need for refurbishment abroad is not an unlikely occurrence, claims by Havana that this was the reason for the shipment were met with scepticism by analysts, suggesting the shipment could have been an attempt to circumvent sanctions against North Korea. Military-to-military relations are unlikely to improve the slowly degrading capabilities of the Cuban armed forces.

ACTIVE 49,000 (Army 38,000 Navy 3,000 Air 8,000) **Paramilitary 26,500**
Conscript liability 2 years

RESERVE 39,000 (Army 39,000) **Paramilitary 1,120,000**
Ready Reserves (serve 45 days per year) to fill out Active and Reserve units; see also Paramilitary.

ORGANISATIONS BY SERVICE

Army ε38,000

FORCES BY ROLE

COMMAND

3 regional comd HQ

3 army comd HQ

MANOEUVRE

Armoured

up to 5 armd bde

Mechanised

9 mech inf bde (1 armd regt, 3 mech inf regt, 1 arty regt, 1 ADA regt)

Light

1 (frontier) bde

Air Manoeuvre

1 AB bde

COMBAT SUPPORT

1 ADA regt

1 SAM bde

Reserves 39,000

FORCES BY ROLE

MANOEUVRE

Light

14 inf bde

EQUIPMENT BY TYPE†

MBT ε900 T-34/T-54/T-55/T-62

LT TK PT-76

RECCE BRDM-1/2

AIFV ε50 BMP-1

APC • APC (W) ε500 BTR-152/BTR-40/BTR-50/BTR-60

ARTY 1,730+

SP 40: **122mm** 2S1 **152mm** 2S3

TOWED 500: **76mm** ZIS-3; **122mm** D-30; M-30; **130mm** M-46; **152mm** D-1; M-1937

MRL • SP 175: **122mm** BM-21 **140mm** BM-14

MOR 1,000: **82mm** M-41; **82mm** M-43; **120mm** M-43; **120mm** M-38

STATIC 122mm 15 JS-2M (hy tk)

AT

MSL • MANPATS 2K16 *Shmel* (AT-1 *Snapper*); 9K11 *Malyutka* (AT-3 9K11 *Sagger*)

GUNS 700+: **100mm** 100 SU-100 SP; **85mm** D-44; **57mm** 600 M-1943

AD • SAM

SP 200+: 200 9K35 *Strela*-10 (SA-13 *Gopher*); 2K12 *Kub* (SA-6 *Gainful*); 9K33 *Osa* (SA-8 *Gecko*); 9K31 *Strela*-1 (SA-9 *Gaskin*)

MANPAD 9K36 *Strela*-3 (SA-14 *Gremlin*); 9K310 *Igla*-1 (SA-16 *Gimlet*); 9K32 *Strela*-2 (SA-7 *Grail*)‡

GUNS 400

SP 57mm ZSU-57-2 SP/**23mm** ZSU-23-4 SP/**30mm** BTR-60P SP

TOWED 100mm KS-19/M-1939/**85mm** KS-12/**57mm** S-60/**37mm** M-1939/**30mm** M-53/**23mm** ZU-23

Navy ε3,000

Western Comd HQ at Cabanas; Eastern Comd HQ at Holquin.

EQUIPMENT BY TYPE

PATROL AND COASTAL COMBATANTS 8

PSO 1 *Rio Damuji* with two single P-15M *Termit* (SS-N-2C *Styx*) AShM, 2 57mm guns, 1 hel landing platform

PCM 1 *Pauk* II† (FSU) with 1 quad lnchr (manual aiming) with 9K32 *Strela*-2 (SA-N-5 *Grail* SAM), 4 single ASTT, 2 RBU 1200, 1 76mm gun

PBF 6 *Osa* II† (FSU) each with 4 single lnchr (for P-15 *Termit* (SS-N-2B *Styx*) AShM – missiles removed to coastal defence units)

MINE WARFARE AND MINE COUNTERMEASURES 5

MHI 3 *Yevgenya*† (FSU)

MSC 2 *Sonya*† (FSU)

LOGISTICS AND SUPPORT 5

ABU 1

AX 1

YTL 3

Coastal Defence

ARTY • TOWED 122mm M-1931/37; **130mm** M-46; **152mm** M-1937

MSL• AShM 2+: *Bandera* IV (reported); 2 P-15 *Rubezh* (SSC-3 *Styx*)

Naval Infantry 550+

FORCES BY ROLE

MANOEUVRE

Amphibious

2 amph aslt bn

Anti-aircraft Defence and Revolutionary Air Force ε8,000 (incl conscripts)

Air assets divided between Western Air Zone and Eastern Air Zone.

Flying hours 50 hrs/year

FORCES BY ROLE

FIGHTER/GROUND ATTACK

3 sqn with MiG-21ML *Fishbed*; MiG-23ML/MF/UM *Flogger*; MiG-29A/UB *Fulcrum*

TRANSPORT

1 (VIP) tpt sqn with An-24 *Coke*; Mi-8P *Hip*; Yak-40

ATTACK HELICOPTER

2 sqn with Mi-17 *Hip H*; Mi-35 *Hind*

TRAINING

2 (tac trg) sqn with L-39C *Albatros* (basic); Z-142 (primary)

EQUIPMENT BY TYPE

AIRCRAFT 45 combat capable

FTR 33: 16 MiG-23ML *Flogger*; 4 MiG-23MF *Flogger*; 4 MiG-23U *Flogger*; 4 MiG-23UM *Flogger*; 2 MiG-29A *Fulcrum*; 3 MiG-29UB *Fulcrum* (6 MiG-15UTI *Midget*; 4+ MiG-17 *Fresco*; 4 MiG-23MF *Flogger*; 6 MiG-23ML *Flogger*; 2 MiG-23UM *Flogger*; 2 MiG-29 *Fulcrum* in store)

FGA 12: 4 MiG-21ML *Fishbed*; 8 MiG-21U *Mongol* A (up to 70 MiG-21bis *Fishbed*; 30 MiG-21F *Fishbed*; 28 MiG-

21PFM *Fishbed;* 7 MiG-21UM *Fishbed;* 20 MiG-23BN *Flogger* in store)
ISR 1 An-30 *Clank*
TPT 11: **Heavy** 2 Il-76 *Candid;* **Light** 9: 1 An-2 *Colt;* 3 An-24 *Coke;* 2 An-32 *Cline;* 3 Yak-40 (8 An-2 *Colt;* 18 An-26 *Curl* in store)
TRG 45: 25 L-39 *Albatros;* 20 Z-326 *Trener Master*
HELICOPTERS
ATK 4 Mi-35 *Hind* (8 more in store)
ASW (5 Mi-14 in store)
MRH 8 Mi-17 *Hip* H (12 more in store)
TPT • Medium 2 Mi-8P *Hip*
AD • SAM SA-3 *Goa;* SA-2 *Guideline* towed
MSL
AAM • IR R-3‡ (AA-2 *Atoll*); R-60 (AA-8 *Aphid*); R-73 (AA-11 *Archer*); **IR/SARH** R-23/24‡ (AA-7 *Apex*); R-27 (AA-10 *Alamo*)
ASM Kh-23‡ (AS-7 *Kerry*)

Paramilitary 26,500 active

State Security 20,000
Ministry of Interior

Border Guards 6,500
Ministry of Interior
PATROL AND COASTAL COMBATANTS 20
PCC: 2 *Stenka*
PB 18 *Zhuk*

Youth Labour Army 70,000 reservists

Civil Defence Force 50,000 reservists

Territorial Militia ε1,000,000 reservists

FOREIGN FORCES

United States US Southern Command: 950 at Guantánamo Bay

Dominican Republic DOM

Dominican Peso pRD		2012	2013	2014
GDP	pRD	2.32tr	2.48tr	
	US$	59bn	60.3bn	
per capita	US$	5,763	5,789	
Growth	%	3.89	2.23	
Inflation	%	3.70	4.45	
Def bdgt	pRD	14.2bn	15.5bn	
	US$	363m	378m	
US$1=pRD		39.27	41.04	

Population 10,219,630

Age	0–14	15–19	20–24	25–29	30–64	65 plus
Male	14.5%	4.9%	4.6%	4.2%	19.3%	3.2%
Female	14.0%	4.7%	4.4%	4.0%	18.6%	3.7%

Capabilities

Lacking a credible external threat, the Dominican military is primarily focused on internal paramilitary duties and counter-narcotics operations. A sizeable proportion of the army is deployed on the Haitian border to bolster security. The army's internal security role is exemplified by an operation in mid-2013 that saw more than 3,000 soldiers deployed to patrol alongside the police following a series of well-publicised attacks. Heavy equipment holdings are minimal and serviceability is questionable. Under the US SOUTHCOM-managed Caribbean Basin Security Initiative, the Dominican Republic received two *Defender*-class sub-10-tonne patrol vessels in 2012. Legislation drafted in 2013 aims to further civilianise and professionalise the armed forces, introducing mandatory retirement for generals after ten years of service, new senior-officer-to-enlisted-personnel ratios, a rank of warrant officer, greater restrictions on promotions, and renaming the Armed Forces Ministry as the Ministry of Defence.

ACTIVE 46,000 (Army 26,000 Navy 10,000 Air 10,000) Paramilitary 15,000

ORGANISATIONS BY SERVICE

Army 26,000
5 Defence Zones

FORCES BY ROLE
SPECIAL FORCES
3 SF bn
MANOEUVRE
Mechanised
1 armd bn
Light
1 (2nd) inf bde (4 inf bn, 1 mtn inf bn)
2 (1st & 3rd) inf bde (3 inf bn)
2 (4th & 5th) inf bde (2 inf bn)
1 (6th) inf bde (1 inf bn)
Air Manoeuvre
1 air cav bde (1 cdo bn, 1 (6th) mtn regt, 1 hel sqn with Bell 205 (op by Air Force); OH-58 *Kiowa;* R-22; R-44 *Raven* II)
Other
1 (Presidential Guard) gd regt
1 (MoD) sy bn
COMBAT SUPPORT
2 arty bn
1 engr bn

EQUIPMENT BY TYPE
LT TK 12 M41B (76mm)
APC (W) 8 LAV-150 *Commando*
ARTY 104
TOWED 105mm 16: 4 M101; 12 *Reinosa* 105/26
MOR 88: **81mm** 60 M1; **107mm** 4 M-30; **120mm** 24 Expal Model L
AT
RCL 106mm 20 M40A1
GUNS 37mm 20 M3

HELICOPTERS

ISR 8: 4 OH-58A *Kiowa*; 4 OH-58C *Kiowa*

TPT • Light 6: 4 R-22; 2 R-44 *Raven* II

Navy 10,000

HQ located at Santo Domingo

FORCES BY ROLE

SPECIAL FORCES

1 (SEAL) SF unit

MANOEUVRE

Amphibious

1 mne sy unit

EQUIPMENT BY TYPE

PATROL AND COASTAL COMBATANTS 17

PCO 1 *Almirante Didiez Burgos* (ex-US *Balsam*)

PCC 2 *Tortuguero* (ex-US *White Sumac*)

PB 14: 2 *Altair* (Swiftships 35m); 4 *Bellatrix* (US Sewart Seacraft); 2 *Canopus* (Swiftships 101); 3 *Hamal* (Damen Stan 1505); 3 *Point*

AMPHIBIOUS 1 *Neyba* (ex-US LCU 1675)

LOGISTICS AND SUPPORT 13

AG 8

YFD 1

YTL 4

Air Force 10,000

Flying hours 60 hrs/year

FORCES BY ROLE

GROUND ATTACK

1 sqn with EMB-314 *Super Tucano**

SEARCH & RESCUE

1 sqn with Bell 205 (UH-1H *Huey II*); Bell 205 (UH-1H *Iroquois*); Bell 430 (VIP); OH-58 *Kiowa* (CH-136); S-333

TRANSPORT

1 sqn with C-212-400 *Aviocar*; PA-31 *Navajo*

TRAINING

1 sqn with T-35B *Pillan*

AIR DEFENCE

1 ADA bn with 20mm guns

EQUIPMENT BY TYPE

AIRCRAFT 8 combat capable

ISR 1 AMT-200 *Super Ximango*

TPT • Light 12: 3 C-212-400 *Aviocar*; 1 Cessna 172; 1 Cessna 182; 1 Cessna 206; 1 Cessna 207; 1 *Commander* 690; 3 EA-100; 1 PA-31 *Navajo*

TRG 13: 8 EMB-314 *Super Tucano**; 5 T-35B *Pillan*

HELICOPTERS

ISR 9 OH-58 *Kiowa* (CH-136)

TPT • Light 16: 8 Bell 205 (UH-1H *Huey* II); 5 Bell 205 (UH-1H *Iroquois*); 1 EC155 (VIP); 2 S-333

AD • GUNS 20mm 4

Paramilitary 15,000

National Police 15,000

Ecuador ECU

US Dollar $[a]		2012	2013	2014
GDP	US$	80.9bn	87bn	
per capita	US$	5,311	5,627	
Growth	%	4.97	4.45	
Inflation	%	5.10	4.66	
Def bdgt	US$	1.51bn	1.51bn	
FMA (US)	US$	0.45m	0.45m	0.45m

[a] The US dollar was adopted as the official currency in 2000

Population 15,439,429

Age	0–14	15–19	20–24	25–29	30–64	65 plus
Male	14.8%	4.9%	4.5%	4.2%	18.0%	3.2%
Female	14.2%	4.8%	4.5%	4.2%	19.1%	3.5%

Capabilities

Border security has long been a priority and a source of friction for the state. Clashes with Peru in the 1990s were only resolved in 1998 with a peace treaty. In recent years there has been tension with Colombia over their shared border and the impact of Colombia's conflict with FARC rebels. Defence policy is predicated on guaranteeing sovereignty and the territorial integrity of the state, with the desire for the armed forces to also participate in international peacekeeping. There has been a growing emphasis on maritime security, with a number of potential acquisitions intended to improve surveillance and patrol capabilities. The services take part in regular domestic exercises, with the army and navy also participating in exercises with international partners. Much of the services' inventory is ageing, with acquisitions often second-hand. The air force purchased ex-South African Air Force *Cheetah* fighter aircraft in 2011, while the navy's frigates were bought from Chile. A 2010 order for seven AS550C3 *Fennec* multi-role helicopters is expected to be complete by 2015. The armed forces have no genuine capacity for sustained power projection beyond national borders.

ACTIVE 58,000 (Army 46,500 Navy 7,300 Air 4,200)
Paramilitary 500

Conscript liability 1 year, selective

RESERVE 118,000 (Joint 118,000)

Ages 18–55

ORGANISATIONS BY SERVICE

Army 46,500

FORCES BY ROLE

gp are bn sized.

COMMAND

4 div HQ

SPECIAL FORCES

1 (9th) SF bde (3 SF gp; 1 SF sqn, 1 para bn,1 sigs sqn, 1 log comd)

MANOEUVRE
Mechanised
1 (11th) armd cav bde (3 armd cav gp, 1 mech inf bn, 1 SP arty gp, 1 engr gp)
1 (5th) inf bde (1 SF sqn, 2 mech cav gp, 2 inf bn, 1 cbt engr coy, 1 sigs coy, 1 log coy)
Light
1 (1st) inf bde (1 SF sqn, 1 armd cav gp, 1 armd recce sqn, 3 inf bn, 1 med coy)
1 (3rd) inf bde (1 SF gp, 1 mech cav gp, 1 inf bn, 1 arty gp, 1 hvy mor coy, 1 cbt engr coy, 1 sigs coy, 1 log coy)
1 (7th) inf bde (1 SF sqn, 1 armd recce sqn, 1 mech cav gp, 3 inf bn, 1 jungle bn, 1 arty gp, 1 cbt engr coy, 1 sigs coy, 1 log coy, 1 med coy)
1 (13th) inf bde (1 SF sqn, 1 armd recce sqn, 1 mot cav gp, 3 inf bn, 1 arty gp, 1 hvy mor coy, 1 cbt engr coy, 1sigs coy, 1 log coy)
Jungle
2 (17th & 21st) jungle bde (3 jungle bn, 1 cbt engr coy, 1 sigs coy, 1 log coy)
1 (19th) jungle bde (3 jungle bn, 1 jungle trg bn, 1 cbt engr coy, 1 sigs coy, 1 log coy)
Aviation
1 (15th) avn bde (2 tpt avn gp, 2 hel gp, 1 mixed avn gp)
COMBAT SUPPORT
1 (27th) arty bde (1 SP arty gp, 1 MRL gp, 1 ADA gp, 1 cbt engr coy, 1 sigs coy, 1 log coy)
1 ADA gp
1 (23rd) engr bde (3 engr bn)
2 indep MP coy
1 indep sigs coy
COMBAT SERVICE SUPPORT
1 (25th) log bde
2 log bn
2 indep med coy

EQUIPMENT BY TYPE
LT TK 24 AMX-13
RECCE 67: 25 AML-90; 10 EE-3 *Jararaca*; 32 EE-9 *Cascavel*
APC 123
APC (T) 95: 80 AMX-VCI; 15 M113
APC (W) 28: 18 EE-11 *Urutu*; 10 UR-416
ARTY 541+
SP 155mm 5 (AMX) Mk F3
TOWED 100: **105mm** 78: 30 M101; 24 M2A2; 24 Model 56 pack howitzer; **155mm** 22: 12 M114; 10 M198
MRL 122mm 24: 18 BM-21; 6 RM-70
MOR 412+: **81mm** 400 M-29; **107mm** M-30 (4.2in); **160mm** 12 M-66 Soltam
AT
RCL 404: **106mm** 24 M40A1; **90mm** 380 M67
AIRCRAFT
TPT • Light 15: 1 Beech 200 *King Air*; 2 C-212; 1 CN-235; 4 Cessna 172; 2 Cessna 206; 1 Cessna 500 *Citation* I; 4 IAI-201 *Arava*;
TRG 6: 2 MX-7-235 *Star Rocket*; 2 T-41D *Mescalero*; 2 CJ-6A
HELICOPTERS
MRH 29: 2 AS550C3 *Fennec*; 6 Mi-17-1V *Hip*; 3 SA315B *Lama*; 18 SA342L *Gazelle* (13 with HOT for anti-armour role)
TPT 11 **Medium** 7: 5 AS332B *Super Puma*; 2 Mi-171E; (3 SA330 *Puma* in store); **Light** 4: 2 AS350B *Ecureuil*; 2 AS350B2 *Ecureuil*
AD
SAM • MANPAD 185+: 75 *Blowpipe*; 20+ 9K32 *Strela*-2 (SA-7 *Grail*)‡; 90 9K38 *Igla* (SA-18 *Grouse*)
GUNS 240
SP 44 M163 *Vulcan*
TOWED 196: **14.5mm** 128 ZPU-1/-2; **20mm** 38: 28 M-1935, 10 M167 *Vulcan*; **40mm** 30 L/70/M1A1

Navy 7,300 (incl Naval Aviation, Marines and Coast Guard)

EQUIPMENT BY TYPE
SUBMARINES • TACTICAL • SSK 2:
2 *Shyri*† (GER T-209/1300, undergoing refit in Chile) each with 8 single 533mm TT each with SUT HWT
PRINCIPAL SURFACE COMBATANTS 2
FRIGATES 2
FFGHM 1 *Presidente Eloy Alfaro*† (ex-UK *Leander* batch II) with 4 single lnchr with MM-40 *Exocet* AShM, 3 twin lnchr with *Mistral* SAM, 1 *Phalanx* CIWS, 1 twin 114mm gun, (capacity 1 Bell 206B *Jet Ranger* II hel)
FFGH 1 *Condell* (mod UK *Leander*) with 4 single lnchr with MM-40 *Exocet* AShM, 2 triple ASTT with Mk 46 LWT, 1 *Phalanx* CIWS, 1 twin 114mm gun, (capacity 1 Bell 206B *Jet Ranger* II hel)
PATROL AND COASTAL COMBATANTS 9
CORVETTES • FSGM 6 *Esmeraldas* (4†) with 2 triple lnchr with MM-40 *Exocet* AShM, 1 quad *Albatros* lnchr with *Aspide* SAM, 2 triple B515 *ILAS-3* 324mm with A244 LWT (removed from two vessels), 1 76mm gun, 1 hel landing platform (upgrade programme ongoing)
PCFG 3 *Quito* (GER Lurssen TNC-45 45m) with 4 single lnchr with MM-38 *Exocet* AShM, 1 76mm gun (upgrade programme ongoing)
LOGISTICS AND SUPPORT 17
AE 1 *Culicuchima*
AGOS 1 *Orion*
AGS 1
AGSC 1 *Rigel*
AK 1 *Galapagos*
AOL 1 *Taurus*
ATF 1
AWT 2: 1 *Quisquis*; 1 *Atahualpa*
AXS 1 *Guayas*
YFD 2 *Rio Napo* (US ARD 12)
YTL 5

Naval Aviation 380

AIRCRAFT
MP 1 CN-235-300M
ISR 3: 2 Beech 200T *King Air*; 1 Beech 300 *Catpass King Air*
TPT • Light 3: 1 Beech 200 *King Air*; 1 Beech 300 *King Air*; 1 CN-235-100
TRG 6: 2 T-34C *Turbo Mentor*; 4 T-35B *Pillan*
HELICOPTERS
TPT • Light 9: 3 Bell 206A; 3 Bell 206B; 1 Bell 230; 2 Bell 430
UAV • ISR 6: **Heavy** 2 *Heron*; **Medium** 4 *Searcher* Mk.II

Marines 2,150

FORCES BY ROLE

SPECIAL FORCES

1 cdo unit

MANOEUVRE

Amphibious

5 mne bn (on garrison duties)

EQUIPMENT BY TYPE

ARTY • MOR 32+ 60mm/81mm/120mm

AD • SAM • MANPAD 64 *Mistral*/9K38 *Igla* (SA-18 *Grouse*)

Air Force 4,200

Operational Command

FORCES BY ROLE

FIGHTER

1 sqn with *Cheetah* C/D; *Mirage* 50DV/EV

FIGHTER/GROUND ATTACK

2 sqn with EMB-314 *Super Tucano**

1 sqn with *Kfir* C-10 (CE); *Kfir* C-2; *Kfir* TC-2

Military Air Transport Group

FORCES BY ROLE

SEARCH & RESCUE/TRANSPORT HELICOPTER

1 sqn with Bell 206B *Jet Ranger* II

1 sqn with *Dhruv*; PA-34 *Seneca*

TRANSPORT

1 sqn with C-130/H *Hercules*; L-100-30

1 sqn with HS-748

1 sqn with DHC-6-300 *Twin Otter*

1 sqn with B-727; EMB-135BJ *Legacy* 600; F-28 *Fellowship*; *Sabreliner* 40/60

TRAINING

1 sqn with Cessna 150/206; DA20-C1; MXP-650; T-34C *Turbo Mentor*

EQUIPMENT BY TYPE

AIRCRAFT 48 combat capable

FGA 31: 10 *Cheetah* C; 2 *Cheetah* D; 4 *Kfir* C-2; 7 *Kfir* C-10 (CE); 2 *Kfir* TC-2; 3 *Mirage* 50DV; 3 *Mirage* 50EV

TPT 35 **Medium** 4: 2 C-130B *Hercules*; 1 C-130H *Hercules*; 1 L-100-30; **Light** 21: 1 Beech E90 *King Air*; 7 Cessna 150; 1 Cessna 206; 3 DHC-6 *Twin Otter*; 1 EMB-135BJ *Legacy* 600; 2 EMB-170; 2 EMB-190; 1 MXP-650; 2 *Sabreliner* 40; 1 PA-34 *Seneca*; **PAX** 10: 2 A320; 2 B-727; 6 HS-748

TRG 35: 6 DA20-C1; 17 EMB-314 *Super Tucano**; 12 T-34C *Turbo Mentor*

HELICOPTERS

MRH 6 *Dhruv*

TPT • Light 8 Bell 206B *Jet Ranger* II

MSL • AAM • IR *Python* III; *Python* IV; R-550 *Magic*; *Shafrir*‡; **SARH** Super 530

AD

MSL

SAM 7 M48 *Chaparral*

SP 6 9K33 *Osa* (SA-8 *Gecko*)

MANPAD 185+: 75 *Blowpipe*; 9K32 *Strela-2* (SA-7 *Grail*)‡; 20 9K310 *Igla-1* (SA-16) *Gimlet*; 90 9K38 *Igla* (SA-18 *Grouse*)

GUNS

SP 20mm 28 M35

TOWED 64: **23mm** 34 ZU-23; **35mm** 30 GDF-002 (twin)

RADAR: 2 CFTC gap fillers; 2 CETC 2D

Paramilitary

All police forces; 39,500

Police Air Service

HELICOPTERS

ISR 3 MD530F

TPT • Light 6: 2 AS350B *Ecureuil*; 1 Bell 206B *Jet Ranger*; 3 R-44

Coast Guard 500

PATROL AND COASTAL COMBATANTS 18

PCC 3 *Isla Fernandina* (*Vigilante*)

PB 12: 1 *10 de Agosto*; 2 *Espada*; 1 *Isla Isabela*; 2 *Manta* (GER Lurssen 36m); 1 *Point*; 4 *Rio Coca*; 1 *Isla Santa Cruz* (Damen Stan 2606)

PBR 3: 2 *Río Esmeraldas*; 1 *Rio Puyango*

DEPLOYMENT

CÔTE D'IVOIRE

UN • UNOCI 2 obs

HAITI

UN • MINUSTAH 67; elm 1 engr coy

LIBERIA

UN • UNMIL 1; 2 obs

SOUTH SUDAN

UN • UNMISS 4 obs

SUDAN

UN • UNISFA 1; 1 obs

El Salvador SLV

El Salvador Colon C		2012	2013	2014
GDP	C	208bn	215bn	
	US$	23.8bn	24.6bn	
per capita	US$	3,823	3,935	
Growth	%	1.60	1.60	
Inflation	%	1.73	1.90	
Def bdgt	C	1.29bn	1.37bn	
	US$	145m	154m	
FMA (US)	US$	1.25m	1.25m	1.8m
US$1=C		8.75	8.75	

Population 6,108,590

Age	0–14	15–19	20–24	25–29	30–64	65 plus
Male	14.8%	5.6%	4.8%	3.9%	16.0%	3.0%
Female	14.1%	5.5%	4.9%	4.2%	19.4%	3.7%

Capabilities

Since the end of the country's civil war in 1992, the Salvadorian military has been dramatically reduced in size. Despite this, El Salvador has been able to deploy small forces to both Iraq and Afghanistan. Challenges for the armed forces include boosting professionalisation, and tackling organised crime and narcotics-trafficking. In 2009, high crime rates led the government to deploy the army in support of the police in high-crime areas, as well as helping to secure prisons and border crossings.

ACTIVE 15,300 **(Army 13,850 Navy 700 Air 750)**
Paramilitary 17,000
Conscript liability 18 months voluntary

RESERVE 9,900 **(Joint 9,900)**

ORGANISATIONS BY SERVICE

Army 9,850; 4,000 conscript (total 13,850)

FORCES BY ROLE
SPECIAL FORCES
1 spec ops gp (1 SF coy, 1 para bn, 1 (naval inf) coy)
MANOEUVRE
Reconnaissance
1 armd cav regt (2 armd cav bn)
Light
6 inf bde (3 inf bn)
Other
1 (special) sy bde (2 border gd bn, 2 MP bn)
COMBAT SUPPORT
1 arty bde (2 fd arty bn, 1 AD bn)
1 engr comd (2 engr bn)
EQUIPMENT BY TYPE
RECCE 5 AML-90; (4 more in store)
APC (W) 38: 30 M37B1 *Cashuat* (mod); 8 UR-416
ARTY 217+
TOWED 105mm 54: 36 M102; 18 M-56 (FRY)
MOR 163+: **81mm** 151 M29; **120mm** 12+: (M-74 in store); 12 UBM 52
AT
RCL 399: **106mm** 20 M40A1 (incl 16 SP); **90mm** 379 M67
AD • GUNS 35: **20mm** 31 M-55; 4 TCM-20

Navy 700 (incl some 90 Naval Inf and SF)

EQUIPMENT BY TYPE
PATROL AND COASTAL COMBATANTS 10
PB 10: 3 *Camcraft* (30m); 1 *Point*; 1 Swiftships 77; 1 Swiftships 65; 4 Type-44 (ex-USCG)
AMPHIBIOUS • LANDING CRAFT
LCM 4

Naval Inf (SF Commandos) 90

FORCES BY ROLE
SPECIAL FORCES
1 SF coy

Air Force 750 (incl 200 Air Defence)

Flying hours 90 hrs/year on A-37 *Dragonfly*

FORCES BY ROLE
FIGHTER/GROUND ATTACK/ISR
1 sqn with A-37B *Dragonfly*; O-2A *Skymaster**
TRANSPORT
1 sqn with BT-67; Cessna 210 *Centurion*; Cessna 337G; *Commander* 114; IAI-202 *Arava*; SA-226T *Merlin* IIIB
TRAINING
1 sqn with R-235GT *Guerrier*; T-35 *Pillan*; T-41D *Mescalero*; TH-300
TRANSPORT HELICOPTER
1 sqn with Bell 205 (UH-1H *Iroquois*); Bell 407; Bell 412EP *Twin Huey*; MD-500E; UH-1M *Iroquois*
EQUIPMENT BY TYPE
AIRCRAFT 16 combat capable
ATK 4 A-37B *Dragonfly*
ISR 11: 6 O-2A/B *Skymaster**; 5 OA-37B *Dragonfly**
TPT • Light 10: 2 BT-67; 2 Cessna 210 *Centurion*; 1 Cessna 337G *Skymaster*; 1 *Commander* 114; 3 IAI-201 *Arava*; 1 SA-226T *Merlin* IIIB
TRG 11: 5 R-235GT *Guerrier*; 5 T-35 *Pillan*; 1 T-41D *Mescalero*
HELICOPTERS
MRH 14: 4 Bell 412EP *Twin Huey*; 8 MD-500E; 2 UH-1M *Iroquois*
TPT• Light 19: 18 Bell 205 (UH-1H *Iroquois*) (incl 4 SAR); 1 Bell 407 (VIP tpt, govt owned)
TRG 5 TH-300
MSL • AAM • IR *Shafrir*‡

Paramilitary 17,000

National Civilian Police 17,000

Ministry of Public Security
AIRCRAFT
ISR 1 O-2A *Skymaster*
TPT • Light 1 Cessna 310
HELICOPTERS
MRH 2 MD-520N
TPT • Light 3: 1 Bell 205 (UH-1H *Iroquois*); 2 R-44 *Raven* II

DEPLOYMENT

AFGHANISTAN
NATO • ISAF 24

CÔTE D'IVOIRE
UN • UNOCI 3 obs

HAITI
UN • MINUSTAH 34

LEBANON
UN • UNIFIL 52; 1 inf pl

LIBERIA
UN • UNMIL 2 obs

SOUTH SUDAN
UN • UNMISS 2 obs

WESTERN SAHARA
UN • MINURSO 3 obs

FOREIGN FORCES

United States US Southern Command: 1 Forward Operating Location (Military, DEA, USCG and Customs personnel)

Guatemala GUA

Guatemalan Quetzal q		2012	2013	2014
GDP	q	391bn	420bn	
	US$	49.9bn	52.9bn	
per capita	US$	3,302	3,415	
Growth	%	3.00	3.30	
Inflation	%	3.78	4.30	
Def bdgt	q	1.65bn	2.04bn	
	US$	212m	256m	
FMA (US)	US$	0.5m	0.5m	1.74m
US$1=q		7.83	7.95	

Population 14,373,472

Age	0–14	15–19	20–24	25–29	30–64	65 plus
Male	18.7%	5.9%	5.2%	4.2%	13.4%	1.9%
Female	18.0%	5.8%	5.3%	4.4%	15.0%	2.2%

Capabilities

After the end of the Guatemalan civil war in 1996, the military was reduced in size and refocused exclusively on external threats. Acquisition of new equipment was extremely limited. Rising levels of organised crime and narcotics trafficking resulted in proposed increases to the defence budget, linked to new procurement and recruitment drives. In 2013, new brigades were established to assist with coastal and border security in San Marcos and Izabal departments. An order for six *Super Tucano* aircraft was put on hold, exacerbating the air force's current serviceability problems. Given the commonly transnational nature of organised criminality and narcotics trafficking in Central America, Guatemala's armed forces engage in close cooperation with their counterparts from Mexico, El Salvador and Honduras. The armed forces retain a limited capability to participate in international operations as well as HA/DR tasks.

ACTIVE 17,300 (Army 15,550 Navy 900 Air 850) **Paramilitary 25,000**

RESERVE 63,850 (Navy 650 Air 900 Armed Forces 62,300)

(National Armed Forces are combined; the army provides log spt for navy and air force)

ORGANISATIONS BY SERVICE

Army 15,550

15 Military Zones

FORCES BY ROLE

SPECIAL FORCES
1 SF bde (1 SF bn, 1 trg bn)
1 SF bde (1 SF coy, 1 ranger bn)
1 SF mtn bde

MANOEUVRE

Light
1 (strategic reserve) mech bde (1 inf bn, 1 cav regt, 1 log coy)
6 inf bde (1 inf bn)

Air Manoeuvre
1 AB bde with (2 AB bn)

Amphibious
1 mne bde

Other
1 (Presidential) gd bde (1 gd bn, 1 MP bn, 1 CSS coy)

COMBAT SUPPORT
1 engr comd (1 engr bn, 1 construction bn)
2 MP bde with (1 MP bn)

Reserves

FORCES BY ROLE

MANOEUVRE

Light
ε19 inf bn

EQUIPMENT BY TYPE

RECCE (7 M8 in store)
APC 47
APC (T) 10 M113 (5 more in store)
APC (W) 37: 30 *Armadillo*; 7 V-100 *Commando*
ARTY 149
TOWED 105mm 76: 12 M101; 8 M102; 56 M-56
MOR 73: **81mm** 55 M1 **107mm** (12 M-30 in store) **120mm** 18 ECIA
AT
RCL 120+: **105mm** 64 M-1974 FMK-1 (ARG); **106mm** 56 M40A1; **75mm** M20
AD • GUNS • TOWED 32: **20mm** 16 GAI-D01; 16 M-55

Navy 900

EQUIPMENT BY TYPE

PATROL AND COASTAL COMBATANTS 10
PB 10: 6 *Cutlass*; 1 *Dauntless*; 1 *Kukulkan* (US *Broadsword* 32m); 2 *Utatlan* (US *Sewart*)
AMPHIBIOUS • LANDING CRAFT • **LCP** 2 *Machete*
LOGISTICS AND SUPPORT • AXS 3

Marines 650 reservists

FORCES BY ROLE

MANOEUVRE

Amphibious
2 mne bn (-)

Air Force 850

2 Air Comd

FORCES BY ROLE

FIGHTER/GROUND ATTACK/ISR

1 sqn with A-37B *Dragonfly*

1 sqn with PC-7 *Turbo Trainer**

TRANSPORT

1 sqn with BT-67; Beech 90/100/200/300 *King Air*; IAI-201 *Arava*

1 (tactical support) sqn with Cessna 206; PA-31 *Navajo*

TRAINING

1 sqn with Cessna R172K *Hawk* XP; T-35B *Pillan*

TRANSPORT HELICOPTER

1 sqn with Bell 206 *Jet Ranger*; Bell 212 (armed); Bell 412 *Twin Huey* (armed); UH-1H *Iroquois*

EQUIPMENT BY TYPE

Serviceability of ac is less than 50%

AIRCRAFT 9 combat capable

ATK 2 A-37B *Dragonfly*

TPT • Light 27: 5 Beech 90 *King Air*; 1 Beech 100 *King Air*; 2 Beech 200 *King Air*; 2 Beech 300 *King Air*; 4 BT-67; 2 Cessna 206; 1 Cessna 208B; 5 Cessna R172K *Hawk* XP; 4 IAI-201 *Arava*; 1 PA-31 *Navajo*

TRG 11: 7 PC-7 *Turbo Trainer**; 4 T-35B *Pillan*

HELICOPTERS

MRH 2 Bell 412 *Twin Huey* (armed)

TPT • Light 18: 2 Bell 205 (UH-1H *Iroquois*); 9 Bell 206 *Jet Ranger*; 7 Bell 212 (armed)

Tactical Security Group

Air Military Police

Paramilitary 25,000 active

National Civil Police 25,000

FORCES BY ROLE

SPECIAL FORCES

1 SF bn

MANOEUVRE

Other

1 (integrated task force) paramilitary unit (incl mil and treasury police)

DEPLOYMENT

CÔTE D'IVOIRE

UN • UNOCI 5 obs

DEMOCRATIC REPUBLIC OF THE CONGO

UN • MONUSCO 151; 1 SF coy

HAITI

UN • MINUSTAH 138; 1 MP coy

LEBANON

UN • UNIFIL 1

SOUTH SUDAN

UN • UNMISS 1; 3 obs

SUDAN

UN • UNISFA 1 obs

Guyana GUY

Guyanese Dollar G$		2012	2013	2014
GDP	G$	575bn	630bn	
	US$	2.79bn	3.01bn	
per capita	US$	3,596	3,872	
Growth	%	3.35	5.51	
Inflation	%	2.97	5.59	
Def bdgt	G$	6.78bn	7.39bn	
	US$	33m	35m	
US$1=G$		206.09	209.13	

Population 739,903

Age	0–14	15–19	20–24	25–29	30–64	65 plus
Male	15.4%	5.8%	4.8%	3.9%	17.9%	2.1%
Female	14.8%	5.5%	4.5%	3.4%	18.9%	3.0%

Capabilities

The country has a very limited military capability based on the Guyana Defence Force, which also undertakes paramilitary and policing tasks. Border issues with Venezuela and Suriname have, in the past, been the focus of security concerns. Brazil is increasingly supportive of the country's modest defence needs.

ACTIVE 1,100 (Army 900 Navy 100 Air 100)

Active numbers combined Guyana Defence Force

RESERVE 670 (Army 500 Navy 170)

ORGANISATIONS BY SERVICE

Army 900

FORCES BY ROLE

SPECIAL FORCES

1 SF coy

MANOUEVRE

Light

1 inf bn

Other

1 (Presidential) gd bn

COMBAT SUPPORT

1 arty coy

1 (spt wpn) cbt spt coy

1 engr coy

EQUIPMENT BY TYPE

RECCE 9: 6 EE-9 *Cascavel* (reported); 3 S52 *Shorland*

ARTY 54

TOWED 130mm 6 M-46†

MOR 48: **81mm** 12 L16A1; **82mm** 18 M-43; **120mm** 18 M-43

Navy 100

EQUIPMENT BY TYPE

PATROL AND COASTAL COMBATANTS 5

PCO 1 *Essequibo* (ex-UK *River)*

PB 4 *Barracuda* (ex-US Type-44)

Air Force 100

FORCES BY ROLE

TRANSPORT

1 unit with Bell 206; Cessna 206; Y-12 (II)

EQUIPMENT BY TYPE

AIRCRAFT • TPT • Light 2: 1 Cessna 206; 1 Y-12 (II)

HELICOPTERS

MRH 1 Bell 412 *Twin Huey*†

TPT • Light 2 Bell 206

Haiti HTI

Haitian Gourde G		2012	2013	2014
GDP	G	329bn	369bn	
	US$	7.9bn	8.54bn	
per capita	US$	759	827	
Growth	%	2.82	6.50	
Inflation	%	6.78	6.75	
FMA (US)	US$			2m
US$1=G		41.64	43.23	

Population 9,893,934

Age	0–14	15–19	20–24	25–29	30–64	65 plus
Male	17.4%	5.7%	5.0%	4.3%	15.4%	1.8%
Female	17.3%	5.7%	5.1%	4.4%	15.7%	2.2%

Capabilities

Haiti has no active armed forces. On 1 June 2004, the United Nations established a multinational stabilisation mission in Haiti (MINUSTAH). Continuing tensions with MINUSTAH, following the 2010 earthquake and the 2011 cholera outbreak, have led to calls for national armed forces to be re-established. Following his election in 2011, President Michel Martelly asked international donors for US$95m to fund a new 3,500-strong army. The first group of eight Haitian recruits arrived in Ecuador in October 2012 for training, followed by a further 30 in January 2013; the military is eventually expected to number approximately 1,500. Given Haiti's history of conflict, natural disasters and lack of external threat, it is likely that the armed force will be given a primarily constabulary and internal security role.

Paramilitary 50

ORGANISATIONS BY SERVICE

Paramilitary 50

Coast Guard ε50

EQUIPMENT BY TYPE

PATROL AND COASTAL COMBATANTS • PB 8: 5 *Dauntless*; 3 3812-VCF

FOREIGN FORCES

Argentina 571; 1 inf bn; 1 hel coy; 1 spt coy; 1 fd hospital

Bolivia 208; 1 mech inf coy

Brazil 1,403; 1 inf bn; 1 engr coy

Canada 39

Chile 464; 1 mech inf bn; 1 hel coy; elm 1 engr coy

Ecuador 67; elm 1 engr coy

El Salvador 34

France 2

Guatemala 138; 1 MP coy

Honduras 1

Indonesia 169: 1 engr coy

Jordan 252; 1 inf coy

Korea, Republic of 2

Nepal 363; 2 inf coy

Paraguay 163; 1 engr coy

Peru 374; 1 inf coy

Philippines 157; 1 HQ coy

Sri Lanka 861; 1 inf bn

United States 8

Uruguay 950; 2 inf bn; 1 mne coy, 1 spt coy

Honduras HND

Honduran Lempira L		2012	2013	2014
GDP	L	360bn	391bn	
	US$	18.4bn	19bn	
per capita	US$	2,242	2,272	
Growth	%	3.30	3.30	
Inflation	%	5.20	5.70	
Def bdgt [a]	L	2.94bn	3.65bn	
	US$	151m	177m	
FMA (US)	US$	1m	1m	4.5m
US$1=L		19.59	20.57	

[a] Defence & national security budget

Population 8,448,465

Age	0–14	15–19	20–24	25–29	30–64	65 plus
Male	18.1%	5.7%	5.1%	4.5%	15.2%	1.7%
Female	17.4%	5.5%	4.9%	4.3%	15.4%	2.2%

Capabilities

Prior to the coup of 2009, the administration of President Manuel Zelaya appeared to have achieved some success in improving the conditions, morale and professionalism of the Honduran armed forces. Although recruitment levels improved, the declared target of a 15,000-strong armed forces was not achieved. Equipment maintenance and procurement still accounts for a tiny fraction of the defence budget, and is largely dependent on foreign aid. In 2011, the Honduran military began to be deployed in a paramilitary role, in conjunction with the police, in order to combat organised crime and narcotics trafficking. A new maritime special forces unit was established in 2012 to assist in this task. The US maintains a small military presence at Soto Cano air base.

ACTIVE 12,000 (Army 8,300 Navy 1,400 Air 2,300) Paramilitary 8,000

RESERVE 60,000 (Joint 60,000; Ex-servicemen registered)

ORGANISATIONS BY SERVICE

Army 8,300

6 Military Zones

FORCES BY ROLE

SPECIAL FORCES

1 (special tac) SF gp (1 SF bn, 1 inf/AB bn)

MANOEUVRE

Mechanised

1 armd cav regt (1 recce sqn, 1 lt tk sqn, 2 mech bn, 1 arty bty, 1 ADA bty)

Light

3 inf bde (3 inf bn, 1 arty bn)

1 inf bde (3 inf bn)

Other

1 (Presidential) gd coy

COMBAT SUPPORT

1 engr bn

Reserves

FORCES BY ROLE

MANOEUVRE

Light

1 inf bde

EQUIPMENT BY TYPE

LT TK 12 *Scorpion*

RECCE 57: 13 RBY-1; 40 *Saladin*; 3 *Scimitar*; 1 *Sultan*

ARTY 118+

TOWED 28: **105mm:** 24 M102**; 155mm:** 4 M198

MOR 90+: **60mm**; **81mm**; **120mm** 60 FMK-2; **160mm** 30 M-66

AT • RCL 170: **106mm** 50 M40A1; **84mm** 120 *Carl Gustav*

AD • GUNS 48: **20mm** 24 M55A2; 24 TCM-20

Navy 1,400

EQUIPMENT BY TYPE

PATROL AND COASTAL COMBATANTS 16

PB 16: 1 *Lempira* (Damen Stan 4207; 1 further vessel in build, expected ISD 2014); 1 *Chamelecon* (Swiftships 85); 1 *Tegucilgalpa* (US *Guardian* 32m); 4 *Guanaja* (ex-US Type-44); 3 *Guaymuras* (Swiftships 105); 5 *Nacaome* (Swiftships 65); 1 *Rio Coco* (US PB Mk III)

AMPHIBIOUS • LANDING CRAFT 3

LCU 1 *Punta Caxinas*

LCM 2

Marines 830

FORCES BY ROLE

MANOEUVRE

Amphibious

1 mne bn

Air Force 2,300

FORCES BY ROLE

FIGHTER/GROUND ATTACK

1 sqn with A-37B *Dragonfly*

1 sqn with F-5E/F *Tiger* II

GROUND ATTACK/ISR/TRAINING

1 unit with Cessna 182 *Skylane*; EMB-312 *Tucano*; MXT-7-180 *Star Rocket*

TRANSPORT

1 sqn with Beech 200 *King Air*; C-130A *Hercules*; Cessna 185/210; IAI-201 *Arava*; PA-42 *Cheyenne*; *Turbo Commander* 690

1 VIP flt with PA-31 *Navajo*; Bell 412SP *Twin Huey*

TRANSPORT HELICOPTER

1 sqn with Bell 205 (UH-1H *Iroquois*); Bell 412SP *Twin Huey*

EQUIPMENT BY TYPE

AIRCRAFT 17 combat capable

FTR 11: 9 F-5E *Tiger* II†; 2 F-5F *Tiger* II†

ATK 6 A-37B *Dragonfly*

TPT 11 **Medium** 1 C-130A *Hercules*; **Light** 10: 1 Beech 200 *King Air*; 2 Cessna 182 *Skylane*; 1 Cessna 185; 2 Cessna 210; 1 IAI-201 *Arava*; 1 PA-31 *Navajo*; 1 PA-42 *Cheyenne; 1 Turbo Commander* 690

TRG 16: 9 EMB-312 *Tucano*; 7 MXT-7-180 *Star Rocket*

HELICOPTERS

MRH 7: 5 Bell 412SP *Twin Huey*; 2 Hughes 500

TPT • Light 3: 2 Bell 205 (UH-1H *Iroquois*); 1 AS350 *Ecureuil*

MSL • AAM • IR *Shafrir*‡

Paramilitary 8,000

Public Security Forces 8,000

Ministry of Public Security and Defence; 11 regional comd

DEPLOYMENT

HAITI

UN • MINUSTAH 1

WESTERN SAHARA

UN • MINURSO 12 obs

FOREIGN FORCES

United States US Southern Command: 360; 1 avn bn with CH-47 *Chinook*; UH-60 *Black Hawk*

Jamaica JAM

Jamaican Dollar J$		2012	2013	2014
GDP	J$	1.35tr	1.45tr	
	US$	15.2bn	15.5bn	
per capita	US$	5,541	5,601	
Growth	%	0.08	0.55	
Inflation	%	7.29	8.49	
Def bdgt	J$	12.3bn	ε12.1bn	
	US$	139m	ε129m	
US$1=J$		88.46	93.86	

Population 2,909,714

Age	0–14	15–19	20–24	25–29	30–64	65 plus
Male	14.7%	5.6%	5.4%	4.5%	15.9%	3.5%
Female	14.2%	5.5%	5.4%	4.6%	16.5%	4.3%

Capabilities

Jamaica retains well-trained armed forces that rank among the most capable in the Caribbean, however the Jamaican Defence Forces (JDF) have little airlift capability and lack any significant capability to deploy internationally. The primary mission of the JDF is focused on internal security and it has been asked on occasion to provide assistance to the Jamaica Constabulary in its activities against organised crime; a role that has proven controversial domestically. Links with major Western armed forces, particularly the UK but also the US and Canada, enable specialist training. In 2011, Canadian forces deployed a small number of CH-146 helicopters to assist training the JDF in SAR missions.

ACTIVE 2,830 (Army 2,500 Coast Guard 190 Air 140)
(combined Jamaican Defence Force)

RESERVE 980 (Army 900 Navy 60 Air 20)

ORGANISATIONS BY SERVICE

Army 2,500

FORCES BY ROLE
MANOEUVRE
Light
2 inf bn
COMBAT SUPPORT
1 engr regt (4 engr sqn)
COMBAT SERVICE SUPPORT
1 spt bn (1 MP coy, 1 med coy, 1 log coy, 1 tpt coy)

EQUIPMENT BY TYPE
APC (W) 4 LAV-150 *Commando*
MOR 81mm 12 L16A1

Reserves

FORCES BY ROLE
MANOEUVRE
Light
1 inf bn

Coast Guard 190

EQUIPMENT BY TYPE
PATROL AND COASTAL COMBATANTS 11
PBF 3
PB 8: 3 *Cornwall* (Damen Stan 4207); 4 *Dauntless*; 1 *Paul Bogle* (US 31m)

Air Wing 140

Plus National Reserve

FORCES BY ROLE
MARITIME PATROL/TRANSPORT
1 flt with BN-2A *Defender*; Cessna 210M *Centurion*
SEARCH & RESCUE/TRANSPORT HELICOPTER
1 flt with Bell 407
1 flt with Bell 412EP
TRAINING
1 unit with Bell 206B3; DA40-180FP *Diamond Star*

EQUIPMENT BY TYPE
AIRCRAFT
TPT • Light 4: 1 BN-2A *Defender*; 1 Cessna 210M *Centurion*; 2 DA40-180FP *Diamond Star*
HELICOPTERS
MRH 2 Bell 412EP
TPT • Light 5: 2 Bell 206B3 *Jet Ranger*; 3 Bell 407

Mexico MEX

Mexican Peso NP		2012	2013	2014
GDP	NP	15.5tr	16.7tr	
	US$	1.18tr	1.27tr	
per capita	US$	10,247	10,989	
Growth	%	3.95	3.39	
Inflation	%	4.11	3.69	
Def bdgt [a]	NP	68.9bn	75.7bn	
	US$	5.24bn	5.78bn	
FMA (US)	US$	7m	7m	7m
US$1=NP		13.17	13.11	

[a] National security expenditure

Population 116,220,947

Age	0–14	15–19	20–24	25–29	30–64	65 plus
Male	14.0%	4.7%	4.4%	4.0%	18.6%	3.1%
Female	13.4%	4.5%	4.4%	4.2%	20.8%	3.8%

Capabilities

Although Mexico's armed forces retain a theoretical national-defence role, they do not train for conventional warfare and their equipment holdings are limited in this regard. Under the Calderón administration operations against drug cartels became the army's primary activity, involving about a quarter of its active strength at any given time, whilst the navy and air force both prioritised procurement of ISR and transport platforms. Whether this situation will continue under President Peña Nieto is unclear. A new National Gendarmerie is being formed, but plans for an initial establishment of 10,000 have been subsequently reduced to 5,000 and activation has been delayed to 2014. A continuing problem with desertion has prompted efforts to improve benefits, training and conditions for serving personnel. The armed forces are constitutionally disbarred from international deployment except in wartime, but have been involved in HA/DR operations.

ACTIVE 270,250 (Army 200,000 Navy 58,500 Air 11,750) Paramilitary 59,500

RESERVE 87,350 (National Military Service)

ORGANISATIONS BY SERVICE

Space

SATELLITES • COMMUNICATIONS 1 *Mexsat*

Army 200,000

12 regions (total: 46 army zones). The army consists of one manoeurvre corps (1st), with three inf bde and one armd bde, one SF corps, one AB corps and one MP corps. Command-and-control functions have been redesigned and decentralised, allowing greater independence for each of the 12 Military Region commanders and establishing C4 units in every region.

FORCES BY ROLE

SPECIAL FORCES
3 SF bde (12 SF bn)
1 amph SF bde (5 SF bn)

MANOEUVRE

Reconnaissance
3 armd bde (2 armd recce bn, 2 lt armd recce bn, 1 (Canon) AT gp)
3 armd recce regt
2 lt armd recce regt
25 mot recce regt

Light
1 (1st) armd corps (1 armd bde (2 armd recce bn, 2 lt armd recce bn, 1 (Canon) AT gp), 3 inf/rapid reaction bde (each: 3 inf bn, 1 arty regt, 1 (Canon) AT gp), 1 cbt engr bde (3 engr bn))
3 indep lt inf bde (2 lt inf bn, 1 (Canon) AT gp)
106 indep inf bn
25 indep inf coy

Air Manoeuvre
1 para bde with (1 (GAFE) SF gp, 3 bn, 1 (Canon) AT gp)

Other
1 (Presidential) gd corps (1 SF gp, 1 mech inf bde (2 inf bn, 1 aslt bn), 1 mne bn (Navy), 1 cbt engr bn, 1 MP bde (3 bn, 1 special ops anti-riot coy))

COMBAT SUPPORT
6 indep arty regt
2 MP bde (3 MP bn)

EQUIPMENT BY TYPE

RECCE 237: 124 ERC-90F1 *Lynx* (4 trg); 40 M8; 41 MAC-1; 32 VBL

APC 706
APC (T) 472: 398 DNC-1 (mod AMX-VCI); 40 HWK-11; 34 M5A1 half-track
APC (W) 234: 95 BDX; 25 DN-4; 19 DN-5 *Toro*; 26 LAV-150 ST; 25 MOWAG *Roland*; 44 VCR (3 amb; 5 cmd post)

ARTY 1,390
TOWED 123: **105mm** 123: 40 M101; 40 M-56; 16 M2A1, 14 M3; 13 NORINCO M-90
MOR 1,267: **81mm** 1,100: 400 M1; 400 Brandt; 300 SB
120mm 167: 75 Brandt; 60 M-65; 32 RT61

AT
MSL • SP 8 *Milan* (VBL)
RCL 1,187+
SP 106mm M40A1
106mm M40A1
GUNS 37mm 30 M3

AD
GUNS 80
TOWED 12.7mm 40 M55; **20mm** 40 GAI-B01
ARV 3 M32 *Recovery Sherman*

Navy 58,500

HQ at Acapulco; HQ (exercise) at Vera Cruz. Two Fleet Commands: Gulf (6 zones), Pacific (11 zones)

EQUIPMENT BY TYPE

PRINCIPAL SURFACE COMBATANTS 7
FRIGATES 7
FFGHM 4 *Allende* (US *Knox*) with 1 octuple Mk16 lnchr with ASROC/RGM-84C *Harpoon* AShM, 1 Mk25 GMLS with *Sea Sparrow* SAM, 2 twin Mk32 324mm ASTT with Mk46 LWT, 1 127mm gun, (capacity 1 MD-902 hel)
FF 3:
1 *Quetzalcoatl* with 2 twin 127mm gun, 1 hel landing platform
2 *Bravo* (US *Bronstein*) with 1 octuple Mk112 lnchr with ASROC, 2 triple Mk32 324mm ASTT with Mk46 LWT, 1 twin 76mm gun, 1 hel landing platform

PATROL AND COASTAL COMBATANTS 127
PSOH 4 *Oaxaca* with 1 76mm gun (capacity 1 AS-565MB *Panther* hel)
PCOH 17:
4 *Durango* (capacity 1 Bo-105 hel)
4 *Holzinger* (capacity 1 MD-902 *Explorer*) with 1 57mm gun
3 *Sierra* (capacity 1 MD-902 *Explorer*) with 1 57mm gun
6 *Uribe* (ESP *Halcon*) (capacity 1 Bo-105 hel)
PCO 10 *Leandro Valle* (US *Auk* MSF) with 1 76mm gun (being withdrawn from service; to be replaced with 4 additional *Oaxaca*-class)
PCG 2 *Huracan* (ISR *Aliya*) with 4 single lnchr with *Gabriel* II AShM, 1 *Phalanx* CIWS
PCC 2 *Democrata*
PBF 75: 6 *Acuario*; 2 *Acuario B*; 4 *Isla* (US *Halter*); 48 *Polaris* (SWE CB90); 15 *Polaris II* (SWE IC 16M; two further under construction, 24 vessels envisaged)
PB 17: 10 *Azteca*; 3 *Cabo* (US *Cape Higgon*); 2 *Punta* (US *Point*); 2 *Tenochtitlan* (Damen Stan 4207; one additonal vessel under construction, two more ordered)

AMPHIBIOUS • LS • LST 2 *Papaloapan* (US *Newport*) with 4 76mm guns

LOGISTICS AND SUPPORT 53

AFD 5

AG 2

AGOR 3: 2 *Altair* (ex-US *Robert D. Conrad*); 1 *Humboldt*

AGS 8: 4 *Arrecife*; 1 *Onjuku*; 1 *Rio Hondo*; 1 *Rio Tuxpan*; 1 *Moctezuma* II (also used as AXS)

AK 4: 1 *Tarasco*; 1 *Rio Suchiate*; 2 *Montes Azules* (can also be used as landing ship, 1 hel landing platform)

ATF 4 *Otomi* with 1 76mm gun

AX 3: 1 *Manuel Azuela*; 2 *Huasteco* (also serve as troop transport, supply and hospital ships)

AXS 1 *Cuauhtemoc* with 2 65mm saluting guns

YTL 6

YM 17

Naval Aviation 1,250

FORCES BY ROLE

MARITIME PATROL

5 sqn with Cessna 404 *Titan*; MX-7 *Star Rocket*; Lancair IV-P

1 sqn with C-212PM *Aviocar**; CN-235-300 MPA *Persuader*

1 sqn with L-90 *Redigo*

TRANSPORT

1 sqn with An-32B *Cline*

1 (VIP) sqn with DHC-8 *Dash 8*; Learjet 24; *Turbo Commander* 1000

TRANSPORT HELICOPTER

2 sqn with AS555 *Fennec*; AS-565MB *Panther*; MD-902; PZL Mi-2 *Hoplite*

2 sqn with Bo-105 CBS-5

5 sqn with Mi-17-1V/V-5 *Hip*

EQUIPMENT BY TYPE

AIRCRAFT 7 combat capable

MP 6 CN-235-300 MPA *Persuader*

ISR 7 C-212PM *Aviocar**

TPT • Light 23: 3 An-32B *Cline*; 4 C-295M; 1 Cessna 404 *Titan*; 1 DHC-8 *Dash 8*; 6 Lancair IV-P; 3 Learjet 24; 5 *Turbo Commander* 1000

TRG 15: 3 L-90TP *Redigo*; 4 MX-7 *Star Rocket*; 8 Z-242L

HELICOPTERS

MRH 29: 2 AS555 *Fennec*; 4 MD-500E; 22 Mi-17-1V *Hip*; 1 Mi-17V-5 *Hip*

SAR 4 AS565MB *Panther*

TPT 23 **Medium** 3 UH-60M *Black Hawk*; **Light** 20: 11 Bo-105 CBS-5; 6 MD-902 (SAR role); 2 PZL Mi-2 *Hoplite*; 1 R-44

Marines 21,500 (Expanding to 26,560)

FORCES BY ROLE

SPECIAL FORCES

3 SF unit

MANOEUVRE

Light

32 inf bn(-)

Air Manoeuvre

1 AB bn

Amphibious

2 amph bde

Other

1 (Presidential) gd bn (included in army above)

COMBAT SERVICE SUPPORT

2 CSS bn

EQUIPMENT BY TYPE

APC (W) 29: 3 BTR-60 (APC-60); 26 BTR-70 (APC-70)

ARTY 122

TOWED 105mm 16 M-56

MRL 122mm 6 Firos-25

MOR 100 **60mm/81mm**

AT • RCL 106mm M40A1

AD • SAM • MANPAD 5+ 9K38 *Igla* (SA-18 *Grouse*)

Air Force 11,750

FORCES BY ROLE

FIGHTER

1 sqn with F-5E/F *Tiger* II

GROUND ATTACK/ISR

4 sqn with PC-7*

1 sqn with PC-7*/PC-9M

ISR/AEW

1 sqn with EMB-145AEW *Erieye*; EMB-145RS; SA-2-37B; SA-227-BC *Metro* III (C-26B)

TRANSPORT

1 sqn with IAI-201 *Arava*; C-295M; PC-6B

1 squadron with B-727; Beech 90

1 sqn with C-27J *Spartan*; C-130E/K *Hercules*; L-100-30

6 (liaison) sqn with Cessna 182/206

1 (anti-narcotic spraying) sqn with Bell 206; Cessna T206H;

1 (Presidential) gp with AS332L *Super Puma*; B-737; B-757; EC225; Gulfstream III; Learjet 35A; Learjet 36A; *Turbo Commander* 680

1 (VIP) gp with B-737; Beech 200 *King Air*; Cessna 500 *Citation*; L-1329 *Jetstar* 8; S-70A-24

TRAINING

1 sqn with Beech F-33C *Bonanza*

1 sqn with PC-7*

1 sqn with SF-260EU

1 sqn (forming) with T-6C *Texan* II

1 unit with PC-7*

TRANSPORT HELICOPTER

1 sqn with Bell 206B; Bell 212; S-65 *Yas'ur* 2000

3 sqn with Bell 206B; Bell 212

1 sqn with MD-530F/MG

1 sqn with Mi-8T; Mi-17; Mi-26T

1 sqn with AS532L *Cougar*; Bell 412EP *Twin Huey*; S-70A-24 *Black Hawk*

ISR UAV

1 unit with *Hermes* 450; *Skylark* MkI

EQUIPMENT BY TYPE

AIRCRAFT 76 combat capable

FTR 10: 8 F-5E *Tiger* II; 2 F-5F *Tiger* II

ISR 6: 2 SA-2-37A; 4 SA-227-BC *Metro* III (C-26B)

ELINT 2 EMB-145RS

AEW&C 1 EMB-145AEW *Erieye*

TPT 124 **Medium** 12: 4 C-27J *Spartan*; 3 C-130E *Hercules*; 2 C-130K *Hercules*; 2 C-130K-30 *Hercules*; 1 L-100-30;

Light 104: 2 Beech 90 *King Air*; 1 Beech 200 *King Air*; 10 C-295M; 59 Cessna 182; 3 Cessna 206; 8 Cessna T206H; 1 Cessna 500 *Citation*; 3 IAI-101B *Arava*; 2 IAI 102 *Arava*; 6 IAI-202 *Arava*; 1 L-1329 *Jetstar* 8; 2 Learjet 35A; 1 Learjet 36; 4 PC-6B; 1 *Turbo Commander* 680; **PAX** 8: 3 B-727; 2 B-737; 1 B-757; 2 Gulfstream III
TRG 122: 20 Beech F33C *Bonanza*; 64 PC-7*; 2 PC-9M*; 7 PT-17; 25 SF-260EU; 4 T-6C *Texan* II

HELICOPTERS
MRH 31: 11 Bell 412EP *Twin Huey*; 20 Mi-17 *Hip* H
ISR 14: 5 MD-530MF; 9 MD-530MG
TPT 107 **Heavy** 7: 2 EC725 *Super Cougar*; 1 Mi-26T *Halo*; 4 S-65C *Yas'ur* 2000; **Medium** 21: 3 AS332L *Super Puma*; 2 AS532UL *Cougar* (on loan); 2 EC225 (VIP); 8 Mi-8T *Hip*; 6 S-70A-24 *Black Hawk*; **Light** 79: 45 Bell 206; 13 Bell 206B *Jet Ranger* II; 7 Bell 206L; 14 Bell 212

UAV • ISR 4 **Medium** 2 *Hermes* 450; **Light** 2 *Skylark* MkI
MSL • AAM • IR AIM-9J *Sidewinder*

Paramilitary 59,500

Federal Police 37,000
Public Security Secretariat
AIRCRAFT
TPT 13 **Light** 7: 2 CN-235M; 2 Cessna 182 *Skylane*; 1 Cessna 500 *Citation;* 2 *Turbo Commander* 695; **PAX** 6: 4 B-727; 1 *Falcon* 20; 1 Gulfstream II
HELICOPTERS
MRH 3 Mi-17 *Hip* H
TPT 24 **Medium** 10: 1 SA330J *Puma;* 6 UH-60L *Black Hawk*; 3 UH-60M *Black Hawk*; **Light** 14: 2 AS350B *Ecureuil*; 1 AS355 *Ecureuil* II; 6 Bell 206B; 5 EC-120
UAV • ISR • Light 2 S4 *Ehécatl*

Federal Ministerial Police 4,500
EQUIPMENT BY TYPE
HELICOPTERS
TPT • Light 35: 18 Bell 205 (UH-1H); 7 Bell 212; 10 Schweizer 333

Rural Defense Militia 18,000
FORCES BY ROLE
MANOEUVRE Light
13 inf unit
13 (horsed) cav unit

Nicaragua NIC

Nicaraguan Gold Cordoba Co		2012	2013	2014
GDP	Co	247bn	275bn	
	US$	10.5bn	11.1bn	
per capita	US$	1,757	1,833	
Growth	%	5.21	4.00	
Inflation	%	7.93	7.02	
Def bdgt	Co	1.55bn	2.1bn	
	US$	66m	85m	
FMA (US)	US$			0.39m
US$1=Co		23.55	24.73	

Population 5,788,531

Age	0–14	15–19	20–24	25–29	30–64	65 plus
Male	15.3%	5.8%	5.5%	4.4%	15.8%	2.1%
Female	14.7%	5.7%	5.5%	4.6%	17.9%	2.6%

Capabilities

The Nicaraguan military is dispersed geographically around the country in order to provide assistance to border- and internal-security operations, with a central reserve focused on a single mechanised brigade. Specialised units focused on disaster relief, coastal security and combatting illegal logging were added in 2010, 2011 and 2012 respectively. Other new units are under discussion, with a focus on new marine and land force contingents to tackle drug traffickers. Major equipment is almost entirely of a Cold War vintage, but has seen some recent modernisation and refurbishment.

ACTIVE 12,000 (Army 10,000 Navy 800 Air 1,200)

ORGANISATIONS BY SERVICE

Army ε10,000
FORCES BY ROLE
SPECIAL FORCES
1 SF bde with (2 SF bn)
MANOEUVRE
Mechanised
1 mech inf bde with (1 armd recce bn, 1 tk bn, 1 mech inf bn, 1 arty bn, 1 MRL bn, 1 AT coy)
Light
1 regional comd with (3 lt inf bn)
4 regional comd with (2 lt inf bn)
2 indep lt inf bn
Other
1 comd regt with (1 inf bn, 1 sy bn, 1 int unit, 1 sigs bn)
COMBAT SUPPORT
1 engr bn
COMBAT SERVICE SUPPORT
1 med bn
1 tpt regt
EQUIPMENT BY TYPE
MBT 62 T-55 (65 more in store)
LT TK (10 PT-76 in store)

RECCE 20 BRDM-2
APC (W) 86: 41 BTR-152 (61 more in store); 45 BTR-60 (15 more in store)
ARTY 796
TOWED 42: **122mm** 12 D-30; **152mm** 30 D-20 in store
MRL 151: **107mm** 33 Type-63**: 122mm** 118: 18 BM-21; 100 GRAD 1P (BM-21P) (single-tube rocket launcher, man portable)
MOR 603: **82mm** 579; **120mm** 24 M-43; (**160mm** 4 M-160 in store)
AT
MSL
SP 12 BRDM-2 *Sagger*
MANPATS 9K11 *Malyutka* (AT-3 *Sagger*)
RCL 82mm B-10
GUNS 281: **100mm** 24 M-1944; **57mm** 174 ZIS-2; (90 more in store); **76mm** 83 ZIS-3
AD • SAM • MANPAD 200+ 9K36 *Strela*-3 (SA-14 *Gremlin*); 9K310 *Igla*-1 (SA-16 *Gimlet*); 9K32 *Strela*-2 (SA-7 *Grail*)‡
AEV T-54/T-55
VLB TMM-3

Navy ε800

EQUIPMENT BY TYPE
PATROL AND COASTAL COMBATANTS • PB 8: 3 *Dabur*; 4 Rodman 101, 1 *Zhuk*

Marines

FORCES BY ROLE
MANOEUVRE
Amphibious
1 mne bn

Air Force 1,200

FORCES BY ROLE
TRANSPORT
1 sqn with An-26 *Curl*; Beech 90 *King Air*; Cessna U206; Cessna 404 *Titan* (VIP)
TRAINING
1 unit with Cessna 172; PA-18 *Super Cub*; PA-28 *Cherokee*
TRANSPORT HELICOPTER
1 sqn with Mi-17 *Hip* H (armed)
AIR DEFENCE
1 gp with ZU-23; C3-*Morigla* M1
EQUIPMENT BY TYPE
AIRCRAFT
TPT • Light 9: 3 An-26 *Curl*; 1 Beech 90 *King Air*; 1 Cessna 172; 1 Cessna U206; 1 Cessna 404 *Titan* (VIP); 2 PA-28 *Cherokee*
TRG 2 PA-18 *Super Cub*
HELICOPTERS
MRH 7 Mi-17 *Hip* H (armed)†
TPT • Medium 2 Mi-171E
AD • GUNS 36: 18 ZU-23; 18 C3-*Morigla* M1
MSL • ASM AT-2 *Swatter*

Panama PAN

Panamanian Balboa B		2012	2013	2014
GDP	B	36.3bn	41.5bn	
	US$	36.3bn	41.5bn	
per capita	US$	9,919	11,150	
Growth	%	10.67	8.98	
Inflation	%	5.70	5.20	
Def bdgt [a]	B	548m	637m	
	US$	551m	637m	
FMA (US)	US$	2.34m	2.34m	1.84m
US$1=B		1.00	1.00	

[a] Public security expenditure

Population 3,559,408

Age	0–14	15–19	20–24	25–29	30–64	65 plus
Male	14.1%	4.6%	4.3%	4.1%	19.8%	3.5%
Female	13.6%	4.4%	4.1%	3.9%	19.6%	4.1%

Capabilities

The Panamanian armed forces were abolished in 1990. A police force and an air/naval coast guard organisation were retained for low-level security activities. Panama would rely on its close relationship with the United States in the face of any significant threats.

Paramilitary 12,000

ORGANISATIONS BY SERVICE

Paramilitary 12,000

National Police Force 11,000

No hy mil eqpt, small arms only
FORCES BY ROLE
SPECIAL FORCES
1 SF unit (reported)
MANOEUVRE
Other
1 (presidential) gd bn (-)
8 paramilitary coy
18 police coy
COMBAT SUPPORT
1 MP bn

National Aeronaval Service ε1,000

FORCES BY ROLE
TRANSPORT
1 sqn with C-212M *Aviocar*; Cessna 210; PA-31 *Navajo*; PA-34 *Seneca*
1 (Presidential) flt with ERJ-135BJ; S-76C
TRAINING
1 unit with Cessna 152; Cessna 172; T-35D *Pillan*
TRANSPORT HELICOPTER
1 sqn with AW139; Bell 205; Bell 205 (UH-1H *Iroquois*); Bell 212; Bell 407; Bell 412; EC145; MD-500E

EQUIPMENT BY TYPE

PATROL AND COASTAL COMBATANTS 23

PCO 1 *Independencia* (ex-US *Balsam*)

PB 22: 3 *Chiriqui* (ex-US PB MkIV); 1 *Escudo de Veraguas;* 1 *Naos;* 1 *Negrita*†; 2 *Panama;* 2 *Panquiaco* (UK Vosper 31.5m); 5 *3 De Noviembre* (ex-US *Point*), 1 *Taboga;* 2 *Saettia;* 4 Type-200

AMPHIBIOUS • LANDING CRAFT • LCU 1 *General Estaban Huertas*

LOGISTICS AND SUPPORT 9

AG 2

YAG 7: 1 *Nombre de Dios* (US MSB 5); 1 *Isla Paridas;* 5 others

AIRCRAFT

TPT • Light 12: 5 C-212M *Aviocar;* 1 Cessna 152, 1 Cessna 172; 1 Cessna 210; 1 ERJ-135BJ; 1 PA-31 *Navajo;* 2 PA-34 *Seneca*

TRG 6 T-35D *Pillan*

HELICOPTERS

MRH 9: 6 AW139; 2 Bell 412; 1 MD-500E

TPT • Light 21: 2 Bell 205; 13 Bell 205 (UH-1H *Iroquois*); 2 Bell 212; 2 Bell 407; 1 EC145; 1 S-76C

Paraguay PRY

Paraguayan Guarani Pg		2012	2013	2014
GDP	Pg	115tr	131tr	
	US$	26bn	30.9bn	
per capita	US$	3,903	4,542	
Growth	%	-1.20	11.00	
Inflation	%	3.79	3.55	
Def bdgt	Pg	1.46tr	1.54tr	
	US$	332m	364m	
FMA (US)	US$	0.35m	0.35m	
US$1=Pg		4413.95	4235.82	

Population	6,623,252

Age	0–14	15–19	20–24	25–29	30–64	65 plus
Male	13.6%	5.4%	5.0%	4.3%	18.7%	3.0%
Female	13.2%	5.3%	5.0%	4.4%	18.5%	3.4%

Capabilities

The potential re-emergence of a territorial dispute with Bolivia over the Chaco region is one of the country's present security concerns. This is contributing to increased interest in renewing elements of the military's equipment inventory, much of which is obsolete. The army continues to use very old land systems, while the air force has a small number of light counter-insurgency aircraft and a variety of utility and tactical transport aircraft. Though land-locked, the country supports a naval force of mainly river patrol craft, reflecting the importance of its river systems. The armed forces have no capacity for power projection. The services train regularly and on a limited scale participate in UN peacekeeping missions.

ACTIVE 10,650 (Army 7,600 Navy 1,950 Air 1,100)

Paramilitary 14,800

Conscript liability 12 months Navy 2 years

RESERVE 164,500 (Joint 164,500)

ORGANISATIONS BY SERVICE

Army 6,100; 1,500 conscript (total 7,600)

Much of the Paraguayan army is maintained in a cadre state during peacetime; the nominal inf and cav divs are effectively only at coy strength. Active gp/regt are usually coy sized.

FORCES BY ROLE

MANOEUVRE

Reconnaissance

1 armd cav sqn

Light

3 inf corps (total: 6 inf div (-), 3 cav div (-), 6 arty bty)

Other

1 (Presidential) gd regt (1 SF bn, 1 inf bn, 1 sy bn, 1 log gp)

COMBAT SUPPORT

1 arty bde with (2 arty gp, 1 ADA gp)

1 engr bde with (1 engr regt, 3 construction regt)

1 sigs bn

Reserves

MANOEUVRE

Light

14 inf regt (cadre)

4 cav regt (cadre)

EQUIPMENT BY TYPE

MBT 3 M4A3 *Sherman*

LT TK 12 M3A1 *Stuart* (6†)

RECCE 28 EE-9 *Cascavel*

APC (T) 20 M9 half-track

APC (W) 12 EE-11 *Urutu*

ARTY 94

TOWED 105mm 14 M101

MOR 81mm 80

AT

RCL 75mm M20

AD • GUNS 19:

SP 20mm 3 M9

TOWED 16: **40mm** 10 M1A1, 6 L/60

Navy 1,100; 850 conscript (total 1,950)

EQUIPMENT BY TYPE

PATROL AND COASTAL COMBATANTS 22

PCR 3: 1 *Itaipú;* 1 *Nanawa*†; 1 *Paraguay*† with 2 twin 120mm gun, 3 76mm gun

PBR 19: 1 *Capitan Cabral;* 2 *Capitan Ortiz* (ROC *Hai Ou*); 2 *Novatec;* 6 Type-701; 3 Croq 15; 5 others

AMPHIBIOUS • LANDING CRAFT • LCVP 3

LOGISTICS AND SUPPORT 5:

YAC 1

YGS 1

YTL 3

Naval Aviation 100

FORCES BY ROLE

TRANSPORT

1 (liaison) sqn with Cessna 150; Cessna 210 *Centurion*; Cessna 310; Cessna 401

TRANSPORT HELICOPTER

1 sqn with AS350 *Ecureuil* (HB350 *Esquilo*); Bell 47 (OH-13 *Sioux*)

EQUIPMENT BY TYPE

AIRCRAFT • TPT • Light 6: 2 Cessna 150; 1 Cessna 210 *Centurion*; 2 Cessna 310; 1 Cessna 401

HELICOPTERS

TPT • Light 2 AS350 *Ecureuil* (HB350 *Esquilo*)

TRG 1 Bell 47 (OH-13 *Sioux*)

Marines 700; 200 conscript (total 900)

FORCES BY ROLE

MANOEUVRE

Amphibious

3 mne bn(-)

Air Force 900; 200 conscript (total 1,100)

FORCES BY ROLE

GROUND ATTACK/ISR

1 sqn with EMB-312 *Tucano**

TRANSPORT

1 gp with B-707; C-212-200/400 *Aviocar*; DHC-6 *Twin Otter*

1 VIP gp with Beech 58 *Baron*; Bell 427; Cessna U206 *Stationair*; Cessna 208B *Grand Caravan*; Cessna 210 *Centurion*; Cessna 402B; PA-32R *Saratoga* (EMB-721C *Sertanejo*); PZL-104 *Wilga* 80

TRAINING

1 sqn with T-25 *Universal*; T-35A/B *Pillan*

TRANSPORT HELICOPTER

1 gp with AS350 *Ecureuil* (HB350 *Esquilo*); Bell 205 (UH-1H *Iroquois*)

EQUIPMENT BY TYPE

AIRCRAFT 6 combat capable

TPT • Light 19: 1 Beech 58 *Baron*; 4 C-212-200 *Aviocar*; 2 C-212-400 *Aviocar*; 2 Cessna 208B *Grand Caravan*; 1 Cessna 210 *Centurion*; 1 Cessna 310; 2 Cessna 402B; 2 Cessna U206 *Stationair*; 1 DHC-6 *Twin Otter*; 1 PA-32R *Saratoga* (EMB-721C *Sertanejo*); 2 PZL-104 *Wilga* 80

TRG 22: 6 EMB-312 *Tucano**; 6 T-25 *Universal*; 7 T-35A *Pillan*; 3 T-35B *Pillan*

HELICOPTERS • TPT • Light 10: 3 AS350 *Ecureuil* (HB350 *Esquilo*); 6 Bell 205 (UH-1H *Iroquois*); 1 Bell 427 (VIP)

Paramilitary 14,800

Special Police Service 10,800; 4,000 conscript (total 14,800)

DEPLOYMENT

CÔTE D'IVOIRE

UN • UNOCI 2; 7 obs

CYPRUS

UN • UNFICYP 14

DEMOCRATIC REPUBLIC OF THE CONGO

UN • MONUSCO 17 obs

HAITI

UN • MINUSTAH 163; 1 engr coy

LIBERIA

UN • UNMIL 1; 2 obs

SOUTH SUDAN

UN • UNMISS 3 obs

SUDAN

UN • UNISFA 1; 3 obs

WESTERN SAHARA

UN • MINURSO 6 obs

Peru PER

Peruvian Nuevo Sol NS		2012	2013	2014
GDP	NS	526bn	577bn	
	US$	199bn	221bn	
per capita	US$	6,530	7,136	
Growth	%	6.28	6.28	
Inflation	%	3.66	2.07	
Def exp	NS	6.47bn		
	US$	2.45bn		
Def bdgt	NS	7bn	7.44bn	
	US$	2.65bn	2.84bn	
FMA (US)	US$	1.98m	1.98m	2.5m
US$1=NS		2.64	2.61	

Population 29,849,303

Age	0–14	15–19	20–24	25–29	30–64	65 plus
Male	14.1%	5.0%	4.7%	4.0%	18.3%	3.2%
Female	13.6%	4.9%	4.8%	4.2%	19.7%	3.5%

Capabilities

The armed forces have been involved in a decades-long conflict with Shining Path leftist guerrillas, which has influenced strongly the focus of the armed services, in particular the army. Territorial disputes have, in the past, also led to clashes, most notably with Ecuador in 1995. The government has a military modernisation programme intended to shape the forces to better meet its perceived future security requirements. The air force is well-equipped by regional standards, and continues to upgrade some of its primary platforms. A further upgrade of the MiG-29 and a possible update of the *Mirage* 2000 were in the pipeline in 2013. Internal security remains the army's focus, and this is reflected by the age of much of its conventional equipment. The development of additional bases was being considered as part of a counter-narcotics effort. The air force has a reasonable tactical airlift capability, though it has no aerial refuelling capacity, while the navy has a modest amphibious operations role. All three services train regularly, while also participating in multinational exercises.

ACTIVE 115,000 (Army 74,000 Navy 24,000 Air 17,000) Paramilitary 77,000

RESERVE 188,000 (Army 188,000)

ORGANISATIONS BY SERVICE

Army 74,000

4 mil region

FORCES BY ROLE

SPECIAL FORCES

1 (1st) SF bde (4 cdo bn, 1 airmob arty gp, 1 MP Coy, 1 cbt spt bn)
1 (3rd) SF bde (3 cdo bn, 1 airmob arty gp, 1 MP coy)
1 SF gp (regional troops)

MANOEUVRE

Armoured

1 (3rd) armd bde (2 tk bn, 1 armd inf bn, 1 arty gp, 1 AT coy, 1 AD gp, 1 engr bn, 1 cbt spt bn)
1 (9th) armd bde (forming - 1 tk bn)

Mechanised

1 (3rd) armd cav bde (3 mech cav bn, 1 mot inf bn, 1 arty gp, 1 AD gp, 1 engr bn, 1 cbt spt bn)
1 (1st) cav bde (4 mech cav bn, 1 MP coy, 1 cbt spt bn)

Light

2 (2nd & 31st) mot inf bde (3 mot inf bn, 1 arty gp, 1 MP coy, 1 log bn)
3 (1st, 7th & 32nd) inf bde (3 inf bn, 1 MP coy, 1 cbt spt bn)

Mountain

1 (4th) mtn bde (1 armd regt, 3 mot inf bn, 1 arty gp, 1 MP coy, 1 cbt spt bn)
1 (5th) mtn bde (1 armd regt, 2 mot inf bn, 3 jungle coy, 1 arty gp, 1 MP coy, 1 cbt spt bn)

Jungle

1 (5th) jungle inf bde (1 SF gp, 3 jungle bn, 3 jungle coy, 1 jungle arty gp, 1 AT coy, 1 AD gp, 1 jungle engr bn)
1 (6th) jungle inf bde (4 jungle bn, 1 engr bn, 1 MP coy, 1 cbt spt bn)

Other

1 (18th) armd trg bde (1 mech cav regt, 1 armd regt, 2 tk bn, 1 armd inf bn, 1 engr bn, 1 MP coy, 1 cbt spt bn)

Aviation

1 (1st) avn bde (1 atk hel/recce hel bn, 1 avn bn, 2 aslt hel/tpt hel bn)

COMBAT SUPPORT

1 (1st) arty bde (4 arty gp, 2 AD gp, 1 sigs gp)
1 (3rd) arty bde (4 arty gp, 1 AD gp, 1 sigs gp)
1 AD gp (regional troops)
1 (22nd) engr bde (3 engr bn, 1 demining coy)

EQUIPMENT BY TYPE

MBT 165 T-55; (75† in store)
LT TK 96 AMX-13
RECCE 95: 30 BRDM-2; 15 Fiat 6616; 50 M9A1
APC 299
APC (T) 120 M113A1
APC (W) 179: 150 UR-416; 25 Fiat 6614; 4 *Repontec*
ARTY 998
SP • 155mm 12 M109A2
TOWED 290
105mm 152: 44 M101; 24 M2A1; 60 M-56; 24 Model 56 pack howitzer; **122mm**; 36 D-30; **130mm** 36 M-46; **155mm** 66: 36 M114, 30 Model 50
MRL • 122mm 22 BM-21 *Grad*
MOR 674+
SP 107mm 24 M106A1
TOWED 650+ **81mm/107mm** 350; **120mm** 300+ Brandt/Expal Model L
AT
MSL 860
SP 22 M1165A2 HMMWV with 9K135 *Kornet* E (AT-14)
MANPATS 838: 350 9K11 *Malyutka* (AT-3 *Sagger*)/HJ-73C, 244 9K135 *Kornet* E (AT-14), 244 *Spike*-ER
RCL 106mm M40A1
AIRCRAFT
TPT • Light 16: 2 An-28 *Cash*; 3 An-32B *Cline*; 1 Beech 350 *King Air*; 1 Beech 1900D; 4 Cessna 152; 1 Cessna 208 *Caravan* I; 2 Cessna U206 *Stationair*; 1 PA-31T *Cheyenne* II; 1 PA-34 *Seneca*
TRG 4 IL-103
HELICOPTERS
MRH 8 Mi-17 *Hip* H
TPT 20 **Heavy** 1 Mi-26T *Halo* (2 more in store); **Medium** 6 Mi-171Sh; **Light** 13: 2 AW109K2; 9 PZL Mi-2 *Hoplite*; 2 R-44
TRG 5 F-28F
AD
SAM • MANPAD 298+: 70 9K36 *Strela*-3 (SA-14 *Gremlin*); 128 9K310 *Igla*-1 (SA-16 *Gimlet*); 100+ 9K32 *Strela*-2 (SA-7 *Grail*)‡
GUNS 165
SP 23mm 35 ZSU-23-4
TOWED 23mm 130: 80 ZU-23-2; 50 ZU-23
ARV M578

Navy 24,000 (incl 1,000 Coast Guard)

Commands: Pacific, Lake Titicaca, Amazon River

EQUIPMENT BY TYPE

SUBMARINES • TACTICAL • SSK 6:
6 *Angamos* (GER T-209/1200 – 2 in refit/reserve) with 6 single 533mm TT with A-185 HWT
PRINCIPAL SURFACE COMBATANTS 9
CRUISERS • CG 1 *Almirante Grau* (NLD *De Ruyter*) with 8 single lnchr with *Otomat* Mk2 AShM, 4 twin 152mm gun
FRIGATES • FFGHM 8:
4 *Aguirre* (ITA *Lupo*) with 8 single lnchr with *Otomat* Mk2 AShM (undergoing upgrade to MM-40 *Exocet* Block III AShM from 2014), 1 octuple Mk29 lnchr with RIM-7P *Sea Sparrow* SAM, 2 triple 324mm ASTT with A244 LWT, 1 127mm gun, (capacity 1 Bell 212 (AB-212)/SH-3D *Sea King*)
4 *Carvajal* (mod ITA *Lupo*) with 8 single lnchr with *Otomat* Mk2 AShM, 1 octuple *Albatros* lnchr with *Aspide* SAM, 2 triple 324mm ASTT with A244 LWT, 1 127mm gun, (capacity 1 Bell 212 (AB-212)/SH-3D *Sea King*)

PATROL AND COASTAL COMBATANTS 14
CORVETTES • FSG 6 *Velarde* (FRA PR-72 64m) with 4 single lnchr with MM-38 *Exocet* AShM, 1 76mm gun
PCR 5:
2 *Amazonas* with 1 76mm gun
1 *Manuel Clavero* (1 additional vessel undergoing acceptance trials; expected ISD end-2013)
2 *Marañon* with 2 76mm gun
PBR 3 *Punta Malpelo*
AMPHIBIOUS
LANDING SHIPS • LST 2 *Paita* (capacity 395 troops) (US *Terrebonne Parish*)
LANDING CRAFT • LCAC 7 Griffon 2000TD (capacity 22 troops)
LOGISTICS AND SUPPORT 32
AFD 3
AGOR 1 *Humboldt*
AGSC 5: 1 *Carrasco*; 2 *Van Straelen*; 1 *La Macha*, 1 *Stiglich* (river survey vessel for the upper Amazon)
AH 4 (river hospital craft)
AO 2 *Noguera*
AOR 1 *Mollendo*
AOT 2 *Bayovar*
ATF 1
AW 1 *Caloyeras*
AXS 1 *Marte*
YPT 1 *San Lorenzo*
YTL 10

Naval Aviation ε800

FORCES BY ROLE
MARITIME PATROL
1 sqn with Beech 200T; Bell 212 ASW (AB-212 ASW); F-27 *Friendship*; F-60; SH-3D *Sea King*
TRANSPORT
1 flt with An-32B *Cline;* Cessna 206
TRAINING
1 sqn with F-28F; T-34C *Turbo Mentor*
TRANSPORT HELICOPTER
1 (liaison) sqn with Bell 206B *Jet Ranger II*; Mi-8 *Hip*

EQUIPMENT BY TYPE
AIRCRAFT
MP 8: 4 Beech 200T; 4 F-60
ELINT 1 F-27 *Friendship*
TPT • Light 4: 3 An-32B *Cline*; 1 Cessna 206
TRG 5 T-34C *Turbo Mentor*
HELICOPTERS
ASW 5: 2 Bell 212 ASW (AB-212 ASW); 3 SH-3D *Sea King*
TPT 11 **Medium** 8: 2 Mi-8 *Hip*; 6 UH-3H *Sea King*; **Light** 3 Bell 206B *Jet Ranger* II
TRG 5 F-28F
MSL • AShM AM-39 *Exocet*

Marines 4,000

FORCES BY ROLE
SPECIAL FORCES
1 cdo gp
MANOEUVRE
Light
2 inf bn
1 inf gp
Amphibious
1 mne bde (1 SF gp, 1 recce bn, 2 inf bn, 1 amph bn, 1 arty gp)
Jungle
1 jungle inf bn

EQUIPMENT BY TYPE
APC (W) 35+: 20 BMR-600; V-100 *Commando*; 15 V-200 *Chaimite*
ARTY 18+
TOWED 122mm D-30
MOR 18+: **81mm**; **120mm** ε18
RCL 84mm *Carl Gustav*; **106mm** M40A1
AD • GUNS 20mm SP (twin)

Air Force 17,000

Divided into five regions – North, Lima, South, Central and Amazon.

FORCES BY ROLE
FIGHTER
1 sqn with MiG-29S/SE *Fulcrum* C; MiG-29UB *Fulcrum* B
FIGHTER/GROUND ATTACK
1 sqn with *Mirage* 2000E/ED (2000P/DP)
2 sqn with A-37B *Dragonfly*
1 sqn with Su-25A *Frogfoot* A†; Su-25UB *Frogfoot* B†
ISR
1 (photo-survey) sqn with *Commander* 690; Learjet 36A; SA-227-BC *Metro* III (C-26B)
TRANSPORT
1 sqn with B-737; An-32 *Cline*
1 sqn with DHC-6 *Twin Otter*; DHC-6-400 *Twin Otter*; PC-6 *Turbo Porter*
1 sqn with L-100-20
TRAINING
2 (drug interdiction) sqn with EMB-312 *Tucano*
1 sqn with MB-339A*
1 sqn with Z-242
1 hel sqn with Schweizer 300C
ATTACK HELICOPTER
1 sqn with Mi-25/Mi-35P *Hind*
TRANSPORT HELICOPTER
1 sqn with Mi-17 *Hip* H
1 sqn with Bell 206 *Jet Ranger;* Bell 212 (AB-212); Bell 412 *Twin Huey*
1 sqn with Bo-105C/LS
AIR DEFENCE
6 bn with S-125 *Pechora* (SA-3 *Goa*)

EQUIPMENT BY TYPE
AIRCRAFT 78 combat capable
FTR 20: 15 MiG-29S *Fulcrum* C; 3 MiG-29SE *Fulcrum C* (8 upgraded to SMP standard by end-2012); 2 MiG-29UB *Fulcrum* B
FGA 12: 2 *Mirage* 2000ED (2000DP); 10 *Mirage* 2000E (2000P) (some†)
ATK 36: 18 A-37B *Dragonfly*; 10 Su-25A *Frogfoot* A†; 8 Su-25UB *Frogfoot* B†
ISR 6: 2 Learjet 36A; 4 SA-227-BC *Metro* III (C-26B)
TPT 19 **Medium** 2 L-100-20; **Light** 13: 4 An-32 *Cline*; 1 *Commander* 690; 3 DHC-6 *Twin Otter*; 4 DHC-6-400 *Twin*

Otter (further 8 on order); 1 PC-6 *Turbo-Porter*; **PAX** 4 B-737
TRG 49: 19 EMB-312 *Tucano*; 10 MB-339A*; 6 T-41A/D *Mescalero*; 14 Z-242
HELICOPTERS
ATK 18: 16 Mi-25 *Hind* D; 2 Mi-35P *Hind* E
MRH 21: 2 Bell 412 *Twin Huey*; 19 Mi-17 *Hip* H
TPT • Light 21: 8 Bell 206 *Jet Ranger*; 6 Bell 212 (AB-212); 1 Bo-105C; 6 Bo-105LS
TRG 4 Schweizer 300C
AD • SAM 100+: S-125 *Pechora* (SA-3 *Goa*); 100+ *Javelin*
MSL
AAM • IR R-3 (AA-2 *Atoll*)‡; R-60 (AA-8 *Aphid*)‡; R-73 (AA-11 *Archer*); R-550 *Magic*; **IR/SARH** R-27 (AA-10 *Alamo*); **ARH** R-77 (AA-12 *Adder*)
ASM AS-30; Kh-29L (AS-14 *Kedge*)
ARM Kh-58 (AS-11 *Kilter*)

Paramilitary 77,000

National Police 77,000 (100,000 reported)

EQUIPMENT BY TYPE
APC (W) 100 MOWAG *Roland*

General Police 43,000

Security Police 21,000

Technical Police 13,000

Coast Guard 1,000

Personnel included as part of Navy
EQUIPMENT BY TYPE
PATROL AND COASTAL COMBATANTS 26
PCC 5 *Rio Nepena*
PB 10: 6 *Chicama* (US *Dauntless*); 1 *Río Chira*; 3 *Río Santa*
PBR 11: 10 *Zorritos*; 1 *Río Viru*
LOGISTICS AND SUPPORT • AH 1 *Puno*
AIRCRAFT
TPT • Light 3: 1 DHC-6 *Twin Otter*; 2 F-27 *Friendship*

Rondas Campesinas

Peasant self-defence force. Perhaps 7,000 rondas 'gp', up to pl strength, some with small arms. Deployed mainly in emergency zone.

DEPLOYMENT

CÔTE D'IVOIRE
UN • UNOCI 3 obs

DEMOCRATIC REPUBLIC OF THE CONGO
UN • MONUSCO 2; 13 obs

HAITI
UN • MINUSTAH 374; 1 inf coy

LIBERIA
UN • UNMIL 2; 2 obs

SOUTH SUDAN
UN • UNMISS 1 obs

SUDAN
UN • UNAMID 4 obs
UN • UNISFA 1; 2 obs

WESTERN SAHARA
UN • MINURSO 2 obs

Suriname SUR

Suriname Dollar srd		2012	2013	2014
GDP	srd	15.6bn	17.3bn	
	US$	4.74bn	5.26bn	
per capita	US$	8,686	9,509	
Growth	%	4.47	4.46	
Inflation	%	4.99	4.83	
Def bdgt	srd	ε134m		
	US$	ε41m		
US$1=srd		3.30	3.30	

Population 566,846

Age	0–14	15–19	20–24	25–29	30–64	65 plus
Male	13.7%	4.5%	4.4%	4.8%	20.5%	2.4%
Female	13.1%	4.3%	4.2%	4.6%	20.2%	3.2%

Capabilities

While assuring sovereignty and territorial integrity are its fundamental roles, the nation's small armed forces would struggle to fulfil either were they ever to face a concerted attack. The army is the largest of the three services, with naval and air units having a very limited capability. Defence ties with Brazil have been growing with the upgrade and supply of a small number of armoured vehicles.

ACTIVE 1,840 (Army 1,400 Navy 240 Air 200)
Paramilitary 100
(All services form part of the army)

ORGANISATIONS BY SERVICE

Army 1,400

FORCES BY ROLE
MANOEUVRE
Mechanised
1 mech cav sqn
Light
1 inf bn (4 coy)
COMBAT SUPPORT
1 MP bn (coy)
EQUIPMENT BY TYPE
RECCE 6 EE-9 *Cascavel*
APC (W) 15 EE-11 *Urutu*
ARTY • MOR 81mm 6
AT • RCL 106mm: M40A1

Navy ε240

EQUIPMENT BY TYPE

PATROL AND COASTAL COMBATANTS 10

PB 5: 3 Rodman 101†; 2 others

PBR 5 Rodman 55

Air Force ε200

EQUIPMENT BY TYPE

AIRCRAFT 3 combat capable

MP 1 C-212-400 *Aviocar**

TPT • Light 2: 1 BN-2 *Defender**; 1 Cessna 182

TRG 1 PC-7 *Turbo Trainer**

Paramilitary ε100

Coast Guard ε100

Formed in November 2013; 3 Coast Guard stations to be formed; HQ at Paramaribo

EQUIPMENT BY TYPE

PATROL AND COASTAL COMBATANTS • PB 1 FPB98 (two FPB72 are on order and expected 2014)

Trinidad and Tobago TTO

Trinidad and Tobago Dollar TT$		2012	2013	2014
GDP	TT$	161bn	171bn	
	US$	25.3bn	26.8bn	
per capita	US$	19,018	20,054	
Growth	%	0.41	2.05	
Inflation	%	9.27	5.59	
Def bdgt	TT$	2.84bn	2.55bn	
	US$	446m	400m	
US$1=TT$		6.38	6.38	

Population 1,225,225

Age	0–14	15–19	20–24	25–29	30–64	65 plus
Male	9.9%	3.2%	3.8%	5.0%	24.8%	3.9%
Female	9.5%	3.0%	3.6%	4.7%	23.4%	5.2%

Capabilities

The Trinidad and Tobago Defence Force faces no external threat, and is primarily tasked with counter-narcotic, border-surveillance and disaster-management roles, though security forces are also preoccupied by issues arising from the flow of weapons and ammunition. The planned purchase of three offshore patrol vessels was cancelled in 2010, however a burgeoning military-to-military relationship with Colombia may lead to an order for an OPV in the future. According to the Chief of Defence in 2012, the country plans to work with its regional counterparts to enhance levels of interoperability across regional armed forces.

ACTIVE 4,050 (Army 3,000 Coast Guard 1,050)

(All services form the Trinidad and Tobago Defence Force)

ORGANISATIONS BY SERVICE

Army ε3,000

FORCES BY ROLE

SPECIAL FORCES

1 SF unit

MANOEUVRE

Light

2 inf bn

COMBAT SUPPORT

1 engr bn

COMBAT SERVICE SUPPORT

1 log bn

EQUIPMENT BY TYPE

MOR 6: **81mm** L16A1

AT

RCL 84mm ε24 *Carl Gustav*

Coast Guard 1,050

FORCES BY ROLE

COMMAND

1 mne HQ

EQUIPMENT BY TYPE

PATROL AND COASTAL COMBATANTS 20

PCO 1 *Nelson* (UK *Island*)

PB 19: 2 *Gasper Grande*; 1 *Matelot*; 4 *Plymouth*; 4 *Point*; 6 *Scarlet Ibis* (Austal 30m); 2 *Wasp*; (1 *Cascadura* (SWE *Karlskrona* 40m) non-operational)

Air Wing 50

AIRCRAFT

TPT • Light 2 SA-227 *Metro* III (C-26)

HELICOPTERS

MRH 2 AW139

TPT • Light 1 S-76

Uruguay URY

Uruguayan Peso pU		2012	2013	2014
GDP	pU	1tr	1.11tr	
	US$	49.4bn	51.7bn	
per capita	US$	14,614	15,254	
Growth	%	3.80	3.80	
Inflation	%	8.10	7.32	
Def bdgt	pU	9.34bn	9.55bn	9.75bn
	US$	460m	445m	
US$1=pU		20.31	21.45	

Population 3,324,460

Age	0–14	15–19	20–24	25–29	30–64	65 plus
Male	10.9%	4.2%	4.0%	3.5%	20.2%	5.5%
Female	10.5%	4.0%	3.8%	3.5%	21.5%	8.3%

Capabilities

Along with the basic aims of assuring sovereignty and territorial integrity, the armed forces have in recent years taken on peacekeeping missions, most notably in Haiti. In regional terms, the services provide competent force, though much of the equipment inventory is second-hand. Air force ambitions to purchase a light fighter aircraft continued to be stymied by a lack of funds. The air force is focused on its counter-insurgency role, with a limited tactical airlift capacity. The army is receiving additional utility vehicles, while two offshore patrol vessels for the navy will likely be built in-country. A defence bilateral agreement on closer collaboration was reached with Argentina at the end of 2012, although the two nations also have a territorial dispute. The military trains regularly, and on a joint basis, as well as participating in multinational exercises. The country has little ability for independent power projection.

ACTIVE 24,650 (Army 16,250 Navy 5,400 Air 3,000) Paramilitary 800

ORGANISATIONS BY SERVICE

Army 16,250

Uruguayan units are sub-standard size, mostly around 30%. Div are at most bde size, while bn are of reinforced coy strength. Regts are also coy size, some bn size, with the largest formation being the 2nd armd cav regt.

FORCES BY ROLE

COMMAND

4 mil region/div HQ

MANOEUVRE

Mechanised

2 armd regt

1 armd cav regt

5 mech cav regt

8 mech inf regt

Light

1 mot inf bn

5 inf bn

Air Manoeuvre

1 para bn

COMBAT SUPPORT

1 (strategic reserve) arty regt

5 fd arty gp

1 AD gp

1 (1st) engr bde (2 engr bn)

4 cbt engr bn

EQUIPMENT BY TYPE

MBT 15 TI-67

LT TK 38: 16 M24 *Chaffee*; 22 M41A1UR

RECCE 110: 15 EE-9 *Cascavel*; 48 GAZ-39371 *Vodnik*; 47 OT-93;

AIFV 18 BMP-1

APC 283

APC (T) 29: 24 M113A1UR; 3 M-93 (MT-LB); 2 PTS

APC (W) 254: 54 *Condor*; 53 OT-64: 147 MOWAG *Piranha*

ARTY 185

SP 122mm 6 2S1

TOWED 44: **105mm** 36: 28 M101A1; 8 M102; **155mm** 8 M114A1

MOR 135: **81mm** 91: 35 M1, 56 LN; **120mm** 44 SL

AT

MSL • MANPATS 15 *Milan*

RCL 69: **106mm** 69 M40A1

UAV • ISR • Light 1 *Charrua*

AD • GUNS • TOWED 14: **20mm** 14: 6 M167 *Vulcan*; 8 TCM-20 (w/Elta M-2016 radar)

AEV MT-LB

Navy 5,400 (incl 1,800 Prefectura Naval Coast Guard)

HQ at Montevideo

EQUIPMENT BY TYPE

PRINCIPAL SURFACE COMBATANTS • FRIGATES 2:

FF 2 *Uruguay* (PRT *Joao Belo*) with 2 triple Mk32 324mm ASTT with Mk46 LWT, 2 100mm gun

PATROL AND COASTAL COMBATANTS 15

PB 15: 2 *Colonia* (US *Cape*); 1 *Paysandu*; 9 Type-44 (coast guard); 3 PS (coast guard)

MINE WARFARE • MINE COUNTERMEASURES 3:

MSO 3 *Temerario* (*Kondor* II)

AMPHIBIOUS 3: 2 **LCVP**; 1 **LCM**

LOGISTICS AND SUPPORT 10

ABU 2

AG 2: 1 *Artigas* (GER *Freiburg*, general spt ship with replenishment capabilities); 1 *Maldonado* (also used as patrol craft)

AGS 1 *Helgoland*

AGSC 1 *Trieste*

ARS 1 *Vanguardia*

AXS 2: 1 *Capitan Miranda*; 1 *Bonanza*

YTB 1

Naval Aviation 210

FORCES BY ROLE

ANTI SUBMARINE WARFARE

1 flt with Beech 200T*; *Jetstream* Mk2

SEARCH & RESCUE/TRANSPORT HELICOPTER
1 sqn with AS350B2 *Ecureuil* (*Esquilo*); Bo-105M; *Wessex* HC2/Mk60
TRANSPORT/TRAINING
1 flt with T-34C *Turbo Mentor*
EQUIPMENT BY TYPE
AIRCRAFT 2 combat capable
MP 2 *Jetstream* Mk2
ISR 2 Beech 200T*
TRG 2 T-34C *Turbo Mentor*
HELICOPTERS
MRH 6 Bo-105M
TPT 2 **Medium** 1 *Wessex* HC2/Mk60; **Light** 1 AS350B2 *Ecureuil* (*Esquilo*)

Naval Infantry 450
FORCES BY ROLE
MANOEUVRE
Amphibious
1 mne bn(-)

Air Force 3,000
Flying hours 120 hrs/year

FORCES BY ROLE
FIGHTER/GROUND ATTACK
1 sqn with A-37B *Dragonfly*
1 sqn with IA-58B *Pucará*
ISR
1 flt with EMB-110 *Bandeirante*
TRANSPORT
1 sqn with C-130B *Hercules*; C-212 *Aviocar*; EMB–110C *Bandeirante*; EMB-120 *Brasilia*
1 (liaison) sqn with Cessna 206H; T-41D
1 (liaison) flt with Cessna 206H
TRAINING
1 sqn with PC-7U *Turbo Trainer*
1 sqn with Beech 58 *Baron* (UB-58); SF-260EU
TRANSPORT HELICOPTER
1 sqn with AS365 *Dauphin*; Bell 205 (UH–1H *Iroquois*); Bell 212
EQUIPMENT BY TYPE
AIRCRAFT 15 combat capable
ATK 15: 10 A-37B *Dragonfly*; 5 IA-58B *Pucará*
ISR 1 EMB-110 *Bandeirante*
TPT 20 **Medium** 2 C-130B *Hercules*; **Light** 18: 2 Beech 58 *Baron* (UB-58); 4 C-212 *Aviocar*; 9 Cessna 206H; 2 EMB-110C *Bandeirante*; 1 EMB-120 *Brasilia*
TRG 21: 5 PC-7U *Turbo Trainer*; 12 SF-260EU; 4 T-41D *Mescalero*
HELICOPTERS
MRH 1 AS365 *Dauphin*
TPT • Light 10: 6 Bell 205 (UH–1H *Iroquois*); 4 Bell 212

Paramilitary 800

Guardia de Coraceros 350 (under Interior Ministry)

Guardia de Granaderos 450

DEPLOYMENT

CÔTE D'IVOIRE
UN • UNOCI 2 obs

DEMOCRATIC REPUBLIC OF THE CONGO
UN • MONUC 1,196; 16 obs; 1 inf bn; 2 mne coy; 1 hel flt; 1 engr coy

EGYPT
MFO 58; 1 engr/tpt unit

HAITI
UN • MINUSTAH 950; 2 inf bn; 1 mne coy, 1 spt coy

INDIA/PAKISTAN
UN • UNMOGIP 2 obs

SUDAN
UN • UNISFA 1

WESTERN SAHARA
UN • MINURSO 1 obs

Venezuela VEN

Venezuelan Bolivar Fuerte Bs		2012	2013	2014
GDP	Bs	1.64tr	2.12tr	
	US$	382bn	346bn	
per capita	US$	12,956	11,527	
Growth	%	5.54	0.07	
Inflation	%	21.07	27.34	
Def bdgt [a]	Bs	21.3bn	32.1bn	
	US$	6.97bn	5.24bn	
US$1=Bs		4.29	6.13	

[a] US dollar conversions should be treated with caution due to effects of currency revaluation and wide differentials between official and parallel exchange rates

Population 28,459,085

Age	0–14	15–19	20–24	25–29	30–64	65 plus
Male	14.6%	4.9%	4.6%	4.0%	18.9%	2.5%
Female	14.0%	4.8%	4.6%	4.0%	19.9%	3.2%

Capabilities

The armed forces are tasked with protecting the sovereignty of the state and assuring territorial integrity. President Nicolas Madura made several changes to the country's military top brass after the death of Hugo Chavez. Madura is also focused on trying to improve domestic security. Equipment deliveries from Russia continued during 2013, including the S-300VM long-range surface-to-air missile system as well as the medium-range *Buk*-M2E. Venezuela is the first export customer for the S-300VM. The air-defence systems will complement the Su-30MKV2, which gives the air force arguably the most capable multi-role fighter aircraft in the region. Delivery of the BMP-3 AFV also resumed last year. The marine corps established three air cavalry groups in 2013. The military trains regularly and there is an increasing focus on joint training. The air force has a tactical airlift capability.

ACTIVE 115,000 (Army 63,000 Navy 17,500 Air 11,500 National Guard 23,000)

Conscript liability 30 months selective, varies by region for all services

RESERVE 8,000 (Army 8,000)

ORGANISATIONS BY SERVICE

Army ε63,000

FORCES BY ROLE

MANOEUVRE

Armoured

1 (4th) armd div (1 armd bde, 1 lt armd bde, 1 AB bde, 1 arty bde, 1 AD bde)

Mechanised

1 (9th) mot cav div (1 mot cav bde, 1 ranger bde, 1 sy bde)

Light

1 (1st) inf div (1 SF bn, 1 armd bde, 1 mech inf bde, 1 ranger bde, 1 inf bde, 1 arty unit, 1 AD bty, 1 spt unit)

1 (2nd) inf div (1 mech inf bde, 1 inf bde, 1 mtn inf bde, 1 AD bty)

1 (3rd) inf div (1 inf bde, 1 ranger bde, 1 sigs bde, 1 MP bde)

Jungle

1 (5th) inf div (1 SF bn, 1 cav sqn, 2 jungle inf bde, 1 engr bn)

Aviation

1 avn comd (1 tpt avn bn, 1 atk hel bn, 1 ISR avn bn)

COMBAT SUPPORT

1 cbt engr corps with (3 engr regt)

COMBAT SERVICE SUPPORT

1 log comd with (2 log regt)

Reserve Organisations 8,000

FORCES BY ROLE

MANOEUVRE

Armoured

1 armd bn

Light

4 inf bn

1 ranger bn

COMBAT SUPPORT

1 arty bn

2 engr regt

EQUIPMENT BY TYPE

MBT 173: 81 AMX-30V; 92 T-72M1M

LT TK 109: 31 AMX-13; 78 *Scorpion* 90

RECCE 441: 42 *Dragoon* 300 LFV2; 10 TPz-1 *Fuchs* (CBRN); 79 V-100/-150; 310 UR-53AR50 *Tiuna*

AIFV 237: 123 BMP-3 (incl variants); 114 BTR-80A (incl variants)

APC 81

APC (T) 45: 25 AMX-VCI; 12 VCI-PC; 8 VACI-TB

APC (W) 36 *Dragoon* 300

ARTY 515+

SP 60: **152mm** 48 2S19 (replacing Mk F3s); **155mm** 12 (AMX) Mk F3

TOWED 92: **105mm** 80: 40 M101A1; 40 Model 56 pack howitzer; **155mm** 12 M114A1

MRL 56: **122mm** 24 BM-21; **160mm** 20 LAR SP (LAR-160); **300mm** 12 9A52 *Smerch*

GUN/MOR 120mm 13 2S23 NONA-SVK

MOR 294+: **81mm** 165; **120mm** 108: 60 Brandt; 48 2S12

SP 21+: **81mm** 21 *Dragoon* 300PM; AMX-VTT

AT

MSL • MANPATS 24 IMI MAPATS

RCL 106mm 175 M40A1

GUNS 76mm 75 M18 *Hellcat*

AD

SAM

SP S-300VM; *Buk*-M2E (SA-17 *Grizzly*)

MANPAD 9K338 *Igla*-S (SA-24 *Grinch*); RBS-70; *Mistral*

GUNS 206+

SP 23mm ε200 ZSU-23-2 **40mm** 6+ AMX-13 *Rafaga*

TOWED 40mm M1; L/70

RADAR • LAND RASIT (veh, arty)

AIRCRAFT

TPT • Light 28: 1 Beech 90 *King Air*; 1 Beech 200 *King Air*; 1 Beech 300 *King Air*; 1 Cessna 172; 6 Cessna 182 *Skylane*; 2 Cessna 206; 2 Cessna 207 *Stationair*; 1 IAI-201 *Arava*; 2 IAI-202 *Arava*; 11 M-28 *Skytruck*

HELICOPTERS

ATK 10 Mi-35M2 *Hind*

MRH 33: 10 Bell 412EP; 2 Bell 412SP; 21 Mi-17V-5 *Hip* H

TPT 9 **Heavy** 3 Mi-26T2 *Halo*; **Medium** 2 AS-61D; **Light** 4: 3 Bell 206B *Jet Ranger*, 1 Bell 206L3 *Long Ranger* II

ARV 5: 3 AMX-30D; 2 *Dragoon* 300RV; *Samson*

VLB *Leguan*

Navy ε14,300; ε3,200 conscript (total 17,500)

EQUIPMENT BY TYPE

SUBMARINES • TACTICAL • SSK 2:

2 *Sabalo* (GER T-209/1300) with 8 single 533mm TT with SST-4 HWT

PRINCIPAL SURFACE COMBATANTS • FRIGATES 6

FFGHM 6 *Mariscal Sucre* (ITA mod *Lupo*) with 8 single lnchr with *Otomat* Mk2 AShM, 1 octuple *Albatros* lnchr with *Aspide* SAM, 2 triple 324mm ASTT with A244 LWT, 1 127mm gun, (capacity 1 Bell 212 (AB-212) hel)

PATROL AND COASTAL COMBATANTS 10

PSOH 4 *Guaiqueri* with 1 *Millennium* CIWS, 1 76mm gun

PBG 3 *Federación* (UK Vosper 37m) with 2 single lnchr with *Otomat* Mk2 AShM

PB 3 *Constitucion* (UK Vosper 37m) with 1 76mm gun

AMPHIBIOUS

LANDING SHIPS • LST 4 *Capana* (capacity 12 tanks; 200 troops) (FSU *Alligator*)

LANDING CRAFT 3:

LCU 2 *Margarita* (river comd)

LCAC 1 Griffon 2000TD

LOGISTICS AND SUPPORT 10

AGOR 1 *Punta Brava*

AGS 2

AK 4 *Los Frailes*

AORH 1 *Ciudad Bolivar*
ATF 1
AXS 1 *Simon Bolivar*

Naval Aviation 500

FORCES BY ROLE
ANTI SUBMARINE WARFARE
1 sqn with Bell 212 (AB-212)
MARITIME PATROL
1 flt with C-212-200 MPA
TRANSPORT
1 sqn with Beech 200 *King Air*; C-212 *Aviocar*; *Turbo Commander* 980C
TRAINING
1 hel sqn with Bell 206B *Jet Ranger* II; TH-57A *Sea Ranger*
TRANSPORT HELICOPTER
1 sqn with Bell 412EP *Twin Huey*; Mi-17V-5 *Hip H*

EQUIPMENT BY TYPE
AIRCRAFT 3 combat capable
MP 3 C-212-200 MPA*
TPT • Light 7: 1 Beech C90 *King Air*; 1 Beech 200 *King Air*; 4 C-212 *Aviocar*; 1 *Turbo Commander* 980C
HELICOPTERS
ASW 5 Bell 212 ASW (AB-212 ASW)
MRH 12: 6 Bell 412EP *Twin Huey*; 6 Mi-17V-5 *Hip*
TPT • Light 1 Bell 206B *Jet Ranger* II (trg)
TRG 1 TH-57A *Sea Ranger*

Marines ε7,000

FORCES BY ROLE
COMMAND
1 div HQ
SPECIAL FORCES
1 spec ops bde
MANOEUVRE
Amphibious
1 (rvn) mne bde
2 (landing) mne bde
COMBAT SUPPORT
1 arty gp (3 arty bty, 1 AD bn)
1 cbt engr bn
1 MP bde
1 sigs bn
COMBAT SERVICE SUPPORT
1 log bn

EQUIPMENT BY TYPE
APC (W) 37 EE-11 *Urutu*
AAV 11 LVTP-7
ARTY • TOWED 105mm 18 M-56
MOR 120mm 12 Brandt
AD • GUNS • SP 40mm 6 M-42
AD • SAM RBS-70
AT•AT-4 *Skip*
RCL 84mm M3 *Carl Gustav*; **106mm** M40A1
AEV 1 AAVR7
AMPHIBIOUS • LANDING CRAFT • 1 **LCM**; 1 **LCU**; 12 **LCVP**
PATROL AND COASTAL COMBATANTS • PBR 23: 18 *Constancia*; 2 *Manaure*; 3 *Terepaima* (*Cougar*)

Coast Guard 1,000

EQUIPMENT BY TYPE
PATROL AND COASTAL COMBATANTS 22
PSOH 3 *Guaicamacuto* with 1 *Millennium* CIWS, 1 76 mm gun, (capacity 1 Bell 212 (AB-212) hel) (1 additional vessel in build)
PB 19: 12 *Gavion*; 1 *Pagalo* (Damen Stan 2606); 4 *Petrel* (US *Point*); 2 *Protector*
LOGISTICS AND SUPPORT 5
AG 2 *Los Tanques* (salvage ship)
AKSL 1
AP 2

Air Force 11,500

Flying hours 155 hrs/year

FORCES BY ROLE
FIGHTER/GROUND ATTACK
1 sqn with F-5 *Freedom Fighter* (VF-5)
2 sqn with F-16A/B *Fighting Falcon*
4 sqn with Su-30MKV
1 sqn with K-8W *Karakorum**
GROUND ATTACK/ISR
1 sqn with K-8W *Karakorum**
1 sqn with EMB-312 *Tucano**; OV-10A *Bronco*
ELECTRONIC WARFARE
1 sqn with *Falcon* 20DC; SA-227 *Metro* III (C-26B)
TRANSPORT
1 sqn with Y-8; C-130H *Hercules*; KC-137
1 sqn with A319CJ; B-737
4 sqn with Cessna T206H; Cessna 750
1 sqn with Cessna 500/550/551; *Falcon* 20F; *Falcon* 900
1 sqn with G-222; Short 360 *Sherpa*
TRAINING
1 sqn with Cessna 182N; SF-260E
1 sqn with EMB-312 *Tucano**
TRANSPORT HELICOPTER
1 VIP sqn with AS532UL *Cougar*; Mi-172
3 sqn with AS332B *Super Puma*; AS532 *Cougar*
2 sqn with Mi-17 *Hip* H
AIR DEFENCE
1 bde with S-125 *Pechora*-2M (SA-3 *Goa*)

EQUIPMENT BY TYPE
AIRCRAFT 95 combat capable
FTR 31: 5 F-5 *Freedom Fighter* (VF-5), 4 F-5B *Freedom Fighter* (NF-5B); 1 CF-5D *Freedom Fighter* (VF-5D); 17 F-16A *Fighting Falcon*; 4 F-16B *Fighting Falcon*
FGA 24 Su-30MKV
ATK 7 OV-10A *Bronco*
EW 4: 2 *Falcon* 20DC; 2 SA-227 *Metro* III (C-26B)
TKR 1 KC-137
TPT 70 **Medium** 12: 5 C-130H *Hercules* (some in store); 1 G-222; 6 Y-8; **Light** 53: 6 Beech 200 *King Air*; 2 Beech 350 *King Air*; 10 Cessna 182N *Skylane*; 12 Cessna 206 *Stationair*; 4 Cessna 208B *Caravan*; 1 Cessna 500 *Citation* I; 3 Cessna 550 *Citation* II; 1 Cessna 551; 1 Cessna 750 *Citation X*; 11 Quad City *Challenger* II; 2 Short 360 *Sherpa*; **PAX** 5: 1 A319CJ; 1 B-737; 1 *Falcon* 20F; 2 *Falcon* 900
TRG 45: 18 EMB-312 *Tucano**; 15 K-8W *Karakorum** ; 12 SF-260E

HELICOPTERS
MRH 8 Mi-17 (Mi-17VS) *Hip* H
TPT • Medium 15: 3 AS332B *Super Puma;* 8 AS532 *Cougar;* 2 AS532UL *Cougar;* 2 Mi-172 (VIP)
AD
SAM S-125 *Pechora*-2M (SA-3 *Goa*)
MANPAD ADAMS; *Mistral*
GUNS • TOWED 228+: **20mm**: 114 TCM-20; **35mm**; **40mm** 114 L/70
RADARS • LAND *Flycatcher*
MSL
AAM • IR AIM-9L/P *Sidewinder;* R-73 (AA-11 *Archer*); PL-5E; *Python* 4; R-27T/ET (AA-10 *Alamo*) **SARH** R-27R/ER (AA-10 *Alamo*); **ARH** R-77(AA-12 *Adder*)
ASM Kh-29L/T (AS-14 *Kedge*); Kh-31A/P (AS-17 *Krypton*); Kh-59M (AS-18 *Kazoo*)
AshM AM-39 *Exocet*

National Guard (Fuerzas Armadas de Cooperacion) 23,000

(Internal sy, customs) 9 regional comd
APC (W) 44: 24 Fiat 6614; 20 UR-416
MOR 50 **81mm**
PATROL AND COASTAL COMBATANTS • PB 34: 12 *Protector;* 12 *Punta;* 10 *Rio Orinoco* II
AIRCRAFT
TPT • Light 34: 1 Beech 55 *Baron;* 1 Beech 80 *Queen Air;* 1 Beech 90 *King Air;* 1 Beech 200C *Super King Air;* 3 Cessna 152 *Aerobat;* 2 Cessna 172; 2 Cessna 402C; 4 Cessna U206 *Stationair;* 6 DA42 MPP; 1 IAI-201 *Arava;* 12 M-28 *Skytruck*
TRG 3: 1 PZL 106 *Kruk;* 2 PLZ M2-6 *Isquierka*
HELICOPTERS
MRH 13: 8 Bell 412EP; 5 Mi-17V-5 *Hip* H
TPT • Light 20: 9 AS355F *Ecureuil* II; 4 AW109; 6 Bell 206B/L *Jet Ranger/Long Ranger;* 1 Bell 212 (AB 212);
TRG 5 F-280C

Table 8 **Selected Arms Procurements and Deliveries, Latin America and the Caribbean**

Designation	Type	Quantity (Current)	Contract Value	Prime Nationality	Prime Contractor	Order Date	First Delivery Due	Notes
Argentina (ARG)								
OPV 80	PSOH	4	ARS619m (US$145m)	ARG/GER	Astillero Rio Santiago	2009	2012	Based on Fassmer OPV 80 design. Project suspended, then resumed in 2010
AT-63 *Pampa* II	Trg ac	10	n.k.	ARG	n.k.	n.k.	2012	First four delivered to Cruz del Sur aerobatic team in 2012
IA-63 *Pampa* III	Trg ac	18	n.k.	ARG	FAdeA	2010	2014	First delivery due 2014
Bell 206	Tpt hel	20	See notes	ITA	Government Surplus	2011	2014	20 ex-Carabinieri hels to be delivered in exchange for three surplus ARG G-222s
Brazil (BRZ)								
VBTP-MR *Guarani*	APC (W)	Up to 2,044	R6bn (€2.5bn)	BRZ/ITA	IVECO Latin America	2009	2012	To replace EE-9 *Cascavel* and EE-11 *Urutu*. Delivery to be complete by 2030
ASTROS 2020	MRL	30	R246m	BRZ	Avibras	2012	2016	–
Gepard 1A2	SPAAGM	34	€37m (US$48.5m)	GER	n/a	2013	2013	34 plus three more used for spares. First delivered mid-2013
SN-BR (Submarino Nuclear Brasileiro)	SSN	1	See notes	BRZ	DCNS	2009	2025	Part of €6.7bn (US$8.3bn) naval programme. Contract covers work on the non-nuclear sections of the submarine
Scorpene-class (S-BR - Submarino Brasileiro)	SSK	4	See notes	FRA	DCNS	2009	2017	Part of €6.7bn (US$8.3bn) naval programme. To be built by Itaguaí Construções Navais (JV between DCNS and Odebrecht). Delivery to be completed 2022
Mi-35M *Hind* (AH-2 *Sabre*)	Atk hel	12	US$150–300m	RUS	Russian Helicopters (Mil)	2008	2010	Contract value incl spares and trg. Nine delivered by mid-2012 with remaining three due in late 2013
AS365K *Panther*	MRH hel	34	R376m (US$215m)	Int'l	EADS (EADS Brazil)	2009	2011	To be manufactured in BRZ by Helibras. Final delivery due 2021
EC725 *Super Cougar*	Tpt hel	50	US$2bn	Int'l	EADS (EADS Brazil)	2008	2010	First three built in FRA. Remainder being manufactured in BRZ by Helibras. Delivery in progress
A-*Darter*	AAM	n.k.	ZAR1bn (US$143m)	RSA	Denel	2007	2015	Progamme schedule has slipped; development to be completed by 2015
Chile (CHL)								
Piloto Pardo-class	PSO	4	n.k.	CHL	ASMAR	2005	2008	Fassmer OPV 80 design. First two in service with Coast Guard. Contract for third vessel signed Dec 2011; delivery due 2014
Colombia (COL)								
LAV III	AIFV	24	US$65m	US	General Dynamics (GDLS Canada)	2013	2013	Equipped with Rafael remote weapon stations. Delivery to be complete by May 2014
Commando Advanced	AIFV	28	US$32m	US	Textron (Textron Marine & Land Systems)	2013	2013	*Commando* Advanced APC variant with 40mm turret. First delivery due by end-2013
20 de Julio-class	PSO	1	pC120bn	COL	Cotecmar shipyard	2011	2013	Second vessel order. Delivery due Dec 2013

Table 8 **Selected Arms Procurements and Deliveries, Latin America and the Caribbean**

Designation	Type	Quantity (Current)	Contract Value	Prime Nationality	Prime Contractor	Order Date	First Delivery Due	Notes
Griffon 2000TD	UCAC	8	n.k.	UK	Griffon Hoverwork	2013	2013	For marines. First delivered Sep 2013
El Salvador (SLV)								
A-37B *Dragonfly*	Atk ac	10	US$860m	CHL	Government Surplus	2013	n.k.	Ex-CHL surplus
Guatemala (GUA)								
EMB-314 *Super Tucano*	Trg ac	6	n.k.	BRZ	Embraer	2013	2014	Order put on hold Jul 2013
Mexico (MEX)								
MEXSAT	Sat	3	US$1bn	US	Boeing	2010	2012	MEXSAT-3 launched Dec 2012. MEXSAT-1 to follow 2013–14
EC725 *Super Cougar*	Tpt hel	6	n.k.	Int'l	Eurocopter	2010	2013	Follow on from similar order signed in 2009. First delivered by Jun 2013
Nicaragua (NIC)								
Molniya-class	PCFG	2	n.k.	RUS	Sredne-Nevsky Shipyard	2013	n.k.	–
Peru (PER)								
Makassar-class	LPD	2	n.k.	ROK	Dae Sun Shipbuilding & Engineering	2012	2015	Construction of first vessel commenced Jul 2013
55m OPV	PCO	5	n.k.	ROK	STX Offshore & Shipbuilding	2013	2015	To be based on ROK *Gumdoksori*-class. First two to be built in ROK; remaining three in PER
DHC-6-400 *Twin Otter*	Tpt ac	12	n.k.	CAN	Viking Air	2010	2011	Four delivered by Apr 2013
KT-1	Trg ac	20	US$200m	ROK	KAI	2012	2014	Ten KT-1 and ten KA-1 variants. First four to be manufactured in ROK, remainder in PER
Venezuela (VEN)								
S-300VM	SAM	n.k.	n.k.	RUS	Almaz-Antey	n.k.	2013	First delivered to 39th AD bde in 2013
Y-8	Tpt ac	8	n.k.	PRC	AVIC	2011	2012	Six delivered by late 2013. Delivery to be complete in 2014

Chapter Nine
Sub-Saharan Africa

The conflict in Mali

The already fragile security situation in Mali rapidly deteriorated in January 2013. A coup in early 2012 had toppled the government, the north of the country had effectively been lost to Tuareg and Islamist rebels, and though there had been pledges of international military assistance in the form of an Economic Community of West African States (ECOWAS) contingent and an EU training mission, the deployments had yet to take place.

On 10 January, more than 1,000 Islamists captured the central town of Konna. Two mobile columns of rebel forces moved towards regional capitals Mopti and Ségou, opening the route to the south – and the capital, Bamako. Resistance from Malian troops gave interim President Dioncounda Traoré time to request assistance from former colonial power, France. Acting under Article 51 of the UN charter, France's President François Hollande ordered immediate military intervention. (See *Survival: Global Politics and Strategy*, April–May 2013.)

Under *Opération Serval*, French special forces helicopters stationed in Burkina Faso attacked rebel forces at Mopti and an air base at Sevaré, and bombing missions were conducted by Chad-based *Mirage* 2000Ds, while light armour drove to Bamako within less than 24 hours from France's *Opération Licorne* in Côte d'Ivoire. Ostensibly supporting Malian troops, the mobility, firepower and training of the French (and the Chadian forces deployed in many cases alongside them) were invaluable in stopping the advance of the Islamists, and in forcing their retreat to the northeastern mountains, where numerous bases and weapons stores were found. As noted in last year's *Military Balance* (see pp. 480–81), rebel activity in Mali's north was given a material boost by the outflow of weaponry from Libya after the fall of the Gadhafi regime.

At the same time, African states pledged immediate troop deployments; the first forces from the African-led International Support Mission in Mali (AFISMA) arrived on 17 January. France's intervention was always intended to be temporary, but with continued rebel activity in some northern towns, as well as doubts as to the capability of AFISMA troops, it was suggested that AFISMA undergo in-country training, as well as convert to a United Nations peacekeeping force. This UN Stabilisation Mission in Mali took over from AFISMA on 1 July. Chad, Nigeria, Niger and Burkina Faso were among the nine regional countries deploying troops, though some of the Nigerian contingent withdrew late in 2013 citing operational priorities at home. The long-planned EU training mission also began in 2013 and is scheduled to last 15 months. A full range of military skills are taught, as well as international humanitarian law and human rights, and in specialist areas such as military intelligence. Two battalions had passed out by September 2013, and a third started training in October. Mentoring continues beyond the initial training: when the *Waraba* battalion departed for the north in June, it was supported by a French detachment.

The French intervention was impressive for the speed with which contingency planning was activated and adapted; rapid entry into theatre and establishment of reliable logistics corridors; the tactics employed; and also the combat effectiveness of the troops deployed. But France's pre-positioned forces in the region proved vital (see Map 2, p. 67), as did the accumulated local knowledge that both these forces and planners back home had accumulated. The intervention did highlight some weaknesses, though. France's air-to-air refuellers were stretched, and with A400M not then in-service, strategic airlift was a problem only surmounted by capability provided by the UK, Canada, the US (with C-17s), Sweden (with C-130) and commercial leases. Intelligence and surveillance assets were also at a premium, and to provide additional capabilities the UK deployed one *Sentinel* aircraft alongside already deployed French *Harfang* unmanned aerial vehicles (UAVs).

The intervention drove the Islamists north and stabilised the government in Bamako, but militant activity continued throughout the year; attacks in Timbuktu and Gao were reported in September and October, and there was a reported breakdown in peace negotiations with ethnic Tuareg groups.

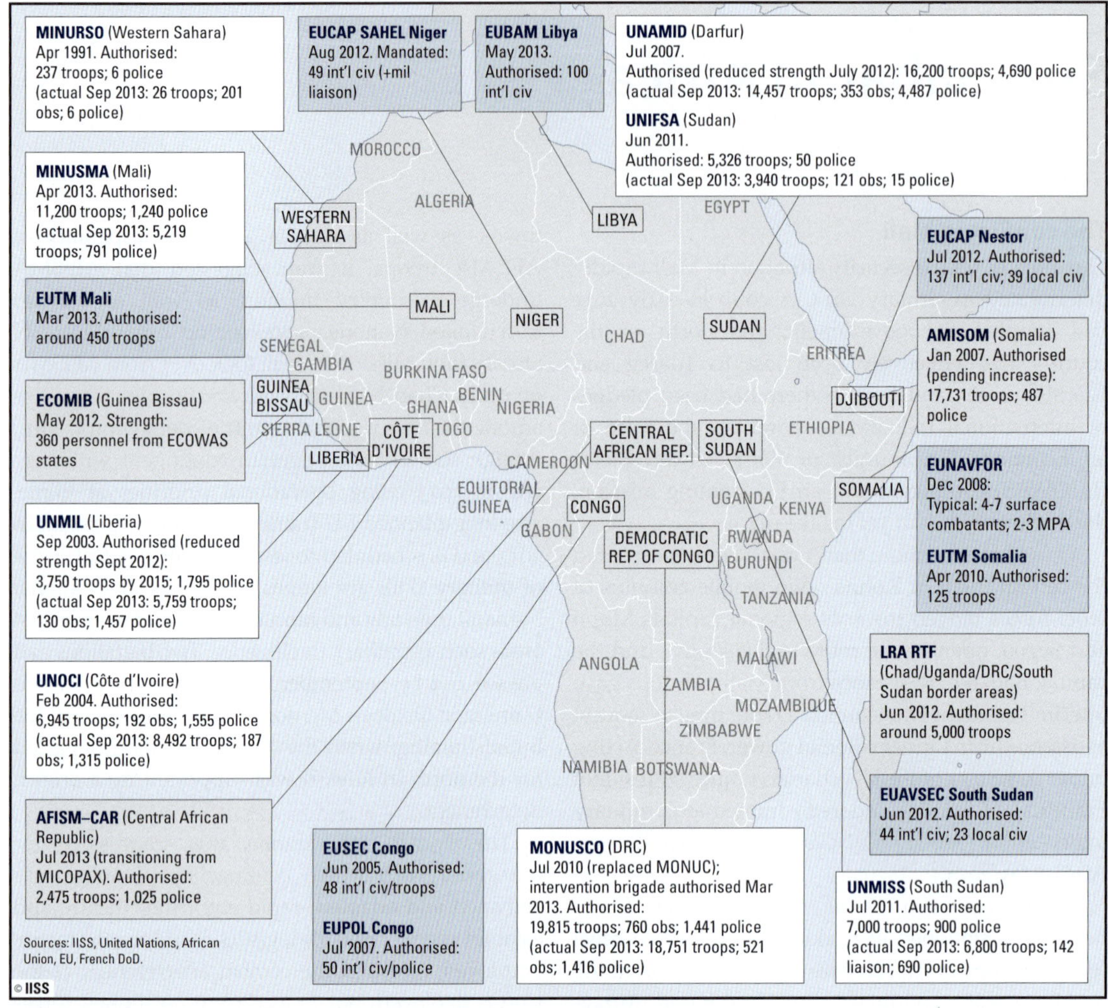

Map 8 **Africa: Selected Peacekeeping and Security Missions**

Durable solutions to the security problems in Mali, and in the wider Sahel to the north, will take years to implement. The capacity of the government and the arms of state, including that of the security forces, to absorb substantial assistance in a short time remains limited. In a situation where the government has not had effective control over a large part of the country for a time, creating the conditions to re-establish sustainable government control involves far more than just effective security forces; a full range of state and local institutions have to take root, and local economies and civil society have to develop. In the north there is an additional factor: numerous areas have seen significant population movements; as a result of the fighting, many ethnic Tuareg have returned to the refugee camps it had taken them years to leave.

Islamist groups used the ungoverned space of the Sahel to their advantage. Mokhtar Belmokhtar – commander of the Signed in Blood battalion, a splinter group of al-Qaeda in the Islamic Maghreb (AQIM) – had threatened to retaliate for efforts to dislodge Islamists in Mali. The attack on the In Amenas gas facility in Algeria that followed in January 2013 was carried out by his group. Signed in Blood is also believed to be responsible for planning attacks in Niger, though experts assess that these were carried out by the Movement for Jihad and Oneness in West Africa. The vast territory involved, and shortage of key capabilities among regional armed forces, places at a premium certain capacities held by Western armed forces, such as persistent wide-area intelligence, surveillance and reconnaissance (ISR). The ability of local armed forces to integrate the product of these assets into their own planning processes remains open to question. A key issue for concerned external states will be how to generate persistent overwatch and how to coordinate with regional armed forces so that potential threats can be addressed rapidly, ideally by local forces.

Opération Serval was, according to media reports, welcomed by Malian civilians, but the picture was perhaps more mixed across the wider continent. There was no desire for Mali to fall to the Islamists, but perhaps some unease that a former colonial power was the only force in the region able to act with such strength, and at such short notice, even after years of work towards building military capacities, and regional standby forces as part of the African Union's (AU) African Peace and Security Architecture, detailed in previous editions of *The Military Balance*.

Continental security initiatives

The aspiration for continent-wide standby forces has not dimmed, although the date for initial operating capability might have slipped to 2015. But the Mali conflict perhaps gave fresh impetus to the desire to create rapid-reaction forces. Though a rapid deployment capability (RDC) was integral to the standby force concept, the AU has said that 'it appears unlikely that we can upgrade the regional RDCs to a satisfactory operational level within a reasonable timeframe'.

As a result, the AU proposed on 25 January an African Immediate Crisis Response Capacity, intended to be 5,000 strong and comprise 1,500-strong battlegroups, capable of deployment within ten days and self-sustaining for 30 days. Operationalising such a force will prove challenging. Personnel can be earmarked, but generating the capacities necessary to deploy, intervene and sustain are more problematic and, while some materials could be drawn from the AU's logistics bases (such as at Douala, Cameroon) and those of the UN, military capabilities such as airlift and integrated ISR are harder to obtain. Nonetheless, the willingness of African states to deploy and engage has been noteworthy in recent years, for instance in the hybrid mission in Darfur, the ad hoc Regional Cooperative Initiative against the Lord's Resistance Army and, particularly, the African Union Mission in Somalia (AMISOM) deployment to Somalia. Outside enablers and sustainment capacities are still required in these missions though, and while the capabilities of deployed ground troops have developed as a result of recent combat experience, deployments on a continental scale require access to a greater range of assets and skills than many states currently possess.

The resources and capabilities of the UN are still drawn upon for many of the continent's peacekeeping missions. Speaking on 29 May 2013, UN Secretary-General Ban Ki-moon said that 'to meet emerging threats and rise to new challenges, [UN] peacekeeping is adjusting its policies to better fulfil its mandates to bring lasting peace to war-torn countries'.

The announcement that the UN was setting up an intervention brigade for deployment to eastern Democratic Republic of the Congo (DRC) was the strongest manifestation of Ban's desire. Spurred by the failure of the United Nations Organization Stabilization Mission in the Democratic Republic of the Congo (MONUSCO) mission to tackle M23 rebels in early 2013, this intervention brigade was deployed by August 2013 to support MONUSCO. Its mandated strength is a three-battalion group with artillery, special forces and reconnaissance companies. The brigade has responsibility for 'neutralising armed groups … and reducing the threat posed by armed groups to state authority and civilian security in eastern DRC'.

In October, the Congolese army (FARDC) and the UN intervention force drove M23 rebels from their final two strongholds. M23 has stated that it will now disarm and pursue political dialogue, though the longer-term prognosis for peace in the east is unclear. The DRC intervention brigade announcement drew some praise, and though there was uncertainty about the precise composition of the combat support package, the mission was reported to have deployed helicopter gunships and artillery in support of FARDC forces. However, it remains to be seen whether UN forces' participation in combat actions will have an effect on other UN personnel in more established peacekeeping deployments. Mali was also noteworthy in this context: there was no peace agreement when the mission was discussed, and the possibility was that UN forces could be entering a conflict zone. These developments come at a time when UN missions more broadly are likely to come under scrutiny, with the UN engaged in its New Horizon Initiative peacekeeping review.

Nigeria: moving beyond Joint Task Forces

Nigeria's armed and security forces remain deployed in the country's northeast to combat Boko Haram. The group was established in 2002, but skirmishes with Nigerian security forces – and the destruction of its base in Kanamma, Yobe State – forced the group underground. When it re-emerged in 2010, now led by Abubakar Shekau, its motivations and modus operandi had changed. Boko Haram strengthened its links with AQIM – and possibly Somalia's al-Shabaab – from which it received weapons, funding and training. This allowed the group to upscale its offensive capability, using improvised explosive devices (IEDs) and rocket-propelled grenades, and conducting drive-by shootings and suicide attacks. Observed weapons systems include technicals mounted with anti-aircraft guns, as well as lighter weapons. In spring 2013, the group grew in strength and confidence, and gained control over parts of Borno State.

Members of both Boko Haram and its offshoot Ansaru travelled to Mali to train in camps organised by AQIM. This experience gave them greater exposure to the tactics and broader jihadist ideology of al-Qaeda sympathisers operating to the north. However, France's *Opération Serval* forced many of these fighters to return to Nigeria. With this infusion

South Africa: deployment lessons

South Africa has the largest economy in Africa and it is one of the top 30 economies worldwide. Its armed forces possess some of the most advanced platforms available on the continent, but it is towards the bottom end of the top ten African contributors to peacekeeping forces. This owes much to a doctrine outlined in the 1996 Defence White Paper and 1998 Defence Review, which suggested that a substantive regional role should be eschewed, limiting deployments to 'one battalion for up to twelve months'. By 2006 the doctrine had been overtaken by continental contingencies: South Africa had joint battalion-strength task forces in Burundi and the DRC; a battalion in Darfur and one, briefly, in the island state of Comoros; and had conducted several smaller missions.

By this time, then-president Thabo Mbeki's strategic view was that Africa had to 'show willing' to win external support, and that South Africa had to take a lead. But his foreign policy was vague: there was no concept of vital interests, there had been no substantive articulation of defence policy since 1998 and, according to analysts, the armed forces had not argued for commensurate capability.

The army's airborne brigade was disbanded (one airborne battalion remains), the air force withdrew half its transports and tankers (the last retiring in the late 2000s) and the navy its only dedicated transport vessel. In 1999, it bought four *Valour*-class frigates, too few, say some analysts, for operations in home and regional waters. Added to this, funding has reduced since 1989, while commitments have increased.

The 2012 Defence Review (due to be finalised by end-2013) is an attempt to reassess doctrine and long-term planning. As noted in *The Military Balance 2013* (p. 489), it accepted the reality of South African involvement in regional security and proposed a level of ambition for it. President Jacob Zuma is keen to follow through on this strategic view, but the current armed forces will find it a challenge to sustain the present operational tempo: army personnel strength means maintaining a consistent deployment cycle (train–deploy–return–rest) is a serious challenge; the air force has difficulty keeping pilots current, has limited airlift and no dedicated maritime patrol capability; the navy has a limited inventory and no sealift; and training and maintenance are hampered by funding levels. Successive defence ministers and parliament's defence committee have repeatedly warned that the South African National Defence Force (SANDF) is, as the latter put it, in a 'fatal downward spiral'.

For Pretoria's foreign deployments, these issues have added urgency. When MONUSCO failed in its defence of Goma, eastern DRC, in November 2012, Pretoria had no options for rapidly reinforcing or extracting South African troops in company and platoon bases in the region. When the protection force for a training contingent in the Central African Republic was attacked by rebels in March 2013, again immediate reinforcement or extraction were impossible. A total of 15 troops died – a number that would have been higher but for hard fighting by the SANDF contingent.

For all this, the armed forces have learned lessons about sustaining forces far from home; operating in deserts, forests and 'among the people' of different cultures; and from other deployed forces during international exercises. Experience has highlighted the need to be both more agile and more effective in smaller force packages, with implications for communications and precision weapons. Active deployment has improved morale and developed the skills and self-confidence of junior officers particularly. The degree to which these lessons have influenced wider government policy will become apparent in the strategic vision of the Defence Review, and in the organisational and capability requirements it sets out (notably around rapid deployment, air and sealift and long-range sustainment), as well as in debates around future defence funding.

of trained personnel, attacks became more audacious and greater geographical and operational overlap was observed, the most notable being Boko Haram's adoption of kidnapping as a tactic.

Military response

Joint Task Force (JTF) *Operation Restore Order* was established in June 2011 with the mandate to restore law and order in the northeast, and Borno State in particular. This army-led force comprised elements of the Department of State Security, the Defence Intelligence Agency, the police, the customs service and the immigration service. Later that year, the federal government approved the establishment of a number of permanent operational bases for JTFs.

Nigerian authorities view Boko Haram as an example of the convergence of terrorist and criminal elements, requiring a full-spectrum counter-insurgency approach, including counter-terrorism (CT) and regular law-enforcement components. To this end, the government created the position of National CT Coordinator in 2012. A new national-security strategy and a national counter-terrorism strategy are also planned. In 2013, the army's Counter-Terrorism and Counter-Insurgency Centre, situated at the Armed Forces Command and Staff College in Jaji, Kaduna State, began training a further 3,000 personnel in skills ranging from urban patrolling and unarmed combat to humanitarian law.

In January 2012, President Goodluck Jonathan declared a state of emergency in 15 local areas as a result of increasing attacks across Borno, Yobe, Niger and Plateau states. Although this lasted only six months, a second state of emergency was declared in May 2013 in Borno, Yobe and Adamawa states. Concerns were expressed that the federal government had effectively lost territorial control of parts of the northeast. This coincided with the deployment to Borno of 2,000 additional security personnel and military assets, while 1,000 extra troops were sent to Adamawa, bringing the deployed total to approximately 8,000. A number of Boko Haram camps in Borno were destroyed, and large amounts of weapons recovered, including locally made rockets, IED components and mobile-communications equipment.

In August 2013, it was announced that the JTF would be replaced by around 8,000 troops sent to the northeast to form a new (7th) army division in Borno State, roled for counter-terrorist tasks. This comprises elements of the 1st Mechanised Brigade (Sokoto, and part of the 1st Division); 21st Armoured Brigade (Maiduguri) and 23rd Armoured Brigade (Yola), both part of the 3rd Armoured Division; plus 1,000 troops recalled from Mali.

As a result of growing military pressure in the northeast, Boko Haram elements have relocated to other northern states including Kano, Kaduna and Katsina; the city of Kano has suffered some particularly bloody attacks; schools and mosques are frequent targets. Substantial numbers of fighters are believed to have escaped after May 2013 into neighbouring Chad and Niger, two countries whose border areas, together with that of Cameroon, have reportedly been used as refuges and recruitment grounds.

DEFENCE ECONOMICS

Relatively robust growth continued across the region, according to the IMF's Regional Economic Outlook, averaging 5% in 2012. Inflation also continued to ease, dropping more than two percentage points to 7.9% in 2012, reflecting the stabilisation of food and fuel prices relative to recent years, tightened monetary policies in some states, and improved weather conditions. However, the sub-regional variations noted in previous editions of *The Military Balance* remain: 2012 growth in oil-exporting countries was 6.1%; in low-income countries (LICs) it was 5.7%; in fragile countries (such as Côte d'Ivoire) it was 7% according to the IMF; and in middle-income countries (MICs) the figure was 3.3%.

The generally positive growth trajectory reflected the relative lack of integration between less-developed African states and financial markets, which served to insulate and 'de-link' growth rates enjoyed by LICs during the global financial crisis from economic conditions in the developed world. Conversely, the slower growth experienced in MICs such as South Africa reflected their ties to the wider global financial system. Oil-exporting states and LICs saw elevated growth rates as a result of foreign investment: the attraction of the former lay in their fast-developing on- and off-shore oil and gas sectors, while both attracted new investment based on the potential of existing and new extractive industries, such as the minerals sector.

Instability and conflict continued to act as a brake on development. This was particularly true of Mali and Guinea-Bissau, according to the IMF. Its staff were unable to update their forecasts for the Central African Republic, which remained highly unstable

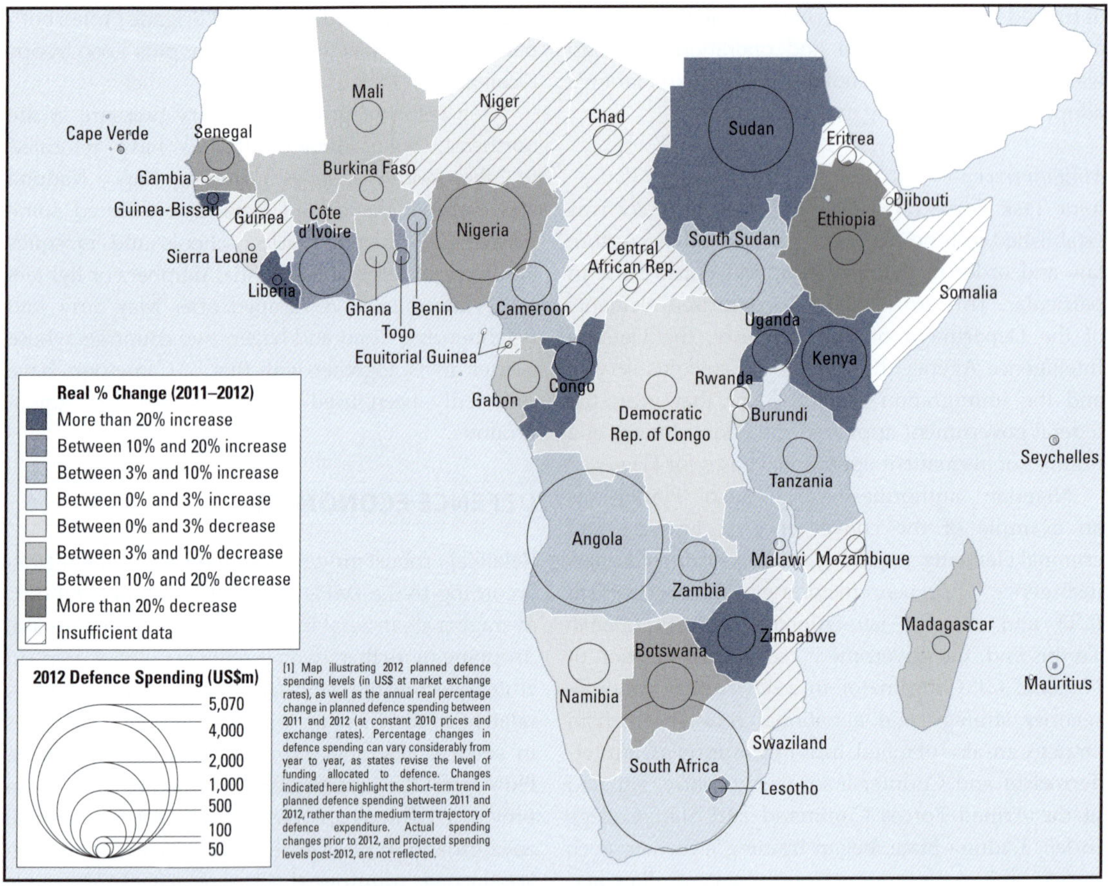

Cape Verde
Senegal
Gambia
Guinea-Bissau
Guinea
Sierra Leone
Liberia
Mali
Burkina Faso
Côte d'Ivoire
Ghana
Togo
Benin
Niger
Nigeria
Chad
Cameroon
Equitorial Guinea
Gabon
Congo
Central African Rep.
Sudan
South Sudan
Eritrea
Djibouti
Ethiopia
Somalia
Uganda
Kenya
Rwanda
Burundi
Democratic Rep. of Congo
Tanzania
Seychelles
Angola
Zambia
Malawi
Mozambique
Madagascar
Zimbabwe
Botswana
Namibia
Mauritius
Swaziland
South Africa
Lesotho

Real % Change (2011–2012)
More than 20% increase
Between 10% and 20% increase
Between 3% and 10% increase
Between 0% and 3% increase
Between 0% and 3% decrease
Between 3% and 10% decrease
Between 10% and 20% decrease
More than 20% decrease
Insufficient data

2012 Defence Spending (US$m)
5,070
4,000
2,000
1,000
500
100
50

[1] Map illustrating 2012 planned defence spending levels (in US$ at market exchange rates), as well as the annual real percentage change in planned defence spending between 2011 and 2012 (at constant 2010 prices and exchange rates). Percentage changes in defence spending can vary considerably from year to year, as states revise the level of funding allocated to defence. Changes indicated here highlight the short-term trend in planned defence spending between 2011 and 2012, rather than the medium term trajectory of defence expenditure. Actual spending changes prior to 2012, and projected spending levels post-2012, are not reflected.

Map 9 **Sub-Saharan Africa Regional Defence Spending[1]**

after a March coup. Sudan, South Sudan and Somalia also suffered from the effects of instability, as did the resource-rich DRC, enduring another year of conflict.

Though the economic impact of climatic conditions such as drought was reportedly moderate in 2012, the floods that took place in Nigeria in mid-2012 slowed growth, despite the country's upward economic trajectory. Continued conflict in parts of the country has the potential to affect economic development, as witnessed in the Niger Delta, where heightened violence has had a detrimental impact on the country's hydrocarbons sector.

While Nigeria remains the continent's major oil producer, other states are also seeing strong growth in this sector, including Angola and a number of East Africa nations, where substantial oil and gas discoveries have been made in recent years. Sudan and South Sudan account for most East African production but, according to the US Energy Information Administration, 'Mozambique, Tanzania, Uganda and Madagascar have shown the most progress toward commercial development of newly discovered reserves'.

Nevertheless, the effect of global commodity prices on regional economies will remain pronounced. While the near-term outlook remains positive, the dependence of some economies on extractive industries, particularly in the non-oil sector, increases their exposure to price fluctuations. Though Sub-Saharan African economies have seen increased growth, and exports of extractive products are increasing, this has not always translated into healthier balance sheets. As the IMF noted, 'budget surpluses declined in many oil exporters, reflecting sharp increases in public spending'. It remains unclear whether such states will, therefore, be willing to divert substantially greater resources to their armed forces or to defence procurements. Defence-spending plans are often formulated with immediate security imperatives in mind, but governments will be conscious of the effect that prolonged instability has on economic

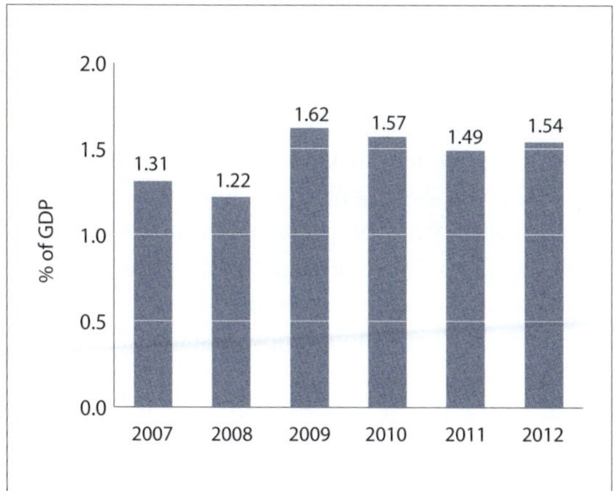

Figure 21 **Sub-Saharan Africa Regional Defence Expenditure** as % of GDP

development and investor confidence. This could provide states, with a sufficiently compelling reason, to still invest in defence and security, despite the sub-optimal economic conditions.

Many procurements in 2012 focused on capabilities that could be used in both military and security roles, and the same was true in 2013. For example, patrol vessels recently purchased by Nigeria, Mauritius, Mozambique and Senegal, though capable of military-related tasks, could also perform constabulary and security roles. Other states continued the trajectory noted in *The Military Balance 2013* of filling in long-held gaps in certain capabilities, such as medium-airlift, of which the ongoing purchase of C-295s by Ghana and Cameroon is an example.

While many African states currently possess light transport aircraft capable of carrying personnel, many do not have aircraft capable of transporting equipment or armour. Some rely on international assistance for such capabilities, as provided by NATO in lifting AMISOM troop contingents.

The number of helicopter deals (see p. 470) is also a reflection of states' awareness of the need to bolster tactical airlift and mobility, while the rising number of advanced turboprop aircraft contracts is also noteworthy. A limited number of countries have either the financial or maintenance/logistics support to make the purchase of advanced combat aircraft cost-effective. Some are seeking to secure more advanced capability from high-end turboprops, such as the EMB-314 *Super Tucano*, as ordered by Burkina Faso and Senegal, while Angola is buying more of these aircraft to fulfil its training requirements.

ETHIOPIA

Ethiopia is a substantial military and economic power in northeast Africa. It is currently engaged in military operations in Somalia, is the major African troop-contributing state for UN peacekeeping operations, and is also engaged in a substantial defence-modernisation programme. Its capital, Addis Ababa, is home to the administrative centre of the AU and numerous other international institutions, a reflection of the development of civil and communications infrastructure in the city since the end of the Ethiopian Civil War in 1991.

The beginning of the civil war is generally held as 1974, when Emperor Haile Selassie was overthrown by a group of military and security officials known as the Derg (committee). Political and military opposition to this new regime came from a variety of sources, including groups that had previously backed the unseating of the emperor, as well as a number of revolutionary groups, such as the eventually victorious Ethiopian People's Revolutionary Democratic Front (EPRDF).

Creating national armed forces

After the downfall of the Derg regime in 1987, a new Ethiopian National Defence Force (ENDF) was created and later established in law. Since then, Ethiopia's armed forces have undergone two extensive demobilisation, disarmament and reintegration (DDR) programmes. The first (1992–95) followed the amalgamation of the revolutionary forces of the EPRDF and elements of the Derg armed forces. The second (2001–03), coming in the wake of the 1998–2000 war with Eritrea, also encompassed some former Derg forces who had rejoined during the conflict. The two DDR programmes, almost entirely locally designed and implemented, have been largely effective in not only disarming and demobilising former combatants, but also reintegrating them back into civilian life.

The secession of Eritrea in 1996 also forced the armed forces to adjust: Ethiopia's navy was disbanded, its ships were sold, and large amounts of equipment and materiel became the property of the Eritrean armed forces. Personnel numbers have fluctuated over the years, from over 500,000 in 1991 to as low as 60,000 in 1998, to nearly 300,000 in 2000 at the end of the Ethiopia–Eritrea war and now to their current strength of approximately 135,000.

Today's armed forces reflect these fluctuations, with large numbers of senior officers who fought both for and against the Derg regime, and with much of their basic equipment based upon the enormous shipments of arms from the Soviet Union in the mid-to-late 1980s.

Defence reform

A ten-year modernisation plan for the defence establishment was implemented in 2005. It is designed to modernise and reorganise the ENDF to fulfil the objectives laid down in the 1995 constitution and the 2002 Foreign Affairs and National Security Policy and Strategy. The intention is that the armed forces will be flexible enough to adapt to political and security developments in the Horn of Africa and across the continent.

Defence policy follows a set of 'principles for national defence' as outlined in the constitution: equitable representation of ethnicities, a civilian minister of defence, protection of the sovereignty of the country, adherence to the constitution and independence from political partisanship. Some of these objectives, such as equitable representation, have yet to be fully realised.

The 2002 strategy document builds on these basic principles and sets out the rationale for and role of the ENDF in supporting both foreign policy and national security. The essential premise is that if Ethiopia is to achieve the development and progress that it seeks, it must work to create a stable region within which it can develop. The emphasis is on early diplomatic engagement, with a strong defence capability as a supporting pillar.

The document also explains the need to conduct a threat assessment before building military capacity, the importance of personnel development in the armed forces, as well as the need to restrict defence expenditure to 2% of GDP unless an imminent threat requires more. Although published in 2002, analysts say the the strategy is still an effective guide to diplomatic and defence activities.

Defence agreements are in place with Sudan, South Sudan, Kenya, Somalia, Somaliland, Djibouti, Uganda, Burundi and Rwanda, as well as a number of more distant African nations. Foreign students from neighbouring countries are to be found in most of Ethiopia's military training schools and colleges, while small numbers of Ethiopian students attend the principal neighbouring staff colleges.

Of the regional states, only Eritrea remains outside the circle of ENDF engagement. Though conflict ended in 2000 with the Algiers Agreement, a territorial dispute remains, centred on the town of Badme (which is subject to a ruling by the internationally mandated Ethiopia–Eritrea Boundary Commission). If rapprochement is achieved, though, an early and constructive engagement by the ENDF with Eritrea's armed forces could be possible. Despite the war of 1998–2000, a number of close friendships still exist between senior figures on both sides; ties in many cases remain warm, though now distant.

Ethiopia's engagements in Somalia (initially unilaterally and now with the endorsement of the AU and UN), in Sudan with UNAMID and as the sole force provider for the UN Interim Stabilisation Force in Abyei, as well as in the Joint Border Verification and Monitoring Mission between Sudan and South Sudan, make sense in the context of the 2002 national security strategy. Addis Ababa has been accused of destabilising ambitions, particularly in light of its movements into Somalia, but for Addis, a stable Somalia is an essential element of its plan to make Ethiopia a middle-income economy by 2025. Similarly, Ethiopia views its engagement in the East African Standby Force (EASF) as a useful tool in developing ties between the armed forces of the Horn of Africa. However, Ethiopian personnel have been frustrated by the lack of progress after hard-won early agreements on structures and basing. They find the predominance of outside advisers, mostly from the West, to be unhelpful in finding regional solutions to the problems of mandating, interoperability and flexibility.

Reform during operations

The aim of the reform process is to have fully professional, all-volunteer armed forces, but there have been substantial challenges in meeting these targets while maintaining large numbers of troops on operations. Up to 50% of total land force personnel are deployed along the border with Eritrea, of whom one third are on the front line; between 5–8% are in Somalia; about 5% are on UN operations; and smaller numbers are deployed on internal operations. The desire to create a more ethnically balanced force has required the early retirement of proportionally larger numbers of Tigrayan personnel and the establishment of soldier-education programmes that take into account regional discrepancies in educational provision. For the air force, pilot selection and training has been an area of particular concern, and the UK's Royal Air Force has provided advice on pilot trainee selection processes.

The future size, shape and roles of the post-transformation ENDF will largely depend upon political and security developments in the region and beyond. When there is no longer a need to station substantial numbers of troops on the border with Eritrea, there will likely be another significant size reduction. A key driver for deciding eventual force strength and capability will be Ethiopia's level of ambition with regard to regional organisations (such as the Intergovernmental Authority for Development and the EASF), and more broadly with the AU and the UN. Glimpses of Ethiopian military developments so far seen – domestically manufactured tactical UAVs, telemedicine between defence hospitals, and information-security developments – indicate a growing capability.

Defence economics

Ethiopia has seen rapid economic growth over the past decade. After a sharp recession in 2003, the country witnessed double-digit rates of economic expansion between 2004 and 2011, averaging 11.4%. Even though growth rates have subsequently fallen, in 2013 the economy was still projected by the IMF to expand by 7%, supported by the government's interventionist approach to economic policymaking.

Sustained government deficits financed directly by the central bank at negative real interest rates, as well as by the forced purchase of treasury bills by private banks, have enabled the adoption of highly expansionist fiscal and monetary policies in support of the government's under-funded five-year Growth and Transformation Plan 2010–2015. It features large-scale state infrastructure projects to upgrade road, rail, power and communications networks. As a result of these policies, the government has had to run down its foreign reserves in order to reduce excess liquidity, which had caused inflation to rise above 20% in 2011 and 2012, although this had stabilised at around 7% in 2013.

Despite its continued reliance on the agricultural sector and soft commodity exports, as well as the crowding-out of the private sector by public investment, Ethiopia has seen GDP per capita quadruple in nominal terms over the last decade (it doubled in real terms), and the IMF forecasts that the country will continue to grow at a healthy 7% over the next five years.

Defence procurement

As part of the transformation plan, the ENDF is investing heavily in new equipment. Almost a third of the US$405m defence budget for FY2013/14 has been earmarked to build mobility and weapons capacity. The purchase of several hundred wheeled and tracked armoured personnel carriers from China in 2007–08 and 200 T-72 main battle tanks from Ukraine in 2011 illustrate the trend towards replacing large amounts of worn-out ex-Soviet equipment with smaller numbers of more capable modern equipment. The overall defence budget has remained within, and often below, the 2% guideline since the end of the Ethiopia–Eritrea war, though with GDP rising, actual annual defence expenditure has risen from 4.4–7.5bn Ethiopian Birr (US$273–405m) between FY2011/12 and FY2013/14.

Defence industry

The ENDF inherited a large but inefficient defence industry. It began under Emperor Menelik II in the early 1900s, when an ammunition factory was set up. By the early 2000s, there were eight military factories refurbishing vehicles and weapons; repairing and overhauling aircraft and building prototype UAVs; and producing uniforms and associated equipment. In 2010, the sector was moved from the defence ministry to become an autonomous government-owned public industrial enterprise, the Metals and Engineering Corporation (METEC). This retains many links to the ministry, including large numbers of personnel employed within elements that have been transferred over, and continues to undertake defence-related work. METEC's core business is to design and manufacture products and facilities for the benefit of the public and the private sector. Currently, METEC is comprised of 15 semi-autonomous and integrated manufacturing companies that operate in more than nine different sectors. This mingling of defence and civil industrial capacity, with defence personnel remaining at the top, has led to speculation that while the separation from the defence ministry might have taken place on paper, it has not happened in practice, and that the ENDF now benefits from control of a large part of the national hi-tech industrial capacity. However, the precise arrangements for government oversight of METEC and its contribution to or benefit from defence finances, if any, remain unclear.

Angola ANG

New Angolan Kwanza AOA		2012	2013	2014
GDP	AOA	11.3tr	12.2tr	
	US$	119bn	126bn	
per capita	US$	5,873	6,033	
Growth	%	8.41	6.18	
Inflation	%	10.28	9.40	
Def bdgt	AOA	396bn	588bn	
	US$	4.15bn	6.05bn	
USD1=AOA		95.42	97.18	

Population 18,565,269

Ethnic groups: Ovimbundu 37%; Kimbundu 25%; Bakongo 13%

Age	0–14	15–19	20–24	25–29	30–64	65 plus
Male	22.2%	5.8%	4.6%	3.8%	12.8%	1.3%
Female	21.3%	5.6%	4.4%	3.7%	12.8%	1.6%

Capabilities

The role of the armed forces is to ensure national sovereignty and territorial integrity. The primary challenge is the continuing activity of secessionist groups in the enclave province of Cabinda. Angola's equipment inventory is largely of Soviet/Russian origin, acquired during the conflict with UNITA over a decade ago. While on paper the army and air force constitute a considerable regional force, combat availability and serviceability of much equipment remains questionable. Force health and education have been investment priorities, although growing defence ties with China might result in equipment recapitalisation. The air force retains a tactical airlift capability, and, unusually for the region, also has a limited capacity for longer-range transport missions. The armed forces train regularly, and participate in multinational exercises.

ACTIVE 107,000 (Army 100,000 Navy 1,000 Air 6,000) Paramilitary 10,000

ORGANISATIONS BY SERVICE

Army 100,000

FORCES BY ROLE

MANOEUVRE

Armoured

1 tk bde

Light

1 SF bde

1 (1st) div (1 mot inf bde, 2 inf bde)

1 (2nd) div (3 mot inf bde, 3 inf bde, 1 arty regt)

1 (3rd) div (2 mot inf bde, 3 inf bde)

1 (4th) div (1 tk regt, 5 mot inf bde, 2 inf bde, 1 engr bde)

1 (5th) div (2 inf bde)

1 (6th) div (3 inf bde, 1 engr bde)

COMBAT SUPPORT

Some engr units

COMBAT SERVICE SUPPORT

Some log units

EQUIPMENT BY TYPE†

MBT 300: ε200 T-54/T-55; 50 T-62; 50 T-72

LT TK 10 PT-76

RECCE 600 BRDM-2

AIFV 250+: 250 BMP-1/BMP-2; BMD-3

APC (W) ε170 BTR-152/BTR-60/BTR-80

ARTY 1,408+

SP 16+: **122mm** 2S1; **152mm** 4 2S3; **203mm** 12 2S7

TOWED 552: **122mm** 500 D-30; **130mm** 48 M-46; **152mm** 4 D-20

MRL 90+: **122mm** 90: 50 BM-21; 40 RM-70 *Dana*; **240mm** BM-24

MOR 750: **82mm** 250; **120mm** 500

AT • MSL • MANPATS 9K11 (AT-3 *Sagger*)

RCL 500: 400 **82mm** B-10/**107mm** B-11 †; **106mm** 100†

GUNS • SP **100mm** SU-100†

AD • SAM • MANPAD 500 9K32 *Strela*-2 (SA-7 *Grail*)‡; 9K36 *Strela*-3 (SA-14 *Gremlin*); 9K310 *Igla*-1 (SA-16 *Gimlet*)

GUNS • TOWED 450+: **14.5mm** ZPU-4; **23mm** ZU-23-2; **37mm** M-1939; **57mm** S-60

ARV T-54/T-55

MW Bozena

Navy ε1,000

EQUIPMENT BY TYPE

PATROL AND COASTAL COMBATANTS 22

PCO 2 *Ngola Kiluange* with 1 hel landing platform (Ministry of Fisheries)

PCC 5 *Rei Bula Matadi* (Ministry of Fisheries)

PBF 5 PVC-170

PB 10: 4 *Mandume;* 5 *Comandante Imperial Santana* (Ministry of Fisheries); 1 Damen 2810 (Ministry of Fisheries)

Coastal Defence

EQUIPMENT BY TYPE

MSL • AShM SS-C-1B *Sepal* (at Luanda)

Air Force/Air Defence 6,000

FORCES BY ROLE

FIGHTER

1 sqn with MiG-21bis/MF *Fishbed*

1 sqn with Su-27/Su-27UB *Flanker*

FIGHTER/GROUND ATTACK

1 sqn with MiG-23BN/ML/UB *Flogger*

1 sqn with Su-22 *Fitter* D

1 sqn with Su-25 *Frogfoot*

MARITIME PATROL

1 sqn with F-27-200 MPA; C-212 *Aviocar*

TRANSPORT

3 sqn with An-12 *Cub*; An-26 *Curl*; An-32 *Cline*; An-72 *Coaler*; BN-2A *Islander*; C-212 *Aviocar*; Do-28D *Skyservant*; EMB-135BJ *Legacy* 600 (VIP); Il-76TD *Candid*

TRAINING

1 sqn with EMB-312 *Tucano*

1 sqn with L-29 *Delfin*; L-39 *Albatros*

1 sqn with PC-7 *Turbo Trainer*; PC-9*
1 sqn with Z-142
ATTACK HELICOPTER
2 sqn with Mi-24/Mi-35 *Hind*; SA342M *Gazelle* (with HOT)
TRANSPORT HELICOPTER
2 sqn with AS565; SA316 *Alouette* III (IAR-316) (incl trg)
1 sqn with Bell 212
1 sqn with Mi-8 *Hip*; Mi-17 *Hip* H
AIR DEFENCE
5 bn/10 bty with S-125 *Pechora* (SA-3 *Goa*); 9K35 *Strela*-10 (SA-13 *Gopher*)†; 2K12 *Kub* (SA-6 *Gainful*); 9K33 *Osa* (SA-8 *Gecko*); 9K31 *Strela*-1 (SA-9 *Gaskin*); S-75M *Volkhov* (SA-2 *Guideline*)

EQUIPMENT BY TYPE†
AIRCRAFT 83 combat capable
FTR 24: 6 Su-27/Su-27UB *Flanker*; 18 MiG-23ML *Flogger*
FGA 42+: 20 MiG-21bis/MF *Fishbed*; 8 MiG-23BN/UB *Flogger*; 13 Su-22 *Fitter* D; 1+ Su-24 *Fencer*
ATK 10: 8 Su-25 *Frogfoot*; 2 Su-25UB *Frogfoot*
ELINT 1 B-707
TPT 50: **Heavy** 4 Il-76TD *Candid*; **Medium** 6 An-12 *Cub*; **Light** 40: 12 An-26 *Curl*; 3 An-32 *Cline*; 8 An-72 *Coaler*; 8 BN-2A *Islander*; 3 C-212-200 *Aviocar*; 4 C-212-300M *Aviocar*; 1 Do-28D *Skyservant*; 1 EMB-135BJ *Legacy* 600 (VIP)
TRG 39: 13 EMB-312 *Tucano*; 3 EMB-314 *Super Tucano** (3 more on order); 6 L-29 *Delfin*; 2 L-39C *Albatros*; 5 PC-7 *Turbo Trainer*; 4 PC-9*; 6 Z-142
HELICOPTERS
ATK 44: 22 Mi-24 *Hind*; 22 Mi-35 *Hind*
MRH 26: 8 AS565 *Panther*; 10 SA316 *Alouette* III (IAR-316) (incl trg); 8 SA342M *Gazelle*
MRH/TPT 27 Mi-8 *Hip*/Mi-17 *Hip* H
TPT • Light 8 Bell 212
AD • SAM 122
SP 70: 10 9K35 *Strela*-10 (SA-13 *Gopher*)†; 25 2K12 *Kub* (SA-6 *Gainful*); 15 9K33 *Osa* (SA-8 *Gecko*); 20 9K31 *Strela*-1 (SA-9 *Gaskin*)
TOWED 52: 40 S-75M *Volkhov* (SA-2 *Guideline*)‡; 12 S-125 *Pechora* (SA-3 *Goa*)
MSL
ASM AT-2 *Swatter*; HOT
ARM Kh-28 (AS-9 *Kyle*)
AAM • IR R-3 (AA-2 *Atoll*)‡; R-60 (AA-8 *Aphid*); R-73 (AA-11 *Archer*); **IR/SARH** R-23/24 (AA-7 *Apex*)‡; R-27 (AA-10 *Alamo*)

Paramilitary 10,000

Rapid-Reaction Police 10,000

Benin BEN

CFA Franc BCEAO fr		2012	2013	2014
GDP	fr	3.79tr	4.08tr	
	US$	7.43bn	8.24bn	
per capita	US$	794	858	
Growth	%	3.85	4.14	
Inflation	%	6.75	3.47	
Def bdgt	fr	39.9bn	42.5bn	
	US$	78m	86m	
US$1=fr		509.99	494.90	

Population 9,877,292

Age	0–14	15–19	20–24	25–29	30–64	65 plus
Male	22.5%	5.6%	4.6%	3.9%	12.5%	1.1%
Female	21.6%	5.4%	4.4%	3.8%	13.0%	1.7%

Capabilities

The country fields a small military, dominated numerically by the army, with the navy and air force limited to providing a handful of platforms for transport and surveillance and inshore patrol respectively. Piracy in the Gulf of Guinea is likely acting as a prompt to the country's renewed interest in maritime patrol. Benin has been designated as the host for a Maritime Multinational Coordination Centre, to coordinate initiatives between Benin, Nigeria, Togo and Niger aimed at combating piracy and other organised crime. The army is predominantly a light infantry force, focused on tasks such as border security and peacekeeping. Capacity building initiatives are underway, with US personnel in 2013 engaged in logistics and 'train-the-trainer' activity in Cotonou. Meanwhile, US marines deployed to Africa Partnership Station 2013 trained Beninese troops in maritime security tasks.

ACTIVE 6,950 (Army 6,500 Navy 200 Air 250)
Paramilitary 2,500
Conscript liability 18 months (selective)

ORGANISATIONS BY SERVICE

Army 6,500

FORCES BY ROLE
MANOEUVRE
Armoured
2 armd sqn
Light
1 (rapid reaction) mot inf bn
8 inf bn
Air Manoeuvre
1 AB bn
COMBAT SUPPORT
1 arty bn
1 engr bn
1 sigs bn
COMBAT SERVICE SUPPORT
1 log bn
1 spt bn

EQUIPMENT BY TYPE

LT TK 18 PT-76 (op status uncertain)
RECCE 31: 14 BRDM-2; 7 M8; 10 VBL
APC (T) 22 M113
ARTY 16+
TOWED 105mm 16: 12 L118 Light Gun; 4 M101
MOR 81mm
AT • RL 89mm LRAC

Navy ε200

EQUIPMENT BY TYPE

PATROL AND COASTAL COMBATANTS
PB 5: 2 *Matelot Brice Kpomasse* (ex-PRC); 3 FPB 98

Air Force 250

AIRCRAFT
TPT 4 **Light** 1 DHC-6 *Twin Otter*†; **PAX** 3: 2 B-727; 1 HS-748†
TRG 2 LH-10 *Ellipse*
HELICOPTERS
TPT • Light 5: 4 AW109BA; 1 AS350B *Ecureuil*†

Paramilitary 2,500

Gendarmerie 2,500

FORCES BY ROLE
MANOEUVRE
OTHER
4 (mobile) paramilitary coy

DEPLOYMENT

CÔTE D'IVOIRE
UN • UNOCI 426; 7 obs; 1 inf bn

DEMOCRATIC REPUBLIC OF THE CONGO
UN • MONUSCO 453; 10 obs; 1 inf bn

LIBERIA
UN • UNMIL 1; 1 obs

MALI
UN • MINUSMA 306; 1 SF coy

SOUTH SUDAN
UN • UNMISS 2 obs

SUDAN
UN • UNISFA 1; 2 obs

Botswana BWA

Botswana Pula P		2012	2013	2014
GDP	P	139bn	155bn	
	US$	17.6bn	18.3bn	
per capita	US$	9,398	9,624	
Growth	%	3.82	4.14	
Inflation	%	7.53	7.23	
Def bdgt [a]	P	3.68bn	3.73bn	
	US$	466m	438m	
FMA (US)	US$	0.2m	0.2m	0.2m
US$1=P		7.90	8.50	

[a] Defence, Justice and Security Budget

Population 2,127,825

Age	0–14	15–19	20–24	25–29	30–64	65 plus
Male	16.9%	5.5%	5.3%	5.0%	16.2%	1.6%
Female	16.3%	5.5%	5.5%	5.2%	14.7%	2.4%

Capabilities

The armed forces are land-dominated, with a small air contingent. Their main task is territorial integrity, increasingly coupled with involvement in regional peacekeeping missions, and the army is developing a limited mechanised capability. Air combat capacity is provided by the CF-5; an obsolescent design, but adequate for the limited roles it is tasked with. The air force also provides tactical airlift. The forces train regularly, and also participate in regional military exercises, but the last significant deployment was to Lesotho in the late 1990s. The operations centre for the SADC Standby Force is located in Gaborone.

ACTIVE 9,000 (Army 8,500 Air 500) **Paramilitary 1,500**

ORGANISATIONS BY SERVICE

Army 8,500

FORCES BY ROLE
MANOEUVRE
Armoured
1 armd bde (-)
Light
2 inf bde (1 armd recce regt, 4 inf bn, 1 cdo unit, 2 ADA regt, 1 engr regt, 1 log bn)
COMBAT SUPPORT
1 arty bde
1 AD bde (-)
1 engr coy
1 sigs coy
COMBAT SERVICE SUPPORT
1 log gp

EQUIPMENT BY TYPE

LT TK 55: ε30 SK-105 *Kuerassier*; 25 *Scorpion*
RECCE 72+: RAM-V-1; ε8 RAM-V-2; 64 VBL
APC 156

APC (T) 6 FV 103 *Spartan*
APC (W) 150: 50 BTR-60; 50 LAV-150 *Commando* (some with 90mm gun); 50 MOWAG *Piranha* III
ARTY 78
TOWED 30: **105mm** 18: 12 L-118 Light Gun; 6 Model 56 pack howitzer; **155mm** 12 Soltam
MRL 122mm 20 APRA-40
MOR 28: **81mm** 22; **120mm** 6 M-43
AT
MSL 6+
SP V-150 TOW
MANPATS 6 TOW
RCL 84mm 30 *Carl Gustav*
AD
SAM • MANPAD 27: 5 *Javelin*; 10 9K310 *Igla*-1 (SA-16 *Gimlet*); 12 9K32 *Strela*-2 (SA-7 *Grail*)‡
GUNS • TOWED 20mm 7 M167 *Vulcan*
ARV *Greif*; M578

Air Wing 500

FORCES BY ROLE
FIGHTER/GROUND ATTACK
1 sqn with F-5A *Freedom Fighter*; F-5D *Tiger* II
ISR
1 sqn with O-2 *Skymaster*
TRANSPORT
2 sqn with BD-700 *Global Express*; BN-2A/B *Defender**; Beech 200 *Super King Air* (VIP); C-130B *Hercules*; C-212-300 *Aviocar*; CN-235M-100; Do-328-110 (VIP)
TRAINING
1 sqn with PC-7 MkII *Turbo Trainer**
TRANSPORT HELICOPTER
1 sqn with AS350B *Ecureuil*; Bell 412EP/SP *Twin Huey*
EQUIPMENT BY TYPE
AIRCRAFT 33 combat capable
FTR 14: 9 F-5A *Freedom Fighter*; 5 F-5D *Tiger* II
ISR 5 O-2 *Skymaster*
TPT 20: **Medium** 3 C-130B *Hercules*; **Light** 16: 4 BN-2 *Defender**; 6 BN-2B *Defender**; 1 Beech 200 *King Air* (VIP); 2 C-212-300 *Aviocar*; 2 CN-235M-100; 1 Do-328-110 (VIP); **PAX** 1 BD700 *Global Express*
TRG 5 PC-7 MkII *Turbo Trainer**
HELICOPTERS
MRH 7: 2 Bell 412EP *Twin Huey*; 5 Bell 412SP *Twin Huey*
TPT • Light 8 AS350B *Ecureuil*

Paramilitary 1,500

Police Mobile Unit 1,500 (org in territorial coy)

Burkina Faso BFA

CFA Franc BCEAO fr		2012	2013	2014
GDP	fr	5.42tr	5.92tr	
	US$	10.5bn	12bn	
per capita	US$	603	673	
Growth	%	8.01	7.03	
Inflation	%	3.60	2.00	
Def bdgt	fr	69.9bn	75.9bn	78.4bn
	US$	135m	153m	
US$1=fr		518.00	494.91	

Population 17,812,961

Age	0–14	15–19	20–24	25–29	30–64	65 plus
Male	22.8%	5.5%	4.6%	3.8%	12.2%	0.9%
Female	22.7%	5.4%	4.5%	3.7%	12.3%	1.5%

Capabilities

The army was involved in the social unrest that troubled the state during the first half of 2011, with protests at barracks in several cities. The aftermath of the upheaval saw the government introduce reform in the army, along with a reported reshuffle of senior officers. The three-month long disturbances, partly at least down to pay and the cost of food, places a question-mark over government–military relations. The army is predominantly infantry, with a limited number of light armoured vehicles. It does provide infantry for UN peacekeeping missions. The small air force has a limited fixed-wing light-attack and transport capacity, with firepower provided by the Mi-35. The acquisition of the *Super Tucano* might bolster its close air support capability. Burkina Faso participates in both the US Africa Contingency Operations Training and Assistance (ACOTA) programme and the Trans-Sahara Counterterrorism Partnership. France also provides military training.

ACTIVE 11,200 (Army 6,400 Air 600 Gendarmerie 4,200) Paramilitary 250

ORGANISATIONS BY SERVICE

Army 6,400

Three military regions. In 2011, several regiments were disbanded and merged into other formations, including the new 24th and 34th *régiments interarmes*.

FORCES BY ROLE
MANOEUVRE
Mechanised
1 cbd arms regt
Light
1 cbd arms regt
6 inf regt
Air Manoeuvre
1 AB regt

COMBAT SUPPORT
1 arty bn (2 arty tp)
1 engr bn

EQUIPMENT BY TYPE

RECCE 83: 19 AML-60/AML-90; 24 EE-9 *Cascavel*; 30 *Ferret*; 2 M20; 8 M8
APC (W) 13 M3 Panhard
ARTY 50+
TOWED 14: **105mm** 8 M101; **122mm** 6
MRL 9: **107mm** ε4 Type-63; **122mm** 5 APRA-40
MOR 27+: **81mm** Brandt; **82mm** 15; **120mm** 12
AT
RCL 75mm Type-52 (M20); **84mm** *Carl Gustav*
RL 89mm LRAC; M20
AD • SAM • MANPAD 9K32 *Strela*-2 (SA-7 *Grail*)‡
GUNS • TOWED 42: **14.5mm** 30 ZPU; **20mm** 12 TCM-20

Air Force 600

FORCES BY ROLE

GROUND ATTACK/TRAINING
1 sqn with SF-260WL *Warrior**; Embraer EMB-314 *Super Tucano**
TRANSPORT
1 sqn with AT-802 *Air Tractor*; B-727 (VIP); Beech 200 *King Air*; CN-235-220; PA-34 *Seneca*
ATTACK/TRANSPORT HELICOPTER
1 sqn with AS350 *Ecureuil*; Mi-8 *Hip*; Mi-17 *Hip* H; Mi-35 *Hind*

EQUIPMENT BY TYPE

AIRCRAFT 5 combat capable
ISR 1 DA42M (reported)
TPT 9 **Light** 8: 1 AT-802 *Air Tractor*; 2 Beech 200 *King Air*; 1 CN-235-220; 1 PA-34 *Seneca*; 3 *Tetras*; **PAX** 1 B-727 (VIP)
TRG 5: 3 EMB-314 *Super Tucano**; 2 SF-260WL *Warrior**
HELICOPTERS
ATK 2 Mi-35 *Hind*
MRH 2 Mi-17 *Hip* H
TPT 2 **Medium** 1 Mi-8 *Hip*; **Light** 1 AS350 *Ecureuil*

Gendarmerie 4,200

Paramilitary 250

People's Militia (R) 45,000 reservists (trained)

Security Company 250

DEPLOYMENT

DEMOCRATIC REPUBLIC OF THE CONGO
UN • MONUSCO 7 obs

MALI
UN • MINUSMA 671; 1 inf bn

SUDAN
UN • UNAMID 804; 10 obs; 1 inf bn

Burundi BDI

Burundi Franc fr		2012	2013	2014
GDP	fr	3.57tr	4.14tr	
	US$	2.48bn	2.59bn	
per capita	US$	282	288	
Growth	%	4.00	4.47	
Inflation	%	11.76	9.02	
Def bdgt	fr	89.6bn	102bn	
	US$	62m	64m	
US$1=fr		1440.73	1596.45	

Population 10,888,321

Ethnic groups: Hutu 85%; Tutsi 14%

Age	0–14	15–19	20–24	25–29	30–64	65 plus
Male	22.9%	5.4%	4.4%	3.8%	12.0%	1.0%
Female	22.7%	5.4%	4.5%	3.8%	12.6%	1.5%

Capabilities

Burundi's armed forces consist predominantly of infantry, supported by some light armour. There is a notional air unit with a handful of light aircraft and helicopters. Border security and counter-insurgency are the main roles for the army. In recent years, the country has deployed both military and police personnel to AMISOM's mission in Somalia, gaining valuable experience in combat as well as specialist military skills. Exercises with US troops have taught skills in IED detection and EOD, as well as patrolling skills, designed to prepare them for operational deployment to AMISOM.

ACTIVE 20,000 (Army 20,000) **Paramilitary 31,000**

DDR efforts continue, while activities directed at professionalising the security forces have taken place, some sponsored by BNUB, the UN mission.

ORGANISATIONS BY SERVICE

Army 20,000

FORCES BY ROLE

MANOEUVRE
Mechanised
2 lt armd bn (sqn)
Light
7 inf bn
Some indep inf coy
COMBAT SUPPORT
1 arty bn
1 AD bn 1 engr bn

Reserves

FORCES BY ROLE

MANOEUVRE
Light
10 inf bn (reported)

EQUIPMENT BY TYPE

RECCE 55: 6 AML-60; 12 AML-90; 30 BRDM-2; 7 S52 *Shorland*

APC 57:

APC (W) 45: 20 BTR-40; 10 BTR-80; 9 M3 Panhard; 6 *Walid*

PPV 12 RG-31 *Nyala*

ARTY 120

TOWED 122mm 18 D-30

MRL 122mm 12 BM-21

MOR 90: **82mm** 15 M-43; **120mm** ε75

AT

MSL • MANPATS *Milan* (reported)

RCL 75mm 60 Type-52 (M-20)

RL 83mm RL-83 *Blindicide*

AD

SAM • MANPAD ε30 9K32 *Strela-2* (SA-7 *Grail*)‡

GUNS • TOWED 150+: **14.5mm** 15 ZPU-4; 135+ **23mm** ZU-23/**37mm** Type-55 (M-1939)

Naval detachment 50

EQUIPMENT BY TYPE

AMPHIBIOUS • LCT 2

LOGISTICS AND SUPPORT • AG 2

Air Wing 200

EQUIPMENT BY TYPE

AIRCRAFT 1 combat capable

TPT 4 **Light** 2 Cessna 150L†; **PAX** 2 DC-3

TRG 1 SF-260W *Warrior**

HELICOPTERS

ATK 2 Mi-24 *Hind*

MRH 2 SA342L *Gazelle*

TPT • Medium (2 Mi-8 *Hip* non-op)

Paramilitary 31,000

General Administration of State Security ε1,000

Local Defence Militia ε30,000

DEPLOYMENT

SOMALIA

AU • AMISOM 5,432; 6 inf bn

SUDAN

UN • UNAMID 2; 8 obs

UN • UNISFA 1 obs

Cameroon CMR

CFA Franc BEAC fr		2012	2013	2014
GDP	fr	12.8tr	13.8tr	
	US$	25bn	28.1bn	
per capita	US$	1,165	1,276	
Growth	%	4.74	5.40	
Inflation	%	3.00	3.00	
Def bdgt	fr	181bn	194bn	
	US$	355m	393m	
US$1=fr		510.00	493.55	

Population 20,549,221

Age	0–14	15–19	20–24	25–29	30–64	65 plus
Male	20.2%	5.3%	4.9%	4.3%	13.9%	1.6%
Female	19.8%	5.2%	4.8%	4.2%	13.8%	1.9%

Capabilities

The ability to meet the potential for regional instability and internal security are tasks for Cameroon's armed forces. Piracy has recently emerged as a threat. A long-running territorial dispute with Nigeria was settled in 2006, though the territory in question, the Bakassi Peninsula, continues to provide security challenges. Land forces are predominantly infantry supported by light vehicles, while the air force operates jet trainers in the ground-attack role. It has a small number of tactical airlift aircraft, supplemented by a handful of utility helicopters. The navy operates both blue water and coastal patrol craft, with concerns over piracy providing the impetus for recent acquisitions. The military has occasionally participated in multinational exercises. It has no ability for power projection beyond its immediate borders, though with the AU developing its continental logistics facility at Douala airbase Cameroon's armed forces will have a model for some of the logistical capacities that could enable deployments.

ACTIVE 14,200 (Army 12,500 Navy 1,300 Air 400)
Paramilitary 9,000

ORGANISATIONS BY SERVICE

Army 12,500

3 Mil Regions

FORCES BY ROLE

MANOEUVRE

Light

1 rapid reaction bde (1 armd recce bn, 1 AB bn, 1 amph bn)

5 mot inf bde (2 mot inf bn, 1 spt bn)

3 (rapid reaction) inf bn (under comd of mil regions)

Air Manoeuvre

1 cdo/AB bn

Other

1 (Presidential Guard) gd bn

COMBAT SUPPORT
1 arty regt (5 arty bty)
1 AD regt (6 AD bty)
1 engr regt

EQUIPMENT BY TYPE

RECCE 70: 31 AML-90; 6 AMX-10RC; 15 *Ferret*; 8 M8; 5 RAM-2000 (reported); 5 VBL
AIFV 22: 8 LAV-150 *Commando* with 20mm gun; 14 LAV-150 *Commando* with 90mm gun
APC 33
APC (T) 12 M3 half-track
APC (W) 21 LAV-150 *Commando*
ARTY 108+
SP 155mm 18 ATMOS 2000
TOWED 52: **105mm** 20 M-101; **130mm** 24: 12 Model 1982 gun 82 (reported); 12 Type-59 (M-46); **155mm** 8 I1
MRL 122mm 20 BM-21
MOR 16+: **81mm** (some SP); **120mm** 16 Brandt
AT
MSL 49
SP 24 TOW (on Jeeps)
MANPATS 25 *Milan*
RCL 53: **106mm** 40 M40A2; **75mm** 13 Type-52 (M-20)
RL 89mm LRAC
AD • GUNS • TOWED 54: **14.5mm** 18 Type-58 (ZPU-2); **35mm** 18 GDF-002; **37mm** 18 Type-63

Navy ε1,300

HQ located at Douala

EQUIPMENT BY TYPE

PATROL AND COASTAL COMBATANTS 11
PCC 2: 1 *Bakassi* (FRA P-48); 1 *L'Audacieux* (FRA P-48)
PB 7: 2 Rodman 101; 4 Rodman 46; 1 *Quartier Maître Alfred Motto*
PBR 2 Swift-38
AMPHIBIOUS • LCU 2 *Yunnan*

Air Force 300-400

FORCES BY ROLE

FIGHTER/GROUND ATTACK
1 sqn with MB-326K; *Alpha Jet**†
TRANSPORT
1 sqn with C-130H/H-30 *Hercules*; DHC-4 *Caribou*; DHC-5D *Buffalo*; IAI-201 *Arava*; PA-23 *Aztec*
1 VIP unit with AS332 *Super Puma*; AS365 *Dauphin* 2; Bell 206B *Jet Ranger*; Gulfstream III
TRAINING
1 unit with *Tetras*
ATTACK HELICOPTER
1 sqn with SA342 *Gazelle* (with HOT)
TRANSPORT HELICOPTER
1 sqn with Bell 206L-3; Bell 412; SA319 *Alouette* III

EQUIPMENT BY TYPE

AIRCRAFT 9 combat capable
ATK 5: 1 MB-326K *Impala* I; 4 MB-326K *Impala* II
TPT 18 **Medium** 3: 2 C-130H *Hercules*; 1 C-130H-30 *Hercules*; **Light** 14: 1 DHC-4 *Caribou*; 1 DHC-5D *Buffalo*; 1 IAI-201 *Arava*; 2 J.300 *Joker*; 2 PA-23 *Aztec*; 7 *Tetras*;
PAX 1 Gulfstream III
TRG 4 *Alpha Jet**†
HELICOPTERS
MRH 8: 1 AS365 *Dauphin* 2; 1 Bell 412 *Twin Huey*; 2 SA319 *Alouette* III; 4 SA342 *Gazelle* (with HOT)
TPT 7 **Medium** 4: 2 AS332 *Super Puma*; 2 SA330J *Puma*; **Light** 3: 2 Bell 206B *Jet Ranger*; 1 Bell 206L3 *Long Ranger*

Paramilitary 9,000

Gendarmerie 9,000

FORCES BY ROLE

MANOEUVRE
Reconnaissance
3 (regional spt) paramilitary gp

DEPLOYMENT

CENTRAL AFRICAN REPUBLIC
AU • AFISM-CAR 500

DEMOCRATIC REPUBLIC OF THE CONGO
UN • MONUSCO 5 obs

Cape Verde CPV

Cape Verde Escudo E		2012	2013	2014
GDP	E	163bn	175bn	
	US$	1.9bn	2.11bn	
per capita	US$	3,604	3,946	
Growth	%	4.29	4.11	
Inflation	%	2.54	3.96	
Def bdgt	E	801m	790m	
	US$	9m	9m	
US$1=E		85.75	83.18	

Population 531,046

Age	0–14	15–19	20–24	25–29	30–64	65 plus
Male	15.7%	5.6%	5.3%	4.7%	15.2%	2.0%
Female	15.5%	5.6%	5.3%	4.7%	17.1%	3.2%

Capabilities

Cape Verde maintains small forces with limited force-projection capacities, driven by policy preoccupations with maritime security in the country's littoral.

ACTIVE 1,200 (Army 1,000 Coast Guard 100 Air 100)
Conscript liability Selective conscription

ORGANISATIONS BY SERVICE

Army 1,000

FORCES BY ROLE

MANOEUVRE
Light
2 inf bn (gp)
COMBAT SUPPORT
1 engr bn

EQUIPMENT BY TYPE

RECCE 10 BRDM-2

ARTY • MOR 18: **82mm** 12; **120mm** 6 M-1943

AT • RL 89mm (3.5in)

AD

SAM • MANPAD 50 9K32 *Strela* (SA-7 *Grail*)‡

GUNS • TOWED 30: **14.5mm** 18 ZPU-1; **23mm** 12 ZU-23

Coast Guard ε100

PATROL AND COASTAL COMBATANTS 5

PCC 2: 1 *Guardião*; 1 *Kondor I*

PB 2: 1 *Espadarte*; 1 *Tainha* (PRC-27m)

PBF 1 *Archangel*

Air Force up to 100

FORCES BY ROLE

MARITIME PATROL

1 sqn with C-212 *Aviocar*; Do-228

EQUIPMENT BY TYPE

AIRCRAFT • TPT • Light 5: 1 C-212 *Aviocar*; 1 Do-228; 3 An-26 *Curl*†

Central African Republic CAR

CFA Franc BEAC fr		2012	2013	2014
GDP	fr	1.11tr	1.18tr	
	US$	2.17bn	2.39bn	
per capita	US$	447	479	
Growth	%	4.11	4.33	
Inflation	%	5.23	1.97	
Def bdgt	fr	ε25.5bn		
	US$	ε50m		
US$1=fr		509.99	494.97	

Population 5,166,510

Age	0–14	15–19	20–24	25–29	30–64	65 plus
Male	20.5%	5.3%	4.8%	4.2%	13.3%	1.4%
Female	20.2%	5.3%	4.8%	4.1%	13.8%	2.2%

Capabilities

The Seleka coalition of rebel groups ousted the president in March 2013, with a rebel leader proclaiming himself president. In May, UN officials were briefed about deteriorating security in the CAR, with 'human rights violations and abuses, increased sexual violence, recruitment of child soldiers and severe humanitarian conditions'. Later, in September, the new president dissolved the Seleka group and ordered their integration into the regular forces. State stability remains fragile, and residual Seleka groups continued to mount attacks on civilian areas, as well as attacks by forces loyal to the deposed president. In July 2013, the Economic Community of Central African States' MICOPAX mission began transitioning to an African-led International Support Mission in the Central African Republic. Reform and restructuring of the defence sector is one of its aims, though this will not be an easy task. Institutional capacity will have been hit hard by ongoing instability. Meanwhile, the CAR armed forces have no capacity for operations other than for internal security. It has no navy, but has some light craft for river patrol, while its small air force has a handful of transport and utility aircraft. France retains a military presence in Bangui, while the UN has indicated it will send a force protection detachment to protect its staff in-country.

ACTIVE 7,150 (Army 7,000 Air 150) **Paramilitary 1,000**

Conscript liability Selective conscription 2 years; reserve obligation thereafter, term n.k.

ORGANISATIONS BY SERVICE

Army ε7,000

FORCES BY ROLE

MANOEUVRE

Mechanised

1 mech bn

Light

1 inf bn

Other

1 (Republican Guard) gd regt (3 gd bn)

1 intervention and spt bn

COMBAT SUPPORT

1 engr bn

COMBAT SERVICE SUPPORT

1 spt bn

EQUIPMENT BY TYPE

MBT 3 T-55†

RECCE 9: 8 *Ferret*†; 1 BRDM-2

AIFV 18 *Ratel*

APC (W) 39+: 4 BTR-152†; 25+ TPK 4.20 VSC ACMAT†; 10+ VAB†

ARTY • MOR 12+: **81mm**†; **120mm** 12 M-1943†

AT • RCL 106mm 14 M40†

RL 89mm LRAC†

PATROL AND COASTAL COMBATANTS 9 **PBR**†

Air Force 150

EQUIPMENT BY TYPE

AIRCRAFT • TPT 7 **Medium** 1 C-130A *Hercules*; **Light** 6: 3 BN-2 *Islander*; 1 Cessna 172RJ *Skyhawk*; 2 J.300 *Joker*

HELICOPTERS

TPT • Light 1 AS350 *Ecureuil*

Paramilitary

Gendarmerie ε1,000

FORCES BY ROLE

MANOEUVRE

Other

8 paramilitary bde

3 (Regional Legion) paramilitary units

FOREIGN FORCES

Cameroon AFISM-CAR 500

Chad AFISM-CAR 800

Congo AFISM-CAR 500

Equatorial Guinea AFISM-CAR 200
France *Operation Boali* 400; 2 inf coy; 1 spt det
Gabon AFISM-CAR 500

Chad CHA

CFA Franc BEAC fr		2012	2013	2014
GDP	fr	5.51tr	5.94tr	
	US$	10.8bn	12bn	
per capita	US$	1,006	1,094	
Growth	%	5.04	8.07	
Inflation	%	7.68	1.52	
Def bdgt	fr	103bn		
	US$	202m		
FMA (US)	US$	0.2m	0.2m	
US$1=fr		510.00	493.57	

Population 11,193,452

Age	0–14	15–19	20–24	25–29	30–64	65 plus
Male	22.9%	5.6%	4.3%	3.6%	10.5%	1.2%
Female	22.3%	5.7%	4.8%	4.2%	13.1%	1.7%

Capabilities

The first decade of this century saw Chad struggling with insurgency as well as conflict with Sudan. A combined EU peacekeeping mission to the Central African Republic and Chad was stationed in Chad until succeeded by a UN force, which concluded in late 2010. The state's military capacity is limited to internal security and border disputes, though the armed forces' ability to deal with significant challenges in either area is questionable. The small air force was bolstered by the acquisition of a few Su-25s for ground attack and Mi-24 *Hind* combat-support helicopters. It has a very limited air transport capacity. Some elements of land forces struggle with obsolescent equipment, the operational readiness of much of which is poor. However, there are exceptions, notably in the units that partnered with French forces on mobile operations in northern Mali in early 2013. These troops covered substantial ground, engaged in combat and took casualties, though media reports at the time of their departure in May said that increasingly asymmetric attacks against Chadian forces was one reason for their departure. Nonetheless, they will have learnt valuable lessons from the operation.

ACTIVE 25,350 (Army 17,000–20,000 Air 350 Republican Guard 5,000) Paramilitary 9,500
Conscript liability Conscription authorised

ORGANISATIONS BY SERVICE

Army ε17,000–20,000 (being reorganised)

7 Mil Regions

FORCES BY ROLE

MANOEUVRE

Armoured

1 armd bn

Light

7 inf bn

COMBAT SUPPORT

1 arty bn
1 engr bn
1 sigs bn

COMBAT SERVICE SUPPORT

1 log gp

EQUIPMENT BY TYPE

MBT 60 T-55
RECCE 309+: 132 AML-60/AML-90; 22 *Bastion Patsas*; ε100 BRDM-2; 20 EE-9 *Cascavel*; 4 ERC-90F *Sagaie*; 31+ RAM-2000
AIFV 92: 83 BMP-1; 9 LAV-150 *Commando* (with 90mm gun)
APC (W) 85: 24 BTR-80; 8 BTR-3E; ε20 BTR-60; 25 VAB-VTT; 8 WZ-523
ARTY 25+
SP 122mm 10 2S1
TOWED 105mm 5 M2
MRL 122mm 10: 4 APRA-40; 6 BM-21 *Grad*
MOR 81mm some; **120mm** AM-50
AT • MSL • MANPATS *Eryx*; *Milan*
RCL 106mm M40A1
RL 112mm APILAS; **89mm** LRAC
AD
SAM
SP 2K12 *Kub* (SA-6 *Gainful*)
MANPAD 9K310 *Igla*-1 (SA-16 *Gimlet*)
GUNS • TOWED 14.5mm ZPU-1/ZPU-2/ZPU-4; **23mm** ZU-23

Air Force 350

FORCES BY ROLE

GROUND ATTACK

1 unit with PC-7; PC-9*; SF-260WL *Warrior**; Su-25 *Frogfoot*

TRANSPORT

1 sqn with An-26 *Curl*; C-130H-30 *Hercules*; Mi-17 *Hip* H; Mi-171
1 (Presidential) Flt with B-737BBJ; Beech 1900; DC-9-87; Gulfstream II

ATTACK HELICOPTER

1 sqn with AS550C *Fennec*; Mi-24V *Hind*; SA316 *Alouette* III

EQUIPMENT BY TYPE

AIRCRAFT 11 combat capable
ATK 8: 6 Su-25 *Frogfoot*; 2 Su-25UB *Frogfoot* B
TPT 8: **Medium** 1 C-130H-30 *Hercules*; **Light** 4: 3 An-26 *Curl*; 1 Beech 1900; **PAX** 3: 1 B-737BBJ; 1 DC-9-87; 1 Gulfstream II
TRG 4: 2 PC-7 (only 1*); 1 PC-9 *Turbo Trainer**; 1 SF-260WL *Warrior**
HELICOPTERS
ATK 3 Mi-24V *Hind*
MRH 11: 6 AS550C *Fennec*; 3 Mi-17 *Hip* H; 2 SA316 *Alouette* III
TPT • Medium 2 Mi-171

Paramilitary 9,500 active

Republican Guard 5,000

Gendarmerie 4,500

DEPLOYMENT

CENTRAL AFRICAN REPUBLIC
AU • AFISM-CAR 800

CÔTE D'IVOIRE
UN • UNOCI 1; 3 obs

MALI
UN • MINUSMA 1,235; 1 SF coy; 2 inf bn

FOREIGN FORCES

France *Operation Epervier* 950; 1 mech inf BG; 1 air unit with 6 *Rafale* F3; 1 C-130H *Hercules*; 1 C-160 *Transall*; 1 C-135FR; 1 hel det with 4 SA330 *Puma*

Congo COG

CFA Franc BEAC fr		2012	2013	2014
GDP	fr	6.98tr	7.32tr	
	US$	13.7bn	14.8bn	
per capita	US$	3,346	3,546	
Growth	%	3.83	6.38	
Inflation	%	5.01	4.54	
Def bdgt	fr	166bn		
	US$	325m		
US$1=fr		510.00	493.55	

Population 4,492,689

Age	0–14	15–19	20–24	25–29	30–64	65 plus
Male	22.7%	5.6%	4.7%	3.8%	11.9%	1.1%
Female	22.4%	5.6%	4.7%	3.8%	12.1%	1.6%

Capabilities

Congo's armed forces have struggled to recover from the brief, but devastating, civil war in the late 1990s. The presence of unofficial militias during that period led to a confusing DDR process, with a lack of clarity, even now, about the defence payroll and the proliferation of small arms in the country. Given the integration of militias into the military, training is inadequate and the level of professionalism low. This is despite a defence budget that fares relatively well in comparison to immediate neighbours. The armed forces' remaining equipment is often outdated or beyond repair. The air force is effectively grounded for lack of spares and serviceable equipment, and the navy is little more than a riverine force despite the need for maritime security on the country's small coastline.

ACTIVE 10,000 (Army 8,000 Navy 800 Air 1,200)
Paramilitary 2,000

ORGANISATIONS BY SERVICE

Army 8,000

FORCES BY ROLE
MANOEUVRE
Armoured
2 armd bn
Light
2 inf bn (gp) each with (1 lt tk tp, 1 arty bty)
1 inf bn
Air Manoeuvre
1 cdo/AB bn
COMBAT SUPPORT
1 arty gp (with MRL)
1 engr bn

EQUIPMENT BY TYPE†
MBT 40: 25 T-54/T-55; 15 Type-59; (some T-34 in store)
LT TK 13: 3 PT-76; 10 Type-62
RECCE 25 BRDM-1/BRDM-2
APC 115+
APC (W) 68+: 20 BTR-152; 30 BTR-60; 18 *Mamba*; M3 Panhard
PPV 47: 15 *Fox*; 32 *Marauder*
ARTY 66+
SP 122mm 3 2S1
TOWED 25+: **100mm** 10 M-1944; **122mm** 10 D-30; **130mm** 5 M-46; **152mm** D-20
MRL 10+: **122mm** 10 BM-21; **122mm** BM-14; **140mm** BM-16
MOR 28+: **82mm**; **120mm** 28 M-43
AT • **RCL 57mm** M18
GUNS 57mm 5 ZIS-2 *M-1943*
AD • **GUNS** 28+
SP 23mm ZSU-23-4
TOWED 14.5mm ZPU-2/ZPU-4; **37mm** 28 M-1939; **57mm** S-60; **100mm** KS-19

Navy ε800

EQUIPMENT BY TYPE
PATROL AND COASTAL COMBATANTS 8
PCC 4 *Février*
PBR 4

Air Force 1,200

FORCES BY ROLE
FIGHTER/GROUND ATTACK
1 sqn with *Mirage* F-1AZ
TRANSPORT
1 sqn with An-24 *Coke*; An-32 *Cline*; CN-235M-100
ATTACK/TRANSPORT HELICOPTER
1 sqn with Mi-8 *Hip*; Mi-35P *Hind*

EQUIPMENT BY TYPE†
AIRCRAFT
FGA 2 *Mirage* F-1AZ
TPT • **Light** 4: 1 An-24 *Coke*; 2 An-32 *Cline*; 1 CN-235M-100
HELICOPTERS†
ATK (2 Mi-35P *Hind* in store)
TPT • **Medium** (3 Mi-8 *Hip* in store)
MSL • **AAM** • **IR** R-3 (AA-2 *Atoll*)‡

Paramilitary 2,000 active

Gendarmerie 2,000

FORCES BY ROLE
MANOEUVRE
Other
20 paramilitary coy

Presidential Guard some

FORCES BY ROLE
MANOEUVRE
Other
1 paramilitary bn

DEPLOYMENT

CENTRAL AFRICAN REPUBLIC
AU • AFISM-CAR 500

Côte D'Ivoire CIV

CFA Franc BCEAO fr		2012	2013	2014
GDP	fr	12.6tr	14tr	
	US$	24.6bn	28.3bn	
per capita	US$	1,054	1,177	
Growth	%	9.84	7.97	
Inflation	%	1.31	3.10	
Def bdgt [a]	fr	324bn	371bn	
	US$	635m	751m	
FMA (US)	US$	0.3m	0.3m	0.2m
US$1=fr		510.01	493.56	

[a] Defence, order and security expenses.

Population 22,400,835

Age	0–14	15–19	20–24	25–29	30–64	65 plus
Male	19.6%	5.6%	5.0%	4.3%	14.5%	1.5%
Female	19.3%	5.5%	5.0%	4.3%	13.8%	1.6%

Capabilities

The UN arms embargo was extended in April 2013. It was first established in 2004 after a civil war that began in 2002. The UN decided, in April 2012, to exempt military training and advice from the broader embargo after elections that year. The army is being formed from personnel from both sides of the conflict, a task that poses obvious challenges. A naval unit with patrol craft exists, at least on paper, but the serviceability of the vessels is uncertain. A small number of helicopters constitute the only air capability. The porous border with Liberia is marked by illicit movement of weapons, and attacks along the border in March 2013 sparked a deployment of UN troops there. According to the UN, the pace of disarmament and security sector reform is uneven, and there have been reports of violence after individuals protested the financial assistance and 'demanded cash benefits'.

ACTIVE ε40,000 target

RESERVE n.k.

Moves to restructure and reform the armed forces continue.

ORGANISATIONS BY SERVICE

Army n.k.

FORCES BY ROLE
MANOEUVRE
Armoured
1 armd bn
Light
4 inf bn
Air Manoeuvre
1 cdo/AB bn
COMBAT SUPPORT
1 arty bn
1 AD bn
1 engr bn
COMBAT SERVICE SUPPORT
1 log bn

EQUIPMENT BY TYPE
MBT 10 T-55†
LT TK 5 AMX-13
RECCE 34: 15 AML-60/AML-90; 13 BRDM-2; 6 ERC-90F4 *Sagaie*
AIFV 10 BMP-1/BMP-2†
APC (W) 31: 12 M3 Panhard; 13 VAB; 6 BTR-80
ARTY 36+
TOWED 4+: **105mm** 4 M-1950; **122mm** (reported)
MRL 122mm 6 BM-21
MOR 26+: **81mm**; **82mm** 10 M-37; **120mm** 16 AM-50
AT • MSL • MANPATS 9K113 *Konkurs* (AT-5 *Spandrel*) (reported); 9K133 *Kornet* (AT-14 *Spriggan*) (reported)
RCL 106mm ε12 M40A1
RL 89mm LRAC
AD • SAM • MANPAD 9K32 *Strela-2* (SA-7 *Grail*)‡ (reported)
GUNS 21+
SP 20mm 6 M3 VDAA
TOWED 15+: **20mm** 10; **23mm** ZU-23-2; **40mm** 5 L/60
VLB MTU
AIRCRAFT • TPT • Medium 1 An-12 *Cub*†

Navy ε900

EQUIPMENT BY TYPE
PATROL AND COASTAL COMBATANTS 3
PB 1 *Intrepide* † (FRA *Patra*)
PBR 2 Rodman (fishery protection duties)
AMPHIBIOUS
LCM 2 *Aby* †
LOGISTICS AND SUPPORT
YT 2

Air Force n.k.

EQUIPMENT BY TYPE†
AIRCRAFT
TPT • PAX 1 B-727

HELICOPTERS
ATK 1 Mi-24 (reported)
TPT • Medium 3 SA330L *Puma* (IAR-330L)

Paramilitary n.k.

Republican Guard unk
APC (W) 4 *Mamba*

Gendarmerie n.k.
APC (W) some VAB
PATROL AND COASTAL COMBATANTS • PB 1 *Bian*

Militia n.k.

DEPLOYMENT

MALI
UN • MINUSMA 126; 1 tpt coy

FOREIGN FORCES

All forces part of UNOCI unless otherwise stated.
Bangladesh 2,168; 13 obs; 2 mech inf bn; 1 avn coy; 1 engr coy; 1 sigs coy; 1 log coy; 1 fd hospital
Benin 426; 7 obs; 1 inf bn
Bolivia 3 obs
Brazil 3; 4 obs
Chad 1; 3 obs
China, People's Republic of 6 obs
Ecuador 2 obs
Egypt 175; 1 engr coy
El Salvador 3 obs
Ethiopia 2 obs
France 6 • *Operation Licorne* 450; 1 armd cav BG; 1 hel unit with 3 SA330 *Puma*
Gambia 3 obs
Ghana 507; 6 obs; 1 inf bn; 1 hel coy; 1 fd hospital
Guatemala 5 obs
Guinea 2 obs
India 8 obs
Ireland 2 obs
Jordan 1,067; 7 obs; 1 SF coy; 1 inf bn
Korea, Republic of 2 obs
Malawi 7; 3 obs
Moldova 3 obs
Morocco 726; 1 inf bn
Namibia 2 obs
Nepal 1; 3 obs
Niger 937; 5 obs; 1 inf bn
Nigeria 10; 4 obs
Pakistan 1,391; 11 obs; 1 inf bn; 1 engr coy; 1 tpt coy
Paraguay 2; 7 obs
Peru 3 obs
Philippines 1; 3 obs
Poland 2 obs
Russia 6 obs
Senegal 495; 10 obs; 1 inf bn
Serbia 3 obs
Tanzania 2; 1 obs
Togo 523; 7 obs; 1 inf bn
Tunisia 3; 7 obs
Uganda 2; 5 obs
Ukraine 38; 1 atk hel flt
Uruguay 2 obs
Yemen, Republic of 1; 9 obs
Zambia 2 obs
Zimbabwe 3 obs

Democratic Republic of the Congo DRC

Congolese Franc fr		2012	2013	2014
GDP	fr	16.3tr	18.3tr	
	US$	17.7bn	19.4bn	
per capita	US$	237	251	
Growth	%	7.11	8.30	
Inflation	%	9.35	6.83	
Def bdgt	fr	213bn	393bn	
	US$	232m	416m	
US$1=fr		918.22	945.02	

Population 75,507,308

Age	0–14	15–19	20–24	25–29	30–64	65 plus
Male	21.9%	5.8%	4.8%	3.9%	12.3%	1.1%
Female	21.6%	5.8%	4.8%	3.9%	12.6%	1.5%

Capabilities

The Democratic Republic of the Congo ostensibly retains the largest armed forces in Central Africa. However, given the country's size and the poor level of training, morale and equipment, the forces are unable to provide security throughout the DRC. The DRC has suffered the most protracted war in the post-Cold War era. For this reason, it is unsurprising that much military equipment is in a poor state of repair and the armed forces, which have since incorporated a number of non-state armed groups, struggle with a variety of loyalties. The latest manifestation of this latter factor was a defection by several hundred soldiers, dubbed M23, in the east of the country in April 2012. This group demonstrated their capability by capturing the eastern city of Goma in November 2012. Amid continuing violence, the UN deployed an 'intervention brigade' to MONUSCO, with artillery and air support. The UN engaged M23 rebels, in conjunction with the armed forces (FARDC), forcing M23 onto the defensive. Many M23 fighters surrendered in October, with their leader calling a ceasefire. Other armed groups are believed to remain in the east. FARDC is heavily dominated by land forces; the air force retains a limited combat capability of mostly Soviet-origin aircraft, and the navy acts as a riverine force. Given the challenges facing the armed forces, the DRC will continue to rely on international peacekeeping deployments for security, in the shape of MONUSCO. International partners, including Belgium, US AFRICOM and MONUSCO have trained personnel.

ACTIVE ε134,250 (Central Staffs ε14,000, Army 103,000 Republican Guard 8,000 Navy 6,700 Air 2,550)

ORGANISATIONS BY SERVICE

Army (Forces du Terre) ε103,000

The DRC has eleven Military Regions. In 2011, all brigades in North and South Kivu provinces were consolidated into 27 new regiments, the latest in a sequence of re-organisations designed to integrate non-state armed groups. The actual combat effectiveness of many formations is doubtful.

FORCES BY ROLE
MANOEUVRE
Light
6 (integrated) inf bde
ε3 inf bde (non-integrated)
27+ inf regt
COMBAT SUPPORT
1 arty regt
1 MP bn

EQUIPMENT BY TYPE†
(includes Republican Guard eqpt)
MBT 149: 12–17 Type-59 †; 32 T-55; 100 T-72
LT TK 40: 10 PT-76; 30 Type-62† (reportedly being refurbished)
RECCE up to 52: up to 17 AML-60; 14 AML-90; 19 EE-9 *Cascavel*; 2 RAM-V-2
AIFV 20 BMP-1
APC 144:
APC (T) 9: 3 BTR-50; 6 MT-LB
APC (W) 135: 30-70 BTR-60PB; 58 M3 Panhard†; 7 TH 390 *Fahd*
ARTY 720+
SP 16: **122mm** 6 2S1; **152mm** 10 2S3
TOWED 119: **122mm** 77 (M-30) M-1938/D-30/Type-60; **130mm** 42 Type-59 (M-46)/Type-59 I
MRL 57: **107mm** 12 Type-63; **122mm** 24 BM-21; **128mm** 6 M-51; **130mm** 3 Type-82; **132mm** 12
MOR 528+: **81mm** 100; **82mm** 400; **107mm** M-30; **120mm** 28: 18; 10 Brandt
AT • RCL 36+: **57mm** M18; **73mm** 10; **75mm** 10 M20; **106mm** 16 M40A1
GUNS 85mm 10 Type-56 (D-44)
AD • SAM • MANPAD 20 9K32 *Strela*-2 (SA-7 *Grail)*‡
GUNS • TOWED 114: **14.5mm** 12 ZPU-4; **37mm** 52 M-1939; **40mm** ε50 L/60† (probably out of service)

Republican Guard 8,000

FORCES BY ROLE
MANOEUVRE
Armoured
1 armd regt
Light
3 gd bde
COMBAT SUPPORT
1 arty regt

Navy 6,700 (incl infantry and marines)

EQUIPMENT BY TYPE
PATROL AND COASTAL COMBATANTS 16
PB 16: 1 *Shanghai* II; ε15 various (all under 50ft)

Air Force 2,550

EQUIPMENT BY TYPE
AIRCRAFT 5 combat capable
FTR 2: 1 MiG-23MS *Flogger;* 1 MiG-23UB *Flogger* C
ATK 3 Su-25 *Frogfoot*
TPT 6 **Medium** 1 C-130H *Hercules;* **Light** 3 An-26 *Curl;* **PAX** 2 B-727
HELICOPTERS
ATK 9: 4 Mi-24 *Hind;* 5 Mi-24V *Hind*
TPT 3 **Heavy** (1 Mi-26 *Halo* non-operational); **Medium** 3: 1 AS332L *Super Puma;* 2 Mi-8 *Hip*

Paramilitary

National Police Force

incl Rapid Intervention Police (National and Provincial forces)

People's Defence Force

FOREIGN FORCES

All part of MONUSCO unless otherwise specified.
Algeria 5 obs
Austria EUSEC RD Congo 1
Bangladesh 2,542; 17 obs; 2 mech inf bn; 1 avn coy; 2 hel coy; 1 engr coy
Belgium 23; 1 avn flt • EUSEC RD Congo 4
Benin 453; 10 obs; 1 inf bn
Bolivia 10 obs
Bosnia and Herzegovina 5 obs
Burkina Faso 7 obs
Cameroon 5 obs
Canada (*Operation Crocodile*) 8 obs
China, People's Republic of 220; 10 obs; 1 engr coy; 1 fd hospital
Czech Republic 3 obs
Denamrk EUSEC RD Congo 3
Egypt 1,006; 21 obs; 1 SF coy; 1 inf bn
France 4 • EUSEC RD Congo 7
Germany EUSEC RD Congo 3
Ghana 466; 23 obs; 1 mech inf bn(-)
Guatemala 151; 1 SF coy
Hungary EUSEC RD Congo 2
India 3,731; 36 obs; 3 mech inf bn; 1 inf bn; 1 hel coy; 1 fd hospital
Indonesia 177; 15 obs; 1 engr coy
Ireland 3 obs
Italy EUSEC RD Congo 1
Jordan 230; 17 obs; 1 SF coy; 1 fd hospital

Kenya 12; 18 obs
Luxembourg EUSEC RD Congo 1
Malawi 118; 9 obs; 1 inf coy
Malaysia 9; 7 obs
Mali 14 obs
Mongolia 2 obs
Morocco 844; 1 obs; 1 mech inf bn; 1 fd hospital
Nepal 1,029; 20 obs; 1 inf bn; 1 engr coy
Netherlands EUSEC RD Congo 3
Niger 1; 17 obs
Nigeria 2; 15 obs
Pakistan 3,715; 43 obs; 3 mech inf bn; 1 inf bn; 1 hel coy
Paraguay 17 obs
Peru 2; 13 obs
Poland 1 obs
Portugal EUSEC RD Congo 2
Romania 22 obs • EUSEC RD Congo 3
Russia 1; 27 obs
Senegal 10; 11 obs
Serbia 5; 3 obs
South Africa (*Operation Mistral*) 1,262; 3 obs; 1 inf bn; 1 avn coy; 1 engr coy
Sri Lanka 4 obs
Sweden 5 obs • EUSEC RD Congo 1
Switzerland 3; 1 obs
Tanzania 1,254; 1 SF coy; 1 inf bn; 1 arty coy
Tunisia 33 obs
Ukraine 254: 11 obs; 2 atk hel sqn
United Kingdom 6 • EUSEC RD Congo 3
United States 3
Uruguay 1,196; 16 obs; 1 inf bn; 2 mne coy; 1 hel flt; 1 engr coy
Yemen, Republic of 5 obs
Zambia 2; 20 obs

Djibouti DJB

Djiboutian Franc fr		2012	2013	2014
GDP	fr	241bn	259bn	
	US$	1.35bn	1.46bn	
per capita	US$	1,523	1,594	
Growth	%	4.84	4.96	
Inflation	%	3.74	2.50	
Def bdgt	fr	ε1.72bn		
	US$	ε10m		
FMA (US)	US$	1.5m	1.5m	1m
US$1=fr		177.67	177.76	

Population 792,198

Ethnic groups: Somali 60%; Afar 35%

Age	0–14	15–19	20–24	25–29	30–64	65 plus
Male	16.8%	5.4%	5.0%	4.0%	13.3%	1.6%
Female	16.8%	5.7%	6.0%	5.3%	18.3%	1.9%

Djibouti's small armed forces are almost entirely dominated by the army, though size and capability has much reduced since the 1990s. Training and external security is bolstered by the presence of US AFRICOM troops and a French base with air combat and transport assets. Clashes with the Eritrean military in 2008 demonstrated the superior nature of the Djiboutian forces' training and skills, but also showed that they would be unable to counter the larger, if less well-equipped, forces of their neighbours. The army has concentrated on mobility in its equipment purchases, suitable for patrol duties but not for armoured warfare, and it is unclear whether the armed forces have the capacity to self-sustain on operations. Djibouti has almost a thousand troops in Somalia as part of AMISOM, and is the lead nation in Sector 4, which covers the Hiiran region.

ACTIVE 10,450 (Army 8,000 Navy 200 Air 250 Gendarmerie 2,000) National Security Force 2,500

ORGANISATIONS BY SERVICE

Army ε8,000

FORCES BY ROLE

4 military districts (Tadjourah, Dikhil, Ali-Sabieh and Obock)

MANOEUVRE

Mechanised

1 armd regt (1 recce sqn, 3 armd sqn, 1 (anti-smuggling) sy coy)

Light

4 inf regt (3-4 inf coy, 1 spt coy)
1 rapid reaction regt (4 inf coy, 1 spt coy)

Other

1 (Republican Guard) gd regt (1 sy sqn, 1 (close protection) sy sqn, 1 cbt spt sqn (1 recce pl, 1 armd pl, 1 arty pl), 1 spt sqn)

COMBAT SUPPORT

1 arty regt

1 demining coy
1 sigs regt
1 CIS sect
COMBAT SERVICE SUPPORT
1 log regt
1 maint coy

EQUIPMENT BY TYPE

RECCE 56: 4 AML-60†; 17 AML-90; 15 VBL; 16-20 *Ratel*
APC (W) 20: 12 BTR-60†; 8 BTR-80
ARTY 104
TOWED 122mm 6 D-30
MRL 8
MOR 45: **81mm** 25; **120mm** 20 Brandt
AT
RCL 106mm 16 M40A1
RL 89mm LRAC
AD • GUNS 15+
SP 20mm 5 M693
TOWED 10: **23mm** 5 ZU-23; **40mm** 5 L/70

Navy ε200

EQUIPMENT BY TYPE

PATROL AND COASTAL COMBATANTS 12
PBF 2 Battalion-17
PB 10: 1 *Plascoa*†; 2 Sea Ark 1739; 1 *Swari*†; 6 others
AMPHIBIOUS • LCM 1 CTM

Air Force 250

EQUIPMENT BY TYPE

AIRCRAFT
TPT • Light 3: 1 Cessna U206G *Stationair*; 1 Cessna 208 *Caravan*; 1 L-410UVP *Turbolet*
HELICOPTERS
ATK (1 Mi-35 *Hind* in store)
MRH 1 Mi-17 *Hip* H
TPT 3 **Medium** 1 Mi-8T *Hip*; **Light** 2 AS355F *Ecureuil* II

Gendarmerie 2,000 +

Ministry of Defence

FORCES BY ROLE

MANOEUVRE
Other
1 paramilitary bn

EQUIPMENT BY TYPE

PATROL AND COASTAL COMBATANTS 1 **PB**

Paramilitary ε2,500

National Security Force ε2,500

Ministry of Interior

Coast Guard 145

EQUIPMENT BY TYPE

PATROL AND COASTAL COMBATANTS 9 **PB**

DEPLOYMENT

SOMALIA

AU • AMISOM 1,000; 1 inf bn

FOREIGN FORCES

France 1,900: 1 (Marine) combined arms regt (2 recce sqn, 2 inf coy, 1 arty bty, 1 engr coy); 1 hel det with 4 SA330 *Puma*; 2 SA342 *Gazelle*; 1 LCT; 1 LCM; 1 air sqn with 7 *Mirage* 2000C/D; 1 C-160 *Transall*; 2 SA330 *Puma*; 1 AS555 *Fennec*

Japan 200; 2 P-3C

United States US Africa Command: 1,200; 1 naval air base

Equatorial Guinea EQG

CFA Franc BEAC fr		2012	2013	2014
GDP	fr	8.78tr	8.21tr	
	US$	17.2bn	16.6bn	
per capita	US$	23,133	21,767	
Growth	%	2.03	-2.05	
Inflation	%	5.50	5.00	
Def exp	fr	ε3.8bn		
	US$	ε7m		
US$1=fr		510.00	493.57	

Population 704,001

Age	0–14	15–19	20–24	25–29	30–64	65 plus
Male	20.9%	5.3%	4.6%	3.9%	13.4%	1.7%
Female	20.2%	5.1%	4.4%	3.8%	14.5%	2.3%

Capabilities

The country's armed forces are dominated by the army, with smaller naval and air components. Equipment is of Soviet or Russian origin, and some fixed- and rotary-wing aircraft may be operated by contractors. Maritime-security concerns in the Gulf of Guinea have resulted in increased emphasis on bolstering its limited coastal patrol capacity. The army's primary role is internal security, while the military has no ability to project power beyond the nation's borders.

ACTIVE 1,320 (Army 1,100 Navy 120 Air 100)

ORGANISATIONS BY SERVICE

Army 1,100

FORCES BY ROLE

MANOEUVRE
Light
3 inf bn (-)

EQUIPMENT BY TYPE

MBT 3 T-55
RECCE 6 BRDM-2
AIFV 20 BMP-1
APC (W) 10 BTR-152

Navy ε120

EQUIPMENT BY TYPE

PATROL AND COASTAL COMBATANTS 10
PSOH 1 *Bata* with 1 76mm gun

PCC 2 OPV 62
PB 7: 1 *Daphne*; 2 *Estuario de Muni*; 2 *Shaldag* II; 2 *Zhuk*
LOGISTICS AND SUPPORT
AKRH 1 *Capitan David Eyama Angue Osa* with 1 76 mm gun

Air Force 100

EQUIPMENT BY TYPE
AIRCRAFT 4 combat capable
ATK 4: 2 Su-25 *Frogfoot;* 2 Su-25UB *Frogfoot* B
TPT 4 **Light** 3: 1 An-32B *Cline*; 2 An-72 *Coaler*; **PAX** 1 *Falcon* 900 (VIP)
TRG 2 L-39C *Albatros*
HELICOPTERS
ATK 5 Mi-24P/V *Hind*
MRH 1 Mi-17 *Hip* H
TPT 4 **Heavy** 1 Mi-26 *Halo*; **Medium** 1 Ka-29 *Helix*; **Light** 2 Enstrom 480

Paramilitary

Guardia Civil

FORCES BY ROLE
MANOEUVRE
Other
2 paramilitary coy

Coast Guard

PATROL AND COASTAL COMBATANTS • PB 1†

DEPLOYMENT

CENTRAL AFRICAN REPUBLIC
AU • AFISM-CAR 200

Eritrea ERI

Eritrean Nakfa ERN		2012	2013	2014
GDP	ERN	47.5bn	54bn	
	US$	3.09bn	3.51bn	
per capita	US$	546	602	
Growth	%	7.02	3.36	
Inflation	%	12.26	12.26	
Def exp	ERN	ε1.2bn		
	US$	ε78m		
USD1=ERN		15.37	15.37	

Population 6,233,682

Ethnic groups: Tigrinya 50%; Tigre and Kunama 40%; Afar; Saho 3%

Age	0–14	15–19	20–24	25–29	30–64	65 plus
Male	20.7%	5.4%	4.6%	3.8%	13.2%	1.6%
Female	20.5%	5.4%	4.6%	3.9%	14.1%	2.1%

Capabilities

Asmara maintains a large standing army (largely conscripted) and an arsenal stocked with outdated but numerous weapons platforms. A UN arms embargo and the age of some of the weapons will render many of them obsolete and it is likely that the platforms will be slowly cannibalised for parts. The Eritrean military appears to have been relatively successful in adapting from an insurgent army (in the 1980s) to standing armed forces. However, the armed forces are still, slowly, formalising lines of command and organisation. The primary focus is defence of its border with Ethiopia, although many troops are used for civilian development and construction tasks. There has been some investment in the nascent air force to produce a regionally comparable fighter wing, though this lacks experienced and trained pilots.

ACTIVE 201,750 (Army 200,000 Navy 1,400 Air 350)
Conscript liability 16 months (4 months mil trg)

RESERVE 120,000 (Army ε120,000)

ORGANISATIONS BY SERVICE

Army ε200,000

Heavily cadreised
FORCES BY ROLE
COMMAND
4 corps HQ
MANOEUVRE
Mechanised
1 mech bde
Light
19 inf div
1 cdo div

Reserve ε120,000

FORCES BY ROLE
MANOEUVRE
Light
1 inf div

EQUIPMENT BY TYPE
MBT 270 T-54/T-55
RECCE 40 BRDM-1/BRDM-2
AIFV 15 BMP-1
APC 35
APC (T) 10 MT-LB†
APC (W) 25 BTR-152/BTR-60
ARTY 208+
SP 45: **122mm** 32 2S1; **152mm** 13 2S5
TOWED 19+: **122mm** D-30; **130mm** 19 M-46
MRL 44: **122mm** 35 BM-21; **220mm** 9 BM-27/9P140 *Uragan*
MOR 120mm/160mm 100+
AT
MSL • MANPATS 200 9K11 *Malyutka* (AT-3 *Sagger*)/ 9K113 Konkurs (AT-5 *Spandrel*)
GUNS 85mm D-44
AD
SAM • MANPAD 9K32 *Strela*-2 (SA-7 *Grail*)‡
GUNS 70+
SP 23mm ZSU-23-4
TOWED 23mm ZU-23

ARV T-54/T-55 reported
VLB MTU reported

Navy 1,400

EQUIPMENT BY TYPE
PATROL AND COASTAL COMBATANTS 12
PBF 9: 5 Battalion-17; 4 *Super Dvora*
PB 3 Swiftships
AMPHIBIOUS 3
LS • LST 2: 1 *Chamo*† (Ministry of Transport); 1 *Ashdod*†
LC • LCU 1 T-4† (in harbour service)

Air Force ε350

FORCES BY ROLE
FIGHTER/GROUND ATTACK
1 sqn with MiG-29/MiG-29SMT/MiG-29UB *Fulcrum*
1 sqn with Su-27/Su-27UBK *Flanker*
TRANSPORT
1 sqn with Y-12(II)
TRAINING
1 sqn with L-90 *Redigo*
1 sqn with MB-339CE*
TRANSPORT HELICOPTER
1 sqn with Bell 412 *Twin Huey*
1 sqn with Mi-17 *Hip H*
EQUIPMENT BY TYPE
AIRCRAFT 20 combat capable
FTR 6: 4 MiG-29 *Fulcrum*; 2 MiG-29UB *Fulcrum*;
FGA 10: 2 MiG-29SMT *Fulcrum*; 5 Su-27 *Flanker*; 3 Su-27UBK *Flanker*
TPT • Light 5: 1 Beech 200 *King Air*; 4 Y-12(II)
TRG 12: 8 L-90 *Redigo*; 4 MB-339CE*
HELICOPTERS
MRH 8: 4 Bell 412 *Twin Huey* (AB-412); 4 Mi-17 *Hip* H
MSL
AAM • IR R-60 (AA-8 *Aphid*); R-73 (AA-11 *Archer*); **IR/SARH** R-27 (AA-10 *Alamo*)

Ethiopia ETH

Ethiopian Birr EB		2012	2013	2014
GDP	EB	726bn	858bn	
	US$	41.9bn	46.3bn	
per capita	US$	483	521	
Growth	%	7.00	6.50	
Inflation	%	22.75	8.28	
Def bdgt	EB	4.4bn	6.5bn	7.5bn
	US$	254m	351m	
FMA (US)	US$	0.84m	0.84m	0.84m
US$1=EB		17.33	18.54	

Population 93,877,025

Ethnic groups: Oromo 40%; Amhara and Tigrean 32%; Sidamo 9%; Shankella 6%; Somali 6%; Afar 4%

Age	0–14	15–19	20–24	25–29	30–64	65 plus
Male	22.2%	5.4%	4.5%	3.7%	12.6%	1.3%
Female	22.2%	5.4%	4.6%	3.8%	12.8%	1.5%

Capabilities

Ethiopia maintains the Horn of Africa's (and one of sub-Saharan Africa's) most effective armed forces. The history of conflict faced by Ethiopia's forces has produced a battle-hardened and experienced force. The country has benefited from some newly procured equipment over the past decade. The country has enough deployable capability to make significant contributions to UN missions in Darfur and South Sudan. Ethiopia has had an increasingly close relationship with Israel, China and the US, which are providing some training and advice. Arms procurement remains largely focused on former Soviet countries, with a June 2011 deal with Ukraine for more than 200 T-72 tanks due to complete in 2013. The air force maintains only a modest lift capacity, which limits the deployability of the forces both within Ethiopia and overseas. Domestically manufactured tactical UAVs, military telemedicine and information security developments indicate the level of developing capability within the armed forces. (See pp. 417–19.)

ACTIVE 138,000 (Army 135,000 Air 3,000)

ORGANISATIONS BY SERVICE

Army 135,000

4 Mil Regional Commands (Northern, Western, Central, and Eastern) each acting as corps HQ

FORCES BY ROLE
MANOEUVRE
Light
1 (Agazi Cdo) SF comd
1 (Northern) corps (1 mech div, 4 inf div)
1 (Western) corps (1 mech div, 3 inf div)
1 (Central) corps (1 mech div, 5 inf div)
1 (Eastern) corps (1 mech div, 5 inf div)
EQUIPMENT BY TYPE
MBT 446+: 246+ T-54/T-55/T-62; 200 T-72
RECCE/AIFV/APC (W) ε450 BRDM/BMP/BTR-60/BTR-152/Type-89/Type-92/*Ze'ev*
ARTY 524+
SP 10+: **122mm** 2S1; **152mm** 10 2S19
TOWED 464+: **122mm** 464 D-30/M-1938 (M-30) M-1938; **130mm** M-46
MRL 122mm ε50 BM-21
MOR 81mm M1/M29; **82mm** M-1937; **120mm** M-1944
AT • MSL • MANPATS 9K11 *Malyutka* (AT-3 *Sagger*); 9K111 *Fagot* (AT-4 *Spigot*)
RCL 82mm B-10; **107mm** B-11
GUNS 85mm εD-44
AD • SAM ε370
TOWED S-75 *Dvina* (SA-2 *Guideline*); S-125 *Pechora* (SA-3 *Goa*)
MANPAD 9K32 *Strela*-2 (SA-7 *Grail*)‡
GUNS
SP 23mm ZSU-23-4
TOWED 23mm ZU-23; **37mm** M-1939; **57mm** S-60
ARV T-54/T-55 reported
VLB MTU reported
MW Bozena

Air Force 3,000

FORCES BY ROLE

FIGHTER/GROUND ATTACK

1 sqn with MiG-21MF *Fishbed* J†; MiG-21UM *Mongol* B†

1 sqn with Su-27/Su-27UB *Flanker*

TRANSPORT

1 sqn with An-12 *Cub*; An-26 *Curl*; An-32 *Cline*; C-130B *Hercules*; DHC-6 *Twin Otter*; L-100-30; Yak-40 *Codling* (VIP)

TRAINING

1 sqn with L-39 *Albatros*

1 sqn with SF-260

ATTACK/TRANSPORT HELICOPTER

2 sqn with Mi-24/Mi-35 *Hind*; Mi-8 *Hip*; Mi-17 *Hip* H; SA316 *Alouette* III

EQUIPMENT BY TYPE

AIRCRAFT 26 combat capable

FGA 26: 15 MiG-21MF *Fishbed* J/MiG-21UM *Mongol* B†; 8 Su-27 *Flanker*; 3 Su-27UB *Flanker*

TPT 10 **Medium** 7: 3 An-12 *Cub*; 2 C-130B *Hercules*; 2 L-100-30; **Light** 4: 1 An-26 *Curl*; 1 An-32 *Cline*; 1 DHC-6 *Twin Otter*; 1 Yak-40 *Codling* (VIP)

TRG 16: 12 L-39 *Albatros*; 4 SF-260

HELICOPTERS

ATK 18: 15 Mi-24 *Hind*; 3 Mi-35 *Hind*

MRH 7: 1 AW139; 6 SA316 *Alouette* III

MRH/TPT 12 Mi-8 *Hip*/Mi-17 *Hip* H

MSL

AAM • IR R-3 (AA-2 *Atoll*)‡; R-60 (AA-8 *Aphid*); R-73 (AA-11 *Archer*); **IR/SARH** R-23/R-24 (AA-7 *Apex*) R-27 (AA-10 *Alamo*)

DEPLOYMENT

CÔTE D'IVOIRE

UN • UNOCI 2 obs

LIBERIA

UN • UNMIL 4; 9 obs

SOMALIA

Army Some

SUDAN

UN • UNAMID 2,539; 16 obs; 3 inf bn

UN • UNISFA 3,912; 78 obs; 2 recce coy; 1 mech inf bn; 2 inf bn; 1 hel sqn; 2 arty coy; 1 engr coy; 1 sigs coy; 1 fd hospital

FOREIGN FORCES

United States some MQ-9 *Reaper*

Gabon GAB

CFA Franc BEAC fr		2012	2013	2014
GDP	fr	9.52tr	10.2tr	
	US$	18.4bn	19.3bn	
per capita	US$	11,929	12,350	
Growth	%	6.21	6.08	
Inflation	%	3.00	3.00	
Def bdgt [a]	fr	115bn	139bn	
	US$	222m	263m	
US$1=fr		518.06	529.48	

[a] Includes funds allocated to Republican Guard

Population 1,640,286

Age	0–14	15–19	20–24	25–29	30–64	65 plus
Male	21.2%	5.4%	4.7%	4.1%	12.7%	1.6%
Female	21.0%	5.4%	4.7%	4.0%	12.9%	2.2%

Capabilities

The country has benefited from the long-term presence of French troops, acting as a security guarantor, while oil revenues have allowed the government to support, in regional terms, capable armed forces. The army is reasonably well equipped, while the navy has a coastal-patrol and fishery protection role. It also maintains an amphibious landing ship. The air force's combat capability was increased with the acquisition of six ex-South African Air Force *Mirage* F1s.

ACTIVE 4,700 (Army 3,200 Navy 500 Air 1,000)
Paramilitary 2,000

ORGANISATIONS BY SERVICE

Army 3,200

Republican Guard under direct presidential control

FORCES BY ROLE

MANOEUVRE

Light

1 (Republican Guard) gd gp (bn)

(1 armd/recce coy, 3 inf coy, 1 arty bty, 1 ADA bty)

8 inf coy

Air Manoeuvre

1 cdo/AB coy

COMBAT SUPPORT

1 engr coy

EQUIPMENT BY TYPE

RECCE 70: 24 AML-60/AML-90; 12 EE-3 *Jararaca*; 14 EE-9 *Cascavel*; 6 ERC-90F4 *Sagaie*; 14 VBL

AIFV 12 EE-11 *Urutu* (with 20mm gun)

APC 52+

APC (W) 28+: 9 LAV-150 *Commando*; 6 Type-92 (reported); 12 VXB-170; M3 Panhard; 1 *Pandur* (Testing)

PPV 24 *Matador*

ARTY 51

TOWED 105mm 4 M101

MRL 140mm 8 *Teruel*
MOR 39: **81mm** 35; **120mm** 4 Brandt
AT • MSL • MANPATS 4 *Milan*
RCL 106mm M40A1
RL 89mm LRAC
AD • GUNS 41
SP 20mm 4 ERC-20
TOWED 37: **23mm** 24 ZU-23-2; **37mm** 10 M-1939; **40mm** 3 L/70

Navy ε500

HQ located at Port Gentil

EQUIPMENT BY TYPE

PATROL AND COASTAL COMBATANTS 15
PCC 2 *General Ba'Oumar* (FRA P-400) with 1 57 mm gun
PBFG 1 *Patra* with 4 SS 12M AShM
PB 12: 4 *Port Gentil* (FRA VCSM); 4 RPB 20; 4 Rodman 66
AMPHIBIOUS 14
LANDING SHIPS • LST 1 *President Omar Bongo* (FRA *Batral*) (capacity 1 LCVP; 7 MBT; 140 troops) with 1 hel landing platform
LANDING CRAFT 13
LCU 1 Mk 9 (ex-UK)
LCVP 12

Air Force 1,000

FORCES BY ROLE

FIGHTER/GROUND ATTACK
1 sqn with *Mirage* F-1AZ
TRANSPORT
1 (Republican Guard) sqn with AS332 *Super Puma*; ATR-42F; *Falcon* 900; Gulfstream IV-SP
1 sqn with C-130H *Hercules*; CN-235M-100
TRAINING
1 (Republican Guard) sqn with T-34 *Turbo Mentor*
ATTACK/TRANSPORT HELICOPTER
1 sqn with Bell 412 *Twin Huey* (AB-412); SA330C/H *Puma*; SA342M *Gazelle*

EQUIPMENT BY TYPE

AIRCRAFT 6 combat capable
FGA 6 *Mirage* F-1AZ
MP (1 EMB-111* in store)
TPT 5 **Medium** 1 C-130H *Hercules*; (1 L-100-30 in store); **Light** 2: 1 ATR-42F; 1 CN-235M-100; **PAX** 2: 1 *Falcon* 900; 1 Gulfstream IV-SP
TRG 3 T-34 *Turbo Mentor*; (4 CM-170 *Magister* in store)
HELICOPTERS
MRH 2: 1 Bell 412 *Twin Huey* (AB-412); 1 SA342M *Gazelle*; (2 SA342L *Gazelle* in store)
TPT 5 **Medium** 4: 1 AS332 *Super Puma*; 3 SA330C/H *Puma*; **Light** 1 EC135

Paramilitary 2,000

Gendarmerie 2,000

FORCES BY ROLE

MANOEUVRE
Armoured
2 armd sqn
Other
3 paramilitary bde
11 paramilitary coy
Aviation
1 unit with AS350 *Ecureuil*; AS355 *Ecureuil* II

EQUIPMENT BY TYPE

HELICOPTERS • TPT • Light 4: 2 AS350 *Ecureuil*; 2 AS355 *Ecureuil* II

DEPLOYMENT

CENTRAL AFRICAN REPUBLIC

AU • AFISM-CAR 500

FOREIGN FORCES

France 900; 1 recce pl with ERC-90F1 Lynx; 1 mtn inf bn; 1 SAR/tpt sqn with 4 SA330 Puma

Gambia GAM

Gambian Dalasi D		2012	2013	2014
GDP	D	28.8bn	33.1bn	
	US$	918m	997m	
per capita	US$	503	532	
Growth	%	3.95	8.90	
Inflation	%	4.65	5.45	
Def bdgt	D	ε189m		
	US$	ε6m		
US$1=D		31.34	33.15	

Population 1,883,051

Age	0–14	15–19	20–24	25–29	30–64	65 plus
Male	19.6%	5.5%	5.0%	4.3%	13.6%	1.5%
Female	19.5%	5.6%	5.1%	4.4%	14.2%	1.7%

Capabilities

The country has a small army supported by an air and marine unit. Its forces have been deployed in support of UN missions, and receive training assistance from the US.

ACTIVE 800 (Army 800)

ORGANISATIONS BY SERVICE

Gambian National Army 800

FORCES BY ROLE

MANOEUVRE
Light
2 inf bn
Other
1 (Presidential Guard) gd coy
COMBAT SUPPORT
1 engr sqn

Marine Unit ε70

EQUIPMENT BY TYPE

PATROL AND COASTAL COMBATANTS 9

PBF 2 Rodman 55
PB 7: 1 *Bolong Kanta*†; 2 *Fatimah* I; 4 *Taipei* (ROC *Hai Ou*) (of which one damaged and in reserve)

Air Wing

EQUIPMENT BY TYPE
AIRCRAFT
TPT 6 **Light** 2 AT-802A *Air Tractor*; **PAX** 4: 1 B-727; 1 CL-601; 2 Il-62M *Classic* (VIP)

DEPLOYMENT

CÔTE D'IVOIRE
UN • UNOCI 3 obs

LIBERIA
UN • UNMIL 2 obs

SUDAN
UN • UNAMID 213; 1 inf coy

Ghana GHA

Ghanaian New Cedi C		2012	2013	2014
GDP	C	70.4bn	84.5bn	
	US$	38.9bn	42.7bn	
per capita	US$	1,562	1,671	
Growth	%	6.98	6.89	
Inflation	%	9.16	8.45	
Def bdgt	C	201m	576m	914m
	US$	111m	291m	
FMA (US)	US$	0.35m	0.35m	0.35m
US$1=C		1.81	1.98	

Population 25,199,609

Age	0–14	15–19	20–24	25–29	30–64	65 plus
Male	19.5%	5.0%	4.4%	3.9%	14.7%	1.9%
Female	19.3%	4.9%	4.5%	4.1%	15.6%	2.2%

Capabilities

In common with other regional militaries, the Ghanaian armed forces are intended to conduct internal security and peacekeeping operations. They are both well-trained and well-funded, with several new equipment programmes undertaken to modernise key capabilities such as airlift and coastal patrol – prompted by the challenge of piracy – as part of a concerted long-term modernisation plan. The small air force is built around the tactical transport role, with a handful of jet trainers available for light attack. The armed forces maintain a strong tradition of military-to-military ties with external partners, a process helped by the KAIPTC centre, hosting numerous regional and international personnel on a range of military and peacekeeping-relevant courses.

ACTIVE 15,500 (Army 11,500 Navy 2,000 Air 2,000)

ORGANISATIONS BY SERVICE

Army 11,500

FORCES BY ROLE
COMMAND
2 comd HQ
MANOEUVRE
Reconnaissance
1 armd recce regt (3 recce sqn)
Light
1 (rapid reaction) mot inf bn
6 inf bn
Air Manoeuvre
2 AB coy
COMBAT SUPPORT
1 arty regt (1 arty bty, 2 mor bty)
1 fd engr regt (bn)
1 sigs regt
1 sigs sqn
COMBAT SERVICE SUPPORT
1 log gp
1 tpt coy
2 maint coy
1 med coy
1 trg bn

EQUIPMENT BY TYPE
RECCE 3 EE-9 *Cascavel*
AIFV 39: 24 *Ratel*-90; 15 *Ratel*-20
APC (W) 56: 50 *Piranha*; 6 Type-05P
ARTY 87+
TOWED 122mm 6 D-30
MRL 3+: **107mm** Type-63; **122mm** 3 Type-81
MOR 78: **81mm** 50; **120mm** 28 *Tampella*
AT • RCL 84mm 50 *Carl Gustav*
AD • SAM • MANPAD 9K32 *Strela*-2 (SA-7 *Grail*)‡
GUNS • TOWED 8+: **14.5mm** 4+: 4 ZPU-2; ZPU-4; **23mm** 4 ZU-23-2
ARV *Piranha* reported

Navy 2,000

Naval HQ located at Accra; Western HQ located at Sekondi; Eastern HQ located at Tema

EQUIPMENT BY TYPE
PATROL AND COASTAL COMBATANTS 14
PCO 2 *Anzone* (US)
PCC 10: 2 *Achimota* (GER Lurssen 57m) with 1 76 mm gun; 2 *Dzata* (GER Lurssen 45m); 2 *Warrior* (GER *Gepard*); 4 *Snake* (PRC 47m)
PBF 1 *Stephen Otu* (ROK *Sea Dolphin*)
PB 1 *David Hansen* (US)

Air Force 2,000

FORCES BY ROLE
GROUND ATTACK
1 sqn with K-8 *Karakorum**; L-39ZO*: MB-326K; MB-339A*
ISR
1 unit with DA-42
TRANSPORT
1 sqn with BN-2 *Defender*; Cessna 172; F-27 *Friendship*; F-28 *Fellowship* (VIP)

TRANSPORT HELICOPTER
1 sqn with AW109A; Bell 412SP *Twin Huey*; Mi-17V-5 *Hip* H; SA319 *Alouette* III

EQUIPMENT BY TYPE†
AIRCRAFT 11 combat capable
ATK 3 MB-326K
TPT 14 **Light** 13: 1 BN-2 *Defender*; 2 C-295; 3 Cessna 172; 3 DA-42; 4 F-27 *Friendship*; **PAX** 1 F-28 *Fellowship* (VIP)
TRG 8: 4 K-8 *Karakorum**; 2 L-39ZO*; 2 MB-339A*
HELICOPTERS
MRH 6: 1 Bell 412SP *Twin Huey*; 3 Mi-17V-5 *Hip* H; 2 SA319 *Alouette* III
TPT 6 **Medium** 4 Mi-171Sh; **Light** 2 AW109A

DEPLOYMENT

CÔTE D'IVOIRE
UN • UNOCI 507; 6 obs; 1 inf bn; 1 hel coy; 1 fd hospital

DEMOCRATIC REPUBLIC OF THE CONGO
UN • MONUSCO 466; 26 obs; 1 mech inf bn

LEBANON
UN • UNIFIL 869; 1 inf bn

LIBERIA
UN • UNMIL 708; 10 obs; 1 inf bn

MALI
UN • MINUSMA 128; 1 construction coy

SOUTH SUDAN
UN • UNMISS 4; 2 obs

SUDAN
UN • UNAMID 17; 8 obs
UN • UNISFA 2; 3 obs

WESTERN SAHARA
UN • MINURSO 7; 10 obs

Guinea GUI

Guinean Franc fr		2012	2013	2014
GDP	fr	39.6tr	45.5tr	
	US$	5.63bn	6.27bn	
per capita	US$	519	564	
Growth	%	3.94	4.51	
Inflation	%	15.23	11.23	
Def bdgt	fr	ε275bn		
	US$	ε39m		
FMA (US)	US$	0.4m	0.4m	0.2m
US$1=fr		7029.53	7249.95	

Population 11,176,026

Age	0–14	15–19	20–24	25–29	30–64	65 plus
Male	21.3%	5.3%	4.5%	3.8%	13.5%	1.6%
Female	20.9%	5.2%	4.4%	3.7%	13.7%	2.0%

Capabilities

The heavily politicised nature of Guinea's armed forces has undermined their professionalism and quality. Much of their inventory of ageing equipment is likely unserviceable.

ACTIVE 9,700 (Army 8,500 Navy 400 Air 800)
Paramilitary 2,600
Conscript liability 2 years

ORGANISATIONS BY SERVICE

Army 8,500

FORCES BY ROLE
MANOEUVRE
Armoured
1 armd bn
Light
1 SF bn
5 inf bn
1 ranger bn
1 cdo bn
Air Manoeuvre
1 air mob bn
Other
1 (Presidential Guard) gd bn
COMBAT SUPPORT
1 arty bn
1 AD bn
1 engr bn

EQUIPMENT BY TYPE
MBT 38: 8 T-54; 30 T-34
LT TK 15 PT-76
RECCE 27: 2 AML-90; 25 BRDM-1/BRDM-2
AIFV 2 BMP-1
APC 50
APC (T) 10 BTR-50
APC (W) 30: 16 BTR-40; 8 BTR-60; 6 BTR-152
PPV 10 *Mamba*†
ARTY 47+
TOWED 24: **122mm** 12 M-1931/37; **130mm** 12 M-46
MRL 220mm 3 BM-27/9P140 *Uragan*
MOR 20+: **82mm** M-43; **120mm** 20 M-1943/M-38
AT
MSL • MANPATS 9K11 *Malyutka* (AT-3 *Sagger*); 9M113 *Konkurs* (AT-5 *Spandrel*)
RCL 82mm B-10
GUNS 6+: **57mm** ZIS-2 *M-1943*; **85mm** 6 D-44
AD • SAM • MANPAD 9K32 *Strela*-2 (SA-7 *Grail)*‡
GUNS • TOWED 24+: **30mm** M-53 (twin); **37mm** 8 M-1939; **57mm** 12 Type-59 (S-60); **100mm** 4 KS-19
ARV T-54/T-55 reported

Navy ε400

EQUIPMENT BY TYPE
PATROL AND COASTAL COMBATANTS 4 • **PB** 1 Swiftships†; 3 RPB 20

Air Force 800

EQUIPMENT BY TYPE†

AIRCRAFT
- **FGA** (3 MiG-21 *Fishbed* non-op)
- **TPT • Light** 2 An-2 *Colt*

HELICOPTERS
- **ATK** 4 Mi-24 *Hind*
- **MRH** 5: 2 MD-500MD; 2 Mi-17-1V *Hip* H; 1 SA342K *Gazelle*
- **TPT** 2 **Medium** 1 SA330 *Puma;* **Light** 1 AS350B *Ecureuil*

MSL
- **AAM • IR** R-3 (AA-2 *Atoll*)‡

Paramilitary 2,600 active

Gendarmerie 1,000

Republican Guard 1,600

People's Militia 7,000 reservists

DEPLOYMENT

CÔTE D'IVOIRE
UN • UNOCI 2 obs

DEMOCRATIC REPUBLIC OF THE CONGO
UN • MONUSCO 1 obs

MALI
UN • MINUSMA 149; 1 inf coy

SOUTH SUDAN
UN • UNMISS 2 obs

WESTERN SAHARA
UN • MINURSO 5 obs

Guinea-Bissau GNB

CFA Franc BCEAO fr		2012	2013	2014
GDP	fr	444bn	464bn	
	US$	870m	940m	
per capita	US$	551	583	
Growth	%	-1.45	4.20	
Inflation	%	2.22	3.00	
Def bdgt	fr	13bn		
	US$	26m		
US$1=fr		510.25	493.37	

Population 1,660,870

Age	0–14	15–19	20–24	25–29	30–64	65 plus
Male	20.0%	5.3%	4.7%	4.0%	13.5%	1.3%
Female	20.0%	5.4%	4.8%	4.1%	14.9%	2.0%

Capabilities

The level of capability and professionalism of the heavily politicised Guinea-Bissau armed forces is uncertain. Most of the equipment holdings are unserviceable. Attempts to improve this suffered a setback after the EU Security Sector Reform Mission withdrew in August 2010, though it had started to lay the groundwork for reform, with elements such as a military census. Angola's MISSANG mission left in 2012. ECOWAS states then deployed a mission, ECOMIB, and are now working with the government on an SSR road map. ECOMIB's mandate has been extended to May 2014. ECOWAS chiefs recommended, in May, that the mission should be bolstered by air and naval assets. The Guinea-Bissau chief of staff earlier requested ECOWAS assistance in patrolling its territorial waters.

ACTIVE ε4,450 (Army ε4,000 (numbers reducing) Navy 350 Air 100) Gendarmerie 2,000

Conscript liability Selective conscription

Manpower and eqpt totals should be treated with caution. A number of draft laws to restructure the armed services and police have been produced.

ORGANISATIONS BY SERVICE

Army ε4,000 (numbers reducing)

FORCES BY ROLE

MANOEUVRE
- **Reconnaissance**
  - 1 recce coy
- **Armoured**
  - 1 armd bn (sqn)
- **Light**
  - 5 inf bn

COMBAT SUPPORT
- 1 arty bn
- 1 engr coy

EQUIPMENT BY TYPE

MBT 10 T-34
LT TK 15 PT-76
RECCE 10 BRDM-2
APC (W) 55: 35 BTR-40/BTR-60; 20 Type-56 (BTR-152)
ARTY 26+
- **TOWED 122mm** 18 D-30/*M-1938*
- **MOR** 8+: **82mm** M-43; **120mm** 8 M-1943

AT
- **RCL 75mm** Type-52 (M20); **82mm** B-10
- **RL 89mm** M20
- **GUNS 85mm** 8 D-44

AD • SAM • MANPAD 9K32 *Strela*-2 (SA-7 *Grail*)‡
- **GUNS • TOWED** 34: **23mm** 18 ZU-23; **37mm** 6 M-1939; **57mm** 10 S-60

Navy ε350

EQUIPMENT BY TYPE

PATROL AND COASTAL COMBATANTS • **PB** 2 *Alfeite*†

Air Force 100

EQUIPMENT BY TYPE

HELICOPTERS • **MRH** 1 SA319 *Alouette* III†

Paramilitary 2,000 active

Gendarmerie 2,000

DEPLOYMENT

MALI
UN • MINUSMA 2

FOREIGN FORCES

Nigeria ECOMIB 160
Senegal ECOMIB 200

Kenya KEN

Kenyan Shilling sh		2012	2013	2014
GDP	sh	3.48tr	3.98tr	
	US$	41.1bn	46.5bn	
per capita	US$	977	1,073	
Growth	%	4.70	5.85	
Inflation	%	9.40	5.17	
Def bdgt [a]	sh	78.6bn	83.5bn	74.4bn
	US$	930m	975m	
FMA (US)	US$	1.5m	1.5m	1.18m
US$1=sh		84.53	85.65	

[a] Excludes allocations for internal security operations.

Population 44,037,656

Ethnic groups: Kikuyu ε22–32%

Age	0–14	15–19	20–24	25–29	30–64	65 plus
Male	21.2%	4.8%	4.6%	4.4%	13.6%	1.2%
Female	21.1%	4.8%	4.6%	4.4%	13.7%	1.5%

Capabilities

Kenya's ground forces with air support moved into southern Somalia in October 2010 as part of *Operation Linda Nchi* to attack al-Shabaab militants. Some foreign logistic support was reportedly required, at least initially. The contingent was incorporated into AMISOM. As of mid-2013, limited fighting continued, with Kenyan and Somali government forces under the banner of the African Union Mission continuing to engage with al-Shabaab fighters in southern Somalia. The army also played a leading role in the counter-attack against militants who seized Nairobi's Westgate mall in September 2013. In regional terms, the armed forces remain capable, but are beginning to suffer as a result of the ageing core elements of their inventories, particularly armoured vehicles and combat aircraft. The air force can provide tactical support and airlift. The small navy undertakes coast guard and counter piracy roles and supported the seaborne attack on al-Shabaab at Kismayu. The country has the ability to project power, albeit on a limited basis, beyond its own territory. Morale among the services is held to be good. The military regularly joins UK troops training in Kenya and takes part in international exercises in Africa.

ACTIVE 24,120 (Army 20,000 Navy 1,600 Air 2,500) **Paramilitary 5,000**
(incl HQ staff)

ORGANISATIONS BY SERVICE

Army 20,000

FORCES BY ROLE
MANOEUVRE
Armoured
1 armd bde (1 armd recce bn, 2 armd bn)
Light
1 spec ops bn
1 ranger bn
1 inf bde (3 inf bn)
1 inf bde (2 inf bn)
1 indep inf bn
Air Manoeuvre
1 air cav bn
1 AB bn
COMBAT SUPPORT
1 arty bde (2 arty bn, 1 mor bty)
1 ADA bn
1 engr bde (2 engr bn)

EQUIPMENT BY TYPE
MBT 78 Vickers Mk 3
RECCE 92: 72 AML-60/AML-90; 12 *Ferret*; 8 S52 *Shorland*
APC 189
APC (W) 84: 52 UR-416; 32 Type-92 (reported); (10 M3 Panhard in store)
PPV 105 *Puma* M26-15
ARTY 110
TOWED 105mm 48: 8 Model 56 pack howitzer; 40 Light Gun
MOR 62: **81mm** 50; **120mm** 12 Brandt
AT • MSL • MANPATS 54: 40 *Milan*; 14 *Swingfire*
RCL 84mm 80 *Carl Gustav*
AD • GUNS • TOWED 94: **20mm** 81: 11 Oerlikon; ε70 TCM-20; **40mm** 13 L/70
ARV 7 Vickers ARV
MW Bozena
HELICOPTERS
MRH 37: 2 Hughes 500D†; 12 Hughes 500M†; 10 Hughes 500MD *Scout Defender*† (with TOW); 10 Hughes 500ME†; 3 Z-9W

Navy 1,600 (incl 120 marines)

EQUIPMENT BY TYPE
PATROL AND COASTAL COMBATANTS 7
PCO 1 *Jasiri* (to be fitted with 1 76 mm gun)
PCFG 2 *Nyayo*
PCC 3: 1 *Harambee* (FRA P400); 2 *Shujaa* with 1 76mm gun
PBF 1 *Archangel*
AMPHIBIOUS • LCM 2 *Galana*
LOGISTICS AND SUPPORT • AP 2

Air Force 2,500

FORCES BY ROLE

FIGHTER/GROUND ATTACK

2 sqn with F-5E/F *Tiger* II

TRANSPORT

Some sqn with DHC-5D *Buffalo*†; DHC-8†; F-70† (VIP); Y-12(II)†

TRAINING

Some sqn with *Bulldog* 103/*Bulldog* 127†; EMB-312 *Tucano*†*; *Hawk* Mk52†*; Hughes 500D†

TRANSPORT HELICOPTER

1 sqn with SA330 *Puma*†

EQUIPMENT BY TYPE†

AIRCRAFT 38 combat capable

FTR 22: 18 F-5E *Tiger* II; 4 F-5F *Tiger* II

TPT 18 **Light** 17: 4 DHC-5D *Buffalo*†; 3 DHC-8†; 10 Y-12(II)†; (6 Do-28D-2† in store); **PAX** 1 F-70† (VIP)

TRG 24: 8 *Bulldog* 103/127†; 11 EMB-312 *Tucano*†*; 5 *Hawk* Mk52†*

HELICOPTERS

TPT • Medium 13: 2 Mi-171; 11 SA330 *Puma*†

MSL

AAM • IR AIM-9 *Sidewinder*

ASM AGM-65 *Maverick;* TOW

Paramilitary 5,000

Police General Service Unit 5,000

PATROL AND COASTAL COMBATANTS • PB 5 (2 on Lake Victoria)

Air Wing

AIRCRAFT • TPT 7 *Cessna*

HELICOPTERS

TPT • Light 1 Bell 206L *Long Ranger*

TRG 2 Bell 47G

DEPLOYMENT

DEMOCRATIC REPUBLIC OF THE CONGO

UN • MONUSCO 12; 18 obs

LEBANON

UN • UNIFIL 1

LIBERIA

UN • UNMIL 2

SOMALIA

AU • AMISOM 3,664: 3 inf bn

SOUTH SUDAN

UN • UNMISS 701; 3 obs; 1 inf bn

SUDAN

UN • UNAMID 81; 6 obs; 1 MP coy

FOREIGN FORCES

United Kingdom Army 170

Lesotho LSO

Lesotho Loti M		2012	2013	2014
GDP	M	20bn	22.6bn	
	US$	2.44bn	2.62bn	
per capita	US$	1,283	1,372	
Growth	%	4.00	3.55	
Inflation	%	5.35	4.90	
Def bdgt	M	454m	466m	
	US$	55m	54m	
US$1=M		8.20	8.65	

Population 1,936,181

Age	0–14	15–19	20–24	25–29	30–64	65 plus
Male	16.6%	4.8%	4.8%	4.8%	15.6%	2.7%
Female	16.5%	5.2%	5.5%	5.6%	15.3%	2.7%

Capabilities

Lesotho's small armed forces are charged with protecting territorial integrity and sovereignty, though South Africa in effect acts as a security guarantor. Most personnel are in infantry units, supported by light vehicles, and the country possesses a small number of tactical transport aircraft and utility helicopters.

ACTIVE 2,000 (Army 2,000)

ORGANISATIONS BY SERVICE

Army ε2,000

FORCES BY ROLE

MANOEUVRE

Reconnaissance

1 recce coy

Light

7 inf coy

Aviation

1 sqn

COMBAT SUPPORT

1 arty bty(-)

1 spt coy (with mor)

EQUIPMENT BY TYPE

RECCE 28: 4 AML-90; 6 RAM-2000; 10 RBY-1; 8 S52 *Shorland*

ARTY 12

TOWED 105mm 2

MOR 81mm 10

AT • RCL 106mm 6 M40

Air Wing 110

AIRCRAFT

TPT • Light 3: 2 C-212-300 *Aviocar;* 1 GA-8 *Airvan*

HELICOPTERS

MRH 3: 1 Bell 412 *Twin Huey;* 2 Bell 412EP *Twin Huey*

TPT • Light 2: 1 Bell 206 *Jet Ranger;* 1 Bo-105LSA-3

Sub-Saharan Africa

DEPLOYMENT

SUDAN

UN • UNAMID 1; 2 obs

Liberia LBR

Liberian Dollar L$		2012	2013	2014
GDP	L$	127bn	148bn	
	US$	1.74bn	1.96bn	
per capita	US$	436	481	
Growth	%	8.35	7.47	
Inflation	%	6.84	6.37	
Def bdgt	L$	24m		
	US$	24m		
FMA (US)	US$	6.5m	6.5m	5.53m
US$1=L$		73.19	75.40	

Population **3,989,703**

Ethnic groups: Americo-Liberians 5%

Age	0–14	15–19	20–24	25–29	30–64	65 plus
Male	22.0%	4.9%	3.7%	4.2%	13.5%	1.5%
Female	21.7%	5.1%	4.0%	4.2%	13.6%	1.5%

Capabilities

Essentially a new force created after the country's 1980s and 1990s civil wars, the Armed Forces of Liberia have, since 2006, gradually developed a nascent defence capacity. However, this force is unable to deliver security throughout the country, and hence Monrovia still relies on the presence of UNMIL for stabilisation. The AFL has no ability to project power beyond its borders, and little ability to do so within areas of the country. There is no air force, and the only maritime security is provided by a small coast guard, reactivated in 2010, equipped entirely with rigid-hulled inflatable boats. The armed forces' first combat mission was launched in October 2012, patrolling the country's southeastern border to prevent cross-border insurgency movements.

ACTIVE 2,050 (Army 2,000, Coast Guard 50)

ORGANISATIONS BY SERVICE

Army 2,000

FORCES BY ROLE

MANOEUVRE

Light

1 (23rd) inf bde with (2 inf bn, 1 engr coy, 1 MP coy)

COMBAT SERVICE SUPPORT

1 trg unit (forming)

Coast Guard 50

10 craft (8 *Zodiac* and 2 *Defender*) under 10t FLD

DEPLOYMENT

MALI

UN • MINUSMA 49; 1 inf pl

FOREIGN FORCES

All under UNMIL comd unless otherwise specified

Bangladesh 529; 13 obs; 2 engr coy; 1 log coy; 1 fd hospital

Benin 1; 1 obs

Bolivia 1; 2 obs

Brazil 2; 2 obs

Bulgaria 2 obs

China, People's Republic of 564; 2 obs; 1 engr coy; 1 tpt coy; 1 fd hospital

Croatia 2

Denmark 2; 3 obs

Ecuador 1; 2 obs

Egypt 7 obs

El Salvador 2 obs

Ethiopia 4; 9 obs

Finland 2

France 1

Gambia 2 obs

Ghana 708; 10 obs; 1 inf bn

Indonesia 1 obs

Jordan 120; 4 obs; 1 fd hospital

Korea, Republic of 1; 1 obs

Kyrgyzstan 3 obs

Malaysia 6 obs

Moldova 2 obs

Montenegro 2 obs

Namibia 3; 1 obs

Nepal 18; 2 obs; 1 MP sect

Niger 2 obs

Nigeria 1,466; 11 obs; 2 inf bn

Pakistan 1,987; 9 obs; 2 inf bn; 2 engr coy; 1 fd hospital

Paraguay 1; 2 obs

Peru 2; 2 obs

Philippines 109; 1 log coy

Poland 1 obs

Romania 2 obs

Russia 4 obs

Senegal 1; 1 obs

Serbia 4 obs

Togo 1; 2 obs

Ukraine 238; 2 obs; 1 hel sqn

United States 5; 4 obs

Yemen, Republic of 1

Zambia 3 obs

Zimbabwe 2 obs

Madagascar MDG

Malagsy Ariary fr		2012	2013	2014
GDP	fr	22tr	24.2tr	
	US$	10.1bn	10.7bn	
per capita	US$	451	466	
Growth	%	1.90	2.62	
Inflation	%	6.45	7.00	
Def bdgt	fr	151bn	163bn	165bn
	US$	69m	72m	
US$1=fr		2172.81	2262.79	

Population 22,599,098

Age	0–14	15–19	20–24	25–29	30–64	65 plus
Male	20.7%	5.6%	4.8%	4.0%	13.6%	1.4%
Female	20.4%	5.5%	4.8%	3.9%	13.8%	1.7%

Capabilities

The military has played a significant role in the island's recent political instability. Elements were involved in the ousting of former-president Marc Ravalomanana in 2009, an abortive coup attempt in 2010 and a mutiny in 2012, which resulted in the temporary closure of the airport at Antananarivo. The army is the dominant force; neither of the small air or naval units has substantive combat capacity, and the state has no power-projection capability.

ACTIVE 13,500 (Army 12,500 Navy 500 Air 500)
Paramilitary 8,100

Conscript liability 18 months (incl for civil purposes)

ORGANISATIONS BY SERVICE

Army 12,500+

FORCES BY ROLE

MANOEUVRE

Light

2 (intervention) inf regt

10 (regional) inf regt

COMBAT SUPPORT

1 arty regt

1 ADA regt

3 engr regt

1 sigs regt

COMBAT SERVICE SUPPORT

1 log regt

EQUIPMENT BY TYPE

LT TK 12 PT-76

RECCE 73: ε35 BRDM-2; 10 *Ferret*; ε20 M3A1; 8 M8

APC (T) ε30 M3A1 half-track

ARTY 25+

TOWED 17: **105mm** 5 M101; **122mm** 12 D-30

MOR 8+: **82mm** M-37; **120mm** 8 M-43

AT • RCL 106mm M40A1

RL 89mm LRAC

AD • GUNS • TOWED 70: **14.5mm** 50 ZPU-4; **37mm** 20 Type-55 (M-1939)

Navy 500 (incl some 100 Marines)

EQUIPMENT BY TYPE

PATROL AND COASTAL COMBATANTS 7

PCC 1 *Chamois*

PB 7: 6 (ex-US); 1 *Daikannon Maru* (fishery protection)

AMPHIBIOUS • LCT 1 (FRA *Edic*)

LOGISTICS AND SUPPORT 3

YT 2 *Aigrette*

YTB 1 *Trozona*

Air Force 500

FORCES BY ROLE

TRANSPORT

1 sqn with An-26 *Curl*; Yak-40 *Codling* (VIP)

1 (liaison) sqn with Cessna 310; Cessna 337 *Skymaster*; PA-23 *Aztec*

TRAINING

1 sqn with Cessna 172; J.300 *Joker*; *Tetras*

TRANSPORT HELICOPTER

1 sqn with SA318C *Alouette* II

EQUIPMENT BY TYPE

AIRCRAFT • TPT 17 **Light** 15: 1 An-26 *Curl*; 4 Cessna 172; 1 Cessna 310; 2 Cessna 337 *Skymaster*; 2 J.300 *Joker*; 1 PA-23 *Aztec*; 2 *Tetras*; 2 Yak-40 *Codling* (VIP); **PAX** 2 B-737

HELICOPTERS • MRH 4 SA318C *Alouette* II

Paramilitary 8,100

Gendarmerie 8,100

PATROL AND COASTAL COMBATANTS • 5 PB

Malawi MWI

Malawian Kwacha K		2012	2013	2014
GDP	K	1.06tr	1.31tr	
	US$	4.21bn	3.82bn	
per capita	US$	253	223	
Growth	%	1.89	5.48	
Inflation	%	21.27	20.20	
Def bdgt	K	7.94bn	8.75bn	17bn
	US$	32m	25m	
US$1=K		250.79	343.43	

Population 16,777,547

Age	0–14	15–19	20–24	25–29	30–64	65 plus
Male	22.4%	5.5%	4.7%	4.0%	12.0%	1.1%
Female	22.3%	5.5%	4.8%	4.1%	12.0%	1.6%

Capabilities

The armed forces' role is to ensure the sovereignty and territorial integrity of the state. The army is the largest force, consisting mainly of infantry supported by light armoured vehicles, and the Chilumba garrison was reorganised as the 11th Battalion, Malawi Rifles early in 2013. The air wing and the naval unit are much smaller supporting services, and the military has no capacity for power projection. The army exercises regularly, participates in multinational exercises, is involved in supporting UN missions, and has received support and deployment training from AFRICOM.

ACTIVE 5,300 (Army 5,300) **Paramilitary 1,500**

ORGANISATIONS BY SERVICE

Army 5,300

FORCES BY ROLE

COMMAND
2 bde HQ
MANOEUVRE
Light
5 inf bn
Air Manoeuvre
1 para bn
COMBAT SUPPORT
1 (general) bn (1+ mne coy, 1 armd recce sqn, 2 lt arty bty, 1 engr unit)
COMBAT SERVICE SUPPORT
8 log coy

EQUIPMENT BY TYPE

Less than 20% serviceability
RECCE 41: 13 *Eland*; 20 FV721 *Fox*; 8 *Ferret*
APC • PPV 10 *Puma* M26-15
ARTY 17
TOWED 105mm 9 lt
MOR 81mm 8 L16
AD • SAM • MANPAD 15 *Blowpipe*
GUNS • TOWED 14.5mm 40 ZPU-4

Navy 220

EQUIPMENT BY TYPE

PATROL AND COASTAL COMBATANTS • PB 1 *Kasungu*†

Air Wing 200

EQUIPMENT BY TYPE

AIRCRAFT • TPT 2 **Light** 1 Do-228; **PAX** 1 *Falcon* 900EX
HELICOPTERS • TPT 3 **Medium** 2: 1 AS532UL *Cougar*; 1 SA330H *Puma*; **Light** 1 AS350L *Ecureuil*

Paramilitary 1,500

Mobile Police Force 1,500

RECCE 8 S52 *Shorland*
AIRCRAFT
TPT • Light 4: 3 BN-2T *Defender* (border patrol); 1 SC.7 3M *Skyvan*
HELICOPTERS • MRH 2 AS365 *Dauphin 2*

DEPLOYMENT

CÔTE D'IVOIRE
UN • UNOCI 7; 3 obs

DEMOCRATIC REPUBLIC OF THE CONGO
UN • MONUSCO 118; 9 obs; 1 inf coy

WESTERN SAHARA
UN • MINURSO 3 obs

Mali MLI

CFA Franc BCEAO fr		2012	2013	2014
GDP	fr	5.26tr	5.65tr	
	US$	10.3bn	11.4bn	
per capita	US$	631	677	
Growth	%	-1.19	4.82	
Inflation	%	5.32	2.92	
Def bdgt	fr	109bn	149bn	
	US$	213m	301m	
US$1=fr		509.99	494.92	

Population 15,968,882

Ethnic groups: Tuareg 6–10%

Age	0–14	15–19	20–24	25–29	30–64	65 plus
Male	24.0%	5.1%	3.9%	3.0%	11.2%	1.5%
Female	23.8%	5.4%	4.5%	3.8%	12.3%	1.5%

Capabilities

Mali's armed forces suffer from low morale, politicisation and outdated equipment. A coup, launched in March 2012, was largely inspired by the army's failing campaign against Tuareg and Islamist rebels in the north of the country. The northern rebellion not only exposed the frailties of the Malian armed forces, but also exacerbated them, as many of the ground forces' armoured vehicles were captured by the insurgents. In January 2013, with columns of jihadi elements judged as preparing to move on Bamako, the government requested French intervention. *Opération Serval*, a high-tempo, joint multinational mission was launched with initial strikes by French forces. The Islamists were driven back into the remote north, though they retain the capacity to attack targets in urban areas. An EU civil and military mission is engaged in training Mali's armed forces, which are still army dominated. The resulting units resemble combined arms battle groups, though apart from some new 4×4s and legacy BTRs, it is hard to tell whether these forces have also benefited from new equipment. The small air force was intermittently capable of delivering limited strike capabilities through its two fighter aircraft and four attack helicopters.

ACTIVE 3,000 (Army 3,000) **Paramilitary 4,800 Militia 3,000**

ORGANISATIONS BY SERVICE

Army ε3,000

FORCES BY ROLE

The remanants of the pre-war Malian army are being reformed into four new combined arms battle groups, each of which will consist of three mot inf coy and additional recce, cdo and cbt spt elms. By late 2013 two of these battle groups had been deployed, and a third was undergoing pre-deployment training.

MANOEUVRE

Light

3 mot inf BG

EQUIPMENT BY TYPE

APC (W) 19: 10 BTR-60PB; 9 BTR-70

Navy

EQUIPMENT BY TYPE

PATROL AND COASTAL COMBATANTS 3 **PBR†**

Air Force

FORCES BY ROLE

FIGHTER

1 sqn with MiG-21MF *Fishbed*; MiG-21UM *Mongol* B

TRANSPORT

1 sqn with An-24 *Coke*; An-26 *Curl*; BN-2 *Islander*; BT-67

TRAINING

1 sqn with L-29 *Delfin*; SF-260WL *Warrior**; *Tetras*

TRANSPORT HELICOPTER

1 sqn with Mi-8 *Hip*; Mi-24D *Hind*; Z-9

EQUIPMENT BY TYPE

AIRCRAFT 4 combat capable

FGA 2: 1 MiG-21MF *Fishbed*; 1 MiG-21UM *Mongol* B

TPT • Light 10: 1 An-24 *Coke*; 2 An-26 *Curl*; 1 BT-67; 2 BN-2 *Islander*; 4 *Tetras*

TRG 8: 6 L-29 *Delfin*; 2 SF-260WL *Warrior**

HELICOPTERS

ATK 2 Mi-24D *Hind*

MRH 1 Z-9

TPT 1 **Medium** 1 Mi-8 *Hip*; **Light** (1 AS350 *Ecureuil* in store)

Paramilitary 4,800 active

Gendarmerie 1,800

FORCES BY ROLE

MANOEUVRE

Other

8 paramilitary coy

Republican Guard 2,000

National Police 1,000

Militia 3,000

DEPLOYMENT

DEMOCRATIC REPUBLIC OF THE CONGO

UN • MONUSCO 14 obs

SUDAN

UN • UNAMID 1; 7 obs

FOREIGN FORCES

All under MINUSMA comd unless otherwise specified

Austria EUTM Mali 8

Bangladesh 5

Belgium EUTM Mali 34

Benin 306; 1 SF coy

Burkina Faso 671; 1 inf bn

Cambodia 2

Chad 1235; 1 SF coy; 2 inf bn

Côte d'Ivoire 126; 1 tpt coy

Czech Republic EUTM Mali 38

Estonia 1 • EUTM Mali 8

Finland 1 • EUTM Mali 10

France 19 • *Operation Serval* 3,200; 1 mech inf BG; 1 log bn; 1 hel unit with 3 EC665 *Tiger*; 8 SA330 *Puma*; 6 SA342 *Gazelle*; 1 FGA det with 3 *Mirage* 2000D • EUTM Mali 207

Germany 61; 1 avn unit • EUTM Mali 73

Ghana 128; 1 construction coy

Guinea 149; 1 inf coy

Guinea-Bissau 2

Hungary EUTM Mali 13

Ireland EUTM Mali 8

Italy EUTM Mali 7

Jordan 1

Latvia EUTM 2

Liberia 49; 1 inf pl

Lithuania EUTM Mali 2

Luxembourg EUTM Mali 1

Mauritania 4

Niger 864; 1 inf bn

Nigeria 115; 1 sigs coy

Poland EUTM Mali 20

Portugal EUTM Mali 1

Romania EUTM Mali 1

Senegal 510; 1 inf coy; 1 arty coy; 1 engr coy

Sierra Leone 5

Slovenia EUTM Mali 3

Spain EUTM Mali 59

Sweden 6 • EUTM Mali 16

Tajikistan 1

Togo 939; 1 inf bn

United Kingdom 2 • EUTM Mali 40

United States 5

Yemen 2

Mauritius MUS

Mauritian Rupee R		2012	2013	2014
GDP	R	345bn	378bn	
	US$	11.5bn	12.1bn	
per capita	US$	8,850	9,307	
Growth	%	3.30	3.72	
Inflation	%	3.85	5.66	
Def bdgt [a]	R	2.15bn	2.59bn	2.58bn
	US$	71m	83m	
US$1=R		30.05	31.17	

[a] Defence and Home Affairs Budget

Population 1,322,238

Age	0–14	15–19	20–24	25–29	30–64	65 plus
Male	10.9%	3.8%	4.1%	3.6%	23.6%	3.2%
Female	10.4%	3.8%	4.0%	3.5%	24.3%	4.8%

Capabilities

The country has no standing armed forces, but the Special Mobile Force (part of the police force) is tasked with providing internal and external security. The coast guard operates a number of patrol craft, including one blue water patrol ship.

ACTIVE NIL Paramilitary 2,500

ORGANISATIONS BY SERVICE

Paramilitary 2,500

Special Mobile Force ε1,750

FORCES BY ROLE

MANOEUVRE

Reconnaissance

2 recce coy

Light

5 (rifle) mot inf coy

COMBAT SUPPORT

1 engr sqn

COMBAT SERVICE SUPPORT

1 spt pl

EQUIPMENT BY TYPE

RECCE 4 *Shorland*

AIFV 2 VAB (with 20mm gun)

APC (W) 16: 7 *Tactica*; 9 VAB

ARTY • MOR 81mm 2

AT • RL 89mm 4 LRAC

Coast Guard ε800

EQUIPMENT BY TYPE

PATROL AND COASTAL COMBATANTS 5

PSOH 1 *Vigilant*† (1 hel landing platform) (vessel has been laid up since 2006 and is for sale)

PB 4: 1 P-2000; 1 SDB-Mk3; 2 *Zhuk* (FSU)

LOGISTICS AND SUPPORT

AGS 1 *Pathfinder*

AIRCRAFT • TPT • Light 3: 1 BN-2T *Defender*; 2 Do-228-101

Police Air Wing

EQUIPMENT BY TYPE

HELICOPTERS

MRH 5: 1 *Dhruv*; 4 SA316 *Alouette* III

TPT • Light 1 AS355 *Ecureuil* II

Mozambique MOZ

Mozambique New Metical M		2012	2013	2014
GDP	M	414bn	483bn	
	US$	14.6bn	15.8bn	
per capita	US$	650	688	
Growth	%	7.50	8.40	
Inflation	%	2.09	5.44	
Def bdgt	M		2.28bn	4.08bn
	US$		75m	
US$1=M		28.38	30.62	

Population 24,096,669

Age	0–14	15–19	20–24	25–29	30–64	65 plus
Male	22.9%	5.7%	4.5%	3.1%	11.2%	1.4%
Female	22.6%	5.9%	5.0%	3.7%	12.5%	1.6%

Capabilities

The armed forces are tasked with combating marine piracy and people-trafficking, as well as assuring the country's territorial integrity. The extent to which they are capable of meeting any of these tasks is doubtful and in general, equipment quality and training remain questionable. However, Mozambique's forces will have learnt lessons from cooperative anti-piracy patrols with South Africa. Budget constraints have severely limited the ability to address areas of weakness, leaving the armed forces dependent on cascaded defence equipment from other nations. However, rising revenues from hydrocarbon exploitation will likely help overall budgets, and it is possible that the need to protect maritime energy infrastructure could drive procurements. There are growing defence ties with China.

ACTIVE 11,200 (Army 10,000 Navy 200 Air 1,000)

Conscript liability 2 years

ORGANISATIONS BY SERVICE

Army ε9,000–10,000

FORCES BY ROLE

SPECIAL FORCES

3 SF bn

MANOEUVRE

Light

7 inf bn

COMBAT SUPPORT

2-3 arty bn

2 engr bn

COMBAT SERVICE SUPPORT
1 log bn

EQUIPMENT BY TYPE†

Equipment at estimated 10% or less serviceability

MBT 60+ T-54
RECCE 30 BRDM-1/BRDM-2
AIFV 40 BMP-1
APC (W) 260: 160 BTR-60; 100 BTR-152
PPV 11 *Casspir*
ARTY 126
TOWED 62; **100mm** 20 M-1944; **105mm** 12 M101; **122mm** 12 D-30; **130mm** 6 M-46; **152mm** 12 D-1
MRL 122mm 12 BM-21
MOR 52: **82mm** 40 M-43; **120mm** 12 M-43
AT
MSL • MANPATS 32: 20 9K11 *Malyutka* (AT-3 *Sagger*); 12 9K111 *Fagot* (AT-4 *Spigot*); (120 9K11 *Malyutka*; 138 9K111 *Fagot* all in store)
RCL 75mm; 82mm B-10; **107mm** 24 B-12
GUNS 85mm 18: 6 D-48; 12 Type-56 (D-44)
AD • SAM • MANPAD 20 9K32 *Strela-2* (SA-7 *Grail*)‡; (230 9K32 *Strela-2* in store)
GUNS 290+
SP 57mm 20 ZSU-57-2
TOWED 270+: **20mm** M-55; **23mm** 120 ZU-23-2; **37mm** 90 M-1939; (10 M-1939 in store); **57mm** 60 S-60; (30 S-60 in store)

Navy ε200

EQUIPMENT BY TYPE

PATROL AND COASTAL COMBATANTS • PB 1 *Pebane* (ex-ESP *Conejera*-class)

Air Force 1,000

FORCES BY ROLE

TRANSPORT
1 sqn with An-26 *Curl*; FTB-337G *Milirole*
ATTACK/TRANSPORT HELICOPTER
1 sqn with Mi-24 *Hind*†
AIR DEFENCE
Some bty with S-75 *Dvina* (SA-2 *Guideline*)†‡

EQUIPMENT BY TYPE

AIRCRAFT
FGA (some MiG-21bis *Fishbed* L & N non-op)
ISR 2 FTB-337G *Milirole*
TPT • Light 2 An-26 *Curl*; (4 PA-32 *Cherokee* non-op)
HELICOPTERS
ATK 2 Mi-24 *Hind*†
TPT • Medium (2 Mi-8 *Hip* non-op)
AD • SAM • TOWED: S-75 *Dvina* (SA-2 *Guideline*)† ‡; (10+ S-125 *Pechora* SA-3 *Goa* non-op‡)

Namibia NAM

Namibian Dollar N$		2012	2013	2014
GDP	N$	101bn	111bn	
	US$	12.3bn	12.9bn	
per capita	US$	5,705	5,920	
Growth	%	4.04	4.15	
Inflation	%	6.70	5.95	
Def bdgt	N$	3.13bn	3.96bn	4.47bn
	US$	381m	458m	
US$1=N$		8.20	8.65	

Population 2,182,852

Age	0–14	15–19	20–24	25–29	30–64	65 plus
Male	16.4%	6.0%	5.6%	5.2%	15.3%	1.9%
Female	16.1%	5.9%	5.5%	5.0%	14.6%	2.4%

Capabilities

The armed forces provide territorial integrity, support civil authorities and participate in peace-support operations. Namibian forces take part in multinational exercises and have also been involved in United Nations and African Union deployments. There is no independent ability to project power beyond national territory, however. Improving mobility remains a priority in terms of both land vehicles and air transport. The air force has turned to China as its main source of combat aircraft and has received helicopters from both China and India. The navy, by contrast, has a long-standing relationship with Brazil, involving both equipment and training.

ACTIVE 9,200 (Army 9,000 Navy 200) **Paramilitary 6,000**

ORGANISATIONS BY SERVICE

Army 9,000

FORCES BY ROLE

MANOEUVRE
Light
6 inf bn
Other
1 (Presidential Guard) gd bn
COMBAT SUPPORT
1 cbt spt bde with (1 arty regt)
1 AT regt
1 AD regt
COMBAT SERVICE SUPPORT
1 log bde

EQUIPMENT BY TYPE

MBT T-54/T-55†; T-34†
RECCE 12 BRDM-2
APC 68
APC (W) 48: 10 BTR-60; 8 Type-05P; 30 *Wolf Turbo 2*
PPV 20 *Casspir*

ARTY 69
TOWED 140mm 24 G2
MRL 122mm 5 BM-21
MOR 40: **81mm**; **82mm**
AT • RCL 82mm B-10
GUNS 12+: **57mm**; **76mm** 12 ZIS-3
AD • SAM • MANPAD 74 9K32 *Strela-2* (SA-7 *Grail*)‡
GUNS 65
SP 23mm 15 *Zumlac*
TOWED 14.5mm 50 ZPU-4
ARV T-54/T-55 reported

Navy ε200

EQUIPMENT BY TYPE
PATROL AND COASTAL COMBATANTS 5
PSO 1 *Elephant*
PCC 1 *Oryx*
PB 3: 1 *Brendan Simbwaye*; 2 *Marlim*
AIRCRAFT • TPT • Light 1 F406 *Caravan II*
HELICOPTERS • TPT • Medium 1 S-61L

Air Force

FORCES BY ROLE
FIGHTER/GROUND ATTACK
1 sqn with F-7 (F-7NM); FT-7 (FT-7NG)
ISR
1 sqn with O-2A *Skymaster*
TRANSPORT
Some sqn with An-26 *Curl*; *Falcon* 900; Learjet 36; Y-12
TRAINING
1 sqn with K-8 *Karakorum**
ATTACK/TRANSPORT HELICOPTER
1 sqn with H425; Mi-8 *Hip*; Mi-25 *Hind* D; SA315 *Lama* (*Chetak*); SA319 *Alouette* III (*Cheetah*)
EQUIPMENT BY TYPE
AIRCRAFT 12 combat capable
FTR 8: 6 F-7 (F-7NM); 2 FT-7 (FT-7NG)
ISR 5 O-2A *Skymaster*
TPT 6: **Light** 5: 2 An-26 *Curl*; 1 Learjet 36; 2 Y-12; **PAX** 1 *Falcon* 900
TRG 4+ K-8 *Karakorum**
HELICOPTERS
ATK 2 Mi-25 *Hind* D
MRH 6: 2 H425; 3 SA315 *Lama* (*Chetak*); 1 SA319 *Alouette* III (*Cheetah*)
TPT • Medium 1 Mi-8 *Hip*

Paramilitary 6,000

Police Force • Special Field Force 6,000 (incl Border Guard and Special Reserve Force)

Ministry of Fisheries

PATROL AND COASTAL COMBATANTS • PCO 3: 2 *Nathanael Maxwilili*; 1 *Tobias Hainyenko*
LOGISTICS AND SUPPORT 5
AGE 1 *Mirabilis*
AGOR 4

DEPLOYMENT

CÔTE D'IVOIRE
UN • UNOCI 2 obs

LIBERIA
UN • UNMIL 3; 1 obs

SOUTH SUDAN
UN • UNMISS 2 obs

SUDAN
UN • UNAMID 3; 10 obs
UN • UNISFA 1; 3 obs

Niger NER

CFA Franc BCEAO fr		2012	2013	2014
GDP	fr	3.35tr	3.62tr	
	US$	6.58bn	7.31bn	
per capita	US$	408	440	
Growth	%	11.24	6.17	
Inflation	%	0.47	1.73	
Def bdgt	fr	35.6bn		
	US$	70m		
FMA (US)	US$	0.4m		
US$1=fr		510.00	494.94	

Population 16,899,327

Ethnic groups: Tuareg 8–10%

Age	0–14	15–19	20–24	25–29	30–64	65 plus
Male	25.2%	5.1%	3.9%	3.2%	11.4%	1.3%
Female	24.8%	5.2%	4.1%	3.3%	11.2%	1.3%

Capabilities

The Nigerien military is smaller, less well-funded and less equipped than almost all of its neighbours. It retains limited capability to deliver security, relying heavily on reconnaissance vehicles to deliver mobility and flexibility. However, given the size of the country and the lack of any significant aerial lift, the armed forces struggle to project their influence throughout Niger and are unable to deploy independently, or with any substantial force, beyond the country's borders. Nonetheless, Niger has participated in international peacekeeping missions, deploying battalion-sized forces. The military is heavily politicised, and retains significant political influence; another coup was launched in 2010, leading to a year-long military junta. Two Tuareg rebellions in the north of the country in the 1990s and 2000s have ensured some experience of counter-insurgency tactics, but capabilities remain limited. As such, the EU launched the two-year EUCAP SAHEL Niger programme in August 2012, which will initially focus on training Nigerien military and security personnel. The mission aims to build capacity to combat non-state armed groups in the Sahel region.

ACTIVE 5,300 (Army 5,200 Air 100) **Paramilitary 5,400**

Conscript liability Selective conscription, 2 years

ORGANISATIONS BY SERVICE

Army 5,200

3 Mil Districts

FORCES BY ROLE

MANOEUVRE

Reconnaissance

4 armd recce sqn

Light

7 inf coy

Air Manoeuvre

2 AB coy

COMBAT SUPPORT

1 AD coy

1 engr coy

COMBAT SERVICE SUPPORT

1 log gp

EQUIPMENT BY TYPE

RECCE 132: 35 AML-20/AML-60; 90 AML-90; 7 VBL

APC (W) 24: 22 M3 Panhard; 2 WZ-523

ARTY • MOR 40: **81mm** 19 Brandt; **82mm** 17; **120mm** 4 Brandt

AT • RCL 14: **75mm** 6 M20; **106mm** 8 M40

RL 89mm 36 LRAC

AD • GUNS 39

SP 20mm 10 M3 VDAA

TOWED 20mm 29

Air Force 100

EQUIPMENT BY TYPE

AIRCRAFT 2 combat capable

ATK 2 Su-25 *Frogfoot*

ISR 2 DA42 MPP *Twin Star*

TPT 7 **Medium** 1 C-130H *Hercules*; **Light** 3: 1 An-26 *Curl*; 2 Cessna 208 *Caravan*; 1 Do-28; 1 Do-228-201; **PAX** 1 B-737-200 (VIP)

HELICOPTERS

MRH 5 ; 2 Mi-17 *Hip* ; 3 SA342 *Gazelle*

Paramilitary 5,400

Gendarmerie 1,400

Republican Guard 2,500

National Police 1,500

DEPLOYMENT

CÔTE D'IVOIRE

UN • UNOCI 937; 5 obs; 1 inf bn

DEMOCRATIC REPUBLIC OF THE CONGO

UN • MONUSCO 1; 17 obs

LIBERIA

UN • UNMIL 2 obs

MALI

UN • MINUSMA 864; 1 inf bn

Nigeria NGA

Nigerian Naira N		2012	2013	2014
GDP	N	43.1tr	48.3tr	
	US$	269bn	284bn	
per capita	US$	1,631	1,676	
Growth	%	6.33	7.16	
Inflation	%	12.22	10.67	
Def bdgt	N	326bn	364bn	
	US$	2.03bn	2.14bn	
FMA (US)	US$	1m	1m	1m
US$1=N		160.55	170.07	

Population 174,507,539

Ethnic groups: North (Hausa and Fulani) Southwest (Yoruba) Southeast (Ibo); these tribes make up ε65% of population

Age	0–14	15–19	20–24	25–29	30–64	65 plus
Male	22.4%	5.3%	4.5%	3.9%	12.6%	1.4%
Female	21.4%	5.1%	4.4%	3.8%	13.6%	1.6%

Capabilities

Nigeria retains the best-funded and -equipped forces in West Africa. Nonetheless, it is alleged to suffer from corruption, poor equipment serviceability and questionable loyalty among ground-level units. On paper, it maintains the broadest spectrum of capabilities in the region, but in reality much of its equipment is unfit to be deployed for prolonged periods of time. Funding problems under decades of military rule until 1999, led to a deterioration in the serviceability of much of Nigeria's equipment. Procurement decisions have arguably not focused on the primary threats to Nigeria, favouring instead equipment designed for state-to-state warfare rather than counter-insurgency roles. These trends have been reversed somewhat in recent years, as refit and repair programmes have attempted to return some of Nigeria's moribund equipment to a useable status. Equally, given the challenges posed by Niger Delta militants and West African pirates, procurement is currently focused on the navy, with offshore patrol vessels, coastal patrol craft and fast patrol boats among the highest priorities. Nevertheless, the difficulties the Nigerian military has faced when tasked with subduing the threat from the Islamist Boko Haram group in the north of the country reflect a lack of effective counter-insurgency and intelligence-gathering capabilities.

ACTIVE 80,000 (Army 62,000 Navy 8,000 Air 10,000) **Paramilitary 82,000**

Reserves planned, none org

ORGANISATIONS BY SERVICE

Army 62,000

FORCES BY ROLE

MANOEUVRE

Armoured

1 (3rd) armd div (1 recce bn, 2 armd bde, 1 arty bde, 1 engr bde)

Mechanised

2 (1st & 2nd) mech div (1 recce bn, 1 mech bde, 1 mot inf bde, 1 arty bde, 1 engr bn)

1 (81st) composite div (1 mech bde)

Light

1 (7th) inf div (forming)

1 (82nd) composite div (1 recce bde, 2 mot inf bde, 1 amph bde, 1 AB bn, 1 arty bde, 1 engr bde)

Other

1 (Presidential Guard) gd bde with (2 gd bn)

COMBAT SUPPORT

1 AD regt

EQUIPMENT BY TYPE

MBT 276: 176 Vickers Mk 3; 100 T-55†

LT TK 157 *Scorpion*

RECCE 452: 90 AML-60; 40 AML-90; 70 EE-9 *Cascavel*; 50 FV721 *Fox*; 20 *Saladin* Mk2; 72 VBL; 110 *Cobra*

APC 484+

APC (T) 317: 250 4K-7FA *Steyr*; 67 MT-LB

APC (W) 167+: 10 FV603 *Saracen*; 110 *Piranha*; 47 BTR-3U; EE-11 *Urutu* (reported)

ARTY 482+

SP 155mm 39 VCA 155 *Palmaria*

TOWED 88: **105mm** 50 M-56; **122mm** 31 D-30/D-74; **130mm** 7 M-46; (**155mm** 24 FH-77B in store)

MRL 122mm 25 APR-21

MOR 330+: **81mm** 200; **82mm** 100; **120mm** 30+

AT • MSL • MANPATS *Swingfire*

RCL 84mm *Carl Gustav*; **106mm** M40A1

AD • SAM 164

SP 16 *Roland*

MANPAD 148: 48 *Blowpipe*; ε100 9K32 *Strela-2* (SA-7 *Grail*)‡

GUNS 90+

SP 30 ZSU-23-4

TOWED 60+: **20mm** 60+; **23mm** ZU-23; **40mm** L/70

RADAR • LAND: some RASIT (veh, arty)

ARV 17: 2 *Greif*; 15 Vickers ARV

VLB MTU-20; VAB

Navy 8,000 (incl Coast Guard)

Western Comd HQ located at Apapa; Eastern Comd HQ located at Calabar;

EQUIPMENT BY TYPE

PRINCIPAL SURFACE COMBATANTS 1

FRIGATES • FFGHM 1 *Aradu* (GER MEKO 360) with 8 single lnchr with *Otomat* AShM, 1 octuple *Albatros* lnchr with *Aspide* SAM, 2 triple STWS 1B 324mm ASTT with A244 LWT, 1 127mm gun, (capacity 1 *Lynx* Mk89 hel)

PATROL AND COASTAL COMBATANTS 107

CORVETTES • FSM 1 *Enymiri* (UK Vosper Mk 9) with 1 triple lnchr with *Seacat* SAM, 1 twin 375mm A/S mor, 1 76mm gun

PSOH 1 *Thunder* (US *Hamilton*) with 1 76 mm gun

PCFG 1 *Ayam* (FRA *Combattante*) with 2 twin lnchr with MM-38 *Exocet* AShM, 1 76mm gun (additional 2 vessels† - 1 used as spares; 1 non-operational; both without *Exocet* AShM)

PCO 4 *Balsam* (buoy tenders (US))

PCC 3 *Ekpe*† (GER Lurssen 57m) with 1 76mm gun

PBF 28: 21 *Manta* (Suncraft 17m); 4 *Manta* Mk II; 3 *Shaldag* II

PB 69: 40 Suncraft 12m; 15 *Stingray* (Suncraft 16m); 4 Swiftships; 3 OCEA FPB 72 MkII; 2 *Sea Eagle* (Suncraft 38m); 2 *Town* (of which one laid up); 2 *Yola;* 1 *Andoni;* (a further 150 small patrol craft under 10 tonnes FLD may be in operation)

MINE WARFARE • MINE COUNTERMEASURES 2:

MCC 2 *Ohue* (mod ITA *Lerici*)

AMPHIBIOUS 5

LS • LST 1 *Ambe*† (capacity 5 tanks; 220 troops) (GER)

LC • LCVP 4 *Stingray 20*

LOGISTICS AND SUPPORT 9

AGHS 1

YFL 2 (ex-GER Damen Stan 1905)

YTB 2 (ex-GER Damen Stan 2909/2608)

YTL 4

Naval Aviation

EQUIPMENT BY TYPE

HELICOPTERS

MRH 2 AW139 (AB-139)

TPT • Light 3 AW109E *Power*†

Air Force 10,000

FORCES BY ROLE

Very limited op capability

FIGHTER/GROUND ATTACK

1 sqn with F-7 (F-7NI); FT-7 (FT-7NI)

MARITIME PATROL

1 sqn with ATR-42MP; Do-128D-6 *Turbo SkyServant*; Do-228-100/200

TRANSPORT

2 sqn with C-130H *Hercules*; C-130H-30 *Hercules*; G-222

1 (Presidential) flt with B-727; B-737BBJ; BAe-125-800; Do-228-200; *Falcon* 7X; *Falcon* 900; Gulfstream IV/V

TRAINING

1 unit with *Air Beetle*†;

1 unit with *Alpha Jet**

1 unit with L-39 *Albatros*†*; MB-339A*

1 hel unit with Mi-34 *Hermit* (trg);

ATTACK/TRANSPORT HELICOPTER

2 sqn with AW109LUH; Mi-24/Mi-35 *Hind*†

EQUIPMENT BY TYPE†

AIRCRAFT 54 combat capable

FTR 15: 12 F-7 (F-7NI); 3 FT-7 (FT-7NI)

MP 2 ATR-42 MP

TPT 30: **Medium** 5: 1 C-130H *Hercules* (4 more in store†); 1 C-130H-30 *Hercules* (2 more in store); 3 G-222† (2 more in store†); **Light** 16: 1 Cessna 550 *Citation*; 8 Do-128D-6 *Turbo SkyServant*; 1 Do-228-100; 6 Do-228-200 (incl 2 VIP); **PAX** 9: 1 B-727; 1 B-737BBJ; 1 BAe 125-800; 2 *Falcon* 7X; 2 *Falcon* 900; 1 Gulfstream IV; 1 Gulfstream V

TRG 107: 58 *Air Beetle*† (up to 20 awaiting repair); 14 *Alpha Jet**; 23 L-39 *Albatros*†*; 12 MB-339AN* (all being upgraded)

HELICOPTERS

ATK 9: 2 Mi-24P *Hind*; 2 Mi-24V *Hind*; 5 Mi-35 *Hind*

MRH 6 AW109LUH

TPT 3: **Medium** 2 AS332 *Super Puma* (4 more in store); **Light** 1 AW109

TRG 5 Mi-34 *Hermit*†

MSL • AAM • IR R-3 (AA-2 *Atoll*)‡; PL-9C

Paramilitary ε82,000

Nigerian Police

Port Authority Police ε2,000

PATROL AND COASTAL COMBATANTS • MISC BOATS/CRAFT 60+ boats

AMPHIBIOUS 5+ ACV

Security and Civil Defence Corps • Police 80,000

EQUIPMENT BY TYPE

APC (W) 74+: 70+ AT105 *Saxon*†; 4 BTR-3U; UR-416

AIRCRAFT • TPT • Light 4: 1 Cessna 500 *Citation* I; 2 PA-31 *Navajo*; 1 PA-31-350 *Navajo Chieftain*

HELICOPTERS • TPT • Light 4: 2 Bell 212 (AB-212); 2 Bell 222 (AB-222)

DEPLOYMENT

CÔTE D'IVOIRE

UN • UNOCI 10; 4 obs

DEMOCRATIC REPUBLIC OF THE CONGO

UN • MONUSCO 2; 15 obs

GUINEA-BISSAU

ECOWAS • ECOMIB 160

LEBANON

UN • UNIFIL 1

LIBERIA

UN • UNMIL 1,466; 11 obs; 2 inf bn

MALI

UN • MINUSMA 115; 1 sigs coy

SOUTH SUDAN

UN • UNMISS 2; 5 obs

SUDAN

UN • UNAMID 2,571; 12 obs; 3 inf bn

UN • UNISFA 3 obs

WESTERN SAHARA

UN • MINURSO 6 obs

Rwanda RWA

Rwandan Franc fr		2012	2013	2014
GDP	fr	4.44tr	5.12tr	
	US$	7.22bn	7.77bn	
per capita	US$	693	730	
Growth	%	7.69	7.60	
Inflation	%	6.29	4.94	
Def bdgt	fr	46.4bn	54.1bn	55.1bn
	US$	76m	82m	
FMA (US)	US$			0.2m
US$1=fr		614.29	658.77	

Population 12,012,589

Ethnic groups: Hutu 80%; Tutsi 19%

Age	0–14	15–19	20–24	25–29	30–64	65 plus
Male	21.3%	4.9%	4.6%	4.3%	13.7%	1.0%
Female	21.0%	4.9%	4.6%	4.4%	13.8%	1.5%

Capabilities

While fielding a comparatively large army in numerical terms, Rwanda's units are lightly equipped, with little mechanisation. A small number of helicopters constitute the air force. The land forces have been involved in combat operations in the Democratic Republic of the Congo as recently as 2009, when a joint operation was conducted with the DRC to combat Democratic Forces for the Liberation of Rwanda rebels. While the stated aim of the military is to defend territorial integrity and national sovereignty, the nature of the armed forces means it would struggle to achieve this against a well-armed and focused opponent.The Rwandan military has, in the past, proved effective in counter-insurgency operations. The army regularly takes part in multinational exercises.

ACTIVE 33,000 (Army 32,000 Air 1,000) Paramilitary 2,000

ORGANISATIONS BY SERVICE

Army 32,000

FORCES BY ROLE

MANOEUVRE

Light

2 cdo bn

4 inf div (3 inf bde)

COMBAT SUPPORT

1 arty bde

EQUIPMENT BY TYPE

MBT 24 T-54/T-55

RECCE 106: ε90 AML-60/AML-90/AML-245; 16 VBL

AIFV 35+: BMP; 15 *Ratel*-90; 20 *Ratel*-60

APC 56+

APC (W) 20+: BTR; *Buffalo* (M3 Panhard); 20 Type-92 (reported)

PPV 36 RG-31 *Nyala*

ARTY 160+
TOWED 35+: **105mm** 29 Type-54 (D-1); **122mm** 6 D-30; **152mm**†
MRL 10: **122mm** 5 RM-70 *Dana;* **160mm** 5 LAR-160
MOR 115: **81mm; 82mm; 120mm**
AD • SAM • MANPAD 9K32 *Strela*-2 (SA-7 *Grail*)‡
GUNS ε150: **14.5mm**; **23mm**; **37mm**
ARV T-54/T-55 reported

Air Force ε1,000

FORCES BY ROLE
ATTACK/TRANSPORT HELICOPTER
1 sqn with Mi-17/Mi-17MD/Mi-17V-5/Mi-17-1V *Hip* H; Mi-24P/V *Hind*
EQUIPMENT BY TYPE
HELICOPTERS
ATK 5: 2 Mi-24V *Hind* E; 3 Mi-24P *Hind*
MRH 10: 1 AW139; 4 Mi-17 *Hip* H; 1 Mi-17MD *Hip* H; 1 Mi-17V-5 *Hip* H; 3 Mi-17-1V *Hip* H
TPT • Light 1 AW109S

Paramilitary

Local Defence Forces ε2,000

DEPLOYMENT

SOUTH SUDAN
UN • UNMISS 980; 2 obs; 1 inf bn

SUDAN
UN • UNAMID 3,236; 10 obs; 4 inf bn
UN • UNISFA 2; 1 obs

Senegal SEN

CFA Franc BCEAO fr		2012	2013	2014
GDP	fr	7.18tr	7.63tr	
	US$	13.9bn	14.4bn	
per capita	US$	1,057	1,068	
Growth	%	3.54	4.02	
Inflation	%	1.10	1.52	
Def bdgt	fr	97.8bn	123bn	
	US$	189m	231m	
FMA (US)	US$	0.325m	0.325m	0.325m
US$1=fr		518.01	530.39	

Population 13,300,410

Ethnic groups: Wolof 36%; Fulani 17%; Serer 17%; Toucouleur 9%; Man-dingo 9%; Diola 9% (of which 30-60% in Casamance)

Age	0–14	15–19	20–24	25–29	30–64	65 plus
Male	21.5%	5.5%	4.7%	3.9%	11.5%	1.3%
Female	21.3%	5.5%	4.8%	4.2%	14.3%	1.6%

Capabilities

Senegal maintains a moderate defence capacity that is tailored towards, although not entirely sufficient to cope with, the primary security threats the country faces, namely the separatist insurgency in Casamance. A close defence relationship with France ensures regular training, and France utilised transport routes from Dakar for its Mali deployment. Fundamentally, the Senegalese armed forces lack funding and equipment. However, they did deploy limited formed units to Guinea-Bissau as part of the ECOWAS mission. Procurement has traditionally favoured the army, with a priority on armoured vehicles.

ACTIVE 13,600 (Army 11,900 Navy 950 Air 750)
Paramilitary 5,000
Conscript liability Selective conscription, 2 years

ORGANISATIONS BY SERVICE

Army 11,900 (incl conscripts)

7 Mil Zone HQ
FORCES BY ROLE
MANOEUVRE
Reconnaissance
4 armd recce bn
Light
1 cdo bn
6 inf bn
Air Manoeuvre
1 AB bn
Other
1 (Presidential Guard) horse cav bn
COMBAT SUPPORT
1 arty bn
1 engr bn
1 sigs bn
COMBAT SERVICE SUPPORT
3 construction coy
1 log bn
1 med bn
1 trg bn
EQUIPMENT BY TYPE
RECCE 118: 30 AML-60; 74 AML-90; 10 M8; 4 M20
AIFV 26 *Ratel*-20
APC 36
APC (T) 12 M3 half-track
APC (W) 16 M3 Panhard
PPV 8 *Casspir*
ARTY 36
TOWED 20: **105mm** 6 HM-2/M101; **155mm** 14: ε6 Model-50; 8 TR-F1
MOR 16: **81mm** 8 Brandt; **120mm** 8 Brandt
AT • MSL • MANPATS 4 *Milan*
RL 89mm 31 LRAC
AD • GUNS • TOWED 33: **20mm** 21 M-693; **40mm** 12 L/60

Navy (incl Coast Guard) 950

EQUIPMENT BY TYPE

PATROL AND COASTAL COMBATANTS 10

PCC 4: 1 *Fouta* (DNK *Osprey*); 1 *Njambour* (FRA SFCN 59m) with 2 76mm gun; 2 *Saint Louis*† (PR-48)

PB 6: 2 *Alioune Samb*; 2 *Alphonse Faye* (operated by Fisheries Protection Directorate); 1 *Conejera*; 1 *Senegal II*

AMPHIBIOUS • LANDING CRAFT 5

LCT 2 *Edic* 700

LCM 3

LOGISTICS AND SUPPORT 3

AG 1

YAG 1 Archangel

YTM 1

Air Force 750

FORCES BY ROLE

MARITIME PATROL/SEARCH & RESCUE

1 sqn with C-212 *Aviocar*; Bell 205 (UH-1H *Iroquois*)

ISR

1 unit with BN-2T *Islander* (anti-smuggling patrols)

TRANSPORT

1 sqn with B-727-200 (VIP); F-27-400M *Troopship*

TRAINING

1 sqn with R-235 *Guerrier**; TB-30 *Epsilon*

ATTACK/TRANSPORT HELICOPTER

1 sqn with AS355F *Ecureuil II;* Bell 206; Mi-35P *Hind;* Mi-171Sh

EQUIPMENT BY TYPE

AIRCRAFT 1 combat capable

TPT 9: **Light** 7: 1 BN-2T *Islander* (govt owned, mil op); 1 C-212-100 *Aviocar*; 2 Beech B200 *King Air*; 3 F-27-400M *Troopship* (3 more in store); **PAX** 2: 1 A319; 1 B-727-200 (VIP)

TRG 3: 1 R-235 *Guerrier**; 2 TB-30 *Epsilon*

HELICOPTERS

ATK 2 Mi-35P *Hind*

TPT 8 **Medium** 2 Mi-171Sh; **Light** 6: 1 AS355F *Ecureuil* II; 1 Bell 205 (UH-1H *Iroquois*); 2 Bell 206; 2 Mi-2 *Hoplite*

Paramilitary 5,000

Gendarmerie 5,000

APC (W) 24: 12 *Gila*; 12 VXB-170

Customs

PATROL AND COASTAL COMBATANTS • PB 2 VCSM

DEPLOYMENT

CÔTE D'IVOIRE

UN • UNOCI 495; 10 obs; 1 inf bn

DEMOCRATIC REPUBLIC OF THE CONGO

UN • MONUSCO 10; 11 obs

GUINEA-BISSAU

ECOWAS • ECOMIB 200

LIBERIA

UN • UNMIL 1; 1 obs

MALI

UN • MINUSMA 510; 1 inf coy; 1 arty coy; 1 engr coy

SOUTH SUDAN

UN • UNMISS 3; 3 obs

SUDAN

UN • UNAMID 812; 17 obs; 1 inf bn

FOREIGN FORCES

France 350; 1 *Atlantique*; 1 C-160 *Transall*

Seychelles SYC

Seychelles Rupee SR		2012	2013	2014
GDP	SR	14.1bn	15.2bn	
	US$	1.03bn	1.13bn	
per capita	US$	11,226	12,207	
Growth	%	2.77	3.22	
Inflation	%	7.11	4.64	
Def bdgt	SR	136m	155m	
	US$	10m	12m	
US$1=SR		13.70	13.39	

Population 90,846

Age	0–14	15–19	20–24	25–29	30–64	65 plus
Male	10.8%	3.7%	4.0%	4.4%	25.5%	2.8%
Female	10.3%	3.4%	3.5%	3.9%	23.2%	4.5%

Capabilities

Piracy is a primary concern for the small People's Defence Forces, with the coast guard and the air force engaged in anti-piracy activities. The coast guard is expanding to meet the challenge, with equipment being donated or offered by concerned nations, including India. The air force's DHC-6 is due to be supplemented by a Dornier 228. The Seychelles' special forces unit is also involved in anti-piracy operations, while an infantry unit is tasked with internal security. The armed forces have no power-projection capability. The US continues to operate MQ-9 *Reaper* UAVs from the country as a contribution to counter-piracy activities in the Indian Ocean.

ACTIVE 420 **(Land Forces 200; Coast Guard 200; Air Force 20)**

ORGANISATIONS BY SERVICE

People's Defence Force

Land Forces 200

FORCES BY ROLE

SPECIAL FORCES

1 SF unit

MANOEUVRE
Light
1 inf coy
Other
1 sy unit
COMBAT SUPPORT
1 MP unit

EQUIPMENT BY TYPE†
RECCE 6 BRDM-2†
ARTY• MOR 82mm 6 M-43†
AD • SAM • MANPAD 10 9K32 *Strela-2* (SA-7 *Grail*) ‡
GUNS • TOWED 14.5mm ZPU-2†; ZPU-4†; **37mm** M-1939†

Coast Guard 200 (incl 80 Marines)

EQUIPMENT BY TYPE
PATROL AND COASTAL COMBATANTS 8
PCC 2: 1 *Andromache* (ITA *Pichiotti* 42m); 1 *Topaz*
PB 6: 2 *Aries*; 1 *Junon*; 2 Rodman *101*; 1 *Fortune* (UK *Tyne*)

Air Force 20

EQUIPMENT BY TYPE
AIRCRAFT
TPT • Light 5: 3 DHC-6-320 *Twin Otter*; 2 Y-12

FOREIGN FORCES

United States US Africa Command: some MQ-9 *Reaper* UAV

Sierra Leone SLE

Sierra Leonean Leone L		2012	2013	2014
GDP	L	16.8tr	20.9tr	
	US$	3.78bn	4.52bn	
per capita	US$	613	716	
Growth	%	19.77	17.14	
Inflation	%	13.81	8.67	
Def bdgt	L	60.4bn	65.3bn	67.6bn
	US$	14m	14m	
US$1=L		4453.96	4619.96	

Population 5,612,685

Age	0–14	15–19	20–24	25–29	30–64	65 plus
Male	20.8%	4.8%	4.4%	3.8%	13.1%	1.6%
Female	21.1%	5.1%	4.7%	4.1%	14.4%	2.1%

Capabilities

The Sierra Leonean Armed Forces are poorly funded and lack any significant combat capability. Since the civil war in the 1990s, there has been little procurement to fill the capability gaps it left. The armed forces' aerial capabilities are largely moribund and the ground forces lack serviceable vehicles. The maritime force has been rejuvenated somewhat by a donated coastal patrol craft and patrol boats, but remains very much a brown-water force. Arguably, the armed forces are currently equipped for its primary role, internal security, and they benefited from an intensive UK training regime in the 2000s. However, should a more significant internal or external threat emerge, it is unlikely that the armed forces would be able to sustain an armed campaign and defeat a committed insurgent group or well-trained adversary. The posting of a battalion to AMISOM will likely lead to improvements in planning and tactics.

ACTIVE 10,500 (Joint 10,500)

ORGANISATIONS BY SERVICE

Armed Forces 10,500

FORCES BY ROLE
MANOEUVRE
Light
3 inf bde (total: 12 inf bn)

EQUIPMENT BY TYPE
ARTY • MOR 31: **81mm** ε27; **82mm** 2; **120mm** 2
AT • RCL 84mm *Carl Gustav*
HELICOPTERS • MRH/TPT 2 Mi-17 *Hip* H/Mi-8 *Hip*†
AD • GUNS 7: **12.7mm** 4; **14.5mm** 3

Navy ε200

EQUIPMENT BY TYPE
PATROL AND COASTAL COMBATANTS • PB 2: 1 *Shanghai* III; 1 *Isle of Man*

DEPLOYMENT

LEBANON
UN • UNIFIL 3

MALI
UN • MINUSMA 5

SOMALIA
AU • AMISOM 850; 1 inf bn

SUDAN
UN • UNAMID 5; 10 obs
UN • UNISFA 3 obs

Somalia SOM

Somali Shilling sh		2012	2013	2014
GDP	US$			
per capita	US$			

*Definitive economic data unavailable

US$1=sh

Population 10,251,568

Age	0–14	15–19	20–24	25–29	30–64	65 plus
Male	22.1%	5.0%	4.6%	3.7%	14.0%	0.9%
Female	22.2%	4.9%	4.4%	3.6%	13.2%	1.4%

Capabilities

With the decline in Somilia-based pirate groups, the principal threat to national stability comes from al-Shabaab jihadists, who utilise small arms, IEDs, light weapons and technicals. The group withdrew from its positions in Mogadishu in 2012 in a self-declared 'tactical retreat' before being ousted from its primary revenue-generating hub of Kismayo in September 2012. However, al-Shabaab remains capable of mounting terrorist attacks that challenge the African Union Mission in Somalia (AMISOM) and the Somali government's authority. Much of the interior of the country is beyond AMISOM control. An internationally backed attempt to forge a standing army has produced a force trained by AMISOM, the EU and private security companies. Since 2010, the EU has trained over 3,600 troops, focusing on NCOs, officers and 'train-the-trainer' initiatives. In some cases, government forces have been accompanied on operations by allied militias. Somaliland and Puntland have their own militias.

ACTIVE 20,000 (Army 20,000)

ORGANISATIONS BY SERVICE

Army ε20,000 (including militias)

FORCES BY ROLE
COMMAND
1 (21st) div HQ
MANOEUVRE
Light
Some cdo unit
6 inf bde (total: ε18 inf bn)

FOREIGN FORCES

Burundi AMISOM 5,432; 6 inf bn
Djibouti AMISOM 1,000; 1 inf bn
Ethiopia some
Kenya AMISOM 3,664; 3 inf bn
Sierra Leone AMISOM 850; 1 inf bn
Uganda AMISOM 6,223; 7 inf bn

TERRITORY WHERE THE RECOGNISED AUTHORITY (SNG) DOES NOT EXERCISE EFFECTIVE CONTROL

Data presented here represent the de facto situation. This does not imply international recognition as a sovereign state.

Somaliland

Population 3.5m

Militia unit strengths are not known. Equipment numbers are generalised assessments; most of this equipment is in poor repair or inoperable.

ORGANISATIONS BY SERVICE

Army ε15,000

FORCES BY ROLE
MANOUEVRE
Armoured
2 armd bde
Mechanised
1 mech inf bde
Light
14 inf bde
COMBAT SUPPORT
2 arty bde
COMBAT SERVICE SUPPORT
1 spt bn

EQUIPMENT BY TYPE†
MBT 33: M47; T54/55
RECCE AML-90; BRDM-2
APC
APC (T) BTR-50
APC(W) 15-20 Fiat 6614
ARTY 69
TOWED 122mm 12 D-30
MRL: 8-12 BM-21 *Grad*
MOR 45: **81mm**; **120mm**
AT • RCL 106mm 16 M40A1
AD • GUNS • TOWED 20mm; some **23mm** ZU-23

Coast Guard 600

Ministry of the Interior

EQUIPMENT BY TYPE
PATROL AND COASTAL COMBATANTS 26
PB 7 *Dolphin 26*
PBR 19

Puntland

Armed Forces ε5,000–10,000; coast guard

South Africa RSA

South African Rand R		2012	2013	2014
GDP	R	3.16tr	3.46tr	
	US$	384bn	376bn	
per capita	US$	7,507	7,257	
Growth	%	2.55	2.84	
Inflation	%	5.65	5.77	
Def bdgt	R	41.6bn	44.6bn	47bn
	US$	5.07bn	4.85bn	
FMA (US)	US$	0.7m	0.7m	0.7m
US$1=R		8.21	9.20	

Population 48,601,098

Age	0–14	15–19	20–24	25–29	30–64	65 plus
Male	14.2%	4.9%	5.5%	5.4%	17.3%	2.4%
Female	14.1%	4.9%	5.3%	5.0%	17.4%	3.6%

Capabilities

The South African National Defence Force (SANDF) remains the most capable force in the region, despite financial and structural problems which have eroded capacity in many areas. Maritime security is a growing concern, illustrated by an ongoing counter-piracy mission in the Mozambique Channel (*Operation Copper*). Equipment recapitalisation efforts in all services have been delayed by funding problems. The armed forces retain some capacity for power projection, limited by the amount of tactical airlift available and by the impact of funding constraints. It still deploys regularly on peacekeeping missions and is a participant in multinational exercises. Historically the SANDF has also played a significant role in training and supporting other African forces, and South Africa is a key contributor to the UN's intervention brigade in the eastern DRC. The third draft of the current Defence Review process, in April 2013, proposes the establishment of a new contingency division, with airborne, air-mobile and amphibious brigades in addition to the currently planned mechanised and motorised divisions. In the short term, however, the priority is to consolidate the army's existing forces into a motorised division, mechanised brigade and contingency brigade.

ACTIVE 62,100 (Army 37,150 Navy 6,250 Air 10,650 South African Military Health Service 8,050)

RESERVE 15,050 (Army 12,250 Navy 850 Air 850 South African Military Health Service Reserve 1,100)

ORGANISATIONS BY SERVICE

Army 37,150

FORCES BY ROLE

Formations under direct command and control of SANDF Chief of Joint Operations: 9 Joint Operational Tactical HQs, troops are provided when necessary by permanent and reserve force units from all services and SF Bde. A new army structure is planned with 2 divisions (1 mechanised, 1 motorised) with 10 bdes (1 armd, 1 mech, 7 motorised and 1 rapid reaction). Training, Support and Land Commands are also planned, while Divisional HQ is to be re-established.

COMMAND
- 2 bde HQ

SPECIAL FORCES
- 1 SF bde (2 SF bn(-))

MANOEUVRE

Reconnaissance
- 1 armd recce bn

Armoured
- 1 tk bn

Mechanised
- 2 mech inf bn

Light
- 10 mot inf bn (1 bn roles as AB, 1 as amph)

COMBAT SUPPORT
- 1 arty bn
- 1 ADA bn
- 1 engr regt

COMBAT SERVICE SUPPORT
- 2 maint units
- 1 construction bn

Reserve 12,250 reservists (under strength)

FORCES BY ROLE

MANOEUVRE

Reconnaissance
- 2 armd recce bn
- 1 recce bn

Armoured
- 3 tk bn

Mechanised
- 6 mech inf bn

Light
- 16 mot inf bn (1 bn roles as AB, 1 as amph)
- 3 lt inf bn (converting to mot inf)

Air Manoeuvre
- 1 AB bn

COMBAT SUPPORT
- 7 arty regt
- 4 AD regt
- 2 engr regt

EQUIPMENT BY TYPE

MBT 34 *Olifant* 1A (133 *Olifant* 1B in store)
RECCE 82 *Rooikat*-76 (94 in store)
AIFV 534 *Ratel*-20/*Ratel*-60/*Ratel*-90
PPV 810: 370 *Casspir*; 440 *Mamba*
ARTY 1,255
- **SP 155mm** 2 G-6 (41 in store)
- **TOWED 140mm** (75 G-2 in store); **155mm** 6 G-5 (66 in store)
- **MRL 127mm** 21: (26 *Valkiri* Mk I in store) (24 tube)); 21 *Valkiri* Mk II MARS *Bataleur* (40 tube); (4 in store (40 tube))
- **MOR** 1,226: **81mm** 1,190 (incl some SP); **120mm** 36

AT
- **MSL • MANPATS** 59: 16 ZT-3 *Swift* (36 in store); 43 *Milan* ADT/ER
- **RCL 106mm** 100 M40A1 (some SP)
- **RL 92mm** FT-5

AD • GUNS 76
- **SP 23mm** 36 *Zumlac*
- **TOWED 35mm** 40 GDF-002

RADAR • LAND ESR 220 *Kameelperd*; 2 Thales *Page*
ARV *Gemsbok*
VLB *Leguan*
UAV • ISR • Light up to 4 *Vulture*

Navy 6,250

Fleet HQ and Naval base located at Simon's Town; Naval stations located at Durban and Port Elizabeth

EQUIPMENT BY TYPE

SUBMARINES • TACTICAL • SSK 3 *Heroine* (Type-209) with 8 533mm TT with AEW SUT 264 HWT (of which one cyclically in reserve/refit)
PRINCIPAL SURFACE COMBATANTS • FRIGATES 4:
- **FFGHM** 4 *Valour* (MEKO A200) with 2 quad lnchr with MM-40 *Exocet* AShM (upgrade to Block III planned); 2 16-cell VLS with *Umkhonto*-IR naval SAM, 1 76mm gun (capacity 1 *Super Lynx* 300 hel)

PATROL AND COASTAL COMBATANTS 6
- **PCC** 3 *Warrior* (ISR *Reshef*) with 2 76mm gun
- **PB** 3 *Tobie*

MINE WARFARE • MINE COUNTERMEASURES 2
MHC 2 *River* (GER *Navors*) (Limited operational roles; training and dive support); (additional vessel in reserve)
AMPHIBIOUS • LCU 6 *Lima*
LOGISTICS AND SUPPORT 7
AORH 1 *Drakensberg* (capacity 4 LCU; 100 troops)
AGHS 1 *Protea* (UK *Hecla*)
YTM 5

Air Force 10,650

Air Force office, Pretoria, and 4 op gps
Command & Control: 2 Airspace Control Sectors, 1 Mobile Deployment Wg
1 Air Force Command Post

FORCES BY ROLE
FIGHTER/GROUND ATTACK
1 sqn with *Gripen* C/D (JAS-39C/D)
TRANSPORT
1 (VIP) sqn with B-737 BBJ; Cessna 550 *Citation* II; *Falcon* 50; *Falcon* 900;
1 sqn with BT-67 (C-47TP)
2 sqn with C-130B/BZ *Hercules*; C-212; Cessna 185; CN-235
9 (AF Reserve) sqn with ε130 private lt tpt ac
TRAINING
1 (Lead-in Ftr Trg) sqn with *Hawk* Mk120*
ATTACK HELICOPTER
1 (cbt spt) sqn with AH-2 *Rooivalk*
TRANSPORT HELICOPTER
4 (mixed) sqn with AW109; BK-117; *Oryx*

EQUIPMENT BY TYPE
AIRCRAFT 50 combat capable
FGA 26: 17 *Gripen* C (JAS-39C); 9 *Gripen* D (JAS-39D)
TPT 35 **Medium** 7 C-130B/BZ *Hercules*; **Light** 24: 3 Beech 200C *King Air*; 1 Beech 300 *King Air*; 3 BT-67 (C-47TP - maritime); 2 C-212-200 *Aviocar*; 1 C-212-300 *Aviocar*; 11 Cessna 208 *Caravan*; 2 Cessna 550 *Citation* II; 1 PC-12; **PAX** 4: 1 B-737BBJ; 2 *Falcon* 50; 1 *Falcon* 900
TRG 74: 24 *Hawk* Mk120*; 50 PC-7 Mk II *Astra*
HELICOPTERS
ATK 11 AH-2 *Rooivalk* (Only 5 in service as of late 2012)
MRH 4 *Super Lynx* 300
TPT 76 **Medium** 39 *Oryx*; **Light** 37: 29 AW109; 8 BK-117
UAV • ISR • Medium *Seeker* II
MSL • AAM • IR V3C *Darter*; **IIR** IRIS-T

Ground Defence

FORCES BY ROLE
MANOEUVRE
Other
12 sy sqn (SAAF regt)

EQUIPMENT BY TYPE
2 Radar (static) located at Ellisras and Mariepskop; 2 (mobile long-range); 4 (tactical mobile). Radar air control sectors located at Pretoria, Hoedspruit

South African Military Health Service 8,050; ε1,100 reservists (total 9,150)

Department of Agriculture, Fisheries and Forestry

EQUIPMENT BY TYPE
PATROL AND COASTAL COMBATANTS 4
PSO 1 *Sarah Baartman*
PBO 3 *Lilian Nyogi*
LOGISTICS AND SUPPORT • AGE 2: 1 *Africana*; 1 *Ellen Khuzmayo*

Department of Environmental Affairs

EQUIPMENT BY TYPE
LOGISTICS AND SUPPORT • AGOS 1 *S A Agulhas* II (used for Antarctic survey)

DEPLOYMENT

DEMOCRATIC REPUBLIC OF THE CONGO
UN • MONUSCO • *Operation Mistral* 1,262; 3 obs; 1 inf bn; 1 avn coy (air med evacuation team, air base control det); 1 engr coy

MOZAMBIQUE CHANNEL
Navy • 1 FFGHM

SUDAN
UN • UNAMID • *Operation Cordite* 808; 16 obs; 1 inf bn

South Sudan SSD

South Sudanese Pound ssp		2011	2012	2013
GDP	ssp	52.48bn	36bn	48.2bn
	US$	17.47bn	12.2bn	13.5bn
per capita	US$	1,644	1,175	1,278
Growth	%	1.44	-52.98	32.06
Inflation	%	47.31	45.08	15.53
Def bdgt	ssp	1.6bn	2.42bn	2.54bn
	US$	533m	819m	714m
FMA (US)	US$			
US$1=ssp		3.00	2.95	3.56

Population 11,090,104

Age	0–14	15–19	20–24	25–29	30–64	65 plus
Male	23.6%	5.8%	4.5%	3.6%	12.0%	1.2%
Female	22.6%	5.1%	4.2%	3.7%	12.7%	0.9%

Capabilities

Reflecting their origin as insurgent forces, the state's armed forces overwhelmingly consist of infantry, with some armour and a small air capability. Security concerns are dominated by continuing friction with Sudan. Ukraine and China have been sources of equipment, and there has been international assistance in establishing the foundations of a security structure, such as NCO academies. There are also plans to downsize personnel numbers, though ongoing conflict means that disarmament, demobilisation and reintegration and security sector reform remain haphazardly applied. A process to draft a national security policy began in September 2012.

ACTIVE 210,000 (Army 210,000)

ORGANISATIONS BY SERVICE

Army ε210,000

FORCES BY ROLE
3 military comd
MANOEUVRE
Light
9 inf div

EQUIPMENT BY TYPE
MBT 110+: Some T-55; 110 T-72M1
ARTY 69+
SP 24 **122mm** 12 2S1 **152mm** 12 2S3
MRL • **122mm** 15 BM-21
MOR **82mm** 30+
AD • **GUNS 23mm** ZU-23-2

Air Force

EQUIPMENT BY TYPE
AIRCRAFT • **TPT** • **Light** 1 Beech 1900
HELICOPTERS
MRH 9 Mi-17 *Hip* H
TPT • **Medium** 1 Mi-172 (VIP)

FOREIGN FORCES

All UNMISS, unless otherwise indicated
Australia 11; 4 obs
Bangladesh 278; 3 obs; 1 engr coy
Belarus 4 obs
Benin 2 obs
Bolivia 3 obs
Brazil 3; 1 obs
Cambodia 147; 3 obs; 1 MP coy; 1 fd hospital
Canada 5; 5 obs
China, People's Republic of 340; 3 obs; 1 engr coy; 1 fd hospital
Denmark 13; 2 obs
Ecuador 4 obs
Egypt 3 obs
El Salvador 2 obs
Fiji 4; 2 obs
Germany 7; 8 obs
Ghana 4; 2 obs
Guatemala 1; 3 obs
Guinea 2 obs
India 1,991; 5 obs; 2 inf bn; 1 fd hospital
Indonesia 3 obs
Italy 1 obs
Japan 271; 1 engr coy
Jordan 3; 3 obs
Kenya 701; 3 obs; 1 inf bn
Korea, Republic of 273; 2 obs; 1 engr coy
Kyrgyzstan 2 obs
Moldova 3 obs
Mongolia 857; 1 inf bn
Namibia 2 obs
Nepal 858; 5 obs; 1 inf bn
Netherlands 7; 2 obs
New Zealand 1; 2 obs
Nigeria 2; 5 obs
Norway 12; 4 obs
Papua New Guinea 2 obs
Paraguay 3 obs
Peru 1 obs
Poland 2 obs
Romania 2; 4 obs
Russia 4; 3 obs
Rwanda 980; 3 obs; 1 inf bn
Senegal 3; 3 obs
Sri Lanka 2 obs
Sweden 2; 4 obs
Switzerland 2; 2 obs
Tanzania 2; 3 obs
Timor-Leste 2 obs
Togo 1
Uganda 1; 1 obs
Ukraine 1; 3 obs
United Kingdom 2
United States 5
Yemen 3; 4 obs
Zambia 3; 3 obs

Sudan SDN

Sudanese Pound sdg		2012	2013	2014
GDP	sdg	221bn	300bn	
	US$	59.9bn	50.6bn	
per capita	US$	1,789	1,472	
Growth	%	-4.40	1.16	
Inflation	%	35.55	28.44	
Def exp	sdg		9bn	
	US$		1.52bn	
US$1=sdg		3.69	5.94	

Population 34,847,910

Ethnic and religious groups: Muslim 70% mainly in North; Christian10% mainly in South; 52% mainly in South; Arab 39% mainly in North

Age	0–14	15–19	20–24	25–29	30–64	65 plus
Male	21.1%	5.6%	4.7%	3.9%	13.4%	1.8%
Female	20.4%	5.2%	4.5%	3.9%	14.1%	1.5%

Capabilities

The end of the civil war resulted in partition in 2011 and the creation of South Sudan. Tensions between the two countries continue, with the Sudanese armed forces also involved in clashes with rebels in the south of the country. Khartoum is also faced with apparently intractable insurgencies in the Blue Nile and South Kordofan provinces. A mixture of Russian and Chinese equipment is operated, and Russian Air Force surplus attack and transport helicopters are reportedly on order. In regional terms, the services are reasonably well-equipped. The air force, though relatively small, fields several comparatively modern combat types, including the MiG-29 and Su-25. Tactical airlift is provided by a variety of transport aircraft. The navy is limited to littoral and river patrol. The country likely has the capacity for limited regional power projection, though its primary military focus remains South Sudan and counter-insurgency.

ACTIVE 244,300 (Army 240,000 Navy 1,300 Air 3,000) Paramilitary 20,000
Conscript liability 2 years for males aged 18–30

RESERVE NIL Paramilitary 85,000

ORGANISATIONS BY SERVICE

Army ε240,000

FORCES BY ROLE
SPECIAL FORCES
5 SF coy
MANOEUVRE
Reconnaissance
1 indep recce bde
Armoured
1 armd div
Mechanised
1 mech inf div
1 indep mech inf bde
Light
11+ inf div
6 indep inf bde
Air Manoeuvre
1 AB div
Other
1 (Border Guard) sy bde
COMBAT SUPPORT
3 indep arty bde
1 engr div (9 engr bn)

EQUIPMENT BY TYPE
MBT 445: 20 M60A3; 60 Type-59/Type-59D; 305 T-54/T-55; 50 T-72M1; 10 *Al-Bashier* (Type-85-IIM)
LT TK 115: 70 Type-62; 45 Type-63
RECCE 248: 6 AML-90; 70 BRDM-1/2; 50–80 *Ferret*; 42 M1114 HMMWV; 30–50 *Saladin*
AIFV 132: 115 BMP-1/2; 10 BTR-3; 7 BTR-80A
APC 412
APC (T) 66: 20-30 BTR-50; 36 M113
APC (W) 346: 10 BTR 70; 50–80 BTR-152; 20 OT-62; 50 OT-64; 10 Type-92 (reported); 55-80 V-150 *Commando*; 96 *Walid*
ARTY 849+
SP 61: **122mm** 51 2S1; **155mm** 10 (AMX) Mk F3
TOWED 123+ **105mm** 20 M101; **122mm** 16+: 16 D-30; D-74; M-30; **130mm** 87: 75 M-46/Type-59-I; 12 M114A1
MRL 665: **107mm** 477 Type-63; **122mm** 188: 120 BM-21; 50 *Saqr*; 18 Type-81
MOR 81mm; **82mm**; **120mm** AM-49; M-43
AT • MSL • MANPATS 4+: 4 *Swingfire*; 9K11 *Malyutka* (AT-3 *Sagger*)
RCL 106mm 40 M40A1
GUNS 40+: 40 **76mm** ZIS-3/**100mm** M-1944; **85mm** D-44
AD • SAM • MANPAD 54 9K32 *Strela-2* (SA-7 *Grail*)‡
GUNS 996+
SP 20: **20mm** 8 M163 *Vulcan*; 12 M3 VDAA
TOWED 946+: 740+ **14.5mm** ZPU-2/**14.5mm** ZPU-4/**37mm** Type-63/**57mm** S-60/**85mm** M-1944; **20mm** 16 M167 *Vulcan*; **23mm** 50 ZU-23-2; **37mm** 80 M-1939; (30 M-1939 unserviceable); **40mm** 60
RADAR • LAND RASIT (veh, arty)

Navy 1,300

EQUIPMENT BY TYPE
PATROL AND COASTAL COMBATANTS 4
PBR 4 *Kurmuk*
AMPHIBIOUS • LANDING CRAFT 7
LCT 2 *Sobat*
LCVP 5
LOGISTICS AND SUPPORT 2
AG 1
AWT 1 *Baraka*

Air Force 3,000

FORCES BY ROLE
FIGHTER
2 sqn with MiG-29SE/UB *Fulcrum*
GROUND ATTACK
1 sqn with A-5 *Fantan*
1 sqn with Su-25/Su-25UB *Frogfoot*
TRANSPORT
Some sqn with An-26 *Curl** (modified for bombing); An-30 *Clank*; An-32 *Cline*; An-72 *Coaler*; An-74TK-200/300; C-130H *Hercules*; Il-76 *Candid*; Y-8
1 VIP unit with *Falcon* 20F; *Falcon* 50; *Falcon* 900; F-27; Il-62M *Classic*
TRAINING
1 sqn with K-8 *Karakorum**
ATTACK HELICOPTER
2 sqn with Mi-24/Mi-24P/Mi-24V/Mi-35P *Hind*
TRANSPORT HELICOPTER
2 sqn with Mi-8 *Hip*; Mi-17 *Hip* H; Mi-171
AIR DEFENCE
5 bty with S-75 *Dvina* (SA-2 *Guideline*)‡

EQUIPMENT BY TYPE
AIRCRAFT 63 combat capable
FTR 22: 20 MiG-29SE *Fulcrum*; 2 MiG-29UB *Fulcrum*
ATK 29+: 15 A-5 *Fantan*; 3+ Su-24 *Fencer*; 9 Su-25 *Frogfoot*; 2 Su-25UB *Frogfoot* B
ISR 2 An-30 *Clank*
TPT 23 **Heavy** 1 Il-76 *Candid*; **Medium** 6: 4 C-130H *Hercules*; 2 Y-8; **Light** 12: 1 An-26 *Curl** (modified for bombing); 2 An-32 *Cline*; 2 An-72 *Coaler*; 4 An-74TK-200;

Sub-Saharan Africa

2 An-74TK-300; 1 F-27 (VIP); **PAX** 4: 1 *Falcon* 20F (VIP); 1 *Falcon* 50 (VIP); 1 Falcon 900; 1 Il-62M *Classic*
TRG 15: 12 K-8 *Karakorum**; 3 UTVA-75
HELICOPTERS
ATK 40: 25 Mi-24 *Hind*; 2 Mi-24P *Hind*; 7 Mi-24V *Hind* E; 6 Mi-35P *Hind*
MRH ε5 Mi-17 *Hip* H
TPT 24 **Medium** 23: 21 Mi-8 *Hip*; 2 Mi-171; **Light** 1 Bell 205
AD • SAM • TOWED: 90 S-75 *Dvina* (SA-2 *Guideline*)‡
MSL • AAM • IR R-3 (AA-2 *Atoll*)‡; R-60 (AA-8 *Aphid*); R-73 (AA-11 *Archer*); **IR/SARH** R-23/24 (AA-7 *Apex*); **ARH** R-77 (AA-12 *Adder*)

Paramilitary 20,000

Popular Defence Force 20,000 (org in bn 1,000); 85,000 reservists (total 102,500)
mil wing of National Islamic Front

FOREIGN FORCES
All UNAMID, unless otherwise indicated
Bangladesh 196; 17 obs; 1 inf coy
Benin UNISFA 1; 2 obs
Bolivia 2 • UNISFA 1; 3 obs
Brazil UNISFA 1; 3 obs
Burkina Faso 804; 10 obs; 1 inf bn
Burundi 2; 8 obs • UNISFA 1 obs
Cambodia 3 • UNISFA 2 obs
China, People's Republic of 233; 1 engr coy
Ecuador UNISFA 1; 1 obs
Egypt 1,055; 32 obs; 1 inf bn; 1 tpt coy
El Salvador UNISFA 1 obs
Ethiopia 2,539; 16 obs; 3 inf bn • UNISFA 3,912; 78 obs; 2 recce coy; 1 mech inf bn; 2 inf bn; 1 hel coy; 2 arty coy; 1 engr coy; 1 sigs coy; 1 fd hospital
Gambia 213; 1 inf coy
Germany 10
Ghana 17; 8 obs • UNISFA 2; 3 obs
Guatemala UNISFA 1; 2 obs
Guinea UNISFA 2 obs
India UNISFA 2; 2 obs
Indonesia 1; 7 obs • UNISFA 1; 1 obs
Iran 2 obs
Jordan 14; 13 obs
Kenya 81; 6 obs; 1 MP coy
Korea, Republic of 2
Kyrgyzstan 2 • UNISFA 1 obs
Lesotho 1; 2 obs
Malaysia 12; 3 obs • UNISFA 1 obs
Mali 1; 7 obs
Mongolia 70; 1 fd hospital • UNISFA 2 obs
Mozambique UNISFA 1 obs
Namibia 3; 10 obs • UNISFA 1 obs
Nepal 365; 20 obs; 1 SF coy; 1 inf coy • UNISFA 2; 3 obs
Nigeria 2,571; 12 obs; 3 inf bn • UNISFA 3 obs
Pakistan 505; 6 obs; 1 engr coy; 1 med pl
Paraguay UNISFA 1 obs
Palau 1; 1 obs
Peru 4 • UNISFA 1; 2 obs
Philippines UNISFA 1; 1 obs
Russia UNISFA 2; 1 obs
Rwanda 3,236; 10 obs; 4 inf bn • UNISFA 2; 2 obs
Senegal 812; 17 obs; 1 inf bn
Sierra Leone 5; 10 obs • UNISFA 3 obs
South Africa 808; 16 obs; 1 inf bn
Sri Lanka UNISFA 1; 5 obs
Tanzania 878; 23 obs; 1 inf bn • UNISFA 1; 1 obs
Thailand 10; 9 obs
Togo 8 obs
Ukraine UNISFA 2; 2 obs
Uruguay UNISFA 1
Yemen, Republic of 5; 49 obs • UNISFA 2 obs
Zambia 5; 13 obs • UNISFA 1 obs
Zimbabwe 2; 7 obs • UNISFA 1; 2 obs

Tanzania TZA

Tanzanian Shilling sh		2012	2013	2014
GDP	sh	44.7tr	51.8tr	
	US$	28.2bn	31.9bn	
per capita	US$	599	663	
Growth	%	6.86	6.98	
Inflation	%	16.00	9.00	
Def exp	sh	483bn		
	US$	305m		
Def bdgt [a]	sh	415bn	531bn	651bn
	US$	262m	327m	
FMA (US)	US$	0.2m	0.2m	0.2m
US$1=sh		1583.11	1624.83	

[a] Excludes expenditure on Ministry of Defence administration and National Service

Population 48,261,942

Age	0–14	15–19	20–24	25–29	30–64	65 plus
Male	22.6%	5.2%	4.5%	3.9%	12.3%	1.3%
Female	22.2%	5.2%	4.5%	3.9%	12.7%	1.7%

Capabilities

While Tanzania has enjoyed comparative stability, security concerns remain, in particular with its neighbour the DRC, piracy, and clashes between Christians and Muslims within its own population. One focus for violence is Zanzibar, a semi-autonomous island territory. In keeping with many other countries in the region, the armed forces' ability to revamp an ageing equipment inventory is hampered by a limited budget. This affects both army and air force. The emerging problem of piracy has focused attention on its naval capability, and its lack of overall capacity to independently meet such a challenge. Tanzania has looked to jointly address anti-piracy tasks with South Africa and

Mozambique. A small tactical transport fleet provides some intra-theatre mobility but otherwise the state has no ability to project power independently beyond its own territory. In recent years, it has received assistance from the UK and US, regularly taken part in multinational exercises in Africa, and has provided some training assistance to other African forces.

ACTIVE 27,000 (Army 23,000 Navy 1,000 Air 3,000) Paramilitary 1,400

RESERVE 80,000 (Joint 80,000)

ORGANISATIONS BY SERVICE

Army ε23,000

FORCES BY ROLE

MANOEUVRE

Armoured

1 tk bde

Light

5 inf bde

COMBAT SUPPORT

4 arty bn

1 mor bn

2 AT bn

2 ADA bn

1 engr regt (bn)

COMBAT SERVICE SUPPORT

1 log gp

EQUIPMENT BY TYPE†

MBT 45: 30 T-54/T-55; 15 Type-59G

LT TK 55: 30 *Scorpion*; 25 Type-62

RECCE 10 BRDM-2

APC (W) 14: ε10 BTR-40/BTR-152; 4 Type-92

ARTY 378

TOWED 170: **76mm** ε40 ZIS-3; **122mm** 100: 20 D-30; 80 Type-54-1 (M-30); **130mm** 30 Type-59-I

MRL 122mm 58 BM-21

MOR 150: **82mm** 100 M-43; **120mm** 50 M-43

AT • RCL 75mm Type-52 (M-20)

GUNS 85mm 75 Type-56 (D-44)

Navy ε1,000

EQUIPMENT BY TYPE

PATROL AND COASTAL COMBATANTS 8

PHT 2 *Huchuan* each with 2 533mm ASTT

PB 6: 2 *Ngunguri*; 2 *Shanghai* II (PRC); 2 VT 23m

AMPHIBIOUS 3

LCU 2 *Yuchin*

LCT 1 *Kasa*

Air Defence Command ε3,000

FORCES BY ROLE

FIGHTER

3 sqn with F-7/FT-7; FT-5; K-8 *Karakorum**

TRANSPORT

1 sqn with Cessna 404 *Titan*; DHC-5D *Buffalo*; F-28 *Fellowship*; F-50; Gulfstream G550; Y-12 (II)

TRANSPORT HELICOPTER

1 sqn with Bell 205 (AB-205); Bell 412 *Twin Huey*

EQUIPMENT BY TYPE†

AIRCRAFT 18 combat capable

FTR 12: 10 F-7TN; 2 FT-7TN

TPT 12: **Medium** 2 Y-8; **Light** 7: 2 Cessna 404 *Titan*; 3 DHC-5D *Buffalo*; 2 Y-12(II); **PAX** 3: 1 F-28 *Fellowship*; 1 F-50; 1 Gulfstream G550

TRG 9: 3 FT-5 (JJ-5); 6 K-8 *Karakorum**

HELICOPTERS

MRH 2 Bell 412 *Twin Huey*

TPT • Light 1 Bell 205 (AB-205)

AD

SAM 160:

SP 40: 20 2K12 *Kub* (SA-6 *Gainful*)†; 20 S-125 *Pechora* (SA-3 *Goa*)†

MANPAD 120 9K32 *Strela*-2 (SA-7 *Grail*)‡

GUNS 200

TOWED 14.5mm 40 ZPU-2/ZPU-4†; **23mm** 40 ZU-23; **37mm** 120 M-1939

Paramilitary 1,400 active

Police Field Force 1,400

18 sub-units incl Police Marine Unit

Air Wing

AIRCRAFT • TPT • Light 1 Cessna U206 *Stationair*

HELICOPTERS

TPT • Light 4: 2 Bell 206A *Jet Ranger* (AB-206A); 2 Bell 206L *Long Ranger*

TRG 2 Bell 47G (AB-47G)/Bell 47G2

Marine Unit 100

PATROL AND COASTAL COMBATANTS • MISC BOATS/CRAFT some boats

DEPLOYMENT

CÔTE D'IVOIRE

UN • UNOCI 2; 1 obs

DEMOCRATIC REPUBLIC OF THE CONGO

UN • MONUSCO 1,254; 1 SF coy; 1 inf bn; 1 arty coy

LEBANON

UN • UNIFIL 158; 2 MP coy

SOUTH SUDAN

UN • UNMISS 2; 3 obs

SUDAN

UN • UNAMID 878; 23 obs; 1 inf bn

UN • UNISFA 1

Togo TGO

CFA Franc BCEAO fr		2012	2013	2014
GDP	fr	1.88tr	2.02tr	
	US$	3.69bn	4.09bn	
per capita	US$	585	635	
Growth	%	5.03	5.13	
Inflation	%	2.58	4.22	
Def bdgt	fr	31.6bn	35.5bn	
	US$	62m	72m	
US$1=fr		510.02	494.96	

Population 7,154,237

Age	0–14	15–19	20–24	25–29	30–64	65 plus
Male	20.4%	5.2%	4.8%	4.2%	13.6%	1.4%
Female	20.3%	5.2%	4.8%	4.2%	14.0%	1.8%

Capabilities

Facing few external or internal threats, the Togolese armed forces are adequate for the internal-security roles for which they might be used. The army is relatively small, fielding a limited light armour capability. The air force and navy are similarly constrained by limited equipment, although, in contrast to other regional states, it is generally well maintained and serviceable. Given the size of the country, there is little requirement for airlift. Togo receives training assistance from France, with occasional visits and support from the US Navy. One possible challenge is the growing trend of piracy in the Gulf of Guinea, in the face of Togo's very limited maritime capability. This explains Togo's participation, along with Benin, Niger and Nigeria, in ECOWAS and international initiatives to improve maritime security in the Gulf of Guinea.

ACTIVE 8,550 (Army 8,100 Navy 200 Air 250)

Paramilitary 750

Conscript liability Selective conscription, 2 years

ORGANISATIONS BY SERVICE

Army 8,100+

FORCES BY ROLE

MANOEUVRE

Reconnaissance

1 armd recce regt

Light

2 cbd arms regt

2 inf regt

1 rapid reaction force

Air Manoeuvre

1 cdo/para regt (3 cdo/para coy)

Other

1 (Presidential Guard) gd regt (1 gd bn, 1 cdo bn, 2 indep gd coy)

COMBAT SUPPORT

1 spt regt (1 fd arty bty, 2 ADA bty, 1 engr/log/tpt bn)

EQUIPMENT BY TYPE

MBT 2 T-54/T-55

LT TK 9 *Scorpion*

RECCE 61: 3 AML-60; 7 AML-90; 36 EE-9 *Cascavel*; 4 M3A1; 6 M8; 3 M20; 2 VBL

AIFV 20 BMP-2

APC (W) 30 UR-416

ARTY 30

SP 122mm 6

TOWED 105mm 4 HM-2

MOR 82mm 20 M-43

AT • RCL 22: **75mm** 12 Type-52 (M-20)/Type-56; **82mm** 10 Type-65 (B-10)

GUNS 57mm 5 ZIS-2

AD • GUNS • TOWED 43 **14.5mm** 38 ZPU-4; **37mm** 5 M-1939

Navy ε200 (incl Marine Infantry unit)

EQUIPMENT BY TYPE

PATROL AND COASTAL COMBATANTS • PB 2 *Kara* (FRA *Esterel*)

Air Force 250

FORCES BY ROLE

FIGHTER/GROUND ATTACK

1 sqn with *Alpha Jet**; EMB-326G*

TRANSPORT

1 sqn with Beech 200 *King Air*

1 VIP unit with DC-8; F-28-1000

TRAINING

1 sqn with TB-30 *Epsilon**

TRANSPORT HELICOPTER

1 sqn with SA315 *Lama*; SA316 *Alouette* III; SA319 *Alouette* III

EQUIPMENT BY TYPE†

AIRCRAFT 10 combat capable

TPT 5 **Light** 2 Beech 200 *King Air*; **PAX** 3: 1 DC-8; 2 F-28-1000 (VIP)

TRG 10: 3 *Alpha Jet**; 4 EMB-326G *; 3 TB-30 *Epsilon**

HELICOPTERS

MRH 4: 2 SA315 *Lama*; 1 SA316 *Alouette* III; 1 SA319 *Alouette* III

TPT • Medium (1 SA330 *Puma* in store)

Paramilitary 750

Gendarmerie 750

Ministry of Interior

FORCES BY ROLE

2 reg sections

MANOEUVRE

Other

1 (mobile) paramilitary sqn

DEPLOYMENT

CÔTE D'IVOIRE

UN • UNOCI 523; 7 obs; 1 inf bn

LIBERIA

UN • UNMIL 1; 2 obs

MALI

UN • MINUSMA 939; 1 inf bn

SOUTH SUDAN

UN • UNMISS 1

SUDAN

UN • UNAMID 8 obs

WESTERN SAHARA

UN • MINURSO 1 obs

Uganda UGA

Ugandan Shilling Ush		2012	2013	2014
GDP	Ush	52.7tr	59tr	
	US$	21bn	21.4bn	
per capita	US$	589	580	
Growth	%	2.57	4.84	
Inflation	%	14.13	5.47	
Def bdgt	Ush	938bn	945bn	1.05tn
	US$	374m	342m	
FMA (US)	US$	0.2m	0.2m	0.2m
US$1=Ush		2507.81	2763.16	

Population 34,758,809

Age	0–14	15–19	20–24	25–29	30–64	65 plus
Male	24.4%	5.8%	4.8%	3.7%	10.1%	0.9%
Female	24.5%	5.8%	4.8%	3.7%	10.2%	1.2%

Capabilities

Uganda's armed forces are relatively large and well equipped. They have, in recent years, seen some advanced capability acquisitions, boosting military capacity, particularly in the air force. Ugandan forces have deployed to Somalia as part of AMISOM since 2007, and in that time will have gained valuable combat experience in terms of planning and tactics, such as in counter-IED and urban patrolling on foot and with armour. The armed forces have a good standard of training, and the country has a number of training facilities, one of which – the camp at Bihanga – is used by the European Union to train Somali security forces. Exercises with US troops have taught skills in IED detection, EOD and counter-terrorist tasks, designed as preparation for operational deployment to AMISOM; US engagement with Uganda is also focused on military support to the regional task force targetting the LRA.

ACTIVE 45,000 (Ugandan People's Defence Force 45,000) **Paramilitary 1,800**

RESERVE 10,000

ORGANISATIONS BY SERVICE

Ugandan People's Defence Force ε40,000–45,000

FORCES BY ROLE

MANOEUVRE

Armoured

1 armd bde

Light

1 cdo bn

5 inf div (total: 16 inf bde)

Other

1 (Presidential Guard) mot bde

COMBAT SUPPORT

1 arty bde

2 AD bn

EQUIPMENT BY TYPE†

MBT 239: 185 T-54/T-55; 10 T-72; 44 T-90S

LT TK ε20 PT-76

RECCE 46: 40 *Eland*; 6 *Ferret*

AIFV 31 BMP-2

APC 79

APC (W) 19: 15 BTR-60; 4 OT-64

PPV 60: 20 *Buffel*; 40 *Mamba*

ARTY 333+

SP 155mm 6 ATMOS 2000

TOWED 243+: **76mm** ZIS-3; **122mm** M-30; **130mm** 221; **155mm** 22: 4 G-5; 18 M-839

MRL 6+: **107mm** (12-tube); **122mm** 6+: BM-21; 6 RM-70

MOR 78+: **81mm** L16; **82mm** M-43; **120mm** 78 *Soltam*

AD

SAM

TOWED 4 S-125 *Pechora* (SA-3 *Goa*)

MANPAD 9K32 *Strela*-2 (SA-7 *Grail*)‡; 9K310 *Igla*-1 (SA-16 *Gimlet*)

GUNS • TOWED 20+: **14.5mm** ZPU-1/ZPU-2/ZPU-4; **37mm** 20 M-1939

ARV T-54/T-55 reported

VLB MTU reported

MW *Chubby*

Air Wing

FORCES BY ROLE

FIGHTER/GROUND ATTACK

1 sqn with MiG-21bis *Fishbed*; MiG-21U/UM *Mongol* A/B; Su-30MK2

TRANSPORT

1 unit with Y-12

1 VIP unit with Gulfstream 550; L-100-30

TRAINING

1 unit with L-39 *Albatros*†*

ATTACK/TRANSPORT HELICOPTER

1 sqn with Bell 206 *Jet Ranger*; Bell 412 *Twin Huey*; Mi-17 *Hip* H; Mi-24 *Hind*; Mi-172 (VIP)

EQUIPMENT BY TYPE

AIRCRAFT 16 combat capable
  FGA 13: 5 MiG-21bis *Fishbed*; 1 MiG-21U *Mongol* A; 1 MiG-21UM *Mongol* B; 6 Su-30MK2
  TPT 4 **Medium** 1 L-100-30; **Light** 2 Y-12; **PAX** 1 Gulfstream 550
  TRG 3 L-39 *Albatros*†*

HELICOPTERS
  ATK 1 Mi-24 *Hind* (2 more non-op)
  MRH 5: 2 Bell 412 *Twin Huey*; 3 Mi-17 *Hip* H (1 more non-op)
  TPT 4: **Medium** 1 Mi-172 (VIP); **Light** 3 Bell 206 *Jet Ranger*

MSL
  AAM • **IR** R-73 (AA-11 *Archer*); **SARH** R-27 (AA-10 *Alamo*); **ARH** R-77 (AA-12 *Adder*) (reported)
  ARM Kh-31P (AS-17A *Krypton*) (reported)

Paramilitary ε1,800 active

Border Defence Unit ε600

Equipped with small arms only

Police Air Wing ε800

HELICOPTERS • **TPT** • **Light** 1 Bell 206 *Jet Ranger*

Marines ε400

PATROL AND COASTAL COMBATANTS 8 **PBR**

Local Militia Forces

Amuka Group ε3,000; ε7,000 (reported under trg) (total 10,000)

DEPLOYMENT

CÔTE D'IVOIRE

UN • UNOCI 2; 5 obs

SOMALIA

AU • AMISOM 6,223; 7 inf bn

SOUTH SUDAN

UN • UNAMID 1; 1 obs

FOREIGN FORCES

(all EUTM, unless otherwise indicated)

Belgium 6
Finland 6
France 23
Germany 3
Hungary 4
Ireland 10
Italy 22
Malta 4
Portugal 5
Spain 16
Sweden 4
UK 2

Zambia ZMB

Zambian Kwacha K		2012	2013	2014
GDP	K	105tr	120tr	
	US$	20.5bn	23.1bn	
per capita	US$	1,474	1,618	
Growth	%	7.33	7.83	
Inflation	%	6.56	6.53	
Def bdgt [a]	K	1.65tr	2.04tr	2.74tr
	US$	321m	390m	
US$1=K		5131.82	5218.32	

[a] Excludes allocations for public order and safety

Population 14,222,233

Age	0–14	15–19	20–24	25–29	30–64	65 plus
Male	23.2%	5.5%	4.5%	3.9%	11.9%	1.0%
Female	23.0%	5.5%	4.6%	3.9%	11.8%	1.4%

Capabilities

Territorial integrity, border security and a commitment to international peacekeeping operations are tenets of the country's armed forces. In common with many of the continent's armed forces, Zambia's forces struggle with obsolescent equipment, limited funding and the challenges of maintaining ageing weapons systems. The army provides forces for UN peacekeeping while the country also supports the Standby Force concept. As a land-locked nation, there is no navy, but a small number of light patrol craft are retained for riverine duties. The air force has a very limited tactical air transport capability, but the armed forces have no independent capacity for power projection. The services have been occasional participants in international exercises.

ACTIVE 15,100 (Army 13,500 Air 1,600) **Paramilitary 1,400**

RESERVE 3,000 (Army 3,000)

ORGANISATIONS BY SERVICE

Army 13,500

FORCES BY ROLE

COMMAND
  3 bde HQ

SPECIAL FORCES
  1 cdo bn

MANOEUVRE
  Armoured
  1 armd regt (1 tk bn, 1 armd recce regt)
  Light
  6 inf bn

COMBAT SUPPORT
  1 arty regt (2 fd arty bn, 1 MRL bn)
  1 engr regt

EQUIPMENT BY TYPE
Some equipment†
MBT 30: 20 Type-59; 10 T-55
LT TK 30 PT-76
RECCE 70 BRDM-1/BRDM-2 (ε30 serviceable)
AIFV 23 *Ratel*-20
APC (W) 33: 13 BTR-60; 20 BTR-70
ARTY 182
TOWED 61: **105mm** 18 Model 56 pack howitzer; **122mm** 25 D-30; **130mm** 18 M-46
MRL 122mm 30 BM-21 (ε12 serviceable)
MOR 91: **81mm** 55; **82mm** 24; **120mm** 12
AT • MSL • MANPATS 9K11 *Malyutka* (AT-3 *Sagger*)
RCL 12+: **57mm** 12 M18; **75mm** M20; **84mm** *Carl Gustav*
AD • SAM • MANPAD 9K32 *Strela*-2 (SA-7 *Grail*)‡
GUNS • TOWED 136: **20mm** 50 M-55 (triple); **37mm** 40 M-1939; **57mm** ε30 S-60; **85mm** 16 M-1939 *KS-12*
ARV T-54/T-55 reported

Reserve 3,000

FORCES BY ROLE
MANOEUVRE
Light
3 inf bn

Air Force 1,600

FORCES BY ROLE
FIGHTER/GROUND ATTACK
1 sqn with K-8 *Karakorum**
1 sqn with MiG-21MF *Fishbed* J†; MiG-21U *Mongol* A
TRANSPORT
1 sqn with MA60; Y-12(II); Y-12(IV); Y-12E
1 (VIP) unit with AW139; CL-604; HS-748
1 (liaison) sqn with Do-28
TRAINING
2 sqn with MB-326GB; MFI-15 *Safari*
TRANSPORT HELICOPTER
1 sqn with Mi-17 *Hip* H
1 (liaison) sqn with Bell 47G; Bell 205 (UH-1H *Iroquois*/AB-205)
AIR DEFENCE
3 bty with S-125 *Pechora* (SA-3 *Goa*)

EQUIPMENT BY TYPE†
Very low serviceability.
AIRCRAFT 25 combat capable
FGA 10: 8 MiG-21MF *Fishbed* J; 2 MiG-21U *Mongol* A
TPT 23: **Light** 21: 5 Do-28; 2 MA60; 4 Y-12(II); 5 Y-12(IV); 5 Y-12E; **PAX** 2: 1 CL-604; 1 HS-748
TRG 41: 15 K-8 *Karakourm**; 10 MB-326GB; 10 MFI-15 *Safari*; 6 SF-260TW
HELICOPTERS
MRH 5: 1 AW139; 4 Mi-17 *Hip* H
TPT • Light 13: 10 Bell 205 (UH-1H *Iroquois*/AB-205); 3 Bell 212
TRG 5 Bell 47G
AD • SAM S-125 *Pechora* (SA-3 *Goa*)
MSL
ASM AT-3 *Sagger*
AAM • IR R-3 (AA-2 *Atoll*)‡; PL-2; *Python* 3

Paramilitary 1,400

Police Mobile Unit 700

FORCES BY ROLE
MANOEUVRE
Other
1 police bn (4 police coy)

Police Paramilitary Unit 700

FORCES BY ROLE
MANOEUVRE
Other
1 paramilitary bn (3 paramilitary coy)

DEPLOYMENT

CÔTE D'IVOIRE
UN • UNOCI 2 obs

DEMOCRATIC REPUBLIC OF THE CONGO
UN • MONUSCO 2; 20 obs

LIBERIA
UN • UNMIL 3 obs

SOUTH SUDAN
UN • UNMISS 3; 3 obs

SUDAN
UN • UNAMID 5; 13 obs
UN • UNISFA 1 obs

Zimbabwe ZWE

Zimbabwe Dollar Z$		2012	2013	2014
GDP	Z$	3.69tr	4.14tr	
	US$	9.8bn	11bn	
per capita	US$	756	837	
Growth	%	4.42	4.96	
Inflation	%	3.72	4.45	
Def bdgt	Z$	120bn	134bn	
	US$	318m	356m	368m
US$1=Z$		376.30	376.30	

Population 13,182,908

Age	0–14	15–19	20–24	25–29	30–64	65 plus
Male	19.9%	5.9%	5.3%	4.8%	12.1%	1.5%
Female	19.5%	5.8%	5.5%	5.4%	12.3%	2.2%

Capabilities

The armed forces' task is notionally to defend the nation's independence, sovereignty and territorial integrity. However, the erosion of the country's already limited military capabilities, as a result of economic problems, suggests that these tasks would likely be beyond it in the face of a committed aggressor. An international deployment on the scale of the approximately 10,000 personnel deployed to the Democratic Republic of the Congo between 1998 and 2002 would now be extremely difficult to replicate. In late 2012, though, elements of the army were deployed to the Mozambique border in preparation for possible operations against Renamo fighters. The armed forces have taken part intermittently in multinational training exercises. China has been the only source of defence equipment for the limited procurement that the country has been able to undertake. A proposed donation of ex-South African *Alouette* III helicopters, ostensibly for spare parts, was blocked by a South African court in early 2013, and both the EU and the US have arms embargoes in place.

ACTIVE 29,000 (Army 25,000 Air 4,000) Paramilitary 21,800

ORGANISATIONS BY SERVICE

Army ε25,000

FORCES BY ROLE

COMMAND
- 1 SF bde HQ
- 1 mech bde HQ
- 5 inf bde HQ

SPECIAL FORCES
- 1 SF regt

MANOEUVRE
- **Armoured**
  - 1 armd sqn
- **Mechanised**
  - 1 mech inf bn
- **Light**
  - 15 inf bn
  - 1 cdo bn
- **Air Manoeuvre**
  - 1 para bn
- **Other**
  - 3 gd bn
  - 1 (Presidential Guard) gd gp

COMBAT SUPPORT
- 1 arty bde
- 1 fd arty regt
- 1 AD regt
- 2 engr regt

EQUIPMENT BY TYPE

MBT 40: 30 Type-59†; 10 Type-69†

RECCE 115: 20 *Eland*; 15 *Ferret*†; 80 EE-9 *Cascavel* (90mm)

APC 85
- **APC (T)** 30: 8 Type-63; 22 VTT-323
- **APC (W)** 55 TPK 4.20 VSC ACMAT

ARTY 254
- **SP 122mm** 12 2S1
- **TOWED 122mm** 20: 4 D-30; 16 Type-60 (D-74)
- **MRL** 76: **107mm** 16 Type-63; **122mm** 60 RM-70 *Dana*
- **MOR** 146: **81mm/82mm** ε140; **120mm** 6 M-43

AD
- **SAM • MANPAD** 30 9K32 *Strela*-2 (SA-7 *Grail*) ‡
- **GUNS • TOWED** 116: **14.5mm** 36 ZPU-1/ZPU-2/ZPU-4; **23mm** 45 ZU-23; **37mm** 35 M-1939

ARV T-54/T-55 reported

VLB MTU reported

Air Force 4,000

Flying hours 100 hrs/year

FORCES BY ROLE

FIGHTER
- 1 sqn with F-7 II†; FT-7†

FIGHTER/GROUND ATTACK
- 1 sqn with K-8 *Karakorum**
- (1 sqn Hawker *Hunter* in store)

GROUND ATTACK/ISR
- 1 sqn with Cessna 337/O-2A *Skymaster**

ISR/TRAINING
- 1 sqn with SF-260F/M; SF-260TP*; SF-260W *Warrior**

TRANSPORT
- 1 sqn with BN-2 *Islander*; CASA 212-200 *Aviocar* (VIP)

ATTACK/TRANSPORT HELICOPTER
- 1 sqn with Mi-35 *Hind*; Mi-35P *Hind* (liaison); SA316 *Alouette* III; AS532UL *Cougar* (VIP)
- 1 trg sqn with Bell 412 *Twin Huey*, SA316 *Alouette* III

AIR DEFENCE
- 1 sqn

EQUIPMENT BY TYPE

AIRCRAFT 46 combat capable
- **FTR** 9: 7 F-7 II†; 2 FT-7†
- **FGA** (12 Hawker *Hunter* in store)
- **ISR** 2 O-2A *Skymaster*
- **TPT • Light** 26: 5 BN-2 *Islander*; 8 C-212-200 *Aviocar* (VIP - 2 more in store); 13 Cessna 337 *Skymaster**; (10 C-47 *Skytrain* in store)
- **TRG** 35: 11 K-8 *Karakorum**; 5 SF-260M; 8 SF-260TP*; 5 SF-260W *Warrior**; 6 SF-260F

HELICOPTERS
- **ATK** 6: 4 Mi-35 *Hind*; 2 Mi-35P *Hind*
- **MRH** 10: 8 Bell 412 *Twin Huey*; 2 SA316 *Alouette* III
- **TPT • Medium** 2 AS532UL *Cougar* (VIP)

MSL • AAM • IR PL-2; PL-5

AD • GUNS 100mm (not deployed); **37mm** (not deployed); **57mm** (not deployed)

Paramilitary 21,800

Zimbabwe Republic Police Force 19,500

incl Air Wg

Police Support Unit 2,300

PATROL AND COASTAL COMBATANTS • PB 5: 3 Rodman 38; 2 Rodman 46 (five Rodman 790 are also operated, under 10 tonnes FLD)

DEPLOYMENT

CÔTE D'IVOIRE

UN • UNOCI 3 obs

LIBERIA

UN • UNMIL 2 obs

SUDAN

UN • UNAMID 2; 7 obs

UN • UNISFA 1

Table 9 **Selected Arms Procurements and Deliveries, Sub-Saharan Africa**

Designation	Type	Quantity	Contract Value (Current)	Prime Nationality	Prime Contractor	Order Date	First Delivery Due	Notes
Angola (ANG)								
Su-30K/MK	FGA ac	18	See notes	RUS	UAC (Sukhoi)	2013	n.k.	Part of reported US$1bn arms package. Ten Su-30MK and eight Su-30K. Ex-Indian Air Force ac
Benin (BEN)								
Casspir NG	PPV	10	n.k.	RSA	Mechem	2013	n.k.	–
Chad (CHA)								
C-27J *Spartan*	Tpt ac	2	n.k.	ITA	Finmeccanica (Alenia Aermacchi)	2013	2013	First delivery due by end-2013
Mauritius (MUS)								
Barracuda-class	PCO	1	US$58.5m	IND	GRSE	2012	2014	Financed by 2005 Indian $100m credit line. Launched Aug 2013 – to commmission Sep 2014
Mozambique (MOZ)								
32m PC	PCC	3	See notes	UAE	Abu Dhabi MAR (CMN)	2013	n.k.	Part of €200m order including three 42m patrol craft
42m PC	PCC	3	See notes	UAE	Abu Dhabi MAR (CMN)	2013	n.k.	Part of €200m order including three 32m patrol craft
Nigeria (NGA)								
P18N (95m OPV)	PSOH	2	US$42m	PRC	CSIC	2012	2015	To be armed with one 76 mm gun. First to be built in China; 50% of second to be built in Nigeria
OPV	PSOH	2	US$200–250m	IND	Pipavav Defence and Offshore Engineering	2012	2015	To be delivered by early 2015. Option for a further two vessels
Mi-35 *Hind*	Atk hel	3	n.k.	RUS	Russian Helicopters (Mil)	2012	n.k.	–
Mi-171Sh	Tpt hel	6	n.k.	RUS	Russian Helicopters (Mil)	2012	n.k.	–
Senegal (SEN)								
EMB-314 *Super Tucano*	Trg ac	3	n.k.	BRZ	Embraer	2013	2013	–
Sudan (SDN)								
Mi-24 *Hind*	Atk hel	12	n.k.	RUS	Government Surplus	2013	2013	Second-hand Russian Air Force surplus
Mi-8MT *Hip*	Tpt hel	12	n.k.	RUS	Government Surplus	2013	2013	Second-hand Russian Air Force surplus
South Africa (RSA)								
Badger (AMV 8x8)	APC (W)	238	ZAR9bn (US$900m)	FIN/RSA	Patria/Denel (Denel Land Systems)	2013	2013	Five variants to be produced: cmd, mor, msl, section, and fire spt vehicles
A-Darter	AAM	n.k.	n.k.	Int'l	Denel	2007	2015	Entry into service now anticipated for 2015

Chapter Ten

Country comparisons – commitments, force levels and economics

Table 10 **Selected Training Activity 2013**

Date	*Title*	Location	Aim	Principal Participants
North America (US and Canada)				
21 Jan–01 Feb 2013	*RED FLAG 13-2*	US	Air cbt ex	NLD, SGP, SWE, UAE, US
11–21 Feb 2013	*TASK GROUP EX*	US	Interop ex	CAN, US
20 Feb–15 Mar 2013	*RED FLAG 13-3*	US	Air cbt ex	AUS, UK, US
03–19 May 2013	*TRIDENT FURY 2013*	CAN	NAVEX	CAN, US
16 May–04 Jun 2013	*MAPLE RESOLVE 1301*	CAN	FTX	CAN, US
27 May–21 Jun 2013	*MAPLE FLAG 46*	CAN	Air cbt ex	BEL, CAN, COL, GER, NLD, SNG, US, UK (obs CHL, IND, OMN, PER, RSA, ROK, UKR)
11–28 Jun 2013	*DAWN BLITZ*	US	Amphib ex	CAN, JPN, NZL, US (obs AUS, CHL, COL, MEX, PER)
05–23 Aug 2013	*NANOOK*	CAN	Disaster relief ex	CAN
13 Jul–17 Aug 2013	*VIBRANT RESPONSE*	US	Disaster relief ex	US
12–13 Aug 2013	*RED FLAG ALASKA 13-3*	US	Air cbt ex	AUS, JPN, NZL, ROK, US
26–28 Aug 2013	*VIGILANT EAGLE 2013*	CAN	CT air ex	CAN, RUS, US
03–19 Sep 2013	*BURMESE CHASE*	US	Land cbt ex	UK, US
Europe				
23 Feb–06 Mar 2013	*PROUD MANTA 13*	Mediterranean	ASW ex	CAN, ESP, FRA, GER, GRC, ITA, NOR, TUR, UK, US
15 Mar 13	*BAGRAM*	POL	FTX	POL, US
15–25 Apr 2013	*JOINT WARRIOR 13-1*	UK	NAVEX	BEL, CAN, DNK, FRA, GER, NLD, NOR, POL, SWE, UK
15–25 Apr 2013	*SABER GUARDIAN*	ROM	CPX	ARM, AZE, BLG, GEO, MOL, ROM, UKR, US
15–26 Apr 2013	*FRISIAN FLAG 13*	NLD	Air cbt ex	BEL, FRA, GER, NLD, POL, SWE
15–26 Apr 2013	*CRYSTAL EAGLE*	DNK	NATO CPX	MNC-NE (and some NATO partners)
24–26 Apr 2013	*LOCKED SHIELDS 2013*	EST (Europe-wide)	Cyber defence ex	ESP, EST, FIN, GER, ITA, LTU, NLD, POL, SVK
09–21 May 2013	*STEADFAST COBALT 2013*	POL	CIS Interop ex	FRA, DNK, GER, ITA, NLD, POL, UK
14–24 May 2013	*TITANIUM FALCON*	CPX	Interop ex	FRA, UK
21 May–07 Jun 2013	*EUROPEAN ADVANCE*	AUT	FTX	AUT, GER, FRA, ITA (EU Battle Group)
28 May–07 Jun 2013	*SHARED RESILIENCE*	BiH, FYROM	HADR ex	ALB, BiH, FYROM, SVN, US
03–14 Jun 2013	*SABER STRIKE 2013*	LVA, EST, LTU	Interop CPX/FTX	EST, LTU, LVA, POL, UK, US, NOR (obs), SWE (obs)
07–22 Jun 2013	*BALTOPS 2013*	Baltic	NAVEX	DNK, EST, FIN, GER, LTU, LVA, NLD, POL, SWE, US
08–26 Jun 2013	*CAPABLE LOGISTICIAN 2013*	SVK	Logistics interop ex	AUS, AUT, BEL, BiH, BLG, CAN, CHE, CRO, ESP, FRA, GEO, GER, GRC, HUN, IND, ITA, JOR, LTU, LVA, MNE, MOR, NLD, NOR, POL, PRT, ROK, ROM, RUS, SVK, SVN, TUR, UK, UKR, US
16–21 Jun 2013	*CANALE*	Mediterranean	NAVEX	ALG, FRA, ITA, LBY, MLT, MOR, TUN
18–21 Jun 2013	*SHARED HORIZONS*	GEO	HADR ex	US, GEO
08–18 Jul 2013	*REGIONAL COOPERATION 2013*	GER	Disaster relief CPX	AFG, KAZ, KGZ, TJK, US
08–19 Jul 2013	*RAPID TRIDENT*	UKR	Interop ex	NATO, PfP states, UKR, US
12–21 Jul 2013	*HELLENIC SPEAR*	GRC	SF FTX	GRC, US
15–24 Jul 2013	*ATLAS VISION*	GER	FTX	RUS, US
17–31 Jul 2013	*HOT BLADE 13*	PRT	Helicopter Interop ex	AUT, BEL, GER, NLD, PRT
17–31 Jul 2013	*NATO TIGER MEET 13*	NOR	Air cbt ex	AUT, BEL, CZE, ESP, FRA, GER, GRC, NLD, NOR, POL, TUR, UK, US
26 Aug–05 Sep 2013	*BRILLIANT ARROW 13*	NOR	Air cbt ex	FRA, GER, GRC, ITA, NED, NOR, POL, PRT, TUR, UK

Table 10 **Selected Training Activity 2013**

Date	*Title*	Location	Aim	Principal Participants
02–20 Sep 2013	*RAMSTEIN ROVER*	CZE	FAC ex	BEL, CZE, DNK, EST, FRA, GER, HUN, ITA, LTU, LVA, NOR, POL, SVK, SVN, TUR, UK, USA
03–17 Sep 2013	*SAUDI-BRITISH GREEN FLAG*	UK	Air cbt ex	SAU, UK
06–09 Sep 2013	*NORTHERN COASTS 2013*	SWE	Interop ex	NATO, EU states
10–20 Sep 2013	*COMBINED ENDEAVOR*	GER	C4I Interop ex	NATO, PfP states
16–26 Sep 2013	*RECCEX 13*	DNK	CBRN ex	DNK, FIN, NOR, SWE
16–27 Sep 2013	*ARCTIC CHALLENGE*	FIN, NOR, SWE	Air cbt ex	FIN, NOR, SWE, UK, US
23 Sep–04 Oct 2013	*NORTHERN CHALLENGE 2013*	ICE	EOD ex	NATO, PfP states
28 Sep–10 Nov 2013	*BALTIC HOST*	EST, LTU, LVA	Host-nation support CPX	EST, LTU, LVA, NATO (Integrated with *Steadfast Jazz 2013*)
05–12 Oct 2013	*ARRCADE CHARGER*	UK	CPX	NATO (ARRC) states
07–11 Oct 2013	*BRTE (BALTIC REGION TRAINING EVENT)*	Baltic states	Air cbt ex	BEL, CZE, EST, FIN, FRA, LTU, US
07–17 Oct 2013	*JOINT WARRIOR 13-2*	UK	NAVEX	DNK, FRA, NOR, UK
08–16 Oct 2013	*CAPABLE EAGLE 13*	UK	Air cbt ex	UK, FRA
02–09 Nov 2013	*STEADFAST JAZZ 2013*	LVA, POL & Europe-wide	Interop ex	NATO Response Force
04–30 Nov 2013	*COBRA 13*	POL	SF ex	CRO, CZE, EST, FIN, FRA, HUN, NLD, LTU, NOR, POL, SVK, UK, US (obs SWE, TUR)
05–09 Nov 2013	*IONEX*	Ionian Sea	NAVEX	ITA, RUS
17–29 Nov 2013	*ARRCADE FUSION*	UK	CPX	NATO members (ARRC and ARRC partner states), AUS, NZL, QTR, UAE
Russia and Eurasia				
03–04 Jul 2013	*AVIADARTS*	RUS	Air cbt ex	RUS
04–12 Jul 2013	*COBALT 2013*	RUS	CT ex	BLR, CSTO states, RUS
05–10 Jul 2013	*MARITIME JOINT EX 2013*	RUS	NAVEX	PRC, RUS
05–12 Jul 2013	*JOINT SEA 2013*	RUS	NAVEX	PRC, RUS
08–20 Jul 2013	*SEA BREEZE*	Black Sea	NAVEX	AZE, BLG, CAN, GEO, GER, ITA, ROM, TUR, UKR, US (obs FRA, LIB, QAT, UAE)
12–21 Jul 2013	n.k.	RUS	Joint ex	RUS Eastern MD snap exercise
27 Jul–15 Aug 2013	*PEACE MISSION 2013*	RUS	CT ex	PRC, RUS
05–23 Aug 2013	*STEPPE EAGLE 13*	KAZ	PSO ex	ITA, KAZ, KGZ, LTU, SWE, TJK, UK, UKR, US (obs BLR, ESP, GER)
19–23 Aug 2013	n.k.	RUS	Air cbt ex	FRA, RUS
01–05 Sep 2013	n.k.	RUS	FTX	KAZ, RUS
20–25 Sep 2013	*INTERACTION 2013*	BLR	CSTO (KSOR) FTX	ARM, BLR, KAZ, KGZ, RUS, TJK
20–26 Sep 2013	*ZAPAD (West) 2013*	BLR, RUS	CSTO FTX	BLR, KAZ, KGZ, RUS, TJK
Asia				
28 Jan–1 Feb 2013	*TAMEX 13–1*	AUS	Air cbt ex	AUS, JPN, NZL, US
04–15 Feb 2013	*COPE NORTH 2013*	US	Interop ex	AUS, JPN, US
11–22 Feb 2013	*COBRA GOLD 13*	THA	PSO/HADR ex	AUS, BRN, CAN, FRA, IDN, ITA, JPN, MNG, MYS, ROK, SGP, THA, US
25 Feb–08 Mar 2013	*EX MALAPURA*	MYS	NAVEX	MYS, SGP
04–08 Mar 2013	*PEACE 13*	PAK	NAVEX	AUS, BGD, IDN, ITA, JPN, MYS, PAK, PRC, SRI, TUR, UAE, UK, US (+obs)
20 Feb–01 Mar 2013	*TROPEX*	IND	NAVEX	FRA, IND
11–21 March 2013	*FOAL EAGLE*	ROK	FTX	ROK, US
11–22 Mar 2013	*COPE TIGER*	THA	Air cbt ex	SGP, THA, US

Table 10 **Selected Training Activity 2013**

Date	*Title*	Location	Aim	Principal Participants
23–25 Mar 2013	*AUSTHAI 13*	THA	NAVEX	AUS, THA
05–17 Apr 2013	*BALIKATAN 13*	PHL	Interop/HADR ex	PHL, US
08–18 April 2013	*BERSAMA LIMA 13*	MYS & SGP	CPX/FTX	AUS, MYS, NZL, SGP, UK
08–18 April 2013	*BERSAMA SHIELD 13*	MYS & SGP	FPDA NAVEX	AUS, MYS, NZL, SGP, UK
03–28 May 2013	*ALAM HALFA*	NZL	FTX	CAN, NZL, UK, US
06–10 May 2013	*TAMEX 13–2*	AUS	Anti Surface Vessel Air cbt ex	AUS, JPN, NZL, US
13–18 May 2013	*MARITIME INFO SHARING EX 2013*	SGP	Interop ex	30 nations incl Western Pacific Naval Symposium states, IMB, ReCAAP-ISC
13–24 May 2013	*BELL BUOY 13*	AUS	NCAGS (Naval CPX)	AUS, CAN, UK, US
16–23 May 2013	*SIMBEX 2013*	SGP	NAVEX	IND, SGP
25 May–19 Aug 2013	*PACIFIC PARTNERSHIP*	Western Pacific Islands	Civil Assitance ex	AUS, CAN, FRA, JPN, MYS, NZL, US
11–21 Jun 2013	*COOPERATION 2013*	RUS	Interop ex	PRC (PAP), RUS (Interior Ministry forces)
17–20 Jun 2013	*2ND ASEAN MILITARIES HADR EX*	BRN	HADR ex	ASEAN states, AUS, IND, JPN, NZL, PRC, ROK, RUS, US
01–05 Jul 2013	*TAMEX 13–3*	AUS	Anti Surface Vessel Air cbt ex	AUS, US, JPN, NZL
15–26 Jul 2013	*CARAT 2013*	SGP	Interop ex	SGP, US
15–26 Jul 2013	*TIGER BALM*	SGP	CPX	SGP, US
15 Jul–05 Aug 2013	*TALISMAN SABRE 13*	AUS	CPX & FTX	AUS, US
03–14 Aug 2013	*KHAAN QUEST*	MNG	PSO ex	AUS, CAN, FRA, GER, JPN, IND, IDN, MNG, NPL, ROK, TAJ, VNM, UK, US (obs KAZ, PRC, RUS, TUR)
02–12 Sep 2013	*SEACAT (Southeast Asia Cooperation Against Terrorism) 2013*	SGP	NAVEX	BRN, IDN, MYS, PHL, SGP, THA, US
02–22 Sep 2013	*SHAHEEN II*	PRC	Air ex	PAK, PRC
16–17 Sep 2013	*EX MATILDA*	AUS	FTX	AUS, SGP
Oct 2013	*MISSION ACTION B 2013*	PRC	FTX	PRC
09–22 Oct 2013	*SHAKTI*	IND	Mtn FTX	FRA, IND
13–25 Oct 2013	*SUMAN WARRIOR*	SGP	FPDA HADR ec	AUS, MYS, NZL, SGP, UK
14–19 Oct 2013	*KONKAN–2013*	IND	Interop ex	IND, UK
19–28 Oct 2013	*INDRA 2013*	IND	CT ex	IND, RUS
04–11 Nov 2013	*SHARP KNIFE AIRBORNE 2013*	IDN	CT ex	IDN, PRC
04–22 Nov 2013	*SOUTHERN KATIPO 13*	NZ	NAVEX/Amph Ex	AUS, NZL, Tonga, PNG
04–26 Nov 2013	*KIWI FLAG*	NZ	Interop air tpt ex	AUS, NZL, PNG, Tonga
05–11 Nov 2013	*MALABAR 2013*	IND	Interop ex	IND, US
05–13 Nov 2013	*HAND-IN-HAND*	PRC	CT ex	IND, PRC
06–17 Nov 2013	*KEEN SWORD*	JPN	NAVEX	JPN, US
11–15 Nov 2013	*ELANG AUSINDO 13*	AUS	Air cbt ex	AUS, IDN
Middle East and North Africa				
27 Jan–07 Feb 2013	*LEADING EDGE*	UAE	PSI ex	UAE, US, 27 other nations
10–26 Feb 2013	*PENINSULA SHIELD EX*	KUW	Interop ex	GCC member states
16 Feb–07 Mar 2013	*GULF FALCON*	QTR	Interop ex	FRA, QTR
09–11 April 2013	n.k.	KWT	NAVEX	KWT, UK
17–27 Apr 2013	*AFRICAN LION*	MOR	CPX/FTX	MOR, US
21 Apr–06 May 2013	*EAGLE RESOLVE*	QTR	FTX	BHR, EGY, FRA, IRQ, ITA, JOR, KWT, LBN, OMN, QTR, SAU, UAE, UK, US
06–30 May 2013	*IMCMEX 13*	Gulf waters	MCM ex	BHR, CAN , FRA, GER, IRQ, JPN, KWT, NLD, NOR, OMN, PAK, QTR, SAU, UAE, UK, US

Table 10 **Selected Training Activity 2013**

Date	*Title*	Location	Aim	Principal Participants
11–23 May 2013	*TABUK 3*	SAU	CBT trg ex	EGY, SAU
Jun 2013	*SHAHEEN STAR 5*	UAE	Air cbt ex	UK, UAE
09–20 Jun 2013	*EAGER LION*	JOR	AD/HADR ex	BHR, CAN, EGY, FRA, IRQ, ITA, JOR, KWT, LBN, PAK, POL, QTR, SAU, TUR, UAE, UK, US
17 Jul–01 Aug 2013	*NOBLE MELINDA*	ISR	MCM ex	ISR, US
17 Jul–01 Aug 2013	*JUNIPER STALLION 13*	ISR	Air cbt ex	ISR, US
12–15 Aug 2013	*RELIANT MERMAID*	Mediterranean Sea	SAR ex	ISR, US
Latin America and the Caribbean				
18 Apr–28 Jun 2013	*BEYOND THE HORIZON/ NEW HORIZONS 2013*	BLZ, PAN, SLV	HADR ex	BLZ, PAN, SLV, US
20 May–06 Jun 2013	*TRADEWINDS 13*	Caribbean Sea	NAVEX	ATG, BHS, Grenada, GUY, HTI, St Kitts & Nevis, St Vincent & Grenadines, TTO, SUR, US
Jun 2013	*INALAF VIII*	ARG/CHL	FTX	ARG, CHL
12–16 Aug 2013	*PANAMAX 13*	PAN, US	Infrastructure protection ex	ARG, BEL, BRZ, CAN, CHL, COL, CRI, DOM, ECU, SLV, FRA, GUA, HND, MEX, NIC, PAN, PER, PRY
20–24 Aug 2013	*VIEKAREN XII*	Beagle Channel	NAVEX	ARG, CHL
08–15 Sep 2013	*UNITAS 13*	COL	NAVEX	BRZ, CAN, CHL, COL, DOM, PER, UK, US
Nov 2013	*NEPTUNO*	PER	NAVEX	CHL, PER
31 Oct–15 Nov 2013	*CRUZEX 2013*	BRZ	Air cbt, CSAR ex	BRZ, CAN, CHL, COL, ECU, URY, US, VEN
04 Nov–15 Nov 2013	*CRUZEIRO DO SUL*	BRZ	CSAR, air-refuelling ex	BRZ, CAN, US
Sub-Saharan Africa				
20 Feb–01 Mar 2013	*CENTRAL ACCORD 13*	CMR	Air / med ex	CMR, US (obs BDI, COG, DRC, STP)
20 Feb–09 Mar 2013	*FLINTLOCK 13*	MRT	CT ex	ALG, BFA, CAN, CHA, ESP, MLI, MRT, NER, NGA, RSA, SEN, TUN, US
25–28 Feb 2013	*OBANGAME*	Gulf of Guinea	NAVEX	BEL, BEN, BRZ, CAM, CIV, EQG, FRA, GAB, NLD, NGA, COG, ESP, TOG, US
07–15 Mar 2013	*SAHARAN EXPRESS 2013*	SEN	NAVEX	CPV, CIV, FRA, GAM, LBR, MRT, MOR, NLD, PRT, SEN, SLE, ESP, UK, US
19–25 May 2013	*MASHARIKI SALAM 2013*	UGA	FTX	East African Standby Force (BUR, COM, DJI, ETH, KEN, RWA, SOM, SDN, SYC, UGA)
24–29 Jun 2013	*WESTERN ACCORD 13*	GHA	CPX/FTX	ECOWAS, US
22 Jul–05 Aug 2013	*SHARED ACCORD*	RSA	HADR interop ex	US, RSA
18 Aug–02 Sep 2013	*ZAMBEZI AZUL*	ANG	FTX	SADC states
04 Sep–10 Oct 2013	*EX WELTWISCHIA*	NAM	SF ex	SADC SF forces
02–22 Nov 2013	*EX SEBOKA*	RSA	FTX	RSA readiness ex
11–18 Nov 2013	*CUTLASS EXPRESS 13*	DJB, KEN, SYC, TZA	MSO ex	DJB, DNK, EASF, EUNAVFOR, KEN, MOZ, MRT, NATO, NLD, RSA, SYC, TZA, US, YEM

Table 11 UN Deployments 2013–14

Europe

Location	CYPRUS	
Operation	UN Peacekeeping Force in Cyprus (UNFICYP)	
Original Mandate	Resolution 186 (4 Mar 1964)	
Mandate Renewed	Resolution 2114 (30 Jul 2013)	
Renewed Until	31 Jan 2014	
Mission	Maintain a buffer zone between the Turkish/ Turkish Cypriot forces and Greek Cypriot forces; supervise the ceasefire lines; undertake humanitarian activities.	
Country	**Forces by role**	**Troops**
United Kingdom	1 inf coy	337
Argentina	2 inf coy, 1 hel pl	266
Slovakia	elms 1 inf coy, 1 engr pl	157
Hungary	1 inf pl	77
Serbia	elms 1 inf coy	46
Chile		14
Paraguay		14
Austria		4
China, People's Republic of		2
Croatia		2
Brazil		1
Canada		1
TOTAL (excluding police)		**921**

Location	SERBIA	
Operation	UN Interim Administration Mission in Kosovo (UNMIK)	
Original Mandate	Resolution 1244 (10 Jun 1999)	
Renewed Until	Cancelled by the Security Council	
Mission	Ensure conditions for a peaceful and normal life for all inhabitants of Kosovo; advance regional stability in the Western Balkans; promote security, stability and respect for human rights; facilitate participation by Kosovan institutions in regional multilateral fora.	
Country		**Military Observers**
Ukraine		2
Czech Republic		1
Moldova		1
Norway		1
Poland		1
Romania		1
Turkey		1
TOTAL (excluding police)		**8**

Asia

Location	AFGHANISTAN	
Operation	UN Assistance Mission in Afghanistan (UNAMA)	
Original Mandate	Resolution 1401 (28 Mar 2002)	
Mandate Renewed	Resolution 2096 (19 Mar 2013)	
Renewed Until	19 Mar 2014	
Mission	Assist the Afghan government in developing and promoting good governance and the rule of law; support human rights; coordinate the delivery of humanitarian aid; promote coherent support for Afghanistan from the international community.	
Country		**Military Observers**
Australia		4
Czech Republic		2

Country	AFGHANISTAN (continued)	
Italy		2
Norway		2
Romania		2
Sweden		2
Denmark		1
Germany		1
Lithuania		1
Mongolia		1
Netherlands		1
New Zealand		1
Poland		1
Portugal		1
Turkey		1
TOTAL (excluding police)		**23**

Location	INDIA AND PAKISTAN	
Operation	UN Military Observer Group in India and Pakistan (UNMOGIP)	
Original Mandate	Resolution 47 (21 Apr 1948)	
Mandate Renewed	Resolution 307 (21 Dec 1971)	
Renewed Until	Cancelled by the Security Council	
Mission	Monitor the ceasefire between India and Pakistan in Kashmir.	
Country		**Military Observers**
Croatia		9
Korea, Republic of		8
Finland		6
Sweden		5
Philippines		4
Italy		3
Thailand		3
Chile		2
Uruguay		2
TOTAL (excluding police)		**42**

Middle East and North Africa

Location	IRAQ		
Operation	UN Assistance Mission in Iraq (UNAMI)		
Original Mandate	Resolution 1500 (14 Aug 2003)		
Mandate Renewed	Resolution 2110 (24 Jul 2013)		
Renewed Until	31 Jul 2014		
Mission	Support government and people of Iraq in the ongoing political process; help to coordinate humanitarian assistance; promote human rights and judicial and legal reform.		
Country	**Forces by role**	**Troops**	**Mil Obs**
Fiji	2 sy units	168	
Nepal	1 sy unit	77	
Australia			2
New Zealand			1
		245	3
TOTAL (excluding police)			**248**

Table 11 **UN Deployments 2013–14**

Location	ISRAEL, SYRIA AND LEBANON
Operation	UN Truce Supervision Organisation (UNTSO)
Original Mandate	Resolution 50 (29 May 1948)
Mandate Renewed	Resolution 339 (23 Oct 1973)
Renewed Until	Cancelled by the Security Council
Mission	Monitor ceasefires; supervise armistice agreements; prevent isolated incidents from escalating; assist other United Nations peacekeeping operations in the region.

Country	Military Observers
Finland	16
Ireland	13
Norway	13
Australia	12
Netherlands	12
Switzerland	12
Denmark	10
Canada	8
New Zealand	8
Italy	7
Austria	6
Sweden	6
Russia	5
Slovenia	5
Argentina	4
China, People's Republic of	4
Chile	3
France	3
Nepal	3
Belgium	2
Estonia	2
Slovakia	2
United States	2
Serbia	1
TOTAL (excluding police)	159

Location	LEBANON
Operation	UNIFIL
Original Mandate	Resolutions 425 and 426 (19 Mar 2008)
Mandate Renewed	Resolution 2115 (29 Aug 2013)
Renewed Until	31 Aug 2014
Mission	Assist the Lebanese government to secure its borders and establish a demilitarised zone in Southern Lebanon; help to ensure access for humanitarian aid.

Country	Forces by role	Troops
Indonesia	1 mech inf bn, 1 MP coy, 1 elm fd hospital; 1 FFGM	1,288
Italy	1 cav bde HQ, 1 amph bn, 1 hel flt, 1 engr coy, 1 sigs coy, 1 CIMIC coy(-)	1,137
India	1 mech inf bn, 1 elm fd hospital	896
Ghana	1 mech inf bn	869
Nepal	1 inf bn	869
France	1 armd cav BG	863
Malaysia	1 mech inf bn, 1 mech inf coy	829
Spain	1 armd inf bde HQ, 1 mech inf BG	587
Ireland	1 mech inf bn(-)	358
China, People's Republic of	1 engr bn, 1 fd hospital	343

Country	LEBANON (continued)	
Bangladesh	1 FFG, 1 PCO	326
Korea, Republic of	1 mech inf bn	321
Brazil	1 FFGHM	260
Cambodia	1 engr coy	219
Finland	1 inf coy	192
Turkey	1 FFGH	190
Austria	1 log coy	168
Tanzania	2 MP coy	158
Sri Lanka	1 inf coy	151
Germany	2 PC	149
Belgium	1 engr coy	104
Greece	1 PB	57
El Salvador	1 inf pl	52
Serbia		49
Brunei		30
Slovenia		14
Belarus		5
Hungary		4
Qatar		3
Sierra Leone		3
Cyprus		2
Armenia		1
Croatia		1
Guatemala		1
Kenya		1
Macedonia (FYROM)		1
Nigeria		1
TOTAL (excluding police)		10,502

Location	SYRIAN GOLAN HEIGHTS
Operation	UN Disengagement Observer Force (UNDOF)
Original Mandate	Resolution 350 (31 May 1974)
Mandate Renewed	Resolution 2108 (27 June 2013)
Renewed Until	31 Dec 2013
Mission	Supervise the continued implemetation of the disengagement of Israeli and Syrian forces; supervise areas of separation and limitation; maintain the ceasefire (mandate renewed every six months).

Country	Forces by role	Troops
Fiji	1 inf bn	500
Philippines	1 inf bn	337
India	1 log bn(-)	194
Ireland	1 inf coy	119
Nepal	1 inf coy	71
Netherlands		2
TOTAL (excluding police)		1,223

Location	WESTERN SAHARA
Operation	UN Mission for the Referendum in the Western Sahara (MINURSO)
Original Mandate	Resolution 690 (29 Apr 1991)
Mandate Renewed	Resolution 2099 (25 Apr 2013)
Renewed Until	30 Apr 2014
Mission	Ensuring compliance with the ceasefire agreed between Morocco and POLISARIO; reduce the threat of mines and unexploded ordnance.

Country	Forces by role	Troops	Mil Obs
Bangladesh	1 fd hospital	19	8
Egypt			21

Table 11 **UN Deployments 2013–14**

Country	WESTERN SAHARA (continued)		
Ghana		7	10
Russia			16
France			13
Honduras			12
Malaysia			12
Yemen			11
China, People's Republic of			10
Pakistan			10
Brazil			9
Croatia			7
Hungary			7
Nigeria			6
Paraguay			6
Guinea			5
Italy			5
Korea, Republic of			4
Mongolia			4
Nepal			4
Argentina			3
El Salvador			3
Ireland			3
Malawi			3
Sri Lanka			3
Austria			2
Peru			1
Poland			1
Togo			1
Uruguay			1
		26	201
TOTAL (excluding police)			**227**

Latin America and the Caribbean

Location	**HAITI**	
Operation	UN Stabilisation Mission in Haiti (MINUSTAH)	
Original Mandate	Resolution 1542 (30 Apr 2004)	
Mandate Renewed	Resolution 2119 (10 Oct 2013)	
Renewed Until	15 Oct 2014	
Mission	Provide logistical support and technical assistance to build the capacity of state institutions; support the work of the Haitian National Police and the National Commission on Disarmament, Dismantlement and Reintegration; public safety and public order; reconstruction and stability efforts following 2010 earthquake.	
Country	**Forces by Role**	**Troops**
Brazil	1 inf bn, 1 engr coy	1,403
Uruguay	2 inf bn, 1 mne coy, 1 spt coy	950
Sri Lanka	1 inf bn	861
Argentina	1 inf bn, 1 hel coy, 1 spt coy, 1 fd hospital	571
Chile	1 mech inf bn, 1 hel coy, elms 1 engr coy	464
Peru	1 inf coy	374
Nepal	2 inf coy	363
Jordan	1 inf coy	252
Bolivia	1 mech inf coy	208
Indonesia	1 engr coy	169
Paraguay	1 engr coy	163

Country	HAITI (continued)	
Philippines	1 HQ coy	157
Guatemala	1 MP coy	138
Ecuador	elms 1 engr coy	67
Canada		39
El Salvador		34
United States		8
France		2
Korea, Republic of		2
Honduras		1
TOTAL (excluding police)		**6,226**

Sub-Saharan Africa

Location	**CÔTE D'IVOIRE**		
Operation	UN Operation in Côte d'Ivoire (UNOCI)		
Original Mandate	Resolution 1528 (27 Feb 2004)		
Mandate Renewed	Resolution 2112 (30 Jul 2013)		
Renewed Until	30 Jun 2014		
Mission	Monitor the ceasefire agreement and arms embargo; assist the Disarmament, Demobilisation and Reintegration programme; security sector reform; promote and protect human rights and law and order; support humanitarian assistance.		
Country	**Forces by role**	**Troops**	**Mil Obs**
Bangladesh	2 mech inf bn, 1 avn coy, 1 engr coy, 1 sigs coy, 1 log coy, 1 fd hospital	2,168	13
Pakistan	1 inf bn, 1 engr coy, 1 tpt bn	1,391	11
Jordan	1 SF coy, 1 inf bn	1,067	7
Niger	1 inf bn	937	5
Morocco	1 inf bn	726	
Togo	1 inf bn	523	7
Ghana	1 inf bn, 1 hel coy, 1 fd hospital	507	6
Senegal	1 inf bn	495	10
Benin	1 inf bn	426	7
Egypt	1 engr coy	175	
Ukraine	1 atk hel flt	38	
Nigeria		10	4
Malawi		7	3
Tunisia		3	7
Yemen		1	9
Paraguay		2	7
India			8
Brazil		3	4
Uganda		2	5
China, People's Republic of			6
France		6	
Russia			6
Guatemala			5
Chad		1	3
Nepal		1	3
Philippines		1	3
Bolivia			3
El Salvador			3
Gambia			3
Moldova			3
Peru			3
Serbia			3
Tanzania		2	1

Table 11 **UN Deployments 2013–14**

Country	CÔTE D'IVOIRE (continued)		
Zimbabwe			3
Ecuador			2
Ethiopia			2
Guinea			2
Ireland			2
Korea, Republic of			2
Namibia			2
Poland			2
Uruguay			2
Zambia			2
		8,492	179
TOTAL (excluding police)			**8,671**

Location	DEMOCRATIC REPUBLIC OF THE CONGO
Operation	UN Organisation Stabilization Mission in the Democratic Republic of Congo (MONUSCO)
Original Mandate	Resolution 1279 (30 Nov 1999)
Mandate Renewed	Resolution 2098 (28 Mar 2013)
Renewed Until	31 Mar 2014
Mission	Maintain a deterrent presence to discourage violence and protect civilians and UN staff; assist in seizing and destroying illegal arms; assist the Congolese government in disarming foreign and local armed groups; specialised 'intervention brigade' tasked with neutralising armed groups; strengthen the presence of military, police and civilian components in eastern DRC and reduce in areas not affected by conflict.

Country	Forces by role	Troops	Mil Obs
India	3 mech inf bn, 1 inf bn, 1 hel coy, 1 fd hospital	3,731	36
Pakistan	3 mech inf bn, 1 inf bn, 1 hel coy	3,715	43
Bangladesh	2 mech inf bn, 1 engr coy, 1 avn coy, 2 hel coy	2,542	17
South Africa	1 inf bn, 1 avn coy, 1 engr coy	1,262	3
Tanzania	1 SF coy, 1 inf bn, 1 arty coy	1,254	
Uruguay	1 inf bn, 1 engr coy, 2 mne coy; 1 hel flt	1,196	16
Nepal	1 inf bn, 1 engr coy	1,029	20
Egypt	1 mech inf bn, 1 SF coy	1,006	21
Morocco	1 mech inf bn, 1 fd hospital	844	1
Ghana	1 mech inf bn	466	23
Benin	1 inf bn	453	10
Ukraine	2 atk hel sqn	254	11
Jordan	1 SF coy, 1 fd hospital	230	17
China, People's Republic of	1 engr coy, 1 fd hospital	220	10
Indonesia	1 engr coy	177	15
Guatemala	1 SF coy	151	
Malawi	1 inf coy	118	9
Tunisia			33
Kenya		12	18
Russia		1	27
Belgium	1 avn flt	23	
Romania			22
Zambia		2	20
Senegal		10	11
Niger		1	17
Nigeria		2	15
Paraguay			17
Malaysia		9	7

Country	DEMOCRATIC REPUBLIC OF THE CONGO (cont.)		
Peru		2	13
Mali			14
Bolivia			10
Canada			8
Serbia		5	3
Burkina Faso			7
Brazil		6	
United Kingdom		6	
Algeria			5
Bosnia-Herzegovina			5
Cameroon			5
Sweden			5
Yemen			5
France		4	
Sri Lanka			4
Switzerland		3	1
Czech Republic			3
Ireland			3
United States		3	
Mongolia			2
Guinea			1
Poland			1
		18,737	534
TOTAL (excluding police)			**19,271**

Location	LIBERIA
Operation	UN Mission in Liberia (UNMIL)
Original Mandate	Resolution 1509 (19 Sep 2003)
Mandate Renewed	Resolution 2116 (18 Sep 2013)
Renewed Until	30 Sep 2014
Mission	Provide support for the peace process and humanitarian assistance; promote human rights; assist in security sector and rule of law reform.

Country	Forces by role	Troops	Mil Obs
Pakistan	2 inf bn, 2 engr coy, 1 fd hospital	1,987	9
Nigeria	2 inf bn	1,466	11
Ghana	1 inf bn	708	10
China, People's Republic of	1 engr coy, 1 tpt coy, 1 fd hospital	564	2
Bangladesh	2 engr coy, 1 log coy, 1 fd hospital	516	13
Ukraine	1 hel sqn	238	2
Jordan	1 med coy	120	4
Philippines	1 log coy	109	
Nepal		18	2
Ethiopia		4	9
United States		5	4
Egypt			7
Malaysia			6
Denmark		2	3
Brazil		2	2
Namibia		3	1
Peru		2	2
Russia			4
Serbia			4
Bolivia		1	2
Ecuador		1	2
Kyrgyzstan			3

Table 11 **UN Deployments 2013–14**

Country	LIBERIA (continued)		
Paraguay		1	2
Togo		1	2
Zambia			3
Benin		1	1
Bulgaria			2
Croatia		2	
El Salvador			2
Finland		2	
Gambia			2
Kenya		2	
Korea, Republic of		1	1
Moldova			2
Montenegro			2
Niger			2
Romania			2
Senegal		1	1
Zimbabwe			2
France		1	
Indonesia			1
Poland			1
Yemen		1	
		5,759	130
TOTAL (excluding police)			5,889

Location	**MALI**	
Operation	United Nations Multidimensional Integrated Stabilization Mission in Mali (MINUSMA)	
Original Mandate	Resolution 2100 (25 Apr 2013)	
Renewed Until	01 Jul 2014	
Mission	Support the transitional authorities in the stabilisation of the country and implementation of the transitional roadmap; carry out security-related tasks; protect civilians; monitor human rights; prepare for free, inclusive and peaceful elections.	
Country	**Forces by role**	**Troops**
Chad	1 SF coy, 2 inf bn	1,235
Togo	1 inf bn	939
Niger	1 inf bn	864
Burkina Faso	1 inf bn	671
Senegal	1 inf coy, 1 arty coy, 1 engr coy	510
Benin	1 SF coy	306
Guinea	1 inf coy	149
Ghana	1 constuction coy	128
Côte d'Ivoire	1 tpt coy	126
Nigeria	1 sigs coy	115
Germany	1 avn unit	61
Liberia	1 inf pl	49
France		19
Sweden		6
Bangladesh		5
Sierra Leone		5
United States		5
Mauritania		4
Cambodia		2
Guinea-Bissau		2
United Kingdom		2
Yemen		2
Estonia		1

Country	MALI (continued)	
Finland		1
Jordan		1
Tajikistan		1
TOTAL (excluding police)		**5,209**

Location	**SOUTH SUDAN**		
Operation	UN Mission in South Sudan (UNMISS)		
Original Mandate	Resolution 1996 (08 Jul 2011)		
Mandate Renewed	Resolution 2109 (11 Jul 2013)		
Renewed Until	15 Jul 2014		
Mission	Support the government in exercising its responsibilties relating to conflict prevention, mitigation, and resolution; support the development of the security and justice sectors; assist the development and implementation of a national Disarmament, Demobilisation and Reintegration strategy; deter violence through proactive deployment.		
Country	**Forces by role**	**Troops**	**Mil Obs**
India	2 inf bn, 1 fd hospital	1,991	5
Rwanda	1 inf bn	980	3
Nepal	1 inf bn	858	4
Mongolia	1 inf bn, 1 engr coy	857	
Kenya	1 inf bn	701	3
China, People's Republic of	1 engr coy, 1 fd hospital	340	3
Bangladesh	1 engr coy	278	3
Korea, Republic of	1 engr coy	273	2
Japan	1 engr coy	271	
Cambodia	1 MP coy, 1 fd hospital	147	3
Norway		12	4
Australia		11	4
Denmark		13	2
Germany		7	8
Canada		5	5
Netherlands		7	2
Nigeria		2	5
Russia		4	3
Yemen		3	4
Fiji		4	2
Ghana		4	2
Jordan		3	3
Romania		2	4
Senegal		3	3
Sweden		2	4
Zambia		3	3
Tanzania		2	3
United States		5	
Belarus			4
Brazil		3	1
Ecuador			4
Guatemala		1	3
Switzerland		2	2
Ukraine		1	3
Bolivia			3
Egypt			3
Indonesia			3
Moldova			3
New Zealand		1	2
Paraguay			3

Table 11 **UN Deployments 2013–14**

Country	SOUTH SUDAN (continued)		
Benin			2
El Salvador			2
Guinea			2
Kyrgyzstan			2
Namibia			2
Papua New Guinea			2
Poland			2
Sri Lanka			2
Timor-Leste			2
Uganda		1	1
United Kingdom		2	
Italy			1
Peru			1
Togo		1	
		6,800	142
TOTAL (excluding police)			**6,942**

Location	**SUDAN (DARFUR REGION)**		
Operation	UN-AU Mission in Darfur (UNAMID)		
Original Mandate	Resolution 1769 (31 Jul 2007)		
Mandate Renewed	Resolution 2113 (30 Jul 2013)		
Renewed Until	31 Aug 2014		
Mission	Protect the local civilian population from violence; monitor the implementation of ceasefire agreements; establish a safe environment for the provision of humanitarian assistance and economic reconstruction; promote human rights and the rule of law.		
Country	**Forces by role**	**Troops**	**Mil Obs**
Rwanda	4 inf bn	3,236	10
Nigeria	3 inf bn	2,571	12
Ethiopia	3 inf bn	2,539	16
Egypt	1 inf bn, 1 tpt coy	1,055	32
Tanzania	1 inf bn	878	23
Senegal	1 inf bn	812	17
South Africa	1 inf bn	808	16
Burkina Faso	1 inf bn	804	10
Pakistan	1 engr coy, 1 med pl	505	6
Nepal	1 SF coy, inf coy	365	20
China, People's Republic of	1 engr coy	233	
Bangladesh	1 inf coy	196	17
Gambia	1 inf coy	213	
Kenya	1 MP coy	81	6
Mongolia	1 fd hospital	70	
Yemen		5	49
Jordan		14	13
Ghana		17	8
Thailand		10	9
Zambia		5	13
Malaysia		12	3
Sierra Leone		5	10
Namibia		3	10
Burundi		2	8
Germany		10	
Zimbabwe		2	7
Indonesia		1	7
Mali		1	7
Togo			8

Country	SUDAN (DARFUR REGION) (continued)		
Peru			4
Cambodia			3
Lesotho		1	2
Bolivia			2
Iran			2
Korea, Republic of		2	
Kyrgyzstan			2
Palau		1	1
		14,457	353
TOTAL (excluding police)			**14,810**

Location	**SUDAN (ABYEI)**		
Operation	United Nations Interim Security Force for Abyei (UNISFA)		
Original Mandate	Resolution 1990 (27 Jun 2011)		
Mandate Renewed	Resolution 2104 (29 May 2013)		
Renewed Until	30 Nov 2013		
Mission	Monitor the border between Sudan and South Sudan; protect civilians and humanitarian workers.		
Country	**Forces by role**	**Troops**	**Mil Obs**
Ethiopia	2 recce coy, 1 mech inf bn, 2 inf bn, 2 arty coy, 1 engr coy, 1 sigs coy, 1 hel sqn, 1 fd hospital	3912	78
Sri Lanka		1	5
Ghana		2	3
Nepal		2	3
Bolivia		1	3
Brazil		1	3
India		2	2
Namibia		1	3
Paraguay		1	3
Yemen		2	2
Benin		1	2
Nigeria			3
Rwanda		2	1
Sierra Leone			3
Cambodia			2
Ecuador		1	1
Mongolia			2
Peru		1	1
Russia		2	
Ukraine			2
Burundi			1
Guatemala			1
Philippines		1	
Tanzania		1	
Uruguay		1	
Zambia		1	
Zimbabwe		1	
		3,937	124
TOTAL (excluding police)			**4,061**

Table 12 **Non-UN Deployments 2013–2014**

Europe

Location	BOSNIA-HERZEGOVINA	
Operation	EUFOR (*Operation Althea*)	
Primary Organisation	EU	
Mission	Ensure continued compliance with the Dayton/Paris agreement; maintain security and stability; provide capacity-building and training support for the armed forces.	
Contributor	**Forces by role (where known)**	**Total:**
Austria	1 inf bn HQ, 1 inf coy, 1 recce pl	314
Turkey	1 inf coy	229
Hungary	1 inf coy	157
Romania		37
Slovakia		35
Poland		34
Switzerland		20
Bulgaria		18
Chile		15
Slovenia		14
Spain		12
Macedonia (FYROM)		11
Finland		8
Ireland		7
United Kingdom		4
Netherlands		3
Czech Republic		2
France		2
Greece		2
Sweden		2
Albania		1
Luxembourg		1
TOTAL		**928**

Location	SERBIA (KOSOVO)	
Operation	KFOR	
Primary Organisation	NATO	
Mission	Contribute to a secure environment and ensure public safety and order; support and coordinate the international humanitarian effort and civil presence; support the development of a stable, democratic, multi-ethnic and peaceful Kosovo; support the development of the Kosovo Security Force.	
Contributor	**Forces by role (where known)**	**Total:**
Germany		741
United States	1 surv bde HQ	669
Italy	1 MRL BG HQ	500
Austria	1 mech inf coy	380
Turkey	1 inf coy	367
France	1 armd cav sqn, 1 log coy	316
Slovenia	2 mot inf coy	303
Poland	1 inf coy	228
Switzerland	1 inf coy	223
Hungary	1 inf coy (Kosovo Tactical Manoeuvre elm)	201
Portugal	1 AB coy (Kosovo Tactical Manoeuvre elm)	173
Morocco	1 inf coy	169
Ukraine	1 inf coy	163
Greece	1 mech inf coy	120
Romania		61

Contributor	SERBIA (KOSOVO) (continued)
Sweden	52
Armenia	36
Denmark	36
Croatia	22
Luxembourg	22
Finland	21
Albania	14
Ireland	12
Bulgaria	11
Czech Republic	7
Netherlands	7
Canada	5
Norway	4
Estonia	2
Lithuania	1
United Kingdom	1
TOTAL	**4,867**

Location	MEDITERRANEAN SEA
Operation	*Active Endeavour*
Primary Organisation	NATO
Mission	Monitor martitime traffic to help deter, defend, disrupt and protect against terrorist activity. (Standing NATO Maritime Group 2)
Contributor	**Forces:**
Germany	1 DDGHM
Italy	1 FFGHM
Spain	1 DDGHM
Turkey	1 FFGHM

Russia and Eurasia

Location	MOLDOVA
Operation	*Trans-dniester Peacekeeping Force*
Primary Organisation	Russia/Moldova/Ukraine
Mission	Peacekeeping operations in the Trans-dniester region under the terms of the 1992 ceasefire agreement, with the aim of contributing to a negotiated settlement between the two sides.
Contributor	**Obs/Troops**
Moldova	400
Russia	350
Ukraine	10
TOTAL	**760**

Table 12 **Non-UN Deployments 2013–2014**

Asia

Location	AFGHANISTAN	
Operation	ISAF/*Operation Enduring Freedom – Afghanistan* (OEF-A)	
Primary Organisation	NATO/United States	
Mission	Counter-insurgency and counter-narcotics operations; training and support for the Afghan National Army; combat operations against al-Qaeda; Afghan security forces training.	
Contributor	**Forces by role (where known)**	**Total:**
United States	1 corps HQ, 2 div HQ, 1 ABCT, 2 SBCT, 5 IBCT, 1 Air Aslt IBCT, 2 cbt avn bde, 1 USMC MEF HQ	67,000
United Kingdom	1 armd bde HQ with (1 armd recce regt, 1 armd regt, 4 inf bn, 1 arty regt, 1 engr regt)	7,700
Germany	1 div HQ, 2 inf BG	4,400
Italy	1 mech inf bde HQ, 1 mech inf regt, 1 para regt	2,825
Georgia	2 inf bn	1,561
Poland	1 air cav bde with (1 inf BG)	1,177
Romania	1 inf bn	1,077
Turkey	1 inf bde HQ, 1 inf bn	1,036
Australia	1 inf bn	1,031
Canada	1 inf bn (trg)	950
Spain		856
Jordan	1 ranger bn	720
Bulgaria	1 mech inf coy	416
Netherlands		400
Hungary	1 lt inf coy	354
Denmark	1 mech inf BG	317
France		266
Sweden		259
Lithuania		240
Slovakia		199
Czech Republic		182
Croatia		181
Belgium		180
Portugal		165
Estonia	1 mech inf coy, 1 mor det	160
Macedonia (FYROM)		158
Latvia		141
Armenia		131
Norway		111
Albania	1 inf coy	105
Finland		100
Azerbaijan	1 engr coy	94
Bosnia-Herzegovina		79
Slovenia		60
Tonga		55
Korea, Republic of		50
Mongolia		40
UAE		35
Montenegro		27
Ukraine		26
El Salvador		24
New Zealand		11
Luxembourg		10
Ireland		7
Austria		3

Contributor	AFGHANISTAN (continued)	
Greece		3
Malaysia		2
TOTAL		**94,924**

Location	NORTH/SOUTH KOREA	
Operation	NNSC	
Mission	Monitor the ceasefire between North and South Korea.	
Contributor		**Total:**
Sweden		5
Switzerland		5
TOTAL		**10**

Middle East and North Africa

Location	EGYPT	
Operation	MFO	
Mission	Supervising implementation of the security provisions of the Egyptian–Israeli peace treaty.	
Contributor	**Forces by role (where known)**	**Total:**
United States	1 inf bn, 1 spt bn	693
Colombia	1 inf bn	354
Fiji	1 inf bn	338
Italy	3 Coastal Patrol unit	78
Uruguay	1 engr/tpt unit	58
Hungary	1 MP unit	42
Canada		28
New Zealand	1 trg unit, 1 tpt unit	28
Australia		25
Czech Republic		3
Norway		3
France		2
TOTAL		**1,652**

Location	ARABIAN SEA
Operation	CTF-150
Primary Organisation	Combined Maritime Forces
Mission	Maritime Security & Counter Terrorism operations in the Arabian Sea.
Contributor	**Forces by role**
Canada	1 FFGHM
France	1 FFGHM
United Kingdom	1 FFGHM

Location	ARABIAN SEA & GULF OF ADEN
Operation	CTF-151
Primary Organisation	Combined Maritime Forces
Mission	Anti-piracy operations off the coast of Somalia.
Contributor	**Forces by role**
Korea, Republic of	1 DDGHM
Australia	1 FFGHM
Pakistan	1 FFGHM
Turkey	1 FFGHM

Table 12 **Non-UN Deployments 2013–2014**

Location:	GULF OF ADEN & INDIAN OCEAN
Operation:	*Operation Atalanta*
Primary Organisation:	EU
Mission:	Maritime Security Operations off the coast of Somalia.
Contributor	**Forces by role**
Germany	1 FFGHM, 1 P-3C
Italy	1 FFGHM
Spain	1 PSO, 1 P-3A
Netherlands	1 LPD
United Kingdom	1 LSD

Location:	GULF OF ADEN & SOMALI BASIN
Operation:	*Operation Ocean Shield*
Primary Organisation:	NATO
Mission:	Anti-piracy operations off the coast of Somalia. (Standing NATO Maritime Group 1)
Contributor	**Forces by role**
Norway	1 FFGHM
Ukraine	1 FFHM
United States	1 FFH
Denmark	1 CL-604 MPA

Location:	PERSIAN GULF
Operation:	CTF-152
Primary Organisation:	Combined Maritime Forces
Mission:	Counter-proliferation and maritime infrastructure protection
Contributor	**Forces by role**
United States	6 MCO, 1 AFSB
United Kingdom	2 MCO, 2 MHC

Sub-Saharan Africa

Country	CENTRAL AFRICAN REPUBLIC
Operation:	AFISM-CAR
Primary Organisation:	AU
Mission:	Provide security; protect civilians; contribute to the national reconciliation process; facilitate political dialogue.
Contributor:	**Total:**
Chad	800
Cameroon	500
Congo	500
Gabon	500
Equatorial Guinea	200
TOTAL	**2,500**

Location:	DEMOCRATIC REPUBLIC OF THE CONGO
Operation:	EUSEC RD CONGO
Primary Organisation:	EU
Mission:	Provide advice and assistance on defence reform; assist the authorities in setting up a defence apparatus capable of guaranteeing the security of the Congolese people; promotion of democratic standards, human rights and the rule of law; promotion of the principles of good governance and transparency; Congolese Army reform.
Contributor:	**Total:**
France	7
Belgium	4
Denmark	3

Contributor	D.R. CONGO (continued)
Germany	3
Netherlands	3
Romania	3
United Kingdom	3
Hungary	2
Portugal	2
Austria	1
Italy	1
Luxembourg	1
Sweden	1
TOTAL	**34**

Location:	GUINEA-BISSAU
Operation:	ECOMIB
Primary Organisation:	ECOWAS
Mission:	Provide security to state institutions; support the government transition process.
Contributor:	**Total:**
Senegal	200
Nigeria	160
TOTAL	**360**

Location:	MALI
Operation:	EUTM Mali
Primary Organisation:	EU
Mission:	Train and advise Mali's armed forces; restore the military capacity of Mali's forces.
Contributor:	**Total:**
France	207
Germany	73
Spain	59
United Kingdom	40
Czech Republic	38
Belgium	34
Poland	20
Sweden	16
Hungary	13
Finland	10
Austria	8
Estonia	8
Ireland	8
Italy	7
Slovenia	3
Latvia	2
Lithuania	2
Luxembourg	1
Portugal	1
Romania	1
TOTAL	**551**

Table 12 **Non-UN Deployments 2013–2014**

Location	SOMALIA	
Operation	AMISOM	
Primary Organisation	AU	
Mission	Support the Somali government's efforts to stabilise the political and security situation; assist implementation of the National Security Stabilization Programme; facilitate the provision of humanitarian assistance.	
Contributor	**Forces (where known):**	**Total:**
Uganda	7 inf bn	6,223
Burundi	6 inf bn	5,432
Kenya	3 inf bn	3,664
Djibouti	1 inf bn	1,000
Sierra Leone	1 inf bn	850
TOTAL		**17,169**

Location	UGANDA
Operation	EUTM Somalia
Primary Organisation	EU
Mission	Strengthen the Somali government and institutions by training members of the Somali National Armed Forces.
Contributor	**Total:**
France	23
Italy	22
Spain	16
Germany	11
Ireland	10
Belgium	6
Finland	6
Portugal	5
Hungary	4
Malta	4
Sweden	4
United Kingdom	2
TOTAL	**113**

Table 13 **International Comparisons of Defence Expenditure and Military Personnel**

	Defence Spending current US$ m			Defence Spending per capita (current US$)			Defence Spending % of GDP			Number in Armed Forces (000)	Estimated Reservists (000)	Paramilitary (000)
	2011	2012	2013	2011	2012	2013	2011	2012	2013	2014	2014	2014
North America												
Canada	20,081	18,445	16,389	590	538	474	1.15	1.04	0.89	66	31	0
United States	687,000	655,388	600,400	2,205	2,088	1,896	4.56	4.19	3.70	1,492	844	0
Total	**707,081**	**673,833**	**616,789**	**2,046**	**1,935**	**1,756**	**4.19**	**3.85**	**3.41**	**1,558**	**875**	**0**
Europe												
Albania[b]	195	185	182	65	62	61	1.51	1.49	1.36	14	0	1
Austria[a]	3,433	3,232	3,232	418	393	393	0.82	0.83	0.76	23	171	0
Belgium[a]	5,546	5,266	5,294	532	504	507	1.08	1.10	1.04	31	7	0
Bosnia-Herzegovina	246	231	n.k.	63	60	n.k.	1.36	1.40	n.k.	11	0	0
Bulgaria[b]	720	723	751	102	103	108	1.34	1.42	1.38	31	303	16
Croatia	776	827	813	173	184	182	1.24	1.44	1.35	17	0	3
Cyprus	511	450	460	456	396	398	2.07	2.01	2.11	12	50	1
Czech Republic[a]	2,513	2,120	2,179	247	208	214	1.17	1.10	1.07	24	0	3
Denmark[a]	4,519	4,422	4,509	817	798	812	1.36	1.43	1.37	17	54	0
Estonia[a]	390	437	480	304	343	379	1.75	2.04	1.99	6	30	0
Finland	3,979	3,601	3,814	757	684	724	1.51	1.46	1.44	22	354	3
France	53,475	50,283	52,352	819	766	794	1.92	1.95	1.91	222	30	103
Germany[a]	46,022	40,994	44,201	565	504	545	1.28	1.22	1.23	186	40	0
Greece[a]	8,520	4,929	5,681	792	458	527	2.85	1.93	2.33	143	217	4
Hungary[b]	1,330	1,323	1,100	133	133	111	0.95	1.03	0.83	27	44	12
Iceland	n.a.	n.a.	n.a.	n.a.	n.a.	n.a.	n.a.	n.a.	n.a.	0	0	0
Ireland[b]	1,320	1,149	1,197	283	243	251	0.60	0.56	0.54	9	5	0
Italy[a]	30,251	26,496	25,229	496	433	410	1.38	1.34	1.22	176	18	184
Latvia[a]	297	256	300	135	117	138	1.05	0.94	0.96	5	8	0
Lithuania[b]	351	329	355	99	93	101	0.82	0.80	0.77	12	7	12
Luxembourg	279	267	249	555	524	484	0.47	0.48	0.41	1	0	1
Macedonia (FYROM)	130	129	n.k.	63	62	n.k.	1.22	1.27	n.k.	8	5	0
Malta[b]	56	50	60	137	122	145	0.63	0.59	0.64	2	0	0
Montenegro[b]	80	52	54	120	79	82	1.76	1.20	1.17	2	0	10
Netherlands[a]	11,659	10,376	10,350	700	620	616	1.39	1.35	1.28	37	3	6

Table 13 **International Comparisons of Defence Expenditure and Military Personnel**

	Defence Spending current US$ m			Defence Spending per capita (current US$)			Defence Spending % of GDP			Number in Armed Forces (000)	Estimated Reservists (000)	Paramilitary (000)
	2011	2012	2013	2011	2012	2013	2011	2012	2013	2014	2014	2014
Norway	7,003	7,143	7,523	1,493	1,518	1,593	1.44	1.43	1.40	26	46	0
Poland[b]	9,227	8,543	9,829	240	222	256	1.79	1.82	1.91	99	0	73
Portugal	2,878	2,640	2,773	267	245	257	1.21	1.25	1.27	43	212	48
Romania[a]	2,315	2,211	2,475	106	101	114	1.22	1.29	1.32	71	45	80
Serbia	972	841	681	133	116	94	2.24	2.26	1.59	28	50	0
Slovakia[a]	1,062	1,016	995	194	185	181	1.10	1.11	1.01	16	0	0
Slovenia[b]	665	509	474	333	255	238	1.32	1.12	1.02	8	2	6
Spain[a]	15,163	13,927	11,593	324	296	245	1.02	1.04	0.84	135	14	80
Sweden[b]	6,160	6,022	6,633	678	661	727	1.13	1.16	1.15	15	0	1
Switzerland[b]	5,431	4,591	5,038	692	579	630	0.82	0.74	0.78	23	161	0
Turkey[f]	10,146	10,167	10,742	129	127	133	1.31	1.30	1.26	511	379	102
United Kingdom	59,978	61,274	57,035	957	972	900	2.47	2.52	2.35	169	79	0
Total**	**296,192**	**276,233**	**279,045**	**481**	**447**	**450**	**1.51**	**1.48**	**1.43**	**2,182**	**2,333**	**748**
Russia and Eurasia												
Armenia	396	402	447	133	135	150	3.86	3.81	4.33	45	210	4
Azerbaijan	1,679	1,761	2,003	179	186	209	2.59	2.48	2.59	67	300	15
Belarus	422	552	n.k.	44	57	n.k.	0.77	0.95	n.k.	48	290	110
Georgia	421	394	389	92	86	85	2.94	2.50	2.29	21	0	12
Kazakhstan	1,766	2,280	2,318	102	130	131	0.95	1.14	1.08	39	0	32
Kyrgyzstan	102	105	102	19	19	18	1.72	1.70	1.41	11	0	10
Moldova[a]	21	22	24	6	6	7	0.30	0.29	0.30	5	58	2
Russia	51,594	58,765	68,163	362	412	478	2.79	3.01	3.08	845	2,000	519
Tajikistan	146	170	189	19	22	24	2.24	2.34	2.21	9	0	8
Turkmenistan[*]	n.k.	539	n.k.	n.k.	107	n.k.	n.k.	1.6	n.k.	22	0	0
Ukraine	1,657	2,050	2,418	37	46	54	1.00	1.14	1.33	130	1,000	85
Uzbekistan[*]	1,422	n.k.	n.k.	51	n.k.	n.k.	3	n.k.	n.k.	48	0	20
Total**	**59,833**	**68,176**	**78,076**	**213**	**242**	**253**	**2.40**	**2.56**	**2.69**	**1,289**	**3,857**	**816**
Asia												
Afghanistan[c]	1,822	2,077	2,898	61	68	93	9.95	10.46	13.81	186	0	152
Australia	25,444	28,269	25,967	1,169	1,284	1,166	1.71	1.83	1.63	56	29	0

Table 13 **International Comparisons of Defence Expenditure and Military Personnel**

	Defence Spending current US$ m			Defence Spending per capita (current US$)			Defence Spending % of GDP			Number in Armed Forces (000)	Estimated Reservists (000)	Paramilitary (000)
	2011	2012	2013	2011	2012	2013	2011	2012	2013	2014	2014	2014
Bangladesh	1,478	1,537	1,652	9	10	10	1.30	1.29	1.22	157	0	64
Brunei	409	411	416	1,017	1,005	1,002	2.50	2.44	2.53	7	1	2
Cambodia[c]	308	346	394	21	23	26	2.39	2.43	2.51	124	0	67
China	90,221	102,643	112,173	67	76	83	1.24	1.24	1.24	2,333	510	660
Fiji	4,693	62	58	5,314	70	65	123.62	1.58	1.39	4	6	0
India[b]	36,115	33,404	36,297	30	28	30	1.98	1.72	1.84	1,325	1,155	1,404
Indonesia	5,826	6,524	8,366	24	26	33	0.69	0.73	0.88	396	400	281
Japan[a]	59,834	59,077	50,977	469	464	401	1.02	0.99	0.99	247	56	13
Korea, DPR of	n.k.	n.k.	n.k.	n.k.	n.k.	n.k.	n.k.	n.k.	n.k.	1,190	600	189
Korea, Republic of	28,335	29,256	31,846	581	599	651	2.54	2.54	2.53	655	4,500	5
Laos	19	20	21	3	3	3	0.23	0.21	0.20	29	0	100
Malaysia	4,693	4,440	5,000	163	152	169	1.63	1.45	1.52	109	52	25
Mongolia	81	114	133	26	36	41	0.93	1.15	1.10	10	137	7
Myanmar	2,415	2,228	2,400	45	41	44	4.69	4.12	4.18	406	0	107
Nepal	269	281	238	9	9	8	1.42	1.45	1.17	96	0	62
New Zealand	2,199	2,207	2,715	512	510	622	1.38	1.32	1.48	9	2	0
Pakistan	5,468	5,814	5,890	29	31	30	2.60	2.52	2.47	644	0	304
Papua New Guinea	77	76	84	12	12	13	0.61	0.50	0.48	2	0	0
Philippines[b]	1,642	1,762	2,205	16	17	21	0.73	0.73	0.78	125	131	41
Singapore	9,362	9,843	9,864	1,784	1,839	1,807	3.60	3.67	3.44	73	313	75
Sri Lanka	1,750	1,533	1,793	82	71	83	2.96	2.57	2.75	161	6	62
Taiwan	9,717	10,452	10,316	419	450	443	2.08	2.24	2.08	290	1,657	17
Thailand[b]	5,520	5,426	6,213	83	81	92	1.60	1.44	1.46	361	200	93
Timor-Leste	52	64	67	47	56	57	1.15	1.52	1.57	1	0	0
Vietnam	2,667	3,295	3,800	29	36	41	2.17	2.39	2.44	482	5,000	40
Total	**293,094**	**309,949**	**321,783**	**77**	**80**	**82**	**1.40**	**1.40**	**1.42**	**9,476**	**14,753**	**3,769**
Middle East and North Africa												
Algeria	8,662	9,324	9,957	236	250	261	4.38	4.51	4.73	130	150	187
Bahrain	943	1,018	1,394	777	816	1,088	3.65	3.84	4.96	8	0	11

Table 13 **International Comparisons of Defence Expenditure and Military Personnel**

	Defence Spending current US$ m			Defence Spending per capita (current US$)			Defence Spending % of GDP			Number in Armed Forces (000)	Estimated Reservists (000)	Paramilitary (000)
	2011	2012	2013	2011	2012	2013	2011	2012	2013	2014	2014	2014
Egypt	4,333	4,582	5,278	53	55	62	1.84	1.80	1.99	439	479	397
Iran	19,510	25,249	17,749	250	320	222	4.04	5.22	4.13	523	350	40
Iraq[c]	12,028	14,727	16,897	396	473	530	10.53	11.28	7.24	271	0	531
Israel	15,163	16,865	15,163	2,029	2,222	1,967	6.22	6.83	5.98	177	465	8
Jordan[e]	1,406	1,520	1,216	216	234	188	4.87	4.85	3.57	101	65	15
Kuwait	4,651	4,761	4,427	1,792	1,799	1,642	2.89	2.73	2.55	16	24	7
Lebanon	1,627	1,735	n.k.	393	419	n.k.	4.17	4.15	n.k.	60	0	20
Libya	n.k.	2,988	4,771	n.k.	532	795	n.k.	3.51	4.95	7	0	0
Mauritania	139	112	145	42	33	42	3	3	3	16	0	5
Morocco	3,343	3,408	3,730	105	105	114	3.37	3.51	3.48	196	150	50
Oman	4,291	6,723	9,246	1,417	2,176	2,931	5.90	8.41	11.73	43	0	4
Palestinian Territories	n.k.	n.k.	n.k.	n.k.	n.k.	n.k.	n.k.	n.k.	n.k.	0	0	56
Qatar*	3,476	n.k.	n.k.	1,880	n.k.	n.k.	2.00	n.k.	n.k.	12	0	0
Saudi Arabia	48,531	56,724	59,560	1,857	2,138	2,211	8.13	8.63	7.99	234	0	16
Syria*	n.k.	n.k.	n.k.	n.k.	n.k.	n.k.	n.k.	n.k.	n.k.	178	0	0
Tunisia	623	705	769	59	66	71	1	1.58	1.55	36	0	12
UAE*	9,320	n.k.	n.k.	1,810	n.k.	n.k.	2.73	n.k.	n.k.	51	0	0
Yemen, Republic of	1,343	1,633	1,812	56	66	71	3.98	4.49	4.65	67	0	71
Total**	**146,295**	**164,492**	**167,832**	**405**	**448**	**450**	**4.75**	**4.91**	**5.01**	**2,562**	**1,683**	**1,431**
Latin America and the Caribbean												
Antigua and Barbuda	29	28	26	329	317	286	2.59	2.40	2.09	0	0	0
Argentina[e]	4,067	4,858	5,104	97	115	120	0.91	1.02	1.02	73	0	31
Bahamas, The	50	55	64	161	174	201	0.65	0.67	0.77	1	0	0
Barbados	33	33	33	116	113	115	0.77	0.72	0.71	1	0	0
Belize	16	16	18	49	48	53	1.09	1.04	1.11	1	1	0
Bolivia	298	336	373	29	33	36	1.24	1.26	1.26	46	0	37
Brazil[a]	36,822	35,266	34,730	186	177	173	1.48	1.45	1.41	318	1,340	395
Chile[a]	4,254	4,274	4,594	251	250	267	1.71	1.59	1.61	61	40	45
Colombia[d]	5,626	6,206	7,016	126	137	153	1.72	1.70	1.81	281	62	159
Costa Rica	271	349	397	59	75	84	0.66	0.78	0.81	0	0	10

Table 13 **International Comparisons of Defence Expenditure and Military Personnel**

	Defence Spending current US$ m			Defence Spending per capita (current US$)			Defence Spending % of GDP			Number in Armed Forces (000)	Estimated Reservists (000)	Paramilitary (000)
	2011	2012	2013	2011	2012	2013	2011	2012	2013	2014	2014	2014
Cuba*	96	n.k.	n.k.	9	n.k.	n.k.	n.k.	n.k.	n.k.	49	39	27
Dominican Republic	342	363	378	34	36	37	0.61	0.61	0.63	46	0	15
Ecuador	1,506	1,509	n.k.	100	99	n.k.	2.27	2.13	n.k.	58	118	1
El Salvador	146	145	154	24	24	25	0.64	0.61	0.62	15	10	17
Guatemala	200	212	256	14	15	18	0.43	0.42	0.48	17	64	25
Guyana	32	33	35	44	44	48	1.26	1.18	1.17	1	1	0
Haiti	n.a.	n.a.	n.a.	n.a.	n.a.	n.a.	n.a.	n.a.	n.a.	0	0	0
Honduras[b]	141	151	177	17	18	21	0.81	0.83	0.93	12	60	8
Jamaica	139	139	129	49	48	44	0.96	0.91	0.83	3	1	0
Mexico	5,051	5,237	5,775	44	46	50	0.44	0.45	0.45	270	87	60
Nicaragua	54	66	85	9	11	15	0.74	0.84	0.76	12	0	0
Panama[c]	490	551	637	142	157	179	1.60	1.58	1.54	0	0	12
Paraguay	233	332	364	36	51	55	0.97	1.27	1.18	11	165	15
Peru	2,034	2,648	2,844	70	90	95	1.15	1.32	1.29	115	188	77
Suriname*	55	n.k.	n.k.	100	n.k.	n.k.	1.21	n.k.	n.k.	2	0	0
Trinidad and Tobago	379	446	400	309	364	326	1.68	1.87	1.49	4	0	0
Uruguay	484	460	445	146	139	134	1.04	0.93	0.86	25	0	1
Venezuela[g]	2,384	6,966	5,240	86	248	184	0.75	2.06	1.52	115	8	0
Total**	**66,685**	**70,837**	**70,944**	**114**	**120**	**119**	**1.18**	**1.23**	**1.18**	**1,538**	**2,183**	**933**
Sub-Saharan Africa												
Angola	3,622	4,147	6,049	206	230	326	3.47	3.61	4.82	107	0	10
Benin	74	78	86	8	8	9	1.01	1.04	1.04	7	0	3
Botswana	540	466	438	261	222	206	3.05	2.64	2.40	9	0	2
Burkina Faso	152	135	153	9	8	9	1.49	1.31	1.28	11	0	0
Burundi	63	62	64	6	6	6	2.68	2.46	2.46	20	0	31
Cameroon	348	355	393	18	18	19	1.36	1.45	1.40	14	0	9
Cape Verde	9	9	9	18	18	18	0.48	0.50	0.45	1	0	0
Central African Republic*	54	n.k.	n.k.	11	n.k.	n.k.	2.47	n.k.	n.k.	7	0	1
Chad*	177	202	n.k.	16	18	n.k.	1.89	2.08	n.k.	25	0	10
Congo*	290	325	n.k.	68	74	n.k.	2.01	2.36	n.k.	10	0	2

Table 13 **International Comparisons of Defence Expenditure and Military Personnel**

	Defence Spending current US$ m			Defence Spending per capita (current US$)			Defence Spending % of GDP			Number in Armed Forces (000)	Estimated Reservists (000)	Paramilitary (000)
	2011	2012	2013	2011	2012	2013	2011	2012	2013	2014	2014	2014
Côte d'Ivoire	587	635	751	27	29	34	2.44	2.61	2.65	n.k.	n.k.	n.k.
Democratic Republic of the Congo	221	232	416	3	3	6	1.41	1.31	2.15	134	0	0
Djibouti*	10	n.k.	n.k.	13	n.k.	n.k.	0.78	n.k.	n.k.	10	0	3
Equatorial Guinea*	8	n.k.	n.k.	12	n.k.	n.k.	0.04	n.k.	n.k.	1	0	0
Eritrea*	78	n.k.	n.k.	13	n.k.	n.k.	2.99	n.k.	n.k.	202	120	0
Ethiopia	273	254	351	3	3	4	0.86	0.61	0.76	138	0	0
Gabon	266	222	263	169	138	161	1.67	1.32	1.36	5	0	2
Gambia*	6	n.k.	n.k.	4	n.k.	n.k.	0.66	n.k.	n.k.	1	0	0
Ghana	128	111	291	5	5	12	0.33	0.28	0.68	16	0	0
Guinea*	42	n.k.	n.k.	4	n.k.	n.k.	0.81	n.k.	n.k.	10	0	3
Guinea-Bissau	20	26	n.k.	13	16	n.k.	2.08	2.89	n.k.	4	0	2
Kenya	629	930	975	15	22	22	1.85	2.22	2.10	24	0	5
Lesotho	50	55	54	26	29	28	2.00	2.12	2.06	2	0	0
Liberia	13	n.k.	n.k.	3	n.k.	n.k.	0.82	n.k.	n.k.	2	0	0
Madagascar	72	69	72	3	3	3	0.73	0.69	0.67	14	0	8
Malawi	43	32	25	3	2	2	0.76	0.71	0.67	5	0	2
Mali	226	213	301	15	14	19	2.13	2.22	2.64	3	0	5
Mauritius	62	71	83	47	54	63	0.55	0.60	0.69	0	0	3
Mozambique	70	n.k.	75	3	n.k.	3	0.55	n.k.	0.47	11	0	0
Namibia	460	381	458	214	176	210	3.67	3.14	3.56	9	0	6
Niger	63	70	n.k.	4	4	n.k.	1.04	1.07	n.k.	5	0	5
Nigeria	2,249	2,033	2,143	14	12	12	0.92	0.75	0.76	80	0	82
Rwanda	74	76	82	6	6	7	1.16	1.09	1.06	33	0	2
Senegal	253	189	231	20	15	17	1.75	1.35	1.61	14	0	5
Seychelles	n.a.	10	12	n.k.	110	127	n.k.	1.02	1.02	0	0	0
Sierra Leone	13	14	14	2	2	3	0.44	0.35	0.31	11	0	0
Somalia	n.k.	n.k.	n.k.	n.k.	n.k.	n.k.	n.k.	n.k.	n.k.	20	0	0
South Africa	5,290	5,069	4,848	108	104	100	1.29	1.30	1.29	62	15	0
South Sudan	533	819	714	53	77	64	3.05	7.16	5.27	210	0	0
Sudan	1,163	n.k.	1,516	35	n.k.	43	1.82	n.k.	3.00	244	0	20

Table 13 **International Comparisons of Defence Expenditure and Military Manpower**

	Defence Spending current US$ m			Defence Spending per capita (current US$)			Defence Spending % of GDP			Number in Armed Forces (000)	Estimated Reservists (000)	Paramilitary (000)
	2011	2012	2013	2011	2012	2013	2011	2012	2013	2014	2014	2014
Tanzania	285	305	327	6	7	7	1.19	1.09	1.03	27	80	1
Togo	59	62	72	9	9	10	1.60	1.71	1.75	9	0	1
Uganda	243	374	342	7	11	10	1.40	1.83	1.60	45	10	2
Zambia	306	321	390	23	23	27	1.59	1.55	1.69	15	3	1
Zimbabwe	198	318	356	16	25	27	2.10	2.95	3.24	29	0	22
Total**	**19,246**	**20,541**	**23,121**	**22**	**23**	**25**	**1.49**	**1.54**	**1.68**	**1,607**	**228**	**246**
Summary												
North America	**707,081**	**673,833**	**616,789**	**2,046**	**1,935**	**1,756**	**4.19**	**3.85**	**3.41**	**1,558**	**875**	**0**
Europe	**296,192**	**276,233**	**279,045**	**481**	**447**	**450**	**1.51**	**1.48**	**1.43**	**2,182**	**2,333**	**748**
Russia and Eurasia	**59,833**	**68,176**	**78,076**	**213**	**242**	**253**	**2.40**	**2.56**	**2.69**	**1,289**	**2,000**	**519**
Asia	**293,094**	**309,949**	**321,783**	**77**	**80**	**82**	**1.40**	**1.40**	**1.42**	**9,476**	**14,753**	**3,769**
Middle East and North Africa	**146,295**	**164,492**	**167,832**	**405**	**448**	**450**	**4.75**	**4.91**	**5.01**	**2,562**	**1,683**	**1,431**
Latin America and the Carribean	**66,685**	**70,837**	**70,944**	**114**	**120**	**119**	**1.18**	**1.23**	**1.18**	**1,538**	**2,183**	**933**
Sub-Saharan Africa	**19,246**	**20,541**	**23,121**	**22**	**23**	**25**	**1.49**	**1.54**	**1.68**	**1,607**	**228**	**246**
Global totals	**1,591,104**	**1,587,578**	**1,557,590**	**230**	**227**	**219**	**2.27**	**2.22**	**2.11**	**20,213**	**24,054**	**7,645**

* Estimates
** Totals include defence spending estimates for states where insufficient official information is available, in order to enable approximate comparisons of regional defence spending between years.
[a] Includes military pensions
[b] Excludes military pensions
[c] Includes public security expenditure
[d] Excludes decentralised expenditures & expenditure on National Police
[e] Excludes expenditure on public order and safety
[f] Excludes allocations for arms procurement, the gendarmerie and coast guard.
[g] Includes estimated value of Russia credit provided for arms procurement, excludes defence funding derived from the National Development Fund (FONDEN). Current US dollar defence spending figures should be treated with caution when compared to spending in previous years, due to effects of currency revaluation in recent years.

PART TWO

Explanatory Notes

The Military Balance is updated each year to provide an assessment of the armed forces and defence expenditures of 171 countries and territories. Each edition contributes to the provision of a unique compilation of data and information, enabling the reader to discern trends by studying editions as far back as 1959. The data in the current edition is accurate according to IISS assessments as at November 2013, unless specified. Inclusion of a territory, country or state in *The Military Balance* does not imply legal recognition or indicate support for any government.

GENERAL ARRANGEMENT AND CONTENTS

The introduction contains analysis of global defence issues and a summary of some themes in the book.

Part I contains essays that analyse important defence trends or debates, followed by the Comparative Defence Statistics graphics section, with features on defence economics, defence industry and military domains.

Regional chapters begin with an overview of the military issues facing the region, trends observed during the preceding year and regional defence economics, followed for select states by country-specific analysis of defence policy and capability issues, and defence economics. These are followed by military capability and defence economics data for regional countries, in alphabetical order. Selected Arms Procurements and Deliveries tables complete each region.

The Chart of Conflict is updated for 2013 to show data on recent and current armed conflicts. The additional theme is women in armed conflict.

USING THE MILITARY BALANCE

The country entries assess personnel strengths, organisation and equipment holdings of the world's armed forces. Force strength and equipment inventory data are based on the most accurate data available, or on the best estimate that can be made. In estimating a country's total capabilities, old equipment may be counted where it is considered that it may still be deployable.

The data presented reflect judgements based on information available to the IISS at the time the book is compiled. Where information differs from previous editions, this is mainly because of changes in national forces, but it is sometimes because the IISS has reassessed the evidence supporting past entries. Given this, care must be taken in constructing time-series comparisons from information given in successive editions.

ABBREVIATIONS AND DEFINITIONS

The large quantity of data in *The Military Balance* has been compressed into a portable volume by the use of abbreviations, a list of which appears on page 501.

The qualification 'some' is used to indicate that while the IISS assesses that a country maintains a capability, a precise inventory is unavailable at time of press. 'About' means the total could be higher than given. In financial data, '$' refers to US dollars unless otherwise stated; billion (bn) signifies 1,000 million (m).

Within the country entries, a number of caveats are employed: the * symbol is used to denote aircraft counted by the IISS as combat capable; † is used when the IISS assesses that the serviceability of equipment is in doubt; and ‡ is used to denote equipment judged obsolescent (weapons whose basic design is more than four decades old and which have not been significantly upgraded within the past decade); these latter two qualitative judgements should not be taken to imply that such equipment cannot be used.

COUNTRY ENTRIES

Information on each country is shown in a standard format, although the differing availability of information and differences in nomenclature result in some variations. Country entries include economic, demographic and military data. Population figures are based on demographic statistics taken from the US Census Bureau. Data on ethnic and religious minorities are also provided in some country entries. Military data includes manpower, length of conscript service where relevant, outline organisation, number of formations and units, and an inventory of the major equipment of each service. Details of national forces stationed abroad and of foreign forces stationed within the given country are also provided.

ARMS PROCUREMENTS AND DELIVERIES

Tables at the end of the regional texts show selected arms procurements (contracts and, in selected cases, major development programmes that may not yet be at contract stage) and deliveries listed by country buyer, together with additional information including, if known, the country supplier, cost, prime contractor and the date on which the first delivery was due to be made. While every effort has been made to ensure accuracy, some transactions may not be fulfilled or may differ – for instance in quantity – from those reported. The information is arranged in the following order: strategic systems; land; sea; air.

DEFENCE ECONOMICS

Country entries include defence expenditures, selected economic performance indicators and demographic aggregates. There are also international comparisons of defence expenditure and military manpower, giving expenditure figures for the past three years in per capita terms and as a % of GDP. The aim is to provide an accurate measure of military expenditure and the allocation of economic resources to defence. All country entries are subject to revision each year as new information, particularly regarding defence expenditure, becomes available. The information is necessarily selective.

Individual country entries show economic performance over the past two years, and current demographic data. Where these data are unavailable, information from the last available year is provided. Where possible, official defence budgets for the current and previous two years are shown, as well as an estimate of actual defence expenditures for those countries where true defence expenditure is thought to be higher than official budget figures suggest. Estimates of actual defence expenditure, however, are only made for those countries where there are sufficient data to justify such a measurement. Therefore, there will be several countries listed in *The Military Balance* for which only an official defence budget figure is provided but where, in reality, true defence related expenditure is almost certainly higher.

All financial data in the country entries are shown both in national currency and US dollars at current year – not constant – prices. US-dollar conversions are generally, but not invariably, calculated from the exchange rates listed in the entry. In some cases a US-dollar purchasing power parity (PPP) rate is used in preference to official or market exchange rates and this is indicated in each case.

Definitions of terms

Despite efforts by NATO and the UN to develop a standardised definition of military expenditure, many countries prefer to use their own definitions (which are often not made public). In order to present a comprehensive picture, *The Military Balance* lists three different measures of military-related spending data.

- For most countries, an official defence-budget figure is provided.
- For those countries where other military-related outlays, over and above the defence budget, are known or can be reasonably estimated, an additional measurement referred to as defence expenditure is also provided. Defence expenditure figures will naturally be higher than official budget figures, depending on the range of additional factors included.
- For NATO countries, an official defence-budget figure as well as a measure of defence expenditure (calculated using NATO's definition) is quoted.

NATO's definition of military expenditure, the most comprehensive, is defined as the cash outlays of central or federal governments to meet the costs of national armed forces. The term 'armed forces' includes strategic, land, naval, air, command, administration and support forces. It also includes other forces if these forces are trained, structured and equipped to support defence forces and are realistically deployable. Defence expenditures are reported in four categories: Operating Costs, Procurement and Construction, Research and Development (R&D) and Other Expenditure. Operating Costs include salaries and pensions for military and civilian personnel; the cost of maintaining and training units, service organisations, headquarters and support elements; and the cost of servicing and repairing military equipment and infrastructure. Procurement and Construction expenditure covers national equipment and infrastructure spending, as well as common infrastructure programmes. R&D is defence expenditure up to the point at which new equipment can be put in service, regardless of whether new equipment is actually procured. Foreign Military Aid (FMA) contributions are also noted.

For many non-NATO countries the issue of transparency in reporting military budgets is fundamental. Not every UN member state reports defence-budget data (even fewer real defence expenditures) to their electorates, the UN, the IMF or other multinational organisations. In the case of governments with a proven record of transparency, official figures generally conform to the standardised definition of defence budgeting, as adopted by the UN, and consistency problems are not usually a major issue. The IISS cites official defence budgets as reported by either national governments, the UN, the OSCE or the IMF.

For those countries where the official defence-budget figure is considered to be an incomplete measure of total military-related spending, and appropriate additional data are available, the IISS will use data from a variety of sources to arrive at a more accurate estimate of true defence expenditure. The most frequent instances of budgetary manipulation or falsification typically involve equipment procurement, R&D, defence-industrial investment, covert weapons programmes, pensions for retired military and civilian personnel, paramilitary forces and non-budgetary sources of revenue for the military arising from ownership of industrial, property and land assets.

Percentage changes in defence spending are referred to in either nominal or real terms. Nominal terms relate to the percentage change in numerical spending figures, and do not account for the impact of price changes (i.e. inflation) on defence spending. By contrast, real terms account for inflationary effects, and may thus be considered a more accurate representation of change over time.

The principal sources for national economic statistics cited in the country entries are the IMF, the Organisation for Economic Cooperation and Development, the World Bank and three regional banks (the Inter-American, Asian and African Development Banks). For some countries, basic economic data are difficult to obtain. The Gross Domestic Product (GDP) figures are nominal (current) values at market prices. GDP growth is real, not nominal, growth, and inflation is the year-on-year change in consumer prices.

Calculating exchange rates

Typically, but not invariably, the exchange rates shown in the country entries are also used to calculate GDP and defence budget and expenditure dollar conversions. Where they are not used, it is because the use of exchange rate dollar conversions can misrepresent both GDP and defence expenditure. For some countries, PPP rather than market exchange rates are sometimes used for dollar conversions of both GDP and defence expenditures. Where PPP is used, it is annotated accordingly.

The arguments for using PPP are strongest for Russia and China. Both the UN and IMF have issued caveats concerning the reliability of official economic statistics on transitional economies, particularly those of Russia, some Eastern European and Central Asian countries. Non-reporting, lags in the publication of current statistics and frequent revisions of recent data (not always accompanied by timely revision of previously published figures in the same series) pose transparency and consistency problems. Another problem arises with certain transitional economies whose productive capabilities are similar to those of developed economies, but where cost and price structures are often much lower than world levels. No specific PPP rate exists for the military sector, and its use for this purpose should be treated with caution. Furthermore, there is no definitive guide as to which elements of military spending should be calculated using the limited PPP rates available. The figures presented here are only intended to illustrate a range of possible outcomes depending on which input variables are used.

GENERAL DEFENCE DATA

Personnel

The 'Active' total comprises all servicemen and women on full-time duty (including conscripts and long-term assignments from the Reserves). When a gendarmerie or equivalent is under control of the defence ministry, they may be included in the active total. Only the length of conscript liability is shown; where service is voluntary there is no entry. 'Reserve' describes formations and units not fully manned or operational in peacetime, but which can be mobilised by recalling reservists in an emergency. Some countries have more than one category of 'Reserves', often kept at varying degrees of readiness. Where possible, these differences are denoted using the national descriptive title, but always under the heading of 'Reserves' to distinguish them from full-time active forces. All personnel figures are rounded to the nearest 50, except for organisations with under 500 personnel, where figures are rounded to the nearest 10.

Other forces

Many countries maintain forces whose training, organisation, equipment and control suggest they may be used to support or replace regular military forces; these are called 'paramilitary'. They include some forces that may have a constabulary role. These are detailed after the military forces of each country, but their manpower is not normally included in the totals at the start of each entry.

Non-state groups

The Military Balance includes some detail on selected non-state groups that pose a militarily significant challenge to state and international security. This information appears in the essays and relevant regional chapters. More detailed information may be obtained from the IISS Armed Conflict Database (*http://acd.iiss.org*).

Cyber

The Military Balance includes detail on selected national cyber capacities, particularly those under the control of, or designed to fulfil the requirements of, defence organisations. Capabilities are not assessed quantitatively. Rather, national organisations, legislation, national security strategies etc. are noted, where appropriate, in an indication of the level of effort states are directing in this area. Generally, civil organisations are not traced here, though in some cases these organisations could have dual civil–military roles.

Units and formation strength

Company	100–200
Battalion	500–1,000
Brigade	3,000–5,000
Division	15,000–20,000
Corps or Army	50,000–100,000

Forces by role and equipment by type

Quantities are shown by function (according to each nation's employment) and type, and represent what are believed to be total holdings, including active and reserve operational and training units. Inventory totals for missile systems relate to launchers and not to missiles. Equipment held 'in store' is not counted in the main inventory totals.

Deployments

The Military Balance mainly lists permanent bases and operational deployments including peacekeeping operations, which are often discussed in the text for each regional section. Information in the country data files details deployments of troops and military observers and, where available, the role and equipment of deployed units. A table of UN and Non-UN Deployments is found on p. 476.

Training activity

Selected exercises, which involve two or more states and are designed to improve interoperability or test new doctrine, forces or equipment, are detailed in tables on p. 472. (Exceptions may be made for particularly important exercises held by single states which indicate important capability or equipment developments.)

LAND FORCES

To make international comparison easier and more consistent, *The Military Balance* categorises forces by role and translates national military terminology for unit and formation sizes. Typical manpower strength, equipment holdings and organisation of formations such as brigades and divisions vary from country to country. In addition some unit terms, such as 'regiment', 'squadron', 'battery' and 'troop' can refer to significantly different unit sizes in different countries. Unless otherwise stated these terms should be assumed to reflect standard British usage where they occur.

NAVAL FORCES

Classifying naval vessels according to role is complex. A post-war consensus on primary surface combatants revolved around a distinction between independently operating cruisers, air-defence escorts (destroyers) and anti-submarine-warfare escorts (frigates). However, new ships are increasingly performing a range of roles. For this reason, *The Military Balance* has drawn up a classification system based on full-load displacement (FLD) rather than a role classification system. These definitions will not necessarily conform to national designations.

AIR FORCES

Aircraft listed as combat capable are assessed as being equipped to deliver air-to-air or air-to-surface ordnance. The definition includes aircraft designated by type as bomber, fighter, fighter ground attack, ground attack, and anti-submarine warfare. Other aircraft considered to be combat capable are marked with an asterisk (*). Operational groupings of air forces are shown where known. Typical squadron aircraft strengths can vary both between aircraft types and from country to country.

When assessing missile ranges, *The Military Balance* uses the following range indicators: Short-Range Ballistic Missile (SRBM), less than 1,000km; Medium-Range Ballistic Missile (MRBM): 1,000–3,000km; Intermediate-Range Ballistic Missiles (IRBM): 3,000–5,000km; Intercontinental Ballistic Missiles (ICBM): over 5,000km.

ATTRIBUTION AND ACKNOWLEDGEMENTS

The International Institute for Strategic Studies owes no allegiance to any government, group of governments, or any political or other organisation. Its assessments are its own, based on the material available to it from a wide variety of sources. The cooperation of governments of all listed countries has been sought and, in many cases, received. However, some data in *The Military Balance* are estimates. Care is taken to ensure that this data is as accurate and free from bias as possible. The Institute owes a considerable debt to a number of its own members, consultants and all those who help compile and check material. The Director-General and Chief Executive and staff of the Institute assume full responsibility for the data and judgements in this book. Comments and suggestions on the data and textual material contained within the book, as well as on the style and presentation of data, are welcomed and should be communicated to the Editor of *The Military Balance* at: IISS, 13–15 Arundel Street, London WC2R 3DX, UK, email: *milbal@iiss.org*. Copyright on all information in *The Military Balance* belongs strictly to the IISS. Application to reproduce limited amounts of data may be made to the publisher: Taylor & Francis, 4 Park Square, Milton Park, Abingdon, Oxon, OX14 4RN. Email: *society.permissions@tandf.co.uk*. Unauthorised use of data from *The Military Balance* will be subject to legal action.

Principal Land Definitions

Forces by role

Command: free-standing, deployable formation HQs.

Special Forces (SF): elite units specially trained and equipped for unconventional warfare and operations in enemy-controlled territory. Many are employed in counter-terrorist roles.

Manoeuvre: combat units and formations capable of maneouvering include:

Reconnaissance: combat units and formations whose primary purpose is to gain information.

Armoured: armoured formations are principally equipped with main battle tanks (MBTs) and heavy armoured infantry fighting vehicles (AIFVs) to provide mounted close combat capability.

Mechanised: mechanised formations use lighter armoured vehicles than armoured formations, and fewer, if any, tanks. They have less mounted firepower and protection, but can usually deploy more infantry than armoured formations.

Light: light formations may have few, if any, organic armoured vehicles. Some may be motorised and equipped with soft-skinned vehicles. Dismounted infantry constitute a primary capability.

Air Manoeuvre: formations and units trained and equipped for delivery by transport aircraft and/or helicopters. Some may have integral aviation assets.

Aviation: army units and formations organically equipped with helicopters and/or fixed-wing aircraft.

Amphibious: amphibious forces are trained and equipped to project force from the sea.

Mountain: formations and units trained and equipped to operate in mountainous terrain.

Other Forces: specifically trained and equipped 'jungle' or 'counter-insurgency' brigades and security units such as 'Presidential Guards', or formations permanently employed in training or demonstration tasks.

Combat Support (CS): includes artillery, engineers, air defence, intelligence, EOD and other CS not integral to manoeuvre formations. They support combat units and formations to enable them to fight and manoeuvre.

Combat Service Support (CSS): includes construction, logistics, maintenance, medical, supply and transport formations and units.

Equipment by type

Light Weapons: include all small arms, machine guns, grenades and grenade launchers and unguided man-portable anti-armour and support weapons. These weapons have proliferated so much and are sufficiently easy to manufacture or copy that listing them would be impractical.

Crew Served Weapons: crew-served recoilless rifles, man-portable ATGW, MANPAD and mortars of greater than 80mm calibre are listed, but the high degree of proliferation and local manufacture of many of these weapons means that estimates of numbers held may not be reliable.

Armoured Fighting Vehicles (AFVs):

Main Battle Tank (MBT): armoured, tracked combat vehicles, armed with a turret-mounted gun of at least 75mm calibre and weighing at least 25 metric tonnes unladen. Lighter vehicles that meet the first three criteria are considered light tanks.

Reconnaissance: combat vehicles designed and equipped to enable reconnaissance tasks.

Armoured Infantry Fighting Vehicle (AIFV): armoured combat vehicles designed and equipped to transport an infantry squad and armed with a cannon of at least 20mm calibre.

Armoured Personnel Carrier (APC): lightly armoured combat vehicles designed and equipped to transport an infantry squad but either unarmed or armed with a cannon of less than 20mm calibre.

Protected Patrol Vehicle (PPV): role-specific armoured vehicles designed to protect troops from small arms, RPG and roadside-bomb threats. Most have little or no cross-country mobility and are not designed for combined-arms manoeuvre.

Artillery: weapons (including guns, howitzers, gun/howitzers, multiple-rocket launchers, mortars and gun/mortars) with a calibre greater than 100mm for artillery pieces and 80mm and above for mortars, capable of engaging ground targets with indirect fire.

Anti-Tank (AT): guns, guided weapons and recoilless rifles designed to engage armoured vehicles and battlefield hardened targets.

Air Defence (AD): guns and missiles designed to engage fixed-wing, rotary-wing and unmanned aircraft.

Combat Support and Combat Service Support Equipment: includes assault bridging, engineer tanks, armoured recovery vehicles and armoured ambulances. Civilian equipment is excluded.

Principal Naval Definitions

To aid comparison between fleets, the following definitions, which do not conform to national definitions, are used:

Submarines: all vessels designed to operate primarily under water. Submarines with a dived displacement below 250 tonnes are classified as midget submarines; those below 500 tonnes are coastal submarines.

Principal surface combatants: all surface ships designed for combat operations on the high seas, with an FLD above 1,500 tonnes. Principal surface combatants include aircraft helicopter carriers, cruisers (with an FLD above 9,750 tonnes), destroyers (with an FLD above 4,500 tonnes) and frigates (with an FLD above 1,500 tonnes).

Patrol and coastal combatants: surface vessels designed for coastal or inshore operations. These include corvettes, which usually have an FLD between 500 and 1,500 tonnes and are distinguished from other patrol vessels by their heavier armaments. Also included in this category are offshore patrol ships, with an FLD greater than 1,500 tonnes, patrol craft, which have an FLD between 250 and 1,500 tonnes and patrol boats with an FLD between ten and 250 tonnes. Vessels with a top speed greater than 35 knots are designated as 'fast'.

Mine warfare vessels: all surface vessels configured primarily for mine laying or countermeasures. Countermeasures vessels are either: sweepers, which are designed to locate and destroy mines in an area; hunters, which are designed to locate and destroy individual mines; or countermeasures vessels, which combine both roles.

Amphibious vessels: vessels designed to transport personnel and/or equipment onto shore. These include amphibious-assault vessels, which can embark fixed-wing and/or rotary-wing air assets as well as landing craft; landing platforms, which can embark rotary-wing aircraft as well as landing craft; landing ships, which are amphibious vessels capable of ocean passage; and landing craft, which are smaller vessels designed to transport personnel and equipment from a larger vessel to land or across small stretches of water. Landing ships have a hold; landing craft are open vessels.

Auxiliary vessels: ocean-going surface vessels performing an auxiliary military role, supporting combat ships or operations. These generally fulfil five roles: under way replenishment (such as tankers and oilers); logistics (such as cargo ships); maintenance (such as cable-repair ships or buoy tenders); research (such as survey ships); and special purpose (such as intelligence-collection ships and ocean-going tugs).

Yard craft/miscellaneous vessels: surface vessels performing a support role in coastal waters or to ships not in service. These vessels often have harbour roles, such as tugs and tenders. Other miscellaneous craft, such as royal yachts, are also included.

Weapons systems: weapons are listed in the following order: land-attack missiles, anti-ship missiles, surface-to-air missiles, torpedo tubes, anti-submarine weapons, CIWS, guns and aircraft. Missiles with a range less than 5km and guns with a calibre less than 57mm are generally not included.

Organisations: naval groupings such as fleets and squadrons frequently change and are shown only where doing so would aid qualitative judgements.

Principal Aviation Definitions

Bomber (Bbr): comparatively large platforms intended for the delivery of air-to-surface ordnance. Bbr units are units equipped with bomber aircraft for the air-to-surface role.

Fighter (Ftr): aircraft designed primarily for air-to-air combat, which may also have a limited air-to-surface capability. Ftr units are equipped with aircraft intended to provide air superiority, which may have a secondary and limited air-to-surface capability.

Fighter/Ground Attack (FGA): multi-role fighter-size platforms with significant air-to-surface capability, potentially including maritime attack, and at least some air-to-air capacity. FGA units are multi-role units equipped with aircraft capable of air-to-air and air-to-surface attack.

Ground Attack (Atk): aircraft designed solely for the air-to-surface task, with limited or no air-to-air capability. Atk units are equipped with fixed-wing aircraft.

Attack Helicopter (Atk Hel): rotary-wing platforms designed for delivery of air-to-surface weapons, and fitted with an integrated fire control system.

Anti-Submarine Warfare (ASW): fixed- and rotary-wing platforms designed to locate and engage submarines, many with a secondary anti-surface-warfare capacity. ASW units are equipped with fixed- or rotary-wing aircraft.

Anti-Surface Warfare (ASuW): ASuW units are equipped with fixed- or rotary-wing aircraft intended for anti-surface-warfare missions.

Maritime Patrol (MP): fixed-wing aircraft and unmanned aerial vehicles (UAVs) intended for maritime surface surveillance, which may possess an anti-surface-warfare capability. MP units are equipped with fixed-wing aircraft or UAVs.

Electronic Warfare (EW): fixed- and rotary-wing aircraft and UAVs intended for electronic countermeasures. EW units are equipped with fixed- or rotary-wing aircraft or UAVs.

Intelligence/Surveillance/Reconnaissance (ISR): fixed- and rotary-wing aircraft and UAVs intended to provide radar, visible light, or infrared imagery, or a mix thereof. ISR units are equipped with fixed- or rotary-wing aircraft or UAVs.

Combat/Intelligence/Surveillance/Reconnaissance (CISR): aircraft and UAVs that have the capability to deliver air-to-surface weapons, as well as undertaking ISR tasks. CISR units are equipped with armed aircraft and/or UAVs for ISR and air-to-surface missions.

COMINT/ELINT/SIGINT: fixed- and rotary-wing platforms and UAVs capable of gathering electronic (ELINT), communication (COMINT) or signals intelligence (SIGINT). COMINT units are equipped with fixed- or rotary-wing aircraft or UAVs intended for the communications-intelligence task. ELINT units are equipped with fixed- or rotary-wing aircraft or UAVs used for gathering electronic intelligence. SIGINT units are equipped with fixed- or rotary-wing aircraft or UAVs used to collect signals intelligence.

Airborne Early Warning (& Control) (AEW (&C)): fixed- and rotary-wing platforms capable of providing airborne early warning, with a varying degree of onboard command-and-control depending on the platform. AEW&C units are equipped with fixed- or rotary-wing aircraft.

Search and Rescue (SAR): units are equipped with fixed- or rotary-wing aircraft used to recover military personnel or civilians.

Combat Search and Rescue (CSAR): units are equipped with armed fixed- or rotary-wing aircraft for recovery of personnel from hostile territory.

Tanker (Tkr): fixed- and rotary-wing aircraft designed for air-to-air refuelling. Tkr units are equipped with fixed- or rotary-wing aircraft used for air-to-air refuelling.

Tanker Transport (Tkr/Tpt): platforms capable of both air-to-air refuelling and military airlift.

Transport (Tpt): fixed- and rotary-wing aircraft intended for military airlift. Light transport aircraft are categorised as having a maximum payload of up to 11,340kg, medium up to 27,215kg, and heavy above 27,215kg. Medium transport helicopters have an internal payload of up to 4,535kg; heavy transport helicopters greater than 4,535kg. PAX aircraft are platforms generally unsuited for transporting cargo on the main deck. Tpt units are equipped with fixed- or rotary-wing platforms to transport personnel or cargo.

Trainer (Trg): a fixed- and rotary-wing aircraft designed primarily for the training role, some also have the capacity to carry light to medium ordnance. Trg units are equipped with fixed- or rotary-wing training aircraft intended for pilot or other aircrew training.

Multi-role helicopter (MRH): rotary-wing platforms designed to carry out a variety of military tasks including light transport, armed reconnaissance and battlefield support.

Unmanned Aerial Vehicles (UAVs): remotely piloted or controlled unmanned fixed- or rotary-wing systems. Light UAVs are those weighing 20–150kg; medium: 150–600kg; and large: more than 600kg.

Reference

Table 14 **List of Abbreviations for Data Sections**

– part of unit is detached/less than
* combat capable
" unit with overstated title/ship class nickname
+ unit reinforced/more than
< under 100 tonnes
† serviceability in doubt
‡ obsolete
ε estimated

AAA anti-aircraft artillery
AAM air-to-air missile
AAV amphibious assault vehicle
AB airborne
ABM anti-ballistic missile
ABU sea-going buoy tender
ac aircraft
ACP airborne command post
ACV air cushion vehicle/armoured combat vehicle
AD air defence
ADA air defence artillery
adj adjusted
AE auxiliary, ammunition carrier
AEV armoured engineer vehicle
AEW airborne early warning
AFS logistics ship
AG misc auxiliary
AGB icebreaker
AGF command ship
AGHS hydrographic survey vessel
AGI intelligence collection vessel
AGOR oceanographic research vessel
AGOS oceanographic surveillance vessel
AGS survey ship
AH hospital ship
AIFV armoured infantry fighting vehicle
AK cargo ship
aka also known as
AKL cargo ship (light)
AKR roll-on/roll-off cargo ship
AKSL stores ship (light)
ALCM air-launched cruise missile
amph amphibious/amphibian
AO oiler
AOE fast combat support ship
AOR fleet replenishment oiler with RAS capability
AORH oiler with hel capacity
AORL replenishment oiler (light)
AORLH oiler light with hel deck
AOT oiler transport
AP armour-piercing/anti-personnel/transport
APC armoured personnel carrier
AR repair ship
ARC cable repair ship
ARG amphibious ready group
ARH active radar homing
ARL airborne reconnaissance low
ARM anti-radiation missile
armd armoured
ARS rescue and salvage ship
arty artillery
ARV armoured recovery vehicle
AS anti-submarine/submarine tender
ASCM anti-ship cruise missile
AShM anti-ship missile
aslt assault
ASM air-to-surface missile
ASR submarine rescue craft
ASTT anti-submarine torpedo tube
ASW anti-submarine warfare
ASuW anti-surface warfare
AT tug/anti-tank
ATBM anti-tactical ballistic missile
ATF tug, ocean going
ATGW anti-tank guided weapon
ATK attack/ground attack
AVB aviation logistic support ship
avn aviation
AWT water tanker
AX training craft
AXL training craft (light)
AXS training craft (sail)
BA budget authority (US)
Bbr bomber
BCT brigade combat team
bde brigade
bdgt budget
BG battle group
BMD ballistic missile defence
BMEWS ballistic missile early warning system
bn battalion/billion
bty battery
C2 command and control
casevac casualty evacuation
cav cavalry
cbt combat
CBRN chemical, biological, radiological, nuclear, explosive
cdo commando
C/G/H/M/N/L cruiser/guided missile/with hangar/with missile/nuclear-powered/light
CISR Combat ISR
CIMIC civil–military cooperation
CIWS close-in weapons system
COIN counter insurgency
comb combined/combination
comd command
COMINT communications intelligence
comms communications
coy company
CPX command post exercise
CS combat support
CSAR combat search and rescue
CSS combat service support
CT counter terrorism
CV/H/L/N/S aircraft carrier/helicopter/light/nuclear powered/VSTOL
CW chemical warfare/weapons
DD/G/H/M destroyer/with AShM/with hangar/with SAM
DDS dry deck shelter
def defence
det detachment
div division
ECM electronic countermeasures
ELINT electronic intelligence
elm element/s
engr engineer
EOD explosive ordnance disposal
eqpt equipment
ESM electronic support measures
est estimate(d)
EW electronic warfare
excl excludes/excluding
exp expenditure
FAC forward air control
fd field
FF/G/H/M fire-fighting/frigate/with AShM/with hangar/with SAM
FGA fighter ground attack
FLD full-load displacement
flt flight
FMA Foreign Military Assistance
FS/G/H/M corvette/with AShM/with hangar/with SAM
FSSG force service support group
Ftr fighter
FTX field training exercise
FW fixed-wing
FY fiscal year
GBU guided bomb unit
gd guard
GDP gross domestic product
GNP gross national product
gp group
HA/DR humanitarian assistance/disaster relief
hel helicopter
HMTV high-mobility tactical vehicle
how howitzer
HQ headquarters
HUMINT human intelligence
HWT heavyweight torpedo
hy heavy

Table 16 **Index of Countries and Territories**

Table 15 **Index of Country/Territory Abbreviations**

AFG	Afghanistan
ALB	Albania
ALG	Algeria
ANG	Angola
ARG	Argentina
ARM	Armenia
ATG	Antigua and Barbuda
AUS	Australia
AUT	Austria
AZE	Azerbaijan
BDI	Burundi
BEL	Belgium
BEN	Benin
BFA	Burkina Faso
BGD	Bangladesh
BHR	Bahrain
BHS	Bahamas
BIH	Bosnia–Herzegovina
BIOT	British Indian Ocean Territory
BLG	Bulgaria
BLR	Belarus
BLZ	Belize
BOL	Bolivia
BRB	Barbados
BRN	Brunei
BRZ	Brazil
BWA	Botswana
CAM	Cambodia
CAN	Canada
CAR	Central African Republic
CHA	Chad
CHE	Switzerland
CHL	Chile
CIV	Côte d'Ivoire
CMR	Cameroon
COG	Congo
COL	Colombia
CPV	Cape Verde
CRI	Costa Rica
CRO	Croatia
CUB	Cuba
CYP	Cyprus
CZE	Czech Republic
DJB	Djibouti
DNK	Denmark
DOM	Dominican Republic
DPRK	Korea, Democratic People's Republic of
DRC	Democratic Republic of the Congo
ECU	Ecuador
EGY	Egypt
EQG	Equitorial Guinea
ERI	Eritrea
ESP	Spain
EST	Estonia
ETH	Ethiopia
FIN	Finland
FJI	Fiji
FLK	Falkland Islands
FRA	France
FYROM	Macedonia, Former Yugoslav Republic
GAB	Gabon
GAM	Gambia
GEO	Georgia
GER	Germany
GF	French Guiana
GHA	Ghana
GIB	Gibraltar
GNB	Guinea-Bissau
GRC	Greece
GRL	Greenland
GUA	Guatemala
GUI	Guinea
GUY	Guyana
HND	Honduras
HTI	Haiti
HUN	Hungary
IDN	Indonesia
IND	India
IRL	Ireland
IRN	Iran
IRQ	Iraq
ISL	Iceland
ISR	Israel
ITA	Italy
JAM	Jamaica
JOR	Jordan
JPN	Japan
KAZ	Kazakhstan
KEN	Kenya
KGZ	Kyrgyzstan
KWT	Kuwait
LAO	Laos
LBN	Lebanon
LBR	Liberia
LBY	Libya
LKA	Sri Lanka
LSO	Lesotho
LTU	Lithuania
LUX	Luxembourg
LVA	Latvia
MDA	Moldova
MDG	Madagascar
MEX	Mexico
MHL	Marshall Islands
MLI	Mali
MLT	Malta
MMR	Myanmar
MNE	Montenegro
MNG	Mongolia
MOR	Morocco
MOZ	Mozambique
MRT	Mauritania
MUS	Mauritius
MWI	Malawi
MYS	Malaysia
NAM	Namibia
NCL	New Caledonia
NER	Niger
NGA	Nigeria
NIC	Nicaragua
NLD	Netherlands
NOR	Norway
NPL	Nepal
NZL	New Zealand
OMN	Oman
PT	Palestinian Territories
PAN	Panama
PAK	Pakistan
PER	Peru
PHL	Philippines
POL	Poland
PNG	Papua New Guinea
PRC	China, People's Republic of
PRT	Portugal
PRY	Paraguay
PYF	French Polynesia
QTR	Qatar
ROC	Taiwan (Republic of China)
ROK	Korea, Republic of
ROM	Romania
RSA	South Africa
RUS	Russia
RWA	Rwanda
SAU	Saudi Arabia
SDN	Sudan
SEN	Senegal
SER	Serbia
SGP	Singapore
SLB	Solomon Islands
SLE	Sierra Leone
SLV	El Salvador
SOM	Somalia
SSD	South Sudan
STP	São Tomé and Príncipe
SUR	Suriname
SVK	Slovakia
SVN	Slovenia
SWE	Sweden
SYC	Seychelles
SYR	Syria
TGO	Togo
THA	Thailand
TJK	Tajikistan
TKM	Turkmenistan
TLS	Timor Leste
TTO	Trinidad and Tobago
TUN	Tunisia
TUR	Turkey
TZA	Tanzania
UAE	United Arab Emirates
UGA	Uganda
UK	United Kingdom
UKR	Ukraine
URY	Uruguay
US	United States
UZB	Uzbekistan
VEN	Venezuela
VNM	Vietnam
YEM	Yemen, Republic of
ZMB	Zambia
ZWE	Zimbabwe

Table 16 **Index of Countries and Territories**